doll at Work

No job is too small for your doll with the cool tools inside!

American Girl®

Published by American Girl Publishing

Questions or comments? Call 1-800-845-0005, visit **americangirl.com**, or write to Customer Service, American Girl, 8400 Fairway Place, Middleton, WI 53562-0497.

Printed in China
13 14 15 16 17 18 19 20 LEO 10 9 8 7 6 5 4 3 2

Editorial Development: Trula Magruder
Art Direction, Design, and Illustration: Sarah Boecher
Production: Tami Kepler, Judith Lary, Paula Moon, Kristi Tabrizi
Set Photography: Jeff Rockwell
Craft Stylist: Trula Magruder
Set Stylist: Kim Sphar
Doll Stylists: Jane Amini, Karen Timm

Dear Doll Lover,

Discover your doll's strongest skills, and put her to work! Does she excel at organizing? Ask her to handle household jobs. Can she hustle? Send her on deliveries. Will she tackle outdoor tasks? Pass her a rake on an autumn day. Inside this book, you'll learn how your doll can start a business or serve her community. The supplies will give your doll a break with initial business costs—and they'll make taking on tasks even more fun. Luckily for you, a doll's work is never done!

Your friends at
American Girl

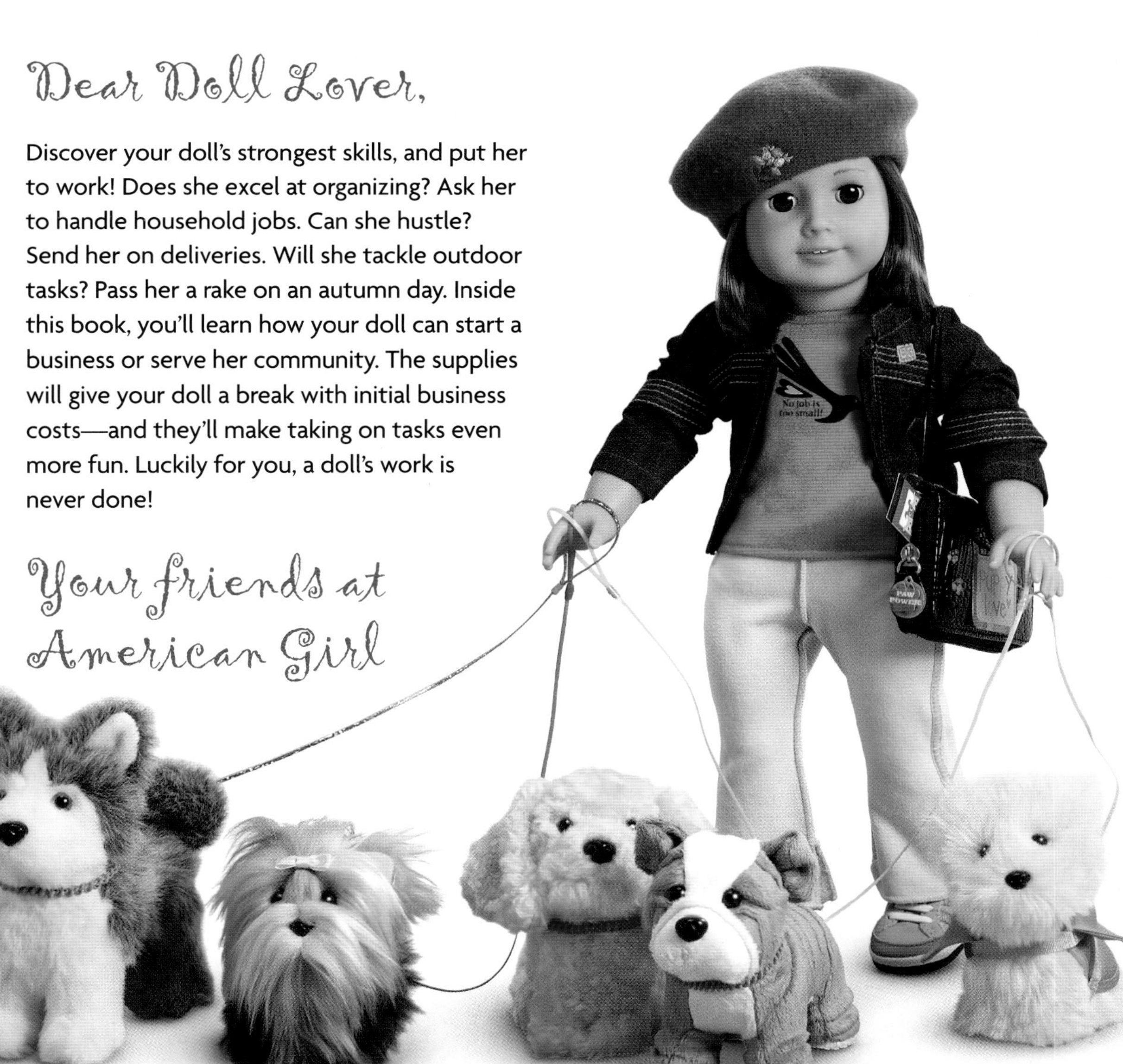

CRAFT WITH CARE!

Keep Your Doll Safe

When creating doll crafts, remember that dyes from ribbons, felt, beads, cords, fabrics, fleece, and other supplies may bleed onto your doll or her clothes and leave permanent stains. To help prevent this, use lighter colors when possible, and check your doll often to make sure the colors aren't transferring to her body, her vinyl, or her clothes. And never get your doll wet! Water and heat greatly increase dye rub-off.

It's Just Pretend

All the doll crafts in this book are for pretend only. So don't put your doll in a real bath—or any water—or expose her or her outfits to sand, sun, or snow.

Get Help!

When you see this symbol ✋ in the book, it means that you need an adult to help you with all or a part of the craft. ALWAYS ask for help before continuing.

Ask First

If a craft asks you to reuse an old item, such as a sock or a shirt, always ask an adult for permission before you use it. Your parent might still need it, so check first.

Craft Smart

If a craft instruction says "cut," use scissors. If it says "glue," use craft glue or Glue Dots®. And if it says "paint," use a nontoxic acrylic paint. Before you use these supplies, ask an adult to check them over—especially the paints and glues. Some crafting supplies are not safe for kids.

Put Away Crafts and Supplies

When you're not using the crafts or craft supplies, put them up high or store them away from little kids and pets. Toddlers and animals might eat your crafts, break them, or even hurt themselves when playing with them.

Search for Supplies

If you can't find an unusual or seasonal craft item (such as a plastic tub or fake snow) at your local stores, ask an adult to help you search online. You can also see if a local store can order the supplies.

Doll Services

Train your doll to do the following jobs, and then put her company logo sticker next to each task she has accomplished. Your doll can use this list to show customers the jobs she's prepared to perform. To promote her company, make sure your doll wears her business tee while she's working.

Inside Work

- Sort mail
- Write invites
- Organize offices
- Decorate cakes
- Arrange albums
- Set tables

Deliveries

- Bring dry cleaning
- Carry flowers
- Get groceries
- Visit vets
- Deliver pizzas

Outdoor Services

- Wash cars
- Plan parties
- Design decks
- Walk dogs
- Rake leaves
- Shovel snow

Business Tools

Get your doll's business started with these cool task tools!

Look for all the kit's accessories **popped in color** throughout the book!

Use the **legal pad, business cards,** and other accessories to promote your doll's business.

Wash Cars

Clean cars or bikes until they gleam.

Give dolls a clean commute! To create a bucket, use a paper punch to make a hole on each side of a spray-paint lid. Slip a silver cord through the holes, and knot each end. Use fiberfill stuffing for suds, and cut a small sponge from a thin, wet sponge. Snip a section off an old orphan ultra-soft sock for a car towel. Display a **car-wash sign.**

Officially licensed by Volkswagen

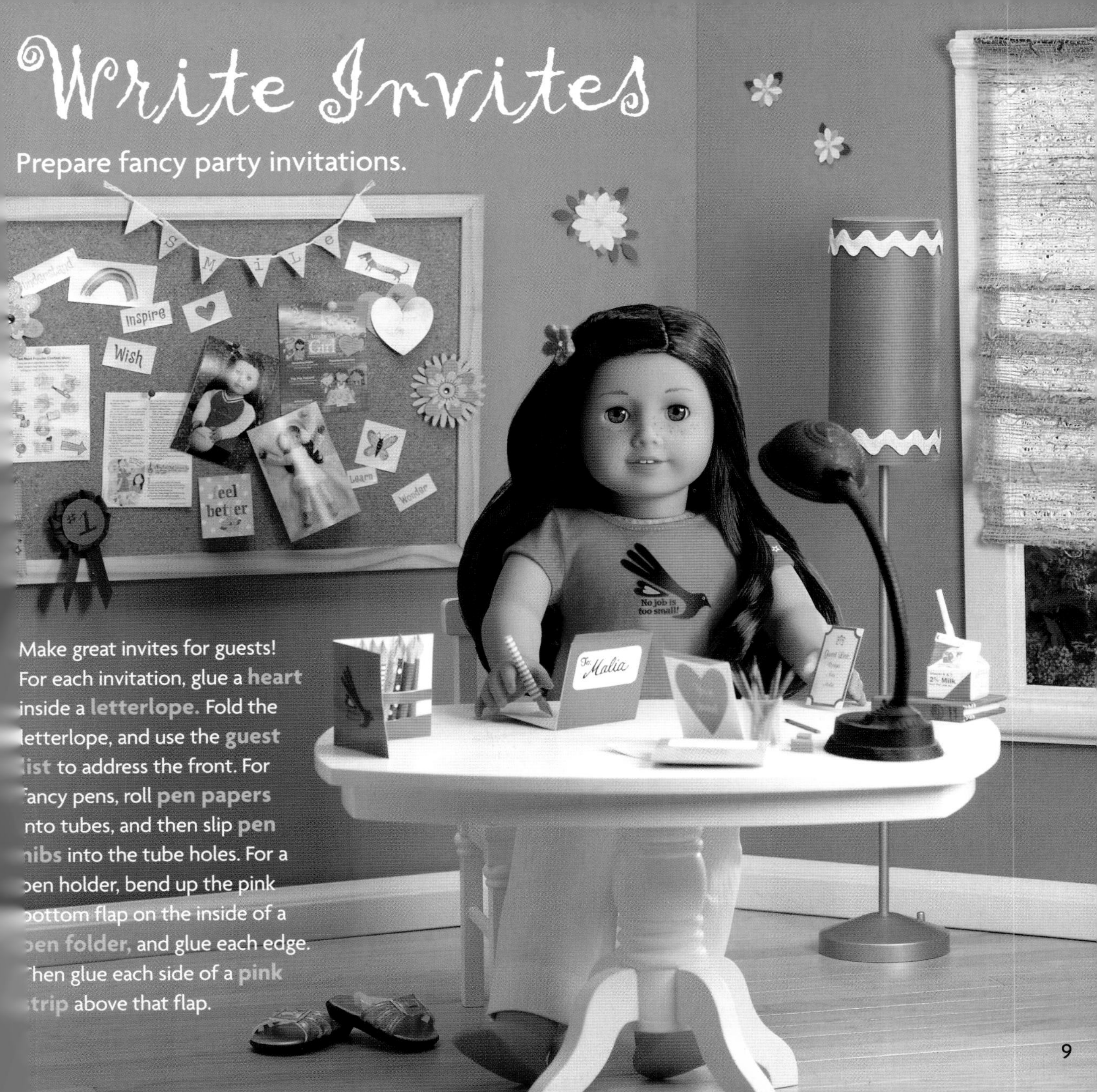

Write Invites

Prepare fancy party invitations.

Make great invites for guests! For each invitation, glue a **heart** inside a **letterlope.** Fold the letterlope, and use the **guest list** to address the front. For fancy pens, roll **pen papers** into tubes, and then slip **pen nibs** into the tube holes. For a pen holder, bend up the pink bottom flap on the inside of a **pen folder,** and glue each edge. Then glue each side of a **pink strip** above that flap.

Carry Flowers

Make a bud feel better with a bitty bouquet.

Cheer up dolls by giving flowers. Slip a rubber band around the stems of mini flowers, wrap the bouquet in tissue paper, and seal the tissue with a **flower seal.** Write a message inside a **greeting card,** and tuck it in the bouquet. Tie on a ribbon.

ɡet Groceries

›eliver food to busy clients.

ep food for quick delivery! First, over your work area. Then soak ıeets of high-quality tissue paper in ater, and shape them into fruits and ɛggies. Make sure the tissue paper is beled "non-bleeding." If the color ıns, the dye could stain your doll! ɛt dry overnight. For jam, wrap aper inside a tiny plastic jar, over the lid with duct tape, nd add a label. For bread, hape loaves from nontoxic ay, brush them with watercolor aint, and let dry. Fill 2 treat acks with the food, nd slip the sacks and ne bread into a box. ttach a **grocery-ox label.**

Plan Parties

Create a pool retreat to beat the heat.

Make a splash putting on an outdoor party! To build a patio, organize matching boxes, leaving an opening for a *pretend* pool. Next, cut cardboard to fit over the boxes and inside the pool. Cover the cardboard on the patio with wrapping paper. Cover the cardboard on the pool floor with blue wrapping paper. Use a mix of papers for the top and bottom of the pool sides. Glue on **pool depth stickers.** To design patio furniture, ask an adult for old plastic dishes and other plasticware. Experiment with shapes, and then glue the pieces together. Let dry. For each frosty treat, cut 2 ice-pop shapes from sparkly self-adhesive craft-foam sheets. Remove the backing sheets, and sandwich 2 blunt-ended toothpicks between the foam. Display the icy treats in lids filled with nontoxic clay. Attach a **pool sign.** Add dolls to the pool, and gently cover them in plastic wrap for water! Promote your work with a **patio tent.**

Enjoy your
new patio!

Bring Dry Cleaning

Deliver fresh-pressed clothes right to the door.

Bring dolls their delicate duds! For bags, remove the holes along the side of a plastic sheet protector, keeping the seam intact, and cut a notch at the top edge. Hang a doll-clothing item on a doll hanger, slip the hanger inside the sheet protector so that it rests in the notch, and tape the top corners down. Attach a **dry-cleaning receipt** to the hanger with a twist tie.

Sort Mail

ack packages, stack them
o, and ship them out.

ep peewee packages for shipping! To start, ld and stack small craft or shipping boxes. r padded envelopes, stuff mini paper cks with tissue, and tape them closed. r mail, use scrapbook embellishments **letters.** For a magazine, cut a small ction from a catalogue, and wrap with a rubber band. For a pboard, cut a rectangle om cardboard. Hold a piece paper from the **legal pad** place with plastic hair clips. r a pencil, color blunt-ended othpicks with markers.

Organize Offices

Help out in a home or business office.

Put your doll to work in a home office! To make a desk, arrange large plastic boxes so that the openings face the doll. To lift the boxes off the floor, balance them on spools. For a chair, open the lid of a small craft box so that the opening faces the floor, and bend the lid back to create a chair back. Tape the lid in place, and cover it with a cup cozy. Slip old-fashioned clothespins onto each box corner for legs. For a laptop, remove the lid from a gift tin, and flip the tin upside down. For the screen, attach the lid to the back edge of the tin with Glue Dots and silver duct tape. Add a **keyboard** and **computer screen.** For office trays, decorate craft-box lids, and label them with **in/out stickers.** Attach **labels** to the **file folders.** Fill a small vase with flowers. To make an invoice pad, glue an **invoice sheet** to a piece of cardboard. Accessorize the office with a decorative globe, an **office-helper sign, business cards,** and other work-related items.

Smile
imagine
Dream
No job is
too small!
URGENT!
OFFICE
HELPER
Ava
IN
OUT

Design Decks

Primp and prune a pretty back patio.

Make a backyard deck dazzle! For bushes, wrap felt around Styrofoam™ cones, accent them with trimmings, and slip them into papier-mâché pots. For a hose, ask an adult if you can cut the handles off an old plastic jump rope. Then add a soap-bottle knob on one end, and cover it with gold duct tape. Display dried flowers, plant pots, **seed packets,** and other gardening supplies. If you don't have a mini deck, make one! Glue faux-wood scrapbook paper to thick cardboard.

Decorate Cakes

Design very fancy cakes for very special occasions!

Create cakes to show and sell! Measure and cut 3 strips and 3 circles from fancy white scrapbook paper to fit the sides and tops of 3 different-sized craft boxes. Cover the boxes with double-stick tape, and press on the paper pieces. Attach a paper doily to a white cardboard circle. Run glue around the bottom rims of the boxes, and stack them on the doily. Decorate the cake with 3-D embellishments. Add a **bakery tent** to the table.

Walk Dogs

Take city dogs for sidewalk strolls.

Parade a pack of pooches along a path! To create leashes, loop plastic lacings around hair elastics, and seal the loops with duct tape. At the opposite ends, make loops large enough to fit around your doll's hand, and tape them closed. For a puppy bag, add a plastic lacing strap to a coin purse, and decorate the purse with pet stickers. Slip in **doggie treats** and other pet essentials.

Arrange Albums

Place precious pics in a photo keeper.

Make an album for peewee pictures. For the covers, look for a pair of plastic luggage tags. To add photo sleeves, slip a sheet of paper into a sheet protector, line up one of the protector's holes with the hole on a tag, and trim the sheet to fit the tag. Repeat to make several sleeves. To construct the album, place the sleeves between the tags, loop a thin cord through all the holes, and tie a bow in front. Organize **doll pictures** inside.

Visit Vets

Take a pet to see the vet.

Deliver pets to an animal clinic. For an exam table, glue silver paper to cardboard, and ask an adult if you can attach a wide-top candleholder under the tabletop with Glue Dots. Hang **pet posters** on walls with removable adhesive strips. For a doctor's coat, ask an adult if you can have an infant's button-up shirt. If so, remove the buttons, fold up the sleeves, and shorten the bottom edge. Make pockets from the trimmed fabric. Re-hem the shirt bottom and attach the pockets with fabric glue or Glue Dots. For a badge, slip a **vet badge** into the corner of a sheet protector, and trim the sheet to fit the ID. Slip the badge onto a pocket with a plastic paper clip. Write the vet's name on the coat with mini letter stickers. Keep white cloth strips and other supplies on hand for injuries.

No job is
too small!
Emily

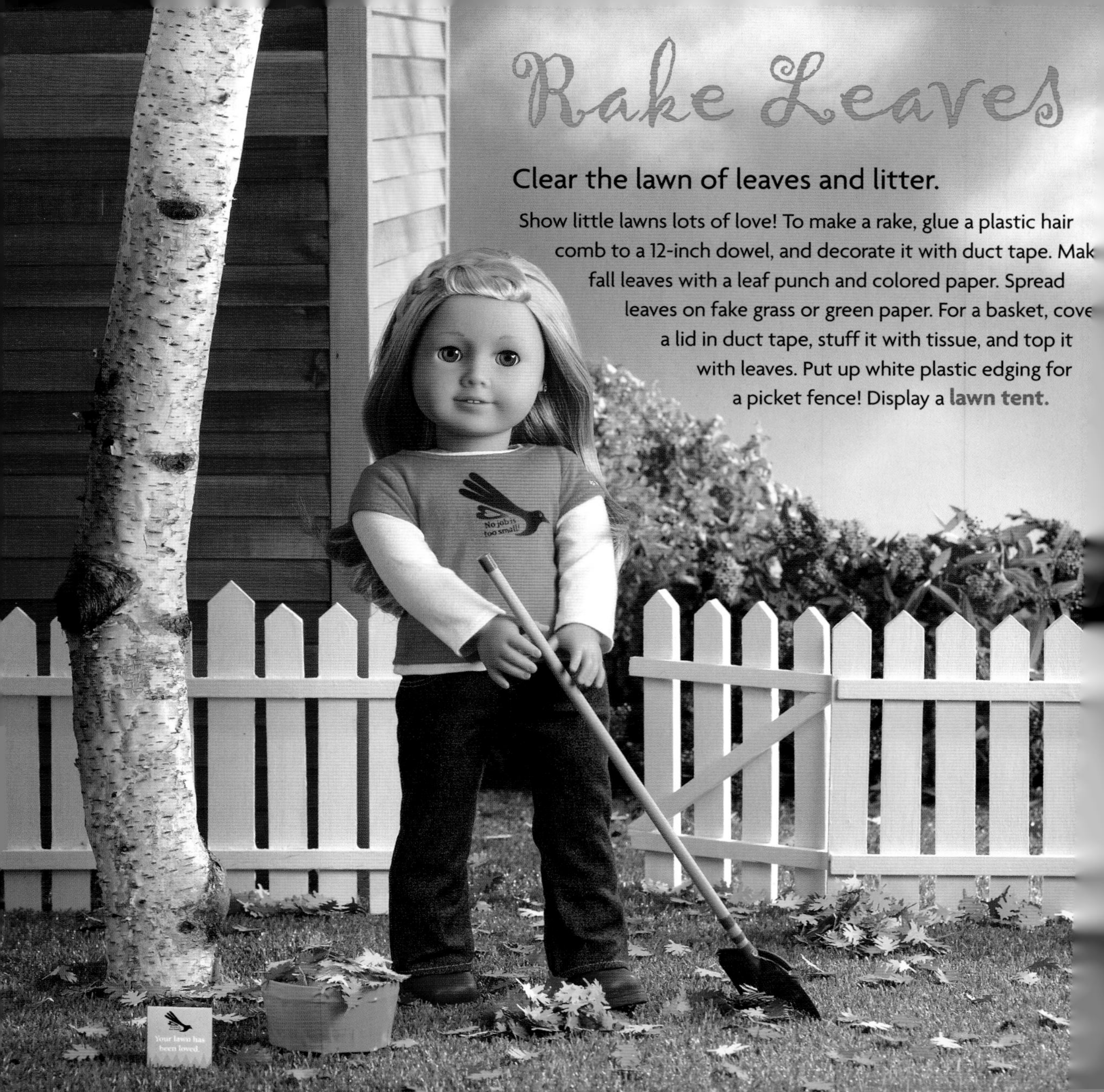

Rake Leaves

Clear the lawn of leaves and litter.

Show little lawns lots of love! To make a rake, glue a plastic hair comb to a 12-inch dowel, and decorate it with duct tape. Mak fall leaves with a leaf punch and colored paper. Spread leaves on fake grass or green paper. For a basket, cove a lid in duct tape, stuff it with tissue, and top it with leaves. Put up white plastic edging for a picket fence! Display a **lawn tent.**

Deliver Pizzas

Make and deliver pizzas in a jiffy.

Bring freshly made pizzas right to the door! To make each pizza, paint the top of a 2½-inch tan craft-foam circle red, leaving an edge showing. Squeeze on craft glue and add strips of white yarn for cheese, black beads for olives, green craft-foam strips for peppers, and red craft-foam circles for pepperoni. Fold up **pizza boxes**, and slip the pizzas inside.

Shovel Snow

Shovel driveways on blustery days.

Keep driveways snowflake-free! Design your snow scene on a large cardboard base to make snow removal easy and neat! *Warning:* Don't use snow anywhere near carpets or rugs. To make a driveway, lay down heavy gray paper, and then load it up with snow. Look for pre-bagged artificial snow at craft or hobby stores (or rub Styrofoam balls together for smaller amounts of snow). To design snowbanks, create mini mounds with fiberfill stuffing, and cover them with the pretend snow. For a snow shovel, cut a shovel shape from thick paper, and cover it with duct tape. Add 3-D silver dot stickers to the blade if you like. Tape the shovel to a 12-inch dowel wrapped in duct tape. For final snow removal, tilt the cardboard base over a garbage bin, or pour the snow into a large plastic bag to reuse it.

No job is
too small!

Set Tables

Create dazzling table designs for special celebrations.

Arrange amazing tables for holidays! Drape fabric over a doll table, and add a ribbon runner. For a centerpiece, paint wood flowerpots with glitter paint. Let dry. For a pretend candle, slip a stirrer straw into each hole, and top with a yellow petal. For dishes, layer dessert plates with plastic and paper plates cut to size. Use mini flying disks for salad bowls and taster cups for glasses. Accent the dishes with strips of gold duct tape. Cut a corner off a paper napkin, roll it, wrap it with a rubber band, and add a decorative sticker. Put names on **place cards** with gold letter stickers. Scatter **gold coins** and gold metallic shreds on the table.

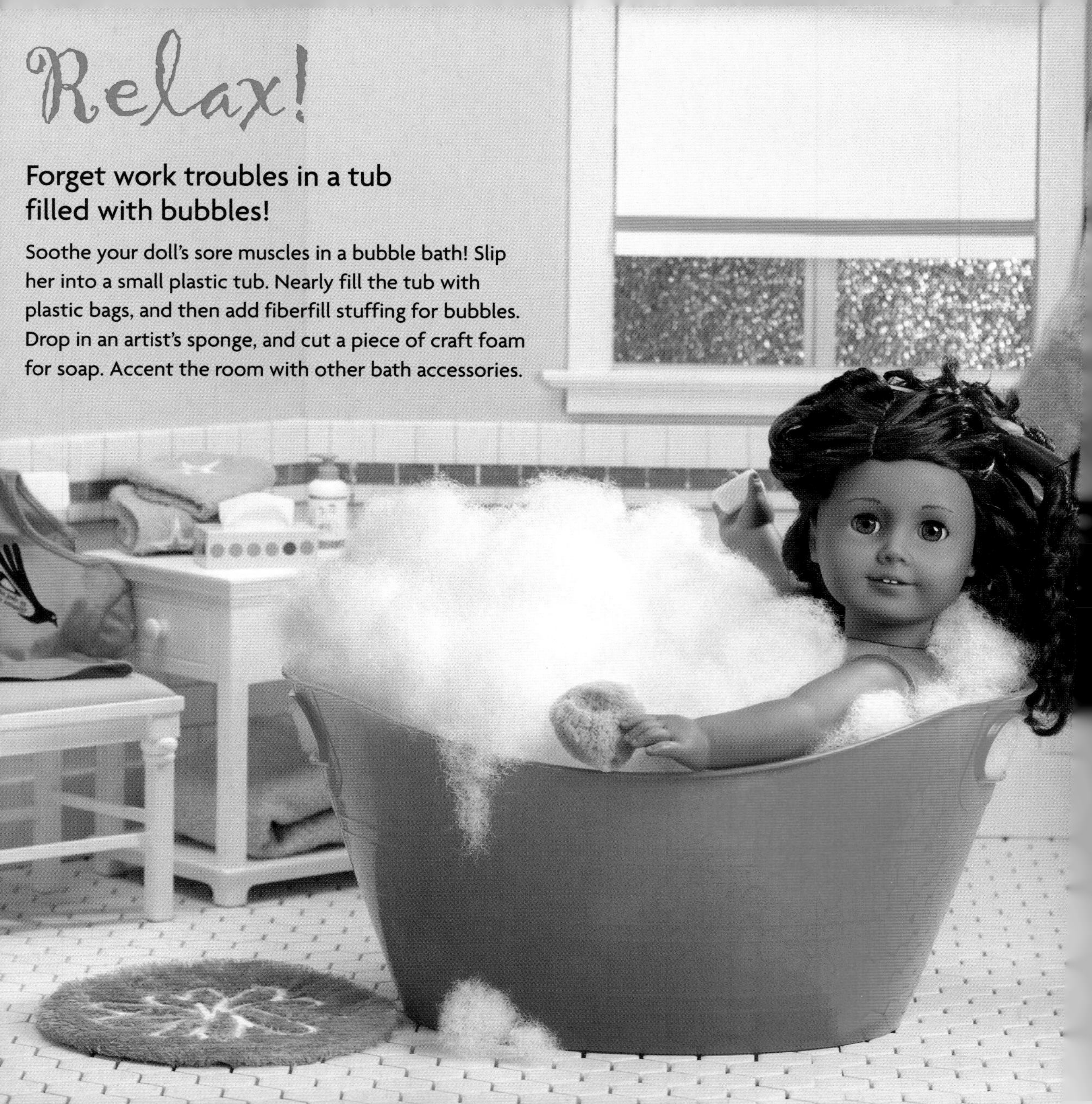

Relax!

Forget work troubles in a tub filled with bubbles!

Soothe your doll's sore muscles in a bubble bath! Slip her into a small plastic tub. Nearly fill the tub with plastic bags, and then add fiberfill stuffing for bubbles. Drop in an artist's sponge, and cut a piece of craft foam for soap. Accent the room with other bath accessories.

MALLOY'S SPORTS COLLECTIBLES VALUE GUIDE

Up-To-Date Prices For Noncard Sports Memorabilia

Roderick A. Malloy

Wallace-Homestead Book Company
Radnor, Pennsylvania

Published in Radnor, Pennsylvania 19089, by Wallace-Homestead,
a division of the Chilton Book Company
Published in association with Attic Books, Ltd.,
Publishers of *Malloy's Sports Cards & Collectibles*

Designed by Stuart W. Wells III

Manufactured in the United States of America

Wallace-Homestead ISBN: 0-87069-689-0
Attic Books ISBN: 0-915018-48-9

1 2 3 4 5 6 7 8 9 0   2 1 0 9 8 7 6 5 4 3

Contents

Field Reports

Listings and Values

Listings and Values (cont.)

Appendices

ACKNOWLEDGMENTS

Special Thanks to the Staff at Attic Books:

Roderick A. Malloy – Editor

Cory Schwartz – Assistant Editor

Dean Sasso – Assistant Editor

Chris Kelman – Assistant Editor

Brian W. Kelly – Copy Editor

Stuart W. Wells III – Graphic Designer

Jay Runningdeer – Graphic Assistant

Louise Girgenti – Production Assistant

Wendy Anne – Intern

Kerri Grady – Intern

Alison James, John Laub,
Evan Wells and Galen Wells – Marketing Team

Alex G. Malloy, Elaine C. Malloy, Allen G. Berman,
Neil Hansen, Christine Nash, Camden Percival
Louis Porter, Jr., Marcy Rickart, Steve Thomas, Evan Wells

Photo Credits and Invaluable Assistance:

Judy Bartolett, Don Bigsby, Warren Cohen, Mark Cooper, John Cummings, Thom Dixon, Pat Flynn, Dennis Goldstein, Dick Hering, Paul Jarrell, Ted Knorr, Debby and Marty Krim, Alex G. Malloy, Richard Moody, Tom Sarro, David Sassman, Thomas D. Slater of The Political Gallery, Sotheby's, Superior Galleries, Bud Tompkins, Mike Wamsley, Richard Wolffers Auctions, Inc., Phil Wood and Jordan Yuter

and to all who sacrificed some of their time for this project:

Jonathan Becker, Beryl Blatt, Craig Campbell, Bob Christianson, Robert Crestohl, Bob Eaton, Marty Falk, Paul Fink, Richard Galasso, Jim Greensfelder, Eiran Harris, Tim Hunter, Michael Jaspersen, Harmer Johnson, Mark Jordan, Bob Kalmuk, Mark Kimball, Paul Kinzer, Frank Kovacs, Rich La Rocca, Lew Lipset, Daniel Lovegrove, Bob Manning, Clay Marston, Cecile Matte, Ralph Paticchio, Wayne Patterson, Steve Prieur, Frank Pulmazik, Don Scott, Jim Stinson, Dave Stuart, Greg Tucker, Pete Wade and Mark Wollin

PREFACE

When we first agreed to put this book together, all those involved realized what a time-consuming project it would be. Just how much time, work and outside assistance we needed could only be determined by going through the whole process. Now that its all over, I would have to say "There's plenty of room for a second volume." If any of the people who assisted on this book heard me say those words, they would probably force me to watch *Harley Davidson and the Marlboro Man* over and over, until I forgot what sports collectibles are all about.

Living and working in the sports collectible industry can be fun, relaxing, aggravating, taxing, confusing and exciting all at the same time! Most of the individuals who pick up this book will undoubtedly be intense collectors of some kind of sports collectible; so the following advice could apply to all of you:
If you ever become disenchanted with the sports collectible industry, take a step back to appreciate the other elements of your life. When you devote the majority of your time and attention to a hobby (or business) as I have done, you are bound to lose sight of some of the other elements of everyday existence. Instead of continuing on this endless tangent about sports collectibles and how they fit into the whole scheme of things, I will receive consultation from that *dirty rotten scoundrel*, Dr. Emil Shüfhausen, and return to give you some insight about this book (which we hope you will read, use and refer to over and over again).

Seriously speaking, this book should prove to be a valuable resource for any sports memorabilia collector or dealer. Our coverage ranges from die-cast replica racing cars to the staple of sports publications, *Sports Illustrated*. Collectors of various items included in this book should be able to locate dealers or fellow collectors who can assist in adding to any collection.

The scope of this book had to be limited because it would be impossible to assemble exhaustive listings on all sports collectibles. We hope to add more listings and categories to future efforts and would welcome any input from outside sources. The next page includes a few interesting examples of semi-obscure items we hope to include in the future.

Before signing off, here is an official plea to any of those who have interest in assisting with a any future endeavors such as *Malloy's Sports Collectibles Value Guide*:

Please send any correspondence regarding future sports collectible publications to:

Attic Books Ltd.
P.O. Box 569
Ridgefield, CT 06877

Best regards to all our fellow sports collectors, Roderick Malloy

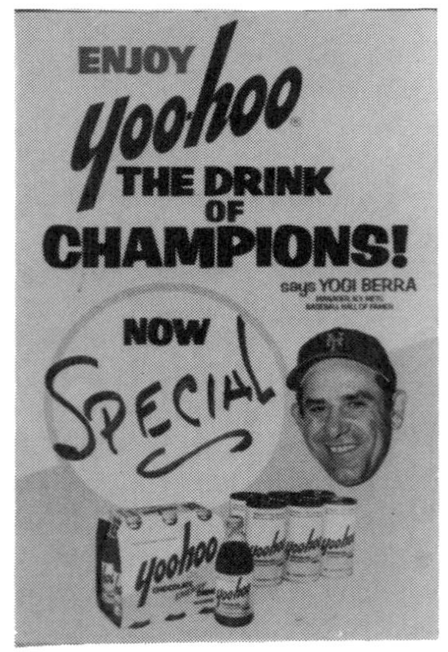

Yoo-Hoo Yogi Berra advertising sign

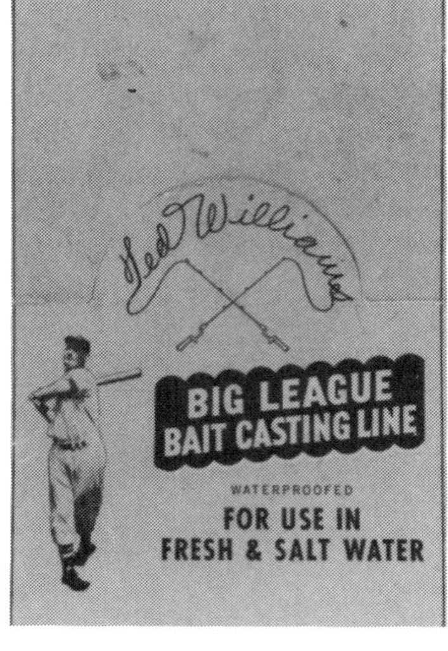

Ted Williams casting line box

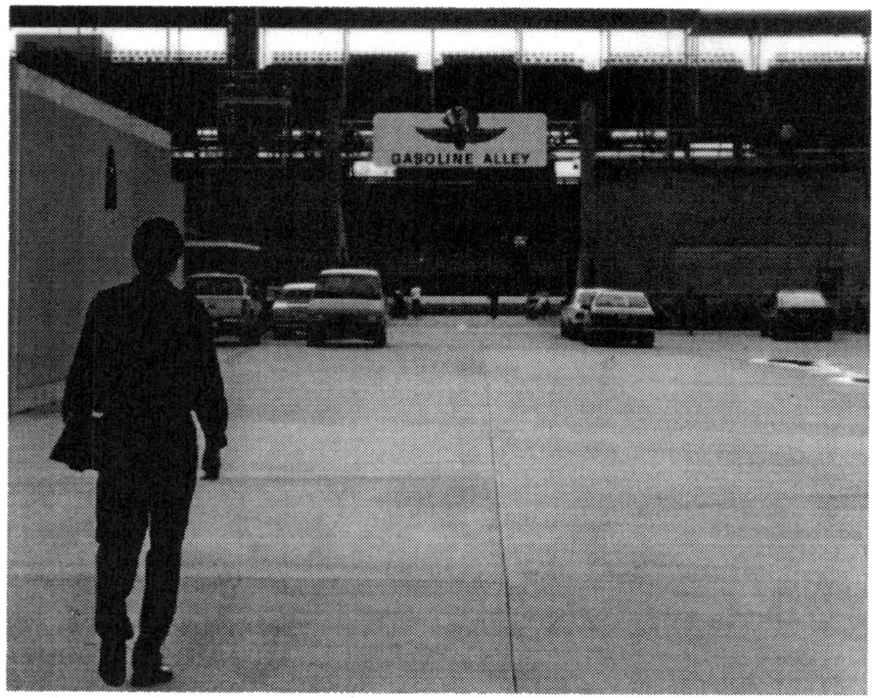

Off to do some additional research for our next project.

A LOOK AT THE SPORTS COLLECTIBLES MARKET

by Roderick A. Malloy

For many individuals, the sports collectible market provides a pleasant release from the hustle and bustle of our hi-tech world. Unfortunately, this market has grown into a monolith few collectors, dealers and outsiders can fathom. Cards continue to hold top billing in the industry, but collectibles such as autographs and game-used equipment have managed to steal many of the headlines.

Enough collectors have entered the market to temporarily support more than fifteen card companies, uncountable sports collectible magazines and thousands of dealers. The increased size and scope of the industry has turned off many investors and dealers who are no longer able to turn a fast buck. Despite the many signs of trouble (dealers going out of business left and right, major card companies declaring bankruptcy, ...) and rumors of the market's demise, there is hope for the sports collectible industry.

This hope comes in the form of the non-card sports collectible segment, which has always been supplementary to the dominant card segment. Non-card collectibles have already secured a significant role in the market and their importance will continue to grow. Dealers and entrepreneurs with foresight have already made the move away from cards, and others are following suit.

Many of the disenchanted members of the sports collectible market have moved from trading, buying and/or selling cards to trading, buying and/or selling anything other than cards. Non-card sports collectibles have been picking up steam for several years; partly because there are many rare items that command big bucks from investors or wealthy collectors and partly because everybody who has ever cared about sports has some collectible item in their closet or tucked away in a box somewhere. The number of hidden and forgotten ticket stubs, pocket schedules, autographed scraps of paper, pins, buttons and other non-card sports collectibles is staggering.

When an individual discovers that he/she already has the makings of a small collection in the closet or basement, he/she is much more likely to catch the collecting virus, because the first steps toward becoming a collector have already been taken. Sports cards may evoke pristine childhood memories for some, but a cherished autograph, baseball glove or ticket stub frequently have the same effect.

Cards have always been the backbone of the sports collectible industry; so why did they drive so many individuals into other segments of the industry? How did this seemingly harmless hobby grow into a highly competitive industry? Will sports collectibles continue to receive attention from major auction houses and companies? The answer to these questions, and any questions regarding the future of the sports collectible market, can only be found after close examination of the market itself.

A Look at the Sports Collectibles Market

Even though many industry analysts reserve serious questions about the future of the sports card industry, we believe that there is room for most of the dealers that are already part of the market. Why do we believe this? Here are our primary reasons:

Diversity. The wide product variety of the sports collectible market allows dealers to specialize in products other than cards, and more importantly, in products other than those the competition is specializing in. There are many dealers who specialize in autographs, several who focus on press pins, game-used equipment, publications, figurines and many other products. Dealers and collectors will continue to diversify until they find a balance between cards and non-card collectibles.

Demand for new products and the existence of untapped collectible niches. Collectors want new products, and many times this demand leads dealers to diversify into other product types. Some dealers help collectors into new areas of collecting, but many times it is the collector who opens the dealer's eyes to a new product or an old product which has increased in popularity. Large companies continue to help fuel this demand for new products by issuing products such as player pennants, cereal boxes, coins and much more. There are always opportunities for new product development as shown by the unusual "POG" milk bottle cap phenomenon in Hawaii [the first cap appeared on a bottle of Passion Orange Guava juice, hence the name POG]. This interesting product has been picked up by SkyBox and other mainland U.S. companies.

Market longevity. Despite the expected downturn in sports collectible sales (part of any product's life cycle), nobody doubts the longevity of the sport-based card and collectible market as a whole. Card companies continue to refresh the collector's interest by issuing new high-quality sets at astounding rates, and other companies and auction houses help in propelling the non-card collectibles to new heights. Three years ago, certain dealers and industry analysts believed that a flooded market would result in a dead market. The market was, without a doubt, flooded by the Spring of 1992. As a result of this flooding, and outside forces such as our nation's coinciding economic downturn, many dealers got pinched out of the industry, a couple of card companies began to falter, and many collectors became fed up with the increasingly intricate industry.

Fortunately, the industry has bounced back. Smaller card shows are no longer the mausoleums they were during the second half of 1992, card company competition is heightening, and collectors are finding more money to put into their rejuvenated hobby. Most importantly, dealers and collectors have begun to realize the importance and potential of the non-card segment of the hobby.

What have we learned from this tough period in the sports collectible industry's history? The sports card industry *is not* immune to a recessionary economy, as previously believed by some short-sighted individuals. But more importantly, we discovered several bright spots which will lead the industry for years to come. The big card companies, such as Upper Deck, Topps and Fleer, have the money and the know-how to champion the next surge in the sports-card market. They realize the importance of other sports collectibles as evidenced by the Upper Deck Authenticated venture. As long as these and other companies remember that the fan/collector is #1, sports memorabilia collecting will persist through the 1990s. This market longevity will result in plenty of collecting opportunities.

Large numbers of resourceful collectors proved to be several steps ahead of the large card companies. Basketball, football and hockey cards gained their rightful spot next to baseball cards in terms of set diversity and short-term popularity — thanks to the collectors who jumped into these sports when baseball cards seemed to be peaking. Now that there are more than *20* football card sets, *10* basketball and *10* hockey sets produced ***each year,*** collectors have begun to dabble in the few auto racing, boxing, golf and other sports' cards. This trend toward sports other than the big four has also taken place in the non-card collectibles market. At Superior Galleries' 1992 National Sports Collectors Convention Auction, three ancillary sports played major roles. Rare boxing items, tennis and Olympic collectibles all played major roles in the auction, even though baseball memorabilia maintained its traditional role of show stealer.

Upper Deck Authenticated's logo. Upper Deck's venture into non-card sports collectibles could be the first of many major changes in the market.

This potential market diversity provided by the untapped sports will help restore the luster to the sports collectible industry. With the World Cup in 1994 and the Summer Olympics in 1996, the United States will be primed for both the emergence of soccer collectibles and the resurgence of Olympics collectibles. Boxing will benefit from the presence of legitimate heavyweights Riddick Bowe and Lennox Lewis, along with the best group of "pound-for-pound" fighters in history (Julio Cesar-Chavez, Pernell Whitaker, Roy Jones, James Toney and Oscar De La Hoya). Competition between Jim Courier, Pete Sampras, Mal Washington, Michael Chang and Goran Ivanisevic should help rejuvenate interest in tennis nationwide.

Potential dynasties should help in maintaining interest in collectibles from the big four sports. Mario Lemieux, Kevin Stevens, Jaromir Jagr & Co. are well on their way to the next hockey dynasty. The Atlanta Braves have plenty of big league talent and even more awaiting their big league call (namely Chipper Jones, Jose Oliva, Mike Kelly, Melvin Nieves, Javy Lopez and Donnie Elliott). Troy Aikman, Emmitt Smith, Ken Norton, Jr. and their youthful teammates could be on their way to a handful of Super Bowl rings. Tony Kukoc may be the ingredient that propels the Chicago Bulls to a few more championship triumphs. Dominant teams always help spur the popularity of professional sports. A perennially great team will earn many faithful supporters, while intensifying the devotion of opposing teams' fans. This process creates two kinds of lifelong fans, i.e.: A) the long-time Yankee fan, or B) the long-time Yankee hater.

Another factor helping to sustain the sports collectible market is the continuous pipeline of future stars. Who knows what would have happened to the card market this past winter if the loaded 1992 rookie class had not descended upon the NBA? Frenzied excitement over Shaquille O'Neal's cards was *the* sports collectible story for many months. In March and April, collectors began to realize that Alonzo Mourning's statistics were only notch or two below Shaq's, while Alonzo's cards were inappropriately selling several notches below his adversary's cards. Rookies such as Mourning and O'Neal are examples of what keeps the card market alive.

While card dealers raked in the dough for Shaq's cards, memorabilia dealers had to wait for other Shaq memorabilia before they could get into the act. This reality presents itself when any young player steals the spotlight. Regardless of the limited supply of collectibles, any hot young star has an impact on the non-card market. After all, whose autograph was hotter than Shaq's in the early part of 1993?

The basic question behind all of this market analysis is: What fuels the industry? Through sports collectibles, people feel an intimate attachment to the athletes they admire. This is the primary reason behind the popularity of sports collectibles. If you like sports or a particular athlete, how could you not appreciate a token of that attachment to the player or sport? Cards by themselves do not have the mystery and history that accompany a torn ticket stub or an autograph scrawled on the back of an airplane napkin. If we could boil away all of the pomp, hype and pseudo extravagance from the sports collectible industry, we would discover that its ingredients are three parts memories and two parts passion for our beloved games.

CATEGORY SUMMARIES

AUTOGRAPHS (pp.17-78)

Gary Carter autograph

The Autograph section of our book is comprised of carefully researched autograph prices from all major sports. The sub-headings in this section cover auto racing, baseball, basketball, boxing, hockey, golf, tennis, the Olympics and professional wrestling. Where it is applicable, these sections are further broken down into Hall of Fame, active and inactive categories. If you're looking for a price on an elusive Jack Dempsey boxing glove, or need to find a value for your signed Ultimate Warrior 8" by 10" glossy photo, you'll find the information you seek in the following pages.

CEREAL BOXES (pp. 84-87)

From its inception in 1935 by the General Mills company, collecting cereal boxes featuring sports personalities has continued to gain popularity. The most notable boxes worth collecting are Wheaties, "The Breakfast of Champions." There is a 58-year history between Wheaties and athletes. The association began in 1933, nine years after the cereal was introduced, when General Mills introduced the slogan "Breakfast of Champions," and began being endorsed by sports stars such as Babe Ruth, Joe DiMaggio, Lefty Grove, Carl Hubbell and Stan Musial.

Companies such as Kellogg's and Post also tried to increase their cereal sales in the 1950s-60s by including baseball cards on the boxes, but it was Wheaties that continued to gain sport star endorsements such as Bob Richards, Bruce Jenner, Mary Lou Retton and Chris Evert. In the last several years, there has been renewed interest in sport personality boxes.

COINS AND MEDALLIONS (pp. 98-107) (pp. 168-172)

Enviromint Bobby Hull collector's coin

This section features values for auto racing, baseball, basketball, football and hockey coins and medallions, as well as values for Summer and Winter Olympic medals. The coins are listed in alphabetical order by sport and maker, and chronologically by year. This list includes older companies such as Armour and Salada tea, and more recent releases from Topps, 7-11 and Enviromint.

Armour coins began inserting plastic coins in their hot dog packages in 1955. They were 1-1/2" in diameter and came in various colors. Many of the fans' favorite players, like Mickey Mantle, Yogi Berra and Pee Wee Reese were included. In fact, the Mantle coin can be found with his last name spelled correctly or misspelled "Mantel." His coin with a correct spelling is valued at $135.00. One of the most rare and highly valued Armour coins is the 1960 Bud Daley, currently priced at $500.00. The reason for its scarcity is unknown, although theories range from a broken printing mold, contract disputes, or that the coin had been used for a brief time as a test product which proved unsuccessful.

1984 7-11 Carlton Fisk coin (L)
& 1992 Enviromint David Robinson coin

Salada coins were first issued in 1962 in packages of Salada Tea and Junket Pudding mix. There are 221 different players available, with variations bringing the total of different coins to 261. One of the most valuable coins is the 1962 Dick Williams, with his name appearing on the right of the coin. It is valued at $800.00.

More contemporary releases have come from 7-11 and the Enviromint company. 7-11 began the production of player coins in 1983 and continued until 1987. Originally, the promotion began as a test in the Los Angeles area, where customers purchasing a large Slurpee drink would be treated to the coin collectible, found underneath the cup. The coins available included six players from the California Angels and six players from the Los Angeles Dodgers. The promotion was deemed a success, and in 1984 the coins were distributed nationally under the name "Slurpee Discs," and they remained in circulation through 1987, and continued to excite and bring a smile to every man, woman and child who purchased a Slurpee.

Chicagoland Processing, which has been in business for 17 years, continues to produce limited edition sport medallions under the Enviromint name. Throughout the years, Enviromint has produced medallions celebrating NFL champions, NHL divisional and Stanley Cup winners, college Final Four victors, and individual players from many professional sports. This year, Enviromint will produce a limited edition Richard Petty fan appreciation set of auto racing coins, and a two piece set featuring Robin Yount and George Brett, to celebrate their 3,000 hits. Although these medallions do not come cheap, many believe that they are a good investment.

Olympic medals are another section of big collecting. There are three different types of Olympic medals: commemorative, participants and winners. First are the commemorative medals, which are normally given away to contributors who raised money for a specific Olympic event. These are the easiest to find, and subsequently, the least valuable. They are still sought however, and may be a good place for the beginning collector to get started. The second-type of medal is the participant's medal, which is given to any athlete who attends the games. Because of the sentimental value, these medals are often hard to find and are very valuable. A participant's medal from the 1992 Barcelona games is currently selling for $125.00. The winners medals are the third, and obviously the most rare and expensive to collect. A winners medal from the Barcelona games is currently selling for $2500.00.

COMIC BOOKS (pp. 108-113)

Sports and comic books are a natural marraige. Perhaps the two most influential mediums of Amercan youth culture, together they offer a varied and sometimes bizarre vision of sporting life in comic form. Fawcett Publications profile baseball heroes Phil Rizzuto, Yogi Berra, Ralph Kiner and Roy Campanella among others, in comics that are all valued in the hundreds. Less valued but just slightly more off-center is D.C.'s *Strangest Sports Stories*, one episode of which featured the country's best baseball team matched on the diamond against Beelzebub himself. Ol' Scratch may not pop up in Amazing Sports's comics, but the company did issue one-shots of Colorado University's football team, UNLV's basketball team and the New Orleans Saints. Auto racing, boxing, unauthorized biographies, even the World Wrestling Federation all found their way into comics, and companies like Dark Horse, Stadium Comics and Gold Key have produced books that should prove to be a devil of a good time.

DIE-CAST CARS (pp. 114-120)

One of the areas of significant growing interest in the collectibles industry in the past sveral years has been found in die-cast cars. Die-cast cars have been around for many years, but a recent rise in the popularity of auto racing collectibles has sparked a renewed interest in these little wheeled gems.

Companies like Hot Wheels and Matchbox are well known for their years of car production, but it is lesser known companies like Ertl, Racing Champs, RCCA, Revell and Funstuff which have produced the most highly collectible cars. In the early 1980's, Ertl became the first major diecast manufacturer to produce 1/64 scale replicas of NASCAR racers in large quantities. The majority of die-cast racing miniatures are offered on three sclaes: 1/64, 1/43 and 1/24. The 1/64 are considered the most valuable by collector's. Cars of long time auto racing champions like Richard Petty, Bobby Allison, Bill Elliott and Darrell Waltrip are produced by almost all die-cast manufacturers, but cars from these lesser

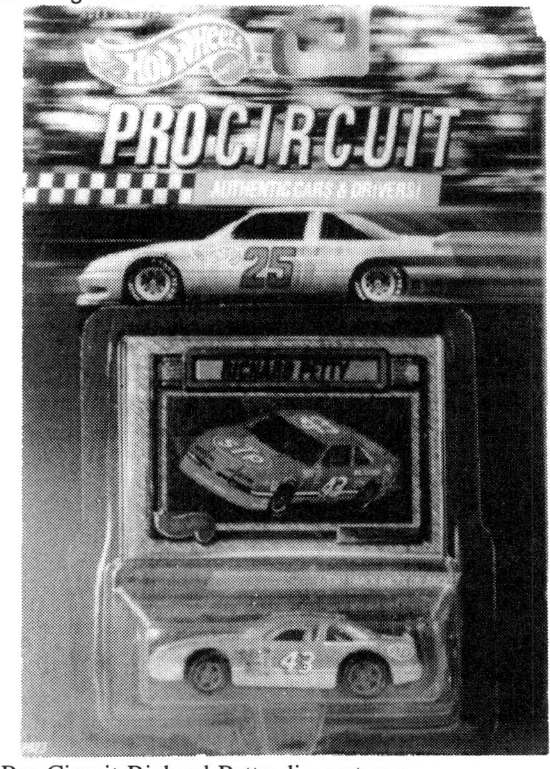

Pro Circuit Richard Petty die-cast car

known companies have the greatest worth.

For example, a Dale Earnhardt ERTL dark blue Wrangler, T-bird is valued at $220.00. A Bill Elliott ERTL, 1985 silver wheels T-bird is worth over $330.00! This year, the most sought after cars will be Richard Petty's. Since Petty has retired from racing, any one of his cars will continue to increase in value for several years. In general, cars that are part of a limited production (10,000 or less) are always considered the most valuable. The reason for this is that limited production cars are individually numbered, so they are self-authenticated. Gentlemen start your engines!

EQUIPMENT (pp. 121-132)

What could be more satisfying than pulling on the old uniform, grabbing the stick or bat and suiting up for a game? How about collecting those uniforms, sticks and bats? Listings for Hall of Famers, active and inactive players in baseball, basketball, football and hockey will guide those interested in collecting the tools of the trade. Lou Gerhig's jersey is vauled in the six figure region, while Kirby Puckett's hat is a bit more affordable. Baseball player endorsed gloves bear monikers like "Ball Hawk," "The Snapper," and "The Trapper" are listed, and are not as pricy as Bronko Nagurski's spikes, which are valued in the tens of thousands. Bobby Hull's jersey, listed at $5,000, might be too hard to come by – maybe Steve Yzerman's stick would be more readily available. Whether it's a Hall of Famer's helmet or an inactive player's basketball sneakers that's desired, these listings come fully equipped to help.

1988 Starting Lineup
Larry Bird figure

FIGURINES (pp. 133-142)

For years, sport figurines had been produced by the Hartland company, which formed in 1950 and produced popular football, western heroes and religious figures. in the last ten years however, companies such as Gartlan, Kenner, Salvino Sports Legends and Sports Impressions began their own sports figure productions which have pushed these molded plastic statues into a very competitive and popular industry.

The most collectible statues are the hand-signed, limited edition models. For example, a Joe DiMaggio hand-signed Gartlan figure is priced at $1,100; while a Hand-signed Larry Bird Salvino Sport Legend figurine is worth $300.00. Kenner Starting Lineup figures are the most reasonably priced due to their production numbers, but the Starting Lineup figures are considered to be the "trading cards" of the 21st century.

PENNANTS (pp. 173-176)

Pennants are a highly collectible sport memorabilia item. Production of pennants began in 1914. They were issued with several popular brands of tobacco and were nicknamed "blankets." The nickname began because the pennants were square felt and were often sewn together to form pillow cases or bed spreads. By 1916, the contemporary triangular design was initiated.

The popularity of pennants continued to grow throughout the years because of the many colors and styles that were manufactured. Some pennants were made for specific players, while others were team oriented. For example, in the 1914 B18 series, Rabbitt Maranville had three different pennants produced. One had a print of a white infield, one had a brown, and the third pictured a red infield. The red infield is the most collectible because it is the most difficult to find. It is valued at $350.00. The others are $40.00 and $150.00.

PINS (pp. 247-263)

Covering almost a century, Olympic and baseball pins highlight this collectibles listing. Encompassing the spectrum from the rare to the sublime, baseball entries range from Chuck Diering's scarce 1956 Topps pin and Mickey Mantle's early 1960's Yellow Basepath pin, to Fun Foods' 1984 Steve Kemp and Ron Davis pins. Listings for Hall of Fame pins, World Series pins and All-Star game pins help round out baseball. Extensive Olympic listings, divided into Summer and Winter sections, contain values for pins from the 1896 games, including judges' and participants' badges, to collectibles of the 1992 Dream Team. Indy 500 pins are listed from 1931 and pins from the Belmont Stakes, Breeder's Cup, Kentucky Derby, and Preakness are included. Boxing and Super Bowl buttons complete this listing, which has been assembled to aid people pin down their collectibles.

PLATES (pp. 264-267)

Ever want to eat lasagna off of Ken Griffey, Jr.? Companies like Sports Impressions, Gartlan USA and Pro Sports Creations have produced collectible plates of famous baseball, basketball, football players and boxers, and some, like Babe Ruth's, are valued in the thousands. Meant for display, these plates come in varied sizes and usually picture the sports figure in action, or capture the athlete in beautiful portrait-style head shots. Whether it's the Kenny Anderson Mini Plate hung on the wall, or the Joe Louis plate valued at $5,000 displayed over the hearth, these collectibles can be anyone's main course.

POSTERS (pp. 284-287)

While *Sports Illustrated* mass produced posters depicting stars from hockey, baseball, football and basketball, some of the most interesting posters are those promoting pugilism. Boxing posters, including LeRoy Neiman's classic *Thrilla in Manila*, commemorating Muhammad Ali's September 1975 defeat of Joe Frazier are highly collectible. Mike Tyson's 1988 Tokyo bout with Tony Tubbs resulted in a beautiful poster, and along with SI's sometimes quite valuable baseball posters, boxing posters, especially those involving Jack Dempsey, can command hundreds of dollars. But monetary concerns aside, the aesthetic values of these posters makes them a commodity that will certainly be hanging around for a while.

PRICE GUIDES (pp. 288-293)

Although it may seem strange to price a price guide, this section does it. *Allan Kaye's Sports Cards, Bank Street Journal, Beckett's, Cartwrights, Legends* and *Malloy's Sports Cards and Collectibles* are featured, along with many others. The sports card and sport memorabilia magazine has been around since the early 1980's, and just to prove that every sports related item is collectible, values for each issue are provided.

For example, the first Beckett's baseball price guide is valued at $145.00! The premiere issue of any price guide is always the most sought after, but covers featuring those in the Hall of Fame or with the potential, also are collected. Issue number six of *Legends Sports Memorabilia* magazine featuring Nolan Ryan, is valued at $325.00.

STAMPS & STICKERS (pp. 325-368)

Since their inception, stamps and stickers, like a sidecar to a motorcycle, have held a supporting role to trading cards. These listings cover the sticky subjects of baseball, basketball and football, ranging from the early sixties to the nineties, with a few sets of particular note. In Topps' 1962 stamp set, first baseman/outfielder Roy Sievers appears on both Kansas City and Philadelphia, and outfielder Johnny Callison's last name is misspelled as "Callizon." Topps also produced sets of cloth stickers in 1972 and 1977, identical to their respective year's cards, and issued sticker sets from 1981 to 1986, their 1984 being collection the company's biggest sticker set ever. Fleer produced stamps and stickers from 1982 until 1986; in 1983, Fleer's stamps could be doled out in a small Vend-A-Stamp dispenser, and stop action sequences of Eddie Murray, Tom Seaver and Mike Schmidt highlight the 1985 Fleer sticker set. Fleer's 1986-87 basketball sticker set contains rookie year stickers of Michael Jordan, Patrick Ewing and Dominique Wilkins, and while Topps boasts the largest assortment (12 sets from 1981 to 1988) of football stickers, in 1988 Italian company Panini, previously licensed in the early eighties by Topps to produce baseball stickers, issued their own set of pigskin peel-backs. These companies, along with collectors, hyave kept stickers and stamps firmly attached to the industry.

YEARBOOKS (pp. 381-421)

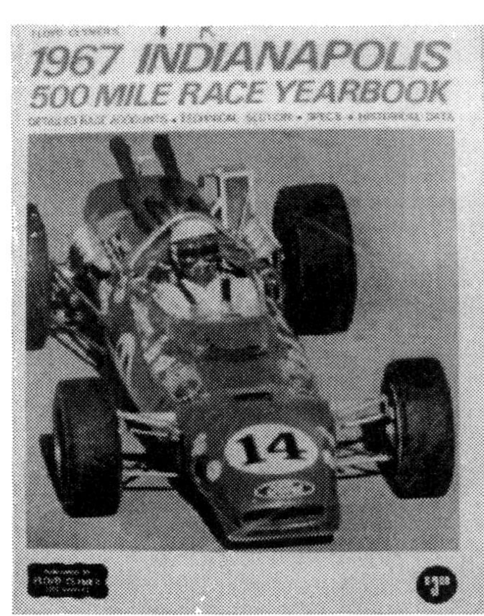

1967 Indianapolis 500 yearbook

Since the early thirties, yearbooks have been sources of information for baseball fans and collectors. The National League has its *Green Book*, while the *Red Book* has served American League zealots. In addition to these two league issued periodicals, each Major League Baseball team has its own yearbook that chronicles exploits of a past year. Basketball, football and hockey all produce various yearbooks, as does auto racing.

Yearbooks have developed and improved in quality in time, many proving to be more valuable than others.

One of the more sought after and highly valued basketball yearbooks is the 1951-52 Celtics media guide; valued at $125.00. In football, one of the more valuable yearbooks is the Green Bay Packers 1960 book which is valued at $50.00. For hockey, the 1947-48 New York Rangers yearbook is valued at $200.00.

MAGAZINE/PERIODICAL GRADING GUIDE

by Louis Porter, Jr.

Assessing the state of preservation of magazines and periodicals is one of the most difficult and highly controversial aspects of collecting them. This system of Grading is broken down into eight different categories:

— **Mint (M)**: The "perfect" book, no matter what its age. A Mint copy of a book has no physical flaws. The pages are perfectly white; there are no marks or blemishes of any kind (e.g.: rust, ink, scratches, etc.) around the staples; and the spine is flat and tight. Mint condition, in reality, is nearly impossible to find in older books, but is more of a possibility in more current publications. Magazines and periodicals in Mint condition often bring a minimum of 100% of the assessed value. Remember that prices arrived at for a Mint copy can be significantly greater than the Near Mint price.

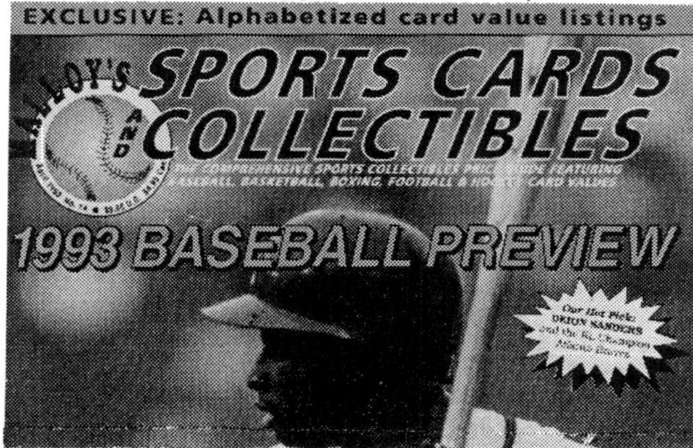

Near Mint - Mint

— **Near Mint (NM)**: Very similar to a Mint copy of a magazine or periodical, but it has very slight luster loss or a minor printing error. Most magazines and periodicals on the newsstand are in Near Mint condition. All the publication values in this book are for items in Near Mint condition.

— **Very Fine (VF)**: This is a very high grade for a magazine or periodical. There is slight wear beginning to show, most likely a small wrinkle or a minor stress line at the staples. Very slight yellowing of the pages is acceptable in this condition. Magazines and periodicals in Very Fine condition bring between 60 and 80% of the Near Mint value.

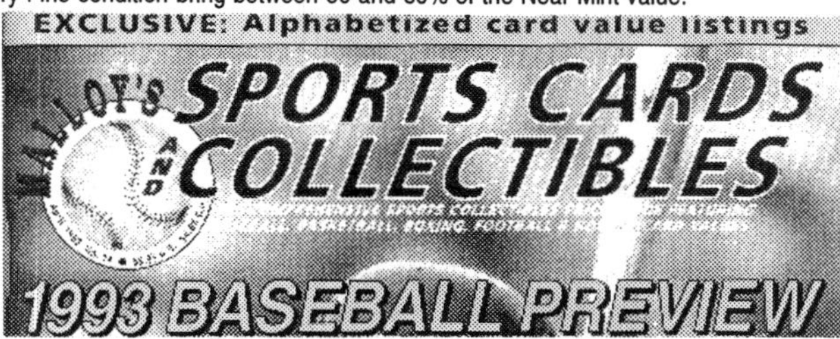

Fine - Very Fine (exhibiting staple stress)

— **Fine (F)**: A book of this grade will most likely display some wear, but will still have a tight cover. Stress lines around the staples are beginning to show, as is a slight yellowing of the pages, and minor color flaking is possible on the covers and edges. Magazines and periodicals in Fine condition bring between 40 and 60% of the Near Mint price.

— **Very Good (VG)**: This is the grade of an obviously read copy, with its original printing luster and gloss almost gone. There are minor areas of wear on the book, but none that deface the cover, and the pages are probably slightly yellowed. Magazines and periodicals in Very Good condition bring between 30 and 40% of the Near Mint price.

— **Good (G)**: This grade denotes an average used copy, still complete with both covers; a well-read copy with nothing missing inside. Magazines and periodicals in Good condition bring between 10 and 20% of the Near Mint price.

— **Fair (Fa)**: This is one of the lower grades, a copy which has been heavily read, is most probably soiled, and the cover of which may even have a small chunk torn out of it. Any magazine or periodical not attached to its interior pages, or which is incomplete (i.e.: is missing pages), is said to be in Fair condition. Key issues can and do bring more than the Good price, but most others are generally priced at between 30 and 70% of Good.

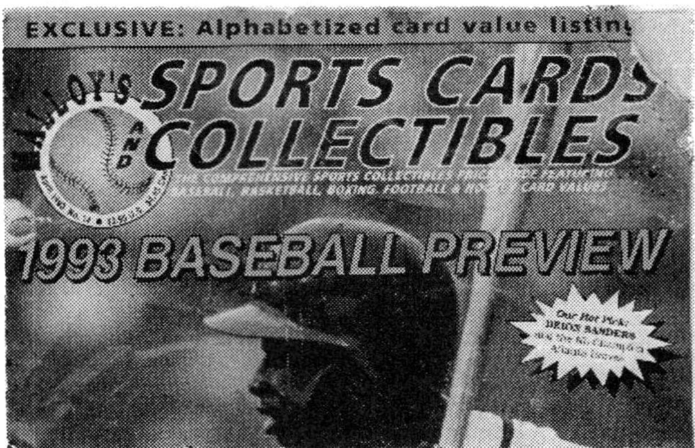

Poor - Fair (plenty of wear along with a torn cover)

— **Poor (Po)**: Damaged by various means such as water or accidental soiling, this type of book is totally unsuited for collecting purposes. At best, magazines and periodicals in Poor condition bring only 10 to 50% of the Good price.

In addition to these Grading terms, there are several general terms which are often used to describe key characteristics that may add to or detract from the Grade of a magazine or periodical. The more respectable dealers will usually fully describe a publication utilizing these abbreviations:

- **NOF, BC** = Name On Front Cover, Back Cover: Hand-written, in either pen or pencil. The size of the letter may also be described (e.g.: 1/2" NOBC,FC = Name On Back Cover, Front Cover, both 1/2" long)
- **RS** = Rusted Staples
- **TOS** = Tape On Spine: Usually characterized by the length of the tape used.
- **SPRL** = Spine Roll: A rolled spine causes "staircasing on the outer edge.
- **LT** = Light; DK = Dark
- **ST** = Stain (e.g.: 1/2" LT ST FC = 1/2" Light Stain on Front Cover)
- **FG** = Fading; BR = Browning
- **SM** = Stress Marks; ST = Stress Tears
- **WS** = Water Stains
- **AR** = Amateur Restoration: Denotes marker bleed through, usually on the spine, seen by looking inside the book. Trimming and AR are unethical, and severely downgrade a book, making it very difficult to sell.
- **M** = Missing
- **SS** = Store Stamp
- **CF** = Centerfold
- **PO** = Piece Out; CO = Chip Out
- **O/W** = Otherwise
- **WP** = White Pages
- **CC** = Corner Crease
- **RC** = Right Corner; LC = Left Corner
- **TR** = Tear
- **PG** = Page
- **BH** = Binder Holes
- **SC** or **SOBSC** = Subscription Crease: In the past, books that were subscribed for were folded in half before they were mailed, leaving a vertical crease down the center. Publications with SC are usually graded at VG.

GRADING GUIDE

Price listings appearing in **Malloy's Sports Collectibles Value Guide** are intended only to serve as a guide. They are not absolute prices at which dealers must sell, nor are they fixed values. These prices also are not a solicitation to buy or sell on the part of the publisher, editors, or any other party.

Paper: ticket stubs, autographs, posters, stamps and stickers

Boxed Items: games, figures, cars, bobbin' heads, cereal boxes

Coins & Medallions: coins and medallions

Books & Magazines: comics, media guides and yearbooks

Non-Paper: glasses, pins, buttons, plate and pennants

◂◂ Mint (Mt) Mint in box ▸▸

- coins = uncirculated

◂◂ Near Mint (NMt) ▸▸

Paper:
- very slight wear or color loss

Boxed Items:
- boxes have little deterioration
- games have been played
- cereal boxes can be flattened

Coins & Medallions:
- coins = **about uncirculated**
- no evidence of wear visible under magnifying glass

Books & Magazines:
- faint spine creases
- most newsstand books = NMt

Non-Paper:
- slightly off center

◂◂ Excellent (Ex) ▸▸

Paper:
- books = very fine
- slight discoloration
- a few minor defects
- slight yellowing of edges

Boxed Items:
- box has visible wear
- game boxes show stress
- contents slightly worn

Coins & Medallions:
- coins = **extremely fine**
- slight loss of detail

Books & Magazines:
- spine wear should not exceed one inch in length
- 1/16th corner creases
- near full cover gloss

Non-Paper:
- minor problems
- slight fading

◂◂ Very Good (VG) ▸▸

Paper:
- no intentional abuse
- slight discoloration
- slight scuffing
- minor rounding or creases of paper

Boxed Items:
- object attractive, minor wear and fading
- boxes may not be present

Coins & Medallions:
- coins = **fine**
- a bold example with all design elements clear, but lacking detail some slight edge nicks or scars.

Books & Magazines:
- obvious visible wear
- spine stress
- multiple corner creases
- very minor tears

Non-Paper:
- fading
- minor paint chips
- minor yellowing
- minor frayed ends

◂◂ Good (G) ▸▸

Paper:
- a well used object
- small creases
- loss of color

Boxed Items:
- object shows wear and fading
- cereal box - front/back only
- games - minor parts missing

Coins & Medallions:
- coins = **very good**
- well worn with slight corrosion or damage

Books & Magazines:
- well worn
- up to 2" tears on spine
- browning
- tape repairs

Non-Paper:
- fading
- definite paint chipping
- yellowing and scratches
- frayed

◂◂ Fair (F) ▸▸

Paper:
- excessive wear
- damaged corners
- heavy creases

Boxed Items:
- no box
- games partially crushed

Coins & Medallions:
- coins = good
- damaged or mutilated
- corroded or broken

Books & Magazines:
- missing some sections
- missing part of cover
- extremely worn

Non-Paper:
- heavy fading
- heavy paint chips
- heavy scratches and wear
- foxing & heavy yellowing

AUTOGRAPH COLLECTING

by Mark Jordan

Collecting sports autographs is something both casual and serious collectors can enjoy equally. Whether you are a fan that gets signatures at a ballpark, goes to shows to meet players, writes players through the mail or uses the services of a dealer, autograph collecting can be fun for all ages.

The biggest segment of the sports autograph market is current players. Whether it is a super star or a common player, active players attract the initial interest among collectors. If you are not able to get an autograph in person, writing requests through the mail may be the next best method. This method, however, is not foolproof.

Most people that receive a reply from an autograph request in the mail feel they have a real autograph of that person, but that can be an erroneous assumption. Sometimes that signature can be signed by another person or by a machine. Some superstars like Nolan Ryan receive over 10,000 pieces of mail a week. It's obviously impossible to sign that many autographs requests – even 200 mail requests a week are tough for a ball player to keep up with. These requests are often answered by the team's public relations department, who send out unsigned photos or an autographed photo signed by someone else. These are called secretarial signatures and although there is no attempt to forge these signatures for profit, they are still considered unauthentic and can find their way onto a dealer's price lists or tables.

It has been estimated that over 50 current players have full or part time help in answering their fan mail. Knowing who actually signs their autograph requests takes knowledgeable dealers and collectors.

The natural progression from collecting current player and living Hall of Fame autographs is to seek signatures of deceased Hall of Famers. Having an autograph is a more personal collectible than a baseball card. The allure of owning an item Babe Ruth actually held in his hands is appealing to many collectors. With the wide publicity about unauthentic autographs surfacing in the hobby, the question facing many collectors is – how can one be sure the deceased Hall of Famer's signature is real?

In my estimation, while only 1-2 percent of all autographs on the market are not genuine, a lot of that percentage is seen in the deceased Hall of Fame category. There are simply far too many examples of non authentic Lou Gehrig, Roger Maris, Babe Ruth and Ty Cobb signatures out on the market.

Several years ago the common forged items were pieces of paper, referred to as "cuts" among collectors. It's fairly easy for a forger to get an old piece of paper and sign the Hall of Famer's name on it. Collectors became suspicious of these items, so forgers began signing team sheets. A typical sheet would have Ruth, Gehrig, and from five to 15 other teammates. Collectors had more confidence in these pieces because they didn't want to believe every signature was forged, when in fact they were. More recently photos, letters and single signed baseballs have surfaced. Many of the premium items on the market now carry prices of $1,000 or more and forging autographs can be quite a lucrative activity for a dishonest person.

Single signed baseballs of Hall of Famers are very popular among collectors right now. Players deceased prior to 1970 are uncommon, and the prices for such balls are many times more than those on an album page. Team baseballs from World Series winners are also in demand and can fetch high prices for the year a team won the Series.

Gold Hall of Fame plaques and Perez Steele postcards are also popular. The gold Hall of Fame plaques can be bought unsigned through the mail, from the Hall of Fame gift shop, and then sent out to get signed. Plaques of deceased stars are available through dealers. These gold plaque cards are an extremely nice and affordable way to start collecting Hall of Famers.

When Dale Murphy won two MVP awards in the mid 1980s, he was one of the first baseball players to use the autopen to answer requests. The autopen, a mechanical device that duplicates a person's signature exactly the same way every time, is made with a matrix from the real signature. Entertainers, public officials, and other people who don't have time to answer their mail use autopens.

The only way to tell if a person is using an autopen is to compare examples of signatures being returned in the mail. If they match *exactly*, then this is an indication of autopen use.

Clubhouse signatures on baseballs is an area about which not much has been reported. Each day a home or visiting player goes into his clubhouse there are dozens of balls, for each member of the team to sign, that are used to keep for themselves, give to friends or charity or to be used as prizes. Every player is supposed to sign each day. In reality players don't sign everyday, and to be truthful, rarely sign at all. The "missing" signatures are then signed by clubhouse personnel, such as the equipment manager, or bat boys who can surprisingly copy players' signatures quite well. Players like Carl Yastrzemski, Mickey Mantle, and Roger Maris were players that often did not sign these balls. Many of these balls make it to dealer tables or price lists without the disclaimer regarding unauthentic signatures on the balls, and this is a tough area to accurately determine what is good and what is not. One must determine which players don't sign, but since many collectors and dealers have clubhouse connections for obtaining material, this information is available for many teams.

Photographs, index cards, baseball cards, checks, letters, and documents such as contracts are other items sought by collectors. The best advice to new collectors is to get particular items signed. While scraps of paper, signatures on programs or other insignificant items have little value, if you find yourself sitting next to Troy Aikman on an airplane, by all means get him to sign your boarding pass. But if you are meeting someone in person, take the time to get something special for the celebrity to sign. It will show your subject that you took the time to find something special and you will be able to enjoy it for years to come.

Many players like Bo Jackson, Ryne Sandberg, Nolan Ryan, Mike Schmidt and Will Clark rarely or never do shows and therefore a big demand for their signatures exist. Often these athlete's signatures are forged. The key to protecting yourself if you can't get in-person signatures is to know what to look for.

Ask dealers questions, such as where they obtained the item. Insist on a lifetime guarantee of authenticity from the dealer; request an invoice. If the dealer is unwilling to provide any of this, shop for a dealer who will provide these guarantees. Dealers who are members of the Sports Collectors Association International all have been screened before they are accepted for membership and have agreed to abide by a strict code of ethics. Ask around at shows or get recommendations from other collectors on who is reputable.

This guide is helpful in helping determine the value of your items. These prices are an estimate of retail values. When selling to a dealer, collectors can only expect to receive 30% to 50 % of price guide value.

AUTOGRAPHS

AUTO RACING: INACTIVE DRIVERS

Allison, Bobby
- Cut signature 6.00
- Personal document 15.00
- 3x5 Card 8.00
- 8x10 Photo 25.00

Baker, Buck
- Cut signature 4.00
- Personal document 10.00
- 3x5 Card 6.00
- 8x10 Photo 18.00

Baker, Buddy
- Cut signature 4.00
- Personal document 9.00
- 3x5 Card 6.00
- 8x10 Photo 20.00

Bettenhausen, Tony
- Cut signature 3.00
- Personal document 10.00
- 3x5 Card 5.00
- 8x10 Photo 15.00

Bonnett, Neil
- Cut signature 4.00
- Personal document 12.00
- 3x5 Card 6.00
- 8x10 Photo 18.00

Bryan, Jimmy
- Cut signature 4.00
- Personal document 10.00
- 3x5 Card 6.00
- 8x10 Photo 18.00

Byron, Red
- Cut signature 4.00
- Personal document 12.00
- 3x5 Card 6.00
- 8x10 Photo 18.00

Cooper, Earl
- Cut signature 4.00
- Personal document 11.00
- 3x5 Card 6.00
- 8x10 Photo 18.00

DePalma, Ralph
- Cut signature 4.00
- Personal document 12.00
- 3x5 Card 6.00
- 8x10 Photo 18.00

Flock, Tim
- Cut signature 4.00
- Personal document 12.00
- 3x5 Card 6.00
- 8x10 Photo 18.00

Harroun, Ray
- Cut signature 4.00
- Personal document 10.00
- 3x5 Card 6.00
- 8x10 Photo 18.00

Isaac, Bobby
- Cut signature 4.00
- Personal document 12.00
- 3x5 Card 6.00
- 8x10 Photo 18.00

Jarrett, Ned
- Cut signature 5.00
- Personal document 11.00
- 3x5 Card 7.00
- 8x10 Photo 20.00

Johnson, Junior
- Cut signature 10.00
- Personal document 19.00
- 3x5 Card 12.00
- 8x10 Photo 29.00

Jones, Parnelli
- Cut signature 5.00
- Personal document 24.00
- 3x5 Card 7.00
- 8x10 Photo 22.00

Lorenzen, Fred
- Cut signature 6.00
- Personal document 12.00
- 3x5 Card 8.00
- 8x10 Photo 18.00

Mays, Rex
- Cut signature 5.00
- Personal document 11.00
- 3x5 Card 7.00
- 8x10 Photo 17.00

Meyer, Louis
- Cut signature 4.00
- Personal document 10.00
- 3x5 Card 6.00
- 8x10 Photo 18.00

Milton, Tommy
- Cut signature 5.00
- Personal document 11.00
- 3x5 Card 7.00
- 8x10 Photo 17.00

Murphy, Jimmy
- Cut signature 4.00
- Personal document 10.00
- 3x5 Card 6.00
- 8x10 Photo 18.00

Parsons, Benny
- Cut signature 5.00
- Personal document 12.00
- 3x5 Card 7.00
- 9x10 Photo 22.00

Paschal, Jim
- Cut signature 4.00
- Personal document 10.00
- 3x5 Card 6.00
- 8x10 Photo 18.00

Pearson, David
- Cut signature 5.00
- Personal document 18.00
- 3x5 Card 7.00
- 8x10 Photo 22.00

Petty, Lee
- Cut signature 5.00
- Personal document 9.00
- 3x5 Card 8.00
- 8x10 Photo 35.00

Petty, Richard

Richard Petty

- Cut signature 10.00
- Personal document 30.00
- 3x5 Card 15.00
- 8x10 Photo 45.00

Rexford, Bill
- Cut signature 4.00
- Personal document 9.00
- 3x5 Card 6.00
- 8x10 Photo 18.00

Roberts, Fireball
- Cut signature 7.00
- Personal document 13.00
- 3x5 Card 10.00
- 8x10 Photo 18.00

Rose, Mauri
- Cut signature 4.00
- Personal document 9.00
- 3x5 Card 6.00
- 8x10 Photo 18.00

Rutherford, Johnny
- Cut signature 6.00
- Personal document 17.00
- 3x5 Card 8.00
- 8x10 Photo 25.00

Shaw, Wilbur
- Cut signature 4.00
- Personal document 9.00
- 3x5 Card 7.00
- 8x10 Photo 18.00

Stewart, Jackie
- Cut signature 7.00
- Personal document 20.00
- 3x5 Card 9.00
- 8x10 Photo 30.00

Thomas, Herb
- Cut signature 4.00
- Personal document 10.00
- 3x5 Card 6.00
- 8x10 Photo 18.00

Unser, Bobby
Cut signature 6.00
Personal document 18.00
3x5 Card 8.00
8x10 Photo 25.00

Ward, Rodger
Cut signature 5.00
Personal document 11.00
3x5 Card 7.00
8x10 Photo 17.00

Weatherly, Joe
Cut signature 4.00
Personal document 9.00
3x5 Card 6.00
8x10 Photo 18.00

White, Rex
Cut signature 4.00
Personal document 9.00
3x5 Card 6.00
8x10 Photo 18.00

Vukovich, Bill
Cut signature 6.00
Personal document 12.00
3x5 Card 8.00
8x10 Photo 23.00

Yarborough, Cale
Cut signature 6.00
Personal document 18.00
3x5 Card 9.00
8x10 Photo 25.00

AUTO RACING: ACTIVE DRIVERS

Allison, Davey
Cut signature 6.00
Personal document 15.00
3x5 Card 8.00
8x10 Photo 25.00

Andretti, John
Cut signature 3.00
Personal document 10.00
3x5 Card 4.00
8x10 Photo 15.00

Andretti, Mario
Cut signature 6.00
Personal document 17.00
3x5 Card 8.00
8x10 Photo 28.00

Andretti, Michael
Cut signature 5.00
Personal document 10.00
3x5 Card 7.00
8x10 Photo 25.00

Bodine, Brett
Cut signature 3.00
Personal document 9.50
3x5 Card 4.00
8x10 Photo 15.00

Bodine, Geoff
Cut signature 4.00
Personal document 11.00
3x5 Card 5.00
8x10 Photo 17.00

Brayton, Scott
Cut signature 3.00
Personal document 6.00
3x5 Card 4.00
8x10 Photo 12.00

Cheever, Eddie
Cut signature 4.00
Personal document 6.00
3x5 Card 5.00
8x10 Photo 15.00

Cope, Derrick
Cut signature 3.00
Personal document 9.50
3x5 Card 4.00
8x10 Photo 15.00

Earnhardt, Dale
Cut signature 7.00
Personal document 22.00
3x5 Card 9.00
8x10 Photo 30.00

Elliott, Bill
Cut signature 6.00
Personal document 15.00
3x5 Card 8.00
8x10 Photo 25.00

Fittipaldi, Emerson
Cut signature 6.00
Personal document 12.00
3x5 Card 8.00
8x10 Photo 25.00

Foyt, A.J.
Cut signature 6.00
Personal document 17.00
3x5 Card 8.00
8x10 Photo 28.00

Gant, Harry
Cut signature 5.00
Personal document 12.00
3x5 Card 6.00
8x10 Photo 18.00

Goodyear, Scott
Cut signature 3.00
Personal document 5.00
3x5 Card 4.00
8x10 Photo 12.00

Gordon, Jeff
Cut signature 5.00
Personal document 5.00
3x5 Card 7.00
8x10 Photo 25.00

Irvan, Ernie
Cut signature 4.00
Personal document 12.00
3x5 Card 6.00
8x10 Photo 20.00

Jarrett, Dale
Cut signature 4.00
Personal document 11.00
3x5 Card 6.00
8x10 Photo 20.00

Johncock, Gordon
Cut signature 4.00
Personal document 20.00
3x5 Card 6.00
8x10 Photo 20.00

Kulwicki, Alan
Cut signature 2.00
Personal document 6.00
3x5 Card 5.00
8x10 Photo 9.00

Labonte, Bobby
Cut signature 3.00
Personal document 7.00
3x5 Card 4.00
8x10 Photo 12.00

Labonte, Terry
Cut signature 3.00
Personal document 7.50
3x5 Card 4.00
8x10 Photo 15.00

Little, Chad
Cut signature 3.00
Personal document 9.50
3x5 Card 4.00
8x10 Photo 15.00

Luyendyk, Arie
Cut signature 4.00
Personal document 6.00
3x5 Card 6.00
8x10 Photo 20.00

Mansell, Nigel
Cut signature 6.00
Personal document 16.00
3x5 Card 8.00
8x10 Photo 30.00

Marlin, Sterling
Cut signature 3.00
Personal document 11.00
3x5 Card 4.00
8x10 Photo 15.00

Martin, Mark
Cut signature 4.00

- Personal document 13.00
- 3x5 Card 6.00
- 8x10 Photo 20.00

Mast, Rick
- Cut signature 4.00
- Personal document 1.00
- 3x5 Card 5.00
- 8x10 Photo 17.00

Mears, Rick
- Cut signature 6.00
- Personal document 16.00
- 3x5 Card 8.00
- 8x10 Photo 25.00

Parsons, Phil
- Cut signature 3.00
- Personal document 13.00
- 3x5 Card 4.00
- 8x10 Photo 15.00

Petty, Kyle
- Cut signature 5.00
- Personal document 15.00
- 3x5 Card 7.00
- 8x10 Photo 25.00

Piquet, Nelson
- Cut signature 4.00
- Personal document 10.00
- 3x5 Card 6.00
- 8x10 Photo 20.00

Prost, Alain
- Cut signature 3.00
- Personal document 15.00
- 3x5 Card 4.00
- 8x10 Photo 12.00

Pruett, Scott
- Cut signature 4.00
- Personal document 12.00
- 3x5 Card 9.00
- 8x10 Photo 19.00

Rahal, Bobby
- Cut signature 4.00
- Personal document 14.00
- 3x5 Card 6.00
- 8x10 Photo 20.00

Rudd, Ricky

Ricky Rudd

- Cut signature 3.00
- Personal document 7.00
- 3x5 Card 5.00
- 8x10 Photo 13.00

Schrader, Ken
- Cut signature 3.00
- Personal document 9.00
- 3x5 Card 4.00
- 8x10 Photo 15.00

Senna, Ayrton
- Cut signature 3.00
- Personal document 13.00
- 3x5 Card 4.00
- 8x10 Photo 12.00

Shepherd, Morgan
- Cut signature 2.00
- Personal document 9.00
- 3x5 Card 3.00
- 8x10 Photo 14.00

Sneva, Tom
- Cut signature 4.00
- Personal document 10.00
- 3x5 Card 6.00
- 8x10 Photo 20.00

Stricklin, Hut
- Cut signature 3.00
- Personal document 8.00
- 3x5 Card 4.00
- 8x10 Photo 12.00

Sullivan, Danny
- Cut signature 7.00
- Personal document 16.00
- 3x5 Card 9.00
- 8x10 Photo 20.00

Trickle, Dick
- Cut signature 3.00
- Personal document 8.00
- 3x5 Card 4.00
- 8x10 Photo 12.00

Unser, Al
- Cut signature 7.00
- Personal document 19.00
- 3x5 Card 9.00
- 8x10 Photo 30.00

Unser Jr., Al
- Cut signature 6.00
- Personal document 12.00
- 3x5 Card 8.00
- 8x10 Photo 25.00

Wallace, Kenny
- Cut signature 3.00
- Personal document 8.00
- 3x5 Card 4.00
- 8x10 Photo 12.00

Wallace, Rusty
- Cut signature 6.00
- Personal document 7.00
- 3x5 Card 8.00
- 8x10 Photo 25.00

Waltrip, Darrell
- Cut signature 6.00
- Personal document 16.00
- 3x5 Card 8.00
- 8x10 Photo 25.00

BASEBALL: HALL OF FAME

Aaron, Hank
- Baseball 40.00
- Cut signature 4.00
- Personal document 35.00
- 3x5 Card 7.00
- 8x10 Photo 30.00
- Perez-Steele Card 47.00
- HOF Plaque 13.00

Alexander, Grover
- Baseball 1,900.00
- Cut signature 210.00
- Personal document 550.00
- 3x5 Card 290.00
- 8x10 Photo 525.00
- HOF Plaque 800.00

Alston, Walter
- Baseball 80.00
- Cut signature 7.00
- Personal document 75.00
- 3x5 Card 20.00
- 8x10 Photo 45.00
- Perez-Steele Card 525.00
- HOF Plaque 55.00

Anson, Cap
- Baseball 5,000.00
- Cut signature 1,275.00
- Personal document 1,500.00
- 3x5 Card 1,000.00
- 8x10 Photo 2,800.00

Aparicio, Luis

Luis Aparicio

- Baseball 21.00
- Cut signature 4.00
- Personal document 18.00
- 3x5 Card 8.00
- 8x10 Photo 14.00
- Perez-Steele Card 27.00
- HOF Plaque 14.00

Luke Appling

Appling, Luke
- Baseball 25.00

Frank "Home Run" Baker

Cut signature	5.00
Personal document	13.00
3x5 Card	11.00
8x10 Photo	24.00
Perez-Steele Card	65.00
HOF Plaque	12.00

Averill, Earl

Baseball	72.00
Cut signature	8.00
Personal document	50.00
3x5 Card	17.00
8x10 Photo	35.00
Perez-Steele Card	660.00
HOF Plaque	22.00

Baker, Frank

Baseball	680.00
Cut signature	55.00
Personal document	105.00
3x5 Card	125.00
8x10 Photo	185.00
HOF Plaque	290.00

Bancroft, Davey

Baseball	420.00
Cut signature	32.00
Personal document	200.00
3x5 Card	55.00
8x10 Photo	170.00
HOF Plaque	390.00

Banks, Ernie

Baseball	22.00
Cut signature	4.00
Personal document	21.00
3x5 Card	6.00
8x10 Photo	20.00
Perez-Steele Card	27.00
HOF Plaque	15.00

Barlick, Al

Baseball	22.00
Cut signature	5.00
Personal document	15.00
3x5 Card	7.00
8x10 Photo	10.00
Perez-Steele Card	37.50
HOF Plaque	17.00

Barrow, Ed

Baseball	850.00
Cut signature	42.00
Personal document	200.00
3x5 Card	80.00
8x10 Photo	190.00

Beckley, Jake

Baseball	3,400.00
Cut signature	1,425.00
Personal document	2,220.00
3x5 Card	1,925.00
8x10 Photo	3,600.00

Bell, Cool Papa

Baseball	55.00
Cut signature	6.00

James "Cool Papa" Bell

Personal document	50.00
3x5 Card	13.00
8x10 Photo	35.00
Perez-Steele Card	85.00
HOF Plaque	20.00

Bench, Johnny

Baseball	24.00
Cut signature	6.00
Personal document	25.00
3x5 Card	5.00
8x10 Photo	18.00
Perez-Steele Card	72.00
HOF Plaque	21.00

Bender, Chief

Baseball	1,100.00
Cut signature	115.00
Personal document	400.00
3x5 Card	175.00
8x10 Photo	425.00
HOF Plaque	925.00

Berra, Yogi

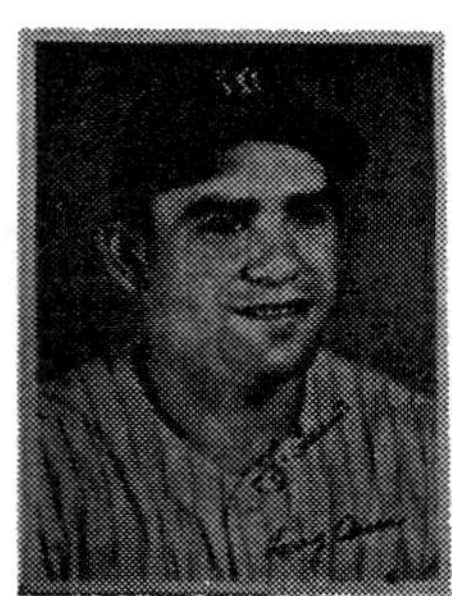

Yogi Berra

Baseball	25.00
Cut signature	5.00
Personal document	21.00
3x5 Card	9.00
8x10 Photo	20.00
Perez-Steele Card	65.00
HOF Plaque	16.00

Bottomley, Jim

Baseball	935.00
Cut signature	110.00
Personal document	250.00
3x5 Card	225.00
8x10 Photo	265.00

Boudreau, Lou

Baseball	16.00
Cut signature	4.00
Personal document	14.00
3x5 Card	6.00
8x10 Photo	9.00
Perez-Steele Card	26.00
HOF Plaque	11.00

Bresnehan, Roger
- Baseball 2,275.00
- Cut signature 360.00
- Personal document 650.00
- 3x5 Card 475.00
- 8x10 Photo 1,175.00

Brock, Lou
- Baseball 19.50
- Cut signature 4.00
- Personal document 16.00
- 3x5 Card 4.50
- 8x10 Photo 13.00
- Perez-Steele Card 42.00
- HOF Plaque 11.00

Brouthers, Dan
- Baseball 3,900.00
- Cut signature 1,550.00
- Personal document 2,200.00
- 3x5 Card 2,700.00
- 8x10 Photo 3,400.00

Brown, Mordecai
- Baseball 2,725.00
- Cut signature 275.00
- Personal document 500.00
- 3x5 Card 410.00
- 8x10 Photo 450.00

Bulkeley, Morgan
- Baseball 4,100.00
- Cut signature 1,500.00
- Personal document 2,300.00
- 3x5 Card 2,450.00
- 8x10 Photo 3,675.00

Burkett, Jesse
- Baseball 3,425.00
- Cut signature 375.00
- Personal document 925.00
- 3x5 Card 775.00
- 8x10 Photo 1,425.00
- HOF Plaque 890.00

Campanella, Roy
- Baseball 1,275.00
- Cut signature 135.00
- Personal document 600.00
- 3x5 Card 235.00
- 8x10 Photo 435.00
- Perez-Steele Card 325.00
- HOF Plaque 615.00

Carew, Rod
- Baseball 775.00
- Cut signature 125.00
- Personal document 275.00
- 3x5 Card 145.00
- 8x10 Photo 250.00
- Perez-Steele Card 400.00
- HOF Plaque 350.00

Carey, Max
- Baseball 77.00
- Cut signature 6.00
- Personal document 60.00
- 3x5 Card 15.00
- 8x10 Photo 45.00
- HOF Plaque 36.00

Cartwright, Alexander
- Cut signature 725.00
- Personal document 2,200.00
- 3x5 Card 875.00
- 8x10 Photo 2625.00

Chadwick, Henry
- Cut signature 1,600.00
- Personal document 1,950.00
- 3x5 Card 1,650.00
- 8x10 Photo 3,575.00

Chance, Frank
- Baseball 3,700.00
- Cut signature 750.00
- Personal document 1,450.00
- 3x5 Card 1,225.00
- 8x10 Photo 1,700.00

Chandler, Happy

Happy Chandler

- Baseball 40.00
- Cut signature 5.00
- Personal document 29.00
- 3x5 Card 11.00
- 8x10 Photo 35.00
- Perez-Steele Card 75.00
- HOF Plaque 15.00

Charleston, Oscar
- Baseball 4,725.00
- Cut signature 1,125.00
- Personal document 975.00
- 3x5 Card 1,725.00
- 8x10 Photo 2,200.00

Chesbro, Jack
- Baseball 5,375.00
- Cut signature 1,200.00
- Personal document 1,475.00
- 3x5 Card 1,875.00
- 8x10 Photo 2,625.00

Clarke, Fred
- Baseball 675.00
- Cut signature 95.00
- Personal document 200.00
- 3x5 Card 150.00
- 8x10 Photo 275.00
- HOF Plaque 325.00

Clarkson, John
- Cut signature 2,100.00
- Personal document 1,975.00
- 3x5 Card 3,375.00
- 8x10 Photo 4,250.00

Clemente, Roberto
- Baseball 810.00
- Cut signature 125.00
- Personal document 225.00
- 3x5 Card 155.00
- 8x10 Photo 275.00

Cobb, Ty
- Baseball 1,850.00
- Cut signature 175.00
- Personal document 750.00
- 3x5 Card 275.00
- 8x10 Photo 575.00
- HOF Plaque 925.00

Cochrane, Mickey
- Baseball 495.00
- Cut signature 65.00
- Personal document 275.00
- 3x5 Card 125.00
- 8x10 Photo 250.00
- HOF Plaque 375.00

Collins, Eddie
- Baseball 1,750.00
- Cut signature 100.00
- Personal document 1500.00
- 3x5 Card 175.00
- 8x10 Photo 3751.00
- HOF Plaque 650.00

Collins, Jimmy
- Baseball 4,100.00
- Cut signature 750.00
- Personal document 1,000.00
- 3x5 Card 1,100.00
- 8x10 Photo 1,800.00

Combs, Earle
- Baseball 2,000.00
- Cut signature 375.00
- Personal document 500.00
- 3x5 Card 550.00
- 8x10 Photo 900.00
- HOF Plaque 1,100.00

Comiskey, Charles
- Baseball 2,800.00
- Cut signature 375.00
- Personal document 450.00
- 3x5 Card 395.00
- 8x10 Photo 690.00

Conlan, Jocko
- Baseball 35.00
- Cut signature 5.00
- Personal document 12.00
- 3x5 Card 10.00
- 8x10 Photo 22.00
- Perez-Steele Card 115.00
- HOF Plaque 25.00

Connolly, Tom
- Baseball 1,300.00
- Cut signature 250.00
- Personal document 650.00
- 3x5 Card 275.00
- 8x10 Photo 750.00
- HOF Plaque 790.00

Connor, Roger
- Baseball 4,900.00
- Cut signature 1,300.00
- Personal document 2,900.00
- 3x5 Card 2,275.00
- 8x10 Photo 3,400.00

Coveleski, Stan
- Baseball 135.00
- Cut signature 11.00
- Personal document 19.00
- 3x5 Card 17.00
- 8x10 Photo 25.00
- Perez-Steele Card 475.00
- HOF Plaque 35.00

Crawford, Sam
- Baseball 1,250.00
- Cut signature 45.00
- Personal document 220.00
- 3x5 Card 70.00
- 8x10 Photo 210.00
- HOF Plaque 225.00

Cronin, Joe
- Baseball 145.00
- Cut signature 14.00

Personal document 450.00
3x5 Card 15.00
8x10 Photo 45.00
Perez-Steele Card 725.00
HOF Plaque 35.00

Cummings, Candy
Cut signature 1,950.00
Personal document 4,100.00
3x5 Card 3,400.00
8x10 Photo 5,500.00

Cuyler, KiKi
Baseball 950.00
Cut signature 100.00
Personal document 350.00
3x5 Card 185.00
8x10 Photo 425.00

Dandridge, Ray
Baseball 35.00
Cut signature 6.00
Personal document 15.00
3x5 Card 7.00
8x10 Photo 17.00
Perez-Steele Card 28.00
HOF Plaque 15.00

Dean, Dizzy
Baseball 600.00
Cut signature 37.00
Personal document 150.00
3x5 Card 60.00
8x10 Photo 125.00
HOF Plaque 110.00

Delahanty, Ed
Cut signature 1,800.00
Personal document 2,100.00
3x5 Card 2,300.00
8x10 Photo 4,700.00

Dickey, Bill
Baseball 35.00
Cut signature 6.00
Personal document 60.00
3x5 Card 12.00
8x10 Photo 27.00
Perez-Steele Card 95.00
HOF Plaque 25.00

Dihigo, Martin
Baseball 3,750.00
Cut signature 750.00
Personal document 1,850.00
3x5 Card 1,200.00
8x10 Photo 2,500.00

DiMaggio, Joe
Baseball 175.00
Cut signature 15.00
Personal document 185.00
3x5 Card 25.00
8x10 Photo 45.00
Perez-Steele Card 325.00
HOF Plaque 45.00

Doerr, Bobby
Baseball 25.00
Cut signature 7.00
Personal document 9.00
3x5 Card 7.00
8x10 Photo 10.00
Perez-Steele Card 25.00
HOF Plaque 11.00

Drysdale, Don
Baseball 15.00
Cut signature 3.00
Personal document 14.00
3x5 Card 6.00
8x10 Photo 12.00
Perez-Steele Card 40.00
HOF Plaque 15.00

Don Drysdale

Duffy, Hugh
Baseball 1,200.00
Cut signature 300.00
Personal document 950.00
3x5 Card 300.00
8x10 Photo 475.00
HOF Plaque 1,200.00

Evans, Billy
Baseball 1,450.00
Cut signature 150.00
Personal document 300.00
3x5 Card 195.00
8x10 Photo 550.00

Evers, Johnny
Baseball 2,800.00
Cut signature 250.00
Personal document 1,150.00
3x5 Card 325.00
8x10 Photo 950.00
HOF Plaque 1,300.00

Ewing, Buck
Cut signature 1,700.00
Personal document 4,000.00
3x5 Card 3,100.00
8x10 Photo 4,900.00

Faber, Red
Baseball 340.00
Cut signature 12.00
Personal document 45.00
3x5 Card 30.00
8x10 Photo 60.00
HOF Plaque 65.00

Feller, Bob

Bob Feller

Baseball 20.00
Cut signature 5.00
Personal document 23.00
3x5 Card 7.00
8x10 Photo 15.00
Perez-Steele Card 35.00
HOF Plaque 10.00

Ferrell, Rick
Baseball 20.00
Cut signature 5.00
Personal document 25.00
3x5 Card 14.00
8x10 Photo 15.00
Perez-Steele Card 45.00
HOF Plaque 15.00

Fingers, Rollie
Baseball 30.00
Cut signature 9.00
3x5 Card 7.00
8x10 Photo 20.00
HOF Plaque 10.00

Flick, Elmer
Baseball 180.00
Cut signature 17.00
Personal document 150.00
3x5 Card 30.00
8x10 Photo 100.00
HOF Plaque 200.00

Ford, Whitey
Baseball 36.00
Cut signature 6.00
Personal document 32.00
3x5 Card 10.00
8x10 Photo 30.00
Perez-Steele Card 50.00
HOF Plaque 15.00

Foster, Rube
Baseball 4,650.00
Cut signature 2,675.00
Personal document 5,650.00
3x5 Card 4,500.00
8x10 Photo 6,750.00

Foxx, Jimmie
Baseball 435.00
Cut signature 75.00
Personal document 425.00
3x5 Card 135.00
8x10 Photo 275.00
HOF Plaque 575.00

Frick, Ford
Baseball 130.00
Cut signature 22.00
Personal document 75.00
3x5 Card 27.00
8x10 Photo 55.00
HOF Plaque 65.00

Frisch, Frankie
Baseball 230.00
Cut signature 22.00
Personal document 125.00
3x5 Card 50.00
8x10 Photo 90.00
HOF Plaque 115.00

Galvin, Pud
Baseball 4,350.00
Cut signature 1,875.00
Personal document 3,350.00
3x5 Card 3,200.00
8x10 Photo 3,675.00

Gehrig, Lou
Baseball 650.00
Cut signature 3,800.00
Personal document 1,400.00
3x5 Card 850.00
8x10 Photo 1,950.00

Gehringer, Charlie
Baseball 35.00
Cut signature 5.00
Personal document 12.00
3x5 Card 8.00
8x10 Photo 15.00
HOF Plaque 15.00

Gibson, Bob
Baseball 27.00
Cut signature 6.00
Personal document 12.00
3x5 Card 7.00
8x10 Photo 20.00
Perez-Steele Card 40.00
HOF Plaque 15.00

Gibson, Josh

Roberto Clemente

Baseball	3,700.00
Cut signature	1,150.00
Personal document	2,300.00
3x5 Card	2,150.00
8x10 Photo	2,500.00

Giles, Warren

Baseball	125.00
Cut signature	17.50
Personal document	42.00
3x5 Card	35.00
8x10 Photo	45.00

Gomez, Lefty

Baseball	60.00
Cut signature	10.00
Personal document	80.00
3x5 Card	15.00
8x10 Photo	35.00
Perez-Steele Card	135.00
HOF Plaque	25.00

Goslin, Goose

Baseball	310.00
Cut signature	45.00
Personal document	315.00
3x5 Card	55.00
8x10 Photo	145.00
HOF Plaque	490.00

Greenberg, Hank

Baseball	75.00
Cut signature	12.00
Personal document	265.00
3x5 Card	22.00
8x10 Photo	45.00
Perez-Steele Card	475.00
HOF Plaque	50.00

Griffith, Clark

Baseball	475.00
Cut signature	110.00
Personal document	40.00
3x5 Card	25.00
8x10 Photo	55.00
HOF Plaque	45.00

Grimes, Burleigh

Baseball	65.00
Cut signature	9.00
Personal document	27.00
3x5 Card	25.00
8x10 Photo	30.00
Perez-Steele Card	395.00
HOF Plaque	25.00

Grove, Lefty

Baseball	195.00
Cut signature	20.00
Personal document	45.00
3x5 Card	35.00
8x10 Photo	55.00
HOF Plaque	60.00

Hafey, Chick

Baseball	175.00
Cut signature	25.00
Personal document	100.00
3x5 Card	30.00
8x10 Photo	60.00
HOF Plaque	70.00

Haines, Jesse

Baseball	245.00
Cut signature	15.00

Bob Gibson, Bob Feller, Charles Gehringer

Joe DiMaggio and Mickey Mantle, and Mickey Mantle

- Personal document 125.00
- 3x5 Card 25.00
- 8x10 Photo 65.00
- HOF Plaque 70.00

Hamilton, Billy

- Baseball 4,250.00
- Cut signature 1,275.00
- Personal document 2,700.00
- 3x5 Card 2,500.00
- 8x10 Photo 2,950.00

Harridge, Will

- Baseball 575.00
- Cut signature 42.00
- Personal document 150.00
- 3x5 Card 70.00
- 8x10 Photo 145.00

Harris, Bucky

- Baseball 245.00
- Cut signature 25.00
- Personal document 65.00
- 3x5 Card 35.00
- 8x10 Photo 80.00
- HOF Plaque 135.00

Hartnett, Gabby

- Baseball 510.00
- Cut signature 31.00
- Personal document 230.00
- 3x5 Card 58.00
- 8x10 Photo 130.00
- HOF Plaque 210.00

Heilmann, Harry

- Baseball 1560.00
- Cut signature 195.00
- Personal document 385.00
- 3x5 Card 275.00
- 8x10 Photo 460.00

Herman, Billy

- Baseball 20.00
- Cut signature 6.00
- Personal document 17.00
- 3x5 Card 5.00
- 8x10 Photo 16.00
- Perez-Steele Card 40.00
- HOF Plaque 11.00

Hooper, Harry

- Baseball 335.00
- Cut signature 15.00
- Personal document 42.00
- 3x5 Card 30.00
- 8x10 Photo 52.00
- HOF Plaque 62.00

Hornsby, Rogers

- Baseball 900.00
- Cut signature 85.00
- Personal document 275.00
- 3x5 Card 125.00
- 8x10 Photo 285.00
- HOF Plaque 520.00

Hoyt, Waite

- Baseball 128.00
- Cut signature 8.00
- Personal document 60.00
- 3x5 Card 18.00
- 8x10 Photo 44.00
- Perez-Steele Card 600.00
- HOF Plaque 35.00

Hubbard, Cal

- Baseball 410.00
- Cut signature 25.00
- Personal document 250.00
- 3x5 Card 51.00
- 8x10 Photo 110.00
- HOF Plaque 340.00

Hubbell, Carl

- Baseball 70.00
- Cut signature 8.00
- Personal document 45.00
- 3x5 Card 11.00
- 8x10 Photo 23.00
- Perez-Steele Card 145.00
- HOF Plaque 24.00

Huggins, Miller

- Baseball 3500.00
- Cut signature 950.00
- Personal document 2500.00
- 3x5 Card 1035.00
- 8x10 Photo 2025.00

Hunter, Catfish

- Baseball 20.00
- Cut signature 5.00
- Personal document 17.00
- 3x5 Card 7.00
- 8x10 Photo 15.00
- Perez-Steele Card 35.00
- HOF Plaque 12.00

Irvin, Monte

- Baseball 20.00
- Cut signature 4.00
- Personal document 17.00
- 3x5 Card 7.00
- 8x10 Photo 15.00
- Perez-Steele Card 27.00
- HOF Plaque 11.00

Jackson, Reggie

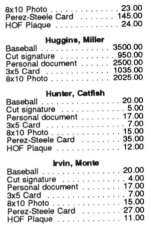

Reggie Jackson

- Baseball 45.00
- Cut signature 15.00
- Personal document 30.00
- 3x5 Card 28.00
- 8x10 Photo 35.00

Jackson, Travis

Baseball 75.00
Cut signature 8.00
Personal document 50.00
3x5 Card 17.00
8x10 Photo 27.00
Perez-Steele Card 220.00
HOF Plaque 22.00

Jenkins, Ferguson

Ferguson Jenkins

Baseball 25.00
Cut signature 6.00
Personal document 75.00
3x5 Card 12.00
8x10 Photo 15.00
Perez-Steele Card 120.00
HOF Plaque 25.00

Jennings, Hugh

Baseball 3650.00
Cut signature 950.00
Personal document 2000.00
3x5 Card 1800.00
8x10 Photo 2300.00

Johnson, Ban

Baseball 1600.00
Cut signature 190.00
Personal document 350.00
3x5 Card 260.00
8x10 Photo 590.00

Johnson, Judy

Baseball 38.00
Cut signature 8.00
Personal document 15.00
3x5 Card 9.00
8x10 Photo 20.00

Johnson, Walter

Baseball 2400.00
Cut signature 290.00
Personal document 750.00
3x5 Card 480.00
8x10 Photo 1000.00

Joss, Addie

Baseball 5200.00
Cut signature 2200.00
Personal document 3700.00
3x5 Card 3000.00
8x10 Photo 4500.00

Kaline, Al

Baseball 19.00
Cut signature 4.00
Personal document 10.00
3x5 Card 7.00
8x10 Photo 12.00
Perez-Steele Card 33.00
HOF Plaque 10.00

Keefe, Tim

Baseball 4500.00
Cut signature 1400.00
Personal document 2900.00
3x5 Card 2400.00
8x10 Photo 3300.00

Keeler, Willie

Baseball 4200.00
Cut signature 1500.00
Personal document 3100.00
3x5 Card 2800.00
8x10 Photo 3500.00

Kell, George

Baseball 20.00
Cut signature 5.00
Personal document 6.00
3x5 Card 7.00
8x10 Photo 12.00
Perez-Steele Card 27.00
HOF Plaque 11.00

Kelley, Joe

Baseball 5100.00
Cut signature 1200.00
Personal document 2400.00
3x5 Card 2100.00
8x10 Photo 3000.00

Kelly, George

Baseball 87.00
Cut signature 8.00
Personal document 17.00
3x5 Card 15.00
8x10 Photo 22.00
Perez-Steele Card 360.00
HOF Plaque 28.00

Kelly, Mike

Baseball 3500.00
Cut signature 2300.00
Personal document 4500.00
3x5 Card 3900.00
8x10 Photo 5500.00

Killebrew, Harmon

Baseball 21.00
Cut signature 4.00
Personal document 10.00
3x5 Card 6.00
8x10 Photo 15.00
Perez-Steele Card 26.00
HOF Plaque 12.00

Kiner, Ralph

Baseball 22.00
Cut signature 5.00
Personal document 10.00
3x5 Card 6.00
8x10 Photo 16.00
Perez-Steele Card 38.00
HOF Plaque 11.00

Klein, Chuck

Baseball 670.00
Cut signature 115.00
Personal document 250.00
3x5 Card 135.00
8x10 Photo 360.00

Klem, Bill

Baseball 1900.00
Cut signature 225.00
Personal document 550.00
3x5 Card 340.00
8x10 Photo 850.00

Koufax, Sandy

Baseball 30.00
Cut signature 6.00

Personal document	8.00
3x5 Card	12.00
8x10 Photo	15.00
Perez-Steele Card	45.00
HOF Plaque	18.00

Lajoie, Nap

Baseball	2225.00
Cut signature	135.00
Personal document	425.00
3x5 Card	195.00
8x10 Photo	625.00
HOF Plaque	650.00

Landis, Kenesaw

Baseball	1500.00
Cut signature	160.00
Personal document	325.00
3x5 Card	240.00
8x10 Photo	450.00

Lazzeri, Tony

Baseball	23.00
Cut signature	8.00
Personal document	15.00
3x5 Card	11.00
8x10 Photo	20.00
Perez-Steele Card	45.00
HOF Plaque	16.00

Lemon, Bob

Baseball	18.00
Cut signature	3.50
Personal document	10.00
3x5 Card	6.00
8x10 Photo	15.00
Perez-Steele Card	35.00
HOF Plaque	11.00

Leonard, Buck

Baseball	34.00
Cut signature	6.00
Personal document	15.00
3x5 Card	11.00
8x10 Photo	19.00
Perez-Steele Card	55.00
HOF Plaque	19.00

Lindstrom, Fred

Baseball	155.00
Cut signature	8.00
Personal document	35.00
3x5 Card	18.00
8x10 Photo	51.00
HOF Plaque	31.00

Lloyd, John

Baseball	5000.00
Cut signature	825.00
Personal document	2600.00
3x5 Card	2100.00
8x10 Photo	3500.00

Lombardi, Ernie

Ernie Lombardi

Baseball	450.00
Cut signature	27.00
Personal document	75.00
3x5 Card	45.00
8x10 Photo	140.00

Lopez, Al

Baseball	50.00
Cut signature	9.00
Personal document	20.00
3x5 Card	11.00
8x10 Photo	27.00
Perez-Steele Card	75.00
HOF Plaque	27.00

Lyons, Ted

Baseball	95.00
Cut signature	87.00
Personal document	25.00
3x5 Card	18.00
8x10 Photo	33.00
Perez-Steele Card	330.00
HOF Plaque	25.00

MacPhail, Larry

Baseball	580.00
Cut signature	62.00
Personal document	85.00
3x5 Card	115.00
8x10 Photo	235.00

Mack, Connie

Baseball	575.00
Cut signature	71.00
Personal document	100.00
3x5 Card	135.00
8x10 Photo	295.00
HOF Plaque	395.00

Mantle, Mickey

Baseball	52.00
Cut signature	9.00
Personal document	22.00
3x5 Card	17.00
8x10 Photo	35.00
Perez-Steele Card	230.00
HOF Plaque	40.00

Manush, Heinie

Baseball	435.00
Cut signature	22.00
Personal document	75.00
3x5 Card	42.00
8x10 Photo	115.00
HOF Plaque	240.00

Maranville, Rabbit

Baseball	1150.00
Cut signature	140.00
Personal document	335.00
3x5 Card	175.00
8x10 Photo	475.00

Marichal, Juan

Baseball	20.00
Cut signature	4.50
Personal document	12.00
3x5 Card	9.00
8x10 Photo	15.00
Perez-Steele Card	35.00
HOF Plaque	14.00

Marquard, Rube

Baseball	265.00
Cut signature	9.00
Personal document	30.00
3x5 Card	15.00
8x10 Photo	45.00
HOF Plaque	32.00

Mathews, Eddie

Baseball	22.00
Cut signature	3.50
Personal document	10.00
3x5 Card	7.00
8x10 Photo	14.00
Perez-Steele Card	27.00

Item	Price
HOF Plaque	12.00

Mathewson, Christy

Item	Price
Baseball	5225.00
Cut signature	800.00
Personal document	1775.00
3x5 Card	910.00
8x10 Photo	2335.00

Mays, Willie

Item	Price
Baseball	45.00
Cut signature	7.00
Personal document	25.00
3x5 Card	11.00
8x10 Photo	28.00
Perez-Steele Card	82.00
HOF Plaque	17.00

McCarthy, Joe

Joe McCarthy

Item	Price
Baseball	315.00
Cut signature	12.00
Personal document	175.00
3x5 Card	32.00
8x10 Photo	47.00
HOF Plaque	51.00

McCarthy, Tommy

Item	Price
Baseball	3500.00
Cut signature	2000.00
Personal document	3500.00
3x5 Card	2800.00
8x10 Photo	5000.00

McCovey, Willie

Item	Price
Baseball	21.00
Cut signature	4.00
Personal document	16.00
3x5 Card	8.00
8x10 Photo	18.00
Perez-Steele Card	27.00
HOF Plaque	14.00

McGinnity, Joe

Item	Price
Baseball	3800.00
Cut signature	1400.00
Personal document	2750.00
3x5 Card	1900.00
8x10 Photo	3500.00

McGraw, John

Item	Price
Baseball	3500.00
Cut signature	475.00
Personal document	750.00
3x5 Card	525.00
8x10 Photo	1200.00

McKechnie, Bill

Item	Price
Baseball	710.00
Cut signature	65.00
Personal document	450.00
3x5 Card	115.00
8x10 Photo	310.00
HOF Plaque	425.00

Medwick, Joe

Item	Price
Baseball	360.00
Cut signature	20.00
Personal document	195.00
3x5 Card	27.00
8x10 Photo	71.00
HOF Plaque	95.00

Mize, Johnny

Item	Price
Baseball	19.00
Cut signature	4.00
Personal document	15.00
3x5 Card	7.00
8x10 Photo	10.00
Perez-Steele Card	27.00
HOF Plaque	9.00

Morgan, Joe

Item	Price
Baseball	25.00
Cut signature	5.00
Personal document	20.00
3x5 Card	10.00
8x10 Photo	15.00
Perez-Steele Card	31.00
HOF Plaque	12.00

Musial, Stan

Item	Price
Baseball	26.00
Cut signature	5.00
Personal document	20.00
3x5 Card	8.00
8x10 Photo	15.00
Perez-Steele Card	65.00
HOF Plaque	13.00

Nichols, Kid

Item	Price
Baseball	2950.00
Cut signature	135.00
Personal document	325.00
3x5 Card	195.00
8x10 Photo	465.00
HOF Plaque	355.00

O'Rourke, Jim

Item	Price
Baseball	4600.00
Cut signature	2100.00
Personal document	3900.00
3x5 Card	3200.00
8x10 Photo	4225.00

Ott, Mel

Item	Price
Baseball	680.00
Cut signature	125.00
Personal document	425.00
3x5 Card	155.00
8x10 Photo	325.00
HOF Plaque	425.00

Paige, Satchel

Item	Price
Baseball	325.00
Cut signature	32.00
Personal document	85.00
3x5 Card	50.00
8x10 Photo	115.00
Perez-Steele Card	1895.00
HOF Plaque	95.00

Satchel Paige

Palmer, Jim

Item	Price
Baseball	25.00
Cut signature	8.00
Personal document	20.00
3x5 Card	15.00
8x10 Photo	19.00
Perez-Steele Card	20.00
HOF Plaque	15.00

Pennock, Herb

Item	Price
Baseball	1200.00
Cut signature	115.00
Personal document	300.00
3x5 Card	185.00
8x10 Photo	425.00

Perry, Gaylord

Item	Price
Baseball	25.00
Cut signature	4.00
Personal document	15.00
3x5 Card	12.00
8x10 Photo	19.00
Perez-Steele Card	22.00
HOF Plaque	18.00

Plank, Eddie

Item	Price
Baseball	4500.00
Cut signature	2200.00
Personal document	3700.00
3x5 Card	3500.00
8x10 Photo	4000.00

Radbourn, Old Hoss

Item	Price
Baseball	4600.00
Cut signature	1600.00
Personal document	3500.00
3x5 Card	2900.00
8x10 Photo	3900.00

Reese, Pee Wee

Item	Price
Baseball	21.00
Cut signature	4.00
Personal document	17.00
3x5 Card	10.00
8x10 Photo	15.00
Perez-Steele Card	54.00
HOF Plaque	13.00

Rice, Sam

Item	Price
Baseball	310.00
Cut signature	17.00
Personal document	100.00
3x5 Card	35.00
8x10 Photo	80.00
HOF Plaque	85.00

Rickey, Branch

Item	Price
Baseball	625.00
Cut signature	82.00
Personal document	425.00
3x5 Card	160.00

8x10 Photo	375.00

Rixey, Eppa

Baseball	375.00
Cut signature	60.00
Personal document	250.00
3x5 Card	100.00
8x10 Photo	225.00

Roberts, Robin

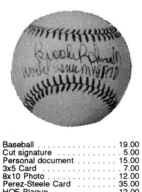

Baseball	20.00
Cut signature	5.00
Personal document	17.00
3x5 Card	8.00
8x10 Photo	13.00
Perez-Steele Card	27.00
HOF Plaque	12.00

Robinson, Brooks

Baseball	19.00
Cut signature	5.00
Personal document	15.00
3x5 Card	7.00
8x10 Photo	12.00
Perez-Steele Card	35.00
HOF Plaque	12.00

Robinson, Frank

Baseball	23.00
Cut signature	4.50
Personal document	17.00
3x5 Card	8.00
8x10 Photo	15.00
Perez-Steele Card	44.00
HOF Plaque	15.00

Robinson, Jackie

Baseball	890.00
Cut signature	110.00
Personal document	385.00
3x5 Card	170.00
8x10 Photo	360.00
HOF Plaque	395.00

Enos Slaughter, Tom Seaver

Robinson, Wilbert

Baseball	2650.00
Cut signature	900.00
Personal document	1700.00
3x5 Card	1225.00
8x10 Photo	2225.00

Roush, Edd

Baseball	70.00
Cut signature	10.00
Personal document	35.00
3x5 Card	12.00
8x10 Photo	27.00
Perez-Steele Card	175.00
HOF Plaque	23.00

Ruffing, Red

Baseball	125.00
Cut signature	11.00
Personal document	75.00
3x5 Card	22.00
8x10 Photo	50.00
Perez-Steele Card	365.00
HOF Plaque	47.00

Rusie, Amos

Baseball	4400.00
Cut signature	1300.00
Personal document	1700.00
3x5 Card	1500.00
8x10 Photo	2300.00

Ruth, Babe

Baseball	2300.00
Cut signature	465.00
Personal document	1500.00
3x5 Card	580.00
8x10 Photo	2100.00
HOF Plaque	3500.00

Schalk, Ray

Baseball	415.00
Cut signature	37.00
Personal document	115.00
3x5 Card	63.00
8x10 Photo	125.00
HOF Plaque	225.00

Schoendienst, Red

Baseball	21.00
Cut signature	4.00
Personal document	17.00
3x5 Card	6.00
8x10 Photo	14.00
Perez-Steele Card	38.00
HOF Plaque	21.00

Seaver, Tom

Baseball	45.00
Cut signature	6.00
Personal document	40.00
3x5 Card	15.00
8x10 Photo	35.00
Perez-Steele Card	45.00
HOF Plaque	18.00

Sewell, Joe

Joe Sewell

Baseball	21.00
Cut signature	4.00
Personal document	16.00
3x5 Card	7.00
8x10 Photo	14.00
Perez-Steele Card	65.00
HOF Plaque	12.00

Simmons, Al

Baseball	550.00
Cut signature	70.00
Personal document	275.00
3x5 Card	125.00
8x10 Photo	250.00
HOF Plaque	422.00

Sisler, George

Baseball	215.00
Cut signature	22.00
Personal document	150.00
3x5 Card	44.00
8x10 Photo	125.00
HOF Plaque	115.00

Slaughter, Enos

Baseball	20.00
Cut signature	3.50
Personal document	14.00

3x5 Card . . . 7.50
8x10 Photo . . . 10.00
Perez-Steele Card . . . 26.00
HOF Plaque . . . 22.00

Snider, Duke

Baseball . . . 26.00
Cut signature . . . 4.50
Personal document . . . 17.00
3x5 Card . . . 7.50
8x10 Photo . . . 15.00
Perez-Steele Card . . . 46.00
HOF Plaque . . . 28.00

Spahn, Warren

Baseball . . . 22.00
Cut signature . . . 4.00
Personal document . . . 17.00
3x5 Card . . . 7.00
8x10 Photo . . . 15.00
Perez-Steele Card . . . 34.00
HOF Plaque . . . 12.00

Spalding, Al

Baseball . . . 4700.00
Cut signature . . . 1500.00
Personal document . . . 2400.00
3x5 Card . . . 2300.00
8x10 Photo . . . 2500.00

Speaker, Tris

Baseball . . . 1300.00
Cut signature . . . 130.00
Personal document . . . 285.00
3x5 Card . . . 225.00
8x10 Photo . . . 375.00
HOF Plaque . . . 570.00

Stargell, Willie

Baseball . . . 22.00
Cut signature . . . 3.00
Personal document . . . 20.00
3x5 Card . . . 8.00
8x10 Photo . . . 17.00
Perez-Steele Card . . . 27.00
HOF Plaque . . . 12.00

Stengel, Casey

Baseball . . . 375.00
Cut signature . . . 20.00
Personal document . . . 175.00
3x5 Card . . . 45.00
8x10 Photo . . . 125.00
HOF Plaque . . . 85.00

Terry, Bill

Baseball . . . 90.00
Cut signature . . . 7.00
Personal document . . . 40.00
3x5 Card . . . 17.00
8x10 Photo . . . 35.00
Perez-Steele Card . . . 200.00
HOF Plaque . . . 28.00

Thompson, Sam

Baseball . . . 7900.00

Casey Stengell

Cut signature . . . 2450.00
Personal document . . . 5500.00
3x5 Card . . . 3900.00
8x10 Photo . . . 6800.00

Tinker, Joe

Baseball . . . 2800.00
Cut signature . . . 295.00
Personal document . . . 555.00
3x5 Card . . . 355.00
8x10 Photo . . . 795.00
HOF Plaque . . . 1200.00

Traynor, Pie

Baseball . . . 545.00
Cut signature . . . 42.00
Personal document . . . 225.00
3x5 Card . . . 75.00
8x10 Photo . . . 195.00
HOF Plaque . . . 355.00

Vance, Dazzy

Baseball . . . 1125.00
Cut signature . . . 80.00
Personal document . . . 355.00
3x5 Card . . . 155.00
8x10 Photo . . . 335.00
HOF Plaque . . . 480.00

Vaughn, Arky

Baseball . . . 1125.00
Cut signature . . . 160.00
Personal document . . . 500.00
3x5 Card . . . 180.00
8x10 Photo . . . 415.00

Veeck, Bill

Baseball . . . 1000.00
Cut signature . . . 240.00
Personal document . . . 600.00
3x5 Card . . . 350.00
8x10 Photo . . . 700.00
Perez-Steele Card . . . 1100.00
HOF Plaque . . . 950.00

Waddell, Rube

Baseball . . . 6800.00
Cut signature . . . 1950.00
Personal document . . . 3500.00
3x5 Card . . . 2225.00
8x10 Photo . . . 4950.00

Wagner, Honus

Baseball . . . 2025.00
Cut signature . . . 175.00
Personal document . . . 425.00
3x5 Card . . . 280.00
8x10 Photo . . . 615.00
HOF Plaque . . . 950.00

Wallace, Bobby

Baseball . . . 1995.00
Cut signature . . . 180.00
Personal document . . . 450.00
3x5 Card . . . 250.00
8x10 Photo . . . 560.00
HOF Plaque . . . 1000.00

Walsh, Ed

Baseball . . . 2800.00
Cut signature . . . 135.00
Personal documen . . . 425.00
3x5 Card . . . 195.00
8x10 Photo . . . 365.00
HOF Plaque . . . 560.00

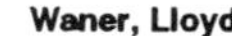

Waner, Lloyd

Ted Williams, Stan Musial, Mickey Mantle

Baseball	165.00
Cut signature	13.00
Personal document	65.00
3x5 Card	22.00
8x10 Photo	45.00
Perez-Steele Card	1990.00
HOF Plaque	38.00

Waner, Paul

Baseball	615.00
Cut signature	55.00
Personal document	350.00
3x5 Card	92.00
8x10 Photo	255.00
HOF Plaque	265.00

Ward, John M.

Baseball	7200.00
Cut signature	1700.00
Personal document	3000.00
3x5 Card	2015.00
8x10 Photo	3900.00

Weiss, George

Baseball	615.00
Cut signature	52.00
Personal document	185.00
3x5 Card	54.00
8x10 Photo	165.00

Welch, Mickey

Baseball	5700.00
Cut signature	2400.00
Personal document	4000.00
3x5 Card	3500.00
8x10 Photo	4600.00

Wheat, Zack

Baseball	450.00
Cut signature	22.00
Personal document	175.00
3x5 Card	45.00
8x10 Photo	145.00
HOF Plaque	165.00

Wilhelm, Hoyt

Baseball	21.00
Cut signature	3.00
Personal document	15.00
3x5 Card	5.50
8x10 Photo	14.00
Perez-Steele Card	27.00
HOF Plaque	11.00

Williams, Billy

Baseball	21.00
Cut signature	4.00
Personal document	10.00
3x5 Card	8.00
8x10 Photo	16.00
Perez-Steele Card	32.00
HOF Plaque	15.00

Williams, Ted

Baseball	54.00
Cut signature	11.00
Personal document	40.00
3x5 Card	16.00
8x10 Photo	33.00
Perez-Steele Card	165.00
HOF Plaque	33.00

Wilson, Hack

Baseball	1700.00
Cut signature	265.00
Personal document	425.00
3x5 Card	340.00
8x10 Photo	595.00

Wright, George

Baseball	3400.00
Cut signature	1000.00
Personal document	2400.00
3x5 Card	1900.00
8x10 Photo	3000.00

Roger Maris and Mickey Mantle

Wright, Harry

Baseball	3400.00
Cut signature	1800.00
Personal document	3100.00
3x5 Card	2700.00
8x10 Photo	3900.00

Wynn, Early

Baseball	20.00
Cut signature	4.00
Personal document	19.00
3x5 Card	7.00
8x10 Photo	17.00
Perez-Steele Card	35.00
HOF Plaque	17.00

Yastrzemski, Carl

Baseball	23.00
Cut signature	4.00
Personal document	17.00
3x5 Card	9.00
8x10 Photo	15.00
Perez-Steele Card	85.00
HOF Plaque	15.00

Yawkey, Tom

Baseball	725.00
Cut signature	80.00
Personal document	250.00
3x5 Card	130.00
8x10 Photo	220.00

Carl Yastrzemski

Young, Cy

Baseball	2100.00
Cut signature	180.00
Personal document	450.00
3x5 Card	250.00
8x10 Photo	375.00
HOF Plaque	950.00

Youngs, Ross

Baseball	4500.00
Cut signature	1225.00
Personal document	1750.00
3x5 Card	1700.00
8x10 Photo	1800.00

BASEBALL: INACTIVE PLAYERS

Allen, Dick	
Baseball	20.00
Cut signature	4.00
Personal document	8.00
3x5 Card	5.00
8x10 Photo	15.00

Ashburn, Richie	
Baseball	20.00
Cut signature	6.00
Personal document	12.00
3x5 Card	6.00
8x10 Photo	8.00

Bauer, Hank	
Baseball	20.00
Cut signature	6.00
Personal document	10.00
3x5 Card	6.00
8x10 Photo	8.00

Bonds, Bobby	
Baseball	24.00
Cut signature	5.00
Personal document	11.00
3x5 Card	6.00
8x10 Photo	18.00

Bouton, Jim	
Baseball	20.00
Cut signature	4.00
Personal document	9.00
3x5 Card	6.00
8x10 Photo	8.00

Boyer, Ken	
Baseball	20.00
Cut signature	2.00
Personal document	6.00
3x5 Card	4.00
8x10 Photo	8.00

Branca, Ralph	
Baseball	30.00
Cut signature	12.00
Personal document	15.00
3x5 Card	10.00
8x10 Photo	20.00

Bunning, Jim	
Baseball	20.00
Cut signature	4.00
Personal document	7.50
3x5 Card	5.00
8x10 Photo	10.00

Burdette, Lou	
Baseball	16.00
Cut signature	4.00
Personal document	6.00
3x5 Card	4.00
8x10 Photo	8.00

Carlton, Steve	
Baseball	45.00
Cut signature	12.00
Personal document	25.00
3x5 Card	18.00
8x10 Photo	35.00

Carter, Gary	
Baseball	30.00
Cut signature	6.00
Personal document	15.00
3x5 Card	10.00
8x10 Photo	20.00

Gary Carter

Cepeda, Orlando	
Baseball	30.00
Cut signature	5.00
Personal document	14.00
3x5 Card	9.00
8x10 Photo	20.00

Cey, Ron	
Baseball	25.00
Cut signature	6.00
Personal document	8.00
3x5 Card	10.00
8x10 Photo	12.50

Colavito, Rocky

Rocky Colavito

Colavito, Rocky	
Baseball	30.00
Cut signature	8.00
Personal document	14.00
3x5 Card	10.00
8x10 Photo	20.00

Concepcion, Dave	
Baseball	27.00
Cut signature	8.00
Personal document	11.00
3x5 Card	8.00
8x10 Photo	17.00

Dark, Alvin	
Baseball	15.00
Cut signature	4.00
Personal document	12.00
3x5 Card	6.00
8x10 Photo	8.00

Doby, Larry	
Baseball	25.00
Cut signature	4.00
Personal document	18.00
3x5 Card	6.00
8x10 Photo	15.00

Evans, Dwight	
Baseball	25.00
Cut signature	5.00
Personal document	12.00
3x5 Card	9.00
8x10 Photo	15.00

Flood, Curt	
Baseball	18.00
Cut signature	3.00
Personal document	12.00
3x5 Card	7.00
8x10 Photo	10.00

Furillo, Carl

Carl Furillo

Furillo, Carl	
Baseball	35.00
Cut signature	6.00
Personal document	30.00
3x5 Card	12.00
8x10 Photo	25.00

Garvey, Steve	
Baseball	22.00
Cut signature	4.00
Personal document	17.00
3x5 Card	8.00
8x10 Photo	12.00

Groat, Dick

Dick Groat

Groat, Dick	
Baseball	15.00
Cut signature	3.00
Personal document	12.00
3x5 Card	6.00
8x10 Photo	8.00

Guidry, Ron	
Baseball	25.00
Cut signature	4.00
Personal document	17.00
3x5 Card	9.00
8x10 Photo	15.00

Hodges, Gil	
Baseball	65.00
Cut signature	15.00
Personal document	25.00
3x5 Card	18.00
8x10 Photo	35.00

Howard, Elston	
Baseball	30.00
Cut signature	4.00
Personal document	12.00
3x5 Card	9.00
8x10 Photo	18.00

Howard, Frank	
Baseball	35.00
Cut signature	4.00
Personal document	17.00
3x5 Card	9.00

8x10 Photo	15.00

Kaat, Jim

Baseball	0.00
Cut signature	0.00
Personal document	0.00
3x5 Card	0.00
8x10 Photo	0.00

Kluszewski, Ted

Ted Kluszewski

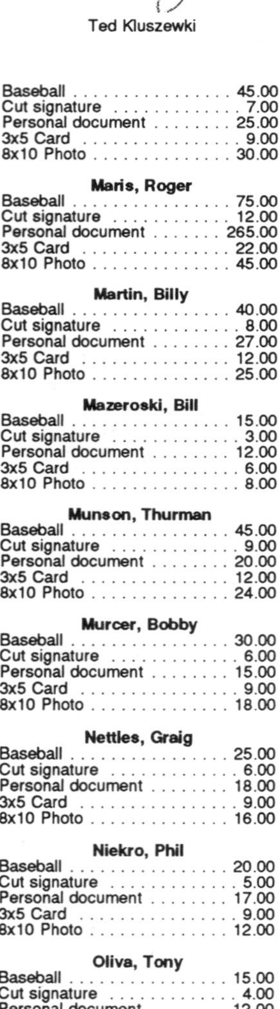

Baseball	45.00
Cut signature	7.00
Personal document	25.00
3x5 Card	9.00
8x10 Photo	30.00

Maris, Roger

Baseball	75.00
Cut signature	12.00
Personal document	265.00
3x5 Card	22.00
8x10 Photo	45.00

Martin, Billy

Baseball	40.00
Cut signature	8.00
Personal document	27.00
3x5 Card	12.00
8x10 Photo	25.00

Mazeroski, Bill

Baseball	15.00
Cut signature	3.00
Personal document	12.00
3x5 Card	6.00
8x10 Photo	8.00

Munson, Thurman

Baseball	45.00
Cut signature	9.00
Personal document	20.00
3x5 Card	12.00
8x10 Photo	24.00

Murcer, Bobby

Baseball	30.00
Cut signature	6.00
Personal document	15.00
3x5 Card	9.00
8x10 Photo	18.00

Nettles, Graig

Baseball	25.00
Cut signature	6.00
Personal document	18.00
3x5 Card	9.00
8x10 Photo	16.00

Niekro, Phil

Baseball	20.00
Cut signature	5.00
Personal document	17.00
3x5 Card	9.00
8x10 Photo	12.00

Oliva, Tony

Baseball	15.00
Cut signature	4.00
Personal document	12.00
3x5 Card	6.00
8x10 Photo	8.00

Mike Schmidt, Phil Rizzuto

Parker, Dave

Baseball	25.00
Cut signature	6.00
Personal document	18.00
3x5 Card	9.00
8x10 Photo	12.00

Piersall, Jimmy

Baseball	15.00
Cut signature	4.00
Personal document	9.00
3x5 Card	5.00
8x10 Photo	8.00

Powell, Boog

Baseball	15.00
Cut signature	4.00
Personal document	12.00
3x5 Card	6.00
8x10 Photo	8.00

Richardson, Bobby

Baseball	18.00
Cut signature	4.00
Personal document	12.00
3x5 Card	10.00
8x10 Photo	8.00

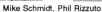

Rizzuto, Phil

Phil Rizzuto

Baseball	20.00
Cut signature	5.00
Personal document	15.00
3x5 Card	12.00
8x10 Photo	10.00

Rose, Pete

Baseball	50.00
Cut signature	6.00
Personal document	35.00
3x5 Card	10.00
8x10 Photo	25.00

Rosen, Al

Baseball	18.00
Cut signature	3.00
Personal document	10.00
3x5 Card	4.00
8x10 Photo	7.00

Santo, Ron

Baseball	20.00
Cut signature	4.00
Personal document	12.00
3x5 Card	6.00
8x10 Photo	8.00

Schmidt, Mike

Baseball	50.00
Cut signature	10.00
Personal document	40.00
3x5 Card	20.00
8x10 Photo	35.00

Skowron, Bill

Baseball	15.00
Cut signature	3.00
Personal document	10.00
3x5 Card	5.00
8x10 Photo	8.00

Staub, Rusty

Baseball	25.00
Cut signature	6.00
Personal document	14.00
3x5 Card	8.00
8x10 Photo	10.00

Sutton, Don

Baseball	17.00
Cut signature	4.00
Personal document	13.00
3x5 Card	7.00
8x10 Photo	10.00

Torre, Joe

Baseball	20.00
Cut signature	4.00
Personal document	12.00
3x5 Card	6.00
8x10 Photo	8.00

Uecker, Bob

Baseball	40.00
Cut signature	7.00
Personal document	23.00
3x5 Card	15.00
8x10 Photo	18.00

White, Bill

Baseball	20.00
Cut signature	4.00
Personal document	12.00
3x5 Card	8.00
8x10 Photo	10.00

Bill White

Wills, Maury
Baseball . . . 18.00
Cut signature . . . 4.00
Personal document . . . 12.00
3x5 Card . . . 6.00
8x10 Photo . . . 9.00

Abbott, Jim
Baseball . . . 25.00
Cut signature . . . 5.00
3x5 Card . . . 7.00
8x10 Photo . . . 15.00

Alomar, Roberto
Baseball . . . 30.00
Cut signature . . . 6.00
3x5 Card . . . 12.00
8x10 Photo . . . 20.00

Alomar, Sandy
Baseball . . . 20.00
Cut signature . . . 4.00
3x5 Card . . . 12.00
8x10 Photo . . . 15.00

Anderson, Brady
Baseball . . . 20.00
Cut signature . . . 4.00
3x5 Card . . . 8.00
8x10 Photo . . . 16.00

Avery, Steve
Baseball . . . 30.00
Cut signature . . . 6.00
3x5 Card . . . 12.00
8x10 Photo . . . 25.00

Baerga, Carlos
Baseball . . . 22.00
Cut signature . . . 5.00
3x5 Card . . . 13.00
8x10 Photo . . . 18.00

Bagwell, Jeff
Baseball . . . 20.00
Cut signature . . . 4.00
3x5 Card . . . 7.00
8x10 Photo . . . 10.00

Baines, Harold
Baseball . . . 24.00
Cut signature . . . 6.00
3x5 Card . . . 14.00
8x10 Photo . . . 19.00

Bell, Derek
Baseball . . . 20.00
Cut signature . . . 4.00
3x5 Card . . . 7.00
8x10 Photo . . . 10.00

Bell, George

Jeff Bagwell

Baseball . . . 20.00
Cut signature . . . 4.00
3x5 Card . . . 8.00
8x10 Photo . . . 10.00

Belle, Albert
Baseball . . . 14.00
Cut signature . . . 3.00
3x5 Card . . . 6.00
8x10 Photo . . . 8.00

Biggio, Craig
Baseball . . . 16.00
Cut signature . . . 4.00
3x5 Card . . . 7.00
8x10 Photo . . . 9.00

Blyleven, Bert
Baseball . . . 25.00
Cut signature . . . 4.00
3x5 Card . . . 9.00
8x10 Photo . . . 12.00

Boggs, Wade
Baseball . . . 27.00
Cut signature . . . 5.00
3x5 Card . . . 8.00
8x10 Photo . . . 20.00

Bonds, Barry
Baseball . . . 35.00
Cut signature . . . 10.00
3x5 Card . . . 15.00
8x10 Photo . . . 20.00

Bonilla, Bobby
Baseball . . . 35.00
Cut signature . . . 7.00
3x5 Card . . . 12.00
8x10 Photo . . . 20.00

Brett, George
Baseball . . . 50.00
Cut signature . . . 10.00
3x5 Card . . . 20.00
8x10 Photo . . . 35.00

Burks, Ellis

Wade Boggs

Baseball 55.00
Cut signature 8.00
3x5 Card 15.00
8x10 Photo 30.00

Butler, Brett
Baseball 28.00
Cut signature 8.00
3x5 Card 15.00
8x10 Photo 18.00

Canseco, Jose
Baseball 45.00
Cut signature 7.00
3x5 Card 15.00
8x10 Photo 30.00

Carter, Joe
Baseball 25.00
Cut signature 5.00
3x5 Card 8.00
8x10 Photo 12.00

Joe Carter

Cedeno, Andujar
Baseball 18.00
Cut signature 4.00
3x5 Card 6.00
8x10 Photo 10.00

Chamberlain, Wes
Baseball 17.00
Cut signature 3.00
3x5 Card 5.00
8x10 Photo 9.00

Clark, Jack
Baseball 25.00
Cut signature 7.00
3x5 Card 10.00
8x10 Photo 14.00

Clark, Will
Baseball 40.00
Cut signature 9.00
3x5 Card 19.00
8x10 Photo 30.00

Clayton, Royce
Baseball 18.00
Cut signature 4.00
3x5 Card 8.00
8x10 Photo 11.00

Clemens, Roger
Baseball 45.00
Cut signature 7.00
3x5 Card 18.00
8x10 Photo 35.00

Coleman, Vince
Baseball 25.00
Cut signature 4.00
3x5 Card 8.00
8x10 Photo 15.00

Cone, David
Baseball 20.00
Cut signature 6.00
3x5 Card 12.00
8x10 Photo 10.00

Cordero, Wilfredo
Baseball 15.00
Cut signature 4.00
3x5 Card 8.00
8x10 Photo 10.00

Cuyler, Milt
Baseball 13.00
Cut signature 2.00
3x5 Card 6.00
8x10 Photo 8.00

Davis, Eric
Baseball 25.00
Cut signature 6.00
3x5 Card 10.00
8x10 Photo 15.00

Davis, Glenn
Baseball 24.00
Cut signature 5.00
3x5 Card 12.00
8x10 Photo 20.00

Dawson, Andre
Baseball 25.00

Andre Dawson

Cut signature 5.00
3x5 Card 15.00
8x10 Photo 20.00

DeShields, Delino
Baseball 25.00
Cut signature 4.00
3x5 Card 12.00
8x10 Photo 20.00

Devereaux, Mike
Baseball 18.00
Cut signature 3.00
3x5 Card 9.00
8x10 Photo 15.00

Dibble, Rob
Baseball 25.00
Cut signature 4.00
3x5 Card 7.00
8x10 Photo 12.00

Drabek, Doug
Baseball 25.00
Cut signature 5.00
3x5 Card 10.00
8x10 Photo 12.00

Dunston, Shawon
Baseball 15.00
Cut signature 4.00
3x5 Card 8.00
8x10 Photo 10.00

Dykstra, Len
Baseball 35.00
Cut signature 4.00
3x5 Card 10.00
8x10 Photo 26.00

Eckersley, Dennis
Baseball 40.00
Cut signature 8.00
3x5 Card 12.00
8x10 Photo 30.00

Erickson, Scott
Baseball 29.00
Cut signature 6.00
3x5 Card 12.00
8x10 Photo 18.00

Fernandez, Tony
Baseball 20.00
Cut signature 3.00
3x5 Card 9.00
8x10 Photo 15.00

Fielder, Cecil
Baseball 30.00
Cut signature 6.00
3x5 Card 12.00
8x10 Photo 18.00

Fisk, Carlton
Baseball 30.00
Cut signature 6.00
3x5 Card 12.00
8x10 Photo 18.00

Fleming, Dave
Baseball 11.00
Cut signature 5.00
3x5 Card 7.00
8x10 Photo 9.00

Franco, Julio
Baseball 15.00
Cut signature 4.00
3x5 Card 6.00
8x10 Photo 10.00

Fryman, Travis
Baseball 11.00
Cut signature 5.00
3x5 Card 7.00
8x10 Photo 9.00

Gant, Ron
Baseball 22.00
Cut signature 6.00
3x5 Card 10.00
8x10 Photo 15.00

Gibson, Kirk
Baseball 24.00
Cut signature 5.00
Personal document 20.00
3x5 Card 10.00
8x10 Photo 16.00

Glavine, Tom
Baseball 35.00
Cut signature 7.00
3x5 Card 12.00
8x10 Photo 28.00

Gonzalez, Juan
Baseball 22.00
Cut signature 5.00
3x5 Card 10.00
8x10 Photo 18.00

Gonzalez, Luis
Baseball 12.00
Cut signature 3.00
3x5 Card 5.00
8x10 Photo 9.00

Rickey Henderson, Fred McGriff, Jack Morris

Gooden, Dwight
Baseball 28.00
Cut signature 5.00
3x5 Card 9.00
8x10 Photo 18.00

Gossage, Goose
Baseball 15.00
Cut signature 3.00
3x5 Card 8.00
8x10 Photo 10.00

Grace, Mark
Baseball 20.00
Cut signature 4.00
3x5 Card 10.00
8x10 Photo 12.00

Greenwell, Mike
Baseball 20.00
Cut signature 4.00
3x5 Card 10.00
8x10 Photo 12.00

Griffey Jr., Ken
Baseball 35.00
Cut signature 6.00
3x5 Card 10.00
8x10 Photo 25.00

Grissom, Marquis
Baseball 20.00
Cut signature 4.00
3x5 Card 12.00
8x10 Photo 16.00

Guerrero, Pedro
Baseball 20.00
Cut signature 4.00
3x5 Card 6.00
8x10 Photo 8.00

Guzman, Juan
Baseball 17.00
Cut signature 3.00
3x5 Card 5.00
8x10 Photo 7.00

Gwynn, Tony
Baseball 25.00
Cut signature 5.00
3x5 Card 12.00
8x10 Photo 18.00

Harnisch, Pete
Baseball 16.00
Cut signature 3.00
3x5 Card 5.00
8x10 Photo 8.00

Harvey, Bryan
Baseball 17.00
Cut signature 4.00
3x5 Card 6.00
8x10 Photo 9.00

Henderson, Rickey
Baseball 45.00
Cut signature 7.00
3x5 Card 20.00
8x10 Photo 38.00

Hershiser, Orel
Baseball 30.00
Cut signature 6.00
3x5 Card 12.00
8x10 Photo 18.00

Hollins, Dave
Baseball 15.00
Cut signature 4.00
3x5 Card 8.00
8x10 Photo 10.00

Hrbek, Kent
Baseball 25.00
Cut signature 4.00
3x5 Card 12.00
8x10 Photo 19.00

Hundley, Todd
Baseball 15.00
Cut signature 4.00
3x5 Card 8.00
8x10 Photo 10.00

Jackson, Bo(see football)
Baseball 35.00
Cut signature 6.00
3x5 Card 15.00
8x10 Photo 28.00

Jefferies, Gregg
Baseball 25.00
Cut signature 5.00
3x5 Card 9.00
8x10 Photo 16.00

Jefferson, Reggie
Baseball 10.00
Cut signature 3.00
3x5 Card 5.00
8x10 Photo 7.00

Johnson, Howard
Baseball 20.00
Cut signature 3.00
3x5 Card 8.00
8x10 Photo 12.00

Jose, Felix
Baseball 16.00
Cut signature 4.00
3x5 Card 6.00
8x10 Photo 9.00

Joyner, Wally
Baseball 29.00
Cut signature 7.00
3x5 Card 10.00
8x10 Photo 20.00

Justice, Dave
Baseball 38.00
Cut signature 6.00
3x5 Card 12.00
8x10 Photo 30.00

Kelly, Pat
Baseball 15.00
Cut signature 3.00
3x5 Card 6.00
8x10 Photo 8.00

Kelly, Roberto
Baseball 21.00
Cut signature 4.00
3x5 Card 8.00
8x10 Photo 12.00

Klesko, Ryan

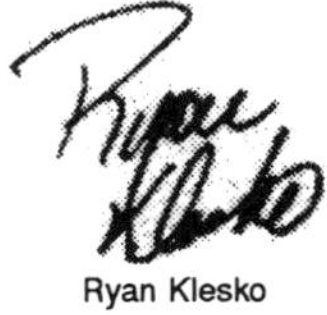

Ryan Klesko

Baseball 6.00
Cut signature 2.00
3x5 Card 3.00
8x10 Photo 4.00

Knoblauch, Chuck
Baseball 22.00
Cut signature 4.00
3x5 Card 10.00
8x10 Photo 18.00

Langston, Mark
Baseball 15.00
Cut signature 3.00
3x5 Card 5.00

8x10 Photo 7.00

Lankford, Ray
Baseball 10.00
Cut signature 3.00
3x5 Card 5.00
8x10 Photo 7.00

Larkin, Barry
Baseball 25.00
Cut signature 5.00
3x5 Card 10.00
8x10 Photo 22.00

Lewis, Mark
Baseball 8.00
Cut signature 1.00
3x5 Card 3.00
8x10 Photo 5.00

Listach, Pat
Baseball 28.00
Cut signature 6.00
3x5 Card 12.00
8x10 Photo 18.00

Lofton, Kenny
Baseball 10.00
Cut signature 2.00
3x5 Card 4.00
8x10 Photo 6.00

Maddux, Greg
Baseball 18.00
Cut signature 4.00
3x5 Card 6.00
8x10 Photo 8.00

Martinez, Dennis
Baseball 20.00
Cut signature 5.00
3x5 Card 8.00
8x10 Photo 12.00

Martinez, Edgar
Baseball 14.00
Cut signature 3.00
3x5 Card 6.00
8x10 Photo 10.00

Martinez, Ramon
Baseball 25.00
Cut signature 6.00
3x5 Card 10.00
8x10 Photo 18.00

Martinez, Tino
Baseball 28.00
Cut signature 6.00
3x5 Card 12.00
8x10 Photo 18.00

Mattingly, Don
Baseball 49.00
Cut signature 9.00
3x5 Card 17.00
8x10 Photo 30.00

McDonald, Ben
Baseball 27.00
Cut signature 6.00
3x5 Card 10.00
8x10 Photo 15.00

McDowell, Jack
Baseball 25.00
Cut signature 7.00
3x5 Card 13.00
8x10 Photo 19.00

McGriff, Fred
Baseball 30.00
Cut signature 7.00
3x5 Card 12.00
8x10 Photo 22.00

Deion Sanders

McGwire, Mark
Baseball 35.00
Cut signature 6.00
3x5 Card 12.00
8x10 Photo 25.00

McRae, Brian
Baseball 10.00
Cut signature 2.00
3x5 Card 4.00
8x10 Photo 6.00

McReynolds, Kevin
Baseball 18.00
Cut signature 4.00
3x5 Card 8.00
8x10 Photo 15.00

Mitchell, Kevin
Baseball 30.00
Cut signature 6.00
3x5 Card 12.00
8x10 Photo 18.00

Molitor, Paul
Baseball 20.00
Cut signature 4.00
3x5 Card 10.00
8x10 Photo 12.00

Morris, Hal
Baseball 22.00
Cut signature 4.00
3x5 Card 8.00
8x10 Photo 10.00

Morris, Jack
Baseball 18.00
Cut signature 3.00
3x5 Card 7.00
8x10 Photo 9.00

Murphy, Dale
Baseball 32.00
Cut signature 7.00
3x5 Card 10.00
8x10 Photo 25.00

Murray, Eddie
Baseball 30.00
Cut signature 8.00
3x5 Card 12.00
8x10 Photo 18.00

Mussina, Mike
Baseball 16.00
Cut signature 4.00
3x5 Card 8.00
8x10 Photo 12.00

Nagy, Charles
Baseball 20.00
Cut signature 4.00
3x5 Card 6.00
8x10 Photo 8.00

Mike Mussina

Offerman, Jose

Baseball	20.00
Cut signature	4.00
3x5 Card	6.00
8x10 Photo	12.00

Olerud, John

Baseball	20.00
Cut signature	4.00
3x5 Card	7.00
8x10 Photo	14.00

Palmeiro, Rafael

Baseball	18.00
Cut signature	6.00
3x5 Card	9.00
8x10 Photo	12.00

Palmer, Dean

Baseball	18.00
Cut signature	4.00
3x5 Card	6.00
8x10 Photo	8.00

Pendleton, Terry

Baseball	28.00
Cut signature	6.00
3x5 Card	12.00
8x10 Photo	20.00

Plantier, Phil

Baseball	14.00
Cut signature	3.00
3x5 Card	5.00
8x10 Photo	7.00

Puckett, Kirby

Baseball	49.00
Cut signature	10.00
3x5 Card	25.00
8x10 Photo	35.00

Raines, Tim

Baseball	20.00
Cut signature	4.00
3x5 Card	6.00
8x10 Photo	8.00

Randolph, Willie

Baseball	25.00
Cut signature	5.00
3x5 Card	9.00
8x10 Photo	12.00

Reardon, Jeff

Jeff Reardon

Baseball	25.00
Cut signature	6.00
3x5 Card	10.00
8x10 Photo	15.00

Ripken, Cal

Baseball	30.00
Cut signature	6.00
3x5 Card	12.00
8x10 Photo	25.00

Rijo, Jose

Baseball	14.00
Cut signature	3.00
3x5 Card	4.00
8x10 Photo	7.00

Rodriguez, Ivan

Baseball	14.00
Cut signature	3.00
3x5 Card	5.00
8x10 Photo	7.00

Ryan, Nolan

Baseball	45.00
Cut signature	4.00
3x5 Card	15.00
8x10 Photo	25.00

Saberhagen, Bret

Baseball	25.00
Cut signature	5.00
3x5 Card	9.00
8x10 Photo	12.00

Sabo, Chris

Baseball	25.00
Cut signature	5.00
3x5 Card	9.00
8x10 Photo	15.00

Sandberg, Ryne

Baseball	40.00
Cut signature	7.00
3x5 Card	15.00
8x10 Photo	35.00

Sanders, Deion

Baseball	38.00
Cut signature	7.00
3x5 Card	18.00
8x10 Photo	25.00

Santiago, Benito

Baseball	20.00
Cut signature	6.00
3x5 Card	8.00
8x10 Photo	12.00

Sax, Steve

Baseball	25.00
Cut signature	6.00
3x5 Card	9.00
8x10 Photo	18.00

Sheffield, Gary

Baseball	30.00
Cut signature	6.00
3x5 Card	12.00
8x10 Photo	18.00

Sierra, Ruben

Baseball	15.00
Cut signature	3.00
3x5 Card	6.00
8x10 Photo	8.00

Smith, Lee

Baseball	20.00
Cut signature	4.00
3x5 Card	7.00
8x10 Photo	10.00

Smith, Ozzie

Baseball	35.00
Cut signature	6.00
3x5 Card	15.00
8x10 Photo	25.00

Smoltz, John

Baseball	28.00
Cut signature	6.00
3x5 Card	15.00
8x10 Photo	18.00

Stewart, Dave

Baseball	25.00
Cut signature	5.00
3x5 Card	9.00
8x10 Photo	12.00

John Smoltz

Stieb, Dave

Baseball	20.00
Cut signature	4.00
3x5 Card	8.00
8x10 Photo	12.00

Strawberry, Darryl

Darryl Strawberry

Baseball	27.00
Cut signature	5.00
3x5 Card	8.00
8x10 Photo	15.00

Tartabull, Danny

Baseball	25.00
Cut signature	5.00
3x5 Card	6.00
8x10 Photo	8.00

Tettleton, Mickey

Baseball	25.00
Cut signature	5.00
3x5 Card	9.00

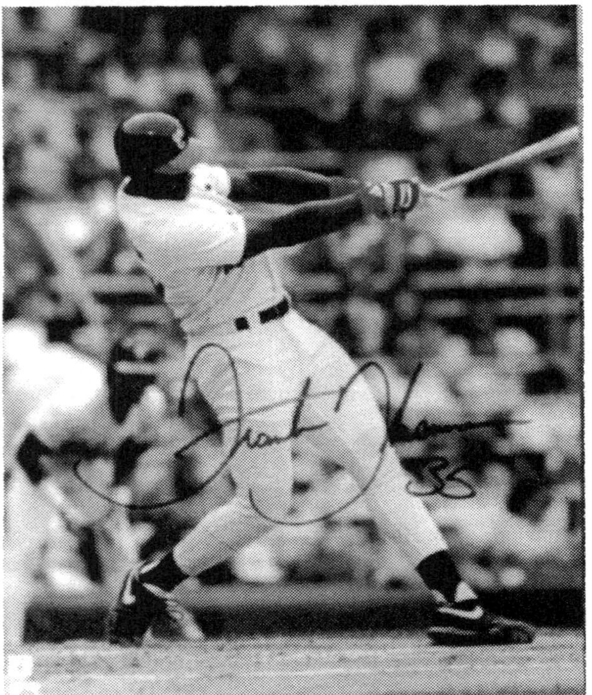

Frank Thomas

8x10 Photo 12.00

Thomas, Frank
Baseball 18.00
Cut signature 4.00
3x5 Card 6.00
8x10 Photo 8.00

Thome, Jim
Baseball 9.00
Cut signature 2.00
3x5 Card 5.00
8x10 Photo 7.00

Trammell, Alan
Baseball 22.00
Cut signature 5.00
3x5 Card 12.00
8x10 Photo 15.00

Valenzuela, Fernando
Baseball 19.00
Cut signature 4.00
Personal document 15.00
3x5 Card 6.00
8x10 Photo 10.00

Van Poppel, Todd
Baseball 15.00
Cut signature 3.00
3x5 Card 4.50
8x10 Photo 8.00

Van Slyke, Andy
Baseball 25.00
Cut signature 5.00
3x5 Card 9.00

8x10 Photo 15.00

Vaughn, Greg
Baseball 22.00
Cut signature 4.00
3x5 Card 8.00
8x10 Photo 12.00

Vaughn, Mo
Baseball 16.00
Cut signature 3.00
3x5 Card 6.00
8x10 Photo 9.00

Ventura, Robin
Baseball 23.00
Cut signature 5.00
3x5 Card 10.00
8x10 Photo 18.00

Viola, Frank
Baseball 22.00
Cut signature 5.00
3x5 Card 8.00
8x10 Photo 15.00

Walker, Larry
Baseball 10.00
Cut signature 2.00
3x5 Card 4.00
8x10 Photo 6.00

Welch, Bob
Baseball 22.00
Cut signature 5.00
3x5 Card 8.00
8x10 Photo 12.00

Whitaker, Lou
Baseball 11.00
Cut signature 3.00
3x5 Card 5.00
8x10 Photo 7.00

Whiten, Mark
Baseball 10.00
Cut signature 2.00
3x5 Card 4.00
8x10 Photo 6.00

Bernie Williams

Williams, Bernie
Baseball 12.00
Cut signature 4.00
3x5 Card 6.00
8x10 Photo 8.00

Williams, Matt
Baseball 22.00
Cut signature 5.00
3x5 Card 8.00
8x10 Photo 15.00

Williams, Mitch
Baseball 45.00
Cut signature 7.00
3x5 Card 20.00
8x10 Photo 35.00

Winfield, Dave
Baseball 45.00
Cut signature 7.00
3x5 Card 18.00
8x10 Photo 30.00

Yount, Robin
Baseball 35.00
Cut signature 7.00
3x5 Card 12.00
8x10 Photo 25.00

Zeile, Todd
Baseball 20.00
Cut signature 5.00
3x5 Card 9.00
8x10 Photo 12.00

BASKETBALL: HALL OF FAME

Archibald, Nate
Basketball 30.00
Cut signature 6.00

3x5 Card 10.00
8x10 Photo 15.00

Arizin, Paul
Basketball 29.00
Cut signature 5.00
3x5 Card 9.00
8x10 Photo 14.00

Auerbach, Red
Basketball 32.00
Cut signature 8.00
3x5 Card 12.00
8x10 Photo 14.00

Barlow, Thomas
Basketball 20.00
Cut signature 4.00
3x5 Card 8.00
8x10 Photo 12.00

Rick Barry

Barry, Rick
Basketball 45.00
Cut signature 7.00
3x5 Card 10.00
8x10 Photo 15.00

Baylor, Elgin

Elgin Baylor

Basketball 42.00
Cut signature 10.00
3x5 Card 15.00
8x10 Photo 20.00

Beckman, John
Basketball 20.00
Cut signature 4.00
3x5 Card 8.00
8x10 Photo 12.00

Bee, Clair
Basketball 24.00
Cut signature 5.00
3x5 Card 10.00
8x10 Photo 14.00

Bing, Dave
Basketball 35.00
Cut signature 4.00
3x5 Card 9.00
8x10 Photo 18.00

Borgmann, Bennie
Basketball 20.00
Cut signature 4.00
3x5 Card 8.00
8x10 Photo 12.00

Bradley, Bill
Basketball 45.00
Cut signature 8.00
3x5 Card 10.00
8x10 Photo 25.00

Brennan, Joseph
Basketball 14.00
Cut signature 2.00
3x5 Card 6.00
8x10 Photo 7.00

Cervi, Alfred
Basketball 20.00
Cut signature 4.00
3x5 Card 8.00
8x10 Photo 12.00

Chamberlain, Wilt
Basketball 125.00
Cut signature 20.00
3x5 Card 45.00
8x10 Photo 75.00

Cooper, Charles
Basketball 45.00
Cut signature 8.00
3x5 Card 12.00
8x10 Photo 24.00

Cousy, Bob

Bob Cousy

Basketball 85.00
Cut signature 10.00
3x5 Card 25.00
8x10 Photo 55.00

Cowens, Dave
Basketball 20.00
Cut signature 5.00
3x5 Card 7.00
8x10 Photo 10.00

Cunningham, Billy
Basketball 30.00
Cut signature 7.00
3x5 Card 9.00
8x10 Photo 14.00

Davies, Robert
Basketball 32.00
Cut signature 8.00
3x5 Card 11.00
8x10 Photo 15.00

DeBernardi, Forrest
Basketball 20.00
Cut signature 5.00
3x5 Card 8.00
8x10 Photo 10.00

DeBusschere, Dave
Basketball 20.00
Cut signature 5.00
3x5 Card 8.00
8x10 Photo 10.00

Dehnert, Henry
Basketball 23.00
Cut signature 7.00
3x5 Card 9.00
8x10 Photo 15.00

Endacott, Paul
Basketball 14.00
Cut signature 6.00
3x5 Card 9.00
8x10 Photo 17.00

Foster, Bud
Basketball 50.00
Cut signature 8.00
3x5 Card 16.00
8x10 Photo 25.00

Frazier, Walt
Basketball 30.00
Cut signature 4.00
3x5 Card 8.00
8x10 Photo 15.00

Friedman, Marty
Basketball 45.00
Cut signature 10.00
3x5 Card 15.00
8x10 Photo 25.00

Fulks, Joe
Basketball 20.00
Cut signature 4.00
3x5 Card 6.00
8x10 Photo 10.00

Gaines, Clarence
Basketball 40.00
Cut signature 7.00
3x5 Card 15.00
8x10 Photo 20.00

Gale, Laddie
Basketball 40.00
Cut signature 7.00
3x5 Card 15.00
8x10 Photo 20.00

Gallatin, Harry
Basketball 45.00
Cut signature 8.00
3x5 Card 15.00
8x10 Photo 24.00

Gates, William
Basketball 50.00
Cut signature 10.00
3x5 Card 15.00
8x10 Photo 25.00

Gola, Tom
Basketball 19.00
Cut signature 3.00
3x5 Card 6.00
8x10 Photo 9.50

Greer, Hal
Basketball 35.00

Earl Monroe

Cut signature 4.00
3x5 Card 6.00
8x10 Photo 17.00

Gruenig, Robert
Basketball 45.00
Cut signature 10.00
3x5 Card 7.00
8x10 Photo 25.00

Hagan, Cliff
Basketball 20.00
Cut signature 4.00
3x5 Card 6.00
8x10 Photo 10.00

Hanson, Victor
Basketball 50.00
Cut signature 10.00
3x5 Card 15.00
8x10 Photo 25.00

Havlicek, John
Basketball 75.00
Cut signature 20.00
3x5 Card 35.00
8x10 Photo 50.00

Hayes, Elvin
Basketball 70.00
Cut signature 18.00
3x5 Card 30.00
8x10 Photo 45.00

Heinsohn, Tommy
Basketball 20.00
Cut signature 6.00
3x5 Card 8.00
8x10 Photo 10.00

Holman, Nat
Basketball 75.00
Cut signature 15.00
3x5 Card 20.00
8x10 Photo 37.00

Holzman, Red
Basketball 55.00
Cut signature 8.00
3x5 Card 15.00
8x10 Photo 27.00

Houbregs, Robert
Basketball 30.00
Cut signature 5.00
3x5 Card 10.00
8x10 Photo 15.00

Hyatt, Chuck
Basketball 40.00
Cut signature 5.00
3x5 Card 10.00
8x10 Photo 20.00

Iba, Henry
Basketball 40.00
Cut signature 5.00
3x5 Card 10.00
8x10 Photo 20.00

Johnson, William
Basketball 40.00
Cut signature 5.00
3x5 Card 10.00
8x10 Photo 20.00

Johnston, Neil
Basketball 35.00
Cut signature 6.00
3x5 Card 9.00
8x10 Photo 17.00

Jones, K.C.
Basketball 18.00
Cut signature 6.00
3x5 Card 8.00
8x10 Photo 10.00

Jones, Sam
Basketball 20.00
Cut signature 6.00
3x5 Card 8.00
8x10 Photo 10.00

Knight, Bobby
Basketball 25.00
Cut signature 5.00
3x5 Card 8.00
8x10 Photo 12.00

Krause, Edward
Basketball 40.00
Cut signature 5.00
3x5 Card 10.00
8x10 Photo 20.00

Kurland, Bob
Basketball 40.00
Cut signature 5.00
3x5 Card 10.00
8x10 Photo 20.00

Lapchick, Joe
Basketball 55.00
Cut signature 9.00
3x5 Card 15.00
8x10 Photo 30.00

Lovellette, Clyde
Basketball 35.00
Cut signature 4.00
3x5 Card 9.00
8x10 Photo 17.00

Lucas, Jerry
Basketball 30.00
Cut signature 5.00
3x5 Card 10.00
8x10 Photo 15.00

Luisetti, Hank
Basketball 50.00
Cut signature 6.00
3x5 Card 12.00
8x10 Photo 25.00

Macauley, Ed
Basketball 30.00
Cut signature 5.00
3x5 Card 10.00
8x10 Photo 15.00

Maravich, Pete
Basketball 40.00
Cut signature 8.00
3x5 Card 14.00
8x10 Photo 20.00

Martin, Slater
Basketball 25.00
Cut signature 4.00
3x5 Card 9.00

8x10 Photo 12.00

McCracken, Branch
Basketball 35.00
Cut signature 7.00
3x5 Card 10.00
8x10 Photo 18.00

McCracken, Jack
Basketball 35.00
Cut signature 7.00
3x5 Card 10.00
8x10 Photo 18.00

McDermott, Bobby
Basketball 40.00
Cut signature 7.00
3x5 Card 15.00
8x10 Photo 20.00

McGuire, Frank
Basketball 35.00
Cut signature 7.00
3x5 Card 9.00
8x10 Photo 18.00

Meyer, Ray
Basketball 40.00
Cut signature 7.00
3x5 Card 15.00
8x10 Photo 20.00

Mikan, George
Basketball 35.00
Cut signature 6.00
3x5 Card 8.50
8x10 Photo 17.00

Mokray, William
Basketball 45.00
Cut signature 8.00
3x5 Card 17.00
8x10 Photo 22.00

Monroe, Earl
Basketball 32.00
Cut signature 8.00
3x5 Card 12.00
8x10 Photo 20.00

Murphy, Charles
Basketball 45.00
Cut signature 7.00
3x5 Card 11.00
8x10 Photo 22.00

Naismith, James
Basketball 2,000.00
Cut signature 600.00
3x5 Card 800.00
8x10 Photo 1,250.00

Page, Harlan
Basketball 35.00
Cut signature 5.00
3x5 Card 10.00
8x10 Photo 20.00

Pettit, Bob
Basketball 40.00
Cut signature 10.00
3x5 Card 15.00
8x10 Photo 20.00

Phillip, Andy
Basketball 25.00
Cut signature 5.00
3x5 Card 7.00
8x10 Photo 15.00

Podoloff, Maurice
Basketball 25.00
Cut signature 5.00
3x5 Card 7.00

8x10 Photo 15.00

Pollard, Jim
Basketball 20.00
Cut signature 5.00
3x5 Card 10.00
8x10 Photo 15.00

Ramsey, Frank
Basketball 27.00
Cut signature 7.00
3x5 Card 10.00
8x10 Photo 15.00

Reed, Willis
Basketball 40.00
Cut signature 9.00
3x5 Card 12.00
8x10 Photo 20.00

Robertson, Oscar
Basketball 35.00
Cut signature 8.00
3x5 Card 12.00
8x10 Photo 17.00

Roosma, John
Basketball 25.00
Cut signature 5.00
3x5 Card 10.00
8x10 Photo 15.00

Rupp, Adolph
Basketball 30.00
Cut signature 5.00
3x5 Card 10.00
8x10 Photo 15.00

Russell, Bill
Basketball . . . . NA
Cut signature . . . . NA
3x5 Card . . . . NA
8x10 Photo 200.00

Saperstein, Abe
Basketball 150.00
Cut signature 20.00
3x5 Card 40.00
8x10 Photo 75.00

Schayes, Dolph
Basketball 65.00
Cut signature 10.00
3x5 Card 15.00
8x10 Photo 30.00

Schmidt, Ernest
Basketball 40.00
Cut signature 6.00
3x5 Card 12.00
8x10 Photo 20.00

Schommer, John
Basketball 30.00
Cut signature 5.00
3x5 Card 10.00
8x10 Photo 15.00

Sedran, Barney
Basketball 25.00
Cut signature 5.00
3x5 Card 7.00
8x10 Photo 12.50

Sharman, Bill

Jerry West

Basketball 25.00
Cut signature 5.00
3x5 Card 7.00
8x10 Photo 12.50

Smith, Dean
Basketball 75.00
Cut signature 15.00
3x5 Card 20.00
8x10 Photo 35.00

Stagg, Amos Alonzo
Basketball 65.00
Cut signature 7.00
3x5 Card 15.00
8x10 Photo 30.00

Steinmetz, Christian
Basketball 30.00
Cut signature 8.00
3x5 Card 12.00
8x10 Photo 20.00

Thompson, John
Basketball 25.00
Cut signature 8.00
3x5 Card 10.00
8x10 Photo 12.00

Thurmond, Nate
Basketball 25.00
Cut signature 6.00
3x5 Card 12.00
8x10 Photo 15.00

Twyman, Jack
Basketball 30.00
Cut signature 6.00
3x5 Card 9.00
8x10 Photo 15.00

Unseld, Wes
Basketball 30.00
Cut signature 6.00
3x5 Card 9.00
8x10 Photo 15.00

Vandivier, Robert
Basketball 35.00
Cut signature 5.00
3x5 Card 7.00
8x10 Photo 20.00

Wachter, Edward
Basketball 20.00
Cut signature 6.00
3x5 Card 8.00
8x10 Photo 15.00

Wanzer, Robert
Basketball 25.00
Cut signature 5.00
3x5 Card 10.00
8x10 Photo 17.00

West, Jerry
Basketball 30.00
Cut signature 7.00
3x5 Card 10.00
8x10 Photo 15.00

Wilkens, Lenny
Basketball 49.00
Cut signature 10.00
3x5 Card 27.00
8x10 Photo 32.00

Wooden, John
Basketball 65.00
Cut signature 8.00
3x5 Card 15.00
8x10 Photo 30.00

BASKETBALL: INACTIVE PLAYERS

Abdul-Jabbar, Kareem
Basketball 78.00
Cut signature 10.00
3x5 Card 25.00
8x10 Photo 40.00

Adams, Alvan
Basketball 18.00
Cut signature 4.00
3x5 Card 6.00
8x10 Photo 9.00

Adelman, Rick
Basketball 12.00
Cut signature 3.00
3x5 Card 5.00
8x10 Photo 6.00

Attles, Al
Basketball 18.00
Cut signature 4.00
3x5 Card 6.00
8x10 Photo 9.00

Barnett, Dick
Basketball 25.00
Cut signature 6.00
3x5 Card 8.00
8x10 Photo 10.00

Beaty, Zelmo
Basketball 30.00
Cut signature 5.00
3x5 Card 10.00
8x10 Photo 15.00

Bellamy, Walt
Basketball 30.00
Cut signature 5.00
3x5 Card 10.00
8x10 Photo 15.00

Bibby, Henry
Basketball 15.00
Cut signature 4.00
3x5 Card 6.00
8x10 Photo 8.00

Don Chaney

Braun, Carl
Basketball 25.00
Cut signature 6.00
3x5 Card 8.00
8x10 Photo 12.00

Brown, Fred
Basketball 24.00
Cut signature 4.00
3x5 Card 8.00
8x10 Photo 12.00

Brown, Larry
Basketball 20.00
Cut signature 4.00
3x5 Card 6.00
8x10 Photo 10.00

Buckner, Quinn
Basketball 12.00
Cut signature 4.00
3x5 Card 6.00
8x10 Photo 8.00

Calverley, Ernie
Basketball 20.00
Cut signature 5.00
3x5 Card 7.00
8x10 Photo 12.00

Carr, Austin
Basketball 15.00
Cut signature 4.00
3x5 Card 6.00
8x10 Photo 10.00

Chaney, Don
Basketball 15.00
Cut signature 4.00
3x5 Card 6.00
8x10 Photo 10.00

Chenier, Phil
Basketball 20.00
Cut signature 5.00
3x5 Card 7.00
8x10 Photo 12.00

Clifton, Nat
Basketball 22.00
Cut signature 5.00
3x5 Card 8.00
8x10 Photo 12.00

Collins, Doug
Basketball 14.00
Cut signature 4.00
3x5 Card 6.00
8x10 Photo 8.00

Dampier, Louie
Basketball 24.00
Cut signature 6.00
3x5 Card 8.00
8x10 Photo 12.00

Dandridge, Bob
Basketball 26.00
Cut signature 6.00
3x5 Card 9.00
8x10 Photo 13.00

Dantley, Adrian
Basketball 30.00
Cut signature 8.00
3x5 Card 10.00
8x10 Photo 12.00

Dawkins, Darryl
Basketball 24.00
Cut signature 4.00
3x5 Card 8.00
8x10 Photo 12.00

Dunleavy, Mike
Basketball 10.00
Cut signature 3.00
3x5 Card 5.00
8x10 Photo 7.00

Embry, Wayne
Basketball 20.00
Cut signature 4.00
3x5 Card 6.00
8x10 Photo 10.00

English, Alex
Basketball 25.00
Cut signature 5.00
3x5 Card 7.00
8x10 Photo 12.00

Erving, Julius
Basketball . . . 100.00
Cut signature . . . 15.00
3x5 Card . . . 30.00
8x10 Photo . . . 50.00

Ford, Chris
Basketball . . . 12.00
Cut signature . . . 4.00
3x5 Card . . . 6.00
8x10 Photo . . . 8.00

Free, World B.
Basketball . . . 20.00
Cut signature . . . 5.00
3x5 Card . . . 7.00
8x10 Photo . . . 12.00

Gallatin, Harry
Basketball . . . 22.00
Cut signature . . . 7.00
3x5 Card . . . 9.00
8x10 Photo . . . 12.00

Gilmore, Artis
Basketball . . . 55.00
Cut signature . . . 10.00
3x5 Card . . . 15.00
8x10 Photo . . . 30.00

Goodrich, Gail
Basketball . . . 65.00
Cut signature . . . 15.00
3x5 Card . . . 10.00
8x10 Photo . . . 30.00

Goukas, Matt
Basketball . . . 14.00
Cut signature . . . 2.00
3x5 Card . . . 4.00
8x10 Photo . . . 7.00

Hairston, Happy
Basketball . . . 18.00
Cut signature . . . 4.00
3x5 Card . . . 7.00
8x10 Photo . . . 9.00

Haskins, Clem
Basketball . . . 12.00
Cut signature . . . 2.00
3x5 Card . . . 4.00
8x10 Photo . . . 6.00

Hawkins, Connie
Basketball . . . 70.00
Cut signature . . . 10.00
3x5 Card . . . 17.00
8x10 Photo . . . 35.00

Haywood, Spencer
Basketball . . . 40.00
Cut signature . . . 8.00
3x5 Card . . . 12.00
8x10 Photo . . . 20.00

Hazzard, Walt
Basketball . . . 8.00
Cut signature . . . 1.00
3x5 Card . . . 3.00
8x10 Photo . . . 6.00

Hudson, Lou
Basketball . . . 24.00
Cut signature . . . 6.00
3x5 Card . . . 8.00
8x10 Photo . . . 14.00

Hundley, Rod
Basketball . . . 24.00
Cut signature . . . 6.00
3x5 Card . . . 8.00
8x10 Photo . . . 14.00

Issel, Dan
Basketball . . . 30.00
Cut signature . . . 5.00
3x5 Card . . . 10.00
8x10 Photo . . . 15.00

Jackson, Phil
Basketball . . . 45.00
Cut signature . . . 7.00
3x5 Card . . . 12.00
8x10 Photo . . . 20.00

Johnson, Dennis
Basketball . . . 30.00
Cut signature . . . 8.00
3x5 Card . . . 10.00
8x10 Photo . . . 15.00

Johnson, Gus
Basketball . . . 25.00
Cut signature . . . 5.00
3x5 Card . . . 10.00
8x10 Photo . . . 15.00

Johnson, Magic
Basketball . . . 100.00
Cut signature . . . 25.00
3x5 Card . . . 35.00
8x10 Photo . . . 50.00

Johnson, Marques
Basketball . . . 45.00
Cut signature . . . 8.00
3x5 Card . . . 12.00
8x10 Photo . . . 25.00

Jones, Bobby
Basketball . . . 20.00
Cut signature . . . 5.00
3x5 Card . . . 10.00
8x10 Photo . . . 15.00

Jones, Caldwell
Basketball . . . 10.00
Cut signature . . . 2.00
3x5 Card . . . 4.00
8x10 Photo . . . 6.00

Kupchak, Mitch
Basketball . . . 11.00
Cut signature . . . 3.00
3x5 Card . . . 5.00
8x10 Photo . . . 7.00

Lanier, Bob
Basketball . . . 35.00
Cut signature . . . 7.00
3x5 Card . . . 10.00
8x10 Photo . . . 15.00

Love, Bob
Basketball . . . 20.00
Cut signature . . . 5.00
3x5 Card . . . 10.00
8x10 Photo . . . 15.00

Lucas, John
Basketball . . . 18.00
Cut signature . . . 5.00
3x5 Card . . . 7.00
8x10 Photo . . . 12.00

Lucas, Maurice
Basketball . . . 30.00
Cut signature . . . 7.00
3x5 Card . . . 10.00
8x10 Photo . . . 15.00

Maxwell, Cedric
Basketball . . . 20.00
Cut signature . . . 5.00
3x5 Card . . . 10.00
8x10 Photo . . . 15.00

McAdoo, Bob
Basketball . . . 35.00
Cut signature . . . 10.00
3x5 Card . . . 15.00
8x10 Photo . . . 20.00

McGinnis, George
Basketball . . . 32.00
Cut signature . . . 9.00
3x5 Card . . . 12.00
8x10 Photo . . . 18.00

Moncreif, Sidney
Basketball . . . 20.00
Cut signature . . . 5.00
3x5 Card . . . 10.00
8x10 Photo . . . 15.00

Murphy, Calvin
Basketball . . . 24.00
Cut signature . . . 6.00
3x5 Card . . . 8.00
8x10 Photo . . . 12.00

Nelson, Don
Basketball . . . 15.00
Cut signature . . . 3.00
3x5 Card . . . 8.00
8x10 Photo . . . 10.00

Nixon, Norm
Basketball . . . 15.00
Cut signature . . . 3.00
3x5 Card . . . 8.00
8x10 Photo . . . 10.00

Paxson, Jim
Basketball . . . 20.00
Cut signature . . . 5.00
3x5 Card . . . 10.00
8x10 Photo . . . 15.00

Porter, Kevin
Basketball . . . 14.00
Cut signature . . . 2.00
3x5 Card . . . 4.00
8x10 Photo . . . 7.00

Rambis, Kurt
Basketball . . . 30.00
Cut signature . . . 8.00
3x5 Card . . . 10.00
8x10 Photo . . . 15.00

Riley, Pat
Basketball . . . 45.00
Cut signature . . . 7.00
3x5 Card . . . 15.00
8x10 Photo . . . 20.00

Sikma, Jack
Basketball . . . 20.00
Cut signature . . . 5.00
3x5 Card . . . 10.00
8x10 Photo . . . 15.00

Silas, Paul
Basketball . . . 18.00
Cut signature . . . 4.00
3x5 Card . . . 6.00
8x10 Photo . . . 8.00

Sloan, Jerry
Basketball . . . 15.00
Cut signature . . . 3.00
3x5 Card . . . 5.00
8x10 Photo . . . 10.00

Theus, Reggie
Basketball . . . 21.00
Cut signature . . . 6.00
3x5 Card . . . 11.00
8x10 Photo . . . 16.00

Thompson, David
Basketball . . . 20.00
Cut signature . . . 5.00

3x5 Card 10.00
8x10 Photo 15.00

Tomjanovich, Rudy
Basketball 19.00
Cut signature 4.00
3x5 Card 9.00
8x10 Photo 12.00

Van Lier, Norm
Basketball 20.00
Cut signature 5.00
3x5 Card 10.00
8x10 Photo 15.00

Walker, Chet
Basketball 27.00
Cut signature 6.00
3x5 Card 10.00
8x10 Photo 15.00

Walton, Bill
Basketball 32.00
Cut signature 6.00
3x5 Card 10.00
8x10 Photo 15.00

Weiss, Bob
Basketball 12.00
Cut signature 2.00
3x5 Card 4.00
8x10 Photo 6.00

Westphal, Paul
Basketball 14.00
Cut signature 3.00
3x5 Card 5.00
8x10 Photo 7.00

White, Jo Jo
Basketball 22.00
Cut signature 7.00
3x5 Card 12.00
8x10 Photo 16.00

Wicks, Sidney
Basketball 18.00
Cut signature 2.00
3x5 Card 5.00
8x10 Photo 7.00

Wilkes, Jamaal
Basketball 18.00
Cut signature 2.00
3x5 Card 5.00
8x10 Photo 7.00

Williams, Gus
Basketball 20.00
Cut signature 5.00
3x5 Card 10.00
8x10 Photo 15.00

Wise, Willie
Basketball 14.00
Cut signature 2.00
3x5 Card 4.00
8x10 Photo 7.00

Zaslofsky, Max
Basketball 45.00
Cut signature 12.00
3x5 Card 17.00
8x10 Photo 25.00

BASKETBALL: ACTIVE PLAYERS

Adams, Michael
Basketball 12.00
Cut signature 4.00
3x5 Card 6.00
8x10 Photo 8.00

Aguirre, Mark
Basketball 12.00
Cut signature 4.00
3x5 Card 6.00
8x10 Photo 8.00

Ainge, Danny
Basketball 30.00
Cut signature 7.00
3x5 Card 11.00
8x10 Photo 15.00

Anderson, Kenny
Basketball 15.00
Cut signature 4.00
3x5 Card 7.00
8x10 Photo 12.00

Anderson, Nick
Basketball 12.00
Cut signature 4.00
3x5 Card 6.00
8x10 Photo 8.00

Anderson, Willie
Basketball 10.00
Cut signature 3.00
3x5 Card 5.00
8x10 Photo 7.00

Larry Bird

Anthony, Greg
Basketball 10.00
Cut signature 3.00
3x5 Card 5.00
8x10 Photo 7.00

Armstrong, B.J.
Basketball 12.00
Cut signature 4.00
3x5 Card 6.00
8x10 Photo 8.00

Augmon, Stacey
Basketball 12.00
Cut signature 4.00
3x5 Card 6.00
8x10 Photo 8.00

Bailey, Thurl
Basketball 12.00
Cut signature 4.00
3x5 Card 6.00
8x10 Photo 8.00

Barkley, Charles
Basketball 40.00
Cut signature 8.00
3x5 Card 15.00
8x10 Photo 20.00

Bird, Larry
Basketball 45.00
Cut signature 5.00
3x5 Card 22.00
8x10 Photo 35.00

Blackman, Rolando
Basketball . . . 20.00
Cut signature . . . 6.00
3x5 Card . . . 8.00
8x10 Photo . . . 10.00

Blaylock, Mookie
Basketball . . . 15.00
Cut signature . . . 4.00
3x5 Card . . . 7.00
8x10 Photo . . . 9.00

Bol, Manute
Basketball . . . 30.00
Cut signature . . . 5.00
3x5 Card . . . 7.00
8x10 Photo . . . 12.00

Brandon, Terrell
Basketball . . . 12.00
Cut signature . . . 4.00
3x5 Card . . . 6.00
8x10 Photo . . . 8.00

Brown, Dee
Basketball . . . 12.00
Cut signature . . . 4.00
3x5 Card . . . 5.00
8x10 Photo . . . 7.00

Burton, Willie
Basketball . . . 11.00
Cut signature . . . 4.00
3x5 Card . . . 5.00
8x10 Photo . . . 7.00

Campbell, Elden
Basketball . . . 14.00
Cut signature . . . 6.00
3x5 Card . . . 6.00
8x10 Photo . . . 9.00

Cartwright, Bill
Basketball . . . 30.00
Cut signature . . . 8.00
3x5 Card . . . 12.00
8x10 Photo . . . 15.00

Causwell, Duane
Basketball . . . 12.00
Cut signature . . . 4.00
3x5 Card . . . 6.00
8x10 Photo . . . 8.00

Ceballos, Cedric
Basketball . . . 12.00
Cut signature . . . 4.00
3x5 Card . . . 6.00
8x10 Photo . . . 8.00

Chambers, Tom
Basketball . . . 12.00
Cut signature . . . 3.00
3x5 Card . . . 5.00
8x10 Photo . . . 7.00

Chapman, Rex
Basketball . . . 11.00
Cut signature . . . 3.00
3x5 Card . . . 5.00
8x10 Photo . . . 7.00

Cheeks, Maurice
Basketball . . . 15.00
Cut signature . . . 5.00
3x5 Card . . . 6.00
8x10 Photo . . . 8.00

Coleman, Derrick
Basketball . . . 35.00
Cut signature . . . 6.00
3x5 Card . . . 12.00
8x10 Photo . . . 15.00

Corbin, Tyrone
Basketball . . . 11.00
Cut signature . . . 3.00
3x5 Card . . . 5.00
8x10 Photo . . . 7.00

Cummings, Terry
Basketball . . . 15.00
Cut signature . . . 5.00
3x5 Card . . . 7.00
8x10 Photo . . . 9.00

Daugherty, Brad
Basketball . . . 20.00
Cut signature . . . 5.00
3x5 Card . . . 7.00
8x10 Photo . . . 10.00

Davis, Walter
Basketball . . . 12.00
Cut signature . . . 4.00
3x5 Card . . . 6.00
8x10 Photo . . . 8.00

Dawkins, Johnny
Basketball . . . 14.00
Cut signature . . . 5.00
3x5 Card . . . 7.00
8x10 Photo . . . 9.00

Day, Todd
Basketball . . . 10.00
Cut signature . . . 2.00
3x5 Card . . . 4.00
8x10 Photo . . . 6.00

Douglas, Sherman
Basketball . . . 12.00
Cut signature . . . 4.00
3x5 Card . . . 6.00
8x10 Photo . . . 8.00

Drexler, Clyde
Basketball . . . 45.00
Cut signature . . . 9.00
3x5 Card . . . 13.00
8x10 Photo . . . 25.00

Dumars, Joe
Basketball . . . 30.00
Cut signature . . . 6.00
3x5 Card . . . 12.00
8x10 Photo . . . 15.00

Chris Mullin

Edwards, Blue
Basketball . . . 14.00
Cut signature . . . 5.00
3x5 Card . . . 7.00
8x10 Photo . . . 9.00

Elliott, Sean
Basketball . . . 12.00
Cut signature . . . 4.00
3x5 Card . . . 6.00
8x10 Photo . . . 8.00

Ellis, Dale
Basketball . . . 14.00
Cut signature . . . 5.00
3x5 Card . . . 7.00
8x10 Photo . . . 9.00

Ellison, Pervis
Basketball . . . 20.00
Cut signature . . . 6.00
3x5 Card . . . 9.00
8x10 Photo . . . 12.00

Ewing, Patrick
Basketball . . . 69.00
Cut signature . . . 12.00
3x5 Card . . . 35.00
8x10 Photo . . . 42.00

Ferry, Danny
Basketball . . . 25.00
Cut signature . . . 5.00
3x5 Card . . . 10.00
8x10 Photo . . . 15.00

Fox, Rick
Basketball . . . 12.00
Cut signature . . . 4.00
3x5 Card . . . 6.00
8x10 Photo . . . 8.00

Gamble, Kevin
Basketball . . . 10.00
Cut signature . . . 3.00
3x5 Card . . . 6.00
8x10 Photo . . . 9.00

Gill, Kendall
Basketball . . . 12.00
Cut signature . . . 4.00
3x5 Card . . . 6.00
8x10 Photo . . . 8.00

Gilliam, Armon
Basketball . . . 20.00
Cut signature . . . 4.00
3x5 Card . . . 7.00
8x10 Photo . . . 12.00

Grant, Harvey
Basketball . . . 20.00
Cut signature . . . 4.00
3x5 Card . . . 9.00
8x10 Photo . . . 13.00

Grant, Horace
Basketball . . . 25.00
Cut signature . . . 4.00
3x5 Card . . . 6.00
8x10 Photo . . . 8.00

Green, A.C.
Basketball . . . 30.00
Cut signature . . . 8.00
3x5 Card . . . 12.00
8x10 Photo . . . 15.00

Gugliotta, Tom
Basketball . . . 12.00
Cut signature . . . 4.00
3x5 Card . . . 6.00
8x10 Photo . . . 8.00

Hardaway, Tim
Basketball . . . 40.00
Cut signature . . . 7.00
3x5 Card . . . 12.00
8x10 Photo . . . 18.00

Harper, Derek

Basketball 14.00
Cut signature 4.00
3x5 Card 6.00
8x10 Photo 8.00

Harper, Ron
Basketball 10.00
Cut signature 2.00
3x5 Card 4.00
8x10 Photo 6.00

Hawkins, Hersey
Basketball 27.00
Cut signature 8.00
3x5 Card 10.00
8x10 Photo 15.00

Hornacek, Jeff
Basketball 30.00
Cut signature 8.00
3x5 Card 10.00
8x10 Photo 15.00

Horry, Robert
Basketball 10.00
Cut signature 2.00
3x5 Card 4.00
8x10 Photo 6.00

Jackson, Chris
Basketball 10.00
Cut signature 2.00
3x5 Card 4.00
8x10 Photo 6.00

Jackson, Mark
Basketball 20.00
Cut signature 4.00
3x5 Card 8.00
8x10 Photo 12.00

Johnson, Kevin
Basketball 30.00
Cut signature 8.00
3x5 Card 11.00
8x10 Photo 15.00

Johnson, Larry
Basketball 35.00
Cut signature 5.00
3x5 Card 10.00
8x10 Photo 15.00

Johnson, Vinnie
Basketball 12.00
Cut signature 4.00
3x5 Card 6.00
8x10 Photo 8.00

Jordan,Michael
Basketball 45.00
Cut signature 6.00
3x5 Card 18.00
8x10 Photo 30.00

Kemp, Shawn
Basketball 20.00
Cut signature 4.00
3x5 Card 8.00
8x10 Photo 12.00

Kersey, Jerome
Basketball 18.00
Cut signature 4.00
3x5 Card 6.00
8x10 Photo 8.00

Kimble, Bo
Basketball 16.00
Cut signature 5.00
3x5 Card 7.00
8x10 Photo 9.00

King, Bernard
Basketball 16.00
Cut signature 5.00
3x5 Card 7.00
8x10 Photo 9.00

King, Stacey
Basketball 19.00
Cut signature 5.00
3x5 Card 7.00
8x10 Photo 9.00

Laettner, Christian
Basketball 35.00
Cut signature 6.00
3x5 Card 12.00
8x10 Photo 25.00

Laimbeer, Bill
Basketball 40.00
Cut signature 10.00
3x5 Card 15.00
8x10 Photo 20.00

Lever, Fat
Basketball 20.00
Cut signature 4.00
3x5 Card 6.00
8x10 Photo 8.00

Lewis, Reggie
Basketball 25.00
Cut signature 6.00
3x5 Card 8.00
8x10 Photo 15.00

Macon, Mark
Basketball 18.00
Cut signature 5.00
3x5 Card 7.00
8x10 Photo 9.00

Majerle, Dan
Basketball 25.00
Cut signature 6.00
3x5 Card 9.00
8x10 Photo 15.00

Malone, Jeff
Basketball 20.00
Cut signature 4.00
3x5 Card 6.00
8x10 Photo 8.00

Malone, Karl
Basketball 45.00
Cut signature 8.00
3x5 Card 12.00
8x10 Photo 25.00

Malone, Moses
Basketball 35.00
Cut signature 8.00
3x5 Card 10.00
8x10 Photo 20.00

Manning, Danny
Basketball 25.00
Cut signature 4.00
3x5 Card 8.00
8x10 Photo 15.00

Marciulionis, Sharunas
Basketball 26.00
Cut signature 4.00
3x5 Card 6.00
8x10 Photo 13.00

Maxwell, Vernon
Basketball 18.00
Cut signature 4.00
3x5 Card 6.00
8x10 Photo 8.00

McDaniel, Xavier
Basketball 35.00
Cut signature 5.00
3x5 Card 12.00
8x10 Photo 25.00

McHale, Kevin
Basketball 30.00
Cut signature 5.00
3x5 Card 11.00
8x10 Photo 17.00

Miller, Reggie
Basketball 12.00
Cut signature 4.00
3x5 Card 6.00
8x10 Photo 8.00

Miner, Harold
Basketball 15.00
Cut signature 4.00
3x5 Card 6.00
8x10 Photo 8.00

Morris, Chris
Basketball 12.00
Cut signature 2.00
3x5 Card 4.00
8x10 Photo 6.00

Mourning, Alonzo
Basketball 28.00

Cut signature 4.00
3x5 Card 6.00
8x10 Photo 10.00

Mullin, Chris
Basketball 28.00
Cut signature 4.00
3x5 Card 6.00
8x10 Photo 10.00

Murdock, Eric
Basketball 12.00
Cut signature 4.00
3x5 Card 6.00
8x10 Photo 8.00

Mutombo, Dikembe
Basketball 59.00
Cut signature 10.00
3x5 Card 22.00
8x10 Photo 27.00

Nance, Larry
Basketball 12.00
Cut signature 4.00
3x5 Card 6.00
8x10 Photo 8.00

Norman, Ken
Basketball 22.00
Cut signature 4.00
3x5 Card 8.00
8x10 Photo 12.00

Oakley, Charles
Basketball 30.00
Cut signature 4.00
3x5 Card 12.00
8x10 Photo 0.00

Olajuwon, Hakeem
Basketball 50.00
Cut signature 8.00
3x5 Card 17.00
8x10 Photo 25.00

O'Neal, Shaquille
Basketball 45.00
Cut signature 10.00
3x5 Card 18.00
8x10 Photo 30.00

Owens, Billy
Basketball 12.00
Cut signature 4.00
3x5 Card 6.00
8x10 Photo 8.00

Parish, Robert
Basketball 35.00
Cut signature 8.00
3x5 Card 15.00
8x10 Photo 20.00

Payton, Gary
Basketball 15.00
Cut signature 3.00
3x5 Card 7.00
8x10 Photo 9.00

Peeler, Anthony
Basketball 12.00
Cut signature 4.00
3x5 Card 6.00
8x10 Photo 8.00

Perkins, Sam
Basketball 20.00
Cut signature 4.00
3x5 Card 10.00
8x10 Photo 13.00

Person, Chuck
Basketball 20.00
Cut signature 4.00

David Robinson

3x5 Card 10.00
8x10 Photo 13.00

Petrovic, Drazen
Basketball 25.00
Cut signature 5.00
3x5 Card 10.00
8x10 Photo 15.00

Pippen, Scottie
Basketball 32.00
Cut signature 7.00
3x5 Card 15.00
8x10 Photo 25.00

Porter, Terry
Basketball 24.00
Cut signature 4.00
3x5 Card 9.00
8x10 Photo 14.00

Reid, J.R.
Basketball 23.00
Cut signature 3.00
3x5 Card 8.00
8x10 Photo 13.00

Rice, Glenn
Basketball 15.00
Cut signature 3.00
3x5 Card 5.00
8x10 Photo 7.00

Richardson, Pooh
Basketball 18.00
Cut signature 4.00
3x5 Card 6.00
8x10 Photo 8.00

Richmond, Mitch
Basketball 20.00
Cut signature 5.00
3x5 Card 7.00
8x10 Photo 9.00

Rivers, Doc
Basketball 20.00
Cut signature 5.00
3x5 Card 7.00
8x10 Photo 9.00

Roberston, Alvin
Basketball 14.00
Cut signature 4.00
3x5 Card 6.00
8x10 Photo 8.00

Robinson, Cliff
Basketball 20.00
Cut signature 5.00
3x5 Card 10.00
8x10 Photo 15.00

Robinson, David
Basketball 42.00
Cut signature 8.00
3x5 Card 15.00
8x10 Photo 20.00

Robinson, Rumeal
Basketball 20.00
Cut signature 5.00
3x5 Card 10.00
8x10 Photo 15.00

Rodman, Dennis
Basketball 19.00
Cut signature 4.00

3x5 Card	9.00
8x10 Photo	14.00

Schrempf, Detlef

Basketball	25.00
Cut signature	5.00
3x5 Card	10.00
8x10 Photo	15.00

Scott, Byron

Basketball	25.00
Cut signature	5.00
3x5 Card	10.00
8x10 Photo	13.00

Scott, Dennis

Basketball	15.00
Cut signature	3.00
3x5 Card	5.00
8x10 Photo	7.00

Seikaly, Rony

Basketball	20.00
Cut signature	8.00
3x5 Card	12.00
8x10 Photo	10.00

Shaw, Brian

Basketball	24.00
Cut signature	5.00
3x5 Card	10.00
8x10 Photo	15.00

Simmons, Lionel

Basketball	30.00
Cut signature	6.00
3x5 Card	9.00
8x10 Photo	15.00

Skiles, Scott

Basketball	20.00
Cut signature	4.00
3x5 Card	8.00
8x10 Photo	12.00

Spud Webb

Smith, Charles

Basketball	25.00
Cut signature	5.00
3x5 Card	10.00
8x10 Photo	15.00

Smith, Steve

Basketball	20.00
Cut signature	4.00
3x5 Card	6.00
8x10 Photo	8.00

Starks, John

Basketball	18.00
Cut signature	3.00
3x5 Card	5.00
8x10 Photo	7.00

Stockton, John

Basketball	24.00
Cut signature	6.00
3x5 Card	8.00
8x10 Photo	10.00

Tisdale, Wayman

Basketball	24.00

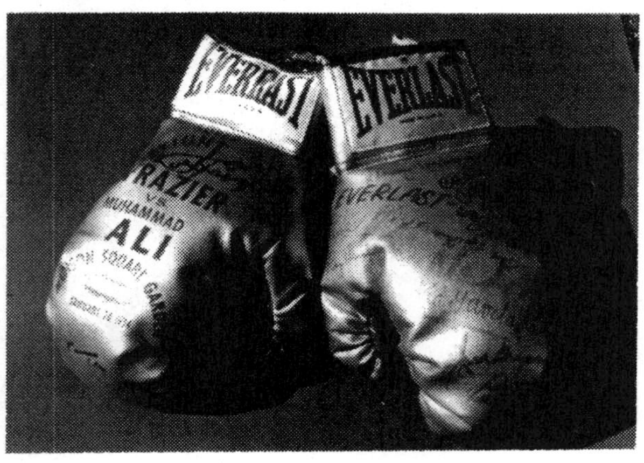

Frazier vs. Ali (1) Commemorative Gloves

Cut signature	6.00
3x5 Card	8.00
8x10 Photo	10.00

Webb, Spud

Basketball	30.00
Cut signature	8.00
3x5 Card	10.00
8x10 Photo	15.00

Wilkins, Dominique

Basketball	35.00
Cut signature	8.00
3x5 Card	12.00
8x10 Photo	20.00

Williams, Buck

Basketball	20.00
Cut signature	4.00
3x5 Card	8.00
8x10 Photo	12.00

Williams, John

Basketball	12.00
Cut signature	2.00
3x5 Card	4.00
8x10 Photo	6.00

Williams, Walt

Basketball	12.00
Cut signature	2.00
3x5 Card	4.00
8x10 Photo	6.00

Worthy, James

Basketball	38.00
Cut signature	6.00
3x5 Card	12.00
8x10 Photo	20.00

INACTIVE BOXERS

Ali, Muhammed

Boxing Gloves	200.00
Cut signature	20.00
Personal document	175.00
3x5 Card	30.00
8x10 Photo	60.00
as ***Cassius Clay***	
Boxing Gloves	350.00
Cut signature	50.00
Personal document	300.00
3x5 Card	65.00
8x10 Photo	125.00

Antuofermo, Vito

Boxing Gloves	100.00
Cut signature	2.00
Personal document	50.00
3x5 Card	5.00
8x10 Photo	15.00

Arguello, Alexis

Boxing Gloves	100.00
Cut signature	5.00
Personal document	45.00
3x5 Card	7.00
8x10 Photo	15.00

Armstrong, Henry

Boxing Gloves	450.00
Cut signature	20.00
Personal document	300.00
3x5 Card	35.00
8x10 Photo	150.00

Attell, Abe

Boxing Gloves	450.00

Muhammed Ali

Cut signature	50.00
Personal document	300.00
3x5 Card	100.00
8x10 Photo	250.00

Baer, Max

Boxing Gloves	450.00
Cut signature	20.00
Personal document	150.00
3x5 Card	50.00
8x10 Photo	200.00

Basilio, Carmen

Boxing Gloves	70.00
Cut signature	2.00
Personal document	50.00
3x5 Card	5.00
8x10 Photo	12.00

Benvenuti, Nino

Boxing Gloves	350.00
Cut signature	10.00
Personal document	200.00
3x5 Card	15.00
8x10 Photo	25.00

Braddock, James J.

Boxing Gloves	500.00
Cut signature	25.00
Personal document	250.00
3x5 Card	50.00
8x10 Photo	150.00

Britton, Jack

Boxing Gloves	500.00
Cut signature	75.00
Personal document	300.00
3x5 Card	100.00
8x10 Photo	150.00

Burns, Tommy

Boxing Gloves	2000.00
Cut signature	200.00
Personal document	700.00
3x5 Card	250.00
8x10 Photo	1000.00

Canzoneri, Tony

Boxing Gloves	400.00
Cut signature	35.00
Personal document	250.00
3x5 Card	50.00
8x10 Photo	200.00

Carnera, Primo

Boxing Gloves	1000.00
Cut signature	100.00
Personal document	250.00
3x5 Card	150.00
8x10 Photo	450.00

Carpentier, Georges

Boxing Gloves	500.00
Cut signature	100.00
Personal document	300.00
3x5 Card	150.00
8x10 Photo	250.00

Cerdan, Marcel

Boxing Gloves	2000.00
Cut signature	250.00
Personal document	700.00
3x5 Card	400.00
8x10 Photo	1000.00

Charles, Ezzard

Boxing Gloves	250.00
Cut signature	25.00
Personal document	200.00
3x5 Card	75.00
8x10 Photo	150.00

Conn, Billy

Boxing Gloves	100.00
Cut signature	6.00
Personal document	80.00
3x5 Card	10.00
8x10 Photo	30.00

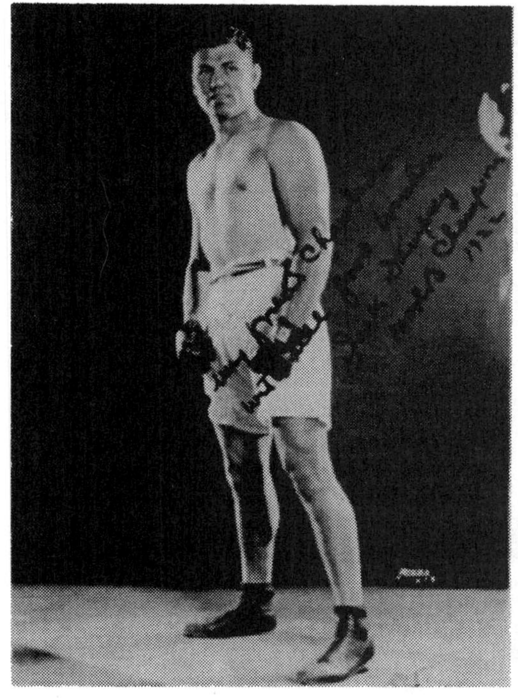

Jack Dempsey

Cooney, Gerry

Boxing Gloves	150.00
Cut signature	2.00
Personal document	50.00
3x5 Card	5.00
8x10 Photo	15.00

Corbett, James J.

Boxing Gloves	2500.00
Cut signature	350.00
Personal document	750.00
3x5 Card	NA
8x10 Photo	1000.00

Dempsey, Jack

Boxing Gloves	450.00
Cut signature	15.00
Personal document	150.00
3x5 Card	35.00
8x10 Photo	150.00

Douglas, Buster

Boxing Gloves	125.00
Cut signature	8.00
Personal document	75.00
3x5 Card	10.00
8x10 Photo	25.00

Duran, Roberto

Boxing Gloves	125.00
Cut signature	10.00
Personal document	100.00
3x5 Card	15.00
8x10 Photo	35.00

Bob Fitzsimmons

Fitzsimmons, Bob

Boxing Gloves	5000.00
Cut signature	1500.00
Personal document	2000.00
3x5 Card	N/A
8x10 Photo	3000.00

Frazier, Joe

Boxing Gloves	125.00
Cut signature	7.00
Personal document	50.00
3x5 Card	9.00
8x10 Photo	25.00

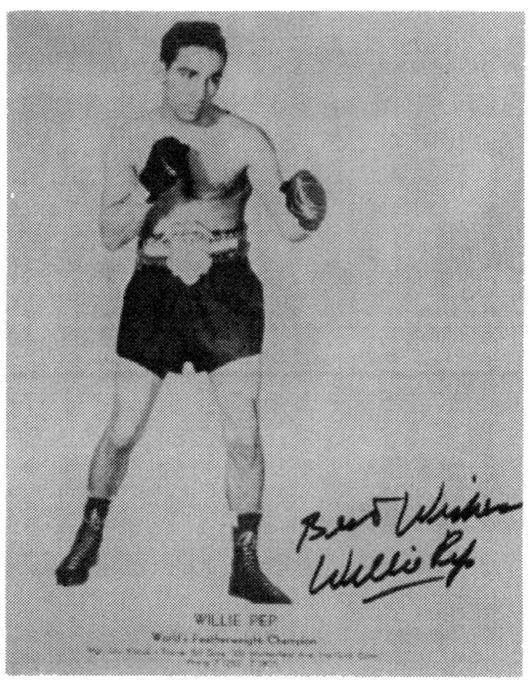

Willie Pep

Gans, Joe

Boxing Gloves	3500.00
Cut signature	600.00
Personal document	1500.00
3x5 Card	N/A
8x10 Photo	2000.00

Gavilan, Kid

Boxing Gloves	100.00
Cut signature	6.00
Personal document	80.00
3x5 Card	8.00
8x10 Photo	25.00

Graziano, Rocky

Boxing Gloves	175.00
Cut signature	10.00
Personal document	100.00
3x5 Card	25.00
8x10 Photo	35.00

Greb, Harry

Boxing Gloves	2700.00
Cut signature	300.00
Personal document	2000.00
3x5 Card	N/A
8x10 Photo	1500.00

Griffith, Emile

Boxing Gloves	65.00
Cut signature	3.00
Personal document	50.00
3x5 Card	5.00
8x10 Photo	15.00

Hagler, Marvin

Boxing Gloves	125.00
Cut signature	7.00
Personal document	100.00
3x5 Card	10.00
8x10 Photo	30.00

Hart, Marvin

Boxing Gloves	5000.00
Cut signature	700.00
Personal document	2000.00
3x5 Card	N/A
8x10 Photo	4000.00

Hearns, Thomas

Boxing Gloves	125.00
Cut signature	5.00
Personal document	100.00
3x5 Card	10.00
8x10 Photo	25.00

Jeffries, James J.

Boxing Gloves	2500.00
Cut signature	200.00
Personal document	600.00
3x5 Card	350.00
8x10 Photo	1000.00

Johansson, Ingemar

Boxing Gloves	175.00
Cut signature	5.00
Personal document	100.00
3x5 Card	10.00
8x10 Photo	20.00

Johnson, Jack

Boxing Gloves	3500.00
Cut signature	250.00
Personal document	650.00
3x5 Card	450.00
8x10 Photo	1500.00

Ketchel, Stanley

Boxing Gloves	5000.00
Cut signature	1000.00
Personal document	3000.00
3x5 Card	N/A
8x10 Photo	3500.00

LaMotta, Jake

Boxing Gloves	75.00
Cut signature	2.00
Personal document	40.00
3x5 Card	10.00
8x10 Photo	15.00

Leonard, Benny

Boxing Gloves	750.00
Cut signature	150.00
Personal document	350.00
3x5 Card	250.00
8x10 Photo	450.00

Leonard, Sugar Ray

Boxing Gloves	125.00
Cut signature	5.00
Personal document	50.00
3x5 Card	10.00
8x10 Photo	18.00

Lesnevich, Gus

Boxing Gloves	250.00
Cut signature	20.00
Personal document	100.00
3x5 Card	50.00
8x10 Photo	125.00

Liston, Sonny

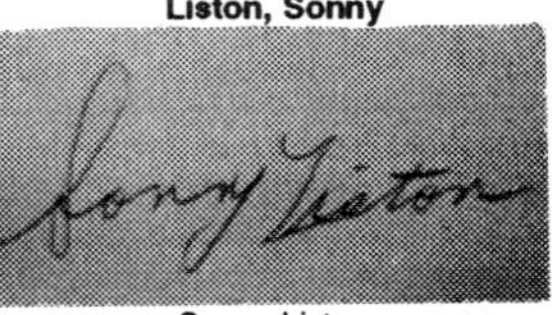

Sonny Liston

Boxing Gloves	2500.00
Cut signature	450.00
Personal document	1000.00
3x5 Card	550.00
8x10 Photo	1000.00

Loughran, Tommy

Boxing Gloves	300.00
Cut signature	25.00
Personal document	150.00
3x5 Card	45.00
8x10 Photo	150.00

Louis, Joe

Boxing Gloves	1000.00
Cut signature	100.00
Personal document	500.00
3x5 Card	150.00
8x10 Photo	350.00

Mancini, Ray

Boxing Gloves	75.00
Cut signature	2.00
Personal document	25.00

Sandy Saddler, Max Schmeling, Leon Spinks

3x5 Card . . . 5.00
8x10 Photo . . . 15.00

Marciano, Rocky
Boxing Gloves . . . 1300.00
Cut signature . . . 350.00
Personal document . . . 750.00
3x5 Card . . . 450.00
8x10 Photo . . . 750.00

Maxim, Joey
Boxing Gloves . . . 45.00
Cut signature . . . 2.00
Personal document . . . 25.00
3x5 Card . . . 5.00
8x10 Photo . . . 15.00

McGovern, Terry
Boxing Gloves . . . 205.00
Cut signature . . . 30.00
Personal document . . . 145.00
3x5 Card . . . 55.00
8x10 Photo . . . 110.00

Monzon, Carlos
Boxing Gloves . . . 250.00
Cut signature . . . 25.00
Personal document . . . 150.00
3x5 Card . . . 45.00
8x10 Photo . . . 100.00

Moore, Archie
Boxing Gloves . . . 50.00
Cut signature . . . 5.00
Personal document . . . 35.00
3x5 Card . . . 8.00
8x10 Photo . . . 18.00

Napoles, Jose
Boxing Gloves . . . 65.00
Cut signature . . . 10.00
Personal document . . . 150.00
3x5 Card . . . 15.00
8x10 Photo . . . 25.00

Norton, Ken
Boxing Gloves . . . 75.00
Cut signature . . . 5.00
Personal document . . . 100.00
3x5 Card . . . 10.00
8x10 Photo . . . 35.00

O'Brien, Philadelphia Jack
Boxing Gloves . . . 500.00
Cut signature . . . 50.00
Personal document . . . 250.00
3x5 Card . . . 75.00
8x10 Photo . . . 250.00

Olson, Carl
Boxing Gloves . . . 45.00
Cut signature . . . 2.00
Personal document . . . 25.00
3x5 Card . . . 5.00
8x10 Photo . . . 15.00

Patterson, Floyd
Boxing Gloves . . . 50.00
Cut signature . . . 2.00
Personal document . . . 35.00
3x5 Card . . . 5.00
8x10 Photo . . . 10.00

Pep, Willie
Boxing Gloves . . . 35.00
Cut signature . . . 2.00
Personal document . . . 45.00
3x5 Card . . . 5.00
8x10 Photo . . . 15.00

Quarry, Jerry
Boxing Gloves . . . 55.00
Cut signature . . . 2.00
Personal document . . . 25.00
3x5 Card . . . 5.00
8x10 Photo . . . 15.00

Robinson, Sugar Ray
Boxing Gloves . . . 450.00
Cut signature . . . 25.00

Jersey Joe Walcott

Personal document . . . 150.00
3x5 Card . . . 35.00
8x10 Photo . . . 150.00

Ross, Barney
Boxing Gloves . . . 450.00
Cut signature . . . 20.00
Personal document . . . 150.00
3x5 Card . . . 35.00
8x10 Photo . . . 150.00

Saddler, Sandy
Boxing Gloves . . . 75.00
Cut signature . . . 15.00
Personal document . . . 100.00
3x5 Card . . . 25.00
8x10 Photo . . . 35.00

Schmeling, Max
Boxing Gloves . . . 125.00
Cut signature . . . 5.00
Personal document . . . 150.00
3x5 Card . . . 10.00
8x10 Photo . . . 50.00

Sharkey, Jack
Boxing Gloves . . . 125.00
Cut signature . . . 15.00
Personal document . . . 150.00
3x5 Card . . . 20.00
8x10 Photo . . . 75.00

Spinks, Leon
Boxing Gloves . . . 110.00
Cut signature . . . 6.00
Personal document . . . 50.00
3x5 Card . . . 8.00
8x10 Photo . . . 20.00

Spinks, Michael
Boxing Gloves . . . 125.00
Cut signature . . . 7.00
Personal document . . . 75.00
3x5 Card . . . 10.00
8x10 Photo . . . 25.00

Sullivan, John L.
Boxing Gloves . . . 2500.00
Cut signature . . . 350.00
Personal document . . . 750.00
3x5 Card . . . NA
8x10 Photo . . . 1000.00

Tunney, Gene
Boxing Gloves . . . 450.00
Cut signature . . . 25.00
Personal document . . . 150.00

3x5 Card	50.00
8x10 Photo	150.00

Walcott, Jersey Joe

Boxing Gloves	150.00
Cut signature	5.00
Personal document	100.00
3x5 Card	10.00
8x10 Photo	35.00

Walker, Mickey

Boxing Gloves	500.00
Cut signature	25.00
Personal document	150.00
3x5 Card	35.00
8x10 Photo	200.00

Willard, Jess

Boxing Gloves	650.00
Cut signature	50.00
Personal document	150.00
3x5 Card	100.00
8x10 Photo	200.00

Zale, Tony

Boxing Gloves	75.00
Cut signature	5.00
Personal document	100.00
3x5 Card	10.00
8x10 Photo	35.00

ACTIVE BOXERS

Barkley, Iran

Boxing Gloves	100.00
Cut signature	4.00
Personal document	50.00
3x5 Card	6.00
8x10 Photo	20.00

Bowe, Riddick

Boxing Gloves	150.00
Cut signature	10.00
Personal document	125.00
3x5 Card	15.00
8x10 Photo	35.00

Carbajal, Michael

Boxing Gloves	100.00
Cut signature	3.00
Personal document	50.00
3x5 Card	5.00
8x10 Photo	15.00

Chavez, Julio Cesar

Boxing Gloves	145.00
Cut signature	10.00
Personal document	250.00
3x5 Card	20.00
8x10 Photo	45.00

De la Hoya, Oscar

Boxing Gloves	125.00
Cut signature	5.00
Personal document	100.00
3x5 Card	7.00
8x10 Photo	20.00

Foreman, George

Boxing Gloves	145.00
Cut signature	8.00
Personal document	75.00
3x5 Card	10.00
8x10 Photo	35.00

Hill, Virgil

Boxing Gloves	100.00
Cut signature	4.00
Personal document	50.00
3x5 Card	6.00
8x10 Photo	15.00

Holmes, Larry

Boxing Gloves	125.00
Cut signature	6.00
Personal document	50.00
3x5 Card	8.00
8x10 Photo	20.00

Holyfield, Evander

Boxing Gloves	150.00
Cut signature	8.00
Personal document	100.00
3x5 Card	10.00
8x10 Photo	35.00

Jackson, Julian

Boxing Gloves	0.00
Cut signature	0.00
Personal document	30.00
3x5 Card	5.00
8x10 Photo	15.00

Jones, Roy

Boxing Gloves	100.00
Cut signature	5.00
Personal document	50.00
3x5 Card	7.00
8x10 Photo	18.00

Lewis, Lennox

Boxing Gloves	125.00
Cut signature	6.00
Personal document	50.00
3x5 Card	10.00
8x10 Photo	30.00

McCallum, Mike

Boxing Gloves	30.00
Cut signature	3.00
Personal document	25.00
3x5 Card	5.00
8x10 Photo	15.00

McGirt, Buddy

Boxing Gloves	100.00
Cut signature	3.00
Personal document	25.00
3x5 Card	5.00
8x10 Photo	15.00

Mercer, Ray

Boxing Gloves	100.00
Cut signature	3.00
Personal document	20.00
3x5 Card	5.00
8x10 Photo	10.00

Moorer, Michael

Boxing Gloves	100.00
Cut signature	5.00
Personal document	50.00
3x5 Card	7.00
8x10 Photo	25.00

Morrison, Tommy

Boxing Gloves	100.00
Cut signature	5.00
Personal document	50.00
3x5 Card	7.00
8x10 Photo	25.00

Nunn, Michael

Boxing Gloves	100.00
Cut signature	3.00
Personal document	25.00
3x5 Card	5.00
8x10 Photo	15.00

Paez, Jorge

Boxing Gloves	100.00
Cut signature	3.00
Personal document	25.00
3x5 Card	5.00
8x10 Photo	15.00

Pazienza, Vinny

Boxing Gloves	35.00
Cut signature	3.00
Personal document	25.00
3x5 Card	2.00
8x10 Photo	15.00

Ruddock, Razor

Boxing Gloves	100.00
Cut signature	5.00
Personal document	50.00
3x5 Card	10.00
8x10 Photo	25.00

Taylor, Meldrick

Boxing Gloves	100.00
Cut signature	3.00
Personal document	25.00
3x5 Card	5.00
8x10 Photo	15.00

Toney, James

Boxing Gloves	65.00
Cut signature	10.00
Personal document	50.00
3x5 Card	10.00
8x10 Photo	25.00

Tyson, Mike

Boxing Gloves	250.00
Cut signature	20.00
Personal document	200.00
3x5 Card	35.00
8x10 Photo	100.00

Whitaker, Pernell

Boxing Gloves	100.00
Cut signature	5.00
Personal document	25.00
3x5 Card	7.00
8x10 Photo	20.00

FOOTBALL: HALL OF FAME

Adderley, Herb

Herb Adderley

Football	20.00
Cut signature	7.00
Personal document	12.00

3x5 Card ... 9.00
8x10 Photo ... 15.00

Alworth, Lance

Football ... 21.00
Cut signature ... 8.00
Personal document ... 13.00
3x5 Card ... 10.00
8x10 Photo ... 15.00

Atkins, Doug

Football ... 19.00
Cut signature ... 6.00
Personal document ... 11.00
3x5 Card ... 9.00
8x10 Photo ... 14.00

Badgro, Morris

Football ... 18.00
Cut signature ... 5.00
Personal document ... 10.00
3x5 Card ... 8.00
8x10 Photo ... 13.00

Battles, Cliff

Football ... 18.00
Cut signature ... 5.00
Personal document ... 10.00
3x5 Card ... 8.00
8x10 Photo ... 13.00

Baugh, Sammy

Football ... 35.00
Cut signature ... 12.00
Personal document ... 20.00
3x5 Card ... 16.00
8x10 Photo ... 20.00

Bednarik, Chuck

Football ... 18.00
Cut signature ... 5.00
Personal document ... 10.00
3x5 Card ... 8.00
8x10 Photo ... 13.00

Bell, Bert

Football ... 20.00
Cut signature ... 7.00
Personal document ... 12.00
3x5 Card ... 10.00
8x10 Photo ... 15.00

Bell, Bobby

Football ... 22.50
Cut signature ... 9.00
Personal document ... 14.00
3x5 Card ... 12.00
8x10 Photo ... 17.00

Berry, Raymond

Football ... 27.00
Cut signature ... 10.00
Personal document ... 15.00
3x5 Card ... 12.00
8x10 Photo ... 17.00

Bidwill, Charles

Football ... 30.00
Cut signature ... 7.00
Personal document ... 17.00
3x5 Card ... 12.00
8x10 Photo ... 20.00

Biletnikoff, Fred

Football ... 35.00
Cut signature ... 6.00
Personal document ... 27.00
3x5 Card ... 9.00
8x10 Photo ... 20.00

Blanda, George

Football ... 35.00
Cut signature ... 9.00
Personal document ... 20.00
3x5 Card ... 11.00

Raymond Berry

8x10 Photo ... 15.00

Blount, Mel

Football ... 25.00
Cut signature ... 5.00
Personal document ... 15.00
3x5 Card ... 9.00
8x10 Photo ... 12.00

Bradshaw, Terry

Football ... 30.00
Cut signature ... 7.00
Personal document ... 22.00
3x5 Card ... 9.00
8x10 Photo ... 15.00

Brown, Jim

Football ... 85.00
Cut signature ... 22.00
Personal document ... 65.00
3x5 Card ... 35.00
8x10 Photo ... 45.00

Brown, Paul

Football ... 45.00
Cut signature ... 10.00
Personal document ... 37.00
3x5 Card ... 18.00
8x10 Photo ... 30.00

Brown, Roosevelt

Football ... 25.00
Cut signature ... 5.00
Personal document ... 15.00
3x5 Card ... 7.00
8x10 Photo ... 12.00

Brown, Willie

Football ... 24.00
Cut signature ... 4.00
Personal document ... 14.00
3x5 Card ... 6.00
8x10 Photo ... 11.00

Buchanan, Buck

Football ... 24.00
Cut signature ... 4.00
Personal document ... 14.00

Jim Brown

3x5 Card ... 6.00
8x10 Photo ... 11.00

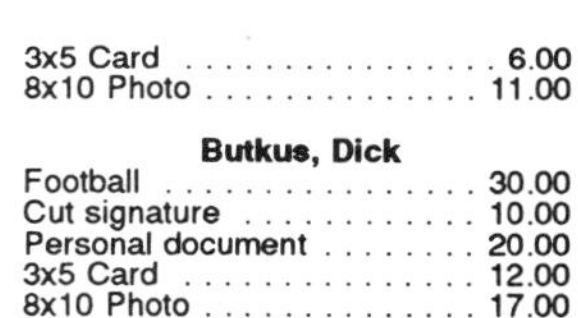

Butkus, Dick

Football ... 30.00
Cut signature ... 10.00
Personal document ... 20.00
3x5 Card ... 12.00
8x10 Photo ... 17.00

Campbell, Earl

Football ... 35.00
Cut signature ... 12.00
Personal document ... 20.00
3x5 Card ... 10.00
8x10 Photo ... 17.00

Canadeo, Tony

Football ... 20.00

Weeb Ewbank

Cut signature 4.00
Personal document 13.00
3x5 Card 7.00
8x10 Photo 10.00

Carr, Joe

Football 22.00
Cut signature 6.00
Personal document 15.00
3x5 Card 9.00
8x10 Photo 12.00

Chamberlin, Guy

Football 21.00
Cut signature 5.00
Personal document 14.00
3x5 Card 8.00
8x10 Photo 11.00

Christiansen, Jack

Football 20.00
Cut signature 4.00
Personal document 13.00
3x5 Card 7.00
8x10 Photo 10.00

Clark, Earl

Football 21.00
Cut signature 5.00
Personal document 14.00
3x5 Card 8.00
8x10 Photo 11.00

Connor, George

Football 20.00
Cut signature 4.00
Personal document 13.00
3x5 Card 6.00
8x10 Photo 10.00

Conzelman, Jimmy

Football 19.00
Cut signature 3.00
Personal document 12.00
3x5 Card 5.00
8x10 Photo 9.00

Csonka, Larry

Football 35.00
Cut signature 12.00
Personal document 24.00
3x5 Card 10.00
8x10 Photo 16.00

Davis, Willie

Football 24.00
Cut signature 7.00
Personal document 18.00
3x5 Card 7.00
8x10 Photo 11.00

Dawson, Len

Football 25.00
Cut signature 8.00
Personal document 19.00
3x5 Card 8.00
8x10 Photo 12.00

Ditka, Mike

Football 35.00
Cut signature 12.00
Personal document 20.00
3x5 Card 10.00
8x10 Photo 17.00

Donovan, Art

Football 35.00
Cut signature 13.00
Personal document 20.00
3x5 Card 13.00
8x10 Photo 17.00

Driscoll, John

Football 20.00
Cut signature 4.00
Personal document 13.00
3x5 Card 6.00
8x10 Photo 10.00

Dudley, Bill

Football 21.00
Cut signature 5.00
Personal document 14.00
3x5 Card 7.00
8x10 Photo 11.00

Edwards, Turk

Football 22.00
Cut signature 6.00
Personal document 15.00
3x5 Card 8.00
8x10 Photo 12.00

Ewbank, Weeb

Football 30.00
Cut signature 14.00
Personal document 20.00
3x5 Card 16.00
8x10 Photo 18.00

Fears, Tom

Football 23.00
Cut signature 7.00
Personal document 13.00
3x5 Card 9.00
8x10 Photo 11.00

Flaherty, Ray

Football 21.00
Cut signature 5.00
Personal document 11.00
3x5 Card 7.00
8x10 Photo 9.00

Ford, Len

Football 24.00
Cut signature 8.00
Personal document 14.00
3x5 Card 10.00
8x10 Photo 12.00

Fortmann, Daniel

Football 20.00
Cut signature 5.00
Personal document 11.00
3x5 Card 6.00
8x10 Photo 8.00

Gatski, Frank

Football 22.00
Cut signature 7.00
Personal document 13.00
3x5 Card 8.00
8x10 Photo 10.00

George, Bill

Football 23.00
Cut signature 8.00
Personal document 14.00
3x5 Card 9.00
8x10 Photo 11.00

Gifford, Frank

Football 35.00
Cut signature 15.00
Personal document 21.00
3x5 Card 15.00
8x10 Photo 18.00

Gillman, Sid

Football 23.00
Cut signature 5.00
Personal document 17.00
3x5 Card 10.00
8x10 Photo 12.00

Graham, Otto

Otto Graham

Football 27.00
Cut signature 9.00
Personal document 21.00
3x5 Card 14.00
8x10 Photo 16.00

Grange, Red

Football 125.00
Cut signature 40.00
Personal document 85.00
3x5 Card 45.00
8x10 Photo 65.00

Greene, Joe

Football 30.00
Cut signature 10.00
Personal document 22.00
3x5 Card 12.00
8x10 Photo 17.00

Gregg, Forrest

Football 24.00
Cut signature 9.00
Personal document 16.00
3x5 Card 10.00
8x10 Photo 13.00

Griese, Bob

Football 35.00
Cut signature 17.00
Personal document 27.00
3x5 Card 14.00
8x10 Photo 22.00

Groza, Lou

Football 25.00
Cut signature 9.00
Personal document 20.00
3x5 Card 12.00
8x10 Photo 15.00

Guyon, Joe

Football 27.00
Cut signature 6.00
Personal document 20.00
3x5 Card 9.00
8x10 Photo 13.00

Halas, George

Football 65.00
Cut signature 20.00
Personal document 50.00
3x5 Card 25.00
8x10 Photo 39.00

Ham, Jack

Jack Ham

Football 35.00
Cut signature 7.00
Personal document 20.00
3x5 Card 10.00
8x10 Photo 15.00

Hannah, John

Football 22.00
Cut signature 7.00
Personal document 13.00
3x5 Card 8.00
8x10 Photo 10.00

Harris, Franco

Franco Harris

Football 40.00
Cut signature 12.00
Personal document 30.00
3x5 Card 15.00
8x10 Photo 25.00

Healey, Ed

Football 20.00
Cut signature 6.00
Personal document 15.00
3x5 Card 7.00
8x10 Photo 13.00

Hein, Mel

Football 24.00
Cut signature 10.00
Personal document 19.00
3x5 Card 11.00
8x10 Photo 17.00

Hendricks, Ted

Football 25.00
Cut signature 11.00
Personal document 20.00
3x5 Card 12.00
8x10 Photo 18.00

Henry, Wilbur

Football 25.00
Cut signature 11.00
Personal document 20.00
3x5 Card 12.00
8x10 Photo 18.00

Herber, Arnie

Football 24.00
Cut signature 10.00
Personal document 18.00
3x5 Card 10.00
8x10 Photo 16.00

Hewitt, Bill

Football 25.00
Cut signature 7.00
Personal document 19.00
3x5 Card 11.00
8x10 Photo 15.00

Hinkle, Clarke

Football 27.00
Cut signature 9.00
Personal document 21.00
3x5 Card 13.00
8x10 Photo 15.00

Hirsch, Elroy

Elroy Hirsch

Football 35.00
Cut signature 10.00
Personal document 25.00
3x5 Card 11.00
8x10 Photo 17.00

Hornung, Paul

Football 37.00
Cut signature 12.00
Personal document 11.00
3x5 Card 27.00
8x10 Photo 19.00

Houston, Ken

Football 24.00
Cut signature 10.00
Personal document 18.00
3x5 Card 16.00
8x10 Photo 10.00

Hubbard, Cal

Football 30.00
Cut signature 10.00
Personal document 23.00
3x5 Card 12.00
8x10 Photo 18.00

Huff, Sam

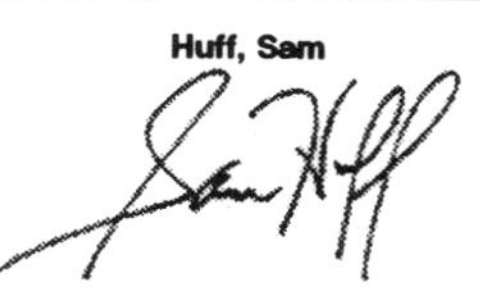

Sam Huff

Football 50.00
Cut signature 20.00
Personal document 35.00
3x5 Card 22.00
8x10 Photo 30.00

Hunt, Lamar

Football 40.00
Cut signature 14.00
Personal document 32.00
3x5 Card 19.00
8x10 Photo 27.00

Hutson, Don

Football 35.00
Cut signature 8.00
Personal document 25.00
3x5 Card 10.00
8x10 Photo 15.00

Johnson, John Henry

Football 30.00
Cut signature 7.00
Personal document 20.00
3x5 Card 8.00
8x10 Photo 13.00

Jones, Deacon

Football 40.00
Cut signature 12.00
Personal document 30.00
3x5 Card 17.00
8x10 Photo 24.00

Jones, Stan

Football 22.00
Cut signature 6.00
Personal document 15.00
3x5 Card 9.00
8x10 Photo 12.00

Jurgensen, Sonny

Football 40.00
Cut signature 12.00
Personal document 30.00
3x5 Card 17.00
8x10 Photo 24.00

Kiesling, Walt

Football 22.00
Cut signature 6.00
Personal document 15.00
3x5 Card 9.00
8x10 Photo 12.00

Kinard, Bruiser

Football 24.00
Cut signature 8.00
Personal document 17.00
3x5 Card 11.00
8x10 Photo 14.00

Lambeau, Curley

Football 25.00
Cut signature 9.00
Personal document 18.00
3x5 Card 12.00
8x10 Photo 15.00

Lambert, Jack

Football 30.00

Cut signature 12.00
Personal document 23.00
3x5 Card 14.00
8x10 Photo 16.00

Landry, Tom

Tom Landry

Football 65.00
Cut signature 24.00
Personal document 50.00
3x5 Card 30.00
8x10 Photo 40.00

Lane, Dick

Football 25.00
Cut signature 9.00
Personal document 18.00
3x5 Card 12.00
8x10 Photo 15.00

Langer, Jim

Football 24.00
Cut signature 8.00
Personal document 17.00
3x5 Card 11.00
8x10 Photo 14.00

Lanier, Willie

Football 25.00
Cut signature 8.00
Personal document 16.00
3x5 Card 10.00
8x10 Photo 14.00

Lary, Yale

Football 23.00
Cut signature 6.00
Personal document 14.00
3x5 Card 8.00
8x10 Photo 12.00

Lavelli, Dante

Football 25.00
Cut signature 8.00
Personal document 16.00
3x5 Card 10.00
8x10 Photo 14.00

Layne, Bobby

Football 40.00
Cut signature 17.00
Personal document 30.00
3x5 Card 21.00
8x10 Photo 29.00

Leemans, Tuffy

Football 25.00
Cut signature 8.00
Personal document 16.00
3x5 Card 10.00
8x10 Photo 14.00

Lilly, Bob

Football 35.00
Cut signature 20.00
Personal document 27.00
3x5 Card 22.00
8x10 Photo 30.00

Lombardi, Vince

Football 125.00
Cut signature 45.00
Personal document 85.00
3x5 Card 55.00
8x10 Photo 65.00

Luckman, Sid

Football 35.00
Cut signature 20.00
Personal document 27.00
3x5 Card 22.00
8x10 Photo 30.00

Lyman, Link

Football 35.00
Cut signature 10.00
Personal document 25.00
3x5 Card 12.00
8x10 Photo 20.00

Mara, Tim

Football 24.00
Cut signature 8.00
Personal document 16.00
3x5 Card 10.00
8x10 Photo 14.00

Marchetti, Gino

Football 35.00
Cut signature 10.00
Personal document 25.00
3x5 Card 12.00
8x10 Photo 20.00

Marshall, George

Football 25.00
Cut signature 8.00
Personal document 18.00
3x5 Card 10.00
8x10 Photo 14.00

Matson, Ollie

Football 25.00
Cut signature 8.00
Personal document 18.00
3x5 Card 10.00
8x10 Photo 14.00

Maynard, Don

Don Maynard

Football 35.00
Cut signature 10.00
Personal document 25.00
3x5 Card 12.00
8x10 Photo 20.00

McAfee, George

Football 32.00
Cut signature 7.00
Personal document 22.00
3x5 Card 9.00
8x10 Photo 17.00

McCormack, Mike

Football 24.00
Cut signature 8.00
Personal document 16.00
3x5 Card 10.00
8x10 Photo 14.00

McElhenny, Hugh

Football 27.00
Cut signature 11.00
Personal document 19.00
3x5 Card 13.00
8x10 Photo 17.00

McNally, John

Football 22.00
Cut signature 6.00
Personal document 14.00
3x5 Card 8.00
8x10 Photo 12.00

Michalske, Mike

Football 23.00
Cut signature 7.00
Personal document 15.00
3x5 Card 9.00
8x10 Photo 13.00

Millner, Wayne

Football 21.00
Cut signature 5.00
Personal document 13.00
3x5 Card 7.00
8x10 Photo 11.00

Mitchell, Bobby

Football 30.00
Cut signature 13.00
Personal document 23.00
3x5 Card 16.00
8x10 Photo 20.00

Mix, Ron

Football 21.00
Cut signature 5.00
Personal document 13.00
3x5 Card 7.00
8x10 Photo 11.00

Moore, Lenny

Football 23.00
Cut signature 7.00
Personal document 15.00
3x5 Card 9.00
8x10 Photo 13.00

Motley, Marion

Football 24.00
Cut signature 8.00
Personal document 16.00
3x5 Card 10.00
8x10 Photo 14.00

Musso, George

Football 29.00
Cut signature 13.00
Personal document 21.00
3x5 Card 15.00
8x10 Photo 19.00

Nagurski, Bronco

Football 125.00
Cut signature 40.00
Personal document 85.00

Bronco Nagurski

3x5 Card	45.00
8x10 Photo	65.00

Namath, Joe

Football	85.00
Cut signature	22.00
Personal document	65.00
3x5 Card	35.00
8x10 Photo	45.00

Neale, Earle

Football	24.00
Cut signature	8.00
Personal document	16.00
3x5 Card	10.00
8x10 Photo	14.00

Nevers, Ernie

Football	23.00
Cut signature	10.00
Personal document	18.00
3x5 Card	17.00
8x10 Photo	12.00

Nitschke, Ray

Football	30.00
Cut signature	13.00
Personal document	23.00
3x5 Card	16.00
8x10 Photo	20.00

Nomellini, Leo

Football	30.00
Cut signature	17.00
Personal document	25.00
3x5 Card	17.00
8x10 Photo	22.00

Olsen, Merlin

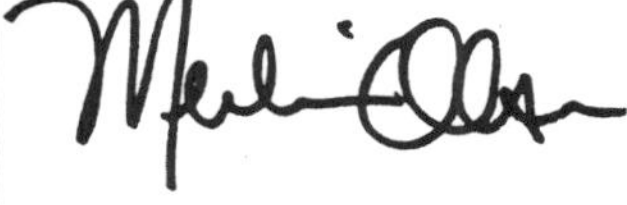

Merlin Olsen

Football	30.00
Cut signature	13.00
Personal document	23.00
3x5 Card	16.00
8x10 Photo	20.00

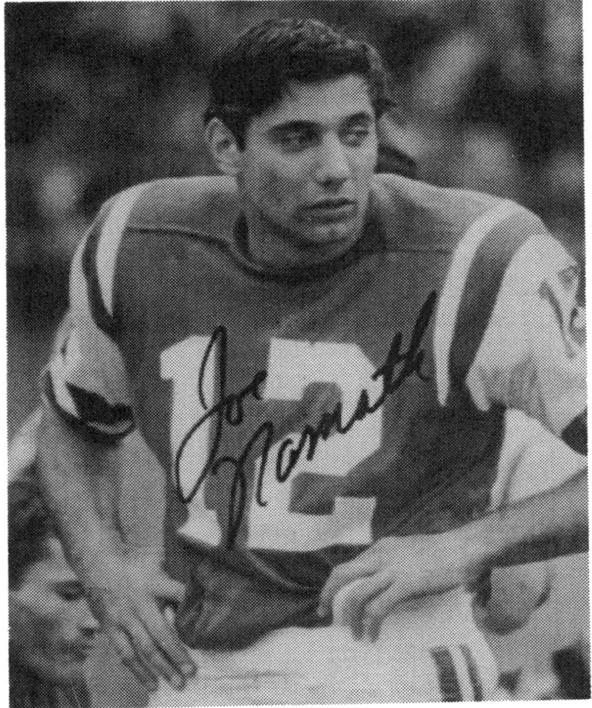

Joe Namath

Otto, Jim

Football	32.00
Cut signature	15.00
Personal document	25.00
3x5 Card	17.00
8x10 Photo	22.00

Alan Page

Owen, Steve

Football	23.00
Cut signature	10.00
Personal document	18.00
3x5 Card	12.00
8x10 Photo	17.00

Page, Alan

Football	32.00
Cut signature	15.00
Personal document	25.00
3x5 Card	17.00
8x10 Photo	22.00

Parker, Ace

Football	30.00
Cut signature	13.00
Personal document	23.00
3x5 Card	15.00
8x10 Photo	20.00

Parker, Jim

Football	25.00
Cut signature	8.00
Personal document	18.00
3x5 Card	10.00
8x10 Photo	15.00

Perry, Joe

Football	25.00
Cut signature	8.00
Personal document	18.00
3x5 Card	10.00
8x10 Photo	15.00

Pihos, Pete

Football	26.00
Cut signature	9.00
Personal document	19.00
3x5 Card	11.00
8x10 Photo	16.00

Ray, Hugh

Football	24.00
Cut signature	7.00
Personal document	17.00
3x5 Card	9.00
8x10 Photo	14.00

Bart Starr

Reeves, Dan

Football	30.00
Cut signature	13.00
Personal document	20.00
3x5 Card	12.00
8x10 Photo	16.00

Ringo, Jim

Football	26.00
Cut signature	9.00
Personal document	19.00
3x5 Card	11.00
8x10 Photo	16.00

Robustelli, Andy

Football	27.00
Cut signature	10.00
Personal document	20.00
3x5 Card	12.00
8x10 Photo	17.00

Rooney, Art

Football	30.00
Cut signature	13.00
Personal document	20.00
3x5 Card	12.00
8x10 Photo	16.00

Rozelle, Pete

Football	35.00
Cut signature	18.00
Personal document	25.00
3x5 Card	17.00
8x10 Photo	21.00

St.Clair, Bob

Football	25.00
Cut signature	8.00
Personal document	15.00
3x5 Card	17.00
8x10 Photo	11.00

Sayers, Gale

Football	40.00
Cut signature	12.00
Personal document	32.00
3x5 Card	17.00
8x10 Photo	25.00

Schmidt, Joe

Football	24.00
Cut signature	7.00
Personal document	17.00
3x5 Card	9.00
8x10 Photo	14.00

Schramm, Tex

Football	65.00
Cut signature	24.00
Personal document	50.00
3x5 Card	30.00
8x10 Photo	40.00

Shell, Art

Football	40.00
Cut signature	12.00
Personal document	32.00
3x5 Card	17.00
8x10 Photo	25.00

Simpson, O.J.

Football	65.00
Cut signature	25.00
Personal document	50.00
3x5 Card	30.00
8x10 Photo	35.00

Starr, Bart

Football	75.00
Cut signature	30.00
Personal document	50.00
3x5 Card	35.00
8x10 Photo	40.00

Staubach, Roger

Football	65.00
Cut signature	25.00
Personal document	50.00
3x5 Card	30.00
8x10 Photo	35.00

Stautner, Ernie

Football	25.00
Cut signature	8.00
Personal document	18.00
3x5 Card	10.00
8x10 Photo	15.00

Stenerud, Jan

Football	30.00
Cut signature	12.00
Personal document	22.00
3x5 Card	14.00
8x10 Photo	19.00

Strong, Ken

Football	28.00
Cut signature	10.00
Personal document	20.00
3x5 Card	12.00
8x10 Photo	17.00

Stydahar, Joe

Football	26.00
Cut signature	12.00
Personal document	18.00
3x5 Card	14.00
8x10 Photo	19.00

Tarkenton, Fran

Football	35.00
Cut signature	17.00
Personal document	27.00
3x5 Card	14.00
8x10 Photo	22.00

Taylor, Charley

Football	28.00
Cut signature	10.00
Personal document	20.00
3x5 Card	12.00
8x10 Photo	17.00

Taylor, Jim

Football	29.00
Cut signature	11.00
Personal document	19.00
3x5 Card	11.00
8x10 Photo	16.00

Thorpe, Jim

Football	125.00
Cut signature	40.00

Jan Stenerud, Art Shell, Fran Tarkenton

Personal document 85.00
3x5 Card 45.00
8x10 Photo 65.00

Tittle, Y.A.

Football 35.00
Cut signature 7.00
Personal document 18.00
3x5 Card 12.00
8x10 Photo 15.00

Trafton, George

Football 25.00
Cut signature 5.00
Personal document 20.00
3x5 Card 10.00
8x10 Photo 15.00

Trippi, Charlie

Football 24.00
Cut signature 4.00
Personal document 18.00
3x5 Card 8.00
8x10 Photo 14.00

Tunnell, Emlen

Football 25.00
Cut signature 5.00
Personal document 20.00
3x5 Card 10.00
8x10 Photo 15.00

Turner, Bulldog

Football 30.00
Cut signature 10.00
Personal document 25.00
3x5 Card 15.00
8x10 Photo 20.00

Unitas, Johnny

Johnny Unitas

Football 40.00
Cut signature 10.00
Personal document 32.00
3x5 Card 15.00
8x10 Photo 25.00

Upshaw, Gene

Football 36.00
Cut signature 12.00
Personal document 30.00
3x5 Card 17.00
8x10 Photo 24.00

Van Brocklin, Norm

Football 40.00

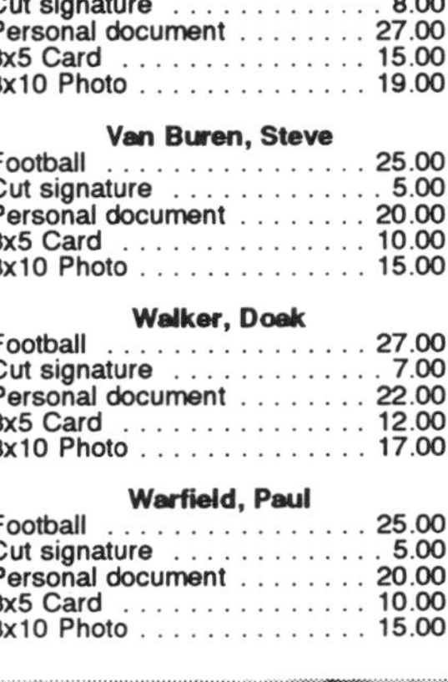

Cut signature 8.00
Personal document 27.00
3x5 Card 15.00
8x10 Photo 19.00

Van Buren, Steve

Football 25.00
Cut signature 5.00
Personal document 20.00
3x5 Card 10.00
8x10 Photo 15.00

Walker, Doak

Football 27.00
Cut signature 7.00
Personal document 22.00
3x5 Card 12.00
8x10 Photo 17.00

Warfield, Paul

Football 25.00
Cut signature 5.00
Personal document 20.00
3x5 Card 10.00
8x10 Photo 15.00

Paul Warfield

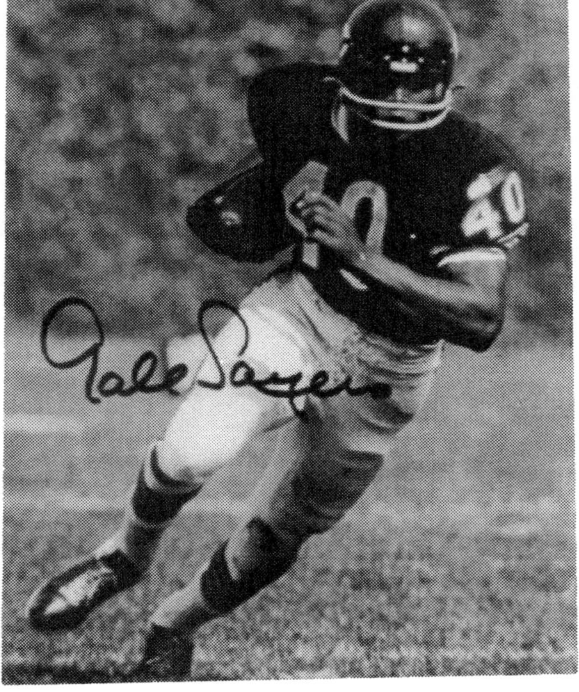

Gale Sayers

Waterfield, Bob

Football 23.00
Cut signature 3.00
Personal document 17.00
3x5 Card 7.00
8x10 Photo 12.00

Weinmeister, Ernie

Football 27.00
Cut signature 7.00
Personal document 21.00
3x5 Card 11.00
8x10 Photo 16.00

Willis, Bill

Football 24.00
Cut signature 4.00
Personal document 15.00
3x5 Card 7.00
8x10 Photo 11.00

Wilson, Larry

Football 25.00
Cut signature 5.00
Personal document 18.00
3x5 Card 8.00
8x10 Photo 13.00

Wojciechowicz, Alex
Football 25.00
Cut signature 5.00
Personal document 18.00
3x5 Card 8.00
8x10 Photo 13.00

Wood, Willie
Football 27.00
Cut signature 7.00
Personal document 20.00
3x5 Card 10.00
8x10 Photo 15.00

FOOTBALL: INACTIVE PLAYERS

Jackson, Bo (see baseball)
Football 35.00
Cut signature 6.00
3x5 Card 15.00
8x10 Photo 28.00

Singletary, Mike
Football 33.00
Cut signature 5.00
3x5 Card 12.00
8x10 Photo 25.00

FOOTBALL: ACTIVE PLAYERS

Aikman, Troy
Football 40.00
Cut signature 5.00
3x5 Card 10.00
8x10 Photo 18.00

Allen, Marcus
Football 30.00
Cut signature 4.00
3x5 Card 9.00
8x10 Photo 14.00

Allen, Terry
Football 20.00
Cut signature 3.00
3x5 Card 4.00
8x10 Photo 7.00

Anderson, Flipper
Football 24.00
Cut signature 3.00
3x5 Card 5.00
8x10 Photo 7.00

Anderson, Neal
Football 25.00
Cut signature 5.00
3x5 Card 10.00
8x10 Photo 15.00

Anderson, Ottis
Football 27.00
Cut signature 5.00
3x5 Card 10.00
8x10 Photo 15.00

Atwater, Steve
Football 21.00
Cut signature 3.00
3x5 Card 5.00
8x10 Photo 7.00

Bailey, Johnny
Football 21.00
Cut signature 3.00
3x5 Card 6.00
8x10 Photo 9.00

Ball, Jerry
Football 20.00
Cut signature 3.00
3x5 Card 6.00
8x10 Photo 9.00

Barnett, Fred
Football 20.00
Cut signature 3.00
3x5 Card 6.00
8x10 Photo 9.00

Bell, Nick
Football 20.00
Cut signature 3.00
3x5 Card 6.00
8x10 Photo 9.00

Bennett, Cornelius
Football 21.00
Cut signature 4.00
3x5 Card 6.00
8x10 Photo 9.00

Bernstine, Rod
Football 20.00
Cut signature 3.00
3x5 Card 6.00
8x10 Photo 9.00

Bieniemy, Eric
Football 20.00
Cut signature 3.00
3x5 Card 6.00
8x10 Photo 9.00

Blades, Brian
Football 20.00
Cut signature 3.00
3x5 Card 6.00
8x10 Photo 9.00

Brooks, James
Football 21.00
Cut signature 4.00
3x5 Card 6.00
8x10 Photo 9.00

Bunch, Jarrod
Football 20.00
Cut signature 3.00
3x5 Card 6.00
8x10 Photo 9.00

Butts, Marion
Football 22.00
Cut signature 4.00
3x5 Card 6.00
8x10 Photo 10.00

Byars, Keith
Football 24.00
Cut signature 5.00
3x5 Card 7.00
8x10 Photo 9.00

Carrier, Mark (DB)
Football 20.00
Cut signature 3.00
3x5 Card 6.00
8x10 Photo 9.00

Carroll, Wesley
Football 20.00
Cut signature 3.00
3x5 Card 6.00
8x10 Photo 9.00

Carter, Anthony
Football 21.00
Cut signature 4.00
3x5 Card 7.00
8x10 Photo 9.00

Clayton, Mark
Football 25.00
Cut signature 5.00
3x5 Card 7.00
8x10 Photo 12.00

Cobb, Reggie
Football 21.00
Cut signature 4.00
3x5 Card 7.00
8x10 Photo 12.00

Coleman, Marco
Football 25.00
Cut signature 5.00
3x5 Card 10.00
8x10 Photo 15.00

Craig, Roger
Football 25.00
Cut signature 5.00
3x5 Card 10.00
8x10 Photo 15.00

Croel, Mike
Football 21.00
Cut signature 4.00
3x5 Card 7.00
8x10 Photo 10.00

Cunningham, Randall
Football 35.00
Cut signature 7.00
3x5 Card 18.00
8x10 Photo 22.00

Dent, Richard
Football 34.00
Cut signature 6.00
3x5 Card 9.00
8x10 Photo 20.00

Dickerson, Eric

Eric Dickerson

Football 24.00
Cut signature 4.00
3x5 Card 8.00
8x10 Photo 10.00

Elway, John
Football 37.00
Cut signature 5.00
3x5 Card 10.00
8x10 Photo 18.00

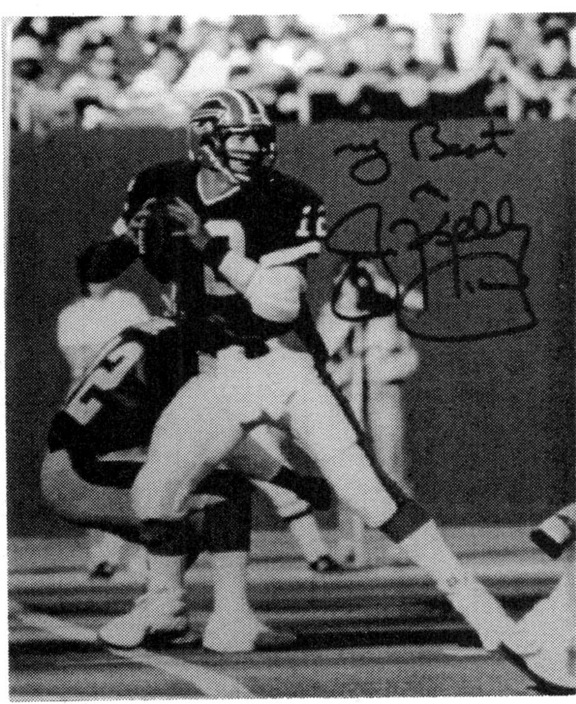

Jim Kelly

Emtman, Steve
Football 27.00
Cut signature 4.00
3x5 Card 9.00
8x10 Photo 17.00

Ervins, Ricky
Football 20.00
Cut signature 3.00
3x5 Card 6.00
8x10 Photo 9.00

Esiason, Boomer
Football 25.00
Cut signature 5.00
3x5 Card 10.00
8x10 Photo 15.00

Everett, Jim
Football 22.00
Cut signature 4.00
3x5 Card 8.00
8x10 Photo 15.00

Favre, Brett
Football 22.00
Cut signature 4.00
3x5 Card 8.00
8x10 Photo 15.00

Foster, Barry
Football 25.00
Cut signature 3.00
3x5 Card 7.00
8x10 Photo 14.00

Gault, Willie
Football 22.00
Cut signature 4.00
3x5 Card 8.00
8x10 Photo 15.00

George, Jeff
Football 21.00
Cut signature 3.00
3x5 Card 5.00
8x10 Photo 9.00

Green, Eric
Football 20.00
Cut signature 3.00
3x5 Card 6.00
8x10 Photo 9.00

Green, Gaston
Football 21.00
Cut signature 4.00
3x5 Card 5.00
8x10 Photo 9.00

Green, Harold
Football 21.00
Cut signature 4.00
3x5 Card 5.00
8x10 Photo 9.00

Hampton, Rodney
Football 22.00
Cut signature 4.00
3x5 Card 6.00
8x10 Photo 10.00

Harbaugh, Jim
Football 21.00
Cut signature 4.00
3x5 Card 6.00
8x10 Photo 9.00

Harper, Alvin
Football 20.00
Cut signature 3.00
3x5 Card 6.00
8x10 Photo 9.00

Haynes, Michael
Football 24.00
Cut signature 5.00
3x5 Card 7.00
8x10 Photo 10.00

Hebert, Bobby
Football 24.00
Cut signature 5.00
3x5 Card 7.00
8x10 Photo 10.00

Heyward, Craig
Football 21.00
Cut signature 4.00
3x5 Card 6.00
8x10 Photo 9.00

Hill, Randall
Football 20.00
Cut signature 3.00
3x5 Card 6.00
8x10 Photo 9.00

Hilliard, Dalton
Football 21.00
Cut signature 4.00
3x5 Card 6.00
8x10 Photo 9.00

Hostetler, Jeff
Football 25.00
Cut signature 5.00
3x5 Card 7.00
8x10 Photo 10.00

Howard, Desmond
Football 25.00
Cut signature 5.00
3x5 Card 7.00
8x10 Photo 10.00

Humphrey, Bobby
Football 20.00
Cut signature 3.00
3x5 Card 6.00
8x10 Photo 9.00

Irvin, Michael
Football 40.00
Cut signature 9.00
3x5 Card 12.00
8x10 Photo 20.00

Ismail, Raghib
Football 30.00
Cut signature 5.00
3x5 Card 8.00
8x10 Photo 10.00

Jeffires, Haywood
Football 24.00
Cut signature 4.00
3x5 Card 7.00
8x10 Photo 10.00

Johnson, Johnny
Football 22.00
Cut signature 4.00
3x5 Card 7.00
8x10 Photo 9.00

Kelly, Jim
Football 40.00
Cut signature 5.00
3x5 Card 9.00
8x10 Photo 14.00

Kennedy, Cortez
Football 27.00
Cut signature 4.00
3x5 Card 7.00
8x10 Photo 11.00

Kosar, Bernie
Football 30.00
Cut signature 6.00
3x5 Card 9.00
8x10 Photo 15.00

Lewis, Greg
Football 21.00
Cut signature 4.00
3x5 Card 7.00
8x10 Photo 9.00

Lofton, James
Football 30.00
Cut signature 6.00
3x5 Card 8.00
8x10 Photo 14.00

Lott, Ronnie
Football 30.00
Cut signature 6.00
3x5 Card 8.00
8x10 Photo 14.00

Majkowski, Don
Football 23.00
Cut signature 4.00
3x5 Card 7.00
8x10 Photo 10.00

Marino, Dan
Football 45.00
Cut signature 7.00
3x5 Card 11.00
8x10 Photo 17.00

Marinovich, Todd
Football 21.00
Cut signature 4.00
3x5 Card 6.00
8x10 Photo 9.00

Maryland, Russell
Football 24.00
Cut signature 5.00
3x5 Card 7.00
8x10 Photo 10.00

McGwire, Dan
Football 20.00
Cut signature 3.00
3x5 Card 6.00
8x10 Photo 9.00

McMahon, Jim
Football 30.00
Cut signature 6.00
3x5 Card 8.00
8x10 Photo 14.00

Meggett, Dave
Football 24.00
Cut signature 3.00
3x5 Card 6.00
8x10 Photo 10.00

Metcalf, Eric

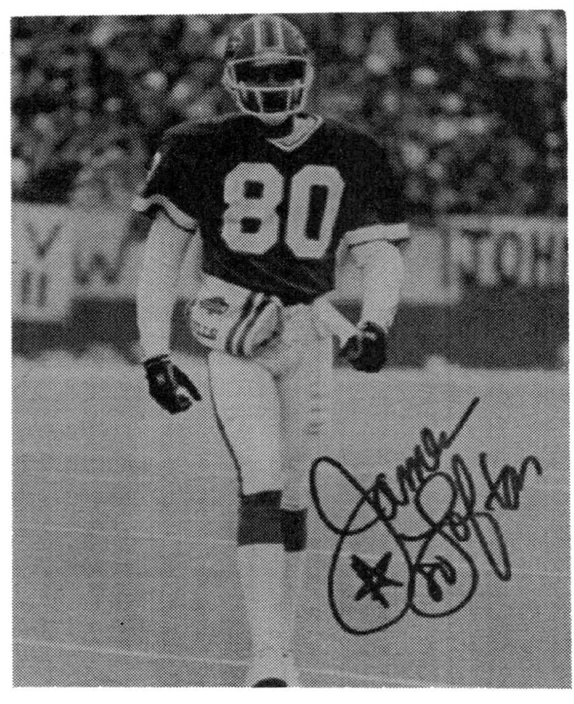

James Lofton

Football 22.00
Cut signature 3.00
3x5 Card 6.00
8x10 Photo 10.00

Miller, Chris
Football 21.00
Cut signature 3.00
3x5 Card 6.00
8x10 Photo 9.00

Monk, Art
Football 30.00
Cut signature 6.00
3x5 Card 8.00
8x10 Photo 14.00

Montana, Joe
Football 45.00
Cut signature 12.00
3x5 Card 15.00
8x10 Photo 25.00

Moon, Warren
Football 35.00
Cut signature 10.00
3x5 Card 12.00
8x10 Photo 20.00

Moore, Herman
Football 21.00
Cut signature 4.00
3x5 Card 6.00
8x10 Photo 9.00

Moore, Rob
Football 22.00
Cut signature 4.00
3x5 Card 6.00
8x10 Photo 10.00

Nagle, Browning
Football 23.00
Cut signature 5.00
3x5 Card 7.00
8x10 Photo 11.00

Okoye, Christian
Football 23.00
Cut signature 4.00
3x5 Card 6.00
8x10 Photo 10.00

Peete, Rodney
Football 24.00
Cut signature 4.00
3x5 Card 6.00
8x10 Photo 10.00

Perry, William
Football 29.00
Cut signature 5.00
3x5 Card 8.00
8x10 Photo 12.00

Joe Montana

Pritchard, Mike
Football 23.00
Cut signature 4.00
3x5 Card 7.00
8x10 Photo 11.00

Proehl, Ricky
Football 22.00
Cut signature 3.00
3x5 Card 6.00
8x10 Photo 9.00

Reed, Andre
Football 30.00
Cut signature 4.00
3x5 Card 6.00
8x10 Photo 14.00

Rice, Jerry
Football 40.00
Cut signature 6.00
3x5 Card 9.00
8x10 Photo 12.00

Rison, Andre
Football 24.00
Cut signature 4.00
3x5 Card 6.00
8x10 Photo 12.00

Rosenbach, Timm
Football 21.00
Cut signature 4.00
3x5 Card 6.00
8x10 Photo 9.00

Russell, Leonard
Football 21.00
Cut signature 4.00
3x5 Card 6.00
8x10 Photo 9.00

Rypien, Mark
Football 25.00
Cut signature 5.00
3x5 Card 7.00
8x10 Photo 10.00

Sanders, Barry
Football 21.00
Cut signature 4.00
3x5 Card 6.00
8x10 Photo 9.00

Sanders, Deion
Football 30.00
Cut signature 5.00
3x5 Card 7.00
8x10 Photo 12.00

Sharpe, Sterling
Football 30.00
Cut signature 8.00
3x5 Card 10.00
8x10 Photo 22.00

Simms, Phil
Football 31.00
Cut signature 6.00
3x5 Card 9.00
8x10 Photo 10.00

Smith, Bruce
Football 25.00
Cut signature 5.00
3x5 Card 7.00
8x10 Photo 10.00

Smith, Emmitt
Football 23.00
Cut signature 4.00
3x5 Card 6.00
8x10 Photo 9.00

Spielman, Chris
Football 22.00
Cut signature 3.00
3x5 Card 6.00
8x10 Photo 9.00

Stephens, John
Football 20.00
Cut signature 3.00
3x5 Card 6.00
8x10 Photo 9.00

Swann, Eric
Football 20.00
Cut signature 3.00
3x5 Card 6.00
8x10 Photo 9.00

Taylor, John
Football 22.00
Cut signature 4.00
3x5 Card 7.00
8x10 Photo 10.00

Taylor, Lawrence
Football 40.00
Cut signature 5.00
3x5 Card 10.00
8x10 Photo 15.00

Testaverde, Vinny
Football 27.00
Cut signature 6.00
3x5 Card 9.00
8x10 Photo 12.00

Thomas, Blair
Football 24.00
Cut signature 4.00
3x5 Card 6.00
8x10 Photo 10.00

Thomas, Derrick
Football 26.00
Cut signature 6.00
3x5 Card 9.00
8x10 Photo 11.00

Thomas, Thurman
Football 40.00
Cut signature 5.00
3x5 Card 9.00
8x10 Photo 14.00

Thompson, Anthony
Football 20.00
Cut signature 3.00
3x5 Card 6.00
8x10 Photo 9.00

Thompson, Darrell
Football 20.00
Cut signature 3.00

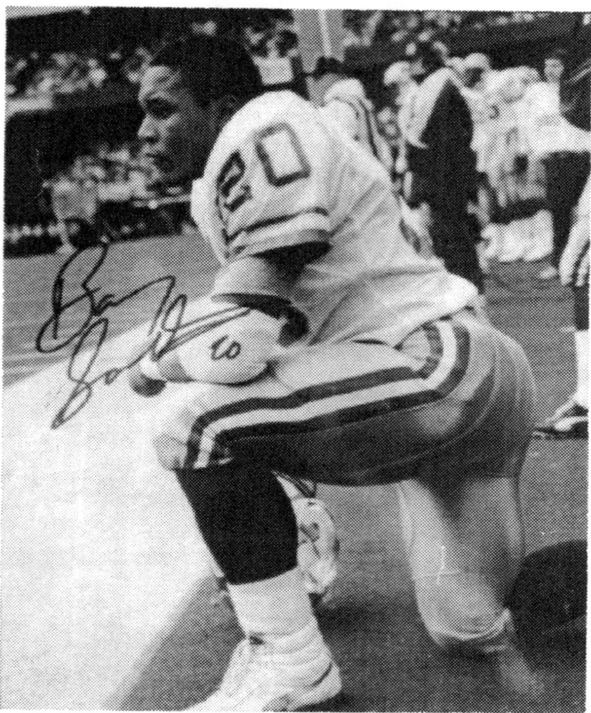

Barry Sanders

3x5 Card . . . 6.00
8x10 Photo . . . 9.00

Toon, Al
Football . . . 23.00
Cut signature . . . 4.00
3x5 Card . . . 7.00
8x10 Photo . . . 9.00

Walker, Herschel
Football . . . 26.00
Cut signature . . . 6.00
3x5 Card . . . 9.00
8x10 Photo . . . 11.00

Walsh, Steve
Football . . . 23.00
Cut signature . . . 5.00
3x5 Card . . . 7.00
8x10 Photo . . . 10.00

Ware, Andre
Football . . . 26.00
Cut signature . . . 6.00
3x5 Card . . . 9.00
8x10 Photo . . . 11.00

Watters, Ricky
Football . . . 22.00
Cut signature . . . 3.00
3x5 Card . . . 5.00
8x10 Photo . . . 7.00

White, Lorenzo
Football . . . 21.00
Cut signature . . . 4.00
3x5 Card . . . 8.00
8x10 Photo . . . 10.00

White, Reggie
Football . . . 26.00
Cut signature . . . 6.00
3x5 Card . . . 9.00
8x10 Photo . . . 11.00

Williams, Harvey
Football . . . 21.00
Cut signature . . . 4.00
3x5 Card . . . 7.00
8x10 Photo . . . 10.00

Williams, John L.
Football . . . 21.00
Cut signature . . . 4.00
3x5 Card . . . 7.00
8x10 Photo . . . 10.00

Woodson, Rod
Football . . . 21.00
Cut signature . . . 3.00
3x5 Card . . . 6.00
8x10 Photo . . . 9.00

Word, Barry
Football . . . 25.00
Cut signature . . . 5.00
3x5 Card . . . 7.00
8x10 Photo . . . 12.00

Young, Steve
Football . . . 30.00
Cut signature . . . 6.00
3x5 Card . . . 9.00
8x10 Photo . . . 12.00

Zorich, Chris
Football . . . 20.00
Cut signature . . . 3.00
3x5 Card . . . 6.00
8x10 Photo . . . 9.00

GOLF

Ballesteros, Seve
Cut signature . . . 5.00
Personal document . . . 10.00
3x5 Card . . . 7.00
8x10 Photo . . . 15.00

Hogan, Ben

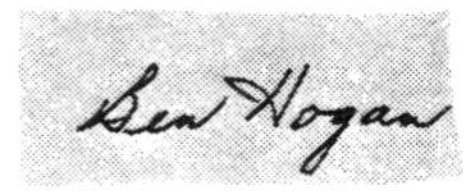

Ben Hogan

Cut signature . . . 10.00
Personal document . . . 30.00
3x5 Card . . . 15.00
8x10 Photo . . . 45.00

Jones, Bobby
Cut signature . . . 10.00
Personal document . . . 19.00
3x5 Card . . . 14.00
8x10 Photo . . . 40.00

Lopez, Nancy
Cut signature . . . 5.00
Personal document . . . 10.00
3x5 Card . . . 7.00
8x10 Photo . . . 15.00

Nelson, Byron
Cut signature . . . 14.00
Personal document . . . 25.00
3x5 Card . . . 15.00
8x10 Photo . . . 30.00

Nicklaus, Jack
Cut signature . . . 15.00
Personal document . . . 27.00
3x5 Card . . . 17.00
8x10 Photo . . . 45.00

Palmer, Arnold

Arnold Palmer

Cut signature . . . 15.00

Personal document 25.00
3x5 Card 17.00
8x10 Photo 45.00

Player, Gary
Cut signature 5.00
Personal document 20.00
3x5 Card 10.00
8x10 Photo 18.00

Rodriguez, Chi Chi
Cut signature 5.00
Personal document 20.00
3x5 Card 10.00
8x10 Photo 18.00

Sarazen, Gene
Cut signature 14.00
Personal document 24.00
3x5 Card 16.00
8x10 Photo 34.00

Snead, Sam
Cut signature 16.00
Personal document 26.00
3x5 Card 18.00
8x10 Photo 45.00

Stephenson, Jan
Cut signature 7.00
Personal document 10.00
3x5 Card 9.00
8x10 Photo 16.00

Trevino, Lee
Cut signature 10.00
Personal document 15.00
3x5 Card 12.50
8x10 Photo 35.00

Watson, Tom
Cut signature 10.00
Personal document 15.00
3x5 Card 12.50
8x10 Photo 25.00

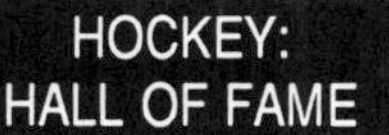

Abel, Sid
Hockey Stick 50.00
Cut signature 5.00
Personal document 20.00
3x5 Card 10.00
8x10 Photo 30.00

Adams, Jack
Hockey Stick 75.00
Cut signature 12.00
Personal document 40.00
3x5 Card 25.00
8x10 Photo 50.00

Apps, Syl
Hockey Stick 50.00
Cut signature 5.00
Personal document 20.00
3x5 Card 10.00
8x10 Photo 30.00

Armstrong, George
Hockey Stick 75.00
Cut signature 12.00
Personal document 40.00
3x5 Card 25.00
8x10 Photo 50.00

Bailey, Ace
Hockey Stick 50.00
Cut signature 5.00
Personal document 20.00
3x5 Card 10.00
8x10 Photo 30.00

Andy Bathgate

Bain, Dan
Hockey Stick 75.00
Cut signature 20.00
Personal document 40.00
3x5 Card 25.00
8x10 Photo 50.00

Baker, Hobey
Hockey Stick 80.00
Cut signature 25.00
Personal document 45.00
3x5 Card 30.00
8x10 Photo 55.00

Barber, Bill
Hockey Stick 25.00
Cut signature 5.00
Personal document 20.00
3x5 Card 10.00
8x10 Photo 15.00

Barry, Marty
Hockey Stick 35.00
Cut signature 9.00
Personal document 24.00
3x5 Card 12.00
8x10 Photo 17.00

Bathgate, Andy
Hockey Stick 37.00
Cut signature 11.00
Personal document 26.00
3x5 Card 14.00
8x10 Photo 19.00

Beliveau, Jean
Hockey Stick 55.00
Cut signature 12.00
Personal document 25.00
3x5 Card 12.00
8x10 Photo 20.00

Benedict, Clint
Hockey Stick 60.00
Cut signature 15.00
Personal document 30.00
3x5 Card 15.00
8x10 Photo 25.00

Bentley, Doug
Hockey Stick 55.00
Cut signature 15.00
Personal document 30.00
3x5 Card 11.00
8x10 Photo 25.00

Bentley, Max
Hockey Stick 57.00
Cut signature 16.00
Personal document 32.00
3x5 Card 12.00
8x10 Photo 45.00

Blake, Toe
Hockey Stick 45.00
Cut signature 12.00

Mike Bossy

Personal document 30.00
3x5 Card 18.00
8x10 Photo 35.00

Boivin, Leo
Hockey Stick 55.00
Cut signature 10.00
Personal document 35.00
3x5 Card 20.00
8x10 Photo 25.00

Boon, Dickie
Hockey Stick 45.00
Cut signature 10.00
Personal document 35.00
3x5 Card 20.00
8x10 Photo 25.00

Bossy, Mike
Hockey Stick 70.00
Cut signature 20.00
Personal document 50.00
3x5 Card 30.00
8x10 Photo 40.00

Bouchard, Butch
Hockey Stick 35.00
Cut signature 10.00
Personal document 25.00
3x5 Card 15.00
8x10 Photo 10.00

Boucher, Frank
Hockey Stick 90.00
Cut signature 30.00
Personal document 65.00
3x5 Card 40.00
8x10 Photo 70.00

Boucher, Buck
Hockey Stick 90.00
Cut signature 30.00
Personal document 65.00
3x5 Card 40.00
8x10 Photo 70.00

Bower, John
Hockey Stick 45.00
Cut signature 15.00
Personal document 39.00
3x5 Card 20.00
8x10 Photo 40.00

Bowie, Russell
Hockey Stick 125.00
Cut signature 45.00
Personal document 75.00
3x5 Card 60.00
8x10 Photo 85.00

Brimsek, Francis
Hockey Stick 75.00
Cut signature 20.00
Personal document 40.00
3x5 Card 25.00
8x10 Photo 50.00

Broadbent, Punch
Hockey Stick 90.00
Cut signature 30.00
Personal document 65.00
3x5 Card 40.00
8x10 Photo 70.00

Broda, Turk
Hockey Stick 90.00
Cut signature 30.00
Personal document 65.00
3x5 Card 40.00
8x10 Photo 70.00

Bucyk, John
Hockey Stick 90.00
Cut signature 30.00
Personal document 65.00
3x5 Card 40.00
8x10 Photo 70.00

Burch, Billy
Hockey Stick 50.00
Cut signature 20.00
Personal document 40.00
3x5 Card 27.00
8x10 Photo 35.00

Cameron, Harry
Hockey Stick 100.00
Cut signature 50.00
Personal document 75.00
3x5 Card 60.00
8x10 Photo 70.00

Cheevers, Gerry
Hockey Stick 45.00
Cut signature 10.00
Personal document 30.00
3x5 Card 20.00
8x10 Photo 25.00

Clancy, King
Hockey Stick 75.00
Cut signature 20.00
Personal document 40.00
3x5 Card 25.00
8x10 Photo 50.00

Clapper, Dit
Hockey Stick 125.00
Cut signature 65.00
Personal document 85.00
3x5 Card 70.00
8x10 Photo 75.00

Clarke, Bobby
Hockey Stick 55.00
Cut signature 25.00
Personal document 45.00
3x5 Card 30.00
8x10 Photo 35.00

Cleghorn, Sprague
Hockey Stick 85.00
Cut signature 45.00
Personal document 65.00
3x5 Card 50.00
8x10 Photo 55.00

Colville, Neil
Hockey Stick 75.00

Cut signature 45.00
Personal document 65.00
3x5 Card 50.00
8x10 Photo 63.00

Conacher, Charles
Hockey Stick 75.00
Cut signature 45.00
Personal document 65.00
3x5 Card 50.00
8x10 Photo 63.00

Connell, Alex
Hockey Stick 55.00
Cut signature 25.00
Personal document 45.00
3x5 Card 30.00
8x10 Photo 35.00

Cook, William
Hockey Stick 75.00
Cut signature 45.00
Personal document 65.00
3x5 Card 50.00
8x10 Photo 63.00

Coulter, Arthur
Hockey Stick 55.00
Cut signature 25.00
Personal document 45.00
3x5 Card 30.00
8x10 Photo 35.00

Cournoyer, Yvan
Hockey Stick 45.00
Cut signature 23.00
Personal document 40.00
3x5 Card 35.00
8x10 Photo 32.00

Cowley, Bill
Hockey Stick 55.00
Cut signature 25.00
Personal document 45.00
3x5 Card 30.00
8x10 Photo 35.00

Crawford, Rusty
Hockey Stick 125.00
Cut signature 50.00
Personal document 75.00
3x5 Card 60.00
8x10 Photo 70.00

Darragh, Jack
Hockey Stick 75.00
Cut signature 45.00
Personal document 65.00
3x5 Card 50.00
8x10 Photo 60.00

Davidson, Scotty
Hockey Stick 75.00
Cut signature 45.00
Personal document 65.00
3x5 Card 50.00
8x10 Photo 60.00

Day, Hap
Hockey Stick 85.00
Cut signature 45.00
Personal document 65.00
3x5 Card 50.00
8x10 Photo 60.00

Delvecchio, Alex
Hockey Stick 75.00
Cut signature 45.00
Personal document 65.00
3x5 Card 50.00
8x10 Photo 60.00

Denneny, Cy
Hockey Stick 100.00
Cut signature 50.00
Personal document 75.00
3x5 Card 60.00
8x10 Photo 70.00

Drillon, Gordie
Hockey Stick 55.00
Cut signature 25.00
Personal document 45.00
3x5 Card 30.00
8x10 Photo 35.00

Drinkwater, Charles
Hockey Stick 75.00
Cut signature 45.00
Personal document 65.00
3x5 Card 50.00
8x10 Photo 60.00

Dryden, Ken
Hockey Stick 55.00
Cut signature 25.00
Personal document 45.00
3x5 Card 30.00
8x10 Photo 35.00

Dunderdale, Thomas
Hockey Stick 100.00
Cut signature 50.00
Personal document 75.00
3x5 Card 60.00
8x10 Photo 70.00

Durnan, Bill
Hockey Stick 75.00
Cut signature 45.00
Personal document 65.00
3x5 Card 50.00
8x10 Photo 60.00

Dutton, Red
Hockey Stick 100.00
Cut signature 50.00
Personal document 75.00
3x5 Card 60.00
8x10 Photo 70.00

Dye, Babe
Hockey Stick 100.00
Cut signature 50.00
Personal document 75.00
3x5 Card 60.00
8x10 Photo 70.00

Esposito, Phil
Hockey Stick 55.00
Cut signature 25.00
Personal document 45.00
3x5 Card 30.00
8x10 Photo 35.00

Esposito, Tony
Hockey Stick 55.00
Cut signature 25.00
Personal document 45.00
3x5 Card 30.00
8x10 Photo 35.00

Farrell, Arthur
Hockey Stick 75.00
Cut signature 45.00
Personal document 65.00
3x5 Card 50.00
8x10 Photo 60.00

Flaman, Fern
Hockey Stick 55.00
Cut signature 25.00
Personal document 45.00
3x5 Card 30.00
8x10 Photo 35.00

Foyston, Frank
Hockey Stick 75.00
Cut signature 45.00
Personal document 65.00
3x5 Card 50.00
8x10 Photo 60.00

Frederickson, Frank
Hockey Stick 75.00
Cut signature 45.00
Personal document 65.00
3x5 Card 50.00
8x10 Photo 60.00

Gadsby, Bill
Hockey Stick 75.00

Rod Gilbert

Cut signature 45.00
Personal document 65.00
3x5 Card 50.00
8x10 Photo 60.00

Gardiner, Chuck
Hockey Stick 100.00
Cut signature 50.00
Personal document 75.00
3x5 Card 60.00
8x10 Photo 70.00

Gardiner, Herb
Hockey Stick 100.00
Cut signature 50.00
Personal document 75.00
3x5 Card 60.00
8x10 Photo 70.00

Gardner, Jimmy
Hockey Stick 75.00
Cut signature 45.00
Personal document 65.00
3x5 Card 50.00
8x10 Photo 60.00

Geoffrion, Boom Boom
Hockey Stick 55.00
Cut signature 25.00
Personal document 45.00
3x5 Card 30.00
8x10 Photo 35.00

Gerard, Eddie
Hockey Stick 100.00
Cut signature 50.00
Personal document 75.00
3x5 Card 60.00
8x10 Photo 70.00

Giacomin, Eddie
Hockey Stick 75.00
Cut signature 45.00
Personal document 65.00
3x5 Card 50.00
8x10 Photo 60.00

Gilbert, Rod
Hockey Stick 55.00
Cut signature 25.00
Personal document 45.00
3x5 Card 30.00
8x10 Photo 35.00

Gilmour, Billy
Hockey Stick 75.00
Cut signature 45.00
Personal document 65.00
3x5 Card 50.00
8x10 Photo 60.00

Stan Mikita

Goheen, Moose
Hockey Stick 100.00
Cut signature 50.00
Personal document 75.00
3x5 Card 60.00
8x10 Photo 70.00

Goodfellow, Ebbie
Hockey Stick 100.00
Cut signature 50.00
Personal document 75.00
3x5 Card 60.00
8x10 Photo 70.00
Hockey Stick 0.00

Grant, Mike
Hockey Stick 75.00
Cut signature 45.00
Personal document 65.00
3x5 Card 50.00
8x10 Photo 60.00

Green, Shorty
Hockey Stick 55.00
Cut signature 25.00
Personal document 45.00
3x5 Card 30.00
8x10 Photo 35.00

Griffis, Si
Hockey Stick 100.00
Cut signature 50.00
Personal document 75.00
3x5 Card 60.00
8x10 Photo 70.00

Hainsworth, George
Hockey Stick 75.00
Cut signature 45.00
Personal document 65.00
3x5 Card 50.00
8x10 Photo 60.00

Hall, Glenn
Hockey Stick 55.00
Cut signature 25.00
Personal document 45.00
3x5 Card 30.00
8x10 Photo 35.00

Hall, Joe
Hockey Stick 75.00
Cut signature 45.00
Personal document 65.00
3x5 Card 50.00
8x10 Photo 60.00

Harvey, Doug
Hockey Stick 75.00
Cut signature 45.00
Personal document 65.00
3x5 Card 50.00
8x10 Photo 60.00

Hay, George
Hockey Stick 100.00
Cut signature 50.00
Personal document 75.00
3x5 Card 60.00
8x10 Photo 70.00

Hern, Riley
Hockey Stick 55.00
Cut signature 25.00
Personal document 45.00
3x5 Card 30.00
8x10 Photo 35.00

Hextall, Bryan
Hockey Stick 75.00
Cut signature 45.00
Personal document 65.00
3x5 Card 50.00
8x10 Photo 60.00

Holmes, Hap
Hockey Stick 75.00
Cut signature 45.00
Personal document 65.00
3x5 Card 50.00
8x10 Photo 60.00

Hooper, Tom
Hockey Stick 75.00
Cut signature 45.00
Personal document 65.00
3x5 Card 50.00
8x10 Photo 60.00

Horner, Red
Hockey Stick 55.00
Cut signature 25.00
Personal document 45.00
3x5 Card 30.00
8x10 Photo 35.00

Horton, Tim
Hockey Stick 45.00
Cut signature 25.00
Personal document 35.00
3x5 Card 30.00
8x10 Photo 40.00

Howe, Gordie
Hockey Stick 75.00
Cut signature 45.00
Personal document 65.00
3x5 Card 50.00
8x10 Photo 60.00

Howe, Sydney
Hockey Stick 85.00
Cut signature 45.00
Personal document 65.00
3x5 Card 50.00
8x10 Photo 60.00

Howell, Harry
Hockey Stick 45.00
Cut signature 25.00
Personal document 35.00
3x5 Card 30.00
8x10 Photo 40.00

Hull, Bobby
Hockey Stick 100.00
Cut signature 50.00
Personal document 75.00
3x5 Card 60.00
8x10 Photo 70.00

Hutton, Bouse
Hockey Stick 65.00
Cut signature 30.00
Personal document 50.00
3x5 Card 30.00
8x10 Photo 40.00

Hyland, Harry
Hockey Stick 100.00
Cut signature 50.00
Personal document 75.00
3x5 Card 60.00
8x10 Photo 70.00

Irvin, Dick
Hockey Stick 100.00
Cut signature 50.00
Personal document 75.00
3x5 Card 60.00
8x10 Photo 70.00

Jackson, Harvey
Hockey Stick 65.00
Cut signature 30.00
Personal document 50.00
3x5 Card 30.00
8x10 Photo 40.00

Johnson, Ching
Hockey Stick 85.00
Cut signature 45.00
Personal document 65.00
3x5 Card 50.00
8x10 Photo 60.00

Johnson, Moose
Hockey Stick 65.00
Cut signature 30.00
Personal document 50.00
3x5 Card 30.00
8x10 Photo 40.00

Johnson, Thomas
Hockey Stick 65.00
Cut signature 30.00
Personal document 50.00
3x5 Card 30.00
8x10 Photo 40.00

Joliat, Aurel
Hockey Stick 100.00
Cut signature 50.00
Personal document 75.00
3x5 Card 60.00
8x10 Photo 70.00

Keats, Duke
Hockey Stick 85.00
Cut signature 45.00
Personal document 65.00
3x5 Card 50.00
8x10 Photo 60.00

Kelly, Red
Hockey Stick 85.00
Cut signature 45.00
Personal document 65.00
3x5 Card 50.00
8x10 Photo 60.00

Kennedy, Teeder
Hockey Stick 85.00
Cut signature 45.00
Personal document 65.00

3x5 Card 50.00
8x10 Photo 60.00

Keon, Dave
Hockey Stick 45.00
Cut signature 25.00
Personal document 35.00
3x5 Card 30.00
8x10 Photo 40.00

Lach, Elmer
Hockey Stick 45.00
Cut signature 25.00
Personal document 35.00
3x5 Card 30.00
8x10 Photo 40.00

Lafleur, Guy
Hockey Stick 35.00
Cut signature 5.00
Personal document 25.00
3x5 Card 12.00
8x10 Photo 20.00

Lalonde, Newsy
Hockey Stick 65.00
Cut signature 30.00
Personal document 50.00
3x5 Card 30.00
8x10 Photo 40.00

Laperriere, Jacques
Hockey Stick 65.00
Cut signature 30.00
Personal document 50.00
3x5 Card 30.00
8x10 Photo 40.00

Laviolette, Jack
Hockey Stick 100.00
Cut signature 50.00
Personal document 75.00
3x5 Card 60.00
8x10 Photo 70.00

Lehman, Hugh
Hockey Stick 65.00
Cut signature 30.00
Personal document 50.00
3x5 Card 30.00
8x10 Photo 40.00

Lemaire, Jacques
Hockey Stick 45.00
Cut signature 25.00
Personal document 35.00
3x5 Card 30.00
8x10 Photo 40.00

LeSueur, Percy
Hockey Stick 65.00
Cut signature 30.00
Personal document 50.00
3x5 Card 30.00
8x10 Photo 40.00

Lewis, Herb
Hockey Stick 85.00
Cut signature 45.00
Personal document 65.00
3x5 Card 50.00
8x10 Photo 60.00

Lindsay, Ted
Hockey Stick 65.00
Cut signature 30.00
Personal document 50.00
3x5 Card 30.00
8x10 Photo 40.00

Lumley, Harry
Hockey Stick 65.00
Cut signature 30.00
Personal document 50.00
3x5 Card 30.00

Bobby Orr

8x10 Photo 40.00

MacKay, Mickey
Hockey Stick 65.00
Cut signature 30.00
Personal document 50.00
3x5 Card 30.00
8x10 Photo 40.00

Mahovlich, Frank
Hockey Stick 70.00
Cut signature 35.00
Personal document 55.00
3x5 Card 35.00
8x10 Photo 45.00

Malone, Joe
Hockey Stick 60.00
Cut signature 25.00
Personal document 45.00
3x5 Card 25.00
8x10 Photo 25.00

Mantha, Sylvio
Hockey Stick 45.00
Cut signature 25.00
Personal document 35.00
3x5 Card 30.00
8x10 Photo 40.00

Marshall, Jack
Hockey Stick 60.00
Cut signature 25.00
Personal document 45.00
3x5 Card 25.00
8x10 Photo 25.00

Maxwell, Steamer
Hockey Stick 45.00
Cut signature 25.00
Personal document 35.00
3x5 Card 30.00
8x10 Photo 40.00

McGee, Frank
Hockey Stick 60.00
Cut signature 25.00
Personal document 45.00
3x5 Card 25.00
8x10 Photo 25.00

McGimsie, Billy
Hockey Stick 150.00
Cut signature 75.00
Personal document 125.00
3x5 Card 85.00
8x10 Photo 95.00

McNamara, George
Hockey Stick 145.00
Cut signature 70.00
Personal document 120.00
3x5 Card 80.00
8x10 Photo 90.00

Mikita, Stan
Hockey Stick 120.00
Cut signature 65.00
Personal document 95.00
3x5 Card 75.00
8x10 Photo 85.00

Moore, Richard
Hockey Stick 60.00
Cut signature 25.00
Personal document 45.00
3x5 Card 25.00
8x10 Photo 25.00

Moran, Paddy
Hockey Stick 45.00
Cut signature 25.00
Personal document 35.00
3x5 Card 30.00
8x10 Photo 40.00

Morenz, Howie
Hockey Stick 120.00
Cut signature 65.00
Personal document 95.00
3x5 Card 75.00
8x10 Photo 85.00

Mosienko, Bill
Hockey Stick 60.00
Cut signature 25.00
Personal document 45.00
3x5 Card 25.00
8x10 Photo 25.00

Nighbor, Frank
Hockey Stick 150.00

Cut signature 75.00
Personal document 125.00
3x5 Card 85.00
8x10 Photo 95.00

Noble, Reg
Hockey Stick 150.00
Cut signature 75.00
Personal document 125.00
3x5 Card 85.00
8x10 Photo 95.00

O'Connor, Buddy
Hockey Stick 45.00
Cut signature 25.00
Personal document 35.00
3x5 Card 30.00
8x10 Photo 40.00

Oliver, Harry
Hockey Stick 120.00
Cut signature 65.00
Personal document 95.00
3x5 Card 75.00
8x10 Photo 85.00

Olmstead, Bert
Hockey Stick 60.00
Cut signature 25.00
Personal document 45.00
3x5 Card 25.00
8x10 Photo 25.00

Orr, Bobby
Hockey Stick 185.00
Cut signature 115.00
Personal document 135.00
3x5 Card 105.00
8x10 Photo 145.00

Parent, Bernie
Hockey Stick 120.00
Cut signature 65.00
Personal document 95.00
3x5 Card 75.00
8x10 Photo 85.00

Park, Brad
Hockey Stick 60.00
Cut signature 25.00
Personal document 45.00
3x5 Card 25.00
8x10 Photo 25.00

Patrick, Joseph
Hockey Stick 120.00
Cut signature 65.00
Personal document 95.00
3x5 Card 75.00
8x10 Photo 85.00

Patrick, Lester
Hockey Stick 120.00
Cut signature 65.00
Personal document 95.00
3x5 Card 75.00
8x10 Photo 85.00

Perreault, Gil
Hockey Stick 60.00
Cut signature 25.00
Personal document 45.00
3x5 Card 25.00
8x10 Photo 25.00

Phillips, Tommy
Hockey Stick 70.00
Cut signature 35.00
Personal document 55.00
3x5 Card 35.00
8x10 Photo 45.00

Pilote, Pierre
Hockey Stick 70.00
Cut signature 35.00
Personal document 55.00
3x5 Card 35.00
8x10 Photo 45.00

Pitre, Pit
Hockey Stick 95.00
Cut signature 35.00
Personal document 65.00
3x5 Card 45.00
8x10 Photo 55.00

Plante, Jacques
Hockey Stick 95.00
Cut signature 35.00
Personal document 65.00
3x5 Card 45.00
8x10 Photo 55.00

Potvin, Denis
Hockey Stick 60.00
Cut signature 25.00
Personal document 45.00
3x5 Card 25.00
8x10 Photo 25.00

Pratt, Babe
Hockey Stick 110.00
Cut signature 65.00
Personal document 95.00
3x5 Card 75.00
8x10 Photo 85.00

Primeau, Joe
Hockey Stick 110.00
Cut signature 65.00
Personal document 95.00
3x5 Card 75.00
8x10 Photo 85.00

Pronovost, Marcel
Hockey Stick 60.00
Cut signature 25.00
Personal document 45.00
3x5 Card 25.00
8x10 Photo 25.00

Pulford, Bob
Hockey Stick 60.00
Cut signature 25.00
Personal document 45.00
3x5 Card 25.00
8x10 Photo 25.00

Pulford, Harvey
Hockey Stick 100.00
Cut signature 55.00
Personal document 85.00
3x5 Card 65.00
8x10 Photo 75.00

Quackenbush, Bill
Hockey Stick 60.00
Cut signature 25.00
Personal document 45.00
3x5 Card 25.00
8x10 Photo 25.00

Rankin, Farnk
Hockey Stick 100.00
Cut signature 55.00
Personal document 85.00
3x5 Card 65.00
8x10 Photo 75.00

Ratelle, Jean
Hockey Stick 60.00
Cut signature 25.00
Personal document 45.00
3x5 Card 25.00
8x10 Photo 25.00

Rayner, Chuck
Hockey Stick 100.00
Cut signature 55.00
Personal document 85.00
3x5 Card 65.00
8x10 Photo 75.00

Reardon, Ken
Hockey Stick 60.00
Cut signature 25.00
Personal document 45.00
3x5 Card 25.00
8x10 Photo 25.00

Richard, Henri
Hockey Stick 60.00
Cut signature 25.00
Personal document 45.00
3x5 Card 25.00
8x10 Photo 25.00

Richard, Maurice

Hockey Stick 100.00
Cut signature 55.00
Personal document 85.00
3x5 Card 65.00
8x10 Photo 75.00

Richardson, George
Hockey Stick 100.00
Cut signature 55.00
Personal document 85.00
3x5 Card 65.00
8x10 Photo 75.00

Roberts, Gordon
Hockey Stick 100.00
Cut signature 55.00
Personal document 85.00
3x5 Card 65.00
8x10 Photo 75.00

Ross, Art
Hockey Stick 200.00
Cut signature 110.00
Personal document 170.00
3x5 Card 130.00
8x10 Photo 150.00

Russel, Blair
Hockey Stick 100.00
Cut signature 55.00
Personal document 85.00
3x5 Card 65.00
8x10 Photo 75.00

Russell, Ernest
Hockey Stick 100.00
Cut signature 55.00
Personal document 85.00
3x5 Card 65.00
8x10 Photo 75.00

Kevin Dineen

Ruttan, Jack
Hockey Stick 100.00
Cut signature 55.00
Personal document 85.00
3x5 Card 65.00
8x10 Photo 75.00

Savard, Serge
Hockey Stick 60.00
Cut signature 25.00
Personal document 45.00
3x5 Card 25.00
8x10 Photo 25.00

Sawchuck, Terry
Hockey Stick 80.00
Cut signature 35.00
Personal document 65.00
3x5 Card 35.00
8x10 Photo 55.00

Scanlan, Fred
Hockey Stick 100.00
Cut signature 55.00
Personal document 85.00
3x5 Card 65.00
8x10 Photo 75.00

Schmidt, Milt
Hockey Stick 80.00
Cut signature 35.00
Personal document 65.00
3x5 Card 35.00
8x10 Photo 55.00

Schriner, Sweeny
Hockey Stick 100.00
Cut signature 55.00
Personal document 85.00
3x5 Card 65.00
8x10 Photo 75.00

Seibert, Earl
Hockey Stick 110.00
Cut signature 65.00
Personal document 95.00
3x5 Card 75.00
8x10 Photo 85.00

Seibert, Oliver
Hockey Stick 110.00
Cut signature 65.00
Personal document 95.00
3x5 Card 75.00
8x10 Photo 85.00

Shore, Eddie
Hockey Stick 150.00
Cut signature 75.00
Personal document 125.00
3x5 Card 85.00
8x10 Photo 95.00

Siebert, Babe
Hockey Stick 100.00
Cut signature 55.00
Personal document 85.00
3x5 Card 65.00
8x10 Photo 75.00

Simpson, Joe
Hockey Stick 100.00
Cut signature 55.00
Personal document 85.00
3x5 Card 65.00
8x10 Photo 75.00

Sittler, Darryl
Hockey Stick 60.00
Cut signature 25.00
Personal document 45.00
3x5 Card 25.00
8x10 Photo 25.00

Smith, Alfred
Hockey Stick 100.00
Cut signature 55.00
Personal document 85.00
3x5 Card 65.00
8x10 Photo 75.00

Smith, Billy
Hockey Stick 60.00
Cut signature 25.00
Personal document 45.00
3x5 Card 25.00
8x10 Photo 25.00

Smith, Clint
Hockey Stick 60.00
Cut signature 25.00
Personal document 45.00
3x5 Card 25.00
8x10 Photo 25.00

Smith, Hooley
Hockey Stick 80.00
Cut signature 35.00
Personal document 65.00
3x5 Card 35.00
8x10 Photo 55.00

Smith, Thomas
Hockey Stick 80.00
Cut signature 35.00
Personal document 65.00
3x5 Card 35.00
8x10 Photo 55.00

Stanley, Allan
Hockey Stick 60.00
Cut signature 25.00
Personal document 45.00
3x5 Card 25.00
8x10 Photo 25.00

Stanley, Barney
Hockey Stick 100.00
Cut signature 55.00
Personal document 85.00
3x5 Card 65.00
8x10 Photo 75.00

Stewart, Jack
Hockey Stick 100.00
Cut signature 55.00
Personal document 85.00
3x5 Card 65.00
8x10 Photo 75.00

Stewart, Nelson
Hockey Stick 100.00
Cut signature 55.00
Personal document 85.00
3x5 Card 65.00
8x10 Photo 75.00

Stuart, Bruce
Hockey Stick 110.00
Cut signature 55.00
Personal document 95.00
3x5 Card 65.00
8x10 Photo 85.00

Stuart, Hod
Hockey Stick 150.00
Cut signature 75.00
Personal document 125.00
3x5 Card 85.00
8x10 Photo 95.00

Taylor, Cyclone
Hockey Stick 150.00
Cut signature 75.00
Personal document 125.00
3x5 Card 85.00
8x10 Photo 95.00

Thompson, Tiny
Hockey Stick 110.00
Cut signature 55.00
Personal document 95.00
3x5 Card 65.00
8x10 Photo 85.00

Tretiak, Vladislav
Hockey Stick 60.00
Cut signature 25.00
Personal document 45.00
3x5 Card 25.00
8x10 Photo 25.00

Trihey, Harry
Hockey Stick 110.00
Cut signature 55.00
Personal document 95.00
3x5 Card 65.00
8x10 Photo 85.00

Ullman, Norm
Hockey Stick 60.00
Cut signature 25.00
Personal document 45.00
3x5 Card 25.00
8x10 Photo 25.00

Vezina, Georges
Hockey Stick 150.00
Cut signature 75.00
Personal document 125.00
3x5 Card 85.00
8x10 Photo 95.00

Walker, Jack
Hockey Stick 100.00
Cut signature 55.00
Personal document 85.00
3x5 Card 65.00
8x10 Photo 75.00

Walsh, Marty
Hockey Stick 100.00
Cut signature 55.00
Personal document 85.00
3x5 Card 65.00
8x10 Photo 75.00

Watson, Harry
Hockey Stick 100.00
Cut signature 55.00
Personal document 85.00
3x5 Card 65.00
8x10 Photo 75.00

Weiland, Cooney
Hockey Stick 85.00

Cut signature 45.00
Personal document 70.00
3x5 Card 50.00
8x10 Photo 60.00

Westwick, Harry
Hockey Stick 100.00
Cut signature 55.00
Personal document 85.00
3x5 Card 65.00
8x10 Photo 75.00

Whitcroft, Fred
Hockey Stick 100.00
Cut signature 55.00
Personal document 85.00
3x5 Card 65.00
8x10 Photo 75.00

Wilson, Phat
Hockey Stick 100.00
Cut signature 55.00
Personal document 85.00
3x5 Card 65.00
8x10 Photo 75.00

Worsley, Gump
Hockey Stick 150.00
Cut signature 75.00
Personal document 125.00
3x5 Card 85.00
8x10 Photo 95.00

Worters, Roy
Hockey Stick 150.00
Cut signature 75.00
Personal document 125.00
3x5 Card 85.00
8x10 Photo 95.00

HOCKEY: INACTIVE PLAYERS

Trottier, Bryan
Hockey Stick 60.00
Cut signature 25.00
Personal document 45.00
3x5 Card 25.00
8x10 Photo 25.00

HOCKEY: ACTIVE PLAYERS

Amonte, Tony
Hockey Stick 25.00
Cut signature 5.00
3x5 Card 10.00
8x10 Photo 15.00

Anderson, Glenn
Hockey Stick 20.00
Cut signature 3.00
3x5 Card 7.00
8x10 Photo 15.00

Belfour, Ed
Hockey Stick 20.00
Cut signature 3.00
3x5 Card 7.00
8x10 Photo 15.00

Bellows, Brian
Hockey Stick 20.00
Cut signature 3.00
3x5 Card 7.00
8x10 Photo 15.00

Brett Hull

Bondra, Peter
Hockey Stick 20.00
Cut signature 3.00
3x5 Card 7.00
8x10 Photo 15.00

Bourque, Ray
Hockey Stick 30.00
Cut signature 6.00
3x5 Card 15.00
8x10 Photo 21.00

Bradley, Shawn
Hockey Stick 20.00
Cut signature 3.00
3x5 Card 7.00
8x10 Photo 15.00

Brind'Amour, Rod
Hockey Stick 30.00
Cut signature 6.00
3x5 Card 15.00
8x10 Photo 21.00

Brown, Rob
Hockey Stick 20.00
Cut signature 3.00
3x5 Card 7.00
8x10 Photo 15.00

Bure, Pavel
Hockey Stick 30.00
Cut signature 6.00
3x5 Card 15.00
8x10 Photo 21.00

Carson, Jimmy
Hockey Stick 20.00
Cut signature 3.00
3x5 Card 7.00
8x10 Photo 15.00

Chelios, Chris
Hockey Stick 30.00
Cut signature 6.00
3x5 Card 15.00
8x10 Photo 21.00

Cheveldae, Tim
Hockey Stick 20.00
Cut signature 3.00
3x5 Card 7.00
8x10 Photo 15.00

Coffey, Paul
Hockey Stick 27.00
Cut signature 6.00
3x5 Card 10.00
8x10 Photo 19.00

Cullen, John
Hockey Stick 20.00

Wayne Gretzky

Cut signature 3.00
3x5 Card 7.00
8x10 Photo 15.00

Damphousse, Vincent
Hockey Stick 30.00
Cut signature 6.00
3x5 Card 15.00
8x10 Photo 21.00

Druce, John
Hockey Stick 20.00
Cut signature 3.00
3x5 Card 7.00
8x10 Photo 15.00

Emerson, Nelson
Hockey Stick 20.00
Cut signature 3.00
3x5 Card 7.00
8x10 Photo 15.00

Essensa, Bob
Hockey Stick 20.00
Cut signature 3.00
3x5 Card 7.00
8x10 Photo 15.00

Falloon, Pat
Hockey Stick 20.00
Cut signature 3.00
3x5 Card 7.00
8x10 Photo 15.00

Fedorov, Sergei
Hockey Stick 27.00
Cut signature 6.00
3x5 Card 10.00
8x10 Photo 19.00

Fleury, Theoren
Hockey Stick 20.00
Cut signature 3.00
3x5 Card 7.00
8x10 Photo 15.00

Gamble, Troy
Hockey Stick 20.00
Cut signature 3.00
3x5 Card 7.00
8x10 Photo 15.00

Garpenlov, Johan
Hockey Stick 20.00
Cut signature 3.00
3x5 Card 7.00
8x10 Photo 15.00

Gartner, Mike
Hockey Stick 27.00
Cut signature 6.00
3x5 Card 10.00
8x10 Photo 19.00

Gelinas, Martin
Hockey Stick 20.00
Cut signature 3.00
3x5 Card 7.00
8x10 Photo 15.00

Gretzky, Wayne
Hockey Stick 85.00
Cut signature 12.00
3x5 Card 35.00
8x10 Photo 65.00

Gusarov, Alexei
Hockey Stick 20.00
Cut signature 3.00
3x5 Card 7.00
8x10 Photo 15.00

Hawerchuk, Dale
Hockey Stick 22.00
Cut signature 5.00
3x5 Card 9.00
8x10 Photo 17.00

Hextall, Ron
Hockey Stick 27.00
Cut signature 6.00
3x5 Card 10.00
8x10 Photo 19.00

Hodge, Ken Jr.
Hockey Stick 20.00
Cut signature 3.00
3x5 Card 7.00
8x10 Photo 15.00

Holik, Bobby
Hockey Stick 22.00
Cut signature 5.00
3x5 Card 9.00
8x10 Photo 17.00

Housley, Phil
Hockey Stick 20.00
Cut signature 3.00
3x5 Card 7.00
8x10 Photo 15.00

Hrudey, Kelly
Hockey Stick 27.00
Cut signature 6.00
3x5 Card 10.00
8x10 Photo 19.00

Hull, Brett
Hockey Stick 80.00
Cut signature 10.00
3x5 Card 30.00
8x10 Photo 60.00

Ing, Peter
Hockey Stick 22.00
Cut signature 5.00
3x5 Card 9.00
8x10 Photo 17.00

Jagr, Jaromir
Hockey Stick 45.00
Cut signature 7.00
3x5 Card 16.00
8x10 Photo 30.00

Janney, Craig
Hockey Stick 22.00
Cut signature 5.00
3x5 Card 9.00
8x10 Photo 17.00

Kamensky, Valerei
Hockey Stick 22.00
Cut signature 5.00
3x5 Card 9.00
8x10 Photo 17.00

Kasparaitis, Darius
Hockey Stick 27.00
Cut signature 6.00
3x5 Card 10.00
8x10 Photo 19.00

Khristich, Dimitri
Hockey Stick 22.00
Cut signature 5.00
3x5 Card 9.00
8x10 Photo 17.00

Kidd, Trevor
Hockey Stick 20.00
Cut signature 3.00
3x5 Card 7.00
8x10 Photo 15.00

Klima, Petr
Hockey Stick 20.00
Cut signature 3.00
3x5 Card 7.00
8x10 Photo 15.00

Kron, Robert
Hockey Stick 22.00
Cut signature 5.00
3x5 Card 9.00
8x10 Photo 17.00

Kurri, Jari
Hockey Stick 20.00
Cut signature 3.00
3x5 Card 7.00
8x10 Photo 15.00

LaChance, Scott
Hockey Stick 27.00
Cut signature 6.00
3x5 Card 10.00
8x10 Photo 19.00

LaFontaine, Pat
Hockey Stick 27.00
Cut signature 6.00
3x5 Card 10.00
8x10 Photo 19.00

Larmer, Steve
Hockey Stick 20.00
Cut signature 3.00
3x5 Card 7.00
8x10 Photo 15.00

Lebeau, Stephan

Scott LaChance

Hockey Stick 20.00
Cut signature 3.00
3x5 Card 7.00
8x10 Photo 15.00

Leetch, Brian
Hockey Stick 22.00
Cut signature 4.00
3x5 Card 9.00
8x10 Photo 16.00

Lemieux, Mario
Hockey Stick 80.00
Cut signature 10.00
3x5 Card 30.00
8x10 Photo 60.00

Lidstrom, Nicklas
Hockey Stick 27.00
Cut signature 6.00
3x5 Card 10.00
8x10 Photo 19.00

Linden, Trevor
Hockey Stick 20.00
Cut signature 3.00
3x5 Card 7.00
8x10 Photo 15.00

Lindros, Eric
Hockey Stick 45.00
Cut signature 7.00
3x5 Card 16.00
8x10 Photo 30.00

MacInnis, Al
Hockey Stick 20.00
Cut signature 3.00
3x5 Card 7.00
8x10 Photo 15.00

Makarov, Sergei
Hockey Stick 27.00
Cut signature 6.00
3x5 Card 10.00
8x10 Photo 19.00

Matteau, Stephane
Hockey Stick 20.00
Cut signature 3.00
3x5 Card 7.00
8x10 Photo 15.00

Messier, Mark
Hockey Stick 22.00
Cut signature 4.00
3x5 Card 9.00
8x10 Photo 16.00

Miller, Kevin
Hockey Stick 22.00
Cut signature 4.00
3x5 Card 9.00
8x10 Photo 16.00

Modano, Mike
Hockey Stick 20.00
Cut signature 3.00
3x5 Card 7.00
8x10 Photo 15.00

Mogilny, Alexander
Hockey Stick 22.00
Cut signature 4.00
3x5 Card 9.00
8x10 Photo 16.00

Morin, Stephane
Hockey Stick 20.00
Cut signature 3.00
3x5 Card 7.00
8x10 Photo 15.00

Mullen, Joe
Hockey Stick 20.00
Cut signature 3.00
3x5 Card 7.00
8x10 Photo 15.00

Muller,Kirk
Hockey Stick 22.00
Cut signature 4.00
3x5 Card 9.00
8x10 Photo 16.00

Murphy, Joe
Hockey Stick 20.00
Cut signature 3.00
3x5 Card 7.00
8x10 Photo 15.00

Nedved, Petr
Hockey Stick 27.00
Cut signature 6.00
3x5 Card 10.00
8x10 Photo 19.00

Neely, Cam
Hockey Stick 22.00
Cut signature 4.00
3x5 Card 9.00
8x10 Photo 16.00

Nemchinov, Sergei
Hockey Stick 20.00
Cut signature 3.00
3x5 Card 7.00
8x10 Photo 15.00

Niedermayer, Scott
Hockey Stick 22.00
Cut signature 4.00
3x5 Card 9.00
8x10 Photo 16.00

Nieuwendyk, Joe
Hockey Stick 22.00
Cut signature 4.00
3x5 Card 9.00
8x10 Photo 16.00

Nolan, Owen
Hockey Stick 20.00
Cut signature 4.00
3x5 Card 9.00
8x10 Photo 15.00

Oates, Adam
Hockey Stick 20.00
Cut signature 3.00
3x5 Card 7.00
8x10 Photo 15.00

Probert, Bob
Hockey Stick 21.00
Cut signature 4.00
3x5 Card 8.00
8x10 Photo 16.00

Ranford, Bill
Hockey Stick 20.00
Cut signature 3.00
3x5 Card 7.00
8x10 Photo 15.00

Recchi, Mark
Hockey Stick 21.00
Cut signature 4.00
3x5 Card 8.00
8x10 Photo 16.00

Reichel, Robert
Hockey Stick 20.00
Cut signature 3.00
3x5 Card 7.00
8x10 Photo 15.00

Rheaume, Manon
Hockey Stick 28.00
Cut signature 6.00
3x5 Card 9.00
8x10 Photo 17.00

Ricci, Mike
Hockey Stick 20.00
Cut signature 3.00
3x5 Card 7.00
8x10 Photo 15.00

Richer, Stephane
Hockey Stick 20.00
Cut signature 3.00
3x5 Card 7.00
8x10 Photo 15.00

Richter, Mike
Hockey Stick 20.00
Cut signature 3.00
3x5 Card 7.00
8x10 Photo 15.00

Robitaille, Luc
Hockey Stick 22.00
Cut signature 4.00
3x5 Card 9.00
8x10 Photo 16.00

Roenick, Jeremy
Hockey Stick 28.00
Cut signature 5.00
3x5 Card 12.00
8x10 Photo 17.00

Roy, Patrick
Hockey Stick 22.00
Cut signature 4.00
3x5 Card 10.00
8x10 Photo 15.00

Ruzicka, Vladimir
Hockey Stick 20.00
Cut signature 3.00
3x5 Card 7.00
8x10 Photo 15.00

Sakic, Joe
Hockey Stick 21.00
Cut signature 4.00
3x5 Card 7.00
8x10 Photo 16.00

Sandstrom, Tomas
Hockey Stick 20.00
Cut signature 3.00
3x5 Card 7.00
8x10 Photo 15.00

Savard, Denis
Hockey Stick 20.00
Cut signature 3.00
3x5 Card 7.00
8x10 Photo 15.00

Semenov, Anatoli
Hockey Stick 20.00
Cut signature 3.00
3x5 Card 7.00
8x10 Photo 15.00

Shanahan, Brendan
Hockey Stick 20.00
Cut signature 3.00
3x5 Card 7.00
8x10 Photo 15.00

Stastny, Peter
Hockey Stick 22.00
Cut signature 4.00
3x5 Card 10.00
8x10 Photo 15.00

Stevens, Kevin
Hockey Stick 21.00
Cut signature 4.00
3x5 Card 7.00
8x10 Photo 12.00

Stevens, Scott
Hockey Stick 20.00
Cut signature 3.00
3x5 Card 7.00
8x10 Photo 15.00

Sundin, Mats
Hockey Stick 20.00
Cut signature 3.00
3x5 Card 7.00
8x10 Photo 15.00

Terreri, Chris
Hockey Stick 20.00
Cut signature 3.00
3x5 Card 7.00
8x10 Photo 15.00

Tikkanen, Esa
Hockey Stick 20.00
Cut signature 3.00
3x5 Card 7.00
8x10 Photo 15.00

Todd, Kevin
Hockey Stick 20.00
Cut signature 3.00
3x5 Card 7.00
8x10 Photo 15.00

Turcotte, Darren
Hockey Stick 22.00
Cut signature 4.00
3x5 Card 10.00
8x10 Photo 15.00

Turgeon, Pierre

Hockey Stick 22.00

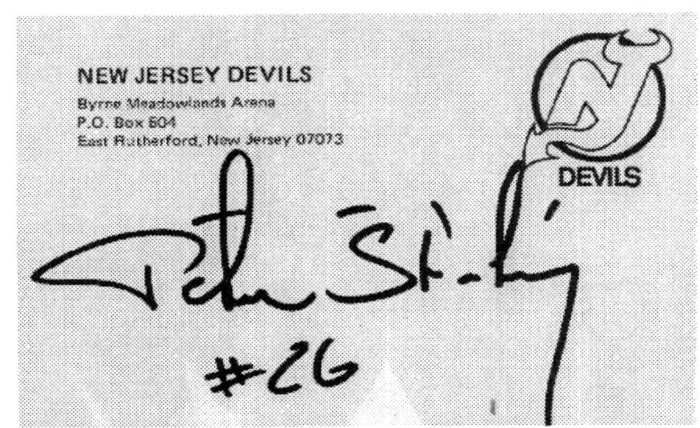

NEW JERSEY DEVILS
Byrne Meadowlands Arena
P.O. Box 504
East Rutherford, New Jersey 07073
DEVILS
#26

Peter Stastny

Cut signature 4.00
3x5 Card 10.00
8x10 Photo 15.00

Vanbiesbrouck, John
Hockey Stick 22.00
Cut signature 4.00
3x5 Card 10.00
8x10 Photo 15.00

Weight, Doug
Hockey Stick 20.00
Cut signature 3.00
3x5 Card 7.00
8x10 Photo 5.00

Weinrich, Eric
Hockey Stick 20.00
Cut signature 3.00
3x5 Card 7.00
8x10 Photo 5.00

Ysebaert, Paul
Hockey Stick 20.00
Cut signature 3.00
3x5 Card 7.00
8x10 Photo 5.00

Yzerman, Steve
Hockey Stick 25.00
Cut signature 5.00
3x5 Card 10.00
8x10 Photo 15.00

Zelepukin, Valerei
Hockey Stick 20.00
Cut signature 3.00
3x5 Card 7.00
8x10 Photo 5.00

OLYMPIC ATHLETES

Albright, Tenley
Cut signature 10.00
Personal document 20.00
3x5 Card 15.00
8x10 Photo 40.00

Ashford, Evelyn
Cut signature 5.00
Personal document 10.00
3x5 Card 8.00
8x10 Photo 20.00

Babashoff, Shirley
Cut signature 5.00
Personal document 10.00
3x5 Card 8.00
8x10 Photo 20.00

Baumann, Alex
Cut signature 5.00
Personal document 10.00
3x5 Card 8.00
8x10 Photo 20.00

Beamon, Bob
Cut signature 10.00
Personal document 20.00
3x5 Card 15.00
8x10 Photo 40.00

Benoit, Joan
Cut signature 8.00
Personal document 18.00
3x5 Card 12.00
8x10 Photo 25.00

Biondi, Matt
Cut signature 8.00
Personal document 18.00
3x5 Card 12.00
8x10 Photo 25.00

Blair, Bonnie
Cut signature 6.00
Personal document 9.00
3x5 Card 11.00
8x10 Photo 19.00

Boitano, Brian
Cut signature 8.00
Personal document 20.00
3x5 Card 15.00
8x10 Photo 30.00

Brisco-Hooks, Valerie
Cut signature 6.00
Personal document 9.00
3x5 Card 11.00
8x10 Photo 19.00

Button, Dick
Cut signature 10.00
Personal document 22.00
3x5 Card 14.00
8x10 Photo 35.00

Campbell, Milt
Cut signature 5.00
Personal document 10.00

3x5 Card 7.00
8x10 Photo 15.00

Caulkins, Tracy
Cut signature 5.00
Personal document 10.00
3x5 Card 7.00
8x10 Photo 15.00

Coe, Sebastian
Cut signature 10.00
Personal document 20.00
3x5 Card 15.00
8x10 Photo 30.00

Comaneci, Nadia
Cut signature 10.00
Personal document 22.00
3x5 Card 19.00
8x10 Photo 35.00

Conner, Bart
Cut signature 8.00
Personal document 18.00
3x5 Card 13.00
8x10 Photo 25.00

Cousins, Robin
Cut signature 5.00
Personal document 15.00
3x5 Card 10.00
8x10 Photo 20.00

Davis, Glenn
Cut signature 5.00
Personal document 10.00
3x5 Card 8.00
8x10 Photo 15.00

Torvill, Jayne / Dean, Christopher
3x5 Card 15.00
8x10 Photo 30.00

Devers, Gail
Cut signature 10.00
Personal document 20.00
3x5 Card 15.00
8x10 Photo 30.00

Didrickson-Zaharias, Babe
Cut signature 75.00
Personal document 350.00
3x5 Card 100.00
8x10 Photo 500.00

Eagan, Eddie
Cut signature 10.00
Personal document 20.00
3x5 Card 15.00
8x10 Photo 30.00

Evans, Janet
Cut signature 8.00
Personal document 18.00
3x5 Card 13.00
8x10 Photo 22.00

Fleming, Peggy
Cut signature 25.00
Personal document 55.00
3x5 Card 35.00
8x10 Photo 75.00

Fosbury, Dick
Cut signature 12.00
Personal document 36.00
3x5 Card 24.00
8x10 Photo 60.00

Haislett, Nicole
Cut signature 8.00
Personal document 18.00
3x5 Card 13.00
8x10 Photo 22.00

Hamill, Dorothy
Cut signature 15.00
Personal document 35.00
3x5 Card 25.00
8x10 Photo 55.00

Heiden, Eric
Cut signature 4.00
Personal document 8.00
3x5 Card 6.00
8x10 Photo 10.00

Heiss, Carol
Cut signature 8.00
Personal document 18.00
3x5 Card 12.00
8x10 Photo 22.00

Henie, Sonja
Cut signature 17.00
Personal document 35.00
3x5 Card 20.00
8x10 Photo 50.00

Jager, Tom
Cut signature 2.00
Personal document 8.00
3x5 Card 6.00
8x10 Photo 10.00

Jenner, Bruce
Cut signature 4.00
Personal document 10.00
3x5 Card 8.00
8x10 Photo 15.00

Johnson, Ben
Cut signature 2.00
Personal document 8.00
3x5 Card 6.00
8x10 Photo 10.00

Johnson, Rafer
Cut signature 2.00
Personal document 8.00
3x5 Card 6.00
8x10 Photo 10.00

Joyner, Florence Griffith
Cut signature 4.00
Personal document 16.00
3x5 Card 12.00
8x10 Photo 20.00

Joyner-Kersee, Jackie
Cut signature 4.00
Personal document 16.00
3x5 Card 12.00
8x10 Photo 20.00

Killy, Jean-Claude
Cut signature 4.00
Personal document 16.00
3x5 Card 12.00
8x10 Photo 20.00

Kingdom, Roger
Cut signature 3.00
Personal document 9.00
3x5 Card 7.00
8x10 Photo 13.00

Korbut, Olga
Cut signature 10.00
Personal document 20.00
3x5 Card 15.00
8x10 Photo 30.00

Lewis, Carl
Cut signature 4.00
Personal document 16.00
3x5 Card 12.00
8x10 Photo 20.00

Louganis, Greg
Cut signature 3.00
Personal document 12.00
3x5 Card 9.00
8x10 Photo 15.00

Lundquist, Steve
Cut signature 2.00
Personal document 8.00
3x5 Card 6.00
8x10 Photo 10.00

Mahre, Phil
Cut signature 2.00
Personal document 6.00
3x5 Card 4.00
8x10 Photo 8.00

Mahre, Steve
Cut signature 2.00
Personal document 6.00
3x5 Card 4.00
8x10 Photo 8.00

Marsh, Mike
Cut signature 2.00
Personal document 6.00
3x5 Card 4.00
8x10 Photo 8.00

Mathias, Bob

Bob Mathias

Cut signature 2.00
Personal document 6.00
3x5 Card 4.00
8x10 Photo 8.00

McCormick, Pat
Cut signature 3.00
Personal document 7.00
3x5 Card 5.00
8x10 Photo 11.00

Meagher, Mary T.
Cut signature 3.00
Personal document 7.00
3x5 Card 5.00
8x10 Photo 11.00

Miller, Shannon
Cut signature 4.00
Personal document 8.00
3x5 Card 6.00
8x10 Photo 12.00

Morales, Pablo
Cut signature 5.00
Personal document 9.00
3x5 Card 7.00
8x10 Photo 14.00

Moses, Edwin
Cut signature . . . 4.00
Personal document . . . 10.00
3x5 Card . . . 7.00
8x10 Photo . . . 15.00

Naber, John
Cut signature . . . 2.00
Personal document . . . 8.00
3x5 Card . . . 4.00
8x10 Photo . . . 10.00

Nurmi, Paavo
Cut signature . . . 20.00
Personal document . . . 70.00
3x5 Card . . . 30.00
8x10 Photo . . . 100.00

Oerter, Al
Cut signature . . . 4.00
Personal document . . . 12.00
3x5 Card . . . 8.00
8x10 Photo . . . 20.00

Owens, Jesse

Jesse Owens

Cut signature . . . 25.00
Personal document . . . 55.00
3x5 Card . . . 35.00
8x10 Photo . . . 75.00

Retton, Mary Lou
Cut signature . . . 4.00
Personal document . . . 12.00
3x5 Card . . . 8.00
8x10 Photo . . . 20.00

Rudolph, Wilma
Cut signature . . . 2.00
Personal document . . . 8.00
3x5 Card . . . 6.00
8x10 Photo . . . 10.00

Sanders, Summer
Cut signature . . . 1.00
Personal document . . . 4.00
3x5 Card . . . 3.00
8x10 Photo . . . 7.00

Schollander, Don
Cut signature . . . 4.00
Personal document . . . 12.00
3x5 Card . . . 8.00
8x10 Photo . . . 20.00

Sheridan, Martin
Cut signature . . . 3.00
Personal document . . . 10.00
3x5 Card . . . 6.00
8x10 Photo . . . 15.00

Shorter, Frank
Cut signature . . . 1.00
Personal document . . . 4.00
3x5 Card . . . 3.00
8x10 Photo . . . 6.00

Spitz, Mark
Cut signature . . . 4.00
Personal document . . . 15.00
3x5 Card . . . 10.00
8x10 Photo . . . 25.00

Stenmark, Ingemar
Cut signature . . . 4.00
Personal document . . . 12.00
3x5 Card . . . 8.00
8x10 Photo . . . 20.00

Thompson, Daley
Cut signature . . . 2.00
Personal document . . . 6.00
3x5 Card . . . 4.00
8x10 Photo . . . 10.00

Tomba, Alberto
Cut signature . . . 4.00
Personal document . . . 12.00
3x5 Card . . . 8.00
8x10 Photo . . . 20.00

Toomey, Bill
Cut signature . . . 4.00
Personal document . . . 12.00
3x5 Card . . . 8.00
8x10 Photo . . . 20.00

Torrence, Gwen
Cut signature . . . 2.00
Personal document . . . 6.00
3x5 Card . . . 4.00
8x10 Photo . . . 10.00

Watts, Quincy
Cut signature . . . 4.00
Personal document . . . 12.00
3x5 Card . . . 8.00
8x10 Photo . . . 20.00

Weissmuller, Johnny
Cut signature . . . 40.00
Personal document . . . 160.00
3x5 Card . . . 80.00
8x10 Photo . . . 200.00

Witt, Katarina
Cut signature . . . 2.00
Personal document . . . 6.00
3x5 Card . . . 4.00
8x10 Photo . . . 10.00

Yamaguchi, Kristi
Cut signature . . . 2.00
Personal document . . . 6.00
3x5 Card . . . 4.00
8x10 Photo . . . 10.00

MEN'S TENNIS

Agassi, Andre
Cut signature . . . 4.00
Personal document . . . 12.00
3x5 Card . . . 8.00
8x10 Photo . . . 20.00

Ashe, Arthur
Cut signature . . . 3.00
Personal document . . . 14.00
3x5 Card . . . 9.00
8x10 Photo . . . 22.00

Becker, Boris
Cut signature . . . 5.00
Personal document . . . 15.00
3x5 Card . . . 10.00
8x10 Photo . . . 30.00

Borg, Bjorn
Cut signature . . . 4.00
Personal document . . . 12.00
3x5 Card . . . 8.00
8x10 Photo . . . 20.00

Chang, Michael
Cut signature . . . 3.00
Personal document . . . 11.00
3x5 Card . . . 7.00
8x10 Photo . . . 15.00

Connors, Jimmy
Cut signature . . . 4.00
Personal document . . . 12.00
3x5 Card . . . 8.00
8x10 Photo . . . 20.00

Courier, Jim
Cut signature . . . 2.00
Personal document . . . 8.00
3x5 Card . . . 6.00
8x10 Photo . . . 10.00

Edberg, Stefan
Cut signature . . . 8.00
Personal document . . . 20.00
3x5 Card . . . 16.00
8x10 Photo . . . 35.00

Laver, Rod
Cut signature . . . 3.00
Personal document . . . 11.00
3x5 Card . . . 7.00
8x10 Photo . . . 15.00

Lendl, Ivan
Cut signature . . . 3.00
Personal document . . . 11.00
3x5 Card . . . 7.00
8x10 Photo . . . 15.00

McEnroe, John
Cut signature . . . 5.00
Personal document . . . 15.00
3x5 Card . . . 10.00
8x10 Photo . . . 25.00

Riggs, Bobby
Cut signature . . . 2.00
Personal document . . . 6.00
3x5 Card . . . 4.00
8x10 Photo . . . 10.00

Tilden, Bill
Cut signature . . . 60.00
Personal document . . . 140.00
3x5 Card . . . 100.00
8x10 Photo . . . 200.00

Wilander, Mats
Cut signature . . . 4.00
Personal document . . . 8.00
3x5 Card . . . 6.00
8x10 Photo . . . 10.00

WOMEN'S TENNIS

Capriati, Jennifer
Cut signature . . . 5.00
Personal document . . . 15.00
3x5 Card . . . 10.00
8x10 Photo . . . 30.00

Court, Margaret
Cut signature . . . 4.00
Personal document . . . 8.00
3x5 Card . . . 6.00
8x10 Photo . . . 10.00

Graf, Steffi
Cut signature . . . 6.00
Personal document . . . 10.00
3x5 Card . . . 8.00
8x10 Photo . . . 12.00

King, Billie Jean

Ric Flair

Cut signature 10.00
Personal document 25.00
3x5 Card 19.00
8x10 Photo 35.00

Navratilova, Martina
Cut signature 5.00
Personal document 15.00
3x5 Card 10.00
8x10 Photo 30.00

Sabatini, Gabriela
Cut signature 6.00
Personal document 12.00
3x5 Card 8.00
8x10 Photo 20.00

Sanchez, Arantxa
Cut signature 4.00
Personal document 8.00
3x5 Card 6.00
8x10 Photo 10.00

Seles, Monica
Cut signature 6.00
Personal document 12.00
3x5 Card 8.00
8x10 Photo 20.00

Wills-Moody, Helen
Cut signature 6.00
Personal document 12.00
3x5 Card 8.00
8x10 Photo 20.00

WRESTLING

Andre the Giant
Cut signature 25.00
3x5 Card 35.00
8x10 Photo 50.00

Backlund, Bob
Cut signature 15.00
3x5 Card 20.00
8x10 Photo 25.00

Beefcake, Brutus
Cut signature 10.00
3x5 Card 14.00
8x10 Photo 20.00

Flair, Ric
Cut signature 5.00
3x5 Card 10.00
8x10 Photo 15.00

Gorgeous George
Cut signature 15.00
3x5 Card 20.00
8x10 Photo 25.00

Hogan, Hulk

Hulk Hogan

Cut signature 8.00
3x5 Card 16.00
8x10 Photo 20.00

Piper, Rowdy Roddy
Cut signature 4.00
3x5 Card 8.00
8x10 Photo 14.00

Samartino, Bruno
Cut signature 5.00
3x5 Card 9.00
8x10 Photo 15.00

Savage, Macho King Randy
Cut signature 9.00
3x5 Card 14.00
8x10 Photo 20.00

Slaughter, Sergeant
Cut signature 9.00
3x5 Card 14.00
8x10 Photo 20.00

Snuka, Jimmy "Superfly"
Cut signature 4.00
3x5 Card 8.00
8x10 Photo 14.00

The Ultimate Warrior

Cut signature 9.00
3x5 Card 14.00
8x10 Photo 20.00

COLLECTING BOBBIN' HEADS

By Brian Kelly

Tim Hunter, in *The Investors Journal*, refers to them as Bobbing Heads; Patrick Flynn, in his Price Guide, prefers the less formal Bobbin' Head Dolls; Denise Tom, in *USA Today*, goes way out on a limb and alludes to these hot collectibles as "annoyingly tacky bobble-headed, sports team dolls." Such a lot of fuss over the little Mr. Met that used to sit on my bureau, right next to my Topps card locker. But at $225.00, that little guy is now significantly more valuable than the Cleon Jones cards I had in my locker.

The first (insert your choice of nomenclature) dolls were manufactured in Japan, in 1960, by Lego Co. They were made out of a paper mache material and were available at ball parks, or by mail order, for $1.00 to $2.98. Dolls were produced for at least twelve major league baseball teams, and four minor league teams, in that first batch.

The 1961-62 Roberto Clemente player caricature doll is the most valuable of the lot, at $1,100.00. This doll was one of a release of four – the other players immortalized with bobbin' heads in this series were Mickey Mantle, Roger Maris, and Willie Mays. The Willie Mays doll is interesting because it was released in two different versions. The original issue featured very dark skin, and is valued at $400; the lighter-skinned variation is more common, and is valued at $175.00.

Pigmentation fluctuations of the Say Hey Kid aside, the most important variation involved with bobbin' heads is the base color. As the serious collector of bobbin' heads will tell you, only the Japanese dolls (produced from 1960-72) will satisfy the true Head fan. Base colors are used to differentiate the years of those dolls.

Various colored square bases were used in 1960-61; 1961-62 were mounted on white square bases (miniatures of this year used white round bases); green round bases were used from 1962-64, and round gold bases were used from 1967-72. There are some variations and subsets like green square bases for 1962, and gold square bases for 1970. Keep in mind these guidelines are only applicable for the Japanese dolls from 1960-72. After 1972, the dolls were manufactured in Hong Kong, Taiwan and Korea. Variations of base colors abound in these non-Japanese dolls.

Lego produced Football bobbin' heads in Japan from 1960-70. These dolls are also identified by their variant bases. 1961-62 came with a wooden or ceramic base; 1966-68 with a gold round base; the NFL merger series from 1968-70 also had round gold bases; AFL teams from 1961-62 had round and square various colored bases; AFC from 1966-67 had gold round bases. There were also NFL boy and girl kissing dolls from 1962, and many colleges had dolls produced during the years 1962-68.

Basketball and hockey dolls were produced in 1961-62; not much is known about the basketball dolls. The assumption is that all NBA teams were produced, along with a Harlem Globetrotter doll. The hockey dolls are only slightly less mysterious. We know they were produced in 1961-62, all with "boy heads", with orange or dark colored hair variations. We also know they were produced from 1966-69, included all expansion teams, and were on gold oval bases.

As with any collectible market, there is always a small group of individuals who attempt to pass counterfeit items. We have heard horror stories of collectors buying black player heads, from years when they were not produced, for exorbitant sums. The collectors had been conned by a quick paint job, and paid the big bucks for a collectible that didn't exist! Try to check for paint consistency inside the head, and compare the doll's paint color to that of a doll you are certain is authentic. This practice is referred to as a "lobotomy" in some head circles.

Once you have mastered the intricacies of identifying heads by their bases, and are able to ascertain the authenticity of variant heads, you are ready to enter the world of collecting bobbin' heads. Good luck, and Happy Head Hunting!

BOBBIN' HEADS

BASEBALL

White Square Base bobbin' heads.

ANGELS

Type	Base	Logo	Value
I	Blue Square	D/E	75.00
II	White Square	D	135.00
II	(Anaheim)	D	110.00
III	White Round Mini	D	125.00
IV	Green Round	D	75.00
V	Gr Round Base, Black		425.00
VI	Gold Round (Cal)	D	50.00
VI	Gold Round (L.A.)	D	40.00

ASTROS

Type	Base	Logo	Value
VI	Gold Round	D	60.00
1970s	Square Gold		150.00

ATHLETICS

Type	Base	Logo	Value
II	White Square	D	275.00
III	White Round Mini	D	125.00
IV	Green Round	D	125.00
V	Gr Round Base, Black		850.00
VI	Gold Round (Gold)	D	25.00
VI	Gold Round (White)	D	125.00
1970s	Square Gold		150.00

BRAVES

Type	Base	Logo	Value
II	White Square	E	200.00
III	White Round Mini	D	225.00
IV	Green Round	D	150.00
V	Gr Round Base, Black		650.00
VI	Gold Round	D	50.00

BREWERS

Type	Base	Logo	Value
VI	Gold Round	D	30.00

CARDINALS

Type	Base	Logo	Value
II	White Square	E	325.00
III	White Round Mini	D	225.00
IV	Green Round	D	135.00
V	Gr Round Base, Black		450.00
VI	Gold Round	D	85.00

COLT 45s

Type	Base	Logo	Value
II	White Square	E	150.00
II	White Sq. (Blue)	E	450.00
III	White Round Mini	D	125.00
IV	Green Round	E	100.00
V	Gr Round Base, Black		850.00

CUBS

Type	Base	Logo	Value
I	Lt. Blue Square	D/E	200.00
II	White Square	E	325.00
III	White Round Mini	D	225.00
IV	Green Round	D	225.00
V	Gr Round Base, Black		475.00
VI	Gold Round	D	85.00

DODGERS

Type	Base	Logo	Value
I	Blue Square	D/E	75.00
II	White Square	E	125.00
III	White Round Mini	D	125.00
IV	Green Round	D	50.00
V	Gr Round Base, Black		275.00
VI	Gold Round	D	40.00
1960s	White Round, Uniform #s		175.00

EXPOS

Type	Base	Logo	Value
VI	Gold Round	D	25.00

GIANTS

Type	Base	Logo	Value
I	Orange Square	D/E	175.00
II	White Square	D/E	225.00
III	White Round Mini	D	125.00
IV	Green Round	D	60.00
V	Gr Round Base, Black		625.00
VI	Gold Round	D	75.00

INDIANS

Type	Base	Logo	Value
II	White Square	E	275.00
III	White Round Mini	D	150.00
IV	Green Round	D	125.00
V	Gr Round Base, Black		275.00
VI	Gold Round	D	85.00
1960s	4 ½" Mini, ballpark doll		60.00

METS

Type	Base	Logo	Value
I	Blue Square	D/E	200.00
II	White Square	D	275.00
III	White Round Mini	D	225.00
IV	Green Round	D	65.00
V	Gr Round Base, Black		350.00
VI	Gold Round	D	60.00
1969	Gold Round, Mr. Met		225.00

ORIOLES

Type	Base	Logo	Value
I	Green Diamond	D/E	175.00
II	White Square	E	250.00
III	White Round Mini	D	150.00
IV	Green Round	D/E	125.00
V	Gr Round Base, Black		375.00
VI	Gold Round	D	65.000

PADRES

Type	Base	Logo	Value
VI	Gold Round	D	75.00

PHILLIES

Type	Base	Logo	Value
II	White Square	E	175.00
III	White Round Mini	D	125.00
IV	Green Round	D/E	75.00
V	Gr Round Base, Black		375.00
VI	Gold Round	D	65.00

PILOTS

VI	Gold Round	D	225.00

PIRATES

I	Orange Square	D/E	175.00
II	White Square	E	400.00
III	White Round Mini	D	225.00
IV	Green Round	D	135.00
V	Gr Round Base, Black		550.00
VI	Gold Round	D	85.00

RANGERS

VI	Gold Round	D	50.00

RED SOX

I	Green Square	D/E	175.00
II	White Square	D	200.00
III	White Round Mini	D	125.00
IV	Green Round	D	85.00
V	Gr Round Base, Black		450.00
VI	Gold Round	D	50.00

REDS

I	Red Square	D/E	200.00
II	White Square	E	375.00
III	White Round Mini	D	275.00
IV	Green Round	D/E	135.00
V	Gr Round Base, Black		550.00
VI	Gold Round	D	85.00

ROYALS

VI	Gold Round	D	60.00

SENATORS

II	White Square	E	225.00
III	White Round Mini	D	150.00
IV	Green Round	D	100.00
VI	Gold Round	D	85.00

TIGERS

I	Green Square	D/E	200.00
II	White Square	E	175.00
III	White Round Mini	D	200.00
IV	Green Round	E	135.00
V	Gr Round Base, Black		450.00
VI	Gold Round	D	100.00

TWINS

I	Blue Square	D	35.00
II	White Square	D	275.00
III	White Round Mini	D	125.00
III	(Minneapolis)	D	150.00
IV	Green Round	D	50.00
V	Gr Round Base, Black		475.00
VI	Gold Round	D	60.00

WHITE SOX

II	White Square	E	175.00
III	White Round Mini	D	100.00
IV	Green Round	D	50.00
V	Gr Round Base, Black		275.00
VI	Gold Round	D	35.00

YANKEES

I	Orange Square	D/E	125.00
II	White Square	E	135.00
III	White Round Mini	D	200.00
IV	Green Round	D/E	100.00
V	Gr Round Base, Black		425.00
VI	Gold Round	D	75.00

BASEBALL PLAYERS

AARON, HENRY

The Aaron bobbin' head was produced in 1975 and depicted him as a Milwaukee Brewer. It was made of plastic and produced in large quantities 20.00

CLEMENTE, ROBERTO

The Clemente bobbin' head is the rarest of the four

The coveted Clemente and dark Mays heads

1961-62 player caricature dolls. Some experts estimate that fewer than 200 were made. The Clemente was sold without a box and there is no miniature 1,100.00

MANTLE, MICKEY

Not the rarest of the four, Mantle is certainly the most popular. It was originally issued in a box, and is found with a Yankee decal or embossed with NY 375.00

Original issue box 50.00

4 ½" miniature 600.00

MARIS, ROGER

The Maris bobbin' head is rarer than the Mantle. It was also issued in a box, and is also found with a Yankee decal or embossed with NY 400.00

Original issue box 50.00

4 ½" miniature 650.00

MAYS, WILLIE

Mays is the most common, but is also found in two variations. One featured very dark skin, and is far more difficult to find; the lighter skin variation is more common. No mini was produced.

Light variation 175.00

Dark variation 300.00

RECENT ISSUES

Yogi Berra	50.00
Ty Cobb	50.00
Whitey Ford	50.00
Ken Griffey Jr.	50.00
Reggie Jackson	40.00
Mickey Mantle	100.00
Roger Maris	80.00
Willie Mays	40.00
Satchell Paige	40.00
Babe Ruth	50.00
Nolan Ryan	80.00
Tom Seaver	50.00

FOOTBALL

Type .. Base .... Logo .... Value

BEARS

I	Wood, Black Square		50.00
II	Black Sq/Rd	E	50.00
III	NFL, Square	E	50.00
IV	"00" Gold Round		45.00
V	Gold Round		30.00
IX	Gold Rd Base, Black	E	115.00
X	Boy/Girl	E	50.00

BENGALS

V	Gold Round		25.00

BILLS

V	Gold Round		30.00
VI	AFL Rd/Sq		350.00
VII	AFL Gold Rd, Ear Pads		115.00
VIII	AFL Gold Rd		75.00

BRONCOS

V	Gold Round		25.00
VI	AFL Rd/Sq		350.00
VII	AFL Gold Rd, Ear Pads		115.00
VIII	AFL Gold Rd		75.00

BROWNS

I	Wood, Brown Square		65.00
II	Brown Sq/Rd	E	75.00
III	NFL, Square	E	90.00
IV	"00" Gold Round		60.00
V	Gold Round		25.00
IX	Gold Rd Base, Black	E	200.00
X	Boy/Girl	E	90.00

CARDINALS

I	Wood, Red Square		35.00
II	Red Sq/Rd	E	35.00
III	NFL, Square	E	50.00
IV	"00" Gold Round		45.00
V	Gold Round		30.00
IX	Gold Rd Base, Black	E	115.00
X	Boy/Girl	E	50.00

CHARGERS

V	Gold Round		45.00
VI	AFL Rd/Sq		350.00
VII	AFL Gold Rd, Ear Pads		100.00
VIII	AFL Gold Rd		75.00

Dan Marino and Terry Bradshaw

CHIEFS

V	Gold Round		25.00
VI	AFL Rd/Sq (Texans)		450.00
VII	AFL Gold Rd, Ear Pads		115.00
VIII	AFL Gold Rd		75.00

COLTS

I	Wood, Blue Square		35.00
II	Blue Sq/Rd	E	35.00
III	NFL, Square	E	50.00
IV	"00" Gold Round		45.00
V	Gold Round		25.00
IX	Gold Rd Base, Black	E	115.00
X	Boy/Girl	E	50.00

COWBOYS

I	Wood, Blue Square		110.00
II	Blue Sq/Rd	E	90.00
III	NFL, Square	E	125.00
IV	"00" Gold Round		125.00
V	Gold Round		80.00
IX	Gold Rd Base, Black	E	250.00
X	Boy/Girl	E	125.00

DOLPHINS

V	Gold Round		90.00

EAGLES

I	Wood, Green Square		35.00
II	Green Sq/Rd	E	35.00
II	(1960 Champs)	E	65.00
III	NFL, Square	E	50.00
IV	"00" Gold Round		45.00
V	Gold Round		35.00
IX	Gold Rd Base, Black	E	115.00
X	Boy/Girl	E	50.00

FALCONS

IV	"00" Gold Round		35.00
V	Gold Round		25.00

49ERS

I	Wood, Red Square		65.00
II	Red Sq/Rd	E	45.00
IV	"00" Gold Round		80.00
V	Gold Round		60.00

GIANTS

I	Wood, Blue/Red Square		65.00
II	Blue/Red Sq/Rd	E	65.00
III	NFL, Square	E	85.00
IV	"00" Gold Round		25.00
V	Gold Round		25.00
IX	Gold Rd Base, Black	E	175.00
X	Boy/Girl	E	85.00

JETS

V	Gold Round		25.00
VI	AFL Rd/Sq (Titans)		450.00
VII	AFL Gold Rd, Ear Pads		125.00
VIII	AFL Gold Rd		75.00

LIONS

I	Wood, Silver Square		25.00
II	Silver Sq/Rd	E	25.00
III	NFL, Square	E	50.00
IV	"00" Gold Round		45.00
V	Gold Round		25.00
IX	Gold Rd Base, Black	E	115.00
X	Boy/Girl	E	50.00

OILERS

V	Gold Round		25.00
VI	AFL Rd/Sq		350.00
VII	AFL Gold Rd, Ear Pads		115.00
VIII	AFL Gold Rd		75.00

PACKERS

I	Wood, Green Square		35.00
II	Green Sq/Rd	E	35.00
III	NFL, Square	E	50.00
IV	"00" Gold Round		45.00
V	Gold Round		30.00

IX	Gold Rd Base, Black	E	115.00
X	Boy/Girl	E	50.00

PATRIOTS

V	Gold Round		30.00
VI	AFL Rd/Sq		350.00
VII	AFL Gold Rd, Ear Pads		115.00
VIII	AFL Gold Rd		75.00

RAIDERS

V	Gold Round		80.00
VI	AFL Rd/Sq		450.00
VII	AFL Gold Rd, Ear Pads		160.00
VIII	AFL Gold Rd		110.00

RAMS

I	Wood, Black Square		50.00
II	Black Sq/Rd	E	35.00
III	NFL, Square	E	50.00
IV	"00" Gold Round		45.00
V	Gold Round		25.00
IX	Gold Rd Base, Black	E	115.00
X	Boy/Girl	E	50.00
XI			

REDSKINS

I	Wood, Maroon Square		90.00
II	Maroon Sq/Rd	E	65.00
III	NFL, Square	E	110.00
IV	"00" Gold Round		80.00
V	Gold Round		80.00
IX	Gold Rd Base, Black	E	225.00
X	Boy/Girl	E	110.00

SAINTS

IV	"00" Gold Round		35.00
V	Gold Round		25.00

STEELERS

I	Wood, Gold Square		110.00
II	Gold Sq/Rd	E	90.00
III	NFL, Square	E	125.00
IV	"00" Gold Round		80.00
V	Gold Round		80.00
IX	Gold Rd Base, Black	E	250.00
X	Boy/Girl	E	125.00

VIKINGS

I	Wood, Purple Square		50.00
II	Purple Sq/Rd	E	35.00
III	NFL, Square	E	85.00
IV	"00" Gold Round		35.00
V	Gold Round		25.00
IX	Gold Rd Base, Black	E	175.00
X	Boy/Girl	E	85.00

FOOTBALL

Terry Bradshaw	40.00
Dan Marino	40.00
Emmitt Smith	40.00
Lawrence Taylor	40.00

HOCKEY

Type .... **Value**

BEARS

61-62	Hershey, boy head	175.00

BLACK HAWKS

61-62	Square base	200.00
66-69	Gold oval base	350.00

BLUES

66-69	Gold oval base	300.00

BRUINS

61-62	Square base	200.00
66-69	Gold oval base	350.00

Assorted Hockey Heads

CANADIENS

61-62	Square base	60.00
66-69	Gold oval base	200.00

CLIPPERS

61-62	Baltimore, Captains head	60.00

CRUSADERS

61-62	Clevland, blue square	75.00

FLYERS

66-69	Gold oval base	200.00

GULLS

61-62	San Diego, Gull head	175.00

KINGS

66-69	Gold oval base	300.00

MAPLE LEAFS

61-62	Square base	60.00
66-69	Gold oval base	200.00

NORTH STARS

66-69	Gold oval base	300.00

PENGUINS

66-69	Gold oval base	200.00

RANGERS

61-62	Square base	75.00
66-69	Gold oval base	225.00

RED WINGS

61-62	Square base	60.00
66-69	Gold oval base	200.00

SEALS

66-69	Gold oval base	300.00

CEREAL BOXES

ALPHA BITS (Post)

1960s Baseball cards on back 50.00

CHEERIOS (General Mills)

1982 Johnny Bench, baseball bench offer 10.00

COOKIE CRISP (Ralston/Purina)

1987 Ozzie Smith on back
Win a Hero For a Day contest 10.00

CORN FLAKES (Kellogg's)

1952 Baseball game ring offer 50.00
1983 Danny White, Dallas Cowboys 25.00
1983 Fernando Valenzuela 35.00
1983 San Diego Chicken 5.00
1992 Team USA w/ Bird, Robinson, etc. 15.00

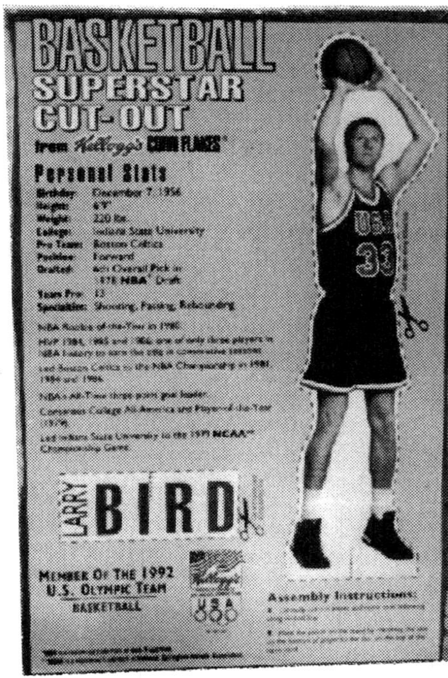

1992 Larry Bird, Team USA 15.00
1992 David Robinson, Team USA 15.00

40% BRAN FLAKES (Post)

1960s Baseball cards on back 50.00

FROSTED MINI WHEATS (Kellogg's)

1992 Larry Bird, Team USA 20.00
1992 Karl Malone, Team USA 20.00
1992 Chris Mullin, Team USA 20.00
1992 David Robinson, Team USA 20.00
1992 John Stockton, Team USA 20.00

FROSTED FLAKES (Kellogg's)

1991 Minnesota Twins, World Champions 20.00

GRAPE NUTS (Post)

1960s Baseball cards on back 50.00

HONEY NUT CRUNCH RAISIN BRAN (Post)

1982 Bob Griese, equipment offer 25.00

POST TOASTIES (Post)

1960s Baseball cards on back 50.00

RAISIN BRAN (Kellogg's)

1960s Baseball cards on back 50.00
1992 Team USA cartoon
w/ Bird, Robinson, Mullin, etc. 15.00

SUGAR CRISP (Post)

1960s Baseball cards on back 50.00

WHEATIES (General Mills)

1935
Fancy Frame with Script Signature

Armstrong, Jack 20.00
Berger, Wally 20.00
Bridges, Tommy 20.00
Cochrane, Mickey 175.00
Collins, James "Rip" 20.00
Dean, Dizzy 55.00
Dean, Paul 22.00
Delancey, William 20.00
Foxx, "Jimmie" 50.00
Frisch, Frank 37.00
Gehrig, Lou 225.00
Goslin, Goose 30.00
Grove, Lefty 45.00
Hubbell, Carl 35.00
Jackson, Travis 30.00
Klein, "Chuck" 30.00
Mancuso, Gus 20.00
Martin, Johnny "Pepper" 20.00
Medwick, Joe 35.00
Ott, Melvin 50.00
Schumacher, Harold 20.00
Simmons, Al 30.00
White, "Jo Jo" 20.00

1936
Fancy Frame with Printed Name and Data

Averill, Earl 30.00
Cochrane, Mickey 40.00
Foxx, Jimmy 45.00
Gehrig, Lou . . . . 225.00.
Greenberg, Hank 40.00
Harnett, "Gabby" 30.00
Hubbell, Carl 35.00
Martin, "Pepper" 17.00
Mungo, Van L. 20.00
Newsom, "Buck" 20.00
Vaughan, "Arky" 30.00
Wilson, Jimmy 20.00

1936
How to Play Winning Baseball

Gomez, Lefty 35.00
Herman, Billy 30.00
Appling, Luke 35.00
Foxx, Jimmie 45.00
Medwick, Joe 35.00
Gehringer, Charles 35.00
Ott, Mel 45.00
Hale, Odell 20.00
Dickey, Bill 50.00
Grove, "Lefty" 50.00
Hubbell, Carl 40.00
Averill, Earl 35.00

1936
Thin Orange Border / Figures in Border

Davis, Curt	20.00
Gehrig, Lou	250.00
Gehringer, Charley	40.00
Grove, Lefty	40.00
Hemsley, Rollie	20.00
Herman, Billy	30.00
Medwick, Joe	30.00
Ott, Mel	45.00
Rowe, Schoolboy	20.00
Vaughn, Arky	30.00
Vosmik, Joe	20.00
Warneke, Lon	20.00

1937
Color Series

Bonura, Zeke	20.00
Bridges, Tom	20.00
Clift, Harland	20.00
Cuyler, Kiki	30.00
DiMaggio, Joe	225.00
Feller, Robert	75.00
Grove, Lefty	50.00
Herman, Billy	30.00
Hubbell, Carl	35.00
Jordan, Buck	20.00
Martin, "Pepper"	20.00
Moses, Wally	20.00
Mungo, Van L.	20.00
Travis, Cecil	20.00
Vaughn, Arky	30.00

1937
How to Star in Baseball

Dickey, Bill	50.00
Ruffing, Red	30.00
Bonura, Zeke	20.00
Gehringer, Charlie	35.00
Vaughn, "Arky"	20.00
Hubbell, Carl	35.00
Lewis, John	20.00
Manush, Heinie	30.00
Grove, "Lefty"	40.00
Herman, Billy	30.00
DiMaggio, Joe	225.00
Mediwick, Joe	30.00

1937
Small Panels with Orange Background Series

Bonura, Zeke	40.00
Bridges, Tom	40.00
Camilli, Dolph	40.00
Demaree, Frank	40.00
DiMaggio, Joe	250.00
Herman, Billy	70.00
Hubbell, Carl	75.00
Lombardi, Ernie	55.00
Martin, "Pepper"	40.00
Moore, Joe	40.00
Mungo, Van L.	40.00.
Ott, Mel	75.00
Radcliff, Raymond	40.00
Travis, Cecil	40.00
Trosky, Harold	40.00
Vaughn, Arky	55.00

1937
Speckled Orange, White, and Blue Series

Appling, Luke	30.00
Averill, Earl	30.00
DiMaggio, Joe	175.00
Feller, Robert	75.00
Gehringer, Charles	40.00
Grove, Lefty	45.00
Hubbbell, Carl	45.00
Medwick, Joe	35.00

1937
29 Series

Bonura, "Zeke"	20.00
Travis, Cecil	20.00
Demaree, Frank	20.00
Moore, Joe	20.00
Lombardi, Ernie	30.00
Martin, John "Pepper"	25.00
Trosky, Harold	20.00
Radcliff, Raymond	20.00
DiMaggio, Joe	225.00
Bridges, Tom	20.00
Mungo, Van L.	20.00
Vaughn, "Arky"	30.00
Statz, Arnold	150.00
Muller, Fred	150.00
Lillard, Gene	150.00

1938
Biggest Thrills in Baseball

Feller, Bob	75.00
Travis, Cecil	20.00
Medwick, Joe	35.00
Walker, Gerald	20.00
Hubbell, Carl	35.00
Johnson, Bob	20.00
Bell, Beau	20.00
Lombardi, Ernie	30.00
Grove, Lefty	40.00
Fette, Lou	20.00
DiMaggio, Joe	250.00
Whitney, Pinky	20.00
Dean, Dizzy	55.00
Gehringer, Charley	40.00
Waner, Paul	30.00
Camilli, Dolf	20.00

1938
Dress Clothes or Civies Series

Fette, Lou	20.00
Foxx, Jimmie	40.00
Gehringer, Charlie	35.00
Grove, Lefty	35.00
Greenberg, Hank	35.00
Lombardi, Ernie	30.00
Medwick, Joe	35.00
Warneke, Lon	20.00

1951 Wheaties George Mikan

1938
Small Panels with Orange, Blue and White Background

Bonura, Zeke	40.00
DiMaggio, Joe	250.00
Gehringer, Charley	80.00
Greenberg, Hank	80.00
Grove, Lefty	80.00
Hubbell, Carl	60.00
Lewis, John "Buddy"	40.00
Manush, Heinie	60.00
Medwick, Joe	60.00
Vaughn, Arky	60.00

1939
100 Years of Baseball

Design of First Diamond	20.00
Gets News of Nomination on Field	20.00

Crowd Boos First Baseball Glove 20.00
Curve Ball Just an Illusion 20.00
Fencer's Mask is Pattern 20.00
Baseball Gets "All Dressed Up" 20.00
Modern Bludgeon Enters Game 20.00
"Casey at the Bat" 20.00

1939
Personal Pointers Series

Lombardi, Ernie 30.00
Allen, Hohnny 20.00
Gomez, Lefty 35.00
Lee, Bill 20.00
Foxx, Jimmie 45.00
Medwick, Joe 35.00
Greenberg, Hank 35.00
Ott, Mell 50.00
Vaughn, Arky 30.00

1940
Champs of the U.S.A.

Feller, Bob
Patrick, Lynn
Ruffing, Charles "Red" 50.00
Durocher, Leo
Patrick, Lynn
Ruffing, Charles "Red" 45.00
DiMaggio, Joe
Duge, John
Greenberg, Hank 150.00
DiMaggio, Joe
Ott, Mel
Vines, Ellsworth 150.00
Bierman, Bernie
Dickey, Bill
Foxx, Jimmie 40.00
Arnovich, Morris
Baker, Capt R.L.
Clark, Earl "Dutch" 20.00
Bell, "Matty"
Jenkins, Ab
Medwick, Joe 20.00
Guldahl, Ralph
Mize, John
O'Brien, Davey 20.00
Guldahl, Ralph
Hartnett, Gabby
O'Brien, Davey 20.00
Feller, Bob
Mize, John
York, Rudy 45.00
Cronin, Joe
Greenberg, Hank
Nelson, Byron 20.00
Lombardi, Ernie
Manders, Jack
Myers, George 20.00
Bartlett, Bob
Hanson, Capt R.C.
Jacobs, Terrell 20.00
Dawson, Lowell "Red"
Herman, Billy
Inge, Adele 20.00
Camili, Dolph
Concello, Antoinette
Wade, Wallace 20.00
Appling, Luke
Hack, Stanley
McManus, Hugh 20.00
Adler, Felix
Trosky, Hal
Vinson, Mabel 20.00

1941
Champs of the U.S.A.

Adler, Felix
Foxx, Jimmie
Hanson, Capt R.G. 45.00
Bierman, Bernie
Feller, Bob
McLeod, Jessie 45.00
Dawson, Lowell "Red"
Greenberg, Hank
Stoker, J.W. 35.00
Concello, Antoinette
Dimaggio, Joe
Nelson, Byron 125.00
Baker, Capt R.L.
"Buck", Frank
McCormick
Reese, Harold "Pee Wee" 45.00
Danning, Harry
McCosky, Barney
Walters, Buck 20.00
Robbins, William
Sarazan, Gene
Walker, Gerald "Gee" 20.00
Gordon, Joe "Flash"
Hack, Stan
Myers, George 20.00

1951

Feller, Bob (Baseball) 100.00
Lujack, John (Football) 60.00
Mikan, George (Basketball) 100.00
Musial, Stan (Baseball) 150.00
Snead, Sam (Golfer) 40.00
Williams, Ted (Baseball) 150.00

1952

Berra, Larry "Yogi" 40.00
Campanella, Roy 40.00
Feller, Bob 30.00
Kell, George 12.00
Kiner, Ralph 20.00
Lemon, Bob 20.00
Musial, Stan 50.00
Rizzuto, Phil 25.00
Roe, Elwin "Preacher" 10.00
Williams, Ted 75.00

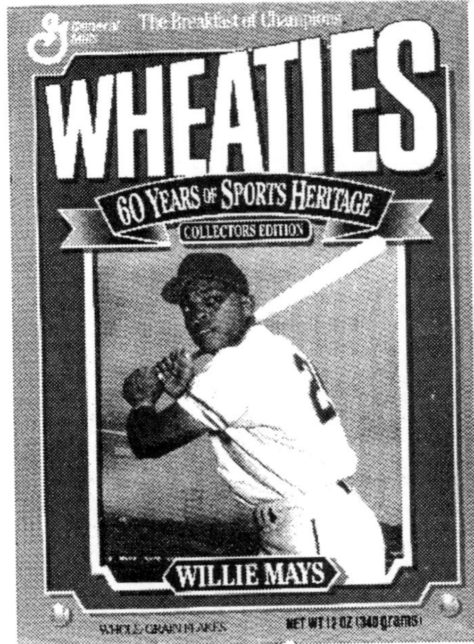

1992 "60 Years of Sports Heritage": Willie Mays

1992
Fleer Wheaties

Coleman, Derrick 25.00
Ewing, Patrick 20.00
Hardaway, Tim 20.00

Johnson, Kevin 20.00
Jordan, Michael 30.00
Miller, Reggie 20.00
Pippen, Scottie 20.00
Robinson, David 20.00

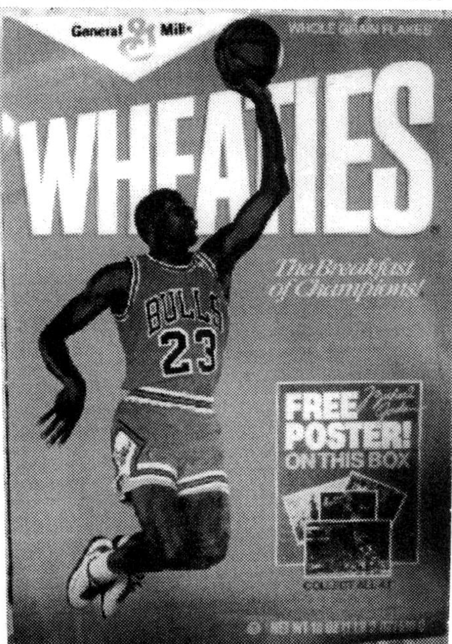

1989 Wheaties Michael Jordan

1992
60 Years of Sports Heritage

Gehrig, Lou 5.00
Mays, Willie 5.00
Ruth, Babe 5.00

Other Wheaties Boxes

Athlete on cover	Value
Aaron, Hank	75.00
Anderson, Sparky	15.00
Baer, Max	60.00
Bench, Johnny (1989)	15.00
Berra, Yogi	75.00
Bird, Larry (1992)	10.00
Boudreau, Lou	50.00
Campanella, Roy	75.00
Carew, Rod (1991)	25.00
Cey, Ron	25.00
Davies, Bob	40.00
Dawkins, Darryl	25.00
Dean, Dizzy	75.00
Dempsey, Jack	75.00
de Varona, Donna	20.00
Didrikson, Babe	50.00
DiMaggio, Joe	100.00
Esiason, Boomer	15.00
Evert, Chris (1987)	15.00
Feller, Bob	75.00
Foxx, Jimmie	100.00
Gehrig, Lou	150.00
Graham, Otto	75.00
Grange, Red	75.00
Greenberg, Hank	100.00
Grove, Lefty	85.00
Hogan, Ben	40.00
Hubbell, Carl	65.00
Jenner, Bruce (1977-79)	15.00
Jordan, Michael (1988-92)	10.00
Kelly, Jim	10.00
Kiner, Ralph	60.00
Largent, Steve (1988)	15.00
Lombardi, Ernie	75.00
Lujack, Johnny	75.00
Mays, Willie	80.00
Meagher, Mary T.	15.00
Mikan, George	65.00
Montana, Joe (1991)	20.00
Musial, Stan	85.00
Nagurski, Bronco	60.00
Newhouser, Hal	75.00
Ott, Mel	100.00
Palmer, Jim (1990)	15.00
Payton, Walter (1988)	20.00
Reese, Pee Wee	60.00
Retton, Mary Lou (1984-86)	10.00
Richards, Bob (1956-70)	20.00
Rizzuto, Phil	60.00
Robinson, Brooks	50.00
Robinson, Jackie	125.00
Rose, Pete (1985-86)	20.00
Rosen, Al	50.00
Ruth, Babe	150.00
Sanders, Barry (1992)	25.00
Snead, Sam	40.00
Spahn, Warren	65.00
Spielman, Chris	15.00
Stanky, Eddie	60.00
Weismuller, Johnny	60.00
Williams, Ted	100.00
Yamaguchi, Kristi (1992)	10.00
1987 World Champion Minnesota Twins	25.00
1988 NBA Champion Los Angeles Lakers	30.00
1988 Super Bowl Champion Washington Redskins	25.00
1990 World Champion Cincinnati Reds	25.00
1991 NBA Champion Chicago Bulls	25.00
1991 NHL Champion Pittsburgh Penguins	25.00
1991 Super Bowl Champion N.Y. Giants	20.00
1991 World Champion Minnesota Twins	20.00
1992 AFC Central Division Champion Pittsburgh Steelers	25.00
1992 NBA Champion Chicago Bulls	20.00
1992 NHL Champion Pittsburgh Penguins	25.00
1992 Super Bowl Champion Washington Redskins	20.00

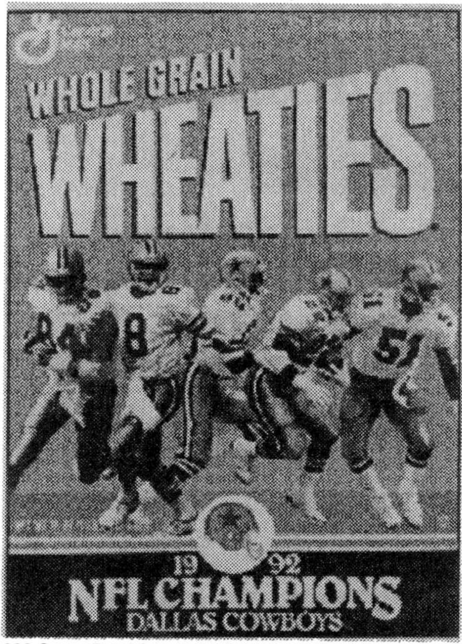

1993 Super Bowl Champion Dallas Cowboys 25.00

OLYMPIC COLLECTIBLES

by Don Bigsby

The entire world, especially the U.S.A., is looking ahead to 1996 when the city of Atlanta hosts the Olympic Centennial Games. The 26th Summer Olympiad will be held exactly 100 years after the modern Games were started in Athens, Greece in 1896.

No one is more excited about the prospect of another Olympics in America than the growing band of Olympic pin collectors. While collecting Olympic memorabilia has been going on in Europe for decades, it was not until the 1980 Winter Games in Lake Placid that pin collecting got its foothold in the United States. When Los Angeles hosted the 23rd Summer games in 1984, the number of collectors increased dramatically! So, the prospect of another Olympic Celebration in the U.S.A. will signal another leap forward for the fastest growing hobby in America.

1920 Olympic program

What is the appeal of collecting memorabilia from the Olympic Games? Most likely it is tied to the worldwide appeal of the Games themselves. Most people who have had the privilege of attending the Super Bowl, World Series, Final Four and the Olympics, say the first three don't come close to the excitement and emotion experienced at the Olympics. Where else can you go and meet people like yourself, with the same dreams and aspirations, who are citizens of nations from all over the world? Dozens of different languages are spoken, yet the language barrier hardly matters when you meet on the street and exchange greetings, and maybe an Olympic pin. Even spectators can become part of this great celebration of the human spirit, by participating in a fringe event of the Games.

Olympic pin collecting is not at all like baseball card collecting. Most Olympic memorabilia was never made for collectors; it was made to identify athletes, officials and press members, or was provided in limited quantities for those working in the Olympic movement. They say the thrill of collecting is in the hunt. Never is this more true than in collecting Olympic memorabilia!

It is recommended that those who want to collect Olympic memorabilia, from pins to winner's medals, should understand the history of the Olympics to give their collection meaning. It usually happens that those who get into Olympic collecting find themselves drawn to the Olympic movement and can't help but learn about this great international phenomenon. Many of today's most knowledgeable Olympic people started out as collectors, and then learned about the organization and history of the Olympics.

So one of the benefits of collecting from the Olympic Games is the knowledge gained about the movement itself. It can also pique interests in world history, and geography. It's been recounted over and over by teachers how the Olympics (and pin collecting) has helped motivate children to learn about the world we live in, and the people we share this small planet with.

Once someone gets involved in Olympic pin collecting, they find out there are many facets to this hobby. There is no boundary to collecting Olympic memorabilia. A collector can take the hobby as far as he/she wishes. For example, pin collecting categories are numerous. One can dabble in the hobby, collecting from only one category or sampling several categories. Or he/she can take their collecting goals much further, trying for many types of Olympic pins. (More about Olympic pin categories later.)

Pins are only a part of the action. People can focus on other collectibles like books, coins, beer mugs, key rings, patches, posters, and stamps. These are generally inexpensive as they were made as souvenirs in large quantity. There are also more expensive items, produced in limited quantity because they were made for official use, or as awards. These include badges, medals, programs, reports, tickets and torches. Most of these items are costly collectibles that could actually be museum pieces. There are other items such as ash trays, official credentials, correspondence, statues, trophies, uniforms, etc.

So, not only does one have many options to select from as far as pin collecting goes, but one can look forward to infinite possibilities if he/she decides to expand from pins into other types of Olympic collectibles. One can dabble in the hobby, or become involved to the point of obsession (as some spouses would attest).

It is important to realize that Olympic memorabilia can be as common as readily available souvenirs, or so rare that only a handful of a certain item exists. This brings us to the collectors who are at opposite ends of the spectrum. For those inclined to find quick success, with little difficulty in growing their collection, many types of pins and certain types of other memorabilia are available. Commemorative pins, patches, key rings, coins, etc. are usually available to meet public demand. Especially if one is fortunate enough to go to, or live near, a host city. It becomes more difficult if the collector decides to try to fill out his/her collection with souvenir items of the past.

Badges, medals, programs, reports, tickets and torches are limited in quantity to meet the needs of the Games themselves. Imagine how much more scarce these items can be when they are from older Olympiads, when the Games were a fraction of the size they are today. Let us now review, in depth, some of the rarer collectibles.

1968 Mexico jury badge

Medals

1956 Stockholm silver winner's medal

There are three types of medals from the Olympic Games. The easiest to find, and therefore the least valuable, of the three are Commemorative Medals. These were usually struck to raise funds for some Olympic organization. They can be as cheap as $10 or $20, but can go quite a bit higher. This article focuses on the other two types of medals. Participation Medals are given to every athlete who takes part in the Games. (This reminds us that "The important thing in the Olympic Games is not to win, but to take part" as Baron Pierre De Coubertin, founder of the Modern Olympics, said.) Therefore these medals are quite meaningful, and can be very scarce and valuable. Barcelona's Participation Medal is selling for $125 currently, and while a 1904 St. Louis Participation Medal is rarely found, it is worth in excess of $3000.

Then there are the Winner's medals. Since 1904 at St. Louis, there have been awards for each event; Gold (first), Silver (second) and Bronze (third). There are more intricacies that can be addressed here, but it is important to know that *generally* Gold Medals are silver, gilded with gold; Silver Medals are bronze, gilded with silver; and Bronze medals are bronze. They have great variations of availability (you might wonder how they're available at all!) considering there were only 44 events at the first Olympics (Athens 1896), compared to 241 at Seoul in 1988. If those numbers seem small, consider that at the first Winter Olympics at Chamonix, France there were 14 events. At Calgary, Canada (1988) there were 46 medal events. A winner's medal from Barcelona could bring around $2500, while a Gold medal from 1956 Stockholm (Equestrian events were held in Sweden due to an animal quarantine in Australia during the year when Melbourne hosted the Summer Olympics) would be worth around $15,000. Estimated values of most Winner's Medals are listed later on.

On the other hand, badges, medals, programs, reports, tickets and torches are limited in quantity to meet the needs of the Games themselves. Imagine how much the scarcity increases for these items when they are from older Olympiads. (The Games were a fraction of the size they are today.) Let us take a look at some of the rarer collectibles.

Badges

This category is the one most closely related to pin collecting. In fact, it was the official badges (made to designate athletes, officials, judges, dignitaries, and press members) that caused pins to become part of the Olympic program. This background will be addressed later under "Pins." It is noteworthy that most European collectors call pins "Badges." For the purposes of this article, when we say badges we mean the official medal designators made in limited quantity by the host Organizing Committee.

The first badges were made for the 1896 Athens Olympiad and were fashioned out of cardboard with a thin blue ribbon tied at top. These were made in three colors: blue for athletes, pink for judges and red for officials. These are worth about $2,000 each.

As the Olympics grew and became more established, the badges were made of metal and were usually engraved to identify the type of person who wore it. Generally, colored ribbons hung from the badges, indicating which sport the wearer was involved with. The existence of badges at the 1900 Paris Olympics is debatable. They were made for the 1904 St. Louis Games (similar to the Participation Medal) and had a loop attached in order to hang from a ribbon. In 1908 in London, several variations were made as identifiers or credentials. At Stockholm in 1912, only two variations were made: competitor and press.

No metal badges of this sort have ever been found from the 1920 Antwerp Olympics. But they were made again in 1924 at Paris and continued to be produced in various styles up through the Montreal Games in 1976. Unexplainably, no badges for the Olympic Games have been made since 1976. Prices for these badges vary greatly, with older ones usually more valuable, particularly Winter Olympic badges. Just for an idea of the price variation, a 1976 Montreal badge sells for about $150, while a 1924 Chamonix Winter Games badge would garner from $1500 to $2000.

Although the Olympic organizing committees ceased to provide badges after Montreal in 1976, there are official badges of one type still made today. These are made for IOC (International Olympic Committee) Sessions, which are held once a year, to plot the future of the Olympic Movement. The first IOC Session was held in 1894 in Paris. The 99th IOC Session was held for the three days preceding the Barcelona Olympics in Spain. The 100th Session will be held in Lausanne, Switzerland, the home of the IOC headquarters. Interestingly, at the same time (June 1993), the new IOC Olympic Museum will be officially opened. Much of the material discussed in this article will be displayed there. It seemed for years that the IOC, as well as National Olympic Committees, were indifferent to the collector world. That is changing now, with possible IOC involvement to organize an international organization for all collectors.

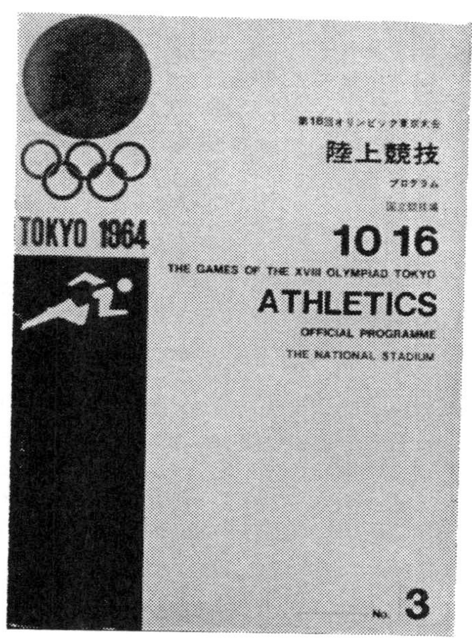

1964 Tokyo program

The badges made for IOC

sessions are usually metal with up to 15 different colored ribbons attached each, designating participants, such as IOC member (white) and press (yellow). Even the most recent badges command a value of about $150, with older session badges escalating in value rapidly. Some estimated values on badges are found at the end of this article.

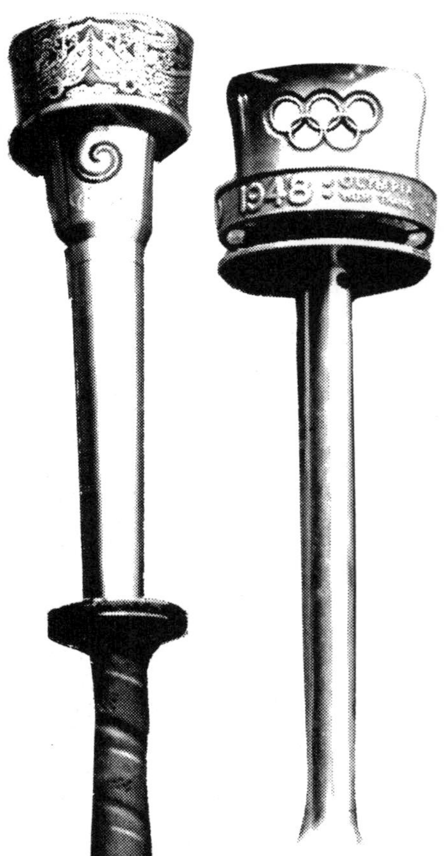

1988 Seoul torch (L), 1948 London torch

Torches

Among the elite Olympic collectibles, torches can be as rare as winners' medals, or more easily available than one might imagine. The first collectible torch used for lighting the modern Olympic flame was from the Berlin games in 1936. The torch is fairly plain, except it has engraved on the handle the major cities it passed through from Athens to Berlin. (The Olympic flame burns continuously at a site near the stadium that held the first modern Olympiad. For each Olympics, the flame is used to light a torch which is carried to the host city, where it then lights a giant cauldron that burns at the main stadium throughout the competition.) The Berlin torches were given to each runner, and many are still obtainable for less than $2000.

In 1984, the Los Angeles Organizing Committee came up with a cross-country torch run that took the flame through almost every state in America. About 3000 segments were sold for $3000 each to raise money for youth sports programs. In most cases, the segments were paid for as tax-deductible donations by large corporations who then awarded the torch to honored employees. The runners got to keep their torches. Several Olympic hosts have followed with a similar plan. Thus a 1984 L. A. torch can be found for about $1000. But, at Calgary in 1988, instead of awarding torches, the runners were given their uniforms. All but 150 of the torches were destroyed, and most of those remaining went to dignitaries, making a Calgary torch tough to obtain.

The value of an Olympic torch is not proportional to how old it is. The determining factor is supply and demand. Since many torches (especially from the Winter Games) were made in small quantity, they are hard to obtain. Estimates of some values are given at the end of this article.

Programs

Program collectors are much more plentiful than medal, badge and torch collectors. There are a lot more of these items out there. For example, if 10,000 seats were available for a soccer match, thousands of that days' program could exist. It's not always as clear cut as that, because each olympiad sets up their own plans for program distribution. It should be noted that the programs usually sought by these hard-core collectors are those given daily at the games, not a souvenir program which can be ordered by mail.

At some Olympics, especially the Winter Games, it seems one daily program was produced to cover all sports on a given day. If the Games covered 12 days, there would be 12 different programs to complete the set. At other Games, there were programs each day for each sport. More recently, there are only one page handouts given as spectators enter the venue. At Barcelona the sponsors did not even provide these!

Each collector has to decide what depth to go into the programs. One suggestion: try to get one program from every Olympics, although it's very difficult and not cheap. A 1896 Athens program has an estimated value of $5000! Programs from the early Games up to 1924 can go as low as $150. Programs for more recent games generally are valued lower. For example, 1976 Montreal programs (there's one for each sport) are only about $10 each. Don't forget, Winter Games programs are less plentiful, and therefore more valuable.

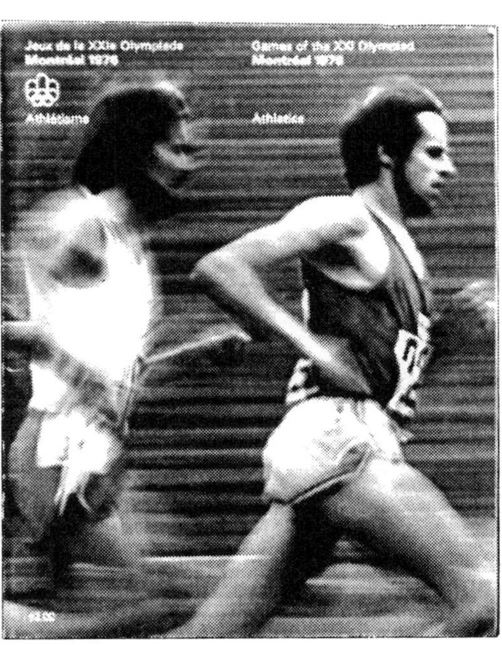

1976 Montreal program

Some collectors have decided rather than collect all programs, or even one from each Olympics, they will specialize and try to get every program from a certain Games. This can be a big project, especially if you choose 1928 Amsterdam, 1932 Los Angeles, 1952 Helsinki or 1956 Melbourne. As with most Olympic collectibles, you have all sorts of possibilities if you do opt to collect programs.

Tickets

Ticket collectors are not as widespread as program collectors. There are probably two reasons for this: (1) Many program collectors use the programs as source documents to find out who competed at an event, what the venues look like, etc., and (2) people tend to leave their tickets, or throw them away after the event. On the plus side, as opposed to varying program distribution at each Olympics, tickets have always been used at each event to the present day. So a collection can be built that encompasses more Olympiads than would be possible for a program collector.

As with programs, sometimes there were tickets that covered all events on a given day, or certain events on all days, or all events on all days. Sometimes there was a single laminated ticket (1932 Lake Placid) or a booklet issued with a packet of tickets to be used (1932 Los Angeles). These types of tickets are rarer and more valuable.

Again, ticket collectors have various options from which to choose what they will collect. One ticket from each Olympics? All tickets from one Olympics? Generally, prices are a little less than programs. Tickets, or ticket stubs, from the last 10 years usually are worth $2 to $10. The prices again climb steeply with age, especially before the 1920s. Of course, Winter Games tickets are usually higher.

Official Reports

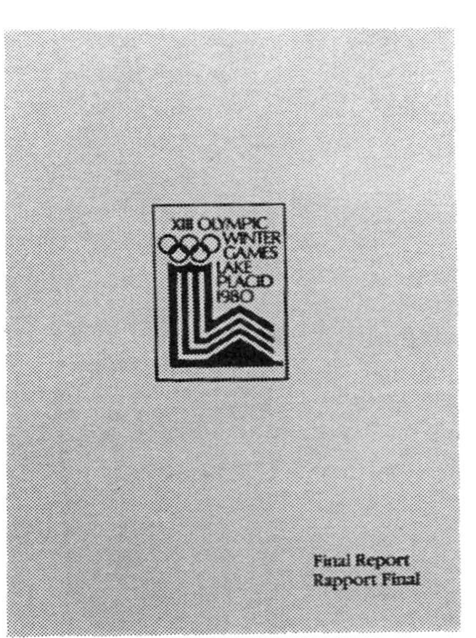

1980 Lake Placid official report

Official reports are prepared by the Organizing Committee that has hosted each Olympics. They usually are prepared, and issued to all IOC members (91 today) and each National Olympic Committee (182 today). In recent years, about 2,000 copies of the official report have been produced. After the required organizations and individuals receive theirs, the excess is put up for sale to help defray the cost of the publication. For example, about 500 extra 1984 Los Angeles official reports were sold for $700 each.

Official reports are almost non-existent from the very first decade of the Olympics. If found, they certainly don't measure up to the 38 pound behemoth prepared after the 184 L.A. Games, but size is not everything. The reason many advanced collectors seek the official reports is to gather information to help them find collectibles in other Olympic fields.

The Organizing Committee's official report tells in detail how they planned, implemented and administered their Olympiad. Its purpose is to assist cities hosting future Olympiads, by sharing all the knowledge learned in their effort. Ideally, each Olympiad should improve on its predecessor. The reports help prevent the recurrence of problems, as well as highlight and suggest what practices should be continued.

Of great interest to the collector is the information on medals, badges, tickets, programs, torch runs, posters, etc. used for that Olympics. Generally there are photographs of the items that are now collectible. Even more important, most reports have valuable statistics like how many medals were made for participants, how much they weigh, and their exact measurement, or how many badges were made and what printing or colored ribbons were used. For example, if there were 20 "IOC" badges made for 1932 Lake Placid, compared to 180 "Official" badges, it is obvious the former is much more scarce and more valuable than the latter.

Official reports are collected by less people than most collectibles mentioned here, except for torches. Although they can get quite expensive (if you can even find them), they are an invaluable source for very serious collectors.

Pins

Finally, a discussion on the most common Olympic collectible – lapel pins. Although pins are far and away the most collected of all Olympic memorabilia, they are being covered last. This was done in hopes that the reader would look over the preceding material to get an overall feel and appreciation of the Olympics; and perhaps a better understanding of where "pins" came from.

The concept of Olympic pin collecting began with the birth of the modern Games. Beginning in Athens (1896) badges were given to athletes, officials, judges, dignitaries and press members to identify participants for the purpose of admittance. These badges were large, ornate pins, usually with ribbons attached.

As the Games continued, athletes from different nations brought their own identifying pins, and gradually began exchanging with each other as a form of good will. This practice occurred as early as the 1908 London Olympics. In 1928, at the Amsterdam Olympiad, several designs of souvenir pins were sold to the public. These pins were made in quantities that are insignificant compared to the souvenir pins of the 1980s and 1990s.

Around 1960, a few corporations made up their own lapel pins. In 1964, several media organizations did likewise. Some pin trading involving non-athletes had begun. The pins were made not so much to identify someone, but as an advertising tool. By the 1970s, more Olympic teams made pins for their athletes to exchange. The organizers of the Olympics began producing logo pins for their Games as a fund-raising tool.

At Lake Placid in 1980, pin trading got its first major recognition. While covering the Olympics, ABC showed some of the frenzied trading between athletes, workers and fans. Suddenly the average sports fan was part of the Olympics! When the Games reached Los Angeles in 1984, the hobby mushroomed. Merchants were loaded with commemorative pins and corporations had made thousands of their sponsor pins to trade. The athletes were ready too, having brought their Olympic team pins to trade with spectators. The hobby received worldwide attention on television.

At the last four Olympic celebrations in 1988 and 1992 the hobby continued to grow, and almost everyone got involved in the craze. Coca-Cola erected giant tents at all four sites and promoted the hobby as the "spectator sport." Looking ahead to Lillehammer, Norway and Atlanta, Georgia it's obvious these host cities will further the craze!

There are three basic types of Olympic pins. These can be broken down further, allowing for many diverse types of Olympic pin collections. The three main categories are:

(1) **Commemorative Pins**. These are the pins authorized by the Organizing Committee to be made and sold in stores as souvenirs. These are generally the most plentiful and usually consist of mascots and logos depicting the various sports, and locations of the venues. One way to get such pins (in a limited quantity) is through the purchase of limited edition framed pin sets.

Otherwise, the pins are usually made to satisfy demand, and never seem to grow much in value.

1994 Lillehamer pins

(2) **Corporate Sponsor Pins**. These pins are made by the various sponsors, suppliers and supporters, usually incorporating the Olympic logo with the corporate name and/or logo. Big business has found that pins are a marvelous means of advertising. The pins in this category are usually not for sale, but are given to employees and VIP's. Many collectors have enjoyed great success in getting corporate pins by writing the companies directly. The most coveted pins from this category are those related to the news media, i.e.: ABC, NBC, CBS, and *Sports Illustrated.*

(3) **National Olympic Team Pins**. These pins are gradually becoming the hottest collectible among Olympic pin collectors. Their allure is more than the simple supply and demand principle. The NOC (National Olympic Committee) pins are made in different countries around the world, and are sometimes hand painted. Most NOC pins are made in small quantities, compared to commemorative and sponsor pins. There is no greater thrill for an NOC pin collector than to get a letter from a remote country with their Olympic Team pin enclosed.

As you may have suspected from the above pin categories, there are many diverse areas for an Olympic pin collector to pursue. Everyone is not looking for the same pins. What one person has for trade may be the very item another collector would cherish.

Usually, beginning collectors look for all pins with the Olympic rings on them, and gradually narrow their field as they become more involved. Sometimes, it takes a long time before one decides which type of pin a collector will specialize in.

Pins can certainly get expensive! The best advice is to shop around, whether you're buying or trading. Nothing is more aggravating than jumping on a pin for $5.00, only to learn it's available elsewhere for $2.00. Many pins can be obtained for free, but the collector has to work for them. New collectors could spend a lot of time at their local library searching for Olympic organizations' addresses, or for a corporation's public relations location because they advertised on television that they are an Olympic sponsor. Sometimes a great deal of work is required to chase down the thinnest of leads, and not all are successful. When all that effort results in adding a rare pin to a collection, there is a great deal of personal satisfaction.

As with any hobby, there are clubs and dealers to find pins through. There are too many dealers to mention, but there is a club that is inexpensive and was formed to promote the hobby and help collectors contact each other. By joining the club, collectors will inevitably be contacted by most of the dealers. The **Olympin Collectors Club** was formed in 1982 and is highly regarded for its integrity and service. The thing that separates Olympin from the others is its goal to bring collectors together and spread Olympic news. Most Olympic pin clubs or newsletters exist solely to sell pins. Olympin exists to promote "Olympism" and lasting friendships between collectors. All dues are returned to the members in benefits.

The annual dues for Olympin is $10.00 (US) or $13.50 (Canadian funds). Members get a quarterly newsletter, a dated member pin, and a member directory listing all members and their collecting interests. To join, write:

Olympin Collectors Club
1386 Fifth Street
Schenectady, NY 12303

Tips On Olympic Collecting

Whatever you decide to collect from the Olympics, here are some basic guidelines or suggestions. First, try to decide as early as possible what your goals are. If you find yourself getting really serious (the Olympics have a way of becoming addictive), it's best to funnel your time, effort and money into the area that most interests you. Try to get past the "anything with 5 rings" concept early on.

Whatever you collect should be displayed for you to look at and enjoy. Believe it or not, many pin collectors put their pins in boxes, and often can't remember if they have certain ones or not. There is no standard way to display Olympic pins or other memorabilia. You'll have to use your own ingenuity to make your collection accessible. Besides being able to quickly determine what you have, displaying your treasures allows you the luxury of remembering how you got things. There can be a *wonderful* story behind each and every pin.

Do not collect Olympic memorabilia in an attempt to make money. It's true that some items appreciate, but many items don't. Pins can be re-made in Taiwan after they have become scarce, thus reducing their salability. If you decide to get into Olympic collecting, you'll find many benefits besides value. Pin collecting should be a hobby that will not only give you great satisfaction in building your collection, but will enlighten you about the world and the people in it.

Try, and this is tough sometimes, to be patient. With any collecting hobby, this is very important. The more you learn about the hobby and the Games, the better you will be able to control your collecting by not making impulsive purchases. Don't try to do your collecting in a vacuum. The more people you meet and know in your hobby, the easier it is to decide what you want to collect, find ways to display your collection, and exhibit patience in acquiring new material.

Don't expect a club or newsletter to tell you how to get all the pins for your collection. What you can expect is for them to help you find other collectors to share knowledge with. If you were given information as to where everything was, what fun would it be? The thrill is in the hunt! Good luck!

COINS

AUTO RACING COINS

MINT COLLECTIBLES OF RACING

No.	Driver	Value
1.	Sterling Marlin	25.00
2.	Ken Schrader	25.00
3.	Bill Elliot	25.00
4.	Harry Gant	25.00
5.	Alan Kulwicki	25.00

ENVIROMINT

Indy 500 - 75th Anniversary . . 35.00

1992 Enviromint Richard Petty coin

1992 Richard Petty fan appreciation tour. 39mm 1.5" 40.00

BASEBALL COINS

1955 ARMOUR COINS

No.	Player	Value
1.	Johnny Antonelli	3.00
2.	Yogi Berra	20.00
3.	Del Crandall	3.00
4.	Larry Doby	5.00
5.	Jim Finigan	3.00
6.	Whitey Ford	12.00
7.	Jim Gilliam	5.00
8.	Harvey Haddix	3.00
9.	Ron Jackson	3.00
10.	Jackie Jensen	5.00
11.	Ted Kluszewski	6.00
12A.	Harvey Kuenn (Error)	8.00
12B.	Harvey Kuenn (Cor)	30.00
13A.	Mickey Mantel (Error)	40.00
13B.	Mickey Mantle (Cor)	135.00
14.	Don Mueller	3.00
15.	Pee Wee Reese	10.00
16.	Allie Reynolds	5.00
17.	Al Rosen	6.00
18.	Curt Simmons	3.00
19.	Duke Snider	25.00
20.	Warren Spahn	15.00
21.	Frank Thomas	3.00
22.	Virgil Trucks	3.00
23.	Robert Turley	3.00
24.	Mickey Vernon	3.00

1959 ARMOUR COINS

No.	Player	Value
1.	Hank Aaron	30.00
2.	Johnny Antonelli	4.00

1955 Armour Jackie Jensen coin

No.	Player	Value
3.	Richie Ashburn	5.00
4.	Ernie Banks	12.00
5.	Don Blasingame	3.50
6.	Bob Cerv	4.00
7.	Del Crandall	3.00
8.	Whitey Ford	12.00
9.	Nellie Fox	5.00
10.	Jackie Jensen	4.50
11.	Harvey Kuenn	5.00
12.	Frank Malzone	3.00
13.	Johnny Podres	4.00
14.	Frank Robinson	12.00

No.	Player	Value
15.	Roy Sievers	3.75
16.	Bob Skinner	4.00
17.	Frank Thomas	4.25
18.	Gus Triandos	3.00
19.	Bob Turley	4.00
20.	Mickey Vernon	3.50

1960 ARMOUR COINS

No.	Player	Value
1A.	Hank Aaron (Milwaukee)	50.00
1B.	Hank Aaron (Braves)	30.00
2.	Bob Allison	4.00
3.	Ernie Banks	12.00
4.	Ken Boyer	6.00
5.	Rocky Colavito	6.00
6.	Gene Conley	3.00
7.	Del Crandall	4.25
8.	Bud Daley	500.00
9.	Don Drysdale	10.00
10.	Whitey Ford	12.00
11.	Nellie Fox	5.00
12.	Al Kaline	12.00
13A.	F. Malzone(Boston)	30.00
13B.	F. Malzone(Red Sox)	5.00
14.	Mickey Mantle	50.00
15.	Eddie Mathews	10.00
16.	Willie Mays	30.00
17.	Vada Pinson	5.00
18.	Dick Stuart	4.00
19.	Gus Triandos	3.50
20.	Early Wynn	8.00

1962 SALADA COINS

No.	Player	Value
1.	Jim Gentile	2.00

No.	Player	Value
2.	Billy Pierce	125.00
3.	Chico Fornandez	1.75
4.	Tom Brewer	22.00
5.	Woody Held	2.00
6.	Ray Herbert	25.00
7A.	K. Aspromonte(Angels)	7.00
7B.	K. Aspromonte(Clev)	3.00
8.	Whitey Ford	20.00
9.	Jim Lemon	0.00
10.	Billy Klaus	2.00
11.	Steve Barber	30.00
12.	Nellie Fox	6.00
13.	Jim Bunning	5.50
14.	Frank Malzone	2.25
15.	Tito Francona	3.00
16.	Bobby Del Greco	2.00
17A.	Steve Bliko (red)	6.50
17B.	Steve Bilko (white)	4.00
18.	Tony Kubek	50.00
19.	Earl Battey	2.00
20.	Chuck Cottier	2.00
21.	Willie Tasby	2.25
22.	Bob Allison	3.50
23.	Roger Maris	30.00
24A.	Earl Averill (red)	6.00
24B.	Earl Averill (white)	3.00
25.	Jerry Lumpe	2.00
26.	Jim Grant	25.00
27.	Carl Yastrzemski	60.00
28.	Rocky Colavito	4.00
29.	Al Smith	2.00
30.	Jim Bushy	30.00
31.	Dick Howser	4.00
32.	Jim Perry	3.00
33.	Yogi Berra	35.00
34A.	Ken Hamlin (red)	7.00
34B.	Ken Hamlin (white)	3.50
35.	Dale Long	2.00

36. Harmon Killebrew 25.00
37. Hal Brown 3.00
38A. Gary Geiger (O on hat) 400.00
38B. G. Geiger (no O on hat) 3.00
39A. Minnie Minoso (ChiSox) 40.00
39B. Minnie Minoso (Cards) 30.00
40. Brooks Robinson 40.00
41. Mickey Mantle 75.00
42. Bernie Daniels 2.00
43. Billy Martin 7.00
44. Vic Power 2.00
45. Joe Pignatano 2.00
46A. Ryne Duren (red) 7.00
46B. Ryne Duren (white) 3.00
47A. Pete Runnels (2nd base) 8.00
47B. Pete Runnels (1st base) 5.00
48A. D.Williams(name right) 800.00
48B. D.Williams(name left) 6.00
49. Jim Landis 2.00
50. Steve Boros 3.00
51A. Zoilo Versalies (red) 6.00
51B. Z. Versalies (white) 3.00
52A. Johnny Temple (Indians) 10.00
52B. Johnny Temple (Orioles) 6.00
53A. Jackie Brandt (Oriole) 7.00
53B. Jackie Brandt (Orioles) 800.00
54. Denny McLain 4.00
55. Sherm Lollar 2.00
56. Gene Stephens 2.25
57A. Leon Wagner (red) 7.00
57B. L. Wagner (white) 3.50
58. Frank Lary 2.00
59. Bill Skowron 4.00
60. Vic Wertz 30.00
61. Willie Kirkland 2.00
62. Leo Posada 2.50
63A. Albie Pearson (red) 7.00
63B. A. Pearson (white) 3.50
64. Bobby Richardson 7.00
65A. Marv Breeding (SS) 8.50
65B. Marv Breeding (2Base) 4.00
66. Roy Sievers 80.00
67. Al Kaline 35.00
68A. Don Buddin (Red Sox) 7.00
68B. Don Buddin (Colt 45's) 5.00

1962 Salada Yogi Berra coin

69A. Lenny Green (red) 6.00
69B. L. Green (white) 4.00
70. Gene Green 30.00
71. Luis Aparicio 8.00
72. Norm Cash 4.00
73. Jackie Jensen 25.00
74 Bubba Phillips 2.00
75. James Archer 3.00
76A. Ken Hunt (red) 7.00
76B. Ken Hunt (white) 3.50
77. Ralph Terry 3.00
78. Camilo Pascual 2.00
79. Marty Keough 30.00
80. Clete Boyer 3.25
81. Jim Pagliaroni 2.00
82A. Gene Leek (red) 6.00
828. Gene Leek (white) 3.00
83. Jake Wood 2.00
84. Coot Veal 25.00
85. Norm Siebern 2.00
86A. Andy Carey (White Sox) 40.00
86B. Andy Carey (Phillies) 5.00
87A. Bill Tuttle (red) 6.00
87B. Bill Tuttle (white) 3.25
88A. J. Piersall (Indians) 7.00
88B. J. Piersall (Senators) 4.00
89. Ron Hansen 35.00
90A. Chuck Stobbs (red) 6.00
90B. C. Stobbs (white) 3.50
91A. Ken McBride (red) 6.00
91B. K. McBride (white) 3.00
92. Bill Bruton 2.00
93. Gus Triandos 2.25
94. John Romano 2.00
95. Elston Howard 4.00
96. Gene Woodling 2.00
97A. Early Wynn (pitching) 35.00
97B. Early Wynn (portrait) 20.00
98. Milt Pappas 2.00
99. Bill Monboquette 2.50
100. Wayne Causey 2.00
101. Don Elston 2.25
102A. Charlie Neal (Dodgers) 8.00
102B. Charlie Neal (Mets) 4.50
103. Don Blasingame 2.00
104. Frank Thomas 25.00
105. Wes Covington 3.00
106. Chuck Hiller 2.00
107. Don Hoak 2.25
108A. Bob Lillis (Cardinals) 13.50
108B. Bob Lillis (Colt 45's) 4.00

1962 Salada Sandy Koufax coin

109. Sandy Koufax 30.00
110. Jerry Coleman 2.00
111. Eddie Matthews 15.00
112. Art Mahaffey 2.00
113A. Ed Bailey (red) 10.00
113B. Ed Bailey (white) 4.00
114. Smokey Burgess 2.00
115. Bill White 3.00
116. Ed Bouchee 30.00
117. Bob Buhl 2.25
118. Vada Pinson 3.00
119. Carl Sawatski 2.00
120. Dick Stuart 2.50
121. Harvey Kuenn 40.00
122. Pancho Herrera 2.00
123A. Don Zimmer (Cubs) 7.50
123B. Don Zimmer (Mets) 4.00
124. Wally Moon 2.50
125. Joe Adcock 2.00
126. Joey Jay 2.00
127A. Maury Wills (blue 3) 9.50
127B. Maury Wills (red 3) 9.50
128. George Altman 2.00
129A. John Buzhardt (Phillies) 7.00
129B. John Buzhardt (ChiSox) 4.00
130. Felipe Alou 3.00
131. Bill Mazeroski 4.00
132. Ernie Broglio 2.00
133. Johnny Roseboro 2.25
134. Mike McCormick 2.50
135A. Charlie Smith (Phil) 8.00
135B. Charlie Smith (ChiSox) 4.00
136. Ron Santo 3.50
137. Gene Freese 2.00
138. Dick Groat 3.00
139. Curt Flood 3.50
140. Frank Bolling 2.00
141. Clay Dalrymple 2.25
142. Willie McCovey 30.00
143. Bob Skinner 2.00
144. Lindy McDaniel 2.50
145. Glenn Hobbie 2.00
146A. Gil Hodges (Dodgers) 45.00
146B. Gil Hodges (Mets) 20.00
147. Eddie Kasko 2.00
148. Gino Cimoli 70.00
149. Willie Mays 60.00
150. Roberto Clemente 50.00
151. Red Schoendienst 3.00
152. Joe Torre 3.50
153. Bob Purkey 2.00
154A. Tommy Davis (Outfield) 6.50
154B. Tommy Davis (3rd Base) 3.25
155A. Andre Rodgers (SS) 7.00
155B. A.Rodgers (1st Base) 3.50
156. Tony Taylor 2.00
157. Bob Friend 2.00
158A. Gus Bell (Reds) 7.00
158B. Gus Bell (Mets) 3.50
159. Roy McMillan 2.00
160. Carl Warwick 2.50
161. Willie Davis 2.25
162. Sam Jones 55.00
163. Ruben Amaro 2.00
164. Sammy Taylor 2.50
165. Frank Robinson 30.00
166. Lew Burdette 3.50
167. Ken Boyer 3.00
168. Bill Virdon 3.50
169. Jim Davenport 2.00
170. Don Demeter 2.00
171. Richie Ashburn 40.00
172. Johnny Podres 4.00
173A. Joe Cunningham (Card) 40.00
173B. Joe Cunningham (Sox) 20.00
174. Elroy Face 2.00
175. Orlando Cepeda 3.00
176A. Bobby Gene Smith (Phil) 7.00
176B. B.Gene Smith (Mets) 3.50
177A. Ernie Banks (Outfield) 35.00
177B. Ernie Banks (SS) 17.50
178A. Daryl Spencer (3rd Base) 7.00
178B. Daryl Spencer (1st Base) 3.50
179. Bob Schmidt 25.00
180. Henry Aaron 60.00
181. Hobie Landrith 4.00
182A. Ed Broussard (Error) 300.00
182B. Ed Bressoud (Cor) 20.00
183. Felix Mantilla 4.00
184. Dick Farrell 4.00
185. Bob Miller 4.50
186. Don Taussig 4.25
187. Pumpsie Green 4.00
188. Bobby Shantz 3.75
189. Roger Craig 5.00
190. Hal Smith 4.00
191. Johnny Edwards 3.75
192. John DeMerit 4.00
193. Joe Amalfitano 3.50
194. Norm Larker 4.00
195. Al Hoist 4.00
196. Al Spangler 3.75
197. Alex Grammas 4.25
198. Jerry Lynch 4.00
199. Jim McKnight 3.75
200. Jose Pagen (sic, Pagan) 4.00
201. Jim Gilliam 13.00
202. Art Ditmar 4.00
203. Bud Daley 4.00
204. John Callison 5.00
205. Stu Miller 3.75
206. Russ Snyder 4.00
207. Billy Williams 25.00
208. Walt Bond 4.25
209. Joe Koppe 4.00
210. Don Schwall 20.00
211. Billy Gardner 4.00
212. Chuck Estrada 3.75
213. Gary Bell 4.00
214. Floyd Robinson 4.25
215. Duke Snider 45.00
216. Lee Maye 4.00
217. Howie Bedell 4.25
218. Bob Will 3.75
219. Dick Green 12.00
220. Carroll Hardy 4.00
221. Danny O'Connoll 4.25

1963 SALADA COINS

No.	Player	Value
1.	Don Drysdale	15.00
2.	Dick Farrell	3.00
3.	Bob Gibson	17.50
4.	Sandy Koufax	40.00
5.	Juan Marichal	15.00
6.	Bob Purkey	3.00
7.	Bob Shaw	3.00
8.	Warren Spahn	20.00
9.	Johnny Podres	3.00
10.	Art Mahaffey	3.50
11.	Del Crandall	4.00
12.	John Roseboro	3.00
13.	Orlando Cepeda	4.50
14.	Bill Mazeroski	5.00
15.	Ken Boyer	4.00
16.	Dick Groat	4.50
17.	Ernie Banks	20.00
18.	Frank Bolling	3.50
19.	Jim Davenport	3.00
20.	Maury Wills	6.00
21.	Willie Davis	3.00
22.	Willie Mays	45.00
23.	Roberto Clemente	50.00
24.	Henry Aaron	50.00
25.	Matty Alou	3.50
26.	John Callison	3.75
27.	Richie Ashburn	6.00
28.	Eddie Mathews	20.00
29.	Frank Robinson	25.00
30.	Billy Williams	14.00
31.	George Altman	3.00
32.	Hank Aguirre	3.00
33.	Jim Bunning	6.00
34.	Dick Donovan	3.00
35.	Bill Monbouquette	3.50
36.	Camilo Pascual	3.00
37.	Dave Stenhouse	2.75
38.	Ralph Terry	3.00
39.	Hoyt Wilhiilm	11.50
40.	Jim Kaat	6.00
41.	Ken McBride	3.00
42.	Ray Herbert	3.50
43.	Milt Pappas	4.00
44.	Earl Battey	3.00
45.	Eiston Howard	4.00
46.	John Romano	3.00
47.	Jim Gentile	3.25
48.	Bill Moran	3.00
49.	Rich Rollins	3.50
50.	Luis Aparicio	12.00
51.	Norm Siebern	3.00
52.	Bobby Richardson	6.00
53.	Brooks Robinson	30.00
54.	Tom Tresh	4.00
55.	Leon Wagnor	3.00
56.	Mickey Mantle	75.00
57.	Roger Maris	30.00
58.	Rocky Colavito	6.00
59.	Frank Thomas	3.00
60.	Jim Landis	3.25
61.	Pete Runnels	3.00
62.	Yogi Berra	30.00
63.	Al Kaline	30.00

1964 TOPPS COINS

No.	Player	Value
1.	Don Zimmer	1.00
2.	Jim Wynn	1.00
3.	Johnny Orsino	0.95
4.	Jim Bouton	1.25
5.	Dick Groat	1.25
6.	Loon Wagner	0.95
7.	Frank Malzone	1.00
8.	Steve Barber	1.00
9.	Johnny Romano	0.95
10.	Tom Tresh	1.00
11.	Folipe Alou	1.25
12.	Dick Stuart	1.00
13.	Claude Osteen	1.00
14.	Juan Pizarro	0.95
15.	Donn Clendenon	1.00
16.	Jimmie Hall	0.85
17.	Al Jackson	1.00

1964 Topps Brooks Robinson coin

1964 Topps Hank Aaron coin

No.	Player	Value
18.	Brooks Robinson	11.50
19.	Bob Allison	1.00
20.	Ed Roebuck	0.85
21.	Pete Ward	0.90
22.	Willie McCovey	10.00
23.	Elston Howard	2.00
24.	Diego Segui	1.00
25.	Ken Boyer	2.00
26.	Carl Yastrzemski	18.00
27.	Bill Mazeroski	2.00
28.	Jerry Lumpe	1.00
29.	Woody Held	0.95
30.	Dick Radatz	1.00
31.	Luis Aparicio	6.00
32.	Dave Nicholson	1.00
33.	Eddie Mathews	8.00
34.	Don Drysdale	10.00
35.	Ray Culp	1.00
36.	Juan Marichal	9.00
37.	Frank Robinson	10.00
38.	Chuck Hinton	1.00
39.	Floyd Robinson	0.95
40.	Tommy Harper	1.00
41.	Ron Hansen	1.00
42.	Ernie Banks	12.00
43.	Jesse Gonder	1.00
44.	Stan Williams	0.95
45.	Vada Pinson	1.25
46.	Rocky Colavito	2.00
47.	Bill Monbouquette	1.00
48.	Max Alvis	1.00
49.	Norm Siebern	0.95
50.	John Callison	1.20
51.	Rich Rollins	1.00
52.	Ken McBride	1.00
53.	Don Lock	0.95
54.	Ron Fairly	1.00
55.	Roberto Clemente	20.00
56.	Dick Ellsworth	1.00
57.	Tommy Davis	1.50
58.	Tony Gonzalez	1.00
59.	Bob Gibson	10.00
60.	Jim Maloney	1.25
61.	Frank Howard	1.75
62.	Jim Pagliaroni	1.00
63.	Orlando Cepeda	2.00
64.	Ron Perranoski	1.00
65.	Curt Flood	1.25
66.	Alvin McBean	1.00
67.	Dean Chance	1.00
68.	Ron Santo	1.25
69.	Jack Baldschun	1.00
70.	Milt Pappas	1.00
71.	Gary Peters	1.00
72.	Bobby Richardson	2.00
73.	Frank Thomas	1.00
74.	Hank Aguirre	1.00
75.	Carlton Willey	0.95
76.	Camilo Pascual	1.00
77.	Bob Friend	0.95
78.	Bill White	1.25
79.	Norm Cash	1.00
80.	Willie Mays	20.00
81.	Leon Carmel	1.00
82.	Pete Rose	25.00
83.	Henry Aaron	20.00
84.	Bob Aspromonte	1.00
85.	Jim O'Toole	1.00
86.	Vic Davalillo	0.95
87.	Bill Freehan	1.25
88.	Warren Spahn	9.00
89.	Ken Hunt	1.00
90.	Denis Menke	1.00
91.	Dick Farrell	0.95
92.	Jim Hickman	1.00
93.	Jim Bunning	2.00
94.	Bob Hendley	1.00
95.	Ernie Brogilo	1.00
96.	Rusty Staub	1.25
97.	Lou Brock	9.00
98.	Jim Fregosi	1.25
99.	Jim Grant	1.00
100.	Al Kaline	13.50
101.	Earl Battey	1.00
102.	Wayne Causey	1.00
103.	Chuck Schilling	0.95
104.	Boog Powell	1.50
105.	Dave Wickersham	1.00
106.	Sandy Koutax	14.00
107.	John Bateman	1.00
108.	Ed Brinkman	1.00
109.	Al Downing	0.95
110.	Joe Azcue	1.00
lll.	Albie Pearson	1.00
112.	Harmon Killebrew	10.00
113.	Tony Taylor	1.00
114.	Larry Jackson	1.00
115.	Billy O'Dell	0.95
116.	Don Demeter	1.00
117.	Ed Charles	1.00
118.	Joe Torre	2.00
119.	Don Nottebart	1.00
120.	Mickey Mantle	35.00
	ALL-STARS (121-164)	
121.	Joe Pepitone	1.00
122.	Dick Stuart	1.00
123.	Bobby Richardson	2.00
124.	Jerry Lumpe	1.00
125.	Brooks Robinson	12.00
126.	Frank Malzone	1.25
127.	Luis Aparicio	6.00
128.	Jim Fregosi	1.75
129.	Al Kaline	12.00
130.	Leon Wagner	1.00
131A.	Mickey Mantle (righty)	35.00
131B.	Mickey Mantle (lefty)	35.00
132.	Albie Pearson	1.00
133.	Harmon Killebrew	7.00
134.	Cart Yastrzemski	17.50
135.	Elston Howard	1.25
136.	Earl Battey	1.00
137.	Camilo Pascual	1.00
138.	Jim Bouton	1.25
139.	Whitey Ford	9.00
140.	Gary Peters	1.00
141.	Bil White	1.25
142.	Orlando Cepeda	1.75
143.	Bill Mazeroski	1.25
144.	Tony Taylor	1.00
145.	Ken Boyer	1.75

146.	Ron Santo	1.50
147.	Dick Groat	1.00
148.	Roy McMillan	1.00
149.	Henry Aaron	17.00

1964 Topps Willie Mays coin

150.	Roberto Clemente	15.00
151.	Willie Mays	17.00
152.	Vada Pinson	1.75
153.	Willie Davis	1.25
154.	Frank Robinson	9.00
155.	Joe Torre	2.25
156.	Tim McCarver	1.25
157.	Juan Marichal	7.50
158.	Jim Maloney	1.25
159.	Sandy Koufax	12.00
160.	Warren Spahn	10.00
161A.	Wayne Causey (NL)	12.00
161B.	Wayne Causey (AL)	1.00
162A.	Chuck Hinton (NL)	12.00
162B.	Chuck Hinton (AL)	1.00
163.	Bob Aspromonte	0.95
164.	Ron Hunt	1.00

1965 OLD LONDON COINS

No.	Player	Value
1.	Hank Aaron	45.00
2.	Richie Allen	5.00
3.	Bob Allison	3.00
4.	Ernie Banks	20.00
5.	Ken Boyer	5.00
6.	Jim Bunning	8.00
7.	Orlando Cepeda	8.00
8.	Dean Chance	2.00
9.	Rocky Colavito	4.50
10.	Vic Davalillo	3.00
11.	Tommy Davis	5.00
12.	Ron Fairly	2.50
13.	Dick Farrell	3.00
14.	Jim Fregosi	4.00
15.	Bob Friend	3.50
16.	Dick Groat	5.00

1965 Old London Carl Yastrzemski

17.	Chuck Hinton	2.50
18.	Ron Hunt	3.00
19.	Ken Johnson	2.50
20.	Al Kaline	25.00
21.	Harmon Killebrew	20.00
22.	Don Lock	2.50
23.	Mickey Mantle	100.00
24.	Roger Maris	25.00
25.	Willie Mays	50.00
26.	Bill Mazeroski	6.00
27.	Gary Peters	3.00
28.	Vada Pinson	5.00
29.	Boog Powell	5.00
30.	Dick Radatz	2.50
31.	Brooks Robinson	25.00
32.	Frank Robinson	25.00
33.	Tracy Stallard	2.50
34.	Joe Torre	6.00
35.	Leon Wagner	3.00
36.	Pete Ward	2.50
37.	Dave Wickersham	2.75
38.	Billy Williams	17.50
39.	John Wyatt	2.50
40.	Carl Yastrzemski	50.00

1971 TOPPS COINS

No.	Player	Value
1.	Clarence Gaston	0.60
2.	Dave Johnson	1.00
3.	Jim Bunning	1.25
4.	Jim Spencer	0.60
5.	Felix Millan	0.70
6.	Gerry Moses	0.60
7.	Fergie Jenkins	1.00
8.	Felipe Alou	1.25
9.	Jim McGlothlin	0.60
10.	Dick McAuliffe	0.70
11.	Joe Torre	1.25
12.	Jim Perry	0.75
13.	Bobby Bonds	1.00
14.	Danny Cater	0.60
15.	Bill Mazeroski	1.00
16.	Luis Aparicio	3.00
17.	Doug Rader	0.75
18.	Vada Pinson	1.00
19.	John Bateman	0.65
20.	Lew Krausse	0.60
21.	Billy Grabarkewitz	0.75
22.	Frank Howard	0.80
23.	Jerry Koosman	0.75
24.	Rod Carew	8.00
25.	Al Ferrara	0.50
26.	Dave McNally	0.60
27.	Jim Hickman	0.50
28.	Sandy Alomar	0.50
29.	Lee May	0.60
30.	Rico Petrocelli	0.60
31.	Don Money	0.50
32.	Jim Rooker	0.55
33.	Dick Dietz	0.50
34.	Roy White	0.60
35.	Carl Morton	0.50
36.	Walt Williams	0.55
37.	Phil Niekro	2.00
38.	Bill Freehan	0.60
39.	Julian Javier	0.50
40.	Rick Monday	0.60
41.	Don Wilson	0.50
42.	Ray Fosse	0.55
43.	Art Shamsky	0.50
44.	Ted Savage	0.50
45.	Claude Osteen	0.60
46.	Ed Brinkman	0.50
47.	Matty Alou	0.60
48.	Al Oliver	1.00
49.	Danny Coombs	0.50
50.	Frank Robinson	5.50
51.	Randy Hundley	0.50
52.	Casar Tovar	0.50
53.	Wayne Simpson	0.50
54.	Bobby Murcer	1.00
55.	Carl Taylor	0.50
56.	Tommy John	1.25
57.	Willie McCovey	5.25
58.	Carl Yastrzemski	12.25
59.	Bob Bailey	0.50
60.	Clyde Wright	0.50
61.	Orlando Cepeda	1.25
62.	Al Kaline	6.25
63.	Bob Gibson	5.25
64.	Bert Campaneris	0.65
65.	Ted Sizemore	0.45
66.	Duke Sims	0.45
67.	Bud Harrelson	0.50
68.	Gerald McNertney	0.45
69.	Jim Wynn	0.55
70.	Ken Bosman	0.45
71.	Roberto Clemente	10.25
72.	Rich Reese	0.45
73.	Gaylord Perry	1.60
74.	Boog Powell	1.00
75.	Billy Williams	1.50
76.	Bill Melton	0.55
77.	Nate Colbert	0.45
78.	Reggie Smith	0.65
79.	Deron Johnson	0.45
80.	Jim Hunter	1.75
81.	Bobby Tolan	0.45
82.	Jim Northrup	0.55
83.	Ron Fairly	0.55
84.	Alex Johnson	0.45
85.	Pat Jarvis	0.45
86.	Sam McDowell	0.55
87.	Lou Brock	6.25
88.	Danny Walton	0.45
89.	Denis Menke	0.55

1971 Topps Jim Palmer coin

90.	Jim Palmer	4.25
91.	Tommy Agee	0.60
92.	Duane Josephson	0.45
93.	Tommy Davis	0.65
94.	Mel Stottlemyre	0.65
95.	Ron Santo	1.00
96.	Amos Otis	0.65
97.	Ken Henderson	0.45
98.	George Scott	0.55
99.	Dock Ellis	0.45
100.	Harmon Killebrew	5.25
101.	Pete Rose	20.00
102.	Rick Reichardt	0.45
103.	Cleon Jones	0.45
104.	Ron Perranoski	0.50
105.	Tony Perez	1.25
106.	Mickey Lolich	0.80
107.	Tim McCarver	0.65
108.	Reggie Jackson	10.25
109.	Chris Cannizzaro	0.45
110.	Steve Hargan	0.45
111.	Rusty Staub	0.80
112.	Andy Messersmith	0.55
113.	Rico Carty	0.65
114.	Brooks Robinson	6.25
115.	Steve Carlton	6.00
116.	Mike Hegan	0.45
117.	Joe Morgan	4.00
118.	Thurman Munson	5.25
119.	Don Kessinger	0.55
120.	Joel Horlen	0.45
121.	Wes Parker	0.55
122.	Sonny Siebert	0.45
123.	Willie Stargell	2.75
124.	Aurelio Rodriguez	0.45
125.	Juan Marichal	4.25
126.	Mike Epstein	0.45
127.	Tom Seaver	8.00
128.	Tony Oliva	1.00
129.	Jim Merritt	0.45
130.	Willie Horton	0.55
131.	Rick Wise	0.45
132.	Sal Bando	0.80
133.	Gates Brown	0.45
134.	Bud Harrelson	0.00

No.	Player	Value
135.	Mack Jones	0.55
136.	Jim Fregosi	0.65
137.	Hank Aaron	10.25
138.	Fritz Peterson	0.45
139.	Joe Hague	0.45
140.	Tommy Harper	0.45
141.	Larry Dierker	0.45
142.	Tony Conigliaro	0.65
143.	Glenn Beckert	0.45
144.	Carlos May	0.45
145.	Don Sutton	1.60
146.	Paul Casanova	0.45
147.	Bob Moose	0.45
148.	Chico Cardenas	0.45
149.	Johnny Bench	7.50
150.	Mike Cuellar	0.55
151.	Donn Clendenon	0.45
152.	Lou Pinielia	1.25
153.	Willie Mays	10.25

1983 7-11 COINS

No.	Player	Value
1.	Rod Carew	1.75
2.	Steve Sax	1.00
3.	Fred Lynn	1.00
4.	Pedro Guerrero	1.50
5.	Reggie Jackson	2.25
6.	Dusty Baker	0.70
7.	Doug DeCinces	0.65
8.	Fernando Valenzuela	2.00
9.	Tommy John	1.25
10.	Rick Monday	0.55

1983 7-11 Bobby Grich coin

No.	Player	Value
11.	Bobby Grich	0.60
12.	Greg Brock	0.65

1984 7-11 COINS

No.	Player	Value
1.	Andre Dawson	0.65
2.	Robin Yount	0.65
3.	Dale Murphy	1.00
4.	Mike Schmidt	1.25
5.	George Brett	1.25
6.	Eddie Murray	1.25
East (E) Players		
7E.	Dave Winfield	1.25
8E.	Tom Seaver	1.25
9E.	Mike Boddicker	0.65
10E.	Wade Boggs	2.00
11E.	Bill Madlock	0.65
12E.	Steve Carlton	1.25
13E.	Dave Stieb	0.65
14E.	Cal Ripken	1.25
15E.	Jim Rice	0.85
16E.	Ron Guidry	0.65
17E.	Darryl Strawberry	2.25
18E.	Tony Pena	0.65
19E.	John Denny	0.55
20E.	Tim Raines	1.00
21E.	Rick Dempsey	0.55
22E.	Rich Gossage	0.65
23E.	Gary Matthews	0.55
24E.	Keith Hernandez	0.85
Central (C) Players		
7C.	Bruce Sutter	0.65
8C.	Cecil Cooper	0.65
9C.	Willie McGee	0.80
10C.	Mike Hargrove	0.55
11C.	Kent Hrbek	1.00
12C.	Carlton Fisk	0.65
13C.	Mario Soto	0.65
14C.	Lonnie Smith	0.55
15C.	Gary Carter	1.25
16C.	Lou Whitaker	0.65
17C.	Ron Kittle	0.80
18C.	Paul Molitor	0.65
19C.	Ozzie Smith	0.80
20C.	Fergie Jenkins	0.55
21C.	Ted Simmons	0.55
22C.	Pete Rose	2.75
23C.	LaMarr Hoyt	0.55
24C.	Dan Quisenberry	0.65
West (W) Players		
7W.	Steve Garvey	1.50
8W.	Rod Carew	1.25
9W.	Fernando Valenzuela	1.00
10W.	Bob Horner	0.80
11W.	Buddy Bell	0.65
12W.	Reggie Jackson	1.75
13W.	Nolan Ryan	1.25
14W.	Pedro Guerrero	0.80
15W.	Atlee Hammaker	0.55
16W.	Fred Lynn	0.80
17W.	Terry Kennedy	0.55
18W.	Dusty Baker	0.55
19W.	Jose Cruz	0.65
20W.	Steve Rogers	0.55
21W.	Rickey Henderson	1.50
22W.	Steve Sax	0.80
23W.	Dickie Thon	0.55
24W.	Matt Young	0.55

1985 7-11 COINS

No.	Player	Value
Central (C) Players		
1C.	Nolan Ryan	1.25

1985 7-11 George Brett coin

No.	Player	Value
2C.	George Brett	1.75
3C.	Dave Winfield	1.25
4C.	Mike Schmidt	1.25
5C.	Bruce Sutter	0.55
6C.	Joaquin Andujar	0.55
7C.	Willie Hernandez	0.65
8C.	Wade Boggs	2.25
9C.	Gary Carter	1.25
10C.	Jose Cruz	0.65
11C.	Kent Hrbek	0.80
12C.	Reggie Jackson	1.75
13C.	Lance Parrish	0.80
14C.	Terry Puhl	0.55
15C.	Dan Quisenberry	0.65
16C.	Ozzie Smith	0.80
Detroit (D) Players		
1D.	Lou Whitaker	0.80

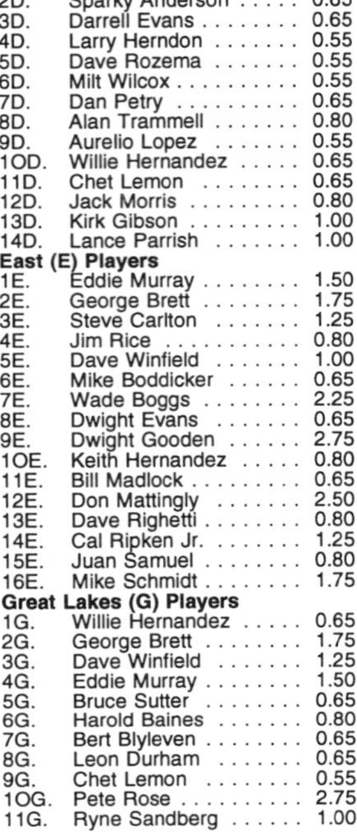

No.	Player	Value
2D.	Sparky Anderson	0.65
3D.	Darrell Evans	0.65
4D.	Larry Herndon	0.55
5D.	Dave Rozema	0.55
6D.	Milt Wilcox	0.55
7D.	Dan Petry	0.65
8D.	Alan Trammell	0.80
9D.	Aurelio Lopez	0.55
10D.	Willie Hernandez	0.65
11D.	Chet Lemon	0.65
12D.	Jack Morris	0.80
13D.	Kirk Gibson	1.00
14D.	Lance Parrish	1.00
East (E) Players		
1E.	Eddie Murray	1.50
2E.	George Brett	1.75
3E.	Steve Carlton	1.25
4E.	Jim Rice	0.80
5E.	Dave Winfield	1.00
6E.	Mike Boddicker	0.65
7E.	Wade Boggs	2.25
8E.	Dwight Evans	0.65
9E.	Dwight Gooden	2.75
10E.	Keith Hernandez	0.80
11E.	Bill Madlock	0.65
12E.	Don Mattingly	2.50
13E.	Dave Righetti	0.80
14E.	Cal Ripken Jr.	1.25
15E.	Juan Samuel	0.80
16E.	Mike Schmidt	1.75
Great Lakes (G) Players		
1G.	Willie Hernandez	0.65
2G.	George Brett	1.75
3G.	Dave Winfield	1.25
4G.	Eddie Murray	1.50
5G.	Bruce Sutter	0.65
6G.	Harold Baines	0.80
7G.	Bert Blyleven	0.65
8G.	Leon Durham	0.65
9G.	Chet Lemon	0.55
10G.	Pete Rose	2.75
11G.	Ryne Sandberg	1.00

1985 7-11 Don Mattingly coin

No.	Player	Value
12G.	Tom Seaver	1.25
13G.	Mario Soto	0.65
14G.	Rick Sutcliffe	0.65
15G.	Alan Trammell	0.80
16G.	Robin Yount	1.25
Southeast (S) Players		
1S.	Dale Murphy	1.50
2S.	Steve Carlton	1.25
3S.	Nolan Ryan	1.25
4S.	Bruce Sutter	0.65
5S.	Dave Winfield	1.25
6S.	Steve Bedrosian	0.55
7S.	Andre Dawson	0.80
8S.	Kirk Gibson	1.00
9S.	Fred Lynn	0.80
10S.	Gary Matthews	0.55
11S.	Phil Niekro	0.80
12S.	Tim Raines	0.80
13S.	Darryl Strawberry	2.25
14S.	Dave Stieb	0.65
15S.	Willie Upshaw	0.65
16S.	Lou Whitaker	0.80
West (W) Players		
1W.	Mike Schmidt	1.75
2W.	Jim Rice	0.80
3W.	Dale Murphy	1.50

4W.	Eddie Murray	1.50
5W.	Dave Winfield	1.25
6W.	Rod Carew	1.25
7W.	Alvin Davis	0.80
8W.	Steve Garvey	1.50
9W.	Rich Gossage	0.80
10W.	Pedro Guerrero	0.80
11W.	Tony Gwynn	1.00
12W.	Rickey Henderson	1.75
13W.	Reggie Jackson	1.75
14W.	Jeff Leonard	0.65
15W.	Alejandro Pena	0.55
16W.	Fernando Valenzuela	1.00

1986 7-11 COINS

No.	Player	Value
1.	Dwight Gooden	2.25
Central (C) Players		
2C.	Wade Boggs	2.25
	George Brett	
	Pete Rose	
3C.	Keith Hernandez	1.25
	Don Mattingly	
	Cal Ripken	
4C.	Harold Baines	0.80
	Pedro Guerrero	
	Dave Parker	
5C.	Dale Murphy	1.25
	Jim Rice	
	Mike Schmidt	
6C.	Ron Guidry	0.80
	Bret Saberhagen	
	Fernando Valenzuela	
7C.	Goose Gossage	0.65
	Dan Quisenberry	
	Bruce Sutter	
8C.	Steve Carlton	1.50
	Nolan Ryan	
	Tom Seaver	
9C.	Keith Hernandez	0.80
	Ryne Sandberg	
	Robin Yount	
10C.	Bert Blyleven	0.65
	Jack Morris	
	Rick Sutcliffe	
11C.	Rollie Fingers	0.55
	Bob James	
	Lee Smith	
12C.	Carlton Fisk	0.65
	Lance Parrish	
	Tony Pena	
13C.	Shawon Dunston	0.65
	Ozzie Guillen	
	Earnie Riles	
14C.	Brett Butler	0.65
	Chet Lemon	
	Willie Wilson	
15C.	Tom Brunansky	0.55
	Cecil Cooper	
	Darrell Evans	
16C.	Kirk Gibson	0.65
	Paul Molitor	
	Greg Walker	
East (E) Players		
2E.	Wade Boggs	2.25
	George Brett	
	Pete Rose	
3E.	Keith Hernandez	1.25
	Don Mattingly	
	Cal Ripken	
4E.	Harold Baines	0.80
	Pedro Guerrero	
	Dave Parker	
5E.	Dale Murphy	1.25
	Jim Rice	
	Mike Schmidt	
6E.	Ron Guidry	0.80
	Bret Saberhagen	
	Fernando Valenzuela	
7E.	Goose Gossage	0.65
	Dan Quisenberry	
	Bruce Sutter	
8E.	Steve Carlton	1.50
	Nolan Ryan	
	Tom Seaver	
9E.	Steve Lyons	0.65
	Rick Schu	
	Larry Sheets	
10E.	Jeff Reardon	0.55
	Dave Righetti	
	Bob Stanley	
11E.	George Bell	1.25
	Darryl Strawberry	
	Dave Winfield	
12E.	Rickey Henderson	1.25
	Tim Raines	
	Juan Samuel	
13E.	Andre Dawson	0.80
	Dwight Evans	
	Edde Murray	
14E.	Mike Boddicker	0.65
	Ron Darling	
	Dave Stieb	
15E.	Tim Burke	0.65
	Brian Fisher	
	Roger McDowell	
16E.	Jesse Barfield	0.80
	Gary Carter	
	Fred Lynn	
Southern (S) Players		
2S.	Wade Boggs	2.25
	George Brett	
	Pete Rose	
3S.	Keith Hernandez	1.25
	Don Mattingly	
	Cal Ripken	
4S.	Harold Baines	0.80
	Pedro Guerrero	
	Dave Parker	
5S.	Dale Murphy	1.25
	Jim Rice	
	Mike Schmidt	
6S.	Ron Guidry	0.80
	Bret Saberhagen	
	Fernando Valenzuela	
7S.	Goose Gossage	0.65
	Dan Quisenberry	
	Bruce Sutter	
8S.	Steve Carlton	1.50
	Nolan Ryan	

1987 Topps Don Mattingly coin

	Tom Seaver	
9S.	Vince Coleman	2.25
	Eric Davis	
	Oddibe McDowell	
10S.	Buddy Bell	0.65
	Ozzie Smith	
	Lou Whitaker	
11S.	Mike Scott	0.65
	Mario Soto	
	John Tudor	
12S.	Jeff Lahti	0.55
	Ted Power	
	Dave Smith	
13S.	Jack Clark	0.65
	Jose Cruz	
	Bob Horner	
14S.	Bill Doran	0.65
	Tommy Herr	
	Ron Oester	
15S.	Tom Browning	1.50
	Joe Hesketh	
	Todd Worrell	
16S.	Willie McGee	1.50
	Jerry Mumphrey	
	Pete Rose	
Western (W) Players		
2W.	Wade Boggs	2.25
	George Brett	
	Pete Rose	
3W.	Keith Hernandez	1.25
	Don Mattingly	
	Cal Ripken	
4W.	Harold Baines	0.80
	Pedro Guerrero	
	Dave Parker	
5W.	Dale Murphy	1.25
	Jim Rice	
	Mike Schmidt	
6W.	Ron Guidry	0.80
	Bret Saberhagen	
	Fernando Valenzuela	
7W.	Goose Gossage	0.65
	Dan Quisenberry	
	Bruce Sutter	
8W.	Steve Carlton	1.50
	Nolan Ryan	
	Tom Seaver	
9W.	Reggie Jackson	0.80
	Dave Kingman	
	Gorman Thomas	
10W.	Rod Carew	1.25
	Tony Gwynn	
	Carney Lansford	
11W.	Phil Bradley	0.65
	Mike Marshall	
	Graig Nettles	
12W.	Andy Hawkins	0.65
	Orel Hershiser	
	Mike Witt	
13W.	Chris Brown	0.80
	Ivan Calderon	
	Mariano Duncan	
14W.	Steve Garvey	0.80
	Bill Madlock	
	Jim Presley	
15W.	Jay Howell	0.55
	Donnie Moore	
	Edwin Nunez	
16W.	Karl Best	0.55
	Stewart Cliburn	
	Steve Ontiveros	

1987 TOPPS COINS

No.	Player	Value
1.	Harold Baines	0.10
2.	Jesse Barfield	0.10
3.	George Bell	0.15
4.	Wade Boggs	0.65
5.	George Brett	0.25
6.	Jose Canseco	0.95
7.	Joe Carter	0.10
8.	Roger Clemens	0.35
9.	Alvin Davis	0.10
10.	Rob Deer	0.10
11.	Kirk Gibson	0.15
12.	Rickey Henderson	0.20
13.	Kent Krbek	0.15
14.	Pete Incaviglia	0.15
15.	Reggie Jackson	0.20
16.	Wally Joyner	0.55
17.	Don Mattingly	1.25
18.	Jack Morris	0.15
19.	Eddie Murray	0.20
20.	Kirby Puckett	0.25
21.	Jim Rice	0.20
22.	Dave Righetti	0.15
23.	Cal Ripken	0.20
24.	Cory Snyder	0.20
25.	Danny Tartabull	0.15
26.	Dave Winfield	0.20
27.	Hubie Brooks	0.10
28.	Gary Carter	0.20
29.	Vince Coleman	0.15

No.	Player	Value
30.	Eric Davis	0.65
31.	Glenn Davis	0.10
32.	Steve Garvey	0.20
33.	Dwight Gooden	0.35
34.	Tony Gwynn	0.25
35.	Von Hayes	0.10
36.	Keith Hernandez	0.15
37.	Dale Murphy	0.25
38.	Dave Parker	0.15
39.	Tony Pena	0.10
40.	Nolan Ryan	0.20
41.	Ryne Sandberg	0.15
42.	Steve Sax	0.10
43.	Mike Schmidt	0.25
44.	Mike Scott	0.10
45.	Ozzie Smith	0.10
46.	Darryl Strawberry	0.35
47.	Femando Valenzuela	0.15
48.	Todd Worrell	0.10

1988 TOPPS COINS

No.	Player	Value
1.	George Bell	0.20
2.	Roger Clemens	0.35
3.	Mark McGwire	0.55
4.	Wade Boggs	0.65
5.	Harold Baines	0.10
6.	Ivan Calderon	0.10
7.	Jose Canseco	0.75
8.	Joe Carter	0.10

1987 Topps Steve Sax coin

No.	Player	Value
9.	Jack Clark	0.10
10.	Alvin Davis	0.10
11.	Dwight Evans	0.10
12.	Tony Fernandez	0.10
13.	Gary Gaetti	0.10
14.	Mike Greenwell	0.35
15.	Charlie Hough	0.10
16.	Wally Joyner	0.25
17.	Jimmy Key	0.10
18.	Mark Langston	0.10
19.	Don Mattingly	0.95
20.	Paul Molitor	0.10
21.	Jack Morris	0.10
22.	Eddie Murray	0.15
23.	Kirby Puckett	0.20
24.	Cal Ripken	0.20
25.	Bret Saberhagen	0.10
26.	Ruben Sierra	0.10
27.	Cory Snyder	0.10
28.	Terry Steinbach	0.10
29.	Danny Tartabull	0.10
30.	Alan Trammell	0.10
31.	Devon White	0.10
32.	Robin Yount	0.10
33.	Andre Dawson	0.10
34.	Steve Bedrosian	0.10
35.	Benito Santiago	0.10
36.	Tony Gwynn	0.20
37.	Bobby Bonilia	0.10
38.	Will Clark	0.25
39.	Eric Davis	0.35
40.	Mike Dunne	0.10
41.	John Franco	0.10
42.	Dwight Gooden	0.35
43.	Pedro Guerrero	0.10
44.	Dion James	0.10
45.	John Kruk	0.10
46.	Jeffrey Leonard	0.10
47.	Carmelo Martinez	0.10
48.	Dale Murphy	0.25
49.	Tim Raines	0.15
50.	Nolan Ryan	0.15
51.	Juan Samuel	0.10
52.	Ryne Sandberg	0.15
53.	Mike Schmidt	0.25
54.	Mike Scott	0.10
55.	Ozzie Smith	0.10
56.	Darryl Strawberry	0.35
57.	Rick Sutcliffe	0.10
58.	Fernando Valenzuela	0.10
59.	Tim Wallach	0.10
60.	Todd Worrell	0.10

ENVIROMINT

Player	Value
Bench, Johnny	30.00
Boggs, Wade	30.00
Brett, George	30.00
Brett, George 3,000 hits	30.00
Canseco, Jose	30.00
Carlton, Steve	30.00
Clark, Will	30.00
Clark, Will (error)	190.00
Clemens, Roger	30.00
Clemente, Roberto	30.00
Cobb, Ty	30.00
Davis, Mark	30.00
Dawson, Andre	30.00
Eckersley, Dennis Cy Young	30.00
Fisk, Carlton	30.00
Garvey, Steve	30.00
Gehrig, Lou	30.00
Gibson, Kirk	30.00
Gooden, Dwight	30.00
Griffey, Jr/Sr. Mariners/Reds.	85.00
Griffey, Jr/Sr. Mariners	30.00
Gwynn, Tony	30.00
Henderson, Rickey	30.00
Hershiser, Orel	30.00
Jackson, Bo Raiders/Royals	50.00
Jackson, Bo White Sox	30.00
Justice, Dave	30.00
Killebrew, Harmon	30.00
Maddux, Greg Cy Young	30.00
Mattingly, Don	30.00
McGwire, Mark	30.00
McGwire, Mark Home Run	30.00
Mitchell, Kevin	30.00
Molitor, Paul	30.00
Olson, Greg	30.00
Puckett, Kirby	30.00
Ripken Jr., Cal MVP	30.00
Robinson, Brooks	30.00
Rookies - McGwire, Canseco	30.00
Rose, Pete	80.00
Ryan, Nolan 300th victory	100.00
Ryan, Nolan 5000th strikeout	125.00
Ryan, Nolan 7th no hitter	75.00
Sabo, Chris	30.00
Sandberg, Ryne	30.00
Seaver, Tom	750.00
Ruth, Babe	30.00
Saberhagen, Bret	30.00
Schmidt, Mike	30.00
Strawberry, Darryl w/ Mets	65.00
Strawberry, Darryl w/Dodgers	30.00
Viola, Frank	30.00
Walton, Jerome	30.00
Williams, Billy	30.00
Yount, Robin	30.00
Yount, Robin 3,000 hits	30.00
Yount, Robin MVP	30.00

Item	Value
Blue Jays 1991 all-star game	30.00
Chicago Cubs	40.00
Colorado Rockies	30.00
Commiskey Park old/new	30.00
Commmiskey Park 75th anniv.	125.00
Dodgers 100th anniv.	30.00
Florida Marlins	30.00
New York Giants	35.00
Oakland A's 25th anniv.	30.00
Wrigley Field 75th anniv.	30.00
Wrigley Field 1st night game	43.00
Team Commemoratives	30.00

Item	Value
1955 Brooklyn Dodgers	35.00
1986 New York Mets World Series Champs	30.00
1987 Minnesota Twins World Series Champs	45.00
1987 Minnesota Twins AL Champs	35.00

Enviromint Cal Ripken Jr. coin

Item	Value
1987 St. Louis Cardinals NL Champs	30.00
1987 Minnesota Twins AL West Champs	35.00
1987 San Francisco Giants NL West Champs	35.00
1987 Detroit Tigers AL East Champs	35.00
1987 St Louis Cardinals NL East Champs	35.00
1987 All-Star Game	30.00
All-Star Game, Commisioners	30.00
1988 Los Angeles Dodgers NL Champs	30.00
1988 Los Angeles Dodgers World Series Champs	30.00
1988 Oakland A's AL West Champs	30.00
1988 Boston Red Sox AL East Champs	35.00
1988 Oakland A's AL West Champs	45.00
1988 New York Mets NL East Champs	35.00
1988 Los Angeles Dodgers NL West Champs	35.00
1988 All-Star Game	75.00
All-Star Game, Commisioners	30.00
1989 Oakland A's World Series Champs	35.00
1989 AL Champs	30.00
1989 NL Champs	30.00
1989 San Francisco Giants NL West Champs	35.00
1989 Oakland A's AL West Champs	35.00
1989 Chicago Cubs NL East Champs	30.00
1989 Toronto Blue Jays AL East Champs	75.00
1989 All-Star Game	45.00
All-Star Game, Commisioners	45.00
1990 Cincinnati Reds NL Champs	30.00
1990 Oakland A's AL Champs	30.00
1990 Boston Red Sox AL East Champs	50.00
1990 Oakland A's AL West Champs	75.00
1990 Pittsburgh Pirates NL East Champs	55.00

1990 Cincinnati Reds NL West Champs	50.00
1990 Cincinnati Reds World Series Champs	30.00
1990 All-Star Game	30.00
All-Star Game, Commisioners	30.00
1991 Minnesota Twins AL Champs	30.00
1991 Minnesota Twins World Series Champs	30.00
1991 Atlanta Braves NL Champs	50.00
1991 Toronto Blue Jays AL East Champs	75.00
1991 Minnesota Twins AL West Champs	30.00
1991 Pitsburgh Pirates NL East Champs	30.00
1991 Atlanta Braves NL West Champs	30.00
1992 Oakland A's NL West Champs	30.00
1992 Toronto Blue Jays World Champs	30.00
1992 Atlanta Braves NL West Champs	30.00
1992 Atlanta Braves NL Champs	30.00
1992 Pittsburgh Pirates NL East Champs	30.00
1992 World Series Set	250.00

BASKETBALL COINS

ENVIROMINT

NBA

Coleman, Derrick ROY	30.00
Johnson, Larry ROY	30.00
Johnson, Magic Assists	30.00
Jordan, Michael 1992 MVP	30.00
Les, Jim 3pt FG percentage	30.00
Miller, Reggie free throw	30.00
Olajuwon, Hakeem blocks	30.00
Robinson, David rebounding	30.00
Stockton, John assists	30.00
Williams, Buck FG percentage	30.00
Chicago Bulls 25th anniv.	30.00
Denver Nuggets 25th anniv.	30.00
Indiana Pacers 25th anniv.	30.00
Seattle Supersonics 25th anniv.	30.00
1991 NBA Champions Bulls	30.00
1991 Central Champs- Bulls	30.00
1991 Eastern Conf.- Bulls	30.00
1992 NBA Champions Bulls	30.00
1992 NBA All-Star Game	30.00
1992 USA Basketball sets	515.00
Set #1	
Bird, Larry	30.00
Ewing, Patrick	30.00
Jordan, Michael	30.00
Laettner, Christian	30.00
Pippen, Scottie	30.00
Robinson, David	30.00
Set #2	
Barkley, Charles	30.00
Drexler, Clyde	30.00
Johnson, Magic	30.00
Malone, Karl	30.00
Mullin, Chris	30.00
Stockton, John	30.00

NCAA

1989 Illinois Final Four	50.00
1989 Michigan Final Four	30.00
1990 Georgia Tech Champs	30.00
1990 Iowa Hawkeyes	50.00
1990 UNLV NCAA Champs	30.00
1990 Duke Final Four	30.00
1991 Kansas Final Four	30.00
1991 North Carolina FF	30.00
1991 UNLV FF Champs	30.00
1991 Duke FF Champs	30.00
1991 Duke NCAA Champs	30.00

FOOTBALL COINS

1963 SALADA COINS

No.	Player	Value
1.	John Unitas	100.00
2.	Lenny Moore	50.00
3.	Jim Parker	15.00
4.	Gino Marchetti	20.00
5.	Dick Szymanski	10.00
6.	Alex Sandusky	10.00
7.	Raymond Berry	35.00
8.	Jimmy Orr	12.00
9.	Ordell Braase	12.00
10.	Bill Pellington	12.00
11.	Bob Boyd	12.00
12.	Paul Hornung	20.00
13.	Jim Taylor	15.00
14.	Henry Jordan	5.00
15.	Dan Currie	5.00
16.	Bill Forester	5.00
17.	Dave Hanner	5.00
18.	Bart Starr	20.00
19.	Max McGee	5.00
20.	Jerry Kramer	6.00
21.	Forrest Gregg	8.00
22.	Jim Ringo	8.00
23.	Billy Kilmer	20.00
24.	Charley Krueger	11.00
25.	Bob St. Clair	20.00
26.	Abe Woodson	11.00
27.	Jimmy Johnson	11.00
28.	Matt Hazeltine	11.00
29.	Bruce Bosley	11.00
30.	Dan Conner	11.00
31.	John Brodie	35.00
32.	J.D. Smith.	11.00
33.	Monte Stickles	11.00
34.	Johnny Morris	5.00
35.	Stan Jones	4.00
36.	J.C. Caroline	4.00
37.	Richie Petitbon	4.00
38.	Joe Fortunato	4.00
39.	Larry Morris	4.00
40.	Doug Atkins	7.00
41.	Billy Wade	5.00
42.	Rick Casares	4.00
43.	Willie Galimore	4.00
44.	Angelo Coia	4.00
45.	Riley Matson	30.00
46.	Carroll Dale	11.00
47.	Eddie Meador	11.00
48.	Jon Arnett	11.00
49.	Joe Marconi	11.00
50.	John Lovetere	11.00
51.	Red Phillips	11.00
52.	Zeke Bratkowski	15.00
53.	Dick Bass	15.00
54.	Les Richter	11.00
55.	Art Hunter	4.00
56.	Jimmy Brown	50.00
57.	Mike McCormack	8.00
58.	Bob Gain	4.00
59.	Paul Wiggin	4.00
60.	Jim Houston	4.00
61.	Ray Renfro	4.00
62.	Galen Fiss	4.00
63.	J.R. Smith	4.00
64.	John Morrow	4.00
65.	Gene Hickerson	4.00
66.	Jim Ninowski	4.00
67.	Tom Tracy	11.00
68.	Buddy Dial	11.00
69.	Mike Sandusky	11.00
70.	Lou Michaels	11.00
71.	Preston Carpenter	11.00
72.	John Reger	11.00
73.	John Henry Johnson	30.00
74.	Gene Lipscomb	20.00
75.	Mike Henry	15.00
76.	George Tarasovic	11.00
77.	Bobby Layne	35.00
78.	Harley Sewell	4.00
79.	Darris McCord	4.00
80.	Yale Lary	8.00
81.	Jim Gibbons	4.00
82.	Gail Cogdill	4.00
83.	Nick Pietrosante	5.00
84.	Alex Karras	10.00
85.	Dick Lane	8.00

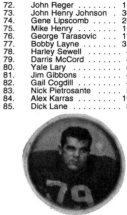

1963 Salada Lou Michaels coin

No.	Player	Value
86.	Joe Schmidt	8.00
87.	John Gordy	4.00
88.	Milt Plum	5.00
89.	Andy Stynchula	11.00
90.	Bob Toneff	11.00
91.	Bill Anderson	11.00
92.	Sam Horner	11.00
93.	Norm Snead	15.00
94.	Bobby Mitchell	25.00
95.	Billy Barnes	11.00
96.	Rod Breedlove	11.00
97.	Fred Hageman	11.00
98.	Vince Promuto	11.00
99.	Joe Rutgens	11.00
100.	Maxie Baughan	4.00
101.	Pete Retzlaff	4.00
102.	Tom Brookshier	5.00
103.	Sonny Jurgensen	11.00
104.	Ed Khayat	4.00
105.	Chuck Bednarik	10.00
106.	Tommy McDonald	5.00
107.	Bobby Walston	4.00
108.	Ted Dean	4.00
109.	Clarence Peaks	4.00
110.	Jimmy Carr	4.00
111.	Sam Huff	10.00
112.	Erich Barnes	4.00
113.	Del Shofner	5.00
114.	Bob Gaiters	4.00
115.	Alex Webster	5.00
116.	Dick Modzelewski	4.00
117.	Jim Katcavage	4.00
118.	Roosevelt Brown	8.00
119.	Y.A. Tittle	20.00
120.	Andy Robustelli	8.00
121.	Dick Lynch	4.00
122.	Don Webb	4.00
123.	Larry Eisenhauer	4.00
124.	Babe Parilli	5.00
125.	Charles Long	4.00
126.	Billy Lott	4.00
127.	Harry Jacobs	4.00
128.	Bob Dee	4.00
129.	Ron Burton	4.00
130.	Jim Colclough	2.00
131.	Gino Cappelletti	5.00
132.	Tommy Addison	4.00
133.	Larry Grantham	4.00
134.	Dick Christy	4.00
135.	Bill Mathis	4.00
136.	Butch Songin	4.00
137.	Dainard Paulson	4.00
138.	Roger Ellis	4.00
139.	Mike Hudock	4.00
140.	Don Maynard	15.00

No.	Player	Value
141.	Al Dorow	4.00
142.	Jack Klotz	4.00
143.	Lee Riley	4.00
144.	Bill Atkins	4.00
145.	Art Baker	4.00
146.	Stew Barber	4.00
147.	Glen Bass	4.00
148.	Al Bemiller	4.00
149.	Richie Lucas	4.00
150.	Archie Matsos	4.00
151.	Warren Rabb	4.00
152.	Ken Rice	4.00
153.	Billy Shaw	4.00
154.	Lavern Torczon	4.00

1983 7-11 COINS

No.	Player	Value
1.	Franco Harris	1.25
2.	Dan Fouts	1.25
3.	Lee Roy Selmon	0.85
4.	Nolan Cromwell	0.60
5.	Marcus Allen	1.50
6.	Joe Montana	3.00
7.	Kellen Winslow	0.60
8.	Hugh Green	0.60
9.	Ted Hendricks	0.90
10.	Danny White	0.85
11.	Wes Chandler	0.60
12.	Jimmie Giles	0.60
13.	Jack Youngblood	0.85
14.	Lester Hayes	0.60
15.	Vince Ferragamo	0.85

1984 7-11 COINS

No.	Player	Value
E1.	Franco Harris	1.00
E2.	Lawrence Taylor	1.25
E3.	Mark Gastineau	0.75
E4.	Lee Roy Selmon	0.75
E5 .	Ken Anderson	0.75
E6.	Walter Payton	2.00
E7.	Ken Stabler	0.75
E8.	Marcus Allen	1.25
E9.	Fred Smerlas	0.50
E10.	Ozzie Newsome	0.75
E11.	Steve Bartkowski	0.50
E12.	Tony Dorsett	1.25
E13.	John Riggins	0.75
E14.	Billy Sims	0.75
E15.	Dan Marino	1.50
E16.	Tony Collins	0.50
E17.	Curtis Dickey	0.50
E18.	Ron Jaworski	0.60
E19.	William Andrews	0.50
E20.	Joe Theismann	1.00
W1.	Franco Harris	1.00
W2.	Joe Montana	2.50
W3.	Matt Blair	0.50
W4.	Warren Moon	1.50
W5.	Marcus Allen	1.25
W6.	John Riggins	0.75
W7.	Walter Payton	2.00
W8.	Vince Ferragamo	0.60
W9.	Billy Sims	0.75
W10.	Ken Anderson	0.75
W11.	Lynn Dickey	0.50
W12.	Tony Dorsett	1.25
W13.	Bill Kenney	0.50
W14.	Ottis Anderson	0.75
W15.	Dan Fouts	1.00
W16.	Eric Dickerson	2.50
W17.	John Elway	1.50
W18.	Ozzie Newsome	0.75
W19.	Curt Warner	0.75
W20.	Joe Theismann	1.00

1992 NOTRE DAME HEISMAN SILVER MEDALLION

No.	Player	Value
1.	Angelo Bertelli	50.00
2.	John Lujack	50.00
3.	Leon Hart	50.00
4.	John Lattner	50.00
5.	Paul Hornung	50.00
6.	John Huarte	50.00
7.	Tim Brown	50.00

1992 Enviromint

Player	Value
Carrier, Mark	30.00
Ditka, Mike	30.00
Elway, John	30.00
Esiason, Boomer	30.00
Jackson, Bo	30.00
Hampton, Dan	30.00
Kelly, Jim	30.00
Kosar, Bernie	30.00
Landry, Tom	30.00
Lombardi, Vince	30.00
Marino, Dan	30.00
Monk, Art	30.00

1984 7-11 Franco Harris coin

Player	Value
Montana, Joe	30.00
Moon, Warren	30.00
Payton, Walter	80.00
Sanders, Barry	30.00
Taylor, Lawrence	30.00

Coin	Value
1985 Chicago Bears NFC Champs	35.00
1985 Chicago Bears Superbowl XX	125.00
1985 New England Patriots AFC Champs	45.00
1986 Cleveland Browns AFC Central Champs	50.00
1986 Denver Broncos AFC Champs	40.00
1986 New York Giants NFC Champs	45.00
1986 New York Giants Superbowl XXI	30.00
1987 Seattle Seahawks AFC Playoffs	250.00
1987 New Orleans Saints NFC Playoffs	55.00
1987 Minnesota Vikings NFC Playoffs	40.00
1987 Denver Broncos AFC West Champs	100.00
1987 Cleveland Browns AFC Central Champs	75.00
1987 San Francisco 49er's NFC West Champs	55.00
1987 Washington Redskins NFC East Champs	45.00
1987 Washington Redskins Superbowl XXII	30.00
1987 Denver Broncos AFC Champs	45.00
1988 San Francisco 49er's NFC West Champs	150.00
1988 San Francisco 49er's SuperBowl XXIII	30.00
1988 Chicago Bears NFC Central Champs	75.00
1988 Philadelphia Eagles NFC East Champs	100.00
1988 Seattle Seahawks AFC West Champs	65.00
1988 Buffalo Bills AFC East Champs	350.00
1988 Cincinnati Bengals AFC Central Champs	45.00
1988 San Francisco 49er's NFC Champs	40.00
1988 Cincinnati Bengals AFC Champs	40.00
1989 Denver Broncos AFC West Champs	30.00
1989 Buffalo Bills AFC East Champs	175.00
1989 Cleveland Browns AFC Central Champs	50.00
1989 San Francisco 49er's NFC West Champs	30.00
1989 San Francisco 49er's Superbowl XXIV	30.00
1989 New York Giants NFC East Champs	30.00
1989 Minnesota Vikings Central Div. Champs	30.00
1989 Denver Broncos AFC Champs	30.00
1989 San Francisco 49er's NFC Champs	30.00
1990 San Francisco 49er's NFC West Champs	30.00
1990 Los Angeles Raiders AFC West Champs	30.00
1990 Chicago Bears NFC Central Champs	30.00
1990 New York Giants NFC East Champs	30.00
1990 New York Giants NFC Champs	30.00
1990 New York Giants Superbowl XXV	30.00
1990 Buffalo Bills AFC East Champs	30.00
1990 Buffalo Bills AFC Champs	30.00
1991 Washington Redskins NFC Champs	30.00
1991 Washington Redskins NFC East Champs	30.00
1991 Washington Redskins SuperBowl XXVI	30.00
1991 New Orleans Saints NFC West Champs	30.00
1991 Detroit Lions NFC Central Champs	30.00
1991 Houstobn Oilers AFC Central Champs	30.00
1991 Denver Broncos AFC West Champs	30.00
1991 Buffalo Bills AFC East Champs	30.00
1991 Buffalo Bills AFC Champs	30.00

Coin	Value
Chicago Bears 75th anniv	35.00
Wash. Redskins 50th anniv	250.00
Dallas Cowboys 25th anniv	30.00
Detroit Lions 50th anniv	30.00
New Orleans Saints 25th anniv	30.00
Dallas Cowboys Super Bowl 1971 & 1977	45.00
Pittsburgh Steelers Super Bowl IX, X, XIII, XIV	175.00
100 Years of Pro Football	30.00

HOCKEY COINS

1961-62 SALADA COINS

No.	Player	Value
1.	Cliff Pennington	2.00
2.	Dallas Smith	2.00
3.	Andre Pronovost	5.00
4.	Charlie Burns	6.00
5.	Leo Boivin	10.00
6.	Don McKenney	2.00
7.	John Bucyk	10.00
8.	Murray Oliver	2.00
9.	Zelio Toppazzini	2.00
10.	Doug Mohns	2.00
11.	Don Head	2.00
12.	Bob Armstrong	2.00
13.	Pat Stapleton	2.00
14.	Orland Kurtenbach	2.00
15.	Dick Meissner	2.00
16.	Ted Green	2.00
17.	Tom Williams	2.00
18.	Aut Erickson	2.00
19.	Phil Watson	2.00
20.	Ed Chadwick	2.00
21.	Wayne Hillman	2.00
22.	Stan Mikita	20.00
23.	Eric Nesterenko	2.00
24.	Reggie Fleming	2.00
25.	Bobby Hull	40.00
26.	Elmer Vasko	2.00
27.	Pierre Pilote	12.00
28.	Chico Maki	2.00
29.	Glenn Hall	10.00
30.	Murray Balfour	2.00
31.	Bronco Horvath	2.00
32.	Ken Wharram	2.00
33.	Ab McDonald	2.00
34.	Billy Hay	2.00
35.	Dollard St. Laurent	2.00
36.	Ron Murphy	2.00
37.	Bob Turner	2.00
38.	Gerry Melnyk	2.00
39.	Jack Evans	2.00
40.	Rudy Pilous	2.00
41.	Johnny Bower	12.00
42.	Allan Stanley	10.00
43.	Frank Mahovlich	20.00
44.	Tim Horton	12.00
45.	Carl Brewer	2.00
46.	Bob Pulford	10.00
47.	Bob Nevin	2.00
48.	Eddie Shack	2.00
49.	Red Kelly	8.00
50.	Bob Baun	2.00
51.	George Armstrong	8.00
52.	Bert Olmstead	8.00
53.	Dick Duff	2.00
54.	Billy Harris	2.00
55.	Larry Keenan	2.00
56.	John MacMillan	2.00
57.	Punch Imlach	2.00
58.	Dave Keon	15.00
59.	Larry Hillman	2.00
60.	Al Arbour	10.00
61.	Sid Abel	20.00
62.	Warren Godfrey	2.00
63.	Vic Stasiuk	2.00
64.	Leo Labine	2.00
65.	Howie Glover	2.00
66.	Gordie Howe	50.00
67.	Val Fonteyne	2.00
68.	Marcel Pronovost	20.00
69.	Parker MacDonald	2.00
70.	Alex Delvecchio	15.00
71.	Ed Litzenberger	2.00
72.	Tom Johnson	8.00
73.	Bruce MacGregor	2.00
74.	Howie Young	2.00
75.	Peter Goegan	2.00
76.	Norm Ullman	15.00
77.	Terry Sawchuk	12.00
78.	Gerry Odrowski	2.00
79.	Bill Gadsby	12.00
80.	Hank Bassen	2.00
81.	Doug Harvey	10.00
82.	Earl Ingarfield	2.00
83.	Pat Hannigan	2.00
84.	Dean Prentice	4.00
85.	Gump Worsley	20.00
86.	Irv Spencer	2.00
87.	Camille Henry	2.00
88.	Andy Bathgate	15.00
89.	Harry Howell	12.00
90.	Andy Hebenton	4.00
91.	Red Sullivan	2.00
92.	Ted Hampson	2.00
93.	Jean Gendron	2.00
94.	Al Langlois	2.00
95.	Larry Cahan	2.00
96.	Bob Cunningham	2.00
97.	Vic Hadfield	4.00
98.	Jean Ratelle	10.00
99.	Ken Schinkel	2.00
100.	Johnny Wilson	2.00
101.	Toe Blake	18.00
102.	Jean Beliveau	25.00
103.	Don Marshall	2.00
104.	Boom Boom Geoffrion	30.00
105.	Claude Provost	6.00
106.	Al Johnson	2.00
107.	Dickie Moore	12.00
108.	Bill Hicke	2.00
109.	Jean Talbot	2.00
110.	Henri Richard	25.00
111.	Louie Fontinanto	2.00
112.	Gilles Tremblay	2.00
113.	Jacques Plante	25.00
114.	Ralph Backstrom	2.00
115.	Marcel Bonin	2.00
116.	Phil Goyette	2.00
117.	Bobby Rousseau	2.00
118.	J.C. Tremblay	2.00
119.	Al MacNeil	2.00
120.	Jean Gauthier	2.00

1992 ENVIROMINT

Belfour, Ed Vezina & Calder	30.00
Bourque, Ray Norris Trophy	30.00
Bure, Pavel Calder Trophy	30.00
Carbonneau, Guy	30.00
Coffey, Paul Norris Trophy	30.00
Fuhr, Grant Vezina Trophy	30.00
Gretzky, Wayne	30.00

1992 Enviromint Brett Hull coin

Hull, Brett	30.00
Hull, Brett/Bobby	30.00
Jagr, Jaromir	30.00
LaFontaine, Pat	30.00
Larmer, Steve	30.00
Lemieux, Mario '91 Smythe	30.00
Lemieux, Mario '92 Smythe	30.00
MacInnis, Al Norris Trophy	30.00
Messier, Mark	30.00
Robitaille, Luc	30.00
Roy, Patrick Vezina	30.00
Sakic, Joe	30.00
Yzerman, Steve	30.00

Canada Cup

United States	30.00
Canada	50.00
Finland	50.00
Sweden	50.00
U.S.S.R	100.00
Czechoslovakia	50.00

1988 Boston Bruins Wales Division	30.00
1988 Detroit Red Wings Norris Division	30.00
1988 Edmonton Oilers Stanley Cup	30.00
1988 New Jersey Devils Patrick Division	75.00
1989 Calgary Flames Campbell Conference	75.00
1989 Calgary Flames Stanley Cup	75.00
1989 Montreal Canadiens Wales Conference	75.00
1990 Calgary Flames Stanley Cup	30.00
1990 Chicago Blackhawks Norris Division	30.00
1990 Edmonton Oilers Stanley Cup	30.00
1990 New York Rangers Patrick Division	30.00
1991 Boston Bruins Adams Divison Champs	30.00
1991 Chicago Blackhawks Norris Division Champs	30.00
1991 Los Angeles Kings Smythe Div. Champs	30.00
1991 Minnesota North Stars Norris Division Champs	30.00
1991 Pittsburgh Penguins Patrick Division Champs	30.00
1991 Pittsburgh Penguins Wales Conference	30.00
1991 Pittsburgh Penguins Stanley Cup	30.00
1992 Chicago Blackhawks Campbell Conference	30.00
1990 Chicago Blackhawks 42nd All-Star game	30.00
1992 Detroit Redwings Norris Division	30.00
1992 Los Angeles Kings 25th anniv.	30.00
1992 Montreal Canadiens Adams Division	30.00
1992 Montreal Canadiens 44th All-Star game	30.00
1992 New York Rangers Patrick Division	30.00
1992 Ottawa Senators	50.00
1991 Philadelphia Flyers 41st All-Star game	30.00
1992 Pittsburgh Penguins 25th anniversary	30.00
1992 Pittsburgh Penguins Wales Conference	30.00
1992 Pittsburgh Penguins Stanley Cup Champs	30.00
1992 San Jose Inaugural	50.00
1992 St Louis Blues 25th anniversary	30.00
1992 Tampa Bay Lightning	30.00
1992 Vancouver Canucks Smythe Division	30.00
1993 All 24 teams each	30.00
1993 All-Star game collector card	90.00
1993 Clarence Campbell Conference collector card	90.00
1993 Prince of Wales Conference collector card	90.00

COMIC BOOKS

A-1 COMICS
Magazine Enterprises
1944

89 BP,Home Run,Stan Musial . 120.00

REAL SPORTS COMICS
Hillman Periodicals
Oct.-Nov. 1948

1 Stanley Ketchel,Boxing(c) .. 175.00

Becomes:

ALL SPORTS

2 Football(c) 125.00
3 Basketball(c) 100.00

Becomes:

ALL-TIME SPORTS

4 Auto Racing(c) 100.00
5 Baseball(c) 100.00
6 Horse Racing(c) 90.00
7 Baseball(c) 90.00

ALL AMERICAN SPORTS
Charlton
October, 1967

1 .... 10.00

ALL-PRO SPORTS
All Pro Sports
(Black & White)

1 Unauthorized Bio-Bo Jackson
Baseball (c) 2.50
1b Football (c) 2.50
2 Unauthorized Bio-Joe Montana . 2.50

All-Star Story of the Dodgers #1,
© Stadium Comics

ALL STAR STORY OF THE DODGERS
Stadium Comics
April, 1979

1 F:Koufax, Robinson,
Campanella 5.00

AMAZING WILLIE MAYS
Famous Funnies
Sept. 1954

1 Willie Mays(c) 400.00

BABE
"The Amazon of the Ozarks"
Prize/Headline Feature
June-July 1948

1 BRo, ... 50.00
2 BRo,Baseball(c) 30.00
3 BRo, ... 25.00
4 BRo,Football(c) 20.00
5 BRo 20.00
6 BRo 20.00
7 BRo,Boxing(c) 20.00
8 BRo 20.00
9 BRo 20.00

BABE RUTH SPORTS COMICS
Harvey Publications
April, 1949

1 BP,Basketball(c) 300.00
2 BP,Baseball(c) 200.00
3 BP,Joe DiMaggio(c) 175.00
4 BP,Bob Feller(c) 150.00
5 BP,Bob Chappuis 125.00
6 BP,George Mikan 150.00
7 BP 125.00
8 BP,Yogi Berra(c) 125.00
9 BP, Stan Musial(c) 135.00
10 .... 100.00
11, February 1951 .... 100.00

BALTIMORE COLTS
American Visuals Corp.
1950 Giveaway

N# Will Eisner(c) 300.00

BASEBALL CLASSICS
Personality

1 Willie Mays 2.95
1a w/trading cards 5.95
2 Lou Gehrig 2.95
2a w/trading cards 5.95

BASEBALL COMICS
Will Eisner Productions
Spring, 1949

1 A:Rube Rooky 500.00

BASEBALL COMICS
Personality

1 Frank Thomas 2.95
1a w/trading cards 5.95
2 Rickey Henderson 2.95
2a w/trading cards 5.95
3 Nolan Ryan 2.95
3a w/trading cards 5.95
4 Cal Ripken, Jr. 2.95
4a w/trading cards 5.95

BASEBALL GREATS
Dark Horse

1 Jimmy Piersall story 2.95

BASEBALL HEROS
Fawcett Publications
1952

N# Babe Ruth(c), Hall
of Fame biographies 500.00

BASEBALL LEGENDS
Revolutionary

1 Babe Ruth 2.50
2 Ty Cobb 2.50
3 Ted Williams 2.50
4 Mickey Mantle 2.50
5 Joe DiMaggio 2.50
6 Jackie Robinson 2.50
7 Sandy Koufax 2.50
8 Willie Mays 2.50
9 Honus Wagner 2.50
10 Roberto Clemente 2.50
11 Yogi Berra 2.50
12 .... 2.50
13 Hank Aaron 2.95
14 Carl Yastremski 2.95
15 Satchel Paige 2.95
16 Johnny Bench 2.95
17 Shoeless Joe Jackson &
the Black Sox Scandal 2.95
18 Lew Gehrig 2.95

BASEBALL SLUGGERS
Personality Comics

1 Ken Griffey, Jr. 2.95
1a Ltd. Edition 5.95
2 Dave Justice 2.95
2a Ltd. Edition 5.95
3 Frank Thomas 2.95
3a Ltd. Edition 5.95
4 Don Mattingly 2.95
4a Ltd. Edition 5.95

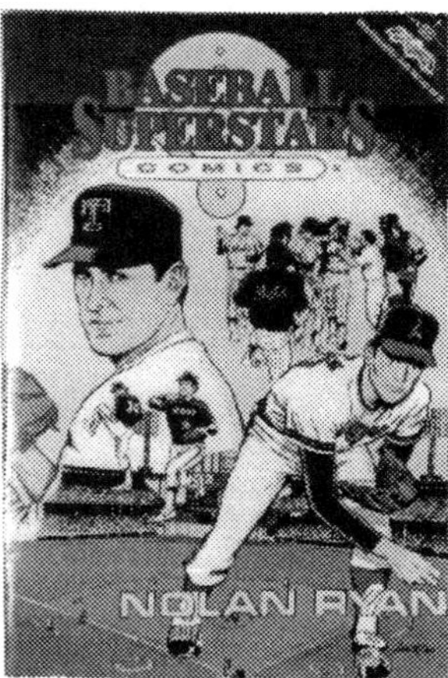

Baseball Superstars #1,
© Revolutionary

BASEBALL SUPERSTARS
Revolutionary

1 Nolan Ryan (B&W comic) 2.50
2 Bo Jackson 2.50
3 Ken Griffey, Jr. 2.50
4 Pete Rose 2.50
5 Rickey Henderson 2.50
6 Jose Canseco 2.50
7 Cal Ripken, Jr. 2.50
8 Carlton Fisk 2.50
9 George Brett 2.50
10 Darryl Strawberry 2.50
11 Frank Thomas 2.50

12 Ryne Sandberg 2.50
13 Kirby Puckett 2.50
14 . . . . 2.50
15 Roger Clemens 2.95
16 Mark McGwire 2.95
17 Steve Avery & Tom Glavine . . 2.95
18 Dennis Eckersley 2.95
19 Dave Winfield 2.95
20 Jim Abbott 2.95
Ann.#1 Nolan Ryan 2.50

BASEBALL THRILLS
ed. Bob Feller
Ziff-Davis Publ. Co.
Summer 1951

10 Bob Feller Predicts Pennant Winners 275.00
2 BP, Yogi Berra story 200.00
3 EK, Joe DiMaggio story, Summer 1952 . . . . 250.00

BASEBALL THRILLS 3-D
3-D Zone
May, 1990

1 Ty Cobb,Ted Williams 2.95

BEST PITCHERS
Personality

1 Nolan Ryan 2.95
1a w/cards 5.95
2 Dwight Gooden 2.95
2a w/cards 5.95
3 Roger Clemens 2.95
3a w/cards 5.95

Bill Stern's Sports Book #Vol 2, #2
© Approved Comics

BILL STERN'S SPORTS BOOK
Approved Comics
Spring-Summer, 1951

1 Ewell Blackwell 100.00
2 . . . . 75.00
Vol 2 #2 . . . . 85.00

BLUE BOLT
Funnies, Inc./Novelty Press/ Premium Service Co
June, 1940

5-2 Boxing cover 20.00
6-5 Soccer cover 22.00
6-9 Iceboat cover 20.00
7-3 Track & Field cover 20.00
8-1 Baseball cover 25.00
8-11 Basketball cover 20.00
9-1 AMc,Baseball cover 22.00
9-6 LbC(c),Football cover 22.00
9-8 Hockey cover 25.00
10-1 Baseball cover,3-D effect . . 25.00

BLUE DEVIL
DC Comics
June, 1984

26 Special Baseball issue 2.00

BO JACKSON Vs. MICHAEL JORDAN
Personality

1 . . . . 2.95
1a Deluxe 6.95
2 . . . . 2.95
2a Deluxe 6.95

BOXING'S BEST COMICS

1 George Foreman 1.95

BRAVE AND THE BOLD
DC Comics
August-September, 1955

45 CI,F:Strange Sports 30.00
46 CI,F:Strange Sports 30.00
47 CI,F:Strange Sports 30.00
48 CI,F:Strange Sports 30.00
49 CI,F:Strange Sports 30.00

BROOKS ROBINSON
Magnum
May, 1992

1 photo(c), JSt 1.75

CALLING ALL BOYS
Parents Magazine Institute
January, 1946

1 Skiing 40.00
5 Fishing 20.00
6 Swimming 20.00
7 Baseball 22.00
9 The Miracle Quarterback . . . 20.00
10 Gary Cooper cover 25.00
12 Baseball,Bob Hope(c) 35.00
14 Football,J.Edgar Hoover(c) . . 25.00

CATHOLIC COMICS
Catholic Publications
June, 1946

5 Football cover 50.00
7 Rose Bowl Game 65.00
8 Basketball cover 50.00

CELEBRITY
Personality

1 Joe DiMaggio 2.95
1a Deluxe 6.95
1 Hank Aaron 2.95
1 Magic Johnson w/cards 5.95
1 Mickey Mantle 2.95
1a w/trading Cards 5.95
1 Nolan Ryan, Living Legend . . . 2.95
2 Nolan Ryan, Living Legend . . . 5.95
1 Sandy Koufax (B&W) 2.95
1a Deluxe 5.95
1 Shaquille O'Neal, sgn 5.00

CHALLENGER, THE
Interfaith Publications
1945

4 JKa,BF, boxing(c) 125.00

CHARLTON SPORT LIBRARY
Charlton
Winter 1969

1 Professional Football 20.00

COLORADO UNIVERSITY
Amazing Sports

1 F:Colorado University football team with four sports cards . . . 4.00

COMICS REVUE
St. John Publ. Co.
June 1947

3 Iron Vic, Baseball cover 35.00

CROWN COMICS
Golfing/McCombs Publ.
Winter 1944

7 JKa,AF,MB(c),Race Car(c) . 150.00

DAREDEVIL COMICS
Lev Gleason Publications
July, 1941

25 CBi(c), baseball cover 225.00
52 CBi(c),Football cover 65.00
58 Football cover 65.00

DC Special #7, © DC Comics

DC SPECIAL
October-December, 1968
[All reprint]

7 Strangest Sports Stories 5.00
13 F:Strange Sports 5.00

DC SUPERSTARS

10 DD,FMc,F:Superhero Baseball Special,A:Joker 5.50

DENVER BRONCOS
Amazing Sports

1 F:John Elway & the Drive . . . ±15.00
1a 2nd printing . . . . ±8.00

DICK COLE
Curtis Publ./ Star Publications
December-January, 1949

1 LbC,LbC(c),CS,All sports cover 85.00
4 LbC, LbC(c),Rowing cover . . 40.00
6 LbC,LbC(c), Rodeo cover . . . 35.00
8 LbC,LbC(c), Football cover . . 35.00
9 LbC,LbC(c), Basketball cover 35.00
10 Joe Louis 50.00

Becomes:

SPORTS THRILLS

11 Ted Williams & Ty Cobb . . . 200.00

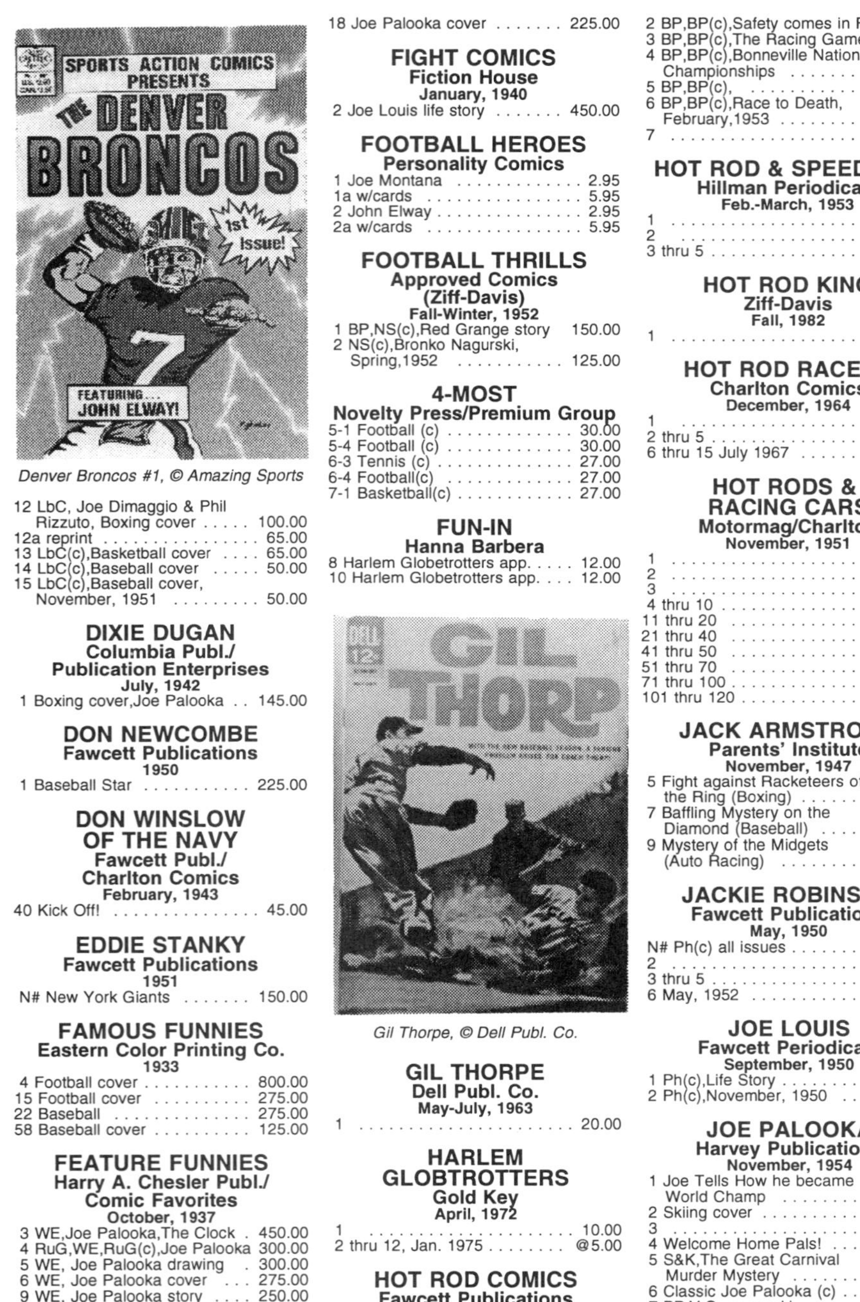

SPORTS ACTION COMICS
PRESENTS
THE DENVER
BRONCOS
1st Issue!
FEATURING...
JOHN ELWAY!
GIL
THORP

Denver Broncos #1, © Amazing Sports

12 LbC, Joe Dimaggio & Phil Rizzuto, Boxing cover 100.00
12a reprint 65.00
13 LbC(c),Basketball cover 65.00
14 LbC(c),Baseball cover 50.00
15 LbC(c),Baseball cover, November, 1951 . . . . 50.00

DIXIE DUGAN
Columbia Publ./ Publication Enterprises
July, 1942

1 Boxing cover,Joe Palooka . . 145.00

DON NEWCOMBE
Fawcett Publications
1950

1 Baseball Star 225.00

DON WINSLOW OF THE NAVY
Fawcett Publ./ Charlton Comics
February, 1943

40 Kick Off! 45.00

EDDIE STANKY
Fawcett Publications
1951

N# New York Giants 150.00

FAMOUS FUNNIES
Eastern Color Printing Co.
1933

4 Football cover 800.00
15 Football cover 275.00
22 Baseball 275.00
58 Baseball cover 125.00

FEATURE FUNNIES
Harry A. Chesler Publ./ Comic Favorites
October, 1937

3 WE,Joe Palooka,The Clock . 450.00
4 RuG,WE,RuG(c),Joe Palooka 300.00
5 WE, Joe Palooka drawing . 300.00
6 WE, Joe Palooka cover . . . 275.00
9 WE, Joe Palooka story 250.00
12 WE, Joe Palooka(c) 250.00
13 WE,LLe, World Series(c) . . 275.00
15 WE,Joe Palooka(c) 225.00
18 Joe Palooka cover 225.00

FIGHT COMICS
Fiction House
January, 1940

2 Joe Louis life story 450.00

FOOTBALL HEROES
Personality Comics

1 Joe Montana 2.95
1a w/cards 5.95
2 John Elway 2.95
2a w/cards 5.95

FOOTBALL THRILLS
Approved Comics (Ziff-Davis)
Fall-Winter, 1952

1 BP,NS(c),Red Grange story 150.00
2 NS(c),Bronko Nagurski, Spring,1952 . . . . 125.00

4-MOST
Novelty Press/Premium Group

5-1 Football (c) 30.00
5-4 Football (c) 30.00
6-3 Tennis (c) 27.00
6-4 Football(c) 27.00
7-1 Basketball(c) 27.00

FUN-IN
Hanna Barbera

8 Harlem Globetrotters app. 12.00
10 Harlem Globetrotters app. . . . 12.00

Gil Thorpe, © Dell Publ. Co.

GIL THORPE
Dell Publ. Co.
May-July, 1963

1 . . . . 20.00

HARLEM GLOBTROTTERS
Gold Key
April, 1972

1 . . . . 10.00
2 thru 12, Jan. 1975 . . . . @5.00

HOT ROD COMICS
Fawcett Publications
February, 1952

N# BP,BP(c),F:Clint Curtis . . . 135.00
2 BP,BP(c),Safety comes in First 75.00
3 BP,BP(c),The Racing Game . 40.00
4 BP,BP(c),Bonneville National Championships 40.00
5 BP,BP(c), ... 40.00
6 BP,BP(c),Race to Death, February,1953 . . . . 40.00
7 . . . . 35.00

HOT ROD & SPEEDWAY
Hillman Periodicals
Feb.-March, 1953

1 . . . . 100.00
2 . . . . 75.00
3 thru 5 . . . . @40.00

HOT ROD KING
Ziff-Davis
Fall, 1982

1 . . . . 125.00

HOT ROD RACERS
Charlton Comics
December, 1964

1 . . . . 35.00
2 thru 5 . . . . @15.00
6 thru 15 July 1967 . . . . @10.00

HOT RODS & RACING CARS
Motormag/Charlton
November, 1951

1 . . . . 100.00
2 . . . . 60.00
3 . . . . 50.00
4 thru 10 . . . . @40.00
11 thru 20 . . . . @30.00
21 thru 40 . . . . @25.00
41 thru 50 . . . . @20.00
51 thru 70 . . . . @15.00
71 thru 100 . . . . @10.00
101 thru 120 . . . . @8.00

JACK ARMSTRONG
Parents' Institute
November, 1947

5 Fight against Racketeers of the Ring (Boxing) 50.00
7 Baffling Mystery on the Diamond (Baseball) 35.00
9 Mystery of the Midgets (Auto Racing) 35.00

JACKIE ROBINSON
Fawcett Publications
May, 1950

N# Ph(c) all issues 500.00
2 . . . . 275.00
3 thru 5 . . . . @250.00
6 May, 1952 . . . . 250.00

JOE LOUIS
Fawcett Periodicals
September, 1950

1 Ph(c),Life Story 300.00
2 Ph(c),November, 1950 . . . . 200.00

JOE PALOOKA
Harvey Publications
November, 1954

1 Joe Tells How he became World Champ 300.00
2 Skiing cover 125.00
3 . . . . 75.00
4 Welcome Home Pals! 75.00
5 S&K,The Great Carnival Murder Mystery 100.00
6 Classic Joe Palooka (c) 80.00
7 BP,V:Grumpopski 75.00
8 BP,Mystery of the Ghost Ship 50.00
9 Drooten Island Mystery 50.00

10 BP 45.00
11 . . . . 40.00
12 BP,Boxing Course 40.00
13 . . . . 35.00
14 BP,Palooka's Toughest Fight 35.00
15 BP,O:Humphrey 52.00
16 BP,A:Humphrey 40.00
17 BP,A:Humphrey 40.00
18 . . . . 40.00
19 BP,Freedom Train(c) 45.00
20 Punch Out(c) 40.00
21 . . . . 30.00
22 V:Assassin 30.00
23 Big Bathing Beauty Issue . . . 30.00
24 . . . . 30.00
25 . . . . 30.00
26 BP,Big Prize Fight Robberies 30.00
27 BP,Mystery of Bald
Eagle Cabin 30.00
28 BP,Fights out West 30.00
29 BP,Joe Busts Crime
Wide Open 30.00
30 BP,V:Hoodlums 25.00
31 BP 25.00
32 BP,Fight Palooka was sure
to Lose 25.00
33 BP,Joe finds Ann 25.00
34 BP,How to Box like a Champ 25.00
35 BP,More Adventures of Little
Max 25.00
36 BP 25.00
37 BP,Joe as a Boy 25.00
38 BP 25.00
39 BP,Original Hillbillies with
Big Leviticus 25.00
40 BP,Joe's Toughest Fight . . . 25.00
41 BP,Humphrey's Grudge Fight 25.00
42 BP 25.00
43 BP 25.00
44 BP,M:Ann Howe 30.00
45 BP 22.00
46 Champ of Champs 22.00
47 BreathtakingUnderwaterBattle 22.00
48 BP,Exciting Indian Adventure 22.00
49 BP 22.00
50 BP,Bondage(c) 22.00
51 BP 22.00
52 BP,V:Balonki 22.00
53 BP 22.00
54 V:Bad Man Trigger McGehee 22.00
55 . . . . 22.00
56 Foul Play on the High Seas . 22.00
57 Curtains for the Champ 22.00
58 V:The Man-Eating Swamp
Terror 22.00
59 The Enemy Attacks 22.00
60 Joe Fights Escaped Convict . 22.00
61 . . . . 20.00
62 S&K 30.00
63 thru 68 . . . . @20.00
69 A Package from Home 20.00
70 BP 20.00
71 . . . . 20.00
72 . . . . 20.00
73 BP 20.00
74 thru 117 . . . . @20.00
118 March, 1961 . . . . 20.00
Giant 1 Body Building 50.00
Giant 2 Fights His Way Back . . 125.00
Giant 3 Visits Lost City 50.00
Giant 4 All in Family 60.00

KING COMICS
David McKay Publications
Starring: Popeye
April, 1936

20 AR,EC,Football(c) 300.00
33 AR,EC,Skiing(c) 225.00
34 AR,Ping Pong(c) 200.00
39 AR,Baseball(c) 200.00
44 AR,Golf(c) 175.00
61 AR,B:Phantom,Baseball(c) . 150.00
156 Baseball(c) 40.00

KRAZY KOMICS
Timely
July, 1942

14 Fishing(c),fa 44.00
15 Ski-Jump(c),fa 45.00
19 Bicycle(c),fa 33.00
24 Baseball(c),fa 33.00

LARRY DOBY, BASEBALL HERO
Fawcett Publications
1950

1 Ph(c),BW 350.00

Legends of Nascar #5, © Vortex

LEGENDS OF NASCAR
Vortex

1 HT,Bill Eliott ($1.50 cover
Price) 15,000 copies . . . . . . ±37.00
1a ($2.00 cover price)
45,000 copies . . . . ±10.00
1b 3rd pr., 80,000 copies 4.00
1c hologram (c) 5.00
2 Richard Petty 4.50
2a hologram (c) error 7.00
2b hologram (c) corrected 7.00
3 Ken Schroder 3.50
3a hologram (c) 5.00
4 Bob Alison 3.00
4a hologram (c) 5.00
5 Sterling Marlin 2.50
5a hologram (c) 5.00
6 Bill Elliot 2.50
6a hologram (c) 5.00
7 Jr. Johnson 2.25
7a hologram (c) 5.00
8 . . . . 2.00
8a hologram (c) 5.00
9 Rusty Wallace 2.00
9a hologram (c) 5.00
10 . . . . 2.00
10a hologram (c) 5.00
11 . . . . 2.00
11a hologram (c) 5.00
12 . . . . 2.00
12a hologram (c) 5.00
13 . . . . 2.00
13a hologram (c) 5.00

LI'L ABNER
Harvey Publications
December, 1947

83 Baseball 60.00

MEL ALLEN SPORTS COMICS
Visual Editions
1949

1 GT 100.00
2 Lou Gehrig 75.00

Mickey Mantle #1, © Magnum Comics

MICKEY MANTLE COMICS
Magnum

1 JSt,Rise to Big Leagues 1.75

NEGRO HEROES
National Urban League
Spring, 1947

2 Jackie Robinson (c) 500.00

NEW ORLEANS SAINTS
Amazing Sports

1 Playoff season(football team) . 6.00

NOLAN RYAN Vs. WAYNE GRETZKY
Personality

1 . . . . 5.95
1a w/cards 10.00

PATCHES
Rural Home Publ./ Patches Publ.
March-April, 1945

5 LbC(c),A:Danny Kaye,Football 50.00

PERSONALITY COMICS

6 Michael Jordan 3.00

PHIL RIZZUTO
Fawcett Publications
1951

Ph(c) The Sensational Story of
The American Leagues MVP 300.00

POWER PACK
August, 1984

13 BA,BWi,Baseball issue 1.50
54 JBg,V:Mad Thinker 1.50
59 TMo,V:Ringmaster 1.50
60 TMo,V:Puppetmaster 1.50

PRIDE OF THE YANKEES
Magazine Enterprises
1949
1 N#,OW,Ph(c),The Life of Lou Gehrig 400.00

RALPH KINER HOME RUN KING
Fawcett Publications
1950
1 N#, Life Story of the Famous Pittsburgh Slugger . 275.00

REAL HEROES COMICS
Parents' Magazine Institiute
September, 1941
6 Lou Gehrig 100.00
14 Pete Gray 30.00

Real Life #49 © Visual Editions

REAL LIFE COMICS
Visual Editions/Better/ Standard/Nedor
September, 1941
24 Babe Ruth 75.00
41 Jimmy Foxx 50.00
45 Olympic Games 30.00
49 ASh(c),GeneBearden 30.00

ROY CAMPANELLA, BASEBALL HERO
Fawcett Publications
1950
N# Ph(c),Life Story of the Battling Dodgers Catcher . . 300.00

SLAM DUNK KINGS
Personality Comics
1 Michael Jordan 2.95
1a w/cards 5.95
2 David Robinson 2.95
2a w/cards 5.95
3 Patrick Ewing 2.95
3a w/cards 5.95
4 Charles Barkley 2.95
4a w/cards 5.95

SMASH HITS SPORTS COMICS
Essankay Publications
January, 1949
1 LbC,LbC(c) 100.00

SPEED SMITH THE HOT ROD KING
Ziff-Davis Publishing Co.
Spring, 1952
1 INS,Ph(c),A:Roscoe the Rascal 100.00

SPORT STARS
Marvel Comics
November, 1949
1 The Life of Knute Rockne . . 200.00
Becomes:

SPORTS ACTION
2 BP(c),The Life of George Gipp175.00
3 BEv,Hack Wilson 100.00
4 Art Houtteman 80.00
5 Nile Kinnick 80.00
6 Warren Gun 80.00
7 Jim Konstanty 80.00
8 Ralph Kiner 90.00
9 Ed "Strangler" Lewis 80.00
10 JMn,'The Yella-Belly' 80.00
11 'The Killers' 80.00
12 'Man Behind the Mask' 90.00
13 Lew Andrews 90.00
14 MWs,Ken Roper, September, 1952 . . . . 80.00

SPORTS CLASSICS
Personality Comics
1 Babe Ruth, ... 2.95
1a w/trading card 5.95
2 Mickey Mantle 2.95
2a w/trading cards 5.95
3 Ty Cobb 2.95
3a w/trading cards 5.95
4 Ted Williams 2.95
4a w/trading cards 5.95
5 Jackie Robinson 2.95
5a w/trading cards 5.95

SPORTS LEGENDS
Revolutionary
1 Joe Namath 2.50
2 Gordy Howe 2.50
3 Arthur Ashe 2.50
4 Muhammed Ali 2.50
5 O. J. Simpson 2.50
6 . . . . 2.50
7 Walter Payton 2.50
8 Wilt Chamberlain 2.50
9 Joe Lewis 2.95
10 Jimmy Connors (B&W) 2.95

SPORTS PERSONALITIES
Personality Comics
1992
1 Bo Jackson 2.95
1a Ltd. Edition 5.95
1b rep. with trading cards 5.95
2 Nolan Ryan 2.95
2a Ltd. Edition 5.95
3 Rickey Henderson 2.95
3a Ltd. Edition 5.95
4 Magic Johnson 2.95
4a Ltd. Edition 5.95
5 Joe Montana 2.95
5a Ltd. Edition 5.95
6 Lawrence Taylor 2.95
6a Ltd. Edition 5.95
7 Wayne Gretzky 2.95
7a Ltd. Edition 5.95
8 George Brett 2.95
8a Ltd. Edition 5.95
9 Mike Tyson 2.95
9a Ltd. Edition 5.95
10 Larry Bird 2.95
10a Ltd. Edition 5.95
11 Bo Jackson 2.95
11a Ltd. Edition 5.95
12 Ken Griffey, Jr. 2.95
12a w/trading cards 5.95
13 Michael Jordan 2.95
13a w/trading cards 5.95
14 Pete Rose 2.95
14a w/trading cards 5.95

SPORTS SUPERSTARS
Revolutionary
1 Michael Jordan 2.50
2 Wayne Gretzky 2.50
3 Magic Johnson 2.50
4 Joe Montana 2.50
5 Mike Tyson 2.50
6 Larry Bird 2.50
7 John Elway 2.50
8 Julius Irving 2.50
9 Barry Sanders 2.50
10 Isiah Thomas 2.75
11 . . . . 2.95
12 Dan Marino 2.95
13 Dieon Sanders 2.95
14 Patrick Ewing 2.95
15 Charles Barkley 2.95
16 Shaquille O'Neal 2.95
Ann.#1 Michael Jordon 2.95

SPORTS STARS
Parents Magazine Institute
Feb.-March 1946
1 Johnny Weissmuller 200.00
2 Baseball greats 150.00
3 and 4 . . . . @100.00

Strange Sports #1, © DC Comics

STRANGE SPORTS STORIES
DC Comics
1 . . . . 2.50
2 thru 7 . . . . 2.00

STRANGE SPORTS STORIES
Adventure
1 thru 3 (B&W) . . . . @2.50

SUPERSNIPE COMICS
Formerly: Army & Navy Comics
12 Football(c) 200.00
2-4 Baseball(c) 150.00
3-1 Ice Skating(c) 125.00
3-3 Baseball(c) 125.00
3-6 Football Hero 125.00
3-10 Plays Basketball 125.00
3-11 Is A Baseball Pitcher 125.00

4-2 Track & Field Athlete 80.00
4-4 Alpine Skiier 80.00
4-5 Becomes a Boxer 80.00
4-6 Race Car Driver 80.00
4-8 Baseball Star 80.00
4-9 Football Hero 80.00

TARGET COMICS
Funnnies Inc./Novelty Publ./ Premium Group/Curtis Circulation Co./Star Publications
February, 1940

8-5 DRi,Track(c) 30.00
8-6 DRi,DRi(c) 30.00
8-11 Boxing(c) 30.00
9-3 Golf(c) 30.00
9-5 DRi,Baseball(c) 30.00
9-9 DRi,Football(c) 30.00

THRILLING TRUE STORY OF THE BASEBALL...
Fawcett Publications
1952

Giants
N# Partial Ph(c),Famous Giants of the Past,inc Mays 450.00
Yankees
2 Yankees Ph(c),Joe DiMaggio, Yogi Berra,Mickey Mantle, Casey Stengel 500.00

TIP TOP COMICS
United Features
1930

19 HF,Football(c) 250.00

TRUE COMICS
True Comics/ Parents' Magazine Press
April, 1941

1 Marathon Run 140.00
3 Baseball Hall of Fame 125.00
4 Track & Field 75.00
5 inc. Brown Bomber 100.00
6 Baseball, World Series 75.00
7 JKa,inc. Football 75.00
15 Bob Feller 65.00
21 Car Racing 65.00
31 Red Grange 50.00
37 Baseball 40.00
38 Water Polo 40.00
39 Wrestling 35.00
44 El Senor Goofy, Baseball . . . 35.00
46 Trotting 35.00
47 Swimming 45.00
48 Track and Field 25.00
49 Baseball 25.00
50 Polo 30.00
52 Speed King 25.00
53 Baseline Booby, Bowling . . . 20.00
56 Ice Skating 20.00
58 inc. Boxing 20.00
60 Car Racing 25.00
63 Motor Boat Racing 25.00
65 inc. Baseball 20.00
66 Easy Guide to Football Formations 25.00
67 inc.Basketball 20.00
71 Story of Joe DiMaggio 150.00
73 The 26 Mile Dash-Story of the Marathon 35.00
74 A Famous Coach's Special Football Tips 30.00
75 inc. Basketball 30.00
77 Lou Boudreau 30.00
78 Stan Musial 50.00
79 Decathalon 20.00
80 inc. Football 25.00
81 Red Grange 125.00
82 Hank Luisetti,Basketball 25.00
84 inc.Baseball 25.00

SPORT COMICS
Street & Smith Publications
October, 1940

1 F:Lou Gehrig 300.00
2 F:Gene Tunney 200.00
3 F:Phil Rizzuto 200.00
4 F:Frank Leahy 200.00
Becomes:

TRUE SPORT PICTURE STORIES

5 Joe DiMaggio 250.00

True Sport #7, © Street & Smith

6 Billy Conn 100.00
7 Mel Ott 150.00
8 Lou Ambers, Pole Vault 100.00
9 Pete Reiser 100.00
10 Frankie Sinkwich 100.00
11 Marty Serfo 80.00
12 JaB(c),Jack Dempsey 75.00
2-1 JaB(c),Willie Pep 75.00
2-2 JaB(c) 75.00
2-3 JaB(c),Carl Hubbell 85.00
2-4 Advs. in Football & Battle . 100.00
2-5 Don Hutson 75.00
2-6 Dixie Walker 100.00
2-7 Stan Musial 150.00
2-8 Famous Ring Champions of All Time 100.00
2-9 List of War Year Rookies . 150.00
2-10 Connie Mack 100.00
2-11 Winning Basketball Plays . . 75.00
2-12 Eddie Gottlieb 75.00
3-1 Bill Conn 85.00
3-2 The Philadelphia Athletics . . 70.00
3-3 Leo Durocher 100.00
3-4 Rudy Dusek 75.00
3-5 Ernie Pyle 75.00
3-6 Bowling with Ned Day 70.00
3-7 Return of the Mighty (Home from War);Joe DiMaggio(c) . 250.00
3-8 Conn V:Louis 200.00
3-9 Reuben Shark 75.00
3-10 BP,BP(c),Don "Dopey" Dillock 50.00
3-11 BP,BP(c),Death Scores a Touchdown 50.00
3-12 Red Sox V:Senators 70.00
4-1 Spring Training in Full Spring 75.00
4-2 BP,BP(c),How to Pitch 'Em Where They Can't Hit 'Em . . 35.00
4-3 BP,BP(c),1947 Super Stars 90.00
4-4 BP,BP(c),Get Ready for the Olympics 100.00
4-5 BP,BP,(c),Hugh Casey 75.00
4-6 BP,BP(c),Phantom Phil Hergesheimer,Hockey (c) . . 100.00
4-7 BP,BP(c),How to Bowl Better 35.00
4-8 Tips on the Big Fight 100.00
4-9 BP,BP(c),Bill McCahan 65.00
4-10 BP,BP(c),Great Football Plays 50.00
4-11 BP,BP(c),Football 50.00
4-12 BP,BP(c),Basketball 50.00
5-1 Satchel Paige 150.00
5-2 History of Boxing, July-August, 1949 . . . . 75.00

TESSIE THE TYPIST
Timely
Summer, 1944

3 Football cover 40.00

UNLV
Amazing Sports

1 Championship season (basketball based on college team) 3.00

VIC VERITY MAGAZINE
Vic Verity Publications
1945

5 CCB,Championship Baseball Game 40.00

WOW COMICS
Fawcett Publications
Winter, 1940

69 A:Tom Mix,Baseball 40.00

WWF BATTLEMANIA
Valiant

1 WWF Action 2.50
2 thru 5 . . . . @2.50

Yogi Berra #1, © Fawcett Publ.

YOGI BERRA
Fawcett Publications
1957

1 Ph(c) 250.00

YOUNG ALL STARS
DC Comics
June, 1987

7 Baseball Game,,A:Tigress 1.25

DIE-CAST CARS

AUTO RACING

 # Maker, Scale, Description . . . . Value

Allison, Bobby

28B ERTL, 1/64, 1340, Hardees 80 Chevy 195.00
88B ERTL, 1/64, 1944, Gatorade/No SVC Buick 100.00
88C ERTL, 1/64, 1944, Gatorade/SVC Buick . . . 63.00
88D ERTL, 1/64, 1944, Gatorade/SVC Buick . . . 65.00
88E ERTL, 1/64, 1944, Gatorade/French/No SVC 70.00

Bobby Allison 1986 Ford by RCCA

22 RCCA, '80s Fords, Allison Racing Ford 6.00
12B R-Champs, 1991 (Petty), Buick 5.00
12B R-Champs, 1992 (Petty), Buick 3.00
29 R-Champs, Ford Torinos 3.00
12A R-Champs, Roaring Racers 6.00

Allison, Davey

28A M-Box, W-Rose, 1/64, Hav. T-Bird 9.00
28B M-Box, W-Rose, 1/64, Hav. T-Bird 4.00
28 RCCA, Revell, 1/64, Hav. (RCCA Club Car) T-Bird 18.00
28 R-Champs, 1989, 1/64, B/White Old T-Bird . 42.00
28A R-Champs, 1990, 1/64, W/Black Old T-Bird . 36.00
28B R-Champs, 1990, 1/64, Black Old T-Bird . . . 18.00
28A R-Champs, 1991 (Earnhardt), Old T-Bird . . . 16.00
28B R-Champs, 1991 (Earnhardt), New T-Bird . . 15.00
28A R-Champs, 1991 (Petty), Old T-Bird 13.00
28B R-Champs, 1991 (Petty), New T-Bird 13.00
28A R-Champs, 1992 (Petty), Hav. New Ford 2.00
28 R-Champs, 1/43, Hav. T-Bird 5.00
28 R-Champs, 1/24, Hav. Ford 10.00
28 R-Champs, Roaring Racers 14.00
28 R-Champs, SupCS, w/ 2 Trucks, Cars, Mini Fords 31.00
28 Promo, 7-Up Promo 1993 T-Bird 10.00
28 Revell, 1/24, Texaco/Hav. T-Bird 9.00

Alsup, B.

12B ERTL, 1/43, 1544, AB Dick Penske Indy . . . 30.00

Andretti, Mario

12A ERTL, 1/43, 1542, Essex Penske PC9 Indy . 27.00
6C R-Champs, Indy Cars, Hav. 3.00
5A R-Champs, Indy Cars, White Helmet 5.00
5B R-Champs, Indy Cars, Black Helmet 5.00

Andretti, Michael

3 R-Champs, Indy Cars, Hav. 3.00
6A R-Champs, Indy Cars, White Helmet 6.00
6B R-Champs, Indy Cars, Black Helmet 5.00

Baker, Buck

300B Legends of Racing, 1/43, 1956 Chrysler . . . 20.00

Baker, Buddy

88F ERTL, 1/64, 9501, Crisco Promo Buick 96.00
21A RCCA, '80s Fords, Valvoline Ford 6.00
10 R-Champs '64 Fords 3.00
6 R-Champs Dodge Daytonas 3.00

Bernstein, Kenny

26A R-Champs, 1990, 1/64, Buick 9.00
26B R-Champs, 1990, 1/64, Oldsmobile 20.00
26C R-Champs, 1990, 1/64, Lumina 33.00
26D R-Champs, 1990, 1/64, Old Pontiac 30.00
26 R-Champs, 1991 (Earnhardt), Buick 3.00
26A R-Champs, 1991 (Petty), New Card Buick . . . 2.00
26B R-Champs, 1991 (Petty), New Card Olds . . . 10.00
26 R-Champs, Roaring Racers 5.00
R-Champs, Draggers Quaker State 9.00
R-Champs, Draggers King Kenny (Red) 6.00
R-Champs, King Quaker State/Mac Tools . . 11.00
R-Champs, King Kenny-w/o Quaker State . . . 9.00

Bodine, Brett

15A ERTL, 1/64, 1329, Crisco Promo T-Bird 16.00
15B ERTL, 1/64, 2450, Crisco/NASCAR T-Bird . . 13.00
26C R-Champs, 1991 (Petty), Buick 4.00
26D R-Champs, 1991 (Petty), Lumina 4.00
26 R-Champs, 1992 (Petty), Quaker State Buick . 3.00
26 R-Champs, 1/43, Quaker State T-Bird 4.00
26 Revell, 1/24, Quaker State T-Bird 10.00

Bodine, Geoff

11A R-Champs, 1991 (Earnhardt), Old T-Bird 3.00
11B R-Champs, 1991 (Earnhardt), New T-Bird . . . 3.00
11 R-Champs, 1991 (Petty), New T-Bird 2.00
11C R-Champs, 1992 (Petty), New Ford 5.00
15 R-Champs, 1992 (Petty), Motorcraft Ford 3.00
11A R-Champs, 1/43, T-Bird 4.00
15B R-Champs, 1/43, Motorcraft T-Bird 5.00
15B R-Champs, 1/24, Motorcraft Ford 10.00
11 R-Champs, Roaring Racers 5.00

Dale Earnhardt 1983 light blue Ford Thunderbird

Cope, Derrike

10 RCCA, Revell, 1/24, Purolator Lumina 10.00
10 R-Champs, 1990, 1/64, 3 Checkers Lumina . 56.00
10A R-Champs, 1991 (Earn), 3 Checkers Lum. . . 18.00
10B R-Champs, 1991 (Earn), 2 Checkers Lumina . 4.00
10A R-Champs, 1991 (Petty), 2 Checkers Lumina . 2.00
10B R-Champs, 1991 (Petty), 3 Checkers Lumina 12.00
10A R-Champs, 1992 (Petty), Puro. (Blue Name) Lumina 2.00
10B R-Champs, 1992 (Petty), Puro. (White Name) Lumina 7.00
10C R-Champs, 1992 (Petty), Puro. (Adams Mark Decal) Lumina 2.00
10 R-Champs, 1/43, Puro. Lumina 5.00
10 R-Champs, 1/24, Puro. Lumina 9.00
10 R-Champs, Roaring Racers 5.00
10 Revell, 1/24, Puro. Lumina 10.00

Crider, C.

9D ERTL, 1/64, 9746, Jimmy Mc's, '36 Ford . . . 13.00

Earnhardt, Dale

15C ERTL, 1/64, 1485, Dark Blue Wrangler T-Bird . . . 220.00
15D ERTL, 1/64, 1485, Light Blue Wrangler T-Bird . . . 210.00
15E ERTL, 1/64, 4077, Wrangler/Pow-R-Pull Buick . . . 225.00
15A ERTL, 1/64 set, 1482, 4-Pc Wrangler Set W/Jeep, P/U T-Bird Lt.Bl . . . 190.00
15B ERTL, 1/64 set, 1482, 4-Pc Wrangler Set W/Jeep, P/U T-Bird Dk.Bi . . . 200.00
3A M-Box, W-Rose, Goodwrench Back Lumina . 38.00
3B M-Box, W-Rose, Quick Lube Back Lumina . . 19.00
3C M-Box, W-Rose, Western Steer Lumina . . . 12.00
3D M-Box, W-Rose, w/o Quick Lube Lumina . . . 9.00
3E M-Box, W-Rose, Mom & Pops Trunk Lumina 11.00
3F M-Box, W-Rose, Lg. Rubber Tires w/ Winross Truck Lumina . . . 31.00
3G M-Box, W-Rose, Flat Black w/ Winross Truck Lumina . . . 31.00
3 RCCA, Revell, 1/64, Goodwrench (RCCA Club Car) Lumina . . . 24.00
15 RCCA, Revell, 1/24, Wrangler '83 T-Bird . . . 14.00
3 R-Champs, 1989, 1/64, Goodwrench Lumina 75.00
3A R-Champs, 1990, 1/64, Goodwrench Lumina 75.00
3B R-Champs, 1990, 1/64, Performance Parts Lumina . . . 22.00
3 R-Champs, 1991 (Earn), Lumina . . . 23.00
3 R-Champs, 1991 (Petty), Lumina . . . 18.00
3 R-Champs, 1992 (Petty), Goodwrench/Quick Lube Lumina . . . 3.00
3 R-Champs, 1/43, Goodwr./Quick Lube Lumina 7.00
3 R-Champs, 1/24, Goodwrench Lumina . . . 10.00
3 R-Champs, Roaring Racers . . . 17.00
3 R-Champs, SupCS, W/ 2 Trucks, cars, No Mini Luminas . . . 31.00
3A Revell, 1/24, Silver Wheels Lumina . . . 12.00
3B Revell, 1/24, Sports Image (Black Wheels) Lumina . . . 23.00

Elliott, Bill

9A ERTL, 1/64, 9408, 1985 Silver Wheels T-Bird . . . 331.00
9B ERTL, 1/64, 9466, 1986 Clear Windows T-Bird . . . 192.00
9C ERTL, 1/64, 9670, 1987 Gold Wheels/Dark Windows T-Bird . . . 56.00
11 M-Box, W-Rose, 1/64, Amoco T-Bird . . . 4.00
11B Pit Row, 1/64, Amoco T-Bird . . . 3.00
11C Pit Row, 1/64, W/out Amoco T-Bird . . . 3.00

Bill Venturini Amoco Promo

11 Pit Row, 1/43, Amoco T-Bird . . . 5.00
9 R-Champs, 1989, 1/64, No Blue Stripe Old T-Bird . . . 54.00
9A R-Champs, 1990, 1/64, Orange, Blue Stripe, No Melling T-Bird . . . 75.00
9B R-Champs, 1990, 1/64, Orange, Blue Stripe, W/ Melling T-Bird . . . 13.00
9C R-Champs, 1990, 1/64, Red, Blue Stripe, W/ Melling T-Bird . . . 20.00
9A R-Champs, 1991 (Earn), Orange/White Old T-Bird . . . 13.00
98 R-Champs, 1991 (Earn), Blue To Top of Back Window New T-Bird . . . 23.00
9C R-Champs, 1991 (Earn), Blue To Back Deck Lid New T-Bird . . . 9.00
9 R-Champs, 1991 (Petty), New T-Bird . . . 3.00
9 R-Champs, 1992 (Petty), Melling (Blue) New Ford . . . 2 00
11A R-Champs, 1992 (Petty), Amoco New Ford . . 2.00
11B R-Champs, 1992 (Petty), Amoco (w/out 11 On Hood) New Ford . . . 2.00
9A R-Champs, 1/43, (Red) Motorcraft T-Bird . . . 7.00
9B R-Champs, 1/43, (Blue) Melling (Also 2-Car Set) T-Bird . . . 4.00
11B R-Champs, 1/43, Amoco T-Bird . . . 4.00
11C R-Champs, 1/43, Budweiser (Ford Motorsport 2-Car Set) T-Bird . . . 13.00
84A R-Champs, 1/43, Melling/Ford Motorsport (Red) T-Bird . . . 10.00
84B R-Champs, 1/43, Melling (Blue) T-Bird . . . 10.00
9 R-Champs, 1/24, Ford . . . 11.00
11 R-Champs, 1/24, Amoco Ford . . . 10.00
9A R-Champs, Roaring Racers, Red . . . 12.00
9B R-Champs, Roaring Racers, Blue . . . 6.00
9A R-Champs, SupCS, W/ 2 Trucks, 2 Cars, Mini Car Fords . . . 31.00
9B R-Champs, SupCS, Ford Motorsports . . . 34.00
9A Promo, Motorcraft New T-Bird . . . 27.00
9B Promo, Coors Light New T-Bird . . . 55.00
9C Promo, Mobil 1 Promo New T-Bird . . . 12.00
9D Promo, Sharp/True Value (1/24 Mobil-1 Promo) March Cosworth . . . 40.00
11 Promo, Milkhouse Cheese New T-Bird . . . 5.00
9A SCM, 1/64 kit, '87 T-Bird . . . 7.00
9B SCM, 1/64 kit, '88 T-Bird . . . 7.00
9C SCM, 1/64 kit, '89 T-Bird . . . 7.00
9D SCM, 1/64 kit, '90 T-Bird . . . 7.00

Fittipaldi, Emerson

1A R-Champs, Indy Cars . . . 4.00
5D Promo, Mobil 1 Promo Indy Car . . . 8.00

Foyt, A.J.

14A R-Champs, 1990, 1/64, Lumina . . . 37.00
14B R-Champs, 1990, 1/64, New Pontiac . . . 14.00

Pole Position Jeff Gordon Baby Ruth Ford

14C R-Champs, 1990, 1/64, Old Pontiac . . . 21.00
14D R-Champs, 1990, 1/64, Olds . . . 11.00
14 R-Champs, 1991 (Earn), Olds . . . 9.00
14A R-Champs, 1991 (Petty), Olds . . . 5.00
14B R-Champs, 1991 (Petty), Buick . . . 9.00
14 R-Champs, 1992 (Petty), Olds . . . 3.00
11 R-Champs Ford Torinos . . . 3.00
14 R-Champs, Roaring Racers . . . 5.00
14 R-Champs, Indy Cars . . . 6.00
14 R-Champs, 2-pack, Indy and Stock Cars . . . 11.00
14A Tonka, 1/24, Gilmore Coyote Indy Car . . . 61.00
14B Tonka, 1/24, Van, Trailer, Car, 2 Figures 5-Piece Set . . . 187.00

Gant, Harry

33 ERTL, 1/64, 1150, Skoal Bandit Buick . . . 260.00
33A ERTL, 1/43, 1721, Skoal Bandit (Taiwan) Buick . . . 141.00
33B ERTL, 1/43, 1721, Skoal Bandit, No Goodyear Buick . . . 118.00
7 RCCA, Revell, 1/24, Mac Tools Buick . . . 14.00
33 R-Champs, 1990, 1/64, New Pontiac . . . 18.00
33A R-Champs, 1991 (Earn), New Pontiac . . . 11.00

No.	Description	Price
33B	R-Champs, 1991 (Earn), Olds	9.00
33A	R-Champs, 1991 (Petty), Olds	4.00
33B	R-Champs, 1991 (Petty), Buick	8.00
33	R-Champs, 1992 (Petty), Olds	2.00
33	R-Champs, 1/43, Olds	4.00
33	R-Champs, 1/24, Olds	10.00
33	R-Champs, Roaring Racers	5.00
7	Pole Position, 1/64, Mac Tools Olds	6.00

Gordon, Jeff

No.	Description	Price
1A	M-Box, W-Rose, 1/64, Baby Ruth (Red Letters) T-Bird	5.00

Jeff McClure "Race for Life" Lumina

No.	Description	Price
1B	M-Box, W-Rose, 1/64, Baby Ruth (Orange Letters) T-Bird	6.00
1	Pit Row, 1/64, Baby Ruth T-Bird	3.00
1	RCCA, Revell, 1/24, Baby Ruth '92 T-Bird	14.00
1B	R-Champs, 1992 (Petty), Baby Ruth Ford	4.00
1	Pole Position, 1/64, Baby Ruth T-Bird	6.00
1D	Promo, Baby Ruth (Motorsports Properties) T-Bird	10.00
1E	Promo, Baby Ruth (R-Champs) T-Bird	10.00
1	Race Daze, 1/64, Baby Ruth T-Bird	7.00

Grissom, S.

No.	Description	Price
31A	Promo, Big Mama's Olds	126.00
31B	Promo, ChannelLock Olds	6.00
31C	Promo, Roddenbery's Olds	6.00

Gurney, Dan

No.	Description	Price
0A	RCCA, Legends, White 1963 Ford	7.00
28B	RCCA, Legends, White 1963 Ford	7.00

Hamilton, Pete

No.	Description	Price
40	P. Hamilton R-Champs, 1991 Superbirds, Plymouth	9.00
40	P. Hamilton R-Champs, 1991 Superbirds, Plymouth By Petty	2.00
5	P. Hamilton R-Champs Ford Torinos	3.00
40	P. Hamilton R-Champs, Superbirds, 1/43, Plymouth	7.00

Hillin, Bobby Jr.

No.	Description	Price
28B	R-Champs, 1992 (Petty), Hav. New Ford	3.00
31	R-Champs, 1992 (Petty), Mondello Parts Lumina	3.00
42B	R-Champs, 1992 (Petty), Mello Yello Pontiac	7.00
42B	R-Champs, 1/43, Mello Yello Pontiac	8.00
42B	R-Champs, 1/24, Mello Yello Pontiac	31.00

Hylton, James

No.	Description	Price
48	Legends of Racing, 1/43, 1971 Mercury	15.00
48	R-Champs Dodge Daytonas	3.00

Irvan, Ernie

No.	Description	Price
4A	M-Box, W-Rose, 1/64, Kodak Lumina	4.00
10B	M-Box, W-Rose, 1/64, Mac Tools Lumina	19.00
4	R-Champs, 1992 (Petty), Kodak Lumina	2.00
4	R-Champs, 1/43, Kodak Lumina	4.00
4	R-Champs, 1/24, Kodak Lumina	9.00
4	R-Champs, Roaring Racers	6.00
4	R-Champs, SupCS, w/ 2 Trucks, 2 Cars, No Mini Car Luminas	31.00
4	Road Champs, 1/64, Kodak Lumina	2.00
4	Road Champs, 1/43 (box), Kodak Lumina	4.00

Jarrett, Dale

No.	Description	Price
21A	ERTL, 1/64, 2467, Citgo/NASCAR T-Bird	9.00
18	Pit Row, 1/64, Interstate Lumina	3.00
21A	Pit Row, 1/64, Citgo (Winston Decal) T-Bird	5.00
21B	Pit Row, 1/64, Citgo (Edelbrock) T-Bird	2.00
18	Pit Row, 1/43, Interslate Batteries Lumina	5.00
18	RCCA, Revell, 1/64, Interstate Batteries Lumina	6.00
21B	R-Champs, 1991 (Earn), New T-Bird	3.00
21	R-Champs, 1991 (Petty), New T-Bird	2.00
18B	R-Champs, 1992 (Petty), Interstate Batteries (No Decals) Lumina	2.00
21A	R-Champs, 1992 (Petty), Citgo New Ford	2.00
18B	R-Champs, 1/43, Interstate Batteries Lumina	4.00
21A	R-Champs, 1/43, Citgo T-Bird	4.00
21A	R-Champs, 1/24, Citgo Ford	11.00
21	R-Champs, Roaring Racers	5.00
18	R-Champs, SupCS, W/ 2 Trucks, 2 Cars, Mini Car Luminas	30.00

Alan Kulwicki 1986 Ford T-Bird

Kulwicki, Alan

No.	Description	Price
7A	M-Box, W-Rose, 1/64, Hooters T-Bird	13.00
7B	M-Box, W-Rose, 1/64, Hooters (New Details) T-Bird	4.00
7	R-Champs, 1992 (Petty), Hooters (No Girls on Card) New Ford	3.00
7	R-Champs, 1/24 Hooters Ford	10.00
7A	Promo, Hooters With Special Card T-Bird	7.00
7B	Promo, Milkhouse Cheese T-Bird	7.00
35	RCCA, Quincy's Steak House T-Bird	10.00

Labonte, Bobby

No.	Description	Price
44	B. Labonte M-Box, W-Rose, 1/64, Penrose (box) Lumina	20.00

Labonte, Terry

No.	Description	Price
94A	Pit Row, 1/64, Sunoco (True Value Decal) Olds	2.00
94B	Pit Row, 1/64, Sunoco (Busch Decal) Olds	6.00
1	R-Champs, 1990, 1/64, Olds	19.00
1	R-Champs, 1991 (Earn), Olds	10.00
94A	R-Champs, 1991 (Petty), Olds	6.00
94B	R-Champs, 1991 (Petty), Buick	7.00
94A	R-Champs, 1992 (Petty), Sunoco Olds	2.00
94B	R-Champs, 1992 (Petty), Sunoco (With Yellow Bumper) Olds	2.00
94	R-Champs, 1/24, Sunoco Olds	9.00
94	R-Champs, Roaring Racers	5.00
94	Pole Position, 1/64, Sunoco	6.00
94	Revell, 1/24, Sunoco Olds	11.00

Lorenzen, Fred

No.	Description	Price
28	Legends, 1/43, 1965 Galaxie	20.00
28A	RCCA, Legends, White 1963 Ford	5.00
28	R-Champs '64 Fords	3.00

Lund, Tiny

No.	Description	Price
0B	RCCA, Legends, Red 1963 Ford	5.00
21B	RCCA, Legends, White/Red (Club Members Car) 1963 Ford	19.00
32	R-Champs '64 Fords	3.00
55	R-Champs Dodge Daytonas	3.00

Marlin, Sterling

No.	Description	Price
22	M-Box, W-Rose, 1/64, Maxwell House T-Bird	3.00
22	Pit Row, 1/64, Maxwell House T-Bird	2.00
22	Pit Row, 1/43, Maxwell House T-Bird	5.00
22	RCCA, Revell, 1/64, Maxwell House T-Bird	6.00
94	R-Champs, 1989, 1/64, Olds	24.00

Fred Lorenzen 1963 Ford

94A R-Champs, 1990, 1/64, Lumina 36.00
94B R-Champs, 1990, 1/64, Olds 12.00
94C R-Champs, 1990, 1/64, Buick 38.00
94D R-Champs, 1990, 1/64, Old Pontiac 36.00
22 R-Champs, 1991 (Earn), Silver Wheels New T-Bird 11.00
94 R-Champs, 1991 (Earn), Olds 6.00
22A R-Champs, 1991 (Petty), Silver Wheels New T-Bird 8.00
22B R-Champs, 1991 (Petty), Black Wheels New T-Bird 2.00
10D R-Champs, 1992 (Petty), Maxwell House (Busch Car) Lumina 3.00
22 R-Champs, 1992 (Petty), Maxwell House New Ford 2.00
22 R-Champs, 1/43, Maxwell House T-Bird 4.00
22 R-Champs, 1/24, Maxwell House Ford 9.00
22 R-Champs, Roaring Racers 5.00
22 Pole Position, 1/64, Maxwell House T-Bird ... 6.00
44 Promo, Piedmont Olds 15.00

Martin, Mark
6 RCCA, Revell, 1/64, Valvoline T-Bird 6.00
6 R-Champs, 1992 (Petty), Valvoline

David Pearson 1959 Chevy

(No Small Decals) New Ford 2.00
60 R-Champs, 1992, Winn Dixie New Ford 3.00
6 R-Champs, 1/43, Valvoline T-Bird 5.00
60 R-Champs, 1/43, Winn Dixie T-Bird 6.00
6 R-Champs, 1/24, Valvoline Ford 10.00
60 R-Champs, 1/24, Winn Dixie Ford 10.00
6 Promo, Milkhouse Cheese T-Bird 5.00
6 Revell, 1/24, Valvoline T-Bird 11.00
6 Road Champs, 1/64, Valvoline T-Bird 2.00
6 Road Champs, 1/43 (box), Valvoline T-Bird .. 5.00
6 Road Champs, 1/43 (pullback), Valvoline T-Bird 5.00
6 Road Champs, 1/43 (sounds), Valvoline T-Bird 7.00
6 Road Champs, 1/25 (sounds), Valvoline T-Bird 12.00

Mast, Rick
1A R-Champs, 1991 (Petty), Olds 2.00
1B R-Champs, 1991 (Petty), Buick 7.00
1A R-Champs, 1992 (Petty), Majik Market Olds .. 2.00
1 R-Champs, 1/24, Majik Market Olds 8.00
1 R-Champs, Roaring Racers 4.00

McEwen, T.
Hot Wheels, 1/64, 1970 #6410 Mongoose (Red) Funny Car 130.00
Hot Wheels, 1/64, 1971 #6410 Mongoose (Blue) Funny Car 124.00
Hot Wheels, 1/64, 1973 #6970 Mongoose (Blue) Funny Car 302.00
Hot Wheels, 1/64, 1979 #2508 Vetty Funny Mongoose Funny Car 20.00
Hot Wheels, 1/64, 1972 #5699 Blue Rear Engine Mongoose Dragger 155.00
R-Champs, Funnys, Mongoose 13.00

Mears, Rick
1 ERTL, 1/43, 1543, Gould Charge Penske PC9 Indy 26.00
2 R-Champs, Indy Cars, Pennzoil 4.00
4A R-Champs, Indy Cars, Yellow Helmet 6.00
4B R-Champs, Indy Cars, Black Helmet 4.00
3 Promo, Mobil 1 Promo Indy Car 8.00

Moroso, Rob
20 R-Champs, 1990, 1/64, Red Stripe To Rear Window Only Olds 27.00
20 R-Champs, 1991 (Earn), Olds 21.00
R-Champs, 3-pack, 1/64 .... 32.00
20 Promo, Crown Olds 23.00

Parsons, Benny
72 Legends of Racing, 1/43, 1973 Chevelle ... 22.00
72 R-Champs Ford Torinos 3.00

Parsons, Phil
55 ERTL, 1/64, 9663, Crown T-Bird 15.00
29A M-Box, W-Rose, 1/64, Matchbox Promo (Box) Lumina 8.00
29B M-Box, W-Rose, 1/64, Phil Parsons Racing (Box) Lumina 20.00
18 Promo, Ford Motorsports Promo Ford 16.00
29 Promo, (With Autograph Add $5.00) Olds .. 19.00

1971 David Pearson Legends of Racing Mercury

Pearson, David
21 Legends of Racing, 1/43, 1971 Mercury 23.00
67 RCCA, Quartzo Legends, 1959 Chevy 18.00
17 R-Champs Ford Torinos 3.00

Pearson, L.
16 R-Champs, 1989, 1/64, Script Pearson Buick 24.00
16A R-Champs, 1990, 1/64, White Bumper Buick 46.00
16B R-Champs, 1990, 1/64, Brown Bumper, Script Pearson Buick 17.00
16C R-Champs, 1990, 1/64, Brown Bumper, Print Pearson Buick 11.00
16D R-Champs, 1990, 1/64, Old Pontiac 34.00
16E R-Champs, 1990, 1/64, New Pontiac 12.00
16F R-Champs, 1990, 1/64, Lumina 32.00
16G R-Champs, 1990, 1/64, Olds 31.00
16 R-Champs, 1991 (Earn), Buick 4.00
16A R-Champs, 1991 (Petty), Buick 3.00
16B R-Champs, 1991 (Petty), Lumina 9.00

Petty, Kyle
7 ERTL, 1/64, 4079, 7-Eleven/Pow-R-Pull Buick 104.00
21B ERTL, 1/64, 9183, Citgo Promo T-Bird 22.00
21C ERTL, 1/64, 2450, Citgo/NASCAR T-Bird ... 16.00
42 M-Box, W-Rose, 1/64, Mello Yello Pontiac ... 3.00
42 RCCA, Revell, 1/64, Mello Yello Pontiac 6.00
7 RCCA, '80s Fords, 7-Eleven Ford 6.00
42A R-Champs, 1990, 1/64, White/Blue Buick .. 104.00

42B R-Champs, 1990, 1/64, White/Blue Olds .. 153.00
42C R-Champs, 1990, 1/64, White/Blue Old Pontiac 89.00
42D R-Champs, 1990, 1/64, White/Blue Lumina 153.00
42E R-Champs, 1990, 1/64, Pink/Blue w/"Sabco Racing" On Trunk New Pontiac .. 17.00
42F R-Champs, 1990, 1/64, Pink/Blue W/out "Sabco Racing" New Pontiac 30.00
42 R-Champs, 1991 (Earn), Peak New Pontiac .. 8.00
42A R-Champs, 1991 (Petty), Peak New Pontiac . 5.00
42B R-Champs, 1991 (Petty), Mello Yello New Pontiac 4.00
42C R-Champs, 1991 (Petty), w/out Mello Yello New Pontiac 5.00
42A R-Champs, 1992 (Petty), Mello Yello Pontiac . 2.00
42A R-Champs, 1/43, Mello Yello Pontiac 5.00
42A R-Champs, 1/24, Mello Yello Pontiac 10.00
42A R-Champs, Roaring Racers, Peak 9.00
42B R-Champs, Roaring Racers, Mello Yello 6.00
42 R-Champs, SupCS, w/ 2 Trucks, 2 Cars, Mini Car Pontiacs 31.00
42 Revell, 1/24, Mello Yello Pontiac 12.00

Petty, Richard

43A ERTL, 1/64, 1599, STP 80 Chevy 126.00
43B ERTL, 1/64, 1942, STP Buick 95.00
43C ERTL, 1/64, 1942, STP/Taiwan Buick 112.00
43D ERTL, 1/64, 1942, STP/French Buick 98.00
43E ERTL, 1/64, 2466, STP/NASCAR Buick 12.00
43F ERTL, 1/64, 4076, STP/Pow-R-Pull Buick . 243.00
43A ERTL, 1/43, 1719, STP (China) Buick 146.00
43B ERTL, 1/43, 1719, STP (Taiwan) Buick ... 169.00
43A ERTL, 1/25, 1679, STP Chevy 158.00
43B ERTL, 1/25, 1827, STP - Red Car Red/Blue Decals Pontiac 165.00

1992 Pro Circuit Richard Petty STP Pontiac

43C ERTL, 1/25, 1827, STP - Blue Car Red/Blue Decal Pontiac 200.00
43D ERTL, 1/25, 8105, Die Cast Kit (Same As 1827) Pontiac 113.00
43 ERTL, 1/18, 7461, STP Pontiac 28.00
43 Franklin Mint, 1/24, STP, 1979 Daytona 500 Winner '77 Olds 154.00
43A M-Box, W-Rose, 1/64, STP Pontiac 4.00
43A Pit Row, 1/64, STP (Winston Decal) Pontiac . 6.00
43B Pit Row, 1/64, STP (Edelbrock Decal) Pontiac 2.00
43 RCCA, Revell, 1/64, STP Pontiac 6.00
43 R-Champs, 1990, 1/64, New Pontiac 21.00
43 R-Champs, 1991 (Earn), New Pontiac 10.00
43 R-Champs, 1991 (Petty), New Pontiac 4.00
43 R-Champs, 1992 (Petty), STP Pontiac 2.00
43 R-Champs, 1992 Tour, Daytona 500 Pontiac 20.00
43 R-Champs, 1992 Tour, Rockingham Pontiac 15.00
43 R-Champs, 1992 Tour, Richmond Pontiac .. 15.00
43 R-Champs, 1992 Tour, Atlanta Pontiac 14.00
43 R-Champs, 1992 Tour, Darlington Pontiac .. 14.00
43 R-Champs, 1992 Tour, Bristol Pontiac 14.00
43 R-Champs, 1992 Tour, N. Wilkesboro Pontiac 14.00
43 R-Champs, 1992 Tour, Martinsville Pontiac . 14.00
43 R-Champs, 1992 Tour, Talladega Pontiac .. 14.00
43 R-Champs, 1992 Tour, One Hot Night Pontiac 14.00
43 R-Champs, 1992 Tour, Charlotte Pontiac ... 14.00
43 R-Champs, 1992 Tour, Dover Pontiac 14.00
43 R-Champs, 1992 Tour, Sonoma Pontiac ... 14.00
43 R-Champs, 1992 Tour, Pocono Pontiac 14.00
43 R-Champs, 1992 Tour, Brooklyn, MI Pontiac 14.00
43 R-Champs, 1992 Tour, Daytona Pepsi 400 Pontiac 14.00
43 R-Champs, 1992 Tour, Pocono Pontiac 13.00
43 R-Champs, 1992 Tour, Talladega Pontiac .. 13.00
43 R-Champs, 1992 Tour, Watkins Glen Pontiac 14.00
43 R-Champs, 1992 Tour, Brooklyn, MI Pontiac 14.00
43 R-Champs, 1992 Tour, Bristol Pontiac 14.00
43 R-Champs, 1992 Tour, Darlington Pontiac .. 13.00
43 R-Champs, 1992 Tour, Richmond Pontiac .. 13.00
43 R-Champs, 1992 Tour, Dover Pontiac 13.00
43 R-Champs, 1992 Tour, Martinsville Pontiac . 13.00
43 R-Champs, 1992 Tour, N. Wilkesboro Pontiac 13.00
43 R-Champs, 1992 Tour, Charlotte Pontiac ... 13.00
43 R-Champs, 1992 Tour, Rockingham Pontiac 13.00
43 R-Champs, 1992 Tour, Phoenix Pontiac ... 13.00
43 R-Champs, 1992 Tour, Atlanta Pontiac 13.00
43 R-Champs, 1991 Superbirds, Plymouth 2.00
43 R-Champs, 1991 Superbirds, Special Edition (Southern Plymouth) Plymouth 22.00
43 R-Champs, 1/43, STP Pontiac 5.00
43 R-Champs, 1/24, STP Pontiac 11.00
43 R-Champs, Petty Collectors Set, Trucks, Superbirds, Figure, Cars Various 37.00
43 R-Champs, Roaring Racers 6.00
43 R-Champs, SupCS, W/ 2 Trucks, 2 Cars, Mini Car Pontiacs 31.00
43 R-Champs, Superbirds, 1/43, Plymouth 7.00
43 R-Champs Ford Torinos, East Tenn. Torino Cobra 3.00
43 Pole Position, 1/64, STP Pontiac 6.00
43 Pro Circuit, w/ card #5 STP Pontiac 5.00
43 Road Champs, 1/64, STP Pontiac 2.00
43 Road Champs, 1/43 (box), STP Pontiac 5.00
43 Road Champs, 1/43 (pullback), STP Pontiac . 5.00
43 Road Champs, 1/43 (sounds), STP Pontiac .. 7.00
43 Road Champs, 1/25 (sounds), STP Pontiac . 12.00
43 SYE, 1992 STP (by Funstuf) Pontiac 6.00
6B SCM, D.K. Ulrich Green/White Monte Carlo 400.00
43 SCM, STP Monte Carlo 92.00

Pressley, R.

59A ERTL, 1/64, 9441, Alliance Racing (1991) Olds 14.00
59B ERTL, 1/64, 2151, Alliance Racing (1992) Olds 7.00
59A Promo, Alliance Racing (1991) Olds 12.00
59B Promo, Alliance Racing (1992 Black Package) Olds 6.00

Prudhomme, Don

Hot Wheels, 1/64, 1982 #2023 Pepsi Challenger Funny Car 23.00

1963 Wendell Scott RCCA Ford series

Hot Wheels, 1/64, 1982 #2023 Pepsi Challenger (w/o snake) Funny Car 23.00

	Hot Wheels, 1/64, 1970 #6409 Snake (Yellow) Funny Car	130.00
	Hot Wheels, 1/64, 1971 #6409 Snake (White) Funny Car	124.00
	Hot Wheels, 1/64, 1973 #6969 Snake (White) Funny Car	302.00
	Hot Wheels, 1/64, 1978 #2023 Army Funny Car	26.00
	Hot Wheels, 1/64, 1972 #5856 Yellow Rear Engine Snake Dragger	155.00
	R-Champs, Draggers, Snake	11.00
	R-Champs, Funnys, Blue "Performance Corner"	12.00
	R-Champs, Funnys, White "Performance Corner"	9.00

Rahal, Bobby

18	R-Champs, Indy Cars, Kraco	4.00

Richmond, Tim

25A	ERTL, 1/64, 9305, Folgers In Coffee Jar Monte Carlo	188.00
25B	ERTL, 1/64, 9305, Folgers Loose Monte Carlo	16.00
25C	ERTL, 1/64, 2450, Folgers/NASCAR Monte Carlo	15.00
250	ERTL, 1/64, 9410, Folgers/T.G. Shepherd Buick	32.00
25	Promo, RCCA Club Car Lumina	19.00

Roberts, Fireball

22	Hot Wheels, 1/64, 1957 # Atlanta Tune up Service Chevrolet	10.00

1963 Fireball Roberts RCCA Ford

22A	RCCA, Legends, 1/64, Dk Purple w/ Name On Roof 1963 Ford	5.00
22B	RCCA, Legends, 1/64, Lt Purple w/ Name On Door 1963 Ford	5.00
22B	RCCA, Quartzo Legends, 1956 Ford	18.00
22	R-Champs '64 Fords	3.00

Roberts, G.

22	Legends of Racing, 1/43, 1962 Pontiac	15.00

Rudd, Ricky

15A	RCCA, '80s Fords, Motorcraft Ford	6.00
5A	R-Champs, 1992 (Petty), Tide (No Small Decals) Lumina	2.00
5	R-Champs, 1/43 Tide Lumina	5.00
5	R-Champs, 1/24 Tide Lumina	10.00
5E	Promo, Tide Promo Lumina	10.00

Ruttman, Joe

75B	Pit Row, 1/64, Dinner Bell T-Bird	2.00
75	Pit Row, 1/43, Dinner Bell T-Bird	5.00
75	Revell, 1/24, Dinner Bell Olds	11.00

Schrader, Ken

90B	RCCA, '80s Fords, Sunny King Ford	6.00
25	R-Champs, 1991 (Petty), Gold Wheels Lumina	2.00
25A	R-Champs, 1992 (Petty), Lumina	2.00
25	R-Champs, 1/43, Lumina	5.00
25	R-Champs, 1/24, Lumina	9.00
25	R-Champs, Roaring Racers	6.00
25	R-Champs, SupCS, w/ 2 Trucks, 2 Cars, Mini Car Luminas	31.00

Schultz, K.

12	Pit Row, 1/64, Piggly Wiggly Pontiac	3.00

Shepherd, Morgan

15A	M-Box, W-Rose, 1/64, Motorcraft T-Bird	12.00
15A	Pit Row, 1/64, Motorcraft (Winston Decal) T-Bird	5.00
15B	Pit Row, 1/64, Motorcraft (Edelbrock Decal) T-Bird	2.00
21	RCCA, Revell, 1/64, Citgo T-Bird	6.00
15A	R-Champs, 1990, 1/64, Red/White Old T-Bird	14.00
15B	R-Champs, 1990, 1/64, Red/Cream Old T-Bird	17.00
15A	R-Champs, 1991 (Earn), Old T-Bird	6.00
15B	R-Champs, 1991 (Earn), Red/White T-Bird	9.00
15C	R-Champs, 1991 (Earn), All Red T-Bird	3.00
15	R-Champs, 1991 (Petty), New T-Bird	2.00
21B	R-Champs, 1992 (Petty), Citgo New Ford	2.00
15A	R-Champs, 1/43, Motorcraft T-Bird	5.00
21B	R-Champs, 1/43, Citgo T-Bird	4.00
15A	R-Champs, 1/24, Motorcraft Ford	9.00
21B	R-Champs, 1/24, Citgo Ford	9.00
15A	R-Champs, Roaring Racers, Red/White	9.00
15B	R-Champs, Roaring Racers, All Red	5.00

1965 Curtis Turner Ford Fairlane

21	Pole Position, 1/64, Citgo T-Bird	6.00
21	Promo, Citgo Promo T-Bird	4.00
21	Revell, 1/24, Citgo T-Bird	8.00

Smith, J.

47	Legends of Racing, 1/43, 1960 Pontiac	20.00

Smith, S.

49	Pit Row, 1/64, Ameritron Batteries Lumina	4.00
49	Pit Row, 1/43, Ameritron Batteries Lumina	5.00
49	R-Champs, 1992 (Petty), Ameritron Lumina	3.00

Speed, Lake

66A	Pit Row, 1/64, TropArtic Pontiac	5.00
83	R-Champs, 1992 (Petty), Purex Ford	3.00

Spencer, Jimmy

98	Pit Row, 1/64, Moly Black Gold Lumina	4.00
98	Pole Position, 1/64, Moly Black Gold Olds	6.00
98	Pole Position, 1/64, Food City Olds	6.00
98	Promo, Moly Black Gold Lumina	8.00
98	Race Daze, 1/64, Moly Black Gold Lumina	7.00

Stricklin, Hut

12	M-Box, W-Rose, 1/64, Raybestos T-Bird	10.00
12	RCCA, Revell, 1/64, Raybestos Lumina	6.00
12A	R-Champs, 1991 (Petty), Buick	5.00
12A	R-Champs, 1992 (Petty), Raybestos Buick	3 00
12B	R-Champs, Roaring Racers	6.00

Trickle, Dick

8	M-Box, W-Rose, Snickers T-Bird	10.00
66	Promo, TropArtic New Pontiac	7.00
66A	Revell, 1/24, Phillips 66 TropArtic Pontiac	33.00

Turner, Curtis

41	Legends of Racing, 1/43, 1965 Galaxie	20.00
26	RCCA, Legends, Red 1963 Ford	5.00
87	RCCA, Legends, Red, White, Blue 1963 Ford	5.00
26	RCCA, Quartzo Legends, 1956 Ford	18.00
26	R-Champs '64 Fords	3.00

Unser, Al Jr.

1B	R-Champs, Indy Cars, Hav., Black Helmet	4.00
5C	R-Champs, Indy Cars, Valvoline	4.00

Unser, Al Sr.

25A R-Champs, Indy Cars, White Helmet 6.00
25B R-Champs, Indy Cars, Black Helmet, w/o Mobil 1 . . . . 5.00

Unser, Bobby

11C ERTL, 1/43, 1541, Norton Spirit Penske PC9 Indy 27.00

Wallace, Kenny

36A RCCA, Revell, 1/64, Cox Lumber Pontiac . . . 6.00
36B RCCA, Revell, 1/64, Dirt Devil Pontiac 6.00
36 R-Champs, 1991 (Petty), New Pontiac 5.00
36A R-Champs, 1992 (Petty), Cox Lumber Pontiac 2.00
36B R-Champs, 1992 (Petty), Dirt Devil Pontiac . . 3.00
36 R-Champs, 1/43, Cox Lumber Pontiac 4.00
36 R-Champs, 1/24, Cox Lumber Pontiac 20.00
36 R-Champs, Roaring Racers 5.00
36 Pole Position, 1/64, Dirt Devil Pontiac 6.00

Wallace, Rusty

2 M-Box, W-Rose, 1/64, Pontiac Excitement . . . 4.00
2 RCCA, Revell, 1/64, Pontiac Excitement 6.00
27A R-Champs, 1990, 1/64, Olds 43.00
27B R-Champs, 1990, 1/64, Old Pontiac 26.00
27C R-Champs, 1990, 1/64, w/ "Miller/Genuine Draft" New Pontiac 22.00
27D R-Champs, 1990, 1/64, w/ "Miller" Only New Pontiac 20.00
27E R-Champs, 1990, 1/64, w/ Silver Decals New Pontiac 28.00
2 R-Champs, 1991 (Earn), New Pontiac 9.00
27A R-Champs, 1991 (Earn), w/ "Miller/Genuine Draft" New Pontiac 25.00
27B R-Champs, 1991 (Earn), w/o "Miller/Genuine Draft" New Pontiac 14.00
27C R-Champs, 1991 (Earn), w/ "Miller" Only New Pontiac 23.00
2 R-Champs, 1991 (Petty), New Pontiac 9.00
2 R-Champs, 1992 (Petty), Pontiac Excitement Pontiac 2.00
2 R-Champs, 1/43, Pontiac 4.00
2A R-Champs, 1/24, AC Delco Pontiac 15.00
2B R-Champs, 1/24, Pontiac Excitement Pontiac 10.00
2 R-Champs, Roaring Racers 10.00
2 R-Champs, SupCS, w/ 2 Trucks, 2 Cars, Mini Car Pontiacs 31.00

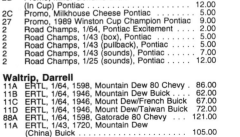

1989 Rusty Wallace NASCAR Champion

27 R-Champs, 1989 NASCAR Champion 15.00
2A Promo, Mobil 1 Promo Pontiac 12.00
2B Promo, Miller Genuine Draft (In Cup) Pontiac 12.00
2C Promo, Milkhouse Cheese Pontiac 5.00
27 Promo, 1989 Winston Cup Champion Pontiac 9.00
2 Road Champs, 1/64, Pontiac Excitement 2.00
2 Road Champs, 1/43 (box), Pontiac 5.00
2 Road Champs, 1/43 (pullback), Pontiac 5.00
2 Road Champs, 1/43 (sounds), Pontiac 7.00
2 Road Champs, 1/25 (sounds), Pontiac 12.00

Waltrip, Darrell

11A ERTL, 1/64, 1598, Mountain Dew 80 Chevy . 86.00
11B ERTL, 1/64, 1946, Mountain Dew Buick 62.00
11C ERTL, 1/64, 1946, Mount Dew/French Buick 67.00
11D ERTL, 1/64, 1946, Mount Dew/Taiwan Buick 72.00
88A ERTL, 1/64, 1598, Gatorade 80 Chevy . . . 121.00
11A ERTL, 1/43, 1720, Mountain Dew (China) Buick 105.00
11B ERTL, 1/43, 1720, Mountain Dew (Taiwan) Buick 145.00
11A ERTL, 1/25, 1683, Mountain Dew Chevy . . 152.00
11B ERTL, 1/25, 1683, Pepsi Challenger Monte Carlo 160.00
88A ERTL, 1/25, 1683, Gatorade Chevy 197.00
88B ERTL, 1/25, 8106, Die Cast Kit (Same As 1683) Chevy 142.00
17 R-Champs, 1992 (Petty), Western Auto Lumina 3.00
17 R-Champs, 1/43, Western Auto Lumina 5.00
17 R-Champs, 1/24, Western Auto (Std. R.C. Packaging) Lumina 10.00
17A Promo, Western Auto (In Cup) Lumina 14.00
17B Promo, Western Auto Promo Lumina 8.00
17C Promo, Milkhouse Cheese Lumina 8.00
17 Revell, 1/24, Western Auto Lumina 10.00

Waltrip, Michael

30 ERTL, 1/64, 2465, Maxwell House/NASCAR T-Bird 9.00
30 M-Box, W-Rose, 1/64, Pennzoil Pontiac 4.00
30 RCCA, Revell, 1/64, Pennzoil Pontiac 6.00
30 R-Champs, 1989, 1/64, Yellow Country Time Old Pontiac 37.00
30A R-Champs, 1990, 1/64, Yellow Country Time New Pontiac 27.00
30B R-Champs, 1990, 1/64, Yellow/Blue Maxwell House New Pontiac 17.00
30A R-Champs, 1991 (Earn), Country Time, No New Decals New Pontiac 20.00
30B R-Champs, 1991 (Earn), Pennzoil, W/ Decals New Pontiac 13.00
30C R-Champs, 1991 (Earn), Pennzoil, No New Decals New Pontiac 10.00
30 R-Champs, 1991 (Petty), Pennzoil, No New Decals New Pontiac 8.00
30 R-Champs, 1992 (Petty), Pennzoil Pontiac . . . 2.00
30 R-Champs, 1/43, Pennzoil T-Bird 5.00
30 R-Champs, 1/24, Pennzoil Pontiac 10.00
30 R-Champs, Roaring Racers 15.00
30 R-Champs, SupCS, W/ 2 Trucks, 2 Cars, Mini Car Pontiacs 30.00
30A Promo, Maxwell House New Pontiac 8.00
30B Promo, Country Time New Pontiac 9.00
30C Promo, Pennzoil Promo New Pontiac 11.00
30 Revell, 1/24, Pennzoil Pontiac 9.00

Wilson, R.

4 ERTL, 1/64, 2464, Kodak/NASCAR Buick . . . 9.00

Yarborough, Cale

27A ERTL, 1/64, 1943, Valvoline Buick 57.00
27B ERTL, 1/64, 1943, Valvoline/Taiwan Buick . . 72.00
27C ERTL, 1/64, 1943, Valvoline/French Buick . . 65.00
28A ERTL, 1/64, 4078, Hardees/ Pow-R-Pull Buick 120.00
52 RCCA, Legends, 1963 Ford 7.00
28 RCCA, '80s Fords, Hardee's Ford 6.00
28 RCCA, Revell, 1/24, Hardee's '86 T-Bird . . . 14.00
66 R-Champs, 1991 (Petty), New Pontiac 3.00
66B R-Champs, 1992 (Petty), TropArtic Pontiac . . 2.00
66C R-Champs, 1992 (Petty), TropArtic New Ford 2.00
06 R-Champs '64 Fords 3.00
21 R-Champs Ford Torinos 3.00
66A R-Champs, TropArtic Pontiac 4.00
66A R-Champs, 1/24, TropArtic (Red) Pontiac . . 10.00
66B R-Champs, 1/24, TropArtic (Black) Pontiac . 10.00
66 R-Champs, Roaring Racers 5.00
29 SYE, 1988 Hardees (by Funstuf) Olds 5.00

1988 Cale Yarborough Funstuff Oldsmobile

EQUIPMENT

All listed equipment values are for *game-used* equipment only. The only exception being the "player endorsed baseball glove" section.

BASEBALL EQUIPMENT

HALL OF FAME PLAYERS

Player	Bat	Hat	Jersey
Aaron, Hank	1,500.00	950.00	15,000.00
Alexander, Grover	7,500.00	2,000.00	45,000.00
Anson, Cap	1,750.00	1,000.00	17,500.00
Aparicio, Luis	400.00	100.00	4,000.00
Appling, Luke	750.00	600.00	8,000.00
Averill, Earl	650.00	500.00	6,750.00
Baker, Frank	2,000.00	1,000.00	17,500.00
Bancroft, Davey	1,000.00	750.00	10,000.00
Banks, Ernie	1,000.00	400.00	10,000.00
Beckley, Jake	1,000.00	800.00	10,000.00
Bench, Johnny	650.00	65.00	6,000.00
Bender, Chief	900.00	750.00	9,500.00
Berra, Yogi	5,000.00	1,900.00	12,000.00
Bottomley, Jim	900.00	450.00	7,500.00
Boudreau, Lou	1,000.00	500.00	9,500.00
Bresnahan, Roger	4,500.00	2,000.00	35,000.00
Brock, Lou	250.00	500.00	2,000.00
Brouthers, Dan	1,250.00	750.00	10,000.00
Brown, Mordecai	1,000.00	1,000.00	15,000.00
Burkett, Jesse	1,250.00	800.00	10,000.00
Campanella, Roy	2,500.00	800.00	15,000.00
Carew, Rod	650.00	350.00	1,000.00
Carey, Max	1,250.00	800.00	10,000.00
Chance, Frank	1,500.00	1,000.00	15,000.00
Chesbro, Jack	1,250.00	1,000.00	16,000.00
Clarke, Fred	1,000.00	700.00	10,000.00
Clarkson, John	1,000.00	800.00	10,000.00
Clemente, Roberto	3,400.00	1,000.00	30,000.00
Cobb, Ty	8,500.00	5,000.00	85,000.00
Cochrane, Mickey	3,750.00	2,500.00	20,000.00
Collins, Eddie	1,500.00	1,000.00	15,000.00
Collins, Jimmy	1,000.00	800.00	10,000.00
Combs, Earle	1,250.00	1,000.00	13,000.00
Connor, Roger	1,000.00	750.00	9,000.00
Coveleski, Stan	1,000.00	750.00	10,000.00
Crawford, Sam	1,250.00	750.00	12,000.00
Cronin, Joe	1,750.00	1,250.00	17,500.00
Cuyler, Kiki	1,750.00	1,200.00	15,000.00
Dean, Dizzy	1,500.00	1,000.00	18,000.00
Delahanty, Ed	1,250.00	1,000.00	11,000.00
DiMaggio, Joe	18,000.00	5,000.00	100,000.00
Dickey, Bill	5,000.00	3,000.00	35,000.00
Doerr, Bobby	750.00	100.00	4,500.00
Drysdale, Don	250.00	300.00	5,500.00
Duffy, Hugh	1,250.00	1,000.00	12,500.00
Evers, Johnny	1,000.00	800.00	11,000.00
Ewing, Buck	2,500.00	1,500.00	18,500.00
Faber, Red	1,000.00	800.00	10,000.00
Feller, Bob	2,250.00	1,000.00	15,000.00
Ferrell, Rick	1,000.00	750.00	8,500.00
Fingers, Rollie	200.00	75.00	4,500.00
Flick, Elmer	1,000.00	900.00	10,000.00
Ford, Whitey	1,500.00	800.00	18,000.00
Foxx, Jimmie	5,000.00	2,000.00	40,000.00
Frisch, Frankie	1,750.00	1,500.00	17,500.00
Galvin, Pud	1,250.00	1,000.00	12,500.00
Gehrig, Lou	14,000.00	10,000.00	125,000.00
Gehringer, Charlie	1,500.00	1,000.00	15,000.00
Gibson, Bob	500.00	200.00	6,000.00
Gomez, Lefty	1,000.00	800.00	13,000.00
Goslin, Goose	1,250.00	1,000.00	12,000.00
Greenberg, Hank	2,500.00	2,250.00	25,000.00
Grimes, Burleigh	1,500.00	800.00	14,000.00

Roger Bresnahan in his road uniform, circa 1911-12

Grove, Lefty	2,500.00	875.00	18,000.00
Hafey, Chick	1,000.00	900.00	10,000.00
Haines, Jesse	1,000.00	800.00	10,000.00
Hamilton, Billy	1,200.00	1,100.00	11,000.00
Hartnett, Gabby	3,000.00	2,750.00	20,000.00
Heilmann, Harry	1,000.00	900.00	10,000.00
Herman, Billy	1,250.00	1,000.00	12,000.00
Hooper, Harry	1,000.00	900.00	9,000.00
Hornsby, Rogers	5,000.00	2,500.00	50,000.00
Hoyt, Waite	1,000.00	750.00	10,000.00
Hubbell, Carl	1,250.00	200.00	10,000.00
Hunter, Catfish	250.00	100.00	6,000.00

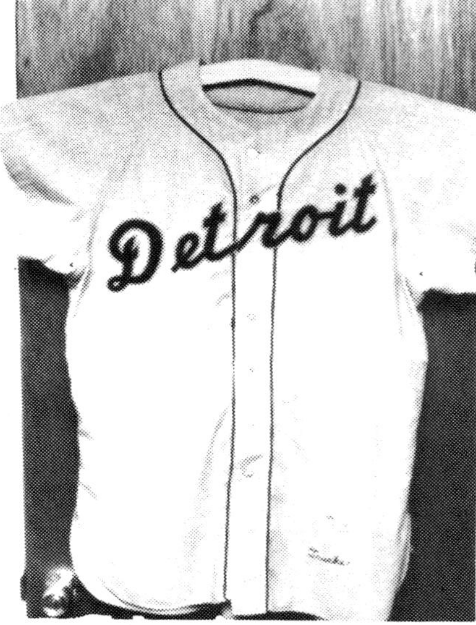

Tigers 1952-57 road jersey

Irvin, Monte	350.00	125.00	2,500.00
Jackson, Travis	1,000.00	900.00	10,000.00
Jenkins, Ferguson	200.00	75.00	5,500.00
Jennings, Hugh	1,250.00	1,000.00	12,000.00
Johnson, Walter	8,500.00	2,500.00	50,000.00
Joss, Addie	1,000.00	800.00	10,000.00
Kaline, Al	1,500.00	500.00	10,000.00
Keefe, Tim	1,000.00	750.00	10,000.00
Keeler, Willie	1,500.00	1,250.00	15,000.00
Kell, George	900.00	700.00	9,000.00
Kelley, Joe	1,750.00	1,250.00	17,000.00
Kelly, George	1,750.00	1,250.00	17,000.00
Kelly, King	1,800.00	1,500.00	18,500.00
Killebrew, Harmon	300.00	250.00	9,000.00
Kiner, Ralph	1,250.00	400.00	10,000.00
Klein, Chuck	1,000.00	900.00	10,000.00
Koufax, Sandy	2,000.00	750.00	16,000.00
Lajoie, Nap	2,000.00	1,500.00	20,000.00
Lazzeri, Tony	1,000.00	900.00	7,500.00
Lemon, Bob	200.00	150.00	1,200.00
Lindstrom, Fred	1,000.00	900.00	10,000.00
Lombardi, Ernie	2,000.00	1,000.00	15,000.00
Lyons, Ted	1,250.00	1,000.00	10,000.00
Mantle, Mickey	7,500.00	2,500.00	95,000.00
Manush, Heinie	1,500.00	1,000.00	14,000.00
Maranville, Rabbit	1,500.00	1,000.00	14,500.00
Marichal, Juan	500.00	150.00	5,500.00
Marquard, Rube	1,000.00	900.00	10,000.00
Mathews, Eddie	2,000.00	1,000.00	15,000.00
Mathewson, Christy	8,250.00	2,500.00	50,000.00
Mays, Willie	3,000.00	1,000.00	20,000.00
McCarthy, Tommy	1,000.00	800.00	10,000.00
McCovey, Willie	750.00	175.00	3,200.00
McGinnity, Joe	1,500.00	1,250.00	15,000.00
Medwick, Joe	1,750.00	1,500.00	16,000.00
Mize, Johnny	1,250.00	1,200.00	10,000.00
Morgan, Joe	500.00	100.00	1,000.00
Musial, Stan	2,500.00	750.00	20,000.00
Nichols, Kid	1,250.00	1,000.00	10,000.00
O'Rourke, Jim	1,250.00	1,000.00	10,000.00
Ott, Mel	3,500.00	2,500.00	25,000.00
Paige, Satchel	1,000.00	1,000.00	15,000.00
Palmer, Jim	400.00	125.00	2,500.00
Pennock, Herb	1,500.00	1,000.00	15,000.00
Perry, Gaylord	200.00	75.00	1,000.00
Plank, Eddie	2,000.00	1,500.00	22,500.00
Radbourn, Old Hoss	1,750.00	1,250.00	20,000.00
Reese, Pee Wee	750.00	700.00	7,000.00
Rice, Sam	1,000.00	900.00	10,000.00
Rixey, Eppa	1,250.00	1,000.00	12,500.00
Roberts, Robin	200.00	125.00	1,500.00
Robinson, Brooks	350.00	125.00	3,500.00
Robinson, Frank	500.00	150.00	5,000.00
Robinson, Jackie	7,500.00	3,000.00	75,000.00
Roush, Edd	1,000.00	900.00	10,000.00
Ruffing, Red	1,250.00	1,000.00	12,000.00
Rusie, Amos	1,000.00	800.00	10,000.00
Ruth, Babe	20,000.00	10,000.00	140,000.00
Schalk, Ray	3,000.00	2,500.00	20,000.00
Schoendienst, Red	650.00	125.00	8,500.00
Seaver, Tom	550.00	500.00	6,500.00
Sewell, Joe	750.00	700.00	7,000.00
Simmons, Al	1,500.00	1,200.00	14,000.00
Sisler, George	1,750.00	1,600.00	16,000.00
Slaughter, Enos	850.00	750.00	8,500.00
Snider, Duke	2,500.00	1,500.00	15,000.00
Spahn, Warren	1,500.00	1,000.00	17,500.00
Speaker, Tris	2,250.00	2,000.00	20,000.00
Stargell, Willie	750.00	200.00	2,500.00
Stengel, Casey	1,200.00	750.00	10,000.00
Terry, Bill	1,250.00	1,000.00	12,000.00
Thompson, Sam	1,000.00	800.00	10,000.00
Tinker, Joe	1,750.00	1,250.00	12,500.00
Traynor, Pie	1,250.00	1,000.00	12,500.00
Vance, Dazzy	1,000.00	900.00	12,500.00
Vaughn, Arky	1,250.00	1,000.00	10,000.00
Waddell, Rube	1,500.00	1,250.00	20,000.00
Wagner, Honus	6,000.00	4,000.00	65,000.00
Wallace, Bobby	1,000.00	750.00	8,000.00
Walsh, Ed	1,500.00	1,000.00	15,000.00
Waner, Lloyd	1,500.00	1,000.00	14,000.00
Waner, Paul	2,000.00	1,500.00	17,500.00
Ward, John M.	1,000.00	750.00	7,500.00
Welch, Mickey	1,000.00	800.00	10,000.00
Wheat, Zack	1,800.00	1,500.00	15,000.00
Wilhelm, Hoyt	350.00	125.00	2,500.00
Williams,Billy	600.00	150.00	6,000.00
Williams, Ted	2,500.00	850.00	20,000.00
Wilson, Hack	1,750.00	1,250.00	15,000.00
Wynn, Early	350.00	100.00	2,250.00
Yastrzemski, Carl	450.00	150.00	3,500.00
Young, Cy	10,000.00	3,000.00	85,000.00
Youngs, Ross	1,000.00	800.00	9,000.00

INACTIVE PLAYERS

Allen, Dick	225.00	100.00	1,000.00
Ashburn, Richie	250.00	150.00	1,250.00
Bauer, Hank	250.00	125.00	1,250.00
Bonds, Bobby	125.00	90.00	350.00
Bouton, Jim	50.00	90.00	950.00
Boyer, Ken	85.00	80.00	875.00
Branca, Ralph	125.00	200.00	1,250.00
Bunning, Jim	75.00	75.00	875.00
Burdette, Lou	65.00	60.00	850.00

1934 Braves home uniform

Carlton, Steve	200.00	200.00	2,000.00
Cash, Norm	75.00	65.00	875.00
Cepeda, Orlando	275.00	200.00	1,100.00
Cey, Ron	175.00	85.00	400.00
Colavito, Rocky	125.00	90.00	900.00
Concepcion, Dave	85.00	65.00	375.00
Dark, Alvin	150.00	100.00	850.00
Doby, Larry	175.00	125.00	950.00
Erskine, Carl	85.00	100.00	900.00
Flood, Curt	90.00	85.00	825.00
Furillo, Carl	550.00	175.00	1,000.00
Garvey, Steve	200.00	100.00	1,000.00
Griffey, Ken	90.00	85.00	300.00
Groat, Dick	75.00	70.00	725.00
Guidry, Ron	25.00	65.00	300.00
Hodges, Gil	650.00	225.00	1,250.00
Howard, Elston	225.00	125.00	875.00
Howard, Frank	175.00	90.00	825.00
Jackson, Reggie	850.00	225.00	1,500.00
Jensen, Jackie	150.00	85.00	825.00
Kaat, Jim	45.00	70.00	300.00
Kluszewski, Ted	175.00	90.00	850.00
Maris, Roger	750.00	250.00	2,000.00
Martin, Billy	825.00	175.00	1,200.00
Mazeroski, Bill	200.00	125.00	700.00
Munson, Thurman	225.00	150.00	550.00
Murcer, Bobby	175.00	100.00	250.00
Nettles, Graig	125.00	100.00	300.00
Niekro, Phil	50.00	75.00	300.00
Oliva, Tony	275.00	95.00	650.00
Parker, Dave	125.00	100.00	450.00
Perez, Tony	90.00	75.00	250.00
Piersall, Jimmy	100.00	75.00	675.00
Powell, Boog	75.00	70.00	300.00
Richardson, Bobby	250.00	100.00	750.00
Rizzuto, Phil	525.00	150.00	900.00
Rose, Pete	900.00	500.00	1,500.00
Rosen, Al	250.00	95.00	750.00
Santo, Ron	75.00	65.00	300.00
Schmidt, Mike	800.00	300.00	1,250.00
Skowron, Bill	250.00	95.00	600.00
Staub, Rusty	150.00	75.00	250.00
Sutton, Don	25.00	90.00	325.00
Torre, Joe	250.00	75.00	325.00
Uecker, Bob	75.00	45.00	200.00
Valenzuela, Fernando	25.00	55.00	250.00
White, Bill	200.00	75.00	325.00
Wills, Maury	75.00	70.00	300.00

ACTIVE PLAYERS

Abbott, Jim	NA	125.00	600.00
Alomar, Roberto	125.00	100.00	350.00
Alomar, Sandy	75.00	50.00	275.00
Avery, Steve	125.00	100.00	650.00
Baerga, Carlos	65.00	50.00	275.00
Bagwell, Jeff	125.00	75.00	425.00
Baines, Harold	100.00	65.00	375.00
Bell, George	125.00	75.00	375.00
Belle, Albert	100.00	65.00	375.00
Biggio, Craig	85.00	65.00	350.00
Blyleven, Bert	25.00	50.00	300.00
Boggs, Wade	300.00	250.00	1,250.00
Bonds, Barry	200.00	150.00	750.00
Bonilla, Bobby	175.00	100.00	700.00
Brett, George	300.00	250.00	1,600.00
Browning, Tom	25.00	50.00	250.00
Burks, Ellis	85.00	65.00	275.00
Butler, Brett	70.00	50.00	225.00
Calderon, Ivan	80.00	65.00	250.00
Canseco, Jose	275.00	150.00	1,500.00
Carter, Gary	150.00	75.00	500.00
Carter, Joe	125.00	60.00	400.00
Cedendo, Andujar	65.00	50.00	200.00
Chamberlain, Wes	65.00	50.00	200.00
Clark, Jack	100.00	55.00	325.00
Clark, Will	250.00	175.00	1,250.00
Clemens, Roger	NA	300.00	1,600.00
Coleman, Vince	100.00	55.00	325.00
Cone, David	25.00	50.00	550.00
Cuyler, Milt	65.00	50.00	200.00
Davis, Eric	150.00	75.00	500.00
Davis, Glenn	125.00	65.00	425.00
Dawson, Andre	200.00	85.00	650.00
DeShields, Delino	75.00	50.00	250.00
Dibble, Rob	25.00	50.00	250.00
Drabek, Doug	25.00	65.00	300.00
Dunston, Shawon	100.00	50.00	300.00
Dykstra, Len	125.00	60.00	425.00
Eckersley, Dennis	25.00	55.00	250.00
Erickson, Scott	25.00	70.00	300.00
Evans, Dwight	125.00	55.00	350.00
Fernandez, Tony	50.00	50.00	175.00
Fielder, Cecil	300.00	125.00	750.00
Fisk, Carlton	200.00	150.00	1,600.00
Franco, Julio	90.00	60.00	275.00
Fryman, Travis	100.00	60.00	325.00
Gant, Ron	175.00	75.00	450.00
Gibson, Kirk	100.00	60.00	325.00
Glavine, Tom	25.00	55.00	325.00
Gonzalez, Juan	85.00	60.00	300.00
Gonzalez, Luis	65.00	50.00	225.00
Gooden, Dwight	25.00	100.00	1,200.00

Original expansion team flannels

Gossage, Goose	25.00	45.00	200.00
Grace, Mark	100.00	50.00	225.00
Greenwell, Mike	100.00	50.00	400.00
Griffey, Ken Jr.	350.00	300.00	1,500.00
Grissom, Marquis	75.00	45.00	225.00
Gruber, Kelly	80.00	55.00	275.00
Guerrero, Pedro	85.00	60.00	280.00
Gwynn, Tony	200.00	100.00	1,000.00
Harnisch, Pete	25.00	60.00	275.00
Harvey, Bryan	NA	45.00	200.00
Henderson, Rickey	450.00	300.00	1,500.00
Hershiser, Orel	50.00	90.00	575.00
Hrbek, Kent	85.00	60.00	400.00
Hundley, Todd	45.00	40.00	175.00
Jackson, Bo	550.00	300.00	1,250.00
Jefferies, Gregg	100.00	65.00	275.00
Jefferson, Reggie	50.00	45.00	175.00
Johnson, Howard	150.00	85.00	450.00
Jordan, Rickey	45.00	45.00	150.00
Jose, Felix	85.00	50.00	150.00
Joyner, Wally	100.00	65.00	500.00
Justice, Dave	175.00	125.00	800.00
Kelly, Pat	100.00	50.00	275.00
Kelly, Roberto	100.00	60.00	325.00
Klesko, Ryan	85.00	55.00	275.00
Knoblauch, Chuck	70.00	55.00	250.00
Langston, Mark	25.00	55.00	225.00
Lankford, Ray	100.00	55.00	250.00
Larkin, Barry	125.00	90.00	450.00
Maas, Kevin	85.00	60.00	275.00
Maddux, Greg	25.00	50.00	225.00
Martinez, Dennis	25.00	50.00	225.00
Martinez, Ramon	25.00	65.00	300.00
Martinez, Tino	45.00	45.00	175.00
Mattingly, Don	600.00	250.00	2,250.00
McDonald, Ben	25.00	65.00	250.00
McDowell, Jack	25.00	60.00	225.00
McGee, Willie	100.00	60.00	250.00
McGriff, Fred	125.00	65.00	325.00
McGwire, Mark	175.00	65.00	800.00
McRae, Brian	50.00	45.00	175.00
McReynolds, Kevin	100.00	65.00	250.00
Merced, Orlando	45.00	45.00	150.00
Mitchell, Kevin	150.00	125.00	500.00
Molitor, Paul	125.00	75.00	350.00
Morris, Hal	50.00	45.00	225.00
Morris, Jack	25.00	100.00	475.00
Murphy, Dale	175.00	80.00	700.00
Murray, Eddie	225.00	100.00	750.00
Mussina, Mike	NA	50.00	250.00
Olerud, John	50.00	45.00	225.00
Palmeiro, Rafael	75.00	50.00	250.00
Pendleton, Terry	80.00	75.00	300.00
Plantier, Phil	150.00	100.00	450.00
Puckett, Kirby	225.00	125.00	1,200.00
Raines, Tim	200.00	100.00	550.00
Randolph, Willie	50.00	45.00	275.00
Reardon, Jeff	25.00	50.00	250.00
Ripken, Cal	400.00	250.00	1,600.00
Rodriguez, Ivan	65.00	50.00	225.00
Ryan, Nolan	500.00	600.00	3,000.00
Saberhagen, Bret	25.00	60.00	300.00
Sabo, Chris	75.00	55.00	275.00
Samuel, Juan	75.00	55.00	225.00
Sandberg, Ryne	450.00	250.00	1,750.00
Santiago, Benito	85.00	50.00	250.00
Sax, Steve	85.00	55.00	250.00
Sierra, Ruben	125.00	75.00	450.00
Smith, Lee	25.00	50.00	250.00
Smith, Ozzie	150.00	80.00	450.00
Smoltz, John	25.00	55.00	275.00
Stewart, Dave	25.00	50.00	200.00

Stieb, Dave	25.00	50.00	175.00
Strawberry, Darryl	300.00	200.00	950.00
Tartabull, Danny	85.00	65.00	275.00
Tettleton, Mickey	60.00	45.00	250.00
Thigpen, Bobby	NA	45.00	250.00
Thomas, Frank	300.00	200.00	1,250.00
Trammell, Alan	100.00	65.00	350.00
Van Poppel, Todd	NA	55.00	250.00
Van Slyke, Andy	125.00	60.00	325.00
Vaughn, Greg	60.00	45.00	225.00
Vaughn, Mo	75.00	60.00	300.00
Ventura, Robin	100.00	75.00	400.00
Viola, Frank	25.00	60.00	275.00
Walker, Larry	75.00	50.00	250.00
Welch, Bob	25.00	50.00	250.00
Whitaker, Lou	125.00	75.00	350.00
Whiten, Mark	50.00	45.00	200.00
Williams, Matt	125.00	100.00	350.00
Williams, Mitch	25.00	50.00	225.00
Winfield, Dave	175.00	125.00	500.00
Yount, Robin	225.00	200.00	950.00
Zeile, Todd	100.00	75.00	300.00

PLAYER ENDORSED BASEBALL GLOVES

Aaron, Hank	MacGregor Special 715 fielder's glove	175.00
Alvis, Max	Wilson Fieldmaster fielder's glove.	35.00
Ashburn, Richie	MacGregor fielder's glove	50.00
Beckert, Glenn	Wilson fielder's glove	40.00
Bell, Gus	MacGregor fielder's glove	50.00
Bench, Johnny	Rawlings catcher's mitt	50.00
Berra, Yogi	Franklin C655 catcher's mitt	85.00
Blanchard, Johnny	Rawlings catcher's mitt	75.00
Bostock, Lyman	Regent fielder's glove	75.00
Boyer, Ken	Rawlings fielder's glove	75.00
Brecheen, Harry	Wilson A2944 fielder's glove	80.00
Bunning, Jim	GRCH fielder's glove	55.00
Burgess, Smokey	J.C. Higgins catcher's mitt	75.00
Campanella, Roy	Wilson catcher's mitt	85.00
Carey, Andy	Rawlings fielder's glove	50.00
Clemente, Roberto	JC Higgins #1633 fielder's.glove.	100.00
Collins, Joe	OK J700 three-finger first baseman's glove	75.00
Collins, Ripper	Goldsmith two-finger first baseman's glove	100.00
Crandall, Del	Franklin catcher's mitt	100.00
Dark, Al	Spalding fielder's glove	50.00
Davenport, Jim	Wilson fielder's glove	40.00
Davis, Spud	Wilson #500 catcher's mitt	75.00
De La Cruz, Tomas	Imperial Mexican MFG fielder's.glove.	75.00
Dickey, Bill	Hawthorne catcher's mitt	200.00
Dickey, Bill	Wilson catcher's mitt	125.00
DiMaggio, Joe	Professional Model F16	400.00
DiMaggio, Joe	Reach fielder's glove	500.00
DiMaggio, Joe	Unknown Mfg fielder's glove	200.00
DiMaggio, Vince	Hutch fielder's glove	125.00
Doerr, Bobby	MacGregor fielder's glove	75.00
Doerr, Bobby	OK SF fielder's glove	55.00
Durocher, Leo	MacGregor G130 fielder's glove.	100.00
Edwards, Johnny	MacGregor catcher's mitt	60.00
Fairly, Ron	Spalding 42-486 first baseman's glove	65.00
Feller, Bob	J.C. Higgins fielder's glove	125.00
Feller, Bob	Starline fielder's glove	100.00
Fonseca, Lew	Wards Marathon fielder's glove.	150.00
Ford, Whitey	Spalding fielder's glove	60.00
Freehan, Bill	Wilson catcher's mitt	75.00
Frisch, Frankie	Spalding fielder's glove	300.00
Gordon, Joe	Marathon fielder's glove	60.00
Gordon, Joe	Wards 60-1205 fielder's glove.	85.00
Gordon, Joe	Wilson fielder's glove	75.00
Gordon, Joe	Wilson fielder's glove	50.00
Grant, Mudcat	Rawlings fielder's glove	60.00
Gustine, Frank	Reach Co. four-finger fielder's.glove.	50.00
Hartnett, Gabby	1911 patent catcher's mitt	200.00
Hassett, Buddy	Processed leather two-finger first baseman's glove	100.00
Herman, Billy	Hutch 40 fielder's glove	75.00
Herman, Billy	J.C. Higgins	

Assorted game-worn flannels

	fielder's glove..	150.00
Higgins, Pinky	Spalding 1939-40 fielder's glove.	80.00
Higgins, Pinky	Spalding #273 fielder's.glove.	90.00
Holtzman, Ken	Rawlings Japan Mfg. fielder's glove..	40.00
Hopp, Johnny	Wilson fielder's glove	65.00
Hornsby, Rogers	Wilson fielder's glove	350.00
House, Frank	J.C. Higgins catcher's mitt	65.00
Jackson, Larry	Rawlings fielder's glove	40.00
Jensen, Jackie	Bufa 3F9 fielder's glove	70.00
Jensen, Jackie	MacGregor fielder's glove	35.00
Kell, George	Wilson A2020 fielder's glove	70.00
Kell, George	Wilson A2932 fielder's glove	80.00
Keltner, Ken	Rawlings KR fielder's glove	75.00
Kiner, Ralph	SNNT fielder's glove	75.00
Kuenn, Harvey	Wilson "Ball Hawk" fielder's glove..	65.00
Kuenn, Harvey	Wilson fielder's glove	60.00
Larsen, Don	Spalding No Hitter model fielder's glove..	75.00
Lemon, Bob	A.H.I. Brand fielder's glove	65.00
Loes, Billy	Nokono Pro Line FG scarce	100.00
Logan, Johnny	Franklin fielder's glove	40.00
Logan, Johnny	Franklin 119 fielder's glove	60.00
Lumpe, Jerry	Spalding fielder's glove	35.00
Mantle, Mickey	Rawlings Triple Crown Winner fielder's glove	135.00
Mantle, Mickey	Rawlings #MM4 FG	125.00
Mantle, Mickey	Rawlings FG later issue	100.00
Maris, Roger	Spalding fielder's glove	100.00
Martin, Billy	Wilson fielder's glove	80.00
Martin, Billy	Wilson four-finger fielder's glove.	85.00
McDougald, Gil	MacGregor fielder's glove	55.00
Medwick, Joe	Marathon Sporting Goods fielder's glove..	75.00
Mejias, Roman	Spalding fielder's glove	40.00
Mize, Johnny	Firestone "Olympians" two-finger first baseman's glove	135.00
Mize, Johnny	O.K. MFG Co. "The Snapper" first baseman's glove	75.00
Morgan, Joe	MacGregor fielder's glove	40.00
Musial, Stan	Franklin fielder's glove	125.00
Newhouser, Hal	Sonnet fielder's glove	80.00
Ott, Mel	Goldsmith fielder's glove	300.00
Owen, Mickey	Rawlings catcher's mitt	80.00
Pearson, Monte	Marathon fielder's glove	85.00
Pesky, Johnny	Rawlings G490 fielder's glove	85.00
Piersall, Jimmy	SNNT JP64 fielder's glove	70.00
Pinson, Vada	Spalding 1st baseman's glove	50.00
Reese, Pee Wee	Denkert fielder's glove	110.00
Reiser, Pete	MacGregor fielder's glove	75.00
Reiser, Pete	OK 758 fielder's glove	75.00
Richardson, Bobby	Denkert fielder's glove	65.00
Richardson, Bobby	Denkert fielder's glove	65.00
Roberts, Robin	MacGregor fielder's glove	65.00
Robinson, Jackie	CPRO - Japanese Mfg. fielder's glove.	75.00
Rowe, Schoolboy	Reach fielder's glove	400.00
Rudi, Joe	Rawlings finger hole fielder's glove..	40.00
Schoendienst, Red	MacGregor fielder's glove	75.00
Seaver, Tom	Rawlings fielder's glove	75.00
Sievers, Roy	Rawlings fielder's glove	78.00
Simmons, Curt	MacGregor fielder's glove	60.00
Skinner, Bob	Rawlings "The Trapper" first baseman's glove	80.00
Snider, Duke	Yale F600 fielder's glove	75.00
Stargell, Willie	Rawlings 626 first baseman's glove	65.00
Stewback, Larry	Hutch catcher's mitt	125.00
Stirnweiss, Snuffy	Spalding #193 fielder's glove	75.00
Stripp, Joe	Spalding 1928-38 two-finger first baseman's glove	125.00
Thompson, Bobby	MacGregor fielder's glove	65.00
Thompson, Hank	Dekert fielder's glove	75.00
Torre, Frank	MacGregor "Trapper" three-finger first baseman's glove	75.00
Traynor, Pie	J.C. Higgins fielder's glove	150.00
Walker, Harry	J.C. Higgins fielder's glove	65.00
Wynn, Early	Wilson fielder's glove	50.00
Yastrzemski, Carl	Spalding fielder's glove	60.00
Young, Pep	Hutch 42 fielder's glove	85.00
Young, Cy	Hutch fielder's glove	650.00

TEAM JERSEY VALUES

Team	Flannel	Knit
American League		
Baltimore Orioles	800.00	200.00
Boston Red Sox	700.00	200.00
California Angels	350.00	175.00
Chicago White Sox	500.00	150.00
Cleveland Indians	500.00	200.00
Detroit Tigers	800.00	300.00
Kansas City Royals	350.00	150.00
Milwaukee Brewers	600.00	250.00
New York Yankees	800.00	350.00
Oakland A's	450.00	250.00
Seattle Mariners		200.00
Texas Rangers	1,000.00	150.00
Toronto Blue Jays		400.00

Note: No flannel listings are entered for Seattle or Toronto, as neither team played during the flannel era. Texas only used flannels for spring training of their first year (1972). The Texas flannels are extremely rare, and are actually re-lettered Washington Senators jerseys.

Team	Flannel	Knit
National League		
Atlanta Braves	500.00	175.00
Chicago Cubs	1,000.00	175.00
Cincinnati Reds	600.00	150.00
Houston Astros	700.00	250.00
Los Angeles Dodgers	600.00	300.00
Montreal Expos	800.00	200.00
New York Mets	1,000.00	250.00
Philadelphia Phillies	750.00	250.00
Pittsburgh Pirates	600.00	250.00
St. Louis Cardinals	650.00	175.00
San Diego Padres	600.00	200.00
San Francisco Giants	750.00	175.00

Note: Generally, a defunct team flannel will be valued at $1,000.00, or higher. The Los Angeles Angels jersey is an exception to this general rule, as the style of the jersey did not change when the team changed from LA to California.

BASKETBALL EQUIPMENT

HALL OF FAME PLAYERS

Player	Sneakers	Jersey
Archibald, Nate	1,000.00	2,250.00
Arizin, Paul	1,000.00	2,000.00
Barry, Rick	1,000.00	2,250.00
Baylor, Elgin	1,500.00	2,500.00
Bing, Dave	750.00	1,250.00
Borgmann, Bennie	1,500.00	2,750.00
Bradley, Bill	1,000.00	2,250.00
Cervi, Alfred	1,750.00	3,500.00
Chamberlain, Wilt	3,000.00	6,000.00
Cooper, Charles	1,500.00	3,000.00
Cousy, Bob	2,750.00	5,750.00
Cowens, Dave	500.00	1,000.00
Cunningham, Billy	750.00	1,500.00
Davies, Robert	1,500.00	2,750.00
DeBusschere, Dave	1,250.00	2,500.00

Dehnert, Henry	2,000.00	4,000.00
Endacott, Paul	2,000.00	4,000.00
Foster, Bud	2,000.00	3,750.00
Frazier, Walt	1,750.00	3,750.00
Friedman, Marty	2,000.00	3,750.00
Fulks, Joe	2,000.00	3,750.00
Gale, Laddie	1,750.00	2,500.00
Gallatin, Harry	1,750.00	2,750.00
Gates, William	1,500.00	2,500.00
Gola, Tom	1,500.00	2,750.00
Greer, Hal	1,500.00	2,750.00
Gruenig, Robert	2,500.00	4,750.00
Hagan, Cliff	2,000.00	3,250.00
Hanson, Victor	2,500.00	4,750.00
Havlicek, John	1,750.00	4,000.00
Hawkins, Connie	1,000.00	1,250.00
Hayes, Elvin	750.00	1,000.00
Heinsohn, Tommy	2,250.00	4,250.00
Holman, Nat	2,500.00	4,750.00
Houbregs, Robert	2,000.00	4,000.00
Hyatt, Chuck	3,000.00	4,750.00
Johnson, William	1,250.00	2,500.00
Johnston, Neil	1,000.00	2,250.00
Jones, K.C.	2,250.00	4,500.00
Jones, Samuel	1,000.00	2,500.00
Krause, Edward	1,250.00	2,500.00
Kurland, Bob	2,750.00	4,250.00
Lanier, Bob	750.00	750.00
Lapchick, Joe	3,000.00	4,750.00
Lovellette, Clyde	750.00	1,500.00
Lucas, Jerry	1,000.00	2,500.00
Luisetti, Hank	2,500.00	4,500.00
Macauley, Ed	2,750.00	4,500.00
Maravich, Pete	1,500.00	4,000.00
Martin, Slater	1,000.00	2,250.00
McCracken, Branch	2,500.00	4,250.00
McCracken, Jack	2,500.00	4,250.00
McDermott, Bobby	1,000.00	1,750.00
Mikan, George	5,000.00	10,000.00
Monroe, Earl	1,750.00	3,500.00
Murphy, Charles	2,250.00	4,000.00
Page, Harlan	2,250.00	3,750.00
Pettit, Bob	2,250.00	4,000.00
Phillip, Andy	2,000.00	3,500.00
Pollard, Jim	1,000.00	1,500.00
Ramsey, Frank	1,500.00	2,500.00
Reed, Willis	1,750.00	3,750.00
Robertson, Oscar	2,250.00	4,250.00
Roosma, John	1,750.00	3,250.00
Russell, Bill	2,750.00	4,750.00
Schayes, Dolph	2,000.00	3,250.00
Schmidt, Ernest	1,750.00	3,000.00
Sedran, Barney	1,500.00	2,750.00
Sharman, Bill	2,250.00	4,500.00
Steinmetz, Christian	2,250.00	4,000.00
Thompson, John (Cat)	2,000.00	4,000.00
Thurmond, Nate	750.00	900.00
Twyman, Jack	750.00	900.00
Unseld, Wes	750.00	1,250.00
Vandivier, Robert	1,500.00	2,250.00
Wachter, Edward	2,500.00	3,500.00
Wanzer, Robert	800.00	1,750.00
West, Jerry	1,000.00	3,500.00
Wilkens, Lenny	750.00	1,250.00
Wooden, John	4,000.00	8,500.00

INACTIVE PLAYERS

Abdul-Jabbar, Kareem	1,250.00	3,750.00
Adams, Alvan	100.00	200.00
Adelman, Rick	125.00	250.00
Attles, Al	150.00	275.00
Barnett, Dick	100.00	200.00
Beaty, Zelmo	100.00	225.00
Bellamy, Walt	125.00	250.00
Bibby, Henry	100.00	200.00
Braun, Carl	125.00	275.00
Brown, Fred	100.00	200.00
Brown, Larry	125.00	225.00
Buckner, Quinn	125.00	225.00
Calverley, Ernie	125.00	275.00
Carr, Austin	125.00	275.00
Chaney, Don	125.00	225.00
Chenier, Phil	100.00	200.00
Clifton, Nat	125.00	275.00
Collins, Doug	125.00	225.00
Dampier, Louie	100.00	200.00
Dandridge, Bob	100.00	200.00
Dantley, Adrian	150.00	250.00
Dawkins, Darryl	150.00	300.00
Dunleavy, Mike	150.00	250.00
Embry, Wayne	100.00	200.00
English, Alex	125.00	225.00
Erving, Julius	1,250.00	3,000.00
Ford, Chris	125.00	250.00
Free, World B.	125.00	225.00
Gallatin, Harry	100.00	200.00
Gilmore, Artis	175.00	275.00
Goodrich, Gail	200.00	375.00
Goukas, Matt	100.00	200.00
Hairston, Happy	100.00	200.00
Haskins, Clem	100.00	200.00
Haywood, Spencer	125.00	225.00
Hazzard, Walt	125.00	250.00
Hudson, Lou	125.00	250.00
Hundley, Rod	150.00	275.00
Issel, Dan	125.00	275.00
Jackson, Phil	125.00	275.00
Johnson, Dennis	150.00	325.00
Johnson, Gus	125.00	225.00
Johnson, Magic	2,500.00	5,000.00
Johnson, Marques	125.00	225.00
Jones, Bobby	200.00	375.00
Jones, Caldwell	100.00	200.00
Kupchak, Mitch	100.00	225.00
Love, Bob	100.00	200.00
Lucas, John	125.00	250.00
Lucas, Maurice	100.00	200.00
Maxwell, Cedric	100.00	200.00
McAdoo, Bob	150.00	275.00
McGinnis, George	100.00	200.00
Moncreif, Sidney	125.00	225.00
Murphy, Calvin	125.00	225.00
Nelson, Don	150.00	250.00
Nixon, Norm	125.00	225.00
Paxson, Jim	100.00	200.00
Porter, Kevin	100.00	200.00
Riley, Pat	200.00	400.00
Sikma, Jack	125.00	225.00
Silas, Paul	125.00	250.00
Sloan, Jerry	100.00	225.00
Theus, Reggie	125.00	250.00
Thompson, David	150.00	275.00
Tomjanovich, Rudy	100.00	200.00
Van Lier, Norm	100.00	200.00
Walker, Chet	100.00	225.00
Walton, Bill	225.00	500.00
Weiss, Bob	100.00	200.00
Westphal, Paul	100.00	200.00
White, Jo Jo	175.00	350.00
Wicks, Sidney	125.00	225.00
Wilkes, Jamaal	175.00	275.00
Williams, Gus	100.00	200.00
Wise, Willie	100.00	200.00
Zaslofsky, Max	100.00	200.00

ACTIVE PLAYERS

Adams, Michael	100.00	175.00
Aguirre, Mark	100.00	200.00
Ainge, Danny	75.00	125.00
Anderson, Kenny	150.00	300.00

Bill Sharman and Dolph Schayes

Anderson, Nick	75.00	125.00
Anderson, Willie	75.00	125.00
Anthony, Greg	75.00	150.00
Armstrong, B.J.	75.00	175.00
Augmon, Stacey	100.00	200.00
Bailey, Thurl	75.00	125.00
Barkley, Charles	400.00	850.00
Bird, Larry	1,000.00	2,750.00
Blackman, Rolando	75.00	175.00
Blaylock, Mookie	100.00	200.00
Bol, Manute	75.00	125.00
Brandon, Terrell	75.00	150.00
Brown, Dee	200.00	450.00
Burton, Willie	75.00	125.00
Campbell, Elden	75.00	150.00
Cartwright, Bill	75.00	150.00
Causwell, Duane	75.00	125.00
Ceballos, Cedric	75.00	125.00
Chambers, Tom	125.00	275.00
Chapman, Rex	75.00	125.00

Cheeks, Maurice	75.00	125.00
Coleman, Derrick	200.00	450.00
Corbin, Tyrone	75.00	125.00
Cummings, Terry	75.00	150.00
Daugherty, Brad	100.00	250.00
Davis, Walter	75.00	125.00
Dawkins, Johnny	75.00	150.00
Douglas, Sherman	75.00	125.00
Drexler, Clyde	350.00	675.00
Dumars, Joe	100.00	225.00
Edwards, Blue	75.00	125.00
Edwards, James	75.00	125.00
Elliott, Sean	75.00	175.00
Ellis, Dale	75.00	175.00
Ellison, Pervis	75.00	175.00
Ewing, Patrick	400.00	875.00
Ferry, Danny	75.00	125.00
Fox, Rick	100.00	175.00
Gamble, Kevin	75.00	125.00
Gill, Kendall	75.00	125.00
Gilliam, Armon	75.00	125.00
Grant, Harvey	75.00	125.00
Grant, Horace	75.00	175.00
Green, A.C.	75.00	150.00
Hardaway, Tim	225.00	475.00
Harper, Derek	100.00	175.00
Harper, Ron	125.00	300.00
Hawkins, Hersey	100.00	200.00
Hodges, Craig	75.00	125.00
Hornacek, Jeff	75.00	175.00
Jackson, Chris	75.00	150.00
Jackson, Mark	100.00	175.00
Johnson, Kevin	225.00	475.00
Johnson, Larry	150.00	350.00
Jordan, Michael	1,250.00	3,000.00
Kemp, Shawn	100.00	225.00
Kersey, Jerome	75.00	175.00
Kimble, Bo	75.00	125.00
King, Bernard	100.00	200.00
King, Stacey	75.00	125.00
Laimbeer, Bill	75.00	175.00
Lever, Fat	75.00	125.00
Lewis, Reggie	100.00	200.00
Macon, Mark	75.00	125.00
Majerle, Dan	75.00	175.00
Malone, Jeff	75.00	125.00
Malone, Karl	225.00	475.00
Malone, Moses	175.00	400.00
Manning, Danny	100.00	225.00
Marciulionis, Sarunas	75.00	175.00
Maxwell, Vernon	75.00	125.00
McDaniel, Xavier	75.00	125.00
McHale, Kevin	125.00	300.00
Miller, Reggie	100.00	225.00
Morris, Chris	75.00	125.00
Mullin, Chris	225.00	475.00
Mutombo, Dikembe	150.00	350.00
Nance, Larry	75.00	150.00
Norman, Ken	75.00	125.00
Oakley, Charles	75.00	125.00
Olajuwon, Hakeem	250.00	550.00
Owens, Billy	125.00	275.00
Parish, Robert	150.00	350.00
Payton, Gary	75.00	175.00
Paxson, John	75.00	175.00
Perkins, Sam	125.00	275.00
Person, Chuck	150.00	300.00
Petrovic, Drazen	75.00	125.00
Pippen, Scottie	250.00	575.00
Porter, Terry	75.00	175.00
Reid, J.R.	75.00	125.00
Rice, Glenn	75.00	175.00
Richardson, Pooh	75.00	150.00
Richmond, Mitch	150.00	325.00
Rivers, Doc	100.00	250.00
Roberston, Alvin	75.00	125.00
Robinson, Cliff	75.00	150.00
Robinson, David	550.00	1,000.00
Robinson, Rumeal	75.00	125.00
Rodman, Dennis	150.00	300.00
Schrempf, Detlef	75.00	175.00
Scott, Byron	100.00	225.00
Scott, Dennis	100.00	250.00
Seikaly, Rony	100.00	200.00
Shaw, Brian	75.00	175.00
Simmons, Lionel	125.00	275.00
Skiles, Scott	75.00	150.00
Smith, Charles	75.00	175.00
Smith, Steve	125.00	275.00
Starks, John	75.00	125.00
Stockton, John	225.00	425.00
Tisdale, Wayman	75.00	125.00
Webb, Spud	75.00	200.00
Wilkins, Dominique	400.00	750.00
Williams, Buck	100.00	175.00
Williams, John	75.00	175.00
Willis, Kevin	75.00	175.00
Worthy, James	250.00	500.00

FOOTBALL EQUIPMENT

HALL OF FAME PLAYERS

Player	Spikes	Helmet	Jersey
Adderley, Herb	100.00	1,000.00	900.00
Alworth, Lance	100.00	1,250.00	1,000.00
Atkins, Doug	100.00	950.00	900.00
Battles, Cliff	125.00	2,750.00	2,500.00
Baugh, Sammy	425.00	15,000.00	14,000.00
Bednarik, Chuck	175.00	4,000.00	3,750.00
Bell, Bobby	100.00	975.00	900.00
Berry, Raymond	125.00	2,500.00	2,300.00
Biletnikoff, Fred	75.00	725.00	650.00
Blanda, George	125.00	3,750.00	3,500.00
Blount, Mel	75.00	700.00	600.00
Bradshaw, Terry	125.00	4,000.00	3,750.00
Brown, Jim	200.00	5,000.00	4,250.00
Brown,Roosevelt	100.00	975.00	900.00
Brown, Willie	100.00	950.00	875.00
Buchanan, Buck	100.00	1,0000.00	925.00
Butkus, Dick	125.00	2,250.00	2,000.00
Campbell, Earl	85.00	850.00	800.00
Canadeo, Tony	100.00	2,000.00	1,750.00
Christiansen, Jack	125.00	2,250.00	2,000.00
Connor, George	100.00	925.00	650.00
Csonka, Larry	80.00	875.00	800.00
Davis, Willie	95.00	850.00	800.00
Dawson, Len	125.00	1,250.00	1,000.00
Ditka, Mike	100.00	1,000.00	900.00
Donovan, Art	100.00	1,500.00	1,250.00
Dudley, Bill	125.00	2,250.00	2,000.00
Edwards, Turk	125.00	2,000.00	1,800.00
Fears, Tom	125.00	2,000.00	1,750.00
Ford, Len	100.00	950.00	900.00
Fortmann, Danny	150.00	2,500.00	2,250.00
Gatski, Frank	85.00	850.00	800.00
George, Bill	125.00	1,750.00	1,500.00
Gifford, Frank	275.00	5,750.00	5,500.00
Graham, Otto	300.00	6,250.00	6,000.00
Grange, Red	400.00	12,000.00	11,500.00
Greene, Joe	80.00	850.00	775.00
Gregg, Forrest	85.00	875.00	725.00
Griese, Bob	90.00	950.00	825.00
Groza, Lou	100.00	1,500.00	1,400.00
Ham, Jack	65.00	675.00	550.00
Hannah, John	75.00	650.00	500.00
Harris, Franco	90.00	1,000.00	850.00

Herber, Arnie	300.00	6,000.00	5,000.00
Hewitt, Bill	125.00	2,000.00	1,850.00
Hinkle, Clarke	350.00	7,000.00	6,000.00
Hirsch, Elroy	225.00	5,400.00	5,200.00
Hornung, Paul	100.00	1,250.00	1,000.00
Houston, Ken	95.00	950.00	900.00
Huff, Sam	100.00	1,250.00	1,000.00
Hutson, Don	450.00	12,500.00	10,000.00
Johnson, John H.	95.00	950.00	875.00
Jones, Deacon	80.00	850.00	775.00
Jones, Stan	90.00	875.00	800.00
Jurgensen, Sonny	125.00	1,500.00	1,250.00
Kinard, Bruiser	150.00	1,750.00	1,500.00
Lambert, Jack	75.00	750.00	700.00
Landry, Tom	200.00	4,500.00	4,250.00
Lane, Dick	95.00	975.00	925.00
Langer, Jim	85.00	800.00	750.00
Lanier, Willie	85.00	850.00	775.00
Lary, Yale	85.00	825.00	750.00
Lavelli, Dante	95.00	975.00	900.00
Layne, Bobby	250.00	7,250.00	7,000.00
Leemans, Tuffy	85.00	950.00	900.00
Lilly, Bob	80.00	850.00	800.00
Luckman, Sid	175.00	4,000.00	3,800.00
Lyman, Link	225.00	NA	8,000.00
Marchetti, Gino	100.00	1,250.00	1,000.00
Matson, Ollie	100.00	1,250.00	1,000.00
Maynard, Don	90.00	950.00	900.00
McAfee, George	125.00	3,000.00	2,800.00
McCormack, Mike	95.00	975.00	900.00
McElhenny, Hugh	125.00	2,750.00	2,600.00
Michalske, Mike	225.00	NA	8,000.00
Millner, Wayne	150.00	3,000.00	2,850.00
Mitchell, Bobby	95.00	900.00	850.00
Mix, Ron	90.00	875.00	800.00
Moore, Lenny	100.00	1,000.00	850.00
Motley, Marion	125.00	2,250.00	2,000.00
Musso, George	95.00	950.00	900.00
Nagurski,Bronko	1,500.00	20,000.00	25,000.00
Namath, Joe	200.00	5,000.00	4,500.00
Nevers, Ernie	750.00	NA	15,000.00
Nitschke, Ray	125.00	1,250.00	1,000.00
Nomellini, Leo	125.00	1,800.00	1,500.00
Olsen, Merlin	100.00	1,500.00	1,350.00
Otto, Jim	100.00	1,250.00	1,000.00
Owen, Steve	650.00	NA	10,000.00
Page, Alan	90.00	900.00	850.00
Parker, Ace	125.00	1,500.00	1,250.00
Parker, Jim	100.00	1,250.00	1,000.00
Perry, Joe	150.00	2,000.00	1,750.00
Pihos, Pete	100.00	1,250.00	1,000.00
Ringo, Jim	95.00	950.00	875.00
Robustelli, Andy	125.00	1,500.00	1,250.00
St.Clair, Bob	90.00	900.00	800.00
Sayers, Gale	200.00	6,000.00	5,000.00
Schmidt, Joe	125.00	1,400.00	1,200.00
Shell, Art	75.00	900.00	850.00
Simpson, O.J.	250.00	5,500.00	4,750.00
Starr, Bart	200.00	6,750.00	6,500.00
Staubach, Roger	175.00	3,500.00	3,250.00
Stautner, Ernie	150.00	2,000.00	1,750.00
Stenerud, Jan	80.00	800.00	700.00
Strong, Ken	125.00	1,500.00	1,250.00
Stydahar, Joe	125.00	1,500.00	1,250.00
Tarkenton, Fran	150.00	2,500.00	2,000.00
Taylor, Charley	90.00	900.00	825.00
Taylor, Jim	100.00	1,250.00	1,000.00
Thorpe, Jim	1,500.00	NA	20,000.00
Tittle, Y.A.	200.00	5,750.00	5,500.00
Trafton, George	250.00	9,000.00	8,500.00
Trippi, Charlie	175.00	4,000.00	3,500.00
Tunnell, Emlen	175.00	3,750.00	3,250.00
Turner, Bulldog	200.00	5,500.00	5,000.00
Unitas, Johnny	200.00	6,750.00	6,500.00
Upshaw, Gene	90.00	900.00	825.00
Van Brocklin, Norm	150.00	4,500.00	4,250.00
Van Buren, Steve	125.00	1,750.00	1,500.00
Walker, Doak	90.00	900.00	825.00
Warfield, Paul	90.00	950.00	875.00
Waterfield, Bob	275.00	10,000.00	9,750.00
Weinmeister, Arnie	90.00	975.00	900.00
Willis, Bill	95.00	950.00	875.00
Wilson, Larry	90.00	925.00	850.00
Wojciechowicz, Alex	125.00	2,000.00	1,800.00
Wood, Willie	90.00	950.00	875.00

1990 Joe Montana helmet

ACTIVE PLAYERS

Aikman, Troy	125.00	1,300.00	1,200.00
Allen, Marcus	100.00	1,250.00	1,100.00
Anderson, Flipper	50.00	425.00	325.00
Anderson, Neal	80.00	850.00	750.00
Anderson, Ottis	60.00	550.00	400.00
Atwater, Steve	50.00	600.00	475.00
Bailey, Johnny	45.00	450.00	325.00
Ball, Jerry	35.00	350.00	250.00
Barnett, Fred	40.00	375.00	275.00
Bell, Nick	45.00	600.00	500.00
Bennett, Cornelius	60.00	800.00	675.00
Bernstine, Rod	40.00	375.00	300.00
Bieniemy, Eric	40.00	400.00	325.00
Blades, Brian	50.00	500.00	375.00
Brooks, James	50.00	450.00	350.00
Broussard, Steve	40.00	425.00	325.00
Brown, Jerome	40.00	375.00	325.00
Bunch, Jarrod	40.00	425.00	300.00
Butts, Marion	45.00	500.00	450.00
Byars, Keith	40.00	400.00	325.00
Carrier, Mark (DB)	45.00	650.00	575.00
Carroll, Wesley	40.00	375.00	300.00
Carter, Anthony	45.00	425.00	350.00
Carter, Dexter	40.00	450.00	350.00
Clayton, Mark	40.00	450.00	375.00
Cobb, Reggie	40.00	500.00	450.00
Craig, Roger	75.00	900.00	800.00
Croel, Mike	45.00	475.00	400.00
Cunningham, Randall	125.00	1,250.00	1,150.00
Dent, Richard	85.00	625.00	475.00
Dickerson, Eric	100.00	1,150.00	1,100.00
Elway, John	125.00	1,200.00	1,100.00
Ervins, Ricky	50.00	700.00	625.00
Esiason, Boomer	75.00	575.00	475.00
Everett, Jim	75.00	750.00	600.00
Favre, Brett	50.00	400.00	300.00
Fenner, Derrick	40.00	350.00	250.00
Gault, Willie	45.00	500.00	375.00

Fenner, Derrick	40.00	350.00	250.00
Gault, Willie	45.00	500.00	375.00
George, Jeff	75.00	600.00	500.00
Green, Eric	45.00	475.00	425.00
Green, Gaston	40.00	475.00	400.00
Green, Harold	40.00	475.00	425.00
Hampton, Rodney	60.00	575.00	450.00
Harbaugh, Jim	55.00	550.00	450.00
Harper, Alvin	45.00	550.00	500.00
Haynes, Michael	40.00	450.00	400.00
Hebert, Bobby	60.00	500.00	450.00
Heyward, Craig	40.00	425.00	375.00
Hill, Randall	40.00	425.00	350.00
Hilliard, Dalton	40.00	400.00	350.00
Hostetler, Jeff	65.00	550.00	475.00
Humphrey, Bobby	40.00	400.00	325.00
Irvin, Michael	75.00	800.00	725.00
Ismail, Raghib (CFL)	200.00	3,000.00	2,750.00
Jackson, Bo	200.00	3,250.00	3,000.00
Jeffires, Haywood	40.00	425.00	325.00
Johnson, Johnny	40.00	400.00	325.00
Joyner, Seth	40.00	375.00	300.00
Kelly, Jim	125.00	1,250.00	1,150.00
Kosar, Bernie	85.00	700.00	600.00
Lewis, Greg	40.00	400.00	300.00
Lofton, James	45.00	550.00	450.00
Lott, Ronnie	75.00	1,100.00	950.00
Majkowski, Don	45.00	450.00	325.00
Marino, Dan	150.00	1,400.00	1,250.00
Marinovich, Todd	60.00	850.00	650.00
Maryland, Russell	40.00	425.00	350.00
McGwire, Dan	50.00	475.00	350.00
McMahon, Jim	65.00	450.00	350.00
Meggett, Dave	45.00	475.00	350.00
Metcalf, Eric	40.00	375.00	250.00
Miller, Chris	50.00	525.00	450.00
Monk, Art	100.00	900.00	750.00
Montana, Joe	225.00	3,500.00	3,250.00
Moon, Warren	85.00	800.00	675.00
Moore, Herman	40.00	375.00	275.00
Moore, Rob	50.00	550.00	450.00
Nagle, Browning	50.00	450.00	350.00
Okoye, Christian	45.00	425.00	325.00
Peete, Rodney	50.00	450.00	350.00
Perry, William	80.00	800.00	700.00
Pritchard, Mike	45.00	450.00	375.00
Proehl, Ricky	40.00	375.00	300.00
Reed, Andre	80.00	1,000.00	850.00
Rice, Jerry	150.00	1,400.00	1,250.00
Rison, Andre	50.00	600.00	450.00
Rosenbach, Timm	45.00	350.00	275.00
Russell, Leonard	50.00	475.00	400.00
Rypien, Mark	100.00	1,100.00	950.00
Sanders, Barry	200.00	2,750.00	2,500.00
Sharpe, Sterling	45.00	450.00	375.00
Simmons, Clyde	40.00	375.00	300.00
Simms, Phil	75.00	700.00	600.00
Smith, Bruce	60.00	800.00	675.00
Smith, Emmitt	200.00	2,200.00	2,000.00
Spielman, Chris	40.00	350.00	275.00
Stephens, John	40.00	350.00	300.00
Swann, Eric	40.00	350.00	275.00
Taylor, John	85.00	850.00	750.00
Taylor, Lawrence	150.00	1,300.00	1,200.00
Testaverde, Vinny	50.00	375.00	300.00
Thomas, Blair	50.00	450.00	350.00
Thomas, Derrick	75.00	800.00	700.00
Thomas, Thurman	175.00	1,800.00	1,600.00
Thompson, Anthony	40.00	400.00	300.00
Thompson, Darrell	40.00	375.00	300.00
Toon, Al	45.00	425.00	325.00
Walker, Herschel	65.00	750.00	675.00
Walsh, Steve	50.00	400.00	350.00
Ware, Andre	45.00	425.00	350.00
Watters, Ricky	40.00	375.00	300.00
White, Reggie	60.00	750.00	650.00
Williams, Harvey	50.00	550.00	475.00
Williams, John L.	40.00	350.00	275.00
Woodson, Rod	45.00	500.00	450.00
Word, Barry	45.00	475.00	425.00
Wright, Alexander	45.00	475.00	400.00
Young, Steve	70.00	850.00	750.00
Zorich, Chris	40.00	350.00	300.00

HOCKEY EQUIPMENT

HALL OF FAME GOALTENDERS

Goaltender	Stick	Jersey
Bower, Johnny	250.00	2,000.00
Cheevers, Gerry	200.00	1,500.00
Dryden, Ken	225.00	1,850.00
Esposito, Tony	200.00	1,750.00
Giacomin, Eddie	200.00	1,600.00
Hall, Glenn	250.00	2,200.00
Parent, Bernie	200.00	1,500.00
Plante, Jacques (Mont.)	325.00	3,500.00
Plante, Jacques (others)	300.00	2,500.00

HALL OF FAME PLAYERS

Player	Skates	Stick	Jersey
Barber, Bill	250.00	100.00	750.00
Bathgate, Andy	400.00	125.00	1,250.00
Beliveau, Jean	800.00	175.00	2,250.00
Boivin, Leo	500.00	100.00	1,250.00
Bossy, Mike	325.00	100.00	1,250.00
Bucyk, John	425.00	100.00	1,000.00
Clarke, Bobby	500.00	200.00	1,500.00
Cournoyer, Yvan	500.00	200.00	1,400.00
Delvecchio, Alex	700.00	125.00	1,250.00
Esposito, Phil	1,550.00	300.00	3,500.00
Flaman, Fern	800.00	175.00	2,000.00
Gadsby, Bill	400.00	125.00	1,250.00
Geoffrion, Boom Boom	850.00	200.00	2,500.00
Gilbert, Rod	625.00	150.00	1,400.00
Harvey, Doug	700.00	125.00	1,450.00
Hextall, Bryan	1,000.00	250.00	2,500.00
Horton, Tim	700.00	125.00	1,300.00
Howe, Gordie (Detroit)	1,750.00	450.00	4,000.00
Howe, Gordie (Hartford)	950.00	200.00	3,500.00
Howell, Harry	450.00	125.00	1,200.00
Hull, Bobby	1,600.00	400.00	5,000.00
Kelly, Red	700.00	125.00	1,350.00
Keon, Dave	550.00	100.00	1,200.00
Lafleur, Guy	625.00	225.00	1,650.00
Laperriere, Jacques	400.00	80.00	1,200.00
Lemaire, Jacques	450.00	100.00	1,300.00
Lindsay, Ted	900.00	200.00	2,500.00
Mahovlich, Frank	700.00	150.00	1,300.00
Mikita, Stan	1,250.00	275.00	3,500.00
Moore, Dickie	500.00	150.00	1,250.00
O'Connor, Buddy	850.00	225.00	2,250.00
Olmstead, Bert	750.00	150.00	2,000.00
Orr, Bobby	700.00	600.00	5,000.00
Park, Brad	475.00	100.00	1,250.00
Perreault, Gil	550.00	150.00	1,300.00
Pilote, Pierre	450.00	125.00	1,250.00
Potvin, Denis	500.00	100.00	1,200.00
Pronovost, Marcel	425.00	125.00	1,250.00
Pulford, Bob	400.00	100.00	1,200.00
Quackenbush, Bill	750.00	175.00	2,100.00
Ratelle, Jean	650.00	150.00	1,400.00
Richard, Henri	650.00	150.00	1,600.00
Savard, Serge	550.00	100.00	1,350.00
Sittler, Darryl	550.00	125.00	1,250.00
Smith, Clint	775.00	225.00	2,250.00
Stanley, Allan	375.00	100.00	1,250.00

Equipment

Player	Skates	Stick	Jersey
Amonte, Tony	200.00	75.00	350.00
Anderson, Glenn	200.00	80.00	425.00
Bellows, Brian	250.00	85.00	425.00
Bondra, Peter	180.00	50.00	250.00
Bourque, Ray	700.00	225.00	1,100.00
Brown, Rob	175.00	65.00	300.00
Bure, Pavel	225.00	85.00	450.00
Carson, Jimmy	175.00	70.00	325.00
Chelios, Chris	275.00	85.00	600.00
Coffey, Paul	700.00	150.00	1,200.00
Cullen, John	150.00	50.00	300.00
Damphousse, Vin	200.00	75.00	350.00
Druce, John	150.00	40.00	250.00
Falloon, Pat	175.00	60.00	275.00
Fedorov, Sergei	275.00	100.00	525.00
Fleury, Theoren	225.00	75.00	360.00
Gamble, Troy	175.00	60.00	300.00
Garpenlov, Johan	175.00	40.00	250.00
Gartner, Mike	275.00	90.00	475.00
Gelinas, Martin	150.00	40.00	225.00
Gretzky, Wayne	1,500.00	350.00	5,000.00
Gusarov, Alexei	150.00	45.00	250.00
Hawerchuk, Dale	225.00	80.00	450.00
Hodge, Ken Jr.	200.00	65.00	325.00
Holik, Bobby	200.00	70.00	350.00
Housley, Phil	225.00	80.00	400.00
Hull, Brett	1,000.00	275.00	2,000.00
Jagr, Jaromir	250.00	85.00	425.00
Janney, Craig	200.00	60.00	300.00
Kamensky, Valerei	200.00	70.00	375.00
Khristich, Dimitri	200.00	65.00	325.00
Kidd, Trevor	175.00	50.00	250.00
Klima, Petr	200.00	75.00	375.00
Kron, Robert	150.00	40.00	250.00
Kurri, Jari	525.00	125.00	900.00
LaFontaine, Pat	350.00	100.00	600.00
Larmer, Steve	300.00	85.00	500.00
Lebeau, Stephan	150.00	40.00	225.00
Leetch, Brian	190.00	200.00	75.00
Lemieux, Mario	1,000.00	275.00	3,000.00
Lidstrom, Nicklas	225.00	75.00	350.00
Linden, Trevor	200.00	75.00	350.00
MacInnis, Al	600.00	150.00	900.00
Makarov, Sergei	150.00	40.00	250.00
Matteau, Stephane	150.00	45.00	260.00
Messier, Mark	800.00	250.00	1,200.00
Miller, Kip	160.00	45.00	270.00
Modano, Mike	165.00	50.00	275.00
Mogilny, Alexander	165.00	45.00	270.00
Morin, Stephane	165.00	45.00	270.00
Mullen, Joey	225.00	75.00	375.00
Muller,Kirk	275.00	80.00	425.00
Murphy, Joe	165.00	40.00	250.00
Nedved, Petr	180.00	50.00	285.00
Neely, Cam	525.00	150.00	875.00
Nemchinov, Sergei	175.00	45.00	250.00
Niedermayer, Scott	190.00	65.00	300.00
Nieuwendyk, Joe	350.00	90.00	500.00
Nolan, Owen	225.00	65.00	550.00
Oates, Adam	500.00	140.00	850.00
Primeau, Keith	165.00	45.00	250.00
Propp, Brian	200.00	75.00	375.00
Recchi, Mark	200.00	60.00	350.00
Reichel, Robert	190.00	60.00	325.00
Ricci, Mike	200.00	60.00	340.00
Richer, Stephane	225.00	80.00	425.00
Robitaille, Luc	525.00	150.00	875.00
Roenick, Jeremy	225.00	80.00	375.00
Ruzicka, Vladimir	180.00	60.00	300.00
Sakic, Joe	350.00	95.00	550.00
Sandstrom, Tomas	325.00	85.00	500.00
Savard, Denis	280.00	80.00	425.00
Semenov, Anatoli	165.00	45.00	250.00
Stastny, Peter	225.00	75.00	400.00
Stevens, Kevin	250.00	80.00	425.00
Stevens, Scott	200.00	75.00	375.00
Sundin, Mats	190.00	60.00	300.00
Tikkanen, Esa	225.00	80.00	425.00
Todd, Kevin	175.00	45.00	225.00
Turcotte, Darren	180.00	50.00	275.00
Turgeon, Pierre	225.00	75.00	375.00
Weight, Doug	180.00	45.00	260.00
Weinrich, Eric	150.00	40.00	250.00
Ysebaert, Paul	180.00	60.00	300.00
Yzerman, Steve	675.00	150.00	925.00

ACTIVE GOALTENDERS

Goaltender	Stick	Jersey
Barrasso, Tom	50.00	325.00
Beaupre, Don	40.00	325.00
Belfour, Ed	150.00	750.00
Cheveldae, Tim	40.00	325.00
Essensa, Bob	50.00	400.00
Fuhr, Grant	75.00	500.00
Hextall, Ron	75.00	450.00
Hrudey, Kelly	40.00	250.00
Ing, Peter	30.00	200.00
Liut, Mike	40.00	300.00
Malarchuk, Clint	40.00	300.00
McLean, Kirk	45.00	325.00
Moog, Andy	60.00	450.00
Ranford, Bill	60.00	450.00
Richter, Mike	75.00	550.00
Roy, Patrick	150.00	900.00
Terreri, Chris	45.00	375.00
Vanbiesbrouck, John	40.00	325.00
Vernon, Mike	45.00	400.00

Jacques Plante (1959).

FIGURINES & STATUES

AUTO RACING FIGURINES

SALVINO SPORT LEGENDS

Driver	# Issued	Value
Foyt, A.J.		
Hand-signed	1,500	250.00
Petty, Richard		
Hand-signed	2,000	265.00
Hand-signed s/e	300	475.00
"Farewell"	2,500	275.00
Waltrip, Darrell		
Hand-signed	1,500	250.00

BASEBALL FIGURINES

GARTLAN USA

Player	# Issued	Value
Aaron, Hank		
Hand-signed	1,982	225.00
Mini	10,000	75.00
Aparicio, Luis		
Hand-signed	1,984	225.00
Mini	10,000	80.00
Barlick, Al		
Hand-signed	1,989	175.00
Bell, "Cool Papa"		
Hand-signed	1,972	195.00
Bench, Johnny		
Hand-signed	1,989	350.00
Hand-signed a/p	250	550.00
Mini	10,000	75.00
Berra, Yogi		
Hand-signed	2,150	225.00
Mini	10,000	80.00
Hand-signed a/p	250	375.00
Brett, George		
Hand-signed	2,250	225.00
Mini	10,000	80.00
Carew, Rod		
Hand-signed	1,991	225.00
Mini	10,000	80.00
Carlton, Steve		
Hand-signed	3,290	210.00
Mini	10,000	80.00
Hand-signed a/p	300	350.00
Dandridge, Ray		
Hand-signed	1,987	195.00
DiMaggio, Joe		
Hand-signed	2,214	1,100.00
AP Hand-signed, pinstripes	325	2,000.00
Fisk, Carlton		
Hand-signed	1,972	225.00
Mini	10,000	80.00
Ford, Whitey		
Hand-signed	2,360	225.00
Mini	10,000	80.00
Hand-signed a/p	250	350.00
Griffey Jr., Ken	10,000	80.00
Hand-signed	1,989	225.00
Irvin, Monte		
Hand-signed	1,973	225.00
Mini	10,000	80.00
Leonard, Buck		
Hand-signed	1,972	195.00
Musial, Stan		
Hand-signed	1,969	325.00
Mini	2,269	100.00
Rose, Pete		
Hand-signed	4,192	1,150.00
Mini	10,000	80.00
Seaver, Tom		
Hand-signed	1,992	225.00
Mini	10,000	80.00
Schmidt, Mike		
Hand-signed	1,987	875.00
Mini	10,000	80.00
Hand-signed a/p	20	1500.00
Spahn, Warren		
Hand-signed	1,973	225.00
Strawberry, Darryl		
Hand-signed	2,500	225.00
Mini	10,000	80.00
Williams, Ted		
Hand-signed	2,654	495.00
Mini	10,000	80.00
Hand-signed a/p	250	650.00
Yastrzemski, Carl		
Hand-signed	1,989	300.00
Hand-signed a/p	250	495.00
Mini	10,000	80.00

Yogi Berra #531

Yogi Berra Hartland

HALL OF FAME 1963

Set of 20 busts	850.00
Alexander, Grover	50.00
Anson, Cap	40.00
Cobb, Ty	65.00
Collins, Eddie	40.00
DiMaggio, Joe	60.00
Evers, Johnny	40.00
Foxx, Jimmie	60.00
Gehrig, Lou	65.00
Gehringer, Charlie	50.00
Hornsby, Rogers	50.00
Johnson, Walter	50.00
Keeler, Willie	40.00
Lajoie, Nap	40.00
Mathewson, Christy	50.00
Ruth, Babe	75.00
Spalding, Al	40.00
Speaker, Tris	40.00
Traynor, Pie	40.00
Wagner, Honus	50.00
Young, Cy	50.00

HARTLAND STATUES 1960-63

Player	(1,000)	Value
Aaron, Henry	150	300.00
Aparicio, Luis	100	400.00
Banks, Ernie	50	400.00
Berra, Yogi (mask)	100	275.00
Berra, Yogi (no mask)		200.00
Colavito, Rocky	10	1,000.00
Drysdale, Don	50	525.00
Fox, Nellie	100	325.00
Groat, Dick	35	2,000.00
Killebrew, Harmon	30	650.00
Mantle, Mickey	150	350.00
Maris, Roger	75	600.00
Mathews, Eddie	150	175.00
Mays, Willie	150	325.00
Musial, Stan	75	300.00
Ruth, Babe	150	300.00
Snider, Duke	75	550.00
Spahn, Warren	150	200.00
Williams, Ted	150	300.00
6" Batboy	15	200.00
4" Minor Leaguer	15	150.00

HARTLAND 1990 RE-ISSUES

Player	(1,000)	Value
Aaron, Henry	10	50.00
Aparicio, Luis	10	50.00
Banks, Ernie	10	50.00
Berra, Yogi	10	50.00
Clemente, Roberto	10	50.00
Colavito, Rocky	10	50.00
Drysdale, Don	10	50.00
Ford, Whitey	10	50.00
Fox, Nellie	10	50.00
Groat, Dick	10	50.00
Killebrew, Harmon	10	50.00
Mantle, Mickey	10	50.00
Maris, Roger	10	50.00
Mathews, Eddie	10	50.00
Mays, Willie	10	50.00
Musial, Stan	10	50.00
Ruth, Babe	10	50.00
Snider, Duke	10	50.00
Spahn, Warren	10	50.00
Williams, Ted	10	50.00
6" Batboy	10	50.00
4" Minor Leaguer	10	50.00

HARTLAND 1993

Nolan Ryan	Open	50.00
Honus Wagner	10	50.00
Cy Young	10	50.00

KENNER STARTING LINEUP

1988 Individual Players

Ashby, Alan	20.00
Baines, Harold	14.00
Bass, Kevin	13.00
Bedrosian, Steve	16.00

Figurines and Statues

Babe Ruth #538

Babe Ruth Hartland Statue

Bell Buddy 24.00
Bell, George 19.00
Boddicker, Mike 17.00
Boggs, Wade 20.00
Bonds, Barry 40.00
Bonilla, Bobby 25.00
Bream, Sid 17.00
Brett, George 32.00
Brown, Chris 18.00
Brunansky, Tom 25.00
Burks, Ellis 42.00
Canseco, Jose 45.00
Carter, Gary 18.00
Carter, Joe 22.00
Clark, Jack 22.00
Clark, Will 35.00
Clemens, Roger 20.00
Coleman, Vince 19.00
Daniels, Kal 17.00
Davis, Alvin 15.00
Davis, Eric 13.00
Davis, Glenn 15.00
Davis, Jody 17.00
Dawson, Andre 17.00
Deer, Rob 18.00
Downing, Brian 15.00
Dunne, Mike 17.00
Dunston, Shawon 27.00
Durham, Leon 15.00
Dykstra, Lenny 25.00
Evans, Dwight 22.00
Fisk, Carlton 50.00
Franco, John 18.00
Franco, Julio 20.00
Gaetti, Gary 17.00
Gooden, Dwight 17.00
Griffey Sr., Ken 33.00
Guerrero, Pedro 13.00
Guillen, Ozzie 20.00
Gwynn, Tony 22.00
Hall, Mel 17.00
Hatcher, Billy 20.00
Hayes, Von 19.00
Henderson, Rickey 25.00
Hernandez, Keith 20.00
Hernandez, Willie 19.00
Herr, Tom 15.00
Higuera, Ted 19.00
Hough, Charlie 15.00
Hrbek Kent 18.00
Incaviglia, Pete 15.00
Johnson, Howard 35.00
Joyner, Wally 14.00
Kennedy, Terry 20.00
Kruk, John 27.00
Langston, Mark 25.00
Lansford, Carney 32.00
Leonard, Jeffrey 15.00
Lynn, Fred 25.00
Maldonado, Candy 15.00
Marshall, Mike 15.00
Mattingly, Don 15.00
McGee, Willie 18.00
McGwire, Mark 45.00
McReynolds, Kevin 20.00
Molitor, Paul 25.00
Moore, Donnie 21.00
Morris, Jack 25.00
Murphy, Dale 15.00
Murray, Eddie 18.00
Nokes, Matt 19.00
O'Brien, Pete 15.00
Oberkfell, Ken 17.00
Parker, Dave 26.00
Parrish, Larry 13.00
Phelps, Ken 16.00
Presley, Jim 15.00
Puckett, Kirby 25.00
Quisenberry, Dan 20.00
Raines, Tim 15.00
Randolph, Willie 17.00
Rawley, Shane 15.00
Reardon, Jeff 32.00
Redus, Gary 19.00
Reuschel, Rick 15.00
Rice, Jim 22.00
Righetti, Dave 15.00
Ripken Jr., Cal 75.00
Rose, Pete 24.00
Ryan, Nolan 200.00
Saberhagen, Bret 24.00
Samuel, Juan 17.00
Sandberg, Ryne 43.00
Santiago, Benito 20.00
Sax, Steve 15.00
Schmidt, Mike 37.00
Scott, Mike 12.00
Seitzer, Kevin 20.00
Sierra, Ruben 42.00
Smith, Ozzie 18.00
Smith, Zane 15.00
Snyder, Cory 15.00
Strawberry, Darryl 16.00
Stubbs, Franklin 15.00
Surhoff, B.J. 24.00
Sutcliffe, Rick 17.00
Tabler, Pat 15.00
Tartabull, Danny 22.00
Trammell, Alan 15.00
Valenzuela, Fernando 12.00
Van Slyke, Andy 33.00
Viola, Frank 20.00
Virgil, Ozzie 14.00
Walker, Greg 15.00
Whitaker, Lou 17.00
White, Devon 20.00
Winfield, Dave 17.00
Witt, Mike 15.00
Worrell, Todd 20.00
Yount, Robin 62.00

1989 Baseball Greats

Ernie Banks, Billy Williams .. 20.00
Johnny Bench, Pete Rose ... 25.00
Roberto Clemente, W. Stargell 20.00
Don Drysdale, Reggie Jackson 15.00
Mickey Mantle, Joe DiMaggio 30.00
Eddie Mathews, Hank Aaron . 40.00
Willie Mays, Willie McCovey . 25.00
Stan Musial, Bob Gibson 70.00
Babe Ruth, Lou Gehrig 35.00

1989 Individual Players

Alomar, Roberto 45.00
Anderson, Brady 22.00
Baines, Harold 15.00
Barrett, Marty 12.00
Bass, Kevin 13.00
Bedrosian, Steve 10.00
Bell, George 15.00
Berryhill, Damon 15.00
Boggs, Wade 15.00
Bonds, Barry 30.00
Bonilla, Bobby 22.00
Bradley, Phil 30.00
Braggs, Glen 16.00
Brantley, Mickey 16.00
Brett, George 27.00
Brookens, Tom 16.00
Brunansky, Tom 15.00
Buechele, Steve 18.00
Burks, Ellis 20.00
Butler, Brett 17.00
Calderon, Ivan 22.00
Canseco, Jose 14.00
Carter, Gary 12.00
Carter, Joe 15.00
Clark, Will 17.00
Clemens, Roger 17.00
Coleman, Vince 12.00
Cone, David 22.00
Daniels, Kal 16.00
Davis, Alvin 17.00
Davis, Chili 37.00
Davis, Eric 13.00
Davis, Glenn 13.00
Davis, Mark 19.00
Dawson, Andre 12.00
Deer, Rob 16.00
Diaz, Bo 17.00
Doran, Billy 22.00
Drabek, Doug 20.00
Dunston, Shawon 17.00
Dykstra, Lenny 15.00
Eckersley, Dennis 27.00
Elster, Kevin 13.00
Fletcher, Scott 12.00
Franco, John 14.00
Gaetti, Gary 11.00
Gant, Ron 60.00
Gibson, Kirk 10.00
Gladden, Dan 15.00
Gooden, Dwight 15.00
Grace, Mark 25.00
Greenwell, Mike 12.00
Gubicza, Mark 10.00
Guerrero, Pedro 9.00
Guillen, Ozzie 20.00
Gwynn, Tony 30.00
Hall, Albert 17.00
Hall, Mel 10.00
Hatcher, Billy 12.00
Hayes, Von 10.00
Henderson, Rickey 20.00
Henneman, Mike 11.00
Hernandez, Keith 11.00
Hershiser, Orel 21.00
Higuera, Ted 20.00
Howell, Jack 35.00
Hrbek, Kent 12.00
Incaviglia, Pete 11.00
Jackson, Bo 45.00
Jackson, Danny 15.00
Jacoby, Brook 12.00
James, Chris 10.00
James, Dion 15.00
Jefferies, Greg 20.00
Jones, Doug 16.00
Joyner, Wally 13.00
Kruk, John 22.00
Langston, Mark 25.00
Lansford, Camey 23.00
Larkin, Barry 32.00
Laudner, Tim 13.00
LaValliere, Mike 15.00
Leiter, Al 12.00
Lemon, Chet 14.00
Lind, Jose 25.00
Maddox, Greg 22.00
Maldonado, Candy 12.00
Marshall, Mike 11.00
Mattingly, Don 15.00
McGee, Willie 15.00
McGwire, Mark 18.00
McReynolds, Kevin 20.00
Molitor, Paul 12.00
Morris, Jack 21.00
Murphy, Dale 14.00

Myers, Randy 20.00
Nokes, Matt 12.00
Pagliarulo Mike 13.00
Parker, Dave 23.00
Pasqua, Dab 20.00
Pena, Tony 17.00
Pendleton, Terry 35.00
Perez, Melido 23.00
Perry, Gerald 16.00
Plesac, Dan 12.00
Puckett, Kirby 21.00
Quinones, Rey 18.00
Raines, Tim 11.00
Ray, Johnny 45.00
Reardon, Jeff 23.00
Reynolds, Harold 18.00
Rice, Jim 14.00
Righetti, Dave 14.00
Ripken Jr., Cal 55.00
Russell, Jeff 17.00
Saberhagen, Brett 20.00
Sabo, Chris 22.00
Salazar, Luis 20.00
Samuel, Juan 13.00
Sandberg, Ryne 22.00
Santiago, Benito 22.00
Schmidt, Mike 62.00
Schofield, Dick 40.00
Sciosca, Mike 15.00
Scott, Mike 12.00
Seitzer, Kevin 12.00
Sheets, Larry 12.00
Shelby, John 12.00
Sierra, Ruben 33.00
Slaught, Don 12.00
Smith, Dave 12.00
Smith, Lee 24.00
Smith, Ozzie 14.00
Smith, Zane 15.00
Snyder, Cory 15.00
Stanicek, Pete 13.00
Steinbach, Terry 30.00
Stewart, Dave 23.00
Stillwell, Kurt 11.00
Strawberry, Darryl 15.00
Surhoff, B.J. 20.00
Sutcliffe, Rick 18.00
Sutter, Bruce 25.00
Swindell, Greg 15.00
Tabler, Pat 15.00
Tartabull, Danny 15.00
Thigpen, Bobby 28.00
Thompson, Milt 18.00
Thompson, Robby 14.00
Trammell, Alan 12.00
Treadway, Jeff 35.00
Uribe, Jose 13.00
Valenzuela, Fernando 13.00
Van Slyke, Andy 19.00
Viola, Frank 12.00
Walk, Bob 13.00
Walker, Greg 19.00
Weiss, Walt 30.00
Welch, Bob 19.00
Whitaker, Lou 14.00
White, Devon 33.00
Winfield, Dave 12.00
Witt, Mike 25.00
Worrell, Todd 16.00
Wynne, Marvell 18.00
Young, Gerald 12.00
Yount, Robin 65.00

1989 One on One

Wade Boggs, R. Henderson . 30.00
Gary Carter, Eric Davis 30.00
Ryne Sandberg, V. Coleman . 50.00
A. Trammell, Jose Canseco . . 35.00

1990 Individual Players

Abbott, Jim 20.00
Alomar Jr., Sandy 18.00
Anderson, Allan 12.00
Backman, Wally 30.00
Ballard, Jeff 11.00

Darryl Strawberry Gartlan Statue

Barfield, Jesse 10.00
Bedrosian, Steve 12.00
Benzinger, Todd 15.00
Berryhil, Damon 10.00
Boggs, Wade 12.00
Bonds, Barry 23.00
Bonilla, Bobby 20.00
Bosio, Chris 12.00
Burks, Ellis 14.00
Canseco, Jose 10.00
Carter, Joe 23.00
Clark, Will
  batting stance 15.00
  swinging 20.00
Clemens, Roger 17.00
Coleman, Vince 10.00
Darling, Ron 11.00
Davis, Eric 10.00
Dawson, Andre 12.00
Dibble, Rob 20.00
Dykstra, Len 27.00
Eckersley, Dennis 27.00
Esasky, Nick 28.00
Gaetti, Gary 12.00
Galarraga, Andres 9.00
Gibson, Kirk 9.00
Gooden, Dwight 10.00
Grace, Mark
  batting stance 15.00
  swinging 27.00
Greenwell, Mike 8.00
Griffey Jr., Ken
  jumping 48.00
  sliding 60.00
Guerrero, Pedro 9.00
Hayes, Von 10.00
Henderson, Dave 15.00
Henderson, Rickey 15.00
Herr, Tom 11.00
Hershiser, Orel 16.00
Hrbek, Kent 10.00
Jackson, Bo 10.00
Jefferies, Greg 12.00
Johnson, Howard 17.00
Jordan, Rickey 14.00
Kelly, Roberto 19.00
Larkin, Barry 23.00
Maddux, Greg 18.00
Magrane, Joe 14.00
Mattingly, Don
  bat in hand 14.00
  swinging 20.00
McDonald, Ben 20.00
McGriff, Fred 15.00
McGwire, Mark 10.00
McReynolds, Kevin 15.00
Mitchell, Kevin 10.00
Molitor, Paul 10.00
Murray, Eddie 20.00
Nokes, Matt 15.00
O'Neill, Paul 17.00
Oquendo, Jose 15.00
Pettis, Gary 30.00
Puckett, Kirby 19.00
Randolph, Willie 15.00
Reed, Jody 14.00
Reuschel, Rick 12.00
Righetti, Dave 10.00
Ripken Jr., Cal 35.00
Ryan, Nolan 30.00
Sabo, Chris 10.00
Samuel, Juan 12.00
Sandberg, Ryne 20.00
Sax, Steve 8.00
Scott, Mike 8.00
Sheffield, Gary 27.00
Smiley, John 15.00
Smith, Ozzie 14.00
Stewart, Dave 15.00
Strawberry, Darryl
  batting stance 10.00
  fielding 18.00
Sutcliffe Rick 14.00
Tettleton, Mickey 14.00
Trammell, Alan 12.00
Van Slyke, Andy 17.00
Viola, Frank 13.00
Walton, Jerome 11.00
Whitaker, Lou 12.00
Williams, Mitch 11.00
Winfield, Dave 16.00
Yount, Robin 40.00

1990 Team Lineup

Boston Red Sox 75.00
Chicago Cubs 50.00
New York Mets 50.00
New York Yankees 50.00
Oakland A's 200.00
American League Team Up . . . 50.00
National League Team Up 50.00

1991 Headliners

Canseco, Jose 18.00
Clark, Will 33.00
Griffey Jr., Ken 30.00
Henderson, Rickey 25.00
Jackson, Bo 15.00
Mattingly, Don 25.00
Ryan, Nolan 35.00

1991 Individual Players

Abbott, Jim 11.00
Alomar Jr., Sandy 11.00
Armstrong, Jack 12.00
Bell, George 10.00
Bonds, Barry 20.00
Bonilla, Bobby 16.00
Browning, Tom 12.00
Canseco, Jose 8.00
Clark, Will 9.00
Coleman, Vince 10.00
Davis, Eric 12.00
Davis, Glenn 9.00
Dawson, Andre 15.00
DeShields, Delino 16.00
Drabek, Doug 14.00
Dunston, Shawon 13.00
Dykstra, Lenny 12.00
Fielder, Cecil 9.00
Franco, John 10.00
Gooden, Dwight 10.00
Grace, Mark 9.00
Griffey Jr., Ken 14.00
Griffey Sr., Ken 17.00
Gruber, Kelly 11.00
Guillen, Ozzie 12.00
Henderson, Rickey 12.00
Jackson, Bo

Player	Value
Royals	9.00
White Sox	18.00
Jefferies, Greg	10.00
Johnson, Howard	15.00
Justice, David	27.00
Kelly, Roberto	15.00
Larkin, Barry	10.00
Maas, Kevin	19.00
Magadan, Dave	10.00
Martinez, Ramon	14.00
Mattingly, Don	10.00
McDonald, Ben	12.00
McGwire, Mark	9.00
Mitchell, Kevin	7.00
Puckett, Kirby	15.00
Raines, Tom	13.00
Ryan, Nolan	25.00
Sabo, Chris	8.00
Sandberg, Ryne	13.00
Santiago, Benito	10.00
Sax, Steve	14.00
Stewart, Dave	15.00
Strawberry, Darryl	14.00
Trammell, Alan	15.00
Viola, Frank	10.00
Williams, Matt	20.00
Zeile, Todd	22.00

1992 Headliners

Player	Value
Brett, George	25.00
Fielder, Cecil	17.00
Griffey Jr., Ken	18.00
Henderson, Rickey	18.00
Jackson, Bo	17.00
Ryan, Nolan	18.00
Sandberg, Ryne	23.00

1992 Individual Players

Player	Value
Alomar, Roberto	13.00
Avery, Steve	9.00
Bell, George	9.00
Belle, Albert	10.00
Biggio, Craig	10.00
Bonds, Barry	15.00
Bonilla, Bobby	8.00
Calderon, Ivan	10.00
Canseco, Jose	8.00
Clark, Will	11.00
Clemens, Roger	14.00
Davis, Eric	10.00
Dibble, Rob	8.00
Erickson, Scott	9.00
Fielder, Cecil	9.00
Finley, Chuck	11.00
Glavine, Tom	19.00
Gonzalez, Juan	18.00
Griffey Jr., Ken	
regular	11.00
spring	11.00
Gwynn, Tony	10.00
Henderson, Dave	7.00
Henderson, Rickey	10.00
Jackson, Bo	
regular	9.00
spring	9.00
Johnson, Howard	10.00
Jose, Felix	10.00
Justice, Dave	14.00
Maas, Kevin	9.00
Martinez, Ramon	9.00
McGriff, Fred	9.00
McRae, Brian	10.00
Puckett, Kirby	8.00
Ripken Jr., Cal	22.00
Ryan, Nolan	10.00
Saberhagen, Bret	8.00
Sabo, Chris	10.00
Sandberg, Ryne	10.00
Seaver, Tom	18.00
Sierra, Ruben	13.00
Strawberry, Darryl	9.00
Tartabull, Danny	12.00
Thomas, Frank	25.00
2nd pose	16.00
Van Poppel Todd	12.00
Williams, Matt	8.00

PRO SPORT CREATIONS

Player	# Issued	Value
Ashburn, Richie		
Hand-signed	1,962	85.00
Mini	3,000	50.00
Dickey, Bill		
Hand-signed	1,954	100.00
a/p	200	150.00
Mini	3,000	55.00
Ford, Whitey		
Hand-signed	1,974	100.00
Mini	3,000	55.00
Garvey, Steve		
Hand-signed	1,987	100.00
Hand-signed a/p	200	100.00
Gibson, Bob		
Hand-signed	1,981	140.00
Mini	3,000	55.00
Gwynn, Tony		
Hand-signed	1,989	100.00
Hand-signed a/p	200	140.00
Killebrew, Harmon		
Hand-signed	1,984	100.00
Hand-signed a/p	200	140.00
Mathews, Eddie		
Hand-signed	1,978	100.00
Hand-signed a/p	200	140.00
Palmer, Jim		
Hand-signed	1,990	125.00
Hand-signed a/p	200	165.00
Mini	3,000	55.00
Robinson, Brooks		
Hand-signed	1,983	100.00
Hand-signed a/p	200	140.00
Stargell, Willie		
Hand-signed	1,988	100.00
Hand-signed a/p	200	140.00

SALVINO SPORT LEGENDS

Player	# Issued	Value
Campanella, Roy		
Hand-signed	2,200	400.00
Hand-signed a/p	200	600.00
Drysdale, Don		
Hand-signed	2,500	175.00
Hand-signed a/p	300	250.00
Henderson, Rickey		
Home signed	600	275.00
Road signed	600	275.00
Hand-signed s/e	550	375.00
Koufax, Sandy		
Hand-signed	2,500	225.00
Hand-signed a/p	300	325.00
Mantle, Mickey		
Batting	682	400.00
Fielding	682	400.00
The Mick	368	700.00
Rookie	368	700.00

Tim Raines Starting Lineup

SPORTS IMPRESSIONS

Player	# Issued	Value
Aaron, Hank		
5"	Open	35.00
7" HR	5,755	100.00
Banks, Ernie		
7" HR	5,512	100.00
5"	Open	35.00
Bench, Johnny		
6"	2,950	45.00
Hand-signed	975	150.00
Branca, Ralph		
Hand-signed	1,951	150.00
Canseco, Jose		
5" stance	Open	35.00
5" swinging	2,950	45.00
3 ¼" ornament	Open	20.00
10" closed	1,990	250.00
Carew, Rod		
7"	3,053	100.00
Carlton, Steve		
9" Ks	500	125.00
Clark, Will		
10"	1,990	200.00
8 ½"	1,990	200.00
5"	Open	35.00
Clemens, Roger		
Hand-signed	975	150.00
5 ½"	2,950	45.00
3 ¼" ornament	Open	20.00
Clemente, Roberto		
7"	5,000	100.00
Cobb, Ty		
7"	5,000	100.00
Davis, Eric		
3 ¼" ornament	Open	20.00
5"	2,950	45.00
Dawson, Andre		
7"	2,500	90.00
Dykstra, Lenny		
5"	2,950	45.00
7"	1,990	100.00
Feller, Bob		
7"	5,000	100.00
Foxx, Jimmie		
7" HR	1,008	100.00
Garvey, Steve		
5"	Open	35.00
7"	2,599	100.00
Gehrig, Lou		
7"	5,000	100.00
Gooden, Dwight		
3 ¼" ornament	Open	20.00
5"	2,950	45.00
7"	5,016	90.00
10"	1,990	195.00
Greenwell, Mike		
5"	2,950	45.00
7"	2,500	90.00
Griffey Jr, Ken		
3 ¼" ornament	Open	20.00
5"	2,950	45.00
7"	1,990	100.00
Gwynn, Tony		
5"	Open	35.00
7"	2,500	90.00
Henderson, Rickey		
3 ¼" ornament	Open	20.00
8 ¼" a/p	94	200.00
Hershiser, Orel		
7"	5,055	90.00
5"	Open	35.00
Jackson, Bo		
3 ¼" ornament	Open	20.00
Jackson, Reggie		
5"	Open	35.00
7" closed	5,000	0.00
Johnson, Howard		
5"	Open	35.00

Ernie Banks #534

Mickey Mantle #539

Ernie Banks Hartland, 1989 Starting Lineup Baseball Greats, Mickey Mantle Hartland

7"	5,020	90.00
Kaline, Al		
7"	2,500	100.00
Killebrew, Harmon		
7" HR	5,573	100.00
Langston, Mark		
7"	1,990	100.00
Mantle, Mickey		
6"	2,950	100.00
5"	Open	35.00
15" doll	1,956	150.00
a/p doll	195	295.00
Mathews, Eddie		
7" HR	5,512	100.00
Mattingly, Don		
7 ½"	1,990	100.00
6" double	2,950	85.00
3 ¼" ornament	Open	20.00
5" batting	Open	35.00
5" fielding	2,950	45.00
10"	1,990	200.00
15" doll	1,990	150.00
a/p doll	195	295.00
Mays, Willie		
7" HR	5,660	100.00
7" catch	5,000	100.00
5"	Open	35.00
4 ¼"	Open	35.00
McCovey, Willie		
7" HR	5,521	100.00
McGwire, Mark		
fig, closed	Open	0.00
9"	1,990	200.00
7" closed	Open	0.00
5"	Open	35.00
Molitor, Paul		
7"	2,500	90.00
Morgan, Joe		
7"	1,990	125.00
5"	Open	35.00
Munson, Thurman		
9 ¾"	995	165.00
7"	5,000	100.00
5"	Open	35.00
Ott, Mel		
7" HR	1,008	100.00
Puckett, Kirby		
3 ¼" ornament	Open	20.00
5"	Open	35.00
7"	1,990	100.00
Ripken, Cal, Jr		
5"	Open	35.00
7"	1,990	100.00
Robinson, Brooks		
7"	2,848	100.00
Robinson, Brooks		
5"	Open	35.00
Robinson, Frank		
7" HR	5,586	100.00
Robinson, Jackie		
7"	5,042	100.00
5"	Open	35.00
Ruth, Babe		
7"	5,000	100.00
4 ¼"	Open	6.00
Ryan, Nolan		
3 ¼" ornament	Open	20.00
9"	1,990	250.00
9" Ks	500	125.00
6 ½" w/ plate		
Mets	3,000	55.00
5" w/ plate		
Angels	3,000	55.00
Astros	3,000	55.00
4 ¼" w/ plate		
Rangers	3,000	55.00
5"	Open	35.00
5"	2,950	45.00
7" a/p	Open	195.00
15" doll	1,992	150.00
a/p doll	199	295.00
Sandberg, Ryne		
Hand-signed	975	150.00
6"	2,950	45.00
3 ¼" ornament	Open	20.00
Seaver, Tom		
5"	Open	35.00
9" Ks	500	125.00
fig, closed	Open	0.00
Snider, Duke		
5"	Open	35.00
Strawberry, Darryl		
5"	2,950	45.00
3 ¼" ornament	Open	20.00
Thomson, Bobby		
Hand-signed	1,951	150.00
Trammell, Alan		
7"	2,500	90.00
7" swinging	2,950	45.00
VanSlyke, Andy		
7"	2,500	90.00
Wagner, Honus		
7"	5,000	100.00
Williams, Ted		
5"	Open	35.00
7" HR	5,521	100.00
Winfield, Dave		
7"	2,500	90.00
Young, Cy		
7"	5,000	100.00

TRANSOGRAM

1969 (one per box)

Common players	18.00
Aaron, Hank	75.00
Allen, Richie	25.00
Alou, Felipe	20.00
Alou, Matty	20.00
Aparicio, Luis	30.00
Azcue, Joe	18.00
Banks, Ernie	50.00
Brock, Lou	40.00
Callison, John	18.00
Cardenal, Jose	18.00
Cater, Danny	18.00
Clemente, Roberto	100.00
Davis, Willie	20.00
Epstein, Mike	18.00
Fregosi, Jim	20.00
Gibson, Bob	40.00
Haller, Tom	18.00
Harrelson, Ken	20.00
Horton, Willie	20.00
Howard, Frank	25.00
John, Tommy	30.00
Kaline, Al	40.00
Killebrew, Harmon	40.00
Knoop, Bobby	18.00
Koosman, Jerry	20.00
Lefebvre, Jim	18.00
Mantle, Mickey	150.00
Marichal, Juan	30.00
May, Lee	20.00
Mays, Willie	75.00
Mazeroski, Bill	25.00
McCarver, Tim	25.00
McCovey, Willie	40.00
McLain, Denny	20.00
McNally, Dave	20.00
Monday, Rick	20.00
Moon Odom, Blue	20.00
Oliva, Tony	25.00
Pascual, Camilo	18.00
Perez, Tony	30.00
Petrocelli, Rico	20.00
Reichardt, Rick	18.00
Robinson, Brooks	50.00
Robinson, Frank	40.00
Rojas, Cookie	20.00
Rose, Pete	75.00
Santo, Ron	20.00
Seaver, Tom	75.00
Staub, Rusty	25.00
Stottlemyre, Mel	20.00
Swoboda, Ron	18.00
Tiant, Luis	20.00
Torre, Joe	25.00
Tovar, Cesar	18.00
Ward, Pete	18.00
White, Roy	20.00
Williams, Billy	25.00
Wilson, Don	18.00
Wynn, Jim	20.00

Yastrzemski, Carl 50.00

1970 (three per box)

Aaron, Hank
Seaver, Tom
Wynn, Jim (box of 3) 150.00
Banks, Ernie
Marichal, Juan
Torre, Joe (box of 3) 75.00
Clemente, Roberto
Gibson, Bob
Koosman, Jerry (box of 3) . . 125.00
Davis, Willie
McCovey, Willie
Santo, Ron (box of 3) 30.00
Fregosi, Jim
Kaline, Al
McDowell, Sam (box of 3) . . . 30.00
Howard, Frank
Reichardt, Rick
Robinson, Frank (box of 3) . . 30.00
Jackson, Reggie
McLain, Denny
Powell, Boog (box of 3) 80.00
Jones, Cleon
Mays, Willie
Rose, Pete (box of 3) 150.00
Killebrew, Harmon
Odom, Blue Moon
Petrocelli, Rico (box of 3) . . . 30.00
Oliva, Tony
Stottlemyre, Mel
Yastrzemski, Carl (box of 3) . 50.00

1970 Mets (three per box)

Kranepool, Ed
Seaver, Tom
Weis, Al (box of 3) 75.00
Boswell, Ken
Grote, Jerry
Koosman, Jerry (box of 3) . . . 25.00
Agee, Tommie
Gentry, Gary
Shamsky, Art (box of 3) 25.00
Clendenon, Donn
Harrelson, Bud
Swoboda, Ron (box of 3) 25.00
Jones, Cleon
McGraw, Tug
Ryan, Nolan (box of 3) 200.00

BASKETBALL FIGURINES

GARTLAN USA

Player	# Issued	Value
Abdul-Jabbar, Kareem		
Hand-signed	1,989	495.00
Hand-signed Purple uniform	33	5,500.00
Mini	10,000	79.00
A/P	100	450.00
Johnson, Magic		
Hand-signed a/p	250	2,650.00
Facsimilie-signed	1,739	465.00
Hand-signed Purple uniform	32	6,500.00
Thomas, Isiah	10,000	75.00
Hand-signed	1,990	225.00
Wooden, John	10,000	80.00
Hand-signed	1,975	175.00
Hand-signed a/p	250	350.00

KENNER STARTING LINEUP

1988 Individual Players

Abdul-Jabbar, Kareem 24.00
Adams, Michael 25.00
Aguirre, Mark 20.00
Ainge, Danny 27.00
Bailey, Thurl 70.00
Barkley, Charles 20.00
Berry, Walter 18.00
Bird, Larry 24.00
Blackmon, Rolando 20.00
Cage, Michael 17.00
Carroll, Joe Barry 20.00
Chambers, Tom 29.00
Cheeks, Maurice 18.00
Cooper, Michael 22.00
Cummings, Terry 22.00
Dantley, Adrian 40.00
Daugherty, Brad 25.00
Dawkins, Johnny 18.00
Drexler, Clyde 45.00
Eaton, Mark 70.00
Ellis, Dale 18.00
English, Alex 17.00
Ewing, Patrick 15.00
Floyd, "Sleepy" 18.00
Garland, Winston 18.00
Gilliam, Armon 16.00
Gminski, Mike 16.00
Greenwood, David 20.00
Harper, Derek 20.00
Harper, Ron 20.00
Higgins, Rod 20.00
Hopson, Dennis 20.00
Hornacek, Jeff 40.00
Jackson, Mark 20.00
Johnson, Dennis 25.00
Johnson, Eddie 16.00
Johnson, Magic 28.00
Johnson, Steve 22.00
Johnson, Vinnie 40.00
Jordan, Michael 20.00
King, Bernard 20.00
Laimbeer, Bill 40.00
Lever, Lafayette 20.00
Malone, Jeff 16.00
Malone, Karl 200.00
Malone, Moses 45.00
Manning, Danny 13.00
McCray, Rodney 20.00
McDaniel, Xavier 25.00
McHale, Kevin 15.00
McKey, Derrick 33.00
Miller, Reggie 30.00
Moncrief, Sidney 20.00
Mullin, Chris 37.00
Olajuwon, Akeem 13.00
Parish, Robert 20.00
Paxson, John 18.00
Perkins, Sam 30.00
Person, Chuck 18.00
Pippen, Scottie 27.00
Porter, Terry 35.00
Pressey, Paul 20.00
Price, Mark 60.00
Rivers, Doc 16.00
Robertson, Alvin 16.00
Robinson, Cliff 20.00
Sampson, Ralph 16.00
Schayes, Danny 20.00
Sikma, Jack 22.00
Smith, Kenny 16.00
Stipanovich, Steve 17.00
Stockton, John 125.00
Thomas, Isiah 18.00
Thompson, LaSalle 20.00
Thorpe, Otis 20.00
Tisdale, Wayman 15.00
Vandeweghe, Kiki 17.00
Webb, Spud 25.00
Wilkins, Dominique 15.00
Wilkins, Gerald 18.00
Williams, Buck 25.00
Williams, John 20.00
Williams, Reggie 15.00
Willis, Kevin 20.00
Worthy, James 25.00

1989 Individual Players

Chapman, Rex 35.00
Curry, Dell 20.00
Harper, Ron 15.00
Nance, Larry 15.00
Tripucka, Kelly 15.00

1989 Legends Collection

Wilt Chamberlain 30.00
Julius Erving 20.00
John Havlicek 10.00
Oscar Robertson 10.00

1989 One on One

Larry Bird, Magic Johnson . . 150.00
Patrick Ewing, K. McHale . . . 35.00
Michael Jordan, I. Thomas . . 90.00
D. Wilkins, Charles Barkley . . 50.00

1989 Slam Dunk Superstars

Larry Bird 50.00
Patrick Ewing 45.00
Magic Johnson 120.00
Michael Jordan 100.00
Isiah Thomas 40.00
Dominique Wilkins 40.00

1990 Individual Players

Barkley, Charles 30.00
Bird, Larry 30.00
Chambers, Tom 20.00
Drexler, Clyde 40.00
Dumars, Joe 20.00
Ewing, Patrick 25.00
Johnson, Magic 30.00
Jordan, Michael 25.00
Malone, Karl 20.00
Mullin, Chris 25.00
Robinson, David 50.00
Scott, Byron 20.00
Stockton, John 25.00
Thomas, Isiah 20.00
Webb, Spud 20.00
Wilkins, Dominique 25.00
Worthy, James 20.00

1991 Individual Players

Barkley, Charles 20.00
Bird, Larry 25.00
Coleman, Derrick 50.00
Drexler, Clyde 30.00
Dumars, Joe 20.00
Ewing, Patrick 20.00
Johnson, Kevin 25.00
Johnson, Magic 25.00
Jordan, Michael
  passing 20.00
  dunking 25.00
Lewis, Reggie 25.00
Robinson, David 20.00
Rodman, Dennis 20.00
Thomas, Isiah 18.00
Webb, Spud 18.00
Wilkins, Dominique 30.00

1992 Individual Players

Barkley, Charles 30.00
Bird, Larry 40.00
Bol, Manute 20.00
Brown, Dee 20.00
Coleman, Derrick 25.00
Divac, Vlade 15.00
Drexler, Clyde 20.00
Dumars, Joe 20.00
Ewing, Patrick 20.00
Hardaway, Tim 40.00
Johnson, Kevin 20.00
Johnson, Larry 100.00
Johnson, Magic 25.00
Jordan, Michael
  regular 20.00
  warm up 25.00
Malone, Karl 25.00
Miller, Reggie 25.00
Mullin, Chris 25.00
Mutombo, Dikembe 25.00

Olajuwon, Hakeem 20.00
Paxson, John 20.00
Pippen, Scottie 25.00
Price, Mark 20.00
Robinson, David
regular 20.00
warmup 25.00
Rodman, Dennis 20.00
Stockton, John 25.00
Thomas, Isiah 25.00

1992 Headliners

Barkley, Charles 14.00
Bird, Larry 16.00
Ewing, Patrick 14.00
Johnson, Magic 15.00
Jordan, Michael 15.00
Mutombo, Dikembe 17.00
Pippen, Scottie 14.00
Robinson, David 14.00

1992 Team Lineups

USA Olympic Team 75.00

SALVINO SPORT LEGENDS

Player	# Issued	Value
Baylor, Elgin		
Hand-signed	700	250.00
Hand-signed s/e	300	350.00
Bird, Larry		
Home signed	500	300.00
Road signed	500	300.00
Home signed s/e	250	375.00
Road signed s/e	250	375.00
West, Jerry		
Hand-signed	700	250.00
Hand-signed s/e	300	350.00

SPORTS IMPRESSIONS

Player	# Issued	Value
Robertson, Oscar		
9"	975	150.00
6"	Open	45.00

BOXING FIGURINES

SALVINO SPORT LEGENDS

Player	# Issued	Value
Ali, Muhammed		
Hand-signed	3,500	275.00
Hand-signed s/e	400	500.00

FOOTBALL FIGURINES

GARTLAN USA

Player	# Issued	Value
Montana, Joe		
Hand-signed	2,250	375.00
Mini	10,000	80.00
Club Mini	Club only	200.00

KENNER STARTING LINEUP

1988 Individual Players

Allen, Marcus 25.00
Anderson, Neal 25.00
Banks, Chip 32.00

Isaiah Thomas Gartlan

Bavaro, Mark 25.00
Bennett, Cornelius 50.00
Bentley, Albert 22.00
Bickett, Duane 22.00
Blackledge, Todd 22.00
Bosworth, Brian 20.00
Brennan, Brian 24.00
Brooks, Bill 24.00
Brooks, James 37.00
Brown, Eddie 35.00
Browner, Joey 22.00
Bruce, Aundray 22.00
Burkett, Chris 35.00
Byars, Keith 22.00
Campbell, Scott 22.00
Carson, Carlos 22.00
Carson, Harry 25.00
Carter, Anthony 35.00
Carter, Gerald 20.00
Carter, Michael 34.00
Casillas, Tony 22.00
Chadwick, Jeff 18.00
Cherry, Deron 23.00
Childress, Ray 30.00
Christiansen, Todd 25.00
Clark, Gary 30.00
Clayton, Mark 25.00
Collinsworth, Cris 35.00
Cosbie, Doug 22.00
Craig, Roger 30.00
Cunningham, Randall 35.00
Davis, Jeff 20.00
Davis, Ken 30.00
Dent, Richard 22.00
Dickerson, Eric 40.00
Dixon, Floyd 20.00
Dorsett, Tony 100.00
Duper, Mark 23.00
Eason, Tony 27.00
Ekern, Carl 22.00
Ellard, Henry 22.00
Elway, John 33.00
Epps, Phillip 25.00
Esiason, Boomer 40.00
Everett, Jim 28.00
Fulwood, Brent 30.00

Gastineau, Mark 24.00
Gault, Willie 50.00
Golic, Bob 20.00
Gray, Jerry 20.00
Green, Darrell 40.00
Green, Jacob 25.00
Green, Roy 32.00
Grogan, Steve 22.00
Harmon, Ronnie 50.00
Hebert, Bobby 35.00
Highsmith, Alonzo 25.00
Hill, Drew 30.00
Jackson, Earnest 18.00
Jackson, Rickey 22.00
Johnson, Vance 23.00
Jones, Ed 22.00
Jones, James 18.00
Jones Rod 20.00
Jones, Rulon 20.00
Jordan, Steve 25.00
Junior, E.J. 33.00
Kelly, Jim 65.00
Kenney, Bill 22.00
Kosar, Bernie 22.00
Kramer, Tommy 30.00
Krieg, Dave 22.00
Krumrie, Tim 30.00
Lee, Mark 30.00
Lippett, Ronnie 30.00
Lipps, Louis 25.00
Lomax, Neil 25.00
Long, Chuck 20.00
Long, Howie 28.00
Lott, Ronnie 45.00
Mack, Kevin 20.00
Malone, Mark 25.00
Manley, Dexter 20.00
Marino, Don 60.00
Martin, Eric 24.00
Mayes, Rueben 24.00
McMahon, Jim 17.00
McNeil, Freeman 19.00
Mecklenburg, Karl 18.00
Merriweather, Mike 18.00
Mitchell, Stump 24.00
Monk, Art 50.00
Montana, Joe 80.00
Moon, Warren 50.00
Morgan, Stanley 20.00
Morris, Joe 20.00
Nelson, Darrin 21.00
Newsome, Ozzie 23.00
O'Brien, Ken 20.00
Offerdahl, John 23.00
Okoye, Christian 50.00
Quick, Mike 20.00
Rice, Jerry 75.00
Riggs, Gerald 18.00
Rogers, Reggie 20.00
Rozier, Mike 25.00
Schroeder, Jay 30.00
Shuler, Mickey 17.00
Simms, Phil 18.00
Singletary, Mike 28.00
Smith, Billy Ray 32.00
Smith, Bruce 50.00
Smith, J.T. 25.00
Stradford, Troy 19.00
Taylor, Lawrence 22.00
Testaverde, Vinnie 20.00
Tippett, Andre 25.00
Toney, Anthony 22.00
Toon, Al 22.00
Trudeau, lack 22.00
Walker, Herschel 19.00
Warner, Curt 22.00
Waymer, Dave 18.00
White, Charles 18.00
White, Danny 23.00
White, Randy 23.00
White, Reggie 22.00
Wilder, James 20.00
Williams, Doug 22.00
Wilson, Marc 50.00
Winder, Sammy 20.00

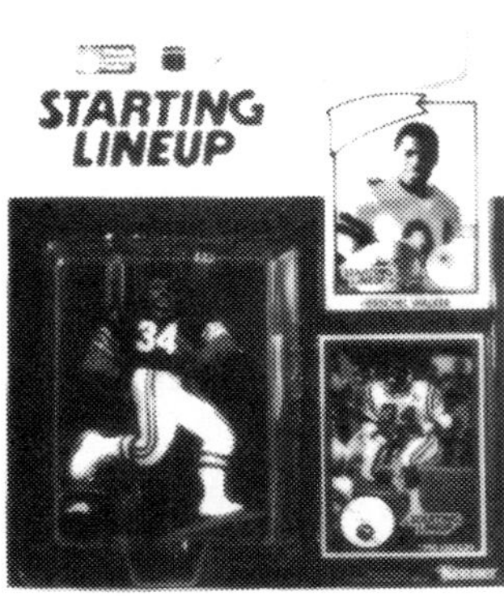

Herschel Walker Starting Lineup

Player	Price
Winslow, Kellen	45.00
Woodson, Rod	20.00
Wright, Randy	25.00

1989 Individual Players

Player	Price
Allen, Marcus	15.00
Anderson, Neal	15.00
Banks, Carl	12.00
Bates, Bill	16.00
Bavaro, Mark	15.00
Bennett, Cornelius	24.00
Bickett, Duane	12.00
Blades, Bennie	14.00
Brister, Bubby	14.00
Brooks, Bill	13.00
Brooks, James	15.00
Brown, Eddie	15.00
Brown, Jerome	25.00
Brown, Tim	14.00
Browner, Joey	15.00
Bryant, Kelvin	12.00
Burt, Jim	18.00
Byars, Keith	15.00
Cadigan, Dave	14.00
Carter, Anthony	15.00
Carter, Michael	20.00
Chandler, Chris	13.00
Clark, Gary	25.00
Conlan, Shane	32.00
Covert, Jimbo	30.00
Craig, Roger	14.00
Cunningham, Randall	15.00
Dent, Richard	15.00
Dixon, Hanford	12.00
Doleman, Chris	16.00
Dorsett, Tony	42.00
Duerson, Dave	14.00
Elway, John	15.00
Esiason, Boomer	15.00
Everett, Jim	15.00
Everett, Thomas	13.00
Farrell, Sean	14.00
Fralic, Bill	17.00
Fryar, Irving	18.00
Fulcher, David	14.00
Givins, Ernest	18.00
Gordon, Alex	13.00
Haley, Charles	22.00
Hebert, Bobby	30.00
Hector, Johnny	12.00
Hill, Drew	21.00
Hilliard, Dalton	16.00
Hinkle, Bryan	12.00
Irvin, Michael	32.00
Jackson, Keith	16.00
James, Gary	12.00
Jones, Sean	13.00
Kelly, Jim	65.00
Kelly, Joe	10.00
Kosar, Bernie	12.00
Krumrie, Tim	16.00
Lipps, Louis	16.00
Lockhart, Eugene	15.00
Lofton, James	25.00
Lomax, Neil	12.00
Long, Chuck	14.00
Long, Howie	12.00
Lott, Ronnie	30.00
Mack, Kevin	12.00
Mandley, Pete	12.00
Manley, Dexter	10.00
Mann, Charles	12.00
Manuel, Lionel	15.00
Marino, Dan	30.00
Marshall, Leonard	13.00
Martin, Eric	15.00
Mayes, Rueben	16.00
McElroy, Vann	14.00
McKinnon, Dennis	12.00
McMahon, Jim	15.00
McMichael, Steve	20.00
McMillan, Eric	13.00
McNeil, Freeman	10.00
Millard, Keith	18.00
Miller, Chris	25.00
Minnifield, Frank	12.00
Monk, Art	25.00
Montana, Joe	40.00
Moon, Warren	22.00
Morris, Joe	14.00
Munoz, Anthony	15.00
Nattiel, Ricky	12.00
Nelson, Darrin	12.00
Noonan, Danny	15.00
O'Brien, Ken	
error "O'Brian"	45.00
correction	12.00
Pelleur, Steve	12.00
Quick, Mike	12.00
Reed, Andre	45.00
Rice, Jerry	38.00
Rozier, Mike	17.00
Schroeder, Jay	15.00
Settle, John	12.00
Shuler, Mickey	12.00
Simms, Phil	12.00
Singletary, Mike	15.00
Slaughter, Webster	15.00
Smith, Bruce	40.00
Spielman, Chris	20.00
Stephens, John	12.00
Stauffer, Kelly	20.00
Swilling, Pat	22.00
Taylor, Lawrence	17.00
Testaverde, Vinny	18.00
Thomas, Thurman	65.00
Tippett, Andre	15.00
Toney, Anthony	14.00
Toon, Al	14.00
Veris, Garin	15.00
Walker, Herschel	14.00
Warner, Curt	15.00
White, Reggie	14.00
Williams, Doug	12.00
Williams, John	15.00
Wilson, Wade	18.00
Woods, Ickey	18.00
Woodson, Rod	14.00
Young, Steve	40.00

1989 One on One

Players	Price
Chris Doleman, J. McMahon	40.00
John Elway, Brian Bosworth	25.00
Howie Long, Herschel Walker	45.00
Lawrence Taylor, K. O'Brien	40.00

1990 Individual Players

Player	Price
Aikman, Troy	20.00
Anderson, Neal	15.00
Bavaro, Mark	15.00
Beuerlein, Steve	14.00
Brister, Bubby	15.00
Brooks, James	13.00
Brown, Tim	11.00
Carter, Cris	19.00
Craig, Roger	10.00
Cunningham, Randall	12.00
Dykes, Hart Lee	12.00
Elway, John	15.00
Esiason, Boomer	14.00
Everett, Jim	14.00
Fletcher, Simon	10.00
Flutie, Doug	26.00
Gentry, Dennis	10.00
Hampton, Dan	20.00
Harbaugh, Jim	20.00
Holman, Rodney	17.00
Humphrey, Bobby	18.00
Irvin, Michael	28.00
Jackson, Bo	16.00
Jackson, Keith	12.00
Johnson, Vance	14.00
Kelly, Jim	15.00
Kosar, Bernie	12.00
Lipps, Louis	12.00
Majkowski, Don	14.00
Mann, Chades	12.00
Manuel, Lionel	10.00
Marino, Dan	25.00
McGee, Tim	12.00
Meggett, David	15.00
Merriweather, Mike	12.00
Metcalf, Eric	15.00
Millard, Keith	10.00
Montana, Joe	15.00
Moon, Warren	20.00
Okoye, Christian	18.00
Rathman, Tom	18.00
Reed, Andre	18.00
Riggs, Gerald	14.00
Rypien, Mark	27.00
Sanders, Barry	40.00
Sanders, Deion	20.00
Sanders, Ricky	15.00
Simmons, Clyde	15.00
Simms, Phil	10.00
Singletary, Mike	12.00
Slaughter, Webster	10.00
Smith, Bruce	16.00
Stephens, John	13.00
Taylor, John	17.00
Thomas, Thurman	36.00
Tomczak, Mike	14.00
Townsend, Greg	12.00
Turner, Odessa	12.00
Walker, Herschel	12.00
Walsh, Steve	17.00
White, Reggie	15.00
Wilson, Wade	12.00
Woods, Ickey	10.00
Woolford, Donnell	14.00
Worley, Tim	15.00
Wright, Felix	12.00

1990 Legends Collection

Player	Price
Bradshaw, Terry	20.00
Ditka, Mike	20.00
Greene, Joe	18.00
Sayers, Gale	25.00
Unitas, Johnny	20.00

1991 Headliners

Player	Price
Elway, John	24.00
Esiason, Boomer	15.00
Marino, Dan	25.00
Montana, Joe	15.00
Rice, Jerry	25.00
Sanders, Barry	22.00

1991 Individual Players

Player	Price
Aikman, Troy	17.00
Anderson, Flipper	11.00
Anderson, Neal	17.00
Brooks, James	16.00
Brown, Eddie	16.00
Carrier, Mark	20.00
Esiason, Boomer	8.00

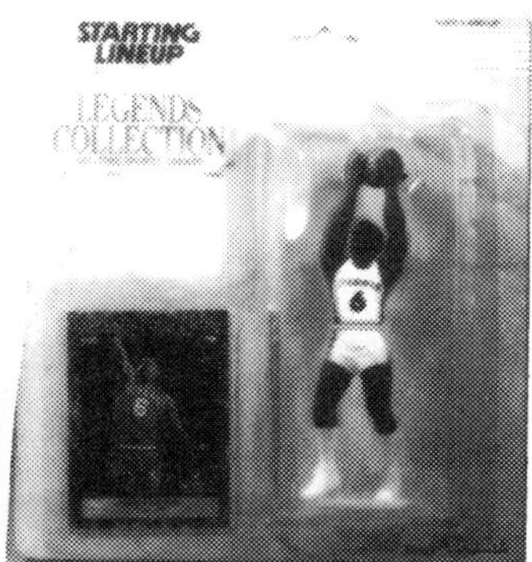

Brett Hull signed Gartlan statue, Magic Johnson Starting Lineup, Julius Erving Starting Lineup Legends

Francis, James	20.00
George, Jeff	20.00
Hampton, Rodney	20.00
Harbaugh, Jim	17.00
Hostetler, Jeff	20.00
Humphrey, Bobby	10.00
Majkowski, Don	15.00
Marino, Dan	20.00
Meggett, Dave	10.00
Montana, Joe	10.00
Moon, Warren	15.00
Okoye, Christian	10.00
Rice, Jerry	10.00
Rison, Andre	25.00
Sanders, Barry	12.00
Simms, Phil	8.00
Smith, Emmitt	65.00
Thomas, Thurman	22.00
Walker, Herschel	12.00

1992 Headliners

Montana, Joe	18.00
Moon, Warren	30.00
Rypien, Mark	15.00
Sanders, Barry	20.00
Smith, Emmitt	30.00
Thomas, Thurman	28.00

1992 Individual Players

Aikman, Troy	20.00
Byner, Earnest	14.00
Cunningham, Randall	18.00
Hampton, Rodney	14.00
Hebert, Bobby	16.00
Hostetler, Jeff	16.00
Irvin, Michael	20.00
Jackson, Bo	14.00
Jeffires, Haywood	14.00
Joyner, Seth	14.00
Kelly, Jim	15.00
Lott, Ronnie	14.00
Marino, Dan	25.00
Montana, Joe	15.00
Moon, Warren	15.00
Moore, Rob	14.00
Rice, Jerry	18.00
Rison, Andre	18.00
Rypien, Mark	14.00
Sanders, Barry	18.00
Sanders, Deion	22.00
Smith, Emmitt	25.00
Swilling, Pat	18.00
Thomas, Derrick	35.00
Thomas, Thurman	20.00
Young, Steve	18.00

SALVINO SPORT LEGENDS

Player	# Issued	Value
Bradshaw, Terry		
Home signed	500	275.00
Road signed	500	275.00
Brown, Jim		
Hand-signed	1,000	325.00
Hand-signed s/e	300	550.00
Hornung, Paul		
Hand-signed	500	250.00
Montana, Joe		
7" signed	2,500	275.00
7" signed s/e	500	375.00
Home signed	500	275.00
Road signed	500	275.00
Home signed ND	500	275.00
Road signed ND	500	275.00
Namath, Joe		
Hand-signed	2,500	275.00
Hand-signed s/e	500	375.00
Sayers, Gale		
Hand-signed	1,000	275.00
Simpson, O.J.		
Home signed	500	250.00
Road signed	500	250.00
Home snd USC	500	275.00
Road snd USC	500	275.00
Starr, Bart		
Hand-signed	500	250.00
Taylor, Jim		
Hand-signed	500	250.00

SPORTS IMPRESSIONS

Player	# Issued	Value
Aikman, Troy		
9"	995	125.00
6"	Open	45.00
3 ¼" ornament	Open	20.00
Cunningham, Randall		
9" home	995	125.00
9" away	995	125.00
6" home	Open	45.00
6" away	Open	45.00
Elway, John		
Hand-snd home	995	125.00
9" away	995	125.00
6" home	Open	45.00
6" away	Open	45.00
Esiason, Boomer		
9" home	995	125.00
9" away	995	125.00
5" home	Open	45.00
5" away	Open	45.00
Everett, Jim		
6"	Open	45.00
Harbaugh, Jim		
6"	Open	45.00
Kelly, Jim		
9"	995	125.00
6"	Open	45.00
3 ¼" ornament	Open	20.00
Kosar, Bernie		
6"	Open	45.00
Lombardi, Vince		
7"	3,926	100.00
Marino, Dan		
9" home	995	125.00
9" away	995	125.00
6" home	Open	45.00
6" away	Open	45.00
3 ¼" ornament	Open	20.00
Montana, Joe		
9" home	995	125.00
9" away	995	125.00
6" home	Open	45.00
6" away	Open	45.00
3 ¼" ornament	Open	20.00
Moon, Warren		
6"	Open	45.00
Okoye, Christian		
6"	Open	45.00
Rice, Jerry		
9" home	995	125.00
9" away	995	125.00
6" home	Open	45.00
6" away	Open	45.00
Rypien, Mark		
6"	Open	45.00
Sanders, Barry		
6"	Open	45.00
3 ¼" ornament	Open	20.00
Taylor, Lawrence		
9" home	995	125.00
9" away	995	125.00
6" home	Open	45.00
6" away	Open	45.00
3 ¼" ornament	Open	20.00
Thomas, Thurman		
6"	Open	45.00
Unitas, John		
5"	Open	45.00
Hand-signed.	Open	150.00

SPORTS IMPRESSIONS

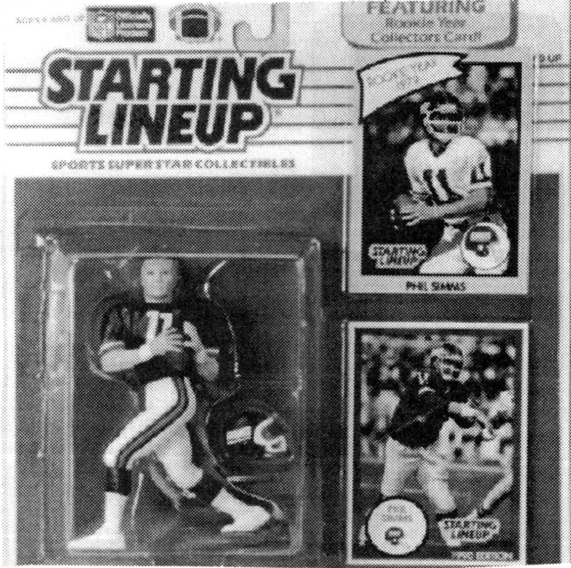

Phil Simms Starting Lineup

Player	# Issued	Value
Palmer, Arnold		
6"	Open	40.00
Player, Gary		
6"	Open	40.00

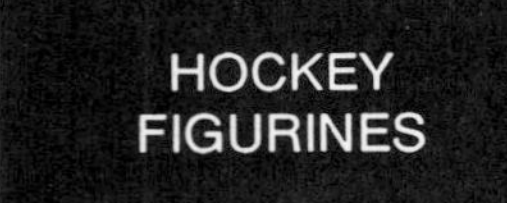

GARTLAN USA

Player	# Issued	Value
Gretzky, Wayne		
Hand-signed	1,851	900.00
Artist's proof, hand-signed, white uniform	300	1,500.00
Gretzky Mini	10,000	80.00
Club Mini	Club only	250.00
Hull, Bobby		
Hand-signed	1,983	250.00
Mini	10,000	80.00
Hull, Brett		
Hand-signed	1,986	250.00
Mini	10,000	80.00

PRO SPORT CREATIONS

Player	# Issued	Value
Howe, Gordie		
Hand-signed	1,972	125.00
Hand-signed a/p	200	165.00

SALVINO SPORT LEGENDS

Player	# Issued	Value
Coffey, Paul		
Home signed	500	275.00
Road signed	500	275.00
Lemieux, Mario		
Home signed	500	275.00
Road signed	500	275.00
Home signed s/e	375	300.00
Road signed s/e	375	300.00
Robitaille, Luc		
Home signed	500	275.00
Road signed	500	275.00

SOCCER FIGURINES

KENNER STARTING LINEUP

1989 English

Player	Value
Adams, T. (Arsenal)	30.00
Aitken, R. (Celtic)	25.00
Aumann, R. (Munich)	25.00
Barnes, John (England)	30.00
Beardsley, P. (England)	25.00
Beardsley, P. (Liverpool)	30.00
Bonner, Pat (Celtic)	37.00
Brehme, A. (W. Germany)	35.00
Bruce, S. (Manchester)	25.00
Buchwald, G. (W. Germ.)	35.00
Butcher, T. (England)	25.00
Careca (Napoli)	55.00
Chapman, L. (Nottingham)	25.00
Clough, N. (Nottingham)	30.00
Cottee, T. (Everton)	30.00
Cowans, G. (Aston Villa)	35.00
Gascoigne, P. (Tottenham)	50.00
Grobbelaar (Liverpool)	35.00
Gullit, Ruud (Dutch Nat.)	62.00
Hughes, M. (Manchester)	25.00
Hughes, M. (Wales)	25.00
Johnston, M. (Scotland)	20.00
Koemen, R. (Dutch)	65.00
Leighton, J. (Manchester)	40.00
Lineker, G. (England)	30.00
Lineker, G. (Tottenham)	42.00
Mabbutt, G. (Tottenham)	20.00
Maradona, D. (Napoli)	65.00
Mathaus, L. (W. Germ. Nat.)	60.00
McClair, B. (Manchester)	30.00
McCoist, A. (Scotland)	25.00
McStay, P. (Celtic)	25.00
McStay, P. (Scotland)	30.00
Merson, P. (Arsenal)	30.00
Mountfield, D. (Aston Villa)	20.00
Nicol, S. (Liverpool)	25.00
Nicol, S. (Scotland)	25.00
Nevin, P. (Everton)	25.00
Pearce, S. (Nottingham)	30.00
Platt, D. (Aston Villa)	30.00
Ratcliffe, K. (Everton)	25.00
Ratcliffe, K. (Wales)	25.00
Rijkaard, F. (Dutch Nat.)	70.00
Robson, B. (England)	25.00
Robson, B. (Manchester)	25.00
Rocastle, D. (Arsenal)	25.00
Rush, I. (Liverpool)	25.00
Rush, I. (Wales)	40.00
Sharpe, G. (Everton)	30.00
Smith, A. (Arsenal)	25.00
Spink, Nigel (Aston Villa)	35.00
Southall, N. (Everton)	40.00
Southall, N. (Wales)	30.00
Stewart, P. (Tottenham)	25.00
Thomas, M. (Arsenal)	25.00
Van Basten, M. (Dutch)	45.00
Van Breukelen, (Dutch)	70.00
Vialli, G. (Milan)	50.00
Waddle, C. (England)	25.00
Walker, D. (Nottingham)	25.00
Walsh, P. (Tottenham)	25.00
Woutters, J. (Dutch)	70.00

1989 German

Player	Value
Allgower, K. (Stuttgart)	35.00
Allots, K. (Marseille)	70.00
Amoros, M. (France)	35.00
Augenthaier, K. (Munchen)	40.00
Aumann, R. (Munchen)	30.00
Beleredorfer, D. (Hamburger)	25.00
Brehme, A. (Mannschatt)	30.00
Buchwald, G. (Mannschaft)	30.00
Buchwald, G. (Stuttgart)	25.00
Burgsmuller, M. (Bremen)	35.00
Careca (Napoli)	40.00
de Beer, W. (Dortmond)	30.00
Dorfner, H. (Munchen)	30.00
Frontzeck, M. (Stuttgart)	30.00
Gaudino, M. (Stuttgart)	70.00
Gullit, R. (Milan)	50.00
Habler, T. (Koln)	30.00
Helmer, T. (Dortmond)	35.00
Hermann, G. (Bremen)	30.00
Immell, E. (Stuttgart)	30.00
Jakobs, D. (Hamburger)	25.00
Jusufi, S. (Hamburger)	30.00
Klinsmann, J. (Mannschaft)	75.00
Kohler, J. (Mannschaft)	45.00
Kohler, J. (Munchen)	30.00
Lineker, G. (England)	35.00
Littbarski, P. (Koln)	30.00
Maradona, D. (Napoli)	60.00
Matthaus, L. (Mannschaft)	90.00
Mill, F. (Dortmond)	30.00
Moeller, A. (Dortmond)	35.00
Pflugler, H. (Munchen)	30.00
Rahn, U. (Koln)	25.00
Reck, O. (Bremen)	30.00
Reuter, S. (Munchen)	35.00
Riedle, K. (Bremen)	35.00
Rijkaard, F (Milan)	45.00
Robson, B. (England)	35.00
Rummenigge, M. (Dortmond)	35.00
Thon, Olaf (Mannschaft)	25.00
Thon, Olaf (Munchen)	35.00
Tigana, J. (France)	40.00
Van Basten, M. (Milan)	35.00
Van Breukelen, H. (Holland)	30.00
Vialli, G. (Italy)	40.00
Voller, R. (Mannschaft)	45.00
von Heesen, T. (Hamburger)	25.00
Zorc, M. (Dorttmond)	35.00

SPORTS GAMES

by Alex G. Malloy

The history of American sports games starts with the most popular spectator sport of the 19th century, horse racing. In 1843, a Boston printer named William Crosby was approached by America's first game entrepreneur, Anne Abbott of Salem, Massachusetts, to produce a simple horse racing game she had designed. Crosby liked the game and agreed to print and distribute the game that year. This game started a tradition of American sports games that has lasted for 150 years.

During the Victorian age, sports games imitated individual participant sports, rather than team sports. Sports games produced during this period include bicycling, golf, yachting, hunting, croquet, and bowling. Chaffee & Selchow, McLoughlin Brothers and Parker Brothers produced the majority of all sports games after 1890. Also during the 1890s, basketball, football, and baseball games started.

New Parlor Game of Baseball, 1879; Debby & Marty Krim Collection

After the Victorian Age, in 1903, the sports game began to rise in popularity. Numerous manufacturers started producing games. The most popular games were the baseball games produced by various companies. This trend continued right up until the time of the Great Depression, when various football games were produced in greater numbers. Other sports games experienced sporadic manufacturing during this period as auto racing, horse racing and golf games began to grow in popularity. The Big Two game companies (Parker Bros. and Milton Bradley) had numerous sports games in their lines. Cadaco-Ellis started producing games in early 1936, and by the 1950s was probably the leading producer of sports games in the United States.

The concept of popular athlete endorsed games began in 1879 with the rare *Running Game of Pedestrianism*, which depicts running stars Rowell and Ennis. Baseball games were the most widely endorsed games. Greats such as Babe Ruth, Christy Mathewson, Lou Gehrig, Walter Johnson, Bob Feller, Carl Yastrzemski, Mickey Mantle, Hank Aaron, and Willie Mays put their names on games. *Jose Canseco's Perfect Baseball Game* is a recent example of this continuing practice.

AUTO RACING

Auto racing games are very popular with toy auto collectors as well as racing fans. Parker Brothers produced the first auto race game in 1904, which depicts an old antique car in a large format. In the Roaring Twenties, All-Fair purchased another popular racing game, *Game of Auto Race* from Urotech Co. and renamed it *Speedem Auto Race*. The playing pieces are six colored metal cars named Stutz, Dodge, Ford,

Max, Buick, and Paige, and players roll six dice with S, D, F, M, B, and P to move the corresponding cars. This game was the first popular auto race game and sold very well throughout the United States.

In 1938, W. Wilbur Shaw produced a little known game which has special significance today. The *Indianapolis 500 Mile Race Game* was packaged in a large manila envelope with Shaw's portrait. A big, accurate board of the famous raceway was played with two sets of cards. Twenty-five trouble cards and twenty-five pit cards depict photos and biographical exploits of 50 greats of the Indy 500 including Gaston Chevrolet, Jimmie Murphy, Eddie Rickenbacker, Earl Cooper, Tommy Milton, Ralph DePalma, Peter DePaolo, and Louis Meyer. These cards show up individually at sports card shows at high prices.

Along the line of the Indy 500 Game is the *United States Auto Club Racing Game* by Avalon Hill-Sports Illustrated. Color picture cards of auto racing greats were also issued and make this game a popular acquisition.

BASEBALL

Baseball games are the most popular of all sports games, with over 320 baseball board and card games having been produced. The premier professional baseball game was produced in 1869, just four years after the Civil War. It includes team rosters and lineup cards. This game, *The New Parlor Game of Baseball*, was published by M.B. Sumner and lithographed by Buford of Boston. A board of this game alone was hammered down at auction with buyer's premium for $8,250 in July 1991, without the implement box. The scarce implement box cover has a line drawing of an early baseball pitcher. This game was touted as the first professional baseball game

Zimmers Baseball Game
Mark Cooper Collection

and includes team rosters and lineup cards.

The period of 1890-1910 saw some of the most beautiful multi-colored lithographed cover baseball games known. McLoughlin Brothers produced the majority of them. The variety of materials used in this era is immense. Masonite, tin, metal, plastic, cardboard, and wood were all used for the game boards.

A quality example of a game from this period was issued in 1912, when the Philadelphia Game Manufacturing Co. produced a fine wood-sided game, *Major League Indoor Baseball.* This game cover has sixteen player photos in ovals, including six Hall-of-Famers: Christy Mathewson, Honus Wagner, Home Run Baker, Ed Walsh, Tris Speaker, and Walter Johnson. The more common version of this cover is plain green with the name of the game in white script. Each year this game was issued with different team lineup cards; in 1916, Babe Ruth is listed in the Boston Red Sox lineup card as a pitcher.

Zimmer Baseball Game, manufactured by McLoughlin Bros., is considered to be the Honus Wagner of table games. Only five examples of this game are known to exist intact, with the fine chromolithographic board depicting greats of the game (including many who became Hall of Famers). This game is valued at $20,000. The 1889 Champion Game of Baseball, put out by A.S. Schultz, depicting a colorful bust of Ho'fer John Clarkson reached a $4,400 price in a recent auction at Superior Galleries in Beverly Hills, CA.

The highly popular *Fan Craze Card Game* was issued in 1904, in four separate editions. The most sought after are the photo card sets of American and National Leaguers. Even single cards of this set bring high values, including the popular Honus Wagner card.

The first game to be endorsed by a player was *The Rube Walker and Harry Davis Baseball Game*, published in 1905 by Champion Athletics. This game was the first of the many player endorsed baseball games that have been issued since.

Though table games based on baseball had been on the market since about 1880, and many were colorfully packaged and fun to play, they did not appeal to devoted diamond fans. The question of how to make a realistic baseball table game stumped most manufacturers. The first really scientific baseball table game was produced by the APBA Game Co. of Lancaster, Pennsylvania.

Introduced in 1950, APBA devised an approach using dice and cards representing the current Major League players of the day; each player's card looked like a computer printout and was different than any other player's card. That was the secret of success for this enterprising company. APBA produced believable results.

The APBA game was never sold in stores. It had to be ordered directly from the company, and it was not (nor is it now) inexpensive. The price is several times that of an ordinary table game. Each year a new set of cards is issued. You do not need to buy the whole game over again; you can merely order the cards. The set consists of player-cards for all the Big League teams, each contained in a small manila envelope. The cards are ordinary playing-card size, and are programmed according to each player's performance from the previous season.

Nobody who played APBA in the 1950s thought about the cards becoming collector's items. But this is precisely what happened. The early sets had rather small printings and some owners discarded the previous year's set when the new one arrived. Low printing and a high mortality rate increased collectibility.

BASKETBALL

Home Court Basketball
Alex G. Malloy Collection

The first basketball game was produced by Chaffee & Selchow only seven years after James Naismith invented the sport in Springfield, Massachusetts. The fascinating part of the very large, gilded-edge board game is the lithographed cover which shows women, not men, at play. The majority of basketball board games, though, were produced after 1940. Cadaco-Ellis produced the popular game *Bas*ket* on a regular basis. *Oscar Robertson's Pro Basketball Strategy* and the rare *Home Court Basketball*, with a photo of Charlie Eckman, are the most valuable games of the post-World War II period.

BOXING

Boxing games are generally not common. The most fascinating boxing game is the 1922 edition of *Tip-Top*, by LaVelle. The game uses two spinning tops in a miniature fight ring. The tops represent the Dempsey vs. Willis heavyweight fight. The top spinning last is the winner. LaVelle also issued later editions with other famous fights. These are considered to be the greatest action sports games produced.

FOOTBALL

Early football games were recognizable by the large and impressive covers of the 1890s. *Yale-Harvard Football* by McLoughlin Brothers, published in 1890, is reportedly the first football game, with its sequel, *Yale-Princeton Football Game*, following five years later. Parker Brothers quickly followed in 1892 with their first football game, called *The Game of Football.* While the insides were often dull, the chromo-lithographic covers were spectacular in these early examples.

In 1923, LaVelle Manufacturing Company introduced a noteworthy game called *Yale-Harvard Football Game*, with the cover depicting a photo of the 1922 Yale-Harvard game. This game has a large, unique, painted iron football player that kicks a wooden football through the metal goal posts. The field is represented by a large green felt field with a white printed gridiron.

In 1932, Howard H. Jones, the coach of 1931 National Champion Southern California, was the first to endorse a football game. This game was produced in Los Angeles by Municipal Service. The large format game depicts photos of Jones and USC at play. In 1936, Notre Dame coach Elmer Layden endorsed a football game produced by Cadaco-Ellis that lasted in different forms through 1970. The cover of the scarce first

The Yale Harvard Game
Debby & Marty Krim Collection

edition contains a picture of Layden against a gold and blue background and a letter from him endorsing the game. The first professional football game, *The Los Angeles Rams Football Game*, was issued in the 1930s by the California Game Company.

Unlike baseball games, where the players give endorsements, football endorsements focus on the great coaches of all-time, including Knute Rockne in 1940, Paul Brown in 1947, Frank Cavanaugh in 1955, and Vince Lombardi in 1970. Some of the great Hall-of-Famers have put their names on football games, however, including Bart Starr and Johnny Unitas in the 1960s, and Roger Staubach in 1973.

GOLF

Substitute Golf, produced by the Quality Toy Manufacturer Shoenhut of Philadelphia and issued in 1906, is the greatest golf game ever issued. The course was created by the players in a large room, using supplied equipment: tees, bunkers, holes, and flags. Each player used a large metal mechanical golfer attached to a handle that enabled the golfer to swing at the ball.

The deluxe edition of *Fore Country Club*, issued by Wilder of St. Louis during the 1930s, is an excellent example of fine game box art. The art deco painting cover depicts a country club golfer swinging away with the club set in the background.

"Light Horse" Harry Cooper was the first golfer to endorse a game, in 1943. This scarce game was made by a small company, Trojan Games. *Arnold Palmer's Inside Golf* and *Tee Off*, by Sam Snead, were produced in the 1960s and 1970s, respectively. Recent golf games have shown considerable improvement; an exceptional quality game called *Ultimate Golf*, produced in 1985, deserves special notice.

HORSE RACING

Horse racing, which dates back to at least the time of the ancient Egyptians, is the oldest sport and table game in America. After William Crosby's 1844 *Game of the Races*, various games were produced during the Victorian era. A later horse racing

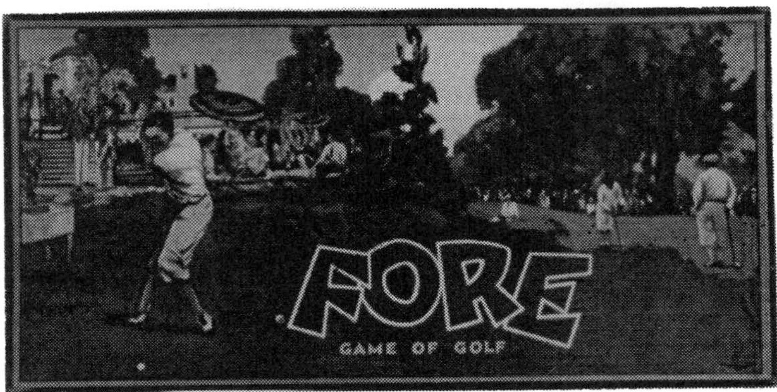

Fore, Game of Golf
Alex G. Malloy Collection

game by a similar name, *The Game of the Race*, produced from the late 1860s to early 1870s, had a colorful board and a fine small wooden implement box with painted metal horses. It was published anonymously.

In the 1890s, various large chromo-lithographic cover games with superb quality art design were issued. McLoughlin Brothers produced the most striking covers, and Parker Brothers, J.H. Singer, and E.O. Clark also produced colorful horse racing games during this period. Most of these games focused on the Steeple Chase.

Jockey endorsed games are few and far between, the only ones of note are *Eddie Arcaro's Riders Up Game* and *Eddie Arcaro's Blue Grass Handicap Horse Race Game* (Transogram). Racing parks, on the other hand, received numerous endorsements, such as *Pimlico*, by Metro, *Saratoga*, by Milton Bradley and J.H. Singer, *Belmont Park* by Marks Brothers, *Hialeah*, by Milton Bradley, *Jerome Park*, by McLoughlin Brothers, and last but not least, *Kentucky Derby* a somewhat common game by Whitman. *Kentucky Derby* was produced over a span of 31 years, from 1938 to 1969.

GENERAL SPORTS GAMES

After most of the big game companies of the turn of the century ceased producing games, Parker Brothers and Milton Bradley continued to produce a great variety. Every game company manufactured some sports games, as they have been popular in every decade. A large quantity of sports games were made by companies that produced just one game, and these games are more scarce and are often regional in availability.

With careful searching, a collector can find the most esoteric sports games. Sports games such as *BMX Cross Challenge Action Game, Grand Master of Martial Arts, Walk the Plank - A Diving and Swimming Game, Young Athlete* (an early gymnastics game), and even *Jai-Alai* (represented in the 1984 game manufactured by Design Origins) are among the more unusual games available.

TABLE GAMES

AUTO RACING GAMES

A&P Motor Car Relay Race, Coast to Coast, Leg 4 (1930's) A&P cereal box 50.00
APBA Saddle Racing Game (APBA 1974) 50.00
Auto Race (D&M CO. 1920's) 75.00
Auto Race (Milton Bradley 1920's) 75.00

1930 Auto Race Game
Alex G. Malloy collection.

Auto Race (Milton Bradley 1930) Radio Series . . . 125.00
Auto Race (Gotham steel 1930) metal mechanical 125.00
Auto Race Game (Milton Bradley 1925) Large, colorful action color 400.00
Auto Race Knapp Electro Game w/air, baseball, football (Knapp, 1929) 175.00
Brownie Auto Race (Jeanette Toy & Novelty 1920s) 150.00
Cannonball Run (Cadaco 1981) Movie adaptation . . 15.00
Car race & Game Hunt (Wilder 1920's) 125.00
Champion Road Race (Champion Spark Plugs premium 1934) 125.00
Circle Racer Board Game (1988) 10.00
Combo 4 games Auto Race, Army & Navy, Game Hunt (Wilder, 1920's) 125.00
Combo board Road and Air Races (Wilder 1928) . 200.00
Cross Country Racer (1940s) wind-up cars 100.00
Daytona 500 Race Game (Milton Bradley 1989) . . . 20.00

1922 Game of Speed King
Alex G. Malloy collection.

Empire Auto Races (Empire 1950s) 30.00
Famous 500 Mile Race Game (1988) 12.50
Flip It, Auto Race & Transcontinental Tour (Deluxe Game Co. 1920s) 75.00
Formula-1 (Parker Brothers 1963) 55.00
Formula-1 (Parker Brothers 1964) 50.00
Formula-1 (Parker Brothers 1968) 35.00
Game of Automobile Race (McLoughlin Bros. 1904) 1,300.00
Game of Auto Race (Orotech Co. 1920s) 200.00
Game of Midget Speedway (Whitman Pub. Co. 1942) 60.00
Game of Speed King (Russell 1922) 150.00
Game of Stock Car Speedway (Johnstone 1965) . . 75.00
Grande Auto Race (Atkins & Co. 1920s) 150.00
Hot Rod (Harett-Gilmar 1953) 30.00
Hot Rod (Donald L. Cranmer 1954) 50.00
Hot Wheels Game (Whitman 1982) 15.00
Hot Wheels Wipe-Out Game (Mattel 1968) 25.00
Indianapolis 500 Mile Race Game (Shaw 1938) Photo, Cards, large speedway board 500.00
Indianapolis 500 75th Running Race Game (International Games Inc 1991) 15.00
Indy Car (S.Alden 1993) 40.00
International Automobile Race (Parker Bros. 1903) 1,200.00
International Grand Prix (Cadaco 1975) 40.00
Junior Motor Race (1930's) Peter Pan Series 40.00
Huggin' The Rail (Selchow & Righter 1948) 75.00
Le Mans (Avalon Hill 1961) 35.00
Midget Auto Race (Cracker Jack Co. 1930s) 25.00
Midget Auto Race (Samuel Lowe 1941) 30.00
Moon Mullins Automobile Race (Milton Bradley 1920s) 125.00
Motor Race (Wolverine Supply & Mfg. Co. 1922) . 125.00

1934 Champion Road Race
Alex G. Malloy collection.

Motor Race Game (1920s) Metal Cars, Germany . 100.00
Nascar Daytona 500 (Milton Bradley 1990) 15.00
Pole Position (Parker Bros. 1983) 18.00
Raceway (B & B Toy Mfg. Co. 1950s) 30.00
Race for the Cup, Auto Racing (Milton Bradley 1910s) 100.00
Race-o-Rama (Built-Rite 1960) 4 race games 35.00
Racing Cars (Ace playing cards 1970s) W. German 10.00
Road Race Game (1930s) UK 75.00
Roll-O Motor Speedway (Supply Sales Co. 1922) . . 50.00

Six Day Race (Holtmann 1986)
German game "6-Tage Rennen" 35.00

1922 Spedem Auto Race
Alex G. Malloy collection.

Spedem Auto Race (All-Fair 1922) 250.00
Spedem Junior Auto Race Game (All-Fair 1929) . . 175.00
Speed Card Game (Pepus 1946) UK 25.00
Speed Circuit (3M 1971) 25.00
Speedway, Big Bopper Game (Ideal 1961) 40.00
Speedway Motor Race (J.Smarkola 1925) 75.00
Speedway Motor Race
(Smith, Kline & French 1920s) 150.00
Sto-Auto Race (Stough Co. 1920s) metal board . . . 50.00
Stock Car Race (Gardner 1950s) 75.00
Stock Car Racing Game (Whitman 1956) 25.00
The Stock Car Racing Game (Ribbit Toy Co. 1981)
w/ Richard Petty & Cale Yarborough 35.00
Straightaway (Selchow & Righter 1961) 50.00
300 Mile Race (Warren Built-Rite 1955) 75.00
Thunder Road (Milton Bradley 1986) 20.00
Tudor Electric Sports Car Race (Tudor 1959) 30.00
USAC Auto Racing (Avalon Hill-Sports
Illustrated 1980) w/ racing cards 100.00
Vallco Pro Drag Racing Game (Zyla 1975) 15.00
Vanderbelt Cup Race Game (Bowers & Hard 1910) 650.00

BASEBALL BOARD GAMES

PRE-1940 BOARD GAMES

ABC Baseball Game 1910s wood side,light board . 375.00
Alexander's Baseball with box 1940s 350.00
All-Star Baseball Game (Whitman Pub. Co 1935) . 100.00
Atkins Real Baseball (Atkins & Co. 1915) 450.00
Auto-Play Baseball Game (Auto-Play Co. 1911) . . 400.00
Aydelott's Parlor Baseball ©1910 . . . . 150.00
Babe Ruth Baseball Game (1933) plain box 750.00
Babe Ruth's Baseball Game (Milton Bradley 1925) 750.00
Babe Ruth National Game of Baseball
(Keiser-Fry 1929) 600.00
Bambino (Johnson Store Equipment Co. 1933)
Made for Chicago World's Fair 200.00
Base Hit (Games Inc. © 1944) card & metal players . .
Baseball (George Parker 1885) 1,000.00
Baseball (George B. Doan & Co. 1920) 100.00
Baseball (J. Ottman Litho Co. 1915) 200.00
Baseball (All-Fair 1926) metal & wood board 150.00
Baseball & Checkers (Milton Bradley 1925) 300.00
Baseball Dominoes (Evans 1910) 300.00
Baseball Game (McLoughlin 1890) 1,000.00
Baseball Game (Brinkman Engineering 1925) 135.00
Baseball Knapp Electro Game Set
(Knapp 1929) w/ air, auto race 175.00

Baseball Mania The Board Game
(Baseball Mania © 1993) 30.00
Baseball Wizard Game (Morehouse Mfg. 1916) . . 250.00
Bases Full, Hand Skill Game. c. 1930 . . . . 60.00
Big League Baseball Game (J. Chein & Co. 1930s) 250.00
Big League Baseball Game (A.E. Gustafson
©1938) Whitman Publishers #3502 . . . . 125.00
Big Six: Christy Mathewson Indoor Baseball
Game (Piroxloid Products Corp ©1922) 750.00

1910 Aydelott's Parlor Baseball
Alex G. Malloy collection.

Boston Baseball Game (Boston Game Co.©1906) 300.00
Broadcast Baseball (Pressman 1938-40) 100.00
The Champion Baseball Game
(New York Games Co. ©1913). 200.00
The Champion Game of Baseball (A.S. Schultz
©1889) Chromolithographic cover, portraits
of John Clarkson, Champion Pitcher and
Dan Brothers,Champion Batter 4,000.00

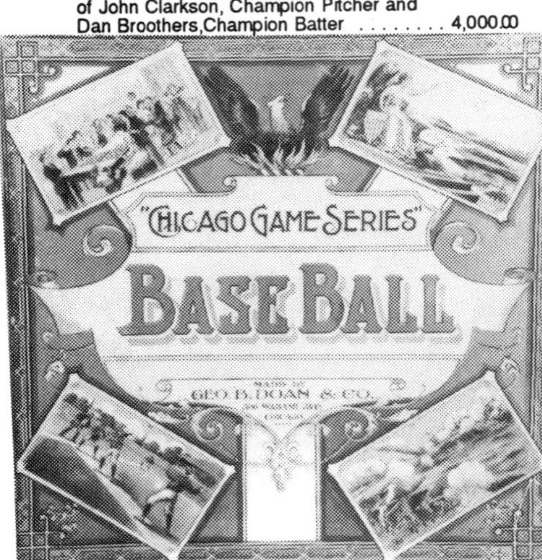

1890's Chicago Game Series Baseball
Debby & Marty Krim Collection

Chicago Game Series Baseball
(George B. Doan & Co. 1890s) 1,200.00
College Baseball Game (Parker Bros. 1890s) . . . 1,000.00
Danny MacFayden's Stove League Baseball

Game (National Game Co. 1935) 350.00
The Diamond Game of Baseball
(McLoughlin Bros. c. 1900) 750.00
Diceball (Ray-Fair Co. ©1938) 100.00
Diceball! (Intellijedx © 1993) 25.00
The Dicex Baseball Game
(Chester S. Howland c. 1925) 250.00
Double Game Board (Parker Bros. 1925) 75.00
Double Header Baseball (Redlich Mfg. Co. 1935) . 175.00
Durgin's New Baseball Game
(Durgin & Palmer 1885) 300.00
Electric Magnetic Baseball (1900) 150.00
Fan-i-Tis (C.W. Marsh 1913) 100.00
Follow the Stars, Watts Indoor League Baseball
(G.H. Allen Watts 1922) 225.00
Game of Base-ball (McLoughlin Bros. 1886) 1,500.00
Game of Baseball (J.H. Singer c. 1890) 500.00
Game of Baseball (Milton Bradley 1910s) 150.00
Game of Baseball (Milton Bradley 1925) 60.00
Game of Baseball (Canada Games Co. 1925) . . . 300.00
Gonfalon Scientific Baseball
(Pioneer Game Co. 1930) 150.00
Goose Goslin Scientific Baseball (Wheeler Toy Co.
© 1935 . . . . 350.00
Graham McNamee World Series Radio Scorebard
Baseball Game (Radio Sports 1930) 350.00
Grand Slam Baseball (Pluto Water) 100.00
Graphic Baseball (Northwestern Products 1930s) . 250.00
The Great American Game (Frantz c. 1925) 150.00
The Great American Game Baseball
(William Dapping c. 1906) 200.00
The Great American Game of Baseball
(Premium for Pittsburgh Brewing Co. 1907) . 200.00
The Great American Game of Baseball
(Hustler Toy Co. 1923) 250.00
Great American Game, Pocket Baseball (Neddy
Pocket Game Co. 1910) dice game 200.00
Great Mails Baseball Game
(Walter Mails Baseball Game Co. c. 1919) . 3,500.00
Grebnelle Championship Parlor Baseball Game
(Grebnelle Game Co. 1914)
Boston Braves park cover 1,500.00
Hatfield Parlor Baseball Game (Hatfield Co. 1914) 200.00
Hening's In-Door Game of Professional Baseball
(Inventor's Co. c. 1889) folding board 750.00
Home Baseball Game (McLoughlin Bros. 1890)
Elongated red baseball 1,500.00
Home Baseball Game (McLoughlin Bros. 1900)
Square & red baseball 1,500.00
Home Baseball Game (McLoughlin Bros. 1910)
Square box & yellow ball 1,100.00
Home Baseball Game (Rosebud Art Co. 1936) . . . 150.00
Home Diamond, The Great Baseball Game
(Philips Co. 1925) 250.00
Variation by the Play Ball Game Co. 250.00
Home Run King (Selrite Prod. 1930s) 400.00
Home Run with Bases Loaded
(T.V. Morrison 1935) John Evers batting . . . 300.00
Home Team Baseball Game
(Rocket Size, Ben Dickenson 1917) 200.00
Home Team Baseball Game
(B. Dikenson, Selchow & Righter 1918) 200.00
Hot Corner Baseball Game
(Pro Sports Action © 1992) 35.00
In-Door Baseball (E. Bommer Playground
Foundation 1926) Premium for Bommer
Spring event 150.00
Inside Baseball Game (Popular Games ©1911)
1911 World Series Giants vs. Athletics 450.00
Junior Baseball Game (Benjamin Seller Mfg. Co. 1915)
Balance Game 150.00
Kellogg's Baseball Game (Kellogg's 1936) 30.00
League Parlor Baseball (Bliss Co. c. 1880s)
Wooden board, ump w/ umbrella 1,500.00
Wooden board, ump w/ scorecard 1,200.00
Leslie's Baseball Game (Perfection Novelty
& Advertising Co. 1909) advertising game . . 200.00
Lew Fonseco, The Carrom Baseball Game
(Carrom Co. 1920s) 750.00
Lou Gehrig's Official Playball (Christy Walsh 1930s) 750.00
Lucky 7 Baseball Game (Ray-Fair Co. ©1937) 75.00
Mac Baseball Game
(Mc Dowell Manufactory Co 1930s) 200.00
Major League Ball (National Game Makers 1921) . 500.00
Major League Baseball (Philadelphia Game Mfg.
Co. 1912) Plain green cover w/ white script . 500.00
Major League Baseball (Philadelphia Game Mfg.
Co. 1916) As above w/ Babe Ruth pitching . 650.00

Major League Indoor Baseball
Debby & Marty Krim collection.

Major League Indoor Baseball Game (Philadelphia
Game Mfg. Co. ©1912): 16 Players Photos inc.
Mathewson, Wagner, Baker, Walsh, Speaker,
Chase, Johnson; Team line-up cards,
wooden hinged box, spinner board 6,000.00
Mathers Parlor Baseball Game (Mathers © 1908) . 500.00
Mathers Parlor Baseball Game (McClurg & Co. 1909) 40.00
Mickey Mouse Baseball
(Post Cereal box premium ©1936) 75.00
The National Game (National Game Co. 1900s)
Small 3 1/2 box 1,200.00
Philadelphia Game Mfg. Co. 750.00
The National Game of Baseball (1900s) 1,200.00
National League Ball Game (Yankee Novelty
Co. 1885) Color cover 500.00
New Baseball Game (Clark & Martin ©1885) 225.00
The New Parlor Game, Baseball (First professional
player baseball game): Team rosters,
line-up cards, 10x10 b&w board 12,500.00
New York Recorder Newspaper Supplement
Baseball Game (1896) 600.00
Nok-Out Baseball Game, Dizzy
& Daffy Dean (1930) 500.00
Our No 7 Baseball Game Puzzle
(Satisfactory Co 1910.) 150.00
Our National Ball Game (McGill & DeLang 1887). . 600.00
Parlor Baseball (Edward Pierce 1878) 3,000.00
Parlor Baseball (American Palor Baseball ©1903) . 250.00
Parlor Baseball Game, Bos vs. Chi (1880s) 3,000.00
Pat Moran's Own Baseball Game
(Smith, Kline & French 1919) 500.00
Peg Baseball (Parker Bros. 1915) 200.00
Pennant Puzzle (L.W.Hardy 1909) Chance photo . 350.00
Pennant Winner (Wolverine Supply Co. 1930s) . . . 250.00
The Philadelphia Inquirer Baseball Game (5/17/1896
art supplement to Philadelphia Inquirer) 200.00
Pinch Hitter (1930s) 150.00
Play Ball (National Game Co., Boston 1920) 200.00
Polar Ball Baseball (Bowline Game Co. 1940) . . . 125.00
Popular Indoor Baseball Game
(Egerton R. Williams ©1896) 1,250.00
Psychic Baseball Game (Parker Bros. ©1935) . . . 250.00
Radio Baseball (Toy Creations 1939) 225.00
Real Baseball Card Game (National Baseball 1900) 250.00
Realistic Baseball
(Realistic Game & Toy Corp. 1925) 300.00
Roll-O Junior Baseball Game (Roll-O Mfg. 1922)
Metal players. 500.00
Roll-Um Baseball (Grg. Co. © 1992) 10.00
Roulette Baseball Game (W. Barthonomae ©1929) 150.00
Rube Bressler's Baseball Game (Bressler ©1936) . 175.00
Rube Walker & Harry Davis Baseball Game (1905)
"Champion Athletics" paddle game 1,200.00
Skor-It Bagatelle (North Western Products 1930s) . 200.00
Slide Kelly! Baseball Game (B.E. Ruth Co. ©1936) 100.00
Slugger Baseball Game (Marks Bros 1930). 150.00
Striker Out (All Fair Inc. 1920s) 250.00
Toto, The New Game (Baseball,
Toto Sales Co. 1925) 75.00

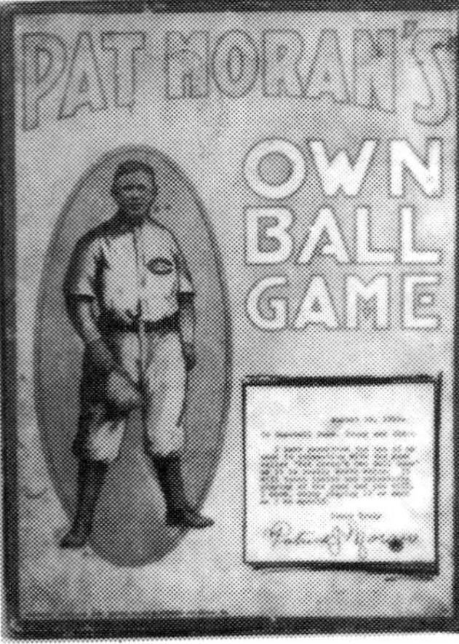

(L-R) Home Diamond, Pat Moran's Own Ball Game, The Diamond Game of Baseball, The National Game of Baseball, Graphic Baseball, Game of Baseball. Debby & Marty Krim collection.

U-Bat-It (Schultz-Ill. Star Co. 1920s) 100.00
Ultimate Sports Trivia (Ram Games ©1992) 35.00
Uncle Sam's Baseball Game (J. C. Bell 1890) . . . 750.00
Wachter's Parlor Baseball (Ragatelle 1925) 200.00
Walter Johnson Baseball Game (1930s) 275.00
Waner's Baseball Game (Waner's Baseball Game, Inc. ©1939) 500.00
World's Championship Baseball (Champion Amusement Co. 1910) 250.00
World's Championship Baseball Game (National Indoor Game and Novelty Co.) 200.00
World's Championship Baseball Game (Beacon Hudson Co. 1930s) 150.00
World Series Parlor Baseball (Clifton E. Hooper 1916) 325.00
Zimmer Baseball Game (McLoughlin Bros. 1885) 18 chromo-litho pictures; considered the finest of baseball games, only 5 known 20,000.00

POST-1939 BOARD GAMES

Alexander's Baseball Game (1940s) 300.00
APBA Baseball (APBA 1960s) 75.00
APBA Baseball (APBA 1970s) 40.00
APBA Baseball (APBA 1980s) 30.00
APBA Baseball Master Game (APBA 1975) 50.00
ASG Major League Baseball (Gerney Games 1973) 75.00
Action Baseball (Pressman 1965) 75.00
All Pro Baseball (Ideal 1950) 60.00
All-Star Baseball (Cadaco 1962) 35.00
All-Star Baseball (Cadaco 1969) 25.00
All-Star Baseball (Cadaco ©1989) w/ card discs . . . 25.00
All-Star Electric baseball & football (Harett-Gilmar 1955) 50.00
All-Time Greats Baseball Game

(Midwest Research 1971) 15.00
Alpha Baseball Game (Realistic Mfg. Co. 1950s) . 150.00
The Approved Little League Baseball Game
(Standard Toy Craft) 75.00
ASG Baseball (3M 1989) 25.00
Autograph Baseball Game (Philadelphia Inquirer Raffle 1948); 36 player autographs on masonite board 150.00
B.B. Ballplayer's Baseball Game (Jon Weber 1955) 40.00
Babe Ruth's Official Baseball Game
(Toytown 1940s) 600.00
(Toytown 1950) 500.00
Bambino Baseball Game
(Mansfield-Zesiger Mfg. Co. 1940) 200.00

Bob Feller's Big League Baseball Game
Alex G. Malloy collection.

Baseball (All-Fair 1946) 60.00
Baseball (Milton Bradley 1941) 50.00
Baseball (Samuel Lowe 1942) w/ basketball, football and hockey games 75.00
Baseball, A Sports Illustrated Game
(Time Inc. 1975) 35.00
Baseball, Football & Checkers
(Parker Bros. ©1957) 50.00
Baseball Action (Ansudon) 8.00
Baseball Card All Star Game (Captoys 1987) 10.00
Baseball Challenge (Tri-Valley Games 1980) 28.00
The Baseball Game (Horatio 1988) 25.00
Baseball Game (Corey Games 1943) 100.00
Baseball Game (Parker Bros. 1949) 25.00
Baseball Game (Parker Bros. 1950) 22.00
Baseball Game & G-Man Target Game
(Marks Bros. ©1940) 150.00
Baseball Greatest Moments (Ashburn Ind. 1979) . . 12.00
Baseball Strategy (Avalon Hill 1973) 12.00
Base Hit! (Games, Inc. 1944) 75.00
Batter-Rou Baseball Game (Memphis Plastic 1950s) Dizzy Dean photo 150.00
Batter Up (Ed-U-Cards 1949) 20.00
Batter Up (M. Hopper 1946) 40.00
Bee Gee Baseball Dart Target (Bee Gee 1935-40) 100.00
Bible Baseball (Schoenferd ©1965) 25.00
Big League Baseball (Saalsfield Art Craft © 1959) . 75.00
Big League Baseball (3M Corporation ©1966) 50.00
Big League Baseball (3M 1971) 30.00
Big League Manager Baseball (BLM) 8.00
Big Six Sports Games (Gardner 1950s): six different sport games including Mickey Mantle's baseball, Verne Gagne's wrestling, All-Star Football, Basketball, Stock Car Race and Golf 250.00
Bileth Baseball (Bileth Enterprises) 18.00
Bob Feller Big League Baseball (Saalfield 1950s) . 100.00
Bob Feller's Big League Baseball (Saalfield 1950) 175.00

Bobby Shantz Baseball Game
(Realistic Games 1955) 200.00
Carl Hubbell Mechanical Baseball
(Gotham Steel Co. 1950) 250.00
Carl Yastrzemski's Action Baseball
(Pressman 1968) 125.00
Casey on the Mound (Kamms 1945) 275.00
Challenge the Yankees (Hasbro 1960s) 250.00
Championship Baseball (Championship Games, T. Lansing ©1966) 40.00
Championship Baseball (Milton Bradley ©1984) . . 100.00
Charlie Brown's All Star Baseball Game
(Parker Bros. 1965) 50.00
Classic Major League Baseball
Green Big Game, 1987 . . . . 250.00
Yellow Update, 1987 . . . . 40.00
Classic Red, 1988 . . . . 15.00
Blue Update, 1988 . . . . 20.00
Big Board, 1989 . . . . 40.00
Travel series, Orange 20.00
Update, 1989 . . . . 15.00
150 Card Game, 1990 . . . . 15.00
Series II Game, 1990 . . . . 13.00
Series III Game, 1990 . . . . 15.00
Series + Game, 1991 . . . . 13.00
Computer Baseball (Epoch Playtime 1966) 35.00
Earl Gillespie Baseball Game (Wei-Gill Inc. 1961) . . 35.00
Electric Baseball by Jim Prentice (1940s) 80.00
Electric Baseball by Jim Prentice (1950s) 65.00
Ethan Allen's All-Star Baseball Game
(Cadaco-Ellis 1942) 100.00
--1943 . . . . 75.00
--1946 . . . . 60.00
--1955 . . . . 50.00
Extra Innings (J Kavanaugh 1975) 15.00
Game of the Week (Hasbro 1969) 35.00
George Brett's 9th-Inning Baseball Game
(Brett Ball ©1981) 35.00
Gil Hodges Pennant Fever
(Research Games ©1970) 175.00
Golden Trivia Game (Western Pub. 1984)
Baseball Edition 10.00
Grand Slam (Sming Game Co. 1979) 30.00
Great Pennant Races (Great Pennant Races 1980) 28.00
Greatest Baseball Teams of Century
(Electronic Design Concepts) 28.00
Hank Aaron Baseball Game (Ideal c. 1970) 70.00
Hank Aaron's Eye Ball Game (1960s) 125.00
Hank Bauer's "Be A Manager" (Barco Games 1960s)
National League edition 150.00
American League edition 150.00

1957 Home Team Baseball Game
Alex G. Malloy Collection.

Home Team Baseball Game
(Selchow & Righter ©1957) 50.00
(Selchow & Righter ©1964) 20.00
Houston Astros Baseball Challenge Game
(Croque Ltd. 1980) 30.00
JDK Baseball (JDK Baseball 1982) 22.00
Jackie Robinson Baseball Game (1940) 600.00
Jackie Robinson Game (1950s) pocket edition . . . 250.00
Jacmar Big League Baseball
(1950s) electric game 200.00
Jose Canseco's Perfect Baseball Game
(Perfect Game Co. 1991) 15.00
KSP Baseball (Koch Sports Products 1983) 28.00
LF Baseball (Len Feder 1980) 25.00
Las Vegas Baseball (Samar Enterprises 1987) 15.00

Line Drive (Lord & Freber Inc. 1953) 85.00
Longball (Ashburn Industries 1975) 40.00
--1980 . . . . 30.00
Look All-Star Baseball Game
(Progressive Research ©1960) 50.00
Main Street Baseball (Main Street Toy Co. 1989) . . 50.00
Major League Baseball (Negamco ©1959) 25.00
Major League Baseball Magnetic Dart Game
(Pressman 1958) 75.00
Manage Your Own Team (Warren Built-Rite 1950s) 75.00
Mickey Mantle's Action Baseball (Pressman 1960) 250.00

1958 Mickey Mantle's Big League Baseball Game
Debby & Marty Krim Collection.

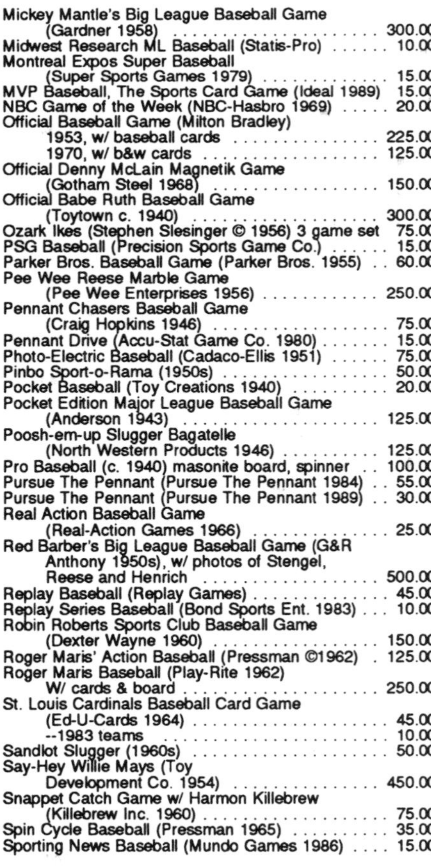

Mickey Mantle's Big League Baseball Game
(Gardner 1958) 300.00
Midwest Research ML Baseball (Statis-Pro) 10.00
Montreal Expos Super Baseball
(Super Sports Games 1979) 15.00
MVP Baseball, The Sports Card Game (Ideal 1989) 15.00
NBC Game of the Week (NBC-Hasbro 1969) 20.00
Official Baseball Game (Milton Bradley)
1953, w/ baseball cards 225.00
1970, w/ b&w cards 125.00
Official Denny McLain Magnetik Game
(Gotham Steel 1968) 150.00
Official Babe Ruth Baseball Game
(Toytown c. 1940) 300.00
Ozark Ikes (Stephen Slesinger © 1956) 3 game set 75.00
PSG Baseball (Precision Sports Game Co.) 15.00
Parker Bros. Baseball Game (Parker Bros. 1955) . . 60.00
Pee Wee Reese Marble Game
(Pee Wee Enterprises 1956) 250.00
Pennant Chasers Baseball Game
(Craig Hopkins 1946) 75.00
Pennant Drive (Accu-Stat Game Co. 1980) 15.00
Photo-Electric Baseball (Cadaco-Ellis 1951) 75.00
Pinbo Sport-o-Rama (1950s) 50.00
Pocket Baseball (Toy Creations 1940) 20.00
Pocket Edition Major League Baseball Game
(Anderson 1943) 125.00
Poosh-em-up Slugger Bagatelle
(North Western Products 1946) 125.00
Pro Baseball (c. 1940) masonite board, spinner . . 100.00
Pursue The Pennant (Pursue The Pennant 1984) . . 55.00
Pursue The Pennant (Pursue The Pennant 1989) . . 30.00
Real Action Baseball Game
(Real-Action Games 1966) 25.00
Red Barber's Big League Baseball Game (G&R Anthony 1950s), w/ photos of Stengel, Reese and Henrich 500.00
Replay Baseball (Replay Games) 45.00
Replay Series Baseball (Bond Sports Ent. 1983) . . . 10.00
Robin Roberts Sports Club Baseball Game
(Dexter Wayne 1960) 150.00
Roger Maris' Action Baseball (Pressman ©1962) . 125.00
Roger Maris Baseball (Play-Rite 1962)
W/ cards & board 250.00
St. Louis Cardinals Baseball Card Game
(Ed-U-Cards 1964) 45.00
--1983 teams 10.00
Sandlot Slugger (1960s) 50.00
Say-Hey Willie Mays (Toy Development Co. 1954) 450.00
Snappet Catch Game w/ Harmon Killebrew
(Killebrew Inc. 1960) 75.00
Spin Cycle Baseball (Pressman 1965) 35.00
Sporting News Baseball (Mundo Games 1986) 15.00

1960 Robin Roberts Sports Club Baseball Game
Debby & Marty Krim Collection.

Sports Illustrated Baseball
(Sports Illustrated 1972) 35.00
Sports Illustrated Pennant Race
(1982 teams; Avalon Hill-Sports Illustrated) . . 15.00
Statis Pro Baseball (Avalon Hill 1979)
First edition 40.00
--1978 player card set 10.00
--1979 player card set 10.00
Strat-O-Matic Baseball (Strat-O-Matic Game Co.)
--1961 . . . . 150.00
--1976 . . . . 45.00
--1960s player card set 25.00
--1970s player card set 15.00
--1980s player card set 12.50
Strategy Manager Baseball
(McGuffin-Ramsey 1967) 25.00
Strike-Lite (Saxon Toy Corp. 1940s) 80.00
Strike Three by Carl Hubbell
(Tone Products Corp. 1948) 400.00
Superstar Baseball (Sports Illustrated 1966) 40.00
Superstar Baseball (Sports Illustrated-Time, Inc. ©1974) 25.00
Superstar Baseball (Avalon Hill-Sports Illustrated) . . 15.00
Swat Baseball (Milton Bradley 1948) 25.00
Tiddle Flip Baseball (Modern Craft Ind. 1949) 25.00
Time Travel Baseball (Time Travel 1979) 18.00
Tom Seaver's Action Baseball (Pressman 1970) . . 250.00
Triple Play (National Games Inc. 1940s) 75.00
Tru-Action Electric Baseball Game (Tudor c. 1955) . 50.00
Whirly Bird Play Catch (Innovation Industries 1960s) w/ Warren Spahn 100.00
Whiz Baseball (Electric Game Co. 1945) 60.00
Wil-Croft Baseball (Wil-Croft 1971) 14.00
Willie Mays Push Button Baseball
(Eldon Champion c. 1965) 250.00
Willie Mays "Say Hey" Baseball
(Centennial Games 1958) 300.00
Winko Baseball (Milton Bradley 1940) 60.00
Win A Card Trading Card Game (Milton Bradley c. 1965) w/ board and "generous (40 of both sports) supply of baseball & football trading cards" 500.00

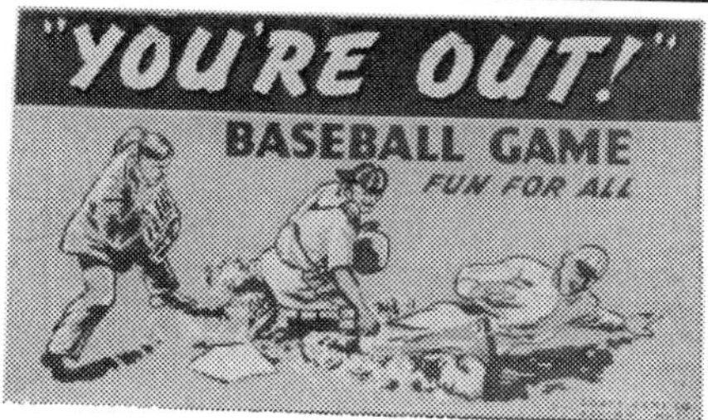

1941 "You're Out!" Baseball Game
Alex G. Malloy collection.

Wiry Dan's Electric Baseball Game
(Harett-Gilmour 1953) 30.00
World Series Baseball Game (Radio Sports 1940s) 300.00
World Series, Big League Baseball Game
(E.S. Lowe c. 1945) 150.00
World's Greatest Baseball Game
(J. Woodlock 1977) 42.00
"You're Out" Baseball Game (Corey Games 1941) 125.00

BASEBALL CARD GAMES

PRE-1940 CARD GAMES

Baseball (Geo. Norris Co. 1905) 200.00
Baseball Game (Liberty League ©1917) 75.00
Baseballitis Card Game (Baseballitis Card Co.
1909) Cartoon players 175.00
Big League Baseball Card Game (Whitman ©1938) 50.00
Egerson R. Williams Popular Indoor Baseball Game
(Popular Indoor Baseball Co. 1889)
19 chromo-litho player portraits 7,500.00
Fan Ball (Fan Ball Co. 1914) felt field 75.00

1904 Fan Craze Card Game
Debby & Marty Krim Collection.

Fan Craze Card Game (Fan Craze Co. 1904)
National League player photo cards 3,000.00
American League player photo cards 2,500.00
Fan Craze Game Drawings (Fan Craze Co. 1904)
-- 3x4 Box 250.00
-- 4x4 Box 250.00
Game of Batter Up (Fenner Game Co. 1914) 125.00
Home Diamond (Phillips c. 1913)
100 photo card packs 250.00

Joe "Ducky" Medwick's Big League
Baseball Game (Johnson 1930s) 500.00
Lawson's Patent Game Baseball
(Lawson's Card Co. 1884) cloth box 1,000.00
Lawson's Baseball Card Game (1910) 175.00
The Major League Baseball Game Card (c. 1910) . 200.00
National American Baseball Game
(Parker Bros. c. 1910) 150.00
The National Baseball Game (National Baseball
Playing Card Co. c. 1913) w/ photo cards . 2,500.00
The National Game (S&S Games 1936)
w/ photo cards 800.00
Psychic Baseball (Psychic Baseball Corp. ©1927) . 300.00
Psychic Baseball (Parker Bros. 1935) 175.00
Tom Barker Card Game (1913) player cards . . . 2,000.00
Williams' Popular Indoor Baseball
(The Hatch Co. 1889) 1,000.00

POST-1939 CARD GAMES

Baseball Card Game (Ed-U-Cards c. 1950s) 25.00
Baseball Game (Parker Bros. ©1949) 50.00
Batter Up Card Game (Ed-U-Cards c. 1940s) 30.00
Big League Baseball Card Game
(State College Game Lab 1940s) 50.00

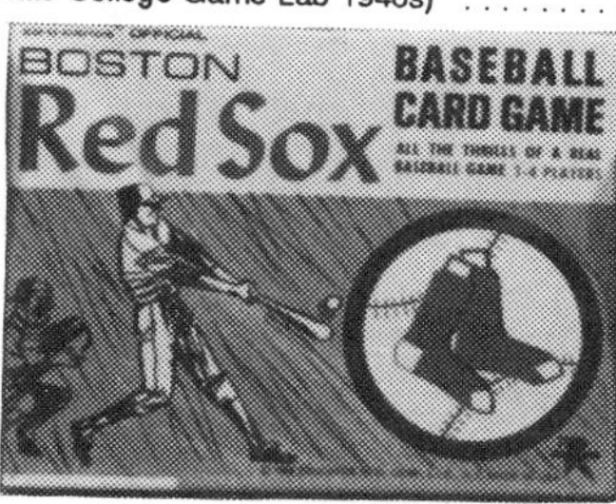

1964 Boston Red Sox Game
Debby & Marty Krim Collection.

Boston Red Sox Game (Ed-U-Cards Mfg. 1964) . . . 75.00
Harry's Grand Slam (Harry Obst 1962) 50.00
Major League Baseball All-Star Playing Cards
(U.S. Playing Card Co. ©1990) 5.00
Mets' Baseball Card Game (Ed-U-Cards 1961) 40.00
Official Baseball Card Game (Milton
Bradley c. 1965) 250.00
Official NY Mets Baseball Card Game
(Ed-U-Cards 1961) 55.00
Pro-Baseball Card Game (Just Games 1980s) 10.00
Scott's Baseball Card Game
(Scott's Baseball Cards ©1989) 25.00
Star Baseball Game (W. P. Ulrich,
Pres. Spokane Club 1941) 100.00

BASKETBALL GAMES

APBA Pro Basketball (APBA) 25.00
All American Basketball (Corey Games 1941) 75.00
All-Pro Basketball (Ideal 1969) 25.00
All Star Basketball. 1950's Gardner 75.00
Basket (Cadaco-Ellis)
--1938 blue box 75.00
--1962 red & yellow box 50.00
--1969 photo cover 35.00
--1973 photo cover 35.00
Basket, Harlem Globetrotter Official Edition
(Cadaco-Ellis, 1970s) 65.00
Basketball (Chaffee & Selchow 1898) Very rare . 3500.00
Basketball (Russell 1929) 65.00
Basketball (Samuel Lowe 1942)
w/ baseball, football & hockey 75.00
Basketball, A Game. 1903 Celluloid ball & hoop . 200.00
Basketball Card Game (Built-Rite Warren 1940s) . . 20.00
Basketball Game (Warren Built-Rite 1950s) 30.00

Basketball Strategy (Avalon Hill-Sports Illustrated) . 10.00
Big League Basketball (Baumgarten & Co. 1920s) 200.00
Big League Manager Basketball (BLM) 14.00
Challenge Basketball All-Stars (Avalon Hill) 16.00
College Basketball (Cadaco-Ellis 1954) 20.00
Computer Basketball (Electric Data Controls Corp. 1969) 65.00
Fastbreak Basketball (Mickey Games) 45.00
Harlem Globetrotters Game (Milton Bradley 1971) . 40.00
Home Court Basketball (Charlie Eckman Photo) 1954 Home Court 200.00

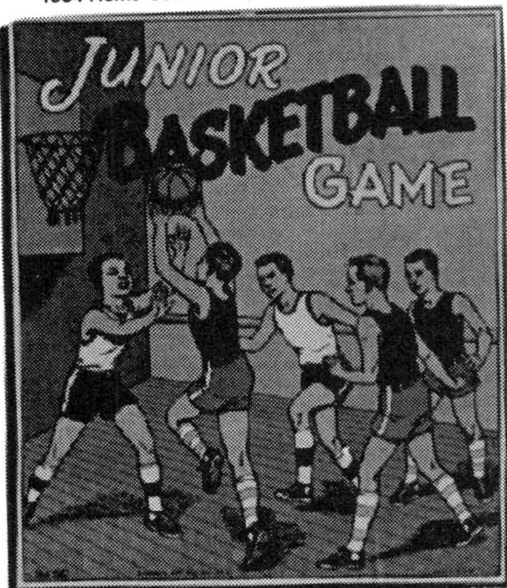

1930's Junior Basketball Game
Alex G. Malloy Collection.

Junior Basketball Game (Rosebud Art Co. 1930s) . . 75.00
KSP Basketball (Koch Sports Products) 20.00
Let's Play Basketball (DMR 1965) 35.00
Mickey Mouse Basketball (Gardner 1950s) 75.00
Negamco Basketball (Nemadji Game Co. 1975) . . . 10.00
Official Basketball Game (Toy Creations 1940) 75.00
The Official Globetrotter Basketball (Meljak 1950s) . 85.00
Official NBA Basketball Game (Gerney Games 1970s) 60.00
Oscar Robertson's Pro Basketball Strategy (Research Games 1964) 100.00
Paris Metro (Infinity Games 1981) 18.00

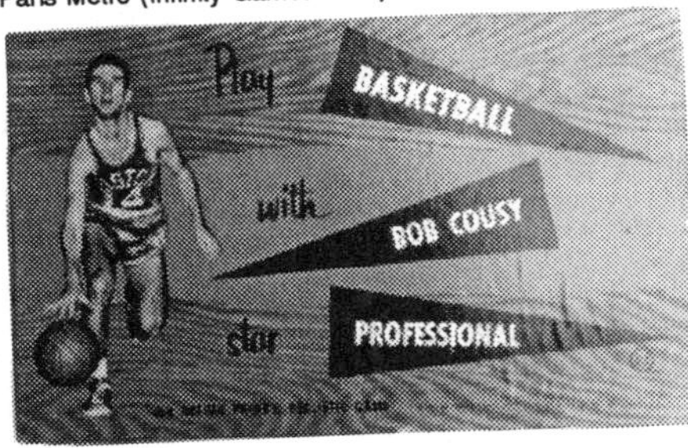

1950's Play Basketball w/ Bob Cousy
Alex G. Malloy collection.

Play Basketball with Bob Cousy (National Games 1950s) 150.00
Quarter Bouncers, Coin Foul Shot Game (Anderson & Association ©1993) 35.00
Real-Life Basketball (Gamecraft 1974) 10.00

Samsonite Basketball (Samsonite 1969) 15.00
Sports Illustrated, All Time, All Star Basketball (Sports Illustrated 1973) 25.00
Sports Illustrated Pro Basketball (Avalon Hill 1981) . 15.00
Star Basketball (Star Paper Products 1926) 175.00
Swish (Jim Hawkers Games Mfg. 1948) 65.00
Tak-Tiks (Midwest Products 1939) 15.00
Top Pro Basketball Quiz Game (Edu-Cards 1970) . 20.00
Top Ten College Basketball (Top Ten Game Co. 1980) 18.00
Tru-Action Electric Basketball (Tudor 1961) 60.00
Ultimate College Basketball (Ultimate Game Co.) . . 50.00
The VCR Basketball Game (Interactive VCR Games 1987) 12.00

BOXING GAMES

The Boxing Game (Kellogg's Stoll & Edwards 1928) 125.00
Century of Great Fights (Research Games 1969) Rocky Graziano endorsement and photo . . . 100.00
Championship Fight Game (Frankie Goodman 1940s) 50.00
Heavy-weight Boxing (Excaliber Games 1979) 25.00
Joe Palooka Boxing Game (Lowell 1950s) 200.00
Jeffries Championship Playing Cards (1904) 54 multi-photo cards of boxers 600.00
Kellogg's Boxing Game (Kellogg's Premium 1936) . 45.00
Knockout (Scarne Games 1937) 75.00
Pug-i-Lo (Pug-i-Lo Games 1960) 75.00

1922 Tip Top Boxing
Alex G. Malloy collection.

Tip-Top Boxing (LaVelle 1922) Dempsey heavyweight fight 300.00
Title Bout (Avalon Hill-Sports Illustrated) 12.00

BOWLING GAMES

APBA Bowling (APBA) 15.00
Bilt-Rite Miniature Bowling Alley (Atwood Momanus 1930s) 100.00
Bowl and Score (E.S. Lowe 1974) 10.00
Bowlem (Parker Bros. 1930s) 25.00
Bowling (Parker Bros. 1896) 200.00
Bowling (Parker Bros. 1900) 3 1/2 square 75.00
Bowling Alley (N.D. Cass 1920) skill & action 50.00
Bowling Board Game (Parker Bros. 1896) 500.00
Donald Duck Pins and Bowling Game (Pressman 1955-9) 50.00

Don Carter & Paula Sperber:
World Bowling Tour (1979) 20.00
Don Carter's Strike Bowling Game (Saalfield 1964) . 75.00
King Pin Deluxe Bowling Alley
(Baldwin Mfg. Co. 1947) 20.00
Let's Bowl A Game (DMR 1960) 25.00
Patent Parlor Bowling Alley
(Thomas Kochka 1899) 100.00
Pocket Size Bowling Card Game (Built-Rite 1950s) . 20.00
Ten Pins (Mason & Parker Mfg. Co. 1920) 50.00

CYCLING GAMES

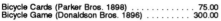

Bicycle Cards (Parker Bros. 1898) 75.00
Bicycle Game (Donaldson Bros. 1896) 300.00

1910 Bicycle Race
Alex G. Malloy collection.

Bicycle Race (Milton Bradley 1910) 125.00
Bicycle Race Game For the Wheelmen (McLoughlin
Bros. 1891) large wheel bicycle 1,000.00
The Bicycle Race Game
(Chaffee & Selchow 1898) 600.00
The Bike Race Game (Master Toy Co. 1930s) 50.00
Boston Globe Bicycle Game of Circulation
(Boston Globe 1895) 75.00
Century Ride (Milton Bradley 1900) 300.00
Century Run Bicycle Game (Parker Bros. 1897) . . 650.00
Game of Bicycle Race (McLoughlin Bros. 1891) . . 900.00
Game of Bicycle Race (McLoughlin Bros. 1895) . . 650.00
Game of Cycling (Parker Bros. 1910) 150.00
The Junior Bicycle Game (Parker Bros. 1897) . . . 350.00
The Merry Game of Bicycling (Parker Bros. 1900) . 150.00
The New Bicycle Game (Parker Bros. 1894) 750.00

DOG RACING GAMES

Dog Race (Transogram 1937) 65.00
Deluxe edition 100.00
Dog Race (Transogram 1940s) smaller box 50.00
Dog Show (J.H. Singer 1890s) 125.00
Dog Sweepstakes (Stoll & Eisen 1935) 150.00
Greyhound Pursuit (N/N Games 1985) 15.00
Greyhound Racing Game (Rex Mfg. Co. 1938) 50.00
Jig Chase (Game Makers Inc. 1930s) Puzzle 50.00
Whippet Race (Pressman & Co. 1940s) 50.00

FOOTBALL GAMES

PRE-1940 GAMES

All-American Foot Ball Game (Parker Bros. 1925) . 150.00

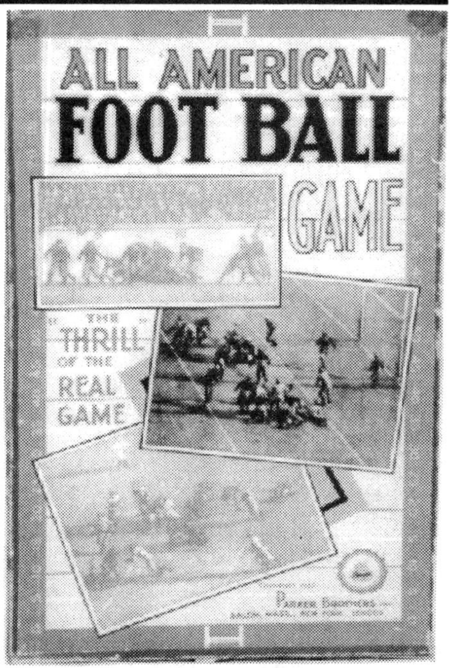

All-American Football Game
Alex G. Malloy collection.

All-American Football Game (National Games 1935) 100.00
American Football Game
(Ace Leather Goods Co. ©1930) 100.00
American Football Game
(American News Co. 1930s) 50.00
American Football Game (Intercollegiate
Football Inc. 1935) 50.00
America's Football (Trojan Games 1939) 75.00
The Benson Football Game (Benson 1930s) 125.00
Big Ten Football Game (Wheaties'
Jack Armstrong Presents 1936) 75.00
Bo McMillan's Indoor Football
(Indiana Game Co. 1939) 75.00
Boys Own Football Game
(McLoughlin Bros. 1901) 750.00
College Football (Milton Bradley 1945) 125.00
Electric Football (Electric Game Co. 1930s) 75.00

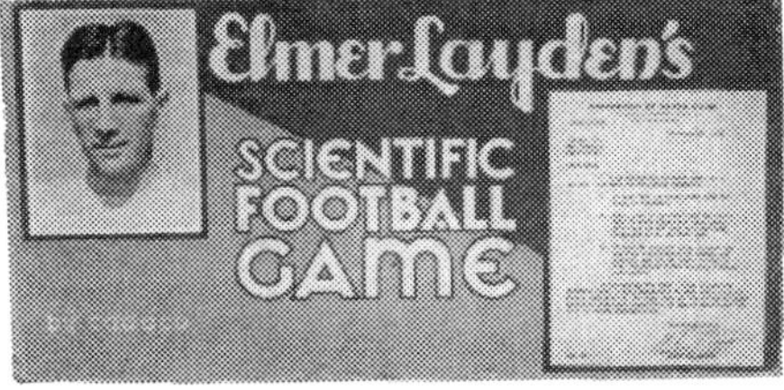

1936 Elmer Layden's Scientific Football Game
Alex G. Malloy collection.

Elmer Layden's Scientific Football
(Cadaco-Ellis 1936) 1st Edition 150.00
Football-As-You-Like-It (Wayne W. Light Co. 1940) 125.00
Football Game (Parker Bros. 1898) 425.00

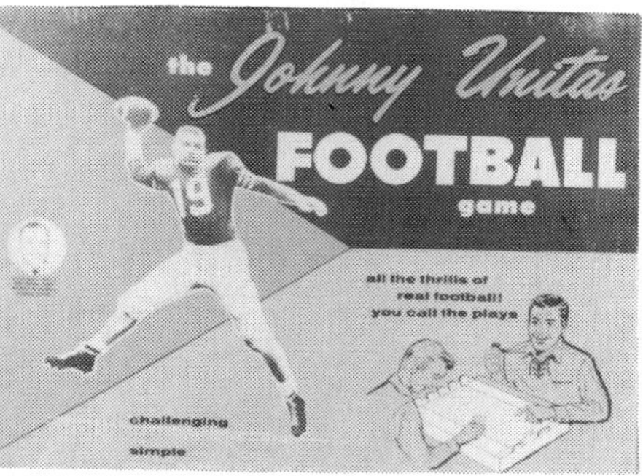

(L-R) Play Football, Touchdown Football Game, The Johnny Unitas Football Game
Alex G. Malloy collection.

Football Game (Parker Bros. 1910)
Popular edition, Princeton-Yale 350.00
The Game of Football (George A. Childs 1895) .. 350.00
The Game of Football (Parker Bros. 1892) 400.00
Game of Touchdown or Parlor Football (Union Mutual Life Ins. Premium, ©1897 J.W.Kelly) . 125.00
Gregg Football Game (Albert A. Gregg 1924)
separate box 250.00
Hit That Line, The All-American Football Game
(La Rue Sales 1930s) 150.00
Howard H. Jones Collegiate Football
(Municipal Service 1932) 150.00
Huddle All-American Football Game (©1931) 150.00
Indoor Football (Underwood 1919) 200.00
Intercollegiate Football (Hustler-Frantz 1923) 125.00
Los Angeles Rams Football Game
(Zondine Game Co. 1930s) 250.00
The New Game, Touchdown
(Hartford Mfg. Co. 1920) 100.00
NFL Stategy (Tudor Games 1935) 60.00
Official Knute Rockne Football Game
(Radio Sports 1930) 350.00
Official Radio Football (Toy Creations ©1939) 100.00
Ot-O-Win Football (Ot-O-Win Toys
and Games 1920s) Wood sides, metal board . 75.00
Parlor Football Game (McLoughlin Bros. 1890s) .. 750.00
Pigskin, Tom Hamilton's Football Game
(Parker Bros. 1934) stadium cover 100.00
Play Football (Whitman 1934) 75.00
Quarterback (Littlefield Mfg. Co. 1914) 150.00
Quarterback (Olympia Games 1914) 50.00
Radio Football Game (Toy Creations 1939) 100.00
Razz-O Dazz-O Six Man Football
(Gruhn & Melton 1938) 85.00
Roll-O Football (Supply Sales Co. 1923) 50.00
Tackle (Tackle Game Co. 1933) 100.00
Thrilling Indoor Football Game
(Cronston Co. 1933) 100.00
Tom Hamilton's Pigskin (Parker Bros. 1935) 100.00
Touchdown (Cadaco 1937) 125.00
Touchdown Football Game
(Wilder Mfg. Co. 1920s) 150.00
21st Century Football (Kerger Co. ©1930) 75.00
Va-Lo Football Card Game (1930s) with board ... 125.00
Varsitee Football Playing Cards (Kerger Co. 1938) 100.00
Varsity Football, PB (Kerger Co. 1925) 75.00
Ward Cuff's Football game
(Continental Sales 1938) 250.00
Wilder's Football Game (Wilder Mfg. Co. 1930s) ... 75.00
Yale Harvard Game (McLoughlin Bros. 1890) ... 1,500.00
Yale-Harvard Football Game
(La Velle Mfg. Co. ©1922) 600.00
Yale and Princeton Football Game
(McLoughlin Bros. 1895) 1,200.00

POST-1939 GAMES

ABC Monday Night Football (Aurora 1972) 35.00
ABC Monday Night Football (Aurora 1973)
Roger Staubach edition 50.00
APBA Pro League Football (APBA 1964) 75.00
APBA 1970s 40.00
APBA 1980s 25.00
Alpha Football Game (Replica Mfg. Co. 1940s) ... 100.00
All-American Football (Cadaco 1969) 50.00
All-Pro Football (Ideal 1967) 25.00
All-Star Football (Gardner & Company c. 1950) ... 75.00
Art Lewis Football Game
(Morgantown Game Co. 1955) 100.00
Bart Starr Quarterback Game (1960s) 250.00
Baseball, Football & Checkers
(Parker Bros. ©1957) 50.00
Big League Manager Football (BLM 1965) 25.00
Big Payoff (Payoff Enterprises Co. 1984) 10.00
Big Time Colorado Football (B.J. Tall 1983) 12.00
Booth's Pro Conference Football (Sher-Co 1977) .. 12.00
Bowl Bound! (Sports Illustrated 1973) 22.00
Bowl Bound! (Avalon Hill-Sports Illustrated 1978) .. 10.00
Bowl and Score (E.S. Lowe 1974) 20.00
Challenge Football (Avalon Hill) 20.00
Chex Ches Football (Chex Ches Games 1971) 18.00
Dan Kersteter's Classic Football (Big League Co.) 18.00

Data Prog. Computerized Pro Football
(Data Prog. Game Co. 1971) 18.00
Elmer Layden's Scientific Football
(Cadaco-Ellis 1940) 90.00
F/11 Armchair Quarterback (James R. Hock 1964) . 18.00
First Down (TGP Games 1970) 15.00
Fobaga (Amer. Football Co. 1942) 70.00
Fooba-Roo Football Game
(Memphis Plastic Ent. 1955) 35.00
Football (J. Pressman & Co. 1940s) 35.00
Football (All-Fair 1946) 70.00
Football (Samuel Lowe 1942)
w/ baseball, basketball and hockey 75.00
Football Fever (Hansen 1985) Game in brief case . 45.00
Football Knapp Electro Game Set
(Knapp Co. 1929) w/air & auto 175.00
Football Strategy (Avalon Hill-Sports Illustrated) . . . 15.00
Football Strategy (Avalon Hill) 12.00
Foto-Electric Football (Cadaco-Ellis ©1950) 75.00
Frank Cavanaugh's American Football
(F. Cavanaugh Assoc. 1955) 30.00
Fut-Bal (The Fut-Bal Co. 1940s) 50.00
Goal Line Stand (Game Shop Inc. 1980) 25.00
Half-Time Football (Lakeside 1979) 10.00
Instant Replay (Parker Bros. 1987) 15.00
Jerry Kramer's Instant Replay
(Emd Enterprises 1970) 20.00
Jim Prentice Electric Football
(Electric Game Co. 1940) 75.00
Jimmy The Greek Oddsmaker Football
(Aurora 1974) 20.00
The Johnny Unitas Football Game (Play-Rite 1960) 150.00
Johnny Unitas' Football (Pro Mentor 1970) 35.00
J.R. Quarterback Football (Built Rite 1950s) 40.00
Kellogg's Football Game (Kellogg's Premium 1936) 35.00
Knute Rockne Football (Radio Sports c. 1940) . . . 300.00
Linebacker Football (Linebacker Inc. 1990) 25.00
Monday Morning Quarterback (A.B. Zbinden 1963) . 22.00
NBC Pro Playoff (NBC-Hasbro 1969) 15.00
NFL Armchair Quarterback (Trade Wind Inc. 1986) . 15.00
NFL Franchise (Rohrwood 1982) 18.00
NFL Game Plan (Tudor Games 1980) 12.00
NFL Play Action (Tudor 1979) 10.00
NFL Quarterback (Tudor 1977) 15.00
NFL Strategy (Tudor 1979) 15.00
NFL Strategy (Tudor 1986) 15.00
Official National Football League Quarterback
(Toy Craft 1965) 70.00
Paul Brown's Football Game (Trikilis 1947) 150.00
Paydirt! (Sports Illustrated 1973) 12.00

1941 Stars on Stripes Football Game
Alex G. Malloy collection.

Paydirt! (Avalon Hill) 10.00
Pigskin (Parker Bros. 1940) 100.00
Parker Bros. 1956 . . . . . 40.00
Parker Bros. 1960 . . . . . 30.00
Pigskin (Parker Bros. 1946)
"Tom Hamilton's Football" 75.00
Playoff Football (Crestline Mfg.Co 1970's) 25.00
Pocket Football (Toy Creations 1940) 35.00
Pocket Football (AMV Publishing) 10.00
Pro Coach Football (Mastermind Sports) 40.00
Pro Draft (Parker Bros. 1974) 20.00
Pro Football (Milton Bradley 1964) 35.00
Pro Football (3M ©1964) 20.00
Pro Football Franchise (Ron Wood 1987) 25.00
Pro Foto-Football (Cadaco 1977) 30.00
Pro Foto-Football (Cadaco 1986) 17.50
Pro Franchise Football (Rohrwood Inc. 1987) 20.00
Pro Quarterback (Tod Lansing 1964) 50.00
Pro Quarterback (Championship Games 1965) 75.00
Pro Replay Football (Pro Replay) 18.00
Quarterback Football Game (Transogram 1969) . . . 35.00
Razzle Dazzle Football Game
(Texantics Unlimited 1954) 70.00
Realistic Football (Match Play 1976) 15.00
Replay Pro Football (Replay Games) 45.00
Rose Bowl Championship Football Game
(E.S. Lowe Co. 1940s) 150.00
Rummy Football (Milton Bradley 1944) 50.00
Samsonite Football (Samsonite 1969) 25.00
Scrimmage (SPI 1973) 15.00
Scrimmage (Scrimmage Inc. 1978) 12.00
Six Points College Football (Six Points) 35.00
Sod Buster (D. Santee 1980) 22.00
Sports Illustrated College Football
(Sports Illustrated 1971) 15.00
Sports Illustrated Pro Football (Time 1970) 18.00
Stars on Stripes Football Game
(Stars & Stripes Games Co. 1941) 80.00
Statis Pro Football (Statis-Pro 1970s) 35.00
Statis Pro Football (Avalon Hill-Sports Illustrated) . . 15.00
Strat-O-Matic College Football (Strat-O-Matic 1976) 30.00
Super Coach TV Football (Coleco 1974) 20.00
Pro Football (Strat-O-Matic 1968) 35.00
--1960s player cards 20.00
--1970s player cards 14.00
--1980s player cards 12.00
T.H.E. Pro Football (T.H.E. Game Co.) 28.00
TSG I: Pro Football (TSG 1971) 45.00
Tackle-Lite (Saxon Toy Corp. 1940s) 75.00
Talking Football (Mattel 1971) 12.00
Talking Monday Night Football (Mattel 1977) 8.00
Thinking Man's Football (3M 1969) 15.00
--3M 1973 . . . . . 12.00
Top Pro Football Quiz Game (Ed-U-Cards 1970) . . 20.00
The VCR Quarterback Game
(Interactive VCR Games 1986) 15.00
Varsity Football Game (Cadaco-Ellis 1942) 65.00
--Cadaco-Ellis 1955 . . . . . 35.00
Vince Lombardi's Game
(Research Games Inc. 1970) 100.00
Whiz Football (Electric Game Co. 1945) 75.00
Win A Card Trading Card Game (Milton Bradley
c. 1965) w/ board and "generous (40 of
both sports) supply of baseball &
football trading cards" 500.00
Wiry Dan's Electric Football Game
(Harett-Gilmar 1953) 50.00

GOLF GAMES

PRE-1940 GAMES

Amateur Golf (Parker Bros. ©1928) 200.00
Bunker Golf (All-Fair 1932) 150.00
Country Club Golf (Franz Mfg. Co. 1923) 150.00
Drive 'n Putt (Carrom Ind. 1940s) wood board 75.00
Fore Country Club (Wilder c. 1929) deluxe edition 250.00
Fore Game of Golf (Wilder c. 1929) 150.00
The Game of Golf (J.H. Singer c. 1890) 200.00
The Game of Golf, Tokalon series
(E.O. Clark c. 1890s) 500.00
The Game of Golf (Clark & Sowdon c. 1905) 650.00
Game of Golf (McLoughlin Bros. 1896) 600.00
Game of Golf Popular Edition
(Parker Bros. c. 1900) 250.00
A Game of Golf (Milton Bradley c. 1930) 200.00
Golf (Shoenhut Phil. 1900) w/ indoor golf tees . . 7,500.00
Golf (Milton Bradley c. 1900) large game 250.00
Golf (Parker Bros. 1907) 200.00
Kellogg's Golf Game (Kellogg's Premium 1936) . . . 35.00
Let's Play Games, Golf (American Toy Works 1939) 70.00
Little Jack Horner Golf Course (1920s)

1930's Nineteenth Hole Golf Game
Alex G. Malloy collection.

Metal/felt course 200.00
Miniature Golf (Miniature Golf Co. 1930s) 50.00
Ninteenth Hole Golf Game (Einson & Freeman 1930s) 125.00
Open Championship Golf Game (Beacon Hudson Co. 1925) 150.00
"Par" Golf Card Game (National Golf Services ©1920) 150.00
Parlor Golf (Chaffee & Selchow 1897) 300.00
"Par" The New Golf Game (Russell Mfg. Co. ©1926) 150.00
Pla-Golf Board Game (Pla-Golf Co. 1938) 75.00
The Popular Game of Golf (Parker Bros. 1896) . . 1,100.00
Rainy Day Golf (Selchow & Righter 1930's) 150.00
Realistic Golf (Parker Bros. 1898) irregular board
32x22 felt field 1,200.00
32x22 wood field 1,000.00
32x22 paper mache 800.00
Roll-O Golf (Supply Sales Co. 1923) 50.00
Substitute Golf (Shoenhut Phil. 1906) 7,500.00
Table Golf (McClurg & Co. 1909) 16.00
Tait's Table Golf (John Tait c. 1914) large box . . . 500.00
Tee Off (Donogof 1935) 150.00
Tiddley Golf Game (Milton Bradley 1928) 100.00
Traps and Bunkers (Milton Bradley 1926-28) 150.00
World's Championship Golf Game (Beacon Hudson Co. 1930s) 200.00
Wyntre Golf (All Fair Games 1920s) board & implement box 250.00

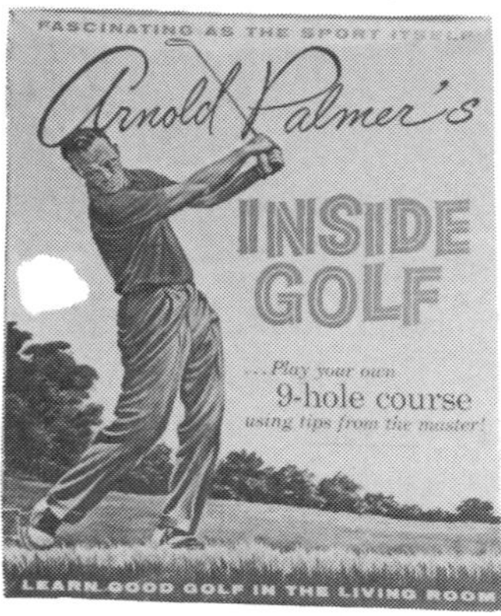

1961 Arnold Palmer's Inside Golf
Alex G. Malloy collection.

POST-1939 GAMES

APBA Golf (APBA) 15.00
Arnold Palmer's Inside Golf (D. B. Remson 1961) . 100.00
Birdie Golf (Barris Corp. 1964) large board 100.00
Break Par Golf Game (Warren-Built Rite 1950s) . . . 30.00
Call It Golf (A. Strauss 1966) 20.00
Challenge Golf At Pebble Beach (3M 1972) 17.00
Country Club Golf (Future Games 1990) 15.00
Cribb Golf (late 1980s) board w/ cards 70.00
Fast Golf (Whitman 1977) 15.00
Fore (Artcraft Paper Prod. 1954) 25.00
Gambler's Golf (Gammon Games 1975) 12.00
The Game of Traps (Traps Mfg. 1950s) action 75.00
Gardner's Championship Golf (Gardner c. 1950s) . . 75.00
Go For The Green! (Sports Illustrated, 1973) 60.00
Let's Go Golfin' (Full-o-Fun Co.) 50.00
Let's Play Golf: The Hawaiian Open (Burlu 1968) . . 30.00
Light Horse H. Cooper Golf Game (Trojan Games 1943) 250.00
Negamco Pro Golf (Nedmadji Game Co.) 7.00
Official Skins Golf Game (O'Connor-Hall 1985) 25.00
Par '73' (Big Top Games 1961) 20.00
Par-A-Shoot Game (Baldwin Mfg. Co. 1947) 25.00
Par Golf (National Games Inc. 1950s) 150.00
Play ABC's Golf (America's Finest Golf Game Co. 1979) 30.00
Pro Golf (Avalon Hill-Sports Illustrated 1982) 12.00
Pro Golf (Avalon Hill 1984) 10.00
Rainy Day Golf (Bryad 1980) 15.00
Roll-a-Par (E.S. Lowe 1964) 20.00
Sports Illustrated Handicap Golf (Sports Illustrated 1971) 16.00

1926-28 Traps & Bunkers
Alex G. Malloy collection.

Tee Off by Sam Snead (Glenn Indust. 1973) 150.00
Thinking Man's Golf (3M 1966) 25.00

Tournament Golf (Rigely Banada 1969) 15.00

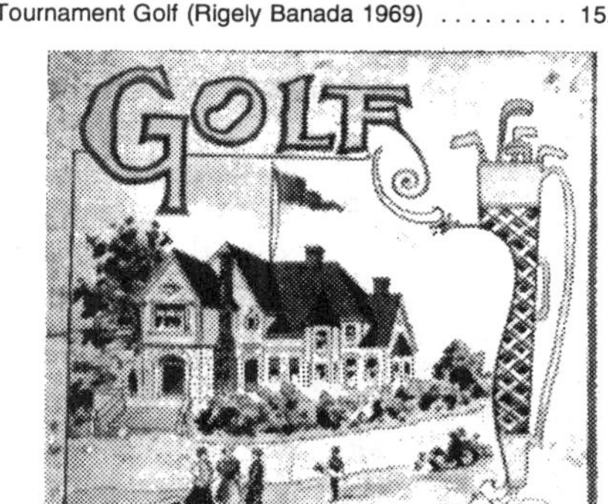

1907 Golf game
Alex G. Malloy collection.

Ultimate Golf (Ultimate Golf Inc. 1985) 50.00
Wide World of Sports Golf (Milton Bradley 1975) . . 90.00

HOCKEY GAMES

Blue Line Hockey (3M 1968) 30.00
Box Hockey (Milton Bradley 1941) 50.00
Face-Off (Con-Fro Game Co.) 35.00
Hockey (Samuel Lowe Co. 1942) w/ baseball, basketball and football games 75.00
Ice Hockey (Milton Bradley 1942) 35.00
The Katzenjammer Kids Hockey (Jaymar 1930s) . . 75.00
NHL All-Pro Hockey (Ideal 1969) 10.00
National Pro Hockey (Sports Action 1985) 35.00
Nip and Tuck Hockey (Parker Bros. 1928) 150.00
Nok-Hockey (Cardinal 1947) 50.00
Official Hockey (Toy Creations 1940) 100.00
Play Hockey Fun with Popeye & Wimpy (Barnum Mfg. 1935) 300.00
Power Play Hockey (Romac Ind 1970) 40.00
Slapshot (Avalon Hill 1982) 12.00
Strat-O-Matic Hockey (Strat-O-Matic 1978) 45.00
Sure Shot Hockey (Ideal 1970) 20.00
Tit for Tat Indoor Hockey (Lemper Novelty Co. 1920s) 65.00

1943 Top Hockey
Alex G. Malloy collection.

Top Hockey (Coren Game Co. 1943) 75.00
The VCR Hockey Game (Interactive VCR Games 1987) 12.00

HORSE RACING GAMES

APBA Saddle Racing Game (APBA 1970s) 18.00
cross The Board Horse Racing Game (MPH Company 1975) 20.00

1931 The American Derby
Alex G. Malloy collection.

American Derby (Henschel Co., Whitman Pub. 1931) 75.00
The American Derby (Cadaco-Ellis 1951) 40.00
The American Derby (Cadaco 1953) 35.00
Belmont Park (Marks Bros Co. 1930) 150.00
Bing Crosby's Game, Call Me Lucky (Parker Bros. ©1954) 75.00
Bookie (Bookie Games Co. 1931) 75.00
Cavalcade (Selchow & Righter 1930s)
--Deluxe wooden pieces 100.00
--Regular set 65.00
Classic Derby (Doremus-Schoen Co., Inc. c. 1935) 150.00
The Crosby Derby (Fishlove Ind. 1947) 50.00
Derby Day Card Game (Parker Bros. 1900) 55.00
Derby Day (Parker Bros. 1930) 125.00
Derby Day (Parker Bros. 1959) 90.00

1888 Derby Steeple Chase
Alex G. Malloy collection.

Derby Steeple Chase (McLoughlin Bros. 1888) . . . 150.00
Derby Steeple Chase (McLoughlin Bros. 1890) . . . 250.00
Eddie Arcaro's Riders Up Game (TS 91) 75.00
Favorite Steeple Chase (J.H. Singer 1895) 150.00
Foto-Finish Horse Race Game (Pressman & Co. 1940s) 75.00
The Game of the Race (unknown early American manufacturer, early 1860s) black, red, embossed gold board 600.00

manufacturer, early 1860s) black, red, embossed gold board 600.00
The Game of the Race (unknown early American manufacturer, 1860s) wooden implement box, painted metal horses 500.00
The Game of the Races (William Crosby 1844) Boston oval track board, lithogrphaed, hand painted; the first American sports game . . . 1,200.00
Game of Racing Stable (D&H Games 1936) 150.00
Game of Steeple Chase (Milton Bradley 1910) 75.00
Game of Steeple Chase, (Parker Bros. 1895)
--Tom Thumb 75.00
--Popular Edition 150.00
Game of Steeple Chasing (McLoughlin Bros. 1903) Playtime Series 500.00
Gee-Wiz Race (Wolverine Supply Co. 1923) 125.00
Giant Wheel Thrills'n Spills Horse Race (Remco 1958) 40.00
Grand National, Sweepstakes (Whitman Publ. c. 1937) 60.00
The Great Horse Race Game (Selchow & Righter 1925) 100.00
Handicap Harness Racing (Hall of Fame Games 1978) 15.00
Hialeah Horse Racing Game (Milton Bradley 1940) . 50.00
Home Stretch Harness Racing (E.S. Lowe 1967) . . 50.00
Horse Race (E.S. Lowe 1943) 35.00
Horce Racing (Milton Bradley 1935) 50.00
Horses (All Fair Inc. ©1927) 70.00
Horses (Modern Makers Inc. 1927) 150.00
Improved Game of Steeple Chase (McLoughlin Bros. 1890s) 275.00
Indoor Horse Racing (Man O' War 1924) 100.00
Jerome Park Steeple Chase, w/Wood sided box (McLoughlin Bros. 1896) 300.00
Jerome Park Steeple Chase, w/cardboard stables (McLoughlin Bros.) 400.00
Jig Race (Game Makers Inc. 1930s) Puzzle Game . 50.00

1920 Saratoga Horse Race Game
Alex G. Malloy collection.

Jockette (Jockette Co. 1950s) 30.00
Kentucky Derby (Whitman 1963) 40.00
Kentucky Derby (Whitman 1969) 30.00
Kentucky Derby Racing Game (Whitman 1938) . . 125.00
Kentucky Derby Racing Game (Whitman 1961) . . . 50.00
Let's Play Games Polo (American Toy Works 1940) 65.00
Magic Race (Habob Co. 1942) 75.00
Merry Steeple Chase (J. Ottmann Lith. 1890's) 60.00
My Word, Horse Race (American Toy Works 1938) 85.00
National Velvet Game (Transogram 1961) 75.00
Neck and Neck (Yaquito 1981) 15.00
Obstacle Race (Wilder Mfg. Co. 1930s) 100.00
Pari, Horse Race Card Game (Pari Sales Co. 1959) 25.00
Pimlico (Metro c. 1940s) 75.00
Ponies & Nags (Vantage Intl. ©1993) 30.00
Saratoga Horse Racing Game (Milton Bradley c. 1920) 125.00
Saratoga Steeple Chase (J.H. Singer 1900) 175.00

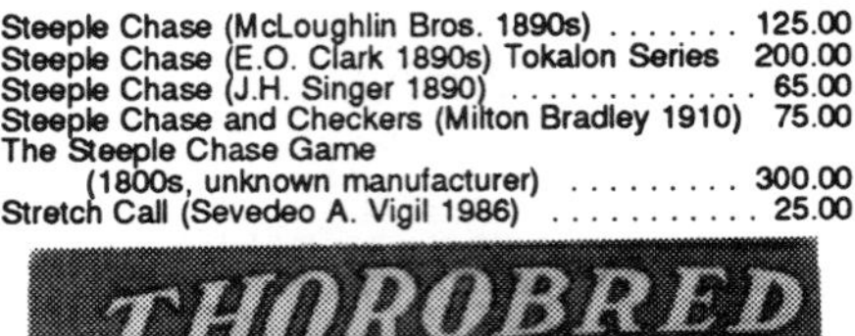

Steeple Chase (McLoughlin Bros. 1890s) 125.00
Steeple Chase (E.O. Clark 1890s) Tokalon Series 200.00
Steeple Chase (J.H. Singer 1890) 65.00
Steeple Chase and Checkers (Milton Bradley 1910) 75.00
The Steeple Chase Game (1800s, unknown manufacturer) 300.00
Stretch Call (Sevedeo A. Vigil 1986) 25.00

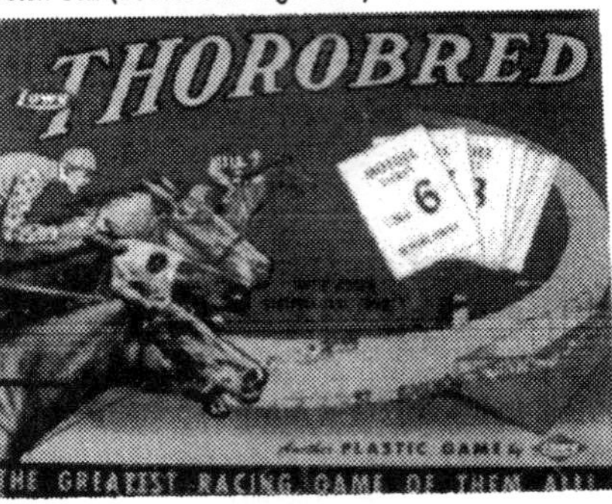

1940's Thorobred game
Alex G. Malloy collection.

Suffolk Downs - Club Edition (Corey Game Co. 1930s) 125.00
Suffolk Downs Racing Game (Corey Games 1947) . 85.00
Sweeps (E.E. Fairchild)
--late 1930s, hand with money on cover 75.00
--1945, two blue horses on cover 65.00
--1945, two brown horses on cover 65.00
Sweepstakes (Haras Mfg. Co. 1930s) 75.00
They're At The Post (MAAS Marketing 1976) 35.00
Thorobred (E.S. Lowe Co. 1940s) 75.00
Tru-Action Electric Horse Race (1960s Tudor) 30.00

1977 Win, Place & Show
Alex G. Malloy collection.

Win, Place & Show (3M 1966) 25.00
Win, Place & Show (3M 1970) 20.00
Win, Place and Show (Milton Bradley 1945-49) 30.00
Win, Place & Show (Avalon Hill w/ Sports Illus. 1977) 15.00

HUNTING GAMES

Buck Fever (L&D Robton Enterprises 1984) 25.00
Buffalo Hunt (Parker Bros. 1900) 75.00
Fox Hunt (Carrom Ind. 1940s) wood board 75.00
Fox Hunt (E.S. Lowe Co. 1940s) 45.00
Fox & Hounds (Parker Bros. 1900)
3 1/2 square box 75.00
Game of Fox and Hounds (Parker Bros. 1948) 35.00
Game of Hunting Hare (McLoughlin 1891)
19 1/2 x 11 . . . . 300.00
8 x 8 . . . . 150.00
Game of Rabbit Hunt (McLoughlin 1870) 250.00
Hare & Hound (Parker Bros. 1895) 350.00
Hounds & Hares (J.W. Keller 1894) card game 50.00
Hunting the Rabbit (Clark & Sowdon 1890s) 200.00
The New Game of Hunting (McLoughlin 1904) . . . 150.00
old Hunter and His Game (c. 1870) card game . . . 250.00

1950's Tally Ho!
Alex G. Malloy collection.

Tally Ho! (Whitman, circa 1950's) 35.00

SAILING & BOATING GAMES

America's Yacht Race (McLoughlin Bros. 1904) . . 875.00
An Exciting Motor Boat Race (American Toy 1930) 150.00
A&P Relay Boat Race Coast to Coast
(A&P Cereal Box 1930s) 35.00
Canoe Race (Milton Bradley 1910) 3 1/2 square . . . 50.00
Clipper Race (Samuel Gabriel 1930s) 100.00
Game of College Boat Race
(McLoughlin Bros. 1896) 500.00
Game of Yachting (S.H. Singer 1900) 75.00

1950's Regatta
Alex G. Malloy collection.

International Yacht Race (McLoughlin Bros. 1890s) 150.00
Navigator-Boat Race (C. Williams Games 1936-7) 100.00
Navigator-Boat Race Game (Whitman Co. 1938)
boards & cards 75.00
Newport Yacht Race (McLoughlin Bros. 1891) . . . 500.00
Outboard Motor Boat (Milton Bradley 1935) 125.00
Regatta (1946) 60.00
Regatta (Whitman, 1950's) 35.00
Regatta (3M 1966) 30.00
Sail Away...A Racing Game (Howard Mullen 1962) . 50.00
Skipper-Race Sailing Game (Cadaco-Ellis 1949) . . . 75.00
Smitty Speed Boat Race Game
(Milton Bradley 1930s) 150.00
Speed Boat (Parker Bros. 1920s) 125.00
Speed Boat Race (Wolverine
Supply & Mfg. Co. 1926) 100.00
Speed Boat Race (Milton Bradley 1930s) 125.00
Varsity Race (Parker Bros. 1899)
College Crew Game 18x11 . . . . 600.00
Vassar Boat Race (Chaffee & Selchow 1899) . . . 1500.00
White Wings (Glevum Games Inc. 1930s) 60.00
Yacht Race (McLoughlin Bros. 1900) 250.00
Yacht Race (Milton Bradley 1905) 100.00
Yacht Race (J. Pressman 1930s) 40.00
Yacht Race (Saturday House & Parker Bros. 1962) 60.00

1930's Yacht Race
Alex G. Malloy collection.

Yacht Race, Tokalon Series
(Clark & Sowdon 1890) 500.00
Yachting (J.H. Singer 1890) 100.00
Yachting (Parker Bros. 1900) 3 1/2" 50.00
"Yachts" the International Race
(Parker Bros. 1910) 200.00

TENNIS GAMES

Pro Tennis (Avalon Hill-Sports Illustrated) 15.00
Set Point, Tennis Strategy Game
(XV Productions 1971) 35.00
Tennis (Parker Bros. 1975) 10.00
Tennis and Baseball (1930) 100.00

TRACK & FIELD GAMES

Athletic Sports (Parker Bros. 1900) 200.00
Bruce Jenner Decathalon Game (1979) 25.00
Cross Country Marathon Game
(Rosebud Art Co. 1930s) 75.00
Decathalon (Sports Illustrated 1972) 15.00

1972 Track Meet
Alex G. Malloy collection.

Endurance Run (Milton Bradley 1930s) 75.00
The Foot Race (Parker Bros. 1900) 3 1/2 square . . 75.00
Hurdle Race (Milton Bradley 1910) 150.00
Official Boston Marathon Game
(Perl Products 1978) 15.00
Olympic Runners (Wolverine Supply Co. 1930) . . . 125.00
Pedestrianism (1879): Very early game with
two stars depicted, rare 500.00
The Torch (S. Alden 1992) 40.00
Track Meet (Sports Illustrated 1972) 18.00

WRESTLING GAMES

1950's Falls, Wrestling Game
Alex G. Malloy collection.

Falls, Wrestling Game (National 1950s) 125.00
Superstar Pro Wrestling Game
(Super Star Game Co. 1984) 18.00
Verne Gagne World Champion Wrestling
(Gardner 1950) 100.00
World Champion Wrestling official Slam o' Rama
card game (International Games, c.1990) 7.00
Wrestling Superstars (Milton Bradley 1985) 15.00
WWF Wrestling Game (Colorforms, c. 1991) 7.00

MISCELLANEOUS SPORTS GAMES

ABC Sports Winter Olympics (Mindscape 1987) . . . 20.00
American Sports (1880s) various depictions
of early sports match cards 150.00
BMX Cross Challenge Action Game
(Cross Challenge Corp. 1988) 10.00
Chicago Sports Trivia Game
(Sports Trivia Inc. 1984) 10.00
Counter Point (Hallmark 1976) 10.00
Demo Derby (Mayfair) 20.00
Game of Pool (1898) 1,000.00

1898 The Young Athlete
Debby & Marty Krim collection.

Gammonball (Fun-Time Products 1980) 20.00
Grand Master of the Martial Arts (Hoyle 1986) 10.00
Hookey: Go Fishin' (Cadaco 1974) 10.00
The Original Home Jai-Alai Game
(Design Origin © 1984) 30.00
Parlor Croquet (Pressman 1940) 25.00
The Skating Race Game
(Chaffee & Selchow 1900) 350.00
Ski Gammon (American Publishing Corp 1962) 10.00
SI: The Sporting Word Game
(Time Inc.-Parker 1961) 10.00
Sla*lom, Ski Run Game (Cadaco-Ellis © 1957) 75.00
Sports Arena No. 1 (Rennoc Games & Toys 1954) . 50.00
Sports Yesteryear (Skor-Mor 1977) 16.00
Sports Yesteryear Game (Samuel Ward Co.) 18.00
Sports Trivia Game (Hoyle 1984) 10.00
Strat-O-Matic Sports "Know-How"
(Strat-O-Matic 1984) 10.00
Superstar TV Sports (ARC 1980) 10.00
Toboggan Slide (Hamilton-Myers 1890) 350.00
Toboggan Slide (J.H. Singer 1890s) 100.00
Walk the Plank (Milton Bradley 1925)
Diving & swimming game 100.00
Walt Disney's Ski Jump Target Game
(American Toy Works 1936-9) 250.00
Young Athlete (gymnastics)
(Chaffee & Selchow 1898) 1,500.00

1890 The Game of Golf
Debby & Marty Krim collection.

Game values are :

Pre-1940	**Very Good Condition**
Post-1940	**Very Fine Condition**
Post-1980	**Near Mint Condition**

HORSE RACING GLASSES

By Dick Hering

The first Kentucky Derby glass was issued in 1938. The 1938 and 1939 glasses were made of glass, while in 1940 there were two variations, one made of glass with a similar design to the 1939 glass, and one made of aluminum. The aluminum was also used in 1941. There was another aluminum version made in 1940 and 1941 issued by the French Lick Hotel Resort. Their version was identical except for the hotel's name appearing on the cup. 1941 was also the year of the introduction of the Bakelite (a.k.a. Beetleware) cup. An early version of plastic, Bakelite was used through 1944, and although the cups came in a variety of colors, there is no way to distinguish one year from another, since they all featured the same horsehead logo and phrase "Kentucky Derby, Churchill Downs."

In 1945 there were three different Kentucky Derby glasses. A "short," which is similar in size to the present day glasses; a "tall," a narrow zombie type glass; and a "jigger," sometimes referred to as a shot glass despite its closer resemblance in size to a juice glass.

In 1946 there was an undecorated glass distributed that was similar to the 1945 tall. This practice was continued in 1947 with an undecorated tall and short version. Some collectors consider these undecorated glasses as part of the set, whereas others consider them meaningless.

From 1948 to the present, all the glasses have been made of glass and are basically the same size, although some years have variations. The 1956 glass pictures three horses running and has a star at the beginning and end of the words "Churchill Downs." Some of the glasses have a missing star and/or a missing tail from one of the horses, so four variations are possible.

There were two variations of the 1958 glass, one being a recycled 1957 with the 1958 winner added on the upper part of the glass, known as the 1958 Iron Leige. The other 1958 version (known as the 1958 Gold Bar) has a large gold bar on each side.

The first Preakness glass, made in 1973, was produced in a very limited quantity and is the most sought after and valuable of the Preakness glasses. In 1974 the number of glasses produced almost doubled that of 1973, but 1974 still proves to be a difficult glass to find. In conjunction with the 100th running of the Preakness, the amount made in 1975 was again significantly increased. In 1976 and 1977 the number of glasses produced again increased substantially, while in 1978 production decreased to the level of 1975. From 1979 through 1984 the number of glasses made increased fractionally. Overproduced in 1985, production levels decreased from 1986 through 1989, but remained steady. In 1990 it was massively overproduced, and the seesaw pattern struck again in 1991 and 1992 as significantly fewer glasses were made. In comparison, the amounts made of Preakness glasses versus Kentucky Derby glasses of corresponding years has always been fractional. Even in 1990, when an all-time high of approximately 40,000 were made, there were 600,000 Derby glasses made that year.

Belmont glasses, like Preakness glasses, were made in very small quantities compared to Kentucky Derby glasses. In some years, production was even smaller than that of corresponding Preakness glasses.

The first Belmont glass was made in 1976, and it is believed that in 1977, 1981, 1982, 1983 and 1988 there were less than 2,300 glasses produced each year. The amount made every year was always under 7,000 until 1991, when a record 14,400 were made. The 1992 figure drops down to 7,920.

Although the first Breeders' Cup was run in 1984, the first glass was not produced until 1985. This glass was produced in a very limited quantity, which explains its high value even though the glass is only 7 years old. The glass has a unique stemmed design that is a break from the traditional shape of the Triple Crown glasses. There were no Breeders' Cup glasses made in 1986 or 1987. Since 1988 they have been continually made in the same shape and size as Triple Crown glasses, but in relatively small quantities. The 1988 & 1991 glasses were slightly overproduced, whereas the 1989 and 1992 were underproduced.

GLASSES

HORSE RACING

BELMONT STAKES GLASSES

1976, 1977 Belmont Stakes glasses

Year	Description	Value
1976	"The Big Apple of Racing"	75.00
1977	Black lettering & stable	325.00
1978	Brown horse shoe & winners listed	100.00
1979	Black horse shoe	65.00
1980	"112th Running," brown racing horses	125.00
1981	"113th Running," color racing horses	300.00
1982	"114th Running," color racing horses	250.00
1983	"115th Running," color racing horses	300.00
1984	"116th Running," color racing horses	175.00
1985	"117th Running," color racing horses	125.00
1986	"118th Running," color racing horses	75.00
1987	Brown & green horse, winners listed	65.00
1988	Brown & green horse, winners listed	75.00
1989	Brown & green horse, winners listed	30.00
	"121" graphic, w/ date	30.00
1990	Brown & green horse, winners listed	15.00
1991	Brown & green horse, winners listed	5.00

BREEDERS CUP GLASSES

Year	Description	Value
1985	Pedestal-style glass, red & blue design	350.00
1986	Not issued	
1987	Not issued	
1988	Churchill Downs, date	10.00
1989	Gulfstream Park, yellow graphic	30.00
1990	Belmont Park, NYC graphic	15.00
1991	Churchill Downs, date black graphic	5.00
	French Glory Error	35.00

KENTUCKY DERBY GLASSES

Officially Licensed Kentucky Derby Shot Glasses have been manufactured since 1987, and are valued at 5-10 dollars.

One other licensed shot glass was available in 1945 and is valued at $700.00.

Year	Description	Value
1938		2500.00
1939	Horses in black racing around base of glass	4400.00
1940	(Glass) Horses in blue racing around base of glass	5200.00
40-41	(Aluminum) "Kentucky Derby Churchill Downs"	450.00
41-44	(Bakelite)	
	Reddish-brown, Derby Emblem	1800.00-3500.00
	Multicolored, Derby Emblem	same
1945	Jigger:	
	"I Have Been to the Kentucky Derby"	900.00
	Tall, Derby Emblem	350.00
	Short, Derby Emblem	850.00

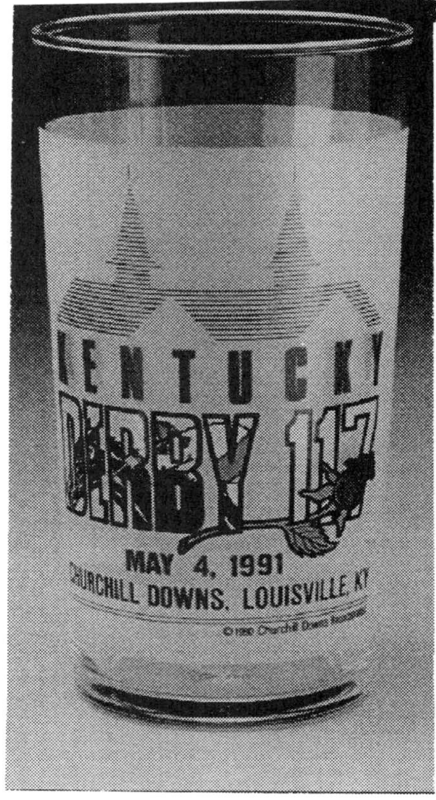

1991 Kentucky Derby julep glass

1946	Undecorated	75.00
1947	Short- undecorated	75.00
	Tall- undecorated	60.00
1948	Clear bottom	125.00
	Frosted bottom	150.00
1949	Matt Winn "He has seen the All"	135.00
1950	Green, horses rounding turn	300.00
1951	"Where Turf Champions are Crowned"	325.00
1952	"Kentucky Derby Gold Cup"	135.00
1953	Derby Emblem, "The Run for the Roses"	100.00
1954	Churchill Downs, winners randomly listed	150.00
1955	Yellow & green, 5 fastest runnings	100.00
1956	Yellow lettering, winners listed	
	1 star, 2 tails	165.00
	1 star, 3 tails	275.00
	2 stars, 2 tails	165.00
	2 stars, 3 tails	175.00
1957	Gold horse & jockey, winners listed	85.00
1958	Iron Liege: gold horse & jockey graphic, winners listed	135.00
	Gold Bar: same as above, w/ gold bar	150.00
1959	Horse & jockey dot portrait, winners listed in gold	50.00
1960	Gold horses, jockeys black, winners	

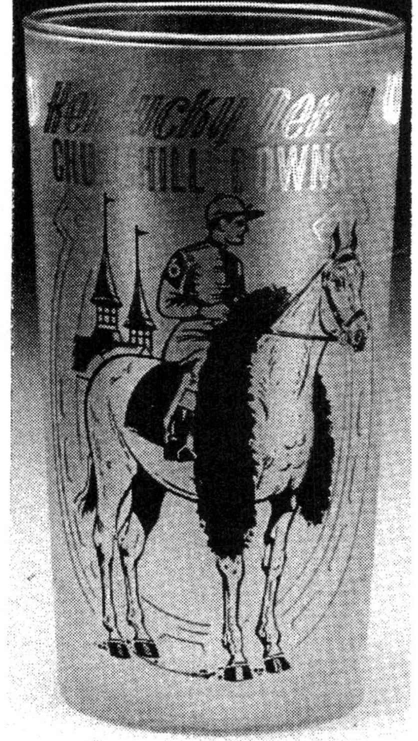

1962 Kentucky Derby julep glass

	listed in black	65.00
1961	Diagonal pict. horse & jockey, winners in gold	85.00
1962	Winning horse & jockey w/ roses	60.00
1963	Black & brown horse & jockey	45.00
1964	Horse head, gold lettering	35.00
1965	Churchill Downs, "Run for the Roses" in red	60.00
1966	Gold lettering, 4 fastest runnings	45.00
1967	Several sm. pics., winners in black	40.00
1968	Red & blue coat of arms, gold lettering	30.00
1969	Jockey #3, horseshoe, horse racers in red	30.00
1970	Green coat of arms, winners listed	50.00
1971	Greens steeples & racers, red lettering	25.00
1972	2 Horses in stretch, orange lettering	25.00
1973	Sign with steeples, red, green lettering	25.00
1974	100th anniversary, gold horse	10.00
	w/ Federal Trademark	100.00
1975	Black & yellow lettering, year in red	4.00
1976	Red, white, blue, stars & stripes base	6.00
1977	Brown & cream colored horse & jockey	3.50
1978	Churchill Downs in brown, red lettering	7.00
1979	Grandstands, horses rounding bend	8.00
1980	Two horses neck & neck, b&w lettering	14.00
1981	Winning horse in yellow shield, green & yellow banner	4.00
1982	Trophy, rose garland, blue banner	5.00
1983	Air brush pict. of Churchill Downs	5.00
1984	Two racers head in, lettering in red, green on back	3.50
1985	"Post Parade Song", orange lettering	4.00
1986	Red roses, lettering, winners in green	6.00
1987	Brown horse & roses in center, winners listed in black	4.50
1988	Two horses head on, red roses	4.00
1989	115 years graphic w/ horse, steeple	3.50
1990	Horse, steeple in back, one red rose	3.00
1991	Derby 117 graphic, one rose	3.00

PREAKNESS GLASSES

Year	Description	Value
1973	Black steeple, black & yellow daisies	500.00
1974	Winners pictured in black	125.00
1975	100th Preakness, black & yellow daisies	100.00
1976	Red, white, blue "Preakness of 76"	65.00

1974, 1975 Preakness glasses

1977	Horse w/ daisies garland	65.00
1978	Horse & jockey, 2 large daisies	100.00
1979	Black & yellow steeple, daisies around rim	65.00
1980	Horses running in front of steeple	65.00
1981	Horses running in front of grandstand	60.00
1982	Jockey w/ "P" silks, daisies garland	55.00
1983	Horse in front of steeple, jockey head	50.00
1984	"Painting the Colors"	40.00
1985	Brown & green horse & jockey graphic	25.00
1986	Steeple, daisies, black bands around base	35.00
1987	Winners list, horses, daisies around glass	25.00
1988	Winners list, large daisies around base	25.00
1989	Large red "114," racing horse, steeple	20.00
1990	Horse head-on, steeple, daisies	5.00
1991	Horse graphic, large daisies	10.00

MEDALLIONS

SUMMER OLYMPICS MEDALLIONS

NOTES: *Values listed are for medallions in their original presentation boxes. Medallions without these boxes are worth 10% less than listed values.*

Documented ownership (provenance) with a medallion will increase the value by 5% or more. If the medallion is accompanied by a famous athlete's or gold medal winner's provenance, the value can be 25-100% greater than the listed value.

1896

Participant's medal, bronze, 50 mm.
OBV: Male figure with laurel and staff, Parthenon in background; inscription Greek lettering
RV: Laurel wreath; inscription Greek lettering . . . 600.00
Gilded Bronze - similar to above. 700.00
Silvered Bronze - similar to above 700.00

1900

Winner's medal, bronze, 41x60 mm.,rectangle .
OBV: Winged figure with laurel; inscription Republic Francaise, Paris 1900, Exposition Universeille.
RV: Male athlete with laurel branches; inscription Exercise Physiques Et Sports 500.00
Pure silver- similar 1,000.00
Silvered bronze 600.00

1904

Participant's medal, copper, 40X40mm, octagon
OBV: Runner with laurel, sunrise; inscription Olympic Games, Saint Louis USA 1904
RV: Three shields, stars, inscription begins Universal Exposition Commemorating ...Looped version worn with ribbon by judges 4,000.00
Non-looped presentation piece 3,000.00

1906

Participant's medal, bronze, 50 mm. Leftover medals from 1896, or restrikes from original dies; a cartouoche with "1906" was soldered over original date.
OBV: Male figure with laurel and staff, Parthenon in background; inscription Greek lettering
RV: Laurel wreath; inscription Greek lettering, 1896 . . . . 350.00
Gilded Bronze- similar to above. 450.00
Silvered Bronze- similar to above 450.00

1908

Participant's medal, pewter, 50 mm.
OBV: Winged figure holding laurel and horn; inscription begins Elis, Athens, Paris, St Louis...
RV: Four horses pulling chariot, no inscription 275.00

1900 Winner's Medallion

Non-competitor Participation medals
Gilt bronze-similar 450.00
Silvered bronze-similar 450.00
Bronze-similar 450.00

1912

Participant's medal, pewter, 50 mm.
OBV: Seated Zeus on column, U.N. building in background; inscription Till Minneaf Olympiksa Spelen Stockholm 1912.
RV: Four horses pulling chariot, same as 1908 . . . . 275.00
Gilt Bronze-similar 500.00
Silvered bronze-similar 500.00
Bronze 500.00

1920

Participant's medal, bronze, 60 mm.
OBV: Three male figures receiving prize from female figure; inscription VII Olympiade Anvers.
RV: Two horse pulling chariot, hovering angel 300.00

1924

Participant's medal, bronze, 55 mm.
OBV: Skyline; Inscription VIII Olympiad Paris 1924.
RV: Winners receiving laurel wreaths from angel; signed Raoul Bernard 250.00

1928

Participant's medal, bronze, 55 mm.
OBV: Stadium with banners; inscription IX Olympiade Amsterdam 1928.
RV: Male and Female figure holding torch on platform, above scale 250.00

1932

1912 Participant's Medallion

Participant's medal, bronze 70mm.
OBV: Male figure holding flag on which is inscribed Xth Olympiad 1932.
RV: Two female figures seated on stairs on either side of U.S.A. shield, figure on left holding smaller shield; inscription Los Angeles, California . . 450.00

1936

1928 Participant's Medallion

Participant's medal, bronze, 70 mm.
OBV: Male figure between two columns, left foot stepping up; inscription XI Olympiade Berlin 1936.
RV: Bell within five concentric circles, German eagle and Olympic rings on bell 225.00

1940, 1944, 1948

Summer Olympics not held, WW II

1948

Participant's medal, bronze, 50 mm.
OBV: London skyline, Olympic rings; inscription XIV Olympiad London 1948.
RV: Four horses pulling chariot, same as 1908 and 1912 . . . . 250.00
Silver plated- similar 350.00

1952

Participant's medal, bronze, 55 mm.
OBV: Two laurel wreathed heads, superimposed over track; inscription Helsinki 1952 Helsinkfors.
RV: Male and female figure holding torches, Olympic rings; inscription XV Olympia 250.00

1956

Participant's medal, bronze, 63 mm.
OBV: Olympic rings above Australian heraldic shield; inscription Olympic Games Melbourne 1956.
RV: 9 Pairs of figures striding on rim of coin, single figure holding Olympic flag; inscription Citius Altius Fortius 300.00

Participant's medal, bronze, 42x50 mm.
OBV: Oval shaped, Horse with rider on platform over Olympic rings; inscription XVI Olympiadens Ryttaravlingar Stockholm 1956.
RV: Blank 800.00

1960

Participant's medal, bronze 55 mm.
OBV: Running female figure with torch, Olympic rings in background.
RV: Abstract design, inscription Giochi Della Olimpiade Roma MCMLX. 350.00

1964

Participant's medal, bronze, 60 mm.
OBV: Artistic rendering of three athletes and laurel.
RV: Olympics rings; inscription XVIII Olympiad, Japanese characters, Tokyo 1964 . . . . 400.00

1968

Participant's medal, copper square, 50x50 mm.
OBV: Pictogram of all Olympic events; inscription Mexico 1968.
RV: Blank, 1 line inscription 225.00

1972

Participant's medal, steel, 50 mm.
OBV: Sunburst; inscription Olympiade Munich 1972.
RV: Olympic rings, laurel, abstract figures. . 300.00

1976

Participant's medal, copper, 45 mm.
OBV: Olympic stadium; inscription XXIe

Olympiade Montreal 1976.
RV: Olympic rings 225.00

1968 Participant's Medallion

1980

Participant's medal, bronze, 55 mm.
OBV: Red Square, Moscow.
RV: Olympic rings, and Olympic logo; inscription XXII, 1 line Cyrillic lettering, Mockba 1980 . . 225.00

1984

Participant's medal, bronze, 60 mm.
OBV: Olympic torch; inscription Citius Altius Fortius, XXIII Olympiad.
RV: Star in motion, Olympic rings, laurel; inscription Los Angeles 1984 . . . . 200.00

1988

Participant's medal, bronze, 60 mm.
OBV: Pagoda, in mountainous setting, bird flying, sun.
. . . . RV: Official games logo, Olympic rings; inscription XXIV Olympiad Seoul 1988 . . . . 175.00

1992

Barcelona participant's medal 125.00

WINTER OLYMPICS MEDALLIONS

1924

Participant's medal, bronze, 4 cm, 3.46 grams.
OBV: Athlete holding skis and skates with Mont Blanc in background;
RV: inscription beginning "Chamonix Mont-Blanc Sports D'Hiver" 4,000.00

Seal medal, bronze, 7 cm.
Same design as participant's medal 35.00

1928

Participant's medal, bronze, 4 cm, 3.5 grams.
OBV: Ice skater among snowflakes;
RV: inscription with Olympic rings and laurel branches on reverse 700.00

Commemorative medal, bronze, 3.7 cm.
OBV: Victory holding laurel branch, on sled pulled by two horses w/ Olympic rings at bottom;
RV: Inscription above laurel branch; by Milo Martin 400.00

Seal medal, bronze, 7 cm.
Same design as participant's medal 35.00

1932

Participant's medal, bronze, 4 cm, 3.3 grams.
OBV: Monument with figure in middle and Olympic rings at top;
RV: Same monument with six shields featuring six different events around top, Lake Placid view at bottom and inscription in center 1,200.00

Seal medal.
OBV: Victory above Lake Placid Sports complex;
RV: Olympic rings above "III Olympic Winter Games Lake Placid 1932", laurel branches at bottom; rim of medal in wave-like pattern 50.00

1936

Participant's medal, bronze, 6 cm.
OBV: "Citius Altius Fortius" above fir tree branch;
RV: Kreuzeck mountain peak w/ski trail running behind Olympic rings 900.00

Seal medal. 3.1 cm (Issued 1977)
OBV: Olympic rings in center;
RV: Three horses pulling Victory on a chariot with hockey stick, skate, ski & sled below . . . 35.00

Aluminum medal in droplet form.
OBV: Peak of Kreuzeck mountain above "Garmisch" and Olympic rings;

RV: Frauenkirche building above "München" . 45.00

1932 Seal medal

1940, 1944, 1948

Winter Olympics not held, WW II

1948

Participant's medal, bronze, 4.0 cm, 3.4 grams.
OBV: Female figure running to left, scarf blowing behind and sun in background;
RV: Various snowflakes of different shapes and sizes around Olympic rings at top, inscription in center and "1•9•4•8" at bottom 900.00

Seal medal.
OBV: Snowflakes above and below inscription;
RV: Hand with Olympic torch, Olympic rings in background 35.00

Commemorative medal, bronze, 3.5 cm.
OBV: Olympic rings over laurel branch w/ inscription along rim;
RV: Kneeling athlete holding Olympic torch .. 75.00

1952

Participant's medal, bronze, 4 cm, 3.5 grams.
OBV: Large snowflake in center with three smaller snowflakes between words "Citius Altius Fortius";
RV: Olympic rings on top of the Oslo symbol with inscription on rim 700.00

Seal medal.
OBV: Olympic torch in center above Olympic rings and Greek "Olympia" with inscription around rim;
RV: Oslo Olympic symbol (two rectangles upon a larger rectangle) with three different snowflakes and an inscription 50.00

Seal medal, bronze.
Same as participant's medal, except smaller in size 35.00

1956

Participant's medal, bronze, 4.0 cm, 3.5 grams.
OBV: Snowflake with mountains behind, "Citius Altius Fortius" and "Cortina 1956" on rim;
RV: Head of athlete with Olympic rings as a crown, torch flame blowing behind and "VII Giochi Olimpici Invernau" on rim 700.00

Bronze opening day medal.
OBV: Stadium with mountains in background;
RV: Star and Olympic emblem on eight snowflakes 150.00

Seal medal, bronze, 7 cm. 30.00

1960

Participant's medal, bronze, 4 cm, 3.4 grams.
OBV: Hand holding Olympic torch with inscription around rim;
RV: Squaw Valley Olympic logo with inscription around rim 700.00

Seal medal.
OBV: Portrait of man and woman facing to the left with inscription on rim;
RV: Olympic rings in center above words "HOCKEY SUR GLACE" with inscription around rim ... 40.00

1964

Participant's medal, bronze, 4 cm, 3.5 grams.
OBV: Innsbruck street scene with mountains in background;
RV: Innsbruck Olympic emblem with inscription around rim 400.00

Seal medal.
OBV: Mountain scene with sharp-cornered inscription "Innsbruck 1964" around top rim and "Torlauf" at bottom 25.00

Commemorative medal, silver, 3 cm, 9.4 grams.
OBV: Town scene with mountains in background and inscription on rim;
RV: Olympic rings above Innsbruck symbol .. 35.00

Commemorative medal, silver, 5 cm, 46.5 grams.
OBV: Old Innsbruck street scene with church and surrounding buildings;
RV: Four sports (bobsledding, skiing, ski jumping and skating) in quadrants with Olympic rings in center 50.00

1968

Participant's medal, bronze, 4 cm, 3.3 grams.
OBV: Athlete's bust facing to left surronded by snowflakes/fir branches;
RV: Panoramic view of Grenoble including "Grenoble 1968" at left and Grenoble logo at right 350.00

Seal medal.
OBV: Grenoble ice crystal symbol above Olympic rings and "GRENOBLE 1968" inscription 20.00

Commemorative medal, silver.
OBV: Ski jumper with Olympic rings below, date and three flowers to right, and inscription around rim;
RV: View of Grenoble with eight winter sportsmen around rim 45.00

1972

Participant's medal, bronze, 4 cm, 3.7 grams.
OBV: Two attached stylized arrows facing upward;
RV: Japanese sun, snowflake, Olympic rings and

"Sapparo '72" in English and Japanese 700.00

Participant's medal for Soviet team members, bronze, 6 cm.
OBV: Sickle in background with Russian inscription in black square on right and Olympic rings on left;
RV: Rounded snowflake (Sapporo logo) with Russian inscription in center 150.00

Fund raising medal, bronze, 3.3 cm.
OBV: Ski jumper above "XI Olympic Winter Games";
RV: Logos in rectangle above inscriptions in Japanese and English 20.00

Commemorative medal, silver, 3.4 cm., 18 grams
OBV: Snowflake logo, Japanese arch and Olympic rings on mountain side with Japanese and English inscriptions on rim;
RV: Eight winter sport events 40.00

Participant's medal, bronze.
OBV: Sapporo logo on Japanese island with Japanese inscriptions on rim;
RV: Japanese sun, snowflake, and Olympic Rings, Sapporo '72, English inscriptions around rim 150.00

1976

Participant's medal, bronze, 4 cm, 3.5 grams.
OBV: Quaint Innsbruck scene with mountains in background and arena in foreground;
RV: Innsbruck emblem among ice crystals with inscription around rim 250.00

Commemorative medal, silver, 3.2 cm, 20 grams.
OBV: Austrian Olympic Committee (ÖOC) logo above Olympic rings with inscription around rim;
RV: ÖOC logo with rings on elaborate snowflake in center with nine winter sports figures accompanied by nine inscriptions of the sports (ex. "BOB," "BIATHLON,". . .) 60.00

Commemorative medal, silver, 3.4 cm, 15 grams.
OBV: Panoramic town scene with inscription over mountains in background;
RV: Olympic rings in center surrounded by nine figures in winter events 30.00

Commemorative medal, silver, 3.5 cm, 15 grams.
OBV: Two speed skaters beneath Olympic rings;
RV: Flame and mountains above Olympic rings with inscription around rim 25.00

1980

Participant's nickel-silver medal, 4 cm, 3.5 grams.
OBV: Nine winter sport figures featuring clockwise from top: ski jumping, biathlon, ice hockey, luge, cross-country skiing, downhill skiing, figure skating, speed skating and bobsled;
RV: Lake Placid logo in center surrounded by four rings featuring an athlete's vow inscription; designed by Marcel Jovine 300.00

Commemorative mascot medal, bronze, 3.7 cm.
OBV: Head of Roni the raccoon with inscription "1980 Lake Placid";
RV: Lake Placid Olympic logo in center with dates at bottom and inscription around rim 20.00

Commemorative bronze medal, 7.6 cm.
OBV: Lake Placid logo in center surrounded by eight "petals" with a different winter sports portrayed in each; sports include cross country and downhill skiing, ski jumping, speed skating, figure skating, ice hockey, bobsled and biathlon;
RV: 1980 calendar with torches at sides and skis and hockey sticks at bottom 40.00

Seal medal.
OBV: Muscular forearm and hand holding torch with Olympic rings to right, inscription to left and mountains in background;
RV: Large pine branch on right with inscription to left and Lake Placid logo at top 25.00

1984

Participant's medal, bronze, one-sided.
Unique design, rectangular shape at top dropping down into circular design -- looks like an elongated keyhole. Sarajevo emblem in center, with "Sarajevo '84" on three lines 400.00

Friendship medal, bronze, 6.4 cm.
Sarajevo to Los Angeles.
OBV: Dove with peace branch flying over Olympic rings and torch, inscribed with "1984" and "Sarajevo - Los Angeles";
RV: Los Angeles Star-in-Motion logo, Olympic rings and Sarajevo logo within oval in center with inscription around rim in English and Slavic . . 50.00

1988

Participant's bronze medal. 6.3 cm.
OBV: Calgary logo above Olympic rings with inscription around rim;
RV: View of Olympic stadium and Calgary buildings with mountains behind, torch at left, "CITIUS ALTIUS FORTIUS" at base 200.00

Volunteer medal.
Similar to above medal, except mountains only on reverse 75.00

Commemorative bronze ceremonies medal, 3.5 cm.
OBV: identical to participant medal;
RV: arc-shaped torch with linear flame, above "CEREMONIES", "MCMLXXXVIII" and Olympic Rings 125.00

Commemorative silver medal. 4.0 cm.
OBV: Skier within three-sided frame which features an inscription and a maple leaf in upper right;
RV: Two hemisphere globes and generic snowflake within same frame as OBV 40.00

1992

Albertville participant's medal 300.00

PENNANTS

BASEBALL PENNANTS

1914 B18 BLANKETS

No.	Player	Value
la.	Babe Adams (Purple pennants)	35.00
lb.	Babe Adams (Red pennants)	40.00
2a.	Sam Agnew (Purple basepaths)	35.00
2b.	Sam Agnew (Red basepaths)	40.00
3a.	Eddie Ainsmith (Green pennants)	15.00
3b.	Eddie Ainsmith (Brown pennants)	15.00
4a.	Jimmy Austin (Purple basepaths)	35.00
4b.	Jimmy Austin (Red basepaths)	40.00
5a.	Del Baker (White infield)	15.00
5b.	Del Baker (Brown infield)	70.00
5c.	Del Baker (Red infield)	270.00
6a.	Johnny Bassler (Purple pennants)	35.00
6b.	Johnny Basaler (Yellow pennants)	70.00
7a.	Paddy Bauman (White infield)	15.00
7b.	Paddy Bauman (Brown infield)	70.00
7c.	Paddy Bauman (Red infield)	270.00
8a.	Luke Boone (Blue infield)	15.00
8b.	Luke Boone (Green infield)	15.00
9a.	George Burns (Brown basepaths)	15.00
9b.	George Burns (Green basepaths)	15.00
10a.	Tioga George Burns (White infield)	15.00
10b.	Tioga George Burns (Brown infield)	70.00
11a.	Max Carey (Purple pennants)	70.00
11b.	Max Carey (Red pennants)	95.00
12a.	Marty Cavanaugh (White infield)	15.00
12b.	Marty Cavanaugh (Brown infield)	120.00
12c.	Marty Cavanaugh (Red infield)	270.00
12d.	Marty Cavanaugh	15.00
13a.	Frank Chance (Green infield)	35.00
13b.	Frank Chance (Brown Pn, Blinfield)	35.00
13c.	Frank Chance (Yellow Pn, Blinfield)	270.00
14a.	Ray Chapman (Purple pennants)	35.00
14b.	Ray Chapman (Yellow pennants)	70.00
15a.	Ty Cobb (White infield)	270.00
15b.	Ty Cobb (Brown infield)	600.00

Ty Cobb blanket

No.	Player	Value
15c.	Ty Cobb	2500.00
16a.	King Cole (Blue infield)	15.00
16b.	King Cole (Green infield)	15.00
17a.	Joe Connolly (White infield)	15.00
17b.	Joe Connolly (Brown infield)	70.00
18a.	Harry Coveleski (White infield)	15.00
18b.	Harry Coveleski (Brown infield)	70.00
19a.	George Cutshaw (Blue infield)	15.00
19b.	George Cutshaw (Green infield)	15.00
20a.	Jake Daubert (Blue infield)	20.00
20b.	Jake Daubert (Green infield)	20.00
21a.	Ray Demmitt (White infield)	15.00
21b.	Ray Demmitt (Brown infield)	70.00
22a.	Bill Doak (Purple pennants)	35.00
22b.	Bill Doak (Yellow pennants)	70.00
23a.	Cozy Dolan (Purple pennants)	35.00
23b.	Cozy Dolan (Yellow pennants)	70.00
24a.	Larry Doyle (Brown basepaths)	20.00
24b.	Larry Doyle (Green basepaths)	20.00
25a.	Art Fletcher (Brown basepaths)	15.00
25b.	Art Fletcher (Green basepaths)	15.00
26a.	Eddie Foster (Brown pennants)	15.00
26b.	Eddie Foster (Green pennants)	15.00
27a.	Del Gainor (White infield)	15.00
27b.	Del Gainor (Brown infield)	70.00
28a.	Chick Gandil (Brown pennants)	20.00
28b.	Chick Gandil (Green pennants)	20.00
29a.	George Gibson (Purple pennants)	35.00
29b.	George Gibson (Red pennants)	40.00
30a.	Hank Gowdy (White infield)	15.00
30b.	Hank Gowdy (Brown infield)	70.00
30c.	Hank Gowdy (Red infield)	275.00
31a.	Jack Graney (Purple pennants)	35.00
31b.	Jack Graney (Yellow pennants)	70.00

Shoeless Joe Jackson blanket

No.	Player	Value
32a.	Eddie Grant (Brown basepaths)	15.00
32b.	Eddie Grant (Green basepaths)	15.00
33a.	Tommy Griffith (White infield)	15.00
33b.	Tommy Griffith (Brown infield)	275.00
34a.	Earl Hamilton (Purple basepaths)	35.00
34b.	Earl Hamilton (Red basepaths)	40.00
35a.	Roy Hartzell (Blue infield)	15.00
35b.	Roy Hartzell (Green infield)	15.00
36a.	Miller Huggins (Purple pennants)	70.00
36b.	Miller Huggins (Yellow pennants)	150.00

37a.	John Hummel (Brown infield)	15.00
37b.	John Hummel (Green infield)	15.00
38a.	Ham Hyatt (Purple pennants)	35.00
38b.	Ham Hyatt (Red pennants)	40.00
39a.	Shoeless J.Jackson (Purple)	1200.00
39b.	Shoeless Joe Jackson (Yellow)	1500.00
40a.	Bill James (White infield)	15.00
40b.	Bill James (Brown infield)	70.00
41a.	Walter Johnson (Brown pennants)	275.00
41b.	Walter Johnson (Green pennants)	275.00
42a.	Ray Keating (Blue infield)	15.00
42b.	Ray Keating (Green infield)	15.00
43a.	Joe Kelley (Purple pennants)	70.00
43b.	Joe Kelley (Red pennants)	100.00
44a.	Ed Konetchy (Purple pennants)	35.00
44b.	Ed Konetchy (Red pennants)	40.00
45a.	Nemo Leibold (Purple pennants)	35.00
45b.	Nemo Leibold (Yellow pennants)	70.00
46a.	Fritz Maisel (Blue infield)	15.00
46b.	Fritz Maisel (Green infield)	15.00
47a.	Les Mann (White infield)	15.00
47b.	Lea Mann (Brown infield)	70.00
48a.	Rabbit Maranville (White infield)	40.00
48b.	Rabbit Maranville (Brown infield)	150.00
48c.	Rabitt Maranville (Red infield)	350.00
49a.	Bill McAllister (Purple pennants)	35.00
49b.	Bill McAllister (Red pennants)	40.00
50a.	George McBride (Brown pennants)	15.00
50b.	George McBride (Green pennants)	15.00
51a.	Chief Meyers (Brown basepaths)	15.00
51b.	Chief Meyers (Green pennants)	15.00
52a.	Clyde Milan (Brown pennants)	15.00
52b.	Clyde Milan (Green pennants)	15.00
53a.	Dots Miller (Purple pennants)	35.00
53b.	Dots Miller (Yellow pennants)	70.00
54a.	Otto Miller (Blue infield)	15.00
54b.	Otto Miller (Green infield)	15.00
55a.	Willie Mitchell (Purple pennants)	35.00
55b.	Willie Mitchell (Yellow pennants)	70.00
56a.	Danny Moeller (Brown pennants)	15.00
56b.	Danny Moeller (Green pennants)	15.00
57a.	Ray Morg (Brown pennants)	15.00
57b.	Ray Morg (Green pennants)	15.00
58a.	George Moriarty (White infield)	15.00
58b.	George Moriarty (Brown infield)	70.00
58c.	George Moriarty (Red infield)	275.00
59a.	Mike Mowrey (Purple pennants)	35.00

59b.	Mike Mowrey (Red pennants)	40.00
60a.	Red Murray (Brown basepaths)	15.00
60b.	Red Murray (Green basepaths)	15.00
61a.	Ivy Olson (Purple pennants)	35.00
61b.	Ivy Olson (Yellow pennants)	70.00
62a.	Steve O'Neill (Purple pennants)	35.00
62b.	Steve O'Neill (Red pennants)	70.00
63a.	Marty O'Toole (Purple pennants)	35.00
63b.	Marty O'Toole (Red pennants)	40.00
64a.	Roger Peckinpaugh (Blue infield)	20.00
64b.	Roger Peckinpaugh (Green infield)	20.00
65a.	Hub Perdue (White infield)	15.00
65b.	Hub Perdue (Brown infield)	70.00
66a.	Del Pratt (Purple pennants)	35.00
66b.	Del Pratt (Yellow pennants)	40.00
67a.	Hank Robinson (Purple pennants)	35.00
67b.	Hank Robinson (Yellow pennants)	70.00
68a.	Nap Rucker (Blue infield)	15.00
68b.	Nap Rucker (Green infield)	15.00
69a.	Slim Sallee (Purple pennants)	35.00
69b.	Slim Sallee (Yellow pennants)	70.00
70a.	Howard Shanks (Brown pennants)	15.00
70b.	Howard Shanks (Green pennants)	15.00
71a.	Burt Shotton (Purple basepaths)	35.00
71b.	Burt Shotton (Red basepaths)	40.00
72a.	Red Smith (Blue infield)	15.00
72b.	Red Smith (Green infield)	15.00
73a.	Fred Snodgrass (Brown basepaths)	20.00
73b.	Fred Snodgrass (Green basepaths)	20.00
74a.	Bill Steele (Purple pennants)	35.00
74b.	Bill Steele (Yellow pennants)	70.00
75a.	Casey Stengel (Blue infield)	125.00
76b.	Casey Stengel (Green infield)	125.00
76a.	Jeff Sweeney (Blue infield)	15.00
76b.	Jeff Sweeney (Green infield)	15.00
77a.	Jeff Teareau (Brown basepaths)	15.00
77b.	Jeff Teareau (Green infield)	15.00
78a.	Terry Turner (Purple pennants)	35.00
78b.	Terry Turner (Yellow pennants)	70.00
79a.	Lefty Tyler (White infield)	15.00
79b.	Lefty Tyler (Brown infield)	70.00
79c.	Lefty Tyler (Red infield)	275.00
80a.	Jim Viox (Purple pennants)	35.00
80b.	Jim Viox (Red pennants)	40.00
81a.	Bull Wagner (Blue infield)	15.00
81b.	Bull Wagner (Green infield)	15.00
82a.	Bobby Wallace (Purple basepaths)	70.00

82b.	Bobby Wallace (Red basepaths)	70.00
83a.	Dee Walsh (Purple basepaths)	35.00
83b.	Dee Walsh (Green basepaths)	40.00
84a.	Jimmy Walsh (Blue infield)	15.00
84b.	Jimmy Walsh (Green infield)	15.00
85a.	Bart Whaling (White infield)	15.00
85b.	Bart Whaling (Brown infield)	70.00
85c.	Bart Whaling (Red infield)	275.00
86a.	Zach Wheat (Blue infield)	70.00
86b.	Zach Wheat (Green infield)	70.00
87a.	Possum Whitted (Purple pennants)	35.00
87b.	Possum Whitted (Yellow pennants)	70.00
88a.	Gus Williams (Purple basepaths)	35.00
88b.	Gus Williams (Red pennants)	40.00
89a.	Owen Wilson (Purple pennants)	35.00
89b.	Owen Wilson (Yellow pennants)	70.00
90a.	Hooks Wiltse (Brown basepaths)	15.00
90b.	Hooks Wiltse (Green basepaths)	15.00

1916 BF2 FELT PENNANTS

No.	Player	Value
1.	Grover Alexander	125.00
2.	Jimmy Archer	35.00
3.	Home Run Baker	125.00
4.	Dave Bancroft	55.00
5.	Jack Barry	35.00
6.	Chief Bender	125.00
7.	Joe Benz	35.00
8.	Mordecai Brown	100.00
9.	George J. Burns	35.00
10.	Donie Bush	35.00
11.	Hick Cady	35.00
12.	Max Carey	35.00
13.	Ray Chapman	45.00
14.	Ty Cobb	500.00
15.	Eddie Collins	125.00
16.	Shano Collins	35.00
17.	Commy Comiskey	125.00
18.	Harry Coveleskie	35.00
19.	Gavvy Cravath	40.00
20.	Sam Crawford	100.00
21.	Jake Daubert	40.00
22.	Josh Devore	35.00
23.	Red Dooin	35.00
24.	Larry Doyle	35.00
25.	Jean Dubuc	35.00
26.	Johnny Evers	125.00
27.	Red Faber	100.00
28.	Eddie Foster	35.00
29.	Del Gainer	35.00
30.	Chick Gandil	45.00
31.	Joe Gedeon	35.00
32.	Hank Gowdy	35.00
33.	Earl Hamilton	35.00
34.	Claude Hendrix	35.00
35.	Buck Herzog	35.00
36.	Harry Hooper	50.00
37.	Miller Huggins	50.00
38.	Shoeless Joe Jackso	700.00
39.	Seattle Bill James	35.00
40.	Hugh Jennings	50.00
41.	Walter Johnson	300.00
42.	Fielder Jones	35.00
43.	Joe Judge	35.00
44.	Benny Kauff	35.00
45.	Bill Killefer	35.00
46.	Nap Lajoie	200.00
47.	Jack Lapp	35.00
48.	Doc Layan	35.00
49.	Jimmy Lavender	35.00
50.	Dutch Leonard	35.00
51.	Duffy Lewis	35.00
52.	Hans Lobert	35.00
53.	Fred Luderus	35.00
54.	Connie Mack	150.00
55.	Sherry Maggee	40.00
56.	Al Mamaux	35.00
57.	Rabbitt Maranville	100.00
58.	Rube Marquard	100.00
59.	George McBride	35.00
60.	John McGraw	75.00
61.	Stuffy McInnes	35.00
62.	Fred Merkle	40.00
63.	Chief Meyers	35.00
64.	Clyde Milan	35.00
65.	Otto Miller	35.00
66.	Pat Moran	35.00
67.	Ray Morgan	35.00
68.	Guy Morton	35.00
69.	Eddie Murphy	35.00
70.	Rube Oldring	35.00
71.	Dode Paskert	35.00
72.	Wally Pipp	50.00
73.	Pants Rowland	35.00
74.	Nap Rucker	35.00
75.	Dick Rudolph	35.00
76.	Reb Russell	35.00
77.	Vic Saier	35.00
78.	Slim Sallee	35.00
79.	Ray Schalk	100.00
80.	Wally Schang	35.00
81.	Wildfire Schulte	35.00
82.	Jim Scott	35.00
83.	George Sisler	125.00
84.	George Stallings	35.00
85.	Oscar Stanage	35.00
86.	Jeff Teareau	35.00
87.	Joe Tinker	125.00
88.	Lefty Tyler	35.00
89.	Hippo Vaughn	35.00
90.	Bobby Veach	35.00
91.	Honus Wagner	300.00
92.	Ed Walsh	100.00
93.	Buck Weaver	50.00
94.	Ivy Wingo	35.00
95.	Joe Wood	50.00
96.	Ralph Young	35.00
97.	Heinie Zimmerman	35.00

1936-37 BF3 FELT PENNANTS TYPE I

No.	Player	Value
1.	Luke Appling (batting)	20.00
2.	Wally Berger (fielding)	10.00
3.	Zeke Bonura (fielding ground ball)	10.00
4.	Dolph Camilli (fielding)	10.00
5.	Ben Chapman (batting)	10.00
6.	Mickey Cochrane (catching)	20.00
7.	Rip Collins (batting)	10.00
8.	Joe Cronin (batting)	20.00
9.	Kiki Cuyler (running)	20.00

(Clockwise) Wally Berger, Charley Grimm, Carl Hubbell

No.	Player	Value
10.	Dizzy Dean (pitching)	35.00
11.	Frank Demaree (batting)	10.00
12.	Paul Derringer (pitching)	10.00
13.	Bill Dickey (catching)	30.00
14.	Jimmy Dykes (fielding)	10.00
15.	Bob Feller (pitching)	30.00
16.	Wes Ferrell (running)	10.00
17.	Jimmy Foxx (batting)	30.00
18.	Larry French (batting)	10.00
19.	Franky Frisch (running)	20.00
20.	Lou Gehrig (fielding at 1st base)	150.00
21.	Charles Gehringer (running)	20.00
22.	Lefty Gomez (pitching)	20.00
23.	Goose Goslin (batting)	20.00
24.	Hank Greenberg (fielding)	20.00
25.	Charlie Grimm (running)	15.00
26.	Lefty Grove (pitching)	20.00
27.	Gabby Hartnett (catching)	20.00
28.	Rollie Hemsley (catching)	10.00
29.	Billy Herman (fielding at 1st base)	20.00
30.	Frank Higgins (rielding)	10.00
31.	Rogers Hornsby (batting)	20.00
32.	Carl Hubbell (pitching)	20.00
33.	Chuck Klein (throwing)	20.00
34.	Tony Lazzeri (batting)	10.00
35.	Hank Leiber (fielding ground ball)	10.00
36.	Ernie Lombardi (catching)	20.00
37.	Al Lopez (throwing)	20.00
38.	Gus Mancuso (running)	10.00
39.	Heinie Manush (batting)	20.00
40.	Pepper Martin (batting)	15.00
41.	Joe McCarthy (kneeling)	20.00
42.	Wally Moses (running)	10.00
43.	Van Mungo (standing)	10.00
44.	Mel Ott (throwing)	30.00
45.	Schoolboy Rowe (pitching)	15.00
46.	Babe Ruth (batting)	250.00
47.	George Selkirk (batting)	10.00
48.	Luke Sewell (sliding)	10.00

49.	Joe Stripp (batting)	10.00
50.	Hal Trosky (rielding)	10.00
51.	Floyd Vaughan (running, script sig.)	20.00
52.	Floyd Vaughan (running, not script sig.)	20.00
53.	Paul Waner (batting)	20.00
54.	Lon Warneke (pitching)	10.00
55.	Jimmy Wilson (fielding ground ball)	10.00
56.	Joe Vosmik (running)	10.00

TYPE II

No.	Player	Value
1.	Luke Appling (batting)	20.00
2.	Zeke Bonura (batting)	10.00
3.	Dolph Camilli (batting)	10.00

No.	Player	Value
4.	Dizzy Dean (batting)	35.00
5.	Frank Demaree (batting)	10.00
6.	Bob Feller (pitching)	35.00
7.	Wes Ferrell (throwing)	10.00
8.	Frank Frisch (fielding)	20.00
9.	Lou Gehrig (batting)	85.00
10.	Lou Gehrig (fielding)	85.00
11.	Hank Greenberg (throwing)	20.00
12.	Charlie Grimm (fielding)	10.00
13.	Charlie Grimm (throwing)	10.00
14.	Lefty Grove (pitching)	20.00
15.	Gabby Hartnett (batting)	20.00
16.	Billy Herman (batting	20.00
17.	Tony Lazzeri (running)	15.00
18.	Tony Lazzeri (throwing)	15.00
19.	Hank Leiber (batting)	10.00
20.	Ernie Lombardi (batting)	20.00
21.	Ducky Medwick (batting)	20.00
22.	Joe Stripp (batting)	10.00
23.	Floyd Vaughan (batting)	20.00
24.	Joe Vosmik (throwing)	10.00
25.	Paul Waner (batting)	20.00
26.	Lon Warneke (batting	10.00
27.	Lon Warneke (pitching)	10.00

1992 Win Craft

Abbot, Jim	4.00
Boggs, Wade	3.00
Brett, George	3.00
Canseco, Jose	4.00
Clark, Will	4.00
Dawson, Andre	3.00
Fielder, Cecil	3.00
Gooden, Dwight	3.00
Grace, Mark	3.00
Griffey Jr., Ken	5.00
Henderson, Rickey	3.00
Hershiser, Orel	3.00
Hrbek, Kent	3.00
Jackson, Bo	3.00
Knoblauch, Chuck	3.00
Mattingly, Don	3.00
McGwire, Mark	4.00
Mitchell, Kevin	3.00
Molitor, Paul	3.00
Puckett, Kirby (1)	5.00
Puckett, Kirby (2)	5.00
Ripken, Cal (MVP)	5.00
Ryan, Nolan	6.00
Sandberg, Ryne	4.00
Smith, Ozzie	3.00
Strawberry, Darryl	3.00
Thomas, Frank	5.00
Trammel, Allan	3.00
Van Slyke, Andy	3.00
Yount, Robin	3.00

BASKETBALL PENNANTS

1992 Win Craft

Barkley, Charles	5.00
Bird, Larry	8.00
Coleman, Derrick	3.00
Divac, Vlade	3.00
Drexler, Clyde	4.00
Dumars, Joe	3.00
Johnson, Kevin	3.00
Johnson, Larry	5.00
Johnson, Larry (2)	5.00
Jordan, Michael	10.00
Kemp, Shawn	4.00
Kimble, Bo	3.00
Malone, Karl	4.00
Manning, Danny	3.00
Miller, Reggie	3.00
Mullin, Chris	4.00
O'Neal, Shaquille	6.00
Pippen, Scottie	4.00
Price, Mark	3.00
Richardson, Pooh	3.00
Robinson, David	5.00

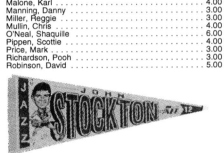

Stockton, John	4.00
Thomas, Isiah	3.00
Wilkens, Dominique	4.00
Worthy, James	3.00

FOOTBALL PENNANTS

1992 Win Craft

Aikman, Troy	6.00
Anderson, Neal	3.00
Anderson, Morten	3.00
Brister, Bubby	3.00
Cunningham, Randall	4.00
Elway, John	4.00
Esiason, Boomer	3.00
Everett, Jim	3.00
Harbaugh, Jim	3.00
Kelly, Jim	5.00
Kosar, Bernie	3.00
Long, Howie	3.00
Marino, Dan	5.00
Monk, Art	4.00
Montana, Joe	7.00
Moon, Warren	4.00
Okoye, Christian	3.00
Rice, Jerry	5.00
Rypien, Mark	4.00
Sanders, Deion	5.00
Simms, Phil	3.00
Smith, Emmitt	8.00
Taylor, Lawrence	5.00
Thomas, Derrick	4.00
Thomas, Thurman	5.00
Young, Steve	4.00

PERIODICAL COLLECTING

by Beryl Blatt

Collecting has certainly become a big business, as the values of baseball, football, basketball and hockey cards have skyrocketed over the past decade. Unfortunately, the hobby's high prices sometimes keep new collectors away. However, another form of collecting has emerged that is gaining popularity due to its affordability – publication collecting. Collecting publications can encompass magazines such as *Sports Illustrated, Sport, Dell Sports, Inside Sports, Street & Smith's*; programs from World Series games, All-Star games, Super Bowls, regular and post season college or pro games; newspapers like *The Sporting News, Baseball Weekly, Hockey News*, and *Pro Football Weekly*; media guides; hard cover books; pocket books and schedules.

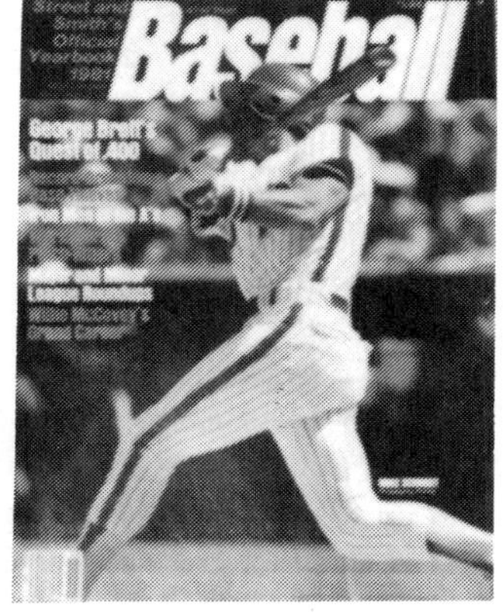

1981 Street & Smith's Baseball Yearbook

Methods of collecting publications and periodicals can vary with each hobbyist. Some may choose to collect only covers featuring their favorite players or team, while others may wish to collect the entire run of a magazine. There are those who only collect the baseball issues or football covers of a publication. Many try to get the covers autographed.

There are also people who collect specific articles appearing in magazines. This aspect of the hobby can prove difficult, as most dealers who handle publications list them by cover subject, not by the index of articles.

The collector who specializes in programs may want all the programs from their favorite team, home and away. They may want specialized programs from World Series or All-Star games. The first game program from a new ball park or a new team is always a desired collectible.

Media guides are usually given only to the media, but collectors have found ways to make them part of their collection. Sought after media guides are usually those that come out the year after a team has won a championship.

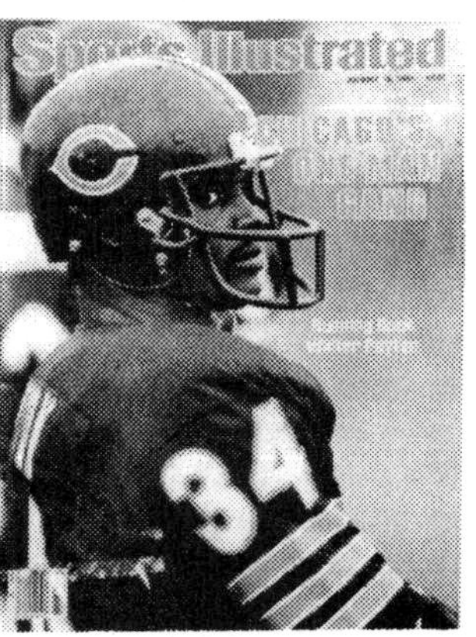

8/16/82 Sports Illustrated

Printed material has become an integral part of collecting for the game player; i.e. "APBA," "Strat-O-Matic," "Pursue the Pennant," and all of the various statistical computer games. These players will use media guides, *Red Books*, *Green Books*, and *The Sporting News Registers and Guides*. All of these publications will help game players get a hold on a team's past performance, essential for re-creation of actual games and seasons.

Rotisserie, or fantasy, sports have grown to such proportions that there are even magazines published just for that purpose. Players or "team owners" of fantasy leagues use league-issued media guides along with stat magazines like *Street & Smith's*, *Bill Mazeroski's*, *Dick Vitale's*, and specialized books to help them draft the best possible team.

College media guides and yearbooks have become popular due to collectors' inclinations to find information about what their favorite player did during his college career. People also find it interesting to see what a player looked like in his younger days. As a matter of fact, high school yearbooks with now-famous players have become a highly sought after collectible.

1948 Street & Smith's Baseball Yearbook

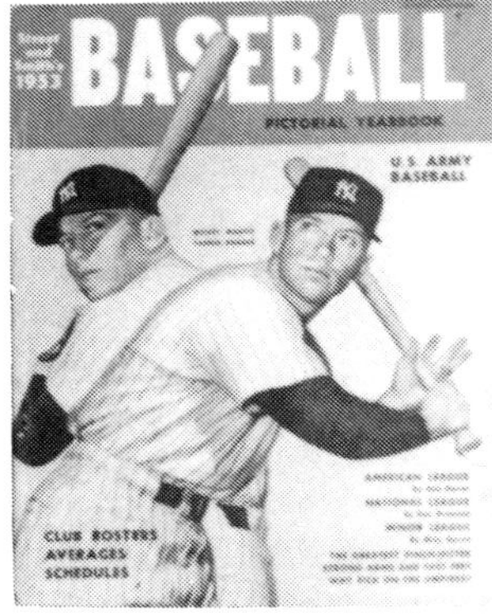

1953 Street & Smith's Baseball Yearbook

Many collectors also try to find specific items in magazines that could make them valuable. One item that fits in this category is the "Faces in the Crowd" section of *Sports Illustrated.* Some of the faces you might find depicted are Vincent Jackson and Don Mattingly. Of course, Jackson is known today as Bo. These sections have caused many of these publications to increase to a greater value.

Chesterfield, Camels, Pall Mall and other brands of cigarettes used athletes to endorse their products. In the '40s, '50s and '60s you may have found your favorite ball player pictured on the back cover of a sports publication advertising these products. Of course, these ads have appeared on the back of non-sport publications which also lend themselves to collecting. There are also times when a ball player will appear on the cover of a publication that has nothing to do with sports, the reason being the star has a direct interest in what the magazine is about. Joe DiMaggio has appeared on the cover of *Overdrive* trucker's magazine because he owns an 18 wheeler. For the collector who likes to collect items bearing his favorite player, this is a great avenue to pursue.

11/14/83 Sports Illustrated

In November 1984, Dr. James Beckett started publishing his *Baseball Card Monthly.* These magazines have become popular collectible items, partly due to their nice photos on both the front and back covers, as well as the artwork on the inside covers. Because of the popularity of the baseball price guide, Beckett added magazines focusing on additional sports such as football, basketball, hockey and future stars. The popularity of the player on the cover will generally determine the value of the magazine.

> Beryl Blatt, known as "The Queen of Publications" after eight years in the publications business, offers an up-to-date computerized listing of all the publications she has available, divided into categories so collectors can request a specific desired list.

PUBLICATIONS

AUTO RACING

1959 Racing Pictorial

RACING PICTORIAL

Year	Cover	Value
1959	USAC emblem, 6 race car drawings	200.00
60-61	Indy & Daytona Photos, race shots & hydroplane boat	50.00
61 Color	Daytona & Indy action photos	70.00
61-62 Ann.	A.J. Foyt (Indy winner) & Ned Jarrett (NASCAR winner)	50.00
62 Color	Indy winner R. Ward, NASCAR photos	70.00
62-63 Ann.	Rodger Ward car, Roger Penske roadster, Parnelli Jones	50.00
63 Color	8 NASCAR photos & 4 Indy photos	70.00
63-64 Ann.	4 Indy & 3 NASCAR drivers	50.00
64 Color	1: A.J. Foyt 2: R.& 6 NASCAR cars	50.00
64-65 Ann.	1: P. Jones, R. Ward & 2 action shots 2: R. Petty, Paul Goldsmith, Stock Cars, A.J. Foyt.	50.00
65 Sum.	1: Langhorne crash, Indy front row. 2: NASCAR, Leroy Yarborough,Fred Lorenzen	40.00
65 Fall	1: Foyt at Atlanta, Unser & Andretti 2: Jr. Johnson at Darlington, Norn Nelson at Milwaukee	40.00
65-66 Ann.	Jim Clark & Colin Chapman (Indy winner)	50.00
66 Spring	1: Jim Hurtibise, Richard Petty 2: D. Hutchinson, Petty, Lloyd Ruby	50.00
66 Sum.	Collage of Indy 500 Photos	40.00
66 Fall	Andretti, Darrel Derringer	40.00
66-67 Ann.	1: Andretti, Jack Brabham car 2: Dave Pearson, Norm Nelson	40.00
67 Spring	Collage of 7 Daytona 500 photos	35.00
67 Sum.	A.J. Foyt	35.00
67 Fall	Mark Donohue, Dennis Hulme	40.00
67-68 Ann.	Petty, Dennis Hulme F-1 racer	40.00
68 Spring	5 Daytona stock car photos	40.00
68 Sum.	6 photos of Indy 500 & Daytona	35.00
68 Fall	Can-Am 5 photos, Foyt dirt car, Andretti Indy car	35.00
68-69 Ann.		40.00
69 Spring	6 Daytona photos, Unser Indy car	35.00
69 Sum.	Indy winner; Andretti	35.00
69 Fall	7 photos of Andretti	35.00
69-70 Ann.	Bobby Isaac & Leroy Yarborough	35.00
70 Spring	9 Daytona 500 photos	40.00
70 Sum.	Sessions crash at Langhorne, Al Unser: Indy winner	30.00
70 Fall	Lothar Motschenbacher Can-Am driver	25.00
70-71 Ann.	Bobby Isaac's superbird, Roger McCluskey superbird	20.00
71 Spring	Al Unser; Indy winner	25.00
71 Sum.	Indy 500 start, Daytona action	20.00
71 Fall	Can-Am driver Pete Robson, Can-AM Jackie Stewart	25.00
71-72 Ann.	6 Daytona photos, Daytona 24 hour photo	35.00
72 Spring	Indy winner; Foyt	30.00
72 Sum.	Michigan NASCAR race, Indy start	22.00
72 Fall	Datsun SCCA cars, midget USAC flips	25.00
72-73 Ann.	A.J. Foyt	30.00
73 Spring	Richard Petty, Daytona winner	20.00
73 Sum.	Michigan Grand Nat. NASCAR photo, Johncock victory	25.00
73 Fall	Bobby & Donny Allison, Mark Donahue Can-Am race	25.00
73-74 Ann.	N.C. Speedway, Parsous, McCluskey	25.00
74 Spring	Petty, Daytona, Unser Ontario 500	25.00
74 Sum.	NASCAR at Atlanta, Indy start	22.00
74 Fall	Hoosier 100 dirt car race	25.00
74-75 Ann.	Cale Yarborough	20.00
75 Spring	Daytona, Foyt victory at Ontario	20.00
75 Sum.	Richard Petty, Daytona	25.00
75 Fall	Hoosier 100 start, Petty at Daytona	25.00
75-76 Ann.	Richard Petty	35.00
76 Spring	Daytona start, Indy start, A.J. Foyt	25.00
76 Sum.	Cale Yarborough, Johnny Rutherford	25.00
76 Fall	D. Pearson, A.J. Foyt	25.00
76-77 Ann.	Gordon Johncock, Cale Yarborough	20.00
77 Spring	Indy start, A.J. Foyt	25.00
77 Sum.	A.J. Foyt	25.00
77 Fall	Tom Sneva, Gordon Johncock	25.00
77-78 Ann.	Cale Yarborough	30.00
78 Spring	A.J. Foyt	25.00
78 Sum.	Al Unser, Cale Yarborough	25.00
78 Fall	A.J. Foyt	25.00
78-79 Ann.	Mario Andretti	25.00
79 Spring	A.J. Foyt	20.00
79 Sum.	Rick Mears	20.00
79 Fall	Al Unser	25.00
79-80 Ann.	A.J. Foyt at Daytona, Petty	30.00
80 Spring	Johnny Rutherford	20.00
80 Sum.	J. Rutherford, C. Yarborough	20.00
80 Fall	Gary Bettenhausen dirt championship car	20.00
80-81 Ann.	Dale Earnhardt	25.00
81 Spring	Johnny Rutherford	20.00
81 Sum.	A.J. Foyt	20.00
81 Fall	Larry Rice dirt champ car	20.00
81-82 Ann.	Darrel Waltrip	25.00
82 Spring	Rick Mears	15.00
82 Sum.	Gordon Johncock	15.00
82-83 Ann.	Darrel Waltrip	25.00
83 Spring	Gordon Johncock	20.00
83 Sum.	Sneva & victory lane, & trophy	15.00
83-84 Ann.	Bobby Allison	20.00
84 Spring	Mario Andretti, Toyota Grand Prix	15.00
85 Spring	Mario Andretti	15.00
86 Spring	Michael Andretti	15.00
86 Final	Bobby Rahal	15.00

1972 Summer: Racing Pictorial

BASEBALL

BASEBALL DIGEST

Issue	Cover	Price
Aug. 42	Elmer Valo	75.00
Sep. 42		15.00
Oct. 42	Pete Reiser	15.00
Nov. 42		15.00
Dec. 42		15.00
Jan.-June 1943		@12.50
July 43	Play at 2nd Base	12.00
Aug. 43	Inside Homer!	12.00
Sep. 43	Stan Musial	22.50
Oct. 43	Spud Chandler	12.00
Nov. 43	Johnny Lindell	12.00
Feb. 44	Bill Johnson	12.00
Mar. 44	Joe Sewell & Bill Nicholson	12.00
Apr. 44	Dixie Walker	12.00
May 44	Lou Boudreau	14.50
July 44	Vern Stephens	12.00
Aug. 44	Bucky Walters	12.00
Sep. 44	Charlie Grimm & G. Barr	12.00
Oct. 44	Walker Cooper	12.00
Nov. 44	Marty Marion	12.00
Feb. 45	Hal Newhouser	13.50
Mar. 45	Grover Hartley	12.00
Apr. 45	Dixie Walker	12.00
May 45	Bill Voiselle	12.00
July 45	Hank Borowy	12.00
Aug. 45	Tommy Holmes	12.00
Sep. 45	Stan Hack	12.00
Oct. 45	Hank Greenberg	14.00
Nov. 45	Al Lopez	12.00
Feb. 46	Charlie Keller	12.00
Mar. 46	B. Considine	12.00
Apr. 46	Bobby Doerr	12.00
May 46	Bob Feller	15.00
July 46	Ted Williams & Joe DiMaggio	20.00
Aug. 46	Joe Cronin	14.00
Sep. 46	Hank Wyse	12.00
Oct. 46	Boo Feriss	12.00
Nov. 46	J. Pesky & R. Schoendienst	12.00
Feb. 47	Bucky Harris	12.00
Mar. 47	J. Rigney & P. Knudsen	12.00
Apr. 47	J. Van Cuyk	12.00
May 47	B. Herman & Hank Greenberg	15.00
July 47	Lou Boudreau & Joe Gordon	14.00
Aug. 47	B. Kerr	12.00
Sep. 47	Ewell Blackwell	12.00
Oct. 47	Joe DiMaggio	20.00
Nov. 47	R. LaPointe	12.00
Jan. 48	Joe Page	12.00
Feb. 48	Leo Durocher & Branch Rickey	14.00
Mar. 48	Meyer, Ennis, Hubbard	10.00
Apr. 48	Joe McCarthy	12.00
May 48	Art Houtteman	12.00
June 48	Willard Marshall	10.00
July 48	Ralph Kiner	15.00
Aug. 48	Lou Boudreau	15.00
Sep. 48	Stan Musial	15.00
Oct. 48	Hank Sauer	12.00
Nov. 48	P. Fagan	10.00
Jan. 49	Jim Hegan	10.00
Feb. 49	Red Rolfe	10.00
Mar. 49	Ted Williams	20.00
Apr. 49	Joe DiMaggio	20.00
May 49	Play at the Plate	12.00
June 49	Robin Roberts	18.00
July 49	J. Groth	9.00
Aug. 49	Frankie Frisch	15.00
Sep. 49	Vic Raschi	10.00
Oct. 49	Mel Parnell, Birdie Tebbetts	10.00
Nov. 49	J. Jorgensen	9.00
Jan. 50	Roy Smalley & Richie Ashburn	12.00
Feb. 50	Dave Koslo	8.00
Mar. 50	1950 Baseball Rules	9.00
Apr. 50	1950 Rosters	10.00
May 50	Stanky, Dark, J. Kramer	10.00
June 50	Joe DiMaggio	15.00
July 50	Phil Rizzuto	12.00
Aug. 50	Dick Sisler	8.00
Sep. 50	Larry Jansen, Art Houtteman	8.00
Oct. 50	Evers	8.00
Nov. 50	Jim Konstanty	8.00
Jan. 51	Yogi Berra, Whitey Ford	12.00
Feb. 51	Gil Hodges	12.00
Mar. 51	Eddie Yost	8.00
Apr. 51	Joe DiMaggio	15.00
May 51	Earnshaw, Fogg	7.00
June 51	Ted Williams	15.00
July 51	Irv Noren	7.00
Aug. 51	Nellie Fox, Paul Richards	12.00
Sep. 51	Stan Musial	15.00
Oct. 51	Gil McDougald	8.00
Nov. 51	Charlie Dressen	7.00
Jan. 52	Eddie Lopat, Phil Rizzuto	12.00
Feb. 52	Eddie Stanky	8.00
Mar. 52	S. Gordan	7.00
Apr. 52	Mike Garcia	7.00
May 52	George Staley	7.00
June 52	Pee Wee Reese	10.00
July 52	Ted Kluzewski	10.00
Aug. 52	Bobby Schantz	7.00
Sep. 52	Sal Maglie	8.00
Oct. 52	Carl Erskine	8.00
Nov. 52	Duke Snider	12.00
Jan. 53	Robin Roberts	12.00
Feb. 53	Eddie Matthews	9.00
Mar. 53	Billy Martin	10.00
Apr. 53	Stan Musial, Mickey Mantle	12.00
May 53	Carl Furillo	10.00
June 53	Bob Lemon	8.00
July 53	Logan, Kellner, Dorish	7.00
Aug. 53	Robin Roberts	12.00
Sep. 53	O'Connell, Strickland, Trucks	7.00
Oct. 53	Casey Stengel	10.00
Jan. 54	Billy Martin	10.00
Mar. 54	Jimmy Piersall	8.00
Apr. 54	Whitey Ford	10.00
May 54	Harvey Kuenn	8.00
June 54	Morgan, E. Matthews	9.00
July 54	Bob Turley	7.50
Aug. 54	Keegan	7.00
Sep. 54	Willie Mays	12.00
Oct. 54	World Series Issue	7.00
N/D. 54	Dusty Rhodes	7.00
J/F. 55	Ralph Kiner, Sarni	10.00
Mar. 55	1955 Rookies	10.00
Apr. 55	Alvin Dark	7.50
May 55	Don Mueller, Bob Lemon	7.50
June 55	Bobby Avila	7.00
July 55	Bill Skowron	7.50
Aug. 55	McMillian, Al Smith	7.00
Sep. 55	Don Newcombe	8.50
Oct. 55	Walter Alston, Tommy Byrne	8.00
Nov. 55	Johnny Podres	8.00
Feb. 56	Al Kaline	10.00
Mar. 56	Rookie Report	9.00
Apr. 56	Luis Aparicio	8.50
May 56	Higgins	7.00
June 56	Clem Labine	7.50
July 56	Mickey Mantle	15.00
Aug. 56	Dale Long	7.50
Sep. 56	Yogi Berra	10.00
Oct. 56	World Series	12.00
N/D. 56	Don Larsen	9.00

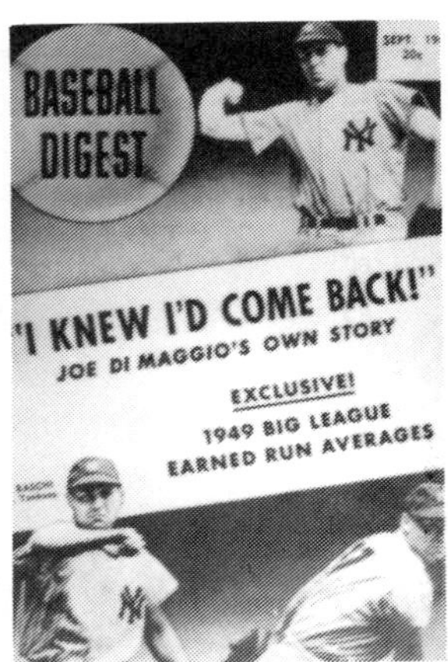

Baseball Digest: August, 1942; July, 1945; September, 1949

Baseball Digest: December, 1956

Issue	Yr	Subject	Price
J/F.	57	Robin Roberts	10.00
Mar.	57	Scouting Reports	10.00
Apr.	57	Farrell, Tighe,Scheffing	8.00
May	57	Don Blasingame	7.00
June	57	Breaking Up the D.P.	7.00
July	57	Don Hoak	7.00
Aug.	57	Stan Musial	10.00
Sep.	57	Bobby Shantz	7.50
O/N.	57	Babe Ruth (World Series)	10.00
D/J.	58	Lew Burdette	7.50
Feb.	58	V. McDaniel	7.00
Mar.	58	Scouting Reports	9.00
Apr.	58	Duke Snider, Willie Mays	12.00
May	58	Ted Williams	15.00
June	58	Stan Musial	15.00
July	58	Warren Spahn	10.00
Aug.	58	Bob Turley	8.00
Sep.	58	Pete Runnels	7.00
O/N.	58	World Series Thrills	8.00
D/J.	59	Turley, J. Jensen, R. Roberts	9.00
Feb.	59	Baseball's Darling Daughters	7.00
Mar.	59	Scouting Reports	9.00
Apr.	59	Ernie Banks	12.00
May	59	Juan Pizarro	7.00
June	59	Antonelli, Pascual, Landis	7.00
July	59	Vada Pinson	7.50
Aug.	59	Hoyt Wilhelm	8.00
Sep.	59	Elroy Face & Rocky Colavito	8.00
O/N.	59	World Series	10.00
D/J.	60	Larry Sherry, John Roseboro	7.00
Feb.	60	Harvey Kuenn	8.00
Mar.	60	Scouting Reports	9.00
Apr.	60	Willie McCovey	9.00
May	60	Early Wynn	8.00
June	60	Bunning, McDaniel, Francona	7.00
July	60	Vern Law	7.00
Aug.	60	Roberto Clemente	10.00
Sep.	60	Ron Hansen	5.50
O/N.	60	Dick Groat	6.50
D/J.	61	Bill Virdon	7.00
Feb.	61	Ralph Houk	6.00
Mar.	61	Scouting Reports	8.00
Apr.	61	Tony Kubek	7.50
May	61	Glenn Hobbie	5.50
June	61	Earl Battey	5.50
July	61	Wally Moon	6.00
Aug.	61	Norm Cash	8.00
Sep.	61	Whitey Ford	9.00
O/N.	61	Koufax,Robinson, M & M Boys	12.00
D/J.	62	Ralph Terry & Elston Howard	7.00
Feb.	62	Joey Jay	6.00
Mar.	62	Scouting Reports	8.00
Apr.	62	Orlando Cepeda	7.00
May	62	Babe Ruth	12.00
June	62	Mickey Mantle	14.00
July	62	Donovan	5.50
Aug.	62	20 Dramatic Home Runs	8.00
Sep.	62	Rich Rollins	5.50
O/N.	62	Tom Tresh & Frank Howard	8.00
D/J.	63	Ralph Terry	6.00
Feb.	63	Ty Cobb & Maury Wills	8.00
Mar.	63	Scouting Reports	8.00
Apr.	63	1963 Rosters	8.00
May	63	Drysdale, Dean, Grove	8.50
June	63	Al Kaline	9.00
July	63	Jim O'Toole	6.00
Aug.	63	Jim Bouton	6.00
Sep.	63	Denny LeMaster	5.50
O,N.	63	Al Downing	6.00
D/J.	64	Dodgers Aces	7.00
Feb.	64	Roger Maris	14.00
Mar.	64	Scouting Reports	8.00
Apr.	64	Sandy Koufax	10.00
May	64	Harmon Killebrew	8.00
June	64	Tommy Davis & C.Yastrzemski	8.50
July	64	Jim Maloney	6.00
Aug.	64	Dave Nicholson	5.50
Sep.	64	Bennett, W. Smith	6.00
O/N.	64	Miracle Braves	8.00
D/J.	65	Dick Groat	6.00
Feb.	65	Winter Trades	7.00
Mar.	65	Scouting Reports	8.00
Apr.	65	Which Tag is Phony?	5.50
May	65	Bill Freehan	5.50
June	65	Tony Conigliaro	8.00
July	65	Yankees' Six Mistakes	8.00
Aug.	65	Don Drysdale	8.00
Sep.	65	Pete Ward & Joe Morgan	6.50
O/N.	65	Biggest W.S. Mysteries	6.00
D/J.	66	Sandy Koufax	9.00
Feb.	66	Willie Mays	9.00
Mar.	66	Scouting Reports	8.00
Apr.	66	1966 Rosters	8.00
May	66	Sam McDowell	6.00
June	66	Should Rules Be Changed?	5.50
July	66	Juan Marichal	7.00
Aug.	66	Gene Alley, Bill Mazeroski	6.00
Sep.	66	George Scott	6.00
O/N.	66	World Series Special	7.00
D/J.	67	Drabowsky, Palmer, W.Bunker	7.00
Feb.	67	Allison, Drysdale, Mathews	6.50
Mar.	67	Scouting Reports	8.00
Apr.	67	1967 Rosters	8.00
May	67	Roger Maris	14.00
June	67	Gaylord Perry, Juan Marichal	10.00
Aug.	67	Joel Horlen	5.00
Sep.	67	Tim McCarver	6.50
O/N.	67	World Series Special	6.00
D/J.	68	Bob Gibson	7.00
Feb.	68	Williams & Others	7.00
Mar.	68	Scouting Reports	8.00
Apr.	68	1968 Rosters	8.00
May	68	R.Carew, J.Johnstone, R. Nye	7.00
June	68	Cookie Rojas & Nelson Briles	5.50
July	68	Jerry Koosman	7.00
Aug.	68	Andy Kosco	5.00
Sep.	68	Matty Alou & Ken Harrelson	6.00
O/N.	68	Bob Gibson, Denny McLain	8.00
D/J.	69	World Series	6.00
Feb.	69	Mickey Mantle	14.00
Mar.	69	Scouting Reports	8.00
Apr.	69	1969 Rosters	8.00
May	69	Al Lopez	6.00
June	69	Ernie Banks	8.00
July	69	Tony Conigliaro	9.00
Aug.	69	Frank Robinson	8.00
Sep.	69	Baseball Flirts With Tragedy	5.00
Oct.	69	World Series Special	6.00
Nov.	69	Super Stars of the 70s	7.00
Dec.	69	Tom Seaver	9.00

Baseball Digest: November, 1968

Issue	Yr	Subject	Price
Jan.	70	Harmon Killebrew	6.50
Feb.	70	Joe Pepitone	4.00
Mar.	70	Gene Alley	4.00
Apr.	70	Tony Perez	5.00
May	70	Roberto Clemente	9.00
June	70	Mel Stottlemyre	4.50
July	70	Ken Holtzman	4.50
Aug.	70	Sal Bando	4.50
Sep.	70	Jim Hickman	4.00
Oct.	70	Jim Palmer	6.50
Nov.	70	Johnny Bench	8.00
Dec.	70	Billy Williams	6.50
Jan.	71	Brooks Robinson	6.50
Feb.	71	Juan Marichal & Sal Bando	6.00
Mar.	71	Carl Yastrzemski	8.00
Apr.	71	Bob Gibson	6.50
May	71	Willie Mays	9.00
June	71	Tony Oliva	6.00
July	71	Hank Aaron	9.00
Aug.	71	Vida Blue	4.50
Sep.	71	Joe Pepitone	4.00
Oct.	71	World Series	6.00
Nov.	71	Bobby Murcer	4.50
Dec.	71	Joe Torre	5.00
Jan.	72	Steve Blass	3.50
Feb.	72	E. Williams	3.50
Mar.	72	Frank Robinson	7.50
Apr.	72	Bill Melton	4.50
May	72	1972 Rosters	5.50
June	72	Reggie Jackson	8.00
July	72	Richie Allen	5.50
Aug.	72	Bud Harrelson	4.00
Sep.	72	Roberto Clemente	8.00
Oct.	72	Gary Nolan	4.00
Nov.	72	Carlton Fisk	7.50
Dec.	72	Richie Allen	5.50
Jan.	73	Pete Rose	8.50
Feb.	73	Cesar Cedeno	5.00
Mar.	73	Harmon Killebrew	6.50
Apr.	73	Don Kessinger	4.00
May	73	Nolan Ryan	10.00
June	73	Tom Seaver	7.00
July	73	Pete Rose	8.00

Aug. 73	C. May, R. Allen, B. Melton	4.50
Sep. 73	Ken Holtzman	4.50
Oct. 73	Bill Russell	4.00
Nov. 73	Jose Cardenal	4.00
Dec. 73	Willie Stargell	5.50
Jan. 74	World Series	6.00
Feb. 74	Willie Mays	8.00
Mar. 74	Bobby Grich	4.00
Apr. 74	Hank Aaron	8.00
May 74	Ted Sizemore	3.50
June 74	Felix Millan	3.50
July 74	Brooks Robinson	5.00
Aug. 74	Tony Perez	4.00
Sep. 74	Tommy John	4.00
Oct. 74	Dick Allen	4.00
Nov. 74	Jackson, Campenaris, Bando	6.00
Dec. 74	Lou Brock	4.50
Jan. 75	Rollie Fingers	4.00
Feb. 75	Steve Garvey	4.00
Mar. 75	Jeff Burroughs	4.00
Apr. 75	Catfish Hunter	4.00
May 75	Mike Schmidt	6.00
June 75	Rod Carew	4.00
July 75	Nolan Ryan	8.00
Aug. 75	Rick Monday	3.50
Sep. 75	Johnny Bench	5.00
Oct. 75	Vida Blue	4.00
Nov. 75	Fred Lynn	4.00
Dec. 75	Joe Morgan	5.00
Jan. 76	Pete Rose	7.00
Feb. 76	Jim Palmer	5.00
Mar. 76	George Brett	6.00
Apr. 76	Carlton Fisk	6.00
May 76	Frank Tanana	3.50
June 76	Rick Manning	3.50
July 76	Bill Madlock	4.00
Aug. 76	Randy Jones	3.50
Sep. 76	Larry Bowa	4.00
Oct. 76	Mickey Rivers	4.00
Nov. 76	Mark Fidrych	5.00
Dec. 76	Joe Morgan	5.00

Baseball Digest: June, 1980

Jan. 77	World Series Highlights	5.00
Feb. 77	Thurman Munson	5.50
Mar. 77	Amos Otis	3.50
Apr. 77	Mark Fidrych	4.00
May 77	John Montefusco	3.50
June 77	Steve Carlton	5.00
July 77	Dave Parker	5.00
Aug. 77	Manny Trillo & Ivan DeJesus	3.50
Sep. 77	Carl Yastrzemski	7.00
Oct. 77	Steve Garvey	4.00
Nov. 77	Bump Wills	3.50
Dec. 77	George Foster	4.00
Jan. 78	Reggie Jackson	7.00
Feb. 78	Willie McCovey	5.00
Mar. 78	Rod Carew	5.00
Apr. 78	Tom Seaver	5.50
May 78	Cesar Cedeno	4.00
June 78	Gary Templeton	4.00
July 78	Dave Kingman	4.00
Aug. 78	Jim Rice	5.00
Sep. 78	Ron Guidry	5.00
Oct. 78	Clint Hurdle, Rich Gale	3.50
Nov. 78	Reggie Smith	4.00
Dec. 78	Dave Parker	5.00
Jan. 79	World Series Highlights	5.00
Feb. 79	Dave Winfield	5.00
Mar. 79	Greg Luzinski	4.00
Apr. 79	Rich Gossage	4.00
May 79	Jack Clark	4.00
June 79	Steve Garvey	4.00
July 79	Al Oliver	3.50
Aug. 79	Bill Buckner	3.50
Sep. 79	Tommy John	4.00
Oct. 79	Mike Schmidt	6.00
Nov. 79	Omar Moreno	3.00
Dec. 79	George Brett	6.00
Jan. 80	Al Oliver	3.50
Feb. 80	Paul Molitor	4.00
Mar. 80	Gary Carter	5.00
Apr. 80	Willie Stargell	5.00
May 80	Don Baylor	4.00
June 80	Nolan Ryan, J.R. Richard	7.00
July 80	Burns, Baumgarten, Trout	3.00
Aug. 80	Ken Landreaux	3.00
Sep. 80	Steve Carlton	5.00
Oct. 80	Reggie Jackson	6.00
Nov. 80	Joe Charboneau	3.00
Dec. 80	George Brett	5.00
Jan. 81	Tug McGraw	4.00
Feb. 81	Eddie Murray	4.00
Mar. 81	Rickey Henderson	6.00
Apr. 81	Mike Schmidt	5.00
May 81	Gary Carter	5.00
June 81	Cecil Cooper	3.00
July 81	Carlton Fisk	5.00
Aug. 81	Fernando Valenzuela	4.00
Sep. 81	Danny Darwin	3.00
Oct. 81	Ron Davis	3.00
Nov. 81	Pete Rose	6.00
Dec. 81	Tim Raines	4.00
Jan. 82	Steve Garvey	4.00
Feb. 82	Carney Lansford	3.50
Mar. 82	Rollie Fingers	4.00
Apr. 82	Dave Winfield	5.00
May 82	Nolan Ryan	7.00
June 82	Jerry Reuss	3.00
July 82	Salome Barojas	2.50
Aug. 82	Dale Murphy	4.50
Sep. 82	Rickey Henderson	5.00
Oct. 82	Robin Yount	5.00
Nov. 82	Kent Hrbek	4.00
Dec. 82	Ozzie & Lonnie Smith	4.00
Jan. 83	Darrell Porter	3.00
Feb. 83	Mario Soto	3.00
Mar. 83	Doug DeCinces	3.00
Apr. 83	Willie McGee	4.00
May 83	Pete Vuckovich	2.50
June 83	Cal Ripken Jr.	5.00
July 83	Tony Pena	3.50
Aug. 83	Dave Stieb	3.50
Sep. 83	Chris Chambliss	3.00
Oct. 83	Ron Kittle	3.00
Nov. 83	Steve Carlton	4.50
Dec. 83	Carlton Fisk	5.00
Jan. 84	Rick Dempsey	3.00
Feb. 84	Wade Boggs	5.00
Mar. 84	Dale Murphy	4.50
Apr. 84	Mike Boddicker	4.00
May 84	Andre Dawson	4.00
June 84	Lance Parrish	3.00
July 84	Bill Madlock	3.00
Aug. 84	Leon Durham	2.50
Sep. 84	Martinez, Gwynn, McReynolds	4.00
Oct. 84	Ryne Sandberg	5.50
Nov. 84	Keith Hernandez	3.50
Dec. 84	Mark Langston	4.00
Jan. 85	Alan Trammell	3.00
Feb. 85	Don Mattingly	5.00
Mar. 85	Frank Viola	3.00
Apr. 85	Jack Morris	3.00
May 85	Tony Gwynn	4.00
June 85	Dwight Gooden	6.00
July 85	Bruce Sutter	2.50
Aug. 85	Pete Rose	5.00
Sep. 85	Lonnie Smith	3.00
Oct. 85	Ron Guidry	3.00
Nov. 85	Pedro Guerrero	3.00
Dec. 85	Dwight Gooden	5.00
Jan. 86	Willie McGee	3.00
Feb. 86	Bret Saberhagen	3.00
Mar. 86	Tom Browning	2.50
Apr. 86	Harold Baines	3.00
May 86	Darryl Strawberry	5.00

Baseball Digest: April, 1985

June 86	Eddie Murray	3.00
July 86	Bert Blyleven	2.50
Aug. 86	Roger Clemens	5.00
Sep. 86	Gary Carter	3.00
Oct. 86	Wally Joyner, Jose Canseco	4.50
Nov. 86	Bill Doran	2.50
Dec. 86	Roger Clemens, Ted Higuera	4.00
Jan. 87	Don Mattingly, Wade Boggs	4.50
Feb. 87	Sid Fernandez	3.00
Mar. 87	Mike Scott	2.50
Apr. 87	Chris Brown	2.00
May 87	Pete O'Brien	2.50
June 87	Eric Davis, Jody Davis	3.50
July 87	Mike Witt	2.00
Aug. 87	Rickey Henderson	4.00
Sep. 87	Jack Clark, Ozzie Smith	3.00
Oct. 87	Mark McGwire	4.00
Nov. 87	George Bell	3.50
Dec. 87	Kevin Seitzer	2.50
Jan. 88	Andre Dawson	3.00
Feb. 88	Frank Viola	2.50
Mar. 88	Jimmy Key	2.00
Apr. 88	Reynolds, Pagliarulo	2.50
May 88	Eric Davis	3.00
June 88	K.C. Royals Pitchers	3.00
July 88	Andy Van Slyke	3.00
Aug. 88	Dave Winfield	3.75
Sep. 88	Greg Maddux	2.75
Oct. 88	Kirby Puckett	3.50
Nov. 88	Jose Canseco	3.50
Dec. 88	Danny Jackson	2.00
Jan. 89	Jose Canseco	3.00
Feb. 89	Orel Hershiser	2.50
Mar. 89	Gregg Jefferies	2.50
Apr. 89	Kirk Gibson	2.50

May 89 Cory Snyder 2.00
June 89 Fred McGriff 3.50
July 89 Will Clark 4.00
Aug. 89 Nolan Ryan 5.00
Sep. 89 Bo Jackson 2.50
Oct. 89 Dave Stewart 2.00
Nov. 89 Howard Johnson 2.00
Dec. 89 Jerome Walton, Dwight Smith 2.00
Jan. 90 . . . . 2.00
Feb. 90 . . . . 2.00
Mar. 90 . . . . 2.00
Apr. 90 . . . . 2.00
May 90 . . . . 2.00
June 90 . . . . 2.00
July 90 Lou Whitaker, Bob Geren 2.00
Aug. 90 Bobby Bonilla, Frank Viola 2.00
Sep. 90 Ozzie Guillen 2.00
Oct. 90 Rickey Henderson 2.25
Nov. 90 Cecil Fielder 2.25

Baseball Digest: July, 1989

Dec. 90 S.Alomar Jr., Dave Justice 2.25
Jan. 91 Bob Welch 2.25
Feb. 91 Chris Sabo 2.25
Mar. 91 Ray Lankford 2.25
Apr. 91 Norm Charlton, Rob Dibble,Randy Myers . . . 2.25
May 91 Darryl Strawberry 2.25
June 91 Tim Raines 2.25
July 91 Kevin Mitchell 2.25
Aug. 91 Roger Clemens 2.25
Sep. 91 Robin Yount 2.25
Oct. 91 Cal Ripken, Jr. 2.25
Nov. 91 Rafael Palmiero & Roberto Alomar 2.25
Dec. 91 Chuck Knoblauch 2.25
Jan. 92 Steve Avery 2.25
Feb. 92 Kirby Puckett 2.25
Mar. 92 Felix Jose 2.25
Apr. 92 Frank Thomas 2.25
May 92 Wade Boggs 2.25
June 92 Greg Olson, Dan Gladen action photo . . . 2.25
July 92 Howard Johnson 2.25
Aug. 92 Mark McGwire 2.25
Sep. 92 Juan Guzman 2.25
Oct. 92 Kirby Puckett 2.25
Nov. 92 Dennis Eckersely & Tom Glavine 2.25
Dec. 92 Pat Listach 2.25
Jan. 93 Roberto Alomar 2.25
Feb. 93 Gary Sheffield 2.25
Mar. 93 Tim Wakefield 2.25
Apr. 93 Jose Canseco 2.25
May 93 Curt Schilling Mike Mussina 2.25

BASEBALL MAGAZINE

1908

May First issue 2,500.00
June 1,000.00
July Uncle Sam pitching . . 600.00
Aug. 400.00
Sep. Cy Young number . . . 500.00
Oct. 300.00
Nov. World Series number . 500.00
Dec. 300.00

1909

Jan-Oct 200.00
Nov. World Series number . 350.00
Dec. World Series recap . . 350.00

1910

Jan-Apr 150.00
May 2nd Anniv. number . . 150.00
Jun-Jul 150.00
Aug. White Sox number . . . 180.00
Nov. World Series number . 300.00
Dec. World Series recap . . 300.00

1911

Jan/May 140.00
June Addie Joss memorial . 160.00
July Detroit number 160.00
Oct. Managers number . . . 200.00
Nov. World Series number . 275.00
Dec. World Series recap . . 275.00

1912

Jan-Feb 130.00
Mar. Ty Cobb number 450.00
Apr. Play Ball 130.00
May-Jul 130.00
Aug. All Star number 150.00
Nov. World Series number . 250.00
Dec. World Series recap . . 250.00

1913

Jan. Magnates Issue 120.00
Feb-Mar 120.00
Apr. Play Ball 120.00
June Horace Fogel 120.00
Jul-Oct 120.00
Nov. World Series number . 225.00
Dec. World Series recap . . 225.00

1914

Jan. 110.00
Feb. Jake Daubert number 130.00
Mar-Oct 110.00
Nov. World Series number . 200.00
Dec. Christy Mathewson number, World Series recap . . 300.00

1915

Jan. Honus Wagner number 200.00
Feb. 100.00
Mar. Eddie Collins number . 175.00
Apr. Walter Johnson num. . 200.00
May-Oct 100.00
Nov. World Series number . 175.00
Dec. World Series recap . . 175.00

1916

Jan-Jul 90.00
Aug. Ty Cobb 350.00
Nov. World Series number . 150.00
Dec. Ruth, Scott, Shore, Gardner, Hooper World Series recap . . 300.00

1917

Jan. John McGraw, N.Y. number 125.00
Feb. Jones, Snyder, Huggins, Plank St. Louis number 125.00
Mar. Tris Speaker number . 125.00
Apr. 80.00
May Who Will Win the Pennants? 80.00
Jun-Oct 80.00
Nov. World Series number . 125.00
Dec. World Series recap . . 125.00

1918

Jan. 70.00
Feb. Grover C. Alexander . 125.00
Mar. Hank Gowdy 70.00
Apr. George Sisler 100.00
May Play Ball 70.00
June Ed Roush 90.00
July Art sliding player 70.00
Aug. Art out sliding 70.00
Sep. Art batter running 70.00
Oct. World Series number . 110.00
Nov. W.S. recap 110.00
Dec. Rube Marquard 90.00

1919

Jan. Ty Cobb 300.00
Feb. John Heydler 60.00
Mar. John Evers 90.00
Apr. Col T.L. Huston 75.00
May John McGraw 100.00
June Pitcher with a "spitter" . 60.00
July Play at the plate 60.00
Aug. Jim Vaughn 60.00
Sep. Play at first 60.00
Oct. Patriotic cover 60.00
Nov. World Series Number 100.00
D./Jan World Series recap . . 200.00

1920

Feb. Ray Schalk 60.00
Mar. Pat Moran 60.00
Apr. Babe Ruth 300.00
May W.R. Johnston 50.00
June Ty Cobb 250.00
July Ross Youngs 75.00
Aug. Grover Alexander . . . 100.00
Sep. Tris Speaker (Inside fc) 60.00
Oct. Babe Ruth 250.00
Nov. World Series number . . 90.00
Dec. Wilbert Robertson, Tris Speaker World Series recap . . 100.00

1921

Jan. Black Sox scandal . . . 100.00
Feb. Judge Kenesaw Landis 75.00
Mar. George Sisler 75.00
Apr. Rogers Hornsby 100.00
May Who Will Win the Pennant? 50.00
June Babe Ruth stories 75.00
July Babe Ruth Stories 75.00
Aug. Plane over park 50.00
Sep. Babe Ruth (inside fc) . 100.00
Oct. Babe Ruth 100.00
Nov. World Series Number . 90.00
Dec. George Bancroft, Peckinpaugh World Series recap 100.00

1922

Jan. Art "Benched" 50.00
Feb. Frank Frisch 75.00
Mar. Harry Heilmann 75.00
Apr. Rogers Hornsby 100.00
May Play Ball 50.00
June Ivy Wingo 50.00
July Catcher 50.00
Aug. Charles Hollocher 50.00
Sep. Pitcher 50.00
Oct. Art- player sliding 50.00
Nov. World Series number . . 90.00
Dec. Miller Huggins, John McGram, World Series recap 125.00

1923

Jan. Art- Play at second . . . 60.00
Feb. Art 60.00
Mar. Art- Batter & catcher . . 60.00
Apr. Art Play at the plate . . . 50.00
May Yankee Stadium 75.00
June Babe Ruth 125.00
July Walter Johnson 125.00
Aug. Fred Williams 50.00
Sep. Art - banner 50.00
Oct. Christy Mathewson (bc) 75.00
Nov. World Series number . . 90.00
Dec. Babe Ruth, Col. Ruppert World Series recap . . 300.00

1924

Jan. George Sisler 60.00
Feb. Edd Roush 60.00
Mar. Eddie Collins 75.00

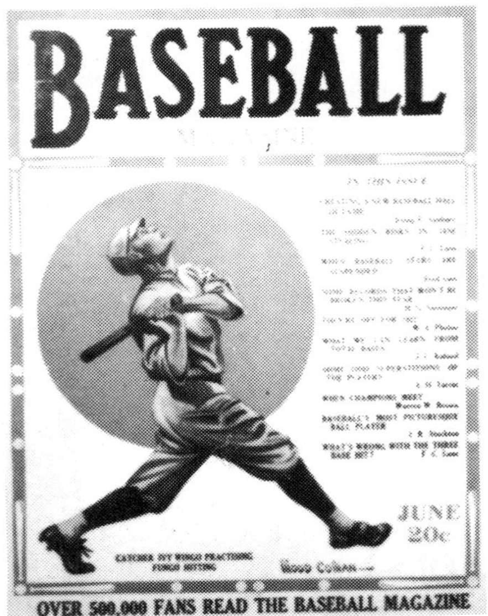

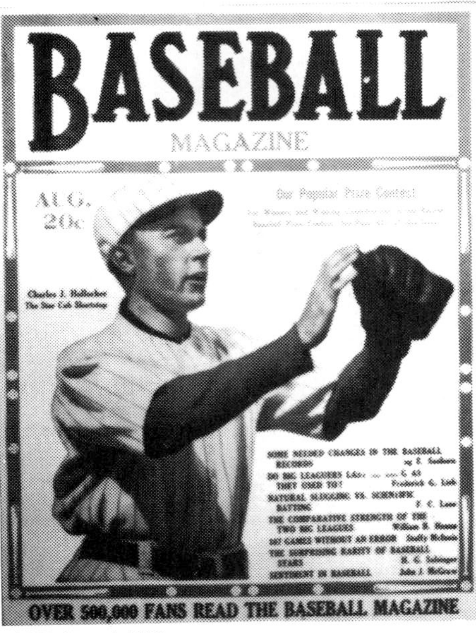

Baseball Magazine: June, 1922; August, 1922

Month	Issue	Price
Apr.	Polo Grounds	50.00
May	Who Will Win the Pennant?	50.00
June	Art- batter & catcher	
July	Art- runner	50.00
Aug.	Grover C. Alexander	85.00
Sep.	Bucky Harris	60.00
Oct.	Max Carey	60.00
Nov.	World Series number	90.00
Dec.	John McGraw, Bill McKechnie; World series recap	85.00
	1925	
Jan.	Dazzy Vance	50.00
Feb.	Bucky Harris (inside bc)	45.00
Mar.	Rogers Hornsby	75.00
Apr.	George Dauss	40.00
May	Who Will Win the Pennant?	40.00
June	Art- batter on deck	40.00
July	Kiki Cuyler (inside bc)	45.00
Aug.	Zach Wheat, Frank Frisch	50.00
Sep.	Jim Bottomley (inside fc)	45.00
Oct.	Bill McKechnie	50.00
Nov.	World Series number	75.00
Dec.	Bucky Harris, Bill McKechnie; World Series recap	250.00
	1926	
Jan.	Rogers Hornsby	75.00
Feb.	Art- fielder	40.00
Mar.	Ted Lyons (inside fc)	45.00
Apr.	Art- play at the plate	40.00
May	Who Will Win the Pennant?	40.00
June	Frank Frisch	50.00
July	Pie Traynor	50.00
Aug	Eddie Collins, George Sisler	60.00
Sep.	Micket Cochrane (inside bc)	45.00
Oct.	Hack Wilson	50.00
Nov.	World Series number	75.00
Dec.	Babe Ruth, Rogers Hornsby World Series recap	250.00
	1927	
Jan.	Ty Cobb	200.00
Feb.	Art- fielder	40.00
Mar.	Art- play at the plate	40.00
Apr.	Art- out at first	40.00
May	Who Will Win the Pennants?	40.00
June	Art- pitcher	40.00
July	Bob O'Farrell	40.00
Aug.	Art- catcher	40.00
Sep.	Lou Gehrig	200.00
Oct.	Joe McCarthy	60.00
Nov.	World Series number	75.00
Dec.	World Series recap	100.00
	1928	
Jan.	E.S. Barnard	40.00
Feb.	Art- pitcher	40.00
Mar.	Art- pitcher	40.00
Apr.	Paul Waner	50.00
May	Who Will Win the Pennant?	40.00
June	Mickey Cochrane (inside bc)	45.00
July	Walter Johnson (inside fc)	50.00
Aug.	Babe Ruth (inside fc)	85.00
Sep.	Art- close play at home	40.00
Oct.	Jim Bottomley	50.00
Nov.	World Series number	75.00
Dec.	Miller Huggins, Lou Gehrig, World Series recap	100.00
	1929	
Jan.	Herb Pennock(inside bc)	45.00
Feb.	Heinie Manush(inside fc)	45.00
Mar.	Jimmie Foxx (inside fc)	50.00
Apr.	Art- runner rounding base	40.00
May	Al Simmons (inside fc)	45.00
June	Grover Alexander (inside bc)	50.00
July	Gabby Hartnett (inside bc)	45.00
Aug.	Mickey Cochrane	60.00
Sep.	Art- batter	40.00
Oct.	Burleigh Grimes	50.00
Nov.	World Series number	75.00
Dec.	Connie Mack, World Series recap	85.00
	1930	
Jan.	Wes Ferrell (inside bc)	35.00
Feb.	Art- pitcher	30.00
Mar.	Left Grove	50.00
Apr.	Art- batter, catcher & ump	30.00
May	Jimmie Foxx (inside bc)	40.00
June	Art- batter	30.00
July	Grover Alexander	50.00
Aug.	Babe Herman (inside fc)	35.00
Sep.	Burleigh Grimes (inside bc)	35.00
Oct.	Walter Johnson (inside bc)	40.00
Nov.	World Series number	50.00
Dec.	Gabby Street, Connie Mack World Series recap	60.00
	1931	
Jan.	Charley Gehringer (inside fc)	35.00
Feb.	Hack Wilson	40.00
Mar.	Art- fielder	30.00
Apr	Art- play at second	30.00
May	Carl Hubbell (inside bc)	35.00
June	Tony Lazzeri (inside bc)	35.00
July	Chick Hafey (inside fc)	35.00
Aug.	Rabbit Maranville	40.00
Sep.	Bucky Harris (inside fc)	35.00
Oct.	Wes Ferrell	35.00
Nov.	World Series number	50.00
Dec.	World Series recap	50.00
	1932	
Jan.	Art- batter	30.00
Feb.	Chuck Klein (inside fc)	40.00
Mar.	Lou Gehrig	60.00
Apr.	Pepper Martin	35.00
May	Walter Johnson (inside bc)	35.00
June	Max Carey	40.00
July	Art- first baseman	30.00
Aug.	O'Doul, Wilson	

Month	Issue	Price
	(inside fc)	35.00
Sep.	George Earnshaw	30.00
Oct.	Earl Averill	40.00
Nov.	World Series number	50.00
Dec.	Gov. Roosevelt, Joe McCarthy World Series recap	75.00
	1933	
Jan.	Lefty O'Doul	40.00
Feb.	Jimmie Foxx	60.00
Mar.	John Heydler	30.00
Apr.	Dale Alexander	30.00
May	25th anniversary number	60.00
June	Bill Terry	50.00
July	Red Faber	40.00
Aug.	Pie Traynor (inside bc)	35.00
Sep.	Walter Johnson	75.00
Oct.	World Series number	50.00
Nov.	Bill Terry, Joe Cronin World Series recap	60.00
Dec.	Carl Hubbell	50.00
	1934	
Jan.	Babe Ruth	200.00
Feb.	William Harridge	35.00
Mar.	Jimmy Wilson	35.00
Apr.	Mickey Cochrane	50.00
May	Who Will Win the Pennant?	30.00
June	Bob O'Farrell	30.00
July	Jimmy Dykes	30.00
Aug.	Casey Stengel	50.00
Sep.	Mel Harder	35.00
Oct.	Landis, World Series number	50.00
Nov.	Mickey Cochrane, Frank Frisch/ World Series recap	60.00
Dec.	Dizy Dean	60.00
	1935	
Jan.	Ford Frick	35.00
Feb.	Joe Cronin	35.00
Mar.	Paul Waner	35.00
Apr.	Lou Gehrig	150.00
May	Babe Ruth, Bill McKechnie	150.00
June	Rogers Hornsby	60.00
July	Charles Dressen	30.00
Aug.	Bob Johnson	25.00
Sep.	Mel Ott	40.00
Oct.	Hank Greenberg	60.00
Nov.	Ruth, Cochrane, Grimm World Series recap	150.00
Dec.	Arky Vaughan	35.00
	1936	
Jan.	Buddy Myer	25.00
Feb.	Gabby Hartnett	35.00
Mar.	Steve O'Neill	25.00
Apr.	Wally Berger	25.00
May	Play Ball	25.00
June	Roger Cramer	25.00
July	Joe Medwick	40.00
Aug.	Bill Dickey	40.00
Sep.	Lon Warneke	25.00
Oct.	World Series number	40.00
Nov.	Joe McCarthy, Bill Terry World Series recap	50.00
Dec.	Luke Appling	35.00
	1937	
Jan.	Jim Ripple	25.00
Feb.	Hal Trosky	25.00
Mar.	Leo Durocher	35.00
Apr.	Johnny Allen	25.00
May	Play Ball	25.00
June	Burleigh Grimes	35.00
July	Wally Moses	25.00
Aug.	Dick Bartell	25.00
Sep.	Joe DiMaggio	125.00
Oct.	Gabby Hartnett	35.00
Nov.	Joe McCarthy, Bill Terry World Series recap	50.00
Dec.	Charley Gehringer	35.00
	1938	
Jan.	Joe Medwick	40.00
Feb.	Gee Walker	25.00
Mar.	Arky Vaughn	35.00
Apr.	Who Will Win the Pennant?	25.00
May	Joe DiMaggio	75.00
June	Woody Jensen, Gus Mancuso	25.00
July	Frank Corsetti, Campbell	25.00
Aug.	Gabby Hartnett	35.00
Sep.	Feller, Rolfe, Trosky	35.00
Oct.	World Series	40.00
Nov.	Joe McCarthy, Gabby Hartnett World Series recap	50.00
Dec.	Dizzy Dean in 38 series	40.00
	1939	
Jan.	Ernie Lombardi	35.00
Feb.	Bob Feller	40.00
Mar.	Cubs, Pirates action	25.00
Apr.	Bobby Doerr	35.00
May	Bartell, Leiber, Mancuso	25.00
June	Centenial Issue (Doubleday)	60.00
July	Ruth, Mathewson (inside c)	50.00
Aug.	Lou Gehrig, Williams	150.00
Sep.	Durocher & Dodgers	30.00
Oct.	'39 All Star Game action	25.00
Nov.	Joe DiMaggio, Bucky Walters World Series recap	100.00
Dec.	Ted Williams	100.00
	1940	
Jan.	Terry Moore	25.00
Feb.	Hand holding ball	20.00
Mar.	Leo Durocher & Dodgers	30.00
Apr.	Joe Gordon's hands	20.00
May	Bill Klem	35.00
June	Bob Feller	35.00
July	John Mize, Ernie Lombardi	30.00
Aug.	Joe Gordon, Cecil Travis	25.00
Sep.	Giants, Dodgers	20.00
Oct.	Joe DiMaggio	75.00
Nov.	'40 Reds, World Series	40.00
Dec.	'40 Series action	25.00
	1941	
Jan.	Jimmy Wilson	20.00
Feb.	Connie Mack	40.00
Mar.	Pete Reiser	25.00
Apr.	McCarthy, Harris, Griffith	30.00
May	Bucky Walters	25.00
June	Bob Johnson	20.00
July	Johnny Hopp	20.00
Aug.	Ted Williams,Lou Gehrig	60.00
Sep.	Enos Slaughter, Camilli	25.00
Oct.	Ump.Summers explains	20.00
Nov.	'41 Yankees,	

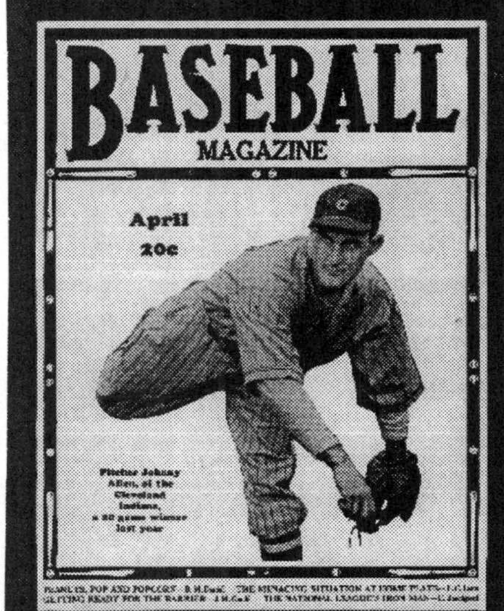

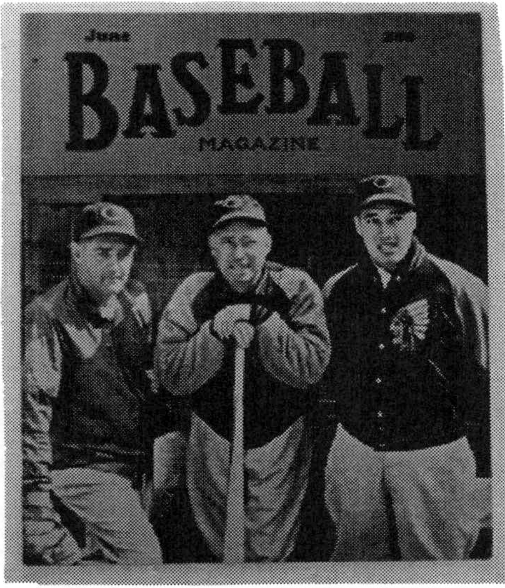

Baseball Magazine: April, 1937; June 1940

	Series recap	50.00
Dec.	Billy Herman, Ted Williams	35.00
	1942	
Jan.	Lou Boudreau	25.00
Feb.	Ott, Stoneham, Brannick	25.00
Mar.	White Sox, Red Sox action	20.00
Apr.	Ebbets Field	20.00
May	Hank Greenberg	35.00
June	Enos Slaughter	25.00
July	Rick Ferrell	25.00
Aug.	Paul Waner	30.00
Sep.	Joe Gordon, Elmer Valo	25.00
Oct.	Walker Cooper, Mickey Owen	20.00
Nov.	Joe McCarthy, Billy Southworth; World Series recap	40.00
Dec.	Clark Griffith	25.00
	1943	
Jan.	Pee Wee Reese	30.00
Feb.	Phil Rizzuto, John Pesky	25.00
Mar.	Jimmy Brown	20.00
Apr.	Chisox, Indians action	15.00
May	Cuyler, Frey, McCullough	20.00
June	Senators in action	15.00
July	Frank Frisch, Rick Sewell	25.00
Aug.	Cullenbine, Siebert	15.00
Sep.	Arky Vaughn, E. Lombardi	25.00
Oct.	Mel Harder, Bill Johnson	20.00
Nov.	McCarthy, Southworth	30.00
Dec.	Crosetti, Cooper, World Series recap	30.00
	1944	
Jan.	Cubs, Braves action	15.00
Feb.	Early Wynn	20.00
Mar.	Yankee batboy	15.00
Apr.	Bob Elliot	18.00
May	Rick Ferrell	20.00
June	War Bond	15.00
July	Jimmie Foxx, Charley Grimm	25.00
Aug.	Tigers, Bosox action	15.00
Sep.	Mel Ott	25.00
Oct.	Mort & Walker Cooper	18.00
Nov.	York, Overmire, O'Neill	18.00
Dec.	'44 Cards team, World Series recap	40.00
	1945	
Jan.	Browns, Yankees action	15.00
Feb.	Ford Frick, Will Harridge	20.00
Mar.	Bosox, Yankees action	15.00
Apr.	N.Y. Giants	15.00
May	Tom Yawkey,Joe Cronin	25.00
June	War appeal letter	15.00
July	Happy Chandler	20.00
Aug.	Chisox, Senators action	15.00
Sep.	Tommy Holmes	18.00
Oct.	Derringer, Borowy, Passeau	20.00
Nov.	Chief Bender, Connie Mack	25.00
Dec.	O'Neill, Grimm, World Series recap	30.00
	1946	
Jan.	Browns, Yankees action	15.00
Feb.	Gionfriddo, Masi	18.00
Mar.	Browns, As action	15.00
Apr.	McCarthy, Ott, Durocher	25.00
May	Bob Feller, Lou Boudreau	30.00
June	Truman, Cronin, Griffith	30.00
July	Reese, Reiser, Griffith	30.00
Aug.	York, Mills	18.00
Sep.	Pirates, Phils action	15.00
Oct.	Ted Williams, Bobby Doerr	40.00
Nov.	Bob Feller, Hal Newhouser	30.00
Dec.	'46 Cards team, World Series recap	40.00
	1947	
Jan.	J. Pesky, Cal Hubbard	20.00
Feb.	George Case, Cal Hubbard	18.00
Mar.	Ed Barrow	25.00
Apr.	Yankees, Bosox action	15.00
May	Rex Barney, Ed Stanky	15.00
June	Ted Williams	35.00
July	Pete Reiser	18.00
Aug.	Luke Appling	25.00
Sep.	Ewell Blackwell	18.00
Oct.	A. Galan, Conlon	18.00
Nov.	John Mize, Ralph Kiner	30.00
Dec.	'47 Series, Jackie Robinson World series recap	40.00
	1948	
Jan.	Ray Coleman	15.00
Feb.	Joe Cronin, Joe McCarthy	25.00
Mar.	Yanks, Indians action	15.00
Apr.	Cubs, Phils action	15.00
May	1948 Braves	15.00
June	Harry S. Truman	25.00
July	Johnny Mize	20.00
Aug.	Steve O'Neill, Dizzy Trout	15.00
Sep.	Stan Musial	40.00
Oct.	Lou Boudreau, Babe Ruth	50.00
Nov.	Connie Mack	25.00
Dec.	Boudreau, Southworth, World Series recap	30.00
	1949	
Jan.	Williams, Doerr, DiMaggio, Stephens	35.00
Feb.	Dobson, Coan, Tebbetts	15.00
Mar.	Pat Mullin	15.00
Apr.	Hitchcock, Swift	15.00
May	Stan Musial, Ted Williams	50.00
June	Washington Opener	15.00
July	Ralph Branca	15.00
Aug.	Stallcup, Rice	15.00
Sep.	Casey Stengel	25.00
Oct.	Ashburn, Seminick	15.00
Nov.	Connie Mack	25.00
Dec.	Harridge, Stengel, Chandler Frick, Shotton, World Series recap	35.00
	1950	
Jan.	Parnell, Kinder, McDermott	15.00
Feb.	Roy Sievers	15.00
Mar.	Henrich, Stengel, Mize	25.00
Apr.	Lollar, Tebbetts, Sievers	15.00
May	Musial, Slaughter, Schoendiest	30.00
June	Earl Torgeson	15.00
July	Chandler, Harridge, Mack	30.00
Aug.	Eddie Sawyer	15.00
Sep.	Johnny Lipon	15.00
Oct.	Richie Ashburn	20.00
Nov.	Al Rosen	20.00
Dec.	Yankee Stadium, World Series recap	30.00
	1951	
Jan.	Hutchinson, Michaels	15.00
Feb.	Billy Goodman	15.00
Mar.	Braves, Cubs action	15.00
Apr.	Garagiola, Jocko Conlon	20.00
May	Spahn, Sain, Bickford	20.00
June	Casey Stengel	25.00
July	Stengel, Sawyer	25.00
Aug.	Rookie Mickey Mantle	200.00
Sep.	Gil Hodges	20.00
Oct.	Worls Series issue	20.00
Nov.	Bob Feller	30.00
Dec.	Cy Young	30.00
	1952	
Jan.	World Series reviewed	15.00
Feb.	Stan Musial, DiMaggio	30.00
Mar.	Ned Garver	15.00
Apr.	Hornsby, Stanky	20.00
May	Ashburn, Ruth, Gehrig	30.00
June	Mays, Houtteman, Stengel	20.00
Jul/Aug	All Star Issue	20.00
Sep.	Ruth, Gehrig, Babe Ruth	50.00
Oct.	Pennant Clincher issue	15.00
N./Dec	World Series issue	25.00
	1953	
Spring	Reese, Shantz, Sauer	15.00
May	Managers' predictions	15.00
June	DiMaggio, Reynolds, Evers	30.00
July	Mantle, Bruton	50.00
Aug.	All Star issue	20.00
Sep.	Mickey Vernon	15.00
Oct.	Gil Hodges	15.00
Nov.	Reese, Roberts, Rizzuto	20.00
	1954	
Aug.		15.00
Sep.	Casey Stengel	25.00
Oct.	World Series Issue	25.00
N./Dec	World Series review	15.00
	1955	
Mar.	Connie Mack	25.00
May	Art- a coach	15.00
June	Pete Runnel	15.00
July	All Star Issue	20.00
	1956	
May	Play Ball	15.00
June	Ted Williams	25.00
July	Mickey Mantle	50.00
Aug.	Bob Friend, Dale Long	15.00
Oct.	Casey Stengel	25.00
	1957	
May	Dob Larson	15.00
Sep.	Bob Feller	50.00
	1964	
Nov.	John Callison	10.00
Dec.	Brooks Robinson	15.00
	1965	
Jan.	'64 cards	15.00
Feb.	Bob Pillinger, etc	10.00
Mar.	Frank Howard	10.00
Apr.	Wally Bunker	10.00

Complete Baseball: Vol. 4 #3

COMPLETE BASEBALL MAGAZINE

1949 Spr.	Vol 1 #1 DiMaggio, Musial, Williams	45.00
1950 Spr.	Vol 1 #2 Kiner, Williams, Musial	35.00
1950 Sum	Vol 2 #2 Berra, Lemon	25.00
1950 Fall	Vol 2 #3 Musial, Roberts, Kell, Jackie Robinson, Rizzuto	30.00
1950 Wint	Vol 2 #4 Musial, Kell, Kiner Rizzuto & 12 others	25.00
1951 Spr.	Vol 3 #1 Kiner	20.00
1951 Sum	Vol 3 #2 Williams,	

Kiner Musial, Hodges & others ... 25.00
1952 Spr. Vol 4 #1 Reese, Irvin, Ashburn, Musial & others ... 20.00
1952 July Vol 4 #2 Ashburn ... 17.50
1952 Sep. Vol 4 #3 Hodges, Kiner ... 17.50
1952 Nov. Vol 4 #4 Allie, Reynolds ... 17.50
1953 Feb. Vol 5 #1 Mantle, Snider, Roberts ... 25.00
1953 Apr. Vol 5 #2 Mantle, Musial ... 25.00
1953 Sum Vol 5 #3 Musial ... 20.00
1953 Sep. Vol 5 #4 CurtSimmons 15.00
1953 Dec. Vol 5 #5 R.Campanella 17.50
1953 Wint Vol 6 #1 Williams ... 20.00

Mazeroski's Baseball: 1983

MAZEROSKI'S BASEBALL

1983 Reggie Jackson-Calif.Angel 8.00
1984 Eddie Murray–Balt.Orioles . 7.50
1985 Ryne Sandberg–Chi.Cubs . 6.00
Dale Murphy–Atlanta Braves 4.50
Doug DeCinces-Cal.Angels 4.00
Dwight Gooden-NY Mets .. 5.00
Kirk Gibson-Detroit Tigers . 4.00
1986 Jack Clark- St.L.Cardinals . 4.00
F. Valenzuela–LA Dodgers 4.00
Lance Parrish–Detroit Tigers 4.00
George Brett–KC Royals .. 6.00
Don Mattingly–NY Yankees 6.00
Pete Rose–Cincinatti Reds 6.00
Jesse Barfield–Tor.B.Jays . 4.00
1987 Ryne Sandberg–Chi.Cubs . 6.00
Sparky Anderson–Det.Tigers 4.00
Tony Fernandez-Toronto B J 4.00
Dwight Evans–Bos.Red Sox 4.00
Mike Scott–Houston Astros 4.00
Gary Carter–NY Mets 4.50
Wally Joyner–Cal. Angels . 4.00
Mike Schmidt–Phi. Phillies . 5.00
1988 Andre Dawson-Chicago Cubs4.50
Will Clark–SF Giants 5.00
Mark McGwire–Oakland ... 4.50
Don Mattingly–NY Yankees 4.50
Dale Murphy–Atlanta Braves 4.00
Alan Trammell-Det.Tigers . 4.00
Wade Boggs–Bos.Red Sox 4.25
Eric Davis–Cincinatti Reds . 4.00
Tim Raines–Montreal 4.00
George Bell–Toronto 4.00
Kirby Puckett–Minn.Twins . 5.00
Ozzie Smith–SL Cardinals . 4.25
Orel Hershiser–LA Dodgers 4.00
1989 Darryl Strawberry-NY Mets 4.00
Fred McGriff–Toronto B Jays4.25
Andres Galaragga-Montreal 4.00
Paul Molitor-Mil Brewers .. 4.00
Greg Maddux-Chicago Cubs 4.00
Kirk Gibson-LA Dodgers .. 4.00
Jose Canseco-Oakland A's 4.25
Mike Greenwell-Bos.Red Sox4.00
1990 Bert Blyleven–Cal. Angels . 4.00
Dave Stewart–Oakland A's 4.00
Kevin Mitchell–SF Giants .. 4.00
Mitch Williams–Chi.Cubs .. 4.00
Howard Johnson–NY Mets . 4.00
Cal Ripken Jr.-Balt.Orioles . 5.00
Ruben Sierra–Tex.Rangers 4.00
Kelly Gruber-Toronto B.Jays 4.00
Bo Jackson–KC Royals ... 4.25
Pedro Guerrero–StL.Cards . 4.00
1991 Frank Viola–NY Mets 4.00
Carlton Fisk–Chi White Sox 4.25
Doug Drabek–Pitt Pirates .. 4.00
Barry Larkin–Cincinatti Reds 4.00
Ken Griffey,Jr.–Sea.Mariners 4.50
Dave Stieb–Toronto B.Jays 4.00
D.Strawberry–LA Dodgers . 4.00
Rickey Henderson–Oak. A's 4.25
1992 Jose Canseco–Oakland A's 4.00
Jim Abbott–Cal Angels ... 4.00
Ryne Sandberg–Chi.Cubs . 4.00
Nolan Ryan–Texas Rangers 4.50
Tom Glavine–Atlanta Braves 4.00
Chris Sabo–Cincinatti Reds 4.00
Joe Carter–Toronto B Jays 4.00
Howard Johnson–NY Mets . 4.00
Len Dykstra–Phi Phillies .. 4.00
Cecil Fielder–Detroit Tigers 4.00
Roger Clemens–Bos.RedSox4.00

NATIONAL LEAGUE GREEN BOOKS

1935 Date January 30, 1935 (First Green Book) 75.00
1936 60th Birthday Edition, date Feb. 2, 1936 ...... 60.00
1937 Title & date Feb. 5, 1937 . 60.00
1938 Title & year 60.00
1939 Centennial Edition 1839-1939 .... 55.00
1940 Title & year 55.00
1941 Title & year 55.00
1942 Baseball diamond 100.00
1943 Title & year 100.00
1944 Title & year 80.00
1945 Title & year 75.00
1946 BBWAA logo 65.00
1947 Title & year in diamond shape 55.00
1948 Runner thrown out at first base 45.00
1949 8 Pennants w/ NL team logos 45.00
1950 8 Baseballs w/ NL team logos 40.00
1951 Ball in Glove, "75th Anniversary" 40.00
1952 8 NL cities, "Our 76th Year"40.00
1953 8 NL cities, "Our 78th Year"40.00
1954 NL All-Star Team (1st glossy cov.) 40.00
1955 8 NL stars (Mays, Musial, Spahn) 40.00
1956 Dodgers' celebration photos35.00
1957 NL logo "82nd Season" .. 35.00
1958 NL salutes the BBWAA .. 35.00
1959 Stan Musial & Warren Spahn clippings 37.50
1960 Musial, Roberts, McCovey, Banks, Snider,etc. 40.00
1961 Groat, F.Robinson, F.Howard, Burdette,Spahn 35.00
1962 Map of U.S. w/10 NL logos 30.00
1963 1958-1962 League Champs' parks 30.00
1964 Stan Musial "...so long, Stan" 35.00
1965 List of past NL Champions 30.00
1966 7 Stadiums of 1960's 25.00
1967 1962-1966 Attendance figures 25.00
1968 1967 Highlights news clippings 25.00
1969 1869 Cincinnati Red Stockings 25.00
1970 Hodges, McCovey, Sizemore, Rose, Mets ... 22.50
1971 Baseball w/ 12 NL team names 20.00
1972 12 bats w/NL team names 20.00
1973 Roberto Clemente memorial 25.00
1974 Hank Aaron & Babe Ruth bust 25.00
1975 Brock,Aaron,Schmidt, Garvey,M.Marshall 18.00
1976 Bench, McEnaney, Reds World Series celebration 16.00
1977 12 NL Team logos 16.00
1978 12 NL Stars 16.00
1979 12 NL Team helmets & 4 baseball bats 16.00
1980 Baseball 12.00
1981 Schmidt, McGraw, All-Stars, Astros 12.00
1982 Rose, Schmidt, Ryan, Valenzuela 15.00
1983 D.Murphy, Carlton, Sax, Oliver,D.Porter 12.00
1984 12 NL team pennants ... 12.00
1985 Sandberg,Sutcliffe, Garvey,Gooden 9.00
1986 Ryan, Gooden, McGee, Rose 10.00
1987 Raines,Scott,Schmidt, Worrell,Mets 8.00
1989 Gibson, Hershiser, Hatcher,LA celebration ... 8.00
1990 NL MVP's & Cy Youngs of 1990's 8.00

PETERSEN'S PRO BASEBALL

1977 Brock, Anderson 10.50
1978 Rod Carew 7.00
1979 Bench, Garvey & others ... 7.00
1980 Willie Stargell 6.00
1981–91 .... @5.00

THE SPORTING NEWS BASEBALL REGISTER

1940 Ty Cobb 75.00
1941 Paul Derringer 35.00
1942 Joe DiMaggio 40.00
1943–44 .... 25.00
1945 .... 20.00
1946 .... 35.00
1947 Walter Johnson 40.00
1948–49 .... 35.00
1950 Joe DiMaggio 35.00
1951–53 .... 25.00
1954–59 .... 15.00
1960–62 .... 12.50
1963–65 .... 8.00
1966 Sandy Koufax 9.00
1967 Frank & Brooks Robinson . 9.00
1968 Red Sox 7.50
1969 Willie Horton 7.50
1970 Tom Seaver 10.00
1971 Willie Mays 10.00
1972 Joe Torre 7.00
1973 Wilbur Wood 6.00
1974 Pete Rose 9.00
1975 Catfish Hunter 7.50
1976 Jim Palmer 7.50
1977 Joe Morgan 7.50
1978 Rod Carew 7.50
1979 Ron Guidry 6.50
1980 Carl Yastrzemski 7.00
1981 George Brett 7.50
1982 Fernando Valenzuela 5.50

Sporting News Baseball Register: 1943

1983 Bruce Sutter 5.00
1984 John Denny 5.00
1985 Willie Hernandez 5.00
1986–92 .... @5.00

THE SPORTING NEWS BASEBALL YEARBOOK

1932 Lefty Grove 20.00
1933 Jimmie Foxx 30.00
1934 Carl Hubbell 25.00
1935 Dizzy Dean 25.00
1936 Hank Greenberg 20.00
1937 Joe McCarthy 20.00
1938 Joe Medwick 20.00
1939 Abner Doubleday 17.50
1940 Bucky Walters 17.50

THE SPORTING NEWS DOPE BOOK

1942 Ted Williams 25.00

One for the Book: 1950

1948 Joe DiMaggio 20.00
1949 Stan Musial 20.00
1950 Ted Williams 20.00
1951 Phil Rizzuto 17.50
1952 Yogi Berra 17.50
1953 Ferris Fain 15.00
1954 Al Rosen 15.00
1955 Willie Mays 17.50
1956 Duke Snider 17.50
1957 Mickey Mantle 25.00
1958 Warren Spahn 35.00
1959 Bob Turley 15.00
1960 .400 Hitters, Aaron 13.50
1961 Rockwell painting 10.00
1962 Team logos 10.00
1963 Don Drysdale 9.00
1964 1st photocover(play at plate) 8.00
1965 Autograph Hounds 8.00
1966 Torre catching pop-up 8.00
1967 Triple Crown winners 8.00
1968 Red Schoendist 8.00
1969 Pete Rose 8.00
1970 Willie McCovey 7.50
1971 Rico Carty 6.00
1972 Mickey Lolich 5.50
1973 Hank Aaron (Art) 5.50
1974 Bobby Bonds 4.50
1975 Jeff Burroughs 4.00
1976 Bill Madlock 4.00
1977 Thurman Munson (Art) 4.00
1978 Steve Carlton 3.75
1979 Jim Rice 3.75
1980 Mike Flanagan 3.25
1981 Cecil Cooper 3.25
1982 Rickey Henderson (1st larger format - 8 x 5-1/8") . 4.40
1983 Dale Murphy 4.50
1984 Lamarr Hoyt 4.00

Sporting News Baseball Guide: 1950

THE SPORTING NEWS BASEBALL GUIDE & RECORD BOOK

1943 Pitcher with Servicemen . 50.00
1944 B.Newsom, B.Dahlgren .. 40.00
1945 Marty Marion 37.50
1946 Hal Newhouser 35.00
1947 Harry Brecheen (Art) 35.00
1948 Ewell Blackwell 50.00
1949 Lou Boudreau 50.00
1950 Phil Rizzuto, Pee Wee Reese 50.00
1951 Red Schoendist 50.00
1952 Stan Musial 50.00
1953 Robin Roberts 45.00
1954 Casey Stengel 45.00
1955 Play at First 45.00
1956 J.Coleman, B.Martin 45.00
1957 Mickey Mantle 50.00
1958 Ted Williams 42.50
1959 Spalding adv. for NL/AL balls 35.00
1960 Mullin "Bum" cartoon 30.00
1961 Relief pitcher award 25.00
1962 Roger Maris, Babe Ruth . 35.00

Becomes:

THE SPORTING NEWS OFFICIAL BASEBALL GUIDE

1963 Mullin cartoon 25.00
1964 Stan Musial 25.00
1965 Robinson, Boyer 17.50
1966 Willie Mays, Sandy Koufax 20.00
1967 Robinson, Koufax, Clemente 20.00
1968 Yaz, Cepeda, Lonborg ... 15.00
1969 Rose, Gibson, McLain ... 17.50
1970 McCovey, Killebrew 10.00
1971 Bench, Gibson, Killebrew . 12.50
1972 Jenkins, Blue, Torre 10.00
1973 Carlton, Bench, Perry ... 12.00
1974 Palmer, Jackson, Bonds . 12.00
1975 Brock, Hunter 10.00
1976 Morgan, Seaver, Palmer . 13.00
1977 Munson, Palmer 8.00
1978 Carew, Ryan, Carlton ... 12.50
1979 Guidry, Rice, Parker 7.00
1980 K.Hernandez, Baylor 6.00
1981 Steve Carlton 8.00
1982 Tom Seaver 10.00

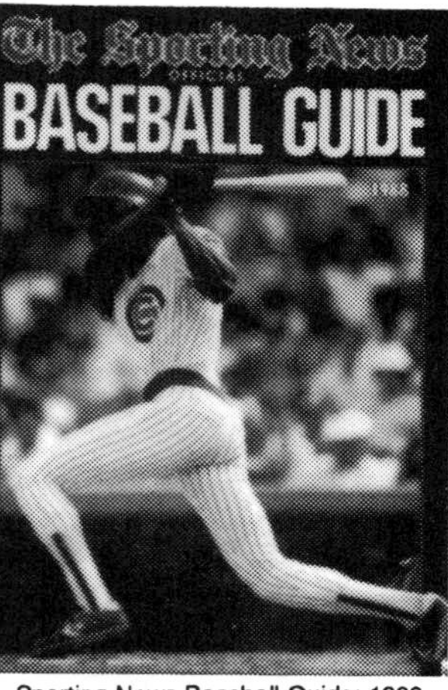

Sporting News Baseball Guide: 1988

1983 Robin Yount 8.00
1984 Cal Ripken, Jr 10.00
1985 Ryne Sandberg 9.00
1986 Willie McGee 5.00
1987 Roger Clemens 8.00
1988 Andre Dawson 6.00
1989 Jose Canseco 6.00
1990 Bret Saberhagen 5.00
1991 Bob Welch 5.00
1992 Will Clark 5.00

THE SPORTING NEWS BASEBALL RECORD BOOK

1981 George Brett, Mike Schmidt 6.00
1982 Valuenzala, Fingers 5.00
1983 Robin Yount, Ozzie Smith . 5.75
1984 Kittle, Strawberry 5.00
1985–92 .... @4.00

THE SPORTING NEWS ONE FOR THE BOOK

1949 Stan Musial 20.00
1950 Luke Appling 15.00
1951 Phil Rizzuto 10.00
1952 Allie Reynolds 10.00
1953 Virgil Trucks 8.00
1954 Roy Campanella 8.00
1955 Joe Adcock 6.50
1956 Robin Roberts 7.00
1957 Pee Wee Reese 6.50
1958 Stan Musial 6.50
1959 Casey Stengel 6.00
1960 Roy Face 5.00
1961 Nellie Fox 5.00

1962 Warren Spahn 4.50
1963 Fox, Apparicio, Hubbs, Wills; new cover design (numeral 1 deleted) 8.00
1964 Julian Javier 3.75
1965 Jim Bunning 3.75
1966 Mets, Dodgers 3.25
1967 Willie Mays 4.00
1968 Mickey Mantle 5.00
1969 Lou Brock 3.25
1970 Hank Aaron 3.25
1971 Hoyt Wilhelm 3.00
1972 Tom Seaver 3.25
1973 Billy Williams 3.00
1974 Nolan Ryan 3.25
1975 Lou Brock 3.00
1976 Rod Carew 3.00
1977 Randy Jones 2.50
1978 George Foster 2.50
1979 Pete Rose 3.00
1980 J.R. Richards 2.50
1981 Mike Schmidt 3.00
1982 Rose, Musial 3.75
1983 Henderson, Yount 3.25

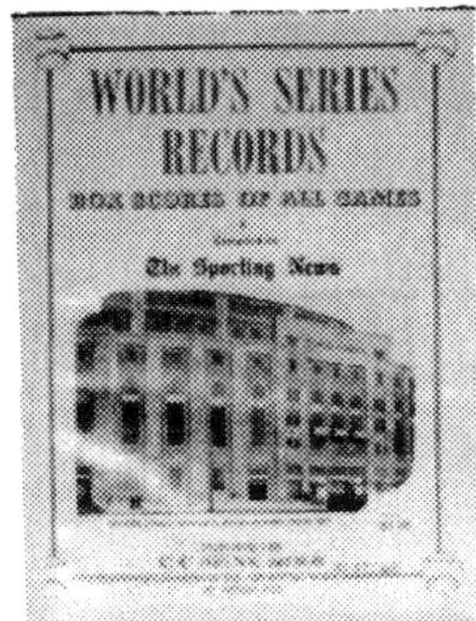

World Series Record Book: 1953

THE SPORTING NEWS WORLD SERIES RECORD BOOK

1953 Yankee Stadium 15.00
1954 Ebbets Field 12.50
1955 World series crowd 7.50
1956 Amoros catch 7.50
1957 Larsen's last pitch 7.50
1958 Browns Deplaning after victory 7.50
1959 Milwaukee Stadium crowd . 7.50
1960 The Screen at LA Coliseum 6.50
1961 Mullin Cartoon of ballplayer 6.00
1962 Yogi Berra 5.50
1963 Ralph Terry 5.50
1964 Sandy Koufax 5.00
1965 Mantle, Richardson, Gibson 6.00
1966 Dodgers vs. Twins; play at 2nd 4.75
1967 F.Robinson HR off Drysdale 5.00
1968 Bob Gibson (1st color photo) 5.00
1969 Mickey Lolich 4.25
1970 David vs. Goliath 4.25
1971 Brooks Robinson 4.25
1972 Manny Sanguillan 3.50
1973 Reds, A's; Anthem at Riverside 3.50
1974 Reggie Jasckson 4.00
1975 Joe Rudi 3.00
1976 Pete Rose 4.00
1977 Johnny Bench 3.50
1978 Reggie Jackson 3.50
1979 Thurman Munson,R.Jackson 3.50
1980 Willie Stargell 3.00

1981 Boone, Porter;Play at the plate 2.75
1982 Lasorda, Guererra, Valenzuela 1st larger format (8x5-1/8") 2.75
1983 Hernandez, Sutter, Porter . 2.75
1984 Rick Dempsey 2.75
1985 (9x6) Gibson, Trammel . . . 2.75
1986 . . . . 2.75
1987 . . . . 2.75
1988 Special "The Series" 336 pages Gaetti, Reardon, Newman 12.95

Street & Smith's: 1941

STREET & SMITH'S BASEBALL

1941 Bob Feller 250.00
1942 Howie Pollet 175.00
1943 N.Y. Giants 110.00
1944 Joe McCarthy 125.00
1945 N.Y. Giants Spr.Training 110.00
1946 Dick Fowler 110.00
1947 Leo Durocher 110.00
1948 Joe DiMaggio 135.00
1949 Lou Boudreau 100.00
1950 Joe DiMaggio & Ted Williams 125.00
1951 Joe DiMaggio & Ralph Kiner 125.00
1952 Stan Musial 110.00
1953 Mickey Mantle 125.00
1954 Eddie Matthews 90.00
1955 Yogi Berra 90.00
1956 Mickey Mantle & Duke Snider 110.00

Street & Smith's: 1955

1957 Mickey Mantle, Don Larson, Yogi Berra 110.00
1958 Bob Buhl & Lew Burdette . 60.00
1959 Mantle, Spahn, Burdette . 70.00
1960 Luis Aparicio & Nellie Fox 50.00
1961 Dick Groat 55.00

Street & Smith's: 1962

1962 Roger Maris 70.00
1963 Tom Tresh 40.00
Stan Musial 50.00
Don Drysdale 40.00
1964 Mickey Mantle 55.00
Warren Spahn 40.00
Sandy Koufax 45.00
1965 Brooks Robinson 45.00
Ken Boyer 40.00
Dean Chance 35.00
1966 Ron Swoboda 30.00
Rocky Colavito 30.00
Sandy Koufax 40.00
1967 Andy Etchebarren 30.00
Harmon Killebrew 30.00
Juan Marichal 30.00
1968 Jim Lonborg 30.00
Orlando Cepeda 30.00
Jim McGlothlin 30.00
1969 Bob Gibson & Denny McLain 30.00
1970 Tom Seaver 35.00
Harmon Killebrew 30.00
Bill Singer 30.00
1971 Boog Powell 25.00
Johnny Bench 30.00
Gaylord Perry 25.00
1972 Roberto Clemente 30.00
Joe Torre 25.00
Vida Blue 25.00
1973 Steve Carlton 25.00
Johnny Bench 25.00
Reggie Jackson 25.00
1974 Hank Aaron 25.00
Pete Rose 25.00
Nolan Ryan 45.00
1975 Lou Brock 22.50
Catfish Hunter 22.50
Mike Marshall 22.50
1976 Fred Lynn 20.00
Joe Morgan 20.00
Davey Lopes 20.00
1977 Thurman Munson 20.00
Mark Fidrych 20.00
Randy Jones 20.00
1978 Reggie Jackson 22.00
Rod Carew 18.00
Steve Garvey 18.00
1979 Ron Guidry 18.00
J.R. Richard 18.00
Burt Hooten 18.00
1980 Mike Flanagan 18.00
Joe Niekro 18.00
Brian Downing 18.00

1981 Mike Schmidt 16.00
all other covers . . . . . @15.00
1982 Nolan Ryan 45.00
Rich Gossage & Pete Rose 18.00
Rollie Fingers &
Tom Seaver 16.00
all other covers . . . . . @15.00
1983 Steve Carlton 15.00
all other covers . . . . . @15.00
1984 Carlton Fisk 15.00
Dale Murphy 14.00
all other covers . . . . . @14.00
1985 Dwight Gooden 15.00
Tigers Take It All 14.00
all other covers . . . . . @14.00
1986 Nolan Ryan 22.50
Gooden & Mattingly 16.00
all other covers . . . . . @14.00
1987 Gary Carter &Jesse Orosco 12.00
Joe Carter 12.00
all other covers . . . . . @12.00
1988 Don Mattingly 13.00

Street & Smith's: 1986

Dale Murphy 12.50
Ozzie Smith 12.50
all other covers . . . . . @12.00
1989 Jose Canseco 12.00
Orel Hershiser 11.00
Mark Grace & Chris Sabo 11.00
Kevin McReynolds 11.00
all other cover . . . . . . @10.00
1990 Anniversary Issue 8.00

WHO'S WHO IN BASEBALL

1912 Generic cover 200.00
1913-15 . . . . not published
1916 Ty Cobb & A's Outfielder 100.00
1917 Tris Speaker 85.00
1918 George Sisler 75.00
1919 Grover Cleveland
Alexander 75.00
1920 Babe Ruth 125.00
1921 Babe Ruth 125.00
1922 Rogers Hornsby 75.00
1923 George Sisler 65.00
1924 Walter Johnson 70.00
1925 Dizzy Vance 50.00
1926 Max Carey 50.00
1927 Frank Frisch 50.00
1928 Hack Wilson 50.00
1929 Bob O'Farrell 45.00
1930 Burleigh Grimes 45.00
1931 Lefty Grove 45.00
1932 Al Simmons 42.50
1933 Chuck Klein 42.50
1934 Bill Terry 42.50
1935 Dizzy Dean 40.00
1936 Hank Greenberg 40.00

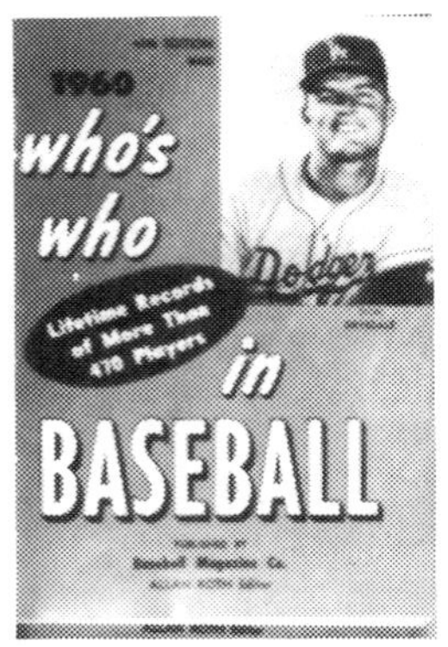

Who's Who in Baseball: 1921; 1960

1937 Lou Gehrig 50.00
1938 Joe Medwick 37.50
1939 Jimmie Foxx 37.50
1940 Bucky Walters 32.50
1941 Bob Feller 32.50
1942 Joe DiMaggio 35.00
1943 Ted Williams 32.50
1944 Stan Musial 30.00
1945 Newhouser, Trout 27.50
1946 Hal Newhouser 25.00
1947 Eddie Dyer 25.00
1948 Ralph Kiner, Johnny Mize 25.00
1949 Lou Boudreau 22.50
1950 Mel Parnell 18.50
1951 Jim Konstanty 18.50
1952 Stan Musial 17.50
1953 Sauer, Shantz 17.50
1954 Al Rosen 16.00
1955 Alvin Dark 17.50
1956 Duke Snider 17.50
1957 Mickey Mantle 20.00
1958 Warren Spahn 17.50
1959 Bob Turley 15.00
1960 Don Drysdale 15.00
1961 Roger Maris 17.50
1962 Whitey Ford 13.50
1963 Don Drysdale 12.50
1964 Sandy Koufax 13.50
1965 Juan Marichal, Klete Boyer 12.50
1966 Willie Mays, Sandy Koufax 13.50
1967 Robinson,Koufax,Clemente 12.50
1968 Carl Yastrzemski 11.00
1969 Rose, Gibson, Yaz, McLain 12.50
1970 Seaver, Killebrew,McCovey 11.00
1971 Johnny Bench,Bob Gibson 10.00
1972 Vida Blue, Joe Torre 8.50
1973 Steve Carlton, Dick Allen . . 8.50
1974 Ryan, Rose, Jackson 10.00
1975 Lou Brock, Steve Garvey . . 8.50
1976 Joe Morgan, Fred Lynn . . . 8.50
1977 Joe Morgan,
Thurman Munson 8.50
1978 Rod Carew, George Foster 8.50
1979 Guidry, Parker, Rice 8.00
1980 Willie Stargell, K.Hernandez 7.50
1981 Mike Schmidt, George Brett 8.00
1982 F. Valenzuela,Rollie Fingers 6.50
1983 Dale Murphy, Robin Yount . 6.50
1984 D. Strawberry, Cal Ripken . 6.50
1985 Ryne Sandberg 6.00
1986 Gooden, Mattingly, McGee . 5.50
1987 Mike Schmidt, R.Clemens . 5.00
1988-92 . . . . @3.50

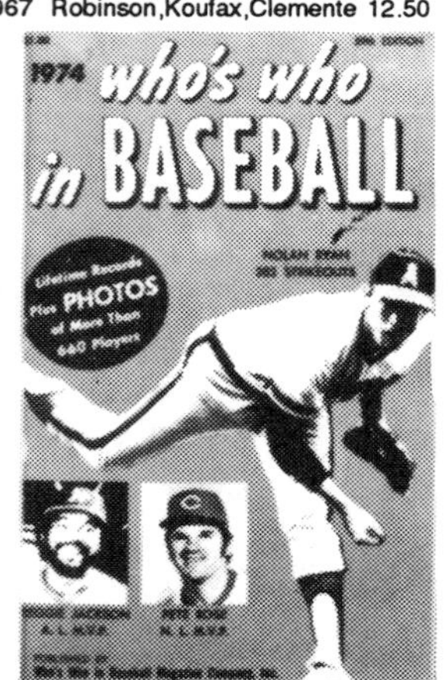

Who's Who in Baseball: 1970; 1974

BASKETBALL

ALL-PRO BASKETBALL STARS

1976	Rick Barry	7.50
1977	John Havlicek	8.00
1978	Julius Erving	10.00
1979	David Thompson	6.00
1981	Larry Bird vs. Julius Erving	15.00
1982	Julius Erving	8.00

BASKETBALL ANNUAL
(Complete Sports)

70-71	Lew Alcindor	15.00
71-72	Pete Maravich	12.50
72-73		7.50
73-74	Bill Walton	7.50
74-75	David Thompson	6.00
75-76	Rick Barry	6.00
76-77		6.00
	Published by Tiger Press	
77-78		5.00
78-79		5.00
79-80		6.50
80-81		10.00
81-82	Sampson; Bagley; John Paxson	5.00
82-83		6.00
83-84		6.00
84-85		5.00
85-86		5.00
86-87	David Robinson	7.50
87-88		6.00
88-89	M.Johnson & Isiah Thomas	8.00
89-90		4.00
90-91		4.00

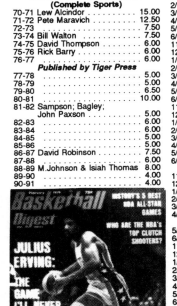

Basketball Digest: February, 1976

BASKETBALL DIGEST

11/73	Artis Gilmore	15.00
12/73	Jerry West	10.00
1/74	Norm Van Lier	6.00
2/74	Kareem Abdul-Jabbar	12.50
3/74	Walt Frazier	8.00
4/74	Dave DeBeusschere	7.50
11/74	John Havlicek	8.00
12/74	Bob McAdoo	6.00
1/75	Bob Lanier	6.00
2/75	Bill Walton	8.00
3/75	Nate Thurmond	6.00
4/75	Rick Barry	6.50
11/75	Kareem Abdul-Jabbar	8.25
12/75	Walt Frazier	6.00
1/76	Pete Maravich	6.75
2/76	Julius Erving	12.00
3/76	Elvin Hayes	6.00
4/76	Dave Cowens	6.00
11/76	Bob McAdoo	5.50
12/76	Julius Erving & David Thompson	9.50
1/77	Artis Gilmore	5.50
2/77	George McGinnis	5.00
3/77	Earl Monroe	5.75
4/77	Bill Walton	6.50
5/77	Jo Jo White	5.00
6/77	Karem Abdul-Jabbar (POY)	7.00
11/77	Maurice Lucas	4.50
12/77	Rick Barry	5.00
1/78	Daryl Dawkins & Moses Malone	6.00
2/78	Alvin Adams	4.50
3/78	Dan Issel	4.50
4/78	Dave Cowens	5.00
5/78	Bob Lanier	5.00
6/78	Bill Walton, (POY)	5.75
11/78	Marvin Webster	4.50
12/78	George Gervin	5.00
1/79	David Thompson	5.00
2/79	Pete Maravich	6.25
3/79	Bob McAdoo	4.50
4/79	Elvin Hayes	5.00
5/79	Artis Gilmore	4.50
6/79	Moses Malone, (POY)	5.50
11/79	Dennis Johnson	4.50
12/79	Kareem Abdul-Jabbar	6.25
1/80	Paul Westphal	4.50
2/80	Julius Erving	7.25
3/80	Larry Bird	12.50
4/80	Marques Johnson	4.00
5/80	Lloyd Free	4.00
6/80	Julius Erving & Magic Johnson	15.00
11/80	Magic Johnson	12.50
12/80	Phil Ford	3.50
1/81	Bill Cartwright	3.50
2/81	Walter Davis	3.50
3/81	Daryl Dawkins	3.50
4/81	Adrian Dantley & Darrell Griffith	4.00
5/81	George Gervin	4.00
6/81	Julius Erving, (POY)	7.75
11/81	Larry Bird	8.50
12/81	Moses Malone	4.25
1/82	Joe Barry Carroll	3.50
2/82	Isiah Thomas	4.25
3/82	Reggie Theus	3.50
4/82	Sidney Moncreif	3.50
5/82	Alex English	3.50
6/82	Kareem Abdul-Jabbar	5.25
11/82	Magic Johnson	10.50
12/82	Buck Williams	3.50
1/83	Robert Parrish	3.50
2/83	Kelly Tripucka	3.00
3/83	Gus Williams	3.00
4/83	Bernard King	3.50
5/83	Artis Gilmore	3.00
6/83	Moses Malone, (POY)	3.50
11/83	Julius Erving	6.50
12/83	Kiki Vandeweghe	3.00
1/84	Larry Bird	8.00
2/84	Mark Aguire	3.00
3/84	Maurice Lucas	3.00
4/84	Jim Paxson	3.00
5/84	Magic Johnson	8.50
6-7/84	Ralph Sampson, (ROY)	3.00
11/84	Larry Bird	7.00
12/84	Jack Sikma	3.00
1/85	Bernard King	3.50
2/85	Isiah Thomas	4.00
3/85	Jeff Ruland	3.00
4/85	Akeem Olajuwon	5.00
5/85	Kareem Abdul-Jabbar	4.75
6-7/85	Michael Jordan, (ROY)	11.00
11/85	Patrick Ewing	5.00
12/85	Rolando Blackman	3.00
1/86	Kevin McHale	3.00
2/86	Dominique Wilkins	3.50
3/86	Ralph Sampson	2.50
4/86	Charles Barkley	4.75
5/86	Magic Johnson	7.75
6-7/86	Larry Bird, (POY)	6.75
11/86	Akeem Olajuwon	4.50
12/86	Xavier McDaniel	3.00
1/87	Michael Jordan	8.50
2/87	Moses Malone	3.50
3/87	Terry Cummings	3.00
4/87	Julius Erving	6.00
5/87	Kevin McHale, Kevin Willis	3.00
6-7/87	Magic Johnson, (POY)	6.50
11/87	Larry Bird	5.75
12/87	Isiah Thomas	3.00
1/88	Karl Malone	3.00
2/88	Charles Barkley	3.50
3/88	Rolando Blackman & Derek Harper	2.50
4/88	Michael Jordan	7.50
5/88	Adrian Dantley	2.50
6-7/88	Magic Johnson	5.50
11/88	Larry Bird	5.25
12/88	Kevin Duckworth	2.50
1/89	Reggie Theus & Moses Malone	2.50
2/89	Kareem Abdul-Jabbar	3.50
3/89	Patrick Ewing & Brad Daugherty	3.00
4/89	Michael Adams	2.00
5/89	Karl Malone & Akeem Olajuwon	3.00
6-7/89	Michael Jordan, (POY)	6.00
11/89	Joe Dumars	3.00
12/89	Chris Mullin	3.00
1/90	Ewing, Jordan, T. Tucker	5.00
2/90	Dennis Rodman	2.50
3/90	Charles Barkley	3.00
4/90	Terry Porter	2.50
5/90	Michael Jordan	5.25
6-7/90	David Robinson, (ROY)	7.50
11/90	Kevin Johnson	3.00
12/90	Mark Price	2.50
1/91	Charles Smith	2.00
2/91	Bill Laimbeer	2.00
3/91	David Robinson & Akeem Olajuwon	5.50
4/91	Brian Shaw & K.McHale	2.00
5/91	Clyde Drexler	2.50
6-7/91	Michael Jordan, (POY)	4.00

Basketball Forecast: 1985-86

BASKETBALL FORECAST

85-86	Michael Jordan & Larry Bird	10.00
86-87	Patrick Ewing vs. Akeem Olajuwon	6.00
87-88	Magic Johnson	7.50
88-89	Michael Jordan	8.00
89-90	Magic Johnson	6.00
90-91		5.00

BASKETBALL NEWS YEARBOOK

1974 Julius Erving 15.00
1975 John Havlicek & Walt Frazier 12.50
1976 Rick Barry 7.50
1977 Julius Erving 12.50
1978 Walton, Maravich, Reed . . . 8.00
1979 Unseld, Walton, Lieberman 7.50

Basketball Scene: 1991

BASKETBALL SCENE

79-80 . . . . 8.00
80-81 Magic Johnson & Larry Bird 15.00
81-82 . . . . 10.00
82-83 . . . . 8.00
83-84 . . . . 6.00
84-85 . . . . 6.00
85-86 Patrick Ewing 6.00
86-87 Jordan, Bird, Olajuwon, D. Wilkins 7.00
87-88 . . . . 5.00
88-89 . . . . 5.00
89-90 . . . . 5.00
90-91 . . . . 4.00
91-92 Jordan, Bird, Magic 3.50

BASKETBALL SPORTS STARS

(Hewfred)

1969 Alcindor, E. Monroe, B.Bradley 20.00
1970 Lew Alcindor 15.00
1971 . . . . 10.00
1972 Pete Maravich 10.00
1973 Wilt Chamberlain 12.50
1974 Walt Frazier 7.50

BASKETBALL WEEKLY

1967

12/4 Alcindor;Will NBA Survive? 15.00
12/11 Butch Van Breda Kolff 5.00
12/21 "No War With ABA" 5.00
12/31 Bing, College Holiday Tourneys 5.00

1968

1/8 UCLA Wins 42nd Straight . 7.50
1/15 1st ABA All-Star Game . . . 7.25
1/22 Houston v.UCLA w/E.Hayes 6.00
1/29 Houston beats UCLA w/Hayes 6.00
2/5 Chamberlain; NBA Expands 8.00
2/12 NCAA Conference Races . 5.00
2/19 76ers Won't Lose Hannum . 5.00
2/26 NCAA Tournament Nears . 5.00
3/11 NCAA All-Americans 7.75
3/18 Kentucky, UNC Dark Horses 5.00
3/25 Can Houston Do It Again? . 5.00
4/30 All-NBA: Russell, Wilt, etc. . 8.00
11/1 Lakers w/Chamberlain, others 8.00
12/2 UCLA Pre-Season Number One 5.25
12/12 Unseld, Monroe, Bullets . . . 5.00
12/23 UCLA After Alcindor 7.00
12/30 NCAA Holiday Tourneys . . 5.00

1969

1/6 Peace on Lakers w/Wilt . . . 7.00
1/13 NBA All-Stars 7.00
1/20 Bullets Most Improved Team 5.00
2/3 NBA Referees; Chamberlain 6.00
2/10 Who is #2 Behind UCLA? . 5.00
2/17 LaSalle on NCAA Probation 4.25
2/24 NCAA Upsets 4.25
3/3 Scouting Reports; Alcindor, etc. 5.00
3/10 NCAA All-Americans 6.00
3/17 Who will Challenge UCLA? 4.25
4/1 UCLA Shoots for #3 . . . . . 4.25
5/1 All-NBA Team 6.00
11/22 NBA vs. ABA w/Barry 5.25
12/8 Many Try to Succeed UCLA 4.25
12/19 Knicks, Kentucky #1 w/Bradley 4.25
12/29 College Holiday Tourneys . 4.00

1970

1/5 Kentucky #1; Dan Issel . . . 4.00
1/12 Kentucky, UCLA #1, 2 . . . . 4.00
1/19 NBA All-Stars, w/Alcindor . . 6.00
1/26 No Merger for NBA, ABA . . 4.00
2/2 Pistol Pete Maravich 7.25
2/9 ABA Makes "War Plans" . . 4.00
2/16 St. Bonaventure; Bob Lanier 4.75
2/23 Controversial World of R.Mount 4.00
3/2 Kentucky, UCLA Tied in Poll 4.25
3/9 NCAA All-Americans; D.Issel 4.50
3/16 NCAA Tourney Previw 4.00
3/23 UCLA Shoots for 4th 4.25
4/6 Pro Cage War Continues . . 4.00
5/10 Lakers-Knicks Showdown . 4.75
11/23 NBA vs.ABA 4.00
11/30 UCLA Pre-Season #1 . . . . 4.00
12/10 Pro Merger Gap Widens . . 3.50
12/21 Bucks Set Record Pace . . . 3.50

1971

1/4 College Holiday Tourneys . 3.50
1/11 Pistons Are For Real 3.50
1/18 NBA All-Star Game w/Wilt, etc. 5.00
1/25 ABA All-Star Game w/Issel, etc. 4.50
2/1 Wicks Omitted in "Secret Draft" 3.50
2/8 #2 USC Looks to Beat #1 UCLA 3.50
2/15 UCLA Number One 3.50
2/22 Every ABA Team Can Win Title 3.50
3/1 Which Player Will Be #1 Pick? 4.00
3/8 NCAA All-Americans 5.00
3/15 NCAA Tournament 3.75
3/22 Kentucky Sentinal Choice . 3.50
2/29 Who Can Topple UCLA? . . 3.50
5/15 Italy Attracting U.S. Players 3.50
11/23 ABA, NBA Start New Seasons 3.50
11/30 USC New #1 . . . . 3.50
12/10 Lakers Crusade w/Wilt 4.50
12/21 UCLA #1 . . . . 3.50

1972

1/11 Marquette's Jim Chones . . 3.00
1/18 NBA All-Star Game 4.75
1/25 Ivy League; UCLA #1 . . . . 3.50
2/1 ABA All-Star Game 4.25
2/8 ABA Draft; Denny Crum . . . 3.50
2/15 Proposed Division After Merger 3.00
2/22 UCLA Favored Again 3.50
2/29 Jim McDaniels to NBA 3.00
3/7 Erving to Jump Leagues? . 5.25
3/14 ABA After Walton 3.50
3/21 Walton (POY) 3.50
3/28 Rupp's Last Game? 3.50
5/15 West (POY) 3.75
11/21 NBA-ABA War Continues . . 3.00
12/5 Doug Collins, Illinois St. . . . 3.50
12/12 New Celts Legend Cowens 3.50
12/19 Kentucky's Joe B. Hall 3.00
12/26 Phil Sellers, David Thompson 3.00

1973

1/4 Jabbar vs. Chamberlain . . . 6.25
1/18 Dwight Lamar, SW La. St. . 2.50
1/25 NBA All-Star Game w/West 3.50
2/1 UCLA Eyes #61 w/Walton . 3.50
2/8 ABA All-Star Game w/Erving 5.00
2/15 The Big Eight 3.00
2/22 Larry Brown 3.00
3/1 Ed Ratleff, Long Beach St. . 2.50
3/8 Phil Chenier, Archie Clark . 3.00
3/15 All-Americans: Walton, others 3.50
3/22 Walton (POY) 3.50
3/29 Meet Me in St. Louis 3.00
5/15 Archibald (POY) 3.00
11/21 Russell w/Sonics 4.50
12/12 Marvin Barnes 2.50
12/19 Geoff Petrie & Sidney Wicks 2.50
12/26 N.C. State: Thompson, others 3.00

1974

1/2 Wilt Chamberlain 5.25
1/9 Kent Benson & Scott May . 2.50
1/16 NBA All-Star Game w/Jabbar 4.25
1/23 Michigan Leads Big 10 . . . 2.50
1/30 Pacers' Mel Daniels 3.00
2/6 Canisius'Larry Fogle 2.00
2/13 So Long Dave (DeBusschere) 3.00
2/20 Referee Ed Rush 2.50
2/27 Road to Greensboro; Walton 3.00
3/6 Willie Wise & James Jones 2.50
3/13 All-Americans w/Walton . . . 3.75
3/20 Bill Walton (POY) 3.00
3/27 David Thompson 2.50
5/15 Dr. J. ABA (POY) 4.75
11/21 ABA 3.00
12/1 NCAA Preview 3.00
12/26 End of an Era: Wilt; others 4.50

1975

1/2 NBA Rookies 3.25
1/9 Hubie Brown 2.50
1/16 Marvin Webster 2.50
1/23 Louisville's Denny Crum . . 2.50
1/30 Moses Malone 4.00
2/6 30 Second Clock in NCAA . 2.00
2/13 Bob McAdoo 2.50
2/20 N.C. State 2.00
2/27 Dave Bing, Norm Van Lier . 2.50
3/6 Wes Unseld 3.50
3/12 Mack Calvin 2.50
3/20 All-Americans: Dantley, others 3.00
3/27 D. Thompson (POY) 2.50
4/3 Kentucky vs. Loisville 2.50
5/15 Dr. J. ABA (POY) 4.25
6/19 Golden State, Kentucky Champs 3.00

1976

11/25 All-Time ABA: Erving,Barry,etc. 4.50
12/9 Marquette Number One . . . 2.00
12/23 Albert King 2.00
12/30 Jim Chones & Campy Russell 2.00

1977

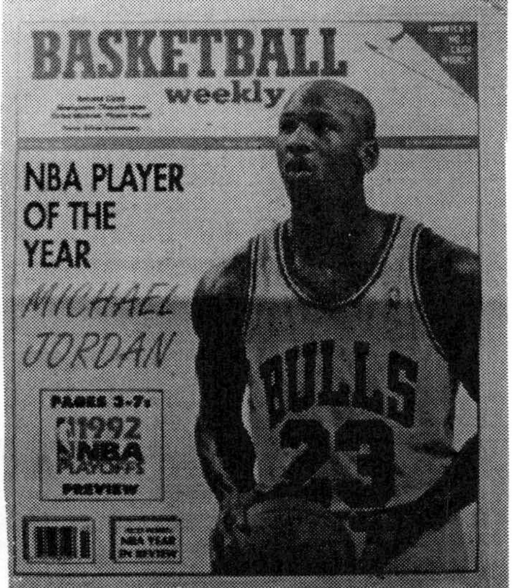

Basketball Weekly:7/6/1992; 5/12/92

1/6 Larry O'Brien, Man of the Year ... 2.00
1/13 Kentucky's Jack Givens ... 2.00
1/20 Bob Lanier ... 2.75
1/27 Dr. J. & George McGinnis . 3.75
2/3 Jerry West as Coach ... 2.50
2/10 Cincinnati Bearcats ... 2.00
2/17 College vs. Pros TV Ratings ... 2.00
2/24 David Thompson ... 2.00
3/3 Michigan's Ricky Green ... 2.00
3/10 U. of San Francisco ... 2.00
3/17 All-Americans Thompson, etc ... 2.50
2/24 M. Thompson (POY) ... 2.50
3/31 The Final Four ... 2.00
4/14 McGuire,Marquette Champs 2.50
11/30 Jabbar vs. Walton ... 3.50
12/14 Dean Smith ... 3.25
12/21 Prep Basketball ... 2.50
12/28 Adolph Rupp, 1901-1977 .. 4.50

1978

1/5 Al McGuire, Man of the Year ... 2.50
1/12 Larry Bird, Indiana St. ... 11.00
1/19 Portland Blazers ... 2.00
1/26 Kyle Macy, Kentucky ... 1.50
2/2 Artis Gilmore ... 2.00
2/9 Arkansas: Moncreif, others . 2.50
2/16 NBA Mid-Season Report .. 2.00
2/23 Jabbar, Lakers ... 3.50
3/2 Marques Johnson, Bucks .. 2.00
3/9 All-Americans: Bird, Ford, etc. ... 6.50
3/16 Butch Lee, (POY) ... 2.00
3/23 Ted Owens, Coach of the Year ... 2.00
3/30 Mike Phillips, Kentucky ... 1.50
4/15 Kentucky Champs ... 2.00
11/29 Bill Walton ... 2.00
12/13 UCLA: Greenwood, others . 2.00
12/20 DeMetha Prep Coach Wooten ... 1.50
12/27 Gene Bartow ... 1.50

1979

1/4 John Havlicek ... 3.25
1/11 George Gervin ... 2.50
1/25 Elvin Hayes ... 2.50
2/1 Jack Ramsey ... 1.50
2/8 Duke University ... 2.25
2/15 Phil Ford, K.C. Kings ... 1.75
2/22 Digger Phelps ... 1.50
3/1 Syracuse's Boeheim, others 1.50
3/8 All-Americans: Bird, Magic, etc. ... 12.00
3/15 Larry Bird (POY) ... 6.50
3/22 Dean Smith Coach of the Year ... 3.25
3/29 Magic, Bird, NCAA Tourney 11.00
4/15 Dick Motta ... 1.50
6/15 Class of '83 w/Sampson .. 1.75
11/28 Havlicek, Dr. J., Kareem .. 4.25
12/12 Ohio St. #1 ... 1.50
12/19 Prep Stars ... 2.00
12/26 76ers' Dr. J., Collins ... 3.50

1980

1/3 Ray Meyer ... 1.50
1/10 Larry Brown ... 1.50
1/17 Hubie Brown, John Drew .. 1.50
1/24 Darrell Griffith ... 1.50
1/31 Moses Malone ... 2.00
2/7 Larry Bird ... 4.25
2/14 Danny Ainge Two Sports .. 2.00
2/21 D. Johnson & Gus Williams 2.00
2/28 Frank McGuire ... 1.50
3/7 All-Americans: Aguirre, others ... 2.50
3/14 Mark Aguirre (POY) ... 2.00
3/21 Denny Crum Coach of the Year ... 1.50
3/28 Final Four ... 1.50
4/15 NBA Playoffs ... 1.50
11/28 NCAA Preview ... 1.50
12/12 Walter Davis ... 1.75
12/26 Magic Johnson, Man of the Year ... 6.50

1981

1/8 Albert King, Maryland ... 1.50
1/15 New Knicks ... 1.50
1/22 Oregon St. ... 1.50
12/29 Ray Meyer ... 1.50
2/5 Marques Johnson ... 1.50
2/12 David Thompson ... 1.75
2/26 Billy Cunningham ... 1.50
3/5 Durand Macklin, LSU ... 1.50
3/12 Bird & Parrish ... 5.25
3/19 All-Americans Isiah, Sampson ... 4.50
3/26 Ralph Miller, Oregon St. .. 1.50
4/2 R. Sampson (POY) ... 1.50
4/15 Paul Westhead ... 1.75
6/15 Patrick Ewing Georgetown Bound ... 4.50
11/20 Kupchak, Birdsong,Edwards 1.50
11/27 Larry Farmer, UCLA Coach 1.50
12/4 Billy Thompson ... 1.50
12/19 Adrian Dantley ... 1.50
12/26 Wes Unseld, Man of the Year ... 1.75

1982

1/7 Antoine Carr ... 1.50
1/21 McCrays, Louisville ... 1.50
1/28 Dr. J., Dawkins, 76ers ... 1.75
2/4 Sleepy Floyd ... 1.50
2/11 Bill Fitch ... 1.25
2/18 Cooper vs. McHale ... 2.00
2/25 Stipanovich, Missouri ... 1.25
3/4 James Worthy, UNC ... 3.25
3/11 George Gervin ... 1.75
3/18 All-Americans Worthy, others ... 2.00
3/25 R. Sampson (POY) ... 1.25
4/1 Dana Kirk Coach of the Year ... 1.25
5/8 The Final Four ... 1.50
5/15 Magic Johnson, Dr. J, others ... 5.25
6/15 Norm Nixon ... 1.25
11/14 Moses Malone ... 1.75
11/21 Ewing, Sampson, Perkins . 2.00
12/9 McGuire, Prep Reggie Williams ... 1.25
12/23 Gus Williams ... 1.25

1983

1/3 Dean Smith Man; of the Year ... 1.50
1/13 Rollie Massimino ... 1.50
1/20 UCLA's Jackson, Wright .. 1.25
1/27 Kareem vs. Parish ... 2.50
2/3 Melvin Turpin ... 1.25
2/10 Dr. J, Moses Malone ... 2.50
2/17 Marques Johnson ... 1.25
2/24 Buck Williams & Larry Brown ... 1.50
3/3 Sampson, Holland, O. Wilson ... 1.25
3/10 Maurice Lucas ... 1.25

Date	Issue	Price
3/17	R. Wittman & Troy Taylor	1.25
3/24	All-Americans Jordan, others	8.50
3/31	R. Sampson (POY)	1.25
4/7	Guy Lewis, Coach of the Year	1.25
4/14	Derrick Floyd	1.25
5/15	Moses Malone vs. Lakers	1.75
11/14	New NBA Coaches	1.25
11/28	Ewing & Georgetown	2.25
12/12	Sikma, Denny Crum	1.25
12/19	Dantley, NCAA Coaches	1.25
	1984	
1/3	World Free, others	1.25
1/16	Dr. J Man of the Year	2.75
1/23	Rookies Sampson, Stipo, others	1.25
1/30	Michael Cage	1.25
2/6	Isiah Thomas & Kelly Tripucka	2.25
2/13	Terry Holland & Othell Wilson	1.25
2/20	Wayman Tisdale, others	1.25
2/27	McHale, Mark Price, etc.	1.75
3/5	Magic Johnson & Isiah Thomas	5.50
3/12	Michael Jordan & Sam Perkins	5.50
3/19	All-Americans Jordan, Mullin,etc	5.50
3/26	NCAA Tournament	1.75
4/2	Billy Tubbs	1.50
4/9	Olajuwon, Final Four	4.25
5/21	Moses Malone, 76ers	1.75
6/18	Jabbar vs. Parish	2.50
11/12	Magic, Toney, D. Stern	3.75
11/26	Mullin, Tisdale, P. Washington	2.25
12/10	Preps	1.75
12/17	Ewing, Georgetown vs. DePaul	2.00
12/31	Larry Bird Man of the Year	3.75
	1985	
1/14	Orlando Woolridge	1.25
1/21	Akeem Olajuwon	2.25
1/28	Dominque Wilkins	3.50
2/4	James Worthy	1.75
2/11	Danny Manning, Kansas	2.25
2/18	NBA All-Stars: Kareem, Dr.J	2.25
2/25	Ed Pickney, Villanova	1.50
3/4	John Williams' 3 Schools	1.25
3/11	Cummings, Nance, Ferry in H.S.	1.75
3/18	All-Americans Ewing, Mullin,etc	2.75
3/25	Patrick Ewing (POY)	2.00
4/1	Bill Frieder, Coach of the Year	1.25
4/8	Ewing, Mullin, Pickney, K. Lee	2.00
5/20	Larry Bird & Robert Parish	2.75
6/24	Tisdale, Mullin, others	1.75
11/11	Ewing, DeBusschere, D. Stern	2.00
11/25	UNC's Daugherty, Smith, Hale	2.00
12/16	J.R. Reid Top Prep	1.75
12/23	Chris Mullin	1.75
	1986-7	
1/6	Kareem Man of the Year	2.50
1/20	J. McCaffrey & M. Martin	1.00
1/27	Reggie Lewis	1.75
2/3	Dr. J & Geroge Gervin	2.50
2/10	Dana Kirk, others	1.00
2/17	Magic, O. Polynice, Guy Lewis	2.75
2/24	Pitino, Webb & M. Bol	1.50
3/3	Akeem Olajuwon, Ron Harper	2.00
3/10	Duke's Alarie, Dawkins, Coach	1.75
3/17	All-Americans Daugherty, others	1.75
3/24	Walter Berry (POY)	1.00
3/31	Krzyzewski, Coach of the Year	1.25
4/7	Final Four Coaches	1.25
4/21	Prep All-Amer. Mills,Reid,etc	1.50
5/19	Larry Bird (POY)	2.75
6/23	Draft Preview: Bias, others	3.25
12/1	Kentucky's Chapman, others	1.50
12/21	Preps Mourning, Owens, others	3.75
	1988	
1/4	Dick Vitale & Bob Knight	2.25
1/11	David Robinson, Man of the Year	5.25
1/25	Pete Maravich Dies	4.75
2/1	W. Hazzard & M. Ray Richardson	1.25
2/8	NBA All-Stars: Jordan, Magic	3.75
2/15	Jordan, M. Sealy, Billy Packer	3.25
2/22	Michael Smith	1.00
2/29	John Chaney, Temple	1.00
3/7	Hersey Hawkins, others	1.50
3/14	Preps Mustaf, Hurley, others	1.50
3/21	All-Americans Elliott,Manning	1.75
3/28	D.Manning (POY)	1.50
4/4	Lute Olson	1.00
4/11	NCAA Final Four Choices	1.25
5/2	Preps Mourning, Owens	2.50
5/16	Jordan, Mark Jackson, Pat Riley	2.75
6/20	NBA Draft: Manning, Seikaly,etc	1.25
11/15	Danny Manning to Clippers	1.25
12/6	Duke #1: Ferry, Coach K	1.50
12/20	Prep Kenny Anderson	2.50
	1989	
1/3	Michael Jordan & Tarkanian	2.50
1/10	Jerry West, Man of the Year	1.25
1/24	Randy White, LA Tech	1.00
1/31	D. Wilkins & Tom Hammonds	1.75
2/7	Cavs Daugherty, Harper, others	1.50
2/14	NBA All-Stars w/Olajuwon	1.50
2/21	Stacey King & Mookie Blaylock	1.50
2/28	Terry Cimmings	1.00
3/7	Chris Jackson	1.25
3/14	Suns' Chambers, Johnson, etc	1.75
3/21	Lute Olson	1.00
3/27	All-Americans S.King,Elliott,etc	1.25
4/3	Sean Elliott (POY)	1.25
4/10	Final Four Preview	1.25
5/29	Michigan's Robinson, Rice, etc	1.50
5/16	Lakers: 3 in a Row?	1.25
6/20	Draft Preview: Ferry,Elliott,etc	1.50
11/14	Isiah Thomas	1.75
12/5	Day, Mayberry, Arkansas #1	1.50
12/19	Preps Montross, Bradley, Wright	2.00
	1990	
1/2	Basketball Cards	1.25
1/10	Chuck Daly, Coach of the Year	1.25
1/23	Gary Payton, others	1.25
1/30	Alonzo Mourning	1.75
2/13	Doug Smith, NBA All-Stars	1.75
2/20	Karl Malone	1.75
2/27	Ga.Tech's Scott, Cremins, etc	1.50
3/6	Charles Barkley	2.00
3/13	Chris Smith, UConn	1.50
3/20	Olajuwon, Kessler T. Hill	1.75
3/26	All-Amers. Coleman, Payton, etc	2.00
4/2	L. Simmons (POY)	1.75
4/9	Leather, Anderson, others	2.25
5/1	UNLV: Johnson, Augmon, Tark, etc	2.75
5/15	NBA Playoffs Preview	1.25
6/1	Draft Preview: Coleman,Scott,etc	1.50
11/13	Michael Jordan	2.75
11/27	Arizona's Rooks, Williams,Stokes	1.50
12/10	Chris Webber Top Prep	2.50
12/17	Paul Westhead	1.00
	1991	
1/14	Shaquille O'Neal	3.00
2/4	Denny Crum & Rick Pitino	1.00
2/11	Bernard King	1.25
2/18	Augmon & Mayberry	1.50
2/25	Michael Jordan	2.00
3/4	Jim Jackson, Cheaney, others	1.75
3/11	Cheeks, English, Moses Malone	1.25
3/18	Dehere, Booth, others	1.25
3/25	All-Amers. Johnson, O'Neal,etc	2.25
4/1	L. Johnson (POY)	2.00
4/8	Final Four Preview	1.25
4/29	Chris Webber H.S. All-American	1.75
5/13	Michael Jordan, Playoff Preview	1.75
7/8	Draft: Johnson, Mutombo,Owens	2.00
11/19	Drexler, 1st Color Photo Cover	2.00
12/3	UCLA's MacLean, Madkins,Martin	1.75
	1992	
1/7	Mike Krzyewski, 1991 Man of the Year	2.95
3/10	LaPhonso Ellis	2.95
5/12	Jordan, NBA POY	2.95
7/6	Magic Johnson, Gold Rush	2.95
11/17	Ewing, NBA Preview	2.95

Basketball's Best: 1951-52

BASKETBALL'S BEST

Season	Issue	Price
51-52	Harry Boykoff	50.00
52-53	George Mikan	65.00
53-54	Mikan, Cousy, Schayes, others	60.00
54-55	Mikan, Cousy, Schayes, others	60.00
55-56	Red Rocha	25.00

56-57 Hand palming basketball . 20.00
57-58 Bob Cousy 35.00
58-59 Tom Heinsohn & Bill Russell 35.00
59-60 Frank Ramsey 15.00
60-61 Elgin Baylor vs. Hawks . . 15.00
61-62 Wilt Chamberlain vs. Knicks 20.00
62-63 Chamberlain, West, Baylor, others 20.00
63-64 Jerry West 20.00
64-65 Wilt Chamberlain 20.00
65-66 Elgin Baylor 15.00
66-67 Rick Barry 12.50
67-68 Chamberlain & Russell . . 17.50
68-69 Bailey, Howell, Havlicek . . 12.50
69-70 L. Alcindor & W. Reed . . 25.00
70-71 W. Chamberlain & W. Reed 10.00
71-72 L. Alcindor & W. Reed . . . 10.00
72-73 L. Alcindor & W. Chamberlain 15.00

COMPLETE SPORTS BASKETBALL

61-62 Bill Russell 25.00
62-63 . . . . 15.00
63-64 Jerry West 20.00

Becomes

PRO BASKETBALL ILLUSTRATED

64-65 Oscar Robertson 20.00
65-66 Wilt Chamberlain 20.00
66-67 . . . . 12.50
67-68 . . . . 12.50
68-69 . . . . 15.00
69-70 Lew Alcindor 15.00
70-71 Lew Alcindor 15.00
71-72 Lew Alcindor 15.00
72-73 John Havlicek 10.00
73-74 Dave Cowens 7.50
74-75 Julius Erving 12.50
75-76 Bob McAdoo 6.00
76-77 Julius Erving 10.00
77-78 . . . . 6.00
78-79 . . . . 6.00
79-80 . . . . 6.00

Published by Lexington Library

80-81 . . . . 15.00
81-82 . . . . 6.00
82-83 . . . . 6.00
83-84 Julius Erving 10.00
84-85 . . . . 6.00
85-86 Larry Bird and Michael Jordan 9.00
86-87 Magic Johnson 10.00
87-88 Michael Jordan 8.00
88-89 . . . . 6.00
89-90 Michael Jordan 6.50
90-91 . . . . 5.00

CORD SPORTFACTS PRO BASKETBALL GUIDE

1973 Jerry West & Kareem Abdul-Jabbar . . . 15.00
1974 Walt Frazier 10.00
1975 Dave Cowens & K. Abdul-Jabbar 12.50
1976 Rick Barry 7.50

COURTSIDE

3/89 Kelly Tripucka 3.50
4/89 Akeem Olajuwon 5.25
5/89 Kiki Vandeweghe 4.00
11/89 David Robinson, Season Preview 7.50
12/89 Magic Johnson 8.50
1/90 Tom Chambers 3.50
2/90 Mr. and Mrs. Bill Laimbeer . 3.00
3/90 Alexander Volkov 2.50
4/90 Sherman Douglas 3.00
5/90 Isiah Thomas vs. Magic Johnson 6.50
11/90 Rodman,Cummings, Season Preview 3.00
12/90 Alvin Robertson vs. Moses . 3.00
1/91 Reggie Lewis 3.50
2/91 Mr. and Mrs. Sarunas Marciolonis 2.50
3/91 Ewing and Moses 3.50
5/91 Pippen v. Dumars, Majerle v. Kersey 4.25
12/91 Robinson, McHale, Season Preview 3.75

Dell Basketball: 1954

DELL BASKETBALL

(Woodward's: 1951)

1950 Don Logfran (Univ. of S. F.) 45.00
1951 Bob Zarvoluk (St. John's) . 40.00
1952 . . . . 25.00
1953 . . . . 20.00
1954 Bob Cousy 50.00
1955 Tom Gola (LaSalle) 15.00
1956 Heinsohn (H. Cross), Russell,Hundley 25.00
1957 Bob Pettit, Chamberlain, Hundley 20.00
1958 Wilt Chamberlain 15.00
1959 O. Robertson, J. West, C. Hawkins 15.00
1960 Wilt Chamberlain, Jerry West 15.00
1961 Jerry Lucas (Ohio St.) . . . 10.00
1962 Chamberlain vs. Russell [Feb.issue] 15.00
1963 Oscar Robertson [Jan.issue] 10.00
1964 Barry Kramer (NYU) [Jan.issue] 7.50

FAST BREAK

(Popular Library)

1970 Alcindor, West, Russell & Havlicek 15.00

Becomes:

BASKETBALL'S ALL-PRO ANNUAL

1971 Alcindor, Reed, Maravich & Mount 15.00
1972 . . . . 10.00
1973 Chamberlain vs. Kareem . 12.50
1974 . . . . 7.50
1975 John Havlicek 7.50

GAME PLAN COLLEGE BASKETBALL YEARBOOK

77-78 Phil Ford (UNC) 7.50
78-79 D. Greenwood (UCLA), Bird, Magic 25.00
87-88 Charles Smith (Pitt) 5.00
88-89 . . . . 5.00
89-90 Coleman,Owens, Thompson,Boeheim 7.00
90-91 . . . . 5.00

GAME PLAN PRO BASKETBALL YEARBOOK

77-78 Julius Erving 12.50
86-87 Mark Price & Kenny Smith 5.00
87-88 David Robinson 8.00
88-89 . . . . 5.00
89-90 . . . . 5.00
90-91 . . . . 5.00

HOOP BASKETBALL YEARBOOK

85-86 Patrick Ewing 10.00
86-87 Larry Bird & Charles Barkley 8.50
87-88 Magic Johnson vs. Kevin McHale 8.50
88-89 . . . . 5.00
89-90 . . . . 5.00
90-91 . . . . 5.00

HOOP "NBA TODAY EDITION"

11/84 Larry Bird 10.00
12/84 Bernard King 5.00
1/85 Michael Jordan 10.00
2/85 Reggie Theus 4.00
3/85 Kareem vs. Walton 6.50

Hoop NBA Today Edition: March, 1990

4/85 Isiah Thomas 6.00
5/85 Larry Bird 7.75
7/85 Bird vs. Kareem 7.75
11/85 Patrick Ewing 6.25
12/85 Julius Erving 6.75
1/86 Terry Cummings 4.00
2/86 Blackman, Schrempf, others 4.25
3/86 Derek Smith 3.50
4/86 Dominique Wilkins 5.00
5/86 Magic w/ trophy 10.00
7/86 Larry Bird 7.75
11/86 Hall of Fame special edition 7.50
12/86 Moses Malone & Larry Bird 6.75
1/87 Michael Jordan 7.75
2/87 Akeem Olajuwon 5.00
3/87 Kiki Vandeweghe 3.50
4/87 . . . . 3.50
5/87 Dr. J Tribute 7.75
6/87 Trophy, ball, shoe and towel 3.50

Issue	Cover	Price
7/87	Magic Johnson	7.75
12/87	Michael Jordan	7.50
1/88	Kareem Adbul-Jabbar	5.50
2/88	Buck Williams	3.50
3/88	Karl Malone	4.50
4/88	Isiah Thomas	4.50
5/88	Charles Barkley	5.25
6/88	Championship trophy	3.00
7/88	Magic, Kareem, Worthy vs. Pistons	6.25
12/88	Danny Manning	3.50
1/89	Dominique Wilkins, Moses, Theus	4.00
2/89	Roy Tarpley	3.00
3/89	Chris Mullin	4.50
4/89	Larry Nance	3.50
5/89	Kareem over Laimbeer	4.25
6/89	Trophy and ball	3.00
7/89	Isiah & Pistons with trophy	3.75
12/89	David Robinson	6.50
1/90	Mark Aguirre	3.00
2/90	Karl Malone	3.50
3/90	Kevin Johnson	4.25
4/90	Patrick Ewing	3.75
5/90	Fat Lever	3.00
6/90	Trophy and basketballs	3.00
7/90	Rodman, Laimbeer vs. Buck Williams	3.50
12/90	Buck Williams & Jerome Kersey	3.00
1/91	Charles Barkley over Bird	4.50
2/91		3.00
3/91	Jordan vs. Rodman and Salley	5.25
4/91	Shawn Kemp	4.00
5/91	Karl Malone vs. Mychal Thompson	3.50
6/91	Isiah Thomas	3.50
7/91	Jordan with trophy	5.50
12/91	Michael Jordan	4.50

INSIDE BASKETBALL
(Sport Magazine)

Year	Cover	Price
1964	Bill Russell & Wilt Chamberlain	25.00
1965		15.00
1966		15.00
1967		15.00
1968		15.00
1969		15.00
1970	P. Maravich, R. Mount, C. Murphy	12.50
1971	Jerry West & Walt Frazier	10.00

MACO'S PRO BASKETBALL ALL-STAR ANNUAL

Year	Cover	Price
1957	Bob Cousy	35.00
1971	Pete Maravich (Sports All-Stars)	20.00

NBA TODAY'S BASKETBALL YEARBOOK

Year	Cover	Price
83-84	Magic Johnson; Larry Bird; Ewing	15.00
84-85	Dr. J & Moses; Bird; Ewing	10.00

PETERSEN'S PRO BASKETBALL

Year	Cover	Price
78-79	Elvin Hayes	7.50
79-80	Dennis Johnson vs. Kareem	8.00
80-81	Magic Johnson	20.00
82-86	Not Published	
87-88	Magic Johnson & Sleepy Floyd	7.50
	Chambers & McDaniel, C. Drexler	6.00
	Akeem Olajuwon & Mark Aguirre	6.00
	Dominique Wilkins	6.00
	Charles Barkley & Moses Malone	6.00
	Larry Bird & Patrick Ewing	7.50
	Michael Jordan & Isiah Thomas	8.00
	Magic Johnson & Larry Bird	8.00
88-89	Magic Johnson & Michael Jordan	10.00
	Magic Johnson & Ralph Sampson	6.50
	Clyde Drexler & Dale Ellis	5.00
	Roy Tarpley & Akeem Olajuwon	6.00
	Dominique Wilkins & Michael Jordan	6.50
	Larry Bird & Patrick Ewing	6.50
	Isiah Thomas & Terry Cummings	5.00
	Karl Malone & Alex English	5.00
89-90	Magic Johnson & Chris Mullin	6.00
	Charles Barkley & Kelly Tripucka	5.00
	Michael Jordan & Magic Johnson	8.00
	Karl Malone & Dale Ellis	5.00
	Moses Malone & Michael Jordan	6.00
	Isiah Thomas & Ron Harper	5.00
	Akeem Olajuwon & Adrian Dantley	5.00
	Patrick Ewing & Robert Parish	5.00

All 90-91 issues include Jordan-Magic poster

Year	Cover	Price
90-91	Michael Jordan & Magic Johnson	10.00
	Magic Johnson & Clyde Drexler	8.00
	Karl Malone & Tom Chambers	6.00
	Akeem Olajuwon & David Robinson	8.00
	Dominique Wilkins & Rony Seikaly	6.00
	Patrick Ewing & Larry Bird	8.00
	Charles Barkley & Muggsy Bogues	6.00
	Michael Jordan & Isiah Thomas	8.00

POPULAR LIBRARY BASKETBALL YEARBOOK

Year	Cover	Price
1960	Jerry West	15.00
1961	Jerry Lucas	12.50
1962	Jerry Lucas	12.50
1963	Ron Bonham (Cincinnati)	10.00
1964	Gary Bradds (Ohio St.)	10.00
1965	Oscar Robertson & Bill Bradley	20.00
1966	Jerry West & Cazzie Russell	15.00
1967	Lew Alcindor	20.00
1968	Bradley, Alcindor, Barry	15.00
1969		10.00
1970		10.00
1971	Lew Alcindor & Willis Reed	10.00
1972	Lew Alcindor	10.00
1973	Bill Walton	7.50
1974	Bill Walton	7.50
1975	Dave Cowens & John Havlicek	7.50
1976	Rick Barry	6.00
1977	Julius Erving	10.00

PRO BASKETBALL ALMANAC
(Sport Magazine)

Year	Cover	Price
1968	Wilt Chamberlain & Bill Russell	15.00
1969		10.00
1970	John Havlicek	10.00

Pro Basketball Almanac: 1971

Year	Cover	Price
1971	Pete Maravich	10.00
1972	Lew Alcindor & Willis Reed	15.00

PRO BASKETBALL FACTBOOK

Year	Cover	Price
71-72	Lew Alcindor	15.00
72-73		10.00
73-74	Wilt Chamberlain vs. Willis Reed	10.00
74-75	Kareem Abdul-Jabbar	10.00

PRO BASKETBALL GUIDEBOOK

Year	Cover	Price
1978	Pete Maravich	15.00
1979	David Thompson	10.00

THE SPORTING NEWS COLLEGE & PRO YEARBOOK

Year	Cover	Price
82-83	Sampson, Ewing, Abdul-Jabbar	10.00
83-84	Jordan, Malone, K.Lee, Abdul-Jabbar	15.00
84-85	Wayman Tisdale & Ralph Sampson	5.00
	Alford, B. Knight, Comegys	5.00
	Patrick Ewing & Larry Bird	10.00
	Patrick Ewing & Magic Johnson	10.00
	Keith Lee & James Worthy	6.00
85-86	Mark Price & Kenny Walker	5.00
	Mark Price & Magic Johnson	8.00
	Michael Jordan & David Rivers	8.00
	Kevin McHale & Pearl Washington	5.00
86-87	Reggie Miller & Charles Barkley	6.00
	Danny Manning & Steve Alford	5.00
	Pervis Ellison & Charles Barkley	6.00
	David Robinson & Charles Barkley	8.00

THE SPORTING NEWS COLLEGE YEARBOOK

Year	Cover	Price
87-88	Rex Chapman	6.00
	Fennis Denbo	5.00
	David Rivers	5.00
	Rony Seikaly	6.00
	Danny Manning	7.00
88-89	Mookie Blaylock & Stacey King	6.00

Year	Cover	Price
	Danny Ferry	6.00
	Alonzo Mourning & Patrick Ewing	8.00
	B.J. Armstrong	6.00
	Dyron Nix & Dwayne Schintzius	5.00
	Todd Lichti & Sean Elliott	6.00
89-90	Chris Jackson	5.00
	Augmon, Tarkanian,Anthony	7.00
	Coleman, Owens, Ellis, Thompson	8.00
	Rumeal Robinson	5.00
	Chris Corchiani & Rodney Monroe	5.00
90-91	Kenny Anderson & Rodney Monroe	5.00
	Shaquille O'Neal & Allan Houston	6.00
	Augmon, L. Johnson, Chris Mills	6.00
	S. Smith, J. Jackson, Eric Anderson	6.00
	B. Owens, Chris Smith, Jim Calhoun	6.00
	B. Owens, Mourning, Darelle Porter	6.00
	S. O'Neal, Lee Mayberry, Todd Day	6.00
	Doug Smith, M. Randall, Henry Iba	4.00

THE SPORTING NEWS OFFICIAL NBA GUIDE

Year	Cover	Price
58-59	Bob Pettit	25.00
59-60	Bill Russell	25.00
60-61	Referee art	10.00
61-62	Bob Pettit	12.50
62-63	Tom Heinsohn	12.50

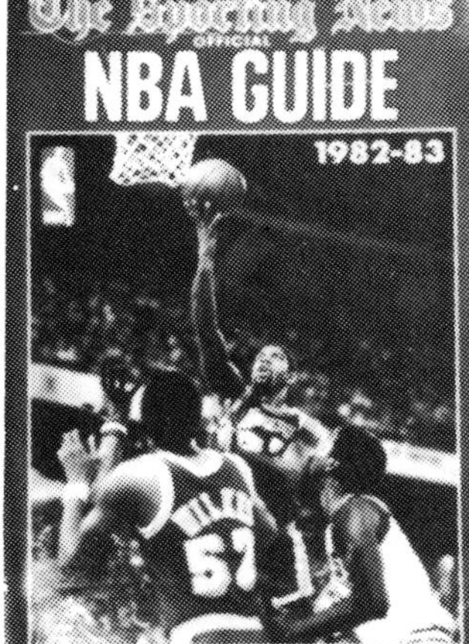

Sporting News Official NBA Guide: 1982-83

Year	Cover	Price
63-64	Hawks vs. Royals action	10.00
64-65	John Havlicek	12.50
65-66	Jerry West & Bill Russell	15.00
66-67	Gene Wiley, Lakers	8.00
67-68	Wilt Chamberlain & Nate Thurmond	12.50
68-69	Jerry West & Oscar Robertson	12.50
69-70	Team logos	7.50
70-71	Willis Reed & Wilt Chamberlain	12.50
71-72	Lew Alcindor IA vs. Unseld	12.50
72-73	Wilt Chamberlain IA vs. Knicks	12.50
73-74	Willis Reed IA vs. Celtics	8.00
74-75	John Havlicek	7.50
75-76	Rick Barry art	6.00
76-77	Jo Jo White	6.00
77-78	Bill Walton	6.00
78-79	Wes Unseld	6.00
79-80	Elvin Hayes	6.00
80-81	Larry Bird IA vs. Magic Johnson	25.00
81-82	Cedric Maxwell	6.00
82-83	Magic Johnson	12.50
83-84	Dr. J IA vs. Kareem	12.50
84-85	Larry Bird	12.50
85-86	Michael Jordan IA vs. Bird	20.00
86-87	Larry Bird	10.00
87-88	Magic Johnson	10.00
88-89	Michael Jordan	10.00
89-90	Joe Dumars	5.00

THE SPORTING NEWS OFFICIAL NBA REGISTER

Year	Cover	Price
80-81	Kareem Abdul-Jabbar	10.00
81-82	Dr. J	10.00
82-83	Moses Malone	7.50
83-84	Moses Malone	6.00
84-85	Kareem IA vs. Sampson	8.00
85-86	Kareem IA vs. Parrish	8.00
86-87	Olajuwon IA vs. Bird, Walton	8.00
87-88	Michael Jordan	10.00
88-89	James Worthy	6.00
89-90	Karl Malone	6.00

Pro Basketball Yearbook: 1988-89

THE SPORTING NEWS PRO BASKETBALL YEARBOOK

Year	Cover	Price
87-88	Magic Johnson	10.00
	Dominique Wilkins	6.00
	Ralph Sampson	4.00
	Michael Jordan	7.00
	Larry Bird	8.00
88-89	Kevin McHale	5.00
	M. Aguirre, I. Thomas, M. Johnson	8.00
89-90	Mark Jackson	4.00
	Joe Dumars	6.00
	Robert Parrish	5.00
	Michael Jordan	8.00
	Akeem Olajuwon	6.00
	Karl Malone	5.00
90-91	Ewing, K. Malone, Bird	7.00
	Michael Jordan & Magic Johnson	8.00
	B.Williams, D.Robinson, M.Johnson	7.00
	Bill Laimbeer & Michael Jordan	6.00
	David Robinson & Akeem Olajuwon	7.00

SPORTS QUARTERLY BASKETBALL EXTRA: COLLEGE

Year	Cover	Price
70-71	Austin Carr	7.50
71-72	Tom McMillen (Maryland)	7.50

SPORTS QUARTERLY PRO BASKETBALL SPECIAL

Year	Cover	Price
69-70	Lew Alcindor, small Cousy (B&W)	12.50
70-71	Willis Reed, small Maravich (B&W)	7.50
71-72	Lew Alcindor	8.00
72-73	Walt Frazier	7.00
73-74	Wilt Chamberlain	8.00
74-75	Julius Erving, John Havlicek	8.00
75-76	Rick Barry	5.00

BASKETBALL ILLUSTRATED

Year	Cover	Price
45-46	College All-Stars / Zollner Pistons	50.00
46-47	Marquette vs. Wisconsin	35.00
1948	LSU vs. Tulane	35.00
1949	Kentucky vs. Phillips 66	20.00

Becomes:

SPORTS REVIEW'S BASKETBALL

Year	Cover	Price
1950	Colorado A & M vs. Utah	15.00
1951	Bradley vs. CCNY	15.00
1952	Colorado A & M vs. Utah	10.00
1953	Michigan vs. Ohio St.	15.00
1954		10.00
1955	Rice vs. St. John's	10.00
1956	Ohio St. vs. Indiana	15.00
1957	R. Hundley, C. Tyra, J. Krebs	10.00
1958	Kentucky vs. Illinois	10.00
1959	Adolph Rupp & John Cox (Kentucky)	10.00
1960	Max Williams (SMU)	10.00
1961	Kentucky team photo	10.00
1962	Jerry Lucas	10.00

STREET & SMITH'S BASKETBALL

Year	Cover	Price
1957	Charlie Tyra (Louisville)	50.00
1958	Tommy Kearns (N. Carolina)	25.00
70-71	Lew Alcindor & Willis Reed	25.00
	Austin Carr & Rudy Tomjanovich	10.00
	Jerry West & Wes Unseld	10.00
71-72	Willis Reed vs. K. Abdul-Jabbar	12.50
72-73	Dave Cowens vs. K. Abdul-Jabbar	10.00
	John McGlockin vs. Gail Goodrich	7.50
	Bill Walton	7.50
73-74	John Havlicek & Pete Maravich	8.00
	Oscar Robertson & Jerry West	8.00
	Gail Goodrich	7.50
74-75	Julius Erving	10.00
75-76	Julius Erving	10.00
	Adrian Dantley & Marques Johnson	6.00
	Paul Silas vs. Rick Barry	5.00
76-77	John Havlicek	6.00
	Pete Maravich	6.00
	P. Westphal, A. Adams, D. Cowens	5.00
77-78	Julius Erving vs. Melvin Bennett	8.00
78-79	Kyle Macy	5.00
	Kareem Abdul-Jabbar	10.00
79-80	Mike O'Koren & Gene Banks	5.00
	Darnell Valentine	5.00

Year	Item	Price
	Bill Walton	6.00
80-81	Larry Bird & Julius Erving	15.00
	Julius Erving, Al Wood, Sam Bowie	8.00
81-82	Sam Bowie	5.00
	John Paxson & Rod Foster	5.00
	Magic Johnson, S. Johnson, Kareem	15.00
82-83	Sam Perkins	5.00
	John Paxson	5.00
	J. Erving, L. Bird, P. Ewing	8.00
83-84	Patrick Ewing	7.50
	Bobby Knight	6.00
84-85	Chris Mullin	6.50
	Milt Wagner	5.00
	Wayman Tisdale	5.00
	Magic Johnson	10.00
85-86	Pearl Washington	5.00
	Danny Manning	6.00
	James Worthy	6.00
86-87	Kenny Smith	5.00
	Michael Jordan	12.50
	Akeem Olajuwon	8.00
87-88	Larry Bird	8.00
	Magic Johnson	10.00
	Bob Knight & Keith Smart	6.00
	Dominique Wilkins	7.00
	Akeem Olajuwon	6.00
	J.R. Reid	5.00
88-89	Mark Macon & Sherman Douglas	5.00
	Danny Ferry	5.00
	Stacey King	5.00
	Tom Hammonds	5.00
	(Pro) M.Jordan, M.Johnson, L.Bird	10.00
89-90	Hank Gathers	6.00
	Rumeal Robinson	5.00
	Alonzo Mourning	7.00
	Chris Jackson	5.00
	(Pro) Isiah Thomas	7.00
	(Pro) Karl Malone	6.00
	(Pro) Michael Jordan	8.00
90-91	Doug Smith	5.00
	Chris Smith	5.00
	Steve Smith	7.00
	Kenny Anderson & Bobby Hurley	7.00
	Don MacLean & Harold Miner	6.00
	Larry Johnson	7.00
	(Pro) Michael Jordan	8.00

TOPICAL MAGAZINE'S PRO BASKETBALL

Year	Item	Price
1964	Wilt Chamberlain	20.00
1965	76ers vs. Hawks	10.00

VITALE'S BASKETBALL

Year	Item	Price
83-84	Michael Jordan (UNC)	25.00
	Moses Malone	7.50
	Magic Johnson	25.00
85-86	Kareem Abdul-Jabbar	10.00
	Kenny Smith & Mark Price	8.00
	Michael Jordan	15.00
	Bernard King & Patrick Ewing	10.00
86-87	David Robinson (Navy)	15.00
	Larry Bird vs. Magic, Lakers	15.00
	Dominique Wilkins	10.00
	Kenny Smith (UNC)	6.00
	Ralph Sampson & Kareem	8.00
	Pervis Ellison & James Blackmon	7.00
	Danny Manning & Steve Alford	7.00
87-88	Derrick Coleman vs. J.R. Reid	10.00
	Larry Bird	10.00
	James Worthy	7.00
	Dominique Wilkins	8.00
	K. Vandeweghe & Xavier McDaniel	5.00
	Danny Manning & Derrick Chievous	5.00
	Bob Knight & Everette Stephens	5.00
	Isiah Thomas	8.00
	Michael Jordan	10.00
	Moses Malone	6.00
	Charles Smith & Rex Chapman	5.00
	Rodney McCray & Mark Aguirre	5.00
88-89	Mark Jackson	5.00
	John Thompson & Sherman Douglas	5.00
	Isiah Thomas & Michael Jordan	10.00
	J.R. Reid & Danny Ferry	5.00
	B.J. Armstrong & Stacey King	5.00
	Pervis Ellison & Dwayne Schintzius	5.00
	Sean Elliott & Todd Lichti	5.00
	James Worthy	6.00
89-90	Magic Johnson & Jerry Tarkanian	10.00
	Joe Dumars & Rumeal Robinson	6.00
	Patrick Ewing & Alonzo Mourning	8.00
	Michael Jordan & Kendall Gill	8.00
	Kevin Johnson & Lute Olson	6.00
	Akeem Olajuwon & Chris Jackson	6.00
	John Stockton & Chris Mullin	6.00
	Scott Williams & Rex Chapman	4.00
90-91	Charles Oakley & Billy Owens	5.00
	Magic Johnson & Larry Bird	8.00
	Kenny Anderson & Rodney Monroe	6.00
	Michael Jordan & Doug Smith	8.00
	Reggie Miller & LaBradford Smith	5.00
	Buck Williams & Tom Chambers	4.00
	Isiah Thomas & Steve Smith	6.00
	David Robinson & Shaquille O'Neal	8.00

Vitale's Basketball: 1992-93

WILT CHAMBERLAIN'S BASKETBALL

Year	Item	Price
1963	Wilt Chamberlain	20.00

POCKET BASKETBALL ANNUALS

BALLANTINE BOOKS PRO BASKETBALL

Year	Item	Price
76-77	Jo Jo White	8.00
77-78	Julius Erving	10.00

BASKETBALL STARS OF...

Year	Item	Price
1961	Wilt Chamberlain	15.00
1962	Three players going for rebound	10.00
1963	Duquesne vs. Bradley	10.00
1964	Wilt Chamberlain	15.00
1965	Bill Russell vs. Knicks	12.50
1966	Bill Russell	12.50
1967	Bill Russell vs. Willis Reed	12.50
1968	Wilt Chamberlain	12.50
1969	Willis Reed	10.00
1970	Lew Alcindor	12.50
1971	Willis Reed	8.00
1972	Lew Alcindor	10.00
1973	Jerry West	8.00

THE COMPLETE HANDBOOK OF COLLEGE BASKETBALL

Year	Item	Price
1979	Kelly Tripucka	6.00
1980	Duke vs. NC State	5.00
1981	Louisville vs. Iowa	5.00

THE COMPLETE HANDBOOK OF PRO BASKETBALL

Year	Item	Price
1975	Julius Erving & John Havlicek	12.50
1976	Jerry West	8.00
1977	Julius Erving	12.50
1978	Bill Walton	8.00
1979	Elvin Hayes	6.00
1980	Dennis Johnson	6.00
1981	Magic Johnson	15.00
1982	Larry Bird vs. Julius Erving	15.00
1983	Magic Johnson vs. Julius Erving	15.00
1984	Kareem vs. Moses	8.00
1985	Larry Bird	10.00
1986	Patrick Ewing	8.00
1987	Larry Bird	8.00
1988	Magic Johnson	10.00
1989	Magic and Isiah kissing	12.50
1990	Dumars, Magic, Worthy and Kareem	8.00
1991	Jordan vs. Laimbeer	6.00

FOOTBALL

AFL YEARBOOK

Year	Cover	Price
1960	Handoff drawing	60.00
1961		50.00
1962	Pro Bowl photo	40.00
1963		35.00
1964	Chiefs vs Oilers	30.00
1965	George Blanda	35.00
1966	Action photos	28.00
1967		25.00
1968	AFL autograph handbook	25.00
1969	Matt Snell	28.00

ALL-PRO FOOTBALL
(Maco Magazine)

Year	Cover	Price
1957	Scrambling QB	55.00
1958		45.00
1959	Johnny Unitas	43.00
1960		35.00
1961	Kyle Rote	32.00
1962	Y.A. Tittle	30.00
1963	Bart Starr	35.00
1964	Johnny Unitas	30.00
1965	Fran Tarkenton	25.00
1966	Frank Ryan	23.00
1967	Carroll Dale	20.00
1968		18.00
1969	Joe Namath	25.00
1970	Stram's victory	18.00
1971		16.00
1972		16.00
1973	Fran Tarkenton	16.00
1974	Fran Tarkenton	15.00

ATHLON'S COLLEGE FOOTBALL

Year	Cover	Price
1987	ACC: Rick Strom	7.50
	Big 8: Steve Taylor	7.50
	Big 10: Chris Spielman	8.00
	East: Penn St. vs Pitt	7.50
	Pac 10: Cal vs Stanford	7.50
	SEC: B. Humphrey & J. Burger	8.50
	SWC: Bret Stafford	7.50
	West: BYU vs Air Force	7.50
1988	All covers	7.00
1989	All covers	7.00
1990	All covers	6.50

ATHLON'S PRO FOOTBALL

Year	Cover	Price
1983	John Riggins	14.00
1984	Brian Sipe	12.00
	All other covers	14.00
1985	All covers	13.00
1986	All covers	12.00
1987	Bernie Kosar	12.00
	All other covers	11.00
1988	Bernie Kosar	10.00
	All other covers	10.00
1989	All covers	10.00
1990	Eric Metcalf	8.00
	All other covers	8.00

COMPLETE SPORTS AFL & NFL YEARBOOK

Year	Cover	Price
1964	Jim Brown	35.00
1965	J. Morris & C. Hennigan	25.00
1966	Jim Brown & Jack Kemp	35.00
1967	Gale Sayers	30.00
1968	Roman Gabriel	18.00
1969	Jurgensen & M. Snell	18.00
1970	Curley Culp	15.00
1971	Dick Butkus	17.00
1972	Csonka & Plunkett	16.00
1973		14.00
1974		14.00
1975		15.00
1976		16.00

Cord Sportfacts Pro Football Guide: 1981

CORD SPORTFACTS' PRO FOOTBALL GUIDE

Year	Cover	Price
1969	John Mackey	18.00
1970		18.00
1971		16.00
1972	Joe Namath	22.00
1973	Larry Brown	15.00
1974	Larry Csonka	17.00
1975	Franco Harris	18.00
1976	Franco Harris	17.00
1977		16.00
1978		16.00
1979		16.00
1980		14.00
1981	Jack Lambert	15.00

CORD SPORTFACTS' PRO FOOTBALL REPORT

Year	Cover	Price
1969	Sonny Jurgensen	18.00
1970		16.00
1971	Ron Johnson, Giants	15.00
1972	Dick Butkus	17.00
1973	Larry Csonka	17.00
1974	O.J. Simpson	22.00

Dell Pro Football Preview: 1973

DELL SPORTS' PRO FOOTBALL PREVIEW

Year	Cover	Price
1958	Bobby Layne	50.00
1959	Johnny Unitas	45.00
1960	Don Meredith & C. Conerly	38.00
1961	Paul Hornung	30.00
1962	Jim Brown & Jim Taylor	35.00
1963	Y.A. Tittle	25.00
1964	Jim Brown	30.00
1965	Namath & Unitas	30.00
1966	Gale Sayers	25.00
1967	Bart Starr	18.00
1968	Donny Anderson	14.00
1969	Leroy Kelly	14.00
1970	Johnny Unitas	14.00
1971	Joe Namath	18.00
1972	Roger Staubach	18.00
1973	Bob Griese	13.00
1974	Larry Csonka	13.00

FAWCETT'S PRO FOOTBALL

Year	Cover	Price
1961	Paul Hornung	35.00
1962	Jim Taylor	30.00
1963	Jim Taylor	25.00

FOOTBALL ACTION

Year	Cover	Price
1976	Joe Namath	20.00
1977		15.00
1978		14.00
1979	Tom Landry (292 pages)	16.00
1980	Mean Joe Greene	15.00
1987	Parcells, Simms & Elway (340)	10.00

Football Digest: 1947

FOOTBALL DIGEST
Simons Publishing

Year	Cover	Price
1947	Johnny Lujack	85.00
1948	Chuck Bednarik	70.00
1949	Sammy Baugh: "My greatest ..."	65.00
1950	Gordon Soltan, Minnesota	60.00
1951	Fred Benners & Sonny Gandee	60.00
1952	Hugh McElhenny, Washington	60.00

Digest Publishing Corp.

Year	Cover	Price
12/67	Don Perkins	30.00
2/68		25.00

4/68 Bart Starr 30.00
8/68 Bobby Bell 22.00
10/68 Leroy Kelly 20.00
11/68 Dave Parks 18.00
12/68 Noland Smith 18.00

Century Publishing Co.

9/71 G. Washington, 49ers 30.00
10/71 Sonny Jurgensen 20.00
11/71 Greg Landry 12.00
12/71 Dick Gordon, Bears vs Vikings 12.00
1/72 John Brodie 14.00
2/72 Dave Osborn, Super Bowl issue 10.00
3/72 John Brockington 8.00
4/72 Duane Thomas 8.50
5/72 Fran Tarkenton 13.00
7/72 Daryle Lamonica 10.50
9/72 Dick Butkus 13.00
10/72 Len Dawson 12.00
11/72 Joe Namath 15.00
12/72 Mercury Morris 8.50
1/73 Larry Brown & Butkus, Nobis 10.00
2/73 Terry Bradshaw 14.00
3/73 John Brockington (full color) 8.00
4/73 Bob Griese 11.50
5/73 Norm Snead 9.00
7/73 O.J. Simpson 15.00
9/73 Larry Csonka 9.00
10/73 Mean Joe Greene 10.00
11/73 Bobby Douglass 6.50
12/73 Daryle Lamonica 7.50
1/74 Chuck Foreman 6.50
2/74 John Hadl 7.00
3/74 O.J. Simpson 12.50
4/74 Larry Csonka 7.50
5/74 Calvin Hill 6.00
7/74 Archie Manning 6.50
9/74 Griese & Hadl 8.50
10/74 Roger Staubach 12.00
11/74 Fran Tarkenton 7.50
12/74 John Brockington 5.00
1/75 Ken Stabler 9.00
2/75 Jim Hart 4.50
3/75 Ken Stabler, POY 7.50
4/75 Super Bowl IX: Noll & Harris 8.00
5/75 Ken Anderson 3.50
7/75 Otis Armstrong 3.00
9/75 Terry Bradshaw 8.00
10/75 Jim Plunkett 5.00
11/75 Wally Chambers 3.00
12/75 Joe Namath 10.00
1/76 Mercury Morris 4.00
2/76 Jeff Siemon 3.00
3/76 O.J. Simpson, POY 10.00
4/76 Lynn Swann 7.50
5/76 Dan Pastorini 3.00
7/76 Bert Jones 3.00
9/76 Lambert crushing Staubach 8.00
10/76 Dallas shotgun w/Staubach 8.00
11/76 Terry Metcalf 3.00
12/76 Billy Kilmer 4.00
1/77 Fran Tarkenton 5.00
2/77 Jim Langer 3.50
3/77 Ken Stabler, POY 6.00
4/77 Super Bowl XI: Clarence Davis 3.50
5/77 Steve Grogan 3.50
7/77 Greg Pruitt 3.00
9/77 Joe Namath, Rams 8.00
10/77 Bradshaw & Stabler 8.00
11/77 Walter Payton 10.00
12/77 Ken Anderson 3.00
1/78 Youngblood stalking Bartkowski 3.50
2/78 Bert Jones 3.00
3/78 Tony Dorsett, ROY 7.50
4/78 SB XII: R.White hitting Morton 4.50
5/78 Jim Zorn 3.00
7/78 Roger Staubach 7.00
9/78 Chuck Foreman 3.00

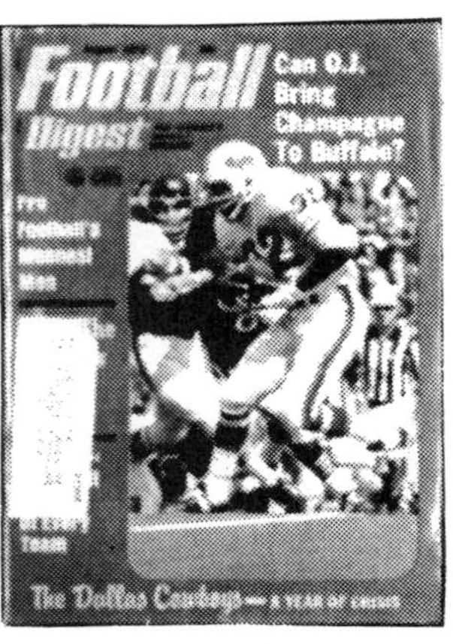

Football Digest: 7/73

10/78 Ron Jaworski 3.00
11/78 O.J. Simpson 7.00
12/78 Franco Harris 6.00
1/79 Pat Haden 2.76
2/79 Don Shula 3.50
3/79 Earl Campbell, POY 5.50
4/79 Super Bowl XIII: Bradshaw 6.50
5/79 Archie Manning 3.00
7/79 Craig Morton 3.00
9/79 Steve Grogan 3.00
10/79 Bill Bergey 2.76
11/79 Dan Fouts 5.50
12/79 David Whitehurst 2.76
1/80 Larry Csonka 3.50
2/80 Terry Bradshaw 6.00
3/80 Dan Fouts, POY 4.50
4/80 Super Bowl XIV: Lynn Swann 4.50
5/80 Lee Roy Selmon 2.80
7/80 Vince Ferragamo 2.80
9/80 Ken Stabler 4.00
10/80 Harry Carson 4.00

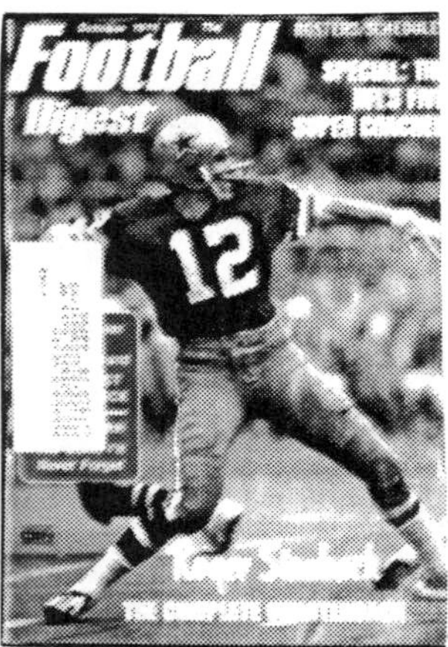

Football Digest: 10/74

11/80 Walter Payton 8.00
12/80 Russ Francis 3.00
1/81 Wilbert Montgomery 2.80
2/81 Bert Jones 2.80
3/81 Brian Sipe, POY 3.00
4/81 Billy Sims, ROY 3.00
5/81 Steve Bartkowski 2.80
7/81 Joe Ferguson 2.80
9/81 Jim Plunkett 5.00
10/81 Tommy Kramer 2.80
11/81 O.J. Anderson 5.00
12/81 Danny White 4.00
1/82 David Woodley 2.50
2/82 Ron Jaworski 2.50
3/82 George Rogers, Off. ROY 2.80
4/82 Ken Anderson, POY 2.80
5/82 Joe Montana 9.00
7/82 Joe Theismann 4.50
9/82 Bert Jones 2.50
10/82 Joe Klecko 3.00
11/82 Terry Bradshaw 4.50
12/82 Montana & Walsh 8.00
1/83 Dan Fouts 3.50
2/83 William Andrews 2.50
3/83 Randy White 4.50
4/83 Marcus Allen, ROY 6.00
5/83 Super Bowl XVII: Riggins 3.50
7/83 Herschel Walker, USFL 5.00
9/83 Lawrence Taylor 7.00
10/83 Doug Williams 3.50
11/83 Kellen Winslow 3.00
12/83 Lynn Dickey 2.50
1/84 Brian Sipe 3.00
2/84 Danny White 3.50
3/84 Eric Dickerson, ROY 5.50
4/84 Joe Theismann, POY 3.50
5/84 Dan Marino 6.00
7/84 Curt Warner 2.50
9/84 Marcus Allen 4.00
10/84 Franco Harris 4.00
11/84 John Elway 6.00
12/84 Billy Sims 2.80
1/85 Tony Dorsett 4.00
2/85 Joe Montana 6.00
3/85 Walter Payton 6.00
4/85 Dan Marino, POY 4.50
5/85 Eric Dickerson 4.00
7/85 Doug Flutie, USFL 3.00
9/85 Dave Krieg 2.50
10/85 Danny White 3.00
11/85 Mark Gastineau 2.50
12/85 Neil Lomax 2.00
1/86 Howie Long 4.00
2/86 Jim McMahon 3.00
3/86 Dieter Brock 2.00
4/86 Marcus Allen, POY 3.80
5/86 Super Bowl XX: O.Wilson,Eason 2.50
7/86 Joe Morris 2.50
9/86 Jim McMahon 2.50
10/86 Louis Lipps 2.80
11/86 James Lofton 3.00
12/86 Dan Fouts 2.50
1/87 Herschel Walker 3.00
2/87 Walter Payton 5.00
3/87 Jay Schroeder 2.50
4/87 Lawrence Taylor, POY 4.00
5/87 Super Bowl XXI: Simms 3.00
7/87 Dan Marino 3.50
9/87 Bernie Kosar 2.50
10/87 Tommy Kramer 2.00
11/87 Tony Eason 2.00
12/87 Curt Warner 2.00
1/88 Joe Montana 5.00
2/88 Walter Payton 4.50
3/88 Eric Dickerson 3.00
4/88 Jerry Rice, POY 4.50
5/88 Super Bowl XXII:D.Williams 2.50
7/88 John Elway 3.00
9/88 Phil Simms 2.50
10/88 Morten Andersen 2.00
11/88 Conlan & Bennett 3.50
12/88 Chris Doleman 2.50
1/89 Brian Bosworth 2.00
2/89 Mike Singletary 3.25

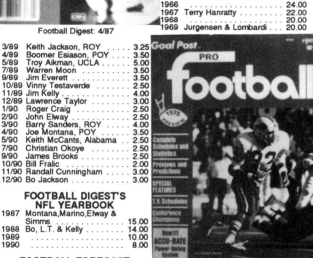

Football Digest: 4/87

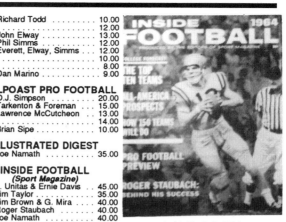

3/89	Keith Jackson, ROY	3.25
4/89	Boomer Esiason, POY	3.50
5/89	Troy Aikman, UCLA	5.00
7/89	Warren Moon	3.50
9/89	Jim Everett	3.50
10/89	Vinny Testaverde	2.50
11/89	Jim Kelly	4.00
12/89	Lawrence Taylor	3.00
1/90	Roger Craig	2.50
2/90	John Elway	2.50
3/90	Barry Sanders, ROY	4.00
4/90	Joe Montana, POY	3.50
5/90	Keith McCants, Alabama	2.50
7/90	Christian Okoye	2.50
9/90	James Brooks	2.50
10/90	Bill Fralic	2.00
11/90	Randall Cunningham	3.00
12/90	Bo Jackson	3.00

FOOTBALL DIGEST'S NFL YEARBOOK

1987	Montana,Marino,Elway & Simms	15.00
1988	Bo, L.T. & Kelly	14.00
1989		10.00
1990		8.00

FOOTBALL FORECAST
(Fawcett Publishing)

1962	Y.A. Tittle	40.00
1963	Bart Starr	35.00

GAME PLAN COLLEGE FOOTBALL

1970	Archie Manning, Mississippi	16.00
1971		13.00
1972	Rich Glover, Nebraska	13.00
1973	Randy Gradishar, Ohio St.	14.00

GAME PLAN PRO FOOTBALL

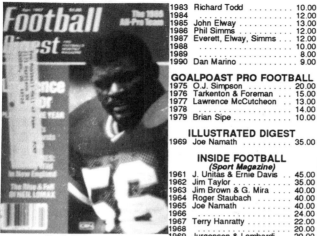

1971	George Blanda	20.00
1972	Roger Staubach	22.00
1973	Larry Csonka	17.00
1974	Fran Tarkenton	16.00
1975	Franco Harris	18.00
1976	Roger Staubach	18.00
1977	Walter Payton	20.00
1978		16.00
1979	Archie Manning	12.00
1980	Joe Ferguson	12.00
1981	Ricky Bell	10.00
1982		15.00
1983	Richard Todd	10.00
1984		12.00
1985	John Elway	13.00
1986	Phil Simms	12.00
1987	Everett, Elway, Simms	12.00
1988		10.00
1989		8.00
1990	Dan Marino	9.00

GOALPOAST PRO FOOTBALL

1975	O.J. Simpson	20.00
1976	Tarkenton & Foreman	15.00
1977	Lawrence McCutcheon	13.00
1978		14.00
1979	Brian Sipe	10.00

ILLUSTRATED DIGEST

1969	Joe Namath	35.00

INSIDE FOOTBALL
(Sport Magazine)

1961	J. Unitas & Ernie Davis	45.00
1962	Jim Taylor	35.00
1963	Jim Brown & G. Mira	40.00
1964	Roger Staubach	40.00
1965	Joe Namath	40.00
1966		24.00
1967	Terry Hanratty	22.00
1968		20.00
1969	Jurgensen & Lombardi	20.00

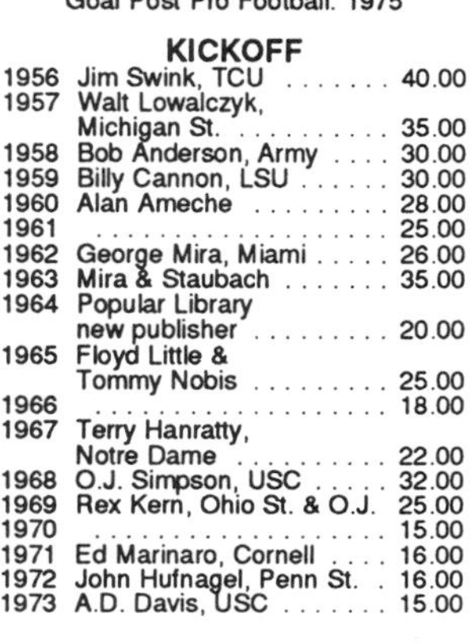

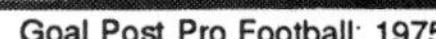

Goal Post Pro Football: 1975

KICKOFF

1956	Jim Swink, TCU	40.00
1957	Walt Lowalczyk, Michigan St.	35.00
1958	Bob Anderson, Army	30.00
1959	Billy Cannon, LSU	30.00
1960	Alan Ameche	28.00
1961		25.00
1962	George Mira, Miami	26.00
1963	Mira & Staubach	35.00
1964	Popular Library new publisher	20.00
1965	Floyd Little & Tommy Nobis	25.00
1966		18.00
1967	Terry Hanratty, Notre Dame	22.00
1968	O.J. Simpson, USC	32.00
1969	Rex Kern, Ohio St. & O.J.	25.00
1970		15.00
1971	Ed Marinaro, Cornell	16.00
1972	John Hufnagel, Penn St.	16.00
1973	A.D. Davis, USC	15.00

Inside Football: 1964

1974	Archie Griffin	18.00

KYLE ROTE'S FOOTBALL PREVIEW

1979	Terry Bradshaw	16.00
1980	Ken Stabler	14.00

LINDY'S COLLEGE FOOTBALL

1987	ACC: D. Fenner & Elkins	8.00
	Big 8: S. Taylor & K. Jones	7.50
	Big 10: Menkhuasen & Davenport	7.50
	Pac 10: Green, Muster & Cotton	8.00
	SEC: James Jackson	7.50
	SWC: E. Metcalf & Tolliver	8.00
1988	All covers	7.00
1989	All covers	7.00
1990	All covers	6.50

LINDY'S PRO FOOTBALL

1987	Kosar & Esiason	9.00
	Simms & Toon	8.00
1988	R. Wright & T. Kramer	7.00
1989	Kosar & Esiason	8.00
1990	E. Metcalf & Esiason	7.00

NFL YEARBOOK

1953	Quarterback w/team logos	95.00
1954	Player in 3-point stance	75.00
1955	Receiver	65.00
1956		60.00
1957		55.00
1958		50.00
1959	Black and White cartoon	45.00
1960	Ball carrier	45.00
1961		40.00
1962		40.00
1963		40.00
1964	Brown Paper cover	35.00
1965		35.00
1966	Tarkenton & Vikings vs Colts	40.00
1967	Donny Anderson	30.00
1968	Now: "NFL autograph handbook"	25.00
1969	Roman Gabriel	20.00

OFFICIAL NFL ANNUALS
Pro Football Yearbook

1979	Payton, Dorsett, Campbell	15.00
1980	Payton, Bradshaw, Fouts	15.00

NFL Team Book

1986	Wiliam Perry	8.00

Preview

1989	Joe Montana	10.00

PETERSEN'S FOOTBALL

1956 "Ram" Ron Waller 75.00
1957 Frank Gifford 75.00
1958 Jon Arnett & Tom Wilson . 50.00
1959 Lenny Moore during Pro Bowl 40.00
1960 Pro Bowl scene 35.00
1961 Bill Anderson during Pro Bowl 30.00
1962 Jim Brown 45.00
1963 Y.A. Tittle 30.00
1964 George Halas & Jim Brown 35.00
1970 Roman Gabriel 18.00
1971 Starr, Blanda & Brodie . . . 20.00
1972 Redskins vs. Rams 17.00
1973 Csonka,Griese,Kiick & L. Brown 20.00
1974 O.J. Simpson 24.00
1975 Lambert & D. White in action 18.00
1976 Bert Jones 15.00
1977 Stabler & Madden 17.00
1978 Staubach & Too Tall Jones 18.00
1979 Terry Bradshaw 17.00
1980 Haden & Ferragamo 10.00
1981 Plunkett, O.J. & Unitas . . 15.00
1982 Joe Montana 20.00

Petersen's Pro Football: 1988

1983 Theismann & Riggins . . . 13.00
1984 Wendell Tyler 10.00
1985 Calvin Muhammad 10.00
1986 Walter Payton 15.00
1987 . . . . 10.00
1988 . . . . 10.00
1989 . . . . 9.00
1990 . . . . 8.00

PRO FOOTBALL ANNUAL
(Reliance Publishing)

1979 Bradshaw & Campbell . . . 18.00
1980 Bradshaw & Campbell . . . 16.00
1981 Plunkett, Campbell & Sims 14.00
1982 Montana & Fouts 18.00
1983 Riggins & M. Allen 15.00

PRO FOOTBALL ANNUAL
(Sport Magazine)

1964 Jim Brown 40.00
1965 Johnny Unitas 35.00
1966 . . . . 30.00
1967 Bart Starr 30.00
1968 Unitas & Jurgensen 28.00
1969 Sayers & Namath 30.00
1970 Gabriel & Namath 25.00
1971 Joe Namath 25.00

PRO FOOTBALL ILLUSTRATED
(Elbak Publishing)

1941 Giants in action 140.00
1942 Ball carrier in action 100.00
1943 Sammy Baugh 95.00
1944 Over-the-shoulder catch . . 85.00
1945 Ball carrier in action 80.00
1946 Wilbur Moore, Redskins . . 75.00
1947 Pat Harder, Cardinals . . . 70.00
1948 Bosh Pritchard, Eagles . . 65.00
1949 Clyde Goodknight,Packers 60.00
1950 Fred Gehrke, Rams 55.00
1951 Billy Vessels, Oklahoma . 50.00

Becomes:

SPORTS REVIEW

1952 . . . . 45.00
1953 Leon Hart & Perry Lowell . 40.00
1954 UCLA vs USC 45.00
1955 Notre Dame vs Texas . . . 50.00
1956 Ted Kress, Michigan 40.00
1957 Clendon Thomas & H. McElhenny 38.00
1958 Sam Williams & Blanche Martin 35.00
1959 Jeff Langston & Donald Norton 32.00
1960 Johnny Unitas 45.00
1961 Colts vs Giants 40.00
1962 Colts vs Bears 38.00
1965 Johnny Unitas 38.00

PRO FOOTBALL ILLUSTRATED
(Complete Sports)

1961 Johnny Unitas 35.00
1962 Paul Hornung 28.00
1963 Jim Brown 37.00
1964 Jim Brown 35.00
1967 Namath & Unitas 28.00
1968 Joe Namath 28.00
1969 Namath & Gabriel 25.00
1970 Sayers & L. Kelly 20.00
1971 Namath & Brodie 22.00
1972 Namath & Tarkenton 22.00
1973 Larry Csonka 18.00
1974 O.J. Simpson 22.00
1975 O.J. & Foreman 20.00
1976 Tarkenton & K. Anderson . 15.00
1977 . . . . 14.00
1978 . . . . 14.00
1979 Terry Bradshaw 17.00
1980 O.J. Anderson 16.00
1981 Billy Sims 13.00
1983 Tony Dorsett & F. McNeil . 15.00

New Publisher: Lexington Library

1985 Montana, Marino & Elway 16.00
1986 McMahon 11.00
1987 Marino, Elway & Simms . . 13.00
1988 Herschel Walker 9.00
1989 Boomer Esiason 9.00
1990 Joe Montana 10.00

PRO FOOTBALL SCENE
(Tiger Press)

1979 . . . . 18.00
1980 . . . . 15.00
1981 . . . . 14.00
1982 . . . . 15.00
1983 . . . . 13.00
1984 . . . . 12.00
1985 Joe Montana 16.00
1986 Marino, M. Allen & McMahon 14.00
1987 . . . . 11.00
1988 . . . . 10.00
1989 . . . . 8.00
1990 Dan Marino 9.00

PRO FOOTBALL STARS
(Whitestone Publishing)

1957 Frank Gifford 75.00

Pro Football Stars: 1957

1960 Johnny Unitas 45.00
1961 Jim Brown 50.00
1962 Bart Starr 40.00
1963 Jim Taylor 32.00

Becomes:

PRO & COLLEGE FOOTBALL

1965 . . . . 30.00
1968 Joe Namath 35.00
1969 Browns vs Giants 20.00
1970 Leroy Kelly 18.00

PROFILE

1974 O.J. Simpson 22.00
1975 Ken Stabler 18.00

PROLOG OFFICIAL NFL ANNUAL

1971 Logo & year (Hardcover) . 35.00
Logo & year (Paperback) . 20.00
1972 Miami vs. Dallas (HC) . . . 30.00
Miami vs. Dallas (PB) . . . 18.00
1973 Larry Brown (last HC) . . . 27.00
Larry Brown (PB) 15.00
1974 Mercury Morris 14.00
1975 Bradshaw handing off to Harris 20.00
1976 Fran Tarkenton 14.00
1977 Bert Jones 12.00
1978 Walter Payton 20.00
1979 Terry Bradshaw 17.00
1980 Jack Youngblood 10.00
1981 Jim Plunkett 12.00
1982 Joe Montana 20.00
1983 Freeman McNeil 10.00
1984 Eric Dickerson 12.00
1985 Walter Payton 17.00
1986 Marcus Allen 12.00
1987 Phil Simms 11.00
1988 Jim McMahon, Kosar & A. Carter 8.00
1989 Montana,J.L.Williams & T.Brown 10.00
1990 Montana, L.T. & Bo 11.00

ROUND-UP PRO & COLLEGE
(Sports Quarterly)

1960 Unitas, Gifford, Ditka 40.00

THE SPORTING NEWS AFL GUIDE

1962 San Diego's Harris 25.00
1963 Incomplete Pass 20.00
1964 Curtis McClinton 20.00
1965 Tobin Rote 15.00
1966 Paul Lowe vs. Buck Buchanan 15.00
1967 Bobby Burnett 15.00

Sporting News: 1962 AFL Guide

- 1968 Lamonica, Nance, Blanda, Sauer . . . 20.00
- 1969 Matt Snell . . . 18.00
- 1970 Lance Alworth . . . 18.00

THE SPORTING NEWS FOOTBALL GUIDE

- 1971 Jim Bakken . . . 15.00
- 1972 Roger Staubach . . . 25.00
- 1973 Mercury Morris . . . 15.00
- 1974 Larry Csonka . . . 16.00
- 1975 Franco Harris . . . 18.00
- 1976 Lynn Swann "The Catch" . 18.00
- 1977 Ken Stabler . . . 17.00
- 1978 Roger Staubach . . . 18.00
- 1979 Terry Bradshaw . . . 18.00
- 1980 Swann and Stallworth . . . 17.00
- 1981 Billy Sims . . . 12.00
- 1982 Ken Anderson . . . 10.00
- 1983 Mark Moseley . . . 9.00
- 1984 Eric Dickerson . . . 11.00
- 1985 Dan Marino . . . 12.00
- 1986 Marcus Allen . . . 11.00
- 1987 Phil Simms . . . 10.00
- 1988 John Elway . . . 10.00
- 1989 Steve Largent . . . 10.00
- 1990 Joe Montana . . . 10.00

THE SPORTING NEWS FOOTBALL RECORD & RULE BOOK

- 1945 Wide Receiver . . . 35.00
- 1946 A.A. Stagg . . . 30.00
- 1947 Pop Warner . . . 30.00
- 1948 Frank Leahy . . . 25.00
- 1949 Sammy Baugh . . . 25.00
- 1950 Greasy Neale . . . 20.00

THE SPORTING NEWS FOOTBALL REGISTER

- 1966 St. Louis Defense . . . 25.00
- 1967 Curt McClinton . . . 15.00
- 1968 George Mira (1st full color) 15.00
- 1969 Bart Starr . . . 18.00
- 1970 Roman Gabriel . . . 15.00
- 1971 Sonny Jurgensen . . . 15.00
- 1972 Eagles vs. Cardinals . . . 10.00
- 1973 Terry Bradshaw . . . 20.00
- 1974 O.J. Simpson . . . 22.00
- 1975 Ken Stabler . . . 15.00
- 1976 Fran Tarkenton . . . 14.00
- 1977 Bert Jones . . . 10.00
- 1978 Walter Payton . . . 20.00
- 1979 Earl Campbell . . . 14.00
- 1980 Dan Fouts . . . 14.00
- 1981 Brian Sipe . . . 9.00
- 1982 George Rogers . . . 9.00
- 1983 Marcus Allen . . . 12.00
- 1984 Dan Marino . . . 13.00
- 1985 Walter Payton . . . 16.00
- 1986 Eddie Brown . . . 8.00
- 1987 Rueben Mayes . . . 8.00
- 1988 Jerry Rice . . . 12.00
- 1989 Boomer Esiason . . . 9.00
- 1990 Barry Sanders . . . 10.00

THE SPORTING NEWS PRO YEARBOOK

- 1981 Brian Sipe . . . 10.00
- 1982 Kellen Winslow . . . 10.00
- 1983 John Riggins . . . 11.00
- 1984 K. Anderson & T. Cousineau . . . 9.00
- All other covers . . . 12.00
- 1985 Montana & Marino . . . 15.00
- 1986 Jim McMahon . . . 10.00
- All other covers . . . 11.00
- 1987 Esiason & Kosar . . . 11.00
- All other covers . . . 11.00
- 1988 Eric Dickerson . . . 10.00
- All other covers . . . 10.00
- 1989 Reggie Williams . . . 8.00
- All other covers . . . 10.00
- 1990 All covers . . . 8.00

THE SPORTING NEWS SUPER BOWL BOOK

- 1981 Jim Plunkett . . . 12.00
- 1982 Joe Montana . . . 18.00
- 1983 Riggins and Grimm . . . 12.00
- 1984 Raiders blocking Redskins punt . . . 10.00
- 1985 Joe Montana . . . 13.00
- 1986 Dan Hampton . . . 10.00
- 1987 Bavaro with McConkey . . 12.00
- 1988 Doug Williams . . . 9.00
- 1989 Jerry Rice . . . 11.00
- 1990 Joe Montana . . . 10.00

SPORTS ALL STARS
(Maco Magazine)

- 1958 Ram running back . . . 40.00
- 1959 . . . 35.00
- 1960 Johnny Unitas . . . 38.00
- 1961 . . . 30.00
- 1962 . . . 28.00
- 1963 Jim Taylor . . . 25.00
- 1964 Jim Brown . . . 30.00
- 1965 Charley Johnson . . . 20.00
- 1966 Dick Butkus . . . 24.00
- 1967 Gale Sayers . . . 25.00
- 1967 All others . . . 20.00
- 1968 Johnny Unitas . . . 22.00
- 1968 Roman Gabriel . . . 20.00
- 1968 All others . . . 18.00
- 1969 Fran Tarkenton . . . 18.00
- 1969 Leroy Kelly . . . 17.00
- 1969 All others . . . 16.00
- 1970 Don Maynard . . . 17.00
- 1971 . . . 16.00
- 1972 Jim Plunkett . . . 16.00
- 1973 Mercury Morris . . . 14.00
- 1974 Roger Staubach . . . 18.00
- 1975 Terry Bradshaw . . . 18.00
- 1976 Terry Bradshaw . . . 17.00
- 1977 . . . 14.00
- 1978 . . . 12.00
- 1979 Ken Anderson . . . 10.00

SPORTS FORECAST
(O'Malley Publishing)

- 1959 LSU team in action (College edition) . . . 50.00
- Eagle receiver (Pro) . . . 50.00

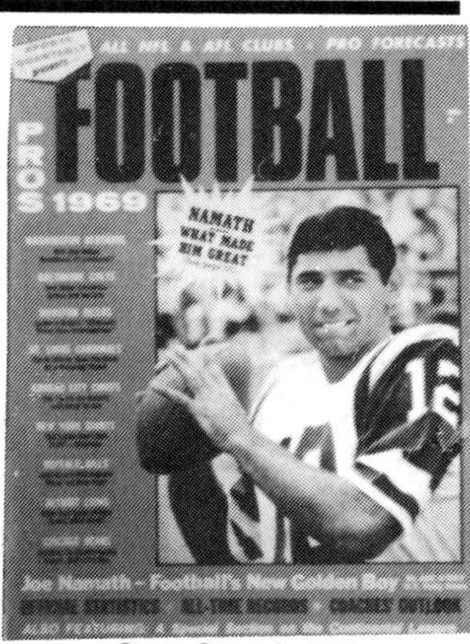

Sports Quarterly: 1969

SPORTS QUARTERLY

- 1968 Donny Anderson . . . 20.00
- 1969 Joe Namath . . . 25.00
- 1970 Sonny Jurgensen . . . 18.00
- 1971 . . . 16.00
- 1972 Raiders vs Rams . . . 16.00
- 1973 Griese, Csonka & Kiick . . 17.00
- 1974 O.J. Simpson . . . 20.00
- 1975 Vikings vs Steelers . . . 15.00
- 1976 Lynn Swann's catch . . . 18.00
- 1977 . . . 14.00
- 1978 Lyle Alzado . . . 14.00
- 1979 Terry Bradshaw . . . 18.00

SPORTS REVIEW

- 1967 Bart Starr . . . 20.00
- 1968 Unitas & Starr . . . 18.00
- 1969 Joe Namath . . . 22.00
- 1970 Joe Kapp . . . 15.00
- 1971 Colts vs Cowboys . . . 16.00
- 1972 . . . 15.00
- 1973 Billy Kilmer . . . 15.00

SPORTS STARS OF PRO & COLLEGE FOOTBALL

- 1972 Jim Plunkett . . . 18.00
- 1973 Bob Griese . . . 16.00
- 1974 Larry Csonka . . . 15.00
- 1975 Ken Stabler . . . 16.00

SPORTS STARS OF PRO FOOTBALL

- 1968 Bart Starr . . . 20.00
- 1969 Joe Namath . . . 25.00
- 1970 . . . 18.00
- 1971 . . . 16.00
- 1972 Joe Namath . . . 20.00
- 1973 Larry Brown . . . 15.00
- 1974 Bob Griese . . . 16.00
- 1975 Terry Bradshaw . . . 18.00

SPORTS TODAY

- 1971 Joe Namath . . . 20.00
- 1972 Roger Staubach . . . 18.00
- 1973 Joe Namath . . . 18.00
- 1974 O.J. Simpson . . . 18.00

STREET & SMITH'S COLLEGE FOOTBALL

- 1940 Center ready to snap ball 225.00
- 1941 Frankie Albert, Stanford . 175.00
- 1942 Alan Cameron, Navy . . . 125.00
- 1943 Seaman Steve Juzwik . . 110.00
- 1944 Bob Kelly, Notre Dame . 110.00
- 1945 Bob Jenkins, Navy . . . 95.00
- 1946 John Ferraro, USC . . . 90.00

1947 Connor of Notre Dame . . 90.00
1948 Jack Cloud, William & Mary 85.00
1949 Charley Justice, North Carolina 80.00
1950 Leon Heath, Oklahoma . . 75.00
1951 Bob Smith, Texas A&M . . 70.00
1952 Johnny Olszewski, California 65.00
1953 "Ike" Eisenhauer, Navy . . 60.00
1954 Ralph Guglielmi, Notre Dame 60.00
1955 Howard Cassidy, Ohio St. 55.00

Street & Smith's Football: 1956

1956 Jim Swink, TCU 52.00
1957 Clendon Thomas, Oklahoma 50.00
1958 Bob White, Ohio St. 47.00
1959 Brennan,Izo,Kuharich, Notre Dame 50.00
1960 Rich Mayo, Air Force 45.00
1961 Ronnie Bull, Baylor 42.00
1962 Jay Wilkinson, Duke 40.00
1963 Tom Myers, Northwestern 38.00
P.Beathard & H.Bedsole, USC 40.00
Paul Martha, Pitt 38.00

Street & Smith's Football:

1964 Roger Staubach, Navy . . . 65.00
Dick Butkus, Illinois 55.00
Craig Morton, California . . 50.00

1965 Roger Bird, Kentucky 35.00
Phil Sheridan, Notre Dame 38.00
Ray Handley, Stanford . . . 36.00
1966 Steve Spurrier, Florida . . . 35.00
Bob Griese, Purdue 45.00
Gary Beban, UCLA 35.00
1967 Ted Hendricks, Miami . . . 38.00
Terry Hanratty, Notre Dame 38.00
Ron Drake, Southern Cal . 32.00
1968 O.J. Simpson, Southern Cal 50.00
Chris Gilbert, Texas 30.00
Larry Smith, Florida 30.00
1969 Rex Kern, Ohio State . . . 25.00
Billy Main 25.00
Steve Kiner, Tennessee . . 25.00
1970 Jim Plunkett, Stanford . . . 35.00
Archie Manning, Mississippi 28.00
Steve Worster, Texas . . . 22.00
1971 Pat Sullivan, Auburn 22.00
Joe Ferguson, Arkansas . 22.00
Sonny Sixkiller, Washington 20.00
1972 Brad Van Pelt, Mich.St. . . 20.00
John Hufnagel, PennState 20.00
Pete Adams, Southern Cal 19.00
1973 Champ Henson, Ohio St. . 18.00
Kermit Johnson, UCLA . . 18.00
Wayne Wheeler, Alabama 18.00
1974 Tom Clements, Notre Dame 20.00
Pat Haden, Southern Cal . 18.00
Brad Davis, Louisiana State 18.00
1975 Archie Griffin, Ohio St. . . . 25.00
Richard Todd, Alabama . . 18.00
John Sciarra, UCLA 16.00
1976 Tony Dorsett, Pittsburgh . 30.00
Rob Lytle, Michigan 16.00
Ricky Bell, Southern Cal . 16.00
1977 Guy Benjamin, Stanford . . 16.00
Ken MacAfee, Notre Dame 17.00
Ben Zambiasi, Georgia . . 16.00
1978 Rick Leach, Michigan . . . 16.00
Jack Thompson, Washington State 16.00
Jeff Rutledge, Alabama . . 16.00
1979 Charles White, Southern Cal 17.00
Mark Herrmann, Purdue . 16.00
Jeff Pyburn, Georgia 16.00
1980 Art Schlichter, Ohio State . 15.00
Rich Campbell, California . 15.00
Scott Woerner, Georgia . . 15.00
1981 Bear Bryant & Herschel Walker 18.00
Anthony Carter & Bob Crable 17.00
Dan Marino & Joe Morris . 22.00
John Elway, Stanford 20.00
1982 Herschel Walker, Georgia 16.00
John Elway, Stanford 18.00
Dan Marino & Curt Warner 20.00
Tony Eason & Marcus Marek 15.00
1983 Mike Rozier, Nebraska . . 17.00
Jacque Robinson, Washington 14.00
Kenny Jackson, Penn State 14.00
Marcus Dupree, Oklahoma 17.00
1984 Bo Jackson, Auburn 25.00
Doug Flutie, Boston Col. . 15.00
Jack Trudeau, Illinois 13.00
Jack Del Rio, So.Cal 13.00
1985 Keith Byars, Ohio State . . 13.00
D.J. Dozier, Penn State . . 14.00
Robbie Bosco, Brigham Young 12.00
Jeff Wickersham, Louisiana State 12.00
1986 Vinny Testaverde, Miami . 14.00
Lorenzo White, Michigan State 13.00
Joe Paterno & D.J. Dozier 15.00
UCLA Bruins 12.00
1987 Tim Brown, Notre Dame . 15.00
Gaston Green, UCLA . . . 13.00
Kerwin Bell, Florida 12.00
Gordie Lockbaum, Holy Cross 12.00
Joe Paterno, Penn State . 12.00
Jamelle Holieway, Oklahoma 11.00
1988 Troy Aikman & Rodney Peete 18.00
Bobby Humphrey,Alabama 15.00
Steve Taylor, Nebraska . . 10.00
Todd Ellis, South Carolina 10.00
Mike Power, Boston College 10.00
1989 Emmitt Smith, Florida . . . 17.00
Mark Carrier,Southern Cal 15.00
Tony Rice, Notre Dame . . 12.00
Troy Taylor, California . . . 10.00
Major Harris, W.Virginia . . 11.00
Demetrius Brown,Michigan 10.00
Bill Musgrave, Oregon . . . 10.00
Mike Gundy, Oklahoma State 10.00
1990 50th Anniversary 8.00

STREET & SMITH'S PRO FOOTBALL

1963 Y.A. Tittle 60.00
Milt Plum 40.00
Roman Gabriel 45.00
1964 Bart Starr 40.00
Jim Katcavage 35.00
Terry Baker 35.00
1965 Johnny Unitas 37.00
Frank Ryan 35.00
Dick Bass 35.00
1966 R. LaLonde & J. Hillebrand 28.00
Ken Willard 28.00
Charley Johnson 28.00
1967 Gale Sayers & Mike Rabold 35.00
Dick Bass 25.00
Tony Lorick & Bob Vogel . 25.00
1968 Don Meredith 28.00
Norm Snead 26.00
Hewritt Dixon 24.00
1969 Joe Namath 35.00
John Brodie 28.00
Jack Concannon & George Seals 22.00

Street & Smith's Pro Football: 1969

Year	Cover	Price
1970	Joe Namath	32.00
	Roman Gabriel	24.00
	Joe Kapp	20.00
1971	Duane Thomas & Ralph Neely	18.00
	Earl Morrall	18.00
	John Brodie & Ken Willard	18.00
1972	Roger Staubach & Duane Thomas	22.00
	Bob Griese	19.00
	John Hadl	18.00
1973	Larry Csonka	17.00
	Chester Marcol	16.00
	Steve Spurrier	16.00
1974	Roger Staubach	22.00
	O.J. Simpson	22.00
	Jim Bertelsen	15.00
1975	Franco Harris	18.00
	Jim Hart	14.00
	Lawrence McCutcheon	14.00
1976	Roger Staubach	20.00
	Terry Bradshaw	20.00
	Ken Stabler	15.00
1977	Walter Payton	20.00
	Bert Jones	12.00
	John Cappelletti	12.00
1978	Tony Dorsett	18.00
	Bob Griese	16.00
	Mark VanEeghen	14.00
1979	Roger Staubach	18.00
	Terry Bradshaw	18.00
	Jim Zorn	12.00
1980	Walter Payton	18.00
	Terry Bradshaw	18.00
	Dan Fouts	14.00
1981	Brian Sipe & Tommy Kramer	10.00
	Jim Plunkett & Jim Zorn	12.00
	E. Campbell & S. Bartkowski	12.00
	Joe Ferguson & Ron Jaworski	10.00
1982	Joe Montana	20.00
	Lawrence Taylor	18.00
	Tony Dorsett	16.00
	Ken Anderson	10.00
1983	Marcus Allen	14.00
	Joe Theismann	12.00
	Ken Anderson	10.00
	A.J. Duhe	10.00
1984	Walter Payton	17.00
	Dan Marino	16.00
	Marcus Allen	13.00
	John Riggins	12.00
1985	Joe Montana	16.00
	Walter Payton	16.00
	Dan Marino	15.00
	Phil Simms	13.00
1986	Dan Marino	14.00
	Eric Dickerson	12.00
	Mike Singletary	11.00
	Joe Morris	10.00
1987	Dan Marino	13.00
	Tony Dorsett	13.00
	John Elway	13.00
	Phil Simms	12.00
	Bernie Kosar	10.00
1988	Jerry Rice	12.00
	Warren Moon	12.00
	John Offerdahl	8.00
	Doug Williams	9.00
	Anthony Carter	9.00
	Ozzie Newsome	10.00
1989	Boomer Esiason	10.00
	Jim Everett	10.00
	Roger Craig	9.00
	Jim Kelly	11.00
	Randall Cunningham	11.00
	Mike Singletary	9.00
	Herschel Walker	8.50
	Morten Andersen	8.00
1990	Joe Montana	9.00

STREET and SMITH'S OFFICIAL Yearbook PRO FOOTBALL 1977

Street & Smith's Pro Football: 1977

TOUCHDOWN ALL-PRO

Year	Cover	Price
1964	Ron Bull, Bears	35.00
1967	Fran Tarkenton	28.00
1968	Lamonica & D. Anderson	20.00
1969	Joe Namath	28.00
1970	Gabriel & C. Hill	18.00
1971	Tarkenton & M. Curtis	17.00
1972	Calvin Hill	16.00
1973	Larry Brown	15.00
1974	O.J. Simpson	20.00

TRUE FOOTBALL YEARBOOK

Year	Cover	Price
1950	Punter in action	80.00
1951	Kyle Rote	75.00
1952	Otto Graham	70.00
1953	Pink cover	65.00
1963	Herb Adderly	30.00
1964	Jim Brown	35.00
1965	Johnny Unitas	28.00
1966		20.00
1967	Bart Starr	20.00
1968	Johnny Unitas	20.00
1969	Earl Morrall	15.00
1970	Len Dawson	17.00
1971	Nowatzke	12.00
1972	Roger Staubach & Alan Page	18.00
1978	Roger Staubach	16.00
1979	Earl Campbell	14.00
1980	Mean Joe Greene	14.00
1981	Jim Plunkett	12.00

WOODWARD'S FOOTBALL YEARBOOK

Year	Cover	Price
1949	Dan Foldberg	75.00
1950		70.00
1951		65.00
1952	Harry Agganis	60.00
1953	Bob Burkhart	55.00
1954		52.00
1955		50.00
1956		48.00
1957	Bobby Cox	45.00
1958	Bob Reifsuyder	40.00
1959	Bob Anderson, Army	35.00
1960	Bob Schloredt,Washington	35.00
1961	Joe Romig, Colorado	35.00

POCKET PRO FOOTBALL ANNUALS

COMPLETE HANDBOOK OF PRO FOOTBALL

(Lancer Books)

Year	Cover	Price
1971	Fran Tarkenton	14.00
1972	Roger Staubach	18.00
1973	Bob Griese	13.00
1974	O.J. Simpson	16.00
1975	Mean Joe Greene	13.00
1976	Terry Bradshaw	14.00
1977	Ken Stabler	12.00
1978	Walter Payton	14.00
1979	Champion Steelers	13.00
1980	Lynn Swann	12.00
1981	Jim Plunkett	11.00
1982	Joe Montana	14.00
1983	Theismann & Riggins	9.00
1984	Marcus Allen	9.00
1985	Joe Montana	12.50
1986	Jim McMahon	8.00
1987	Phil Simms	8.50
1988	Bo Jackson	10.00
1989	Jerry Rice	9.00
1990	Bradshaw & Montana	9.00

NFL REPORT

Year	Cover	Price
1972	Jim Plunkett (Signet)	15.00
1973	Bradshaw & Harris (Signet)	18.00
1974	Larry Csonka (Signet)	14.00
1975	Lawrence McCutcheon (Dell)	10.00
1976	Franco Harris (Dell)	14.00
1977	Ken Stabler (Dell)	13.00
1978	Mark Van Eeghen (Dell)	10.00
1979	Tony Dorsett (Dell)	13.00
1980	Earl Campbell (Dell)	12.00
1981	Wilbert Montgomery (Dell)	8.00
1982	Kellen Winslow (Dell)	8.50
1983	James Lofton (Dell)	9.00
1984	Todd Christensen (Dell)	8.00
1987	Eric Dickerson (Signet)	8.50
1988	John Elway (Signet)	8.50

PRO FOOTBALL

(Ballantine Books)

Year	Cover	Price
1976	Lynn Swann	15.00
1977	O.J. Simpson	18.00

PRO FOOTBALL ALMANAC

(Fawcett Gold Medal Books)

Year	Cover	Price
1964	Jim Brown	30.00
1965	Bill Brown & Tarkenton	20.00

PRO FOOTBALL HANDBOOK

(Pocket Books)

Year	Cover	Price
1960	Johnny Unitas	35.00
1961	Sonny Jurgensen	30.00
1962	Football action	25.00
1963	Cleats and ball	20.00
1964	Ball carrier	18.00
1965	Jim Brown	28.00
1966		15.00
1967	Ball bursting through paper	34.00
1968	White helmet	12.00
1969	Jets wool cap on ball	12.00

Becomes:

THE POCKET BOOK OF PRO FOOTBALL

Year	Cover	Price
1974	O.J. Simpson	15.00
1975	Mean Joe Greene	12.00
1976	Terry Bradshaw	13.00
1977	Ken Stabler	12.00
1978	Walter Payton	13.00
1979	Terry Bradshaw	12.00
1980	Earl Campbell	10.00

HOCKEY PUBLICATIONS

ACTION SPORTS HOCKEY

Issue	Cover	Price
1/72	Dave Keon	15.00
2/72	Keith Magnuson	8.00
3/72	Jean Ratelle	10.00
4/72	Frank & Pete Mahovlich	10.00
5/72	Bobby Hull	15.00
10/72	Brad Park	12.00
11/72	Bobby Orr	15.00
12/72	Marcel Dionne	8.00
1/73	Bobby Clarke	8.00
2/73	Garry Unger	7.50
3/73	Bobby Hull	12.00
4/73		7.50
5/73	Jacques Lemaire	8.00
11/73	Bobby Clarke	8.50
12/73	Brad Park	9.00
1/74	Tony Esposito	8.00
2/74	Paul Henderson	7.50

Action Sports Hockey: February, 1980

Issue	Cover	Price
3/74	Phil Esposito	9.00
4/74	Bobby Orr	10.00
5/74	Yvan Cournoyer	8.50
12/74	Bobby Clarke	8.00
1/75		6.00
2/75	Derek Sanderson	5.00
3/75	Bobby Orr & Brad Park	9.50
4/75	Rangers vs. Canadiens	6.00
5/75		5.00
12/75	Guy Lafleur	8.00
1/76		5.00
2/76	Denis Potvin	7.00
3/76	Brad Park & Phil Esposito	8.00
4/76		5.00
5/76	Flyers vs. USSR	6.00
11/76	Guy Lafleur & Reggie Leach	6.50
1/77	Darryl Sittler	7.00
2/77	Bobby Orr & Denis Potvin	8.00
3/77	Pete McNab & Ken Dryden	6.00
4/77		5.00
5/77	Bobby Clarke & Brad Park	6.00
11/77	Guy Lafleur	6.00
1/78	Borje Salming	5.50
2/78	Gil Perreault	6.00
3/78	Larry Robinson	5.00
4/78	Gordie Howe & Mike Palmateer	8.00
11/78	Tiger Williams	5.00
1/79	Guy Lafleur	6.00
2/79		5.00
3/79	Borje Salming	5.00
4/79	Terry O'Reilly	4.50
11/79	Guy Lafleur	5.00
1/80	Ulf Nilsson	4.00
2/80	Darryl Sittler	5.00
3/80	Black Hawks vs. Islanders	4.00
4/80	Marcel Dionne	5.00

COMPLETE HANDBOOK OF PRO HOCKEY

Issue	Cover	Price
71-72	Black Hawks vs. Bruins action	15.00
72-73	Rangers vs. Bruins action	10.00
73-74	Rangers vs. Canadiens action	10.00
74-75	Bobby Clarke	12.00
75-76		8.00
76-77	Paul Newman in *Slapshot*	12.00
77-78	Guy Lafleur	12.00
78-79	Canadiens vs. Bruins action	8.00
79-80	Bob Gainey action vs. Rangers	10.00
80-81	Islanders w/ Stanley Cup	8.00
81-82	Wayne Merrick action vs. Oilers	6.00
82-83	Wayne Gretzky	15.00
83-84	Billy Smith	6.00
84-85	Gretzky, Oilers w/ Stanley Cup	10.00
85-86	Wayne Gretzky action vs. Flyers	10.00
86-87	Flyers vs. Flames action	5.00
87-88	Ron Hextall action vs.Oilers	5.00

CORD SPORTFACTS HOCKEY GUIDE

Issue	Cover	Price
69-70	Norm Ullman	15.00
70-71	Bobby Orr	18.00
71-72	Bobby Orr	18.00
72-73	Bobby Orr	18.00
73-74	Frank Mahovlich	12.00

Hockey Blueline Magazine:

HOCKEY BLUELINE MAGAZINE

Issue	Cover	Price
10/54	Gordie Howe	75.00
11/54		50.00
12/54	Al Rollins	50.00
1/55	Milt Schmidt	65.00
2/55	Jim Thomson	40.00
5/55	Edgar Laprade	35.00
6/55	Bill Quackenbush	50.00
10/55	Toe Blake	50.00
11/55	Tony Leswick	35.00
12/55	Jacques Plante	50.00
1/56	Ted Lindsay & ref	45.00

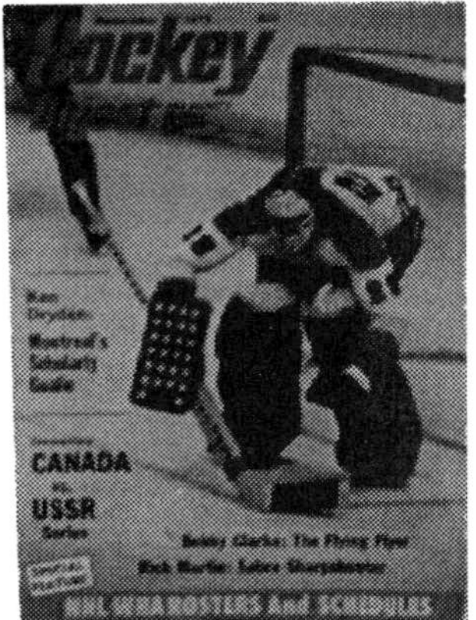

Hockey Digest: 12/72

Issue	Cover	Price
3/56	Gil Mayer	30.00
5/56	Moore, Geoffrion, Plante, Blake	40.00
9/56	Maurice Richard	45.00
10/56	Gordie Howe	50.00
11/56	Maurice Richard	45.00
12/56	Ted Sloan	30.00
1/57	Ted Lindsay	40.00
2/57	Doug Mohns	30.00
3/57	Jean Beliveau	40.00
4/57	Gump Worsley	40.00
5/57	Gordie Howe	45.00
11/57	Ed Litzenberger	25.00
12/57	Boom Boom Geoffrion	35.00
1/58	Lou Fontinato	25.00
2/58	Don McKenney	25.00
3/58	Andy Bathgate	35.00
4/58	Frank Mahovlich	35.00
5/58	Maurice Richard	40.00
10/58	Henri Richard	35.00
11/58	Fleming Mackell	20.00
12/58	Bill Gadsby	35.00
1/59	Dickie Duff	20.00
2/59	Andy Bathgate	30.00
3/59	Hockey fights	20.00
4/59	Jean Beliveau	30.00
5/59	Beliveau, Bathgate, Plante, others	30.00

HOCKEY DIGEST

Issue	Cover	Price
11/72	Bobby Orr	30.00
12/72	Ken Dryden	15.00
1/73	North Stars vs. Rangers	6.00
6/73	Keith Magnuson	6.00
3/73	Brad Park	7.50
4/73	Derek Sanderson	6.00
5/73	Gary Unger	6.00
6/73	Phil Esposito	7.50
11/73	Rick MacLeish	6.00
12/73	Henri Richard	8.00
1/74	Bobby Hull	10.00
2/74	Mickey Redmond	5.50
3/74	Gil Perreault	6.00
4/74	Steve Vickers	5.50
5/74	Tony Esposito	6.00
6/74	Tom Lysiak	5.50
11/74	Dave Schultz	5.50
12/74	Mike Walton	5.50
1/75	Bobby Orr	8.00
2/75	Stan Mikita	6.00
3/75	Marcel Dionne	6.00
4/75	Rick Martin	5.00
5/75	Derrick Sanderson	5.00
6/75	Guy Lafleur	7.50
11/75	Bobby Clarke	6.50

Hockey Digest: 6/78

12/75 Gil Perreault 5.50
1/76 Dennis Potvin 5.00
2/76 Bobby Hull 7.50
3/76 Bobby Sheehan 4.50
4/76 Gary Unger 4.50
5/76 Jean Ratelle 5.00
6/76 Ken Dryden 5.50
11/76 Bobby Orr 6.00
12/76 Phil Esposito 6.00
1/77 Larry Robinson,Guy Lafleur 6.00
2/77 Dave Schultz 4.50
3/77 Peter McNab 4.50
4/77 Steve Shutt vs. Bruins 4.50
5/77 Borje Salming 5.00
6/77 Glenn Resch 5.00
11/77 S. Savard, Habs
w/ Stanley Cup 5.00
12/77 Willy Plett 4.00
1/78 Rick MacLeish 4.50
2/78 Wayne Cashman vs. Flyers 4.00
3/78 Mike Bossy 5.50
4/78 Rick Martin 4.00
5/78 Darryl Sittler 4.50
6/78 Guy Lafleur 5.00
11/78 Terry O'Reilly 4.00
12/78 Ulf Nilsson &
Anders Hedberg 4.00
1/79 Danny Gare 4.00
2/79 Dale McCourt 4.00
3/79 Clark Gillies 4.00
4/79 Rangers vs. Flyers 4.00
5/79 Ken Dryden
vs. Bryan Trottier 4.50
6/79 Guy Lafleur 5.00
11/79 Rangers vs.
Gainey, Canadiens 4.00
12/79 Marcel Dionne 4.50
1/80 Bobby Clarke 4.50
2/80 Islanders vs. Oilers 4.00
3/80 Phil Esposito vs.North Stars 4.50
4/80 Gil Perreault 4.00
5/80 Wayne Gretzky 10.00
6/80 Tony Esposito 4.50
11/80 Islanders w/ Stanley Cup . . 4.00
12/80 Ray Bourque 4.00
1/81 Gillies, Islanders vs. Flyers 3.50
2/81 Flyers fighting Blues 3.00
3/81 Mike Bossy 3.50
4/81 Bob Gainey vs.Phil Esposito 3.50
5/81 Charlie Simmer 3.00
6/81 Dennis Savard 3.00
11/81 Wayne Gretzky vs.Rangers 7.50
12/81 Bryan Trottier 3.50
1/82 Rick Kehoe 3.00
2/82 Reed Larson 3.00
3/82 Bobby Smith 3.00
4/82 Normand Leveille 3.00
5/82 Wayne Gretzky 7.50
6/82 Mark Acton 3.00
11/82 Bryan Trottier 3.50
12/82 Doug Wilson 3.00
1/83 Bobby Carpenter 3.00
2/83 Peter Stastny 3.50
3/83 Denis Savard 3.50
4/83 Dino Ciccarelli 3.00
5/83 Pete Peeters 3.00
6/83 Wayne Gretzky 6.50
11/83 Billy Smith 3.00
12/83 Barry Pederson 3.00
1/84 Phil Housley 3.50
2/84 Mark Pavelich 3.00
3/84 Richard Brodeur 3.00
4/84 Larry Robinson 3.00
5/84 Wayne Gretzky 6.00
6/84 Denis Potvin 3.50
11/84 Mark Messier 5.00
12/84 Tom Barrasso 3.00
1/85 Michel Goulet 3.00
2/85 Dino Ciccarelli 3.00
3/85 Herb Brooks 3.00
4/85 Tim Kerr 3.00
5/85 Mike Bossy 3.50
7/85 Wayne Gretzky 5.50
11/85 Paul Coffey 3.50
12/85 Pelle Lindbergh 3.00
1/86 Rod Langway 2.50

Hockey Digest: 3/86

2/86 Marcel Dionne 3.00
3/86 Mario Lemieux 6.50
4/86 Barry Pederson 2.50
5/86 Kelly Hrudey 2.50
7/86 Wayne Gretzky 5.00
11/86 Patrick Roy 3.00
12/86 John Vanbiesbrouck 2.50
1/87 Wendel Clark 2.50
2/87 Bernie Federko 2.50
3/87 Mark Howe 2.50
4/87 Scott Stevens 2.50
5/87 Mike Bossy 3.00
6/87 Wayne Gretzky 5.00
11/87 Ron Hextall 2.50
12/87 Glen Hanlon 2.50
1/88 Dale Hawerchuk 3.00
2/88 Mario Lemieux 6.00
3/88 Kevin Dineen 2.50
4/88 Denis Potvin 2.50
5/88 Canadiens vs. Bruins 2.00
6/88 Grant Fuhr 2.00
11/88 Wayne Gretzky 5.00
12/88 Sean Burke 2.00
1/89 Mike Keenan 2.00
2/89 Al MacInnis 2.50
3/89 Cam Neely 2.50
4/89 Brian Leetch 2.50
5/89 Steve Yzerman 2.50
6/89 Mario Lemiuex 5.00
11/89 Joe Mullen 2.50
12/89 Wayne Gretzky 4.50
1/90 Chris Chelios 2.00
2/90 Mick Vukota &
Kevin Hatcher 2.00
3/90 Sergei Makarov 2.50
4/90 Doug Wilson 2.00
5/90 Flyers vs. Rangers rivalry . 2.00
6/90 Ray Bourque 2.50
11/90 Mark Messier 2.50
12/90 John Druce 2.00
1/91 Jon Casey 2.00
2/91 Dale Hawerchuk 2.00
3/91 Brett Hull 4.50
4/91 John Vanbiesbrouck 2.00
5/91 Chris Chelios 2.00
6/91 Wayne Gretzky 3.50
11/91 Mario Lemieux 3.50
12/91 Stephane Richer 2.00

HOCKEY ILLUSTRATED

11/62 Jacques Plante 30.00
12/62 Andy Bathgate 25.00
1/63 Jean Beliveau 25.00
2/63 Bobby Hull 25.00
3/63 Gordie Howe 40.00
11/63 . . . . 15.00
12/63 Dave Keon &
Terry Sawchuck 20.00
1/64 Boom Boom Geoffrion . . 20.00
2/64 Henri Richard 20.00
3/64 Glenn Hall & Elmer Vasko 18.00
4/64 Bobby Hull 30.00
11/64 . . . . 15.00
12/64 Marcel Pronovost &
Johnny Bower 18.00
1/65 Jean Beliveau 18.00
2/65 Dave Keon 16.00
3/65 Canadiens vs.Black Hawks 14.00
4/65 Bobby Hull 20.00
11/65 Jean Beliveau 15.00
12/65 Hull, Mahovlich,H.Richard 15.00
1/66 Gordie Howe 18.00
2/66 Bobby Hull &
Johnny Bower 16.00
3/66 Henri Richard 12.00
4/66 Jean Beliveau 12.00
11/66 Henri Richard 12.00
12/66 Bobby Hull &
Gordie Howe 20.00
1/67 Bobby Hull 15.00
2/67 Jean Beliveau 12.00
3/67 Bobby Rousseau 10.00
4/67 Henri Richard &
Dave Keon 12.00
11/67 Bobby Hull 15.00
12/67 Henri Richard 12.00
1/68 Ed Giacomin 12.00
2/68 Bobby Hull 15.00
3/68 Gordie Howe 15.00
4/68 Frank Mahovlich 12.00
5/68 Bobby Hull 14.00
11/68 . . . . 10.00
12/68 . . . . 10.00
1/69 Rod Gilbert 12.00
2/69 Gordie Howe 14.00
3/69 . . . . 10.00
4/69 Bobby Hull 14.00
5/69 . . . . 10.00
11/69 . . . . 10.00
12/69 . . . . 10.00
1/70 . . . . 10.00
2/70 Stan Mikita 14.00
3/70 Alex Delvecchio 12.00
4/70 Bobby Orr 18.00
5/70 Ed Giacomin 12.00
11/70 Bobby Orr 16.00
12/70 Tony Esposito 12.00
1/71 Gordie Howe 12.00
2/71 Keith Magnuson 9.00
3/71 Yvan Cournoyer &
Jean Beliveau 12.00

Hockey Illustrated: December, 1966

Date	Cover	Price
4/71	Brad Park & Ed Westfall	12.00
5/71	Derek Sanderson	9.00
11/71	Ken Dryden	12.00
12/71	Phil Esposito	15.00
1/72	Gil Perreault	12.00
2/72	Dennis Hull	9.00
3/72	Garry Unger	9.00
4/72	Hadfield, Ratelle, Gilbert	10.00
5/72	Gump Worsley	12.00
6/72	John McKenzie	8.00
11/72	Walt Tkaczuk	8.00
12/72	Phil Esposito vs. USSR	12.00
1/73		8.00
2/73		8.00
3/73		8.00
4/73		8.00
5/73		8.00
6/73		8.00
11/73		8.00
12/73		8.00
1/74	Cournoyer, Robert, Redmond	8.50
2/74	Orr, Favell, Tullan	9.50
3/74	Hull, Schultz, Gilbert	10.00
4/74	Tony Esposito	9.00
5/74	Gil Perreault & Norm Ullman	9.00
6/74	H.Richard, Park, Martin, Taylor	8.50
1/75	Bobby Orr	9.00
2/75	Ken Dryden	9.00
3/75	Bobby Clarke	9.00
4/75	Phil Esposito	9.00
5/75	Rogie Vachon	8.50
1/76	Bobby Orr	9.00
2/76	Guy Lafleur	9.00
3/76	Tony Esposito	8.50
4/76	Ken Dryden	9.00
5/76	Bobby Clarke & Guy Lafleur	9.00
1/77	Denis Potvin	8.50
2/77	Darryl Sittler	8.00
3/77	Larry Robinson	7.00
4/77	Bernie Parent	7.50
5/77	Guy Lafleur	8.00
1/78	Rick Martin	7.00
2/78	Ken Dryden	8.00
3/78	Bobby Clarke	7.50
4/78	Rogie Vachon	7.50
5/78	Guy Lafleur	7.50
1/79	Jacques Lemaire	7.00
2/79	Darryl Sittler	7.50
3/79	Marcel Dionne	7.50
4/79	Bryan Trottier	7.50
1/80	Mike Palmateer	6.50
2/80	Real Cloutier	6.50
3/80	Reggie Leach	7.00
4/80	Anders Hedbert	6.50
1/81	Jim Schoenfeld	6.00
2/81	Bobby Smith	6.50
3/81	Borje Salming	6.50
4/81		6.00

HOCKEY ILLUSTRATED YEARBOOK

Season	Cover	Price
61-62	Boom Boom Geoffrion	35.00
62-63		25.00
63-64		25.00
64-65	Eddie Shack	25.00
65-66		20.00
66-67		20.00
67-68		18.00
68-69		18.00
69-70		15.00
70-71		15.00
71-72		15.00
72-73		12.00
73-74	Bobby Clarke	14.00
74-75	Bernie Parent	12.00
75-76	Bobby Clarke	12.00
76-77	Ken Dryden	12.00
77-78	Guy Lafleur	12.00
78-79	Mike Bossy	10.00
79-80	Guy Lafleur	10.00
80-81	Wayne Gretzky	20.00
81-82		10.00
82-83	Wayne Gretzky	15.00

HOCKEY NEWS YEARBOOK

Season	Cover	Price
82-83	Wayne Gretzky	15.00
83-84	Wayne Gretzky, Pete Peeters	12.00
84-85		8.00
85-86		8.00
86-87	Coffey,Gretzky, C.Lemieux	10.00
87-88		7.00
88-89	Mario Lemieux	8.00
89-90	MacInnis, Gretzky, Lemieux, others	8.00
90-91		5.00

Hockey Pictorial: 5/76

HOCKEY PICTORIAL

Date	Cover	Price
10/55	Jean Beliveau, others	70.00
11/55	Red Kelly, others	60.00
12/55	Leo Labine	50.00
1/56	Tod Sloan, others	45.00
2/56	Andy Bathgate	50.00
3/56	Richard brothers	50.00
4/56	Glenn Hall	45.00
5/56	Henri Richard,Stanley Cup	50.00
10/56	Beliveau, Lindsay, Howe, others	60.00
11/56	Worsley, Howe, Ullman	50.00
12/56	Jean Beliveau	40.00
1/57	Leo Labine	35.00
2/57	Ted Lindsay & Gordie Howe	50.00
3/57	Doug Harvey	40.00
4/57	Harvey, Howe, Hall, Lindsay, etc	45.00
5/57	Henri Richard vs. Bruins	35.00
10/57	Rocket Richard	45.00
11/57	Bill Gadsby	40.00
12/57	Gordie Howe	45.00
1/58	Real Chevrefils	25.00
2/58	Camille Henry	25.00
3/58	Ed Chadwick	25.00
4/58	Henri Richard	30.00
5/58	Allan Stanley	30.00
10/58	Frank Mahovlich	30.00
11/58	Ed Litzenberger	22.00
12/58	Norm Ullman	26.00
1/59	Andy Bathgate	26.00
2/59	Doug Mohns	22.00
3/59	Tom Johnson	20.00
4/59	Glenn Hall	22.00
5/59	Canadiens w/Stanley Cup	22.00
10/59	Dickie Moore	22.00
11/59	Bobby Hull	40.00
12/59	Alex Delvecchio	25.00
1/60	Carl Brewer	20.00
2/60	Vic Stasiuk	20.00
3/60	"Kid Hockey Flourishes"	15.00
4/60	Jean Beliveau	25.00
9/60	Bob Pulford	15.00
10/60	Dean Prentice	16.00
11/60	Bill Hay	15.00
12/60	Don McKenney	15.00
1/61	Murray Oliver	15.00
2/61	Ralph Blackstrom	15.00
3/61	Bobby Hull	30.00
4/61	Frank Mahovlich	20.00
9/61	Boom Boom Geoffrion	20.00
10/61	Dave Keon	18.00
11/61	Doug Mohns	16.00
12/61	Beliveau, Hall, others	18.00
1/62	Geoffrion, Pronovost, Hall, others	18.00
2/62	Carl Brewer	15.00
3/62	Detroit v. Boston, Mon. vs. Tor	15.00
4/62	Kelly, Tremblay, Plante, Pulford	18.00
9/62	Maple Leafs vs. Bruins	16.00
10/62	Henri Richard	16.00
11/62	Black Hawks vs.Canadiens	15.00
12/62	Black Hawks vs. Maple Leafs	15.00
1/63	Gordie Howe	25.00
2/63	Stan Mikita	25.00
3/63	Don Simmons	15.00
4/63	Bobby Hull	20.00
9/63	Johnny Bower & Bobby Hull	20.00
10/63	Jacques Plante	18.00
11/63	Gordie Howe	20.00
12/63	Black Hawks bench	15.00
1/64	Milt Schmidt & Leo Boivin	18.00
2/64	Jean Beliveau	18.00
3/64	Pierre Pilote	16.00
4/64		12.00
9/64	Charlie Hodge	12.00
10/64		12.00
11/64		12.00
12/64		12.00
1/65		12.00
2/65		12.00
3/65		12.00
4/65	Charlie Hodge & Ron Ellis	12.00
5/65	Gordie Howe & Norm Ullman	20.00
10/65	Henri Richard & Frank Mahovlich	16.00
11/65	Rod Gilbert	15.00
12/65	Gordie Howe &	

Hockey Pictorial: 4/57

- Bill Gadsby 18.00
- 1/66 Frank Mahovlich 15.00
- 2/66 Stan Mikita 18.00
- 3/66 Roger Crozier 14.00
- 4/66 Hull, Mikita, Hall, Pilote . . 18.00
- 5/66 . . . . . 12.00
- 10/66 Canadiens goalies 12.00
- 11/66 Bob Pulford 12.00
- 12/66 Gordie Howe & Alex Delvecchio 18.00
- 1/67 Gerry Cheevers 12.00
- 2/67 Ed Giacomin 12.00
- 3/67 Bobby Rousseau 10.00
- 4/67 Bobby Hull 18.00
- 10/67 NHL expansion 10.00
- 11/67 Bobby Orr 18.00
- 12/67 Crisp, Roberts, Bassen, others 12.00
- 1/68 Cesare Maniago & Bob Woytowich 10.00
- 2/68 Stan Mikita 15.00
- 3/68 Henderson, Ullman, McGregor 12.00
- 4/68 Stanley Cup 12.00
- 10/68 St. Louis Blues 10.00
- 11/68 Clauede Ruel 10.00
- 12/68 Wayne Connelly & Wren Blair 10.00
- 1/69 Gump Worsley 12.00
- 2/69 Stan Mikita 14.00
- 3/69 Brad Park & Gordie Howe 15.00
- 4/69 . . . . . 10.00
- 11/69 Montreal vs. St. Louis . . . 10.00
- 12/69 Ken Hodge 12.00
- 1/70 . . . . . 10.00
- 2/70 Yvan Cournoyer 12.00
- 3/70 Bobby Orr 15.00
- 4/70 Mike Laughton & Juha Widing 10.00
- 5/70 St. Louis Blues 10.00
- 11/70 Carol Vadnais 10.00
- 12/70 Tony Esposito 12.00
- 1/71 Roger Crozier 10.00
- 2/71 Phil Esposito 18.00
- 3/71 Keith Magnuson 9.50
- 4/71 Bobby Orr 14.00
- 5/71 Ken Dryden 15.00
- 11/71 Chicago vs. Montreal 10.00
- 12/71 Norm Ullman 12.00
- 1/72 . . . . . 9.50
- 2/72 Jacques Plante & Frank Mahovlich 12.00
- 3/72 . . . . . 9.50
- 4/72 P. Mahovlich, Hull, T. Esposito 12.00

Hockey Pictorial: 4/58

- 5/72 Rod Gilbert 12.00
- 11/72 . . . . . 9.50
- 12/72 Brad Park 12.00
- 1/73 Villemure, Nielson, Tullen 10.00
- 2/73 Richard Martin & Gil Perreault 12.00
- 3/73 Dan Awrey & Phil Esposito 12.00
- 4/73 Dryden, Oliver, Prentice . . 10.00
- 5/73 Bobby Orr 12.00
- 11/73 Gil Perreault 12.00
- 12/73 Steve Vickers & Jim Nielsen 9.00
- 1/74 Bobby Orr 12.00
- 2/74 Dave Keon 10.00
- 3/74 Richard Martin 9.50
- 4/74 Tony Esposito 10.00
- 5/74 Frank Mahovlich 10.00
- 11/74 Phil Esposito 12.00
- 12/74 Denis Potvin 9.50
- 1/75 Bobby Orr 10.00
- 2/75 Gary Smith 8.00
- 3/75 Phil Russell 8.00
- 4/75 Danny Grant 8.00
- 5/75 Ken Dryden 10.00
- 11/75 Rod Gilbert 10.00
- 12/75 Stan Mikita 10.00
- 1/76 Bobby Clarke 9.00
- 2/76 Phil Esposito 9.50
- 3/76 Rogie Vachon 9.00
- 4/76 Gerry Cheevers 8.50
- 5/76 Bobby Clarke 9.00
- 11/76 Bobby Clarke 9.00
- 12/76 Phil Esposito 8.50
- 1/77 Brad Park 8.50
- 2/77 Don Murdoch 7.50
- 3/77 Marcel Dionne 8.50
- 4/77 Steve Shutt 7.50
- 5/77 Reggie Leach 8.00
- 6/77 Guy Lafleur 10.00
- 10/77 Larry Robinson 7.00
- 11/77 Lanny McDonald 7.00
- 12/77 Denis Potvin 7.50
- 1/78 Guy LaPointe & Richard Martin 7.00
- 2/78 Bryan Trottier 8.00
- 3/78 Keith Magnuson 7.00
- 4/78 Gil Perreault 7.50
- 5/78 Guy Lafleur 8.50
- 10/78 Guy Lafleur 8.50
- 11/78 Terry O'Reilly 7.00
- 12/78 Orr, Park, Salming 9.50
- 1/79 Hedberg, Martin, Resch, Watson 7.00

Hockey Pictorial: 4/79

- 2/79 Tretiak, McCourt, Robinson, etc. 8.00
- 3/79 Vachon,T.Esposito, Lysiak,Sargeant 8.50
- 4/79 Mike Bossy & Garry Unger 8.00
- 5/79 Stan Mikita & Denis Potvin 8.50

HOCKEY TIMES

- 11/70 Bobby Orr & Gordie Howe 25.00
- 12/70 Ken Hodge 12.00
- 1/71 Bruins vs. Black Hawks . . 10.00
- 2/71 Bobby Orr 18.00
- 3/71 Blues vs. Bruins 10.00
- 4/71 Bruins w/ Stanley Cup . . . 12.00
- 5/71 Johnston 10.00
- 6/71 Canadiens w/ Stanley Cup 12.00
- 7/71 Jean Beliveau retires 15.00
- 8/71 Gordie Howe & Tony Esposito 15.00
- 9/71 Bobby Orr 15.00
- 10/71 Bobby Orr 15.00
- 11/71 Phil Esposito 15.00
- 12/71 Derek Sanderson 10.00
- 1/72 Reggie Leach 10.00
- 2/72 Orr, Hull, Hodge 18.00
- 3/72 Canadiens vs. Bruins 12.00
- 4/72 Ken Dryden 12.00
- 5/72 Bobby Orr vs. Blues 15.00
- 6/72 Bobby Orr 15.00
- 7/72 Bruins executives 8.00
- 8/72 Johnston 9.00
- 9/72 Bobby Orr 14.00
- 10/72 John Bucyk 12.00
- 11/72 Bobby Orr 14.00
- 12/72 Tony Esposito 10.00
- 1/73 Bruins art 8.00
- 2/73 Fred Stanfield 8.00
- 3/73 Bobby Orr 12.00
- 4/73 Bobby Orr 12.00
- 5/73 Ted Green 8.00
- 6/73 . . . . . 8.00
- 7/73 . . . . . 8.00
- 8/73 . . . . . 8.00
- 9/73 . . . . . 8.00

HOCKEY TODAY

Published by CAHA

- 77-78 Darryl Sittler 15.00
- 78-79 Guy Lafleur 12.00
- 79-80 . . . . . 10.00
- 80-81 Bobby Smith 8.00

Issue	Cover	Price
81-82		10.00
82-83		10.00
83-84	Trottier, Gretzky, J.Patrick	12.00
84-85		7.00
85-86	Lanny McDonald	6.00
86-87		6.00
87-88	Mario Lemieux & Wayne Gretzky	10.00
88-89	Sean Burke	5.00
89-90	75th Anniv. w/ Howe, Gretzky, etc.	7.50
90-91	Messier, Lindros, Ricci	6.50

HOCKEY TODAY

Published by Ideal Sports

Issue	Cover	Price
76-77	Guy Lafleur	15.00
77-78	Guy Lafleur	12.00
78-79		12.00
79-80	Guy Lafleur	10.00

HOCKEY WORLD

Issue	Cover	Price
5/66	Jean Beliveau	25.00
10/66	Boom Boom Geoffrion	20.00
11/66	Mikita, Hull, Reay	20.00
1/67	Worsley, Ullman, MacGregor	18.00
2/67	Gilbert, Goyette, Marshall	15.00
3/67	Yvan Cournoyer	15.00
4/67	Bobby Orr & Bobby Hull	25.00
5/67	Henri Richard	16.00
10/67	Glenn Hall	14.00
11/67	Dave Keon & Eddie Johnston	15.00
12/67	Rangers vs. Maple Leafs	12.00
1/68	Bobby & Dennis Hull	16.00
2/68	Eddie Shack	12.00
3/68		12.00
4/68	Vam Impe, Orr,Hull,Favell	14.00
5/68	Beliveau, Orr, Hull, Mikita, etc.	18.00
5/71	Gerry Cheevers & Jean Ratelle	15.00
10/71		10.00
11/71	Gil Parreault	12.00
12/71		10.00
1/72		10.00
3/72	Doug Favell	10.00
4/72		10.00
5/72		10.00
10/72	North Stars action	10.00
11/72	Ken Dryden	12.00
12/72	Dunc Wilson	9.00
1/73	Cournoyer vs. Johnston	10.00
3/73		9.00
4/73		9.00
5/73	Keith Magnuson	9.00
10/73		8.50
11/73	Tony Esposito	9.50
12/73		8.00
1/74		8.00
3/74		8.00
4/74		8.00
5/74		8.00
10/74	Bobby Clarke	9.00
11/74	Darryl Sittler	9.00
12/74		7.50
1/75		7.50
3/75		7.50
4/75	Dennis Hextall	7.50
5/75		7.50
10/75	Bernie Parent	8.50
11/75	Bobby Orr	9.00

INSIDE HOCKEY

Issue	Cover	Price
11/87	Dale Hawerchuk	4.50
1/88	Mark Messier	5.00
3/88	Scott Stevens	3.00
5/88	Stephane Richer	3.00
10/88	Sean Burke	3.00
11/88	The courts and Hockey violence	2.50
1/89	Naslund, Robinson, others	3.00
2/89	Glenn Anderson	2.50
4/89	Claude Lemieux	2.50
5/89	25 People You Should Know	5.00
10/89	Sittler, Eagleson, Lewis	2.50
11/89	Wayne Gretzky	5.00
12/89	Trevor Linden	3.00
1/90	Paul Coffey & Mike Ricci	3.50
2/90	Tomas Sandstrom	2.50
4/90	Hockey fighting	2.00
5/90	Oates, Messier, Gilmour	4.00
10/90	Bourque & Hull	5.00
11/90	Eric Lindros (Canada)	8.00
	Kirk Muller (U.S.)	2.50
1/91	Esa Tikkanen	2.50
2/91	Chris Chelios	3.00
4/91	Theoren Fleury	2.50
5/91	Don Cherry (Canada)	2.50
	Brett Hull (U.S.)	4.00
10/91	Belfour, Recchi, Gagner	3.50
11/91	Mario Lemieux	4.00
12/91	Joe Sakic	2.50

INSIDE HOCKEY YEARBOOK

Issue	Cover	Price
90-91	Ranford, Richer, Yzerman	6.00
91-92	Brett Hull (U.S.)	5.50
	Patrick Roy (Canada)	5.50

OFFICIAL NHL GUIDE

Issue	Cover	Price
32-33	Howie Morenz	250.00
33-34		225.00
34-35		200.00
35-36	Action art	175.00
36-37		150.00

1969-70 NHL Guide

Issue	Cover	Price
37-38		150.00
38-39		150.00
39-40		125.00
40-41		125.00
41-42		125.00
42-43		115.00
43-44		115.00
44-45		100.00
45-46	Action art	100.00
46-47		95.00
47-48	NHL logo	95.00
48-49	NHL logo	90.00
49-50	NHL logo	90.00
50-51	NHL logo	85.00
51-52	NHL logo	85.00
52-53	NHL logo	80.00
53-54	NHL logo	75.00
54-55	NHL logo	70.00
55-56	NHL logo	70.00
56-57	NHL logo	65.00
57-58	NHL logo	65.00
58-59	NHL logo	60.00
59-60	NHL logo	60.00
60-61	NHL logo	55.00

1970-71 NHL Guide

Issue	Cover	Price
61-62	NHL logo	50.00
62-63	NHL logo	45.00
63-64	NHL logo	40.00
64-65	NHL logo	40.00
65-66	NHL logo	35.00
66-67	50th Anniversary NHL logo	45.00
67-68	NHL logo	25.00
68-69	NHL logo	20.00
69-70	P.Esposito, S.Savard, Worsley	30.00
70-71	Gordie Howe & Clarence Campbell	30.00
71-72	Richard, Geoffrion, Hull, Espo, Bucyk	30.00
72-73	Esposito vs. Worsley	25.00
73-74	Clarke,Cournoyer, Orr,Esposito,etc	25.00
74-75	Phil Esposito vs. Bobby Clarke	20.00
75-76	Ken Dryden vs. Ed Westfall	20.00
76-77	Curt Bennett, Garry Unger	15.00
77-78	Clarence Campbell photos	12.00
78-79	Bob Gainey & Selke Trophy	12.00
79-80	NHL team logos	10.00
80-81	Wayne Gretzky	35.00
81-82	Mike Liut	10.00
82-83	Wayne Gretzky	20.00
83-84	Islanders 4 in a row	10.00

Becomes:

OFFICAL NHL GUIDE & RECORD BOOK

Issue	Cover	Price
84-85	Gretzky, Oilers w/ Stanley Cup	15.00
85-86	Paul Coffey & Wayne Gretzky	12.00
86-87	Gainey, Robinson, Habs w/ Stanley	10.00
87-88	Gretzky vs. Howe; M. Goulet	12.00
88-89	Mario Lemieux & Wayne Gretzky	15.00
89-90	Lanny McDonald w/ Stnaley Cup	7.00
90-91	Hull, Messier, Bourque	8.00

OFFICIAL NHL RECORD BOOK

Issue	Cover	Price
50-51	Terry Sawchuck	85.00
51-52		65.00
52-53		55.00
53-54		50.00
54-55		40.00
55-56		40.00

56-57 35.00
57-58 Howe, Beliveau, Gadsby, others 50.00
58-59 Bathgate, Hall, Howe, others 40.00
59-60 30.00
60-61 Geoffrion, Hull, Howe, others 45.00
61-62 30.00
62-63 30.00
63-64 Beliveau, Howe, Mikita, others 35.00
64-65 25.00
65-66 Beliveau, Howe, Hull, Bucyk, etc 30.00
66-67 25.00
67-68 20.00
68-69 20.00
69-70 20.00
70-71 15.00
71-72 15.00
72-73 12.00
73-74 12.00
74-75 10.00
75-76 10.00
76-77 10.00
77-78 10.00
78-79 10.00
79-80 12.00
80-81 12.00
81-82 12.00
82-83 NHL logo & year 10.00
83-84 Wayne Gretzky 15.00
Becomes Offical NHL Guide & Record Book

PETERSEN'S HOCKEY

79-80 Guy Lafleur 12.00
80-81 Wayne Gretzky 20.00

POPULAR LIBRARY'S FACE-OFF HOCKEY YEARBOOK

69-70 Bobby Orr 20.00
70-71 Bobby Orr vs.Black Hawks 16.00
71-72 Phil Esposito, Ken Dryden 16.00

PROUDFOOT'S PRO HOCKEY

68-69 Black Hawks vs. Canadiens action 12.00
69-70 Hockey skate 8.00
70-71 Hockey cartoon 8.00
71-72 Hockey cartoon 8.00
72-73 Hockey cartoon 8.00
73-74 Hockey cartoon 8.00
74-75 Bernie Parent 10.00
75-76 Hockey caroon 8.00
76-77 8.00
77-78 Guy Lafleur 12.00
78-79 8.00
79-80 7.00
80-81 7.00
81-82 Dino Ciccarelli 7.50
82-83 Mike Bossy 8.00
83-84 6.50
84-85 Wayne Gretzky 12.00
85-86 Bobby Carpenter 6.00

RINKSIDE

11/89 Calgary Flames 4.00
12/89 Tom Barrasso 3.00
1/90 Mario Lemieux 6.00
2/90 Kevin Dineen 2.50
3/90 Bob Kudelski 2.50
4/90 Don Beaupre 2.50
11/90 Paul Cavallini 2.50
12/90 Luc Robitaille 3.00
1/91 Doug Wilson 2.50
2/91 Bobby Holik 2.50
3/91 Jimmy Carson 3.00
4/91 Playoff Preview 2.50

THE SPORTING NEWS HOCKEY YEARBOOK

90-91 Brian Leetch &

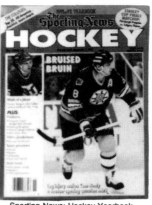

Sporting News: Hockey Yearbook

Pat LaFontaine 6.00
Mike Keenan & Brett Hull 6.00
Wayne Gretzky & Mario Lemieux 7.00
Patrick Roy & Ray Bourque 6.00
Patrick Roy & Mark Messier 6.00

THE SPORTING NEWS NHL GUIDE

67-68 45.00
68-69 Bobby Hull & Johnny Bower 35.00
69-70 Bobby Orr 30.00
70-71 Gordie Howe 30.00
71-72 Phil Esposito 25.00
72-73 15.00
73-74 Yvan Cournoyer 16.00
74-75 Bernie Parent 16.00
75-76 Bobby Clarke 16.00
76-77 12.00
77-78 Guy Lafleur 15.00
78-79 Robinson, Habs w/ Stanley Cup 12.00
79-80 Bob Gainey 10.00
80-81 8.50
81-82 Mike Bossy 10.50
82-83 8.50
83-84 8.00
84-85 7.50
85-86 Coffey, Gretzky, Kurri 10.00
86-87 6.50
87-88 6.00
88-89 Mario Lemieux 7.50
89-90 6.00
90-91 6.00

THE SPORTING NEWS NHL REGISTERS

72-73 25.00
73-74 15.00
74-75 Stan Mikita 18.00
75-76 12.00
76-77 Marcel Dionne 12.00
77-78 10.00
78-79 10.00
79-80 Bryan Trottier 10.00
80-81 Wayne Gretzky 20.00
81-82 Mike Liut 8.00
82-83 8.00
83-84 8.00
84-85 7.50
85-86 Tim Kerr vs. Islanders 7.50
86-87 7.50
87-88 6.00
88-89 Grant Fuhr 6.00
89-90 6.00
90-91 6.00

SPORTS EXTRA HOCKEY

1/72 Bobby Orr 15.00
3/72 Phil Esposito 15.00
5/72 Gilles Villemure & Ed Giacomin 12.00
12/72 Bobby Hull 16.00
2/73 V.Hadfield vs. Canadiens; B. Orr 12.00
4/73 Brad Park & Bobby Orr 12.00
12/73 Esposito bros., G. Howe 12.00
1/74 Walt Tkaczuck vs. Black Hawks 8.00
3/74 Phil Esposito 10.00
11/74 Bobby Clarke, Bobby Orr 12.00
3/75 Red Wings vs. Rangers, Orr, etc. 9.00

SPORTS QUARTERLY INSIDE HOCKEY

67-68 Hull, Vachon, Mikita, Beliveau, etc 25.00
68-69 20.00
69-70 15.00
70-71 12.00
71-72 Dryden, Park, H. Richard 15.00
72-73 Orr, Cournoyer, Ratelle 14.00
73-74 Cournoyer, P. Esposito, Redmond 12.00
74-75 10.00
75-76 10.00
76-77 8.00
77-78 8.00
78-79 8.00
79-80 Mike Bossy, Guy Lafleur 9.50
80-81 Billy Smith,Wayne Gretzky 15.00

SPORTS SPECIAL HOCKEY

12/68 Bobby Hull 25.00
2/69 Gordie Howe 20.00
5/69 Jean Beliveau 14.00
12/69 Bobby Orr 20.00
4/70 Ed Giacomin 12.00
12/70 Bobby Hull, Bobby Orr 20.00
2/71 Bobby Hull 16.00
4/71 Stan Mikita 18.00
12/71 Ken Dryden 16.00
2/72 Bobby Hull 14.00
4/72 Jean Ratelle 12.00
12/72 Jean Ratelle 12.00
2/73 Derek Sanderson 9.00
4/73 Phil Esposito 12.00
12/73 Cournoyer, Hull, Clarke 14.00
1/74 Bobby Orr, Gil Perreault 12.00
3/74 Bobby Clarke 10.00
11/74 Parent, P.Esposito, Howe 12.00
3/75 Phil Esposito 10.00

ALL SPORTS

Inside Sport: April, 1980

INSIDE SPORTS

Date	Cover	Value
Oct. 79	Lemon wearing Yankees hat	30.00
Apr. 80	Nolan Ryan	40.00
May 80	Magic Johnson, Fidrych, Bench	15.00
June 80	Ray Leonard & Roberto Duran	6.00
July 80	Ken Reitz	5.00
Aug. 80	W.Randolph, S.Garvey, R.Duran	6.00
Sep. 80	Ken Stabler & Art Schlichter	5.00
Oct. 80	H.Cosell, D.Meredith, F.Gifford	5.00
Nov. 80	Muhammed Ali	6.00
Dec. 80	Ray Meyer & BearBryant	5.00
Jan. 81	Jimmy the Greek	4.00
Feb. 81	JayneModean(Swimsuit)	15.00
Mar. 81	Ronald Reagan	4.50
Apr. 81	George Brett	7.50
May 81	Outlaw Pitchers	4.00
June 81	Jan Stephenson & Jim Palmer	5.00
July 81	Joe Namath	5.00
Aug. 81	Salary Survey (inc. Magic, Rose)	6.00
Sep. 81	Herschel Walker	4.50
Oct. 81	John Matuszek	4.00
Nov. 81	Tony Dorsett	5.00
Dec. 81	Terry Bradshaw	5.00
Jan. 82	Randy White	4.00
Feb. 82	Amy Hardin (Swimsuit)	5.50
Mar. 82	Gerry Cooney	4.00
Apr. 82	Steve Garvey	5.00
May 82	Pete Rose	6.00
June 82	Gerry Cooney & Larry Holmes	4.00
July 82	What's Hot & What's Not	4.00
Aug. 82	Joe Montana	10.00
Sep. 82	Kellen Winslow	4.00
Oct. 82	Jack Lambert	4.00
Nov. 82	Ed "Too Tall" Jones	4.50
Oct. 83	John Riggins	4.00
Nov. 83	Lawrence Taylor	8.00
Dec. 83	Marvin Hagler & Roberto Duran	4.00
Jan. 84	Ken Stabler	4.00
Feb. 84	Heather Locklear (Swimsuit)	6.00
Mar. 84	Darryl Strawberry	6.00
Apr. 84	Ripken, Fisk, Murray, Oz.Smith	5.00
May 84	Fernando Valenzuela	5.00
June 84	Mike Schmidt	5.50
July 84	Steve Garvey & Rich Goosage	5.00
Aug. 84	Winfield & Steinbrenner	5.75
Sep. 84	Danny White	3.50
Oct. 84	Walter Payton	5.00
Nov. 84	Joe Theismann	4.00
Dec. 84	Marcus Allen & Eric Dickerson	4.00
Jan. 85	Joe Montana	4.50
Feb. 85	TracyScoggins(Swimsuit)	8.00
Mar. 85	John McEnroe & Gus Williams	3.50
Apr. 85	Gibson,Sandberg, Garvey,Quiz	4.50
May 85	Rick Sutcliffe & Gary Carter	4.00
June 85	Rickey Henderson & 6 Dodgers	5.00
July 85	T.Seaver, N.Ryan, J. Koosman	8.50
Aug. 85	NFL Ratings & Inside Stuff	3.50
Sep. 85	NFL & College Preview	3.50
Oct. 85	Mark Gastineau & Cheerleader	3.50
Nov. 85	Pat Ewing & Michael Jordan	5.00
Dec. 85	'85-'86 College All-Americans	4.00
Jan. 86	Jim McMahon	3.50
Feb. 86	Lisa Hartman (Swimsuit)	8.00
Mar. 86	Baseball's Best Player (Rickey #1)	5.50
Apr. 86	1986 Baseball Preview	4.00
May 86	Baseball Ratings & Inside Stuff	4.50
June 86	Larry Bird & Magic Johnson	6.00
July 86	How to Beat the Bears (Payton)	4.00
Aug. 86	Football Ratings & Inside Stuff	3.50
Sep. 86	NFL & College Preview	3.50
Oct. 86	Football's Best Players	4.00
Nov. 86	NBA Preview (Jordan, Bird, Magic, Dr.J)	7.50
Dec. 86	David Robinson & Steve Alford	7.00
Jan. 87	NFL Playoffs	3.00
Feb. 87	ChristyFichtner(Swimsuit)	4.50
Mar. 87	Baseball's Best by Position	4.50
Apr. 87	1987 Baseball Preview	3.00
May 87	Baseball Ratings & Inside Stuff	3.00
June 87	NBA Playoffs (Jordan)	5.00
July 87	Jim McMahon & Phil Simms	3.00
Aug. 87	Football Ratings & Inside Stuff	3.00
Sep. 87	NFL & College Preview	3.00
Oct. 87	Football's Best Players	3.50
Nov. 87	NBA & College Preview	3.00
Dec. 87	Basketball Ratings & Inside Stuff	5.00
Jan. 88	How to Beat the Best	3.00
Feb. 88	Emma Samms(Swimsuit)	7.50
Mar. 88	Baseball's Best Players	4.00
Apr. 88	1988 Baseball Preview	3.00
May 88	Ewing, Magic (Playoff Preview)	5.50
June 88	Baseball Ratings & Inside Stuff	3.00
July 88	100 Football Questions	3.00
Aug. 88	Football Ratings & Inside Stuff	3.00
Sep. 88	Simms, Peete, Kosar, S.Smith	3.00
Nov. 88	M. Johnson, L. Bird, M. Jordan	6.50
Dec. 88	Mark Jackson & Magic Johnson	5.00
Mar. 89	Total Average	3.00
Apr. 89	Baseball Preview	3.50
May 89	NBA Playoff Preview	4.00
July 89	Montana, Rice, Jimmy Johnson	6.00
Aug. 89	Football '89 (Singletary, Aikman)	2.50
Sep. 89	Football '89 (Cunningham, Moon)	3.50
Oct. 89	Michael Jordan	5.00
Nov. 89	Jordan, Magic, etc (NBA Preview)	5.50
Dec. 89	Akeem Olajuwon & Patrick Ewing	4.50

LIFE MAGAZINE

Date	Cover	Value
10/11/37	USC football captain	35.00
4/25/38	Brooklyn Dodger	35.00
10/24/38	Sid Luckman	35.00
5/1/39	Joe DiMaggio	75.00
6/19/39	USC sprinter	15.00
1/15/40	USC basketball	25.00
4/1/40	New York Giant	20.00
11/11/40	Michigan'sTomHarmon	25.00
9/1/41	Ted Williams	65.00
11/17/41	Texas football	15.00
1/22/45	St. John's basketball	15.00
10/22/45	Ohio State football	15.00
4/1/46	StL. Cardinal baseball	15.00
9/16/46	Army's Blanchard & Davis	30.00
9/29/47	Johnny Lujack	25.00
4/5/48	Dodgertown	15.00
8/2/48	Sprinter Mel Patton	10.00
9/27/48	Doak Walker	15.00
5/2/49	West Point baseball	10.00
5/16/49	Boxing kids	10.00
7/11/49	Bob Mathias	20.00
8/1/49	Joe DiMaggio	30.00
10/3/49	College Football roundup	10.00
5/8/50	Jackie Robinson	50.00
11/13/50	Kyle Rote	15.00
2/11/52	Olympic skiing	10.00
6/8/53	Roy Campanella	20.00
9/14/53	Casey Stengel	20.00
8/8/55	Ben Hogan	15.00
6/25/56	Mickey Mantle	75.00
12/10/56	Olympic sprinter Bobby Morrow	15.00
10/14/57	Milwaukee celebrates World Series	10.00
4/7/58	Sugar Ray Robinson	20.00
4/28/58	Willie Mays in San Francisco	25.00
7/21/58	Roy Campanella	20.00
2/29/60	Winter Olympics	10.00
8/22/60	Olympic swimmers	10.00
9/12/60	Olympic gymnasts	10.00
12/5/60	Pro football kickoff	10.00
8/18/61	Mantle & Maris	75.00
11/17/61	Minnesota Vikings	10.00
9/28/62	Don Drysdale	20.00
8/2/63	Sandy Koufax	30.00
2/14/64	Winter Olympics	10.00
3/6/64	Cassius Clay	50.00
7/31/64	Olympic diver	10.00
10/9/64	Donna de Varona	10.00
10/30/64	Don Schollander	10.00
7/30/65	Mickey Mantle	50.00
12/10/65	Tommy Nobis	10.00
10/14/66	Browns vs. Packers	10.00
9/8/67	Carl Yastrzemski	20.00
2/23/68	Peggy Fleming	10.00
9/20/68	Arthur Ashe	20.00
12/13/68	Baltimore Colts	8.00
6/20/69	Joe Namath	20.00
9/26/69	Jerry Koosman	15.00
10/23/70	Muhammad Ali	20.00
3/5/71	Ali vs. Frazier	20.00
3/19/71	Frazier beats Ali	20.00
12/3/71	Pro football's most violent men	8.00
1/14/72	Staubach & Landry	20.00
2/18/72	Winter Olympics	8.00

Date	Cover	Value
3/24/72	Kareem vs. Wilt	15.00
5/5/72	Cathy Rigby	8.00
8/18/72	Mark Spitz	15.00
9/15/72	Olympic tragedy in Munich	8.00
9/22/72	Frank Shorter	8.00
10/6/72	Pro football	8.00
11/3/72	Joe Namath	12.00
1984	Special: Olympics	10.00
2/88	Winter Olympics	6.00
1988	Special: Blacks in America includ. Magic Johnson	12.00

NEWSWEEK

Date	Cover	Value
4/15/33	Catcher tagging sliding runner	20.00
4/29/33	Carl Hubbell	30.00
7/29/33	House of David signs girl pitcher	15.00
9/9/33	Connie Mack	25.00
9/30/39	Clark Giffith	20.00
12/23/33	Judge Landis	25.00
2/17/34	Babe Ruth contest	35.00
3/17/34	Mel Ott in spring training	25.00
10/6/34	Mickey Cochrane	25.00
4/20/35	Judge Kenesaw Mountain Landis	25.00
10/3/36	Carl Hubbell	25.00
10/11/37	Carl Hubbell	22.00
4/18/38	Rudy York	15.00
10/10/38	Yankee-Cub World Series	30.00
6/19/39	Abner Doubleday and Cooperstown	30.00
9/16/46	Ted Williams	30.00
6/2/47	Bob Feller	20.00
10/6/47	Bruce Edwards & Dodger Farm system	12.00
4/26/48	Billy Southworth & Joe McCarthy	15.00
8/8/49	Branch Rickey	15.00
4/17/50	Mel Parnell	10.00
3/24/52	Dodgers' spring training	10.00
10/4/54	Bob Feller & Bob Lemon	15.00
10/3/55	Baseball and color television	8.00
6/25/56	Mickey Mantle	40.00
7/1/57	Stan Musial	20.00
8/3/59	Casey Stengel	15.00
8/14/61	Year of the Home Run	10.00
4/26/65	The Astrodome	8.00
10/11/65	Sandy Koufax	15.00
10/2/67	Carl Yastrzemski	12.00
8/13/75	Aaron and Ruth	18.00
6/16/75	Nolan Ryan	25.00
7/28/76	Vida Blue and Big Salaries	7.00
8/6/90	George Steinbrenner	4.00

THE SPORTING NEWS

1932

Date	Cover	Value
1/2	Bud Tinning, Cubs	30.00
1/14	Les Mallon, Wash. Nats	30.00
1/21	Oscar Roettger, A's	30.00
1/28	Joyner White, Tigers	30.00
2/4	Horace Ford, Cardinals	30.00
2/11	Lee Mangum, Braves	30.00
2/18	Cubs prepare for Catalina Island	30.00
2/25	M. Olson (Red Sox), Bill Terry	35.00
3/3	S. Gibson (Giants), Waite Hoyt	35.00
3/10	Edward Madjeski, A's	30.00
3/17	Leonard Koenecke, Giants	30.00
3/24	William Brenzel, Pirates	30.00
3/31	J. Smead Jolley, White Sox	32.00
4/7	Burleigh Grimes, Cubs	35.00
4/14	Monte Weaver, Senators	30.00
4/21	Harold Anderson, White Sox	30.00
4/28	Samuel Byrd, Yankees	30.00
5/5	William Rogell, Tigers	30.00
5/12	Walter Betts, Braves	30.00
5/19	Ernie Lombardi, Reds	35.00
5/26	Bill Dickey, Yankees	50.00
6/2	F. Knothe (Braves), Pie Traynor	35.00
6/9	Jimmy Foxx, Bill Terry	65.00
6/16	Mel Ott	65.00
6/23	Dizzy Dean	75.00
6/30	Lefty Gomez	50.00
7/7	William Clark, Dodgers	30.00
7/14	Larry French, Pirates	30.00
7/21	Oscar Melillo, Browns	30.00
7/28	Lloyd Brown, Senators	30.00
8/4	Earl Grace, Pirates	30.00
8/11	John Jones, A's	30.00
8/18	Ernie Orsatti, Cardinals	30.00
8/25	Baxter Jordan, Braves	30.00
9/1	Red Ruffing & Pepper Martin	45.00
9/8	Tony Freitas, A's	30.00
9/15	Billy Herman & Joe Medwick	35.00
9/22	Evar Swanson, White Sox	30.00
9/29	Yankees v. Cubs (Ruth, Gehrig, etc)	150.00
10/6	Babe Ruth & Lou Gehrig	350.00
10/13	H. Smith (Pirates), Joe Cronin	32.00
10/20	Howard Maple, Senators	30.00
10/27	John Hogan, Giants	30.00
11/3	Del Bissonette, Dodgers	30.00
11/10	Fred Lindstrom, Giants	32.00
11/17	George Susce, Tigers	30.00
11/24	George Grantham, Reds	30.00
12/1	Harry Taylor, Cubs	30.00
12/8	Babe Herman, Cubs	32.00
12/15	Travis Jackson	32.00
12/22	Hal Rhyne, White Sox	30.00
12/29	Sam West, Browns	30.00

1933

Date	Cover	Value
1/5	Henry Johnson, Red Sox	30.00
1/12	Gus Mancuso, Giants	30.00
1/19	Paul Andrews, Red Sox	30.00
1/26	Woody English, Cubs	30.00
2/2	Ossie Bluege, Senators	30.00
2/9	J.Moore (Giants), Honus Wagner	35.00

The Sporting News: 2/7/35

Date	Cover	Value
2/16	Harry Rice, Reds	30.00
2/23	Carl Reynolds, Browns	30.00
3/2	Bud Parmelee, Giants	30.00
3/9	Bob Boken, Senators	30.00
3/16	Beryl Richmond, Cubs	30.00
3/23	Schumacher (Giants), Appling	35.00
3/30	Don Brennan, Yankees	30.00
4/6	Frank Reiber, Tigers	30.00
4/13	Bill Werber, Yankees	30.00
4/20	Schoolboy Rowe	35.00
4/27	Clinton Brown, Indians	30.00
5/4	Carl Hubbell, Luke Appling	45.00
5/11	Schoolboy Rowe & Pete Fox	35.00
5/18	Russell Van Atta, Yankees	30.00
5/25	Wally Berger, Braves	32.00
6/1	J. Walter Miller, White Sox	30.00
6/8	Bobby Coombs, Athletics	30.00
6/15	Harley Boss, Indians	30.00
6/22	Bill McAfee, Senators	30.00
6/29	John Jackson, Phillies	30.00
7/6	First All-Star Issue (Ruth, Gehrig, Foxx, etc.)	300.00
7/13	Chuck Fullis, Phillies	30.00
7/20	Dib Williams, Athletics	30.00
7/27	S. Leslie (Dodgers), R. Hornsby	45.00
8/3	Dizzy Dean	50.00
8/10	Pearson (Indians), C. Hubbell	40.00
8/17	D. Chapman (Nationals), Mel Ott	40.00
8/24	Dolph Camilli, Cubs	32.00
8/31	Dizzy & Paul Dean	50.00
9/7	Gus Mancuso, Giants	30.00
9/14	Travis Jackson, Giants	32.00
9/21	Joey Kuhel, Nationals	30.00
9/28	Al Lopez, Dodgers	32.00
10/5	Nationals vs. Giants W.S. (Ott, Hubbell, etc.)	125.00
10/12	Giants team photo	85.00
10/19	Babe Phelps, Cubs	30.00
10/26	Fritz Ostermueller, Red Sox	30.00
11/2	Tony Piet, Pirates	30.00
11/9	Red Rolfe, Yankees	35.00
11/16	John Pomorski, White Sox	30.00
11/23	Spud Davis, Cardinals	30.00
11/30	George Steinback, Cubs	30.00
12/7	Reggie Grabowski, Phillies	30.00
12/14	Raymond Prim, Senators	30.00
12/21	John Stone, Senators	30.00
12/28	Joseph Glenn, Yankees	30.00

1934

Date	Cover	Value
1/4	Lou Chiozza, Phillies	28.00
1/11	Pete Fox, Tigers	28.00
1/18	Benny Tate, Cubs	28.00
1/25	Glenn Spencor, Pirates	28.00
2/1	Forrest Twogood, Indians	28.00
2/8	Edward Baecht, Browns	28.00
2/15	Henry Johnson, Red Sox	28.00
2/22	Cy Blanton, Pirates	28.00
3/1	Dick Ward, Cubs	28.00
3/8	John Krider, Phillies	28.00
3/15	Giants' catchers	28.00
3/22	L.Stine & O.Nitcholas, White Sox	28.00
3/29	Al Lopez, Dodgers	30.00
4/5	Bill & George Dickey	40.00
4/12	Augie Galan, Cubs	28.00
4/19	Jack Rothrock, Cardinals	28.00
4/26	Johnny Pasek, White Sox	28.00
5/3	Al Spohrer, Braves	28.00
5/10	Daniel MacFayden, Yankees	28.00
5/17	Carl Reynolds, Red Sox	28.00
5/24	Joe Cascarella, Athletics	28.00
5/31		28.00

6/7	Linus Frey, Dodgers	28.00
6/14	Al Benton, Athletics	28.00
6/21	William Urbanski, Braves	28.00
6/28	Billy Knickerbocker, Indians	28.00
7/5	Second All-Star Issue (Ruth, Gehrig, others)	250.00
7/12	Johnny Broaca, Yankees	28.00
7/19	Fred Ostermueller, Red Sox	28.00
7/26	Hal Lee, Braves	28.00
8/2	James Weaver, Cubs	28.00
8/9	Alex Kampouris, Reds	28.00
8/16	Bill Myers, Giants	28.00
8/23	Zeke Bonura, White Sox	28.00
8/30	Buzz Boyle, Dodgers	28.00
9/6	Jo Jo White, Tigers	28.00
9/13	Leslie Tietje, White Sox	28.00
9/20	Johnny McCarthy, Dodgers	28.00
9/27	Beryl Richmond, Reds	28.00
10/4	Tigers vs. Cardinals World Series (Dean, Greenberg, Gehringer,)	125.00
10/11	Cards Win World Series (Dean, Medwick, Frisch)	75.00
10/18	George Hockette,Red Sox	28.00
10/25	Pat Malone, Cubs	28.00
11/1	Oscar Melillo	28.00
11/8	Lynford Lary, Senators	28.00
11/15	George Watkins, Phillies	28.00
11/22	D. Bartell & J. Vergez, Phillies	28.00
11/29	Todd (Phillies), Joe DiMaggio	150.00
12/6	George Stumpf, Red Sox	28.00
12/13	Bill Dietrich, Athletics	28.00
12/20	Dutch Leonard, Dodgers	28.00
12/27	Marvin Duke, Yankees	28.00
	1935	
1/3	Wally Moses, Athletics	28.00
1/10	Steve Sundra, Indians	28.00
1/17	Roy Hansen, Phillies	28.00
1/24	Hal Finney, Pirates	28.00
1/31	Walter Millies, Dodgers	28.00
2/7	Francis Parker, Tigers	28.00
2/14	Larry Bettencourt,Browns	28.00
2/21	Edward Durham, White Sox	28.00
2/28	Eugene Schott, Reds	28.00
3/7	Leon Chagnon, Giants	28.00
3/14	Clif Bolton, Senators	28.00
3/21	Todd Moore, Cardinals	28.00
3/28	Luke Sewell, Cubs	28.00
4/4	Clyde Hatter, Tigers	28.00
4/11	Babe Dahlgren, Red Sox	28.00
4/18	Leslie Tietje, White Sox	28.00
4/25	Tony Lazzeri, Yankees	35.00
5/2	Joseph Stripp, Dodgers	28.00
5/9	Johny Whitehead, White Sox	28.00
5/16	Dolph Camilli, Phillies	30.00
5/23	Whitey Whitehead, Cards	28.00
5/30	Bucky Harris & Bobo Newsome	30.00
6/6	Whitey Wilshere,Athletics	28.00
6/13	Pep Young, Pirates	28.00
6/20	Leon Chagnon, Giants	28.00
6/27	Tommy Bridges, Tigers	28.00
7/4	Cleveland Municipal Stadium, All-Star Issue	150.00
7/11	Slick Castleman, Giants	28.00
7/18	William Myers, Reds	28.00
7/25	Pete Fox, Tigers	28.00
8/1	Roy Henshaw, Cubs	28.00
8/8	Lewis Riggs, Cardinals	28.00
8/15	Jose Gomez	28.00
8/22	Joe Vosmik, Indians	28.00
8/29	Joseph Bowman, Phillies	28.00
9/5	Roxie Lawson, Tigers	28.00
9/12	Bud Hafey, Pirates	28.00
9/19	Ivy Andrews, Browns	28.00
9/26	Paul Derringer, Reds	28.00
10/3	Tigers vs. Cubs World Series	95.00

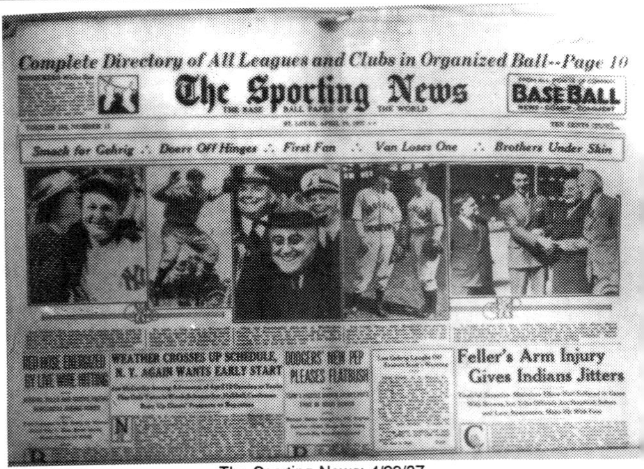

Complete Directory of All Leagues and Clubs in Organized Ball--Page 10

The Sporting News

BASEBALL

Smash for Gehrig ∴ Doors Off Hinges ∴ First Fan ∴ Van Loses One ∴ Brothers Under Skin

WEATHER CROSSES UP SCHEDULE; N. Y. AGAIN WANTS EARLY START

DODGERS' NEW PEP PLEASES FLATBUSH

Feller's Arm Injury Gives Indians Jitters

The Sporting News: 4/29/37

10/10	Tigers win W.S. (Greenberg, Gehringer, Cochrane, others)	75.00
10/17	Hal Lee, Braves	28.00
10/24	William McGee,Cardinals	28.00
10/31		28.00
11/7	Eugene Lillard, Cubs	28.00
11/14	Dennis Galehouse, Indians	28.00
11/21	Frank Pytlok, Indians	28.00
11/28	Whitey Whitehead, Giants	28.00
12/5	Donald McNair, Athletics	28.00
12/12	Leroy Parmelee,Cardinals	28.00
12/19		28.00
12/26	Monte Pearson, Yankees	28.00
	1936	
1/2	George McQuinn, Reds	28.00
1/9	Frank Gabler, Giants	28.00
1/16	Jack Knott, Browns	28.00
1/23	Roy Johnson, Tigers	28.00
1/30	Babe Phelps, Dodgers	28.00
2/6	Elbert Fletcher, Braves	28.00
2/13	James DeShong, Senators	28.00
2/20	Orville Jorgens, Phillies	28.00
2/27	Roy Hughes, Indians	28.00
3/5	Samuel Leslie, Giants	28.00
3/12	Rudy York, Tigers	28.00
3/19	Alfred Todd, Pirates	28.00
3/26	James Oglesby, Athletics	28.00
4/2	Hank Greenberg	50.00
4/9	Lee John Norris, Phillies	28.00
4/16	Albert Butcher, Dodgers	28.00
4/23	Charlie Grimm, Cubs	28.00
4/30	Bill & George Dickey	45.00
5/7	Bill Terry, Giants	40.00
5/14	Dusty Rhodes, Athletics	28.00
5/21	50th Anniversary Issue, w/ FDR congrats letter	75.00
5/26	Frankie Frisch, Cardinals	40.00
6/4	Steve O'Neill, Indians	28.00
6/11	Stuart Martin, Cardinals	28.00
6/18	Gabby Hartnett, Cubs	35.00
6/25	Monte Pearson, Yankees	28.00
7/2	All-Star Game Issue	150.00
7/9	A. Galan (Cubs), Lou Gehrig	85.00
7/16	Jimmy Foxx, Lefty Grove, others	75.00
7/23	Dizzy Dean	45.00
7/30	Jimmy Foxx	50.00
8/6	Tom Yawkey	28.00
8/13	Italo Chelini, White Sox	28.00

8/20	Rip Radcliff, White Sox	28.00
8/27	Women baseball fans	28.00
9/3	Joe McCarthy, Jimmy Foxx	50.00
9/10	Bob Feller	100.00
9/17	Branch Rickey	35.00
9/24	John McCarthy, Giants	28.00
10/1	Yankees vs. Giants (Gehrig,)	200.00
10/8	Lou Gehrig, Yanks win Series	150.00
10/15	James Mosolf, Boston Bees	28.00
10/22	Earl Averill, other Indians	35.00
10/29	Joe DiMaggio w/ family	125.00
11/5	Six comeback players	28.00
11/12	Burleigh Grimes	32.00
11/19	American League officials	28.00
11/26	Gehrig, Gomez,stars w/ wives	100.00
12/6	George Caster, Athletics	28.00
12/10	Winter Meetings	28.00
12/17	Lavagetto, other traded players	30.00
12/24	Ruth, Cronin, Dean, other salary increases	40.00
12/31	Hubbell, VanderMeer, McCarthy, Rickey (#1 MEN OF THE YEAR)	100.00
	1937	
1/7	Frisch, Goslin, Cuyler others, then and now	40.00
1/14	P. Dean, Cochrane, other injured players	35.00
1/21	Ival Goodman, Reds	26.00
1/28	Paul Dean & Branch Rickey	30.00
2/4	V. DiMaggio, other minor leaguers	28.00
2/11	Off-season training (Goslin, P. Dean, P.Waner, others)	40.00
2/18	Gabby Hartnett	28.00
2/25	St. Louis Browns	26.00
3/4	Giants in Havana	26.00
3/11	Bob Feller	75.00
3/18	A's & Chi Sox in spring training	26.00
3/25	Greenberg, DiMaggio, others	75.00
4/1	Jeff Heath	26.00

Story of John Vander Meer, New No-Hit King
The Sporting News
BASE BALL
RUTH, AS COACH, PUTS NEW LIFE IN DODGERS
BABE IS BACK
WITH BRAND-NEW SUIT
AND SAME OLD SMILE

The Sporting News: 6/23/38

- 4/8 Pepper Martin, Cardinals . 28.00
- 4/15 Roxie Lawson, Tigers . . . 26.00
- 4/22 Hefty ballplayers 26.00
- 4/29 Gehrig & wife, Doerr, Mungo, DiMaggio, FDR . 100.00
- 5/6 Cochrane, Greenberg, Tigers 50.00
- 5/13 Lamar Newsome, Athletics 26.00
- 5/20 Gerry Walker, Tigers 26.00
- 5/27 Cubs trainer 26.00
- 6/3 Lloyd Waner, short players 35.00
- 6/10 Branch Rickey 28.00
- 6/17 Dick Bartell, Giants 26.00
- 6/24 J. Dykes & White Sox . . . 26.00
- 7/1 Griffith Stadium, All-Star Issue 100.00
- 7/8 P. Dean, Hubbell, no-hitters 40.00
- 7/15 Hartnett, Root, other Cubs 28.00
- 7/22 Bucky Jordan, Reds 26.00
- 7/29 Del Baker, Tigers coach . 26.00
- 8/5 Heinie Manush 28.00
- 8/12 John Wilson, Red Sox . . . 26.00
- 8/19 Ott, Hartnett, players & families 40.00
- 8/26 Jim Turner, Bees 26.00
- 9/2 Rudy York, Tigers 26.00
- 9/9 Joe Medwick, Cardinals . . 30.00
- 9/16 Kid fans 26.00
- 9/23 Lou Gehrig 100.00
- 9/30 "Body Parts of the Stars," DiMaggio eyes, Gehrig legs, etc. . . . 75.00
- 10/7 Yankees vs. Giants 150.00
- 10/14 Yankees win World Series 100.00
- 10/21 Major League trainers . . . 26.00
- 10/28 Mgr. Vitt, Indians 26.00
- 11/4 Pirate bosses 26.00
- 11/11 Gehringer party 35.00
- 11/18 Dodger bosses 26.00
- 11/25 DiMaggio, Lazzeri, more-at home 60.00
- 12/2 Indian bosses 26.00
- 12/9 Milwaukee Winter Meetings 26.00
- 12/16 More Winter Meetings . . . 26.00
- 12/23 Joe Medwick MVP celebration 30.00
- 12/30 Keller, J.T. Allen, E. Barrow (#1 MEN OF THE YEAR) 75.00

1938

- 1/6 Florida players at home . . 26.00
- 1/13 Like father, like son 26.00
- 1/20 Grover Alexander elected: HOF 35.00
- 1/27 Cecil Travis 26.00
- 2/3 St. Petersburg players at home 26.00
- 2/10 August Mancuso 26.00
- 2/17 Joe Gordon, other rookies 35.00
- 2/24 Harry Danning 26.00
- 3/3 Lefty Gomez 32.00
- 3/10 Cubs at Catalina Island . . 26.00
- 3/17 Indians in New Orleans . . 26.00
- 3/24 Browns players (Newsom, more) 26.00
- 3/31 Spalding factory making balls 26.00
- 4/7 V. DiMaggio, other Bees . 28.00
- 4/14 Clay Bryant, Cubs 26.00
- 4/21 1st Ball Presidents, Taft to FDR 32.00
- 4/28 Bobby Doerr, Red Sox . . . 30.00
- 5/5 Bobo Newsom 26.00
- 5/12 Bob Feller in action 65.00
- 5/19 Three umpires 26.00
- 5/26 Bill Dickey 35.00
- 6/2 Forest Pressnell, Dodgers 26.00
- 6/9 Casey Stengel managing Bees 45.00
- 6/16 Siebert & Chapman, Athletics 26.00
- 6/23 Babe Ruth, Dodger coach 125.00
- 6/30 All-Star Issue (Gehrig, others) 150.00
- 7/7 Crosley Field 26.00
- 7/14 Babe Ruth & 6'9" John Gee 125.00
- 7/21 Fastest ballplayers 26.00
- 7/28 Ballplayers' wives 28.00
- 8/4 Hank Greenberg 45.00
- 8/11 Ernie Lombardi 30.00
- 8/18 Major League musicians . 26.00
- 8/25 Joe Glenn, Yankees 26.00
- 9/1 Lynn Myers, Cardinals . . . 26.00
- 9/8 Vance Page, Cubs 26.00
- 9/15 Miguel Gonzalez, Cardinals 26.00
- 9/22 Red Ruffing 35.00
- 9/29 Hank Greenberg 40.00
- 10/6 Yankee team picture . . . 100.00
- 10/13 Faces in W.S. crowd, w/ Ruth 75.00
- 10/28 Major league scouts 26.00
- 10/27 Off-season hunting, w/ Foxx 35.00
- 11/8 Foxx & Lombardi 35.00
- 11/10 Mack's 1913 $100,000 infield 28.00
- 11/17 PCL Presidents 26.00
- 11/24 Gehrig, Goslin, Simmons, vets 75.00
- 12/1 New Orleans Winter Meetings 26.00
- 12/8 MLB President Bramham . 26.00
- 12/15 New Orleans Winter Meetings 26.00
- 12/22 New York Winter Meetings 26.00
- 12/29 VanderMeer, J. McCarthy, Giles (#1 MEN OF THE YEAR) 50.00

1939

- 1/5 D.Dean, P.Waner, others golfing 35.00
- 1/12 Baseball historians 24.00
- 1/19 Triumvirate to rule Yankees 24.00
- 1/26 New owners of Yankees . 24.00
- 2/2 Dizzy Trout, "Bengal Kittens" 24.00
- 2/9 Off-season player homes . 24.00
- 2/16 Tris Speaker, others 30.00
- 2/23 Hornsby, A.A. managers . 28.00
- 3/2 Hot Springs, AR, Giants camp 24.00
- 3/9 Cubs at Catalina Island . . 24.00
- 3/16 Camilli, Lazzeri, Lavagetto 30.00
- 3/23 "Identify these Yankees" . 24.00
- 3/30 Marty Marion, Cards' SS shuffle 26.00
- 4/6 Browns photos 24.00
- 4/13 ROY favorites, w/ T. Williams 125.00
- 4/20 McKechnie, Reds coaching staff 24.00
- 4/27 Zeke Bonura, Giants 24.00
- 5/4 Barney McCosky, Tigers . 24.00
- 5/11 Babe Dahlgren 24.00
- 5/18 traded Tigers, Browns . . . 24.00
- 5/25 Lon Warneke & father . . . 24.00
- 6/1 Cardinals manager 24.00
- 6/8 Bill Cissell 24.00
- 6/15 Doubleday Field 24.00
- 6/22 Greenberg, Terry, Ruffing, others 40.00
- 6/29 Browns firemen 24.00
- 7/6 All-Star Issue w/ 52 photos 150.00
- 7/13 Players w/ complicated names 24.00
- 7/20 Johnny Mize 30.00
- 7/27 Donald McNair, White Sox 24.00
- 8/3 Derringer & Walters, Reds 24.00
- 8/10 Tony Cuccinello, Bees . . . 24.00
- 8/17 Garter Dykes, White Sox . 24.00
- 8/24 Branch Rickey 26.00
- 8/31 Bourdreau, Mack, Vitt, Indians 28.00
- 9/7 Gabby Hartnett 26.00
- 9/14 Bob Feller 60.00
- 9/21 A.A. pitchers 24.00
- 9/28 White Sox coaches 24.00
- 10/5 Yankees vs. Reds: W. Series 100.00
- 10/12 World Series fans 50.00
- 10/19 Yankee minor leaguers . . 24.00
- 10/26 Short major leaguers (Durocher, Waners, etc.) . 50.00
- 11/2 Minor league managers . . 24.00
- 11/9 Tall major leaguers

(Greenberg, etc) 26.00
11/16 Bullpen buddies 24.00
11/23 Connie Mack alumni 26.00
11/30 Cincinnati Winter Meetings 24.00
12/7 Larry MacPhail 24.00
12/14 Winter Meetings 24.00
12/21 Lefty Grove 28.00
12/28 DiMaggio, Durocher, MacPhail (#1 MEN OF THE YEAR) 125.00

1940

1/4 Young Redbirds on the Rise 24.00
1/11 Yankee talent finders 24.00
1/18 Landis rules on farm teams 24.00
1/25 Reds promise to stay in pink 24.00
2/1 Landis proposes plan to stabalize minors 24.00
2/8 Bucky Walters 24.00
2/15 Anaheim photos 24.00
2/22 Winter Haven, Giants camp 24.00
2/29 Nationals training in Orlando 24.00
3/7 Dodgers in Belleair, FL 24.00
3/14 Reds in Tampa 24.00
3/21 Indians in Ft. Myers, FL 24.00
3/28 Minor league managers 24.00
4/4 Hank Greenberg, others 30.00
4/11 Mickey Haris & Mickey Witek 24.00
4/18 Gabby Hartnett, other vets 26.00
4/25 Managers' wives 24.00
5/2 Goose Goslin, others 26.00
5/9 Pee Wee Reese, other Dodgers 28.00
5/16 Hal Newhouser 28.00
5/23 Clyde Shown, Cardinals 24.00
5/30 Athletics infield 24.00
6/6 P. Waner, V. DiMaggio, others 26.00
6/13 Fathers of ballplayers 24.00
6/20 Ducky Medwick 28.00
6/27 Rollie Hemsley 24.00
7/4 All-Star Issue, w/52 photos 150.00
7/11 "Return Selections of All-Star Game to Fans" 26.00
7/18 DiMaggio, Mize, Greenberg, 85.00
7/25 Billy Southworth, Cardinals 24.00
8/1 Female baseball fans' clothing 24.00
8/8 Frankie Frisch, Pirates 28.00
8/15 Barney McCoskey, Tigers 24.00
8/22 T. Williams wants out of Boston 80.00
8/29 Learning from Their Dads 24.00
9/5 Phil Rizzuto & Gerald Priddy 30.00
9/12 Lou Novikoff & Lou Stringer 24.00
9/19 Texas League Standouts 24.00
9/26 Jimmy Foxx 40.00
10/3 Schoolboy Rowe, WS 45.00
10/10 Reds win W.S., team photo 65.00
10/17 Jimmy Wilson 24.00
10/24 DiMaggio & Feller register for draft 75.00
10/31 Dodgers of yesteryear 24.00
11/7 Hank Greenberg, AL MVP 40.00
11/14 Frank McCormick, NL MVP 24.00
11/21 Ray Schalk 24.00
11/28 Atlanta Winter Meetings 24.00
12/5 Charley Grimm 24.00
12/12 Winter Meetings 24.00
12/19 Bob Feller 50.00

The Sporting News: 4/13/44

12/26 Debs Garms 24.00

1941

1/2 Feller, Rizzuto, others (#1 MEN OF THE YEAR) 80.00
1/9 Bill Klem 24.00
1/16 Leading Relief Hurlers 24.00
1/23 William C. Tuttle 24.00
1/30 Ted Lyons 24.00
2/6 Cardinal Newcomers 24.00
2/13 Bob Newsom 24.00
2/20 Al Simmons, Newsom, others 25.00
2/27 Dodgers in Cuba 24.00
3/6 Giants in Miami 24.00
3/13 Reds in Tampa 24.00
3/20 Browns & Bees in San Antonio 24.00
3/27 Front-office families 24.00
4/3 Minor league managers 24.00
4/10 Cobb, Frisch, others 35.00
4/17 FDR throwing out first pitch 30.00
4/24 Landis, Frick, Harridge, Bramham 24.00
5/1 Bob Feller 45.00
5/8 Larry MacPhail, others 24.00
5/15 Baseball husbands & wives 24.00
5/22 Connie Mack 30.00
5/29 Branch Rickey 28.00
6/5 Jimmy Dykes 24.00
6/12 "Brooklyn Dodgers Issue" 65.00
6/19 Ted Williams 75.00
6/26 SS: Reese, Rizzuto, Appling, Boudreau, others 45.00
7/3 Briggs Stadium, All-Star Issue 85.00
7/10 Jeff Heath 24.00
7/17 Sportsman's Park scoreboard 24.00
7/24 1B: Gehrig, Foxx, Mize, others 80.00
7/31 300 Game Winners: Young, Grove, Johnson, Mathewson, others 50.00
8/7 5 pitchers: "Stoppers" 24.00
8/14 Honus Lobert 24.00
8/21 "All-Star Noismatics" 24.00
8/28 Rizzuto & Gordon 30.00
9/4 Lon Warneke 24.00
9/11 Hal Chase 24.00
9/18 Hal Chase 24.00
9/25 Joe McCarthy 28.00
10/2 W.S. Issue: Rizzuto, others 75.00
10/9 World Champion Yanks photo 75.00
10/16 3B: Traynor, Rolfe, Baker, etc. 28.00
10/23 John Wyatt 24.00
10/30 Minor league managers 24.00
11/6 Dolph Camilli 24.00
11/13 Joe DiMaggio 100.00
11/20 .400 hitters: Williams, Hornsby, Cobb, Jackson, others 75.00
11/27 Jacksonville Winter Meetings 24.00
12/4 Lou Boudreau 35.00
12/11 Winter Meetings 24.00
12/18 Sgt. Hank Greenberg 40.00
12/25 Rogers Hornsby 35.00

1942

1/1 Ted Williams, others (#1 MEN OF THE YEAR) 100.00
1/8 Mel Ott 40.00
1/15 2B: Hornsby, Gehringer, Frisch, others 40.00
1/22 FDR to Landis: Keep Playing 30.00
1/29 Ted Williams 75.00
2/5 Musial, others as minor leaguers 35.00
2/12 Jimmie Foxx, others 40.00
2/19 C: Cochrane, Dickey, others 35.00
2/26 Bill McKechnie, Cardinals mgr. 24.00
3/5 Six Yankee pitchers 24.00
3/12 Bruce Campbell 24.00
3/19 Burt Shotton & Lou Boudreau 28.00
3/26 Mel Ott & Mrs. McGraw 35.00
4/2 Ty Cobb 45.00
4/9 Nine major league coaches 24.00
4/16 FDR: "Play Ball!" 28.00
4/23 Vern Stephens 24.00
4/30 Player-Managers: Cronin, Boudreau, Ott, others 35.00
5/7 Feller, Greenberg, others: "V" 40.00
5/14 Navy photos 24.00
5/21 Four players wearing #13 24.00
5/28 Bobby Doerr 26.00
6/4 3 Phillies wearing glasses 24.00
6/11 Joe Gordon 26.00
6/18 Edgar Smith 24.00
6/25 Paul Waner 26.00
7/2 All-Star Issue: Ruth, Gehrig, Foxx, Williams, others 150.00
7/9 Don Gutteridge, Browns 24.00
7/16 Players at new positions 24.00
7/23 Chet Laabs 24.00
7/30 Rollie Hemsley 24.00
8/6 Lou Boudreau, others 30.00
8/13 Hitting Pitchers: Ruth, others 60.00
8/20 Headhunting cartoon 24.00
8/27 Lou Novikoff caricature 24.00
9/3 SS: Rizzuto, Reese, others 30.00
9/10 24.00
9/17 James Sewell 24.00
9/24 Joe Jackson 50.00
10/1 W.S. Issue: Joe McCarthy 100.00
10/8 Famous "Babes": Ruth, others 65.00
10/15 Musial, Champions at home 40.00
10/22 Ossie Bluege 24.00
10/29 Mort Cooper 24.00
11/5 Branch Rickey 26.00
11/12 Bobo Newsom 24.00
11/19 Sam Breadon 24.00
11/26 Nick Altrock 24.00
12/3 Judge Landis 26.00

- 12/10 Al Schacht . . . 24.00
- 12/17 Lefty Grove . . . 28.00
- 12/24 Major leaguers help war effort . . . 24.00
- 12/31 Williams, Veeck, Southworth, others (#1 MEN OF THE YEAR) 100.00

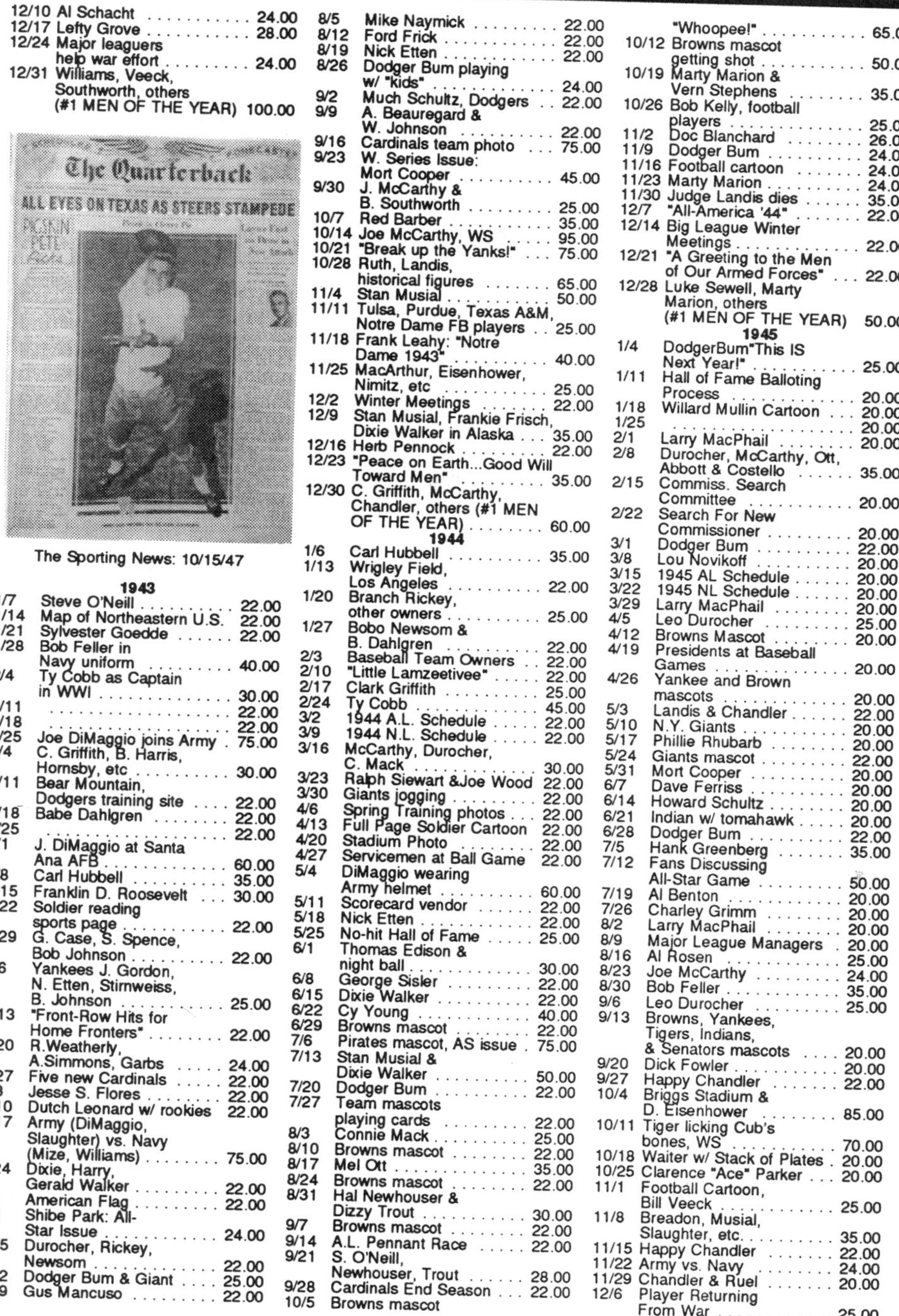

The Sporting News: 10/15/47

1943

- 1/7 Steve O'Neill . . . 22.00
- 1/14 Map of Northeastern U.S. 22.00
- 1/21 Sylvester Goedde . . . 22.00
- 1/28 Bob Feller in Navy uniform . . . 40.00
- 2/4 Ty Cobb as Captain in WWI . . . 30.00
- 2/11 . . . 22.00
- 2/18 . . . 22.00
- 2/25 Joe DiMaggio joins Army . 75.00
- 3/4 C. Griffith, B. Harris, Hornsby, etc . . . 30.00
- 3/11 Bear Mountain, Dodgers training site . . . 22.00
- 3/18 Babe Dahlgren . . . 22.00
- 3/25 . . . 22.00
- 4/1 J. DiMaggio at Santa Ana AFB . . . 60.00
- 4/8 Carl Hubbell . . . 35.00
- 4/15 Franklin D. Roosevelt . . . 30.00
- 4/22 Soldier reading sports page . . . 22.00
- 4/29 G. Case, S. Spence, Bob Johnson . . . 22.00
- 5/6 Yankees J. Gordon, N. Etten, Stirnweiss, B. Johnson . . . 25.00
- 5/13 "Front-Row Hits for Home Fronters" . . . 22.00
- 5/20 R.Weatherly, A.Simmons, Garbs . . . 24.00
- 5/27 Five new Cardinals . . . 22.00
- 6/3 Jesse S. Flores . . . 22.00
- 6/10 Dutch Leonard w/ rookies 22.00
- 6/17 Army (DiMaggio, Slaughter) vs. Navy (Mize, Williams) . . . 75.00
- 6/24 Dixie, Harry, Gerald Walker . . . 22.00
- 7/1 American Flag . . . 22.00
- 7/8 Shibe Park: All-Star Issue . . . 24.00
- 7/15 Durocher, Rickey, Newsom . . . 22.00
- 7/22 Dodger Bum & Giant . . . 25.00
- 7/29 Gus Mancuso . . . 22.00
- 8/5 Mike Naymick . . . 22.00
- 8/12 Ford Frick . . . 22.00
- 8/19 Nick Etten . . . 22.00
- 8/26 Dodger Bum playing w/ "kids" . . . 24.00
- 9/2 Much Schultz, Dodgers . . 22.00
- 9/9 A. Beauregard & W. Johnson . . . 22.00
- 9/16 Cardinals team photo . . . 75.00
- 9/23 W. Series Issue: Mort Cooper . . . 45.00
- 9/30 J. McCarthy & B. Southworth . . . 25.00
- 10/7 Red Barber . . . 35.00
- 10/14 Joe McCarthy, WS . . . 95.00
- 10/21 "Break up the Yanks!" . . . 75.00
- 10/28 Ruth, Landis, historical figures . . . 65.00
- 11/4 Stan Musial . . . 50.00
- 11/11 Tulsa, Purdue, Texas A&M, Notre Dame FB players . . 25.00
- 11/18 Frank Leahy: "Notre Dame 1943" . . . 40.00
- 11/25 MacArthur, Eisenhower, Nimitz, etc . . . 25.00
- 12/2 Winter Meetings . . . 22.00
- 12/9 Stan Musial, Frankie Frisch, Dixie Walker in Alaska . . . 35.00
- 12/16 Herb Pennock . . . 22.00
- 12/23 "Peace on Earth...Good Will Toward Men" . . . 35.00
- 12/30 C. Griffith, McCarthy, Chandler, others (#1 MEN OF THE YEAR) . . . 60.00

1944

- 1/6 Carl Hubbell . . . 35.00
- 1/13 Wrigley Field, Los Angeles . . . 22.00
- 1/20 Branch Rickey, other owners . . . 25.00
- 1/27 Bobo Newsom & B. Dahlgren . . . 22.00
- 2/3 Baseball Team Owners . . 22.00
- 2/10 "Little Lamzeetivee" . . . 22.00
- 2/17 Clark Griffith . . . 25.00
- 2/24 Ty Cobb . . . 45.00
- 3/2 1944 A.L. Schedule . . . 22.00
- 3/9 1944 N.L. Schedule . . . 22.00
- 3/16 McCarthy, Durocher, C. Mack . . . 30.00
- 3/23 Ralph Siewart &Joe Wood 22.00
- 3/30 Giants jogging . . . 22.00
- 4/6 Spring Training photos . . . 22.00
- 4/13 Full Page Soldier Cartoon 22.00
- 4/20 Stadium Photo . . . 22.00
- 4/27 Servicemen at Ball Game 22.00
- 5/4 DiMaggio wearing Army helmet . . . 60.00
- 5/11 Scorecard vendor . . . 22.00
- 5/18 Nick Etten . . . 22.00
- 5/25 No-hit Hall of Fame . . . 25.00
- 6/1 Thomas Edison & night ball . . . 30.00
- 6/8 George Sisler . . . 22.00
- 6/15 Dixie Walker . . . 22.00
- 6/22 Cy Young . . . 40.00
- 6/29 Browns mascot . . . 22.00
- 7/6 Pirates mascot, AS issue . 75.00
- 7/13 Stan Musial & Dixie Walker . . . 50.00
- 7/20 Dodger Bum . . . 22.00
- 7/27 Team mascots playing cards . . . 22.00
- 8/3 Connie Mack . . . 25.00
- 8/10 Browns mascot . . . 22.00
- 8/17 Mel Ott . . . 35.00
- 8/24 Browns mascot . . . 22.00
- 8/31 Hal Newhouser & Dizzy Trout . . . 30.00
- 9/7 Browns mascot . . . 22.00
- 9/14 A.L. Pennant Race . . . 22.00
- 9/21 S. O'Neill, Newhouser, Trout . . . 28.00
- 9/28 Cardinals End Season . . . 22.00
- 10/5 Browns mascot "Whoopee!" . . . 65.00
- 10/12 Browns mascot getting shot . . . 50.00
- 10/19 Marty Marion & Vern Stephens . . . 35.00
- 10/26 Bob Kelly, football players . . . 25.00
- 11/2 Doc Blanchard . . . 26.00
- 11/9 Dodger Bum . . . 24.00
- 11/16 Football cartoon . . . 24.00
- 11/23 Marty Marion . . . 24.00
- 11/30 Judge Landis dies . . . 35.00
- 12/7 "All-America '44" . . . 22.00
- 12/14 Big League Winter Meetings . . . 22.00
- 12/21 "A Greeting to the Men of Our Armed Forces" . . . 22.00
- 12/28 Luke Sewell, Marty Marion, others (#1 MEN OF THE YEAR) 50.00

1945

- 1/4 DodgerBum"This IS Next Year!" . . . 25.00
- 1/11 Hall of Fame Balloting Process . . . 20.00
- 1/18 Willard Mullin Cartoon . . . 20.00
- 1/25 . . . 20.00
- 2/1 Larry MacPhail . . . 20.00
- 2/8 Durocher, McCarthy, Ott, Abbott & Costello . . . 35.00
- 2/15 Commiss. Search Committee . . . 20.00
- 2/22 Search For New Commissioner . . . 20.00
- 3/1 Dodger Bum . . . 22.00
- 3/8 Lou Novikoff . . . 20.00
- 3/15 1945 AL Schedule . . . 20.00
- 3/22 1945 NL Schedule . . . 20.00
- 3/29 Larry MacPhail . . . 20.00
- 4/5 Leo Durocher . . . 25.00
- 4/12 Browns Mascot . . . 20.00
- 4/19 Presidents at Baseball Games . . . 20.00
- 4/26 Yankee and Brown mascots . . . 20.00
- 5/3 Landis & Chandler . . . 22.00
- 5/10 N.Y. Giants . . . 20.00
- 5/17 Phillie Rhubarb . . . 20.00
- 5/24 Giants mascot . . . 22.00
- 5/31 Mort Cooper . . . 20.00
- 6/7 Dave Ferriss . . . 20.00
- 6/14 Howard Schultz . . . 20.00
- 6/21 Indian w/ tomahawk . . . 20.00
- 6/28 Dodger Bum . . . 22.00
- 7/5 Hank Greenberg . . . 35.00
- 7/12 Fans Discussing All-Star Game . . . 50.00
- 7/19 Al Benton . . . 20.00
- 7/26 Charley Grimm . . . 20.00
- 8/2 Larry MacPhail . . . 20.00
- 8/9 Major League Managers . 20.00
- 8/16 Al Rosen . . . 25.00
- 8/23 Joe McCarthy . . . 24.00
- 8/30 Bob Feller . . . 35.00
- 9/6 Leo Durocher . . . 25.00
- 9/13 Browns, Yankees, Tigers, Indians, & Senators mascots . . . 20.00
- 9/20 Dick Fowler . . . 20.00
- 9/27 Happy Chandler . . . 22.00
- 10/4 Briggs Stadium & D. Eisenhower . . . 85.00
- 10/11 Tiger licking Cub's bones, WS . . . 70.00
- 10/18 Waiter w/ Stack of Plates . 20.00
- 10/25 Clarence "Ace" Parker . . . 20.00
- 11/1 Football Cartoon, Bill Veeck . . . 25.00
- 11/8 Breadon, Musial, Slaughter, etc. . . . 35.00
- 11/15 Happy Chandler . . . 22.00
- 11/22 Army vs. Navy . . . 24.00
- 11/29 Chandler & Ruel . . . 20.00
- 12/6 Player Returning From War . . . 25.00

12/13 Two Baseball Owners ... 20.00
12/20 "Peace on Earth...Good Will Toward Men" cartoon ... 30.00
12/27 Hal Newhouser, M.L. (POY) ... 30.00

1946

1/3 Hall of Fame Elections ... 22.00
1/10 Sam Breadon ... 20.00
1/17 Larry MacPhail ... 22.00
1/24 Happy Chandler ... 22.00
1/31 Joe DiMaggio & Ted Williams ... 150.00
2/7 Mel Ott ... 25.00
2/14 Grapefruit League ... 20.00
2/21 Hank Greenberg ... 30.00
2/28 Mexican League ... 20.00
3/7 Bob Feller ... 30.00
3/14 Ted Williams ... 50.00
3/21 Leo Durocher ... 25.00
3/28 Cardinal outfielders ... 20.00
4/4 Johnny Mize ... 25.00
4/11 Mickey Owen ... 20.00
4/18 Peacetime baseball begins 50.00
4/25 Spud Chandler ... 25.00
5/2 Tommy Henrich ... 25.00
5/9 J.Cronin & Joe McCarthy . 25.00
5/16 '46 Red Sox sluggers ... 25.00
5/23 Ted Williams ... 30.00
6/5 Bill Dickey & Ted Lyons .. 28.00
6/12 Babe Ruth ... 50.00
6/19 Red Sox Tear League Apart ... 20.00
6/26 Joe Garagiola ... 25.00
7/3 Veeck Buys Cleveland Indians ... 20.00
7/10 Bill Veeck, AS issue ... 50.00
7/17 Ted Williams ... 40.00
7/24 Larry MacPhail ... 20.00
7/31 Hal Newhouser ... 25.00
8/7 Dizzy Dean ... 25.00
8/14 M.Owen, Mexican league . 20.00
8/21 Mickey Owen ... 20.00
8/28 Feller's 98.6 mph pitch .. 30.00
9/4 Larry MacPhail ... 20.00
9/11 Jackie Robinson ... 50.00
9/18 Ted Williams & Mickey Vernon ... 30.00
9/25 T. Williams & S. Musial .. 60.00
10/2 Eddie Collins retires ... 20.00
10/9 Frank Frisch resigns, WS . 60.00
10/16 DiMaggio, MacPhail, Gordon ... 50.00
10/23 Harry "The Cat" Brecheen, WS ... 50.00
10/30 TSN 60 year chronology 250.00
11/6 Bob Feller ... 25.00
11/13 Bucky Harris ... 20.00
11/20 Ted Williams MVP ... 50.00
11/27 Stan Musial MVP ... 50.00
12/4 Leo Durocher ... 40.00
12/18 Walter Johnson dies ... 40.00
12/25 Billy Evans ... 20.00

1947

1/1 Stan Musial, Eddie Dyer, Tom Yawkey (#1 MEN OF THE YEAR) 60.00
1/8 Little Baseball Stars ... 20.00
1/15 Joe DiMaggio ... 40.00
1/22 Branch Rickey ... 30.00
1/29 Bob Feller ... 30.00
2/5 Pepper Martin ... 25.00
2/12 Stan Musial & Sam Breadon ... 25.00
2/19 Hank Greenberg ... 25.00
2/26 Speaker, Hornsby, McKechnie ... 25.00
3/5 Ted Williams & Stan Musial ... 40.00
3/12 Leo Durocher & H. Chandler ... 40.00
3/19 Larry MacPhail & Leo Durocher ... 40.00
3/26 Durocher, MacPhail, Chandler ... 40.00
4/2 Hank Greenberg ... 30.00
4/9 Yogi Berra & Joe Medwick ... 25.00
4/16 Durocher Suspended One Year ... 60.00
4/23 Babe Ruth ... 300.00
4/30 Pete Reiser ... 20.00
5/7 Babe Ruth Day ... 50.00
5/14 Hank Greenberg ... 25.00
5/21 Johnny Mize ... 25.00
5/28 Hal Chase dies ... 20.00
6/4 Dugout Jockeys ... 20.00
6/11 George McQuinn ... 20.00
6/18 Bobby Thomson ... 22.00
6/25 Warren Spahn ... 35.00
7/2 Ewell Blackwell ... 20.00
7/9 P.K. Wrigley, AS issue ... 60.00
7/16 L. Doby Breaks AL Color Line ... 60.00
7/23 Bobo Newsom ... 25.00
7/30 15 inducted in HOF ... 25.00
8/6 Burt Shotton ... 20.00
8/13 Harry "The Hat" Walker .. 20.00
8/20 Stan Musial ... 35.00
8/27 Connie Mack ... 25.00
9/3 Dan Bankhead (1st Negro ML Pitcher) ... 25.00
9/10 Frank McCormick ... 20.00
9/17 Jackie Robinson: ROY ... 75.00
9/24 Dixie & Harry Walker ... 20.00
10/1 Burt Shotton & Bucky Harris ... 75.00
10/8 Joe McCarthy & Tom Yawkey ... 60.00
10/15 George Weiss ... 50.00
10/22 Joe Kuhel ... 20.00
10/29 Larry MacPhail ... 20.00
11/5 Red Ruffing retires ... 20.00
11/12 Mudd Ruel & Zack Taylor ... 20.00
11/19 Snuffy Stirnweiss ... 20.00
11/26 Bob Elliott MVP ... 20.00
12/3 Joe DiMaggio MVP ... 50.00
12/10 Sam Breadon ... 25.00
12/17 Leo Durocher ... 25.00
12/24 Hugh Casey ... 20.00
12/31 Ted Williams, B. Harris, B. Rickey (#1 MEN OF THE YEAR) 75.00

1948

1/7 Phil Masi ... 35.00
1/14 Stars Salaries ... 20.00
1/21 Sam Breadon retires ... 20.00
1/28 Bill Veeck & Bob Feller .. 30.00
2/4 Joe McCarthy ... 20.00
2/11 Herb Pennock dies ... 20.00
2/18 Eddie Miller ... 20.00
2/25 Spring Training ... 20.00
3/3 H. Pennock, P. Traynor in HOF ... 25.00
3/10 Joe McCarthy ... 22.00
3/17 Pat Seerey ... 20.00
3/24 Babe Ruth ... 30.00
3/31 McCarthy, Stephens, Pesky ... 22.00
4/7 Hank Greenberg ... 30.00
4/14 Joe McCarthy ... 22.00
4/21 '48 Predictions ... 50.00
4/28 Dixie Walker ... 20.00
5/5 Schoolboy Rowe ... 20.00
5/12 Bill Meyer ... 20.00
5/19 Newhouser, Feller, Blackwell, Branca ... 30.00
5/26 Ken Keltner ... 20.00
6/2 Stan Musial ... 35.00
6/9 50 Home Run Club ... 30.00
6/16 Yankee Stadium 25th Anniv. ... 25.00
6/23 Babe Ruth ... 300.00
6/30 Ted Williams ... 40.00
7/7 Bob Lemon no-hitter ... 20.00
7/14 R. Campanella Newest Dodger ... 40.00
7/21 Vic Raschi, AS ... 25.00
7/28 L. Durocher Dodgers to Giants ... 22.00
8/4 Joe Tinker dies ... 20.00
8/11 Tinker, Evers, Chance ... 22.00
8/18 Lou Boudreau ... 24.00
8/25 Babe Ruth dies at 53 ... 500.00
9/1 Carl Erskine ... 100.00
9/8 Phil Rizzuto ... 22.00
9/15 Richie Ashburn ... 22.00
9/22 Satchel Paige ... 25.00
9/29 B. Southworth & G. Stallings ... 20.00
10/6 '14 Miracle Braves, WS .. 50.00
10/13 TSN All-Star team, WS .. 50.00

The Sporting News: 4/13/49

10/20 George Weiss & Casey Stengel ... 50.00
10/27 Casey Stengel ... 25.00
11/3 Happy Chandler ... 20.00
11/10 Lefty Gomez ... 20.00
11/17 Steve O'Neill ... 20.00
11/24 Red Rolfe ... 20.00
12/1 Lou Boudreau MVP ... 25.00
12/8 Stan Musial MVP ... 35.00
12/15 Baseball meetings ... 20.00
12/22 Baseball meetings ... 20.00
12/29 Lou Boudreau, Bill Meyer, Bill Veeck (#1 MEN OF THE YEAR) 40.00

1949

1/5 Pete Reiser ... 30.00
1/12 20-Game Winners a Vanishing Breed ... 18.00
1/19 Earl Torgeson ... 18.00
1/26 Dick Manville ... 18.00
2/2 Bill Veeck ... 20.00
2/9 Murray Dickson ... 18.00
2/16 Joe DiMaggio & Bob Feller ... 30.00
2/23 Spring Training ... 18.00
3/2 Honus Wagner at 75 ... 20.00
3/9 Casey Stengel & '49 Yanks ... 20.00
3/16 Fred Sanford ... 18.00
3/23 George Earnshaw ... 18.00
3/30 Joe McCarthy ... 18.00
4/6 Gene Woodling ... 18.00
4/13 Joe DiMaggio & Ted Williams ... 200.00
4/20 Joe DiMaggio ... 50.00
4/27 Lou Boudreau ... 20.00
5/4 Chuck Connors ... 18.00
5/11 Charlie Gehringer in HOF 20.00
5/18 Bobby Shantz ... 18.00
5/25 Sam Breadon ... 18.00
6/1 Sam Breadon ... 18.00
6/8 Sam Breadon ... 18.00
6/15 Jumpers to Mexican League Reinstated ... 18.00

Date	Issue	Price
6/22	Frank Frisch	18.00
6/29	Ray Boone	18.00
7/6	Joe DiMaggio returns	50.00
7/12	Ebbets Field, AS issue	50.00
7/20	Billy Southworth, AS	20.00
7/27	Casey Stengel	25.00
8/3	Stan Musial	30.00
8/10	Joe Page	25.00
8/17	Luke Appling	20.00
8/24	Yogi Berra	25.00
8/31	Connie Mack Day	18.00
9/7	Joe DiMaggio	50.00
9/14	Bill Klem at 75	18.00
9/21	Enos Slaughter	22.00
9/28	Billy Southworth	18.00
10/5	Williams, Slaughter Top Players	50.00
10/12	Casey Stengel, WS	45.00
10/19	Branch Rickey, WS	50.00
10/26	Casey Stengel	30.00
11/2	Phil Rizzuto	20.00
11/9	My Life With Leo/ Laraine Day	18.00
11/16	Yogi Berra & Joe Garagiola	25.00
11/23	Jackie Robinson MVP	40.00
11/30	Ted Williams MVP	40.00
12/7	Ted Williams & Vern Stephens	25.00
12/14	Bobby Thomson	18.00
12/21	TSN All-Star Team	20.00
12/28	T. Williams, C. Stengel, B. Carpenter (#1 MEN OF THE YEAR)	60.00
	1950	
1/4	Joe DiMaggio	35.00
1/11	Branch Rickey	18.00
1/18	Bob Dillinger	18.00
1/25	Virgil Trucks	18.00
2/1	Jackie Robinson	25.00
2/8	Gerry Priddy	18.00
2/15	Ty Cobb Player of Half Century	30.00
2/22	Spiraling Salaries	18.00
3/1	Hank Greenberg	22.00
3/8	Del Crandall	20.00
3/15	Branch Rickey	20.00
3/22	Connie Mack	20.00
3/29	Sam Jethroe	20.00
4/5	Connie Mack	20.00
4/12	Billy Martin & Jackie Jensen	25.00
4/19	B. Rickey & Jackie Robinson	35.00
4/26	Luke Easter	20.00
5/3	Jack Banta	20.00
5/10	Yogi Berra	25.00
5/17	Edward G. Barrow	18.00
5/24	Ty Cobb saga begins	25.00
5/31	Robin Roberts & Curt Simmons	20.00
6/7	Phil Rizzuto	20.00
6/14	Bob Feller	25.00
6/21	Boston Beats Browns 29-4	18.00
6/28	Joe McCarthy retires	20.00
7/5	George Kell	20.00
7/12	Babe Ruth, All-Star game	50.00
7/19	Luke Easter	25.00
7/26	Ruth Versus Cobb A Dead Heat	30.00
8/2	Casey Stengel	25.00
8/9	Eddie Collins & Larry Lajoie	18.00
8/16	Sam Jethroe	18.00
8/23	Vern Bickford no-hittter	25.00
8/30	Preacher Roe	20.00
9/6	Hank Bauer	18.00
9/13	Gil Hodges' 4 HR game	20.00
9/20	Lou Boudreau	20.00
9/27	Sal Maglie	20.00
10/4	B. Rickey, WS issue	50.00
10/11	Whitey Ford, WS	50.00
10/18	Jerry Coleman, WS	40.00
10/25	Connie Mack retires	18.00
11/1	W. O'Malley & Branch Rickey	25.00
11/8	P. Rizzuto, J. Konstanty MVPs	20.00
11/15	Grover C. Alexander dies	30.00
11/22	Honus Wagner	22.00
11/29	Al Lopez	18.00
12/6	Winter baseball meetings	18.00
12/13	Marty Marion	18.00
12/20	Happy Chandler	18.00
12/27	Happy Chandler	18.00
	1951	
1/3	Phil Rizzuto, Red Rolfe, George Weiss (#1 MEN OF THE YEAR)	40.00
1/10	Yogi Berra & Phil Rizzuto	25.00
1/17	Phil Rizzuto	20.00
1/24	Tom Henrich	18.00
1/31	Mickey Mantle	100.00
2/7	Jimmie Foxx, Mel Ott in HOF	25.00
2/14	N.L. Celebrates 75th Birthday	25.00
2/21	Happy Chandler	18.00

The Sporting News: 12/19/51

Date	Issue	Price
2/28	Stan Musial	25.00
3/7	Red Ruffing	18.00
3/14	Stan Musial	25.00
3/21	Happy Chandler retires	18.00
3/28	Fred Clarke	18.00
4/4	Mickey Mantle	50.00
4/11	Bobby Avila	25.00
4/18	PLAY BALL	40.00
4/25	Mickey Mantle	300.00
5/2	Grover Alexander	25.00
5/9	Leo Durocher, Giants 11-game losing streak	18.00
5/16	Gil McDougald	18.00
5/23	Leo Durocher	20.00
5/30	Robinson,Snider, Hodges,Furillo	35.00
6/6	Branch Rickey	18.00
6/13	Ed Lopat	18.00
6/20	Minnie Minoso	18.00
6/27	Walter O'Malley & B. Bavasi	20.00
7/4	'26 Cardinals	18.00
7/11	Cobb, Cochrane, Gehringer	50.00
7/18	Roy Campanella	25.00
7/25	Allie Reynolds no-hitter	18.00
8/1	Dizzy & Paul Dean	20.00
8/8	'51 Dodgers	25.00
8/15	Willie Mays	50.00
8/22	Charley Gehringer	30.00
8/29	Bob Feller	30.00
9/5	Casey Stengel	30.00
9/12	Johnny Sain	18.00
9/19	Bobby Thomson	25.00
9/26	Bill Klem dies	18.00
10/3	Home Run Baker, WS issue	50.00
10/10	Musial, Feller, Roe, Fain	200.00
10/17	Warren Giles, WS	45.00
10/24	Gabe Paul	18.00
10/31	Lou Boudreau	20.00
11/7	Alvin Dark	18.00
11/14	Stan Musial & Ted Williams	45.00
11/21	Yogi Berra	25.00
11/28	Gil Hodges	20.00
12/5	Bill Bevens	18.00
12/12	Minnie Minoso	25.00
12/19	Joe DiMaggio retires	100.00
12/26	Joe DiMaggio	40.00
	1952	
1/2	S. Musial, L. Durocher, G. Weiss (#1 MEN OF THE YEAR)	75.00
1/9	Leo Durocher & Eddie Stanky	18.00
1/16	Tommy Holmes	16.00
1/23	Walter Briggs dies	16.00
1/30	Gus Zernial	16.00
2/6	'51 Clubs Using Negroes	30.00
2/13	B. Thomson & R. Branca	30.00
2/20	Johnny Mize	20.00
2/27	Paul Waner	16.00
3/5	Casey Stengel	18.00
3/12	Ruth, DiMaggio, Dickey, etc.	30.00
3/19	Ty Cobb	25.00
3/26	Ty Cobb	25.00
4/2	Clem Labine	16.00
4/9	Monte Irvin	18.00
4/16	PLAY BALL	40.00
4/23	Wilmer Mizell	16.00
4/30	Walter O'Malley	20.00
5/7	Walter O'Malley	20.00
5/14	Ty Cobb	22.00
5/21	Jackie Jensen	15.00
5/28	Dale Mitchell	15.00
6/4	Davey Williams	15.00
6/11	Ty Cobb & Rogers Hornsby	25.00
6/18	B. Veeck, R. Hornsby firing	18.00
6/25	Jimmy Piersall	15.00
7/2	Carl Erskine	15.00
7/9	Leo Durocher & Casey Stengel	35.00
7/16	Solly Hemus, AS	20.00
7/23	Clark Griffith	16.00
7/30	Clark Griffith	16.00
8/6	Clark Griffith	16.00
8/13	Jackie Jensen	16.00
8/20	Bill Veeck	18.00
8/27	Billy Loes	16.00
9/3	Robin Roberts	18.00
9/10	Early Wynn	18.00
9/17	Hank Sauer	16.00
9/24	Joe Black & Clint Courtney	16.00
10/1	'41 Dodgers, WS issue	40.00
10/8	'52 Yankees & '52 Dodgers	40.00
10/15	Johnny Mize, WS	40.00
10/22	Mickey Mantle	40.00
10/29	Phil Rizzuto	18.00
11/5	Bill Veeck & Frank Lane	16.00
11/12	Mickey Mantle Life Story	50.00
11/19	Duke Snider	25.00
11/26	TSN All-Star team	20.00
12/3	Del Webb: Yankee Builder	16.00
12/10	Jackie Robinson	25.00
12/17	Ferris Fain	16.00

12/24 Johnny Allen 16.00
12/31 R. Roberts, E. Stanky, G. Weiss (#1 MEN OF THE YEAR) 30.00

The Sporting News

VEECK'S L. A. MAJOR ROCKET SIZZLING

The Sporting News: 3/17/54

1953

1/7 '52 Baseball Thrills section 30.00
1/14 Johnny Mize 18.00
1/21 Eddie Stanky 16.00
1/28 Johnny Mize 18.00
2/4 Dizzy Dean & Al Simmons 20.00
2/11 Ed Yost 16.00
2/18 Eddie Robinson 16.00
2/25 August A. Busch Jr. 16.00
3/4 Russ Meyer 16.00
3/11 Mickey Grasso 16.00
3/18 Braves Move to Milwaukee, Browns to Baltimore 16.00
3/25 Braves and Browns shift . 16.00
4/1 E. Wynn, B. Lemon, M. Garcia 20.00
4/8 Casey Stengel 18.00
4/15 PLAY BALL 30.00
4/22 Milwaukee opener 16.00
4/29 Mickey Mantle Hits 565 foot HR 100.00
5/6 Brawls (Martin/Courtney) . 16.00
5/13 Bobo Holloman no-hitter . 16.00
5/20 Cobb, Mize ,Slaughter . . . 20.00
5/27 Dave Philley 16.00
6/3 Roy Campanella 25.00
6/10 Hoyt Wilhelm 16.00
6/17 Mickey Mantle 45.00
6/24 '53 Yanks Win 18 straight 16.00
7/1 Ed Mathews & Mickey Mantle 45.00
7/8 A. Rosen, L. Doby, L. Easter 20.00
7/15 Dressen & Stengel, AS . . 30.00
7/22 Carl Furillo & Monte Irvin 20.00
7/29 Robin Roberts 18.00
8/5 Ted Williams 30.00
8/12 Mickey Vernon 18.00
8/19 Allie Reynolds 18.00
8/26 '53 Dodger Sluggers 20.00
9/2 Vic Raschi, Preacher Roe 18.00
9/9 Red Schoendienst 18.00
9/16 Ed Mathews 25.00
9/23 Yankees & Dodgers Clinch 20.00
9/30 '49-'53 Yankees, WS issue 45.00
10/7 Gilliam & Kuenn Top Rookies 20.00
10/14 Bill Veeck, WS 40.00
10/21 Rogers Hornsby 18.00
10/28 Rogers Hornsby 18.00
11/4 Jimmy Piersall 18.00
11/11 Nap Lajoie 18.00
11/18 Jimmie Dykes 18.00
11/25 Eddie Joost 18.00
12/2 Atlanta Crackers 16.00
12/9 Walt Alston 18.00
12/16 Bob Feller 20.00
12/23 Ed Barrow dies 16.00
12/30 Al Rosen, Casey Stengel, Lou Perini (#1 MEN OF THE YEAR) 35.00

1954

1/6 '53 Baseball Thrills 20.00
1/13 Bobo Newsome 16.00
1/20 Danny O'Connell 16.00
1/27 Maranville, Terry, Dickey: HOF 20.00
2/3 Spring training 16.00
2/10 Bobby Thomson 18.00
2/17 Paul Krichell 16.00
2/24 Willie Mays 30.00
3/3 Enos Slaughter 16.00
3/10 Johnny Antonelli 16.00
3/17 Walt Alston 18.00
3/24 J.A. Robert Quinn 16.00
3/31 Don Newcombe 18.00
4/7 '54 Dodgers 16.00
4/14 Baseball's Back in Baltimore 35.00
4/21 Ted Williams 30.00
4/28 Hal Jeffcoat 16.00
5/5 Bucky Harris 16.00
5/12 Stan Musial 5 HR Day . . . 75.00
5/19 Johnny Temple 16.00
5/26 Ernie Banks & Gene Baker 22.00
6/2 Art Houtteman 16.00
6/9 Ed Lopat 16.00
6/16 Roy Campanella 25.00
6/23 Wagner, Hornsby, Musial . 25.00
6/30 Frank Thomas 16.00
7/7 Willie Mays & Duke Snider 45.00
7/14 Dusty Rhodes, AS issue . 30.00
7/21 Willie Mays 35.00
7/28 Eddie Stanky 16.00
8/4 Bob Feller 25.00
8/11 Branch Rickey 16.00
8/18 Bob Lemon 16.00
8/25 Don Mueller 16.00
9/1 Jack Harshman 16.00
9/8 Smokey Burgess 16.00
9/15 Willie Mays & Johnny Antonelli 50.00
9/22 Casey Stengel 18.00
9/29 Leo Durocher & Al Lopez, WS 45.00
10/6 Wally Moon & Bob Grim, WS 25.00
10/13 Mays, Avila, Lemon, Antonelli 100.00
10/20 Pinky Higgins 16.00
10/27 Connie Mack 16.00
11/3 Joe McCarthy 16.00
11/10 Joe McCarthy 16.00
11/17 A's Move to K.C. 16.00
11/24 Joe Garagiola 16.00
12/1 Bob Turley 16.00
12/8 Bob Feller 15.00
12/15 TSN All-Star team 20.00
12/22 Ted Kluszweski 18.00
12/29 Stan Lopata 16.00

1955

1/5 W. Mays, L. Durocher, H. Stoneham (#1 MEN OF THE YEAR) 60.00
1/12 Nellie Fox 16.00
1/19 Ken Boyer 18.00
1/26 Joe Nuxhall 16.00
2/2 J. DiMaggio, G. Hartnett, D. Vance, T. Lyons Elected to HOF 25.00
2/9 HR Baker, Ray Schalk Elected to HOF 16.00
2/16 Home Run Baker 16.00
2/23 Sad Sam Jones 16.00
3/2 Roy Campanella 20.00
3/9 Jim Busby 16.00
3/16 Gil Hodges 18.00
3/23 Herb Score 16.00
3/30 Mike Higgins 16.00
4/6 Warren Spahn 20.00
4/13 Herb Score & Ken Boyer 35.00
4/20 Ralph Kiner 18.00
4/27 25-Game Winners 16.00
5/4 '55 Yanks 20.00
5/11 Don Mueller 16.00
5/18 Harvey Kuenn 16.00
5/25 Duke Snider 20.00
6/1 Harry Chiti 16.00
6/8 Al Kaline 25.00
6/15 Roy Campanella & Yogi Berra 25.00
6/22 Don Newcombe 16.00
6/29 Jim Konstanty 16.00
7/6 Dick Donovan 16.00
7/13 Stan Musial, AS issue . . . 30.00
7/20 Ernie Banks 25.00
7/27 Preacher Roe & The Spitter 20.00
8/3 Sherm Lollar 50.00
8/10 Spitball debate 16.00
8/17 Jimmy Piersall 16.00
8/24 Del Ennis 16.00
8/31 Hank Bauer 18.00
9/7 Al Smith 16.00
9/14 Mickey Mantle 30.00
9/21 Don Mossi & Ray Narleski 18.00
9/28 Past Yankees-Dodgers World Series 60.00
10/5 H. Score, B. Virdon Top Rookies 25.00
10/12 Johnny Podres, WS 200.00
10/19 Snider, Kaline, Ford, Roberts 35.00
10/26 Roy Campanella 20.00
11/2 Clark Griffith dies 16.00
11/9 Bobby Bragan 16.00
11/16 Cy Young dies 18.00
11/23 Double Play Duos 16.00
11/30 Bucky Walters 16.00
12/7 TSN All-Star team 18.00
12/14 Roy Campanella MVP . . . 20.00
12/21 Earl Torgeson 16.00
12/28 Bob Feller 20.00

1956

1/4 D. Snider, W. Alston, W. O'Malley (#1 MEN OF THE YEAR) 60.00
1/11 Gil Coan 14.00
1/18 Randy Jackson 14.00
1/25 Pepper Martin 14.00
2/1 Hank Greenberg & Joe Cronin Elected to HOF 15.00
2/8 Hank Greenberg & Joe Cronin 18.00
2/15 Connie Mack dies at 93 . . 16.00
2/22 Calvin Griffith 14.00
2/29 Robin Roberts 16.00
3/7 Hank Greenberg 18.00
3/14 Vern Law 14.00
3/21 10 Greatest Players of '46-'55 Decade 25.00
3/28 Stan Musial 25.00
4/4 Earl Averill 14.00
4/11 Marty Marion 14.00
4/18 Yanks vs. Bums Again in '56 . . . . 35.00
4/25 Minnie Minoso 14.00

Date	Issue	Price
5/2	Top Relief Pitchers	14.00
5/9	Bob Friend	14.00
5/16	Bill Sarni	14.00
5/23	Vic Wertz	14.00
5/30	Dale Long	14.00
6/6	Murray Dickson	14.00
6/13	Mickey Mantle	75.00
6/20	Gabe Paul	14.00
6/27	Alvin Dark	14.00
7/4	Williams, Musial, DiMaggio	100.00
7/11	Stan Musial, Player of Decade	100.00
7/18	Gabe Paul, AS	20.00
7/25	Tigers Sold for $5.5 Million	20.00
8/1	Bill Skowron	20.00
8/8	Fred Haney	14.00
8/15	Ted Williams Fined $5000	25.00
8/22	Braves Hurlers	20.00
8/29	Joe Adcock	20.00
9/5	Frank Robinson, Luis Aparicio Lead Rookies	25.00
9/12	The Home Run	20.00
9/19	Birdie Tebbets	25.00
9/26	Babe Ruth	45.00
10/3	Casey Stengel, WS issue	60.00
10/10	Mantle,Aaron, Newcombe,Pierce	150.00
10/17	Don Larsen: Perfect WS Game	400.00
10/24	Frank Robinson, Luis Aparicio Top Rookies	20.00
10/31	No-Hit Pitchers who Faded Fast	14.00
11/7	Al Lopez	14.00
11/14	Mickey Mantle	30.00
11/21	Frank Lary	30.00
11/28	Mickey Mantle	30.00
12/5	Baseball's 15 Greatest Feats	15.00
12/12	Bob Scheffing	14.00
12/19	Jackie Robinson to Giants	20.00
12/26	Harvey Kuenn	14.00

The Sporting News

Snider, Roberts, Kaline, Ford Best in '55

The Sporting News: 10/19/55

1957

Date	Issue	Price
1/2	M. Mantle, B. Tebbets, G. Paul (#1 MEN OF THE YEAR)	75.00
1/9	Bob Feller retires	18.00
1/16	Jackie Robinson retires	20.00
1/23	Mickey Mantle, George Weiss	30.00
1/30	Duke Snider	18.00
2/6	Stan Musial	20.00
2/13	Joe McCarthy, Sam Crawford Elected to HOF	15.00
2/20	Ted Williams	25.00
2/27	Yank, A's trade	14.00
3/6	Phil Rizzuto	15.00
3/13	Gil Hodges	15.00
3/20	Frank Sullivan	14.00
3/27	Marv Throneberry	14.00
4/3	Ty Cobb	16.00
4/10	Ted Williams	20.00
4/17	Kubek, Rodgers Top Rookies	30.00
4/24	Roy Campanella	20.00
5/1	Roger Maris	25.00
5/8	Tom Yawkey	14.00
5/15	Ted Williams	25.00
5/22	Ted Williams	20.00
5/29	Whitey Ford	18.00
6/5	Dodgers and Giants to move	25.00
6/12	O'Malley	14.00
6/19	Stan Musial	20.00
6/26	Baseball Brawls & Beanballs	14.00
7/3	Danny McDevitt	14.00
7/10	Musial & T. Williams, AS	30.00

The Sporting News: 4/17/57

Date	Issue	Price
7/17	Ford Frick	15.00
7/24	Yankees Success System	14.00
7/31	Giants to S.F. in '58	14.00
8/7	Polo Grounds History	15.00
8/14	Polo Grounds History	20.00
8/21	Roy Sievers	14.00
8/28	Giants Shift	14.00
9/4	Nellie Fox	14.00
9/11	Frank Malzone	14.00
9/18	Walt Moryn	14.00
9/25	Al Kaline	20.00
10/2	Warren Spahn, WS issue	35.00
10/9	Ted Williams & Stan Musial	35.00
10/16	Dodgers to L.A. in '58, WS	30.00
10/23	Lew Burdette	14.00
10/30	L.A. Franchise Battle	15.00
11/6	Yogi Berra	18.00
11/13	Yogi Berra	18.00
11/20	Frank Lane	14.00
11/27	Frank Lane	20.00
12/4	Winter Baseball meetings	14.00
12/11		14.00
12/18	Al Lopez	14.00
12/25	L.A. Dodgers	15.00

1958

Date	Issue	Price
1/1	T. Williams, F. Hutchinson, F. Lane (#1 MEN OF THE YEAR)	35.00
1/8	Mickey Mantle & Ted Williams	15.00
1/15	Ed Mathews	18.00
1/22	George Weiss & Frank Lane	14.00
1/29	L.A. Dodgers	14.00
2/5	Campy's Career Ends: Crash	20.00
2/12	Stars' Salaries Then & Now	14.00
2/19	Billy Martin	15.00
2/26	Willie Mays	20.00
3/5	Duke Snider & Gil Hodges	18.00
3/12	Deron Johnson	14.00
3/19	Leadoff Hitters	14.00
3/26	'58 Braves to Repeat?	15.00
4/2	'58 Giants	15.00
4/9	'58 Batting Derby	15.00
4/16	CALIFORNIA HERE WE COME	30.00
4/23	Ike at Opener	14.00
4/30	L.A. Dodgers	16.00
5/7	Chinese Home Runs	14.00
5/14	Stan Musial 3000 Hits	60.00
5/21	Branch Rickey	14.00
5/28	'58 Yankee pitchers	14.00
6/4	S.F. Giants	14.00
6/11	Ryne Duren	14.00
6/18	Yanks/K.C. Deals	14.00
6/25	Walter O'Malley	14.00
7/2	Gabe Paul	14.00
7/9	All-Time All-Stars	25.00
7/16	Casey Stengel & Kefauver	15.00
7/23	Jackie Jensen	14.00
7/30	Phil Wrigley	14.00
8/6	Bob Turley	14.00
8/13	Philly Whiz Kids	14.00
8/20	Yank Old-Timers	15.00
8/27	Ted Williams	25.00
9/3	Ernie Banks	18.00
9/10	Jensen, Turley, Spahn, Banks	16.00
9/17	Pete Runnels	14.00
9/24	Aaron, Musial, Mays, Ashburn	35.00
10/1	George Weiss, WS issue	30.00
10/8	Top Rookies in '58	16.00
10/15	Player-Manager's Success, WS	25.00
10/22	Mighty Mites	14.00
10/29	Casey Stengel	15.00
11/5	Stan Musial	20.00
11/12	Max Carey	14.00
11/19	Lee MacPhail	14.00
11/26	Houston bids for franchise	14.00
12/3	Winter baseball meetings	14.00
12/10	Will Harridge retires	14.00
12/17	Will Harridge & Joe Cronin	14.00
12/24	N.Y. Yankees' Homes	14.00
12/31	B. Turley, C. Stengel, J. Brown (#1 MEN OF THE YEAR)	25.00

1959

Date	Issue	Price
1/7	Will Harridge retires	14.00
1/14	Marty Marion	14.00
1/21	Bill Norman	14.00
1/28	Willie Mays	20.00
2/4	Soaring player salaries	14.00
2/11	Zack Wheat in HOF	14.00
2/18	Spring Training	14.00
2/25	Bill Veeck	15.00
3/4	J. McGraw, F. Frisch, Stallings, L. Durocher	15.00
3/11	Solly Hemus	14.00
3/18	Frank Lary	14.00
3/25	Ty Cobb	18.00

Date	Issue	Price
4/1	Ray Narleski & Don Mossi	14.00
4/8	PLAY BALL	25.00
4/15	HOF historian Lee Allen	14.00
4/22	Clint Courtney	14.00
4/29	Woodie Held	14.00
5/6	Paul Richards	14.00
5/13	'59 Yanks' Woes	14.00
5/20	Ernie Banks	18.00
5/27	'25 Yanks	14.00
6/3	Hank Aaron	20.00
6/10	Ed Mathews & Rocky Colavito	16.00
6/17	Hoyt Wilhelm	14.00
6/24	Roy Face	14.00
7/1	Harmon Killebrew	15.00
7/8	Ted Williams & Hubbell, AS	25.00
7/15	Billy Jurges	14.00
7/29	Zack Wheat into HOF	14.00
8/5	Don Drysdale	15.00
8/12	Willie McCovey	20.00
8/19	Eppa Rixey	14.00
8/26	Al Lopez	14.00
9/2	Ty Cobb	18.00
9/9	'59 White Sox, Bill Veeck	20.00
9/16	Al Lopez & Tony Cuccinello	14.00
9/23	'59 Yankees Flop	15.00
9/30	Bill Veeck, WS issue	30.00
10/7	Early Wynn	15.00
10/14	'59 Series Sum-up	25.00
10/21	Larry Sherry	14.00
10/28	Wally Moon	14.00
11/4	Chuck Dressen	14.00
11/11	TSN's '59 All-Stars	18.00
11/18	Nellie Fox MVP	15.00
11/25	Bob Allison	14.00
12/2	Winter Baseball meetings	14.00
12/9	'59 Williams & Musial decline	15.00
12/16	Billy Jurges	15.00
12/23	Great HOF 1st Sackers	18.00
12/30	E. Wynn, W. Alston, B. Bavasi (#1 MEN OF THE YEAR)	30.00
	1960	
1/6	Walt Alston	14.00
1/13	Joe Cronin	12.00
1/20	Willie Mays	25.00
1/27	Clark Griffith	12.00
2/3	Johnny Temple	12.00
2/10	E. Rixey, S. Rice, E. Roush	12.00
2/17	Ernie Banks	18.00
2/24	Walter O'Malley	12.00
3/2	Pete Reiser	12.00
3/9	'60 Chisox Graybeards	12.00
3/16	Walt Alston	12.00
3/23	Chuck Dressen	12.00
3/30	'60 Yankees analysis	15.00
4/6	Ed Lopat	12.00
4/13	PLAY BALL	25.00
4/20	C. Young, C. Mathewson, W. Johnson, E. Wynn, W. Spahn	20.00
4/27	Colavito & Kuenn trade	14.00
5/4	Bill DeWitt	12.00
5/11	Ken Boyer	12.00
5/18	Lou Boudreau	12.00
5/25	Roger Maris	25.00
6/1	Bill Veeck	12.00
6/8	Frank Howard	12.00
6/15	Bill Mazeroski	13.00
6/22	Comiskey Dynasty	12.00
6/29	Ted Williams Hits 500th HR	40.00
7/6	Roberto Clemente	25.00
7/13	Roger Maris, AS issue	25.00
7/20	New Franchises for '62	15.00
7/27	Del Crandall	12.00
8/3	Cookie Lavagetto	12.00
8/10	Casey Stengel & Jim Piersall	12.00
8/17	T. Williams Player of Decade	100.00
8/24	Dick Groat	12.00
8/31	Roger Maris & Dick Groat	20.00
9/7	Roy Sievers	12.00
9/14	1890s Stars	12.00
9/21	D. Murtaugh, P. Richards, S. Hemus, C. Lavagetto	12.00
9/28	Stan Musial	25.00
10/5	'27 Yankees, WS issue	30.00
10/12	Lindy McDaniel & M. Fornieles	15.00
10/19	Bobby Richardson, WS	25.00
10/26	Casey Stengel Fired	15.00
11/2	A.L. Expansion for '61	12.00
11/9	George Weiss	12.00
11/16	Roger Maris MVP	25.00
11/23	Roy Harney	12.00
11/30	Winter baseball meetings	12.00
12/7	Ralph Houk	12.00
12/14	L.A. Angels	12.00
12/21	John Galbreath	12.00
12/28	Billy Bruton	12.00
	1961	
1/4	B. Mazeroski, D. Murtaugh, G. Weiss (#1 MEN OF THE YEAR)	30.00
1/11	Ted Kluszewski	13.00
1/18	Florida Flingers	12.00
1/25	Billy Hamilton & Max Carey	12.00
2/1	Walt Alston	12.00
2/8	Lindy McDaniel	12.00
2/15	Stars Swan Songs	14.00
2/22	Max Carey	12.00
3/1	Ralph Houk	12.00
3/8	Leo Durocher	13.00
3/15	Best OF: Yankees or Tigers?	15.00

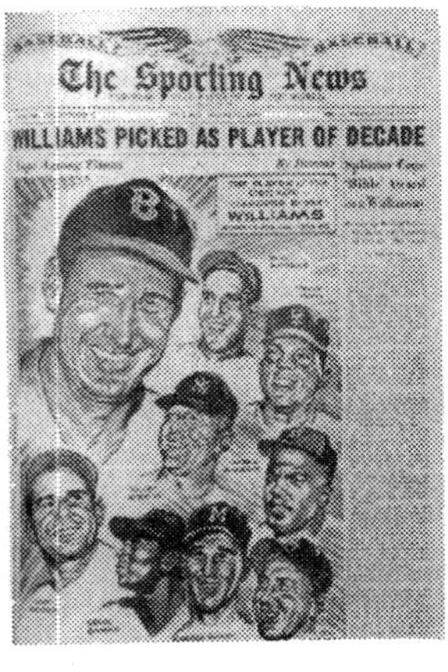

The Sporting News: 8/17/60

Date	Issue	Price
3/22	Joe DiMaggio	18.00
3/29	Mickey Mantle	30.00
4/5	'61 Managers	12.00
4/12	Presidents / Opening Day	40.00
4/19	Carl Yastrzemski & Willie Davis	30.00
4/26	Whitey Ford	16.00
5/3	Babe Herman	14.00
5/10	Wally Moon	25.00
5/17	Jim Gentile	14.00
5/24	Alvin Dark	14.00
5/31	Charles O. Finley	14.00
6/7	Pitching coach Jim Turner	14.00
6/14	Johnny Temple	14.00
6/21	Sandy Koufax	20.00
6/28	Mickey Mantle & Roger Maris	100.00
7/5	300-Game-Winners (c)	20.00
7/12	Mantle, Maris, Ford, Cash, Koufax, Cepeda, Jay, F. Robinson	60.00
7/19	George Weiss, AS	20.00
7/26	Ty Cobb dies at 74	50.00
8/2	Red Sox immortals	40.00
8/9	Ford Frick's HR-record ruling	25.00
8/16	Elston Howard	15.00
8/23	Whitey Ford	25.00
8/30	Top '61 Rookies	30.00
9/6	Mantle & Maris HR Race	75.00
9/13	W. Ford, W. Spahn, L. Arroyo	40.00
9/20	Ralph Houk	40.00
9/27	B. Ruth, M. Mantle, R. Maris	100.00
10/4	'39 Yankees vs. Reds, WS	50.00
10/11	Casey Stengel, N.Y. Mets	200.00
10/18	Hail the Champs!	45.00
10/25	Yogi Berra	15.00
11/1	Top '61 Rookies	15.00
11/8	Ron Santo	12.00
11/15	Johnny Temple	12.00
11/22	Roger Maris MVP	60.00
11/29	Winter baseball meetings	12.00
12/6	Walter O'Malley	12.00
12/13	The Ty Cobb That I Knew-Spink	14.00
12/20	Best No. 2 Hitters	14.00
12/27	George Sisler	12.00
	1962	
1/3	R. Maris, Houk, D. Topping, Spahn (#1 MEN OF THE YEAR)	40.00
1/10	Al Kaline	18.00
1/17	Rogers Hornsby	14.00
1/24	HOF prospects	15.00
1/31	Pie Traynor	12.00
2/7	Elston Howard	13.00
2/14	Gil Hodges	13.00
2/21	Sophomore Jinx	12.00
2/28	Roger Maris	18.00

The Sporting News: 7/21/62

Date	Issue	Price
3/7	M. Mantle, W. Mays, S. Musial, T. Williams, W. Spahn	50.00
3/14	HOFers Who Remained	

With One Team . . . 25.00
3/28 Ray Schalk . . . 12.00
4/4 Minnie Minoso . . . 12.00
4/11 PLAY BALL . . . 20.00
4/18 '62 Giants . . . 12.00
4/25 Ford Frick . . . 12.00
5/2 Felipe & Matty Alou . . . 12.00
5/9 Mets' Casey Stengel . . . 12.00
5/16 Ralph Terry . . . 12.00
5/23 Sandy Koufax . . . 15.00
6/2 Dick Howser & Luis Aparicio . . . 12.00
6/9 '62 Giant Hurlers . . . 12.00
6/16 Bob Purkey . . . 12.00
6/23 Carl Sawatski . . . 12.00
6/30 Don Drysdale . . . 14.00
7/7 All-Star Goats . . . 18.00
7/14 Maury Wills . . . 12.00
7/21 Mays, T.Davis, Mantle, Wagner . . . 25.00
7/28 Cub Immortals . . . 20.00
8/4 Bob Gibson . . . 20.00
8/11 '62 Reds . . . 12.00
8/18 Yogi Berra . . . 20.00
8/25 Juan Marichal . . . 20.00
9/1 Tom Tresh . . . 12.00
9/8 New York Mets . . . 20.00
9/15 Frank Howard & Ron Fairly . . . 12.00
9/22 Mantle, Marichal, Wills, Donovan . . . 20.00
9/29 George Weiss . . . 12.00
10/6 Walter O'Malley, WS issue . . . 20.00
10/13 Ralph Houk rates '62 Yankees . . . 20.00
10/20 '62 Baseball Thrills . . . 20.00
10/27 Tresh & Hubbs Top Rookies . . . 20.00
11/2 Birdie Tebbetts . . . 12.00
11/10 Brooks & Frank Robinson . . . 30.00
11/17 Don Drysdale . . . 14.00
11/24 Stan Musial . . . 18.00
12/1 George Sisler Jr. . . . 12.00
12/8 Tom Tresh . . . 12.00
12/15 Jack Sanford . . . 12.00
12/22 Walter O'Malley . . . 12.00
12/29 Drysdale & Wills (#1 MEN) . . . 25.00

1963

1/5 '62 World Series seventh game . . . 15.00
1/12 Top rookie prospects for '63 . . . 14.00
1/19 Jim Piersall . . . 12.00
1/26 Dean Chance . . . 12.00
2/2 Same Mele . . . 12.00
2/9 Chicago White Sox . . . 12.00
2/16 Sandy Koufax . . . 16.00
2/23 Johnny Pesky . . . 12.00
3/2 Dan Topping . . . 12.00
3/9 . . . 12.00
3/16 Mickey Mantle & Willie Mays . . . 35.00
3/23 '63 Yankees . . . 15.00
3/30 Ralph Terry . . . 12.00
4/6 Don Hoak . . . 12.00
4/13 PLAY BALL . . . 18.00
4/20 Duke Snider . . . 14.00
4/27 Ernie Broglio . . . 12.00
5/4 Bobby Richardson, Tony Kubek . . . 14.00
5/11 Luis Aparicio & Al Smith . 13.00
5/18 . . . 12.00
5/25 Sandy Koufax pitches no-hitter . . . 16.00
6/1 Ron Fairly . . . 12.00
6/8 Casey Stengel & Jim Piersall . . . 12.00
6/15 Gil Hodges . . . 13.00
6/22 Billy O'Dell . . . 12.00
6/29 Juan Marichal's no-hitter . 14.00
7/6 N.Y. Yankees . . . 14.00
7/13 Casey Stengel, AS issue . 18.00
7/20 Koufax, Aaron, Ford, Wagner . . . 20.00
7/27 Hal Woodenshick . . . 12.00
8/3 Rich Rollins . . . 12.00
8/10 Carl Yastrzemski & F. Malzone . . . 16.00
8/17 Dick Ellsworth . . . 12.00
8/24 '63 Dodgers . . . 12.00
8/31 Warren Spahn . . . 14.00
9/7 Dick Groat . . . 12.00
9/14 Jimmy Hall . . . 12.00
9/21 Top Rookies of '63 . . . 14.00
9/28 20 game winners . . . 12.00
10/5 Yankees vs. Dodgers: past WS . . . 25.00
10/12 Ford, Koufax, Kaline, Aaron . . . 30.00
10/19 Dodgers Sweep Yankees . 25.00
10/26 Pete Rose . . . 30.00
11/2 Dick Stuart . . . 12.00
11/9 Y. Berra New Yankees Manager . . . 14.00
11/16 Carl Yastrzemski . . . 16.00
11/23 Hank Aaron . . . 18.00
11/30 Elston Howard . . . 12.00
12/7 Rocky Colavito . . . 12.00
12/14 Sandy Koufax Player of Year . . . 25.00
12/21 Leon Wagner . . . 12.00
12/28 Jim Bouton . . . 12.00

1964

1/4 '63 L.A. Dodgers . . . 20.00
1/11 Albie Pearson . . . 10.00
1/18 Sandy Koufax . . . 18.00
1/25 Walter Alston . . . 10.00
2/1 Jim "Mudcat" Grant . . . 10.00
2/8 Luman Harris . . . 15.00
2/15 Chuck Hinton . . . 10.00
2/22 Eddie Mathews . . . 12.00
2/29 Casey Stengel . . . 12.00
3/7 Burleigh Grimes . . . 10.00
3/14 Al Kaline . . . 15.00
3/21 Willie McCovey . . . 14.00
3/28 Branch Rickey . . . 10.00
4/4 Jim Gilliam . . . 10.00
4/11 Sandy Koufax & Don Drysdale . . . 20.00
4/18 PLAY BALL . . . 18.00
4/25 Spahn, E. Matthews, Aaron . . . 20.00
5/2 McCovey, Mays, Cepeda . 20.00
5/9 Frank Howard . . . 10.00
5/16 Tony Oliva . . . 12.00
5/23 Richie Allen . . . 12.00
5/30 Ron Hansen . . . 10.00
6/6 Dave Wickersham . . . 10.00
6/13 Ron Santo . . . 10.00
6/20 Wally Bunker . . . 10.00
6/27 Whitey Ford . . . 15.00
7/4 Billy Williams . . . 12.00
7/11 Willie Mays . . . 25.00
7/18 Dick Radatz . . . 10.00
7/25 Gene Mauch . . . 10.00
8/1 Boog Powell . . . 10.00
8/8 Ron Hunt . . . 10.00
8/15 Bill Freehan . . . 10.00
8/22 Johnny Callison . . . 10.00
8/29 Harmon Killebrew & Bob Allison . . . 14.00
9/5 Roberto Clemente . . . 20.00
9/12 Elston Howard . . . 12.00
9/19 Brooks Robinson . . . 15.00
9/26 Ken Boyer . . . 12.00
10/3 Dean Chance . . . 10.00
10/10 Oliva, Allen, Bunker, WS . 20.00
10/17 Yankees vs. Cardinals, WS . . . 15.00
10/24 Bing Devine, WS . . . 20.00
10/31 Johnny Keane . . . 10.00
11/7 Ara Parseghian . . . 15.00
11/14 Dick Butkus . . . 12.00
11/21 Johnny Unitas . . . 15.00
11/28 Bob Pettit (1st Hoops cover) . . . 14.00
12/5 Mel Stottlemyre & Harry Walker . . . 10.00
12/12 Jim Brown . . . 18.00
12/19 Gino Cappelletti . . . 10.00
12/26 Jerry Hill & Jim Parker . . . 10.00

1965

1/2 Bob Gibson & Ken Boyer . . . 16.00
1/9 John Unitas & Don Shula . . . 18.00
1/16 Red Auerbach . . . 12.00
1/23 Bill Bradley . . . 14.00
1/30 Jerry West . . . 12.00
2/6 Baseball to Elect New Commissioner . . . 12.00
2/13 Sam Jones & Walt Hazzard . . . 10.00
2/20 Joe Lapchick . . . 10.00
2/27 Spring Training . . . 10.00
3/6 Bill Bradley . . . 12.00
3/13 Bill Russell . . . 15.00
3/20 Rocky Colavito . . . 10.00
3/27 Juan Marichal . . . 14.00
4/3 Bo Belinsky & Dick Stuart . . . 10.00
4/10 The Houston Astrodome . 10.00
4/17 PLAY BALL . . . 15.00
4/24 LBJ Visits Astrodome . . . 12.00
5/1 John Romano . . . 10.00
5/8 Eddie Mathews . . . 12.00
5/15 Tony Conigliaro . . . 10.00
5/22 Frank Robinson . . . 15.00
5/29 White Sox Pitchers . . . 10.00
6/5 Bob Gibson . . . 15.00
6/12 Felix Mantilla . . . 10.00
6/19 Wes Parker . . . 10.00
6/26 Vic Davalillo . . . 10.00
7/3 Hank Aaron . . . 18.00
7/10 . . . 10.00
7/17 Sandy Koufax & Don Drysdale . . . 20.00
7/24 Willie Horton . . . 10.00
7/31 Deron Johnson . . . 10.00
8/7 Sonny Siebert . . . 10.00
8/14 Richie Allen . . . 12.00
8/21 Pete Rose . . . 25.00
8/28 Curt Blefary . . . 10.00

The Sporting News: 1/15/66

9/4 Vern Law . . . 10.00
9/11 Sam McDowell . . . 10.00
9/18 Jim Bunning . . . 10.00
9/25 Sandy Koufax' perfect game . . . 25.00
10/2 Willie McCovey . . . 12.00
10/9 Jim "Mudcat" Grant, WS . 12.00
10/16 Lou Johnson . . . 10.00
10/23 Maury Wills, WS . . . 12.00
10/30 Koufax, Mays,

Oliva, Grant 20.00
11/6 Cal Griffith's Greatest Year 10.00
11/13 Charlie Johnson 10.00
11/20 Paul Lowe 10.00
11/27 Mike Garrett 10.00
12/4 Don Anderson & Jim Grabowski 10.00
12/11 All-America Offense 10.00
12/18 Jim Brown 15.00
12/25 Gale Sayers 15.00

1966

1/1 Joe Namath 25.00
1/8 Sandy Koufax 20.00
1/15 Vince Lombardi & Packers 15.00
1/22 Ted Williams 16.00
1/29 Thad Jaracz 10.00
2/5 Cazzie Russell 10.00
2/12 Guy Rodgers 10.00
2/19 Doug Wardlaw & Corky Bell 10.00
2/26 Wilt Chamberlain 15.00
3/5 Hank Aguirre 10.00
3/12 Cazzie Russell 12.00
3/19 Dick Stuart 10.00
3/26 Willie Davis 10.00
4/2 Camilo Pascual 10.00
4/9 Brooks & Frank Robinson 20.00
4/16 Atlanta & Anaheim Stadiums 15.00

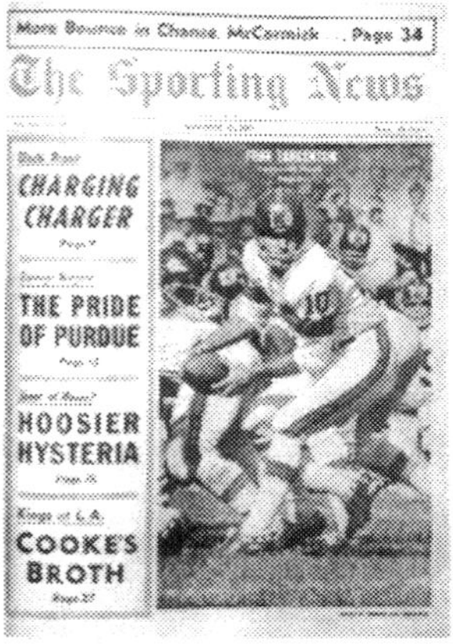

The Sporting News: 11/25/67

4/23 Emmett Ashford 10.00
4/30 Mil. Braves move to Atlanta 10.00
5/7 Fred Whitfield & Larry Brown 10.00
5/14 Don Sutton 11.00
5/21 Willie Mays 20.00
5/28 Luis Tiant 10.00
6/4 Rick Reichardt 10.00
6/11 Joe Morgan 12.00
6/18 Sandy Koufax & Juan Marichal 18.00
6/25 Sonny Siebert 10.00
7/2 Richie Allen 10.00
7/9 Jim Northrup 10.00
7/16 August A. Busch, Jr, AS . 15.00
7/23 Gaylord Perry 12.00
7/30 Jack Aker 10.00
8/6 Woodie Fryman 10.00
8/13 Boog Powell 10.00
8/20 Orlando Cepeda 10.00
8/27 Baltimore Orioles 12.00
9/3 Phil Regan 10.00
9/10 Jim Kaat 10.00
9/17 Willie Stargell 14.00
9/24 Felipe & Matty Alou 10.00
10/1 Jim Nash 10.00
10/8 Hank Bauer, WS issue . . 15.00
10/15 Jim Lefebvre 10.00
10/22 Luis Aparicio 12.00
10/29 Don Meredith 12.00
11/5 Terry Hanratty 10.00
11/12 George Gross & Keith Lincoln 10.00
11/19 Larry Wilson 10.00
11/26 Johnny Robinson 10.00
12/3 Bob Gladieux 10.00
12/10 Steve Spurrier 10.00
12/17 Bill Russell 14.00
12/24 Elijah Pitts 10.00
12/31 Rick Barry 12.00

1967

1/7 Bart Starr 12.00
1/14 Hank Stram 8.00
1/21 Lew Alcindor 16.00
1/28 Alex Hannum 8.00
2/4 Tom & Dick Van Ardsdale 8.00
2/11 Mendy Rudolph 8.00
2/18 Harry Howell 8.00
2/25 Baseball Cartoons 10.00
3/4 Bob Cousy 10.00
3/11 Stan Mikita 10.00
3/18 Hoyt Wilhelm 8.00
3/25 Andy Etchebarren 8.00
4/1 J. Kaat, D. Chance, J. Grant 9.00
4/8 Frank Robinson (color) . . 15.00
4/15 PLAY BALL 12.00
4/22 Jim Fregosi 8.00
4/29 Roger Maris (color) 25.00
5/6 Whitey Ford 12.00
5/13 Steve Hargan 8.00
5/20 Rick Reichardt (color) 8.00
5/27 Walter Alston (color) 8.00
6/3 Gary Nolan (color) 8.00
6/10 Rod Carew 10.00
6/17 Juan Marichal 9.00
6/24 Al Dark & E. Stanky (color) 8.00
7/1 Jim Lonborg 8.00
7/8 Bob Veale 8.00
7/15 Jim McGlothlin, AS issue . 15.00
7/22 Tim McCarver, AS 10.00
7/29 Tommy John & Gary Peters 8.00
8/5 Dick Williams 8.00
8/12 Joe Torre 9.00
8/19 Paul Blair 8.00
8/26 Mike McCormick 8.00
9/2 Gil Hodges & Frank Howard 9.00
9/9 Rusty Staub 8.00
9/16 Jack Kemp 8.00
9/23 Carl Yastrzemski 12.00
9/30 Earl Wilson 8.00
10/7 Stan Musial & Schoendienst 12.00
10/14 Carl Yastrzemski (color) . . 25.00
10/21 Jim Lonborg, WS 15.00
10/28 Bob Gibson, WS (color) . . 20.00
11/4 Len Dawson (color) 8.00
11/11 Jim Hart 8.00
11/18 Gary Beban (color) 8.00
11/25 Fran Tarkenton 9.00
12/2 Leroy Kelly 8.00
12/9 Lew Alcindor 14.00
12/16 Vince Lombardi 10.00
12/23 Daryle Lamonica 8.00
12/30 Roman Gabriel 8.00

1968

1/6 Green Bay Packers 8.00
1/13 Vince Lombardi & Bart Starr 10.00
1/20 Wes Unseld (color) 8.00
1/27 Donny Anderson 8.00
2/3 Phil Esposito 10.00
2/10 Lenny Wilkins 8.00
2/17 Don May 8.00
2/24 Elvin Hayes 9.00
3/2 Carl Yastrzemski (color) . . 15.00
3/9 Dick Hughes 8.00
3/16 Mark Belanger 8.00
3/23 Jim Bunning 8.00
3/30 Don Wert 8.00
4/6 Mickey Mantle & family . . 25.00
4/13 Lou Brock 12.00
4/20 Pete Rose (color) 25.00
4/27 Jim Fregosi & Bobby Knoop 8.00
5/4 Harmon Killebrew (color) . 12.00
5/11 Jerry Koosman 8.00
5/18 Mickey Lolich 8.00
5/25 Orlando Cepeda (color) . . . 9.00
6/1 Frank Howard 8.00
6/8 Don Drysdale 9.00
6/15 Woody Fryman 8.00
6/22 Jim Hardin 8.00

The Sporting News: 8/17/68

6/29 Tony Horton (color) 8.00
7/6 Denny McLain 8.00
7/13 Willie McCovey, AS issue 12.00
7/20 Willie Horton (color) 9.00
7/27 Matty Alou (color) 8.00
8/3 Luis Tiant (color) 8.00
8/10 Glenn Beckert 8.00
8/17 Reggie Jackson & Rick Monday 25.00
8/24 Dal Maxvill 8.00
8/31 Ted Uhlaender 8.00
9/7 Phil Regan 8.00
9/14 Roman Gabriel (color) 8.00
9/21 Bill Freehan (color) 8.00
9/28 Mike Shannon 8.00
10/5 D. McLain & L. Grove, WS 15.00
10/12 Roger Maris & family, WS 25.00
10/19 Bob Gibson, WS (color) . . 18.00
10/26 Don Meredith (color) 8.00
11/2 Sonny Jurgenson (color) . . 8.00
11/9 Terry Hanratty 8.00
11/16 B. Bell, J. Lynch, W. Lanier 8.00
11/23 Bart Starr (color) 9.00
11/30 Earl Morrall (color) 8.00
12/7 College Basketball Preview 8.00
12/14 O.J. Simpson (color) 15.00
12/21 John Hadl (color) 8.00
12/28 Joe Namath 14.00

1969

1/4 Denny McLain (color) 8.00
1/11 John Mackey 8.00

1/18 Elvin Hayes (color) 9.00
1/25 Joe Namath 14.00
2/1 Norm Ullman 8.00
2/8 Bobby Hull 10.00
2/15 Phil Esposito 10.00
2/22 Gordie Howe (color) 10.00
3/1 Willie Mays (color) 15.00
3/8 Billy Caspar (color) 8.00
3/15 Ted Williams 15.00
3/22 Denny McLain 8.00
3/29 Tony Conigliaro 8.00
4/5 100 Years of Baseball 20.00
4/12 L. Brock, Flood, Pinson (color) 12.00
4/19 Don Buford 8.00
4/26 Tug McGraw 8.00
5/3 Mel Stottlemyre 8.00
5/10 Bill Sudakis 8.00
5/17 Dave McNally (color) 8.00
5/24 Richie Hebner 8.00
5/31 Bobby Murcer 8.00
6/7 Don Kessinger 8.00
6/14 Blue Moon Odom (color) 8.00
6/21 Lee May (color) 8.00
6/28 Ray Culp (color) 8.00
7/5 Ken Holtzman (color) 8.00
7/12 Rod Carew 10.00
7/19 B. Powell, Robinsons (color) 12.00
7/26 Reggie Jackson (color) 20.00
8/2 Matty Alou (color) 8.00
8/9 Willie McCovey (color) 14.00
8/16 Rico Petrocelli 8.00
8/23 Phil Niekro 9.00
8/30 Steve Carlton (color) 15.00
9/6 Ron Santo (color-art) 8.00
9/13 Mike Cuellar 8.00
9/20 Gale Sayers (color-art) 10.00
9/27 Bobby Tolan (color) 8.00
10/4 Billy Martin (color-art) 9.00
10/11 Tom Seaver (color-art) 20.00
10/18 Boog Powell (color-art) 8.00
10/25 Harmon Killebrew (color) 10.00
11/1 David (Mets) & Goliath (Orioles) 15.00
11/8 Rex Kern (color-art) 8.00
11/15 George Allen (color-art) 8.00
11/22 M. Garrett, R.Holmes, W. McVea 8.00
11/29 Mike Phipps (color) 8.00
12/6 Rick Mount (Last B&W cover) 8.00
12/13 Bobby Orr 15.00
12/20 Daryle Lamonica 8.00
12/27 Roman Gabriel 8.00

1970

1/3 James Street 8.00
1/10 Bill Bradley 15.00
1/17 Willie Mays 12.00
1/24 Rogie Vachon 8.00
1/31 Mike Pratt 8.00
2/7 Lou Hudson 8.00
2/14 Pete Maravich 15.00
2/21 Tony Esposito 8.00
2/28 Roberto Clemente 12.00
3/7 John Vallely 8.00
3/14 Bill Russell 9.00
3/21 Stan Mikita 9.00
3/28 Lew Alcindor 12.00
4/4 Arnold Palmer 8.00
4/11 Yaz, T. Conigliaro, R. Smith 15.00
4/18 Johnny Bench 10.00
4/25 Bert Campenaris 8.00
5/2 Rusty Staub 8.00
5/9 Brant Alyea 8.00
5/16 Tony Perez 8.00
5/23 Hank Aaron 20.00
5/30 Dave Johnson 8.00
6/6 Richie Allen 8.00
6/13 Vada Pinson 8.00
6/20 Jim Merritt 8.00
6/27 Danny Walton 8.00
7/4 Rico Carty 8.00
7/11 Felipe Alou 8.00

The Sporting News: 9/20/69

7/18 Pete Rose 12.00
7/25 Willie Mays 12.00
8/1 Billy Grabarkewitz 8.00
8/8 Al Kaline 10.00
8/15 Ray Fosse 8.00
8/22 Roy White 8.00
8/29 Dave Giusti 8.00
9/5 Bud Harrelson 8.00
9/12 Bernie Carbo 8.00
9/19 Len Dawson 8.00
9/26 Joe Pepitone 8.00
10/3 Gaylord & Jim Perry 10.00
10/10 Danny Murtaugh 8.00
10/17 J. Palmer, M. Cuellar, D. McNally 10.00
10/24 Johnny Bench 15.00
10/31 World Series Wrap-Up 9.00
11/7 Archie Manning 8.00
11/14 Bill Munson 8.00
11/21 Jim Johnson 8.00
11/28 Joe Theismann 9.00
12/5 Gary Cuozzo 8.00
12/12 Austin Carr 8.00
12/19 Keith Magnuson 8.00
12/26 Johnny Robinson 8.00

1971

1/2 Rex Kern 7.00
1/9 John Wooden 8.00
1/16 John Unitas 8.50
1/23 Dan Issel 7.00
1/30 Super Bowl V 7.00
2/6 Brad Park 7.00
2/13 Lew Alcindor 9.50
2/20 Phil Esposito 8.50
2/27 Palmer, Bamberger, Etchebarren 8.00
3/6 Pete Maravich 8.00
3/13 Sidney Wicks 7.00
3/20 John Havlicek 7.00
3/27 Mel Daniels 7.00
4/3 Yvan Cournoyer 7.00
4/10 Johnny Bench & Boog Powell 15.00
4/17 Reggie Jackson 14.00
4/24 Tony Conigliaro 7.00
5/1 Manny Sanguillen 7.00
5/8 Steve Carlton 9.50
5/15 Canonero II 7.00
5/22 Willie Stargell 9.00
5/29 Indianapolis 500 7.00
6/5 Vida Blue 7.00
6/12 Jerry Grote 7.00
6/19 Sonny Siebert 7.00
6/26 Dick Dietz 7.00
7/3 Fergie Jenkins 8.00
7/10 Bobby Murcer 7.00
7/17 Willie Mays 10.00

7/24 Joe Torre 8.00
7/31 Frank Robinson 9.00
8/7 Tony Oliva 7.50
8/14 Amos Otis 7.00
8/21 Dock Ellis 7.00
8/28 Jack Nicklaus 7.00
9/4 Bill Melton 7.00
9/11 College Football Preview 7.00
9/18 John Brodie 7.00
9/25 Mickey Lolich 7.00
10/2 Wilbur Wood 7.00
10/9 Al Downing 7.00
10/16 Brooks Robinson 12.00
10/23 Joe Torre 7.50
10/30 Roberto Clemente, WS 15.00
11/6 Walt Patulski 7.00
11/13 Billy Kilmer 7.00
11/20 Terry Beasley & Pat Sullivan 7.00
11/27 Greg Pruitt 7.00
12/4 Bob Griese 7.50
12/11 Otis Taylor 7.00
12/18 Allan Hornyak & Luke Witts 7.00
12/25 Garry Unger 7.00

1972

1/1 Jerry Tagge 7.00
1/8 Lee Trevino 7.00
1/15 Roger Staubach 8.50
1/22 Wilt Chamberlain & Gail Goodrich 8.00
1/29 Artis Gilmore 7.00
2/5 Tyler Palmer 7.00
2/12 Ted Harris 7.00
2/19 Dave Cowens 7.50
2/26 Jean Ratelle 7.00
3/4 Cuellar, Dobson, McNally, Palmer 8.50
3/11 Chris Evert 7.00
3/18 Bill Walton 7.00
3/25 Marc Tardi 7.00
4/1 Jack Nicklaus 7.00

The Sporting News: 5/21/71

4/8 Roberto Clemente 15.00
4/15 Kareem Abdul-Jabbar 8.50
4/22 Bobby Hull 8.00
4/29 Play Ball 7.00
5/6 Gerry Cheevers 7.00
5/13 Don Sutton 7.00
5/20 Riva Ridge 7.00
5/27 Milt Wilcox 7.00
6/3 Dave Kingman 7.00
6/10 Mickey Lolich 7.00
6/17 Gary Nolan 7.00
6/24 D. Baylor, T. Crowley, B. Grich 7.00
7/1 Danny Frisella &

Date	Issue	Price
	Tug McGraw	7.00
7/8	Lou Piniella	7.50
7/15	Manny Sanguillen	7.00
7/22	Joe Rudi	7.00
7/29	Hank Aaron	9.50
8/5	Jack Nicklaus	7.00
8/12	Sparky Lyle	7.00
8/19	Cesar Cedeno	7.00
8/26	Mark Spitz	7.00
9/2	Steve Carlton	8.00
9/9	Bob Devaney	7.00
9/16	Len Dawson	7.00
9/23	Carlton Fisk	8.00
9/30	Al Oliver	7.00
10/7	Joe Namath	9.00
10/14	Luis Tiant	7.00
10/21	Billy Williams	8.00
10/28	Johnny Bench	8.50
11/4	Dick Williams	7.00
11/11	Jerrel Wilson	7.00
11/18	Larry Csonka	8.00
11/25	Larry Brown	7.00
12/2	Gilbert Perreault	7.00
12/9	Terry Bradshaw	8.00
12/16	Bill Walton	8.00
12/23	Jacques Lemaire	7.00
12/30	Nate "Tiny" Archibald	7.00
	1973	
1/6	Charlie Finley	7.00
1/13	Super Bowl VII, Clemente dies	8.00
1/20	J.P.Parise, Clemente tribute	9.00
1/27	Spencer Haywood	7.00
2/3	Zelmo Beatty	7.00
2/10	Mickey Redmond	7.00
2/17	UCLA Bruins basketball	8.00
2/24	George McGinnis	7.00
3/3	Rollie Fingers	8.00
3/10	Bobby Clarke	7.00
3/17	Bill Walton & John Wooden	8.00
3/24	Nate "Tiny" Archibald	7.00
3/31	Billy Cunningham	7.00
4/7	Jack Nicklaus	7.00
4/14	Steve Carlton	8.00
4/21	Phil Esposito	8.00
4/28	Chris Speier	7.00
5/5	Nolan Ryan	20.00
5/12	Fred Patek & Cookie Rojas	7.00
5/19	Joe Morgan	8.00
5/26	Indianapolis 500	7.00
6/2	Wilbur Wood	7.00
6/9	Joe Ferguson	7.00
6/16	Joe Coleman	7.00
6/23	Ron Santo	7.00
6/30	Ron Blomberg	7.00
7/7	Bobby Bonds	7.50
7/14	John Mayberry	7.00
7/21	Bob Watson	7.00
7/28	P. Rose, J. Bench, J. Morgan	10.00
8/4	Bert Blyleven	7.00
8/11	Bobby Bonds	7.50
8/18	Thurman Munson	7.50
8/25	Del Unser	7.00
9/1	Orlando Cepeda	7.50
9/8	Darrell Evans	7.00
9/15	W. Hayes, R. Gradishar, J. Hicks	7.00
9/22	Larry Csonka	7.00
9/29	Lou Brock	8.00
10/6	Willie Mays	9.00
10/13	Jim Palmer	7.50
10/20	J. Hunter, V. Blue, K. Holtzman	7.50
10/27	Jon Matlack	7.00
11/3	Mike Andrews	7.00
11/10	John Hadl	7.00
11/17	Fran Tarkenton	7.50
11/24	Archie Griffin	7.00
12/1	Tom Clements	7.00
12/8	Bill Walton	7.50
12/15	Bob Lee	7.00

Date	Issue	Price
12/22	O.J. Simpson	8.50
12/29	Nick Buoniconti	7.00
	1974	
1/5	Pete Maravich	6.00
1/12	Julius Erving	9.00
1/19	Bob Griese	6.00
1/26	David Thompson	6.00
2/2	George Gervin	6.00
2/9	Kerry & Kim Hughes	6.00
2/16	Johnny Miller	6.00
2/23	Bill Walton	7.00
3/2	Dick Green	6.00
3/9	John Shumate	6.00
3/16	Dave Shultz	6.00
3/23	Bob McAdoo	6.00
3/30	Rick Barry	6.00
4/6	Play Ball	6.50
4/13	Jack Nicklaus	6.00
4/20	Hank Aaron & Babe Ruth	25.00
4/27	Ted Simmons	6.00
5/4	Roy White	6.00
5/11	Jim Wynn	6.00
5/18	Jeff Burroughs	6.00
5/25	Ken Singleton	6.00
6/1	John Hiller	6.00
6/8	Mike Schmidt	10.00
6/15	Gaylord Perry	7.00
6/22	Tommy John	6.00
6/29	Rod Carew	7.50
7/6	Ralph Garr	6.00
7/13	Carlton Fisk	7.00

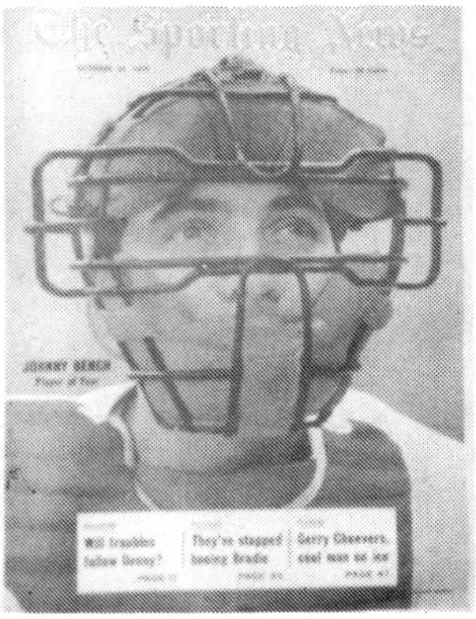

The Sporting News: 10/28/72

Date	Issue	Price
7/20	Dick Williams	6.00
7/27	Mike Marshall	6.00
8/3	Steve Busby	6.00
8/10	Greg Gross	6.00
8/17	Reggie Jackson	8.50
8/24	Lou Brock	7.00
8/31	Jorge Orta	6.00
9/7	Cornelius Green & Archie Griffin	6.00
9/14	Richie Zisk	6.00
9/21	O.J. Simpson	7.50
9/28	Reggie Smith	6.00
10/5	Rod Shoate	6.00
10/12	Jim Plunkett	6.00
10/19	Bill Virdon	6.00
10/26	Steve Garvey	6.50
11/2	L. Brock, J. Burroughs, J. Hunter, M. Marshall	7.00
11/9	Jim Hart	6.00
11/16	Reggie McKenzie	6.00
11/23	Dennis Franklin	6.00
11/30	George Blanda	6.00
12/7	Ken Anderson	6.00
12/14	Monty Towe	6.00
12/21	Marv Hubbard	6.00
12/28	Rick Barry	6.00

Date	Issue	Price
	1975	
1/4	Lou Brock	7.00
1/11	Bob McAdoo	6.00
1/18	Terry Bradshaw, Fran Tarkenton	7.50
1/25	Swen Nater	6.00
2/1	Guy Lafleur	7.00
2/8	Steve Green	6.00
2/15	Walt Frazier	6.00
2/22	Steve Vickers	6.00
3/1	Adrian Dantley	6.00
3/8	Bobby Bonds & Catfish Hunter	7.00
3/15	Julius Erving	8.50
3/22	Dave Cowens	6.00
3/29	George McGinnis	6.00
4/5	Rogie Vachon	6.00
4/12	Opening Day	6.00
4/19	Elvin Hayes	6.00
4/26	Dave Concepcion	6.00
5/3	Frank Robinson	8.00
5/10	Greg Luzinski	6.00
5/17	Nolan Ryan	17.00
5/24	Ken Reitz	6.00
5/31	Jim Palmer	7.00
6/7	Madlock, Monday, J. Morales	6.00
6/14	Ron LeFlore	6.00
6/21	Andy Messersmith	6.00
6/28	Hal McRae	6.00
7/5	Joe Morgan	7.00
7/12	Fred Lynn	6.00
7/19	Mays, Musial, Ruth, Williams, etc	12.00
7/26	Robin Yount	10.00
8/2	Dave Parker	6.50
8/9	Claudell Washington	6.00
8/16	Al Hrabosky	6.00
8/23	Jim Kaat	6.00
8/30	Larry Bowa & Dave Cash	6.00
9/6	Randy Jones	6.00
9/13	Archie Griffin	6.00
9/20	John Mayberry	6.00
9/27	Terry Bradshaw	6.50
10/4	R. Fingers, P. Lindblad, J. Todd	6.00
10/11	Sparky Anderson	6.00
10/18	Fred Lynn	6.00
10/25	Rick Barry	6.50
11/1	Roger Staubach	7.00
11/8	Pete Johnson	6.00
11/15	Curley Culp	6.00
11/22	Lynn Swann	7.00
11/29	Fran Tarkenton	7.00
12/6	Jim Bakken	6.00
12/13	Richard Washington	6.00
12/20	Bert Jones	6.00
12/27	Ray Guy	6.00
	1976	
1/3	John Sciarra	6.00
1/10	Archie Griffin	6.00
1/17	Adrian Dantley	6.00
1/24	Franco Harris	6.50
1/31	Scotty May	6.00
2/7	Alvin Adams	6.00
2/14	Kareem Abdul-Jabbar	7.50
2/21	John Lucas	6.00
2/28	George McGinnis	6.00
3/6	Fred Lynn	6.00
3/13	David Thompson	6.00
3/20	Jim Cleamons, Bill Fitch, Bobby Smith, Dick Snyder	6.00
3/27	Phil Smith	6.00
4/3	John Havlicek	6.50
4/10	Fergie Jenkins	6.50
4/17	Don Gullett	6.00
4/24	Frank Tanana	6.00
5/1	Larry Bowa	6.00
5/8	Dave Kingman	6.00
5/15	Toby Harrah	6.00
5/22	Willie Horton	6.00
5/29	Ron Cey	6.00
6/5	George Brett	10.00
6/12	Chris Chambliss	6.00

The Sporting News: 4/3/76

6/19 Randy Jones . . . 6.00
6/26 Ron LeFlore . . . 6.00
7/3 George Foster . . . 6.00
7/10 John Montefusco . . . 6.00
7/17 Johnny Bench . . . 10.00
7/24 Jim Slaton . . . 6.00
7/31 Al Oliver . . . 6.00
8/7 Dennis Leonard . . . 6.00
8/14 Mark Fidrych . . . 7.00
8/21 Dave Cash . . . 6.00
8/28 Rico Carty . . . 6.00
9/4 Tony Dorsett . . . 7.00
9/11 Jack Lambert . . . 6.00
9/18 Rick Rhoden . . . 6.00
9/25 Mickey Rivers . . . 6.00
10/2 Rick Leach . . . 6.00
10/9 Billy Kilmer . . . 6.00
10/16 Rawley Eastwick . . . 6.00
10/23 Cincinnati "Big Red Machine" . . . 10.00
10/30 Jo Jo White . . . 6.00
11/6 Steve Grogan . . . 6.00
11/13 Ricky Bell . . . 6.00
11/20 Conrad Dobler . . . 6.00
11/27 Wally Chambers . . . 6.00
12/4 Marques Johnson . . . 6.00
12/11 Dave Caspar . . . 6.00
12/18 Isaac Curtis . . . 6.00
12/25 Bert Jones . . . 6.00

1977

1/1 Tony Dorsett . . . 7.00
1/8 David Thompson . . . 6.50
1/15 Ken Stabler . . . 6.50
1/22 Bill Walton . . . 6.50
1/29 Rudy Tomjanovich . . . 6.00
2/5 Rick Robey . . . 6.00
2/12 Julius Erving . . . 8.50
2/19 Pete Maravich . . . 7.00
2/26 Billy Knight . . . 6.50
3/5 D. Baylor, B. Grich, J. Rudi . . . 6.00
3/12 Paul Westphal . . . 6.00
3/19 Elvin Hayes . . . 6.50
3/26 Wayne Garland . . . 6.00
4/2 Mike Schmidt . . . 7.50
4/9 Don Gullett & Reggie Jackson . . . 8.00
4/16 Bert Campenaris . . . 6.00
4/23 Rick Monday . . . 6.00
4/30 Rollie Fingers . . . 6.50
5/7 Amos Otis . . . 6.00
5/14 Joe Rudi . . . 6.00
5/21 Ted Simmons . . . 6.00
5/28 Ron Cey . . . 6.00
6/4 Mitchell Page . . . 6.00
6/11 Dave Parker . . . 6.50
6/18 Richie Zisk . . . 6.00
6/25 Bruce Sutter . . . 6.00
7/2 Hubie Green . . . 6.00
7/9 Butch Wynegar . . . 6.00
7/16 Jeff Burroughs . . . 6.00
7/23 Frank Tanana . . . 6.00
7/30 Steve Carlton . . . 7.50
8/6 Joe Morgan . . . 7.50
8/13 Jim Rice . . . 6.50
8/20 A. Dawson, Cromartie, Valentine . . . 6.50
8/27 Billy Hunter & Bump Wills . . . 6.00
9/3 Tommy John . . . 6.00
9/10 Ross Browner . . . 6.00
9/17 Tony Dorsett . . . 6.50
9/24 Graig Nettles . . . 6.00
10/1 Greg Luzinski . . . 6.00
10/8 Al Cowens . . . 6.00
10/15 Rod Carew . . . 7.00
10/22 Ron Cey, Steve Garvey, D.Baker, Reggie Smith . . . 7.00
10/29 Pete Maravich . . . 10.00
11/5 Earl Campbell . . . 10.00
11/12 Craig Morton . . . 6.00
11/19 Walter Payton . . . 9.50
11/26 Drew Pearson . . . 6.00
12/3 Reggie Theus . . . 6.00
12/10 Jack Ham . . . 6.00
12/17 Pat Haden . . . 6.00
12/24 Bob Griese . . . 6.00
12/31 Bear Bryant & Woody Hayes . . . 6.00

1978

1/7 Steve Cauthen . . . 5.00
1/14 Butch Lee . . . 5.00
1/21 Roger Staubach & Craig Morton . . . 6.00
1/28 Dave Twardzik . . . 5.00
2/5 Jack Givens . . . 5.00
2/12 Julius Erving . . . 6.00
2/19 Walter Davis . . . 5.00
2/26 Larry Bird . . . 12.00
3/4 Rod Carew & George Foster . . . 6.00
3/11 D. Greenwood & Roy Hamilton . . . 5.00
3/18 David Thompson . . . 5.00
3/25 Kareem Abdul-Jabbar . . . 6.00
4/1 Bernard King . . . 5.00
4/8 Salute to '78 Season . . . 6.00
4/15 Lyman Bostock . . . 5.00
4/22 Garry Templeton . . . 5.00
4/29 Steve Kemp & Jason Thompson . . . 5.00
5/6 Don Money . . . 5.00
5/13 Ross Grimsley . . . 5.00
5/20 Pete Rose . . . 10.00
5/27 Jim Rice . . . 5.00
6/3 Blue, Barr, Knepper, Montefusco . . . 5.00
6/10 Gary Alexander . . . 5.00
6/17 Ron Guidry . . . 5.00
6/24 Vic Davalillo & Manny Mota . . . 5.00
7/1 Paul Splittorff . . . 5.00
7/8 J. Palmer, D. Martinez, M. Flanagan, S. McGregor . 6.00
7/15 R. Carew, G. Foster, S. Garvey, R. Guidry, T. Seaver, J. Rice . . . 8.50
7/22 Larry Bowa . . . 5.00
7/29 Jim Sundberg . . . 5.00
8/5 Terry Puhl . . . 5.00
8/12 Paul Molitor . . . 5.00
8/19 Jack Clark . . . 5.00
8/26 Davey Lopes . . . 5.00
9/2 Roger Staubach . . . 6.00
9/9 Joe Montana . . . 10.00
9/16 Carlton Fisk . . . 6.00
9/23 Dave Parker . . . 5.50
9/30 Rich Gossage . . . 5.00
10/7 Chuck Fusina . . . 5.00
10/14 Elvin Hayes . . . 5.00
10/21 Steve Garvey . . . 10.00
10/28 Ron Guidry . . . 10.00
11/4 Joe Theismann . . . 5.50
11/11 Billy Simms . . . 5.00
11/18 Jack Thompson . . . 5.00
11/25 Terry Bradshaw . . . 5.50
12/2 Mike Gminski . . . 5.00
12/9 Earl Campbell . . . 5.50
12/16 Steve Grogan . . . 5.00
12/23 Matt Bahr . . . 5.00
12/30 Jeff Rutledge . . . 5.00

1979

1/6 Ron Guidry . . . 5.00
1/13 Kelly Tripucka . . . 5.00
1/20 Walter Davis & Paul Westphal . . . 5.00
1/27 Franco Harris . . . 5.50
2/3 Moses Malone . . . 6.00
2/10 George Gervin . . . 5.00
2/17 Darrell Griffith . . . 5.00
2/24 John Drew . . . 5.00
3/3 Spring Training . . . 5.00
3/10 Lloyd Free & Randy Smith . . . 5.00
3/17 Larry Bird . . . 10.00
3/24 Phil Ford . . . 5.00
3/31 Magic Johnson . . . 17.00
4/7 G. Perry, Guidry, Madlock, Rice . . . 6.50
4/14 Bobby Dandridge . . . 5.00
4/21 Pete Rose . . . 6.50
4/28 Rod Carew . . . 6.00
5/5 Reggie Jackson . . . 7.00
5/12 Vida Blue . . . 5.00
5/19 Al Oliver . . . 5.00
5/26 J.R. Richard . . . 5.00
6/2 Mike Marshall . . . 5.00
6/9 Gary Carter . . . 5.00
6/16 Fred Lynn . . . 5.00
6/23 L. Brock, G. Hendrick, K. Hernandez, T. Simmons, G. Templeton . . . 5.50
6/30 Tommy John . . . 5.00
7/7 Roy Smalley . . . 5.00
7/14 Terry Bradshaw . . . 5.50
7/21 Brett, Lynn, Parker, Rose . 10.00
7/28 Joe Niekro . . . 5.00
8/4 Don Baylor . . . 8.00
8/11 Willie Stargell . . . 8.00
8/18 Mike Flanagan . . . 5.00
8/25 Dave Kingman & Mike Schmidt . . . 8.00
9/1 Walter Payton . . . 6.50
9/8 Mark Herrmann . . . 5.00
9/15 Carl Yastrzemski . . . 8.00
9/22 Lou Brock . . . 8.00
9/29 Tom Seaver . . . 6.00
10/6 Darrell Porter . . . 5.00
10/13 Dennis Johnson . . . 5.00
10/20 P. Rose, R. Jackson, J. Bench, R. Fingers, B. Dent . . . 8.00
10/27 Wilbert Montgomery . . . 10.00
11/3 Art Schlichter . . . 5.00
11/10 Paul McDonald . . . 5.00
11/17 Dan Fouts . . . 5.00
11/24 Lee Roy Selmon . . . 5.00
12/1 Gminski, D. Griffith, M. O'Koren . . . 5.00
12/8 Ottis Anderson . . . 5.00
12/15 John Stallworth . . . 5.00
12/22 Brian Sipe . . . 5.00
12/29 Pete Rose . . . 6.50

1980

1/5 Steadman Shealy . . . 5.00
1/12 Willie Stargell . . . 8.00
1/19 Kyle Macy . . . 5.00
1/26 J. Lambert & Jack Youngblood . . . 5.00
2/2 L. Swann & B. Cunningham . . . 5.50
2/9 Larry Bird . . . 10.00
2/16 Joe Barry Carroll . . . 5.00
2/23 Truck Robinson . . . 5.00
3/1 Mark Aguirre & Ray Meyer . . . 5.00
3/8 Keith Hernandez . . . 5.00
3/15 Magic Johnson . . . 15.00

3/22 Darrell Griffith 5.00
3/29 Joe Barry Carroll 5.00
4/5 Bobby Clarke & Guy Lafleur 5.00
4/12 Mike Flanagan & Dave Winfield 5.00
4/19 Nolan Ryan 10.00
4/26 George Brett 6.00
5/3 Billy Simms & Marc Wilson 5.00
5/10 Kent Tekulve 5.00
5/17 George Foster 5.00
5/24 Gorman Thomas 5.00
5/31 Ken Reitz & Champ Summers 5.00
6/7 Dave Kingman 5.00
6/14 Carlton Fisk 6.00
6/21 Steve Carlton 6.00
6/28 Reggie Smith 5.00
7/5 Billy Martin 6.00
7/12 Steve Garvey 5.50
7/19 Franco Harris 5.50
7/26 Jim Palmer & Earl Weaver 6.00
8/2 Reggie Jackson 6.50
8/9 Willie Wilson 5.00
8/16 Lee Mazzilli 5.00
8/23 Jim Bibby & Steve Stone 5.00
8/30 Andre Dawson & Ron LeFlore 5.00
9/6 Ken Stabler 5.00

The Sporting News: 1/7/78

9/13 Hugh Green & Major Oglivie 5.00
9/20 George Brett 6.00
9/27 Jose Cruz & Walter Payton 5.50
10/4 Pete Rose 10.00
10/11 K. Abdul-Jabbar & Magic 15.00
10/18 Ron Jaworski 5.00
10/25 D. Quisenberry & Mike Schmidt 10.00
11/1 Willie Mays Aikens 5.00
11/8 John Jefferson 8.00
11/15 Bear Bryant & Vince Ferragamo 5.00
11/22 Herschel Walker 5.50
11/29 Conrad Dobler 5.00
12/6 Albert King 5.00
12/13 Steve Bartkowski 5.00
12/20 Joe Cribbs & Billy Simms 5.00
12/27 Earl Campbell 5.50

1981

1/3 Bob Crable & Herschel Walker 5.50
1/10 George Brett 8.00
1/17 Tommy Kramer & Jerry Robinson 5.00
1/24 W. Montgomery & J. Plunkett 5.00
1/31 Bill Bergey & Ted Hendricks 5.00
2/7 Jim Plunkett 5.00
2/14 Steve Johnson & Ralph Sampson 5.00
2/21 NBA Headaches 5.00
2/28 M. Bossy, D. Potvin, B. Trottier 5.00
3/7 Rick Langford & Billy Martin 8.00
3/14 J.B. Carroll, L. Free, B. King 5.00
3/21 Mark Aguirre 5.00
3/28 Fred Lynn & Don Sutton 5.50
4/4 Jeff Lamp & Isiah Thomas 5.50
4/11 R. Yount, C. Cooper, B. Oglivie, T. Simmons, G. Thomas 10.00
4/18 Ty Cobb & Nap Lajoie 8.00
4/25 Bruce Sutter 5.00
5/2 Bum Phillips 5.00
5/9 Tony Armas & Matt Keough 9.00
5/16 C. Fisk, R. LeFlore, G. Luzinski 6.00
5/23 T. Raines & F. Valenzuela 8.50
5/30 B. Kuhn, M. Miller, R. Grebey 5.00
6/6 Gary Matthews 5.00
6/13 Ken Singleton 5.00
6/20 Stan Musial & Pete Rose 10.00
6/27 Baseball On Strike 7.00
7/4 David Graham 5.00
7/11 Tony Dorsett 5.50
7/18 C. Evert Lloyd & John McEnroe 5.50
7/25 Chuck Tanner 5.00
8/1 L. Taylor, H. Green, E.J. Junior 6.00
8/8 B. Gibson, J. Mize, R. Foster 6.00
8/15 Baseball's Back 6.00
8/22 Goose Gossage 5.00
8/29 T. Seaver, J. Bench, Concepcion 8.00
9/5 Anthony Carter 5.00
9/12 Kellen Winslow 5.00
9/19 Sugar Ray Leonard 7.00
9/26 David Woodley 5.00
10/3 Doug James & Tim Koegel 8.00
10/10 Nolan Cromwell 8.00
80/17 Ed Jones & Harvey Martin 8.50
10/24 L. Bennett, C. Knox, D. Vermiel 8.00
10/31 Dave Winfield 8.50
11/7 Larry Bird & Cedric Maxwell 8.00
11/14 Tommy Kramer 5.00
11/21 Fred Dean & Joe Montana 7.50
11/28 Dan Marino 6.00
12/5 D. Crum, J. Eaves, D. Smith 5.00
12/12 Ken Anderson 5.00
12/19 Marcus Allen 5.00
12/26 Mark Gastineau & Joe Klecko 5.00

1982

1/2 Herschel Walker 4.50
1/9 Wayne Gretzky 8.50
1/16 Dan Fouts & Doug Wilkerson 4.00
1/23 K. Anderson, P. Johnson, R. Lott 4.00
1/30 J. Montana, K. Anderson, J. Namath, D. Shula, J. Stallworth 6.50
2/6 Joe Montana & Eddie Edwards 6.00
2/13 Sam Perkins 4.00
2/20 Isiah Thomas 5.00
2/27 Moses Malone 4.50
3/6 Steve Garvey 4.50
3/13 Lafleur, Trottier, Smith, Bossy 4.50
3/20 Ralph Sampson 4.00
3/27 Garry Templeton, Ozzie Smith 4.50
4/3 Sam Perkins, Eric Floyd, Lynden Rose, Rodney McCray 4.00
4/10 Stargell, Rose, Yaz, Perry 7.50
4/17 D. Collins, G. Foster, K. Griffey 4.00
4/24 Al Oliver 4.00
4/26 Kenneth Sims, Ron Meyer 4.00
5/3 Rafael Ramirez 4.00
5/10 Eddie Murray 4.50
5/17 Keith Hernandez 4.00
5/24 Craig Stadler 4.00
5/31 LaMarr Hoyt, Keith Moreland 4.00
6/7 Gerry Cooney & Larry Holmes 4.50
6/14 Rickey Henderson 6.50
6/21 John McEnroe 4.00
6/28 Carl Yastrzemski 5.00
7/5 Gene Mauch 4.00
7/12 Gary Carter & Andre Dawson 4.50
7/19 Mike Ditka & Frank Kush 4.00
7/26 Earl Weaver 4.50
8/2 H. Aaron, F. Robinson, H. Chandler, T. Jackson Inducted into HOF 5.50
8/9 Cecil Cooper & Robin Yount 4.50
8/16 Vince Ferragamo & Bert Jones 4.00
8/23 Steve Sax & Reggie Jackson 5.50
8/30 Herschel Walker 4.00
9/6 Randy White, Rickey Henderson 5.00
9/13 Marcus Allen 4.00
9/20 Dale Murphy 4.50
9/27 John Elway 4.50
10/4 Todd Blackledge 4.00
10/11 Robin Yount, Don Sutton, others 4.50
10/18 Bruce Sutter & Cecil Cooper 4.00
10/25 Robin Yount 4.50
11/1 Moses Malone & Julius Erving 5.00
11/8 Pitt Football Team 4.00
11/15 Gerry Faust 4.00
11/22 Sugar Ray Leonard 5.00
11/29 Neil Lomax & Jim Stuckey 4.00
12/6 Terry Bradshaw 4.50
12/13 Herschel Walker 4.00
12/20 Ken Stabler 4.00
12/27 Bruce Hughes & James Brooks 4.00

1983

1/3 Whitey Herzog, Man of the Year 4.00
1/10 M. Moseley, Riggins, Theismann 4.50
1/17 Don Shula & Tom Landry 4.00
1/24 Riggins, J. Jacoby, F. McNeill 4.00
1/31 Manley, A.J. Duhe, B. Brudzinski 4.00
2/7 John Riggins & Ross Grimm 4.00

Date	Issue	Price
2/14	Wayman Tisdale	4.00
2/21	Wayne Gretzky & Pete Peeters	6.00
2/28	Cheeks, Moncreif, Jim Paxson	4.00
3/7	Billy Martin	4.50
3/14	Minniefield, Sundvold, S.Granger	4.00
3/21	Steve Garvey	4.00
3/28	Michael Jordan	12.00
4/4	Porter, O. Smith, L. Smith, Sutter	4.00
4/11	Carl Yastrzemski	4.50
4/18	Steve Kemp	4.00
4/25	John Elway	4.50
5/2	Reggie Jackson	5.50
5/9	Nolan Ryan	8.00
5/16	George Brett	5.00
5/23	Mike Marshall & Greg Brock	4.00
5/30	Moses Malone & K. Abdul-Jabbar	5.00
6/6	Steve Carlton	4.50
6/13	Dave Steib	4.00
6/20	Rod Carew	4.50
6/27	D.Evans, T.O'Malley, Hammaker	4.00
7/4	All-Time All-Stars	4.00
7/11	Fernando Valenzuela	4.00
7/18	Joe Theismann	4.00
7/25	Pete Rose	5.00
8/1	B. Robinson, G. Kell, Alston, Marichal Inducted Into HOF	4.50
8/8	Billy Martin, George Brett, Lee McPhail, Joe Brinkman	5.00
8/15	Franco Harris & Jack Lambert	4.00
8/22	Nancy Lopez & Ray Knight	4.00
8/29	Blair Keil	4.00
9/5	R. Todd, W. Walker, Lam Jones	4.00
9/12	Floyd Bannister	4.00
9/19	Walter Payton	5.00
9/26	Cecil Cooper & Andre Dawson	4.50
10/3	Danny White	4.00
10/10	B. Mazeroski, D. Larsen, C. Fisk, G. Alexander	5.00
10/17	Lyle Alzado & Ted Hendricks	4.00
10/24	Cal Ripken Jr. & Lenn Sakata	7.00
10/31	Ralph Sampson	4.00
11/7	Marvin Hagler	4.00
11/14	Eric Dickerson	4.00
11/21	Mike Rozier	4.00
11/28	Akeem Olajuwon	4.50
12/5	Dan Marino & Tony Nathan	4.50
12/12	Roy Green & Cal Ripken Jr.	6.00
12/19	Mike Rozier	4.00
12/26	John Riggins	4.00
	1984	
1/2	Bowie Kuhn	4.00
1/9	Dave Krieg, Doug Betters	4.00
1/16	Riggins, L. Pillars, W. Harper	4.00
1/23	Mark Aguirre	4.00
1/30	J. Hayes, D. Jensen, J. Squirek	4.00
2/6	1984 U.S. Olympic Hockey Team	5.00
2/13	UNC Basketball Team (Jordan, Perkins, Daugherty, etc.)	8.00
2/20	Larry Bird & Robert Parrish	5.00
2/27	Mike Rozier	4.00
3/5	Cal Ripken Jr.	5.50
3/12	Patrick Ewing	5.00
3/19	Trottier, B. Bourne, B. Smith	4.00
3/26	Michael Jordan	7.00
4/2	Pete Rose	5.00
4/9	Rich Gossage	4.00
4/16	Kareem Abdul-Jabbar	5.00
4/23	Wade Boggs	5.00
4/30	Bill Madlock	4.00
5/7	Phil Niekro & Jose Rijo	4.00
5/14	Dave Kingman	4.00
5/21	Darryl Strawberry	5.00
5/28	Parrish, Trammell, Lemon, Whitaker	4.00
6/4	USFL Cartoon	4.00
6/11	Mike Schmidt	5.00
6/18	Leon Durham	4.00
6/25	Eddie Murray	4.50
7/2	Rickey Henderson	5.00
7/9	1934 A.S. Game Anniversary (Hubbell, Ruth, Gehrig, Foxx, etc.)	5.00
7/16	Warren Moon	4.50
7/23	Tony Gwynn	4.50
7/30	Carl Lewis	4.00
8/6	Drysdale, Ferrell, Reese, Killebrew, Aparicio Inducted Into HOF	4.50
8/13	U.S. Women's 4 x 100 freestyle relay Olympic Team	4.00

The Sporting News: 2/25/78

Date	Issue	Price
8/20	Ryne Sandberg, Carl Lewis	5.00
8/27	University of Texas Longhorns	4.00
9/3	Ed Jones, Landry, D. White	4.00
9/10	Dickey, R. McMillan, G. Bracelin	4.00
9/17	Kirk Gibson & Willie Hernandez	4.00
9/24	Kirby Puckett	4.50
10/1	Walter Payton	4.50
10/8	Willie Mays	4.50
10/15	Steve Garvey & Alan Trammell	4.00
10/22	K. Gibson, Trammell, Whitaker	4.50
10/29	Michael Jordan	6.00
11/5	Dan Marino	4.50
11/12	Doug Flutie	4.00
11/19	Mark Gastineau	4.00
11/26	Wayman Tisdale & Robbie Bosco	4.00
12/3	Seahawks & Broncos	4.00
12/10	Eric Dickerson	4.00
12/17	Bill Walsh & Roger Craig	4.00
12/24	No Issue	
12/31	Peter Ueberroth	4.00
	1985	
1/7	W.Bennett, Stephenson, J.Toews	4.00
1/14	Mark Clayton	4.00
1/21	Joe Montana	5.50
1/28	Joe Montana & Wendell Tyler	5.00
2/4	Wayne Gretzky	5.50
2/11	R. Henderson, Steinbrenner, Berra, J. Torborg, others	4.50
2/18	Chris Mullin	4.50
2/25	Larry Bird & Derek Smith	4.50
3/4	Ryne Sandberg	4.50
3/11	Akeem Olajuwon & R. Sampson	4.50
3/18	Carpenter, Langway, Christian	4.00
3/25	Bruce Sutter	4.00
4/1	Patrick Ewing	4.50
4/8	D. Mattingly & Rickey Henderson	5.00
4/15	S. Anderson, A. Trammell, K. Gibson, W. Hernandez, J. Morris	4.50
4/22	LaMarr Hoyt & Dale Murphy	4.00
4/29	Dale Murphy	4.00
5/6	James Worthy & Magic Johnson	5.50
5/13	T. Armas, J. Rice, M. Easler, D. Evans, W. Boggs	4.50
5/20	Billy Martin	4.50
5/27	Terry Whitfield	4.00
6/3	Kelly, Bryant, Walker, Anderson	4.50
6/10	Schuerholz, Brett, W. Wilson, Quisenberry	4.00
6/17	Joaquin Andujar	4.00
6/24	J. Clark, D. Green, D. LaPoint	4.00
7/1	Dale Murphy & Eddie Murray	4.50
7/8	Vince Coleman	4.00
7/15	Bill Caudill & Gary Lavelle	4.00
7/22	Foot kicking a football	4.00
7/29	D. Gooden & '85 HOF Inductees	4.50
8/5	Namath, Simpson, Staubach	5.50
8/12	Tom Seaver	5.00
8/19	Peter Ueberroth	4.00
8/26	Bo Jackson	5.00
9/2	Curt Warner	4.00
9/9	Three Rivers Stadium	4.00
9/16	Pete Rose	5.00
9/23	Neil Lomax	4.00
9/30	Mets and Yankees	4.00
10/7	Pedro Guerrero	4.00
10/14	Tudor, T. Nieto, M. Jorgenson	4.00
10/21	Julius Erving & K. Abdul-Jabbar	5.00
10/28	Jim McMahon	4.00
11/4	Bret Saberhagen	4.00
11/11	Chuck Long	4.00
11/18	N. Cromwell, L. Irvin, J. Johnson, G. Green	4.00
11/25	Gerry Faust	4.00
12/2	L. Taylor & F. McNeil	4.50
12/9	Kirk Gibson	4.00
12/16	Payton, Craig, Allen, Wilder	4.50
12/23	Oklahoma, Penn St., Iowa, & Miami helmets	4.00
	1986	
1/6	Pete Rose, Man of the Year	4.50
1/13	Dan Marino, NFL Playoffs	4.00
1/20	Richard Dent, Super Bowl Preview	3.50
1/27	Akeem Olajuwon	3.50
2/3	Dan Hampton, "Super Bears"	3.50
2/10	Ken Harrelson	3.50
2/17	Candlestick Park	3.50

2/24 K. Smith, D. Ferrell, J. Dawkins, T. Landry, C. Barkley 3.50
3/3 G. Brett, J. Clark, R. Henderson 4.00
3/10 Bol, Webb, Flutie, H. Walker 3.50
3/17 R. Jackson, F. Zoeller, D. Manning, K. Walker 3.50
3/24 Dave Parker & Darryl Strawberry 4.00
3/31 Larry Bird & Magic Johnson 6.00
4/7 Ozzie Smith, Joe Montana . 4.00
4/14 Gretzky, Kurri, Coffey, Anderson 4.00
4/21 Jose Canseco, Will Clark, Pete Incaviglia, Andres Galarraga 5.00
4/28 Dick Williams & LaMarr Hoyt 3.50
5/5 Bill Walton 3.50
5/12 R. Jackson, D. Sutton, B. Boone 3.50
5/19 Phil Niekro 3.50
5/26 N. Ryan, P. Rose, S. Carlton 6.00
6/2 Robin Yount 3.50
6/9 D. Gooden & K. Hernandez 4.00
6/16 Bill Walton 3.50
6/23 Ray Floyd 3.50
6/30 Len Bias 4.00
7/14 Wade Boggs 4.00
7/21 Dieter Brock 3.50
7/28 C. Snyder, B. Witt, S. Bankhead, W. Clark, O. McDowell ... 4.00
8/4 Bill Bradley & Jack Kemp 3.50
8/11 Pete Rozelle & Frank Rothman 3.50
8/18 Jose Canseco 4.00
8/25 Earl Weaver 3.50
9/1 Don Mattingly 4.00
9/8 Jay Schroeder 3.50
9/15 Herschel Walker 3.50
9/22 Lou Holtz 3.50
9/29 Roger Clemens & Gary Carter 4.00
10/6 Patrick Roy, Vinny Testaverde 3.50
10/13 Glenn Davis, Keith Hernandez, Doug DeCinces, Jim Rice . 3.50
10/20 J. Elway, P. Rozelle 3.50
10/27 Schmidt, Dykstra, A. Ashby. 4.00
11/3 Marty Barrett & Gary Carter 3.50
11/10 Jim McMahon 3.50
11/17 Lawrence Taylor 4.00
11/24 Eric Dickerson 3.50
12/1 Vinny Testaverde 3.50
12/8 Joe Montana 4.50
12/15 Jerry Rice 4.50
12/22 Bernie Kosar 3.50
12/29 No issue

1987

1/5 Larry Bird, Man of the Year 4.50
1/12 Penn St. Number One 3.50
1/19 Jim Burt, Leonard Marshall 3.50
1/26 John Elway 3.50
2/2 Phil McConkey 3.50
2/9 L.A. Clippers, Mike Tyson . 6.00
2/16 Bobby Knight 3.50
2/23 David Robinson 6.50
3/2 Dwight Gooden 4.00
3/9 Steve Alford 3.50
3/16 Tito Horford & J.R. Reid .. 3.50
3/23 Julius Erving & Michael Jordan 6.00
3/30 Mike Schmidt 4.00
4/6 Reggie Jackson 4.00
4/13 Ron Guidry 3.50
4/20 Larry Mize 3.50
4/27 Magic Johnson 4.50
5/4 What's Wrong w/ College Sports? 3.50
5/11 Andre Dawson 3.75
5/18 Pete Rose 4.00
5/25 Bret Saberhagen 3.50
6/1 R. Henderson & C. Hudson 4.00
6/8 Jack Clark 3.50
6/15 Eric Davis 3.75
6/22 Kareem Abdul-Jabbar 4.00
6/29 Scott Simpson 3.50
7/6 Harold Baines & Jody Davis 3.50
7/13 Jack Morris & Alan Trammell 3.75
7/20 New Look For NFL? 3.50
7/27 Bert Blyleven & Jeff Reardon 3.50
8/3 Whitey Herzog 3.50
8/10 R. Henderson, L. Durham, Strawberry, Guidry, G. Pettis, V. Coleman 4.00
8/17 J. McMahon, R. Reuschel, L. Dawson, J. Greene 3.50
8/24 Greg Louganis, Cal Ripken Sr. 3.50
8/31 J. Clark, E. Davis, A. Dawson, G. Bell, M. McGwire, D. Mattingly 4.00
9/7 Will Clark 4.00
9/14 Jamelle Holieway 3.50
9/21 B. Bosworth & V. Testaverde 3.50
9/28 Baltimore: Life After Football 3.50
10/5 Alan Trammell & George Bell 3.50
10/12 Wayne Gretzky, Muhammed Ali 4.50
10/19 Mets & Red Sox 3.50
10/26 Willie McGee & Greg Gagne 3.50
11/2 Kirby Puckett & Kent Hrbek 4.00
11/9 Danny White & Gaston Green 3.50
11/16 Athletes & Agents 3.50
11/23 Payton, O.Newsome, D.Sanders 4.00
11/30 Emmitt Smith, others 4.50
12/7 Bo Jackson, Pat LaFontaine 4.50
12/14 Tim Brown, George Bell, M. Bol 3.50
12/21 Hebert, Ueberroth, T. Richmond 3.50
12/28 No Issue

1988

1/4 Jerry Rice 4.00
1/11 Jimmy Johnson 3.50
1/18 D. Williams, J. Bostic, W. Perry 3.50
1/25 Doug Williams & John Elway 3.50
2/1 Mets & Yankees hats 3.50
2/8 Doug Williams, Rulon Jones, Raleigh McKenzie 3.50
2/15 Ron Hextall 3.50
2/22 Charles Barkley & Magic 4.00
2/29 J.R. Reid & Danny Ferry .. 3.50
3/7 Kirk Gibson & Tommy Lasorda 3.75
3/14 Paul Coffey & Mario Lemieux 4.00
3/21 Danny Ainge 3.50
3/28 Hersey Hawkins 3.50
4/4 B. Horner, L. Mize, Stacey King 3.50
4/11 Hrbek, Larry Brown, W. Garland 3.50
4/18 Sandy Lyle 3.50
4/25 P. Riley, F. Robinson, E. Murray 3.50
5/2 Billy Martin & Dave Winfield 4.00
5/9 Roger Clemens 4.00
5/16 Canseco, McGwire, Parker 4.50
5/23 Larry Bird & Dennis Johnson 4.00
5/30 Wrigley Field 3.50
6/6 N. Ryan, D. Gooden, D. Robinson 6.50
6/13 Michael Spinks 3.50
6/20 Greg Maddux & Mark Grace 3.50
6/27 Curtis Strange & Nick Faldo 3.50
7/4 B. Martin, Galarraga, Magic 4.00
7/11 Baseball Cards, Andy Van Slyke, Danny Manning 3.50
7/18 Tony Dorsett 3.50
7/25 G. Brett, C. Sabo, T. Steinbach 3.50
8/1 Frank Viola 3.50
8/8 Darryl Strawberry 4.00
8/15 Darryl Stingley, Joe Morgan 3.50
8/22 Alan Trammell 3.50
8/29 Joe Montana 4.50
9/5 Kirby Puckett, D. Rasmussen 3.75
9/12 B. Beathard, J. Cooke, J.Gibbs 3.50
9/19 Cornelius Bennett 3.50
9/26 Michael Irvin 3.50
10/3 Matt Biondi & Janet Evans 3.50
10/10 F. Griffith-Joyner, J. Joyner-Kersee, C. Lewis, B. Johnson 3.50
10/17 Wade Boggs, Jose Canseco, Darryl Strawberry, Kirk Gibson 4.50
10/24 Kirk Gibson & Orel Hershiser 4.00
10/31 Orel Hershiser 4.00
11/7 Larry Bird & Magic Johnson 4.50
11/14 Vinny Testaverde, Dick Shultz, Broderick Thomas 3.50
11/21 Boomer Esiason 3.50
11/28 L. Holtz, T. Landry, C. Noll . 3.50
12/5 Notre Dame Football Team 3.50
12/12 Neil Lomax & J.T. Smith .. 3.50
12/19 Barry Sanders 4.50
12/26 No Issue

1989

1/2 Jackie Joyner-Kersee 3.50
1/9 Neal Anderson 3.50
1/16 Joe Montana & Boomer Esiason 4.00
1/23 Yaz & Bench 4.50
1/30 Jerry Rice & David Fulcher 3.50
2/6 Wayne Gretzky 4.00
2/13 Nick Anderson, Marcus Allen, Karl Malone 3.50
2/20 Chris Jackson, Wayne Gretzky 4.00
2/27 Danny Ferry, Sean Elliott, Pervis Ellison, Stacey King 3.50
3/6 B. Valentine, A. Van Slyke, P. Molitor, E. Murray 3.50
3/13 Stacey King 3.50
3/20 C. Barkley & Michael Jordan 4.50
3/27 Chris Mullin & Stacey King 3.50
4/3 J. Clark, B. Hurst, J. McKeon 3.50

4/10 Ken Griffey Jr. & Ken Griffey Sr. 6.50
4/17 Nick Faldo, Troy Aikman .. 4.00
4/24 P. Rose, T. Cummings, E. Burks 4.00
5/1 Kareem Abdul-Jabbar, Greg Jefferies, Barry Sanders 4.50
5/8 Kevin Mitchell 3.75
5/15 Brady Anderson & Cal Ripken 3.75
5/22 Tommy John, Jose DeLeon 3.50

The Sporting News: 2/20/89

5/29 Isiah Thomas & Dennis Rodman 3.50
6/5 Ernie Whitt & Fred McGriff 3.50
6/12 Schmidt, Blyleven, Deion Sanders 4.00
6/19 Baseball Hall of Fame 3.50
6/26 J. Salley, A.C. Green, J. Edwards 3.50
7/3 Don Zimmer, Neil Lomax, Barry Switzer, John Franco 3.50
7/10 Pervis Ellison, David Stern . 3.50
7/17 Bill Walsh 3.50
7/24 O. Hershiser & Howard Johnson 4.00
7/31 R. Palmeiro, R. Sierra, J. Franco 4.00
8/7 Lonnie Smith & Tom Watson 3.50
8/14 Kevin Mitchell & Will Clark 4.00
8/21 Nolan Ryan 5.00
8/28 Mike Scott, Lou Holtz, J. Oquendo 3.50
9/4 Pete Rose 3.75
9/11 Carl Peterson, Marty Schottenheimer, Bo Schembechler 3.50
9/18 Wade Boggs & Tony Gwynn 4.00
9/25 Notre Dame vs. Michigan .. 3.50
10/2 Gregg Olson, Krumrie, McMahon 3.50
10/9 Reggie White, Randall Cunningham, Mario Lemieux 4.00
10/16 Kevin Mitchell, Ryne Sandberg, Mark McGwire, Fred McGriff 4.00
10/23 Terry Kennedy & Terry Steinbach 3.50
10/30 San Francisco Earthquake 4.00
11/6 Oakland Athletics 3.50
11/13 Phil Simms, Emmitt Smith 4.00
11/20 Bill McCartney 3.50
11/27 Sugar Ray Leonard 3.50
12/4 Duran, Marinovich, D. Dawkins 3.50
12/11 Kevin Mitchell 3.50
12/18 Steve Largent 3.50
12/25 No Issue

1990

1/1 Joe Montana 4.00
1/8 Joe Carter, Mark Langston, Mark Davis, Dave Parker .. 3.50
1/15 B. Sanders, P. Simms, P. Ewing 4.00
1/22 Joe Montana & John Elway 4.00
1/29 M. Schmidt, Player of the Decade 4.00
2/5 Joe Montana 4.00
2/12 Paul Tagliabue & Fay Vincent 3.50
2/19 Brett Hull & Alonzo Mourning 3.75
2/26 Chris Jackson, Isiah Thomas 3.50
3/5 Baseball Lockout 3.50
3/12 Pete Rose, Dwight Gooden 3.75
3/19 Jackie Jones, John McVay 3.50
3/26 Charles Barkley, Dennis Scott 3.75
4/2 Alaa Abdelnaby 3.50
4/9 Jack McKeon, Darryl Strawberry 3.50
4/16 Nick Faldo, Blair Thomas 3.50
4/23 David Robinson 4.50
4/30 G. Davis, K. Puckett, K. Hrbek 3.50
5/7 Piniella, P. O'Neill, B. Larkin, C. Sabo, E. Davis 3.50
5/14 Magic Johnson, Mark Jackson 3.75
5/21 Will Clark & Jose Canseco 4.00
5/28 Michael Jordan 4.00
6/4 Mike Tyson, Cecil Fielder 4.00
6/11 Viola, M. Schooler, M. Williams 3.50
6/18 Len Dykstra 3.50
6/25 Bill Laimbeer, Nolan Ryan 4.00
7/2 Charlie Fox, Barry Bonds 3.50
7/9 B. Saberhagen & D. Gooden 3.50
7/16 Mouse Davis, Lyle Alzado 3.50
7/23 Bert Blyleven & Don Drysdale 3.50
7/30 Dave Parker, Mark Davis, Neal Heaton, David Wells 3.50
8/6 Strawberry, Tapani, Gant 3.75
8/13 George Steinbrenner, Nolan Ryan 4.00
8/20 Comiskey Park, Hurst, Mattingly 3.50
8/27 John Elway, Bob Welch ... 3.50
9/3 Roger Craig (FB), Ramon Martinez, Jeff Ballard 3.50
9/10 Jose Canseco & Barry Larkin 4.00
9/17 Jeff George 3.75
9/24 George Williams, R. Henderson 3.50
10/1 Welch, McGwire, Canseco, McGee, Baines, Weiss, Lansford 3.50
10/8 Buster Douglas 3.75
10/15 Andy Van Slyke & Chris Sabo 3.50
10/22 Dennis Eckersley 3.50
10/29 Lou Piniella & Rob Dibble 3.50
11/5 E. Holyfield & B. Douglas 4.00
11/12 George Welsh, Warren Moon 3.50
11/19 Orland Woolridge, Paul Westhead 3.50
11/26 Esa Tikkanen & Wayne Gretzky 4.00
12/3 Lawrence Taylor & Joe Montana 4.00
12/10 Clyde Drexler, Boomer Esiason 3.50
12/17 Fred McGriff & Joe Carter 3.50
12/24 Bobby Knight, Norm Ellenberger, Pete Peeters, Jerry Rice 3.50
12/31 Baseball glove full of money 3.50

1991

1/7 Nolan Ryan, Lawrence Tisch 3.50
1/14 George Ackles, Ed Belfour 3.00
1/21 Brett Hull, J. Williams, B. Ryan 3.00
1/28 Darryl Talley, Scott Radecic 3.00
2/4 E. Walls, P. Williams, J. Lofton 3.00
2/11 Magic Johnson, K. Johnson 3.50
2/18 Rick Pitino, Sam Perkins .. 3.00
2/25 Bernard King, L. Robinson 3.00
3/4 Dave Parker, M. Jordan, Pippen 3.50
3/11 Jim Palmer, Doc Rivers, Gretzky 3.00
3/18 Expansion Big Bang 3.00
3/25 Richmond basketball players 3.00
4/1 Bruce Froemming 3.00
4/8 Christian Laettner, Johanning 3.00
4/15 Evander Holyfield 3.50
4/22 Scott Sanderson, George Bell, Rickey Henderson, Jack Clark 3.00
4/29 Portland Trailblazers 3.00
5/6 Rod Brind'amour, Casey, Jordan 3.00
5/13 Strike/gold, N. Ryan, Henderson 3.50
5/20 Rob Dibble 3.00
5/27 Dave Justice, A.J. Foyt ... 3.00
6/3 Rick Mears, Mario Lemieux 3.50
6/10 Michael Jordan, Magic Johnson 4.00
6/17 Andre Dawson 3.00
6/24 Denver, Miami, M. Jordan 3.50
7/1 Gambling in Baseball 3.00
7/8 T. Van Poppel, Hundley, Lankford 3.00
7/15 Ronnie Lott, Roger Craig .. 3.00
7/22 Michael Jordan 3.50
7/29 Peter Ueberroth 3.00
8/5 Tiger Stadium 3.00
8/12 Batting Orders, Dennis Martinez 3.00
8/19 Wounded baseball, H. Walker 3.00
8/26 David Klingler, Pedro Guerrero 3.00
9/2 Jim Kelly, Robert Bailey ... 3.00
9/9 Bobby Cox,

Date	Cover	Value
	Randall Cunningham	3.00
9/16	Don Shula, Bobby Bonilla	3.00
9/23	Jackie Sherrill, Terry Pendleton	3.00
9/30	J. Carter, W. Gretzky, R. Ismail	3.00
10/7	Howard Dinkins, Sam Mills	3.00
10/14	John Smoltz, Cale Gundy	3.00
10/21	Kirby Puckett, Jim Mora	3.00
10/28	Jeff Hostetler, Ray Handley	3.00
11/4	Jack Morris, Ty Detmer, Drexler	3.00
11/11	Bommer Esiason, Bobby Bonilla	3.00
11/18	Magic Johnson	3.50
11/25	Darryl Spencer, Kindred	3.00
12/2	M. Guyton, P. Johnson, Rathman	3.00
12/9	Derrick Thomas, Kevin Loughery	3.00
12/16	Coll. Athlete Criminals, Bonilla	3.00
12/23	Steve Palermo, Whitey Herzog, Gino Torretta, Steve Emtman	3.00
12/30	Mark Rypien, Guy Carbonneau	3.00
	1992	
1/6	Michael Jordan	3.00
1/13	John Elway, Tim Hardaway	2.50
1/20	Jeff Wright, B. Smith, R. Hextall	2.50
1/27	Kenny Smith, Thurman Thomas	2.50
2/3	B. Edwards, A. Reed, A. Mogilny	2.50
2/10	Jerry Tarkanian	2.50
2/17	M. Jordan, Gretzky, Mourning	2.50
2/24	Charles Barkley (image)	2.50
3/2	Tom Glavine, Sam Wyche	2.50
3/9	Christian Laettner, K. Puckett	2.50
3/16	Dennis Rodman, George Brett	2.50
3/23	Mark Messier, Shaquille O'Neal	3.50
3/30	Jim Jackson, Cal Ripken	2.50
4/6	Ron Dibble, Joe Carker	2.50
4/13	Laettner, Jose Canseco	2.50
4/20	Oriole Park at Camden Yards	2.50
4/27	Scottie Pippen, Butch Hobson	2.50
5/4	Barry Bonds, Steve Emtman	2.50
5/11	Tony Gwynn, John Bagley	2.50
5/18	Clyde Drexler, Craig Biggio	2.50
5/25	Lenny Harris, Chris Miller	2.50
6/1	Terry Porter, Todd Hundley	2.50
6/8	Jeff Reardon, Scottie Pippen	2.50
6/15	Michael Jordan, Gary Scheffield	3.00
6/22	David Cone, Chicago Bulls	2.50
6/29	W. Randolph, Durocher, Rypien	2.50
7/6	Norm Charlton, Dibble, O'Neal	2.50
7/13	Eric Dickerson	2.50
7/20	Carlton Fisk, Barkley, Ewing	2.50
7/27	Robin Yount, Jeff George	2.50
8/3	El Beisbol se poncha, John Daly	2.50
8/10	Pablo Morales, Jackie Autry	2.50
8/17	Quincy Watts	2.50
8/24	Bill Walsh	2.50
8/31	John Smoltz, Larry Bird	3.00
9/7	Randall Cunningham, John Wetteland	2.50
9/14	Minnesota Vikings, Joe Carter	2.50
9/21	Fay Vincent, Paul Tagliabue	2.50
9/28	Jay Bell, Darrin Fletcher, Krieg	2.50
10/5	T. Thomas, Lindros, Glavine	2.50
10/12	Dennis Eckersley, Bill Cowher	2.50
10/19	Don Majkowski, Steve Avery	2.50
10/26	Ed Sprague, Dan Marino	2.50
11/2	J. Carter, O. Nixon, B. McCartney	2.50
11/9	Robert Parish, Frank Broyles	2.50
11/16	Gino Torretta, Jimmy Johnson	2.50
11/23	Football helmet, Mark McGwire	2.50
11/30	Jamal Mashburn, Elvis Grbac	2.50
12/7	Bill Bidwill, Dennis Rodman	2.50
12/14	Mike Singetary, Dick Butkus	2.50
12/21	Paul Tagliabue	2.50
12/28	Mike Krzyzewski	2.50

Sport Magazine: March, 1980

SPORT

Date	Cover	Value
Sep. 46	Joe DiMaggio	450.00
Oct. 46	Glen Davis & Doc Blanchard	75.00
Nov. 46	College Football	75.00
Dec. 46	Tom Harmon	75.00
Jan. 47	Andy Phillips	18.00
Feb. 47	Bentley Brothers	18.00
Mar. 47	Alex Groza	18.00
Apr. 47	Leo Durocher	22.50
May 47	Horse Racing	18.00
June 47	Bob Feller	25.00
July 47	E. Dyer & Joe Cronin	20.00
Aug. 47	Ted Williams	45.00
Sep. 47	Vince & Joe DiMaggio	75.00
Oct. 47	Harry Gilmer	18.00
Nov. 47	Johnny Lujack	20.00
Dec. 47	Charlie Trippi	20.00
Jan. 48	Ralph Beard	14.00
Feb. 48	Frank Brimsek	14.00
Mar. 48	George Kaftan	14.00
Apr. 48	Ted Williams	40.00
May 48	Babe Ruth	45.00
June 48	Joe Louis	22.00
July 48	Ewell Blackwell	20.00
Aug. 48	Stan Musial	35.00
Sep. 48	Joe DiMaggio & Ted Williams	60.00
Oct. 48	Lou Gehrig	45.00
Nov. 48	Doak Walker	20.00
Dec. 48	Johnny Lujack	20.00
Jan. 49	Ed Macavky	15.00
Feb. 49	Lou Boudreau	20.00
Mar. 49	R. Beard	15.00
Apr. 49	Bob Feller	25.00
May 49	Enos Slaughter	25.00
June 49	Hal Newhouser	25.00
July 49	Lou Boudreau & Joe Gordon	25.00
Aug. 49	Jackie Robinson	35.00
Sep. 49	Joe DiMaggio	55.00
Oct. 49	Christy Mathewson	22.00
Nov. 49	Charlie Justice	15.00
Dec. 49	Johnny Lujack & Sid Luckman	20.00
Dec. 49	Sport Annual	15.00
Jan. 50	University of San Francisco	15.00
Feb. 50	Tommy Henrich	16.00
Mar. 50	George Mikan	20.00
Apr. 50	Casey Stengel	25.00
May 50	Ralph Kiner	30.00
June 50	Bob Lemon	25.00
July 50	Stan Musial	30.00
Aug. 50	Art Houteman	15.00
Sep. 50	Don Newcombe	20.00
Oct. 50	World Series	25.00
Nov. 50	Harry Agganis	15.00
Dec. 50	Football	15.00
Dec. 50	Sport Annual	25.00
Jan. 51	Basketball	12.00
Feb. 51	Nat Holman	12.00
Mar. 51	Sports Special	12.00
Apr. 51	Baseball	25.00
May 51	Baseball Jubilee	25.00
June 51	Sugar Ray Robinson	25.00
July 51	Ewell Blackwell	14.00
Aug. 51	Yogi Berra	25.00
Sep. 51	Ted Williams	35.00
Oct. 51	Jackie Robinson	35.00
Nov. 51	B. McColl	12.00
Dec. 51	Johnny Lujack	12.00
Jan. 52	No Issue Published	
Feb. 52	Sugar Ray Robinson	15.00
Mar. 52	Gil McDougald	15.00
Apr. 52	Chico Carrasquel	10.00
May 52	Alvin Dark	15.00
June 52	Ralph Kiner	16.00
July 52	Stan Musial	25.00
Aug. 52	Allie Reynolds	12.00
Sep. 52	Mike Garcia	12.00
Oct. 52	J. Robinson & Pee Wee Reese	35.00
Nov. 52	Jackie Robinson	14.00
Dec. 52	J. Olszewski	10.00
Jan. 53	Rocky Marciano	20.00
Feb. 53	Bobby Shantz	10.00
Mar. 53	Bob Cousy	17.50
Apr. 53	Mickey Mantle	40.00
May 53	Bob Lemon	14.00
June 53	Hank Sauer	12.00
July 53	Ferris Fain	10.00
Aug. 53	Warren Spahn	15.00
Sep. 53	Robin Roberts	12.00
Oct. 53	Roy Campanella	18.00
Nov. 53	Phil Rizzuto	14.00
Dec. 53	Michigan Football	10.00
Jan. 54	Eddie LeBaron	12.00
Feb. 54	Eddie Matthews	15.00
Mar. 54	Casey Stengel	20.00
Apr. 54	Don Newcombe	10.00
May 54	Ted Kluzewski	12.50

Issue	Cover	Price
June 54	Rocky Marciano	18.00
July 54	Stan Musial	22.50
Aug. 54	Minnie Minoso	14.00
Sep. 54	Duke Snider	18.00
Oct. 54	Al Rosen	14.00
Nov. 54	L. Morris	10.00
Dec. 54	Army Football	12.00
Jan. 55	Pete Pihos	12.00
Feb. 55	Alvin Dark	14.00
Mar. 55	Rocky Marciano	15.00
Apr. 55	Bob Turley	14.00
May 55	Bobby Thompson	12.00
June 55	Johnny Antonelli	10.00
July 55	Ned Garver	10.00
Aug. 55	Paul Richards	12.00
Sep. 55	Duke Snider	15.00
Oct. 55	Yogi Berra	20.00
Nov. 55	E. Eredelatz	10.00
Dec. 55	Hugh McElhenny	10.00
Jan. 56	Doak Walker	10.00
Feb. 56	Sihugo Green	8.00
Mar. 56	Walt Alston	14.00
Apr. 56	Larry Doby	12.00
May 56	Bob Lemon	14.00
June 56	Willie Mays	25.00
July 56	Ted Williams	25.00
Aug. 56	Vinegar Bend Mizell	8.00
Sep. 56	Anniversary Issue	18.00
Oct. 56	Mickey Mantle	30.00
Nov. 56	Paul Hornung	15.00
Dec. 56	B. Morrow	8.00
Jan. 57	Wilt Chamberlain	13.00
Feb. 57	Jacques Plante	12.00

Sport Magazine: January, 1958

Issue	Cover	Price
Mar. 57	Mickey Mantle	30.00
Apr. 57	Eddie Matthews	12.00
May 57	Roy Campanella	12.00
June 57	Early Wynn	10.00
July 57	Al Kaline	15.00
Aug. 57	Joe Adcock	8.00
Sep. 57	Duke Snider	15.00
Oct. 57	Billy Pierce	10.00
Nov. 57	D. Stephenson	8.00
Dec. 57	Chicago Bears	8.00
Jan. 58	Baseball Stars	8.00
Feb. 58	Carmen Basilio	8.00
Mar. 58	Lew Burdette	10.00
Apr. 58	Nellie Fox	12.00
May 58	Yogi Berra	15.00
June 58	Willie Mays	10.00
July 58	Herb Score	10.00
Aug. 58	Billy Martin	12.00
Sep. 58	Eddie Matthews	14.00
Oct. 58	Bob Turley	12.00
Nov. 58	B. Anderson	9.00
Dec. 58	Johnny Unitas	12.50
Jan. 59	Maurice "Rocket" Richard	12.50
Feb. 59	Lew Burdette & R. Johnson	10.00
Mar. 59	Al Kaline	15.00
Apr. 59	Rocky Colavito	12.00
May 59	Hank Bauer & Gil Hodges	10.00
June 59	Mickey Mantle & Ted Williams	30.00
July 59	D. Newcombe & J. Piersall	12.00
Aug. 59	Mickey Mantle	25.00
Sep. 59	Ted Wiliams & Stan Musial	25.00
Oct. 59	Warren Spahn	12.00
Nov. 59	Coach Dietzel of LSU	9.00
Dec. 59	Johnny Unitas	11.00
Jan. 60	Bob Cousy	10.00
Feb. 60	Ingemar Johansson	9.00
Mar. 60	Jackie Robinson & Willie Mays	15.00
Apr. 60	Duke Snider	12.00
May 60	W. McCovey & H. Killebrew	14.00
June 60	Don Drysdale	12.00
July 60	Frank Howard & Luis Aparicio	10.00
Aug. 60	Mickey Mantle	22.50
Sep. 60	Rocky Colavito	8.00
Oct. 60	Babe Ruth	10.00
Nov. 60	Roger Maris	15.00
Dec. 60	Johnny Unitas	10.00
Jan. 61	Bobby Layne	10.00
Feb. 61	Danny Murtaugh	8.00
Mar. 61	Oscar Robertson	15.00
Apr. 61	Frank Howard	10.00
May 61	Dick Groat	8.00
June 61	Willie Mays	15.00
July 61	Rocky Colavito	8.00
Aug. 61	Warren Spahn	10.00
Sep. 61	Joe DiMaggio & Mickey Mantle	30.00
Oct. 61	N. Moon	8.00
Nov. 61	Paul Hornung	10.00
Dec. 61	Sam Huff	9.00
Jan. 62	Jim Brown	12.50
Feb. 62	Roger Maris	15.00
Mar. 62	Wilt Chamberlain	12.50
Apr. 62	Norm Cash & Vada Pinson	8.00
May 62	Baseball Sluggers	10.00
June 62	Hank Aaron	14.00
July 62	Mickey Mantle	22.00
Aug. 62	Rocky Colavito & Harvey Kuenn	10.00
Sep. 62	Ken Boyer & Stan Musial	14.00
Oct. 62	Willie Mays	14.00
Nov. 62	Tommy Davis & Jim Taylor	8.00
Dec. 62	Johnny Unitas & Jim Brown	10.00
Jan. 63	Paul Hornung	8.50
Feb. 63	Maury Wills	7.50
Mar. 63	Bob Cousy	9.00
Apr. 63	Wilt Chamberlain	10.00
May 63	Mickey Mantle & Yogi Berra	25.00
June 63	Maury Wills	8.00
July 63	Rocky Colavito & Al Kaline	10.00
Aug. 63	Willie Mays	14.00
Sep. 63	Sandy Koufax	12.00
Oct. 63	Mickey Mantle	18.00
Nov. 63	Whitey Ford	15.00
Dec. 63	Del Shafner	7.50
Dec. 63	Sport Annual	10.00
Jan. 64	Jim Taylor	8.00
Feb. 64	Sandy Koufax	12.00
Mar. 64	Cassius Clay	11.00
Apr. 64	Oscar Robertson	9.00
May 64	Warren Spahn	10.00
June 64	Dick Stuart	9.00
July 64	Carl Yastrzemski	15.00
Aug. 64	Joe DiMaggio & Willie Mays	25.00
Sep. 64	Mickey Mantle	14.00
Oct. 64	Willie Mays	12.00
Nov. 64	Harmon Killebrew	11.00

Sport Magazine: September, 1961

Issue	Cover	Price
Dec. 64	Jim Brown	9.00
Jan. 65	Johnny Unitas	9.00
Feb. 65	Fred Hutchinson	7.50
Mar. 65	Jerry West	9.00
Apr. 65	Dean Chance	8.00
May 65	Sandy Koufax	11.00
June 65	Willie Mays	12.50
July 65	Johnny Callison	7.50
Aug. 65	Mickey Mantle	15.00
Sep. 65	Lou Gehrig	15.00
Oct. 65	Sandy Koufax & Maury Wills	11.00
Nov. 65	Johnny Unitas & 'T. Mason	8.00
Dec. 65	F. Tarkenton & S. Jurgenson	9.00
Jan. 66	Charley Johnson	5.00
Feb. 66	Sandy Koufax	15.00
Mar. 66	Bill Russell	9.00
Apr. 66	Willie Mays & Paul Hornung	11.00
May 66	Maury Wills	7.50
June 66	Joe Namath	10.00
July 66	Mickey Mantle	15.50
Aug. 66	Frank Robinson	9.00
Sep. 66	Willie Mays	11.00
Oct. 66	Sandy Koufax	10.00
Nov. 66	John Brodie	7.50
Dec. 66	Gale Sayers	10.00
Jan. 67	Don Meredith	8.00
Feb. 67	Frank Robinson	8.50
Mar. 67	Wilt Chamberlain	9.00
Apr. 67	Lew Alcindor	11.00
May 67	Mickey Mantle	15.00
June 67	Willie Mays	12.50
July 67	Dick Allen & J. Ryan	8.00
Aug. 67	Roberto Clemente	17.50
Sep. 67	Pete Rose	17.50
Oct. 67	Orlando Cepeda & Johnny Unitas	8.00
Nov. 67	Joe Namath	9.50
Dec. 67	Bart Starr	9.00
Jan. 68	Mike Garrett	5.00
Feb. 68	Carl Yastrzemski	10.00
Mar. 68	Lew Alcindor	9.00
Apr. 68	Bobby Hull	9.00
May 68	Willie Mays	10.00
June 68	Carl Yastrzemski	9.00
July 68	Hank Aaron	10.00
Aug. 68	Pete Rose	10.00
Sep. 68	Don Drysdale	8.00
Oct. 68	Fran Tarkenton	6.00
Nov. 68	Don Meredith	5.00
Dec. 68	O.J. Simpson	10.00
Jan. 69	Deacon Jones	4.50
Feb. 69	John Havlicek &	

Sport Magazine: May, 1967

O.J. Simpson 10.00
Mar. 69 West, Baylor, Chamberlain 10.00
Apr. 69 Mickey Mantle 15.00
May 69 Hall of Famers 10.00
June 69 Ted Williams 15.00
July 69 Tony Conigliaro 6.00
Aug. 69 O.J. Simpson 10.00
Sep. 69 Cubs Stars 10.00
Oct. 69 Sonny Jurgenson 5.00
Nov. 69 Gale Sayers 9.00
Dec. 69 O.J. Simpson & Others 10.50
Jan. 70 Calvin Hill 7.00
Feb. 70 K. Abdul-Jabbar & Gil Hodges 9.00
Mar. 70 Jerry West 8.00
Apr. 70 Willis Reed 7.00
May 70 Tom Seaver 12.00
June 70 Harmon Killebrew 9.00
July 70 Bart Starr & Johnny Unitas 7.50
Aug. 70 Hank Aaron 10.00
Sep. 70 Johnny Bench 11.00
Oct. 70 Top Quarterbacks 9.00
Nov. 70 Dick Butkus 7.00
Dec. 70 Roman Gabriel 4.00
Jan. 71 L. Brown & M. Lucci ... 4.00
Feb. 71 Dave Bing & Dave DeBusschere 5.00
Mar. 71 Pete Maravich 10.00
Apr. 71 John Havlicek 9.00
May 71 Ted Williams 12.00
June 71 Boog Powell 5.00
July 71 Carl Yastrzemski 8.00
Aug. 71 M. Curtis 5.00
Sep. 71 Willie Mays 10.00
Oct. 71 Vida Blue 5.00
Nov. 71 K. Willard 5.00
Dec. 71 Bob Griese 6.00
Jan. 72 Larry Brown 5.50
Feb. 72 Spencer Haywood 5.00
Mar. 72 Wilt Chamberlain 7.00
Apr. 72 Bobby Orr 7.50
May 72 Bobby Hull 7.00
June 72 Brooks Robinson 8.00
July 72 Joe Namath 9.00
Aug. 72 Tom Seaver 10.00
Sep. 72 Frank Robinson 8.00
Oct. 72 Jim Plunkett 6.00
Nov. 72 Otis Taylor 5.00
Dec. 72 Fran Tarkenton 5.00
Jan. 73 Merlin Olson 5.00
Feb. 73 Rick Barry 5.00
Mar. 73 Ken Dryden 5.00
Apr. 73 Oscar Robertson 7.00
May 73 Dave Cowens 6.00
June 73 A.J. Foyt 6.00
July 73 George Foreman 8.50
Aug. 73 Bobby Murcer 5.00
Sep. 73 Gaylord Perry 6.50
Oct. 73 Pennant Time 7.00
Nov. 73 Franco Harris 7.00
Dec. 73 Joe Namath 8.50
Jan. 74 L. Little & M. Fernandez 8.00
Feb. 74 Kareem Abdul-Jabbar .. 8.50
Mar. 74 Basketball Coaches ... 6.00
Apr. 74 Dave DeBusschere 5.50
May 74 Hank Aaron 10.00
June 74 Pete Rose 10.50
July 74 Chris Evert & Jimmy Connors 6.00
Aug. 74 Larry Csonka 7.00
Sep. 74 Muhammed Ali 10.00
Oct. 74 Reggie Jackson 10.00
Nov. 74 Joe Namath 8.50
Dec. 74 O.J. Simpson 7.50
Jan. 75 Fran Tarkenton 5.00
Feb. 75 Muhammed Ali 10.00
Mar. 75 Julius Erving 10.00
Apr. 75 Rick Barry 5.00
May 75 Frank Robinson 5.00
June 75 Johnny Miller 4.00
July 75 Bobby Bonds 5.00
Aug. 75 Billy Martin 5.00
Sep. 75 Jimmy Connors 5.00
Oct. 75 James Harris 4.00

Sport Magazine: September, 1971

Nov. 75 Joe Namath 6.00
Dec. 75 Joe Greene 6.00
Jan. 76 Super Bowl Preview ... 6.00
Feb. 76 Fran Tarkenton 6.00
Mar. 76 George McGinnes 5.00
Apr. 76 Steve Garvey 6.00
May 76 Tom Seaver 7.00
June 76 Next Jock in the White House 4.50
July 76 Bruce Jenner 5.00
Aug. 76 Pete Rose & Joe Morgan 7.50
Sep. 76 Franco Harris 5.00
Oct. 76 Bert Jones 4.00
Nov. 76 O.J. Simpson 5.00
Dec. 76 Pill-Popping 4.50
Jan. 77 Roger Staubach 7.00
Feb. 77 Julius Erving 7.00
Mar. 77 Joe Namath 8.00
Apr. 77 Bill Walton 4.00
May 77 Jan Stephenson 4.50
June 77 Greed 4.00
July 77 Mark Fidrych 4.00
Aug. 77 Boxing 4.50
Sep. 77 Leonard Willis 5.50
Oct. 77 Rod Carew 6.50
Nov. 77 Earl Monroe 6.00
Dec. 77 Ken Stabler 6.50
Jan. 78 Tony Dorsett 7.00
Feb. 78 Kareem Abdul-Jabbar .. 8.00
Mar. 78 Maurice Lucas 4.00
Apr. 78 Reggie Jackson & Catfish Hunter 7.00
May 78 Graig Nettles 5.00
June 78 Juluis Erving 7.00
July 78 Jim Rice 4.50
Aug. 78 Tom Seaver 7.00
Sep. 78 Cliff Branch 4.50
Oct. 78 Carl Yastrzemski 5.50
Nov. 78 O.J. Simpson 5.00
Dec. 78 Jack Lambert 4.50
Jan. 79 Harvey Martin 4.00
Feb. 79 Julius Erving 6.00
Mar. 79 John Drew 5.50
Apr. 79 Pete Rose 6.00
May 79 Ron Guidry 5.00
June 79 Dave Parker 5.00
July 79 Graig Nettles 5.00
Aug. 79 Rod Carew 6.00
Sep. 79 Tony Dorsett 7.00
Oct. 79 Reggie Jackson 7.50
Nov. 79 Oakland Raiders 5.00
Dec. 79 Pat Haden 4.50
Jan. 80 Jack Ham 5.50
Feb. 80 Magic Johnson 9.00
Mar. 80 Larry Bird 9.00
Apr. 80 Willie Stargell 5.50
May 80 Lou Piniella 4.50
June 80 Bill Russell 4.50
July 80 Gorman Thomas 4.50
Aug. 80 Terry Bradshaw 6.00
Sep. 80 Tommy John 5.50
Oct. 80 Earl Campbell 5.50
Nov. 80 Lee Roy Selmon 4.00
Dec. 80 Football's Special Teams 4.00
Jan. 81 Billy Simms 4.00
Feb. 81 Danny White 4.00
Mar. 81 Kelly Tripucka 4.00
Apr. 81 Tug McGraw 5.50
May 81 Billy Martin 5.00
June 81 Don Sutton 5.50
July 81 Goose Gossage & Bruce Sutter 5.00
Aug. 81 Jim Plunkett 4.00
Sep. 81 Earl Campbell 5.50
Oct. 81 Doug Plank 4.00
Nov. 81 Lester Hayes 4.50
Dec. 81 Steve Bartkowski 4.00
Jan. 82 Tony Dorsett 5.50
Feb. 82 Magic Johnson 8.50
Mar. 82 Gerry Cooney 4.00
Apr. 82 Fernando Valenzuela .. 5.00
May 82 Reggie Jackson 7.00
June 82 Tom Seaver 5.50
July 82 Billy Martin 5.50

Sport Magazine: Jan, 1980

Aug. 82 Joe Montana 5.5
Sep. 82 Herschel Walker 5.0
Oct. 82 L.A. Rams 4.0
Nov. 82 Lawrence Taylor 7.5
Dec. 82 Patrick Ewing 6.0
Jan. 83 Fearless Predictions ... 4.0
Feb. 83 Tony Dorsett 5.0

Mar. 83 Top 100 Salaries 4.50
Apr. 83 Steve Garvey 5.00
May 83 Steve Carlton 7.50
June 83 Schmdit, Dawson, Carter, Yount 7.00
July 83 Reggie Jackson 8.50
Aug. 83 Marcus Allen 5.00
Sep. 83 Marcus Dupree 4.00
Oct. 83 Mark Gastineau 4.00
Nov. 83 Franco Harris 4.50
Dec. 83 Lyle Alzado 4.50
Jan. 84 Dan Marino 5.50
Feb. 84 Fearless Predictions ... 4.00
Mar. 84 Top 100 Salaries 4.00
Apr. 84 Cal Ripken Jr. 6.50
May 84 Wayne Gretzky 10.00
June 84 Dale Murphy 4.50
July 84 Baseball Managers 4.00
Aug. 84 Eric Dickerson 4.00
Sep. 84 Darryl Clack 4.00
Oct. 84 Walter Payton 6.00
Nov. 84 Betting Football 4.00
Dec. 84 Chris Mullin & Patrick Ewing 5.50
Jan. 85 Dan Marino 5.50
Feb. 85 Fearless Predictions ... 4.00
Mar. 85 Gary Carter 5.00
Apr. 85 Dwight Gooden 6.50
May 85 G. Matthews & K. Hernandez 4.00
June 85 George Brett 5.00
July 85 Kirk Gibson 5.00
Aug. 85 Joe Montana 7.50
Sep. 85 Maryland Football 4.00
Oct. 85 Dan Marino 5.00
Nov. 85 Lawrence Taylor & Marcus Allen 5.50
Dec. 85 Patrick Ewing 5.00

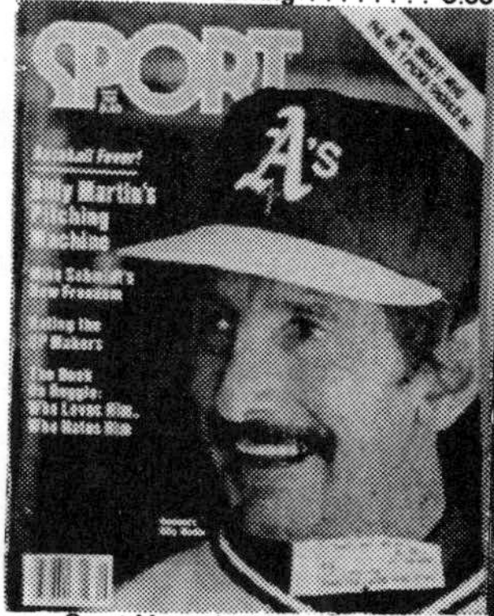

Sport Magazine: March, 1981

Jan. 86 Jim McMahon 4.00
Feb. 86 William Perry 3.00
Mar. 86 Dwight Gooden 4.00
Apr. 86 Bret Saberhagen 4.00
May 86 George Brett 4.50
June 86 Top 100 Salaries 3.00
July 86 P. Rose, R. Jackson, G.Carter 5.00
Aug. 86 Howie Long 3.00
Sep. 86 Jim Harbaugh 3.00
Oct. 86 Dan Marino 4.50
Nov. 86 Pervis Ellison 3.00
Dec. 86 40th Anniversary Issue . 4.00
Jan. 87 John Elway 3.00
Feb. 87 Joe Montana & Marcus Allen 4.00
Mar. 87 Clemens, E. Davis, Schmidt 6.00
Apr. 87 Darryl Strawberry 4.00
May 87 Dominique Wilkins 3.00
June 87 Top 100 Salaries 3.00
July 87 Dave Parker 4.00
Aug. 87 Roger Craig 3.00
Sep. 87 Lawrence Taylor 4.50
Oct. 87 Jim Kelly 3.50
Nov. 87 Larry Bird 5.50
Dec. 87 Dawson, Raines, Simms,Leonard 3.50
Jan. 88 BoomerEsiason 3.50
Feb. 88 NFL Coaches 2.50
Mar. 88 Jefferies, J. McDowell, D. Lovell 4.00
Apr. 88 Will Clark & Keith Hernandez 4.00
May 88 Isiah Thomas 3.50
June 88 Top 100 Salaries 3.00
July 88 Mike Tyson 5.00
Aug. 88 L.A. Raiders 3.00
Sep. 88 Troy Aikman 3.00
Oct. 88 Cornelius Bennett 2.50
Nov. 88 Michael Jordan 7.00
Dec. 88 Stacey King 2.50
Jan. 89 Dennis Gentry 2.50
Feb. 89 Cindy Crawford (Swimsuit) 6.00
Mar. 89 Orel Hershiser 4.00
Apr. 89 Baseball Preview 4.00
May 89 Magic Johnson 5.00
June 89 Top 100 Salaries 3.00
July 89 Jose Canseco 4.00
Aug. 89 Montana, Aikman, Cunningham 5.00
Sep. 89 College Football Preview 3.00
Oct. 89 43rd Anniversary Issue . 4.00
Nov. 89 Bird, Jordan, M. Johnson 7.00
Dec. 89 College Basketball Preview 3.00

Sports Illustrated: 8/16/54

SPORTS ILLUSTRATED

1954

Date	Cover	Value
8/16	Eddie Matthews (Topps card insert)	250.00
8/23	19th Hole (Topps card insert)	225.00
8/30	Vacationing(Swimsuit cov.)	15.00
9/6	Sailing	15.00
9/13	Auto Racing	15.00
9/20	Calgary Stampede	12.00
9/27	Calvin Jones	10.00
10/4	Estes Park, Colorado	10.00
10/11	Oklahoma Bandsmen	10.00
10/18	Steeplechase	10.00
10/25	Hunting Preview	10.00
11/1	Oklahoma Football	15.00
11/8	Fishing at Montauk Point	10.00
11/15	Spoonbill Duck	10.00
11/22	Y.A. Tittle	25.00
11/29	1900 Peugeot	10.00
12/6	African Lion	10.00
12/13	Royal Horse Show	10.00
12/20	Ken Sears (Horseshow)	10.00
12/27	Switzerland Ski Resort	10.00

1955

Date	Cover	Value
1/3	Roger Bannister (SOY)	25.00
1/10	Santa Anita, CA	8.00
1/17	Rafael Rodriquez (Bullfighter)	8.00
1/24	Swedish Gymnast	8.00
1/31	Jill Kinmont	8.00
2/7	Carol Heiss	8.00
2/14	Great Dane	8.00
2/21	Caribbean Vacation (Swimsuit)	10.00
2/28	Hialeah Park	8.00
3/7	Joe Alston (Badminton)	8.00
3/14	Buddy Werner (Skier)	8.00
3/21	Parry O'Brien	8.00
3/28	Steve Nagy (Bowler)	8.00
4/4	Augusta National	10.00
4/11	Mays, Durocher, D. Day (Card insert)	100.00
4/18	Al Rosen	40.00
4/25	Tenzing Norgay	8.00
5/2	Tom Courtney	8.00
5/9	Ballooning	8.00
5/16	American Bird Watching	8.00
5/23	Zale Parry (Skin Diver)	8.00
5/30	Herb Score	15.00
6/6	Trout Fishing	8.00
6/13	Sailing	8.00
6/20	Ed Furgol (US Open)	10.00
6/27	Duke Snider	30.00
7/4	Kippax Fearnought(Bulldog)	8.00
7/11	Yogi Berra	40.00
7/18	Swaps	8.00
7/25	Matterhorn (Mountain Climbing)	8.00
8/1	Ted Williams (FC)	50.00
8/8	Ann Marston (Archery)	8.00
8/15	Anniversary Issue	15.00
8/22	Don Newcombe	15.00
8/29	Tony Trabert	10.00
9/5	Fred, Art Pinder (Spearfishing)	8.00
9/12	Bud Wilkinson	10.00
9/19	Rocky Marciano	40.00
9/26	Walter Alston	20.00
10/3	Doak Walker	12.00
10/10	Upland Birds (Hunting Preview)	8.00
10/17	Princeton Marching Band	8.00
10/24	Howard "Hopalong" Cassidy	9.00
10/31	National Horse Show Preview	8.00
11/7	Bob Pelligrini	8.00
11/14	Ernest Burton (Hunting)	8.00
11/21	Skeeter Werner (Skiing)	8.00
11/28	Don Holleder (Army Football)	10.00
12/5	Louise Dyer	8.00
12/12	Dachsunds	8.00
12/19	Skiing Resorts	8.00
12/26	Jim Swink	8.00

1956

Date	Cover	Value
1/2	Johnny Podres (SOY)	25.00
1/9	Bob Cousy (FC)	30.00
1/16	Mike Souchak	7.50
1/23	Jean Beliveau	20.00
1/30	Jenkins Albright (Skating)	7.50
2/6	Ralph Miller	7.50
2/13	Indoor Track	7.50
2/20	Great White Heron (Everglades)	7.00
2/27	Hialeah Race Track	7.50
3/5	Stan Musial	30.00
3/12	Taejon of Crown Crest	7.00
3/19	Fishing	7.50
3/26	Jim Kimberly	7.50
4/2	Al Wiggins	7.50

Sports Illustrated: 6/18/56

Date	Issue	Price
4/9	Baseball Preview	22.00
4/16	Barbara Romack	7.00
4/23	Billy Martin	25.00
4/30	Brown Trout Fishing	7.50
5/7	Kentucky Derby Preview	9.00
5/14	Al Kaline, Harvey Kuenn	25.00
5/21	John Landy	7.50
5/28	Bob Sweikert (Indy 500)	9.00
6/4	Floyd Patterson	15.00
6/11	Sam Snead	15.00
6/18	Mickey Mantle (FC)	50.00
6/25	Warren Spahn	25.00
7/2	Sime, Morrow	7.50
7/9	Mantle, Banks, Musial	40.00
7/16	T. Kluzewski, G. Bell, W. Post	25.00
7/23	Adios, Harry	7.50
7/30	Joe Adcock	15.00
8/6	Jeanne Stunyo (Diving)	7.00
8/13	Olympic Sailing	7.50
8/20	Second Anniversary Issue	25.00
8/27	Illinois State Fair (Horseriding)	7.00
9/3	Lew Hoad	7.50
9/10	Whitey Ford (FC)	25.00
9/17	Willie Hartack	7.50
9/24	College Football Preview	12.00
10/1	Mickey Mantle/ World Series	45.00
10/8	Coach Brown, Ratterman	7.50
10/15	Harold Vanderbilt	7.00
10/22	Dr. John Chambers (Duckhunting)	7.00
10/29	Paul Hornung (FC)	15.00
11/5	Yale-Dartmouth Football	9.00
11/12	Maentz, Kramer	7.50
11/19	Olympic Preview	90.00
11/26	UCLA vs. USC	9.00
12/3	Chuck Conerly	8.00
12/10	Olympic Track	8.00
12/17	Olympic Results	9.00
12/24	Christmas Double Issue	9.00

1957

Date	Issue	Price
1/7	Bob Morrow (SOY)	9.00
1/14	Skiing in Utah	7.00
1/21	Johnny Lee	7.00
1/28	Boston Bruins	10.00
2/4	Hugh Schaddelee (Yachting)	6.50
2/11	Boxer Dog	6.50
2/18	Jim Krebs	7.00
2/25	Saxton vs. Basilio	8.00
3/4	Mickey Mantle	40.00
3/11	Ben Hogan, Golf Fundamentals	9.00
3/18	Ted Lindsay, Gordie Howe (FC)	15.00
3/25	Carroll Shelby	7.00
4/1	Dan Hodge (Wrestling)	7.00
4/8	A. Wells Peck (Fishing)	6.50
4/15	Baseball Preview	20.00
4/22	Wally Moon	10.00
4/29	Fullmer vs. Robinson	15.00
5/6	Kentucky Derby	8.00
5/13	Billy Pierce	15.00
5/20	Gussie Busch	7.00
5/27	Jim Bryan (Indy 500)	8.00
6/3	Clem Labine	15.00
6/10	Cary Middlecoff	7.00
6/17	Eddie Arcaro	7.50
6/24	Bob Gutowski	7.00
7/1	Yachting Flags	6.00
7/8	S. Musial & T. Williams	35.00
7/15	Animal Moods	6.00
7/22	Hank Bauer	9.00
7/29	Patterson vs. Jackson	10.00
8/5	Bonnie Prudden (Fitness)	6.00
8/12	Russell Schleeh (Hydroplane)	7.00
8/19	Hambletonian Preview	7.00
8/26	Countess Consuelo Crespi	6.00
9/2	Althea Gibson	7.50
9/9	Roy McMillan	8.00
9/16	Carmen Basilio	9.00
9/23	Football Preview Issue	12.00
9/30	World Series Issue	15.00
10/7	Ollie Matson	7.00
10/14	Charles Goren	7.00
10/21	Duck Hunting	6.00
10/28	Walk Into Autumn	6.00
11/4	Bobby Cox	9.00
11/11	The Lemon Drop Kid	7.00
11/18	Oklahoma Sooners	9.00
11/25	Willy Schaeffler	7.00
12/2	Russian Physical Fitness	6.00
12/9	College Basketball Issue	15.00
12/16	Skiing Fashions	7.00
12/23	Stan Musial (SOY)	25.00

1958

Date	Issue	Price
1/6	Winter Vacation Guide	6.00
1/13	Family Fun (Caribbean Tour)	6.00
1/20	NBA All-Star Game Preview	10.00
1/27	Willie Shoemaker	8.00
2/3	Guadalupe Islands Seals	6.00
2/10	Salaun, Mateer (Squash Champs)	6.00
2/17	Jacques Plante	9.00
2/24	Phil Reavis (AAU Track)	6.00
3/3	Yankees, Spring Training Issue	9.00
3/10	Surfing in Australia	6.00
3/17	Sal Maglie	12.00
3/24	Basilio vs. Robinson	10.00
3/31	Roy Sievers	10.00
4/7	The Masters	6.00
4/14	Baseball Issue	20.00
4/21	Del Crandall	12.00
4/28	Silky Sullivan (Kentucky Derby)	9.00
5/5	Gil McDougald	10.00
5/12	America's Cup	6.50
5/19	Richie Ashburn	15.00
5/26	Pat O'Connor (Indy 500)	6.50
6/2	Eddie Mathews	15.00
6/9	Dick Mayer (U.S. Open)	6.50
6/16	Hoad Meets Gonzalez	6.50
6/23	Jackie Jensen	10.00
6/30	Mixed Doubles Tennis	6.00
7/7	Baseball All-Star Game	15.00
7/14	Educating Your Dog	5.00
7/21	Chris Von Saltza (Swimming)	5.00
7/28	Frank Thomas	10.00
8/4	Nantucket	6.00
8/11	Scuba Diving	5.00
8/18	Roy Harris	6.00
8/25	Pine Valley	5.00
9/1	Patterson Beats Harris	7.00
9/8	Mirimachi Salmon Fishing	5.00
9/15	America's Cup	6.50
9/22	College Football Issue	10.00
9/29	The World Series	15.00
10/6	North Carolina Outer Banks	5.00
10/13	Ohio State Buckeyes	8.00
10/20	James McCarthy (Mountaineer)	6.00
10/27	Chick Zimmerman	6.50
11/3	Hugh Wiley	6.50
11/10	Herb Elliot	6.50
11/17	Mr. & Mrs. John Olin (Hunting)	6.00
11/24	Dawkins, Walters, Anderson	6.50
12/1	Sun Valley, Idaho	5.00
12/8	College Basketball Issue	12.00
12/15	Wagner & Paul (Ice Skating)	6.00
12/22	Holiday Issue (Bowl Preview)	8.00

1959

Date	Issue	Price
1/5	Ingemar Johansson	7.00
1/12	Andy Bathgate	6.50
1/19	Pheasant Hunting	6.00
1/26	Hialeah Race Track	6.50
2/2	Ron Delaney	6.50
2/9	Skiing in Colorado	6.00
2/16	Johnny Longden	6.50
2/23	Small Boat Sailing	5.00
3/2	Casey Stengel (Spring Training)	15.00
3/9	Ed Sullivan	6.50
3/16	Phil Hill (Auto Racing)	6.50
3/23	Aly Khan (Horse Racing)	6.50
3/30	Tommy Armour	6.50
4/6	Robert Tyre Jones	6.50
4/13	Willie Mays (Baseball Issue)	30.00
4/20	Bill Talbert	7.00
4/27	Silver Spoon (Kentucky Derby)	7.00
5/4	Bob Turley	10.00
5/11	Gambling in Las Vegas	6.50
5/18	Bob Mosbacher (Sailing)	6.00
5/25	Indy 500	7.00
6/1	Gary Cooper	6.50
6/8	U.S. Open Golfers	6.50
6/15	L.A. Coliseum	8.00
6/22	Ingemar Johansson	7.00
6/29	The Golden Eagle	6.50
7/6	Johansson vs. Patterson	7.50
7/13	Becky Collins	6.50
7/20	Vasiliy Kuznetscov	6.50
7/27	Toots Shor	6.50
8/3	First International Trot	6.00
8/10	Nellie Fox & Luis Aparicio	25.00
8/17	Anne Quast	6.50
8/24	S. Niarchos (Yaz "Faces")	20.00
8/31	Perry O'Brien	6.50
9/7	Alex Olmedo	6.50
9/14	Charlie Coe	7.00
9/21	College Football Preview	10.00
9/28	Chicago White Sox	10.00
10/5	Johnny Unitas	12.00
10/12	Dawn of Duck Hunting Season	5.00
10/19	Little Le Mans	6.50
10/26	George Izo (Notre Dame)	7.50
11/2	Ryder Cup	6.50
11/9	College Football	12.00
11/16	Daytona Speedway	7.00
11/23	Alta, Utah Ski Season	5.00
11/30	National Field Trials (Hunting)	5.00
12/7	College Basketball Preview	12.00
12/14	Tom Watson (Skiing)	6.00
12/21	Special Holiday Issue	9.00

1960

Date	Issue	Price
1/4	Ingemar Johansson (SOY)	7.00
1/11	Jerry Lucas	10.00
1/18	Art Wall	6.00

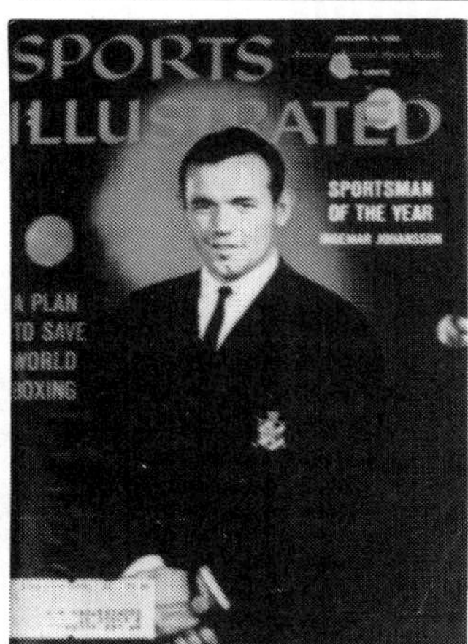

Sports Illustrated: 1/4/60

Date	Issue	Price
1/25	USSR Hockey	6.50
2/1	Betsy Suite	6.00
2/8	Bedlington Dog Show	5.00
2/15	Winter Olympics Preview	8.00
2/22	Horse Racing	6.00
2/29	Squaw Vally Olympic Report	7.00
3/7	Spring Training	8.00
3/14	Bowling	5.00
3/21	Maurice "Rocket" Richard	9.00
3/28	James Leisenring (Fishing)	5.00
4/4	The Masters	6.50
4/11	Baseball Preview	15.00
4/18	Carin Cone	5.00
4/25	Dallas Long	5.00
5/2	Kentucky Derby	8.00
5/9	Alaska's Northwest Passage	5.00
5/16	Australia	5.00
5/23	Charles Goren	5.00
5/30	Herb Elliot	5.00
6/6	Red Schoendienst	10.00
6/13	Palmer, Venturi, Finsterwald	7.00
6/20	Johansson vs. Patterson	8.00
6/27	Glen Davis	7.00
7/4	Comiskey Park Scoreboard	8.00
7/11	Jim Beatty	5.00
7/18	Candlestick Park	7.00
7/25	Southern California Regatta	5.00
8/1	Mike Troy	6.00
8/8	Dick Groat	10.00
8/15	Olympics	8.00
8/22	Barbara McIntire (Golf)	5.00
8/29	Mt. Dhaulagiri (Himalayas)	7.00
9/5	Rome Olympics ceremonies	6.00
9/12	Jack Nicklaus (FC)	10.00
9/19	College Football Preview	7.00
9/26	Jim Brown	15.00
10/3	Bob Schloredt	6.00
10/10	Vernon Law	8.00
10/17	Sportswear (Swimsuit cov.)	9.00
10/24	Violence in Football	5.00
10/31	Jack Brabham (Racing)	6.00
11/7	Stanley Walker Gourmet	5.00
11/14	Bobby Hull (FC)	15.00
11/21	Skiing Season Preview	5.00
11/28	Joe Bellino	5.00
12/5	Sam Snead	8.00
12/12	College Basketball Spec.	10.00
12/19	Norm Van Brocklin	9.00
12/26	John F. Kennedy	15.00
	1961	
1/9	Arnold Palmer (SOY)	9.00
1/16	Bob Cousy	12.00
1/23	Bing Crosby Pebble Beach Golf	6.00
1/30	Safe Freeway Driving	5.00
2/6	Indoor Track	5.50
2/13	Laurence Owen (Skating)	5.00
2/20	Billy Casper	5.50
2/27	World Bobsledding	5.50
3/6	Spring Training	10.00
3/13	Floyd Patterson	7.00
3/20	Skydiving	5.00
3/27	NCAA Basketball Championship	10.00
4/3	The Masters	5.50
4/10	Baseball Preview	10.00
4/17	Golden Gate Fishing	5.00
4/24	Hot Rod World	5.00
5/1	Kentucky Derby Preview	5.50
5/8	Gary Player	5.50
5/15	Cookie Lavagetto	7.00
5/22	Claire Boothe Luce (Snorkeling)	5.00
5/29	Indy 500	5.50
6/5	Ocean Racing	5.00
6/12	U.S. Open	5.50
6/19	Earl Young	5.00
6/26	Ernie Broglio & Willie Mays	12.50
7/3	Underwater Swimming	5.00
7/10	World Tennis Crisis	5.50
7/17	Valeri Brumel	5.00
7/24	How & Why a Fish Strikes	5.00
7/31	Stop-Action Baseball	7.00
8/7	Lisa Lane (Chess)	5.00
8/14	Murray Rose	5.00
8/21	Judy Torluemke	5.00
8/28	John Sellers	5.00
9/4	Forest Hills	5.00
9/11	Deane Berman	5.00
9/18	College Football Issue	9.00
9/25	Bart Starr (FC)	12.00
10/2	Roger Maris	30.00
10/9	Joey Jay	7.00
10/16	Terry Baker	5.00
10/23	Hord & Arnett	5.00
10/30	Wilt Chamberlain (FC)	13.00
11/6	Kelso	6.00
11/13	Tom McNeeley	5.00
11/20	Y.A. Tittle, N.Y. Giants	9.00
11/27	Jimmy Saxton	5.00
12/4	Skiing	5.00
12/11	Basketball Preview	8.00
12/18	Dan Currie	5.00
12/25	Francine Breaud (Skiing)	5.00
	1962	
1/8	Jerry Lucas (SOY)	9.00
1/15	NHL Goaltenders	7.50
1/22	Doug & Joan Sanders	5.00
1/29	Chet Jastremski (Swimming)	5.00
2/5	Joan Hannah (Skiing)	5.00
2/12	Sonny Liston	8.00
2/19	Mikey Wright	5.00
2/26	John Uelses	5.00
3/5	Casey Stengel	12.00
3/12	Kentucky Derby Preview	6.00
3/19	UCLA Beats USC (Basketball)	7.50
3/26	Ricardo Rodriquez (Auto Racing)	5.50
4/2	Arnold Palmer	8.50
4/9	Frank Lary	6.50
4/16	Donna DeVarona	5.50
4/23	Johns Hopkins Lacrosse	5.50
4/30	Luis Aparicio	10.00
5/7	Kentucky Derby	6.00
5/14	Gene Littler	5.50
5/21	Water Skiing	5.00
5/28	Floyd Patterson	7.00
6/4	Willie Mays	15.00
6/11	U.S. Open Preview	5.50
6/18	Cornell Crew	5.00
6/25	Jack Nicklaus	9.00
7/2	Mickey Mantle	25.00
7/9	America's Cup	5.00
7/16	Igor TerOvanesyan	5.00
7/23	Barbara McAlister	5.00
7/30	Ken Boyer	10.00
8/6	Paul Runyan	5.00

Sports Illustrated: 10/2/61

Date	Issue	Price
8/13	Dick Fortenberry	5.00
8/20	Don Drysdale	12.00
8/27	Helga Schultze	5.00
9/3	California Beaches	5.00
9/10	Jim Taylor	9.50
9/17	Liston vs. Patterson	9.00
9/24	College Football Preview	9.00
10/1	World Series	15.00
10/8	Tommy McDonald	7.00
10/15	Sonny Gibbs	5.00
10/22	Big Game Hunting	5.00
10/29	Fran Tarkenton	9.00
11/5	Diving in California	5.00
11/12	Sam Snead & Arnold Palmer	8.00
11/19	Nick Pietrosante	5.00
11/26	Paul Dietzel	5.00
12/3	Montana Winter Winterland	5.00
12/10	Cotton Nash (College Hoops)	7.00
12/17	Hubbard & Gifford	8.00
12/24	Sky Diving (Double Issue)	5.50
	1963	
1/7	Terry Baker (SOY)	5.50
1/14	Phil Rodgers	5.00
1/21	Women In Water	4.50
1/28	Howie Young	5.00
2/4	Valeri Brumel	5.00
2/11	Cathy Nagel	5.00
2/18	Jerry Barber	5.00
2/25	Rex Ellsworth	5.00
3/4	Sandy Koufax (FC)	20.00
3/11	Chuck Ferriers	5.00
3/18	College Hoop Championships	7.50
3/25	Liston vs. Patterson	7.50
4/1	Masters Golf Preview	5.00
4/8	Baseball Preview	15.00
4/15	Two Golf Strokes	4.50
4/22	Marlin Fishing	4.50
4/29	Art Mahaffy	4.50
5/6	Kentucky Derby	5.00
5/13	Cruise Guest	4.50
5/20	Paul Hornung	10.00
5/27	Dan Gurney (Indy 500)	6.00
6/3	Bob Hope	8.00
6/10	Cassius Clay (FC)	30.00
6/17	Jack Nicklaus	8.50
6/24	Roy Face	7.50
7/1	Julius Boros	5.00
7/8	Good Casting (Fishing)	4.50
7/15	Arnold Palmer	1.00
7/22	Dick Groat	8.50
7/29	Sonny Liston	7.00
8/5	Nancy Vonderheide (Archery)	4.50

Sports Illustrated: 8/20/62; 10/19/64; 4/5/65

Date	Cover	Price
8/12	Alfred C. Vanderbilt	4.50
8/19	Ron Vanderkelen	4.00
8/26	Dennis Ralston	5.00
9/2	Ron Fairly	7.50
9/9	Pro Football Preview	9.00
9/16	5.5 Meter Yachting	4.50
9/23	George Mira (College Football)	7.00
9/30	Whitey Ford	15.00
10/7	Deer Hunting	4.50
10/14	Ronnie Bull	4.50
10/21	Duke Carlisle	5.00
10/28	Art Heymann & Jerry Lucas	6.50
11/4	Jack Cvercko	4.50
11/11	Violence in Football	5.00
11/18	Skiing Weekends	4.50
11/25	Willie Galimore	4.50
12/2	Roger Staubach (FC)	12.50
12/9	F. Ramsey (College Basktball)	7.50
12/16	Tobin Rote	5.00
12/23	C.K. Yang	4.50
	1964	
1/6	Pete Rozelle (SOY)	9.00
1/13	Dempsey vs. Willis	6.00
1/20	Skin Diving (Swimsuit)	6.00
1/27	Winter Olympics Preview	5.00
2/3	Bobby Hull	12.00
2/10	Egon Zimmerman	5.00
2/17	Bridge	4.50
2/24	Cassius Clay	15.00
3/2	Casey Stengel & Yogi Berra	15.00
3/9	Clay vs. Liston	15.00
3/16	Gordie Howe	10.00
3/23	Tony Lema	5.00
3/30	Walt Hazzard	5.00
4/6	Jack Nicklaus	8.00
4/13	Sandy Koufax	10.00
4/20	Texas Women's Track	5.00
4/27	C. Harmon (L. Alcindor "Faces")	20.00
5/4	Kentucky Derby Preview	5.00
5/11	Al Kaline	10.00
5/18	Joey Giardello	5.00
5/25	Frank Howard	9.00
6/1	A.J. Foyt (FC)	10.00
6/8	Bill Hartack	4.50
6/15	U.S. Open Preview	4.50
6/22	Tom O'Hara	4.50
6/29	Ken Venturi	5.00
7/6	Alvin Dark	8.00
7/13	Bill Talbert	4.50
7/20	Shirley McLaine	4.50
7/27	Tommy McDonald	7.00
8/3	Betsy Rawls	4.50
8/10	Johnny Callison	7.00
8/17	Don Trull	4.50
8/24	America's Cup	5.00
8/31	Brooks Robinson (FC)	15.00
9/7	Pro Football Preview	9.00
9/14	Jim Ryan	5.00
9/21	College Football Preview	8.00
9/28	Tommy Mason	6.50
10/5	Tokyo Olympic Preview	6.00
10/12	Dick Butkus (FC)	10.00
10/19	Tokyo Olympics	6.00
10/26	Tommy Heinsohn (FC)	10.00
11/2	John Huarte	4.50
11/9	John David Crow	5.00
11/16	Clay vs. Liston	12.50
11/23	Skiing	4.50
11/30	Alex Karras	6.50
12/7	Bill Bradley (FC)	10.00
12/14	Charley Johnson	5.00
12/21	Ken Venturi (SOY)	5.00
12/28	Charley Johnson	5.00
	1965	
1/4	Frank Ryun	4.50
1/11	Ernie Koy	4.50
1/18	Sue Peterson (1st swimsuit cover)	30.00
1/25	Bobby Hull	10.00
2/1	Chuvalo vs. Patterson	6.00
2/8	Jerry West (FC)	8.00
2/15	Top 18 Golf Courses (Part I)	8.00
2/22	Top 18 Golf Courses (Part II)	8.00
3/1	Jim Bunning & Bo Belinsky	8.00
3/8	Billy Kidd (Skiing)	5.00
3/15	Tony Lema	5.00
3/22	Willie Pastrano	5.00
3/29	Gail Goodrich	6.00
4/5	Arnold Palmer & Jack Nicklaus	10.00
4/12	Wilt Chamberlain	10.00
4/19	Baseball Preview	15.00
4/26	Sonny Liston	7.00
5/3	Kentucky Derby	5.00
5/10	Mulder & Smith	5.00
5/17	Bill Veeck	8.00
5/24	Clay vs. Liston	10.00
5/31	Indy 500	5.00
6/7	Clay vs. Liston	10.00
6/14	U.S. Open	5.00
6/21	Mickey Mantle	25.00
6/28	Henry Parker (Rowing)	4.50
7/5	Bill Talbert	5.00
7/12	Maury Wills	9.00
7/19	Joe Namath (FC)	20.00
7/26	Arnold Palmer	7.50
8/2	Powerboating & Fishing	4.50
8/9	Juan Marichal	12.00
8/16	Y.A. Tittle	8.00
8/23	Tony Oliva	10.00
8/30	Michael Jazy	4.50
9/6	Sugar Ray Robinson	8.00
9/13	F. Tarkenton	9.00
9/20	College Football Preview	5.00
9/27	Frank Ryun	5.00
10/4	Zoilo Versalles (World Series)	10.00
10/11	Ken Willard	5.00
10/18	Tommy Nobis	5.00
10/25	Bill Russell (FC)	12.00
11/1	Randell & Johnson	6.00
11/8	Harrry Jones	5.00
11/15	Skiing	4.50
11/22	Clay vs. Patterson	10.00
11/29	Dennis Gabatz	5.00
12/6	UCLA Basketball	7.50
12/13	Lance Alworth	7.00
12/20	Sandy Koufax (SOY)	16.00
	1966	
1/3	College Bowl Games	8.00
1/10	Jim Taylor	9.00
1/17	Sonny Bippus (Swimsuit)	25.00
1/24	Iowa Basketball	5.00
1/31	Stan Mikita (FC)	8.00
2/7	Billy Casper	5.00
2/14	Rick Mount	5.00
2/21	Jean Claude Killy	5.00
2/28	Leo Durocher & Eddie Stanky	9.00
3/7	Adolph Rupp	7.00
3/14	Richman Flowers (Track)	5.00
3/21	Gary Player	5.00
3/28	NCAA Basketball Championship	6.00
4/4	Nicklaus, Player, Palmer	12.00
4/11	Chuvalo vs. Ali	10.00
4/18	Dick Groat (Baseball Preview)	9.00
4/25	Chicago vs. Detroit (Stanley Cup)	8.00
5/2	Peggy Fleming	8.00
5/9	John Havlicek (FC)	11.00
5/16	Kentucky Derby Preview	7.00
5/23	Sam McDowell	8.00

5/30 Indy 500 . . . 5.00
6/6 Joe Morgan & Sonny Jackson . . . 10.50
6/13 Ken Venturi (U.S. Open) . . 5.00
6/20 Jim Ryun . . . 5.00
6/27 Billy Casper . . . 5.00
7/4 Ocean Sailing . . . 4.00
7/11 Andy Etchebarren . . . 7.00
7/18 Surfing . . . 4.00
7/25 Otto Graham . . . 8.00
8/1 Jim Ryun . . . 5.00
8/8 Frank Emanual . . . 5.00
8/15 Bear Bryant . . . 8.00
8/22 Paul Hornung & Jim Taylor . . . 8.00
8/29 Arthur Ashe (FC) . . . 10.00
9/5 Harry Walker . . . 7.00
9/12 Gale Sayers (FC) . . . 15.00
9/19 Gary Beban . . . 5.00
9/26 Gaylord Perry (FC) . . . 12.00
10/3 Roman Gabriel . . . 8.00
10/10 Brooks & Frank Robinson (FC) . . . 15.00
10/17 Joe Namath . . . 10.00
10/24 Elgin Baylor (FC) . . . 9.00
10/31 Bart Starr . . . 8.00
11/7 Terry Hanratty . . . 5.00
11/14 Ski Runs . . . 4.00
11/21 Ross Fichtner . . . 5.00
11/28 Notre Dame vs. Michigan State . . . 9.00
12/5 L. Alcindor (FC; College Hoops) . . . 25.00
12/12 Jim Nance . . . 6.00
12/19 Jim Ryun (SOY) . . . 8.00

1967

1/2 College Bowl Previews . . . 7.00
1/9 Bart Starr . . . 8.00
1/16 Marilyn Tindall (Swimsuit) 15.00
1/23 Max McGee(Super Bowl I) 20.00
1/30 Rod Gilbert . . . 7.00
2/6 Ernie Terrell . . . 8.00
2/13 Rick Barry . . . 7.00
2/20 Bob Seagren . . . 5.00
2/27 Walters & Thomforde . . . 5.00
3/6 Arnold Palmer . . . 7.00
3/13 Jim Nash . . . 6.00
3/20 Mikita, Wharram, Mohns . . 9.00
3/27 Jean Claude Killy . . . 6.00
4/3 Lew Alcindor . . . 14.00
4/10 Jack Nicklaus . . . 8.00
4/17 Maury Wills . . . 7.00
4/24 Rick Barry . . . 6.00
5/1 Jim Hall (Auto Racing) . . . 5.00
5/8 Mickey Mantle . . . 25.00
5/15 Buzzie Bavasi . . . 7.00
5/22 Tommy Smith . . . 5.00
5/29 Indy 500 . . . 5.00
6/5 Al Kaline . . . 10.00
6/12 Bill Casper . . . 5.00
6/19 Joe Harris . . . 5.00
6/26 Jack Nicklaus . . . 8.00
7/3 Roberto Clemente (FC) . . 25.00
7/10 Muhammed Ali . . . 10.00
7/17 Fran Tarkenton . . . 9.00
7/24 Surfing in Hawaii . . . 4.00
7/31 The Spitball . . . 6.00
8/7 Gay Brewer . . . 4.50
8/14 Taylor & Cuozzo . . . 8.00
8/21 Carl Yastrzemski (FC) . . . 15.00
8/28 The Intrepid . . . 4.50
9/4 Tim McCarver . . . 8.00
9/11 College Football Preview . . 7.00
9/18 Pro Football Preview . . . 6.00
9/25 Nino Benvenuti . . . 5.00
10/2 Texas vs. USC . . . 7.00
10/9 Mike Phipps . . . 4.00
10/16 Lou Brock (FC) . . . 12.00
10/23 Pro Basketball . . . 8.00
10/30 Tenessee vs. Alabama . . . 7.00
11/6 Dan Reeves . . . 7.00
11/13 Skiing Fashions . . . 4.00
11/20 Gary Beban & O.J. Simpson (FC) . . . 15.00
11/27 Jim Hart . . . 7.00

12/4 The 12 Foot Basket . . . 4.00
12/11 Bobby Orr (FC) . . . 12.00
12/18 Roman Gabriel . . . 7.00
12/25 Carl Yastrzemski (SOY) . . 15.00

1968

1/8 Packers vs. Raiders . . . 9.00
1/15 Turia Mau (Swimsuit) . . . 10.00
1/22 Vince Lombardi (Super Bowl II) . . . 20.00
1/29 Elvin Hayes & Lew Alcindor . . . 9.00
2/5 Billy Kidd . . . 5.00
2/12 Bobby Hull . . . 8.00
2/19 Peggy Fleming . . . 5.50
2/26 Curtis Turner . . . 5.00
3/4 Pete Maravich . . . 14.00

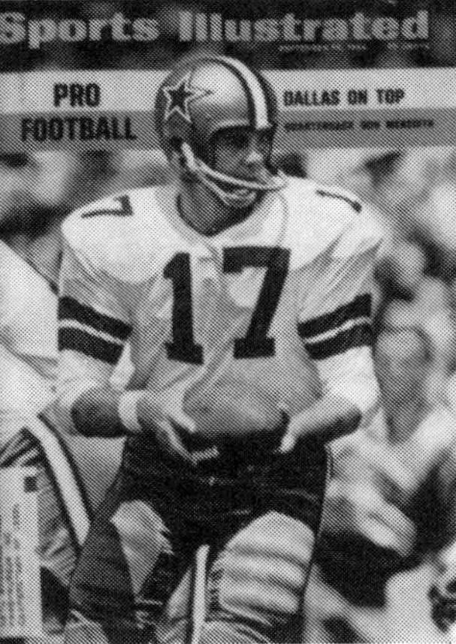

Sports Illustrated: 9/16/68

3/11 Johnny Bench (FC), Rookies . . . 15.00
3/18 Bill Bradley . . . 9.00
3/25 Julius Boros (Golf) . . . 5.00
4/1 UCLA vs. Houston . . . 9.00
4/8 Stanley Cup . . . 8.00
4/15 Lou Brock (Baseball) . . . 10.00
4/22 Bob Goalby . . . 5.00
4/29 Jerry West & Elgin Baylor . . . 9.00
5/6 Ron Swoboda . . . 9.50
5/13 Indy 500 . . . 5.00
5/20 Kentucky Derby Drug Mystery . . . 5.00
5/27 Pete Rose (FC) . . . 25.00
6/3 Dave Patrick . . . 5.00
6/10 U.S. Open Preview . . . 5.00
6/17 Don Drysdale . . . 9.00
6/24 Lee Trevino . . . 7.00
7/1 The Black Athlete . . . 6.00
7/8 Ted Williams . . . 12.00
7/15 Ray Nitschke . . . 9.00
7/22 Mark Spitz . . . 6.00
7/29 Denny McClain . . . 9.00
8/5 Nevele Pride (Horse Racing) . . . 5.00
8/12 Paul Brown . . . 8.00
8/19 Curt Flood . . . 9.00
8/26 Rod Laver . . . 5.00
9/2 Ken Harrelson . . . 6.00
9/9 College Football Preview . . 7.00
9/16 Don Meredith . . . 7.00
9/23 Denny McLain (30th Win) . . 9.00
9/30 Mexico City Olympics . . . 6.00
10/7 St. Louis Cardinals . . . 10.00
10/14 O.J. Simpson . . . 10.00
10/21 Olympics . . . 7.00
10/28 Forrest Gregg & Paul Brown . . . 6.00
11/4 Earl Monroe . . . 7.00

Sports Illustrated: 9/8/69

11/11 Bruce Jankowski . . . 4.00
11/18 Jean Claude Killy . . . 6.00
11/25 Earl Morrall . . . 7.00
12/2 College Basketball Preview 6.00
12/9 Joe Namath . . . 9.00
12/16 Colts vs. Packers . . . 7.00
12/23 Bill Russell . . . 10.00

1969

1/6 Tom Matte . . . 6.00
1/13 Jamee Becker (Swimsuit) 10.00
1/20 Joe Namath (Super Bowl III) . . . 20.00
1/27 Wilt Chamberlain . . . 10.00
2/3 Bobby Orr . . . 10.00
2/10 Bob Ogden . . . 5.00
2/17 Bob Lunn . . . 4.00
2/24 Knicks vs. Philadelphia . . . 6.00
3/3 Vince Lombardi . . . 8.00
3/10 Track Scandal . . . 4.50
3/17 Ted Williams . . . 10.00
3/24 Guerin & Mullins . . . 6.00
3/31 Lew Alcindor . . . 9.00
4/7 Red Berenson . . . 5.00
4/14 Bill Freehan (Baseball Preview) . . . 8.00
4/21 Tommy Archer . . . 5.00
4/28 Bill Russell . . . 8.50
5/5 Muhammed Ali . . . 9.00
5/12 John Havlicek . . . 9.00
5/19 Walter Alston . . . 8.00
5/26 Grizzly Bear . . . 4.50
6/2 Fun in Water . . . 4.00
6/9 Lee Trevino . . . 5.00
6/16 Joe Namath . . . 8.00
6/23 Drug Scandal . . . 4.50
6/30 Ron Santo . . . 8.00
7/7 Reggie Jackson (FC) . . . 22.50
7/14 O.J. Simpson . . . 9.00
7/21 Billy Martin . . . 6.00
7/28 S. Jurgenson & V. Lombardi . . . 8.00
8/4 Bill Russell . . . 8.50
8/11 Joe Namath . . . 8.00
8/18 Hank Aaron (FC) . . . 22.50
8/25 O.J. Simpson . . . 9.00
9/1 Arnold Palmer . . . 7.00
9/8 Pete Rose & Ernie Banks . . . 16.00
9/15 Ohio State . . . 7.00
9/22 Jim Turner . . . 7.00
9/29 Jimmy Jones . . . 5.00
10/6 Frank Robinson . . . 9.00
10/13 Bruce Kemp . . . 5.00
10/20 Brooks Robinson

(World Series) 12.00
10/27 Lew Alcindor 9.00
11/3 Vikings 5.00
11/10 Steve Owens 6.00
11/17 Skiing 4.50
11/24 Len Dawson 6.00
12/1 Pete Maravich 10.00
12/8 Walt Frazier 7.00
12/15 Texas vs. Arkansas 5.00
12/22 Tom Seaver (FC; SOY) 22.50

1970

1/5 Dave Osborn 5.00
1/12 Cheryl Tiegs (Swimsuit) 15.00
1/19 Len Dawson (Super Bowl IV) 12.00
1/26 Bob Cousy 9.00
2/2 Last Chance 4.00
2/9 Terry Bradshaw (FC) 15.00
2/16 Tom McMillen 6.00
2/23 Denny McLain 8.00
3/2 New York Rangers 7.00
3/9 Lew Alcindor 9.00
3/16 Collins, Vallely, Issel, Lanier 7.00
3/23 Richie Allen 6.50
3/30 UCLA Wins NCAA Championship 7.00
4/6 Keith Magnuson 5.00
4/13 Jerry Koosman 8.00
4/20 Billy Casper 4.50
4/27 Lew Alcindor 8.00
5/4 Bobby Orr 9.00
5/11 Super Hippie 4.00
5/18 Dave DeBusschere 7.00
5/25 Hank Aaron 10.00
6/1 Jack Nicklaus & Arnold Palmer 6.00
6/8 Al Unser (Indy 500) 7.50
6/15 Steve Prefontaine 4.00
6/22 Tony Conigliaro 10.00
6/29 Tony Jacklin 4.50
7/6 George Frenn 4.50
7/13 Johnny Bench 10.00
7/20 Joe Kapp 6.00
7/27 Willie Mays (3000 Hits) 15.00
8/3 Frank Shorter 4.50
8/10 Mike Garrett 6.00
8/17 Joe Namath 8.00
8/24 Rick Barry 6.50
8/31 Les Shy (Dallas Cowboys) 6.00
9/7 Buddy Harrelson & Pete Rose 10.00
9/14 Archie Manning 7.50
9/21 Dick Butkus 7.00
9/28 Durocher, Murtaugh, Hodges 8.00
10/5 Colorado vs. Penn State 6.00
10/12 Alex Karras 6.00
10/19 World Series 10.00
10/26 O. Robertson (FC) 8.50
11/2 Monday Night Football 5.00
11/9 Theismann, Tatum, Worster 7.00
11/16 Calvin Murphy 6.00
11/23 George Blanda 7.00
11/30 Sidney Wicks 6.00
12/7 Roman Gabriel 5.00
12/14 Woo Woo Worster 4.00
12/21 Bobby Orr (SOY) 9.50

1971

1/4 John Roche 4.50
1/11 Joe Theisman 6.50
1/18 Craig Morton (Super Bowl) 6.50
1/25 Jim O'Brien (Super Bowl V) 10.00
2/1 Tannia Rubiano(Swimsuit) 10.00
2/8 Lew Alcindor & Willis Reed 6.50
2/15 Jim Plunkett 6.00
2/22 Dr. Merriweather 4.00
3/1 Frazier vs. Ali 10.00
3/8 Jack Nicklaus 5.50
3/15 Frazier Beats Ali 12.00
3/22 Wes Parker 6.00
3/29 Phil & Tony Esposito 8.00
4/5 Steve Patterson 5.00
4/12 Boog Powell 7.00
4/19 Willis Reed & Lew Alcindor 7.00
4/26 Montreal vs. Boston 7.00
5/3 Dave Duncan & Jim Fregosi 6.00
5/10 Oscar Robertson 7.00
5/17 James McAlister 5.00
5/24 Marty Liquori (Track) 4.50
5/31 Vida Blue 9.00
6/7 Al Unser & Pete Revson 6.50
6/14 Canonero (Horse Racing) 5.00
6/21 Jerry Grote 6.00
6/28 Lee Trevino 6.00
7/5 Alex Johnson 6.00
7/12 Evonne Goolagong 4.00
7/19 George Blanda 6.00
7/26 Muhammed Ali 10.00
8/2 Willie Stargell (FC) 10.00
8/9 Mike Peterson 5.00
8/16 Calvin Hill 6.00
8/23 Steve McQueen 5.00
8/30 Ferguson Jenkins 8.50
9/6 Jackie Stewart 5.00
9/13 College Football Preview 5.00
9/20 John Brodie 6.00
9/27 Maury Wills 6.00
10/4 Sonny Sixkiller 4.00
10/11 Joe Greene 6.50
10/18 Frank Robinson 8.00
10/25 Johnson & DeBusschere 6.00
11/1 Ed Marinaro 6.00
11/8 Norm Bulaich 4.00
11/15 Olympics 5.00
11/22 Oklahoma vs. Nebraska 6.00
11/29 Tom Burleson 5.50
12/6 Johnny Musso 4.50
12/13 Gail Goodrich 5.50
12/20 Lee Trevino (SOY) 6.00

1972

1/3 Garo Yepremian 6.00
1/10 Awesome Nebraska 4.50
1/17 Swimsuit Issue 10.00
1/24 Duane Thomas (Super Bowl VI) 10.00
1/31 Ann Henning 4.00
2/7 Walt Frazier & Dave Cowens 6.00
2/14 Ken Dryden 5.00
2/21 Al McGuire 4.50
2/28 A.J. Foythoe 6.50
3/6 Bill Walton (FC) 8.00
3/13 Johnny Bench 10.00
3/20 NCAA Basketball Championship 6.50
3/27 Vida Blue 7.00
4/3 Bill Walton 7.50
4/10 Joe Torre 7.50
4/17 Jack Nicklaus 5.50
4/24 Lew Alcindor 6.50
5/1 Willie Davis 6.00
5/8 Phil Esposito & Bobby Orr 9.00
5/15 Wilt Chamberlain 8.00
5/22 Willie Mays 10.00
5/29 Louie Jacobs 4.00
6/5 Mark Donohue (Indy 500) 4.50
6/12 Dick Allen 6.00
6/19 Bobby Hull 7.50
6/26 Jack Nicklaus 5.50
7/3 Steve Blass 5.50
7/10 Johnny Unitas 6.00
7/17 Jim Ryun 4.50
7/24 Football Playbook 4.00
7/31 Robyn Smith (Horse Racing) 4.50
8/7 Larry Csonka & Jim Kiick 7.50
8/14 Bobby Fisher 4.50
8/21 Sparky Lyle 6.00
8/28 Olympics 5.00
9/4 Mark Spitz 6.00
9/11 B. Devaney (College Football) 4.50
9/18 Walt Garrison 5.00
9/25 Carlton Fisk (FC) 10.00
10/2 Greg Pruitt 6.00
10/9 Joe Namath 7.00
10/16 Wilt Chamberlain 7.00
10/23 Catfish Hunter (World Series) 9.00
10/30 Dave & Don Buckley 5.00

Sports Illustrated: 2/5/73

11/6 Larry Brown 5.50
11/13 John Havlicek 7.00
11/20 Terry Davis 5.00
11/27 Walter Luckett 4.50
12/4 Steve Spurrier 5.00
12/11 Campy Russell 5.50
12/18 Lee Roy Jordan 6.00
12/25 John Wooden & B.J. King (SOY) 7.00

1973

1/8 Mercury Morris 5.50
1/15 Doug Collins 5.50
1/22 Bob Griese (Super Bowl VII) 10.00
1/29 Dayle Haddon (Swimsuit) 10.00
2/5 Bill Walton 7.00
2/12 Steve Smith 4.50
2/19 Kareem & Wilt Chamberlain 8.00
2/26 Gil Perreault 5.50
3/5 Sports On Broadway 4.00
3/12 Bill Melton 6.50
3/19 Olga Korbut 4.50
3/26 Bill Walton & UCLA 7.00
4/2 Henri Richard 5.00
4/9 Steve Carlton 9.00
4/16 Earl Monroe 5.50
4/23 Muhammed Ali 9.00
4/30 Chris Speier 5.00
5/7 Jerry West & Walt Frazier 6.00
5/14 Mark Spitz 5.00
5/21 Bobby Riggs 4.50
5/28 Women In Sports 4.50
6/4 Wilbur Wood 5.50
6/11 Secretariat 6.00
6/18 George Foreman (FC) 10.00
6/25 Jack Nicklaus 5.00
7/2 Bobby Murcer & Ron Blomberg 6.00
7/9 George Allen 6.00
7/16 Billie Jean King 4.00
7/23 Tom Weiskopf 4.50
7/30 Carlton Fisk 9.00
8/6 John Matuszek 5.00
8/13 Dirt Bike Racing 4.00
8/20 Bill Russell &

Date	Cover	Price
	Claude Osteen	7.00
8/27	Duane Thomas	4.50
9/3	Bob Rigby	4.00
9/10	Texas Football (College Preview)	6.00
9/17	Larry Csonka	6.00
9/24	Danny Murtaugh	6.00
10/1	Anthony Davis	5.00
10/8	Fran Tarkenton	6.50
10/15	Nate Archibald	6.00
10/22	John Milner & Bert Campenaris	6.00
10/29	O.J. Simpson	7.00
11/5	Anthony Davis	5.00
11/12	Pete Maravich	7.00
11/19	Phil Esposito	7.00
11/26	David Thompson	6.00
12/3	Bear Bryant & Alabama	6.00
12/10	Len Elmore	5.00
12/17	Marv Hubbard	4.50
12/24	Jackie Stewart	5.00
1974		
1/7	Fran Tarkenton	6.50
1/14	Julius Erving (FC)	12.00
1/21	Larry Csonka (Super Bowl VIII)	10.00
1/28	Ann Simonton (Swimsuit)	10.00
2/4	Ali Beats Frazier	10.00
2/11	Ben Crenshaw	4.50
2/18	John Havlicek	6.50
2/25	Bill Walton & UCLA	6.00
3/4	Jimmy Connors (FC)	10.00
3/11	Gordie Howe	7.00
3/18	Babe Ruth	10.00
3/25	Bill Walton & Tom Burleson	6.00
4/1	UCLA vs. N.C. State	6.00
4/8	Pete Rose	12.00
4/15	Hank Aaron (HR #715)	22.00
4/22	Gary Player	5.00
4/29	Bruce Hardy	4.50
5/6	Flyers vs. Rangers	5.00
5/13	Kentucky Derby	5.00
5/20	John Havlicek	6.50
5/27	Jim Wynn	5.00
6/3	Johnny Rutherford (Indy 500)	4.50
6/10	Johnny Miller (U.S. Open)	4.50
6/17	Reggie Jackson	10.00
6/24	Hale Irwin	4.50
7/1	Rod Carew (FC)	9.00
7/8	Gerald Ford	6.00
7/15	Jimmy Connors & Chris Evert	7.50
7/22	Lou Brock	8.00
7/29	Terry Bradshaw	7.00
8/5	Pro Football Strike	4.50
8/12	Mike Marshall	6.50
8/19	Lee Trevino	5.00
8/26	John Newcombe	4.50
9/2	Evil Knievel	5.00
9/9	Archie Griffin	5.00
9/16	O.J. Simpson	7.00
9/23	Joe Gilliam	5.00
9/30	Tom Clements	4.50
10/7	Catfish Hunter	8.00
10/14	Bill Walton & Kareem	6.50
10/21	Dodgers vs. Athletics	8.00
10/28	Ali vs. Foreman	12.50
11/4	Oklahoma Football	5.00
11/11	Ali Beats Foreman	8.00
11/18	Wood Green	12.50
11/25	Ken Dryden	5.00
12/2	College Basketball	5.00
12/9	Anthony Davis & USC	5.00
12/16	Rick Barry	5.00
12/23	Muhammed Ali (SOY)	10.00
1975		
1/6	Franco Harris (FC)	7.00
1/13	Bill Tilden	5.50
1/20	Terry Bradshaw (Super Bowl IX)	10.00
1/27	Cheryl Tiegs (Swimsuit)	15.00
2/3	John Laskowski	4.00
2/10	Rogie Vachon	4.50
2/17	Dave Meyers	4.00
2/24	Dog Champion	4.00
3/3	Cincinnati Reds (Spring Training)	8.00
3/10	Lee Elder	5.00
3/17	Phil Ford	6.00
3/24	Ali vs. Wepner	7.50
3/31	Kentucky vs. Indiana	5.00
4/7	Steve Garvey	6.50

Sports Illustrated: 5/2/77

Date	Cover	Price
4/14	Vasili Alexeyev (Weighlifting)	4.50
4/21	Jack Nicklaus	5.00
4/28	NBA Playoffs	5.00
5/5	Jimmy Connors	5.00
5/12	Kentucky Derby	4.50
5/19	A.J. Foyt (Indy 500)	5.50
5/26	Filbert Bayi	4.00
6/2	Billy Martin	6.00
6/9	Rocky Bleier	5.00
6/16	Nolan Ryan (FC)	30.00
6/23	Pele	5.00
6/30	Lou Graham	6.50
7/7	Fred Lynn	7.50
7/14	Arthur Ashe	5.00
7/21	Jim Palmer & Tom Seaver	11.00
7/28	Csonka, Kiick, Warfield (WFL)	6.00
8/4	Tim Shaw	4.50
8/11	The Baseball Boom	5.50
8/18	Jack Nicklaus	5.00
8/25	Bart Starr	5.00
9/1	Brian Oldfield	4.50
9/8	College Football	5.00
9/15	M. Ali, J. Frazier, Don King	7.50
9/22	Joe Greene	5.50
9/29	Rick Slager	4.50
10/6	Reggie Jackson	8.00
10/13	Ali vs. Frazier	7.50
10/20	Red Sox vs. Reds	10.00
10/27	George McGinnis	5.00
11/3	Bench,McEnaney (Reds Win WS)	10.00
11/10	Fran Tarkenton	5.00
11/17	Pro Hockey Violence	4.50
11/24	Chuck Muncie	4.50
12/1	Kent Benson & Indiana	6.00
12/8	Bubba Bean & Texas A&M	4.50
12/15	George Foreman	8.00
12/22	Pete Rose (SOY)	12.00
1976		
1/5	Preston Pearson	5.00
1/12	Franco Harris	5.00
1/19	The Sylvanders(Swimsuit)	10.00
1/26	Lynn Swann (Super Bowl X)	1.00
2/2	Sheila Young (Olympics)	4.50
2/9	Ernie Grunfeld & Bernard King	5.00
2/16	Franz Klammer	4.00
2/23	Bobby Clarke	5.00
3/1	Muhammed Ali	7.50
3/8	Bob McAdoo	5.00
3/15	Bill Veeck	6.50
3/22	Tracy Austin	4.50
3/29	Kent Benson	5.00
4/5	Scott May (NCAA Championship)	5.00
4/12	Joe Morgan	8.50
4/19	Ray Floyd	4.00
4/26	Evonne Goolagong	4.00
5/3	Mike Schmidt (FC)	10.00
5/10	Angel Cordero	4.50
5/17	Julius Erving	9.00
5/24	Larry Robinson (Stanley Cup)	5.00
5/31	Carlton Fisk (Yankees vs. Red Sox)	7.50
6/7	Alvin Adams	4.50
6/14	Dwight Stones	4.00
6/21	George Brett (FC)	12.00
6/28	Bowie Kuhn	4.50
7/5	Frank Shorter	4.00
7/12	Randy Jones	5.00
7/19	Olympic Preview	5.00
7/26	Olympics	4.50
8/2	Nadia Comaneci	6.00
8/9	Bruce Jenner	7.50
8/16	Calvin Hill	5.00
8/23	Steve Spurrier	5.00
8/30	Reggie Jackson	8.00
9/6	Rick Leach	4.50
9/13	Bert Jones	4.00
9/20	Jimmy Connors	5.00
9/27	Ken Norton	4.00
10/4	Mark Manges	4.00
10/11	George Foster	5.00
10/18	Chuck Foreman	4.00
10/25	Dave Cowens & Julius Erving	6.00
11/1	Johnny Bench (World Series)	8.50
11/8	Tony Dorsett (FC)	8.00
11/15	David Thompson	5.50
11/22	Walter Payton (FC)	10.00
11/29	Ricky Green	4.50
12/6	Rocky Bleier	4.50
12/13	Bill Walton	4.50
12/20	Chris Evert (SOY)	5.00
1977		
1/3	Clarence Davis	4.50
1/10	Tony Dorsett	7.50
1/17	Ken Stabler (Super Bowl XI, FC)	9.00
1/24	Lena Kansbod (Swimsuit)	8.00
1/31	Bill Cartwright	4.50
2/7	Guy Lafleur	5.50
2/14	Kareem Abdul-Jabbar	6.00
2/21	NBC Olympic TV Deal	3.50
2/28	Cale Yarbrough	4.50
3/7	Steve Cauthen	4.50
3/14	Tom Lasorda	5.50
3/21	George McGinnis	4.00
3/28	Bump Wills	3.50
4/4	Butch Lee	4.50
4/11	Joe Rudi	5.00
4/18	Tom Watson (FC)	4.50
4/25	Sidney Wicks	5.00
5/2	Reggie Jackson	7.00
5/9	Brad Parks	4.00
5/16	Kentucky Derby	4.00
5/23	Bill Walton	4.50
5/30	Dave Parker	6.50
6/6	Mark Fidrych & Big Bird	7.00
6/13	Bill Walton	4.50
6/20	Seattle Slew	5.00
6/27	Tom Seaver	8.00
7/4	Ted Turner	4.00
7/11	Bjorn Borg	4.00
7/18	Rod Carew & Ted Williams	9.00
7/25	Conrad Dobler	4.00

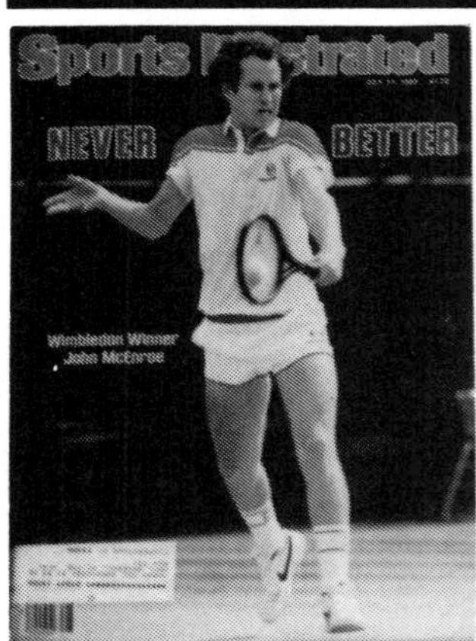

Sports Illustrated: 7/11/83

Date	Issue	Price
8/1	Boating the Colorado Rapids	3.50
8/8	Carlos Monzon	4.00
8/15	Sadaharu Oh	6.50
8/22	Lanny Wadkins	4.00
8/29	Greg Luzinski	5.00
9/5	Ross Browner	3.50
9/12	Alberto Juantorena (Track)	3.50
9/19	Ken Stabler	8.00
9/26	Roberto Duran	4.50
10/3	Billy Simms	4.50
10/10	Ali Beats Shavers	6.50
10/17	Rubin Carter	4.00
10/24	Russell & Munson (World Series)	8.00
10/31	Maurice Lucas	4.00
11/7	Semi-Though, The Movie	3.50
11/14	Belmont Swindle	3.50
11/21	AFC vs. NFC	3.50
11/28	Larry Bird (FC)	14.00
12/5	Earl Campbell	6.00
12/12	Bryan Trottier	4.50
12/19	Steve Cauthen (SOY)	4.00
	1978	
1/2	Mark Van Eeghen	4.50
1/9	Terry Eurick	4.00
1/16	Maia Joao (Swimsuit)	8.00
1/23	White & Martin (Super Bowl XII)	7.50
1/30	Duran Beats Dejesus	4.50
2/6	Dick Buerkle (Track & Field)	3.50
2/13	Sidney Moncreif	5.00
2/20	Walter Davis	4.00
2/27	Leon Spinks	5.00
3/6	Houston McTear	3.50
3/13	Gene Banks	4.00
3/20	Clint Hurdle	4.00
3/27	Jack Nicklaus	4.50
4/3	J. Givens (NCAA Championship)	5.00
4/10	George Foster & Rod Carew	6.50
4/17	Gary Player	4.00
4/24	Mark Fidrych	4.00
5/1	Gary Player	4.00
5/8	Elvin Hayes	5.00
5/15	Steve Cauthen & Affirmed	4.50
5/22	Marvin Webster	4.00
5/29	Canadiens vs. Bruins	4.50
6/5	Al Unser (Indy 500)	5.00
6/12	Ken Norton	4.50
6/19	Affirmed Wins Belmont	4.50
6/26	Andy North (U.S. Open)	4.00
7/3	Argentina Wins World Cup	4.00
7/10	Nancy Lopez	4.00
7/17	Is Money Ruining Sports?	3.50
7/24	Jack Nicklaus	4.50
7/31	Billy Martin	5.00
8/7	Pete Rose	10.00
8/14	Brutality in Football	4.00
8/21	Bill Walton	4.50
8/28	Eagle II (Ballooning)	3.50
9/4	Roger Staubach	5.50
9/11	Lou Holtz (College Football)	5.00
9/18	Jimmy Connors	5.00
9/25	Muhammed Ali	7.50
10/2	Charles White	4.00
10/9	Terry Bradshaw	6.00
10/16	Marvin Webster	4.00
10/23	Graig Nettles (World Series)	7.50
10/30	Bill Rodgers	4.00
11/6	Horse Racing	3.50
11/13	Chuck Fusina	4.00
11/20	Rick Berns	4.00
11/27	Magic Johnson (FC)	25.00
12/4	Earl Campbell	5.00
12/11	Mountain Climbing	3.50
12/18	John McEnroe (FC)	8.00
12/25	Jack Nicklaus (SOY)	4.50
	1979	
1/8	Alabama Beats Penn State	4.50
1/15	Terry Bradshaw (Year In Sports)	6.50
1/22	Ohio State vs. Illinois	4.00
1/29	Rocky Bleier (Super Bowl XIII)	8.00
2/5	Christie Brinkley (Swimsuit)	10.00
2/12	Danny Lopez	4.00
2/19	Moses Malone	5.00
2/26	Eamonn Coghlan (Track)	3.50
3/5	Spring Training	5.00
3/12	Dudley Bradley	4.00
3/19	Harry Chappas	4.00
3/26	Larry Bird	12.50
4/2	Magic Johnson	12.50
4/9	Rice & Parker (Baseball Preview)	6.00
4/16	Denis Potvin	4.50
4/23	Fuzzy Zoeller	4.00
4/30	George Bamberger	4.00
5/7	Elvin Hayes	4.00
5/14	Kentucky Derby	4.00
5/21	Giorgio Chinaglia	4.00
5/28	Pete Rose	8.00
6/4	Tom Watson	4.00
6/11	Gus Williams	4.00
6/18	Earl Weaver	4.50
6/25	Hale Irwin	4.00
7/2	Duran Beats Palomino	4.00
7/9	Eamonn Coghlan (Track)	3.50
7/16	Bjorn Borg (Mattingly "Faces")	20.00
7/23	Nolan Ryan	25.00
7/30	Sebastian Coe	4.00
8/6	Ken Stabler	4.00
8/13	Silver Anniversary Issue	7.00
8/20	John Jefferson	4.00
8/27	Baseball's Golden Oldies	5.00
9/3	Earl Campbell	4.50
9/10	Billy Simms (College Football)	4.00
9/17	Tracy Austin	4.00
9/24	Vagas Ferguson	4.00
10/1	Dewey Selmon	4.00
10/8	Holmes Beats Shavers	4.50
10/15	Bill Walton	4.50
10/22	Pirates vs. Orioles	5.00
10/29	Bill Rogers	4.00
11/5	Franco Harris	4.50
11/12	Heisman Candidates	4.50
11/19	Magic Johnson	10.00
11/26	Art Schlichter	4.00
12/3	Indiana (College Basketball)	4.50
12/10	Sugar Ray Leonard (FC)	8.00
12/17	Ralph Sampson	4.50
12/24	Stargell & Bradshaw (SOY)	6.50
	1980	
1/7	Ricky Bell	4.00
1/14	L.C. Greenwood	4.00
1/21	Gordie Howe	5.00
1/28	John Stallworth (Super Bowl XIV)	8.00
2/4	Christie Brinkley (Swimsuit)	10.00
2/11	Eric Heiden	3.50
2/18	Mary Decker	3.50
2/25	Eric Heiden (Winter Olympics)	3.50
3/3	USA Olympic Hockey Team	10.00
3/10	Jim Craig	3.50
3/17	Albert King	3.50
3/24	Kirk Gibson	4.50
3/31	Louisville Wins NCAAs	5.50
4/7	K. Hernandez (Baseball Preview)	5.00
4/14	Muhammed Ali	7.00
4/21	Seve Ballesteros	3.50
4/28	Julius Erving & Larry Bird	10.00
5/5	Kareem Abdul-Jabbar	6.00
5/12	Kentucky Derby	4.00
5/19	Shame Or Education	3.00
5/26	Magic Johnson	10.00
6/2	Johnny Rutherford	3.50
6/9	Darrell Porter	4.00
6/16	Roberto Duran	3.50
6/23	Jack Nicklaus	4.00
6/30	Duran vs. Leonard	4.50
7/7	Steve Scott	3.50
7/14	Bjorn Borg	4.00
7/21	Steve Carlton (FC)	7.00
7/28	Olympics	4.00
8/4	Reggie Jackson	7.00
8/11	Sebastian Coe	3.50
8/18	J.R. Richard	4.50
8/25	Orioles vs. Yankees	4.50
9/1	Hugh Green (College Football)	4.00
9/8	Pro Football Preview	4.50
9/15	John McEnroe	4.00
9/22	Billy Simms	4.00
9/29	Muhammed Ali	7.00
10/6	Gary Carter	6.00
10/13	Muhammed Ali	7.00
10/20	Paul Westphal	4.00
10/27	Mike Schmidt (World Series)	6.50
11/3	Alberto Salazar	3.00
11/10	L.C. Greenwood	3.50
11/17	Herschel Walker	4.00
11/24	Sugar Ray Leonard	4.50
12/1	College Basketball Preview	5.00
12/8	Vince Ferragamo	3.50
12/15	Lloyd Free	3.50
12/22	USA Hockey Team (SOY)	7.50
	1981	
1/5	Dave Winfield (FC)	7.50
1/12	Chuck Muncie	3.50
1/19	Mark Van Eeghen	3.50
1/26	Bobby Knight	4.00
2/2	Rod Martin (Super Bowl XV)	7.00
2/9	Christie Brinkley (Swimsuit)	15.00
2/16	Point Shaving Scheme	3.50
2/23	Bobby Carpenter	3.50
3/2	J.R. Richard	4.00
3/9	Magic Johnson	10.00
3/16	Rollie Fingers	6.00
3/23	Rolando Blackman	3.50
3/30	Ralph Sampson	4.00
4/6	Isiah Thomas (NCAA Championship)	6.50
4/13	Brett & Schmidt	

(Baseball) 8.00
4/20 Tom Watson 3.50
4/27 Oakland A's Five Starters 5.00
5/4 Gerry Cooney 3.50
5/11 K. McHale, L. Bird, M. Cheeks 10.00
5/18 Fernando Valenzuela 5.50
5/25 A.J. Foyt 4.50
6/1 Marvis & Joe Frazier 4.50
6/8 Greg Luzinski 4.00
6/15 Bjorn Borg 3.50
6/22 Baseball Strike 3.50
6/29 David Graham 3.50
7/6 Leonard vs. Kalule 4.00
7/13 John McEnroe 4.50
7/20 V. Ferragamo (Bo Jackson "Faces") 15.00
7/27 Tom Seaver 7.00
8/3 John Hannah 3.50
8/10 George Brett & Mike Schmidt 8.00
8/17 Gary Carter 5.50
8/24 Wendell Tyler 3.50
8/31 Herschel Walker (College Football) 4.50
9/7 Jim Plunkett 3.50
9/14 Thomas Hearns 3.50
9/21 John McEnroe 4.00
9/28 Leonard vs. Hearns 4.50
10/5 Marcus Allen 4.50
10/12 Wayne Gretzky (FC) 15.00
10/19 Texas vs. Oklahoma 4.00
10/26 Graig Nettles 5.00
11/2 World Series 6.00
11/9 Larry Bird 8.50
11/16 Holmes vs. Snipes 3.50
11/23 Bear Bryant 4.00
11/30 Dean Smith (College Basketball) 4.00
12/7 Tony Dorsett 3.50
12/14 Cris Collinsworth 3.50
12/21 Earl Cooper 3.50
12/28 Sugar Ray Leonard (SOY) 4.00

Sports Illustrated: 11/28/83

1982

1/11 Perry Tuttle 3.50
1/18 Dwight Clark('The Catch') 10.00
1/25 Joe Montana (FC) 17.50
2/1 Earl Cooper (Super Bowl XVI) 5.00
2/8 Carol Alt (Swimsuit) 15.00
2/15 Wayne Gretzky 7.00
2/22 Sidney Moncreif 3.50
3/1 Herschel Walker (FC) 4.50
3/8 Pipeline surfing 3.00
3/15 Reggie Jackson 6.00
3/22 Patrick Ewing (FC) 6.50
3/29 Sam Perkins 4.00
4/5 James Worthy 4.50
4/12 Steve Garvey (Baseball Preview) 6.00
4/19 Craig Stadler 3.50
4/26 Renaldo Nehemiah 3.50
5/3 Jack Sikma 3.50
5/10 Georgia Frontiere & Bert Jones 3.50
5/17 Gaylord Perry 4.00
5/24 Magic Johnson 8.50
5/31 Julius Erving 6.50
6/7 Gerry Cooney 3.50
6/14 Special Report: Cocaine 3.00
6/21 Holmes Beats Cooney 4.00
6/28 Tom Watson 3.50
7/5 Kent Hrbek 4.00
7/12 Jimmy Connors (V.Coleman "Faces") 5.00
7/19 Pete Rose & Yastrzemski 8.00
7/26 Mary Decker 3.50
8/2 Ray Mancini 3.50
8/9 Dale Murphy 6.00
8/16 Walter Payton 6.50
8/23 Franco Harris 4.00
8/30 Tom Cousineau 3.50
9/6 Rickey Henderson (FC) 10.00
9/13 Wayne Peace 3.50
9/20 Jimmy Connors 4.00
9/27 NFL Strike 3.50
10/4 Todd Blackledge 3.50
10/11 Robin Yount (FC) 7.00
10/18 Marvin Hagler 3.50
10/25 Robin Yount (World Series) 7.00
11/1 Moses Malone 4.00
11/8 John Elway (FC) 7.00
11/15 Sugar Ray Leonard 4.00
11/22 Ray Mancini 3.50
11/29 Ralph Sampson & Pat Ewing 4.00
12/6 Redskins Beat Eagles 3.50
12/13 Marcus Allen 3.50
12/20 Ralph Sampson 3.50
12/27 Wayne Gretzky (SOY) 8.00

1983

1/10 Penn State Number One 3.50
1/17 Chuck Muncie 3.50
1/24 Andra Franklin 3.50
1/31 Redskins Beat Dallas 4.00
2/7 John Riggins (Super Bowl XVII) 5.00
2/14 Cheryl Tiegs (Swimsuit) 7.50
2/21 Terry Cummings 3.50
2/28 Julius Erving 5.00
3/7 Herschel Walker 4.00
3/14 P. Rose, J. Morgan, T. Perez 7.00
3/21 Billy Goodwin (St. John's) 3.50
3/28 Michael Spinks 3.50
4/4 Gary Carter 4.00
4/11 N.C. State Wins NCAA Championship 7.50
4/18 Tom Seaver 7.00
4/25 Steve Garvey 5.00
5/2 Larry Bird & Dominique Wilkins 8.00
5/9 Kareem Abdul-Jabbar 8.00
5/16 Kentucky Derby 3.50
5/23 Billy Smith (Stanley Cup) 3.50
5/30 Larry Holmes 3.50
6/6 Moses Malone 3.50
6/13 Rod Carew 6.00
6/20 Marcus Dupree 3.50
6/27 Roberto Duran 3.50
7/4 Dale Murphy 5.00
7/11 John McEnroe 4.00
7/18 Andre Dawson & Dave Stieb 5.00
7/25 Tom Watson 3.50
8/1 Richard Todd 3.50
8/8 Howard Cosell 3.50
8/15 John Elway 4.00
8/22 Carl Lewis 3.50
8/30 Tony Dorsett 3.50
9/5 Mike Rozier 3.50
9/12 Edwin Moses 3.50
9/19 Martina Navratilova (U.S. Open) 3.50
9/26 Doug Flutie 4.00
10/3 Steve Carlton 5.50
10/10 Joe Washington 3.50
10/17 Eric Dickerson 4.00
10/24 Rick Dempsey (World Series) 4.00
10/31 Ralph Sampson 3.50
11/7 Hagler vs. Duran 4.00
11/14 Dan Marino (FC) 7.00
11/21 Hagler Beats Duran 4.00

Sports Illustrated: 9/2/85

11/28 M. Jordan (FC) & S. Perkins 25.00
12/5 Sam Bowie 3.50
12/12 Jim Brown 4.00
12/19 John Riggins 4.00
12/26 Mary Decker (SOY) 3.50

1984

1/9 Keith Griffin 3.50
1/16 Joe Theisman 3.50
1/23 Wayne Gretzky 7.00
1/30 Jack Squirek (Super Bowl XVIII) 4.50
2/6 Winter Olympics 3.50
2/13 Paulina Porizkova (Swimsuit) 7.00
2/20 Debbie Armstrong (Skiing) 3.00
2/27 Bill Johnson (Skiing) 3.00
3/5 Magic Johnson 7.50
3/12 George Brett 7.00
3/19 Patrick Ewing 5.00
3/26 Sam Perkins 3.50
4/2 Yogi Berra 5.50
4/9 Georgetown vs. Houston 4.00
4/16 Rich Gossage & Graig Nettles 5.00
4/23 Darryl Strawberry (FC) 7.00
4/30 Navratilova Beats Lloyd 3.50
5/7 Bernard King 3.50
5/14 Mike Bossy 3.50
5/21 Soviets Boycott Olympics 3.00
5/28 Alan Trammell 5.00
6/4 Magic Johnson 7.00
6/11 Leon Durham 3.50
6/18 Martina Navratilova 3.50
6/25 Carl Lewis 3.50
7/2 Dwight Stones 3.00
7/9 Jeff Float (Swimming) 3.00
7/16 John McEnroe 3.50
7/23 Michael Jordan 15.00
7/30 Jack Lambert 3.50
8/6 Rafer Johnson (Olympics) 3.50
8/13 Mary Lou Retton (Olympics) 3.50

8/20 Carl Lewis 3.50
8/27 Pete Rose 6.00
9/3 Joe Theisman 3.50
9/10 Dolphins vs. Redskins 3.50
9/17 John McEnroe 3.50
9/24 Dwight Gooden (FC) & R. Sutcliffe 8.00
10/1 Jeff Smith 3.50
10/8 Sammy Winder 3.50
10/15 Walter Payton 6.00
10/22 Alan Trammell 5.00
10/29 Larry Bird & Bill Russell ... 7.50
11/5 Gerry Faust 3.50
11/12 What's Wrong with the NFL 3.00
11/19 Mark Duper 3.50
11/26 Reagan, Ewing, Thompson 5.00
12/3 Doug Flutie 3.50
12/10 Michael Jordan (FC) 12.50
12/17 Eric Dickerson 3.50
12/24 Mary Lou Retton & Edwin Moses (SOY) 3.50

1985

1/7 Walter Abercrombie 3.50
1/14 Dan Marino 6.00
1/21 Dan Marino &Joe Montana 10.00
1/28 Roger Craig (Super Bowl XIX) 5.00
2/4 Walter Berry 3.50
2/11 Paulina Porizkova (Swimsuit) 7.50

Sports Illustrated: 2/10/86

2/18 Wayne Gretzky 7.00
2/25 Doug Flutie 3.50
3/4 Mike Schmidt (Baseball Salaries) 6.50
3/11 Jack Nicklaus & Son 4.00
3/18 Fred Lynn 5.00
3/25 Mantle, Mays, Ueberroth . 8.00
4/1 Ewing, Mullin, McClain 5.50
4/8 Ed Pinckney (NCAAs) 3.50
4/15 Dwight Gooden 6.00
4/22 Hagler Beats Hearns 3.50
4/29 Hulk Hogan 3.50
5/6 Billy Martin 5.00
5/13 Magic Johnson 7.00
5/20 Patrick Ewing 4.50
5/27 Herschel Walker 4.00
6/3 Danny Sullivan (Indy 500) . 3.50
6/10 Kareem Abdul-Jabbar 4.50
6/17 Abdul-Jabbar & C. Evert .. 4.50
6/24 Andy North 3.50
7/1 Larry Holmes 3.50
7/8 Fernando Valenzuela 5.00
7/15 Boris Becker 3.50
7/22 Howie Long 3.50
7/29 Mary Decker Slaney 3.50
8/5 Pedro Guerrero 4.50
8/12 Tony Dorsett 3.50
8/19 Pete Rose 6.00
8/26 Bernie Kosar 3.50
9/2 Dwight Gooden 5.00
9/9 Bill Elliott 3.50
9/16 Joe Louis 4.00
9/23 Ozzie Smith (FC) 5.50
9/30 Spinks vs. Holmes 3.50
10/7 Tony Robinson 3.50
10/14 Eddie Robinson 3.50
10/21 Jim McMahon 4.00
10/28 Ozzie Smith (World Series) 6.00
11/4 Royals Win World Series .. 5.00
11/11 Florida & Penn State 3.50
11/18 Dale Brown 3.50
11/25 Bears Beat Dallas 4.00
12/2 Bo Jackson (FC), Long, Dudek 8.00
12/9 Kirk Gibson 5.00
12/16 Marcus Allen 3.50
12/23 Kareem Abdul-Jabbar (SOY) 4.00

1986

1/6 Mike Tyson (FC) 10.00
1/13 Craig James 3.00
1/20 Jim McMahon 4.00
1/27 Bears vs. Patriots 5.00
2/3 Bears Win Super Bowl XX . 6.00
2/10 Elle MacPherson(Swimsuit) 7.50
2/17 Danny Manning 6.00
2/24 Network Sports Coverage . 2.50
3/3 Larry Bird 7.50
3/10 Gambling 2.50
3/17 Mark Alarie 3.00
3/24 Hagler vs. Mugabi 3.00
3/31 Final Four 3.00
4/7 P. Ellison (NCAA Championship) 3.50
4/14 Wade Boggs (FC) 6.00
4/21 Jack Nicklaus 3.50
4/28 Dominique Wilkins 3.50
5/5 Ernest Hemingway 2.50
5/12 Roger Clemens (FC) 7.00
5/19 James Worthy 4.00
5/26 Akeem Olajuwon (FC) 4.00
6/2 Canadiens Win Stanley Cup 3.50
6/9 Larry Bird 7.50
6/16 Kevin McHale 3.50
6/23 Raymond Floyd 2.50
6/30 Len Bias 3.50
7/7 Diego Maradona 2.50
7/14 Bo Jackson 7.00
7/21 Jim Kelly (FC) 6.00
7/28 Rickey Henderson 7.00
8/4 Oil Can Boyd 3.00
8/11 "Too Tall" Jones & William Perry 3.50
8/18 Herschel Walker 4.00
8/25 Ron Darling 3.00
9/1 Kristie Phillips (Gymnastics) 2.50
9/8 Sugar Ray Leonard 3.50
9/15 Ivan Lendl 3.00
9/22 Notre Dame Beats Michigan 3.50
9/29 M. Gastineau & L. Taylor(FC) 8.50
10/6 Darryl Strawberry 5.00
10/13 John Elway 4.00
10/20 Bobby Grich & Doug DeCinces 3.50
10/27 Rice & Carter (World Series) 5.00
11/3 Ray Knight (Mets Win Series) 4.50
11/10 NFL Injuries 2.50
11/17 Michael Jordan 10.00
11/24 Vinny Testaverde 3.00
12/1 Mike Tyson 6.00
12/8 Walter Payton 4.00
12/15 Mark Bavaro 3.00
12/22 Joe Paterno (SOY) 3.00

1987

1/5 Brian Bosworth 3.00

Sports Illustrated: 1/6/86

1/12 Ozzie Newsome 3.00
1/19 Rich Karlis 2.50
1/26 Lawrence Taylor 7.00
2/2 Phil Simms (Super Bowl XXI) 4.00
2/9 Elle MacPherson (Swimsuit) 7.50
2/16 Dennis Conner & Ronald Reagan 3.00
2/23 Magic Johnson 7.50
3/2 J.R. Reid 3.00
3/9 The Ripkens (Cal Jr.,FC) . 10.00
3/16 Gary McLain 2.50
3/23 Bobby Knight 4.00
3/30 Hagler vs. Leonard 3.00
4/6 Joe Carter & Cory Snyder 5.00
4/13 Leonard Beats Hagler 3.50
4/20 Player Salaries 2.50
4/27 Rob Deer 3.00
5/4 Julius Erving 4.50
5/11 Reggie Jackson 4.50
5/18 Isiah Thomas 3.00
5/25 Eric Davis 4.00
6/1 Wayne Gretzky 6.00
6/8 Larry Bird 7.00
6/15 Lakers vs. Celtics 3.50
6/22 Kareem Abdul-Jabbar 4.00
6/29 Watson & Simpson 2.50
7/6 A Day In Baseball 2.50
7/13 D. Strawberry & Don Mattingly (FC) 7.50
7/20 Andre Dawson 5.00
7/27 Pit Bull 2.50
8/3 Vinny Testaverde 3.00
8/10 Mike Tyson 5.00
8/17 Alan Trammell 4.00
8/24 Jim McMahon 4.00
8/31 Tim Brown 3.00
9/7 Surf's Up 2.50
9/14 Jackie Joyner-Kersee 2.50
9/21 John Elway 3.00
9/28 Ozzie Smith 5.00
10/5 Lloyd Moseby 3.50
10/12 Steve Walsh 3.00
10/19 Greg Gagne 4.00
10/26 Dan Gladden 4.00
11/2 Twins Win World Series ... 5.00
11/9 Eric Dickerson 3.00
11/16 F. Denbo (College Basketball) 3.00
11/23 Dexter Manley 3.00
11/30 Oklahoma vs. Nebraska ... 2.50
12/7 Arnold Schwarzenegger ... 4.00
12/14 Bo Jackson 7.00
12/21 Athletes Who Care (SOY) . 3.50
12/28 Michael Jordan 8.00

1988

1/11 Miami Beats Oklahoma ... 3.00
1/18 Anthony Carter ... 3.00
1/25 John Elway ... 3.00
2/1 Mike Tyson ... 5.00
2/8 Doug Williams (Super Bowl XXII) ... 4.00
2/15 Elle MacPherson (Swimsuit) ... 7.50
2/22 Wilt Chamberlain & Bill Russell ... 3.50
2/29 Brian Boitano (Figure Skating) ... 2.50
3/7 Kirk Gibson ... 5.00
3/14 Pam Postema ... 2.50
3/21 Larry Bird ... 6.00
3/28 Mark Macon ... 3.00
4/4 Will Clark & Mark McGwire ... 8.00
4/11 Danny Manning ... 3.00
4/18 How Good Are the Lakers? 3.00
4/25 Muhammed Ali ... 4.00
5/2 Billy Ripken ... 3.00
5/9 Pete Rose ... 5.00
5/16 Michael Jordan ... 7.00
5/23 Magic Johnson ... 6.00
5/30 Wayne Gretzky ... 6.00

Sports Illustrated: 10/12/81

6/6 Fired Coaches & Managers ... 2.50
6/13 Mike Tyson & Robin Givens ... 5.00
6/20 Michael Spinks ... 3.00
6/27 Magic Johnson & Bill Laimbeer ... 5.50
7/4 Mike Tyson ... 5.00
7/11 Darryl Strawberry ... 4.00
7/18 Casey At the Bat ... 2.50
7/25 Florence Griffith-Joyner ... 2.50
8/1 Tony Dorsett ... 3.00
8/8 Beer and Sports ... 2.50
8/15 Sports in China ... 2.50
8/22 Wayne Gretzky & Magic Johnson ... 7.50
8/29 Bernie Kosar ... 3.00
9/5 Florida Football ... 2.50
9/12 Jim McMahon ... 3.50
9/19 Steffi Graf ... 3.00
9/26 Dwight Evans ... 4.00
10/3 Ben Johnson ... 3.00
10/10 Florence Joyner & Jackie Kersey ... 2.50
10/17 Jose Canseco (FC) ... 8.00
10/24 Tony Rice ... 3.00
10/31 Orel Hershiser (FC; World Series) ... 7.00
11/7 Karl Malone (FC) ... 3.00
11/14 Tom Landry & Chuck Noll . 7.00
11/21 Saints vs. Rams ... 2.50
11/28 Rodney Peete ... 3.00
12/5 Tony Rice ... 3.00
12/12 Charles Barkley (FC) ... 8.00
12/19 Orel Hershiser (SOY) ... 6.00
12/26 Florence Griffith-Joyner ... 2.50

1989

1/9 Tony Rice ... 3.00
1/16 Ickey Woods ... 2.50
1/23 Kareem Abdul-Jabbar ... 4.00
1/30 Jerry Rice (Super Bowl XXIII) ... 8.00
2/6 Mario Lemieux (FC) ... 4.00
2/13 Patrick Ewing ... 7.00
2/20 Chris Jackson ... 3.00
2/27 Charles Thompson ... 2.50
3/6 Wade Boggs ... 3.50
3/13 Michael Jordan ... 7.50
3/20 Jimmy Johnson ... 2.50
3/27 Steffi Graf ... 3.00
4/3 Pete Rose ... 4.00
4/10 Glen Rice (Michigan Wins NCAAs) ... 3.00
4/17 Nick Faldo ... 2.50
4/24 Tony Mandarich ... 3.00
5/1 Nolan Ryan ... 9.50
5/8 Jon Peters ... 3.00
5/15 Michael Jordan ... 6.50
5/22 Julie Krone ... 2.50
5/29 Kentucky's Shame ... 2.50
6/5 James Worthy ... 3.50
6/12 Bo Jackson ... 6.00
6/19 Leonard vs. Hearns ... 3.00
6/26 Curtis Strange ... 2.50
7/3 Pete Rose ... 4.50
7/10 Rick Reuschel ... 2.50
7/17 George Foreman ... 5.50
7/24 Gregg Jefferies ... 3.50
7/31 Greg Lemond (Tour de France) ... 2.50
8/7 Boomer Esiason ... 3.00
8/14 Michael Jordan ... 6.00
8/21 Troy Aikman (FC) ... 6.00
8/28 Chris Evert ... 3.00
9/4 College Football Preview .. 3.00
9/11 Randall Cunningham ... 3.50
9/18 Boris Becker ... 3.00
9/25 Raghib Ismail (FC) ... 3.50
10/2 Joe Montana ... 6.00
10/9 Sergei Starikov ... 2.50
10/16 Rickey Henderson ... 5.00
10/23 Herschel Walker ... 3.50
10/30 Earthquake World Series .. 4.00
11/6 Joe Dumars & Michael Jordan ... 6.00
11/13 Deion Sanders (FC) ... 5.00
11/20 Rumeal Robinson ... 3.00
11/27 Heisman Candidates ... 3.00
12/4 Stephen McGuire ... 2.50
12/11 Larry Bird ... 6.00
12/18 Montana, Gretzky, Johnson ... 8.00
12/25 Greg Lemond (SOY) ... 2.50

1990

1/8 Miami National Champs ... 3.00
1/15 Jerry Rice ... 5.00
1/22 John Elway ... 3.00
1/29 David Robinson (FC) ... 8.00
2/5 Joe Montana (Super Bowl XXIV) ... 10.00
2/12 Judit Masco (Swimsuit) .. 6.00
2/19 Mike Tyson KO'd ... 6.00
2/26 Buster Douglas ... 2.50
3/5 Gary Payton (College Basketball) ... 3.00
3/12 Tony Larussa ... 3.00
3/19 Jennifer Capriati ... 3.00
3/26 Bo Kimble ... 3.00
4/2 UNLV Runnin' Rebels ... 5.00
4/9 UNLV Wins NCAA Championship ... 5.00
4/16 Ted Williams ... 4.50
4/23 Tomas Sandstrom ... 2.50
4/30 Jeff George ... 3.00
5/7 Ken Griffey Jr (FC) ... 7.50
5/14 Your Sneakers Or Your Life? ... 2.50
5/21 Michael Jordan ... 5.50
5/28 Will Clark ... 4.00
6/4 Len Dykstra ... 3.50
6/11 Isiah Thomas ... 3.00
6/18 Seles, Steinbrenner, Nicklaus ... 2.50
6/25 Hale Irwin ... 2.50
7/2 Marvin Hagler ... 2.50
7/9 Darryl Strawberry ... 3.00

Sports Illustrated: 2/4/80

7/16 Martina Navratilova ... 2.50
7/23 Minor League Baseball ... 3.00
7/30 G. Lemond Wins Tour De France ... 2.50
8/6 Joe Montana ... 5.00
8/13 Autograph Madness ... 2.50
8/20 Jose Canseco ... 4.50
8/27 Troy Aikman ... 4.00
9/3 Todd Marinovich ... 3.00
9/10 Barry Sanders (FC) ... 5.00
9/17 Pete Sampras ... 2.50
9/24 Rick Mirer ... 4.00
10/1 Bobby Bonilla ... 3.50
10/8 O.J. Simpson ... 3.00
10/15 Burt Grossman ... 2.50
10/22 Dennis Eckersley (FC) ... 5.00
10/29 Chris Sabo (World Series) . 4.00
11/5 Bill Laimbeer (NBA Preview) ... 2.50
11/12 William Bell ... 2.50
11/19 S. Augmon/Larry Johnson (FC) ... 6.00
11/26 Notre Dame falls from Number 1 ... 2.50
12/3 Magic Johnson ... 4.50
12/10 Ty Detmer Wins Heisman . 2.50
12/17 Michael Jordan ... 4.00
12/24 Joe Montana (SOY) ... 5.00
12/31 Pictures '90 ... 3.00

1991

1/14 Dan Marino ... 4.00
1/21 Shaquille O'Neal (FC) ... 7.00
1/28 Ottis Anderson ... 2.50
2/4 Everson Walls ... 2.50
2/11 Ashley Montana(Swimsuit) . 3.00
2/18 Dream Team, Barkley, Ewing, Malone, Magic, Jordan ... 5.00
2/25 Rocket Ismail ... 2.75
3/4 Darryl Strawberry ... 2.50
3/11 Robert Parish ... 2.50
3/18 Brett Hull ... 2.75
3/25 Mike Tyson & Razor Ruddock ... 3.00
4/1 Mark Randall ... 2.50
4/8 Grant Hill (FC) ... 3.00
4/15 Baseball Issue: Nolan Ryan ... 4.00

Date	Cover	Value
4/22	Ian Woosnam	2.00
4/29	Evander Holyfield & G. Foreman	2.75
4/6	Bjorn Borg	2.00
5/13	Roger Clemens, Ryan	4.00
5/20	Michael Johnson	2.75
5/27	Mickey Mantle & Roger Maris	3.00
6/3	Michael Jordan	4.00
6/10	Magic & Michael Jordan	5.00
6/17	Michael Jordan	4.00
6/24	Mike Tyson & Michael Jordan	4.00
7/1	Orel Hershiser	2.50
7/8	Lyle Alzado	2.00
7/15	Steffi Graf	2.25
7/22	2001: A Fan's World	2.00
7/29	Cal Ripken	3.00
8/5	The Black Athlete (Jordan, J. Joyner-Kersee in college)	2.75
8/12	Eric Dickerson	2.50
8/19	John Daly (George Bush insert)	2.50
8/26	David Klingler	2.50
9/2	Bruce Smith [NFL Preview 1991]	2.25
9/9	Mike Powell (long jump record)	2.00
9/16	Jimmy Connors	3.00
9/23	Desmond Howard	3.25
9/30	Ramon Martinez	3.00
10/7	Bobby Hebert	2.75
10/14	Gary Clark	3.00
10/21	Kirby Puckett (FC)	4.00
10/28	Dan Gladden, Greg Olson (WS)	3.00
11/4	Twins Celebration	3.00
11/11	Jordan, Pippen, P. Jackson	4.00
11/18	Magic Johnson (Special Tribute)	6.00
11/25	Christian Laettner	3.25
12/2	Jim McMahon	2.50
12/9	Desmond Howard	3.00
12/16	Bills defense on Jay Shroeder	2.00
12/30	Pictures of 1991	2.25
	1992	
1/13	Muhammed Ali (50th birthday)	4.00
1/20	Thurman Thomas	3.00
1/27	Winter Olympic Preview	2.00
2/3	Mark Rypien (Superbowl XXVI)	2.00
2/10	Patric Ewing (Mullin insert)	2.25
2/17	Tyson "Guilty" (Olympics)	2.50
2/24	Bonnie Blair (Olympics)	2.25
3/2	Kristi Yamaguchi (Olympic)	2.00
3/9	Kathy Ireland (Swimsuit)	2.50
3/16	Ryne Sandberg	2.25
3/23	Larry Bird	3.00
3/30	Malcolm Mackey	2.00
4/6	Kirby Puckett	2.25
4/13	Bobby Hurley	2.00
4/20	Fred Couples	2.00
4/27	Deion Sanders (Emtman insert)	2.50
5/4	Barry Bonds	2.25
5/11	Jordan vs. Drexler (Playoffs)	3.00
5/18	Baseball 92: Comedy of Errors	2.50
5/25	Jordan, Pippen vs. Ewing, Knicks	2.50
6/1	Mark McGwire	2.25
6/8	Mario Lemieux	3.00
6/15	Michael Jordan (NBA Finals)	3.00
6/22	Jordan w/ cigar	3.00
6/29	Tom Kite	2.00
7/6	Steve Palermo	2.00
7/13	Andre Agassi	2.75
7/20	Jackie Joyner (Summer Olympic)	2.50
7/27	Joe Montana	3.00
8/3	Nelson Diebel (Olympics)	2.00
8/10	Gail Devers (Olympics)	2.00
8/17	Carl Lewis (Olympics)	2.25
8/24	Deion Sanders	3.00
8/31	College Football: Best & Worst	2.00
9/7	1992 Football Preview: Jery Rice	2.00
9/14	Jim Harbaugh	2.00
9/21	Stefan Edberg	2.00
9/28	Tony Mandarich	2.00
10/5	George Brett	2.25
10/12	Randall Cunningham	2.25
10/19	Walt Weiss, Dave Winfield	2.25
10/26	Roberto Alomar, John Smoltz (WS)	2.25
11/2	Blue Jays Celebration	2.00
11/9	Charles Barkley (NBA Preview)	2.25
11/16	Dallas Defense - Everett, Norton	2.00
11/23	Riddick Bowe, Evander Holyfield	3.00
11/30	Shaquille O'Neal	3.00
12/7	NFL 1992: Carnage Continues	2.00

Sports Illustrated: 2/24/87

Date	Cover	Value
12/14	Larry Bird & Magic Johnson	4.00
12/21	Sportsman of Year: Arthur Ashe	2.00
12/28	Carl Lewis	2.00

SPECIAL ISSUES

Date	Cover	Value
1977	The Year In Sports	7.00
2/9/78	The Year In Sports	6.00
2/15/79	The Year In Sports	6.00
3/1/80	The Year In Sports	6.00
2/12/81	The Year In Sports	5.00
2/10/82	The Year In Sports	5.00
9/1/82	College & Pro Football Spectac.	5.00
2/16/83	The Year In Sports	5.00
9/1/83	College & Pro Football Spectac.	5.00
2/8/84	The Year In Sports	5.00
7/18/84	Special 1984 Olympics Preview	8.00
9/5/84	College & Pro Football Spectac.	6.00
9/4/85	College & Pro Football Spectac.	5.00
11/20/85	College Basketball 85-86	5.00
9/8/86	College & Pro Football Spectac.	5.00
11/19/86	College Basketball 86-87	5.00
9/9/87	Pro Football Spectacular	5.00
11/18/87	College Basketball 87-88	5.00
1/22/88	1988 Winter Olympics Preview	5.00
9/14/88	Summer Olympics Preview	5.00
11/20/88	College Basketball 88-89	5.00
4/5/89	Baseball 1989 Special	5.00
1989	Swimsuit Anniversary	8.00
1989	Swimsuit 25th Anniv.	8.00
1991	Michael Jordan SOY (Hologram)	20.00
Fall 1991	SI's 25 Unforgettable Moments	3.50
Fall 1992	Willie Mays	3.00

TIME MAGAZINE

Date	Cover	Value
1929	Bill Wrigley	75.00
1930	Wilbert Robinson	75.00
1932	Col. Jacob Ruppert	75.00
1934	Lefty Gomez	70.00
10/7/35	Mickey Cochrane	50.00
1936	Lou Gehrig/ Carl Hubbell	85.00
12/21/36	Bob Feller	65.00
7/18/38	Happy Chandler	50.00
4/21/47	Leo Durocher	45.00
10/4/48	Joe DiMaggio	75.00
4/10/50	Ted Williams	75.00
4/28/52	Eddie Stanky	40.00
6/13/53	Mickey Mantle	100.00
7/26/54	Willie Mays	45.00
6/13/55	Broadway play "Damn Yankees"	25.00
7/11/55	Augie Busch	25.00
10/3/55	Casey Stengel	30.00
5/28/56	Robin Roberts	25.00
7/8/57	Birdie Tebbetts	20.00
4/28/58	Walter O'Malley	20.00
8/24/59	Rocky Colavito	20.00
9/13/68	Denny McLain	15.00
9/5/69	N.Y. Mets	30.00
5/24/71	Vida Blue	15.00
7/10/72	Johnny Bench	20.00
6/3/74	Reggie Jackson	20.00
8/18/75	Charley Finley	10.00
4/26/76	Babe Ruth	20.00
7/18/77	Rod Carew	20.00
7/23/79	Earl Weaver	10.00
5/11/81	Billy Martin	10.00
7/26/82	Carl Yastrzemski /Pete Rose	15.00
1/7/85	Peter Ueberroth	8.00
8/19/85	Pete Rose	10.00
4/7/86	Dwight Gooden	10.00
7/10/89	Pete Rose	8.00

TOPPS MAGAZINE

Date	Cover	Value
Winter '91	Jose Canseco	10.00
Spring '91	Nolan Ryan	5.00
Summer '91	Bo Jackson	5.00
Fall '91	The Griffeys	5.00
Winter '91	Cecil Fielder	5.00
Spring '91	Barry Bonds & Bobby Bonilla	5.00
Summer '91	Rickey Henderson	5.00
Fall '91	Cal Ripken, Jr.	5.00
Winter '92	Ken Griffey, Jr.	5.00
Spring '92	Howard Johnson	3.00
Spring '92	Frank Thomas	3.00
Summer '92	Mark McGwire	5.00
Fall '92	Gary Sheffield	5.00
Winter '93	Barry Bonds	5.00

PINS & BUTTONS

AUTO RACING PINS

INDY 500 PIT BADGES

Pit badges were paper prior to 1938 except for the 1931 celluloid pin. For badges with "Race Day Backups" add $10.00

Year	Style	Value
1931	Celluloid pin	2,000.00
1938	Bronze pin	2,200.00
1939	Bronze pin	2,500.00
1940	Bronze pin	1,500.00
1941	Bronze pin	1,250.00
1946	Bronze pin	3,000.00
1947	Silver pin	1,500.00
	Bronze pin	750.00
1948	Silver pin	250.00
	Bronze pin	200.00
1949	Silver pin	400.00
	Bronze pin	200.00
1950	Silver pin	300.00
	Bronze pin	150.00
1951	Silver pin	250.00
	Bronze pin	150.00
1952	Silver pin	250.00
	Bronze pin	125.00
1953	Silver pin	200.00
	Bronze pin	100.00
1954	Silver pin	180.00
	Bronze pin	90.00
1955	Silver pin	175.00
	Bronze pin	85.00
1956	Silver pin	175.00
	Bronze pin	80.00
1957	Silver pin	165.00
	Bronze pin	80.00
1958	Silver pin	145.00
	Bronze pin	80.00
1959	Silver pin	150.00
	Bronze pin	80.00
1960	Silver pin	100.00
	Bronze pin	50.00
1961	Bronze badge-gold color (Gold Anniver.)	100.00
1962	Silver pin	100.00
	Bronze pin	50.00
1963	Silver pin	100.00
	Bronze pin	50.00
1964	Silver pin	100.00
	Bronze pin	50.00
1965	Silver pin	100.00
	Bronze pin	45.00
1966	Silver pin	95.00
	Bronze pin	45.00
1967	Silver pin	90.00
	Bronze pin	45.00
1968	Silver pin	90.00
	Bronze pin	45.00
1969	Silver pin	90.00
	Bronze pin	45.00
1970	Silver pin	85.00
	Bronze pin	40.00
1971	Bronze Badge, "NATO" at bottom	500.00
	Silver Badge, number at bottom	85.00
	Bronze Badge, number at bottom	35.00

(Clockwise from upper left) Indianapolis 500 pit badges: 1931 celluloid; 1959, 1967 & 1965 metal pit badges.

Year	Pin	Value
1975	Silver pin	80.00
	Bronze pin	35.00
1976	Silver pin	75.00
	Bronze pin	35.00
1977	Silver pin	75.00
	Bronze pin	35.00
1978	Silver pin	75.00
	Bronze pin	35.00
1979	Silver pin	75.00
	Bronze pin	35.00
1980	Silver pin	75.00
	Bronze pin	35.00
1981	Silver pin	75.00
	Bronze pin	35.00
1982	Silver pin	75.00
	Bronze pin	35.00
1983	Silver pin	75.00
	Bronze pin	35.00
1984	Silver pin	70.00
	Bronze pin	35.00
1985	Silver pin	70.00
	Bronze pin	35.00
1986	Silver pin	70.00
	Bronze pin	35.00
1987	Silver pin	70.00
	Bronze pin	35.00
1988	Silver pin	65.00
	Bronze pin	35.00
1989	Silver pin	65.00
	Bronze pin	35.00
1990	Silver pin	65.00
	Bronze pin	35.00
1991	Silver pin	65.00
	Bronze pin	35.00
1992	Silver pin	65.00
	Bronze pin	35.00

BASEBALL PINS

1932-34 ORBIT GUM NUMBERED PINS

No.	Player	Value
1.	Ivy Andrews (Red Sox)	12.00
2.	Carl Reynolds (Browns)	12.00
3.	R. Stephenson (Cubs)	15.00
4.	Lon Warneke (Cubs)	12.00

No.	Player	Value
5.	Frank Grube (W. Sox)	12.00
6.	"Kiki" Cuyler (Cubs)	25.00
7.	M. McManus (Red Sox)	12.00
8A.	"Lefty" Clark (Giants)	15.00
8B.	"Lefty" Clark (Dodgers)	30.00
9.	G. Blaeholder (Browns)	12.00
10.	Willie Kamm (Indians)	12.00
11.	Jimmy Dykes (W. Sox)	15.00
12.	Earl Averill (Indians)	25.00
13.	Pat Malone (Cubs)	12.00
14.	"Dizzy" Dean (Cards)	65.00
15.	Dick Bartell (Phillies)	12.00
16.	Guy Bush (Cubs)	12.00
17.	Bud Tinning (Cubs)	12.00
18.	Jimmy Foxx (Athletics)	50.00
19.	"Mule" Haas (W. Sox)	12.00
20.	Lew Fonseca (W. Sox)	12.00
21.	"Pepper" Martin (Cards)	15.00
22.	Phil Collins (Phillies)	12.00
23.	Bill Cissell (Indians)	12.00
24.	Bump Hadley (Browns)	12.00
25.	Smead Jolley (Red Sox)	12.00
26.	Burleigh Grimes (Cubs)	20.00
27.	D. Alexander (Red Sox)	12.00
28.	Mickey Cochrane (A's)	30.00
29.	Mel Harder (Indians)	14.00
30.	Mark Koenig (Cubs)	12.00
31A.	Lefty O'Doul (Giants)	15.00
31B.	Lefty O'Doul (Dodgers)	25.00
32A.	Woody English (Cubs)	12.00
32B.	W. English (Cubs, w/out bat)	20.00
33A.	Billy Jurges (Cubs)	12.00
33B.	Billy Jurges (Cubs, w/out bat)	20.00
34.	B. Campbell (Browns)	12.00
35.	Joe Vosmik (Indians)	12.00
36.	Dick Porter (Indians)	12.00
37.	Charlie Grimm (Cubs)	15.00
38.	George Earnshaw (A's)	12.00
39.	Al Simmons (W. Sox)	25.00
40.	"Red" Lucas (Reds)	12.00
51.	Wally Berger (Braves)	12.00
52.	Jim Levey (Browns)	12.00
58.	Ernie Lombardi (Reds)	25.00
64.	Jack Burns (Browns)	12.00
67.	Billy Herman (Cubs)	20.00
72.	Bill Hallahan (Cards)	12.00
92.	Don Brennan (Yankees)	12.00
96.	Sam Byrd (Yankees)	12.00
99.	B. Chapman (Yankees)	12.00
103.	John Allen (Yankees)	12.00
107.	Tony Lazzeri (Yankees)	18.00
111.	Earl Combs (Yankees)	20.00
116.	Joe Sewell (Yankees)	20.00
120.	Lefty Gomez (Yankees)	30.00

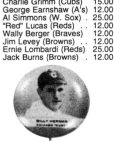

1932-34 ORBIT GUM UNNUMBERED PINS

No.	Player	Value
1.	D. Alexander (Red Sox)	25.00
2.	Andrews (Red Sox)	25.00
3.	Earl Averill (Indians)	35.00
4.	Dick Bartell (Phillies)	25.00
5.	Wally Berger (Braves)	25.00
6.	G. Blaeholder (Browns)	25.00
7.	Jack Burns (Browns)	25.00
8.	Guy Bush (Cubs)	25.00
9.	Campbell (Browns)	25.00
10.	Cissell (Indians)	25.00
11.	"Lefty" Clark (Dodgers)	25.00
12.	Mickey Cochrane (A's)	45.00
13.	Phil Collins (Phillies)	25.00
14.	Kiki Cuyler (Cubs)	35.00
15.	Dizzy Dean (Cardinals)	65.00
16.	Jimmy Dykes (W. Sox)	30.00
17.	George Earnshaw (A's)	25.00
18.	Woody English (Cubs)	25.00
19.	Lew Fonseca (W. Sox)	25.00
20.	Jimmie Foxx (Athletics)	55.00
21.	Burleigh Grimes (Cubs)	35.00
22.	Charlie Grimm (Cubs)	30.00
23.	"Lefty" Grove (Athletics)	45.00
24.	Frank Grube (W. Sox)	25.00
25.	Mule Haas (White Sox)	25.00
26.	Hadley (Browns)	25.00
27.	"Chick" Hafey (Reds)	35.00
28.	J. Haines (Cardinals)	35.00
29.	Bill Hallahan (Cardinals)	25.00
30.	Mel Harder (Indians)	30.00
31.	"Gabby" Hartnett (Cubs)	35.00
32.	"Babe" Herman (Cubs)	30.00
33.	Billy Herman (Cubs)	35.00
34.	Rogers Hornsby (Cards)	65.00
35.	Johnson (Red Sox)	25.00
36.	Smead Jolley (Red Sox)	25.00
37.	Billy Jurges (Cubs)	25.00
38.	Willie Kamm (Indians)	25.00
39.	Mark Koenig (Cubs)	25.00
40.	Levey (Browns)	25.00
41.	Ernie Lombardi (Reds)	35.00
42.	Red Lucas (Reds)	20.00
43.	Ted Lyons (White Sox)	35.00
44.	Connie Mack (Athletics)	45.00
45.	Pat Malone (Cubs)	25.00
46.	P. Martin (Cardinals)	30.00
47.	M. McManus (Red Sox)	25.00
48.	Lefty O'Doul (Dodgers)	30.00
49.	Porter (Indians)	25.00
50.	Reynolds (Browns)	25.00
51.	Charlie Root (Cubs)	25.00
52.	Seeds (Red Sox)	25.00
53.	Al Simmons (White Sox)	35.00
54.	R. Stephenson (Cubs)	30.00

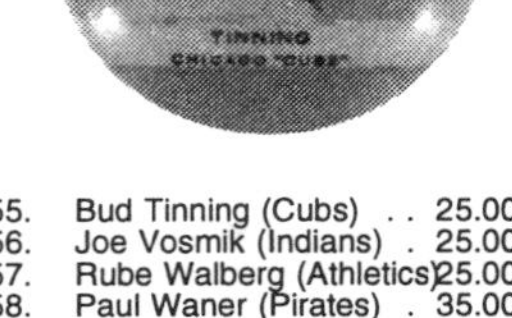

No.	Player	Value
55.	Bud Tinning (Cubs)	25.00
56.	Joe Vosmik (Indians)	25.00
57.	Rube Walberg (Athletics)	25.00
58.	Paul Waner (Pirates)	35.00
59.	Lon Warneke (Cubs)	25.00
60.	Pinky Whitney (Phillies)	25.00

1956 TOPPS PINS

No.	Player, position	Value
1.	Aaron, Hank (Outfield)	55.00
2.	Amoros, Sandy (OF)	12.00
3.	Arroyo, Luis (Pitcher)	12.00
4.	Banks, Ernie (SS)	25.00
5.	Berra, Yogi (Catcher)	40.00
6.	Black, Joe (Pitcher)	12.00
7.	Boone, Ray (3rd base)	12.00

1956 Art Fowler Topps pin

No.	Player, position	Value
8.	Boyer, Ken (Third base)	15.00
9.	Collins, Joe (First base)	12.00
10.	Conley, Gene (Pitcher)	12.00

11. Diering, Chuck (OF) . 110.00
12. Donovan, Dick (Pitcher) 12.00
13. Finigan, Jim (Second) 12.00
14. Fowler, Art (Pitcher) .. 12.00
15. Gomez, Ruben (Pitcher) 12.00
16. Groat, Dick (Shortstop) 15.00
17. Haddix, Harvey (Pitcher) 12.00
18. Harshman, Jack (P) .. 12.00
19. Hatton, G. (Third base) 12.00
20. Hegan, Jim (Catcher) . 12.00
21. Hodges, Gil (First base) 25.00
22. Hofman, Bobby (Infield) 12.00
23. House, Frank (Catcher) 12.00
24. Jensen, Jackie (OF) .. 15.00
25. Kaline, Al (Outfield) .. 30.00
26. Kennedy, B. (3B) 12.00
27. Kluszewski, T. (1B) .. 15.00
28. Long, Dale (First base) 12.00
29. Lopez, H. (Third base) 12.00
30. Mathews, Eddie (3B) . 25.00
31. Mays, Willie (Outfield) 60.00
32. McMillan, Roy (SS) .. 12.00
33. Miranda, W. (Shortstop) 12.00
34. Moon, Wally (Outfield) 12.00
35. Mossi, Don (Pitcher) .. 12.00
36. Negray, Ron (Pitcher) . 12.00
37. O'Brien, J. (2B) 12.00
38. Paula, Carlos (Outfield) 12.00
39. Power, Vic (First base) 12.00
40. Rivera, Jim (Outfield) . 12.00
41. Rizzuto, Phil (Shortstop) 25.00
42. Robinson, J. (3B) 45.00
43. Rosen, Al (Third base) 15.00
44. Sauer, Hank (Outfield) 10.00
45. Sievers, Roy (Outfield) 12.00
46. Skowron, Bill (1B) ... 15.00
47. Smith, Al (Outfield) ... 12.00
48. Smith, Hal (Catcher) .. 12.00
49. Smith, Mayo (Manager) 12.00
50. Snider, Duke (Outfield) 40.00
51. Spahn, Warren (Pitcher) 25.00
52. Spooner, Karl (Pitcher) 12.00
53. Stobbs, Chuck (Pitcher) 60.00
54. Sullivan, Frank (Pitcher) 12.00
55. Tremel, Bill (Pitcher) .. 12.00
56. Triandos, Gus (1B) ... 12.00

57. Turley, Bob (Pitcher) 12.00
58. Wehmeier, H. (Pitcher) 12.00
59. Williams, Ted (Outfield) 60.00
60. Zernial, Gus (Outfield) 12.00

1950s YELLOW BASEPATH PINS

No.	Player	Value
1.	Aaron, Hank	110.00
2.	Adcock, Joe	30.00
3.	Aparicio, Luis	55.00
4.	Ashburn, Richie	40.00
5.	Baker, Gene	25.00
6.	Banks, Ernie	55.00
7.	Berra, Yogi	65.00
8.	Bruton, Bill	25.00
9.	Doby, Larry	35.00
10.	Friend, Bob	25.00
11.	Fox, Nellie	40.00
12.	Greengrass, Jim	25.00
13.	Gromek , Steve	25.00
14.	Groth, Johnny	25.00
15.	Hodges, Gil	45.00
16.	Kaline, Al	65.00
17.	Kluszewski, Ted	35.00
18.	Logan, Johnny	25.00
19.	Long, Dale	25.00
20.	Mantle, Mickey	200.00

Gene Baker Yellow Basepath pin

No.	Player	Value
21.	Mathews, Ed	45.00
22.	Minoso, Orestes	35.00
23.	Musial, Stan	110.00
24.	Newcombe, Don	30.00
25.	Porterfield, Bob	25.00
26.	Reese, Pee Wee	55.00
27.	Roberts, Robin	45.00
28.	Schoendienst, Red	35.00
29.	Snider, Duke	85.00
30.	Stephens, Vern	25.00
31.	Woodling, Gene	25.00
32.	Zernial, Gus	25.00

1969 MLBPA PINS

No.	Player	Value
1.	Aaron, Hank	10.00
2.	Allen, Richie	3.00
3.	Alou, Felipe	3.00
4.	Alvis, Max	2.00
5.	Aparicio, Luis	5.00
6.	Banks, Ernie	10.00

No.	Player	Value
7.	Bench, Johnny	12.00
8.	Brock, Lou	10.00
9.	Brunet, George	2.00
10.	Callison, Johnny	2.00
11.	Carew, Rod	10.00
12.	Cepeda, Orlando	2.00
13.	Chance, Dean	2.00
14.	Clemente, Roberto	10.00
15.	Davis, Willie	2.00
16.	Drysdale, Don	10.00
17.	Fairly, Ron	2.00
18.	Flood, Curt	3.00
19.	Freehan, Bill	3.00
20.	Fregosi, Jim	3.00
21.	Gibson, Bob	9.00
22.	Harrelson, Bud	2.00
23.	Harrelson, Ken	3.00
24.	Hart, Jim Ray	2.00
25.	Helms, Tommy	2.00
26.	Horlen, Joel	2.00
27.	Horton, Tony	2.00
28.	Horton, Willie	3.00
29.	Howard, Frank	2.00

No.	Player	Value
30.	Kaline, Al	8.00
31.	Kessinger, Don	3.00
32.	Killebrew, Harmon	10.00
33.	Koosman, Jerry	3.00
34.	Lolich, Mickey	3.00
35.	Lonborg, Jim	2.00
36.	Maloney, Jim	3.00
37.	Marichal, Juan	8.00
38.	Mays, Willie	10.00
39.	McCarver, Tim	3.00
40.	McCovey, Willie	8.00
41.	McDowell, Sam	2.00
42.	McLain, Denny	3.00
43.	Monday, Rick	2.00
44.	Oliva, Tony	2.00
45.	Pepitone, Joe	3.00
46.	Powell, Boog	3.00
47.	Reichardt, Rick	2.00
48.	Richert, Pete	2.00
49.	Robinson, Frank	10.00
50.	Robinson, Brooks	8.00
51.	Rose, Pete	30.00
52.	Santo, Ron	7.00
53.	Stottlemyre, Mel	3.00
54.	Swoboda, Ron	2.00
55.	Tiant, Luis	3.00
56.	Torre, Joe	3.00
57.	Ward, Pete	2.00
58.	Williams, Billy	3.00
59.	Wynn, Jim	2.00
60.	Yastrzemski, Carl	18.00

1983 MLBPA REPRINT PINS

No.	Player	Value
1.	Aaron, Hank	6.00
2.	Allison, Bob	1.00
3.	Berra, Yogi	3.00
4.	Campanella, Roy	6.00
5.	Cash, Norm	3.00
6.	Cepeda, Orlando	3.00
7.	Clemente, Roberto	5.00
8.	DiMaggio, Joe	8.00
9.	Doerr, Bobby	4.00
10.	Drysdale, Don	4.00
11.	Feller, Bob	6.00
12.	Ford, Whitey	3.00
13.	Fox, Nelson	3.00
14.	Howard, Frank	1.00
15.	Hunter, Jim (Catfish)	4.00
16.	Kaline, Al	3.00

1983 Stan Musial MLPBA pin

No.	Player	Value
17.	Koufax, Sandy	3.00

Z18.	Mantle, Mickey	10.00
19.	Marichal, Juan	4.00
20.	Mathews, Eddie	4.00
21.	Mays, Willie	6.00
22.	McCovey, Willie	3.00
23.	Musial, Stan	3.00
24.	Oliva, Tony	3.00

25.	Paige, Satchel	3.00
26.	Rizzuto, Phil	3.00
27.	Roberts, Robin	4.00
28.	Robinson, Brooks	3.00
29.	Robinson, Jackie	6.00
30.	Santo, Ron	3.00
31.	Skowron, Bill	3.00
32.	Snider, Duke	3.00
33.	Spahn, Warren	3.00
34.	Williams, Billy	4.00
35.	Williams, Ted	6.00
36.	Wills, Maury	4.00

1984 FUN FOODS PINS

No.	Player	Value
1.	Dave Winfield	0.30
2.	Lance Parrish	0.20
3.	Gary Carter	0.30
4.	Pete Rose	0.60
5.	Jim Rice	0.25
6.	George Brett	0.40
7.	Fernando Valenzuela	0.25
8.	Darryl Strawberry	0.40
9.	Steve Garvey	0.35
10.	Rollie Fingers	0.17
11.	Mike Schmidt	0.35
12.	Kent Tekulve	0.13
13.	Ryne Sandberg	0.30
14.	Bruce Sutter	0.17
15.	Tom Seaver	0.30
16.	Reggie Jackson	0.40
17.	Rickey Henderson	0.40
18.	Mark Langston	0.15
19.	Jack Clark	0.15
20.	Willie Randolph	0.13
21.	Kirk Gibson	0.30
22.	Andre Dawson	0.20
23.	Dave Concepcion	0.15
24.	Tony Armas	0.15
25.	Dan Quisenberry	0.17
26.	Pedro Guerrero	0.25
27.	Dwight Gooden	1.50
28.	Tony Gwynn	0.35
29.	Robin Yount	0.30
30.	Steve Carlton	0.30
31.	Bill Madlock	0.17
32.	Rick Sutcliffe	0.15
33.	Willie McGee	0.25
34.	Greg Luzinski	0.15
35.	Rod Carew	0.30
36.	Dave Kingman	0.17
37.	Alvin Davis	0.20
38.	Chili Davis	0.17
39.	Don Baylor	0.17
40.	Alan Trarnmell	0.20
41.	Tim Raines	0.30
42.	Cesar Cedeno	0.15
43.	Wade Boggs	0.60
44.	Frank White	0.13
45.	Steve Sax	0.17
46.	George Foster	0.17
47.	Terry Kennedy	0.15
48.	Cecil Cooper	0.17
49.	John Denny	0.13
50.	John Candelaria	0.13
51.	Jody Davis	0.15
52.	George Hendrick	0.13
53.	Ron Kittle	0.17
54.	Fred Lynn	0.20
55.	Carney Lansford	0.15
56.	Gorman Thomas	0.15
57.	Manny Trillo	0.13
58.	Steve Kemp	0.15
59.	Jack Morris	0.20
60.	Dan Petry	0.17
61.	Mario Soto	0.15
62.	Dwight Evans	0.17
63.	Hal McRae	0.15
64.	Mike Marshall	0.20
65.	Mookie Wilson	0.15
66.	Graig Nettles	0.20
67.	Ben Oglivie	0.15
68.	Juan Samuel	0.20
69.	Johnny Ray	0.17
70.	Gary Matthews	0.15
71.	Ozzie Smith	0.20
72.	Carlton Fisk	0.20
73.	Doug DeCinces	0.15
74.	Joe Morgan	0.25
75.	Dave Stieb	0.20
76.	Buddy Bell	0.17
77.	Don Mattingly	0.85
78.	Lou Whitaker	0.20
79.	Willie Hernandez	0.17
80.	Dave Parker	0.25
81.	Bob Stanley	0.15
82.	Willie Wilson	0.20
83.	Orel Hershiser	0.25
84.	Rusty Staub	0.15
85.	Goose Gossage	0.20
86.	Don Sutton	0.20
87.	Al Holland	0.13
88.	Tony Pena	0.17
89.	Ron Cey	0.17
90.	Joaquin Andujar	0.17
91.	LaMarr Hoyt	0.15
92.	Tommy John	0.20
93.	Dwayne Murphy	0.15
94.	Willie Upshaw	0.15
95.	Gary Ward	0.15
96.	Ron Guidry	0.20
97.	Chet Lemon	0.13
98.	Aurelio Lopez	0.13
99.	Tony Perez	0.17

100.	Bill Buckner	0.15
101.	Mike Hargrove	0.13
102.	Scott McGregor	0.15
103.	Dale Murphy	0.50
104.	Keith Hernandez	0.30
105.	Paul Molitor	0.17
106.	Bert Blyleven	0.17
107.	Leon Durham	0.17
108.	Lee Smith	0.15
109.	Nolan Ryan	0.30
110.	Harold Baines	0.25
111.	Kent Hrbek	0.25
112.	Ron Davis	0.13
113.	George Bell	0.20
114.	Charlie Hough	0.15
115.	Phil Niekro	0.25
116.	Dave Righetti	0.20
117.	Darrell Evans	0.15
118.	Cal Ripken Jr.	0.40
119.	Eddie Murray	0.40
120.	Storm Davis	0.17
121.	Mike Boddicker	0.17
122.	Bob Horner	0.25
123.	Chris Chambliss	0.15
124.	Ted Simmons	0.17
125.	Andre Thornton	0.15
126.	Larry Bowa	0.15
127.	Bob Dernier	0.13
128.	Joe Niekro	0.15
129.	Jose Cruz	0.17
130.	Tom Brunansky	0.20
131.	Gary Gaetti	0.20
132.	Lloyd Moseby	0.20
133.	Frank Tanana	0.15

ANONYMOUS MANUFACTURERS

INDIVIDUAL PLAYERS

Aaron, Hank

715 April 8, 1974 (3 ¼")	50.00
Atlanta Salutes (2 ¼")	10.00
Thanks Milwaukee (2 3/8")	10.00
Magnavox, 715 (3")	50.00
500, August 23, 1968 (2 ¼")	35.00

Banks, Ernie

Day, August 15, 1964 (1 ¾")	50.00

Berra, Yogi

Day, April 14, 1964 (1 ½")	75.00

Boudreau, Lou

Day, October 28, 1948 (1 ½")	35.00
Border with B&W Photo (1 ½")	5.00

DiMaggio, Joe

Color Border 1960's (1 ¾")	30.00
Buitoni Foods, Club (1 ½")	75.00

Doby, Larry

Congratulations, (1 ¼")	35.00

Drysdale, Don

Portrait (3 ½")	15.00
Pitching (3 ½")	15.00

Feller, Bob

Pitching (3")	35.00
Author of How to Pitch (1 ½")	50.00
Club (1")	30.00

Gehrig, Lou

Never Forgotten (3")	75.00

Hodges, Gil
Gil Hodges Lanes (1 ½") . . . 45.00
Portrait (3 ½") 15.00
Jackson, Reggie
Portrait (1 ½") 10.00
Kaline, Al
Day, August 2, 1970 (3") . . . 75.00
Kiner, Ralph
Batting (2 ½") 10.00
Mantle, Mickey
Bust (2 ½") 35.00
I Love Mickey (2 ½") 75.00
Maris, Roger
Batting (3 ½") 20.00
I'm For Maris, 60 in '61 (2 ½") 50.00
Bust w/bat (3 ½") 20.00
Mays, Willie
MVP 1965 (3 ½") 50.00
'Say Hey' The News (3 ½") . 60.00
McLain, Denny
31 Wins, with Wilson 25.00
Neal, Charlie
Bust (3 ½") 10.00
Page, Satchel
Bust (1 ½") 20.00
Robinson, Frank
Blue Ribbon Batting (3") . . . 20.00
Blue Ribbon Bread, Head (3") 20.00
Robinson, Jackie
Congratulations 1947 (1 ½") 100.00
Brooklyn Eagle (1 ½") 100.00
I'm Rooting (1 ½") 45.00
I'm Rooting Border (1 ½") . . 45.00
Rose, Pete
Portrait (1 ½") 10.00
Ruth, Babe
Club Jordan Marsh (1 ¼") . . 75.00
Ask Me, Sunoco Gasoline (3") 75.00
Never Forgotten (2 ½") 50.00
Santo, Ron
Day, Aug 28, 1971 . . . . 35.00
Snider, Duke
Bust (3 ½") 20.00
Spahn, Warren
Spahnie, Sept 17, 1963 (2 ½")60.00
Williams, Billy
Day, June 29, 1969 (2 ½") . . 35.00

Williams, Ted
Batting (1 ½") 15.00
Bust Line Drawing (1 ¼") . . . 20.00
Wills, Maury
Bust (3") 10.00
Wynn, Early
300 Club (2 ½") 35.00
Yastrzemski, Carl
Bust (3 ½") 15.00

INDIVIDUAL TEAMS

Atlanta Braves
Head of Indian (3") 15.00
Baltimore Orioles
Logo (3") 15.00
Boston Braves
League Champions, Indian . 25.00
League Champions 1948 . . . 25.00
Boston Red Sox
World Champions 1946 (1½") 25.00
Go Red Sox (1") 5.00
Nine Color Portraits (4") . . . 25.00
Team Portrait (6") 25.00
Brooklyn Dodgers
1953 League Champions (4") 50.00
This is the Year (3") 40.00
Champions (1 ½") 15.00
Beat Them Yanks (3") 35.00
Dodgerette Dodger Fan Club (1 ½") 25.00
Chicago Cubs
Jr Booster Club (1") 12.00
Chicago White Sox
Logo (1 ½") 15.00
World Series 1959 (1 ½") . . 25.00
Standard Oil, Go, Go, Sox (1 ½") 20.00
Chicago American Go Go Club (1") 20.00
Cincinnati Reds
Logo (3") 20.00
Beat the Bombers (2 ½") . . . 35.00
Cleveland Indians
1954 League Champions, Team (3") 40.00
1952 Lopez Limited (1 ½") . . 30.00
Alumco, Inc "Knothole Club" 25.00
Detroit Tigers
Iffy Club (1") 20.00
Los Angeles Dodgers
Logo (2") 10.00
League Champs (2") 25.00
Los Angeles Angels
Logo (2 ½") 15.00
Milwaukee Braves
Let's Beat em' Again (2 ½") . 25.00
Logo - Boosters (1 ½") 20.00
Minnesota Twins
Logo (1 ½") 15.00
New York Giants
Giants in 1948 (1") 25.00
I'm For the Giants (1") 20.00
Champions (2") 35.00

New York Mets
The Amazin'Mets, We're No 1 (2 ½") . . . 35.00
Logo "Mr Met" (2 ½") 25.00
Let's Go Mets (1 ½") 15.00
New York Yankees
Champions (1 ½") 20.00
Booster (1") 15.00
1953 Champions Team Portrait (4") 75.00
1949 Logo Brass (1 ¼) 75.00
Beat Dem Bums (2") 35.00
Logo (1") 10.00
1962 World Series, Shell Oil (3") 50.00
Philadelphia Phillies
League Champs 14 Cameos (4") 50.00
Silco Philco, Phabulous Phillies (1 ½") 25.00
Opening Day, 1953 (1 ½") . . 25.00
Opening Day, 1954 (1 ½") . . 25.00
Phillies Cap (1 ½") 5.00
Tasty Kake (1 ½") 25.00
Pittsburgh Pirates
Booster (1 ¼") 15.00
World Champions (3") 25.00
St Louis Cardinals
League Champs 1968 (1 ½") 25.00
Logo (1") 10.00
Washington Senators
Logo (2") 15.00

BASEBALL PRESS PINS

ALL-STAR GAME PRESS PINS

Year	Site	Maker	Value
1938	Cincinnati	Bastian	7,500.00
1941	Detroit	Dodge	2,500.00
1943	Philadelphia	Unkn.	1,500.00

Year	Site	Maker	Value
1946	Boston	Balfour	1,000.00
1947	Chicago	Unkn.	1,750.00
1948	St. Louis	Button	2,000.00
1949	Brooklyn	Balfour	500.00
1950	Chicago	Balfour	400.00
1951	Detroit	Unkn.	300.00
1952	Philadelphia	Martin	400.00
1953	Cincinnati	Robbins	425.00
1954	Cleveland	Balfour	300.00
1955	Milwaukee	Balfour	275.00
1956	Washington	Balfour	350.00
1957	St. Louis	Balfour	500.00
1958	Baltimore	Balfour	550.00
1959	Los Angeles	Balfour	200.00
1959	Pittsburgh	Balfour	300.00
1960	Kansas City	Balfour	350.00
1960	N. York (AL)	Balfour	375.00
1961	Boston	Balfour	600.00
1961	San Fran.	Balfour	650.00
1962	Chicago	Balfour	450.00
1962	Washington	Balfour	300.00
1963	Cleveland	Balfour	100.00
1964	N. York (NL)	Balfour	250.00
1965	Minnesota	Balfour	125.00
1966	St. Louis	Balfour	50.00
1967	California	Balfour	100.00
1968	Houston	Balfour	125.00
1969	Washington	Balfour	100.00
1970	Cincinnati	Balfour	50.00
1971	Detroit	Balfour	100.00
1972	Atlanta	Balfour	50.00
1973	Kansas City	Balfour	75.00
1974	Pittsburgh	Balfour	75.00
1975	Milwaukee	Unkn.	50.00
1976	Philadelphia	Balfour	50.00
1977	N. York (AL)	Balfour	25.00
1978	San Diego	Balfour	45.00
1979	Seattle	Balfour	40.00
1980	Los Angeles	Balfour	30.00
1981	Cleveland	Balfour	25.00
1982	Montreal	Balfour	30.00
1983	Chicago	Balfour	20.00

Year	Team	Maker	Value
1984	San Fran.	Balfour	35.00
1985	Minnesota	P. David	40.00
1986	Houston	Balfour	65.00
1987	Oakland	Josten	80.00
1988	Cincinnati	Josten	100.00
1989	California		75.00
1990	Chicago		125.00
1991	Toronto		125.00

HALL OF FAME PINS

Year	Inductees	Value
1982	Aaron, Chandler, Jackson, Robinson	700.00
1983	Alston, Kell, Marichal, Robinson	675.00
1984	Aparicio, Drysdale, Killebrew, Ferrell, Reese	450.00
1985	Brock, Slaughter, Vaughan, Wilhelm	425.00
1986	Doerr, McCovey	425.00
1987	Dandridge, Hunter, Williams	650.00
1988	Stargell	650.00
1989	Barlick, Bench, Schoendienst, Yastrzemski	650.00
1990	Morgan, Palmer	650.00
1991	Carew, Jenkins, Perry	625.00

Note: All pins, beginning in 1982, produced by Balfour. Veterans Committee Electees not included.

WORLD SERIES PRESS PINS

Year	Teams	Maker	Value
1911	N. Y. (NL)	NA	
	Phila. (AL)	A.Kerr	18,000.00
1912	Boston(AL)	Unkn.	5,000.00
	N. Y. (NL)	W&Hoag	12,500.00
1913	N. Y. (NL)	W&Hoag	10,000.00
	Phila. (AL)	Caldwell	6,800.00
1914	Boston(NL)	B.&Bush	5,500.00
	Phila. (AL)	Caldwll.	11,000.00
1915	Boston(AL)	B.&Bush	5,500.00
	Phila. (NL)	Caldwll.	11,000.00
1916	Boston(AL)	B.&Bush	5,000.00
	Brooklyn	D.&Clust	4,400.00
1917	Chic.(AL)	Grnduck.	9,500.00
	N.Y. (NL)	Unkn.	7,000.00
1918	Boston(AL)	B.&Bush	5,500.00
	Chic.(NL)	NA	
1919	Chic.(AL)	Grnduck	12,500.00
	Cincinnati	G. Fox	4,750.00
1920	Brooklyn	Unkn.	3,000.00
	Cleveland	Unkn.	3,000.00
1921	N.Y.(Both)	W.&Hoag	4,000.00
1922	N.Y.(Both)	W.&Hoag	4,000.00
1923	N.Y.(Both)	D.&Clust	3,800.00
1924	N.Y.(NL)	D.&Clust	2,600.00
	Washington	D.&Clust	2,400.00
1925	Pittsburgh	W.&Hoag	2,200.00
	Washington	D.&Clust	2,200.00
1926	N.Y.(AL)	D.&Clust	2,850.00
	St.L.(NL)	Unkn.	2,400.00

Year	Teams	Maker	Value
1927	N.Y.(AL)	D.&Clust	3,600.00
	Pittsburgh	W.&Hoag	2,400.00
1928	N.Y.(AL)	D.&Clust	2,400.00
	St.L(NL)	Button	1,200.00
1929	Chic.(NL)	Coburn	2,200.00
	Phila.(AL)	Unkn.	1,750.00
1930	Phila.(AL)	Unkn.	5,000.00
	St.L.(NL)	Button	1,000.00
1931	Phila.(AL)	Unkn.	1,300.00
	St.L.(NL)	Button	900.00
1932	Chic.(NL)	D.&Clust	2,200.00
	N.Y.(AL)	D.&Clust	1,200.00
1933	N.Y.(NL)	D.&Clust	850.00
	Wash.	D.&Clust	950.00
1934	Detroit	D.&Clust	700.00
	St.L.(NL)	Button	800.00
1935	Chic.(NL)	Childs	2,200.00
	Detroit	Unknown	850.00
1936	N.Y.(NL)	D. & Clust	400.00
	N.Y.(AL)	D. & Clust	800.00
1937	N.Y.(NL)	D. & Clust	700.00
	N.Y.(AL)	D. & Clust	800.00
1938	Chic.(NL)	Lambert	2,250.00
	N.Y.(AL)	D. & Clust	750.00
1939	Cincinnati	Bastian	450.00
	N.Y.(AL)	D. & Clust	750.00
1940	Cincinnati	Bastian	475.00
	Detroit	Unknown	650.00
1941	Brooklyn	D. & Clust	725.00
	N.Y.(AL)	D. & Clust	475.00
1942	N.Y.(AL)	D. & Clust	500.00
	St.L.(NL)	Button	2,400.00

Year	Teams	Maker	Value
1943	N.Y.(AL)	D. & Clust	500.00
	St.L.(NL)	Button	2,400.00
1944	St.L.(AL)	Button	575.00
	St.L.(NL)	Button	575.00
1945	Chic.(NL)	Unknown	550.00
	Detroit	Unknown	575.00
1946	Boston(AL)	Balfour	600.00
	St.L.(NL)	Button	500.00

Year	Teams	Maker	Value
1947	Brooklyn	D. & Clust	800.00
	N.Y.(AL)	D. & Clust	775.00
1948	Boston(NL)	Balfour	500.00
	Cleveland	Balfour	400.00
1949	Brooklyn	D. & Clust	575.00
	N.Y.(AL)	D. & Clust	550.00
1950	N.Y.(AL)	D. & Clust	350.00
	Phila.(NL)	Martin	325.00
1951	N.Y.(AL)	D. & Clust	250.00
	N.Y.(NL)	D. & Clust	175.00
1952	Brooklyn	D. & Clust	600.00
	N.Y.(AL)	Balfour	275.00
1953	Brooklyn	D. & Clust	325.00
	N.Y.(AL)	Balfour	325.00
1954	Cleveland	Balfour	225.00
	N.Y.(NL)	D. & Clust	135.00
1955	Brooklyn	D. & Clust	450.00
	N.Y.(AL)	Balfour	250.00
1956	Brooklyn	D.&Clust	1,800.00
	N.Y.(AL)	Balfour	250.00
1957	Milwaukee	Balfour	150.00
	N.Y.(AL)	Balfour	200.00
1958	Milwaukee	Balfour	150.00
	N.Y.(AL)	Balfour	200.00
1959	Chic.(AL)	Balfour	200.00
	L.A.	Balfour	300.00
1960	N.Y.(AL)	Balfour	225.00
	Pittsburgh	Josten	375.00
1961	Cincinnati	Balfour	175.00
	N.Y.(AL)	Balfour	275.00
1962	N.Y.(AL)	Balfour	175.00
	San Fran.	Balfour	350.00
1963	L.A.(NL)	Balfour	200.00
	N.Y.(AL)	Balfour	200.00
1964	N.Y.(AL)	Balfour	200.00
	St.L.	Josten	150.00

Year	Teams	Maker	Value
1965	L.A.(NL)	Balfour	100.00
	Minnesota	Balfour	90.00
1966	Baltimore	Balfour	150.00
	L.A.	Balfour	100.00
1967	Boston	Balfour	150.00
	St. Louis	Balfour	75.00
1968	Detroit	Balfour	165.00
	St. Louis	Balfour	65.00
1969	Baltimore	Balfour	125.00
	N.Y.(NL)	Balfour	400.00
1970	Baltimore	Jenkins	100.00
	Cincinnati	G.B. Miller	100.00
1971	Baltimore	Balfour	100.00
	Pittsburgh	Balfour	100.00
1972	Cincinnati	Balfour	75.00
	Oakland	Balfour	275.00
1973	N.Y. (NL)	Balfour	175.00
	Oakland	Josten	325.00
1974	L.A.	Balfour	125.00
	Oakland	Josten	400.00
1975	Boston	Balfour	325.00
	Cincinnati	Balfour	125.00
1976	Cincinnati	Balfour	150.00
	N.Y.(AL)	Balfour	125.00

Year	Teams	Maker	Value
1977	L.A.	Balfour	80.00
	N.Y.(AL)	Balfour	125.00
1978	L.A.	Balfour	70.00
	N.Y.(AL)	Balfour	100.00
1979	Baltimore	Balfour	65.00
	Pittsburgh	Balfour	55.00
1980	K.C.	Green Co.	75.00
	Phila.	Balfour	35.00
1981	L.A.	Balfour	60.00
	N.Y.(AL)	Balfour	60.00
1982	Milwaukee	Balfour	50.00
	St. Louis	Balfour	20.00
1983	Baltimore	Balfour	30.00
	Phila.	Balfour	35.00
1984	Detroit	Balfour	55.00

Year	Teams	Maker	Value
	San Diego	Balfour	50.00
1985	K.C.	Green Co.	75.00
	St. Louis	Balfour	85.00
1986	Boston	Balfour	75.00
	N.Y.(NL)	Balfour	100.00
1987	Minnesota	Josten	60.00
	St. Louis	Balfour	65.00
1988	L.A.		50.00
	Oakland		50.00

Year	Teams	Maker	Value
1989	Oakland		95.00
	San Fran		95.00
1990	Cincinnati		130.00
	Oakland		95.00
1991	Atlanta		0.00
	Minnesota		0.00
1992	Atlanta		0.00
	Toronto		0.00

PHANTOM WORLD SERIES PRESS PINS

Year	Teams	Maker	Value
1935	St.L.(NL)		NYP
1938	Pitt.(NL)	W.&Hoag	1,000.00
1944	Detroit (AL)	Unknown	750.00
1945	St.L.(NL)	Button	600.00
1946	Brook.(NL)	D.&Clust	175.00
1948	Boston(AL)	Balfour	1,800.00
	N.Y.(AL)	D.&Clust	1,800.00
1949	Boston(AL)	Balfour	1,800.00
	St.L.(NL)	Unknown	725.00
1950	Boston(AL)		1,800.00
	Brook.(NL)	Balfour	2,400.00
1951	Brook.(NL)	D.&Clust	400.00
	Cleve.(AL)	Balfour	1,750.00
1952	N.Y.(NL)	D.&Clust	500.00
1955	Chic.(AL)	Unknown	800.00
	Cleve.(AL)	Balfour	800.00
1956	Milw.(NL)	Balfour	85.00
	N.Y.(AL)		NA
1959	Milw.W(NL)	Balfour	650.00
	Milw.R(NL)	Balfour	800.00
	S Fran.(NL)	Balfour	800.00
1960	Balt.(AL)	Balfour	1,250.00
	Chic.(AL)	Balfour	1,600.00
1963	St.L.(NL)	Josten	150.00
1964	Balt. B (AL)	Balfour	850.00
	Balt.HP(AL)	Balfour	850.00
	Chic.(AL)	Balfour	1,100.00
	Cinc.(NL)	Balfour	125.00
	Phila.(NL)	Martin	25.00
1965	S Fran.(NL)	Balfour	150.00
1966	Pitts.(NL)	Balfour	450.00
	S Fran.(NL)	Balfour	1,400.00
1967	Chic.(AL)	Balfour	75.00
	Minn.(AL)	Balfour	50.00
1969	Atlanta(NL)	Josten	75.00
	Minn.(AL)	Balfour	35.00
	S Fran.(NL)	Balfour	150.00
1970	Calif.(AL)	Balfour	450.00
	Chic.(NL)	Balfour	450.00
1971	Oak.Lg(AL)	Balfour	750.00
	Oak.S(AL)	Unknown	150.00
	S Fran.(NL)	Balfour	150.00
1972	Chic.(AL)	Balfour	1,000.00
	Pitts.(NL)	Balfour	1,000.00
1974	Texas (AL)	Balfour	550.00
1975	Oak.(AL)	Josten	450.00
1976	Phila.(NL)	Balfour	50.00
1977	Boston(AL)	Balfour	75.00
1978	Calif.(AL)		NA
	Cinc.(NL)	Balfour	75.00
	S Fran.(NL)	Balfour	35.00
1979	Calif.(AL)	Balfour	300.00
	Cinc.(NL)		NA
	Houst.(NL)	Balfour	850.00
	Montr.(NL)	Balfour	50.00
1980	Houst.(NL)	Balfour	125.00
	Montr.(NL)		NA
1981	Chic.(NL)	Balfour	200.00
	Oak.AL)	Balfour	100.00
	Phila.(NL)	Balfour	65.00
1982	Atlanta(NL)		NA
	L.A.(NL)	Balfour	150.00
1983	Chic.(AL)	Balfour	35.00
	Milw.(AL)	Balfour	225.00
	Pitt.(NL)	Balfour	200.00
1984	Chic.(NL)	Balfour	250.00
1985	Tor.(AL)	Balfour	200.00
1986	Cal.(AL)	G. Peddler	175.00
	Houst.(NL)	Balfour	175.00
1987	Boston(AL)		150.00
	Detroit (AL)	Balfour	150.00
	N.Y.(AL)	Balfour	200.00
	N.Y.(NL)	Balfour	200.00
	S Fran.(NL)	Balfour	60.00
1988	Boston(AL)		75.00
1990	Boston(AL)		60.00
	Pitt.(NL)		300.00

BOXING PINS

ANONYMOUS MANUFACTURERS
INDIVIDUAL BOXERS

Muhammad Ali
Sting Like a Bee (3 ½") 20.00
Frazier vs Ali, March 8, 1971 (1 ¾") 20.00
Hey Kids, Fights Mr. Tooth Decay (1974) 20.00
Various fight buttons, ea. . $5-25.00

Hurricane Johnson
Polo Grounds July 29 (1 ¾") . 25.00

Joe Louis
World's Heavyweight Champion (1 ¾") 30.00
WW II - We'll Win (1 ½") 30.00
Punch (1 ½") 15.00

Floyd Patterson
Polo Grounds July 29 (1 ¾") . 25.00

Ray Robinson
Portrait (1 ¾") 25.00

FOOTBALL PINS

SUPER BOWL PRESS PINS

#	Year	Result	Value
I	1967	GB35, KC10	1,200.00
II	1968	GB 33, Oak.14	950.00
III	1969	Jets 16, Balt. 7	850.00
IV	1970	KC 23, Minn. 7	NA
V	1971	Bal. 16, Dal. 13	NA
VI	1972	Dal. 24, Mia.3	400.00
VII	1973	Mia. 14, Was.7	375.00
VIII	1974	Mia. 24, Min.7	375.00
IX	1975	Pit. 16, Min.6	275.00
X	1976	Pit.21, Dal.17	325.00
XI	1977	Oak.32, Min.14	250.00
XII	1978	Dal.27, Den.10	225.00
XIII	1979	Pit.35, Dal.31	200.00

#	Year	Result	Value
XIV	1980	Pit.31, Ram 19	200.00
XV	1981	Oak.27, Phi.10	175.00
XVI	1982	S.F.26, Cin.21	150.00
XVII	1983	Was.27, Mia.17	150.00
XVIII	1984	Raid.38, Was.9	140.00
XIX	1985	S.F.38, Mia.16	135.00

#	Year	Result	Value
XX	1986	Chi.46, N.E.10	150.00
XXI	1987	NYG 39, Den.20	135.00
XXII	1988	Was.42, Den.10	125.00
XXIII	1989	S.F.20, Cin.16	125.00
XXIV	1990	S.F.55, Den.10	125.00
XXV	1991	NYG 20, Buf.19	125.00
XXVI	1992	Was.37, Buf.24	125.00

Note: Press pins for Super Bowls I, II, and III were issued as tie bars; formal press pins were not issued for Super Bowls IV and V, instead, patches were acceptable for members of the media. Super Bowl IV patch: $75, Super Bowl V patch: $60.

HORSE RACING PINS

BELMONT STAKES PINS

Year	Value
1987	10.00
1988	10.00
1989	15.00
1990	10.00
1991	8.00
1992	6.00

BREEDERS CUP PINS

Year	Value
1985	20.00
1986	NA
1987	NA
1988	10.00
1989	12.00
1990	8.00
1991	3.00
1992	15.00

KENTUCKY DERBY FESTIVAL PINS

Year	Pin	Value
1973	Pegasus Pin (Plastic)	650.00
1974	Pegasus Pin (Plastic)	100.00
1975	Pegasus Pin (Plastic)	275.00
1976	Pegasus Pin (Plastic)	65.00

1977 Pegasus Pin (Plastic) .. 50.00
1978 Pegasus Pin (Plastic) .. 50.00
1979 Pegasus Pin (Plastic) .. 50.00
1980 Pegasus Pin (Plastic) .. 40.00
1981 Pegasus Pin (Plastic) .. 15.00
1982 Pegasus Pin (Plastic) .. 15.00
1983 Pegasus Pin (Plastic) .. 10.00
1984 Pegasus Pin (Plastic) .. 10.00
1985 Pegasus Pin (Plastic) ... 8.00
1986 Pegasus Pin (Plastic) ... 6.50
1987 Pegasus Pin (Plastic) ... 5.00
1988 Enamel Lapel Pin 4.00
1989 Enamel Lapel Pin 3.50
1990 Enamel Lapel Pin 3.00
1991 Enamel Lapel Pin 2.50
1992 Enamel Lapel Pin 2.00

KENTUCKY DERBY PINS

1987 .... 4.00
1988 .... 10.00
1989 .... 10.00
1990 .... 5.00
1991 .... 3.00
1992 .... 3.00

PREAKNESS PINS

1987 .... 10.00
1988 .... 10.00
1989 .... 10.00
1990 .... 10.00
1991 .... 15.00
1992 .... 6.00

SUMMER OLYMPIC PINS & BADGES

1896 Athens, Greece

BADGES

Participant's badge, 49mm.:
Athletes, blue badge, blue ribbons, Greek letters 2,000.00
Judge's badge, pink w/ blue ribbons, Greek lettering 2,000.00
Official's badge, red w/ blue ribbons, Greek lettering 2,000.00

1900 Paris, France

BADGES

Judge's badge, silver:
Seated female figure, holding trumpet, winged torch overhead; inscription 1900 Jury, signed L. Rotter 600.00

1904 St. Louis, Missouri

PINS

Souvenir pin, silver 500.00
French team pin, oval athlete w/ javelin 250.00
Participant's Badge 4,000.00

1906 Athens, Greece

BADGES

Participant's badge:
blue with gold trim, stylized gold "A" in center on white background, 1906 in gold on bottom 1,000.00

PINS

Team Pins - first team pins given by host country, Athens 1906 inscribed on individual country flags 150-400.00

1908 London, England

BADGES

Judge's badge:
resembles 4 flower petals, with blue circular band in center inscribed Olympic Games London 1908 Judge; Helmeted figure, profile bust, inside circular band with laurel 750.00
Steward's badge:
same design on shield, on inscription Steward replaces Judge 750.00
Competitor's badge:
exactly like Judge's badge except for flower petals, Competitor replaces Judge 400.00

1912 Stockholm, Sweden

BADGES

Participant badges:
front view of male face, encircled with laurel. Bottom inscription Olympiska Spelen Stockholm 1912, with three crowns 300.00
Press Badge:
blue background, trimmed in gold, Stadion Pressen and gold star 350.00

PINS

Czechoslovakian pin. Gold lion on red, white and blue background 200.00
First souvenir pin available to public.
Naked athlete waving flag; inscription Olympiska Spelen Stockholm 1912 ..... 150.00
Flag stick pin.
Red, white and blue w/"Olympiska Spelen 1912" 100.00
Souvenir pin.
silver w/ three crowns . 150.00

1908 Steward's Badge

1924 Paris, France

BADGES

Press Badge:
Shield with colored Olympic rings on top, letters COF, and tri -masted ship in center. Blue border around shield - Presse VIII Olympiade Paris 1924, in gold letters 400.00
Official's badge:
Similar, white border, gold letters, Officiel VIII Olympiade Paris 1924 .... 400.00
Concurrent red 300.00

PINS

White, blue and red flag. Gold lettering viv Pariz 1924 125.00
Colombes Villa pin, gold triangular shape with laurel leaves around circle of sports equipment;

inscription VIIIme Olympiade Paris Colombes 150.00

1928 Amsterdam Olympic official's badge

1928
Amsterdam, Holland

BADGES

Competitor's Badge:
Circular, with red, white and blue bars on top. Gold lettering in bars IXe Olympiade Amsterdam. Colored rings on bronze background, inscription "1928 Concurrent" on circular part 300.00

Official's badge, similar, substitute "Officiel" for concurrent 350.00

Press Badge:
Oval, green band on outside, gold lettering IXe Olympiade Amsterdam. Dark interior oval, colored Olympic rings, inscription 1928 Presse 400.00

PINS

Czechoslovakian bronze enamel pin: w/ Olympic rings and olive branch 150.00

Flag, gold trim, colored Olympic rings on yellow background, black "J.I. IXe Olympiade" .. 100.00

1932
Los Angeles, California

BADGES

Press Badge:
Triangular shaped badge with shield inscription "Xth Olympiad Los Angeles, 1932", Olympic rings w/ laurel leaf. Red & yellow ribbon attached to badge ... 350.00

PINS

Donator's pin, shield with red, white and blue shield and Olympic rings. Outer ring inscription "Xth Los Angeles 1932 Olympiad" 100.00

Souvenir pin, octagonal with male athlete draped with laurel,

1932 Los Angeles Press badge

inscription Xth Olympiad 1932 Los Angeles 100.00

Souvenir pin, round, outer circle black, gold laurel, gold lettering Olympiade 1932. Inside circle red, inscription D.A.S.G., Olympic rings 125.00

U.S. Olympic committee pin, similar to above; U.S. Olympic Committee 150.00

1936
Berlin, Germany

BADGES

Judge's Badge, bronze:
Olympic rings above Brandenburg Gate inscription XI Olympiade Berlin 1936 400.00

PINS

Czechoslovakian die-cut pin:
Red, white and blue enameled flag next to a shield w/ lion facing to left 200.00

Czechoslovakian bronze enamel pin:
Pigeon flying to left w/ Czech flag behind 135.00

Souvenir pin:
White w/ gold outline. Eagle with swastika above colored Olympic rings. Gold "1936 XI Olympiade Berlin" 65.00

Souvenir pin:
Nazi swastika above columns, Olympic rings below columns, all cut out. White with gold outline and gold "1936 XI. Olympiade Berlin" 50.00

1940, 1944

Summer Olympics not held, WW II

1948
London, England

BADGES

Official's badges:
Big Ben above colored Olympic rings, inscription XIV Olympiad London 1948. Hanging ribbon with blue Official tag, ribbon in Olympic colors, white ribbon gold lettering National Olympic Committee 250.00

PINS

Souvenir pin, similar to above, no ribbons 45.00

1952
Helsinki, Finland

BADGES

Official's badge:
Blue badge, colored Olympic rings, U.N. Building, silver outline; inscription (on bottom) XV Olympia Helsinki Helsinkfors. Red ribbon, black letters, F.I.G. Tuomart 300.00

Competitor's badge:
Similar to above, Bronze color. Yellow ribbon, gold lettering, Yoeosurheilu Athletisme 200.00

Press Badge
. . . . 200.00

PINS

Czechoslovakian enamel pin:
Lion facing left on red background w/ banner at top and color Olympic rings at bottom 100.00

Gold enamel lapel pin:
Green background on a shield design, white enamel moon and three stars at top . 100.00

Hungarian enamel pin:
Gold eagle at top w/ Hungarian colors behind, dove in center and color Olympic rings on white enamel triangle 75.00

Russian team pin:
Soviet flag, red marble enamel with gold mast 75.00

1948 London official's badge

Souvenir pins:
Similar to above, colored Olympic rings, red background . . 35.00

1956
Melbourne, Australia

BADGES

Participant's Badge:
Oval, red outline, white center with torch, green shape of Australia, colored Olympic rings. Olympic Games Melbourne 1956, white lettering on red outline w/ red ribbon 300.00

Guest of Honor badge:
Similar to above, white outline, gold center. White ribbon, red "Guest of Honor" 500.00

1956 Participant's badge

Official's badge:
Similar to above, blue background on rings, two blue and yellow ribbons . . . 300.00

PINS

Romanian gold die-cut enamel pin:
White enamel flame at top color Olympic rings below . . . 30.00

Souvenir pin:
Blue in shape of Australia, torch; inscription XVIth Olympiad Melbourne 1956 . . . . . . 40.00

1960
Rome, Italy

BADGES

Official's badge:
Gold laurel leaf outline, green background, gold Trojan horse on platform above Olympic rings; inscription Roma MCMLX. Red tag below, gold lettering Ufficiale 300.00

Athlete's Badge:
Similar to above. White tag below, Atleta 300.00

PINS

Great Britain gold enamel
shield pin: 85.00

Souvenir pin:
Blue, tag shaped. Trojan horse above Olympic rings; inscription Roma MCMLX 50.00

1964
Tokyo, Japan

PINS

First mascot pin:
White figure standing behind sign with red Japanese rising sun symbol, Olympic rings, and inscription Tokyo . . . . . . 30.00.

Press pin:
Square, gold outline, white background. Radio tower with rising sun at apex, emanating concentric circles. Black "UER-EBU." At bottom "Tokyo (Olympic rings) 1964". 100.00

1968
Mexico City, Mexico

BADGES

Security badge:
White metal, rectangle, enamel, 86.5 x 31 mm. 100.00

C.N.O. badge:
Gold enamel badge
37 x 63mm. 250.00

Mission Chief badge:
Gold enamel, 37 x 63mm.
"Jefe de Mision" 250.00

PINS

Great Britain gold enamel shield pin:
Flag w/ Olympic rings . . 60.00

Great Britain gold enamel rectangular pin:
Union jack at left w/ rings and "GB" at right on white enamel 100.00

Soviet Union silver enamel pin:
"CCCP" in basketball above date and Olympic rings which form basketball hoop 20.00

Souvenir pin, rectangle:
White background, gold Olympic rings, gold Aztec calender; inscription Mexico, mexican flag on bottom 30.00

Similar half white, half red background, colored rings, different flags 30.00

Colored cut out Olympic Rings:
Above tag with red background; inscription Mexico 1968 . 30.00

1972
Munich, Germany

BADGES

Official's badge:
Silver color, sunburst. Blue tag below, dark blue lettering Mannschafts-offizieller . 150.00

Guest Badge:
Similar to above, all gold colored. White lettering Gast . . 175.00

PINS

Gold enamel oval pin:
Rings on white background "Munich, 1972" 22.50

Great Britain gold enamel rectangular pin:
Large flag at left, white enamel field to right w/ Olympic rings at top 100.00

Great Britain gold enamel shield pin:
Union jack w/ gold stripes in place of white all on white background 50.00

Kenya team enamel pin:
Shield w/ crossed spears on white field 75.00

Poland gold enamel stick pin:
White enamel eagle on red enamel background . . . 25.00

Souvenir pin:
Oblong, aqua background. Gold Olympic rings, sunburst. Gold lettering Munchen 10.00

White metal enamel rectangular pin:
Light blue field w/ Munich spiral emblem 13 x 32 mm. . . 12.00

Same as above: 9 x 22 mm . 10.00

1976
Montreal, Canada

BADGES

Competitor's badge:
Oblong, metallic, red Olympic rings in motion, small aqua square with Concurrent in middle; inscription XXIe Olympiade Montreal 1976 . . . . 60.00

Participant's Badge:
Montreal's Olympic logo/concurrent/Montreal 1976 29 x 56 mm 150.00

Also found with "Medecin" (doctor), "Invite" (guest) "Presse Officiel D'Equipe" (Team Official), and many others.

PINS

Corporate pin:
Orto 1976, Montreal's Olympic logo 30 x 50 mm 85.00

Die-cut tie tack:
(Montreal's Olympic logo) 3 sizes goldplated 18x17.5mm, 17 x 16 mm, 11 x 10.5 mm 5.00

Mascot pin (Amik):
Black beaver shape, with red stripe, Olympic rings in motion 15.00

Radio-TV Badge:
Emblem of Canadian Broadcasting ABC TV pin: ABC within circle/ Montreal's Olympic logo/ Montreal 1976.
24 x 29 mm 125.00

ABC TV Pin:
"ABC" (within circle)/Montreal's Olympic logo/"Montreal 1976"/"ABC guest".
39 x 44 mm 150.00

Radio & TV Pin:
Spain/RTVE/Olympic Rings/Montreal/76
15 x 18 mm 65.00

British TV Pin:
BBC TV/Montreal's Olympic logo/Montreal/1976
26 x 34 mm 150.00

West German Radio & TV Pin:
Montreal Olympic logo/ "ARD, ZDF" 32 x 26 mm 50.00

Souvenir pin:
Silver cut out Olympic rings in motion 5.00

TEAM PINS

Austrian Pin:
Montreal's Olympic logo/ "Osterreich" 29 x 37 mm 60.00

Bulgarian Pin:
Montreal (in cyrillic)/1976/Olympic Rings 13 x 16 mm 7.00
Canadian Pin:
Olympic rings/"1976 Can(Maple Leaf)ada". 33 x 30 mm . 30.00
Czechoslovakian Pin:
(national flag)/(olympic rings)/CSSR/1976/Montreal/Mont. olympic logo 15x30mm . 15.00
Identical 10X20MM 10.00
Field Hockey Pin:
Map outline/Montreal's Olympic logo /TheIndian /Maharadja /crossed field-hockey sticks. 32x30mm 40.00
Great Britain's Team Pin:
Great Britain/Union Jack/olympic rings/Montreal/1976 26x32mm 75.00
Great Britain Female Team Members Pin:
(olympic rings)/1976/G.B. 51x26mm 100.00
Hong Kong N.O.C. Pin:
HongKong/crowned lion/ 1976/ olympic rings 26mm . . . 40.00
Hungarian pin:
Olympic Rings, Maple Leaf/ Montreal 1976/ Hungarian Flag Colors 33x16mm 25.00

1976 Olympic Great Britain team pin

Hungarian pin:
Maple Leaf, Olympic Rings Hungarian flag colors, Montreal/1976 . . . . 15.00
India Boxing Federation Pin:
India/ Chakra emblem/ I.A.B.F./ boxing glove/ Montreal 1976 16x32 . . . . 15.00
Japan. Canadian flag with Montreal's Olympic logo/ Montreal/ 1976/ Japanese flag 35.00
Kenya's Team Pin:
Kenya/ (Shield with crossed spears)/ Montreal/ 1976 27x34mm 85.00
Korean Pin:
Korea/Montreal's Olympic Logo/Amateur Boxing Federation 19mm 35.00
Korean Team Pin:
Montreal 1976/ Korea/ yin-yang emblem/ Olympic rings 19mm 30.00
Another identical 27mm . 50.00
Malaysia Pin:
Malaysian Hockey Federation/ coat of arms & crossed field -hockey sticks/Montreal/olympic rings/Canada 25.00
Malaysia. Montreal's Olympic Logo/ Montreal 1976. 19mm 50.00
Netherlands Pin:
(olympic rings)/(Lion Rampant)/1976 . . . . . . 10.00
Poland's Soccer Team Pin:
XXI Olympiade/Olympic rings/Montreal's logo/soccer ball/1976 Montreal 37x37mm 35.00
Republic of China Pin
(Montreal's Olympic logo)/ Rep. of China Flag (olympic rings)/ Chinese letters) 46x25mm 40.00
Soviet Team Pin:
Star, hammer & sickle/Olympic Rings/1976 39x24mm . . 75.00
Spain Team Pin:
Espana/Montreal's Olympic Logo 27x42mm 50.00
Sudan Team Pin:
Sudanese flag/Sudan/Olympic rings/1976 25mm 65.00
Swiss National. 19(OLYMPIC RINGS)76 on Flag 13x17mm 40.00
Trinidad and Tobago. Montreal/ Olympic rings/national flag. 45.00
West German Pin:
Olympic rings/Montreal/ 1976/Eagle 23x11 . . . . . 25.00

1980
Moscow, CIS

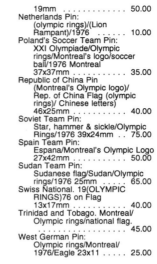

1980 Moscow souvenir pin

PINS

Souvenir pin:
Oblong shape, red background. Cyrillic lettering and 80 in gold lettering on black background on top. Official Olympic logo rings on bottom 5.00

Souvenir pin:
Rectangular, gold official Olympic logo in upper left hand corner on red background, Mockba 1980 in gold on white background on bottom, Olympic colors trailing gold medal in center . . . 5.00
Souvenir pins:
Russian maiden in traditional dress, Olympic colors, maiden holding loaf of bread with Olympic logo and rings . 10.00
Misha the bear souvenir pins:
Misha standing on box depicting athlete(s) . . . . . each @ 3.00

1984
Los Angeles, California

MEDIA PINS

ABC Television:
ABC LA corporate logo 15.25
ABC Sarajevo corporate logo 30.00
ABC LA guest badge 45.00
ABC Sarajevo guest badge . 60.00
ABC LA executive design . . 45.00
ABS Sarajevo exe. design . . 35.00
ABC/Sam - cloisonne 75.00
ABC/Stars - cloisonne 55.00
ACM Internat.(LA Licensee) . 55.00
Adidas (LA Licensee) 30.00
American Express (Sponsor) . 6.00
AMF- Athletic Equipment 6.00
Sports Illustrated. green . . . 8.00

1988
Seoul, South Korea

PINS

Souvenir pin:
Hodori official mascot . . 3.00
Olympic logo in red, white and blue Olympic rings 5.00

Similar to above, with inscription Seoul 1988 . . . . 5.00

MEDIA PINS

Associated Press, cloisonne, rectangle, Seoul 88 indicated 20.00
ARD ZDF, domed, rectangle, rings on top 15.00
ARD ZDF, domed, rectangle, rings on bottom 50.00
ITV, cloisonne, rectangle, with mascot 20.00
RAI (Italian media) square, w/mascot 50.00
BBC, cloisonne, rectangle. with

mascot 50.00
TVE (Spanish media), medal, irregular, with mascot . . 15.00
USA Today cloisonne, blue background, Seoul 88 indicated 20.00
AP Communications, cloisonne, rectangle, with mascot . 25.00
Washington Post, flat enamel, square, white background, Seoul 88 indicated 20.00
AFP (French media), cloisonne, Seoul 88 indicated 30.00
Sports Illustrated, cloisonne, rectangle, blue background, Seoul 88 indicated 25.00
Sports Illustrated, cloisonne, rectangle, white background, Seoul 88 indicated 25.00
BILD, cloisonne, Seoul 88 indicated 50.00
ESPN, plastic oval, Seoul 88 indicated 25.00
RFE/RL, cloisonne, Seoul 88 indicated 20.00
Reuters, domed, rectangle, with mascot 15.00
CBC Sports, domed, with mascot 15.00
SRC Sports, domed, with mascot 15.00
UPI, domed, rectangle, Seoul 88 indicated 25.00
NBC Guest badge, rectangle, blue and white 75.00
Television New Zealand, cloisonne, with kiwi and Seoul 88 indicated 20.00
Radio New Zealand, cloisonne, with kiwi and Seoul 88 . . . . 20.00
NOS Netherlands, domed, with mascot 10.00
Radio France, cloisonne, Seoul 88 indicated 20.00
TVR Japan, cloisonne, with mascot 20.00
Voice of America, cloisonne, round, with Seoul 88 indicated . 15.00
ABC Sports Australia, cloisonne, with kangaroo 50.00
Swiss-SRG SSR, metal, with Seoul 88 indicated 15.00

Areco Algerian rectangular enamel pin:
map of Algeria in green and white enamel w/ red star and moon and color Olympic rings 10.00

1992 Barcelona, Spain

MEDIA PINS

NBC Barcelona pin:
Gold colored Barcelona 92 at top, colored peacock in middle, rectanglular with bottom cut to resemble rings, domed 10.00
NBC affiliate Barcelona pin:
Similar to above, w/appendage on side 1/2" inch long with with station call letters, city name, or station number (60 different) 15.00
NBC radio affiliate pin:
similar 10.00
NBC Cablevision pin:
Round domed with white background with red NBC at top, gold rings in middle, black Cablevision at bottom, about 5/8" 10.00
TVA enamel pin:

1992 Barcelona TVA enamel pin

TVA logo in rectangle at top Barcelona logo and rings in diamond at bottom 10.00

CORPORATE SPONSOR

IBM PIN SET
Barcelona logo at top, IBM at bottom, 3/4" cut out enamel 5.00
Cobi at computer terminal, IBM at bottom (5/8" cut out enamel) 5.00
Rectangular upright pin:
3/4" by 1/2, Barcelona logo, IBM running across bottom enamel 5.00
Cobi at computer 1/2" round, domed 5.00
All pins come in three combos: silver and blue/black, gold and blue/black, gold with colored symbols and Cobi.
M&M: similar to winter game pins, depicting 25 summer sports, name of sport across bottom, cloisonne . . . . . . each @ 5.00
Pedigree: set of 28 different sports, pins each about 3/4" by 1". Sports at the top in color on white background. Pedigree on blue ribbon, USA rings at bottom edging is gold . . . each @ 3.00

SPONSOR SERIES: 1/2" high with Barcelona cut out at top and name of company at bottom Time, Phillips, Seiko, Kodak, Sony, Coca-Cola in gold; Xerox and Sony in silver each @ 5.00
Uncle Ben's Rice: rectangular enamel with orange and black border color Barcelona logo . . . 5.00
Coca-Cola: with Barcelona logo in color at top, Coca- Cola logo in red at bottom 5.00
Kodak: cloisonne triangular with red background, gold Barcelona logo on top, red Kodak logo on bottom. Official Sponsor written on one side of logo, Olympic Games 1992 on other . . . 5.00
McDonald's: round top colored red, blue and gold. 19 Barcelona 92 at top. Cut out rings in the center, square bottom with golden arches 5.00
McDonald's: similar, except for squared top with gymnast 5.00
Seiko: rectangular pin 3/4" by 1" with white background and Barcelona logo in color. Official Timer & SEIKO on bottom of pin, domed 5.00
Cloisonne 8.00

COBI MASCOT PINS

Cobi Mascot series in gold, and silver depicting 32 different sporting events. Comes in small plasic box on card with Barcelona logo. All pins are 1/2" to 3/4" in size, logos are on some but not on others according to size. All metal with black enamel; discontinued in favor of more colorful pins . . . . each @ 5.00
Cobi designs, similar to mascot series sports pins, with colored enamel 5.00
Cobi Media pins, similar to above, depicting photographer, video cameraman, radio announcer, reporter with pad. Also discontinued . . . . each @ 8.00

COMMEMORATIVE

Barcelona 92 under rings, USA cut out at top 1" by 1", enamel 3.00
Cloisonne 5.00
Barcelona 1992 on black background, under cut out colored rings 1" by 3/4" high enamel 5.00
Barcelona logo on 1 1/4" on white background, made by Albertville official pin, square 10.00
round 10.00
Sports pins by Official USA pin licencsee, each depicting one of several sports; Barcelona '92 at top cut out, a rectangular white

background in the middle, sport picture in gold at bottom.
Enamel 5.00
Cloisonne 7.00
Basketball & Baseball add 2.00
USA Basketball Team Pin: 1" by 1 1/2" white background, ten players at top with Barcelona Bound in red. Barcelona logo and 1992 at bottom. RV:Player names/jersey numbers . 15.00

WINTER OLYMPIC

PINS AND BADGES

1924
Chamonix, France
Press Badge 2000.00

1928
St. Moritz, Switzerland
Press Badge 500.00

1932
Lake Placid, New York
Press Badge 600.00

1936
Garmisch-Partenkirchen Germany

Press Badge 500.00
Olympic Committee Pin:
3.4 cm, nickel-silver and enamel featuring "KREUZECK -GARMISCH" above mountain peak, ski trail and Olympic rings; surrounded by silver pine branches and cones . . 150.00
Edelweiss badge:
3.2 cm x 2.7 cm. Openwork of edelweiss flower w/ "Garmisch -Partenkirchen" & Olympic rings 45.00
Same as above, with swastika 75.00
Commemorative badge. Silver enamel, 4 cm. Swastika in center of black and white mountain, with blue enamel sky and colored Olympic rings 100.00

Commemorative badge:
Silver enamel, 3.5 cm. Same badge as above, no swastika 75.00
Commemorative badge:
Same as above, but smaller size (4.7 x 2.7 cm), with edelweiss decorations on each side 50.00

1940
Commemorative pin:
Round light blue and white enamel with stylized skate blade and Olympic rings 150.00
Same pin as above, white color only 150.00
Press Badge 2000.00

1944
Winter Olympics not held, WW II

1948
St. Moritz, Switzerland

PINS AND BADGES

Bronze, colored enamel, 3.3 cm pin:
Olympic rings on sun rays within an inscribed circle . . . 125.00
Bronze, colored enamel, 2.7 x 1.3 cm pin:
Rooster perched on Olympic rings 40.00

Bronze uniface, 2.7 x 1.7 cm pin:
Radiant sun with "1948" above and Olympic rings and "St. Moritz" below; with 7.5 inch yellow/blue twisted cord and tassels 180.00
Silver enamel pin:
Olympic rings attached by two rings to black, white and blue enamel shield inscribed with "St. Moritz" and featuring a mountain goat at bottom 160.00
Press Badge 400.00

1952
Oslo, Norway
PINS AND BADGES
Bronze iron pin:
Bar/Ski with colored Olympic rings in center, "1952" to right and "NORGE" to left . . 45.00
Press Badge 500.00

1956
Cortina d'Ampezzo, Italy
Press Badge 500.00

1960
Sqaw Valley, California

1964
Innsbruck, Austria

PINS AND BADGES
ABC media pin:
Silver shield with red diagonal line between red ABC logo and red Innsbruck logo . . . 200.00
Reproduction of above pin, unauthorized and of inferior quality 2.00
Brass and enamel press badge:
4.2 x 3.0 cm, rounded corners. White square featuring Innsbruck symbol (same as pin above) with "PRESS" below--all on black enamel background . . 300.00
Commemorative brass/enamel pin:
4.8 x 3.4 cm. "Welcome in Austria . . ." inscription within ring, lying on pair of skis with red-white enamel shield containing Olympic rings 85.00
Commemorative brass/enamel pin:
2.6 x 2.6 cm. Olympic rings over Innsbruck symbol on black background with white border featuring inscription "IX OLYMP WINTER SPIELE" 40.00
Press Badge 250.00

1968
Grenoble, France

PINS AND BADGES
ABC media pin:
ABC logo on black within silver triangle at top, Grenoble logo and Olympic rings on light blue enamel -- all in shield with "Grenoble - 1968" in banner at bottom 125.00
Official's bronze and enamel badge:
2.2 x 1.4 cm. Grenoble logo in white enamel on bronze background with Olympic rings and "Grenoble 1968" at bottom 60.00
Commemorative red and white pin:
Olympic rings on white background above flame and "1968" 35.00
Commemorative red, white and blue enamel on white metal pin, 3.7 x 3.1 cm. Grenoble symbol and Olympic rings surrounded by white inscribed rim 35.00
Stick pin:
"1968" on the bottom two rings of five colored-enamel Olympic rings 35.00
Press Badge 350.00

1972
Sapporo, Japan
Press Badge 450.00

1976
Innsbruck, Austria

PINS
ABC media pin:
Red, blue and green ABC logo in white circle within a red triangle at top, Innsbruck logo below on white background; "Innsbruck

1976" in black banner below shield; gold finish 150.00
Same as above/silver finish 150.00
ABC guest badge:
Same design as pins above within black shield and featuring "ABC GUEST" in gold at bottom 200.00
Stick pin:
2 cm x 2 cm square, brass & enamel. Innsbruck symbol and Olympic rings in center surrounded by white box-outline with inscription "XII OLYMP WINTER SPIELE"; similar to 1964 design 15.00
Press Badge 200.00

1980 Lake Placid, New York

PINS

ABC media pin:
Lake Placid logo in blue enamel on white background with red ABC logo/circle in upper right; "Lake Placid 1980" in black banner beneath shield; silver finish 60.00
ABC guest badge:
Identical design as pin above within black shield and with "ABC GUEST" in gold 150.00
ABC Good Morning America pin:
Black and white enamel shield 100.00
Lake Placid Olympic logo pin:
Nickel-silver and enamel, 5.1 x 3.5 cm. Logo with Olympic rings in white-blue enamel and words "Lake Placid" at bottom . 10.00
Lake Placid Olympic logo pin:
White metal, 5 x 3.7 cm. Olympic rings in pale blue and white enamel, inscribed with "TM" (trademark initials) 20.00
Lake Placid Olympic logo pin:
White metal enamel, 2 x 1.5 cm. Official white metal logo pin cut-out Olympic rings with red, white colored enamel "slopes" leading up to rings 20.00
Common press/radio-TV pins 35.00
Common N.O.C. pins 15.00
Common Lake Placid logo pins 5.00
Common Olympic village pins 4.00
Toyota Sponsor pin:
2.1 x 2.2 cm, white metal. Red-blue enamel U.S. shield with "Toyota" at top and "USA" in center 15.00
Common Sponsor pins 10.00
Roni raccoon buttons:
5.75 cm, Trench mfg., Buffalo, NY. Roni participating in various sports, all with "1980 LAKE PLACID"; each 1.00

1984 Sarajevo, Yugoslavia

PINS

Sarajevo logo stick pin:
Gold-finish, 1.8 x 1 cm. Olympic rings, Sarajevo logo and "Sarajevo '84" in rectangle 2.00
Same as above, silver or bronze finish 2.00

Mascot pins featuring Voochko the wolf; all include Sarajevo logo, Olympic rings and "Sarajevo '84" in gold:

Voochko carrying U.S. flag .. 5.00
Voochko carrying Olympic torch 5.00

15 various pins portraying Voochko in different Winter sports: including ice hockey, bobsled, figure skating, skiing, ski jumping, etc.; each 5.00

Framed Voochko sets:
16 pin set including keystone pin of Sarajevo logo in number-black colored enamel beneath gold Olympic rings. The other 15 pins include: Voochko with torch, Voochko with U.S. flag and Voochko participating in 13 different Winter sports. In center of frame lies a black nameplate with gold lettering featuring the serial # of the set, the Olympic rings, the Sarajevo logo & "Sarajevo '84 XIV Olympic Winter Games" 100.00

17 pin Pan Am set with same 16 pins as above set, in addition to a keystone domed enamel pin featuring the blue Pan Am logo in the center of the red Sarajevo logo, all on a white background with cut-out Olympic rings at top 275.00

Sponsor pins:
ABC executive shield:
ABC Olympic logo in navy blue enamel triangle at top, orange-red Sarajevo logo on white background at bottom of shield and "Sarajevo 1984" on black banner beneath shield 25.00
ABC media enamel shield:
Official ABC pin featuring ABC Olympic logo on black enamel above Sarajevo logo on white background; red and blue lines run along sides and bottom of shield 25.00
Unofficial ABC cloisonne shield:
Same style as above, except ABC logo on blue 10.00
ABC enamel guest badge:
Same design as above within a black enamel shield; includes words "ABC GUEST" in gold 100.00
Campbell's soup domed enamel pins:
Sarajevo logo, Olympic rings and "OFFICIAL SOUP . . ." in red on white 5.00
Campbell's kids playing 5 different sports featuring Olympic rings, Sarajevo logo and "Sarajevo '84" in blue on white background; sports featured include hockey, ski jumping, speed and figure skating and bobsledding. Each 5.00
Chevrolet domed enamel:
Chevrolet logo in blue at top, Olympic rings and red Sarajevo logo beneath with "TM" and "Sarajevo '84" 7.50
Coca-Cola cloisonne:
Coke logo to left, red Sarajevo logo to right on white beneath Olympic rings (only 1,000 produced) 100.00
Reproduction of Coke Sarajevo pin: inferior quality 5.00
Flying Tigers domed enamel:
"Flying Tigers" in gold on blue background at bottom; cut-out Olympic rings at top; red Sarajevo logo on white with "Sarajevo '84" in middle . 7.00
Landau Associates domed enamel:
Red, white and blue, horizontal design. "RLA" logo to left on blue, red Sarajevo logo to right beneath cut-out Olympic rings, corporate name spelled out on red enamel across bottom 9.00
Same as above, brown & white enamel. 9.00
Landau Associates domed enamel:
Red, white and blue, vertical design. "RLA" logo at bottom on red enamel, blue Sarajevo logo on white with cut-out Olympic rings above 8.00
Same as above, brown & white enamel 8.00
Merrill Lynch fine enamel:
Blue with gold detail. Rectangular pin with cut-out rings at top left, Sarajevo logo at left and gold outline of bull at right .. 10.00
Same as above, blue, black and white enamel. Blue snowflake, black bull on white 20.00
Same as above, blue and white enamel. Blue snowflake, white bull on white 20.00
Miller High Life domed enamel:
Orange, red, white and blue. Shield shape with Miller logo at top, orange Sarajevo logo in center on white background with red line along left border and blue line along right border 8.00
Motorola domed enamel:
Blue, gold and white. Shield shape featuring Motorola logo at top in white on gold, Sarajevo logo below on blue background 10.00
Motorola/Voochko domed enamel:
Blue, brown, red and white. Voochko at left holding blue Motorola flag 8.00
Pan Am domed enamel:
Red, white and blue. Cut-out Olympic rings above red Sarajevo logo with blue Pan Am logo in center 5.00
Pageantry World/Voochko domed enamel:
Red, white, blue and black. Voochko to left of red and white flag with Sarajevo logo; "Pageantry World, Inc." appears in blue oval at base ... 10.00

Roman Meal domed enamel:
Red, white and blue. "Roman Meal" in gold on blue banner at bottom, blue Sarajevo logo in center of circle with red outline and Olympic rings at top . 7.50

Sports Illustrated cloisonne:
Red, white and blue. Rectangle w/ Sports Illustrated in blue at top, large, red "1984" in middle with generic snowflake between the "9" and "8", "Winter Olympics" and "Sarajevo" at bottom; all on white 10.00

Stanley domed enamel shield:
Red, white, blue, black and yellow. Stanley logo at bottom with red Olympic rings at top and red Sarajevo logo in center; on white with red and blue outlines 7.50

1988 Calgary, Canada

PINS

Calgary logo cloisonne pin:
Logo and "Calgary '88" in gold on red background 10.00

Calgary Olympic village pin:
Gold pin with arch forming top 100.00

Common emblem pins 5.00

Mascot pins:

Howdy and Hidy mascot pins, cloisonne:
Howdy participating in various sports including biathlon, skiing and others. Pins with both Howdy and Hidy include figure skating and a welcome pin which portrays Howdy waving the Canadian flag. Calgary logo appears somewhere on the mascots' uniforms on each pin. Each 4.00

Howdy and Hidy circular pins, cloisonne.
Similar to pins above except all on pale blue circular background. Eleven different featuring: bobsled, luge, ice hockey, biathlon, ski jumping, cross country skiing, downhill skiing, slalom skiing, figure skating, speed skating and welcome pin. Each 7.50
Mounted and framed complete set with red-white-black inscription on gold nameplate 100.00

Sponsor pins:

ABC enamel pin:
Original pin issued one year before Games, blue and white shield with one union bug on back 25.00

ABC domed enamel pin:
Similar to pin above; one union bug on back 10.00

ABC thin metal. Similar design to above pins, multiple union bugs on back 5.00

ABC Holiday enamel pin:
ABC Olympic logo with "Calgary '88": two varieties; one with red enamel the other with green, each 5.00

Coca-Cola poster pin:
Domed enamel, red and gold. "Calgary '88'" at top, Calgary logos in center and Coke logo at bottom 5.00

Coca-Cola poster pins:
Domed enamel. Different pin for each of first fifteen Winter Olympic Games. Pins feature Coke logo with symbols, site names and years from each Games. Each 5.00

Michelob Dark enamel pin:
Michelob Dark logo at top with Calgary logo and "Calgary '88" below 5.00

Same pin as above, Michelob logo 5.00

Same pin as above, Michelob Light logo 5.00

Same pin as above, Natural Light logo 5.00

1992 Albertville, France

PINS

USA Albertville enamel pin:
Cut-out colored Olympic rings with "USA" above and "Albertville" below 2.50

Original bid pin:
Heavy metal. "Savoie Olympique Albertville 1992" on white background, no Olympic rings 25.00

Mascot pins:

Original chamois goat mascot cloisonne pins:
"Magic" participating in various Winter sports in stylized designs, made by Stadium Paris; only © on back. Each 20.00

Sponsor pins:

Bausch & Lomb cloisonne pin:
Rectangular pin with Albertville logo, "Albertville '92", Olympic rings and "Bausch & Lomb" 4.00

CBS domed enamel pin:
Rectangular pin with colored Olympic rings above three mountain peaks and "CBS", "Albertville '92" on gold at bottom 5.00

1992 M&M Mars pin

Chrysler enamel pin:
Chrysler corporation logo at top, "1992 Albertville" in center, "USA" and Olympic rings 4.00

Kodak enamel pin:
Diamond/square-shape with "Kodak" in triangle at bottom, Albertville logo above, "Official Sponsor Olympic Games 1992" in bands across top 3.00

M & M enamel pins:
M & M character participating in various Winter sports. M & M logo at top with Olympic rings beneath and name of sport across bottom. Each . . . 4.00

Renault white metal pin:
Rectangular pin featuring Renault logo on white 25.00

Visa enamel pin:
Rectangular pin with "Visa" across top Albertville logo in center, "Albertville '92" & Olympic rings at bottom 5.00

NOC PINS

Afghanistan, round, black & green 65.00
Algeria, small rectangle, silver, dove design 30.00
Algeria, small rectangle, gold, dove design 30.00
American mascotoa, domed, Olympiad Seoul 25.00
Andorra, cloisonne, shield, red, yellow, blue 10.00
Antigua, domed, red & black, with sun 32.00
Argentina, blue shield, Seoul 15.00
Australia, silver & gold boomerang, with rings 15.00
Austria, cloisonne, blue oval, red & white 20.00
Bahrain, domed oval, mascot 32.00
Bangladesh, domed, gold XXIV Olympiad 27.00
Barbados, domed, irregular shape, Bar. Flag 15.00
Belgium, domed, black & red lion 20.00
Belize, domed, red, blue, white shield 15.00
Benin, cloisonne, white shield, w/country 25.00
Bermua, domed,aqua & white,mascot 20.00
Bhutan, domed, orange & yellow, dragons 55.00
Burma, plastic, lg shield, white peacock 55.00
Bolivia, domed, small green rectangle 65.00
Botswana, round, gold, zebras 30.00
Botswana, round, zebras . . . 30.00
Botswana, round, bronze, zebras 30.00
Brazil, cloisonne, rectangle,

mascot 20.00
British Virgin Isles, white circle,green 40.00
Similar, Seoul symbol . . 45.00
Brunei, gold, with crown . . . 75.00
Bulgaria, domed, yellow background, with mascot 5.00
Bulgaria, similar, green background 10.00
Canada, cloisonne,white background, with mascot 15.00
Cameroon, gold rectangle . . 20.00
Cayman Islands, cloisonne, white shield 25.00
Chad, circle, gold, with map . 65.00
Chile, small, red, white and blue shield 20.00
People's Republic of China, cloissone, dark red, red flag with rings 40.00
Similar, small flag over rings 30.00
Colombia, domed, very small, dark blue 15.00
Congo, silver circle, map . . 20.00
Cook Islands, domed, small, white 25.00
Costa Rica, maroon circle, with flat bottom 15.00
Costa Rica, red, white and blue shield, black background 25.00
Cyprus, domed, white shield 6.00
Czechoslovakia, red, white, blue, flag 5.00
Denmark, cloisonne, red with white cross 10.00
Dominican Republic, round, white, red and blue 20.00
Djibouti, antelope head 60.00
East Germany, rectangle, gold, red, black 10.00
Ecuador, domed, shield, Seoul 88 10.00 Egypt, blue background, black, white, red, shield . 32.00
El Salvador, blue, white & blue shield 15.00
Fiji Island, domed, rectangle, white & blue 27.00
Finland, Olympic rings colored 15.00
France, traditional rooster . . 15.00
Gabon, cloisonne, green, yellow, & blue shield 70.00
Painted metal, similar . . 90.00
Domed, small, similar . . 55.00
Ghana, dark blue shield, w/ bird & black star 60.00
Tiny variation 50.00
Great Britain, white shield, with flag 27.00
Greece, cloisonne, blue . . . 20.00
Guam, domed, elliptic, palm tree 12.00
Guatemala, domed, blue circle, with bird 15.00
Guinea, small shield with elephant 60.00
Guyana, rectangle, red, yellow, green, white, map of country 27.00
Burkina Faso, red, & green circle, with gold horses 115.00
Honduras, gold circle, with blue flag 20.00
Hong Kong, domed, lions and crest 10.00
Hungary, cloisonne, white diamond, rings 45.00
India, rectangle, white 40.00
Indonesia, cloisonne, red & yellow, with torch 37.00
Domed, large, brown . . . 42.00
Iraq, domed, flag design, gold 45.00
Red, similar 35.00
Blue, similar 35.00
White, similar 35.00
Green, similar 35.00
Iran, cloisonne, rectangle, shield, ... 25.00
Ireland, small white shield . . 10.00
Iceland, white, geyser design 10.00
Israel, domed, rectangle, blue & white 15.00
Italy, red, yellow, green 10.00
Ivory Coast, domed, green, with elephant 20.00
Jamaica, domed, black, yellow & green 30.00
Japan, flag design 10.00
Jordan, domed, rectangle, flag 20.00
Kenya, domed, white shield, lion 10.00
Korea, blue circle with Seoul symbol 20.00
Kuwait, domed, gold shield . 35.00
Laos, domed, flag 20.00
Lebanon, rectangle, gold . . . 32.00
Liberia, gold circle with ship design 32.00
Silver, similar 32.00
Libya, round, gold, torch . . 100.00
Liechtenstein silver oval . . . 15.00
Malaysia, small white & blue circle 40.00
Rectangle, silver 35.00
Malawi, rectangle, small, blue, Seoul 88 . . . . 37.00
Mali, domed, green, yellow, red shield 35.00
Malta, heraldic cross, rings . 10.00
Mauritius, domed, shield with map in blue 62.00
Mexico, cloisonne, round, black background, Seoul 88 . . 12.00
Small gold metal square, Seoul 88 . . . . 20.00
Monaco, shield, monks, crest 25.00
Mongolia, flag, rings 42.00
Morocco, domed, large white circle, Seoul symbol 40.00
Mozambique, domed, triangle design 22.00
Nepal, domed, circle with hat 10.00
Netherlands Antilles, round, white circle, red, white, and blue shield 45.00
Nicarauga, rectangle, blue, white, blue 37.00
Niger, large green shield, animal, flag 105.00
Small shield, Seoul 88 110.00
Nigeria, white & green shield 25.00
Small, gold, with Flag, Seoul 80.00
Netherlands, orange design . 15.00
Norway, domed, red, white, and blue oval 15.00
New Zealand, fern with rings 15.00
Oman, domed, gold circle with crossed swords . . . 37.00
available 47.00
Papua New Guinea, cloisonne, rectangle . . . 20.00
Pakistan, metal, small, round, gold, with mascot 20.00
Metal, medium, round, gold, with mascot 45.00
Metal, large, round, gold, with mascot 60.00
Panama, red, white and blue design 10.00
Paraguay, cloisonne, rectangle, gold with red, white, and blue 20.00
Peru, cloisonne, red, white, red design 30.00
Phillipines, domed flag, Seoul symbol 32.00
Poland, torch design 5.00
Puerto Rico white shield with Seoul symbol 22.00
Portugal, rectangle, metal . . 35.00
Qatar, maroon/gold circle . . 37.00
Republic of China, white circle 20.00
Rectangle with Seoul symbol 20.00
Romania, red, yellow, blue . 10.00
Saint Vincent, domed rectangle, flag 20.00
San Marino, domed, shield, blue, yellow, gold 15.00
Saudi Arabia, small gold shield, green wreath 22.00
Saudi Arabia, domed, small shield 20.00
Senegal, white painted, lion . 45.00
Sierra Leone, cloisonne, Seoul 88 . . . . 90.00
Singapore, domed, rectangle, white 10.00
Solomon Islands, domed, shield crest 32.00
Somalia, painted blue design 45.00
Spain traditional design 10.00
Surinam, round design 20.00
Swaziland, domed, blue, with hatchet 25.00
Sweden, cloisonne, 3 Swedish crowns 15.00
Switzerland, metal, with Seoul symbol 90.00
Syria, Flag with rings 25.00
Taiwan, domed rectangle, flag 15.00
Tanzania, cloisonne, small rectangle 27.00
With Seoul symbol 45.00
Thailand, small elephant . . . 25.00
Large elephant 35.00
Very large elephant, over rings 45.00
Togo, torch 25.00
Tonga, domed, red flag with cross 50.00
Trinidad and Tobago, cloison, Hodori,white . . . 30.00
Similar, black 30.00
Tunisia, rings, over shield . . 35.00
Turkey, red flag design 20.00
Uganda domed, white circle, 2 birds 35.00
United Arab Emirate, domed, shield 25.00
USA set of light blue with Statue of Liberty, one for each sport . . . . @15.00
USSR, large red flag 45.00
Fake, non-raised version 25.00
Uruguay, blue, white, blue . 20.00
Venezuela, domed, white . . 20.00
Vietnam, plastic, silver with red flag 20.00
West Germany, domed, rectangle, Seoul 15.00
Yemen, South. Large gold, Seoul symbol 85.00
Yemen, North. gold circle, castle & star 75.00
Zaire, pewter, hand with torch 10.00
Zambia, pewter, with bird . . 10.00
Zimbabwe, white map shape, Seoul 88 . . . . 35.00

PLATES

BASEBALL PLATES

ARMSTRONG

Player	No. Issued	Value
Rose, Pete		
Hand-signed	1,000	600.00
10¼"	10,000	45.00

D.H. USSHER LTD.

Player	No. Issued	Value
Carter, Joe		
Hand-signed	1,000	200.00
Gruber, Kelly		
Signed 10¼"	1,000	200.00
Signed 8½"	5,000	65.00

GARTLAN USA

Player	No. Issued	Value
Aparicio, Luis		
Hand-signed	1,984	125.00
8½"	10,000	45.00
Mini	Open	19.00
a/p	250	150.00
Barlick, Al		
Mini	Open	19.00
Club	Club only	45.00
Bench, Johnny		
Hand-signed	1,989	175.00
Mini	Open	19.00
Berra, Yogi		
Hand-signed	2,150	125.00
8½"	10,000	45.00
Mini	Open	45.00
a/p	250	175.00
Brett, George		
Hand-signed	2,000	250.00
Mini	Open	19.00
Carew, Rod		
Hand-signed	950	150.00
8½"	10,000	45.00
Mini	Open	19.00
Fisk, Carlton		
Hand-signed	950	150.00
8½"	10,000	45.00
Mini	Open	19.00
a/p	300	200.00
Ford, Whitey		
Hand-signed	2,360	125.00
8½"	10,000	45.00
Mini	Open	19.00
a/p	250	175.00
Griffey Jr., Ken		
Club	Club only	30.00
10¼"	1,992	125.00
8½"	10,000	45.00
Jackson, Reggie		
Mini	Open	19.00
Rose, Pete		
Farewell, a/p	50	550.00
Hand-signed	950	300.00
Mini	Open	19.00
Club 1989	Club only	65.00
Platinum	4,192	650.00
Platinum, Mini	Open	19.00
Schmidt, Mike		
Hand-signed	1,987	500.00
Mini	Open	19.00
a/p	56	750.00
Seaver, Tom		
Hand-signed	1,992	125.00
8½"	10,000	45.00
Strawberry, Darryl		
Hand-signed	2,500	125.00
8½"	10,000	45.00
Mini	Open	19.00

GREAT EVENT SERIES

Player	No. Issued	Value
Clemens, Roger		
Signed decal	200	900.00
10¼"	2,000	200.00
Jackson, Reggie		
Signed decal	537	350.00
10¼"	537	100.00
Joyner, Wally		
Signed decal	313	300.00
10¼"	313	75.00
Sutton, Don		
Signed decal	300	300.00
10¼"	300	75.00

HACKETT AMERICAN

Player	No. Issued	Value
Aaron, Hank		
Hand-signed	755	425.00
8½"	5,000	60.00
Carlton, Steve		
Hand-signed	600	325.00
8½"	5,000	60.00
Cobb, Ty		
8½"	5,000	75.00
Ford, Whitey		
Hand-signed	472	300.00
8½"	5,000	60.00
Garvey, Steve		
Hand-signed	1,207	225.00
10¼"	8,973	60.00
Jackson, Reggie		
Hand-signed	464	900.00
10¼"	9,536	60.00
Killebrew, Harmon		
Signed decal	573	325.00
8½"	5,000	60.00
Koufax, Sandy		
Hand-signed	1,000	475.00
Mathews, Eddie		
Signed decal	540	300.00
Mays, Willie		
Hand-signed	660	450.00
8½"	5,000	60.00
Ruth, Babe		
8½"	10,000	95.00
Ryan, Nolan		
10¼"	1,598	700.00
8½"	5,000	125.00
Seaver, Tom		
Hand-signed	3,272	350.00
8½"	5,000	60.00
Signed "300"	1,200	250.00
8½ "300"	5,000	60.00

Gartlan 8½" Ken Griffey, Jr. plate

MARIGOLD

Player	No. Issued	Value
DiMaggio, Joe		
Hand-signed	325	1,650.00
10¼"	10,000	200.00
Hand-signed a/p	50	2,500.00
Facsimilie-signed	2000	450.00

Mantle, Mickey		
Hand-signed	1,000	550.00
10¼"	10,000	150.00

PRO SPORTS CREATIONS

Player	No. Issued	Value
Palmer, Jim		
Hand-signed	1,000	150.00
Hand-signed a/p	200	200.00
10¼"	5,000	60.00
Mini	15,000	20.00

SPORTS IMPRESSIONS

Player	No. Issued	Value
Banks, Ernie		
8½"	5,000	60.00
Mini	Open	20.00
Bench, Johnny		
8½"	5,000	60.00
Mini	Open	20.00
10¼"	975	150.00
Boggs, Wade		
Mini	Open	20.00
10¼"	2,000	75.00
10¼"	1,000	150.00
Branca, Ralph		
Mini	Open	20.00
Hand-signed w/ Thomson	1,951	75.00
Canseco, Jose		
Mini	Open	20.00
10¼"	10,000	75.00
Clark, Will		
Mini	Open	20.00
10¼"	10,000	75.00
Hand-signed	2,500	200.00
Clemens, Roger		
Mini	Open	20.00
10¼"	975	150.00
8½"	5,000	60.00
Clemente, Roberto		
Mini	Open	20.00
10¼"	10,000	75.00
Cobb, Ty		
Mini	Open	20.00
10¼"	10,000	75.00
Dawson, Andre		
Mini	Open	20.00
10¼"	10,000	75.00
10¼" gold	1,000	150.00
Dykstra, Len		
Mini	Open	20.00
10¼"	2,000	75.00
10¼" gold	1,000	150.00
Feller, Bob		
Mini	Open	20.00
10¼" gold	1,000	150.00
10¼"	10,000	75.00
Gehrig, Lou		
Mini	Open	20.00
10¼"	10,000	75.00
Gooden, Dwight		
Mini	Open	20.00
10¼"	3,500	150.00
Griffey Jr., Ken		
Mini w/ Dad	Open	20.00
10¼" w/ Dad	1,991	150.00
Henderson, Rickey		
Mini	Open	20.00
10¼"	1,990	150.00
Hershiser, Orel		
Mini	Open	20.00
10¼"	10,000	75.00
Hand-signed	2,500	150.00
Kaline, Al		
Mini	Open	20.00
10¼"	10,000	75.00
10¼" gold	1,000	150.00
Mantle, Mickey		
Mini	Open	40.00
Mini	Open	20.00
Mini "life"	Open	20.00
Mini "50s"	Open	20.00
Mini "60s"	Open	20.00
10¼" gold	1,500	300.00
10¼"	3,500	75.00
10¼" "50s"	1,951	150.00
10¼" "60s"	1,961	150.00
8½" "life"	5,000	60.00
12" oval	1,968	195.00
Mattingly, Don		
Mini "23"	Open	20.00
Mini "PoY"	Open	20.00
10¼" "23"	1,991	150.00
10¼" "Pride"	3,500	150.00
Mays, Willie		
Mini	Open	20.00
10¼"	2,500	150.00
Mini "Gold"	Open	20.00
8½" "Gold"	5,000	30.00
McGwire, Mark		
Mini	Open	20.00
10¼" gold	1,000	150.00
Molitor, Paul		
Mini	Open	20.00
10¼" gold	1,000	150.00
10¼"	10,000	75.00
Morgan, Joe		
Mini	Open	20.00
10¼" gold	1,990	150.00
Munson, Thurman		
Mini	Open	20.00
10¼"	10,000	75.00
Musial, Stan		
Mini	Open	20.00
10¼"	1,963	150.00
Robinson, Brooks		
Mini	Open	20.00
10¼" gold	1,000	150.00
10¼"	2,000	75.00
Robinson, Jackie		
Mini	Open	20.00
10¼" gold	1,956	150.00

Sports Impressions 10¼" Andre Dawson plate

Ruth, Babe		
Mini (2 styles)	Open	20.00
10¼"	10,000	75.00
8½"	5,000	60.00
Ryan, Nolan		
Mini Miracle	Open	20.00
Mini No-hit	Open	20.00
Mini 300 win	Open	20.00
Mini 5,000	Open	20.00
8½" Miracle	3,000	60.00
8½" No-hit	5,000	60.00
10¼" No-hit	1,992	150.00
10¼" 300 win	1,990	150.00
10¼" 5,000	5,000	150.00
Sandberg, Ryne		
Mini	Open	20.00
10¼" gold	975	150.00
8½"	5,000	60.00
Seaver, Tom		
Mini	Open	20.00
10¼"	3,311	150.00
Snider, Duke		
10¼" gold	1,500	150.00
10¼"	5,000	75.00
Hand-signed	50	250.00
Mini	Open	20.00
Mini "Gold"	Open	20.00
8½"	5,000	60.00
Thomson, Bobby		
Mini	Open	20.00
Hand-signed w/ Branca	1,951	75.00
Trammell, Alan		
Mini	Open	20.00
10¼" gold	1,000	150.00
10¼"	10,000	75.00
Wagner, Honus		
Mini	Open	20.00
10¼"	10,000	75.00
Williams, Ted		
Mini plate	Open	20.00
10¼" gold	1,150	275.00
Hand-signed	350	400.00
10¼"	3,000	75.00
"Splinter"	1,960	150.00
Yastremzski, Carl		
Mini	Open	20.00
10¼" gold	1,500	150.00
10¼"	3,000	75.00
Young, Cy		
Mini	Open	20.00
10¼"	10,000	75.00

BASKETBALL PLATES

GARTLAN USA

Player	No. Issued	Value
Abdul-Jabbar, Kareem		
Hand-signed	1,989	275.00
Mini	Open	18.00
Johnson, Magic		
Hand-signed	1,987	800.00
Mini	Open	25.00
Wooden, John		
Hand-signed	1,975	100.00
8½"	10,000	45.00
Mini	Open	19.00

SPORTS IMPRESSIONS

Player	No. Issued	Value
Anderson, Kenny		
10¼"	Open	150.00
Mini	Open	20.00
Barkley, Charles		
10¼"	1,991	150.00
8½"	5,000	60.00
Mini	Open	20.00
Bird, Larry		
10¼"	1,991	150.00
10¼" tribute	1,992	150.00
8½" (2 styles)	5,000	60.00
Mini (3 styles)	Open	20.00
Coleman, Derrick		
Mini	Open	20.00
Daugherty, Brad		
Mini	Open	20.00
Dream Team		
10¼" 1st 10	1,992	200.00
10¼" Dream	1,992	200.00
8½" 1st 10	7,500	60.00
8½" Dream	7,500	60.00
8¼" 1st 10	7,500	60.00
Mini (5 styles)	Open	20.00
Drexler, Clyde		
10¼"	1,991	150.00
8½"	5,000	60.00
Mini (2 styles)	Open	20.00
Dumars, Joe		
Mini	Open	20.00
Ewing, Patrick		
10¼"	1,991	150.00
8½"	5,000	60.00
Mini	Open	20.00
Hardaway, Tim		
Mini	Open	20.00
Johnson, Kevin		
10¼"	1,991	150.00
8½"	5,000	60.00
Mini	Open	20.00
Johnson, Larry		
10¼"	Open	150.00
Mini	Open	20.00
Johnson, Magic		
10¼" gold	1,991	250.00
8½" (2 styles)	5,000	60.00
Mini (3 styles)	Open	20.00
10¼"	1,992	150.00
Jordan, Michael		
10¼" gold	1,991	275.00
10¼"	1,992	150.00
8½" (2 styles)	5,000	75.00
Mini (2 styles)	Open	20.00
Kemp, Shawn		
Mini	Open	20.00
King, Bernard		
10¼"	Open	150.00
Mini	Open	20.00
Laettner, Christian		
Mini	Open	20.00
Lewis, Reggie		
Mini	Open	20.00
Malone, Karl		
10¼"	1,991	150.00
8½"	5,000	60.00
Mini	Open	20.00
Manning, Danny		
Mini	Open	20.00
McHale, Kevin		
10¼"	Open	150.00
Mini	Open	20.00
Miller, Reggie		
10¼"	Open	150.00
Mini	Open	20.00
Mullin, Chris		
10¼"	1,991	150.00
8½"	5,000	60.00
Mini (2 styles)	Open	20.00
Mutombo, Dikembe		
10¼"	1,991	150.00
Mini	Open	20.00
Olajuwon, Hakeem		
10¼"	1,991	150.00
Mini	Open	20.00
O'Neal, Shaquille		
Mini	Open	20.00
Paxson, John		
Mini	Open	20.00
Pippen, Scottie		
10¼"	Open	150.00
Mini	Open	20.00
Porter, Terry		
Mini	Open	20.00
Price, Mark		
10¼"	Open	150.00
Mini	Open	20.00
Richmond, Mitch		
Mini	Open	20.00
Robertson, Oscar		
10¼"	1,991	150.00
8½"	5,000	60.00
Mini	Open	20.00
Robinson, David		
10¼"	1,991	150.00
8½"	5,000	60.00
Mini (2 styles)	Open	20.00
Seikaly, Rony		
10¼"	Open	150.00
Mini	Open	20.00
Skiles, Scott		
10¼"	Open	150.00
Mini	Open	20.00
Thomas, Isiah		
10¼"	1,991	150.00
8½"	5,000	60.00
Mini	Open	20.00
Wilkins, Dominique		
10¼"	1,991	150.00
8½"	5,000	60.00
Mini	Open	20.00
Worthy, James		
10¼"	Open	150.00
Mini	Open	20.00

Sports Impressions 8½" David Robinson plate

BOXING PLATES

SPORTS IMPRESSIONS

Boxer	No. Issued	Value
Louis, Joe		
10¼"	5,000	75.00
Mini	Open	20.00
Marciano, Rocky		
10¼"	5,000	75.00
Mini	Open	20.00

FOOTBALL PLATES

GARTLAN USA

Player	No. Issued	Value
Montana, Joe		
Hand-signed	2,250	250.00
8½"	10,000	45.00
3¼"	Open	19.00
Club 1991	Club only	34.00
a/p	250	295.00
Staubach, Roger		

Hand-signed	1,979	200.00
Mini	Open	19.00

SPORTS IMPRESSIONS

Player	No. Issued	Value
Aikman, Troy		
10¼"	1,990	150.00
8½"	5,000	60.00
Mini	Open	20.00
Cunningham, Randall		
10¼"	1,990	150.00
8½"	5,000	60.00
Mini	Open	20.00
Elway, John		
10¼"	1,990	150.00
8½"	5,000	60.00
Mini	Open	20.00
Esiason, Boomer		
Mini	Open	20.00
8½"	5,000	60.00
10¼"	1,990	150.00
Everett, Jim		
Mini	Open	20.00
8½"	5,000	60.00
10¼"	1,990	150.00
Harbaugh, Jim		
10¼"	1,992	150.00
8½"	5,000	60.00
Mini	Open	20.00
Kelly, Jim		
10¼"	1,990	150.00
8½"	5,000	60.00
Mini	Open	20.00
Kosar, Bernie		
Mini	Open	20.00
8½"	5,000	60.00
10¼"	1,990	150.00
Lombardi, Vince		
8½"	3,926	60.00
Mini	Open	20.00
Marino, Dan		
10¼"	1,990	150.00
8½"	5,000	60.00
Mini	Open	20.00
Montana, Joe		
10¼"	1,992	150.00
8½"	5,000	60.00
Mini	Open	20.00
Moon, Warren		
10¼"	1,990	150.00
8½"	5,000	60.00
Mini	Open	20.00
Okoye, Christian		
10¼"	1,992	150.00
8½"	5,000	60.00
Mini	Open	20.00
Payton, Walter		
10¼"	1,988	150.00
8½"	5,000	60.00
Mini	Open	20.00
Rice, Jerry		
10¼"	1,990	150.00
8½"	5,000	60.00
Mini	Open	20.00
Rypien, Mark		
10¼"	1,992	150.00
8½"	5,000	60.00
Mini	Open	20.00
Sanders, Barry		
10¼"	1,992	150.00
8½"	5,000	60.00
Mini	Open	20.00
Taylor, Lawrence		
10¼"	1,992	150.00
8½"	5,000	60.00
Mini	Open	20.00
Thomas, Thurman		
10¼"	1,992	150.00
8½"	5,000	60.00
Mini	Open	20.00
Unitas, John		
10¼"	1,973	150.00
8½"	5,000	60.00
Mini	Open	20.00

Sports Impressions 10¼" Troy Aikman plate

GOLF PLATES

SPORTS IMPRESSIONS

Golfer	No. Issued	Value
Palmer, Arnold		
Mini	Open	20.00
8½"	5,000	60.00
10¼"	1,500	150.00
Player, Gary		
Mini	Open	20.00
8½"	5,000	60.00
10¼"	1,500	150.00

HOCKEY PLATES

D.H. USSHER LTD.

Player	No. Issued	Value
Howe, Gordie		
Hand-signed	2,421	140.00
LaFleur, Guy		
Signed 10¼"	1,991	145.00
Signed 8½"	3,500	65.00
Sittler, Darryl		
Hand-signed	1,989	130.00
Tretiak, Vladislav		
Hand-signed	Open	130.00
Williams, Tiger		
Signed 10¼"	2,200	130.00
Signed 8½"	2,200	65.00
Yzerman, Steve		
Hand-signed	1,000	200.00
8½"	5,000	65.00

ENOR

Player	No. Issued	Value
Messier, Mark		
Hand-signed	3,000	85.00

GARTLAN USA

Player	No. Issued	Value
Gretzky, Wayne		
Hand-signed a/p	300	550.00
Hand-signed	1,851	400.00
8½"	10,000	45.00
Mini	Open	19.00
Howe, Gordie		
Hand-signed	2,358	150.00
8½"	10,000	45.00
Mini	Open	19.00

Gartlan Gordie Howe plate

Player	No. Issued	Value
Hull, Bobby and Brett		
Hand-signed	950	275.00
8½"	10,000	45.00
Mini	Open	19.00
McDonald, Lanny		
a/p	75	300.00
Hand-signed	1,500	175.00
4¼"	Open	30.00
Sittler, Darryl		
a/p	75	250.00
Hand-signed	1,989	135.00
4¼"	Open	30.00

LYNEL STUDIOS

Player	No. Issued	Value
Gretzky, Wayne		
8½"	Open	200.00

POCKET SCHEDULES

By Judy Bartolett

As long as there have been games, there have been schedules to let the fans know when the game was taking place. Over the years the schedule has taken on many different shapes and forms and has grown in popularity as a collectible (rather than a practical) item.

Why collect schedules? In many cases, schedule collecting is less expensive than collecting cards or other types of sports memorabilia. Schedules are promotional items designed to gain as much exposure as possible for the team (and the sponsor of the schedule) so they are usually available for free. Often the only expense involved in schedule collecting is postage for writing to teams, sponsors, and other collectors.

1993 Yankees Sked

In recent years many teams have showcased a star player, or the manager, on the schedule. These schedules contain artwork and photographs that rival those found on sports cards. Older schedules are not as aesthetically pleasing as current ones, but they are unique pieces of sports history and are generally in shorter supply than their sports card counterparts from the same years.

Schedules are available for just about any sport you might be interested in, and for any level of that sport. While this is not a comprehensive list, just take a look at a few of the sports featured on schedules: auto racing, baseball, basketball, field hockey, football, golf, gymnastics, horse racing, ice hockey, jai-alai, lacrosse, rodeo, rugby, soccer, softball, swimming, tennis, track, volleyball, and wrestling.

In addition to the major leagues, colleges and universities produce schedules for men's and women's athletics, as do minor leagues, semi-pro leagues, and even high schools.

Countless objects have been used as schedules in the past. Some quite innovative and interesting examples are: banks, coins (usually with a sponsor on the obverse, and the schedule on the reverse), decals and stickers (with the schedule either on the backing paper or the sticker itself), hockey pucks, paper napkins, plastic cups (often available with a beverage purchase at the stadium), rulers, seat cushions, street maps, and can coolers.

These stories are all true: In 1988-89, the University of North Dakota printed its basketball, football, and hockey schedules on seat cushions sold at home games; the 1990 Chicago Bears had their schedules printed on plastic cups; the 1983-84 Milwaukee Bucks schedule was featured on a coin bank shaped like a beer can; and the 1963 Minnesota Twins found their games listed on a twelve-inch metal ruler.

These oddball schedules are obviously not the most common varieties available. The most common type of schedule is the pocket schedule, known to collectors as a "sked." A fan might keep a sked posted on his refrigerator or in his wallet for easy reference, so as to always know when a favorite team's games are. These schedules (often measuring about the size of a standard sports card) have many variations regarding color, design, and overall quality.

Pocket schedules are known to have been issued for most of the twentieth century. A number of older schedules appear in a small booklet form, often with spaces for fans to keep track of a team's record. An example of this is the 1950 Chicago White Sox schedule (sponsor A.J Reach). This was a schedule of the entire American League, with day-by-day listings for every team, and a special section on the White Sox which lists their game times, ticket prices, doubleheaders, and night games.

While many recent skeds include three or more folded panels and are printed on glossy paper, most older skeds were printed on thick paper and had two panels (one listed home games, the other listed away games).

The types of sponsors for some of the older skeds are very similar to the sponsors today. In 1949 the *Cincinnati Enquirer* issued a Reds pocket schedule, and in 1959 the *Detroit News* sponsored the Tigers schedule. Other typical sponsors include gas stations, restaurants, hotels, banks and credit unions, and insurance companies.

While the sponsors have remained surprisingly the same, schedule designs have changed dramatically over the years. As stated earlier, star players have recently been showcased on a large number of schedules. A few recent notable star skeds were Ken Griffey, Jr. (Seattle Mariners 1991), Larry Bird (Boston Celtics 1990-91), Troy Aikman (Dallas Cowboys 1992), and Brett Hull (St. Louis Blues 1990-91, 1991-92).

In addition to the pocket sked, there is an almost infinite number of items that might be classified as a sked. Matchbook schedules date back to the pre-Depression era, and are still in use today. Matchbooks usually have a team logo on the front, an advertisement on the back, and the games listed inside. Some types of matchbook schedules even picture individual players on the front or back, rather than just a logo.

A few examples of recent matchbook schedules include a 1982 sked for the Milwaukee Brewers and a 1984 release for the St. Louis Cardinals. The skeds show their team logos on the front and list the home games on the inside. The Brewers matchbook is sponsored by WPRE Radio in Prairie Du Chein, Wisconsin, and the Cardinals matchbook was issued by the Lou Brock Sports Shop at Lambert International Airport in St. Louis.

Another rather common item is the brochure schedule. These are usually obtained from a team's ticket office and serve a number of purposes. Some schedules showcase all of the different ticket options for a particular team, while other teams may produce different brochures for season tickets, package plans, group tickets, and single-game tickets.

Brochures can run from bland to beautiful. Most major league teams print their single-game ticket order brochures on white paper, with one or two different ink colors, and might show a team logo. Season ticket and group ticket brochures, on the other hand, are often heading towards the beautiful end of the

1990-91 Magic Sked

1991-92 Flyers Sked

spectrum.

In 1991 the Minnesota Twins treated collectors to two beautiful brochures. The season ticket brochure featured a photograph of autographed baseballs, signed by Twins stars of past and present. In addition to the signed balls, a Twins logo ball, and an All-Star Game baseball are also represented. On the group ticket order brochure is a collage of baseball cards (mostly Topps) which not only showcases stars like Rod Carew, Harmon Killebrew, and Kirby Puckett, but includes lesser lights like Al Newman, Bombo Rivera and Rob Wilfong. Both brochures have wraparound cover photographs.

Posters are often released with schedules printed on them. Sometimes they are ballpark giveaways, but often they are promotional devices designed for display at ticket outlets or other retail establishments, like liquor stores and sporting goods shops.

Like any other type of sked, the quality of poster schedules vary; some feature full color player photographs, others showcase team logos, and others seem to be nothing more than a giant listing of games.

In 1984, Super America teamed up with the Minnesota Twins to sponsor a Twins poster schedule. The poster is red, white, and blue and has photos of Tom Brunansky, Kent Hrbek, and Ken Schrom, all surrounded by press clippings from the previous season. Hardware Hank sponsored a Twins poster sked for their silver anniversary season in 1986. In addition to the silver anniversary logo, the poster shows a large black-and-white photo of a number of Twins players congratulating each other after a game.

A recent trend, taking sked collecting by storm, is the magnet schedule (printed on thick magnet stock). These skeds are almost always early season giveaways, usually during the first home weekend or game, or sometimes they are given away later in the season, on fan appreciation day.

The *Chicago Tribune* and Sports Channel teamed up to sponsor a Chicago White Sox magnet sked in 1990. The four by seven inch schedule includes a calendar listing of Sox games, along with a listing of Comiskey Park promotional days. Old Style Beer sponsored a magnet sked for the Cubs the following year.

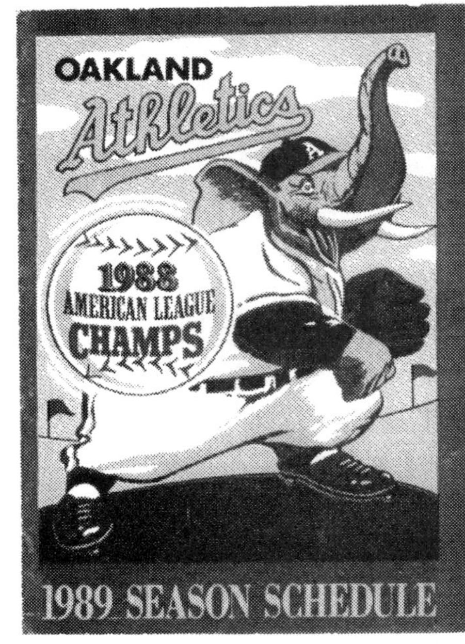

1989 Athletics Sked

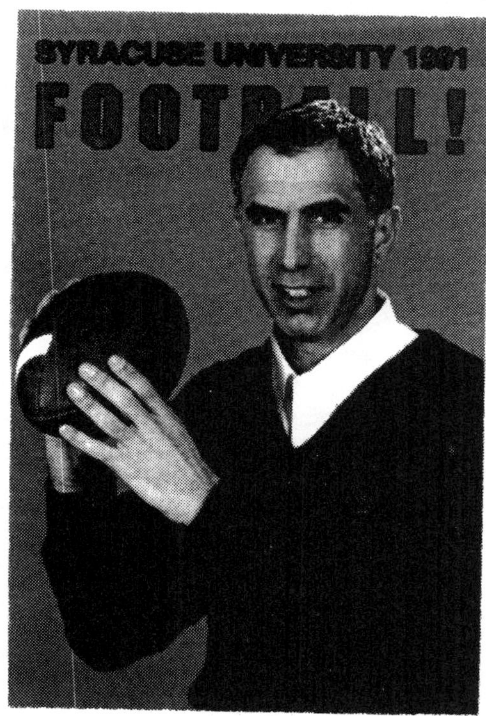

1991 Syracuse Sked

Like the Sox magnet, the sked had a chronological listing of Cubs games, along with 1991 promotional games.

In probably the most unusual sked, the 1986 Minnesota Twins were featured on a schedule of epic proportions, 35 feet high and 106 feet wide. Sponsored by WCCO Radio, Midwest Federal, Naegele Advertising and the Minneapolis Athletic Club, this sked was painted on an outside wall of the club.

Schedules are rarely bought and sold among collectors (which is good news for the Athletic Club). The majority of collectors build collections through trade, so selling is not necessary. If schedules are seen for sale, they are most often in the hands of a non-schedule collector.

The older the schedule, for the most part, the more valued it is. Before 1975, few schedule collectors existed. Most schedules were probably not saved from year to year because their usefulness expired at the end of a given season.

However, always remember a simple fact of sked collecting, namely; schedules are free promotional items, so they are designed without an eye to value, unlike a pack of sports cards intended for retail sale. The only value schedules have is in the hands of an interested collector. For these reasons, most post-1975 schedules are considered "common" and are traded one-for-one among collectors.

Schedules that are in special demand include those from defunct teams and leagues, as well as first year expansion teams (like the 1977 Toronto Blue Jays and Seattle Mariners). Instead of assigning a monetary value to these skeds, these premium skeds are usually traded for a handful of commons.

Non-schedule collectors put a premium on schedules picturing star players. However, most of these schedules are quite common and are traded freely among schedule collectors.

Schedule collecting is a fun, relatively inexpensive way to follow sports. It allows the collector the freedom to collect only the schedules she or he wants to specialize in, be it a team, league, sport, sponsor, or other category. Sports schedules (pocket and the infinite number of other varieties) are an economical alternative or addition to any sports collection. They are often attractive and inexpensive, and the contact with teams and collectors make schedule collecting a more personal segment of the sports collecting world. If you have only looked at schedules in the past to check game times, next time you might want to stop for a closer look. You might find that schedules deserve a place in your collection, not just on your refrigerator.

BASEBALL SCHEDULES

by Paul E. Jarrell

Fans can not attend games if they don't know when to go, so clubs have always put out schedules. A team issue schedule is one put out by the team that can be picked up when attending the games or by mail correspondence. Several of the early team owners owned private businesses like breweries and clothing stores whose advertisements were on the schedules. However, many of the team issue schedules had no advertisement and this practice is still in use for some of the teams today. All teams put out a league booklet schedule for the National and American Leagues.

Many companies in the Major League cities see schedules as an inexpensive way to advertise. Advertising also appeared on match covers, place mats, menus, ink blotters, pencils, posters, and baseball tickets on occasion. The railroad was the main way of travel for the ball clubs in the early years and many railroads put schedules out for various teams. Newspapers printed team schedules as well. You could find schedules in places ranging from pool parlors to your local cafeteria. Roster type schedules were popular. They featured spring training and sometimes the home season schedule. This type of schedule began as early as the 1920s.

Schedules printed in two different languages (Spanish and English) originated in the mid-1970s. The 1993 Marlins have them (as you might expect) as well as the following teams: Dodgers, Angels, Padres, White Sox, and Cubs. Strangely, I have never seen or heard of any at the New York clubs.

Many different graphics are drawn on schedule covers. They range from a simple baseball and bat to cartoon baseball scenes, drawings of ballparks, likeness of famous players, photos and drawings of banks, cafeterias and whatever business sponsored that particular schedule along with a very plain type that had only the team and year on the front. Willard Mullin, a famous cartoonist that worked for the *New York World Telegram,* did a combination schedule for the New York teams in the 1950s. A combination schedule is one with two or more teams on the same schedule and it always had only the home games listed. Probably the most desirable schedule would be one with a photo of an HOF player. They include: Ty Cobb 1912 Tigers, Babe Ruth 1933 Yankees roster, Christy Mathewson 1913 Reds, Hugh Jennings 1910 and 1911 Tigers Michigan journal, and Lefty Grove 1926 athletics.

In 1993, there will be upwards of 10,000 different sponsored schedules and a serious schedule collector will obtain about 1500. If he can get all the team issues and major sponsored ones, he will have had a good year.

POCKET SCHEDULES

BASEBALL

Availability ...... A
Cover Artwork C
Tradability .... T
[Ratings: A (best) - D (worst)]

ANGELS

1966 California Angels Sked

1960s .... A ... A ... A
1970s .... B ... C ... B
1980s .... B ... C ... B
1990s .... A ... C ... B

ASTROS

1960s .... B ... B ... B
1970s .... B ... C ... B
1980s .... B ... C ... B
1990s .... B ... B ... B

ATHLETICS

Philadelphia Athletics

1900s .... A ... B ... A
1910s .... A ... B ... B
1920s .... A ... A ... A
1930s .... B ... A ... A
1940s .... B ... A ... A
1950s .... B ... B ... A

Kansas City Athletics

1950s .... A ... B ... A
1960s .... A ... B ... A

Oakland Athletics

1960s .... B ... B ... A
1970s .... B ... C ... B
1980s .... B ... C ... B
1990s .... B ... B ... B

BLUE JAYS

1970s .... B ... B ... A
1980s .... B ... B ... B
1990s .... B ... B ... B

BRAVES

Boston Braves

1900s .... A ... B ... A
1910s .... A ... B ... A
1920s .... A ... B ... A
1930s .... A ... B ... A
1940s .... A ... B ... A
1950s .... A ... B ... A

Milwaukee Braves

1950s .... B ... A ... A
1960s .... B ... A ... A

Atlanta Braves

1960s .... B ... A ... A
1970s .... B ... B ... B
1980s .... A ... B ... B
1990s .... A ... B ... B

BREWERS

Seattle Pilots

1960s .... B ... A ... A

Milwaukee Brewers

1970s .... B ... C ... B
1980s .... A ... C ... B
1990s .... A ... A ... B

CARDINALS

1900s .... A ... B ... A
1910s .... A ... B ... A
1920s .... A ... A ... A
1930s .... A ... A ... A
1940s .... A ... A ... A
1950s .... A ... A ... A

1965 St. Louis Cardinals Sked

1960s .... A ... A ... A
1970s .... B ... B ... B
1980s .... A ... B ... B
1990s .... A ... B ... B

CUBS

1900s .... A ... B ... A
1910s .... A ... B ... A
1920s .... A ... B ... A
1930s .... A ... A ... A
1940s .... B ... A ... A

1960 Chicago Cubs Sked

1950s .... B ... A ... A
1960s .... C ... A ... A
1970s .... C ... A ... A
1980s .... D ... A ... A
1990s .... D ... A ... A

DODGERS

Brooklyn Dodgers

1900s .... A ... B ... A
1910s .... A ... B ... A
1920s .... A ... B ... A
1930s .... A ... C ... A
1940s .... A ... C ... A
1950s .... A ... B ... A

Los Angeles Dodgers

1950s .... A ... A ... A
1960s .... B ... A ... A
1970s .... B ... C ... A
1980s .... A ... B ... A
1990s .... A ... B ... B

EXPOS

1960s .... B ... B ... A
1970s .... C ... B ... A
1980s .... C ... B ... A
1990s .... B ... B ... A

GIANTS

New York Giants

1900s .... A ... B ... A
1910s .... A ... B ... A
1920s .... A ... B ... A
1930s .... A ... C ... A
1940s .... A ... C ... A
1950s .... A ... C ... A

San Francisco Giants

1950s .... A ... A ... A
1960s .... A ... A ... A
1970s .... B ... C ... B
1980s .... A ... C ... B
1990s .... A ... C ... B

INDIANS
1900s .... A ... A ... A
1910s .... A ... A ... A
1920s .... A ... A ... A
1930s .... A ... A ... A
1940s .... A ... A ... A
1950s .... C ... C ... A
1960s .... A ... A ... A
1970s .... B ... C ... B
1980s .... A ... C ... B
1990s .... A ... C ... B

MARINERS
1970s .... B ... C ... A
1980s .... B ... B ... B
1990s .... B ... A ... A

MARLINS

1993 Florida Marlins Sked

1990s .... C ... A ... A

METS
1960s .... A ... B ... A
1970s .... B ... C ... B
1980s .... B ... B ... B
1990s .... A ... A ... B

ORIOLES
St. Louis Browns
1900s .... A ... B ... A
1910s .... A ... B ... A
1920s .... A ... A ... A
1930s .... A ... A ... A
1940s .... A ... A ... A
1950s .... A ... A ... A
Baltimore Orioles
1950s .... A ... A ... A
1960s .... B ... A ... A
1970s .... B ... B ... B
1980s .... B ... C ... B
1990s .... A ... A ... B

PADRES
1960s .... B ... B ... B
1970s .... B ... C ... B
1980s .... B ... C ... B
1990s .... A ... C ... B

PHILLIES
1900s .... A ... B ... A
1910s .... A ... B ... A
1920s .... A ... A ... A
1930s .... B ... A ... A
1940s .... B ... A ... A
1950s .... B ... A ... A
1960s .... B ... B ... A
1970s .... A ... C ... B
1980s .... A ... C ... B
1990s .... A ... B ... B

PIRATES
1900s .... A ... B ... A
1910s .... A ... B ... A
1920s .... A ... A ... A
1930s .... A ... A ... A
1940s .... A ... A ... A

1952 Pittsburgh Pirates Sked

1950s .... A ... A ... A
1960s .... A ... A ... A
1970s .... A ... C ... B
1980s .... A ... C ... B
1990s .... A ... B ... B

RANGERS
Washington Senators
1960s .... A ... B ... A
1970s .... B ... B ... A
Texas Rangers
1970s .... B ... C ... B
1980s .... A ... B ... B
1990s .... A ... B ... B

REDS
1900s .... A ... B ... A
1910s .... A ... B ... A
1920s .... A ... A ... A
1930s .... A ... A ... A
1940s .... D ... B ... A
1950s .... A ... A ... A
1960s .... A ... A ... A
1970s .... B ... C ... B
1980s .... B ... C ... B
1990s .... B ... B ... B

RED SOX
1900s .... A ... B ... A
1910s .... A ... B ... A
1920s .... A ... A ... A
1930s .... A ... A ... A
1940s .... A ... A ... A
1950s .... A ... A ... A
1960s .... B ... A ... A
1970s .... B ... A ... B
1980s .... B ... A ... B
1990s .... A ... B ... B

ROCKIES
1990s .... C ... A ... A

ROYALS
1960s .... B ... B ... B
1970s .... B ... C ... B
1980s .... A ... C ... B
1990s .... A ... C ... B

TIGERS
1900s .... A ... B ... A
1910s .... A ... B ... A
1920s .... A ... A ... A
1930s .... A ... A ... A
1940s .... A ... A ... A
1950s .... C ... B ... A
1960s .... C ... B ... A
1970s .... A ... C ... B
1980s .... A ... B ... B
1990s .... A ... A ... B

TWINS
Washington Senators
1900s .... A ... B ... A
1910s .... A ... B ... A
1920s .... A ... A ... A
1930s .... A ... A ... A
1940s .... A ... A ... A
1950s .... A ... A ... A
1960s .... B ... B ... A
Minnesota Twins
1960s .... C ... C ... A
1970s .... C ... C ... B
1980s .... A ... B ... B
1990s .... A ... A ... B

WHITE SOX
1900s .... A ... B ... A
1910s .... A ... B ... A
1920s .... A ... A ... A
1930s .... A ... A ... A
1940s .... A ... A ... A
1950s .... A ... A ... A
1960s .... B ... B ... A
1970s .... B ... C ... B
1980s .... A ... B ... B
1990s .... A ... B ... B

YANKEES
1900s .... A ... B ... A
1910s .... A ... B ... A
1920s .... A ... C ... A
1930s .... A ... C ... A
1940s .... A ... B ... A
1950s .... A ... B ... A
1960s .... B ... B ... A
1970s .... C ... C ... A
1980s .... C ... C ... A
1990s .... C ... B ... A

BASKETBALL

BUCKS
1960s .... A ... A ... A
1970s .... B ... C ... B
1980s .... B ... A ... B
1990s .... A ... A ... B

BULLETS
Chicago Bullets
1960s .... A ... B ... A
Baltimore Bullets
1960s .... A ... A ... A
Washington Bullets
1960s .... A ... A ... A
1970s .... B ... A ... B
1980s .... B ... B ... B
1990s .... B ... B ... B

BULLS
1960s .... A ... B ... A
1970s .... B ... B ... B
1980s .... B ... A ... A

1990s . . . . B . . . A . . . A

CAVALIERS

1970s . . . . C . . . D . . . C
1980s . . . . B . . . B . . . C
1990s . . . . B . . . C . . . C

CELTICS

1940s . . . . A . . . B . . . A
1950s . . . . A . . . B . . . A
1960s . . . . A . . . B . . . A
1970s . . . . B . . . C . . . A
1980s . . . . B . . . A . . . A

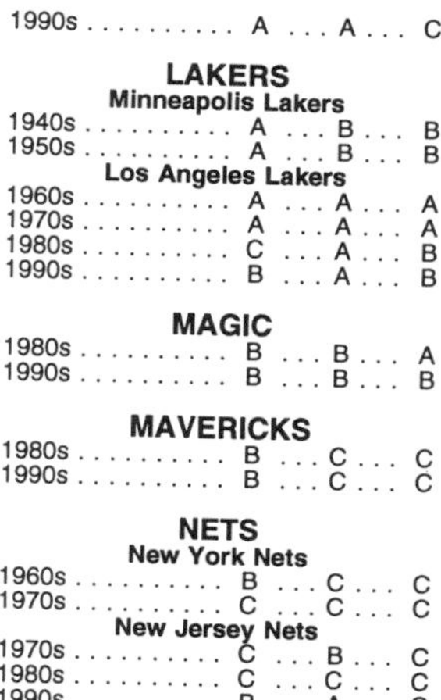

1992 Boston Celtics Sked

1990s . . . . B . . . A . . . A

CLIPPERS

Buffalo Braves

1970s . . . . B . . . B . . . C

San Diego Clippers

1970s . . . . C . . . C . . . B
1980s . . . . C . . . B . . . C

Los Angeles Clippers

1980s . . . . B . . . C . . . B
1990s . . . . B . . . A . . . B

HAWKS

Tri-Cities Hawks

1940s . . . . A . . . B . . . B
1950s . . . . A . . . B . . . B

Milwaukee Hawks

1950s . . . . A . . . A . . . B

St. Louis Hawks

1950s . . . . A . . . A . . . A
1960s . . . . A . . . A . . . A

Atlanta Hawks

1960s . . . . A . . . A . . . A
1970s . . . . B . . . C . . . C
1980s . . . . B . . . C . . . C
1990s . . . . B . . . C . . . C

HEAT

1980s . . . . B . . . B . . . C
1990s . . . . B . . . B . . . C

HORNETS

1980s . . . . B . . . C . . . A
1990s . . . . B . . . C . . . B

JAZZ

New Orleans Jazz

1970s . . . . C . . . B . . . B

Utah Jazz

1970s . . . . B . . . B . . . C
1980s . . . . C . . . B . . . C

1990s . . . . C . . . B . . . C

KINGS

Rochester Royals

1940s . . . . A . . . B . . . B
1950s . . . . A . . . B . . . B

Cincinnati Royals

1950s . . . . A . . . A . . . A
1960s . . . . B . . . A . . . A
1970s . . . . B . . . B . . . A

KC-Omaha Kings

1970s . . . . B . . . B . . . C

Kansas City Kings

1970s . . . . B . . . C . . . B
1980s . . . . C . . . B . . . C

Sacramento Kings

1980s . . . . C . . . B . . . C
1990s . . . . B . . . B . . . C

KNICKS

1940s . . . . A . . . B . . . A
1950s . . . . A . . . C . . . A
1960s . . . . A . . . C . . . A
1970s . . . . B . . . B . . . C
1980s . . . . A . . . B . . . C

1992-93 New York Knicks Sked

1990s . . . . A . . . A . . . C

LAKERS

Minneapolis Lakers

1940s . . . . A . . . B . . . B
1950s . . . . A . . . B . . . B

Los Angeles Lakers

1960s . . . . A . . . A . . . A
1970s . . . . A . . . A . . . A
1980s . . . . C . . . A . . . B
1990s . . . . B . . . A . . . B

MAGIC

1980s . . . . B . . . B . . . A
1990s . . . . B . . . B . . . B

MAVERICKS

1980s . . . . B . . . C . . . C
1990s . . . . B . . . C . . . C

NETS

New York Nets

1960s . . . . B . . . C . . . C
1970s . . . . C . . . C . . . C

New Jersey Nets

1970s . . . . C . . . B . . . C
1980s . . . . C . . . C . . . C
1990s . . . . B . . . A . . . C

1991-92 New Jersey Nets Sked

NUGGETS

1960s . . . . A . . . A . . . A
1970s . . . . C . . . B . . . C
1980s . . . . C . . . C . . . C
1990s . . . . B . . . C . . . C

PACERS

1960s . . . . B . . . A . . . A
1970s . . . . C . . . C . . . C
1980s . . . . B . . . A . . . C
1990s . . . . B . . . A . . . C

PISTONS

Ft. Wayne Pistons

1940s . . . . A . . . B . . . A
1950s . . . . B . . . A . . . C

Detroit Pistons

1950s . . . . A . . . A . . . A
1960s . . . . A . . . A . . . A
1970s . . . . B . . . D . . . C
1980s . . . . B . . . C . . . C
1990s . . . . B . . . A . . . B

ROCKETS

San Diego Rockets

1960s . . . . A . . . A . . . C
1970s . . . . B . . . A . . . C

Houston Rockets

1970s . . . . C . . . B . . . C
1980s . . . . B . . . B . . . C
1990s . . . . B . . . B . . . C

76ERS

Syracuse Nationals

1940s . . . . A . . . B . . . A
1950s . . . . A . . . B . . . A
1960s . . . . A . . . B . . . A

Philadelphia 76ers

1960s . . . . A . . . B . . . A
1970s . . . . C . . . C . . . C
1980s . . . . C . . . C . . . B
1990s . . . . B . . . C . . . C

SPURS

Dallas Spurs

1960s . . . . A . . . C . . . B
1970s . . . . A . . . C . . . B

San Antonio Spurs

1970s . . . . C . . . C . . . C
1980s . . . . C . . . C . . . C
1990s . . . . B . . . A . . . B

SUNS
1960s . . . . A . . . B . . . A
1970s . . . . B . . . C . . . C
1980s . . . . B . . . B . . . C
1990s . . . . B . . . B . . . C

SUPERSONICS
1960s . . . . A . . . A . . . A
1970s . . . . C . . . B . . . B
1980s . . . . B . . . B . . . C
1990s . . . . B . . . B . . . C

TIMBERWOLVES
1980s . . . . B . . . C . . . A

1990-91 Minnesota T-Wolves Sked

1990s . . . . B . . . B . . . B

TRAILBLAZERS
1970s . . . . A . . . A . . . C
1980s . . . . A . . . A . . . C
1990s . . . . A . . . A . . . C

WARRIORS
Philadelphia Warriors
1940s . . . . A . . . B . . . A
1950s . . . . A . . . B . . . A
1960s . . . . B . . . B . . . A
Golden State Warriors
1960s . . . . B . . . B . . . A
1970s . . . . C . . . C . . . C
1980s . . . . B . . . A . . . C
1990s . . . . B . . . B . . . C

FOOTBALL

BEARS
1920s . . . . A . . . B . . . A
1930s . . . . A . . . B . . . A
1940s . . . . A . . . B . . . A
1950s . . . . A . . . A . . . A
1960s . . . . B . . . A . . . A
1970s . . . . C . . . B . . . B
1980s . . . . B . . . B . . . A
1990s . . . . A . . . A . . . A

BENGALS
1960s . . . . A . . . A . . . A
1970s . . . . B . . . C . . . B
1980s . . . . B . . . B . . . B
1990s . . . . B . . . B . . . B

1964 Chicago Bears Sked

BILLS
1960s . . . . B . . . B . . . A
1970s . . . . B . . . B . . . B
1980s . . . . B . . . C . . . B
1990s . . . . A . . . C . . . B

BRONCOS
1960s . . . . A . . . A . . . A
1970s . . . . B . . . C . . . B
1980s . . . . B . . . C . . . B
1990s . . . . B . . . C . . . B

BROWNS
1940s . . . . A . . . A . . . A
1950s . . . . A . . . A . . . A
1960s . . . . A . . . A . . . A
1970s . . . . B . . . C . . . B
1980s . . . . B . . . B . . . B
1990s . . . . A . . . B . . . B

BUCCANEERS
1970s . . . . B . . . C . . . B
1980s . . . . B . . . B . . . B
1990s . . . . B . . . B . . . B

CARDINALS
Chicago Cardinals
1920s . . . . A . . . B . . . A
1930s . . . . A . . . B . . . A
1940s . . . . A . . . A . . . A
1950s . . . . A . . . A . . . A
St. Louis Cardinals
1960s . . . . A . . . B . . . A
1970s . . . . B . . . C . . . B
1980s . . . . B . . . C . . . B
Phoenix Cardinals
1980s . . . . B . . . B . . . B
1990s . . . . B . . . B . . . C

CHARGERS
Los Angeles Chargers
1960s . . . . A . . . A . . . A
San Diego Chargers
1960s . . . . A . . . A . . . A
1970s . . . . B . . . B . . . B
1980s . . . . C . . . B . . . C
1990s . . . . C . . . A . . . C

CHIEFS
Dallas Texans
1960s . . . . A . . . A . . . A
Kansas City Chiefs
1960s . . . . A . . . A . . . A
1970s . . . . B . . . B . . . B
1980s . . . . B . . . B . . . B
1990s . . . . B . . . B . . . B

COLTS
Baltimore Colts
1950s . . . . A . . . A . . . A
1960s . . . . A . . . A . . . A
1970s . . . . B . . . C . . . A
1980s . . . . C . . . C . . . C
Indianapolis Colts
1980s . . . . B . . . B . . . B
1990s . . . . B . . . B . . . B

COWBOYS
1960s . . . . A . . . A . . . A
1970s . . . . B . . . A . . . A

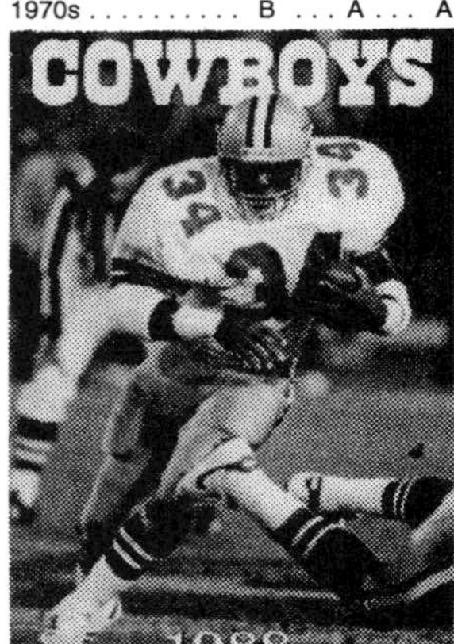

1988 Dallas Cowboys Sked

1980s . . . . B . . . A . . . B
1990s . . . . A . . . A . . . B

DOLPHINS
1960s . . . . A . . . A . . . A
1970s . . . . B . . . B . . . A
1980s . . . . B . . . B . . . A
1990s . . . . B . . . B . . . B

EAGLES
1930s . . . . A . . . B . . . A
1940s . . . . A . . . B . . . A
1950s . . . . A . . . A . . . A
1960s . . . . A . . . A . . . A
1970s . . . . B . . . C . . . B
1980s . . . . A . . . C . . . B
1990s . . . . B . . . B . . . B

FALCONS
1960s . . . . A . . . A . . . A
1970s . . . . B . . . A . . . B
1980s . . . . B . . . A . . . B
1990s . . . . B . . . B . . . B

49ERS
1940s . . . . A . . . A . . . A
1950s . . . . A . . . A . . . A
1960s . . . . A . . . A . . . A
1970s . . . . B . . . A . . . B
1980s . . . . B . . . A . . . A
1990s . . . . B . . . A . . . A

GIANTS
1920s . . . . A . . . B . . . A
1930s . . . . A . . . B . . . A
1940s . . . . A . . . B . . . A
1950s . . . . A . . . A . . . A

1960s .... A ... A ... A
1970s .... B ... B ... B
1980s .... B ... B ... B
1990s .... B ... C ... B

JETS

1960s .... A ... A ... A
1970s .... B ... B ... B
1980s .... B ... C ... B
1990s .... A ... C ... C

LIONS

1930s .... A ... B ... A
1940s .... A ... B ... A
1950s .... A ... A ... A
1960s .... A ... A ... A
1970s .... B ... B ... B
1980s .... B ... A ... B
1990s .... A ... A ... B

OILERS

1960s .... A ... A ... A
1970s .... B ... C ... A
1980s .... B ... B ... B
1990s .... B ... A ... B

PACKERS

1920s .... A ... B ... A
1930s .... A ... B ... A
1940s .... A ... B ... A
1950s .... A ... A ... A
1960s .... A ... A ... A
1970s .... B ... C ... B
1980s .... B ... C ... B

1990 Green Bay Packers Sked

1990s .... A ... B ... B

PATRIOTS
Boston Patriots

1960s .... A ... A ... A
1970s .... B ... A ... B

New England Patriots

1970s .... B ... B ... B
1980s .... B ... B ... B
1990s .... A ... B ... C

RAIDERS
Oakland Raiders

1960s .... A ... A ... A
1970s .... C ... B ... A
1980s .... B ... A ... A

Los Angeles Raiders

1980s .... B ... B ... A
1990s .... B ... B ... B

RAMS
Cleveland Rams

1930s .... A ... B ... A
1940s .... A ... B ... A

Los Angeles Rams

1940s .... A ... A ... A
1950s .... A ... A ... A
1960s .... A ... A ... A
1970s .... B ... C ... B
1980s .... B ... A ... B
1990s .... B ... A ... B

REDSKINS
Boston Redskins

1930s .... A ... A ... A

Washington Redskins

1930s .... A ... A ... A
1940s .... A ... A ... A
1950s .... A ... A ... A
1960s .... A ... B ... A
1970s .... B ... C ... B
1980s .... B ... B ... A
1990s .... B ... A ... A

SAINTS

1960s .... A ... A ... A
1970s .... B ... B ... B
1980s .... B ... B ... B
1990s .... B ... B ... B

SEAHAWKS

1970s .... B ... B ... B
1980s .... B ... A ... B
1990s .... B ... A ... B

STEELERS

1930s .... A ... B ... A
1940s .... A ... B ... A
1950s .... A ... A ... A
1960s .... A ... A ... A
1970s .... B ... C ... A
1980s .... B ... C ... B
1990s .... A ... C ... B

VIKINGS

1960s .... A ... A ... A
1970s .... B ... C ... B
1980s .... A ... B ... B

1992 Minnesota Vikings Sked

1990s .... A ... A ... B

HOCKEY

BARONS

1970s .... C ... B ... A

BLACKHAWKS

1920s .... A ... B ... A
1930s .... A ... B ... A
1940s .... A ... B ... A
1950s .... B ... B ... A
1960s .... B ... B ... A
1970s .... C ... B ... C
1980s .... A ... B ... B
1990s .... A ... C ... B

BLUES

1960s .... A ... A ... A
1970s .... C ... C ... B
1980s .... B ... C ... B
1990s .... B ... A ... B

BRUINS

1920s .... A ... B ... A
1930s .... A ... B ... A
1940s .... A ... A ... A
1950s .... A ... A ... A
1960s .... A ... A ... A
1970s .... C ... B ... B

1988-89 Boston Bruins Sked

1980s .... B ... B ... B
1990s .... B ... A ... B

CANADIENS

1920s .... A ... B ... A
1930s .... A ... B ... A
1940s .... A ... B ... A
1950s .... A ... B ... A
1960s .... A ... B ... A
1970s .... B ... A ... B
1980s .... C ... A ... A
1990s .... C ... A ... A

CANUCKS

1960s .... B ... C ... B
1970s .... C ... B ... A
1980s .... C ... B ... A
1990s .... C ... B ... C

CAPITALS

1970s .... B ... B ... B
1980s .... B ... B ... B
1990s .... B ... A ... B

DEVILS
Kansas City Scouts

1970s .... C ... B ... A

Colorado Rockies

1970s .... C ... B ... C
1980s .... C ... A ... A

New Jersey Devils

1980s .... B ... B ... B
1990s .... A ... C ... B

FLAMES
Atlanta Flames

1970s .... B ... C ... C
1980s .... C ... C ... C

Calgary Flames

1980s . . . . C . . . B . . . B
1990s . . . . C . . . B . . . B

FLYERS

1967-68 Philadelphia Flyers Sked

1960s . . . . A . . . A . . . A
1970s . . . . B . . . A . . . A
1980s . . . . A . . . B . . . B
1990s . . . . A . . . A . . . B

ISLANDERS

1970s . . . . C . . . C . . . B
1980s . . . . B . . . C . . . B
1990s . . . . A . . . B . . . B

JETS

1970s . . . . C . . . A . . . B
1980s . . . . C . . . B . . . B
1990s . . . . C . . . B . . . B

KINGS

1960s . . . . B . . . B . . . A
1970s . . . . C . . . B . . . B
1980s . . . . B . . . A . . . B
1990s . . . . B . . . A . . . A

MAPLE LEAFS

1920s . . . . A . . . B . . . A
1930s . . . . A . . . B . . . A
1940s . . . . A . . . B . . . A
1950s . . . . A . . . B . . . A
1960s . . . . A . . . B . . . A
1970s . . . . B . . . B . . . B
1980s . . . . B . . . C . . . B
1990s . . . . B . . . B . . . B

NORDIQUES

1970s . . . . C . . . B . . . B
1980s . . . . C . . . B . . . B
1990s . . . . C . . . B . . . B

NORTH STARS

1960s . . . . A . . . B . . . B
1970s . . . . B . . . C . . . B
1980s . . . . B . . . B . . . B
1990s . . . . B . . . A . . . B

OILERS

1970s . . . . B . . . B . . . B
1980s . . . . C . . . B . . . A
1990s . . . . C . . . B . . . B

PENGUINS

1990-91 Minnesota North Stars Sked

1960s . . . . A . . . B . . . A
1970s . . . . C . . . B . . . B
1980s . . . . B . . . B . . . B

1992-93 Pittsburgh Penguins Sked

1990s . . . . B . . . A . . . B

RANGERS

1920s . . . . A . . . B . . . A
1930s . . . . A . . . B . . . A
1940s . . . . A . . . B . . . A
1950s . . . . A . . . C . . . D
1960s . . . . A . . . C . . . A
1970s . . . . B . . . B . . . B
1980s . . . . A . . . B . . . B
1990s . . . . A . . . B . . . B

RED WINGS

1920s . . . . A . . . B . . . A
1930s . . . . A . . . B . . . A
1940s . . . . A . . . B . . . A
1950s . . . . A . . . A . . . A
1960s . . . . A . . . A . . . A
1970s . . . . B . . . A . . . B
1980s . . . . B . . . C . . . B
1990s . . . . A . . . C . . . B

SABRES

1970s . . . . B . . . C . . . B
1980s . . . . B . . . B . . . B
1990s . . . . A . . . A . . . B

SEALS

1970s . . . . B . . . B . . . B

WHALERS

1970s . . . . B . . . B . . . B
1980s . . . . B . . . A . . . B
1990s . . . . A . . . A . . . B

COLLEGE BASEBALL

ALABAMA

1970s . . . . C . . . C . . . B
1980s . . . . B . . . B . . . B
1990s . . . . B . . . B . . . B

ARIZONA

1980s . . . . B . . . C . . . B
1990s . . . . B . . . C . . . B

ARIZONA STATE

1960s . . . . C . . . B . . . A
1970s . . . . C . . . B . . . A
1980s . . . . B . . . A . . . B
1990s . . . . B . . . A . . . B

ARKANSAS

1970s . . . . B . . . C . . . B
1980s . . . . B . . . C . . . B
1990s . . . . B . . . B . . . B

AUBURN

1980s . . . . B . . . A . . . B
1990s . . . . B . . . A . . . B

CALIFORNIA

1970s . . . . B . . . B . . . C
1980s . . . . B . . . B . . . C
1990s . . . . B . . . B . . . C

CAL-STATE FULLERTON

1980s . . . . B . . . A . . . B
1990s . . . . B . . . A . . . B

CLEMSON

1970s . . . . B . . . B . . . B
1980s . . . . B . . . A . . . B
1990s . . . . B . . . A . . . B

CREIGHTON

1970s . . . . B . . . B . . . A
1980s . . . . B . . . B . . . A
1990s . . . . B . . . B . . . A

EASTERN MICHIGAN

1970s . . . . B . . . C . . . B
1980s . . . . B . . . C . . . B
1990s . . . . B . . . B . . . B

FLORIDA

1970s . . . . B . . . B . . . B
1980s . . . . B . . . B . . . B
1990s . . . . B . . . A . . . B

FLORIDA STATE

1970s . . . . B . . . B . . . B
1980s . . . . B . . . A . . . A
1990s . . . . B . . . A . . . B

GEORGIA

1970s . . . . B . . . C . . . C
1980s . . . . B . . . C . . . B
1990s . . . . B . . . B . . . B

GEORGIA TECH

1970s . . . . B . . . B . . . B

1980s .... A ... B ... B
1990s .... B ... B ... A

HAWAII

1980s .... B ... A ... B
1990s .... B ... A ... B

LONG BEACH ST.

1980s .... B ... B ... B
1990s .... B ... A ... B

L.S.U.

1970s .... B ... B ... B
1980s .... B ... B ... A
1990s .... A ... B ... A

MIAMI

1970s .... B ... B ... A
1980s .... B ... B ... A
1990s .... B ... A ... A

MICHIGAN

1960s .... B ... B ... B
1970s .... B ... B ... B
1980s .... B ... A ... A
1990s .... B ... A ... A

MINNESOTA

1960s .... B ... B ... B
1970s .... B ... B ... B
1980s .... B ... B ... B

1992-93 Minnesota Sked

1990s .... B ... A ... B

MISSISSIPPI ST.

1970s .... B ... B ... B
1980s .... C ... B ... A
1990s .... B ... B ... B

MISSOURI

1960s .... C ... C ... B
1970s .... B ... C ... B
1980s .... B ... C ... B
1990s .... B ... C ... B

NORTH CAROLINA

1970s .... B ... C ... C
1980s .... B ... C ... C
1990s .... B ... B ... C

NOTRE DAME

1980s .... A ... B ... A
1990s .... A ... B ... A

OHIO ST.

1960s .... B ... C ... B
1970s .... B ... C ... B
1980s .... B ... B ... B
1990s .... B ... B ... B

OKLAHOMA ST.

1960s .... B ... C ... B
1970s .... B ... C ... B
1980s .... B ... B ... A
1990s .... B ... B ... B

PEPPERDINE

1970s .... B ... B ... B
1980s .... B ... B ... B
1990s .... B ... A ... A

SETON HALL

1980s .... A ... C ... B
1990s .... A ... B ... C

SOUTH CAROLINA

1970s .... B ... C ... B
1980s .... B ... B ... B
1990s .... B ... B ... C

SOUTHERN ILLINOIS

1960s .... B ... C ... C
1970s .... B ... B ... C
1980s .... B ... B ... B
1990s .... B ... B ... B

STANFORD

1960s .... B ... B ... B
1970s .... B ... B ... A
1980s .... B ... A ... A
1990s .... B ... A ... A

TEXAS

1960s .... A ... B ... A
1970s .... B ... B ... A
1980s .... B ... A ... A
1990s .... B ... A ... A

U.S.C.

1950s .... B ... C ... A
1960s .... B ... C ... B
1970s .... B ... B ... B
1980s .... B ... B ... B
1990s .... A ... B ... B

VILLANOVA

1980s .... B ... C ... C
1990s .... B ... B ... B

WAKE FOREST

1970s .... B ... C ... B
1980s .... B ... B ... B
1990s .... B ... B ... B

WICHITA STATE

1970s .... C ... B ... A
1980s .... C ... B ... A
1990s .... B ... A ... A

COLLEGE BASKETBALL

ALABAMA

1950s .... C ... B ... A
1960s .... C ... B ... A
1970s .... B ... B ... B
1980s .... B ... A ... B
1990s .... A ... A ... B

ARIZONA

1970s .... B ... B ... B
1980s .... B ... A ... A
1990s .... B ... A ... B

ARIZONA ST.

1980s .... B ... B ... B
1990s .... B ... A ... B

ARKANSAS

1970s .... C ... B ... A
1980s .... B ... A ... B
1990s .... B ... A ... B

AUBURN

1970s .... B ... B ... C
1980s .... B ... A ... B
1990s .... B ... A ... B

BOSTON COLLEGE

1960s .... B ... B ... B
1970s .... B ... B ... B
1980s .... B ... A ... B
1990s .... A ... B ... B

CINCINNATI

1960s .... C ... C ... A
1970s .... B ... B ... A
1980s .... B ... B ... B
1990s .... B ... A ... B

CLEMSON

1970s .... B ... B ... B
1980s .... B ... A ... B
1990s .... B ... A ... B

COLORADO

1950s .... C ... C ... B
1960s .... B ... C ... B
1970s .... B ... B ... C
1980s .... B ... B ... C
1990s .... B ... B ... C

CONNECTICUT

1970s .... C ... B ... B
1980s .... B ... A ... B

1991-92 Connecticut Sked

1990s .... B ... A ... B

DePAUL

1960s .... C ... B ... B
1970s .... B ... B ... B
1980s .... B ... A ... B
1990s .... B ... A ... B

DUKE

1950s .... C ... C ... A
1960s .... C ... B ... A
1970s .... B ... B ... A
1980s .... B ... A ... A
1990s .... B ... A ... A

FLORIDA STATE

1970s .... B ... B ... B
1980s .... B ... A ... B
1990s .... B ... A ... A

GEORGETOWN

Decade			
1970s	C	B	A
1980s	B	A	A
1990s	B	A	A

GEORGIA

Decade			
1970s	B	B	B
1980s	B	A	B
1990s	B	A	B

GEORGIA TECH

Decade			
1970s	B	B	B
1980s	B	A	B
1990s	B	A	B

HOUSTON

Decade			
1960s	B	C	B
1970s	B	B	B
1980s	B	A	A
1990s	B	B	B

ILLINOIS

Decade			
1950s	C	C	A
1960s	C	B	A
1970s	B	B	B
1980s	B	B	B
1990s	A	A	B

INDIANA

Decade			
1950s	C	C	A
1960s	C	C	A
1970s	B	B	A
1980s	B	B	A
1990s	B	A	A

INDIANA ST.

Decade			
1970s	C	B	A
1980s	B	B	C
1990s	B	B	C

IOWA

Decade			
1950s	C	C	B
1960s	C	C	B
1970s	B	B	B
1980s	B	B	B
1990s	B	A	B

KANSAS

Decade			
1950s	C	C	A
1960s	C	B	A
1970s	B	B	A
1980s	B	A	A
1990s	B	A	A

KANSAS ST.

Decade			
1950s	C	C	B
1960s	C	C	B
1970s	B	B	B
1980s	B	A	B
1990s	B	A	B

KENTUCKY

Decade			
1950s	C	C	A
1960s	C	C	A
1970s	C	B	A
1980s	B	B	B
1990s	B	A	A

LaSALLE

Decade			
1950s	C	C	B
1960s	B	B	B
1970s	B	B	B
1980s	B	A	B
1990s	B	A	B

L.S.U.

Decade			
1950s	C	C	B
1960s	C	C	B
1970s	B	B	B
1980s	B	A	A
1990s	B	A	A

LOUISVILLE

Decade			
1950s	C	C	A
1960s	C	B	A
1970s	B	A	A
1980s	B	A	A
1990s	B	A	B

LOYOLA MARYMOUNT

Decade			
1980s	B	A	A
1990s	B	A	B

MARQUETTE

Decade			
1950s	C	B	B
1960s	B	B	B
1970s	B	B	A
1980s	B	B	B
1990s	B	A	B

1992-93 NCAA Sked

MARYLAND

Decade			
1950s	C	B	B
1960s	B	B	B
1970s	B	B	B
1980s	B	A	A
1990s	B	B	C

MASSACHUSETTS

Decade			
1980s	B	A	B
1990s	B	A	B

MEMPHIS ST.

Decade			
1960s	C	B	B
1970s	B	B	B
1980s	B	A	A
1990s	A	A	B

MIAMI

Decade			
1980s	A	C	B
1990s	B	B	B

MICHIGAN

Decade			
1950s	C	B	A
1960s	C	B	A
1970s	B	B	B
1980s	B	A	A
1990s	B	A	A

MICHIGAN ST.

Decade			
1950s	C	B	B
1960s	C	B	B
1970s	B	A	A
1980s	B	A	B
1990s	B	A	B

MINNESOTA

Decade			
1950s	C	B	B
1960s	B	B	B
1970s	B	B	B
1980s	A	A	B
1990s	A	A	B

MISSISSIPPI

Decade			
1970s	B	C	B
1980s	B	C	B
1990s	B	B	B

MISSOURI

Decade			
1970s	B	C	B
1980s	B	B	B
1990s	B	A	B

NAVY

Decade			
1980s	B	B	B

NEBRASKA

Decade			
1980s	B	A	A
1990s	B	A	B

NORTH CAROLINA

Decade			
1950s	C	B	A
1960s	C	B	A
1970s	B	B	A
1980s	B	B	A
1990s	B	A	A

NORTH CAROLINA ST.

Decade			
1950s	C	C	B
1960s	B	B	B
1970s	B	B	A
1980s	B	A	A
1990s	B	A	B

NOTRE DAME

Decade			
1950s	C	B	A
1960s	B	B	A
1970s	B	B	A
1980s	B	A	A
1990s	B	A	A

OHIO ST.

Decade			
1960s	C	B	[illegible]
1970s	B	B	[illegible]
1980s	B	A	[illegible]
1990s	B	A	[illegible]

OKLAHOMA

Decade			
1970s	B	B	
1980s	B	B	
1990s	B	A	

OKLAHOMA ST.

Decade			
1970s	B	B	
1980s	B	A	
1990s	B	A	

OREGON ST.

Decade			
1950s	C	C	
1960s	C	B	
1970s	B	B	
1980s	B	A	
1990s	B	A	

PITTSBURGH

Decade			
1970s	B	B	
1980s	B	A	
1990s	B	A	

PRINCETON

Decade			
1960s	B	C	
1970s	B	B	
1980s	B	B	
1990s	B	B	

PROVIDENCE

Decade			
1960s	C	B	
1970s	B	B	
1980s	B	A	
1990s	B	A	

PURDUE
1960s .... C ... B ... B
1970s .... B ... B ... B
1980s .... B ... A ... B
1990s .... B ... A ... B

RHODE ISLAND
1980s .... B ... B ... B
1990s .... B ... B ... B

RICHMOND
1980s .... B ... A ... B
1990s .... B ... A ... B

SAN FRANCISCO
1950s .... C ... A ... A
1960s .... C ... B ... B
1970s .... B ... B ... C

ST. JOHN'S
1950s .... C ... C ... A
1960s .... B ... B ... B
1970s .... B ... B ... B
1980s .... B ... A ... B
1990s .... B ... A ... B

SETON HALL
1970s .... B ... B ... B
1980s .... B ... A ... B
1990s .... B ... A ... B

STANFORD
1960s .... B ... B ... B
1970s .... B ... A ... B
1980s .... B ... A ... B
1990s .... B ... A ... B

SYRACUSE
1970s .... B ... B ... B
1980s .... A ... A ... B

1991-92 Syracuse Sked

1990s .... A ... A ... B

TEMPLE
1950s .... C ... B ... B
1960s .... B ... B ... B
1970s .... B ... B ... B
1980s .... B ... A ... B
1990s .... B ... A ... B

TENNESSEE
1960s .... C ... B ... B
1970s .... B ... B ... B
1980s .... B ... B ... B
1990s .... B ... A ... B

TEXAS
1980s .... B ... B ... B
1990s .... B ... A ... B

U.C.L.A.
1950s .... C ... B ... A
1960s .... C ... B ... A
1970s .... C ... B ... A
1980s .... C ... A ... A
1990s .... B ... A ... B

U.N.L.V.
1970s .... C ... B ... A
1980s .... B ... A ... A
1990s .... B ... A ... A

U.S.C.
1950s .... C ... B ... A
1960s .... B ... B ... A
1970s .... B ... B ... A
1980s .... B ... A ... B
1990s .... B ... A ... B

UTAH
1950s .... C ... C ... A
1960s .... C ... C ... A
1970s .... C ... B ... B
1980s .... B ... A ... B
1990s .... B ... A ... B

VANDERBILT
1950s .... C ... C ... A
1960s .... C ... C ... A
1970s .... B ... B ... B
1980s .... B ... A ... B
1990s .... B ... A ... B

VILLANOVA
1960s .... C ... B ... B
1970s .... B ... B ... B
1980s .... B ... A ... B
1990s .... B ... A ... B

VIRGINIA
1970s .... B ... B ... B
1980s .... B ... B ... B
1990s .... B ... A ... B

WAKE FOREST
1960s .... C ... B ... B
1970s .... B ... B ... B
1980s .... B ... A ... B
1990s .... B ... A ... B

WEST VIRGINIA
1960s .... B ... B ... B
1970s .... B ... B ... B
1980s .... B ... A ... B
1990s .... B ... A ... B

XAVIER
1980s .... B ... A ... B
1990s .... B ... A ... B

COLLEGE FOOTBALL

AIR FORCE
1980s .... B ... A ... A
1990s .... B ... B ... B

ALABAMA
1950s .... C ... B ... A
1960s .... B ... B ... A
1970s .... B ... A ... A
1980s .... B ... A ... B
1990s .... B ... A ... B

ARIZONA
1980s .... B ... B ... B
1990s .... B ... A ... B

ARKANSAS
1950s .... C ... C ... B
1960s .... B ... B ... B
1970s .... B ... B ... B
1980s .... B ... A ... B
1990s .... B ... A ... B

ARMY
1950s .... B ... B ... A
1960s .... B ... B ... B
1970s .... A ... B ... B
1980s .... A ... C ... B
1990s .... A ... A ... B

AUBURN
1960s .... B ... B ... B
1970s .... B ... B ... B
1980s .... B ... A ... B
1990s .... B ... B ... B

BOSTON COLLEGE
1960s .... C ... B ... B
1970s .... B ... B ... B
1980s .... B ... A ... B
1990s .... B ... A ... B

B.Y.U.
1970s .... B ... B ... B
1980s .... B ... A ... B
1990s .... B ... A ... B

CALIFORNIA
1950s .... C ... B ... A
1960s .... B ... B ... B
1970s .... B ... A ... B
1980s .... B ... A ... B
1990s .... B ... A ... B

CLEMSON
1960s .... B ... B ... B
1970s .... B ... B ... B
1980s .... B ... A ... B
1990s .... B ... A ... B

COLORADO
1960s .... C ... B ... B
1970s .... B ... B ... B
1980s .... B ... B ... B
1990s .... B ... B ... B

EAST CAROLINA
1990s .... B ... B ... B

FLORIDA
1960s .... C ... B ... B
1970s .... B ... B ... B
1980s .... B ... A ... B
1990s .... B ... A ... B

FLORIDA STATE
1960s .... C ... B ... B
1970s .... B ... A ... B
1980s .... B ... A ... A
1990s .... B ... B ... B

GEORGIA
1950s .... C ... C ... B
1960s .... B ... B ... B
1970s .... B ... B ... B
1980s .... B ... B ... A
1990s .... B ... A ... B

GEORGIA TECH
1970s .... B ... B ... B
1980s .... B ... A ... B
1990s .... B ... A ... B

HAWAII
1980s .... B ... B ... B

1990s . . . . B . . . B . . . B

HOUSTON
1960s . . . . C . . . C . . . C
1970s . . . . B . . . B . . . B
1980s . . . . B . . . B . . . B
1990s . . . . B . . . B . . . B

ILLINOIS
1960s . . . . B . . . C . . . B
1970s . . . . B . . . B . . . B
1980s . . . . B . . . B . . . B
1990s . . . . A . . . A . . . B

INDIANA
1960s . . . . C . . . C . . . B
1970s . . . . B . . . B . . . B
1980s . . . . B . . . B . . . B
1990s . . . . B . . . B . . . B

IOWA
1960s . . . . C . . . B . . . A
1970s . . . . B . . . B . . . B
1980s . . . . B . . . B . . . B
1990s . . . . B . . . A . . . B

L.S.U.
1960s . . . . B . . . C . . . B
1970s . . . . B . . . B . . . B
1980s . . . . B . . . B . . . B
1990s . . . . B . . . A . . . B

LOUISVILLE
1960s . . . . C . . . C . . . B
1970s . . . . B . . . B . . . B
1980s . . . . B . . . A . . . B
1990s . . . . A . . . A . . . C

MARYLAND
1960s . . . . C . . . B . . . B
1970s . . . . B . . . B . . . B
1980s . . . . B . . . A . . . B
1990s . . . . B . . . A . . . B

MIAMI
1950s . . . . C . . . C . . . B
1960s . . . . B . . . C . . . B
1970s . . . . B . . . C . . . B
1980s . . . . B . . . C . . . A
1990s . . . . B . . . C . . . A

MICHIGAN
1950s . . . . C . . . B . . . A
1960s . . . . B . . . B . . . A
1970s . . . . B . . . B . . . A
1980s . . . . B . . . A . . . A
1990s . . . . B . . . A . . . A

MICHIGAN ST.
1950s . . . . C . . . C . . . B
1960s . . . . B . . . B . . . B
1970s . . . . B . . . B . . . B
1980s . . . . B . . . A . . . B
1990s . . . . B . . . A . . . B

MINNESOTA
1950s . . . . C . . . B . . . B
1960s . . . . B . . . B . . . B
1970s . . . . B . . . B . . . B
1980s . . . . A . . . A . . . B
1990s . . . . A . . . B . . . B

MISSISSIPPI
1950s . . . . C . . . B . . . B
1960s . . . . B . . . B . . . B
1970s . . . . B . . . B . . . B
1980s . . . . B . . . C . . . B
1990s . . . . B . . . C . . . B

NAVY
1950s . . . . C . . . B . . . A
1960s . . . . B . . . A . . . A
1970s . . . . B . . . A . . . B
1980s . . . . A . . . A . . . B
1990s . . . . B . . . A . . . B

NEBRASKA
1950s . . . . C . . . B . . . A
1960s . . . . B . . . B . . . A
1970s . . . . B . . . B . . . A
1980s . . . . B . . . B . . . A
1990s . . . . B . . . A . . . B

NORTH CAROLINA
1970s . . . . B . . . B . . . B
1980s . . . . B . . . A . . . B
1990s . . . . B . . . A . . . B

NORTH CAROLINA ST.
1960s . . . . C . . . B . . . B
1970s . . . . B . . . B . . . B
1980s . . . . B . . . B . . . B
1990s . . . . B . . . A . . . B

NOTRE DAME
1950s . . . . C . . . B . . . A
1960s . . . . B . . . B . . . A
1970s . . . . B . . . B . . . A
1980s . . . . B . . . B . . . A
1990s . . . . B . . . B . . . A

OHIO ST.
1960s . . . . B . . . B . . . B
1970s . . . . B . . . B . . . B
1980s . . . . B . . . B . . . B
1990s . . . . A . . . B . . . B

OKLAHOMA
1950s . . . . C . . . B . . . A
1960s . . . . B . . . B . . . A
1970s . . . . B . . . B . . . A
1980s . . . . B . . . B . . . A
1990s . . . . A . . . A . . . B

OKLAHOMA ST.
1950s . . . . C . . . C . . . B
1960s . . . . B . . . B . . . B
1970s . . . . B . . . B . . . B
1980s . . . . B . . . B . . . B
1990s . . . . B . . . A . . . B

OREGON
1960s . . . . C . . . C . . . B
1970s . . . . B . . . B . . . B
1980s . . . . B . . . B . . . B
1990s . . . . B . . . A . . . B

PENN ST.
1950s . . . . C . . . B . . . A
1960s . . . . B . . . B . . . A
1970s . . . . B . . . A . . . A
1980s . . . . B . . . A . . . B
1990s . . . . A . . . A . . . B

PITTSBURGH
1950s . . . . C . . . B . . . B
1960s . . . . B . . . B . . . B
1970s . . . . B . . . B . . . B
1980s . . . . B . . . A . . . B
1990s . . . . B . . . A . . . B

PURDUE
1950s . . . . C . . . B . . . B
1960s . . . . B . . . B . . . B
1970s . . . . B . . . B . . . B
1980s . . . . B . . . A . . . B
1990s . . . . A . . . A . . . B

SAN DIEGO ST.
1980s . . . . B . . . A . . . C
1990s . . . . B . . . A . . . B

SOUTH CAROLINA
1950s . . . . C . . . C . . . B
1960s . . . . B . . . B . . . B
1970s . . . . B . . . B . . . B
1980s . . . . B . . . A . . . B
1990s . . . . B . . . A . . . B

S.M.U.
1950s . . . . C . . . B . . . B
1960s . . . . B . . . B . . . A
1970s . . . . B . . . B . . . A
1980s . . . . B . . . B . . . B
1990s . . . . B . . . A . . . B

STANFORD
1950s . . . . C . . . B . . . A
1960s . . . . C . . . B . . . B
1970s . . . . B . . . B . . . B
1980s . . . . B . . . B . . . B

1991 Stanford Sked

1990s . . . . B . . . B . . . B

SYRACUSE
1950s . . . . B . . . B . . . B
1960s . . . . B . . . B . . . B
1970s . . . . B . . . B . . . B
1980s . . . . A . . . A . . . B
1990s . . . . A . . . B . . . B

TENNESSEE
1950s . . . . C . . . B . . . B
1960s . . . . B . . . B . . . B
1970s . . . . B . . . B . . . B
1980s . . . . B . . . A . . . B
1990s . . . . B . . . A . . . B

TEXAS
1950s . . . . C . . . B . . . A
1960s . . . . B . . . B . . . A
1970s . . . . B . . . B . . . A
1980s . . . . B . . . A . . . A
1990s . . . . A . . . A . . . A

TEXAS A&M
1950s . . . . C . . . C . . . B
1960s . . . . B . . . C . . . B
1970s . . . . B . . . B . . . B
1980s . . . . B . . . B . . . B
1990s . . . . B . . . B . . . B

TEXAS TECH
1960s . . . . C . . . C . . . B
1970s . . . . B . . . B . . . B
1980s . . . . B . . . B . . . B
1990s . . . . B . . . B . . . B

U.C.L.A.

1950s . . . . C . . . B . . . B

1960s . . . . B . . . B . . . B

1970s . . . . B . . . B . . . A

1980s . . . . B . . . A . . . A

1990s . . . . B . . . A . . . B

U.N.L.V.

1970s . . . . B . . . C . . . B

1980s . . . . B . . . B . . . B

1990s . . . . B . . . B . . . B

U.S.C.

1950s . . . . B . . . B . . . A

1960s . . . . B . . . A . . . A

1970s . . . . B . . . A . . . A

1980s . . . . B . . . A . . . A

1990s . . . . B . . . A . . . B

VIRGINIA

1970s . . . . B . . . B . . . B

1980s . . . . B . . . A . . . B

1990s . . . . B . . . A . . . B

WASHINGTON

1960s . . . . C . . . B . . . B

1970s . . . . B . . . B . . . B

1980s . . . . B . . . B . . . B

1990s . . . . B . . . B . . . B

WASHINGTON ST.

1970s . . . . B . . . B . . . B

1980s . . . . B . . . B . . . B

1990s . . . . B . . . A . . . B

WEST VIRGINIA

1960s . . . . B . . . C . . . B

1970s . . . . B . . . B . . . B

1980s . . . . B . . . B . . . B

1990s . . . . B . . . B . . . B

COLLEGE HOCKEY

BOSTON COLLEGE

1970s . . . . B . . . A . . . B

1980s . . . . B . . . A . . . B

1990s . . . . B . . . A . . . B

BOSTON UNIVERSITY

1970s . . . . B . . . B . . . B

1980s . . . . B . . . A . . . B

1990s . . . . B . . . A . . . B

BOWLING GREEN

1970s . . . . B . . . C . . . B

1980s . . . . B . . . B . . . B

1990s . . . . B . . . B . . . B

BROWN

1970s . . . . B . . . B . . . B

1980s . . . . B . . . B . . . B

1990s . . . . B . . . A . . . B

CLARKSON

1970s . . . . B . . . B . . . B

1980s . . . . B . . . A . . . B

1990s . . . . A . . . A . . . B

COLGATE

1970s . . . . B . . . B . . . B

1980s . . . . B . . . A . . . B

1990s . . . . B . . . A . . . B

COLORADO COLLEGE

1950s . . . . C . . . C . . . B

1960s . . . . C . . . B . . . B

1970s . . . . C . . . B . . . B

1980s . . . . C . . . B . . . B

1990s . . . . C . . . A . . . B

CORNELL

1970s . . . . B . . . B . . . B

1980s . . . . B . . . B . . . B

1990s . . . . B . . . A . . . B

DARTMOUTH

1970s . . . . B . . . B . . . B

1980s . . . . B . . . A . . . B

1990s . . . . B . . . A . . . B

DENVER

1970s . . . . C . . . B . . . B

1980s . . . . B . . . B . . . A

1990s . . . . B . . . A . . . B

HARVARD

1970s . . . . C . . . C . . . B

1980s . . . . B . . . A . . . B

1990s . . . . B . . . A . . . B

LAKE SUPERIOR ST.

1980s . . . . C . . . B . . . A

1990s . . . . C . . . A . . . A

MAINE

1970s . . . . B . . . B . . . B

1980s . . . . B . . . A . . . B

1990s . . . . B . . . A . . . B

MIAMI-OHIO

1980s . . . . B . . . A . . . B

1990s . . . . B . . . A . . . B

MICHIGAN

1970s . . . . C . . . A . . . B

1980s . . . . B . . . A . . . B

1990s . . . . B . . . A . . . B

MICHIGAN ST.

1970s . . . . C . . . B . . . B

1980s . . . . B . . . A . . . B

1990s . . . . B . . . A . . . B

MINNESOTA

1970s . . . . B . . . B . . . B

1980s . . . . B . . . A . . . B

1992-93 Minnesota Sked

1990s . . . . A . . . A . . . B

MINNESOTA-DULUTH

1970s . . . . C . . . B . . . B

1980s . . . . B . . . A . . . B

1990s . . . . A . . . A . . . B

NEW HAMPSHIRE

1970s . . . . C . . . A . . . B

1980s . . . . B . . . A . . . B

1990s . . . . B . . . A . . . B

NORTH DAKOTA

1970s . . . . C . . . B . . . B

1980s . . . . C . . . A . . . B

1990s . . . . C . . . A . . . B

NORTHERN MICHIGAN

1970s . . . . C . . . B . . . B

1980s . . . . B . . . A . . . B

1990s . . . . B . . . A . . . B

NOTRE DAME

1970s . . . . B . . . B . . . B

1980s . . . . B . . . B . . . B

1990s . . . . B . . . B . . . B

PROVIDENCE

1970s . . . . C . . . B . . . B

1980s . . . . B . . . A . . . B

1990s . . . . B . . . A . . . B

R.P.I.

1970s . . . . B . . . B . . . B

1980s . . . . B . . . B . . . B

1990s . . . . B . . . A . . . B

ST. LAWRENCE

1970s . . . . C . . . A . . . B

1980s . . . . B . . . A . . . B

1990s . . . . B . . . B . . . B

VERMONT

1970s . . . . C . . . A . . . B

1980s . . . . B . . . A . . . B

1990s . . . . B . . . B . . . B

WISCONSIN

1970s . . . . B . . . A . . . B

1980s . . . . A . . . A . . . B

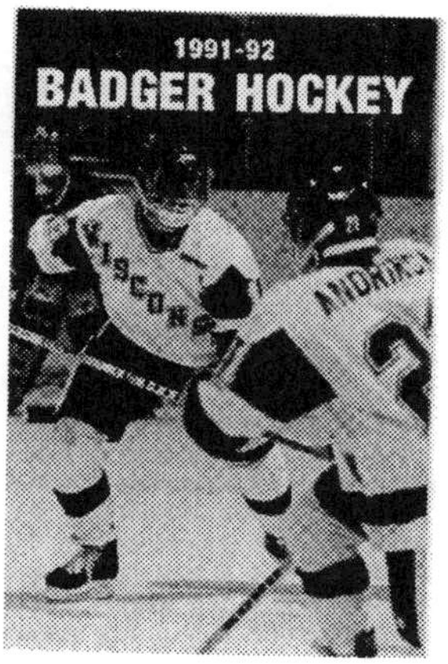

1991-92 Wisconsin Sked

1990s . . . . A . . . A . . . B

YALE

1970s . . . . C . . . B . . . B

1980s . . . . B . . . B . . . B

1990s . . . . B . . . B . . . B

POSTERS

BASEBALL POSTERS

SPORTS ILLUSTRATED POSTERS

Player	Year Issued	Value
Aaron, Hank	1968	40.00
Agee, Tommy	68-71	10.00
Allen, Richie	1968	12.00
Alley, Gene	1968	10.00
Alou, Felipe	1968	10.00
Alvis, Max	1968	10.00
Andrews, Mike	1969	10.00
Aspromonte, Bob	68-71	12.00
Banks, Ernie	1968	25.00
Beckert, Glen	1970	14.00
Bell, Gary	1968 (Indians)	12.00
Bell, Gary	1968 (Pilots)	15.00
Bonds, Bobby	1970	14.00
Boyer, Clete	1968	10.00
Brock, Lou	1968	22.00
Callison, Johnny	1968	12.00
Campaneris, Bert	1968	12.00
Cardenas, Leo	1968	12.00
Carew, Rod	1970	35.00
Casanova, Paul	1968	12.00

1968 Sports Illustrated Orlando Cepeda poster

Player	Year Issued	Value
Cepeda, Orlando	1968	14.00
Clemente, Roberto	1968	175.00
Conigliaro, Tony	1968	16.00
Cuellar, Mike	1970	10.00
Davis, Tommy	1968	15.00
Davis, Willie	1968	12.00
Drysdale, Don	1968	24.00
Epstein, Mike	1970	10.00
Ferrara, Al	1968	10.00
Flood, Curt	1968	12.00
Freehan, Bill	1968	12.00
Fregosi, Jim	1968	10.00
Gibson, Bob	1968	22.00
Harrelson, Buddy	1968	10.00
Harrelson, Ken	1968	10.00
Holtzman, Ken	1970	10.00
Horlen, Joe	1968	10.00
Horton, Tony	1968	10.00
Howard, Frank	1968	16.00
Jackson, Reggie	1969	110.00
Jenkins, Ferguson	68-71	35.00

1968 Sports Illustrated Tommy John poster

Player	Year Issued	Value
John, Tommy	1968	14.00
Jones, Cleon	1970	10.00
Kaline, Al	1968	22.00
Killebrew, Harmon	1968	30.00
Koosman, Jerry	1968	14.00
Let's Go Mets	1969	35.00
Lolich, Mickey	1970	14.00
Londborg, Jim	1968	12.00
Maloney, Jim	1968	10.00
Mantle, Mickey	1968	200.00
Marichal, Juan	1968	30.00
Mays, Willie	1968	175.00
Mazeroski, Bill	1968	15.00
McCarver, Tim	1968	12.00
McCormick, Mike	1968	10.00
McCovey, Willie	1968	125.00
McDowell, Sam	1970	10.00
McLain, Denny	1968	15.00

Mincher, Don	1968 (Angels)	10.00
Mincher, Don	1968 (Pilots)	14.00
Monday, Rick	1968	12.00
Murcer, Bobby	68-71	14.00
Niekro, Phil	1970	16.00
Odom, John	68-71	12.00
Oliva, Tony	1968	15.00
Parker, Wes	1970	10.00
Perez, Tony	1970	16.00
Petrocelli, Rico	1968	10.00
Powell, Boog	68-71	14.00
Reichart, Rick	1968	10.00

1968 Sports Illustrated Brooks Robinson poster

Robinson, Brooks	1968	75.00
Robinson, Frank	1968	40.00
Rose, Pete	1968	35.00
Santo, Ron	1968	12.00
Seaver, Tom	1968	75.00
Short, Chris	1968	10.00
Singer, Bill	1970	10.00
Smith, Reggie	1968	10.00
Staub, Rusty	1968	14.00
Stottlemyre, Mel	1968	12.00
Swoboda, Ron	1968	10.00
Tovar, Cesar	1968	12.00
White, Roy	68-71	10.00
Williams, Walt	1970	10.00
Wilson, Earl	1968	12.00
Wynn, Jimmy	1968	10.00
Yastrzemski, Carl	1968	35.00

BASKETBALL POSTERS

SPORTS ILLUSTRATED POSTERS

Player	Year Issued	Value
Bradley, Bill	68-71	65.00
Cunningham, Billy	68-71	12.00
Havlicek, John	68-71	30.00
Hayes, Elvin	1970	35.00
Haywood, Spencer	1971	12.00
Reed, Willis	68-71	20.00
Robertson, Oscar	1971	45.00

BOXING FIGHT POSTERS

HEAVYWEIGHT BOUTS

Date	Result	Value
07/04/19	J. Dempsey def. J. Willard	750.00
09/06/20	J. Dempsey def. B. Miske	600.00
12/14/20	J. Dempsey def. B. Brennan	750.00
07/02/21	J. Dempsey def. G. Carpentier	600.00
07/04/23	J. Dempsey def. T. Gibbons	500.00
09/14/23	J. Dempsey def. L. Firpo	500.00
09/23/26	G. Tunney def. J. Dempsey	750.00
07/21/27	J. Dempsey def. J. Sharkey	500.00
09/22/27	G. Tunney def. J. Dempsey	700.00
07/26/28	G. Tunney def. T. Heeney	350.00
06/12/30	M. Schmeling def. J. Sharkey	450.00
07/03/31	M. Schmeling def. Y. Stribling	250.00
06/21/32	J. Sharkey def. M. Schmeling	250.00
09/26/32	M. Schmeling def. Walker	325.00
06/25/35	J. Louis def. P. Carnera	400.00
09/24/35	J. Louis def. M. Baer	350.00
06/19/36	M. Schmeling def. J. Louis	325.00
08/18/36	J. Louis def. J. Sharkey	300.00
06/22/37	J. Louis def. J. Braddock	450.00

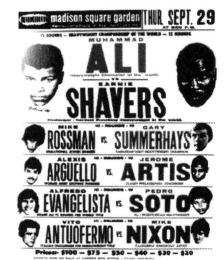

9/29/77 Muhammad Ali vs. Earnie Shavers

06/22/38	J. Louis def. M. Schmeling	325.00
07/13/39	B. Conn def. J. Bettina	200.00
09/25/39	B. Conn def. J. Bettina	150.00
11/17/39	B. Conn def. G. Lesnevich	150.00
06/05/40	B. Conn def. G. Lesnevich	150.00
05/23/41	J. Louis def. B. Baer	350.00
06/18/41	J. Louis def. B. Conn	250.00
01/09/42	J. Louis def. B. Baer	150.00
06/19/46	J. Louis def. B. Conn	100.00
12/05/47	J. Louis def. J. Walcott	165.00
06/25/48	J. Louis def. J. Walcott	150.00
06/22/49	E. Charles def. J. Walcott	75.00
09/27/50	E. Charles def. J. Louis	100.00
03/07/51	E. Charles def. J. Walcott	75.00
07/18/51	J. Walcott def. E. Charles	75.00
10/26/51	R. Marciano def. J. Louis	250.00
06/05/52	J. Walcott def. E. Charles	75.00

9/21/55 Rocky Marciano vs. Archie Moore

09/23/52	R. Marciano def. J. Walcott	225.00
05/15/53	R. Marciano def. J. Walcott	150.00
06/17/54	R. Marciano def. E. Charles	150.00
09/17/54	R. Marciano def. E. Charles	150.00
05/16/55	R. Marciano def. D. Cockell	150.00
09/21/55	R. Marciano def. A. Moore	150.00
11/30/56	F. Patterson def. A. Moore	150.00
06/26/59	I. Johansson def. F. Patterson	100.00
06/20/60	F. Patterson def. I. Johansson	75.00
03/13/61	F. Patterson def. I. Johansson	75.00
09/25/62	S. Liston def. F. Patterson	85.00
11/15/62	C. Clay def. A. Moore	450.00
07/22/63	S. Liston def. F. Patterson	125.00
02/25/64	C. Clay def. S. Liston	225.00

9/30/75 Muhammad Ali vs. Joe Frazier

05/25/65	M. Ali def. S. Liston	100.00
11/22/65	M. Ali def. F. Patterson	85.00
03/04/68	J. Frazier def. B. Mathis	45.00
11/28/70	J. Frazier def. B. Foster	50.00
03/08/71	J. Frazier def. M. Ali	85.00
09/20/72	M. Ali def. F. Patterson	75.00

3/20/88 Mike Tyson vs. Tony Tubbs

2/25/89 Mike Tyson vs. Frank Bruno

Date	Bout	Price
11/21/72	M. Ali def. B. Foster	60.00
01/22/73	G. Foreman def. J. Frazier	65.00
03/31/73	K. Norton def. M. Ali	75.00
09/01/73	G. Foreman def. J. Roman	40.00
09/10/73	M. Ali def. K. Norton	65.00
01/28/74	M. Ali def. J. Frazier	75.00
03/26/74	G. Foreman def. K. Norton	50.00
10/30/74	M. Ali def. G. Foreman	85.00
09/30/75	M. Ali def. J. Frazier	65.00
06/15/76	G. Foreman def. J. Frazier	50.00
09/28/76	M. Ali def. K. Norton	50.00
09/29/77	M. Ali def. E. Shavers	60.00
02/15/78	L. Spinks def. M. Ali	60.00
06/09/78	L. Holmes def. K. Norton	40.00
09/15/78	M. Ali def. L. Spinks	60.00
10/02/80	L. Holmes def. M. Ali	50.00
06/12/81	L. Holmes def. L. Spinks	35.00
06/11/82	L. Holmes def. G. Cooney	35.00
05/20/83	L. Holmes def. T. Witherspoon	40.00
09/21/85	M. Spinks def. L. Holmes	35.00
04/19/86	M. Spinks def. L. Holmes	30.00
11/22/86	M. Tyson def. T. Berbick	85.00
03/07/87	M. Tyson def. Bonecrusher Smith	60.00
05/30/87	M. Tyson def. P. Thomas	50.00
05/30/87	T. Tucker def. B. Douglas	30.00
08/01/87	M. Tyson def. T. Tucker	60.00
10/16/87	M. Tyson def. T. Biggs	50.00
01/22/88	M. Tyson def. L. Holmes	50.00
03/20/88	M. Tyson def. T. Tubbs	50.00
06/27/88	M. Tyson def. M. Spinks	50.00
02/25/89	M. Tyson def. F. Bruno	50.00
07/21/89	M. Tyson def. C. Williams	45.00
02/10/90	B. Douglas def. M. Tyson	85.00
10/25/90	E. Holyfield def. B. Douglas	35.00
03/18/91	M. Tyson def. R. Ruddock	40.00
04/19/91	E. Holyfield def. G. Foreman	35.00
06/28/91	M. Tyson def. R. Ruddock	40.00
10/18/91	R. Mercer def. T. Morrison	20.00
11/23/91	E. Holyfield def. B. Cooper	25.00
02/07/92	L. Holmes def. R. Mercer	20.00
05/15/92	M. Moorer def. B. Cooper	20.00
06/19/92	E. Holyfield def. L. Holmes	30.00
07/18/92	R. Bowe def. P. Coetzer	30.00
10/31/92	L. Lewis def. R. Ruddock	25.00
11/13/92	R. Bowe def. E. Holyfield	35.00

FOOTBALL POSTERS

SPORTS ILLUSTRATED POSTERS

Name	Year	Price
Alworth, Lance	68-71	20.00
Bakken, Jim	68-71	8.00
Banaszak, Pete	68-71	12.00
Barney, Lem	68-71	14.00
Battle, Mike	68-71	8.00
Biletnikoff, Fred	68-71	18.00
Blanda, George	68-71	20.00
Brockington, John	68-71	12.00
Brodie, John	1968	20.00
Brown, Bill	68-71	8.00
Brown, Larry	68-71	18.00
Bulaich, Norm	68-71	8.00
Butkus, Dick	68-71	65.00
Carter, Vince	68-71	8.00
Coffey, Junior	68-71	8.00
Cook, Greg	68-71	8.00
Csonka, Larry	68-71	20.00
Curtis, Mike	68-71	14.00
Davidson, Ben	68-71	12.00
Dawson, Len	68-71	20.00
Eller, Carl	68-71	18.00
Farr, Mel	1969	8.00
Gabriel, Roman	1968	15.00
Garrett, Mike	68-71	8.00
Grabowski, Jim	68-71	12.00
Greene, Joe	68-71	18.00
Griese, Bob	68-71	30.00
Hadl, John	1969	14.00
Hawkins, Ben	68-71	8.00
Hayes, Bob	68-71	12.00
Jackson, Rich	68-71	8.00
Johnson, Charley	68-71	8.00
Johnson, Ron	68-71	8.00
Jones, Deacon	1969	14.00
Jones, Homer	1969	8.00
Jorgensen, Sonny	1968	25.00
Kapp, Joe	68-71	12.00
Karras, Alex	1970	12.00
Kelly, Leroy	68-71	12.00
Kemp, Jack	1968	35.00
Kilmer, Billy	68-71	14.00
Lamonica, Daryle	68-71	20.00
Landry, Greg	1971	12.00
Lilly, Bob	68-71	18.00
Little, Floyd	68-71	14.00
Lockhart, Spider	68-71	8.00
Mackey, John	1968	14.00
Manning, Archie	68-71	18.00
Matte, Tom	1969	8.00
Maynard, Don	68-71	18.00
Morton, Craig	1970	12.00
Nance, Jim	68-71	12.00
Nelson, Bill	1970	12.00
Nix, Kent	68-71	8.00
Nitschke, Ray	68-71	18.00
Nobis, Tommy	68-71	14.00
Namath, Joe	68-71	100.00
Olsen, Merlin	68-71	30.00
Page, Alan	68-71	18.00
Plunkett, Jim	1971	14.00
Reeves, Dan	1968	12.00
Rossovich, Tim	68-71	8.00
Russell, Andy	68-71	7.00
Ryan, Frank	1968	10.00
Sauer, George	68-71	7.00
Sayers, Gale	68-71	30.00
Sellers, Ron	68-71	8.00
Shaw, Dennis	68-71	8.00
Simpson, O.J.	68-71	85.00
Smith, Jackie	68-71	12.00
Snead, Norm	68-71	10.00
Snell, Matt	68-71	12.00
Starr, Bart	68-71	30.00
Staubach, Roger	68-71	65.00
Taylor, Charley	68-71	18.00
Taylor, Otis	68-71	18.00
Warfield, Paul	68-71	18.00
Washington, Gene	68-71	12.00
Webster, George	1969	8.00
Wilson, Larry	68-71	18.00
Woodson, Marv	68-71	8.00

HOCKEY POSTERS

SPORTS ILLUSTRATED POSTERS

Name	Year	Price
Berenson, Red	1970	30.00
Esposito, Phil	1971	20.00
Giscomin, Ed	1970	14.00
Hadfield, Vic	68-71	8.00
Howe, Gordie	68-71	35.00
Hull, Bobby	68-71	40.00
Keon, Dave	68-71	8.00
Orr, Bobby	68-71	40.00
Sanderson, Derek	68-71	12.00
Worsley, Gump	68-71	12.00

PRICE GUIDES

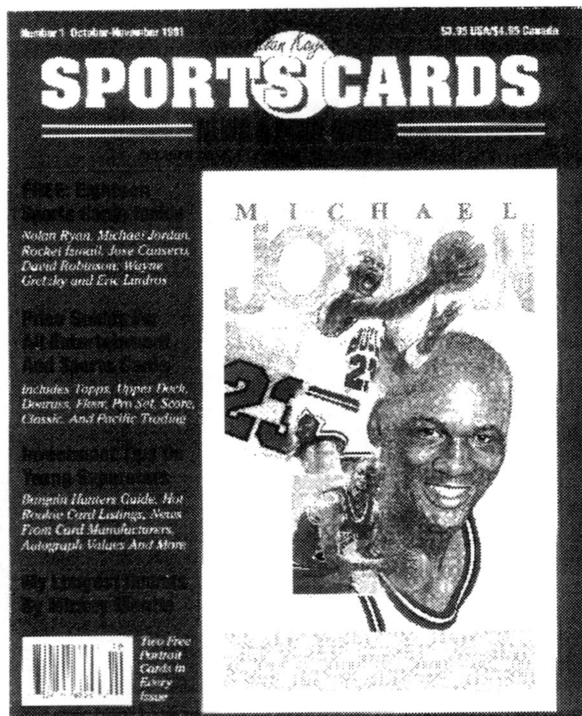

(Clockwise) Oct/Nov. 1991 Allan Kayes Sports Cards, Jan. 1990 Beckett's, May/June 1991 Legends

ALLAN KAYE'S SPORTS CARDS

ISSUE	COVER	VALUE
1	Michael Jordan	15.00
1	Nolan Ryan	14.00
2	Pete Rose	6.00
2	Wayne Gretzky	8.00
3	Jim Kelly	6.00
3	Magic Johnson	9.00
4	Cal Ripken Jr.	9.00
4	Brett Hull	7.00
5	Bobby Bonilla	7.00
5	Eric Lindros	8.00
6	Frank Thomas	8.00
6	Jose Canseco	7.00
7	Roger Clemens	7.00
7	David Robinson	6.00
8	Ken Griffey Jr.	9.00
8	Mickey Mantle	10.00
9	Ryne Sandberg	7.00
9	Hank Aaron	7.00
10	Will Clark	7.00
10	Joe DiMaggio	7.00
11	Dave Justice	6.00
11	Joe Montana	8.00

BALL STREET JOURNAL

ISSUE	COVER	VALUE
1	Nolan Ryan	40.00
2	Bo Jackson	30.00
3	Ken Griffey, Jr.	30.00
4	Rickey Henderson	20.00
5	Cal Ripken, Jr.	15.00
6	Frank Thomas	15.00
2-1	Michael Jordan	10.00
2-2	Dave Justice	7.00
2-3	Dikembe Mutombo	10.00
SD	Nolan Ryan/Diamond Edition	15.00
2-4	Babe Ruth - Hall of Fame	10.00
2-5	Michael Jordan/Olympics	10.00
2-6	Frank Thomas	8.00
OS	Olympic Supplement	4.00
2-7	Shaquille O'Neal	8.00
2-8	Deion Sanders	7.00
2-9	Joe Montana	7.00
2-10	Gary Sheffield	7.00
2-11	Emmitt Smith	8.00
2-12	Shaquille O'Neal	7.00

BECKETT'S BASEBALL

Front and Back cover photos are listed for all *Beckett's*

ISSUE	COVER	VALUE

No.	Cover	Price
1	Clemente/Murphy, Sandberg	145.00
2	Mantle/Ripken, Palmer	75.00
3	Mays/Winfield, Clemente	45.00
4	Aaron/G.Carter, Gwynn	35.00
5	Musial/Murray, Trammel	30.00
6	Bench/Boggs, Murphy	25.00
7	Garvey, Schmidt	25.00
8	Sutcliffe, Yastrzemski	25.00
9	Ripken, Franco	25.00
10	R.Jackson,Durham	25.00
11	Rose, Musial	25.00
12	Gooden, Banks	25.00
13	Coleman/McGee, Guidry	20.00
14	Mattingly/Saberhagen	20.00
15	Gooden, G.Carter	20.00
16	Brett, R.Henderson	20.00
17	Boggs, Canseco/Robidoux	20.00
18	Murphy, Winfield	20.00
19	Mantle,Strawberry	20.00
20	Clemens, Incaviglia/Canseco	15.00
21	Rose,Puckett	15.00
22	Joyner,Schmidt	15.00
23	Mattingly,Gooden	15.00
24	Boggs, E.Davis	15.00
25	Clemens, R.Henderson	15.00
26	Schmidt,Snyder	15.00
27	Puckett, Coleman	15.00
28	E.Davis, Strawberry	15.00
29	Mays, Incaviglia	15.00
30	B.Jackson, McGwire/Canseco	10.00
31	Dawson, Mattingly	10.00
32	McGwire, Gwynn	5.00
33	Bell, Seitzer/Brett	5.00
34	Puckett, McGwire/E.Davis	7.50
35	Mattingly, W.Clark	7.50
36	Seitzer, Boggs/Clemens	5.00
37	Santiago, Murphy	5.00
38	E.Davis, Greenwell	5.00
39	Nokes, Gooden	5.00
40	Canseco, DiMaggio	7.50
41	Winfield, Grace	5.00
42	Strawberry, Sabo/Bonilla	5.00
43	Mattingly, Galaragga/Raines	5.00
44	Canseco, Jefferies	7.50
45	Hershiser, McGire	5.00
46	W.Clark, Cone	7.50
47	Greenwell, Gibson	5.00
48	Grace, Bench	7.50
49	Jefferies, Sheffield	5.00
50	Clemente, Canseco	7.50
51	B.Jackson, Burks	7.50
52	W.Clark, Banks	7.50
53	Mitchell, Griffey Jr.	7.50
54	J.Abbott, Yastrzemski	5.00
55	Ryan, McGriff	7.50
56	Mitchell/Clark, J.Walton	5.00
57	R.Henderson, M. Williams	7.50
58	Sierra, Saberhagen	5.00
59	B.Jackson, G.Olson	5.00
60	Yount, Zeile	5.00
61	Grace, H.Johnson	5.00
62	Mattingly, E.Anthony	5.00
63	B.Jackson, Raines	6.00
64	Griffey, Jr.,Viola	6.00
65	Sandberg, Clemens/Ryan	5.00
66	R.Henderson, Fisk	5.00
67	Canseco, Jefferies	2.50
68	Bonds, S. Alomar Jr.	2.50

(Clockwise) January 1992 Tuff Stuff, Dec. 1991 Beckett's, August 1991 Beckett's

No.	Title	Price
69	Ryan, Justice	5.00
70	Fielder, Larkin	2.50
71	Brett, Maas	2.50
72	Griffey Jr., Strawberry	3.00
73	R.Henderson, R. Martinez	5.00
74	Ripken, Bonilla	3.00
75	DiMaggio/Mantle, Gehrig/Ruth	3.00
76	Clemens, B. Robinson	3.00
77	Gwynn/McGriff, Dawson	3.00
78	Justice, Erickson	3.00
79	F.Thomas, Winfield	3.00
80	B.Jackson, H. Johnson	3.00
81	Fielder, Ventura	2.95
82	Ryan, Avery/Glavine	3.00
83	O.Smith, Bagwell	3.00
84	Ripken, Plantier	3.00
85	F.Thomas, Gant	3.00
86	Avery, R.Alomar	3.00
87	Puckett, Sierra	3.00
88	D.Sanders, Perez/Rose/Bench	3.00
89	McGwire, McDowell	3.00
90	Yount, Kruk	3.00
91	Sheffield, Juan Guzman/R.Alomar	3.00
92	Glavine, Mussina	3.00
93	Gonzalez, Karros	3.00
94	F.Thomas, Knoblauch	3.00
95	Griffey Jr., Listach	3.00

BECKETT'S BASKETBALL

No.	Title	Price
1	Jordan,Ewing	14.00
2	Robinson, K. Malone	5.00
3	Magic Johnson, K. Johnson	12.50
4	Barkley, Dumars, Green	3.00
5	Robinson, Olajuwan	5.00
6	Ewing, Stockton	3.00
7	Bird, Kemp	3.00
8	Drexler, R.Miller	3.00
9	D.Wilkins, Hardaway	3.00
10	Jordan, Coleman	5.00
11	K.Johnson, B.King	3.00
12	Abdul-Jabbar, Pippen	5.00
13	Magic Johnson, Shaw	3.00
14	Jordan, L.Johnson	5.00
15	K.Malone, I. Thomas	3.00
16	Robinson, Drexler	3.00
17	Coleman, Mullin	3.00
18	Mutombo, S.Smirth	3.00
19	Hardaway, Simmons	3.00
20	L.Johnson, D.Brown	5.00
21	Pippen, Price	3.00
22	Augmon, Rodman	3.00
23	Owens, O'Neal, Laettner	3.00
24	Magic, K.Malone,Ewing,Jordan,Barkley	12.50
25	Jorddan, Bird, Parrish, McHale	5.00
26	Magic Johnson, Gill	3.00
27	O'Neal, Barkley	2.95
28	Bird, Kemp	3.00
29	L.Johnson, K.Malone	3.00
30	Laettner, L.Ellis	3.00
31	Jordan, W.Williams	3.00

(Clockwise) Fall 1992 Cartwrights , Feb. 1993 Beckett's, March 1989 Beckett's

BECKETT'S FOOTBALL

1	B.Jackson,Marino	12.50
2	Montana,Dickerson	12.50
3	Elway,Cunningham	5.00
4	B.Sanders, Okoye	10.00
5	Ware, Taylor	5.00
6	Rice, Everett	5.00
7	Majkowski, Payton	3.00
8	B.Jackson, Moon	3.00
9	Montana, Humphrey	3.00
10	B.Jackson, Lombardi/Starr	11.00
11	Cunningham, N.Anderson	3.00
12	T.Thomas, E.Smith	3.00
13	Ismail, Lott	3.00
14	B.Smith, J.Johnson	3.00
15	Esiason, Butts	3.00
16	Rice, George	3.00
17	B.Sanders, D.Thomas	3.00
18	Moon, Rison	3.00
19	Aikman, Carrier	3.00
20	Lott/Craig, Sharpe	3.00
21	E.Smith, B.Thomas	3.00
22	Kelly, Namath	3.00
23	Rypien, H.Williams	3.00
24	Marino, Russell	3.00
25	T.Thomas, Elway	3.00
26	Howard, Swilling	3.00
27	Ervins, Irvin	3.00
28	B.Sanders, D.Sanders	3.00
29	D.Thomas, McGwire	3.00
30	E.Smith, Cunningham	3.00
31	Monk, Nagle	3.00
32	D.Sanders, Moon	3.00
33	Marino, H.Walker	3.00

January 1993 Beckett's

34	Watters, L. Taylor	3.00

BECKETT'S FUTURE STARS

1	Van Poppel/Ryan,K.Anderson	5.00
2	F.Thomas, O'Neal	3.00
3	Sierra/Gonzalez, L Johnson	3.00
4	Morris, D.Sanders	3.00
5	D.Bell,T.Martinez	3.00
6	Ismail,Bagwell	3.00
7	McRae, Owens	3.00
8	O'Neal, Croel	3.00
9	Howard, Plantier	3.00
10	Klesko, Motumbo	3.00
11	MacLean/T.Murray, Buckley	3.00
12	F.Thomas, Avery	3.00
13	Griffey Jr.,Rodriguez	3.00
14	Taylor, Von Poppel	3.00
15	R.Sanders, McCarty	3.00
16	Mussina, Lofton	3.00
17	Knoblauch, Salmon	3.00
18	Nagle, Karros	3.00
19	J.Gonzalez, D.McGwire	3.00
20	Faulk, B.Sanders, Eldred	3.00
21	O'Neal, Watters	3.00

BECKETT'S HOCKEY

1	Gretzky, Roy	12.50
2	Brett Hull, Messier	10.00
3	Yzerman, Bobby Hull	3.00
4	Lemieux, Sakic	10.00
5	Bourque, Bossy	3.00
6	Roy, Oates	3.00
7	Federov, MacInnis	7.50

December 1992 Beckett's

8	Lindros, Cullen	12.00
9	Belfour, Recchi	3.00
10	Lemieux, Potvin, Messier	5.00
11	Jagr, Fleury	3.00
12	Kurri, Stastny	3.00
13	Brett Hull, Robitaille	3.00
14	Fuhr, Savard	3.00
15	Messier, Falloon	5.00
16	Linden, Nolan	3.00
17	Bure, Stevens	3.00
18	Roenick, Lidstrom	3.00
19	Gretzky, Amonte	3.00
20	G.Dionne, Lachance	3.00
21	LaFontaine, Brind'Amour	3.00
22	Pittsburgh Celebration, Cherry	3.00
23	Lindros, T.Esposito	3.00
24	Bure, Oates	3.00
25	Gretzky, Lafleur	3.00
26	Rheaume, Niedermayer	3.00
27	Leetch, Mogilny	3.00

BECKETT'S MINOR LEAGUE MONTHLY

1	Jefferies, Finley	10.00
2	Hershiser, M.Marshall	9.00
3	S. Alomar Jr., Gordon	7.00
4	Greenwell, Jordan	6.50
5	J.Canseco, O.Canseco	5.00
6	Jefferies, Davis	5.00
7	Griffey Jr., Rose Jr.	5.00
8	Ventura, Zeile	5.00
9	Mitchell, Belle/Allred	5.00
10	W.Clark, McGwire	5.00
11	Walton, M.Pina	5.00
12	Grace, D.Bell	5.00
13	Superstars of the '90s, Deion Sanders	5.00
14	Ansley/E.Jones, Anthony	5.00
15	McDonald, Vaughan	5.00
16	Bo Jackson, Ripken Jr.	5.00
17	Boggs, Naehring	5.00
18	Zeile, Musial	5.00
19	Sierra, K.Brown	5.00
20	Griffey, Jr., K.Jones	5.00
21	Maas, Gonzalez	5.00
22	Justice, Thomas	5.00

CARTWRIGHTS

ISSUE	COVER	VALUE
1	Dave Justice	29.00
2	Ken Griffey, Jr.	10.00
3	Roger Clemens	10.00
4	Frank Thomas	10.00

	Vol. 2-1 Nolan Ryan	10.00

SPECIAL COLLECTORS EDITION

	Vol.1-4 Frank Thomas-Teal Foil	35.00
	Vol.2-1 Nolan Ryan-Blue Foil	20.00

Signature Series

(Special Stamp with number on cover)

	Vol.1-4 Frank Thomas	90.00

DIAMOND SPORTS MEMORABILIA

1	Dan Marino	8.00
2	Olympic Basketball Team	5.00
3	Cal Ripken, Jr.	5.00

THE INVESTORS JOURNAL

ISSUE	COVER	VALUE
1	Eric Lindros	29.00
2	Gretzky, McNall, Ismail, Candy	20.00
3	Michael Jordan	15.00
4	Ryne Sandberg	10.00
5	Shaquille O'Neal	19.00
6	Mickey Mantle	10.00
7	Magic Johnson	10.00
	1st Ann. Cal Ripken, Jr.	13.00
8	Manon Rheaume	10.00
8	Clyde Drexler (Regional Cover)	10.00

Special Foil Editions

3S	Silver Edition	60.00
4B	Blue Edition	50.00
5P	Purple Edition	70.00
6R	Red Edition	40.00
7LB	Light Blue Edition	50.00
	1st Ann. Copper Edition	60.00
8MRH	Holofoil Edition	60.00
8CDR	Rainbow Foil Edition	60.00

LEGENDS SPORTS MEMORABILIA

Hobby Edition

ISSUE	COVER	VALUE
1	Mantle, Ruth, DiMaggio	46.00
2	Garvey, Koufax, Hershiser	19.00
3	Yastrzemski, Bench	42.00
4	Lou Gehrig	20.00
5	Tony Gwynn	150.00

July/Aug. 1992 Legends

6	Nolan Ryan	325.00
7	Mitchell, Mays, McCovey	19.00
8	Bo Jackson	94.00
9	Morgan, Palmer	115.00
10	Clark, Ott	29.00
11	Mattingly, DiMaggio	27.00
12	Banks, Sandberg	24.00
13	Joe Montana	25.00
14	Cecil Fielder	40.00
15	Wayne Gretzky	25.00
16	Rickey Henderson	23.00
17	Michael Jordan	24.00
18	12th National Program	15.00
	12th National Gold Program	175.00
19	Ken Griffey, Jr.	14.00
20	Carew, Jenkins, Perry	11.00
21	Nolan Ryan	10.00
22	David Robinson	8.00
23	Cal Ripken, Jr	9.00
24	Brett Hull	8.00
25	Jose Canseco	75.00
26	Pete Rose	10.00
27	Dan Marino	10.00
28	Frank Thomas	9.00
29	Magic Johnson	14.00
30	Roger Clemens	8.00
31	Mario Lemieux	9.00
32	13th National Program	9.00
	13th National Program Gold	60.00
33	Dave Justice	8.00
34	Seaver, Fingers	9.00
35	Nolan Ryan – Anaheim	30.00
36	Darryl Strawberry	7.00
37	Mark Messier	8.00
38	Michael Jordan	35.00
39	Roberto Alomar	7.00
40	Emmitt Smith	8.00
41	Robin Ventura/Hobby	8.00
42	Larry Bird/Hobby	15.00
43	Arnold Palmer/Hobby	13.50
44	Kirby Puckett/Hobby	12.00
45	Muhammad Ali/Hobby	12.00

Newsstand Edition

N1	Robin Ventura	8.00
N2	Larry Bird	15.00
N3	Robin Yount	8.00
N4	Arnold Palmer	13.50
N5	Kirby Puckett	12.00
N6	Muhammad Ali	12.00

22-Karat Series

	Nolan Ryan	160.00
	Roberto Alomar	70.00
	Larry Bird	90.00
	Arnold Palmer	70.00
	Muhammad Ali	70.00
	Mickey Mantle	70.00

Special Issues

	Fishing Issue/Gwynn	10.00
	Fishing Issue/Marlin	10.00

Autographed Issues

3-4	Ernie Banks	35.00
3-4	Joe Montana	75.00
4.1	Cecil Fielder	45.00
4.3	Ken Griffey, Jr.	45.00
4.5	Jose Canseco	95.00
5.1	Pete Rose	40.00
5.4	Dave Justice	40.00
5.4	Rollie Fingers	40.00
5.6	Roberto Alomar	40.00
6.1	Robin Ventura	40.00

MALLOY'S SPORTS CARDS & COLLECTIBLES

ISSUE	COVER	VALUE
1	Sports Publications	5.00
2	World Series pins & programs	3.00
3	Boxing collectibles	3.00
4	Winter Olympics & Super Bowl memorabilia	3.00
5	Basketball & Hockey annuals	3.00
6	Sports equipment issue	3.00
7	Indy 500 & Kentucky Derby memorabilia	3.00
8	Olympic Issue	3.00
9	Football issue	3.00
10	Hockey issue	3.00
11	Basketball issue	3.00
12	Shaquille O'Neal, Hot Rookies	4.00
13	Brien Taylor, Baseball rookies	3.00
14	Deion Sanders, Baseball Preview	3.00
15	Shaquille O'Neal Special Issue	5.00

MVP

ISSUE	COVER	VALUE
	Prototype Nolan Ryan	17.00
1	Michael Jordan	17.00

May 1993 Malloy's Sports Cards & Collectibles

PROFILES

ISSUE	COVER	VALUE
1	Frank Thomas	30.00
2	Ken Griffey, Jr.	25.00

RBI

ISSUE	COVER	VALUE
	Prototype Michael Jordan(White Sox)	17.00
1	Ronald Reagan	15.00
2	Frank Thomas	7.00
3	Dave Justice	10.00
	Cactus League Frank Thomas	10.00
	Grapefruit League Ryne Sandberg	10.00
4	Nolan Ryan	17.00
5	Mickey Mantle	10.00

SHOWCASE

ISSUE	COVER	VALUE
1	Frank Thomas	10.00
2	Steve Avery	6.00

SPEEDWAY

ISSUE	COVER	VALUE
1	Dale Earnhardt	17.50
1	Richard Petty	12.00
2	Harry Gant	10.00
3	Bill Elliot	10.00
4	Davey Allison	10.00
5	Earnie Ivan	10.00
6	Richard Petty	10.00

January/February 1993 Legends

SPORTS EDUCATIONAL

ISSUE		COVER	VALUE
1991	Baseball	Nolan Ryan	8.00
1991	Football	Emmitt Smith	8.00
1991	Hockey	Wayne Gretzky	8.00
1992	Baseball	Magic Johnson	8.00

THE SPORTS REPORT

ISSUE	COVER	VALUE
Prototype	Frank Thomas	12.00
1	Michael Jordan	10.00
2	Shaquille O'Neal	10.00

THE SPORTS REPORT LIMITED ISSUES

ISSUE	COVER	VALUE
Prototype	Limited Silver Edition	40.00
1	Limited Holofoil Edition	40.00
2	Limited Holofoil Edition	50.00

SUPERSTARS

ISSUE	COVER	VALUE
1	Nolan Ryan 9.00	
2	Frank Thomas	9.00
3	Brien Taylor 9.00	

TUFF STUFF

ISSUE	COVER	VALUE
June 90	Bo Jackson (baseball)	10.00
July 90	Nolan Ryan	6.00
Aug. 90	Ken Griffey, Jr.	5.00
Sept 90	Jose Canseco	5.00
Oct. 90	Jerry Rice	5.00
Nov. 90	Bo Jackson (football)	8.00
D/Jan 91	Barry Sanders	5.00

August 1992 Tuff Stuff

ISSUE	COVER	VALUE
Feb. 91	Michael Jordan	6.00
Mar. 91	Wayne Gretzky	6.00
Apr. 91	Rickey Henderson	6.00
May 91	David Robinson	6.00
June 91	George Brett	6.00
July 91	Roger Clemens	6.00
Aug. 91	Cal Ripken, Jr.	6.00
Sept 91	Emmitt Smith	7.00
Oct. 91	Darryl Strawberry	6.00
Nov. 91	Tyson/Holyfield	6.00
Dec. 91	Jim Kelly	6.00
Jan. 92	Magic Johnson	7.00
Feb. 92	Warren Moon.	6.00
Mar. 92	Larry Bird	6.00
Apr. 92	David Justice	6.00
May 92	Ryne Sandberg	6.00
June 92	Nolan Ryan	7.00
July 92	Olympic Basketball Dream Team	7.00
Aug. 92	Frank Thomas	6.00
Sept 92		5.00
Oct. 92	Babe Ruth	5.00
Nov. 92	Joe Montana	5.00
Dec. 92		5.00
Jan. 93		5.00
Feb. 93	Magic Johnson	5.00
Apr. 93	Shaquille O'Neal	5.00

HORSE RACING PROGRAMS

By Dick Hering

The first Kentucky Derby was run on May 17, 1875, at Churchill Downs Racetrack, in Louisville, Kentucky. Although not the oldest, it is the only of the three Triple Crown races that has run continuously.

The person who made the Derby what it is today was Colonel Matt Winn, who took over the management of Churchill Downs in 1902, and continued as president until his death at the age of 88 in 1949. It is said that Col. Winn was in attendance when the first Derby was run in 1875, and that he boasted he had seen every Derby since then until his death. He is pictured on the 1949 glass with the caption "He Has Seen Them All."

The Kentucky Derby was considered a local race until 1915, when Harry Payne Whitney sent his undefeated filly Regret from the east to win the race. This started the trend of other big Eastern stables sending their top three year-olds every year to compete.

The oldest known Derby program to have changed hands in recent years is one from 1899, which sold for $1,250. Derby program prices listed in this guide prior to 1899 are a general consensus by dealers and collectors of what they would sell for if they were available.

The Preakness Stakes was first run on May 27, 1873, at the Maryland Jockey Club (now known as Pimlico Race Course) in Baltimore, Maryland. Although two years older then the Kentucky Derby, the Preakness was not run from 1891 to 1893. It was run at New York's Morris Park 1890, and at Gravesend in New York from 1894 to 1908. The Preakness Stakes was named for the horse Preakness who won the 1870 Dinner Party Stakes, the first stakes race ever run at Pimlico. In some years, the Preakness was run before the Derby, as in 1930, when Gallant Fox won the Preakness on May 9th and won the Derby on May 17th. Some years the Derby and Preakness were run on the same day, as in 1917, when both races were run on May 12th. Until recent years Preakness programs were not sought after by collectors as much as Derby programs. For various reasons most Preakness programs, even those as recent as the late 1980s, are in short supply and in great demand, explaining their higher values over corresponding Derby programs.

The Belmont Stakes, the oldest of the Triple Crown races, was first run in 1867 at New York's Jerome Park. The race was named for August Belmont I, the first President of Jerome Park, and a monarch of the American turf. It continued to be run at Jerome Park until 1890, when it was switched to Morris Park in New York and ran there until 1904. Since 1904 it has been run at Belmont Park with the exception of 1963 to 1967, when it was run at Aqueduct while Belmont Park was being reconstructed. The Belmont Stakes was not run in the years 1911 and 1912.

Belmont programs, like Preakness programs, have become much more popular i recent years, and are also in short supply and great demand.

The Breeders' Cup is a chamionship event like the World Series or Super Bowl and is moved to a different location each year. The idea of the Breeders' Cup was first conceived in 1982 by Lexington, Kentucky breeder John R. Gaines, who formed a committee to cultivate the idea. This committee was spear-headed by John Nerud, President of Tartan Farm, Ocala, Florida, and former trainer of Dr. Fager, considered by many the greatest horse of this century. The first Breeders' Cup was run on November 10, 1984, at Hollywood Park in Calfornia. The Breeders' Cup is a series of seven races run in different divisions on the same afternoon that attract the best horses in the world. The popularity and prestige of this event in its short nine year history has increased so dramatically that it overshadows the Triple Crown races.

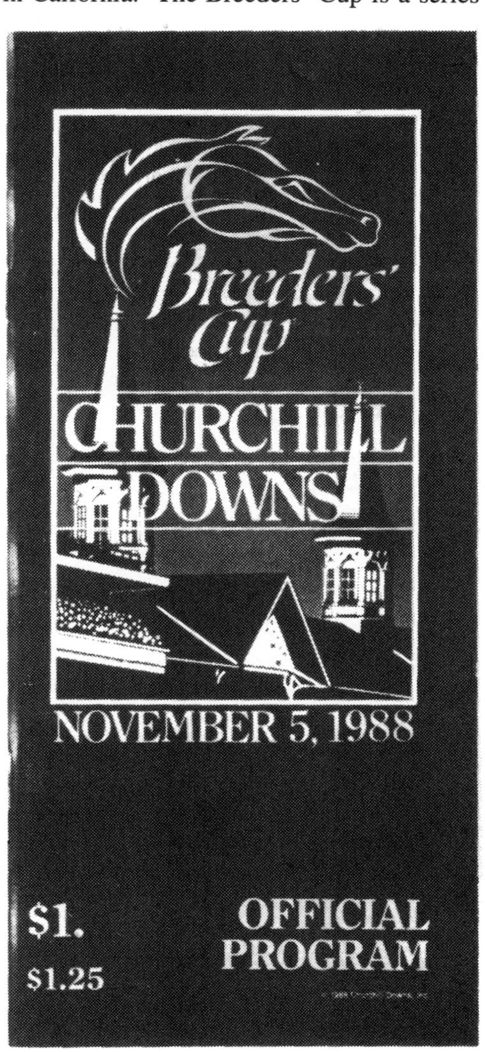

1988 Breeders' Cup

Breeders' Cup programs did not really start to gain interest with collectors until after the 1988 running. Although all Breeders' Cup programs are still available through dealers in mint condition, the 1986 and 1987 bring a premuim price. In 1986 the crowd was much smaller than expected, and although there were plenty of programs leftover, the host track Santa Anita mistakenly threw them away. In 1987 the host track, Hollywood Park, anticipated a small crowd as in 1986, but the opposite occured and they ran out before the day ended.

Other than Kentucky Derby, Preakness, Belmont, and Breeders' Cup, many other thoroughbred racing programs are collected to a lesser degree (programs of a particular horse, a certain race, Triple Crown winners, and match race programs which are prized collectibles). Some programs are extremely valuable, such as any Man 0' War program that would be worth a minimum of $1,400 in average condition.

PROGRAMS

AUTO RACING PROGRAMS

DAYTONA 500 PROGRAMS

Date	Winner	Car Type	Value
1959	Lee Petty	Oldsmobile	200.00
1960	Junior Johnson	Chevrolet	100.00
1961	Marvin Panch	Pontiac	75.00
1962	Fireball Roberts	Pontiac	75.00
1963	Tiny Lund	Ford	50.00
1964	Richard Petty	Plymouth	200.00
1965	Fred Lorenzen	Ford	30.00
1966	Richard Petty	Plymouth	75.00
1967	Mario Andretti	Ford	30.00
1968	Cale Yarborough	Mercury	15.00
1969	L.R. Yarborough	Ford	15.00
1970	Pete Hamilton	Plymouth	15.00
1971	Richard Petty	Plymouth	30.00
1972	A.J. Foyt	Mercury	25.00
1973	Richard Petty	Dodge	25.00
1974	Richard Petty	Dodge	25.00
1975	Benny Parsons	Chevrolet	10.00
1976	David Pearson	Mercury	10.00
1977	Cale Yarborough	Chevrolet	10.00
1978	Bobby Allison	Ford	15.00
1979	Richard Petty	Oldsmobile	20.00
1980	Buddy Baker	Oldsmobile	10.00
1981	Richard Petty	Buick	15.00
1982	Bobby Allison	Buick	10.00
1983	Cale Yarborough	Pontiac	10.00
1984	Cale Yarborough	Chevrolet	10.00
1985	Bill Elliott	Ford	10.00
1986	Geoff Bodine	Chevrolet	10.00
1987	Bill Elliott	Ford	10.00
1988	Bobby Allison	Buick	10.00
1989	Darrell Waltrip	Chevrolet	10.00
1990	Derrike Cope	Chevrolet	10.00
1991	Ernie Irvan	Chevrolet	10.00
1992	Davey Allison	Ford	10.00

INDY 500 PROGRAMS

Date	Winner	Car Type	Value
1911	Ray Harroun	Marmon "Wasp"	1,500.00
1912	Joe Dawson	National	1,250.00
1913	Jules Goux	Peugeot	1,250.00
1914	Rene Thomas	Delage	1,100.00
1915	Ralph DePalma	Mercedes	1,000.00
1916	Dario Resta	Peugeot	900.00
1917-18	Race not held due to WWI		
1919	Howard Wilcox	Peugeot	875.00
1920	Gaston Chevrolet	Monroe Special	875.00
1921	Tommy Milton	Frontenac Special	800.00
1922	Jimmy Murphy	Murphy Special	800.00
1923	Tommy Milton	H.C.S. Special	750.00
1924	L.L Corum & Joe Boyer	Duesenberg Special	750.00
1925	Peter DePaolo	Duesenberg Special	650.00
1926	Frank Lockhart	Miller Special	600.00
1927	George Sounders	Duesenberg Special	650.00
1928	Louis Meyer	Miller Special	550.00
1929	Ray Keech	Simplex Special	475.00
1930	Billy Arnold	Miller-Hartz Special	475.00
1931	Louis Schneider	Bowes Special	400.00
1932	Fred Frame	Miller-Hartz Special	400.00
1933	Louis Meyer	Tydol Special	350.00
1934	Bill Cummings	Boyle Special	350.00
1935	Kelly Petillo	Gilmore Special	350.00
1936	Louis Meyer	Ring Free Special	300.00
1937	Wilbur Shaw	Shaw Gilmor Special	300.00
1938	Floyd Roberts	Burd Special	200.00
1939	Wilbur Shaw	Boyle Special	200.00
1940	Wilbur Shaw	Boyle Special	200.00
1941	Floyd Davis & Mauri Rose	Noc-Out Special	150.00
1942-45	Race not held due to WWII		
1946	George Robson	Thorne Special	50.00
1947	Mauri Rose	Blue Crown Special	50.00
1948	Mauri Rose	Blue Crown Special	50.00
1949	Bill Holland	Blue Crown Special	50.00
1950	Johnnie Parsons	Wynn's Special	40.00
1951	Lee Wallard	Belanger Special	40.00
1952	Troy Ruttman	Agajanian Special	40.00
1953	Bill Vukovich	Fuel Injection Special	35.00
1954	Bill Vukovich	Fuel Injection Special	35.00
1955	Bob Sweikert	John Zink Special	35.00
1956	Pat Flaherty	John Zink Special	30.00
1957	Sam Hanks	Belond Special	30.00
1958	Jimmy Bryan	Belond AP Special	30.00
1959	Rodger Ward	Leader 500 Roadster	25.00
1960	Jim Rathmann	Ken-Paul Special	25.00
1961	A.J. Foyt, Jr.	Bowes Seal Fast	30.00
1962	Rodger Ward	Leader 500 Roadster	20.00
1963	Parnelli Jones	Willard Battery	20.00
1964	A.J. Foyt, Jr.	Sheraton-Thompson	30.00

1911 Indy 500 program

1919 Indy 500 program

1938 Indy 500 program

1965	Jim Clark	Lotus by Ford	15.00
1966	Graham Hill	American Red Ball	15.00
1967	A.J. Foyt, Jr.	Sheraton-Thompson	30.00
1968	Bobby Unser	Rislone Special	15.00
1969	Mario Andretti	STP Special	12.00
1970	Al Unser	Johnny Lightning	15.00
1971	Al Unser	Johnny Lightning	15.00
1972	Mark Donohue	Sunoco McLaren	10.00
1973	Gordon Johncock	STP Special	10.00
1974	J. Rutherford	McLaren	10.00
1975	Bobby Unser	Jorgensen Eagle	10.00
1976	J. Rutherford	Hy-Gain McLaren	10.00
1977	A.J. Foyt, Jr.	Gilmore Special	25.00
1978	Al Unser	First National	10.00
1979	Rick Mears	The Gould Charge	10.00
1980	J. Rutherford	Pennzoil Chaparral	10.00
1981	Bobby Unser	Norton Spirit	10.00
1982	Gordon Johncock	STP Special	15.00
1983	Tom Sneva	Texaco Star	10.00
1984	Rick Mears	Pennzoil Z-7 Special	10.00
1985	Danny Sullivan	Miller Special	10.00
1986	Bobby Rahal	Budweiser	10.00
1987	Al Unser	Cummins Holset	10.00
1988	Rick Mears	Penske-Chevrolet V-8	10.00
1989	E. Fittipaldi	Penske-Chevrolet V-8	10.00
1990	Arie Luyendyk	Domino's Chevrolet	10.00
1991	Rick Mears	Penske-Chevrolet	10.00
1992	Al Unser, Jr.	Galmer-Chevrolet	10.00

BASEBALL PROGRAMS

ALL-STAR GAME PROGRAMS

Year	Site	Value
1933	Comiskey Park, Chicago	2,000.00
1934	Polo Grounds, New York	3,500.00
1935	Cleveland Stadium	450.00
1936	Braves Field, Boston	3,750.00
1937	Griffith Stadium, Washington	750.00
1938	Crosley Field, Cincinnati	1,000.00
1939	Yankee Stadium, New York	2,250.00
1940	Sportsman's Park, St. Louis	800.00
1941	Briggs Stadium, Detroit	650.00
1942	Polo Grounds, New York	4,750.00
1943	Shibe Park, Philadelphia	800.00
1944	Forbes Field, Pittsburgh	1,500.00
1945	No game	
1946	Fenway Park, Boston	1,750.00
1947	Wrigley Field, Chicago	325.00
1948	Sportsman's Park, St. Louis	375.00
1949	Ebbets Field, Brooklyn	975.00
1950	Comiskey Park, Chicago	375.00
1951	Briggs Stadium, Detroit	150.00
1952	Shibe Park, Philadelphia	175.00
1953	Crosley Field, Cincinnati	300.00
1954	Cleveland Stadium	225.00
1955	County Stadium, Milwaukee	175.00
1956	Griffith Stadium, Washington	175.00
1957	Busch Stadium, St. Louis	225.00
1958	Memorial Stadium, Baltimore	250.00
1959	Game 1: Forbes Field, Pittsburgh	275.00
	Game 2: Memorial Coliseum, L.A.	100.00
1960	Game 1: Municipal Stadium, Kansas City	150.00
	Game 2: Yankee Stadium, New York	140.00
1961	Game 1: Candlestick Park, San Fran.	400.00
	Game 2: Fenway Park, Boston	325.00
1962	Game 1: D.C. Stadium, Washington	125.00
	Game 2: Wrigley Field, Chicago	100.00
1963	Cleveland Stadium	100.00
1964	Shea Stadium, New York	275.00
1965	Metropolitan Stadium, Minnesota	75.00
1966	Busch Memorial Stadium, St. Louis	125.00
1967	Anaheim Stadium, California	175.00
1968	The Astrodome, Houston	100.00
1969	RFK Stadium, Washington	75.00
1970	Riverfront Stadium, Cincinnati	150.00
1971	Tiger Stadium, Detroit	100.00
1972	Atlanta Stadium	40.00
1973	Royals Stadium, Kansas City	125.00
1974	Three Rivers Stadium, Pittsburgh	35.00
1975	County Stadium, Milwaukee	35.00
1976	Veterans Stadium, Philadelphia	25.00
1977	Yankee Stadium, New York	25.00
1978	San Diego Stadium	40.00
1979	The Kingdome, Seattle	25.00
1980	Dodger Stadium, Los Angeles	20.00
1981	Cleveland Stadium	20.00
1982	Olympic Stadium, Montreal	20.00
1983	Comiskey Park, Chicago	15.00
1984	Candlestick Park, San Francisco	15.00
1985	H. H. Humphrey Metrodome, Minnesota	15.00
1986	The Astrodome, Houston	15.00
1987	Oakland Coliseum	10.00
1988	Riverfront Stadium, Cincinnati	10.00
1989	Anaheim Stadium, California	10.00
1990	Wrigley Field, Chicago	10.00
1991	SkyDome, Toronto	10.00
1992	Jack Murphy Stadium, San Diego	10.00

AMERICAN LEAGUE PLAYOFF PROGRAMS

1969	Baltimore Orioles	50.00
	Minnesota Twins	60.00
1970	Baltimore Orioles	35.00
	Minnesota Twins	35.00
1971	Baltimore Orioles	20.00
	Oakland A's	25.00
1972	Oakland A's	20.00
	Detroit Tigers	20.00
1973	Oakland A's	20.00
	Baltimore Orioles	20.00
1974	Oakland A's	15.00
	Baltimore Orioles	15.00
1975	Boston Red Sox	20.00

1947 All-Star Game Program

1951 All-Star Game Program

1961 All-Star Game Program

1969 N.L.C.S. program

1973 N.L.C.S. program

1990 N.L.C.S. program

Year	Team	Value
	Oakland A's	15.00
1976	New York Yankees	25.00
	Kansas City Royals	15.00
1977	New York Yankees	20.00
	Kansas City Royals	15.00
1978	New York Yankees	20.00
	Kansas City Royals	15.00
1979	Baltimore Orioles	10.00
	California Angels	10.00
1980	Kansas City Royals	10.00
	New York Yankees	10.00
1981	New York Yankees	10.00
	Oakland A's	10.00
1982	Milwaukee Brewers	10.00
	California Angels	10.00
1983	Baltimore Orioles	15.00
	Chicago White Sox	15.00
1984	Detroit Tigers	8.00
	Kansas City Royals	8.00
1985	Kansas City Royals	8.00
	Toronto Blue Jays	15.00
1986	Boston Red Sox	10.00
	California Angels	8.00
1987	Minnesota Twins	10.00
	Detroit Tigers	8.00
1988	Oakland A's	8.00
	Boston Red Sox	8.00
1989	Oakland A's	8.00
	Toronto Blue Jays	8.00
1990	Oakland A's	8.00
	Boston Red Sox	8.00
1991	Minnesota Twins	8.00
	Toronto Blue Jays	8.00
1992	Toronto Blue Jays	10.00
	Oakland A's	8.00

NATIONAL LEAGUE PLAYOFF PROGRAMS

Year	Team	Value
1969	New York Mets	100.00
	Atlanta Braves	75.00
1970	Cincinnati Reds	40.00
	Pittsburgh Pirates	45.00
1971	Pittsburgh Pirates	30.00
	San Francisco Giants	30.00
1972	Cincinnati Reds	20.00
	Pittsburgh Pirates	20.00
1973	New York Mets	50.00
	Cincinnati Reds	25.00
1974	Los Angeles Dodgers	15.00
	Pittsburgh Pirates	20.00
1975	Cincinnati Reds	15.00
	Pittsburgh Pirates	15.00
1976	Cincinnati Reds	15.00
	Philadelphia Phillies	15.00
1977	Los Angeles Dodgers	15.00
	Philadelphia Phillies	15.00
1978	Los Angeles Dodgers	10.00
	Philadelphia Phillies	10.00
1979	Pittsburgh Pirates	15.00
	Cincinnati Reds	10.00
1980	Philadelphia Phillies	10.00
	Houston Astros	15.00
1981	Los Angeles Dodgers	10.00
	Montreal Expos	20.00
1982	St. Louis Cardinals	10.00
	Atlanta Braves	15.00
1983	Philadelphia Phillies	10.00
	Los Angeles Dodgers	10.00
1984	San Diego Padres	10.00
	Chicago Cubs	10.00
1985	St. Louis Cardinals	10.00
	Los Angeles Dodgers	8.00
1986	New York Mets	10.00
	Houston Astros	10.00
1987	St. Louis Cardinals	8.00
	San Francisco Giants	8.00
1988	Los Angeles Dodgers	8.00
	New York Mets	8.00
1989	San Francisco Giants	8.00
	Chicago Cubs	8.00
1990	Cincinnati Reds	8.00
	Pittsburgh Pirates	8.00
1991	Atlanta Braves	10.00
	Pittsburgh Pirates	8.00
1992	Atlanta Braves	10.00
	Pittsburgh Pirates	8.00

WORLD SERIES PROGRAMS

Year	Team	League	Value
1903	Boston	American	30,000.00
	Pittsburgh	National	35,000.00
1904	No series		
1905	New York	National	17,500.00
	Philadelphia	American	16,000.00
1906	Chicago	National	15,000.00
	Chicago	American	16,000.00
1907	Chicago	National	14,000.00
	Detroit	American	14,000.00
1908	Chicago	National	12,500.00
	Detroit	American	12,000.00
1909	Detroit	American	10,000.00
	Pittsburgh	National	12,000.00
1910	Chicago	National	7,500.00
	Philadelphia	American	6,500.00
1911	New York	National	5,000.00
	Philadelphia	American	6,000.00
1912	Boston	American	4,500.00
	New York	National	5,000.00
1913	New York	National	4,000.00
	Philadelphia	American	4,500.00
1914	Boston	National	3,000.00
	Philadelphia	American	3,000.00
1915	Boston	American	3,500.00
	Philadelphia	National	3,500.00
1916	Boston	American	4,500.00

Year	Team	League	Price
	Brooklyn	National	6,000.00
1917	Chicago	American	4,500.00
	New York	National	3,000.00
1918	Boston	American	5,500.00
	Chicago	National	5,000.00
1919	Chicago	American	7,000.00
	Cincinnati	National	6,000.00
1920	Brooklyn	National	4,500.00
	Cleveland	American	4,000.00
1921	New York	Both	3,250.00
1922	New York	Both	2,750.00
1923	New York	American	4,000.00
1923	New York	National	3,000.00
1924	New York	National	3,000.00
	Washington	American	1,000.00
1925	Pittsburgh	National	4,000.00
	Washington	American	1,000.00
1926	New York	American	1,500.00
	St. Louis	National	1,750.00
1927	New York	American	3,250.00
	Pittsburgh	National	4,000.00
1928	New York	American	2,750.00
	St. Louis	National	1,500.00
1929	Chicago	National	750.00
	Philadelphia	American	1,250.00
1930	Philadelphia	American	750.00
	St. Louis	National	600.00
1931	Philadelphia	American	500.00
	St. Louis	National	500.00
1932	Chicago	National	600.00
	New York	American	1,250.00

1913 World Series program

Year	Team	League	Price
1933	New York	National	850.00
	Washington	American	650.00
1934	Detroit	American	350.00
	St. Louis	National	450.00
1935	Chicago	National	450.00
	Detroit	American	600.00
1936	New York	National	375.00
	New York	American	375.00
1937	New York	National	375.00
	New York	American	375.00
1938	Chicago	National	425.00
	New York	American	425.00
1939	Cincinnati	National	350.00
	New York	American	350.00
1940	Cincinnati	National	300.00
	Detroit	American	325.00
1941	Brooklyn	National	350.00
	New York	American	300.00
1942	New York	American	275.00
	St. Louis	National	250.00
1943	New York	American	200.00
	St. Louis	National	225.00
1944	St. Louis	American	250.00
	St. Louis	National	200.00
1945	Chicago	National	150.00
	Detroit	American	250.00

Year	Team	League	Price
1946	Boston	American	175.00
	St. Louis	National	175.00
1947	Brooklyn	National	250.00
	New York	American	225.00
1948	Boston	National	175.00
	Cleveland	American	75.00
1949	Brooklyn	National	225.00
	New York	American	200.00
1950	New York	American	150.00
	Philadelphia	National	125.00
1951	New York	American	200.00
	New York	National	150.00
1952	Brooklyn	National	200.00
	New York	American	150.00
1953	Brooklyn	National	150.00
	New York	American	125.00
1954	Cleveland	American	125.00
	New York	National	150.00
1955	Brooklyn	National	200.00
	New York	American	150.00
1956	Brooklyn	National	200.00
	New York	American	150.00
1957	Milwaukee	National	125.00
	New York	American	100.00

1958 World Series program

Year	Team	League	Price
1958	Milwaukee	National	125.00
	New York	American	75.00
1959	Chicago	American	150.00
	Los Angeles	National	100.00
1960	New York	American	75.00
	Pittsburgh	National	100.00
1961	Cincinnati	National	100.00
	New York	American	125.00
1962	New York	American	75.00
	San Francisco	National	125.00
1963	Los Angeles	National	55.00
	New York	American	50.00
1964	New York	American	60.00
	St. Louis	National	100.00
1965	Los Angeles	National	35.00
	Minnesota	American	50.00
1966	Baltimore	American	100.00
	Los Angeles	National	40.00
1967	Boston	American	100.00
	St. Louis	National	100.00
1968	Detroit	American	125.00
	St. Louis	National	90.00
1969	Baltimore	American	65.00
	New York	National	125.00
1970	Baltimore	American	30.00
	Cincinnati	National	40.00
1971	Baltimore	American	40.00
	Pittsburgh	National	35.00
1972	Cincinnati	National	35.00
	Oakland	American	45.00
1973	New York	National	20.00
	Oakland	American	50.00

Year	Team	League	Value
1974	Los Angeles	National	35.00
	Oakland	American	35.00
1975	Boston	American	25.00
	Cincinnati	National	25.00
1976	Cincinnati	National	20.00
	New York	American	20.00
1977	Los Angeles	National	15.00
	New York	American	15.00
1978	Los Angeles	National	15.00
	New York	American	15.00
1979	Baltimore	American	15.00
	Pittsburgh	National	20.00
1980	Kansas City	American	15.00
	Philadelphia	National	15.00
1981	Los Angeles	National	12.00
	New York	American	12.00
1982	Milwaukee	American	15.00
	St. Louis	National	15.00
1983	Baltimore	American	12.00
	Philadelphia	National	12.00
1984	Detroit	American	10.00
	San Diego	National	10.00
1985	Kansas City	American	10.00
	St. Louis	National	10.00
1986	Boston	American	12.00
	New York	National	12.00
1987	Minnesota	American	10.00
	St. Louis	National	10.00
1988	Los Angeles	National	10.00
	Oakland	American	10.00
1989	Oakland	American	10.00
	San Francisco	National	10.00

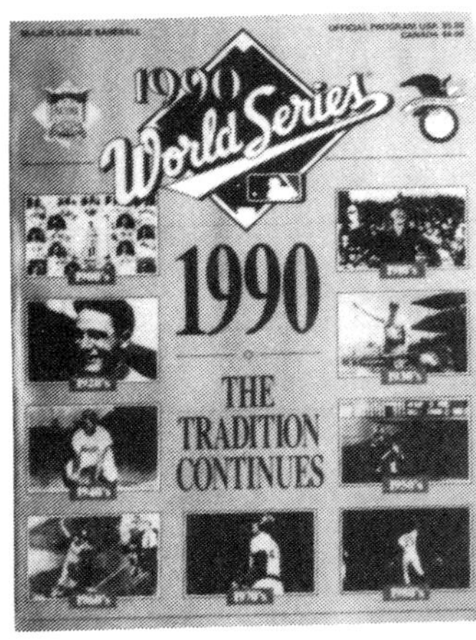

1990 World Series program

Year	Team	League	Value
1990	Cincinnati	National	10.00
	Oakland	American	10.00
1991	Atlanta	National	10.00
	Minnesota	American	10.00
1992	Atlanta	National	10.00
	Toronto	American	10.00

BASKETBALL PROGRAMS

NBA ALL-STAR GAME

Year	Score	Site	Value
1951	East 111, West 94	Boston	150.00
1952	East 108, West 91	Boston	150.00
1953	West 79, East 75	Fort Wayne	150.00
1954	East 98, West 93 OT	New York	125.00
1955	East 100, West 91	New York	100.00
1956	West 108, East 94	Rochester	100.00
1957	East 109, West 97	Boston	75.00
1958	East 130, West 118	St. Louis	60.00
1959	West 124, East 108	Detroit	50.00
1960	East 125, West 115	Philadelphia	60.00
1961	West 153, East 131	Syracuse	50.00
1962	West 150, East 130	St. Louis	40.00
1963	East 115, West 108	Los Angeles	40.00
1964	East 111, West 107	Boston	30.00
1965	East 124, West 123	St. Louis	30.00
1966	East 137, West 94	Cincinnati	30.00
1967	West 135, East 120	San Francisco	25.00
1968	East 144, West 124	New York	25.00
1969	East 123, West 112	Baltimore	30.00
1970	East 142, West 135	Philadelphia	20.00
1971	West 108, East 107	San Diego	20.00
1972	West 112, East 110	Los Angeles	15.00
1973	East 104, West 84	Chicago	15.00
1974	West 134, East 123	Seattle	15.00
1975	East 108, West 102	Phoenix	15.00
1976	East 123, West 109	Philadelphia	15.00
1977	West 125, East 124	Milwaukee	15.00
1978	East 133, West 125	Atlanta	12.00
1979	West 134, East 129	Detroit	12.00
1980	E. 144, W. 135 OT	Washington	20.00
1981	East 123, West 120	Cleveland	12.00
1982	East 120, West 118	New Jersey	12.00
1983	East 132, West 123	Los Angeles	12.00
1984	E. 154, W. 145 OT	Denver	12.00
1985	West 140, East 129	Indiana	10.00
1986	East 139, West 132	Dallas	10.00
1987	W. 154, E. 149 OT	Seattle	10.00
1988	East 138, West 133	Chicago	10.00
1989	West 143, East 134	Houston	10.00
1990	East 130, West 113	Miami	10.00
1991	East 116, West 114	Charlotte	10.00
1992	West 153, East 113	Orlando	10.00

NCAA DIVISION I FINAL FOUR BASKETBALL TOURNAMENT

Year	Champion	Site	Value
1952	Kansas	Seattle	250.00
1953	Indiana	Kansas City	150.00
1954	La Salle	Kansas City	125.00
1955	San Francisco	Kansas City	150.00
1956	San Francisco	Evanston, IL	150.00
1957	North Carolina	Kansas City	125.00
1958	Kentucky	Louisville	100.00
1959	California	Louisville	90.00
1960	Ohio St.	San Francisco	75.00
1961	Cincinnati	Kansas City	75.00
1962	Cincinnati	Louisville	75.00
1963	Loyola (IL)	Louisville	65.00
1964	UCLA	Kansas City	80.00
1965	UCLA	Portland	80.00
1966	Texas Western	College Park, MD	50.00
1967	UCLA	Louisville	50.00
1968	UCLA	Los Angeles	40.00
1969	UCLA	Louisville	40.00
1970	UCLA	College Park, MD	40.00
1971	UCLA	Houston	25.00
1972	UCLA	Los Angeles	25.00
1973	UCLA	St. Louis	25.00
1974	N.C. State	Greensboro, NC	20.00
1975	UCLA	San Diego	20.00
1976	Indiana	Philadelphia	20.00
1977	Marquette	Atlanta	15.00
1978	Kentucky	St. Louis	15.00
1979	Michigan St.	Salt Lake City	25.00
1980	Louisville	Indianapolis	10.00
1981	Indiana	Philadelphia	10.00
1982	North Carolina	New Orleans	10.00
1983	N.C. State	Albuquerque	10.00
1984	Georgetown	Seattle	10.00
1985	Villanova	Lexington, KY	10.00
1986	Louisville	Dallas	10.00
1987	Indiana	New Orleans	10.00
1988	Kansas	Kansas City	10.00
1989	Michigan	Seattle	10.00
1990	UNLV	Denver	10.00
1991	Duke	Indianapolis	10.00
1992	Duke	Minneapolis	10.00

NATIONAL JUNIOR COLLEGE BASKETBALL TOURNAMENT

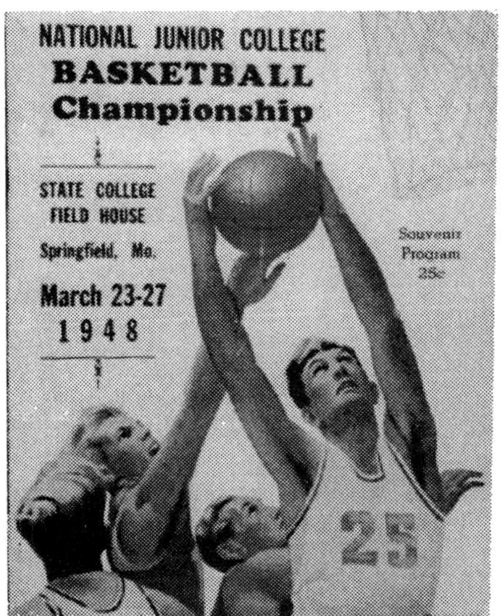

1948 National Jr. College Basketball Tournament program

Year	Notable participants	Value
1948		150.00
1949	Jim Loscutoff	100.00
1950		80.00
1951	Maury John (coach)	80.00
1952	Dick Garmaker, Cotton Fitzsimmons	80.00
1953	Ray Shumann, Cotton Fitzsimmons	80.00
1954	Billy Tubbs	75.00
1955	Maury John (coach)	60.00
1956	Jack Hartman (coach), Gene Keady (player)	40.00
1957	Maury John (coach)	35.00
1958	Ted Owens (coach)	35.00
1959	Ted Owens (coach)	35.00
1960	Ted Owens (coach)	30.00
1961	Dick Motta (coach)	25.00
1962	Dick Motta, Jack Hartman, Cotton Fitzsimmons Larry Mantle (Mickey's brother)	25.00
1963	Cotton Fitzsimmons, Larry Mantle	25.00
1964	Mel Daniels	25.00
1965	Cotton Fitzsimmons	20.00
1966	Cotton Fitzsimmons	15.00
1967	Cotton Fitzsimmons, Oliver Taylor	15.00
1968	Artis Gilmore, Fred Brown, Oliver Taylor	15.00
1969	Artis Gilmore, Fred Brown, Bob Nash	15.00
1970	Bob McAdoo, Slick Watts, Ron Behagen	15.00
1971	Ron Behagen, Benny Clyde	10.00
1972	Ricky Sobers, Foots Walker	10.00
1973	Ricky Sobers, Bob Elmore, Lionel Hollins	8.00
1974	Rickey Green, Ray Williams	8.00
1975	Rickey Green, Ray Williams	8.00
1976	Vinnie Johnson	6.00
1977	Alton Lister, Johnny High	6.00
1978		6.00
1979	Paul Pressey, James "Buster" Douglas	6.00
1980	Paul Pressey, Darrell Walker	5.00
1981		5.00
1982	Gerald Wilkins, Spud Webb	5.00
1983	Spud Webb, Armon Gilliam	5.00
1984	Nate McMillan, Walter Berry	5.00
1985	Mitch Richmond	5.00
1986	Mitch Richmond, Mookie Blaylock	5.00
1987	Mookie Blaylock	5.00
1988		8.00
1989		4.00
1990	Latrell Sprewell	4.00
1991		4.00
1992		4.00

BOXING PROGRAMS

HEAVYWEIGHT BOUTS

Date	Bout	Value
07/04/19	J. Dempsey def. J. Willard	1,500.00
09/06/20	J. Dempsey def. B. Miske	1,250.00
12/14/20	J. Dempsey def. B. Brennan	1,250.00
07/02/21	J. Dempsey def. G. Carpentier	1,200.00
07/04/23	J. Dempsey def. T. Gibbons	1,100.00
09/14/23	J. Dempsey def. L. Firpo	1,000.00
09/23/26	G. Tunney def. J. Dempsey	1,500.00
07/21/27	J. Dempsey def. J. Sharkey	1,000.00
09/22/27	G. Tunney def. J. Dempsey	1,500.00
07/26/28	G. Tunney def. T. Heeney	350.00
06/12/30	M. Schmeling def. J. Sharkey	400.00
07/03/31	M. Schmeling def. Y. Stribling	350.00
06/21/32	J. Sharkey def. M. Schmeling	350.00
09/26/32	M. Schmeling def. Walker	375.00
06/25/35	J. Louis def. P. Carnera	500.00
09/24/35	J. Louis def. M. Baer	475.00
06/19/36	M. Schmeling def. J. Louis	425.00
08/18/36	J. Louis def. J. Sharkey	400.00
06/22/37	J. Louis def. J. Braddock	500.00
06/22/38	J. Louis def. M. Schmeling	425.00
07/13/39	B. Conn def. J. Bettina	275.00
09/25/39	B. Conn def. J. Bettina	250.00
11/17/39	B. Conn def. G. Lesnevich	250.00
06/05/40	B. Conn def. G. Lesnevich	250.00
05/23/41	J. Louis def. B. Baer	375.00
06/18/41	J. Louis def. B. Conn	375.00
01/09/42	J. Louis def. B. Baer	350.00
06/19/46	J. Louis def. B. Conn	300.00
12/05/47	J. Louis def. J. Walcott	265.00
06/25/48	J. Louis def. J. Walcott	250.00
06/22/49	E. Charles def. J. Walcott	75.00
09/27/50	E. Charles def. J. Louis	100.00
03/07/51	E. Charles def. J. Walcott	50.00
07/18/51	J. Walcott def. E. Charles	50.00
10/26/51	R. Marciano def. J. Louis	250.00
06/05/52	J. Walcott def. E. Charles	50.00
09/23/52	R. Marciano def. J. Walcott	200.00
05/15/53	R. Marciano def. J. Walcott	100.00
06/17/54	R. Marciano def. E. Charles	100.00
09/17/54	R. Marciano def. E. Charles	100.00
05/16/55	R. Marciano def. D. Cockell	100.00
09/21/55	R. Marciano def. A. Moore	100.00
11/30/56	F. Patterson def. A. Moore	100.00
06/26/59	I. Johansson def. F. Patterson	80.00
06/20/60	F. Patterson def. I. Johansson	75.00
03/13/61	F. Patterson def. I. Johansson	75.00
09/25/62	S. Liston def. F. Patterson	80.00
11/15/62	C. Clay def. A. Moore	250.00
07/22/63	S. Liston def. F. Patterson	110.00
02/25/64	C. Clay def. S. Liston	200.00
05/25/65	M. Ali def. S. Liston	100.00
11/22/65	M. Ali def. F. Patterson	75.00
03/04/68	J. Frazier def. B. Mathis	35.00
11/28/70	J. Frazier def. B. Foster	50.00
03/08/71	J. Frazier def. M. Ali	75.00
09/20/72	M. Ali def. F. Patterson	65.00
11/21/72	M. Ali def. B. Foster	50.00
01/22/73	G. Foreman def. J. Frazier	65.00
03/31/73	K. Norton def. M. Ali	60.00
09/01/73	G. Foreman def. J. Roman	40.00
09/10/73	M. Ali def. K. Norton	50.00
01/28/74	M. Ali def. J. Frazier	65.00
03/26/74	G. Foreman def. K. Norton	50.00
10/30/74	M. Ali def. G. Foreman	45.00
10/01/75	M. Ali def. J. Frazier	50.00
06/15/76	G. Foreman def. J. Frazier	40.00
09/28/76	M. Ali def. K. Norton	35.00
09/29/77	M. Ali def. E. Shavers	45.00
02/15/78	L. Spinks def. M. Ali	45.00
06/09/78	L. Holmes def. K. Norton	20.00
09/15/78	M. Ali def. L. Spinks	40.00
10/02/80	L. Holmes def. M. Ali	30.00
06/12/81	L. Holmes def. L. Spinks	15.00

06/11/82 L. Holmes def. G. Cooney 15.00
05/20/83 L. Holmes def. T. Witherspoon 25.00
09/21/85 M. Spinks def. L. Holmes 15.00
04/19/86 M. Spinks def. L. Holmes 10.00
11/22/86 M. Tyson def. T. Berbick 45.00
03/07/87 M. Tyson def. Bonecrusher Smith 30.00
05/30/87 M. Tyson def. P. Thomas 25.00
05/30/87 T. Tucker def. B. Douglas 25.00
08/01/87 M. Tyson def. T. Tucker 30.00
10/16/87 M. Tyson def. T. Biggs 20.00
01/22/88 M. Tyson def. L. Holmes 25.00
03/20/88 M. Tyson def. T. Tubbs 25.00

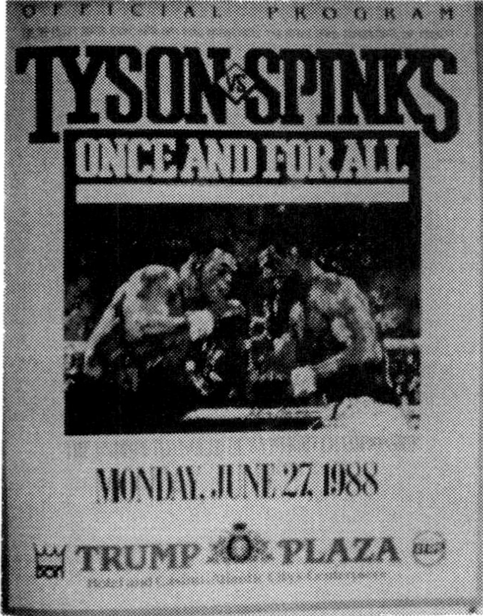

June 27, 1988: Mike Tyson vs. Michael Spinks

06/27/88 M. Tyson def. M. Spinks 25.00
02/25/89 M. Tyson def. F. Bruno 40.00
07/21/89 M. Tyson def. C. Williams 15.00
02/10/90 B. Douglas def. M. Tyson 25.00
10/25/90 E. Holyfield def. B. Douglas 20.00
03/18/91 M. Tyson def. R. Ruddock 20.00
04/19/91 E. Holyfield def. G. Foreman 15.00
06/28/91 M. Tyson def. R. Ruddock 15.00
10/18/91 R. Mercer def. T. Morrison 8.00
11/23/91 E. Holyfield def. B. Cooper 8.00
02/07/92 L. Holmes def. R. Mercer 8.00
05/15/92 M. Moorer def. B. Cooper 8.00
06/19/92 E. Holyfield def. L. Holmes 8.00
07/18/92 R. Bowe def. P. Coetzer 10.00
10/31/92 L. Lewis def. R. Ruddock 10.00
11/13/92 R. Bowe def. E. Holyfield 10.00

FOOTBALL: COLLEGE BOWL GAMES

ALL-AMERICAN BOWL

Known as Hall-of-Fame Classic from 1977-84
All games played in December

1977 Maryland 17, Minnesota 7 . . . . 15.00
1978 Texas A&M 28, Iowa St. 12 . . . . 10.00
1979 Missouri 24, S. Carolina 14 . . . . 10.00
1980 Arkansas 34, Tulane 15 . . . . 8.00
1981 Mississippi St. 10, Kansas 0 . . . . 8.00
1982 Air Force 36, Vanderbilt 28 . . . . 8.00
1983 W. Virginia 20, Kentucky 16 . . . . 8.00
1984 Kentucky 20, Wisconsin 19 . . . . 8.00
1985 Georgia Tech 17, Mich. St. 14 . . . . 5.00
1986 Florida St. 27, Indiana 13 . . . . 5.00
1987 Virginia 22, BYU 16 . . . . 5.00
1988 Florida 14, Illinois 10 . . . . 5.00
1989 Texas Tech 49, Duke 21 . . . . 5.00
1990 N.C. State 31, So. Mississippi 27 . . . . 5.00

ALOHA BOWL

All games played in December

1982 Washington 21, Maryland 20 . . . . 10.00
1983 Penn St. 13, Washington 10 . . . . 8.00
1984 SMU 27, Notre Dame 20 . . . . 8.00
1985 Alabama 24, USC 3 . . . . 8.00
1986 Arizona 30, N. Carolina 21 . . . . 5.00
1987 UCLA 20, Florida 16 . . . . 5.00
1988 Washington St. 24, Houston 22 . . . . 5.00
1989 Michigan St. 33, Hawaii 13 . . . . 5.00
1990 Syracuse 28, Arizona 0 . . . . 5.00
1991 Georgia Tech 18, Stanford 17 . . . . 5.00

BLOCKBUSTER BOWL

All games played in December

1990 Florida St. 24, Penn St. 17 . . . . 8.00
1991 Alabama 30, Colorado 25 . . . . 5.00

BLUEBONNET BOWL

All games played in December

1959 Bluebonnet Bowl program

1959 Clemson 23, TCU 7 . . . . 45.00
1960 Alabama 3, Texas 3 . . . . 25.00
1961 Kansas 33, Rice 7 . . . . 20.00
1962 Missouri 14, Georgia Tech 10 . . . . 15.00
1963 Baylor 14, LSU 7 . . . . 15.00
1964 Tulsa 14, Mississippi 7 . . . . 15.00
1965 Tennessee 27, Tulsa 6 . . . . 15.00
1966 Texas 19, Mississippi 0 . . . . 15.00
1967 Colorado 31, Miami, FL 21 . . . . 15.00
1968 SMU 28, Oklahoma 27 . . . . 12.00
1969 Houston 36, Auburn 7 . . . . 12.00
1970 Alabama 24, Oklahoma 24 . . . . 12.00
1971 Colorado 29, Houston 17 . . . . 12.00
1972 Tennessee 24, LSU 17 . . . . 12.00
1973 Houston 47, Tulane 7 . . . . 10.00
1974 Houston 31, N.C. State 31 . . . . 10.00
1975 Texas 38, Colorado 21 . . . . 10.00
1976 Nebraska 27, Texas Tech 24 . . . . 10.00
1977 USC 47, Texas A&M 28 . . . . 10.00
1978 Stanford 25, Georgia 22 . . . . 10.00

Year	Game	Price
1979	Purdue 27, Tennessee 22	8.00
1980	N. Carolina 16, Texas 7	8.00
1981	Michigan 33, UCLA 14	8.00
1982	Arkansas 28, Florida 24	8.00
1983	Okahoma St. 24, Baylor 14	8.00
1984	W. Virginia 31, TCU 14	8.00
1985	Air Force 24, Texas 16	5.00
1986	Baylor 21, Colorado 9	5.00
1987	Texas 32, Pittsburgh 27	5.00

CALIFORNIA BOWL

All games played in December

Year	Game	Price
1981	Toledo 27, San Jose St. 25	10.00
1982	Fresno St. 29, Bowling Green 28	8.00
1983	N. Illinois 20, Cal St. Fullerton 13	8.00
1984	UNLV 30, Toledo 13	8.00
1985	Fresno St. 51, Bowling Green 7	8.00
1986	San Jose St. 37, Miami, OH 7	5.00
1987	E. Michigan 30, San Jose St. 27	5.00
1988	Fresno St. 35, W. Michigan 30	5.00
1989	Fresno St. 27, Ball St. 6	5.00
1990	San Jose St. 48, Cent. Michigan 24	5.00
1991	Bowling Green 28, Fresno St. 21	5.00

COPPER BOWL

All games played in December

Year	Game	Price
1989	Arizona 17, N.C. State 10	8.00
1990	California 17, Wyoming 15	5.00
1991	Indiana 24, Baylor 0	5.00

COTTON BOWL

All games played in January, except where * indicated, which is a December game

Year	Game	Price
1937	TCU 16, Marquette 6	250.00
1938	Rice 28, Colorado 14	150.00
1939	St. Mary's 20, Texas Tech 13	150.00
1940	Clemson 6, Boston College 3	100.00
1941	Texas A&M 13, Fordham 12	100.00
1942	Alabama 29, Texas A&M 21	75.00
1943	Texas 14, Georgia Tech 7	75.00
1944	Randolph Field 7, Texas 7	75.00
1945	Oklahoma A&M 34, TCU 0	65.00
1946	Texas 40, Missouri 27	65.00
1947	Arkansas 0, LSU 0	65.00
1948	Penn St. 13, SMU 13	50.00
1949	SMU 21, Oregon 13	50.00
1950	Rice 27, N. Carolina 13	50.00
1951	Tennessee 20, Texas 14	40.00
1952	Kentucky 20, TCU 7	40.00
1953	Texas 16, Tennessee 0	40.00
1954	Rice 28, Alabama 6	30.00
1955	Georgia Tech 14, Arkansas 6	25.00
1956	Mississippi 14, TCU 13	25.00
1957	TCU 28, Syracuse 17	25.00
1958	Navy 20, Rice 7	25.00
1959	Air Force 0, TCU 0	25.00
1960	Syracuse 23, Texas 14	20.00
1961	Duke 7, Arkansas 6	20.00
1962	Texas 12, Mississippi 7	20.00
1963	LSU 13, Texas 0	20.00
1964	Texas 28, Navy 6	20.00
1965	Arkansas 10, Nebraska 7	15.00
1966	LSU 14, Arkansas 7	15.00
*1966	Georgia 24, SMU 9	15.00
1968	Texas A&M 20, Alabama 16	15.00
1969	Texas 36, Tennessee 13	15.00
1970	Texas 21, Notre Dame 17	15.00
1971	Notre Dame 24, Texas 11	12.00
1972	Penn St. 30, Texas 6	12.00
1973	Texas 17, Alabama 13	10.00
1974	Nebraska 19, Texas 3	10.00
1975	Penn St. 41, Baylor 20	10.00
1976	Arkansas 31, Georgia 10	10.00
1977	Houston 30, Maryland 21	8.00
1978	Notre Dame 38, Texas 10	10.00
1979	Notre Dame 35, Houston 34	10.00
1980	Houston 17, Nebraska 14	8.00
1981	Alabama 30, Baylor 2	8.00
1982	Texas 14, Alabama 12	8.00
1983	SMU 7, Pittsburgh 3	8.00
1984	Georgia 10, Texas 9	8.00
1985	Boston College 45, Houston 28	6.00
1986	Texas A&M 36, Auburn 16	5.00
1987	Ohio St. 28, Texas A&M 12	5.00
1988	Texas A&M 35, Notre Dame 10	8.00
1989	UCLA 17, Arkansas 3	5.00
1990	Tennessee 31, Arkansas 27	5.00
1991	Miami, FL 46, Texas 3	6.00
1992	Florida St. 10, Texas A&M 2	5.00

FIESTA BOWL

All games played in January, except where * indicated, which are December games

Year	Game	Price
*1971	Arizona St. 45, Florida St. 38	20.00
*1972	Arizona St. 49, Missouri 35	15.00
*1973	Arizona St. 28, Pittsburgh 7	15.00
*1974	Oklahoma St. 16, BYU 6	10.00
*1975	Arizona St. 17, Nebraska 14	10.00
*1976	Oklahoma 41, Wyoming 7	10.00
*1977	Penn St. 42, Arizona St. 30	10.00
*1978	Arkansas 10, UCLA 10	10.00
*1979	Pittsburgh 16, Arizona 10	8.00
*1980	Penn St. 31, Ohio St. 19	8.00
1982	Penn St. 26, USC 10	8.00
1983	Arizona St. 32, Oklahoma 21	8.00
1984	Ohio St. 28, Pittsburgh 23	5.00
1985	UCLA 39, Miami, FL 37	6.00
1986	Michigan 27, Nebraska 23	5.00
1987	Penn St. 14, Miami, FL 10	5.00
1988	Florida St. 31, Nebraska 28	5.00
1989	Notre Dame 34, W. Virginia 21	6.00
1990	Florida St. 41, Nebraska 17	5.00
1991	Louisville 34, Alabama 7	5.00
1992	Penn St. 42, Tennessee 17	5.00

FLORIDA CITRUS BOWL

Known as Tangerine Bowl from 1947-82
All games played in January except where * indicated, which are December games

Year	Game	Price
1947	Catawba 31, Maryville 6	50.00
1948	Catawba 7, Marshall 0	40.00
1949	Murray St. 21, S. Ross St. 21	40.00

1962 Cotton Bowl program

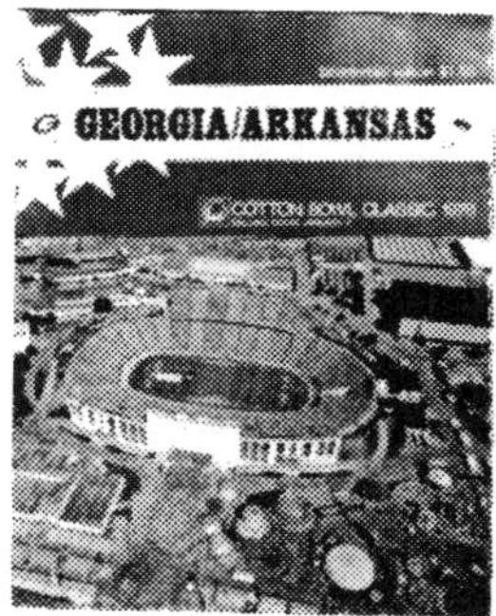

1976 Cotton Bowl program

1971 Fiesta Bowl program

1950	St. Vincent 7, Emory & Henry 6	40.00
1951	M. Harvey 35, Emory & Henry 14	35.00
1952	Stetson 35, Arkansas St. 20	35.00
1953	E. Texas St. 33, Tenn. Tech 0	35.00
1954	Arkansas St. 7, E. Texas St. 7	30.00
1955	Nebraska-Omaha 7, E. Kentucky 6	30.00
1956	Juniata 6, Missouri Valley 6	30.00
1957	W. Texas St. 20, So. Miss 13	25.00
1958	E. Texas St. 10, So. Miss 9	25.00
*1958	E. Texas St. 26, Miss. Valley 7	25.00
1960	Mid. Tenn. St. 21, Presbyterian 12	20.00
*1960	Citadel 27, Tennessee Tech 0	20.00
*1961	Lamar 21, Mid. Tenn. St. 14	15.00
*1962	Houston 49, Miami, OH 21	15.00
*1963	W. Kentucky 27, Coast Guard 0	15.00
*1964	E. Carolina 14, Mass. 13	15.00
*1965	E. Carolina 31, Maine 0	15.00
*1966	Morgan St. 14, Westchester 6	15.00
*1967	Tenn.-Martin 25, Westchester 8	15.00
*1968	Richmond 49, Ohio U. 42	15.00
*1969	Toledo 56, Davidson 33	10.00
*1970	Toledo 40, William & Mary 12	10.00
*1971	Toledo 28, Richmond 3	8.00
*1972	Tampa 21, Kent St. 18	8.00
*1973	Miami, OH 16, Florida 7	8.00
*1974	Miami, OH 21, Georgia 10	8.00
*1975	Miami, OH 20, S. Carolina 7	8.00
*1976	Oklahoma 49, BYU 21	10.00
*1977	Florida St. 40, Texas Tech 17	10.00
*1978	N.C. State 30, Pittsburgh 17	8.00
*1979	LSU 34, Wake Forest 10	8.00
*1980	Florida 35, Maryland 20	8.00
*1981	Missouri 19, So. Mississippi 17	8.00
*1982	Auburn 33, Boston College 26	8.00
*1983	Tennessee 30, Maryland 23	8.00
*1984	Florida St. 17, Georgia 17	8.00
*1985	Ohio St. 10, BYU 7	5.00
1987	Auburn 16, USC 7	5.00
1988	Clemson 35, Penn St. 10	5.00
1989	Clemson 13, Oklahoma 6	5.00
1990	Illinois 31, Virginia 21	5.00
1991	Georgia Tech 45, Nebraska 21	5.00
1992	California 37, Clemson 13	5.00

FREEDOM BOWL

All games played in December

1984	Iowa 55, Texas 17	10.00
1985	Washington 20, Colorado 17	5.00
1986	UCLA 31, BYU 10	5.00
1987	Arizona St. 33, Air Force 28	5.00
1988	BYU 20, Colorado 17	5.00
1989	Washington 34, Florida 7	5.00
1990	Colorado St. 32, Oregon 31	5.00
1991	Tulsa 28, San Diego St. 17	5.00

GATOR BOWL

All games played in January except where * indicated, which are December games

1946	Wake Forest 26, S.Carolina 14	100.00
1947	Oklahoma 34, N.C. State 13	75.00
1948	Georgia 20, Maryland 20	50.00
1949	Clemson 24, Missouri 23	50.00
1950	Maryland 20, Missouri 7	40.00
1951	Wyoming 20, Washington & Lee 7	40.00
1952	Miami, FL 14, Clemson 0	40.00
1953	Florida 14, Tulsa 13	35.00
1954	Texas Tech 35, Auburn 13	30.00
*1954	Auburn 33, Baylor 13	30.00
*1955	Vanderbilt 25, Auburn 13	25.00
*1956	Georgia Tech 21, Pittsburgh 14	25.00
*1957	Tennessee 3, Texas A&M 0	20.00
*1958	Mississippi 7, Florida 3	20.00
1960	Arkansas 14, Georgia Tech 7	20.00
*1960	Florida 13, Baylor 12	20.00
*1961	Penn St. 30, Georgia Tech 15	15.00
*1962	Florida 17, Penn St. 7	15.00
*1963	N. Carolina 35, Air Force 0	15.00
1965	Florida St. 36, Oklahoma 19	15.00
*1965	Georgia Tech 31, Tex. Tech 21	15.00
*1966	Tennessee 18, Syracuse 12	15.00
*1967	Florida St. 17, Penn St. 17	15.00
*1968	Missouri 35, Alabama 10	15.00
*1969	Florida 14, Tennessee 13	10.00
1971	Auburn 35, Mississippi 28	10.00
*1971	Georgia 7, N. Carolina 3	10.00
*1972	Auburn 24, Colorado 3	10.00
*1973	Texas Tech 28, Tenn. 19	10.00
*1974	Auburn 27, Texas 3	10.00
*1975	Maryland 13, Florida 0	10.00
*1976	Notre Dame 20, Penn St. 9	15.00
*1977	Pittsburgh 34, Clemson 3	8.00
*1978	Clemson 17, Ohio St. 15	8.00
*1979	N. Carolina 17, Michigan 15	8.00

1951 Gator Bowl program

*1980	Pittsburgh 37, S. Carolina 9	8.00
*1981	N. Carolina 31, Arkansas 27	8.00
*1982	Florida St. 31, W. Virginia 12	6.00
*1983	Florida 14, Iowa 6	6.00
*1984	Okla. St. 21, S. Carolina 14	6.00
*1985	Florida St. 34, Okla. St. 23	5.00
*1986	Clemson 27, Stanford 21	5.00
*1987	LSU 30, S. Carolina 13	5.00
1989	Georgia 34, Michigan St. 27	5.00
1990	Clemson 27, W. Virginia 7	5.00
1991	Michigan 35, Mississippi 3	5.00
*1991	Oklahoma 48, Virginia 14	5.00

HALL-OF-FAME BOWL

All games played in January, except where * indicated, which is a December game

*1986	Boston College 27, Georgia 24	8.00
1988	Michigan 28, Alabama 24	6.00
1989	Syracuse 23, LSU 10	5.00
1990	Auburn 31, Ohio St. 14	5.00
1991	Clemson 30, Illinois 0	5.00
1992	Syracuse 24, Ohio St. 17	5.00

HOLIDAY BOWL

All games played in December

1978	Navy 23, BYU 16	15.00
1979	Indiana 38, BYU 37	8.00
1980	BYU 46, SMU 45	8.00
1981	BYU 38, Washington St. 36	8.00
1982	Ohio St. 47, BYU 17	6.00
1983	BYU 21, Missouri 17	6.00
1984	BYU 24, Michigan 17	5.00
1985	Arkansas 18, Arizona St. 17	5.00
1986	Iowa 39, San Diego St. 38	5.00
1987	Iowa 20, Wyoming 19	5.00
1988	Oklahoma St. 62, Wyoming 14	5.00
1989	Penn St. 50, BYU 39	5.00
1990	Texas A&M 65, BYU 14	5.00
1991	Iowa 13, BYU 13	5.00

JOHN HANCOCK BOWL

Known as Sun Bowl from 1936-86
All games played in December, except where * indicated, which are January games

Year	Game	Price
*1936	Hardin-Simmons 14, New Mexico St. 14	150.00
*1937	Hardin-Simmons 34, Texas Mines 6	100.00
*1938	W. Virginia 7, Texas Tech 6	75.00
*1939	Utah 26, New Mexico 0	50.00
*1940	Arizona St. 0, Catholic U. 0	50.00
*1941	W. Reserve 26, Arizona St. 13	50.00
*1942	Tulsa 6, Texas Tech 0	50.00
*1943	Air Force 13, Hardin-Simmons 7	50.00
*1944	SW Texas 7, New Mexico 0	50.00
*1945	SW Texas 35, New Mexico 0	45.00
*1946	New Mexico 34, Denver 24	45.00
*1947	Cincinnati 18, Virginia Tech 6	45.00
*1948	Miami, OH 13, Texas Tech 12	45.00
*1949	W. Virginia 21, Texas Mines 12	45.00
*1950	Tex.Western 33, Georgetown 20	40.00
*1951	West Texas 14, Cincinnati 13	40.00
*1952	Texas Tech 25, Pacific 14	40.00
*1953	Pacific 26, So. Mississippi 7	35.00
*1954	Tex. Western 37, So. Miss. 14	35.00
*1955	Tex. Western 47, Florida St. 20	30.00
*1956	Wyoming 21, Texas Tech 14	30.00
*1957	G. Wash. 13, Tex.Western 0	30.00
*1958	Louisville 34, Drake 20	25.00
1958	Wyoming 14, Hard.-Simmons 6	25.00
1959	New Mex. St. 28, N. Texas 6	25.00
1960	New Mex. St. 20, Utah St. 13	25.00
1961	Villanova 17, Wichita 9	20.00
1962	West Texas 15, Ohio U. 14	20.00
1963	Oregon 21, SMU 14	20.00
1964	Georgia 7, Georgia Tech 0	15.00
1965	Texas Western 13, TCU 12	15.00
1966	Wyoming 28, Florida St. 20	15.00
1967	UTEP 14, Mississippi 7	15.00
1968	Auburn 34, Arizona 10	15.00
1969	Nebraska 45, Georgia 6	15.00
1970	Ga. Tech 17, Texas Tech 9	10.00
1971	LSU 33, Iowa St. 15	10.00
1972	N. Carolina 32, Texas Tech 28	10.00
1973	Missouri 34, Auburn 17	10.00
1974	Miss. St. 26, N. Carolina 24	8.00
1975	Pittsburgh 33, Kansas 19	8.00
*1977	Texas A&M 37, Florida 14	8.00
1977	Stanford 24, LSU 14	8.00
1978	Texas 42, Maryland 0	8.00
1979	Washington 14, Texas 7	8.00

1980 Sun Bowl program

Year	Game	Price
1980	Nebraska 31, Mississippi St.17	6.00
1981	Oklahoma 40, Houston 14	6.00
1982	N. Carolina 26, Texas 10	5.00
1983	Alabama 28, SMU 7	5.00
1984	Maryland 27, Tennessee 26	5.00
1985	Arizona 13, Georgia 13	5.00
1986	Alabama 28, Washington 6	5.00
1987	Oklahoma St. 35, W. Virginia 33	5.00
1988	Alabama 29, Army 28	5.00
1989	Pittsburgh 31, Texas A&M 28	5.00
1990	Michigan St. 17, USC 16	5.00
1991	UCLA 6, Illinois 3	5.00

INDEPENDENCE BOWL

All games played in December

Year	Game	Price
1976	McNeese St. 20, Tulsa 16	15.00
1977	La. Tech 24, Louisville 14	8.00
1978	E. Carolina 35, La. Tech 13	8.00
1979	Syracuse 31, McNeese St. 7	8.00
1980	So. Miss. 16, McNeese St. 14	6.00
1981	Texas A&M 33, Okla. St. 16	6.00
1982	Wisconsin 14, Kansas St. 3	5.00
1983	Air Force 9, Mississippi 3	5.00
1984	Air Force 23, Va. Tech 7	5.00
1985	Minnesota 20, Clemson 13	5.00
1986	Mississippi 20, Tex. Tech 17	5.00
1987	Washington 24, Tulane 12	5.00
1988	So. Mississippi 38, UTEP 18	5.00
1989	Oregon 27, Tulsa 24	5.00
1990	La. Tech 34, Maryland 34	5.00
1991	Georgia 24, Arkansas 15	5.00

LIBERTY BOWL

All games played in December

Year	Game	Price
1959	Penn St. 7, Alabama 0	75.00
1960	Penn St. 41, Oregon 12	65.00
1961	Syracuse 15, Miami, FL. 14	55.00
1962	Oregon St. 6, Villanova 0	35.00
1963	Mississippi St. 16, N.C. State 12	25.00
1964	Utah 32, W. Virginia 6	20.00
1965	Mississippi 13, Auburn 7	20.00
1966	Miami, FL 14, Va. Tech 7	20.00
1967	N.C. State 14, Georgia 7	15.00
1968	Mississippi 34, Va. Tech 17	15.00
1969	Colorado 47, Alabama 33	15.00
1970	Tulane 17, Colorado 3	10.00
1971	Tennessee 14, Arkansas 13	10.00
1972	Georgia Tech 31, Iowa St. 30	10.00
1973	N.C. State 31, Kansas 18	10.00
1974	Tennessee 7, Maryland 3	10.00
1975	USC 20, Texas A&M 0	8.00
1976	Alabama 36, UCLA 6	8.00
1977	Nebraska 21, N. Carolina 17	8.00
1978	Missouri 20, LSU 15	8.00
1979	Penn St. 9, Tulane 6	8.00
1980	Purdue 28, Missouri 25	6.00
1981	Ohio St. 31, Navy 28	6.00
1982	Alabama 21, Illinois 15	6.00
1983	Notre Dame 19, Boston Col. 18	8.00
1984	Auburn 21, Arkansas 15	5.00
1985	Baylor 21, LSU 7	5.00
1986	Tennessee 21, Minnesota 14	5.00
1987	Georgia 20, Arkansas 17	5.00
1988	Indiana 34, S. Carolina 10	5.00
1989	Mississippi 42, Air Force 29	5.00
1990	Air Force 23, Ohio St. 11	5.00
1991	Air Force 38, Mississippi St. 15	5.00

ORANGE BOWL

All games played in January

Year	Game	Price
1935	Bucknell 26, Miami, FL. 0	500.00
1936	Catholic U. 20, Mississippi 19	250.00
1937	Duquesne 13, Miss. St. 12	150.00
1938	Auburn 6, Michigan St. 0	150.00
1939	Tennessee 17, Oklahoma 0	100.00
1940	Georgia Tech 21, Missouri 7	75.00
1941	Mississippi St. 14, Georgetown 7	75.00
1942	Georgia 40, TCU 26	50.00
1943	Alabama 37, Boston Col. 21	50.00
1944	LSU 19, Texas A&M 14	50.00
1945	Tulsa 26, Georgia Tech 12	45.00
1946	Miami, FL 13, Holy Cross 6	50.00
1947	Rice 8, Tennessee 0	45.00
1948	Georgia Tech 20, Kansas 14	45.00
1949	Texas 41, Georgia 28	40.00
1950	Santa Clara 21, Kentucky 13	30.00
1951	Clemson 15, Miami, FL 14	40.00
1952	Georgia Tech 17, Baylor 14	25.00

1975 Liberty Bowl program

1958 Orange Bowl program

1962 Orange Bowl program

1953	Alabama 61, Syracuse 6	30.00
1954	Oklahoma 7, Maryland 0	30.00
1955	Duke 34, Nebraska 7	30.00
1956	Oklahoma 20, Maryland 6	25.00
1957	Colorado 27, Clemson 21	25.00
1958	Oklahoma 48, Duke 21	25.00
1959	Oklahoma 21, Syracuse 6	25.00
1960	Georgia 14, Missouri 0	20.00
1961	Missouri 21, Navy 14	20.00
1962	LSU 25, Colorado 7	20.00
1963	Alabama 17, Oklahoma 0	20.00
1964	Nebraska 13, Auburn 7	15.00
1965	Texas 21, Alabama 17	15.00
1966	Alabama 39, Nebraska 28	15.00
1967	Florida 27, Georgia Tech 12	15.00
1968	Oklahoma 26, Tennessee 24	15.00
1969	Penn St. 15, Kansas 14	15.00
1970	Penn St. 10, Missouri 3	15.00
1971	Nebraska 17, LSU 12	12.00
1972	Nebraska 38, Alabama 6	12.00
1973	Nebraska 40, Notre Dame 6	15.00
1974	Penn St. 16, LSU 9	10.00
1975	Notre Dame 13, Alabama 11	15.00
1976	Oklahoma 14, Michigan 6	10.00
1977	Ohio St. 27, Colorado 10	10.00
1978	Arkansas 31, Oklahoma 6	10.00
1979	Oklahoma 31, Nebraska 24	10.00
1980	Oklahoma 24, Florida St. 7	10.00
1981	Oklahoma 18, Florida St. 17	10.00
1982	Clemson 22, Nebraska 15	10.00
1983	Nebraska 21, LSU 20	10.00
1984	Miami, FL 31, Nebraska 30	10.00
1985	Washington 28, Oklahoma 17	10.00
1986	Oklahoma 25, Penn St. 10	10.00
1987	Oklahoma 42, Arkansas 8	8.00
1988	Miami, FL 20, Oklahoma 14	10.00
1989	Miami, FL 23, Nebraska 3	10.00
1990	Notre Dame 21, Colorado 6	10.00
1991	Colorado 10, Notre Dame 9	10.00
1992	Miami, FL 22, Nebraska 0	10.00

PEACH BOWL

All games played in December, except where * indicated, which are January games

1968	LSU 31, Florida St. 27	50.00
1969	W. Virginia 14, S. Carolina 3	25.00
1970	Arizona St. 48, N. Carolina 26	15.00
1971	Mississippi 41, Georgia Tech 18	15.00
1972	N.C. State 49, W. Virginia 13	15.00
1973	Georgia 17, Maryland 16	15.00
1974	Texas Tech 6, Vanderbilt 6	10.00
1975	W. Virginia 13, N.C. State 10	10.00
1976	Kentucky 21, N. Carolina 0	10.00
1977	N.C. State 24, Iowa St. 14	10.00
1978	Purdue 41, Georgia Tech 21	10.00
1979	Baylor 24, Clemson 18	8.00
*1981	Miami, FL 20, Virginia Tech 10	10.00
1981	W. Virginia 26, Florida 6	8.00
1982	Iowa 28, Tennessee 22	8.00
1983	Florida St. 28, N. Carolina 3	8.00
1984	Virginia 27, Purdue 24	5.00
1985	Army 31, Illinois 29	5.00
1986	Virginia Tech 25, N.C. State 24	5.00
*1988	Tennessee 27, Indiana 22	5.00
1988	N.C. State 28, Iowa 23	5.00
1989	Syracuse 19, Georgia 18	5.00
1990	Auburn 27, Indiana 23	5.00
*1992	East Carolina 37, N.C. State 34	5.00

ROSE BOWL

All games played in January

1902	Michigan 49, Stanford 0	7,500.00
1916	Washington St. 14, Brown 0	2,000.00
1917	Oregon 14, Penn 0	1,750.00
1918	Mare Island 19, Camp Lewis 7	1,650.00
1919	Great Lakes 17, Mare Island 0	1,500.00
1920	Harvard 7, Oregon 6	1,250.00
1921	California 28, Ohio St. 0	1,250.00
1922	California 0, Wash. & Jeff. 0	1,000.00
1923	USC 14, Penn St. 0	1,250.00
1924	Navy 14, Washington 14	750.00
1925	Notre Dame 27, Stanford 10	1,000.00
1926	Alabama 20, Washington 19	750.00
1927	Alabama 7, Stanford 7	750.00
1928	Stanford 7, Pittsburgh 6	750.00
1929	Georgia Tech 8, California 7	700.00
1930	USC 47, Pittsburgh 14	700.00
1931	Alabama 24, Washington St. 0	700.00
1932	USC 21, Tulane 12	675.00
1933	USC 35, Pittsburgh 0	650.00
1934	Columbia 7, Stanford 0	500.00
1935	Alabama 29, Stanford 13	500.00
1936	Stanford 7, SMU 0	475.00
1937	Pittsburgh 21, Washington 0	450.00
1938	California 13, Alabama 0	400.00
1939	USC 7, Duke 3	300.00
1940	USC 14, Tennessee 0	200.00
1941	Stanford 21, Nebraska 13	225.00
1942	Oregon St. 20, Duke 16 (Durham)	2,000.00
1943	Georgia 9, UCLA 0	225.00
1944	USC 29, Washington 0	200.00
1945	USC 25, Tennessee 0	225.00
1946	Alabama 34, USC 14	150.00
1947	Illinois 45, UCLA 14	125.00
1948	Michigan 49, USC 0	175.00
1949	Northwestern 20, California 14	150.00
1950	Ohio St. 17, California 14	100.00
1951	Michigan 14, California 6	80.00
1952	Illinois 40, Stanford 7	75.00
1953	USC 7, Wisconsin 0	75.00
1954	Michigan St. 28, UCLA 20	65.00
1955	Ohio St. 20, USC 7	65.00
1956	Michigan St. 17, UCLA 14	60.00
1957	Iowa 35, Oregon St. 19	60.00
1958	Ohio St. 10, Oregon 7	50.00
1959	Iowa 38, California 12	50.00
1960	Washington 44, Wisconsin 8	50.00
1961	Washington 17, Minnesota 7	55.00

1938 Rose Bowl program

1955 Rose Bowl program

1964 Rose Bowl program

1962	Minnesota 21, UCLA 3	45.00
1963	USC 42, Wisconsin 37	50.00
1964	Illinois 17, Washington 7	35.00
1965	Michigan 34, Oregon St. 7	30.00
1966	UCLA 14, Michigan St. 12	30.00
1967	Purdue 14, USC 13	25.00
1968	USC 14, Indiana 3	25.00
1969	Ohio St. 27, USC 16	25.00
1970	USC 10, Michigan 3	20.00
1971	Stanford 27, Ohio St. 17	20.00
1972	Stanford 13, Michigan 12	25.00
1973	USC 42, Ohio St. 17	20.00
1974	Ohio St. 42, USC 21	20.00
1975	USC 18, Ohio St. 17	15.00
1976	UCLA 23, Ohio St. 10	15.00
1977	USC 14, Michigan 6	15.00
1978	Washington 27, Michigan 20	15.00
1979	USC 17, Michigan 10	15.00
1980	USC 17, Ohio St. 16	15.00
1981	Michigan 23, Washington 6	10.00
1982	Washington 28, Iowa 0	10.00
1983	UCLA 24, Michigan 14	12.00
1984	UCLA 45, Illinois 9	12.00
1985	USC 20, Ohio St. 17	12.00
1986	UCLA 45, Iowa 28	10.00
1987	Arizona St. 22, Michigan 15	10.00
1988	Michigan St. 20, USC 17	10.00
1989	Michigan 22, USC 14	10.00
1990	USC 17, Michigan 10	10.00
1991	Washington 46, Iowa 34	10.00
1992	Washington 34, Michigan 14	10.00

SUGAR BOWL

All games played in January, except where * indicated, which are December games

1935	Tulane 20, Temple 14	450.00
1936	TCU 3, LSU 2	350.00
1937	Santa Clara 21, LSU 14	250.00
1938	Santa Clara 6, LSU 0	250.00
1939	TCU 15, Carnegie Tech 7	150.00
1940	Texas A&M 14, Tulane 13	125.00
1941	Boston College 19, Tennessee 13	125.00
1942	Fordham 2, Missouri 0	75.00
1943	Tennessee 14, Tulsa 7	60.00
1944	Georgia Tech 20, Tulsa 18	50.00
1945	Duke 29, Alabama 26	50.00
1946	Oklahoma A&M 33, St. Mary's 13	50.00
1947	Georgia 20, N. Carolina 10	40.00
1948	Texas 27, Alabama 7	35.00
1949	Oklahoma 14, N. Carolina 6	35.00
1950	Oklahoma 35, LSU 0	35.00
1951	Kentucky 13, Oklahoma 7	30.00
1952	Maryland 28, Tennessee 13	30.00
1953	Georgia Tech 24, Miss. 7	30.00
1954	Ga. Tech 42, W. Virginia 19	30.00
1955	Navy 21, Mississippi 0	30.00
1956	Georgia Tech 7, Pittsburgh 0	25.00
1957	Baylor 13, Tennessee 7	25.00
1958	Mississippi 39, Texas 7	25.00
1959	LSU 7, Clemson 0	25.00
1960	Mississippi 21, LSU 0	25.00
1961	Mississippi 14, Rice 6	25.00
1962	Alabama 10, Arkansas 3	20.00
1963	Mississippi 17, Arkansas 13	20.00
1964	Alabama 12, Mississippi 7	20.00
1965	LSU 13, Syracuse 10	20.00
1966	Missouri 20, Florida 18	20.00
1967	Alabama 34, Nebraska 7	20.00
1968	LSU 20, Wyoming 13	15.00
1969	Arkansas 16, Georgia 2	15.00
1970	Mississippi 27, Arkansas 22	15.00
1971	Tennessee 34, Air Force 13	15.00
1972	Oklahoma 40, Auburn 22	15.00
*1972	Oklahoma 14, Penn St. 0	15.00
*1973	Notre Dame 24, Alabama 23	15.00
*1974	Nebraska 13, Florida 10	10.00
*1975	Alabama 13, Penn St. 6	10.00
1977	Pittsburgh 27, Georgia 3	10.00
1978	Alabama 35, Ohio St. 6	10.00
1979	Alabama 14, Penn St. 7	10.00

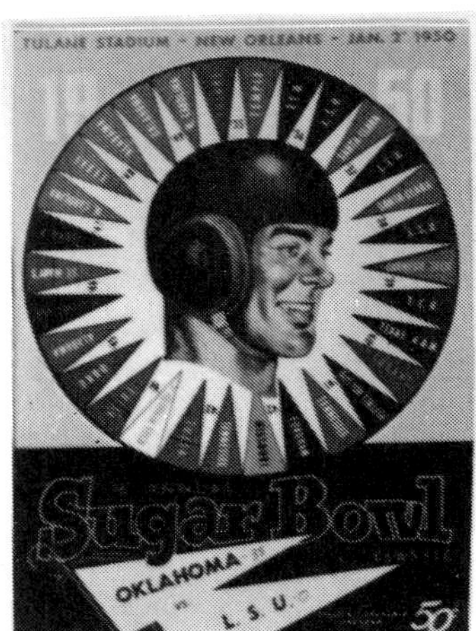

1950 Sugar Bowl program

1980	Alabama 24, Arkansas 9	10.00
1981	Georgia 17, Notre Dame 10	12.00
1982	Pittsburgh 24, Georgia 20	10.00
1983	Penn St. 27, Georgia 23	8.00
1984	Auburn 9, Michigan 7	8.00
1985	Nebraska 28, LSU 10	8.00

1986	Tennessee 35, Miami, FL 7	8.00
1987	Nebraska 30, LSU 15	8.00
1988	Auburn 16, Syracuse 16	8.00
1989	Florida St. 13, Auburn 7	8.00
1990	Miami, FL 33, Alabama 25	8.00
1991	Tennessee 23, Virginia 22	8.00
1992	Notre Dame 39, Florida 28	8.00

SUN BOWL

see John Hancock Bowl

TANGERINE BOWL

see Florida Citrus Bowl

FOOTBALL: PRO PLAYOFF GAMES

Round	Result	Value
	1933	
NFL Champ.	Chi. Bears 23, N.Y. Giants 21	1,500.00
	1934	
NFL Champ.	N.Y. Giants 30, Chi. Bears 13	1,250.00
	1935	
NFL Champ.	Detroit Lions 26, N.Y. Giants 7	900.00
	1936	
NFL Champ.	Green Bay 21, Boston Redskins 6	850.00
	1937	
NFL Champ.	Was. Redskins 28, Chi. Bears 21	800.00
	1938	
NFL Champ.	N.Y. Giants 23, Green Bay 17	750.00
	1939	
NFL Champ.	Green Bay 27, N.Y. Giants 0	750.00
	1940	
NFL Champ.	Chi. Bears 73, Was. Redskins 0	900.00
	1941	
NFL Champ.	Chicago Bears 37, N.Y. Giants 9	650.00
	1942	
NFL Champ.	Was. Redskins 14, Chi. Bears 6	650.00
	1943	
NFL Champ.	Chi. Bears 41, Was. Redskins 21	600.00
	1944	
NFL Champ.	Green Bay 14, N.Y. Giants 7	600.00
	1945	
NFL Champ.	Clev. Rams 15, Was. Redskins 14	500.00
	1946	
NFL Champ.	Chicago Bears 24, N.Y. Giants 14	425.00
	1947	
NFL Champ.	Chi. Cardinals 28, Philadelphia 21	350.00
	1948	
NFL Champ.	Philadelphia 7, Chi. Cardinals 0	350.00
	1949	
NFL Champ.	Philadelphia 14, L.A. Rams 0	375.00
	1950	
NFL Champ.	Clev. Browns 30, L.A. Rams 28	350.00
	1951	
NFL Champ.	L.A. Rams 24, Clev. Browns 17	300.00
	1952	
NFL Champ.	Detroit Lions 17, Clev. Browns 7	300.00
	1953	
NFL Champ.	Detroit Lions 17, Clev. Browns 16	175.00
	1954	
NFL Champ.	Clev. Browns 56, Detroit Lions 10	175.00
	1955	
NFL Champ.	Clev. Browns 38, L.A. Rams 14	250.00
	1956	
NFL Champ.	N.Y. Giants 47, Chicago Bears 7	175.00
	1957	
NFL Champ.	Detroit Lions 59, Clev. Browns 14	125.00
	1958	
NFL Champ.	Baltimore Colts 23, N.Y. Giants 17	125.00
	1959	
NFL Champ.	Baltimore Colts 31, N.Y. Giants 16	125.00
	1960	
NFL Champ.	Philadelphia 17, Green Bay 13	125.00
AFL Champ.	Houston Oilers 24, L.A. Chargers 16	300.00
	1961	
NFL Champ.	Green Bay 37, N.Y. Giants 0	150.00
AFL Champ.	Houston Oilers 10, S.D. Chargers 3	250.00
	1962	
NFL Champ.	Green Bay 16, N.Y. Giants 7	100.00
AFL Champ.	Dallas Cowboys 20, Houston Oilers 17	250.00
	1963	
NFL Champ.	Chicago Bears 14, N.Y. Giants 10	75.00

Super Bowl II program

Super Bowl III program

Super Bowl X program

AFL Champ.	San Diego 51, Boston Patriots 10	125.00

1964

NFL Champ.	Clev. Browns 27, Baltimore Colts 0	65.00
AFL Champ.	Buffalo 20, San Diego 7	75.00

1965

NFL Champ.	Green Bay 23, Clev. Browns 12	60.00
AFL Champ.	Buffalo 23, San Diego 0	60.00

1966

NFL Champ.	Green Bay 34, Dallas 27	55.00
AFL Champ.	Kansas City 31, Buffalo 7	45.00
Super Bowl I	**Green Bay 35, Kan. City 10**	**350.00**

1967

NFL Conf.	Dallas 52, Cleveland 14	30.00
NFL Conf.	Green Bay 28, L.A. Rams 7	30.00
NFL Champ.	Green Bay 21, Dallas 17	35.00
AFL Champ.	Oakland 40, Houston 7	35.00
S. Bowl II	**Green Bay 33, Oakland 14**	**275.00**

1968

NFL Conf.	Cleveland 31, Dallas 20	25.00
NFL Conf.	Baltimore 24, Minnesota 14	25.00
NFL Champ.	Baltimore 34, Cleveland 0	30.00
AFL Champ.	N.Y. Jets 27, Oakland 23	30.00
S. Bowl III	**N.Y. Jets 16, Baltimore 7**	**200.00**

1969

NFL Conf.	Cleveland 38, Dallas 14	20.00
NFL Conf.	Minnesota 23, L.A. Rams 20	20.00
NFL Champ.	Minnesota 27, Cleveland 7	20.00
AFL Div.	Kansas City 13, N.Y. Jets 6	20.00
AFL Div.	Oakland 56, Houston 7	20.00
AFL Champ.	Kansas City 17, Oakland 7	20.00
S. Bowl IV	**Kansas City 23, Minnesota 7**	**200.00**

1970

AFC Div.	Baltimore 17, Cincinnati 0	15.00
AFC Div.	Oakland 21, Miami 14	15.00
AFC Champ.	Baltimore 27, Oakland 17	17.50
NFC Div.	Dallas 5, Detroit 0	15.00
NFC Div.	San Francisco 17, Minn. 14	15.00
NFC Champ	Dallas 17, San Francisco 10	17.50
S. Bowl V	**Baltimore 16, Dallas 13**	**150.00**

1971

AFC Div.	Miami 27, Kan. City 24 (OT)	20.00
AFC Div.	Baltimore 20, Cleveland 3	15.00
AFC Champ.	Miami 21, Baltimore 0	15.00
NFC Div.	Dallas 20, Minnesota 12	15.00
NFC Div.	San Francisco 24, Wash. 20	15.00
NFC Champ	Dallas 14, San Francisco 3	20.00
S. Bowl VI	**Dallas 24, Miami 3**	**125.00**

1972

AFC Div.	Pittsburgh 13, Oakland 7	12.00
AFC Div.	Miami 20, Cleveland 14	12.00
AFC Champ.	Miami 21, Pittsburgh 17	12.00
NFC Div.	Dallas 30, San Fran. 28	15.00
NFC Div.	Washington 16, Green Bay 3	12.00
NFC Champ	Washington 26, Dallas 3	12.00
S. Bowl VII	**Miami 14, Washington 7**	**100.00**

1973

AFC Div.	Oakland 33, Pittsburgh 14	10.00
AFC Div.	Miami 34, Cincinnati 16	12.00
AFC Champ.	Miami 27, Oakland 10	15.00
NFC Div.	Minnesota 27, Washington 20	10.00
NFC Div.	Dallas 27, L.A. Rams 16	12.00
NFC Champ	Minnesota 27, Dallas 10	12.00
S. Bowl VIII	**Miami 24, Minnesota 7**	**100.00**

1974

AFC Div.	Oakland 28, Miami 26	12.00
AFC Div.	Pittsburgh 32, Buffalo 14	12.00
AFC Champ.	Pittsburgh 24, Oakland 13	15.00
NFC Div.	Minnesota 30, St. Louis 14	10.00
NFC Div.	L.A. Rams 19, Washington 10	10.00
NFC Champ	Minnesota 14, L.A. Rams 10	10.00
S. Bowl IX	**Pittsburgh 16, Minnesota 6**	**75.00**

1975

AFC Div.	Pittsburgh 28, Baltimore 10	12.00
AFC Div.	Oakland 31, Cincinnati 28	12.00
AFC Champ.	Pittsburgh 16, Oakland 10	20.00
NFC Div.	L.A. Rams 35, St. Louis 23	10.00
NFC Div.	Dallas 17, Minnesota 14	12.00
NFC Champ	Dallas 37, L.A. Rams 7	12.00
S. Bowl X	**Pittsburgh 21, Dallas 17**	**50.00**

1976

AFC Div.	Oakland 24, New England 21	10.00
AFC Div.	Pittsburgh 40, Baltimore 14	10.00
AFC Champ.	Oakland 24, Pittsburgh 7	15.00
NFC Div.	Minnesota 35, Washington 20	10.00
NFC Div.	L.A. Rams 14, Dallas 12	12.00
NFC Champ	Minnesota 24, L.A. Rams 13	10.00
S. Bowl XI	**Oakland 32, Minnesota 14**	**50.00**

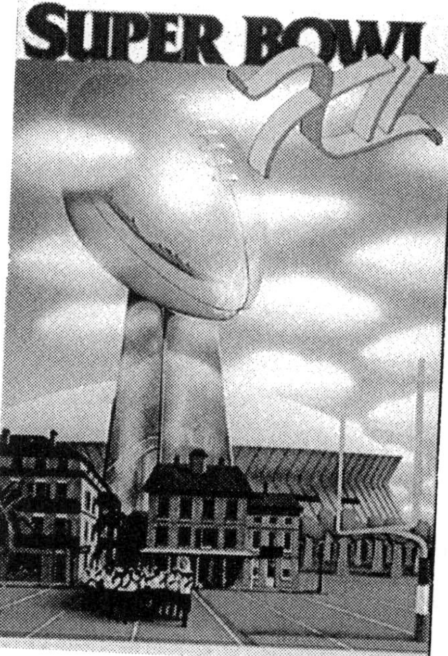

Super Bowl XII program

1977

AFC Div.	Denver 34, Pittsburgh 21	10.00
AFC Div.	Oakland 37, Baltimore 31 (OT)	12.00
AFC Champ.	Denver 20, Oakland 17	10.00
NFC Div.	Dallas 37, Chicago 7	12.00
NFC Div.	Minnesota 14, L.A. Rams 7	10.00
NFC Champ	Dallas 23, Minnesota 6	10.00
S. Bowl XII	**Dallas 27, Denver 10**	**40.00**

1978

AFC W. Card	Houston 17, Miami 9	10.00
AFC Div.	Houston 31, New England 14	10.00
AFC Div.	Pittsburgh 33, Denver 10	12.00
AFC Champ.	Pittsburgh 34, Houston 5	12.00
NFC W. Card	Atlanta 14, Philadelphia 13	10.00
NFC Div.	Dallas 27, Atlanta 20	12.00
NFC Div.	L.A. Rams 34, Minnesota 10	10.00
NFC Champ.	Dallas 28, L.A. Rams 0	12.00
S. Bowl XIII	**Pittsburgh 35, Dallas 31**	**35.00**

1979

AFC W. Card	Houston 13, Denver 7	10.00
AFC Div.	Houston 17, San Deigo 14	10.00
AFC Div.	Pittsburgh 34, Miami 14	12.00
AFC Champ.	Pittsburgh 27, Houston 13	12.00

NFC W. Card	Philadelphia 27, Chicago 17	10.00
NFC Div.	Tampa Bay 24, Phil. 17	10.00
NFC Div.	L.A. Rams 21, Dallas 19	10.00
NFC Champ.	L.A. Rams 9, Tampa Bay 0	10.00
S. Bowl XIV	**Pittsburgh 31, L.A. Rams 19**	**30.00**

1980

AFC W. Card	Oakland 27, Houston 7	10.00
AFC Div.	San Diego 20, Buffalo 14	10.00
AFC Div.	Oakland 14, Cleveland 12	10.00
AFC Champ.	Oakland 34, San Diego 27	10.00
NFC W. Card	Dallas 34, L.A. Rams 13	10.00
NFC Div.	Philadelphia 31, Minnesota 16	10.00
NFC Div.	Dallas 30, Atlanta 27	12.00
NFC Champ.	Philadelphia 20, Dallas 7	12.00
S. Bowl XV	**Oakland 27, Philadelphia 10**	**25.00**

1981

AFC W. Card	Buffalo 31, N.Y. Jets 27	8.00
AFC Div.	San Diego 41, Miami 38 (OT)	10.00
AFC Div.	Cincinnati 28, Buffalo 21	8.00
AFC Champ.	Cincinnati 27, San Diego 7	8.00
NFC W. Card	Giants 27, Philadelphia 21	8.00
NFC Div.	Dallas 38, Tampa Bay 0	10.00
NFC Div.	San Fran. 38, N.Y. Giants 24	12.00
NFC Champ.	San Francisco 28, Dallas 27	12.00
S. Bowl XVI	San Francisco 26, Cinci. 21	20.00

1982

AFC 1st Rd.	L.A. Raiders 27, Cleveland 10	8.00
AFC 1st Rd.	Miami 28, New England 3	8.00
AFC 1st Rd.	N.Y. Jets 44, Cincinnati 17	8.00
AFC 1st Rd.	San Diego 31, Pittsburgh 28	8.00
AFC 2nd Rd.	N.Y. Jets 17, L.A. Raiders 14	8.00
AFC 2nd Rd.	Miami 34, San Diego 13	8.00
AFC Champ.	Miami 14, N.Y. Jets 0	8.00
NFC 1st Rd.	Washington 31, Detroit 7	8.00
NFC 1st Rd.	Dallas 30, Tampa Bay 17	8.00
NFC 1st Rd.	Green Bay 41, St. Louis 16	8.00
NFC 1st Rd.	Minnesota 30, Atlanta 24	8.00
NFC 2nd Rd.	Washington 21, Minnesota 7	8.00
NFC 2nd Rd.	Dallas 37, Green Bay 26	8.00
NFC Champ.	Washington 31, Dallas 17	10.00
S. Bowl XVII	**Washington 27, Miami 17**	**20.00**

1983

AFC W. Card	Seattle 31, Denver 7	6.00
AFC Div.	Seattle 27, Miami 20	6.00
AFC Div.	L.A. Raiders 38, Pittsburgh 10	8.00
AFC Champ.	L.A. Raiders 30, Seattle 14	6.00
NFC W. Card	L.A. Rams 24, Dallas 17	6.00
NFC Div.	San Francsico 24, Detroit 23	8.00
NFC Div.	Washington 51, L.A. Rams 7	6.00
NFC Champ.	Washington 24, San Fran. 21	8.00
S. Bowl XVIII	**L.A. Raiders 38, Washington 9**	**15.00**

1984

AFC W. Card	Seattle 13, L.A. Raiders 7	6.00
AFC Div.	Miami 31, Seattle 10	6.00
AFC Div.	Pittsburgh 24, Denver 17	6.00
AFC Champ.	Miami 45, Pittsburgh 28	8.00
NFC W. Card	N.Y. Giants 16, L.A. Rams 13	6.00
NFC Div.	San Fran. 21, N.Y. Giants 10	8.00
NFC Div.	Chicago 23, Washington 19	6.00
NFC Champ.	San Francisco 23, Chicago 0	8.00
S. Bowl XIX	**San Francisco 38, Miami 16**	**18.00**

1985

AFC W. Card	New England 26, N.Y. Jets 14	6.00
AFC Div.	Miami 24, Cleveland 21	6.00
AFC Div.	New Eng. 27, L.A. Raiders 20	6.00
AFC Champ.	New England 31, Miami 14	6.00
NFC W. Card	N.Y. Giants 17, San Fran. 3	6.00
NFC Div.	L.A. Rams 20, Dallas 0	6.00
NFC Div.	Chicago 21, N.Y. Giants 0	8.00
NFC Champ.	Chicago 24, L.A. Rams 0	8.00
S. Bowl XX	**Chicago 46, New England 10**	**16.00**

1986

AFC W. Card	N.Y. Jets 35, Kansas City 15	5.00
AFC Div.	Cleveland 23, N.Y. Jets 20 (OT)	6.00
AFC Div.	Denver 22, New England 17	5.00
AFC Champ.	Denver 23, Cleveland 20 (OT)	15.00
NFC W.Card	Washington 19, L.A. Rams 7	6.00
NFC Div.	Washington 27, Chicago 13	6.00
NFC Div.	N.Y. Giants 49, San Fran. 3	8.00
NFC Champ.	N.Y. Giants 17, Washington 0	8.00
S. Bowl XXI	**N.Y. Giants 39, Denver 20**	**15.00**

1987

AFC W.Card	Houston 23, Seattle 20 (OT)	6.00
AFC Div.	Cleveland 38, Indianapolis 21	5.00
AFC Div.	Denver 34, Houston 10	5.00
AFC Champ.	Denver 38, Cleveland 33	10.00
NFC W.Card	Minnesota 44, N. Orleans 10	5.00
NFC Div.	Minnesota 36, San Fran. 24	5.00
NFC Div.	Washington 21, Chicago 17	6.00
NFC Champ.	Washington 17, Minnesota 10	6.00
S. Bowl XXII	**Washington 42, Denver 10**	**14.00**

1988

AFC W. Card	Houston 24, Cleveland 23	5.00
AFC Div.	Buffalo 17, Houston 10	5.00
AFC Div.	Cincinnati 21, Seattle 13	5.00
AFC Div.	Cincinnati 21, Buffalo 10	6.00
NFC W. Card	Minnesota 28, L.A. Rams 17	5.00
NFC Div.	San Francisco 34, Minnesota 9	5.00
NFC Div.	Chicago 20, Philadelphia 12	5.00
NFC Champ.	San Francisco 28, Chicago 3	6.00
S. Bowl XXIII	**San Francisco 20, Cinci. 16**	**12.00**

1989

AFC W. Card	Pittsburgh 26, Houston 23	5.00
AFC Div.	Cleveland 34, Buffalo 30	5.00
AFC Div.	Denver 24, Pittsburgh 23	5.00
AFC Champ.	Denver 37, Cleveland 21	8.00
NFC W. Card	L.A. Rams 21, Philadelphia 7	5.00
NFC Div.	L.A. Rams 19, Giants 13 (OT)	5.00

1974 AFC Conf. Championship program

Super Bowl XX program

1987 AFC Conf. Championship program

NFC Div.	San Francisco 41, Minn. 13	5.00
NFC Champ.	San Francisco 30, L.A. Rams 3	6.00
S. Bowl XXIV	**San Francisco 55, Denver 10**	**12.00**

1990

AFC W. Card	Miami 17, Kansas City 16	5.00
AFC W. Card	Cincinnati 41, Houston 14	5.00
AFC Div.	Buffalo 44, Miami 34	5.00
AFC Div.	L.A. Raiders 20, Cincinnati 10	5.00
AFC Champ.	Buffalo 51, L.A. Raiders 3	6.00
NFC W. Card	Chicago 16, New Orleans 6	5.00
NFC W. Card	Washington 20, Philadelphia 6	5.00
NFC Div.	N.Y. Giants 31, Chicago 3	5.00
NFC Div.	San Francisco 28, Wash. 10	5.00
NFC Champ.	N.Y. Giants 15, San Fran. 13	8.00
S. Bowl XXV	**N.Y. Giants 20, Buffalo 19**	**10.00**

1991

AFC W. Card	Kansas City 10, L.A. Raiders 6	5.00
AFC W. Card	Houston 17, N.Y. Jets 10	5.00
AFC Div.	Denver 26, Houston 24	5.00
AFC Div.	Buffalo 37, Kansas City 14	5.00
AFC Champ.	Buffalo 10, Denver 7	6.00
NFC W. Card	Atlanta 27, New Orleans 20	5.00
NFC W. Card	Dallas 17, Chicago 13	5.00
NFC Div.	Washington 24, Atlanta 7	5.00
NFC Div.	Detroit 38, Dallas 6	5.00
NFC Champ.	Washington 41, Detroit 10	6.00
S. Bowl XXVI	**Washington 37, Buffalo 24**	**10.00**

1992

AFC W. Card	Buffalo 41, Houston 38	10.00
AFC W. Card	San Diego vs. Kansas City	5.00
AFC Div.	Miami vs. San Diego	5.00
AFC Div.	Buffalo vs. Pittsburgh	5.00
AFC Champ.	Buffalo vs. Miami	5.00
NFC W. Card	Washington vs. Minnesota	5.00
NFC W. Card	Philadelphia vs. New Orleans	5.00
NFC Div.	Dallas vs. Philadelphia	6.00
NFC Div.	San Francisco vs. Washington	5.00
NFC Champ.	Dallas vs. San Francisco	8.00
S. Bowl XXVII	**Dallas vs. Buffalo**	**5.00**
	w/ Troy Aikman *GameDay* insert card on p. 168	**25.00**

PRO BOWL PROGRAMS

1951 Pro Bowl program

1951	American 28, National 27 (L.A. Coliseum)	175.00
1952	National 30, American 13 (L.A. Coliseum)	100.00
1953	National 27, American 7 (L.A. Coliseum)	100.00
1954	East 20, West 9 (L.A. Coliseum)	75.00
1955	West 26, East 19 (L.A. Coliseum)	65.00
1956	East 31, West 30 (L.A. Coliseum)	65.00
1957	West 19, East 10 (L.A. Coliseum)	50.00
1958	West 26, East 7 (L.A. Coliseum)	45.00
1959	East 28, West 21 (L.A. Coliseum)	45.00
1960	West 38, East 21 (L.A. Coliseum)	40.00
1961	West 35, East 31 (L.A. Coliseum)	25.00
1962	West 31, East 30 (L.A. Coliseum)	25.00
1963	East 30, West 20 (L.A. Coliseum)	25.00
1964	West 31, East 17 (L.A. Coliseum)	25.00
1965	West 34, East 14 (L.A. Coliseum)	20.00
1966	East 36, West 7 (L.A. Coliseum)	20.00
1967	East 20, West 10 (L.A. Coliseum)	20.00
1968	West 38, East 20 (L.A. Coliseum)	20.00
1969	West 10, East 7 (L.A. Coliseum)	20.00
1970	West 16, East 13 (L.A. Coliseum)	15.00
1971	NFC 27, AFC 6 (L.A. Coliseum)	15.00
1972	AFC 26, NFC 13 (L.A. Coliseum)	15.00
1973	AFC 33, NFC 28 (Texas Stadium)	10.00
1974	AFC 15, NFC 13 (Arrowhead Stadium)	10.00
1975	NFC 17, AFC 10 (Orange Bowl)	8.00
1976	NFC 23, AFC 20 (Superdome)	8.00
1977	AFC 24, NFC 14 (Kingdome)	8.00
1978	NFC 14, AFC 13 (Tampa Stadium)	8.00
1979	NFC 13, AFC 7 (L.A. Coliseum)	8.00
1980	NFC 37, AFC 27 (Aloha Stadium)	5.00
1981	NFC 21, AFC 7 (Aloha Stadium)	5.00
1982	AFC 16, NFC 13 (Aloha Stadium)	5.00
1983	NFC 20, AFC 19 (Aloha Stadium)	5.00
1984	NFC 45, AFC 3 (Aloha Stadium)	5.00
1985	AFC 22, NFC 14 (Aloha Stadium)	5.00
1986	NFC 28, AFC 24 (Aloha Stadium)	5.00
1987	AFC 10, NFC 6 (Aloha Stadium)	5.00
1988	AFC 15, NFC 6 (Aloha Stadium)	5.00
1989	NFC 34, AFC 3 (Aloha Stadium)	5.00
1990	NFC 27, AFC 21 (Aloha Stadium)	5.00
1991	AFC 23, NFC 21 (Aloha Stadium)	5.00
1992	NFC 21, AFC 15 (Aloha Stadium)	5.00

HOCKEY PROGRAMS

NHL ALL-STAR GAME

Year	Final Score	Site	Value
1947	All-Stars 4, Toronto 3	Toronto	150.00
1948	All-Stars 3, Toronto 1	Chicago	125.00
1949	All-Stars 3, Toronto 1	Toronto	125.00
1950	Detroit 7, All-Stars 1	Detroit	125.00
1951	1st Team 2, 2nd Team 2	Toronto	75.00
1952	1st Team 1, 2nd Team 1	Detroit	75.00
1953	All-Stars 3, Montreal 1	Montreal	75.00
1954	All-Stars 2, Detroit 2	Detroit	45.00
1955	Detroit 3, All-Stars 1	Detroit	45.00
1956	All-Stars 1, Montreal 1	Montreal	45.00
1957	All-Stars 5, Montreal 3	Montreal	45.00
1958	Montreal 6, All-Stars 3	Montreal	45.00
1959	Montreal 6, All-Stars 1	Montreal	40.00
1960	All-Stars 2, Montreal 1	Montreal	40.00
1961	All-Stars 3, Chicago 1	Chicago	15.00
1962	Toronto 4, All-Stars 1	Toronto	10.00
1963	All-Stars 3, Toronto 3	Toronto	10.00
1964	All-Stars 3, Toronto 2	Toronto	10.00
1965	All-Stars 5, Montreal 2	Montreal	15.00
1966	Game moved from start of season to mid-season		
1967	Montreal 3, All-Stars 0	Montreal	15.00
1968	Toronto 4, All-Stars 3	Toronto	10.00
1969	West 3, East 3	Montreal	10.00
1970	East 4, West 1	St. Louis	10.00
1971	West 2, East 1	Boston	10.00
1972	East 3, West 2	Minnesota	10.00
1973	East 5, West 4	New York	10.00
1974	West 6, East 4	Chicago	10.00
1975	Wales 7, Campbell 1	Montreal	10.00
1976	Wales 7, Campbell 5	Philadelphia	8.00
1977	Wales 4, Campbell 3	Vancouver	8.00
1978	Wales 3, Campbell 2 OT	Buffalo	8.00
1979	Challenge Cup vs. USSR	New York	10.00
1980	Wales 6, Campbell 3	Detroit	8.00
1981	Campbell 4, Wales 1	Los Angeles	8.00

1979 NHL Challenge Cup program

1988 NHL All-Star Game program

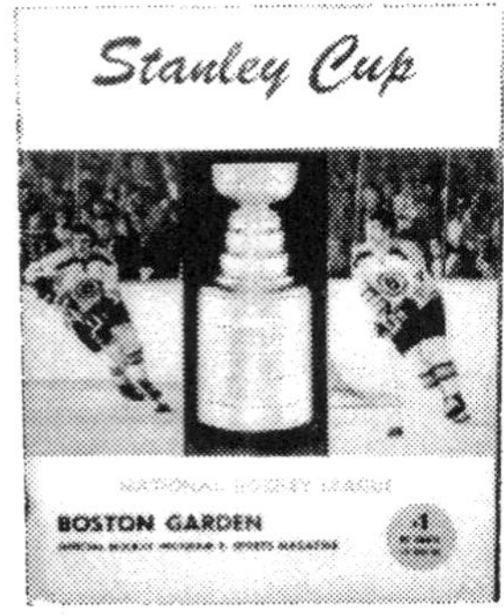

1972 Stanley Cup Playoff program

1982	Wales 4, Campbell 2	Washington	8.00
1983	Campbell 9, Wales 3	N.Y. Islanders	8.00
1984	Wales 7, Campbell 6	New Jersey	8.00
1985	Wales 6, Campbell 4	Calgary	8.00
1986	Wales 4, Campbell 3 OT	Hartford	8.00
1987	Rendez-Vous'87 vs. USSR	Quebec	10.00
1988	Wales 6, Campbell 5 OT	St. Louis	8.00
1989	Campbell 9, Wales 5	Edmonton	8.00
1990	Wales 12, Campbell 7	Pittsburgh	8.00
1991	Campbell 11, Wales 5	Chicago	8.00
1992	Campbell 10, Wales 6	Philadelphia	8.00

NHL STANLEY CUP PLAYOFFS

Year	Champion vs. runner-up	Value
1930	Montreal Canadiens vs. Boston	450.00
1931	Montreal Canadiens vs. Chicago	450.00
1932	Toronto vs. N.Y. Rangers	350.00
1933	N.Y. Rangers vs. Toronto	300.00
1934	Chicago vs. Detroit	225.00
1935	Montreal Maroons vs. Toronto	250.00
1936	Detroit vs. Toronto	200.00
1937	Detroit vs. N.Y. Rangers	200.00
1938	Chicago vs. Toronto	175.00
1939	Boston vs. Toronto	175.00
1940	N.Y. Rangers vs. Toronto	250.00
1941	Boston vs. Detroit	150.00
1942	Toronto vs. Detroit	150.00
1943	Detroit vs. Boston	125.00
1944	Montreal vs. Chicago	125.00
1945	Toronto vs. Detroit	100.00
1946	Montreal vs. Boston	125.00
1947	Toronto vs. Montreal	100.00
1948	Toronto vs. Detroit	75.00
1949	Toronto vs. Detroit	75.00
1950	Detroit vs. N.Y. Rangers	75.00
1951	Toronto vs. Montreal	65.00
1952	Detroit vs. Montreal	60.00
1953	Montreal vs. Boston	60.00
1954	Detroit vs. Montreal	45.00
1955	Detroit vs. Montreal	45.00
1956	Montreal vs. Detroit	45.00
1957	Montreal vs. Boston	45.00
1958	Montreal vs. Boston	45.00
1959	Montreal vs. Toronto	30.00
1960	Montreal vs. Toronto	30.00
1961	Chicago vs. Detroit	20.00
1962	Toronto vs. Chicago	15.00
1963	Toronto vs. Detroit	15.00
1964	Toronto vs. Detroit	15.00
1965	Montreal vs. Chicago	25.00
1966	Montreal vs. Detroit	25.00
1967	Toronto vs. Montreal	20.00
1968	Montreal vs. St. Louis	15.00
1969	Montreal vs. St. Louis	15.00
1970	Boston vs. St. Louis	10.00
1971	Montreal vs. Chicago	12.00
1972	Boston vs. N.Y. Rangers	10.00
1973	Montreal vs. Chicago	10.00
1974	Philadelphia vs. Boston	10.00
1975	Philadelphia vs. Buffalo	10.00
1976	Montreal vs. Philadelphia	8.00
1977	Montreal vs. Boston	8.00
1978	Montreal vs. Boston	8.00
1979	Montreal vs. N.Y. Rangers	8.00
1980	N.Y. Islanders vs. Philadelphia	8.00
1981	N.Y. Islanders vs. Minnesota	8.00
1982	N.Y. Islanders vs. Vancouver	8.00
1983	N.Y. Islanders vs. Edmonton	8.00
1984	Edmonton vs. N.Y. Islanders	10.00
1985	Edmonton vs. Philadelphia	10.00
1986	Montreal vs. Calgary	8.00
1987	Edmonton vs. Philadelphia	10.00
1988	Edmonton vs. Boston	10.00
1989	Calgary vs. Montreal	8.00
1990	Edmonton vs. Boston	8.00
1991	Pittsburgh vs. Minnesota	8.00
1992	Pittsburgh vs. Chicago	8.00

HORSE RACING PROGRAMS

NOTE: Triple Crown winners in CAPS

BELMONT STAKES PROGRAMS

Year	Winning Horse	Jockey	Value
1867	Ruthless	J. Kilpatrick	2,000.00
1868	General Duke	Bobby Swim	1,200.00
1869	Fenian	C. Miller	1,000.00
1870	Kingfisher	W. Dick	1,000.00
1871	Harry Bassett	W. Miller	1,000.00
1872	Joe Daniels	James Roe	1,000.00
1873	Springbok	James Roe	1,000.00
1874	Saxon	G. Barbee	1,000.00
1875	Calvin	Bobby Swim	1,000.00
1876	Algerine	Billy Donohue	1,000.00
1877	Cloverbrook	C. Holloway	1,000.00
1878	Duke of Magenta	L. Hughes	1,000.00
1879	Spendthrift	George Evans	1,000.00
1880	Grenada	L. Hughes	1,000.00
1881	Saunterer	T. Costello	1,000.00
1882	Forester	Jim McLaughlin	1,000.00
1883	George Kinney	Jim McLaughlin	1,000.00
1884	Panique	Jim McLaughlin	950.00
1885	Tyrant	Paul Duffy	950.00
1886	Inspector B	Jim McLaughlin	950.00
1887	Hanover	Jim McLaughlin	900.00
1888	Sir Dixon	Jim McLaughlin	900.00
1889	Eric	W. Hayward	900.00
1890	Burlington	Pike Barnes	850.00
1891	Foxford	Ed Garrison	850.00
1892	Patron	W. Hayward	850.00
1893	Comanche	Willie Simms	800.00
1894	Henry of Navarre	Willie Simms	900.00
1895	Belmar	Fred Taral	800.00

1896	Hastings	H. Griffin	800.00
1897	Scottish Chieftain	J. Scherrer	800.00
1898	Bowling Brook	F. Littlefield	800.00
1899	Jean Bereaud	R. Clawson	800.00
1900	Ildrim	Nash Turner	750.00
1901	Commando	H. Spencer	750.00
1902	Masterman	John Bullman	750.00
1903	Africander	John Bullman	750.00
1904	Delhi	George Odom	750.00
1905	Tanya	E. Hildebrand	750.00
1906	Burgomaster	Lucien Lyne	700.00
1907	Peter Pan	G. Mountain	750.00
1908	Colin	Joe Notter	950.00
1909	Joe Madden	E. Dugan	700.00
1910	Sweep	James Butwell	700.00
1911-12	Not held		

1940 Belmont Stakes program

1913	Prince Eugene	Roscoe Troxler	650.00
1914	Luke McLuke	Merritt Buxton	650.00
1915	The Finn	George Byrne	650.00
1916	Friar Rock	E. Haynes	600.00
1917	Hourless	James Butwell	600.00
1918	Johren	Frank Robinson	550.00
1919	SIR BARTON	John Loftus	1,100.00
1920	Man O' War	Clarence Kummer	1,750.00
1921	Grey Lag	Earl Sande	550.00
1922	Pillory	C.H. Miller	450.00
1923	Zev	Earl Sande	500.00
1924	Mad Play	Earl Sande	450.00
1925	American Flag	Albert Johnson	450.00
1926	Crusader	Albert Johnson	450.00
1927	Chance Shot	Earle Sande	450.00
1928	Vito	Clarence Kummer	450.00
1929	Blue Larkspur	Mack Garner	450.00
1930	GALLANT FOX	Earle Sande	600.00
1931	Twenty Fox	Charles Kurtsinger	500.00
1932	Faireno	Tom Mally	400.00
1933	Hurryoff	Mack Garner	400.00
1934	Peace Chance	W.D. Wright	375.00
1935	OMAHA	Willie Saunders	550.00
1936	Granville	James Stout	325.00

1987 Belmont Stakes program

1937	WAR ADMIRAL	Charles Kurtsinger	500.00
1938	Pasteurized	James Stout	350.00
1939	Johnstown	James Stout	375.00
1940	Bimelech	Fred Smith	350.00
1941	WHIRLAWAY	Eddie Arcaro	500.00
1942	Shout Out	Eddie Arcaro	325.00
1943	COUNT FLEET	Johnny Longden	475.00
1944	Bounding Home	G.L. Smith	300.00

1945	Pavot	Eddie Arcaro	300.00
1946	ASSAULT	Warren Mehrtens	450.00
1947	Phalanx	R. Donoso	275.00
1948	CITATION	Eddie Arcaro	500.00
1949	Capot	Ted Atkinson	250.00
1950	Middleground	William Boland	275.00
1951	Counterpoint	David Gorman	250.00
1952	One Count	Eddie Arcaro	250.00
1953	Native Dancer	Eric Guerin	300.00
1954	High Gun	Eric Guerin	225.00
1955	Nashua	Eddie Arcaro	250.00
1956	Needles	David Erb	250.00
1957	Gallant Man	Bill Shoemaker	300.00
1958	Cavan	Pete Anderson	175.00
1959	Sword Dancer	Bill Shoemaker	200.00
1960	Celtic Ash	Bill Hartack	175.00
1961	Sherluck	Braulio Baeza	175.00
1962	Jaipur	Bill Shoemaker	150.00
1963	Chateaugay	Braulio Baeza	150.00
1964	Quadrangle	Manuel Ycaza	150.00
1965	Hail to All	John Sellers	125.00
1966	Amberoid	William Boland	125.00
1967	Damascus	Bill Shoemaker	150.00
1968	Stage Door Johnny	Gus Gustines	125.00
1969	Arts and Letters	Braulio Baeza	125.00
1970	High Echelon	John Rotz	100.00
1971	Pass Catcher	Walter Blum	100.00
1972	Riva Ridge	Ron Turcotte	100.00
1973	SECRETARIAT	Ron Turcotte	115.00
1974	Little Current	Miguel Rivera	65.00
1975	Avatar	Bill Shoemaker	75.00
1976	Bold Forbes	Angel Cordero Jr.	75.00
1977	SEATTLE SLEW	Jean Cruget	75.00
1978	AFFIRMED	Steve Cauthen	135.00
1979	Coastal	Ruben Hernandez	50.00
1980	Temperence Hill	Eddie Maple	35.00
1981	Summing	George Martens	30.00
1982	Conquistador Cielo	Laffit Pincay Jr.	35.00
1983	Caveat	Laffit Pincay Jr.	35.00
1984	Swale	Laffit Pincay Jr.	40.00
1985	Creme Fraiche	Eddie Maple	30.00
1986	Danzig Connection	Chris McCarron	25.00
1987	Bet Twice	Craig Perret	20.00
1988	Risen Star	Eddie Delahoussaye	20.00
1989	Easy Goer	Pat Day	15.00
1990	Go and Go	Michael Kinane	10.00
1991	Hansel	Jerry Bailey	6.00
1992	A.P. Indy	Eddie Delahoussaye	5.00

BREEDERS CUP PROGRAMS

Year	Cover	Value
1984		15.00
1985		12.00
1986		30.00
1987		25.00
1988		5.00
1989		7.00
1990		5.00
1991		4.00
1992		4.00

KENTUCKY DERBY PROGRAMS

Year	Winning Horse	Jockey	Value
1875	Aristides	Oliver Lewis	3,500.00
1876	Vagrant	Bobby Swim	2,250.00
1877	Baden Baden	Billy Walker	2,000.00
1878	Day Star	Jimmy Carter	2,000.00
1879	Lord Murphy	Charlie Shauer	1,900.00
1880	Fonso	George Lewis	1,800.00
1881	Hindoo	Jim McLaughlin	1,800.00
1882	Apollo	Babe Hurd	1,750.00
1883	Leontaus	Billy Donohue	1,750.00
1884	Buchanan	Isaac Murphy	1,700.00
1885	Joe Cotton	Babe Henderson	1,650.00
1886	Ben Ali	Paul Duffy	1,650.00
1887	Montrose	Isaac Lewis	1,600.00
1888	Macbeth II	George Covington	1,600.00
1889	Spokane	Thomas Kiley	1,500.00
1890	Riley	Isaac Murphy	1,500.00
1891	Kingman	Isaac Murphy	1,400.00
1892	Azra	Lonnie Clayton	1,350.00
1893	Lookout	Eddie Kunze	1,350.00
1894	Chant	Frank Goodale	1,300.00
1895	Halma	Soup Perkins	1,300.00
1896	Ben Brush	Willie Simms	1,300.00
1897	Typhoon II	Buttons Garner	1,250.00
1898	Plaudet	Willie Simms	1,250.00
1899	Manuel	Fred Taral	1,250.00
1900	Lieut. Gibson	Jimmy Boland	950.00
1901	His Eminence	Jimmy Winkfield	900.00

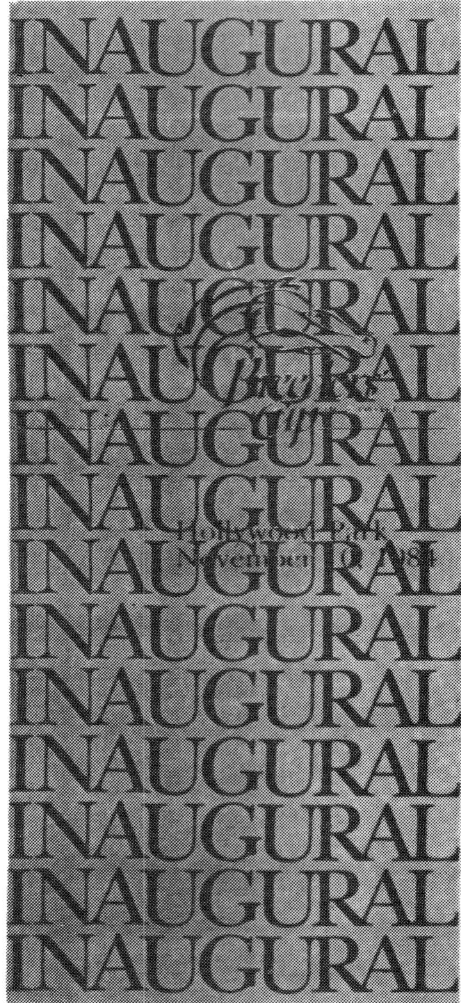

1984 Breeder's Cup program

1902	Alan-a-Dale	Jimmy Winkfield	875.00
1903	Judge Himes	Hal Booker	850.00
1904	Elwood	Shorty Prior	825.00
1905	Agile	Jack Martin	800.00
1906	Sir Huon	Roscoe Troxler	800.00
1907	Pink Star	Andy Minder	775.00
1908	Stone Street	Arthur Pickens	775.00
1909	Wintergreen	Vincent Power	750.00
1910	Donau	Fred Herbert	700.00
1911	Meridian	George Archibald	675.00
1912	Worth	C.H.Shilling	600.00

1913	Donerail	Roscoe Goose	675.00
1914	Old Rosebud	John McCabe	650.00
1915	Regret	Joe Notter	800.00
1916	George Smith	Johnny Loftus	600.00
1917	Omar Khayyam	Charles Borel	600.00
1918	Exterminator	William Knapp	700.00
1919	SIR BARTON	Johnny Loftus	950.00
1920	Paul Jones	Ted Rice	500.00
1921	Behave Yourself	Charles Thompson	475.00
1922	Morvich	Albert Johnson	500.00
1923	Zev	Earl Sande	525.00

FIFTY-EIGHTH
KENTUCKY DERBY

·OFFICIAL·
PROGRAM

TWENTY GRAND
WINNER OF THE KENTUCKY DERBY 1931

CHURCHILL DOWNS
1875 DERBY DAY 1932
Saturday, May 7
FIRST RACE AT 1:45 P. M.
Churchill Downs
INCORPORATED
PRICE TEN CENTS
C. T. DEARING PRINTING COMPANY, Incorporated

1932 Kentucky Derby program

1924	Black Gold	John Mooney	550.00
1925	Flying Ebony	Earl Sande	475.00
1926	Bubbling Over	Albert Johnson	450.00
1927	Whiskery	Linus McAtee	425.00
1928	Reigh Count	Chick Lang	375.00
1929	Clyde Van Dusen	Linus McAtee	375.00
1930	GALLANT FOX	Earl Sande	425.00
1931	Twenty Grand	Charles Kurtsinger	400.00
1932	Burgoo King	Eugene James	350.00
1933	Brokers Tip	Don Meade	325.00
1934	Cavalcade	Mack Garner	325.00
1935	OMAHA	Willie Saunders	375.00
1936	Bold Venture	Ira Hanford	300.00

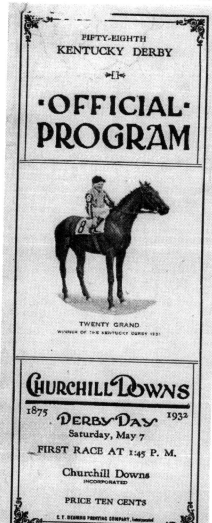

1974 Kentucky Derby program

1937	WAR ADMIRAL	Charles Kurtsinger	375.00
1938	Lawrin	Eddie Arcaro	275.00
1939	Johnstown	James Stout	250.00
1940	Gallahadion	Carroll Bierman	225.00
1941	WHIRLAWAY	Eddie Arcaro	275.00
1942	Shut Out	Wayne Wright	200.00
1943	COUNT FLEET	Johnny Longden	275.00
1944	Pensive	Conn McCreary	175.00
1945	Hoop Jr.	Eddie Arcaro	150.00
1946	ASSAULT	Warren Mehrtens	175.00
1947	Jet Pilot	Eric Guerin	125.00

1948	CITATION	Eddie Arcaro	250.00
1949	Ponder	Steve Brooks	125.00
1950	Middleground	William Boland	100.00
1951	Count Turf	Conn McCreary	90.00

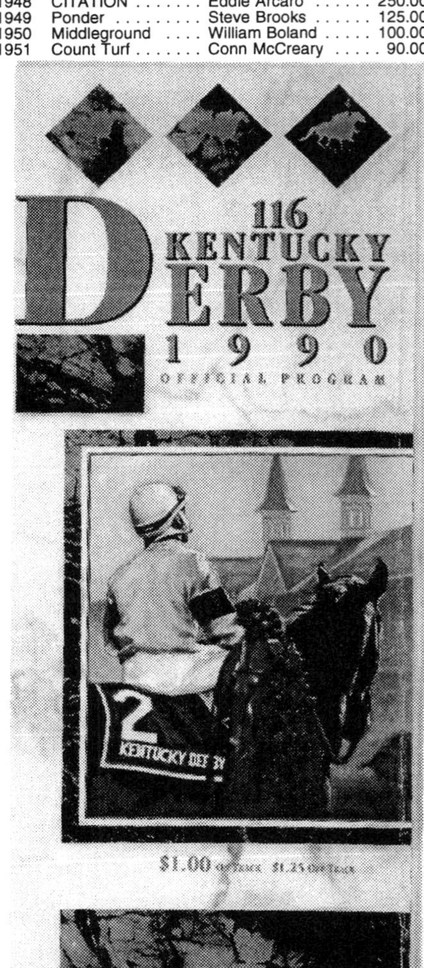

1990 Kentucky Derby program

1952	Hill Gail	Eddie Arcaro	85.00
1953	Dark Star	Hank Moreno	100.00
1954	Determine	Raymond York	85.00
1955	Swaps	Bill Shoemaker	115.00
1956	Needles	David Erb	80.00
1957	Iron Liege	Bill Hartack	100.00
1958	Tim Tam	I. Valenzuela	75.00
1959	Tommy Lee	Bill Shoemaker	75.00
1960	Venetian Way	Bill Hartack	65.00
1961	Carry Back	John Sellers	95.00
1962	Decidedly	Bill Hartack	65.00
1963	Chateaugay	Braulio Baeza	55.00
1964	Northern Dancer	Bill Hartack	75.00
1965	Lucky Debonair	Bill Shoemaker	55.00
1966	Kauai King	Don Brumfield	45.00
1967	Proud Clarion	Bobby Ussery	45.00
1968	Forward Pass	I. Valenzuela	40.00
1969	Majestic Prince	Bill Hartack	40.00
1970	Dust Commander	Mike Manganello	35.00
1971	Canonero II	Gustavo Avila	30.00
1972	Riva Ridge	Ron Turcotte	25.00
1973	SECRETARIAT	Ron Turcotte	75.00
1974	Cannonade	Angel Cordero Jr.	20.00
1975	Foolish Pleasure	Jacinto Vasquez	25.00
1976	Bold Forbes	Angel Cordero Jr.	20.00
1977	SEATTLE SLEW	Jean Cruguet	20.00
1978	AFFIRMED	Steve Cauthen	20.00
1979	Spectacular Bid	Ron Franklin	20.00
1980	Genuine Risk	Jacinto Vasquez	18.00
1981	Pleasant Colony	Jorge Velasquez	10.00
1982	Gato Del Sol	Eddie Delahoussaye	8.00
1983	Sunny's Halo	Eddie Delahoussaye	8.00
1984	Swale	Laffit Pincay Jr.	9.00
1985	Spend A Buck	Angel Cordero Jr.	6.00
1986	Ferdinand	Bill Shoemaker	7.00
1987	Alysheba	Chris McCarron	6.00
1988	Winning Colors	Gary Stevens	6.00
1989	Sunday Silence	Pat Valenzuela	6.00
1990	Unbridled	Craig Perret	5.00
1991	Strike the Gold	Chris Antley	4.00
1992	Lil E. Tee	Pat Day	4.00

PREAKNESS STAKES PROGRAMS

Year	Winning Horse	Jockey	Value
1873	Survivor	G. Barbee	2,000.00
1874	Culpepper	W. Donohue	1,000.00
1875	Tom Ochiltree	L. Hughes	1,250.00
1876	Shirley	G. Barbee	1,000.00
1877	Cloverbrook	C. Holloway	1,000.00
1878	Duke of Magenta	C. Holloway	1,000.00
1879	Harold	L. Hughes	1,000.00
1880	Grenada	L. Hughes	950.00
1881	Saunterer	T. Costello	950.00
1882	Vanguard	T. Costello	950.00
1883	Jacobus	G. Barbee	950.00
1884	Knight of Ellerslie	S. Fisher	950.00
1885	Tecumseh	Jim McLaughlin	900.00
1886	The Bard	S. Fisher	900.00
1887	Dunboyne	W. Donohue	900.00
1888	Refund	F. Littlefield	900.00
1889	Buddhist	W. Anderson	850.00
1890	Mintague	W. Martin	850.00
1891-93	Not held		
1894	Assignee	Fred Taral	800.00
1895	Belmar	Fred Taral	800.00
1896	Margrave	H. Griffin	800.00
1897	Paul Kauvar	T. Thorpe	800.00
1898	Sly Fox	W. Simms	800.00
1899	Half Time	R. Clawson	800.00
1900	Hindus	H. Spencer	750.00
1901	The Parader	F. Landry	750.00
1902	Old England	L. Jackson	750.00
1903	Flocarline	W. Gannon	750.00
1904	Bryn Mawr	E. Hildebrand	750.00
1905	Cairngorm	W. Davis	750.00
1906	Whimsical	Walter Miller	750.00
1907	Don Enrique	G. Mountain	750.00
1908	Royal Tourist	Eddie Dugan	750.00
1909	Effendi	Willie Doyle	700.00
1910	Layminster	R. Estep	700.00
1911	Watervale	Eddie Dugan	700.00
1912	Colonel Holloway	C. Turner	700.00
1913	Buskin	James Butwell	700.00
1914	Holiday	A. Schuttinger	650.00
1915	Rhine Maiden	Douglas Hoffman	650.00
1916	Damrosch	Linus McAtee	600.00
1917	Kalitan	E. Haynes	600.00
1918	War Cloud	Johnny Loftus	550.00
	Jack Hare	Charles Peak	
1919	SIR BARTON	Johnny Loftus	1,200.00
1920	Man O' War	Clarence Kummer	2,000.00
1921	Broomspun	John Maiben	500.00
1922	Pillory	Whitey Abel	500.00
1923	Vigil	B. Marinelli	500.00
1924	Nellie Morse	John Merimee	600.00
1925	Conventry	Clarence Kummer	450.00
1926	Display	John Maiben	500.00
1927	Bostonian	Whitey Abel	450.00
1928	Victorian	Sonny Workman	450.00
1929	Dr. Freeland	Louis Schaefer	450.00
1930	GALLANT FOX	Earl Sande	650.00
1931	Mate	George Ellis	400.00
1932	Burgoo King	John Maiben	400.00

1955 Preakness program

1933	Head Play	Charles Kurtsinger	400.00
1934	High Quest	Robert Jones	400.00
1935	OMAHA	Willie Saunders	500.00
1936	Bold Venture	George Woolf	375.00
1937	WAR ADMIRAL	Charles Kurtsinger	500.00
1938	Dauber	Maurice Peters	375.00
1939	Challedon	George Seabo	350.00
1940	Bimelech	F.A. Smith	350.00
1941	WHIRLAWAY	Eddie Arcaro	475.00
1942	Alsab	Basil James	350.00
1943	COUNT FLEET	Johnny Longden	475.00
1944	Pensive	Conn McCreary	325.00
1945	Polynesian	W.D. Wright	350.00
1946	ASSAULT	Warren Mehrtens	425.00
1947	Faultless	Doug Dobson	300.00
1948	CITATION	Eddie Arcaro	550.00
1949	Capot	Ted Atkinson	250.00
1950	Hill Prince	Eddie Arcaro	250.00

The Preakness

108th Running

1873-1983

PIMLICO

MAY 21, 1983

1983 Preakness program

1951	Bold	Eddie Arcaro	250.00
1952	Blue Man	Conn McCreary	250.00
1953	Native Dancer	Eric Guerin	300.00
1954	Hasty Road	Johnny Adams	225.00
1955	Nashua	Eddie Arcaro	250.00
1956	Fabius	Bill Hartack	225.00

1957	Bold Ruler	Eddie Arcaro	275.00
1958	Tim Tam	Ismael Valenzuela	200.00
1959	Royal Orbit	William Harmatz	200.00
1960	Bally Ache	Bobby Ussery	175.00
1961	Carry Back	Johnny Sellers	225.00
1962	Greek Money	John Rotz	150.00
1963	Candy Spots	Bill Shoemaker	150.00
1964	Northern Dancer	Bill Hartack	200.00
1965	Tom Rolfe	Ron Turcotte	135.00
1966	Kauai King	Don Brumfield	125.00
1967	Damascus	Bill Shoemaker	150.00
1968	Forward Pass	Ismael Valenzuela	125.00
1969	Majestic Prince	Bill Hartack	135.00
1970	Personality	Eddie Belmonte	125.00
1971	Canonero II	Gustavo Avila	100.00
1972	Bee Bee Bee	Eldon Nelson	100.00
1973	SECRETARIAT	Ron Turcotte	110.00
1974	Little Current	Miguel Rivera	65.00
1975	Master Derby	Darrel McHargue	75.00
1976	Elocutionist	John Lively	85.00
1977	SEATTLE SLEW	Jean Cruguet	75.00
1978	AFFIRMED	Steve Cauthen	125.00
1979	Spectacular Bid	Ron Franklin	50.00
1980	Codex	Angel Cordero Jr.	35.00
1981	Pleasant Colony	Jorge Velasquez	30.00
1982	Aloma's Ruler	Jack Kaenel	30.00
1983	Deputed Testamony	Donald Miller	30.00
1984	Gate Dancer	Angel Cordero Jr.	25.00
1985	Tank's Prospect	Pat Day	25.00
1986	Snow Chief	Alex Solis	28.00
1987	Alysheba	Chris McCarron	22.00
1988	Risen Star	Eddie Delahoussaye	20.00
1989	Sunday Silence	Pat Valenzuela	22.00
1990	Summer Squall	Pay Day	15.00
1991	Hansell	Jerry Bailey	8.00
1992	Pine Bluff	Chris McCarron	6.00

OLYMPIC PROGRAMS

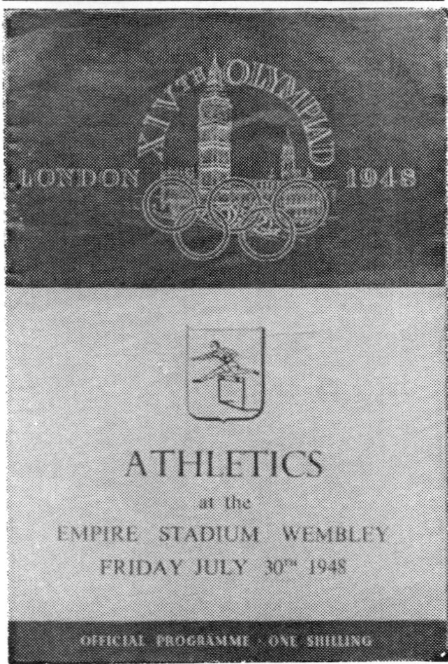

1948 Summer Olympics program

Olympic program values are for official daily programs *or* common event-specific programs.

SUMMER OLYMPICS PROGRAMS

1896	Athens, Greece	5,000.00
1904	St. Louis, Missouri	3,000.00
1908	London, England	200.00
1912	Stockholm, Sweden	200.00
1920	Antwerp, Belgium	150.00
1924	Paris, France	100.00
1928	Amsterdam, Holland	40.00
1932	Los Angeles, California	25.00
1936	Berlin, Germany	50.00
1948	London, England	30.00
1952	Helsinki, Finland	25.00
1956	Melbourne, Australia	25.00
1956	Stockholm, Sweden	75.00
1960	Rome, Italy	25.00
1964	Tokyo, Japan	25.00
1968	Mexico City, Mexico	25.00
1972	Munich, Germany	15.00
1976	Montreal, Quebec	10.00
1980	Moscow, Soviet Union	20.00
1984	Los Angeles, California	10.00
1988	Seoul, South Korea	10.00
1992	Barcelona, Spain	5.00

WINTER OLYMPICS PROGRAMS

1932	Lake Placid, New York	50.00
1936	Garmisch-Partenkirchen, Germany	150.00
1948	St. Moritz, Switzerland	75.00
1952	Oslo, Norway	60.00
1956	Cortina d'Ampezzo, Italy	60.00
1960	Squaw Valley, California	50.00
1964	Innsbruck, Austria	50.00
1968	Grenoble, France	40.00
1972	Sapporo, Japan	40.00
1976	Innsbruck, Austria	25.00
1980	Lake Placid, New York	10.00
1984	Sarajevo, Yugoslavia	10.00
1988	Calgary, Alberta	5.00
1992	Albertville, France	2.00

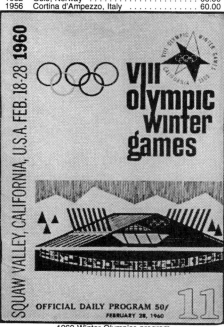

1960 Winter Olympics program

BASEBALL PROGRAMS

by Dennis Goldstein

Baseball programs were first put out in the 1850s or 1860s in order to score the games. Sporting goods dealers produced programs as foldover scorecards prominently advertising their baseball equipment. Since the late nineteenth century, each year most professional baseball teams have either put out or authorized an official program or scorecard for the team.

A small but fervent group of collectors seek baseball programs. Programs from the World Series and All Star games capture most collectors' attention. Consequently, these programs, especially pre-1920 World Series programs, command high prices.

Some program collectors search for "regular season" baseball programs, usually from the major league teams. Due to the sheer number of these various annual programs and to the difficulty of finding earlier ones, it is virtually impossible to collect old programs for each year from every major league team. Thus, regular season program collectors usually focus on one or more areas of program collecting.

Some of the more popular areas include programs from a favorite team or featuring favorite players, special event programs, minor league programs, and programs from the Players League, Federal League, and Negro Leagues.

Many factors affect the level of desirability and price of baseball programs. The condition of a program is extremely important. Most collectors want programs in nice condition. Unless a program in lesser condition (torn, badly stained, missing pages) is rare, generally it's value is low.

1901, 1909 and 1946 Dodger Programs

The inherent qualities of a program also affect its desirability and price. The overall design and attractiveness of a program, especially of the front cover, is a big factor. Some collectors seek covers depicting a player, team or stadium. Inside, player pictures and eye-catching advertising also enhance the program. The number of pages and the paper quality of the program matter. Glossy paper is better than cheap, brownish paper.

Since many program collectors want programs from special events or special professional leagues, these programs command premium prices. Due to number, variety and rarity of some of these programs, their values are not contained in the price guide. Still, be aware of special programs that are worth a lot. These programs include the following: the opening game of a stadium, city or team; and programs from the Union League, Players League, Federal League and Negro Leagues.

1953 Yankees Program

Our price guide provides a price range for programs in excellent condition for each major team by decades. An excellent program is free of any significant wear or defects. Since the values of a team's programs do not vary significantly from year to year, a price range for each decade has been uses. Generally, the higher end of the range reflects values a the beginning of the decade and the lower end reflects values at the lower end of the decade. Also, the range reflects price variations among market areas and dealers. For example, Yankees' and Mets' programs sell at a premium in the northeast. Finally, the use of the price ranges and open ended values ($500.00+ for pre-1930 programs) reflects their scarcity. Since some of these programs pop up so infrequently, they do not have established prices.

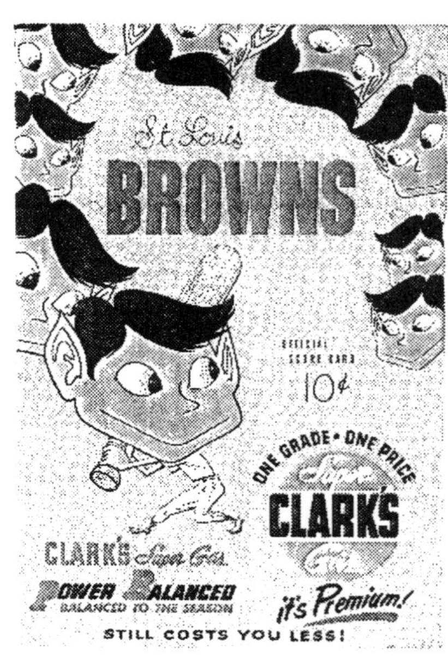

St. Louis Browns Program

The price guide contains values only for pre-1970 major league teams. Since few collectors seek recent major league programs or non-professional baseball programs (semi-pro, college, high school, and amateur), most have nominal values. While minor league,exhibition game, and pre-1920 college baseball programs are valuable, the programs are too numerous to list in the price guide.

REGULAR SEASON BASEBALL PROGRAMS

ANGELS

1961-69 .... 5.00-25.00

ASTROS (COLT 45s)

1962-69 .... 5.00-35.00

ATHLETICS

Philadelphia Athletics

1901-09 .... 200.00-500.00
1910-19 .... 75.00-150.00
1920-29 .... 35.00-65.00
1930-39 .... 20.00-35.00

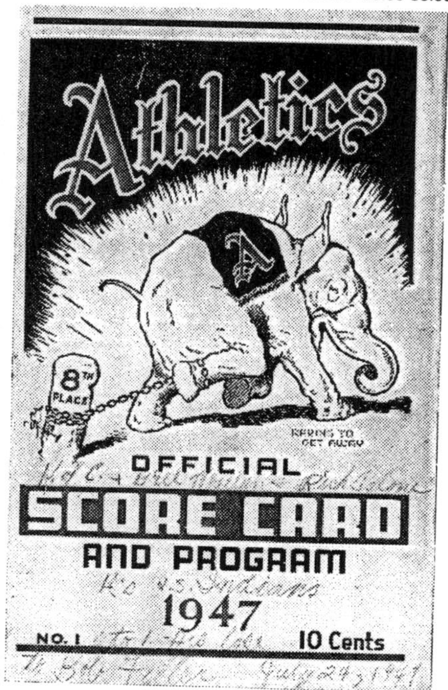

1947 Athletics program

1940-49 .... 15.00-20.00
1950-54 .... 10.00-15.00

Kansas City Athletics

1955-59 .... 10.00-15.00
1960-67 .... 5.00-10.00

Oakland Athletics

1968-69 .... 5.00-10.00

BLUE JAYS

1970-79 .... 5.00-7.50

BRAVES

Boston Braves

1958 Athletics program

pre-1900 .... 500.00-750.00
1900-09 .... 200.00-500.00
1910-19 .... 100.00-200.00
1920-29 .... 40.00-75.00
1930-39 .... 20.00-35.00
1940-49 .... 15.00-25.00
1950-52 .... 10.00-20.00

Milwaukee Braves

1953-59 .... 10.00-20.00
1960-65 .... 5.00-10.00

Atlanta Braves

1966-69 .... 5.00-10.00

BREWERS

Seattle Pilots

1969 .... 10.00-15.00

Milwaukee Brewers

1970-79 .... 5.00-7.50

BROWNS
(became ORIOLES in 1954)

1902-09 .... 250.00-500.00
1910-19 .... 100.00-200.00
1920-29 .... 40.00-75.00
1930-39 .... 25.00-35.00
1940-49 .... 15.00-25.00
1950-59 .... 15.00-25.00

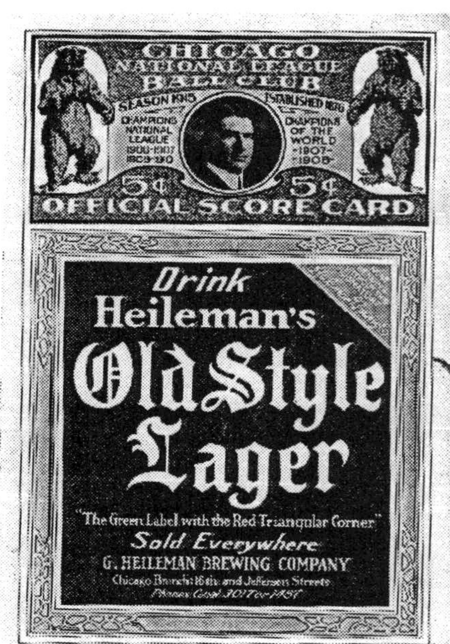

1915 Cubs program

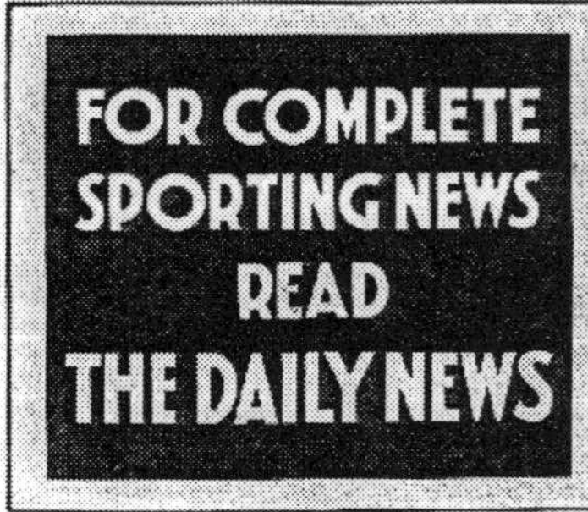

1922 Cubs program

CARDINALS

pre-1900	500.00-750.00
1900-09	200.00-500.00
1910-19	100.00-200.00
1920-29	40.00-75.00
1930-39	20.00-35.00
1940-49	15.00-20.00
1950-59	10.00-15.00
1960-69	5.00-10.00

CUBS

pre-1900	500.00-750.00
1900-09	250.00-500.00
1910-19	100.00-250.00
1920-29	40.00-75.00
1930-39	20.00-35.00

1947 Cubs program

1940-49	15.00-25.00
1950-59	10.00-15.00
1960-69	5.00-10.00

DODGERS

Brooklyn Dodgers

pre-1900	500.00-750.00
1900-09	250.00-400.00
1910-19	100.00-200.00
1920-29	40.00-100.00
1930-39	25.00-50.00
1940-49	20.00-30.00
1950-57	10.00-25.00

Los Angeles Dodgers

1958-59	10.00-25.00
1960-69	5.00-10.00

EXPOS

1969	5.00-10.00

GIANTS

New York Giants

pre-1900	500.00-750.00
1900-09	250.00-500.00

1910-19 . . . . . 100.00-200.00
1920-29 . . . . . 40.00-75.00
1930-39 . . . . . 20.00-35.00
1940-49 . . . . . 15.00-20.00
1950-57 . . . . . 10.00-20.00

San Francisco Giants

1958-59 . . . . . 10.00-20.00
1960-69 . . . . . 5.00-10.00

INDIANS

pre-1900 . . . . . 500.00-750.00
1900-09 . . . . . 250.00-500.00
1910-19 . . . . . 150.00-250.00
1920-29 . . . . . 50.00-100.00
1930-39 . . . . . 25.00-40.00
1940-49 . . . . . 15.00-20.00
1950-59 . . . . . 10.00-15.00
1960-69 . . . . . 5.00-10.00

MARINERS

1977-79 . . . . . 5.00-7.50

METS

1962-69 . . . . . 5.00-50.00

ORIOLES

pre-1900 . . . . . 500.00-750.00
1902-03 . . . . . 500.00-600.00
1954-59 . . . . . 10.00-35.00

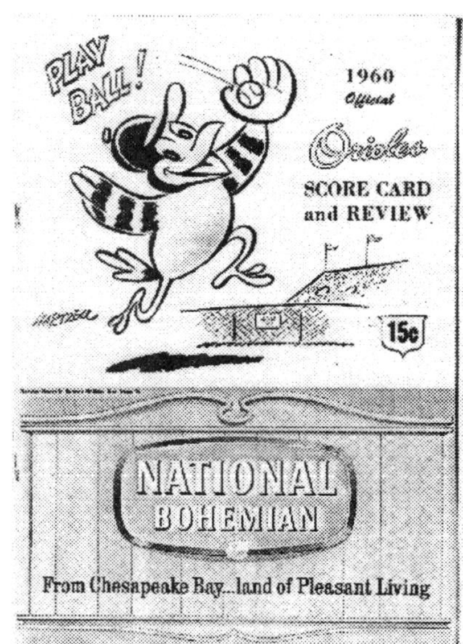

1960 Orioles program

1960-69 . . . . . 5.00-10.00

PADRES

1969 . . . . . 5.00-10.00

PHILLIES

pre-1900 . . . . . 500.00-750.00
1900-09 . . . . . 250.00-500.00
1910-19 . . . . . 100.00-200.00
1920-29 . . . . . 50.00-100.00
1930-39 . . . . . 25.00-40.00
1940-49 . . . . . 15.00-25.00
1950-59 . . . . . 10.00-20.00
1960-69 . . . . . 5.00-10.00

PIRATES

pre-1900 . . . . . 500.00-750.00
1900-09 . . . . . 200.00-500.00
1910-19 . . . . . 100.00-200.00
1920-29 . . . . . 40.00-100.00

1939 Pirates program

1930-39 . . . . . 25.00-40.00
1940-49 . . . . . 15.00-20.00
1950-59 . . . . . 10.00-15.00
1960-69 . . . . . 5.00-10.00

RANGERS

1972-79 . . . . . 5.00-10.00

REDS

pre-1900 . . . . . 500.00-750.00
1900-09 . . . . . 250.00-500.00
1910-19 . . . . . 150.00-250.00
1920-29 . . . . . 40.00-100.00
1930-39 . . . . . 25.00-50.00
1940-49 . . . . . 15.00-20.00
1950-59 . . . . . 10.00-15.00
1960-69 . . . . . 5.00-10.00

RED SOX

1901-09 . . . . . 200.00-500.00
1910-19 . . . . . 100.00-200.00
1920-29 . . . . . 40.00-75.00
1930-39 . . . . . 20.00-35.00
1940-49 . . . . . 15.00-25.00
1950-59 . . . . . 10.00-20.00
1960-69 . . . . . 5.00-10.00

ROYALS

1969 . . . . . 5.00-10.00

1950-59	10.00-25.00
1960-69	5.00-15.00

1967 Red Sox program

1944 Tigers program

SENATORS
(became Twins in 1961)
(became Rangers in 1972)

pre-1900	500.00-750.00
1900-09	250.00-500.00
1910-19	150.00-250.00
1920-29	40.00-100.00
1930-39	20.00-35.00
1940-49	15.00-25.00
1950-59	10.00-20.00
1960-69	5.00-10.00

TIGERS

pre-1900	500.00-750.00
1900-09	300.00-500.00
1910-19	150.00-250.00
1920-29	50.00-100.00
1930-39	20.00-40.00
1940-49	15.00-25.00
1950-59	10.00-15.00
1960-69	5.00-10.00

TWINS

1961-69	5.00-25.00

WHITE SOX

1901-09	200.00-500.00
1910-19	100.00-200.00
1920-29	40.00-75.00
1930-39	20.00-35.00
1940-49	15.00-20.00
1950-59	10.00-15.00
1960-69	5.00-10.00

YANKEES

1903-09	250.00-500.00
1910-19	100.00-200.00
1920-29	50.00-100.00
1930-39	25.00-50.00
1940-49	20.00-35.00

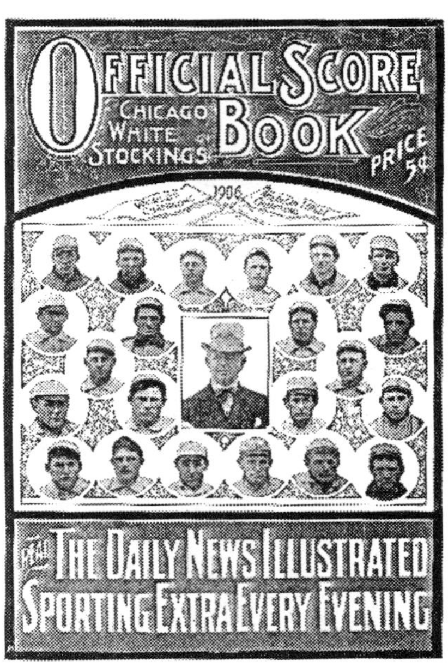

1906 White Sox program

STAMPS & STICKERS

BASEBALL STAMPS

1961 TOPPS STAMPS

No.	Player	Value
BALTIMORE ORIOLES		
1.	Steve Barber	0.30
2.	Jackie Brandt	0.30
3.	Marv Breeding	0.30
4.	Chuck Estrada	0.30
5.	Jim Gentile	0.45
6.	Ron Hansen	0.30
7.	Milt Pappas	0.45
8.	Brooks Robinson	1.75
9.	Gene Stephens	0.30
10.	Gus Triandos	0.45
11.	Hoyt Wilhelm	1.10
BOSTON RED SOX		
12.	Tom Brewer	0.30
13.	Gene Conley	0.30
14.	Ike Delock	0.30
15.	Gary Geiger	0.30
16.	Jackie Jensen	0.45
17.	Frank Malzone	0.45
18.	Bill Monbouquette	0.30
19.	Russ Nixon	0.30
20.	Pete Runnels	0.45
21.	Willie Tasby	0.30
22.	Vic Wertz	0.30
23.	Carl Yastrzemski	4.00
CHICAGO CUBS		
24.	George Altman	0.30
25.	Bob Anderson	0.30
26.	Richie Ashburn	0.60
27.	Ernie Banks	1.50
28.	Ed Bouchee	0.30
29.	Jim Brower	0.30
30.	Dick Ellsworth	0.30
31.	Don Elston	0.30
32.	Ron Santo	0.45
33.	Sam Taylor	0.30
34.	Bob Will	0.30
35.	Billy Williams	0.85
CHICAGO WHITE SOX		
36.	Luis Aparicio	1.00
37.	Russ Kemmerer	0.30
38.	Jim Landis	0.30
39.	Sherm Lollar	0.30
40.	J.C. Martin	0.30
41.	Minnie Minoso	0.45
42.	Billy Pierce	0.45
43.	Bob Shaw	0.30
44.	Al Smith	0.30
45.	Gerry Staley	0.30
46.	Early Wynn	1.00
CINCINNATI REDS		
47.	Ed Bailey	0.30
48.	Gus Bell	0.45
49.	Jim Brosnan	0.30
50.	Chico Cardenas	0.30
51.	Gene Freese	0.30
52.	Eddie Kasko	0.30
53.	Jerry Lynch	0.30
54.	Billy Martin	0.85
55.	Jim O'Toole	0.30
56.	Vada Pinson	0.45
57.	Wally Post	0.30
58.	Frank Robinson	1.50
CLEVELAND INDIANS		
59.	John Antonelli	0.45
60.	Ken Aspromonte	0.30
61.	Tito Francona	0.45
62.	Jim Grant	0.30
63.	Woody Held	0.30
64.	Barry Latman	0.30
65.	Jim Perry	0.45
66.	Jimmy Piersall	0.45
67.	Bubba Phillips	0.30
68.	Vic Power	0.30
69.	John Romano	0.30
70.	Johnny Temple	0.30
DETROIT TIGERS		
71.	Hank Aguirre	0.30
72.	Frank Bolling	0.30
73.	Steve Boros	0.45
74.	Jim Bunning	0.85
75.	Norm Cash	0.45
76.	Harry Chiti	0.30
77.	Chico Fernandez	0.30
78.	Dick Gernert	0.30
79.	Al Kaline (green)	2.50
80.	Al Kaline (brown)	2.50
81.	Frank Lary	0.45
82.	Charlie Maxwell	0.30
83.	Dave Sisler	0.30
KANSAS CITY A'S		
84.	Hank Bauer	0.45
85.	Bob Boyd	0.30
86.	Andy Carey	0.30
87.	Bud Daley	0.30
88.	Dick Hall	0.30
89.	J.C. Hartman	0.30
90.	Ray Herbert	0.30
91.	Whitey Herzog	0.45
92.	Jerry Lumpe	0.30
93.	Norm Siebern	0.30
94.	Marv Throneberry	0.45
95.	Bill Tuttle	0.30
96.	Dick Williams	0.45
LOS ANGELES ANGELS		
97.	Jerry Casale	0.30
98.	Bob Cerv	0.30
99.	Ned Garver	0.30
100.	Ron Hunt	0.30
101.	Ted Kluszewski	0.60
102.	Bob Sadowski	0.30
103.	Eddie Yost	0.30
LOS ANGELES DODGERS		
104.	Tom Davis	0.45
105.	Don Drysdale	1.50
106.	Frank Howard	0.45
107.	Norm Larker	0.30
108.	Wally Moon	0.45
109.	Charlie Neal	0.30
110.	Johnny Podres	0.45
111.	Ed Roebuck	0.30
112.	Johnny Roseboro	0.30
113.	Larry Sherry	0.30
114.	Duke Snider	2.50
115.	Stan Williams	0.30
MILWAUKEE BRAVES		
116.	Hank Aaron	4.00
117.	Joe Adcock	0.45
118.	Bill Bruton	0.30
119.	Bob Buhl	0.30
120.	Wes Covington	0.30
121.	Del Crandall	0.45
122.	Joey Jay	0.30
123.	Felix Mantilla	0.30
124.	Eddie Mathews	1.50
125.	Roy McMillan	0.30
126.	Warren Spahn	1.50
127.	Carlton Wiley	0.30
MINNESOTA TWINS		
128.	Bob Allison	0.45
129.	Earl Battey	0.30
130.	Reno Bertoia	0.30
131.	Billy Gardner	0.45
132.	Jim Kaat	0.60
133.	Harmon Killebrew	1.50
134.	Jim Lemon	0.45
135.	Camilo Pascual	0.45
136.	Pedro Ramos	0.30
137.	Chuck Stobbs	0.30
138.	Zoilo Versalles	0.30
139.	Pete Whisenant	0.30
NEW YORK YANKEES		
140.	Luis Arroyo	0.30
141.	Yogi Berra	3.00
142.	John Blanchard	0.30
143.	Clete Boyer	0.45
144.	Art Ditmar	0.30
145.	Whitey Ford	2.00
146.	Elston Howard	0.60
147.	Tony Kubek	0.60
148.	Mickey Mantle	10.50
149.	Roger Maris	2.50
150.	Bobby Shantz	0.45
151.	Bill Stafford	0.30
152.	Bob Turley	0.30
PHILADELPHIA PHILLIES		
153.	John Buzhardt	0.30

No.	Player	Value
154.	Johnny Callison	0.45
155.	Tony Curry	0.30
156.	Clay Dalrymple	0.30
157.	Bobby Del Greco	0.30
158.	Dick Farrell	0.30
159.	Tony Gonzales	0.30
160.	Pancho Herrera	0.30
161.	Art Mahaffey	0.30
162.	Robin Roberts	1.50
163.	Tony Taylor	0.30
164.	Lee Walls	0.30
PITTSBURGH PIRATES		
165.	Smokey Burgess	0.45

166. Elroy Face 0.45
167. Bob Friend 0.45
168. Dick Groat 0.45
169. Don Hoak 0.30
170. Vernon Law 0.45
171. Bill Mazeroski 0.60
172. Rocky Nelson 0.30
173. Bob Skinner 0.30
174. Hal Smith 0.30
175. Dick Stuart 0.45
176. Bill Virdon 0.45

ST. LOUIS CARDINALS

177. Ken Boyer 0.60
178. Curt Flood 0.60
179. Alex Grammas 0.30
180. Larry Jackson 0.30
181. Julian Javier 0.30
182. Ron Kline 0.30
183. Lindy McDaniel 0.30
184. Stan Musial 4.00
185. Curt Simmons 0.45
186. Hal Smith 0.30
187. Deryl Spencer 0.30
188. Bill White 0.45

SAN FRANCISCO GIANTS

189. Don Blasingame 0.30
190. Eddie Bressoud 0.30
191. Orlando Cepeda 0.85
192. Jim Davenport 0.45
193. Harvey Kuenn 0.45
194. Hobie Landrith 0.35
195. Juan Marichal 1.50
196. Willie Mays 4.00
197. Mike McCormick 0.45
198. Willie McCovey 1.50
199. Billy O'Dell 0.35
200. Jack Sanford 0.35

WASHINGTON SENATORS

201. Bud Daley 0.30
202. Dick Donovan 0.30
203. Bobby Klaus 0.30
204. Johnny Klippstein 0.30
205. Dale Long 0.30
206. Ray Semproch 0.30
207. Gene Woodling 0.45

1962 TOPPS STAMPS

No. Player .... Value

BALTIMORE ORIOLES

1. Baltimore Emblem 0.30
2. Jerry Adair 0.30
3. Jackle Brandt 0.30
4. Chuck Estrada 0.30
5. Jim Gentile 0.45
6. Ron Hansen 0.30
7. Milt Pappas 0.45
8. Brooks Robinson 1.50
9. Gus Triandos 0.45
10. Hoyt Wilhelm 1.00

BOSTON RED SOX

11. Boston Emblem 0.30
12. Mike Forniales 0.30
13. Gary Geiger 0.30
14. Frank Malzone 0.45
15. Bill Monboquette 0.30
16. Russ Nixon 0.30
17. Pete Runnels 0.45
18. Chuck Schilling 0.30
19. Don Schwall 0.30
20. Carl Yastrzemski 5.25

CHICAGO CUBS

21. Chicago Emblem 0.30
22. George Altman 0.30
23. Ernie Banks 1.50
24. Dick Bertell 0.30
25. Don Cardwell 0.30
26. Dick Ellsworth 0.30

1962 Topps Carl Yastrzemski

27. Glen Hobbie 0.30
28. Ron Santo 0.60
29. Barney Schultz 0.30
30. Billy Williams 0.85

CHICAGO WHITE SOX

31. Chicago Emblem 0.30
32. Luis Aparicio 1.00
33. Camilo Carreon 0.30
34. Nellie Fox 0.85
35. Ray Herbert 0.30
36. Jim Landis 0.30
37. J.C. Martin 0.30
38. Juan Pizzaro 0.30
39. Floyd Robinson 0.30
40. Early Wynn 1.00

CINCINNATI REDS

41. Cincinnati Emblem 0.30
42. Gordon Coleman 0.30
43. John Edwards 0.30
44. Gene Frease 0.30
45. Joe Jay 0.30
46. Eddie Kasko 0.30
47. Jim O'Toole 0.30
48. Vada Pinson 0.45
49. Bob Purkey 0.30
50. Frank Robinson 1.50

CLEVELAND INDIANS

51. Cleveland Emblem 0.30
52. Ty Cline 0.30
53. Dic Donovan 0.30
54. Tito Francona 0.45
55. Woody Held 0.30
56. Barry Latman 0.30
57. Jim Perry 0.45
58. Bubba Phillips 0.30
59. Vic Power 0.30
60. Johnny Romano 0.30

DETROIT TIGERS

61. Detroit Emblem 0.30
62. Steve Boros 0.45
63. Bill Bruton 0.30
64. Jim Bunning 0.85
65. Norm Cash 0.45
66. Rocky Colavito 0.60
67. Al Kaline 2.00
68. Frank Lary 0.45
69. Don Mossi 0.45
70. Jake Wood 0.30

HOUSTON COLT 45'S

71. Houston Emblem 0.30
72. Joe Amalfitano 0.30
73. Bob Aspromonte 0.30
74. Dick Farrell 0.30
75. Al Heist 0.30
76. Sam Jones 0.30
77. Bobby Shantz 0.45
78. Hal W. Smith 0.30
79. Al Spangler 0.30
80. Bob Tiefenauer 0.30

KANSAS CITY A'S

81. Kansas City Emblem 0.30
82. Jim Archer 0.30
83. Dick Howser 0.45
84. Jerry Lumpe 0.30
85. Leo Posada 0.30
86. Bob Shaw 0.30
87. Norm Siebern 0.30
88. Roy Sievers (also 169) 0.60
89. Gene Stephens 0.30
90. Haywood Sullivan 0.45
91. Jerry Walker 0.30

LOS ANGELES ANGELS

92. Los Angeles Angels 0.30
93. Steve Bilko 0.30
94. Ted Bowsfield 0.30
95. Ken Hunt 0.30
96. Ken McBride 0.30
97. Albie Pearson 0.30
98. Bob Rodgers 0.30
99. George Thomas 0.30
100. Lee Thomas 0.30
101. Leon Wagner 0.30

LOS ANGELES DODGERS

102. Los Angeles Emblem 0.30
103. Don Drysdale 1.50
104. Ron Fairly 0.30
105. Frank Howard 0.45
106. Sandy Koufax 3.00
107. Wally Moon 0.45
108. Johnny Podres 0.45
109. John Roseboro 0.30
110. Duke Snider 2.50
111. Daryl Spencer 0.30

MILWAUKEE BRAVES

112. Milwaukee Emblem 0.30
113. Hank Aaron 4.00
114. Joe Adcock 0.45
115. Frank Bolling 0.30
116. Lou Burdette 0.45
117. Del Crandall 0.45
118. Ed Mathews 1.50
119. Roy McMillan 0.30
120. Warren Spahn 2.00
121. Joe Torre 0.60

MINNESOTA TWINS

122. Minnesota Emblem 0.30
123. Bob Allison 0.45
124. Earl Battey 0.30
125. Lenny Green 0.30
126. Harmon Killebrew 1.60
127. Jack Kralick 0.30
128. Camilo Pascual 0.45
129. Pedro Ramos 0.30
130. Bill Tuttle 0.30
131. Zoilo Versailles 0.30

NEW YORK METS

132. Now York Emblem 0.30
133. Gus Bell 0.45
134. Roger Craig 0.45
135. Gil Hodges 1.50
136. Jay Hook 0.30
137. Hobie Landrith 0.30
138. Felix Mantilla 0.30
139. Bob L. Miller 0.30
140. Leo Walls 0.30
141. Don Zimmer 0.45

NEW YORK YANKEES

142. New York Emblem 0.30
143. Yogi Berra 2.50
144. Clete Boyer 0.45

145. Whitey Ford 2.00
146. Elston Howard 0.60
147. Tony Kubek 0.60
148. Mickey Mantle 10.00
149. Roger Maris 2.50
150. Bobby Richardso 0.60
151. Bill Skowron 0.45

PHILADELPHIA PHILLIES

152. Philadelphia Emblem 0.30
153. Ruben Amaro 0.30
154. Jack Baldschun 0.30
155. Johnny Callison 0.45
156. Clay Dalrymple 0.30
157. Don Demeter 0.30
158. Tony Gonzalez 0.30
159. Roy Sievers (also 58) 0.60
160. Tony Taylor 0.30
161. Art Mahaffy 0.30

PITTSBURGH PIRATES

162. Pittsburgh Emblem 0.30
163. Smoky Burgess 0.45
164. Bob Clements 3.50
165. Roy Face 0.45
166. Bob Friend 0.45
167. Dick Groat 0.45
168. Don Hoak 0.30
169. Bill Mazeroski 0.60
170. Dick Stuart 0.45
171. Bill Virdon 0.45

ST. LOUIS CARDINALS

172. St. Louis Emblem 0.30
173. Ken Boyer 0.60
174. Larry Jackson 0.30
175. Julian Javier 0.30
176. Tim McCarver 0.45
177. Lindy McDaniel 0.30
178. Minnie Minoso 0.45
179. Stan Musial 3.50
180. Ray Sadecki 0.30
181. Bill White 0.45

SAN FRANCISCO GIANTS

182. San Francisco Emblem 0.30
183. Felipe Alou 0.45
184. Ed Bailey 0.30
185. Orlando Cepeda 0.85
186. Jim Davenport 0.45
187. Harvey Kuenn 0.45
188. Juan Marichal 1.50
189. Willie Mays 4.00
190. Mike McCormick 0.45
191. Stu Miller 0.30

WASHINGTON SENATORS

192. Washington Emblem 0.30
193. Chuck Cottier 0.45
194. Pete Daley 0.30
195. Bennie Daniels 0.30
196. Chuck Hinton 0.30
197. Bob Johnson 0.30
198. Joe McClain 0.30
199. Danny O'Connell 0.30
200. Jimmy Piersall 0.45
201. Gene Woodling 0.30

1964 TOPPS STAMPS

No. Player .... Value

SHEET ONE

1. Ed Charles 0.55
2. Vada Pinson 0.85
3. Jimmy Hall 0.55
4. Milt Pappas 0.65
5. Dick Ellsworth 0.55
6. Frank Malzone 0.65
7. Max Alvis 0.55
8. Pete Ward 0.55
9. Tony Taylor 0.55
10. Bill White 0.70

SHEET TWO

1964 Topps Felipe Alou

11. Don Zimmer 0.70
12. Bobby Richardson 0.85
13. Larry Jackson 0.55
14. Norm Siebern 0.55
15. Frank Robinson 2.50
16. Bob Aspromonte 0.55
17. Al McBean 0.55
IS. Floyd Robinson 0.55
19. Bill Monbouquette 0.55
20. Willie Mays 6.00

SHEET THREE

21. Brooks Robinson 3.00
22. Joe Pepitone 0.70
23. Carl Yastrzemski 6.00
24. Don Lock 0.55
25. Ernie Banks 2.50
26. Dave Nicholson 0.55
27. Bob Clemente 6.00
28. Curt Flood 0.85
29. Woody Held 0.55
30. Jesse Gonder 0.55

SHEET FOUR

31. Juan Pizarro 0.55
32. Jim Maloney 0.70
33. Ron Santo 0.85
34. Harmon Killebrew 2.50
35. Ed Roebuck 0.55
36. Boog Powell 0.85
37. Jim Grant 0.55
38. Hank Aguirre 0.55
39. Juan Marichal 2.00
40. Bill Mazeroski 0.85

SHEET FIVE

41. Dick Radatz 0.70
42. Albie Pearson 0.55
43. Tommy Harper 0.70
44. Carl Willey 0.55
45. Jim Bouton 0.85
46. Ron Perranoski 0.60
47. Chuck Hinton 0.60
48. John Romano 0.60
49. Norm Cash 0.85
50. Orlando Cepeda 1.00

SHEET SIX

51. Dick Stuart 0.70
52. Rich Rollins 0.55
53. Mickey Mantle 10.00
54. Steve Barber 0.55
55. Jim O'Toole 0.55
56. Gary Peters 0.55
57. Warren Spahn 2.50
58. Tony Gonzalez 0.55
59. Joe Torre 0.85
60. Jim Fregosi 0.70

SHEET SEVEN

61. Ken Boyer 0.85
62. Felipe Alou 0.85
63. Jim Davenport 0.70
64. Tommy Davis 0.85

65. Rocky Colavito 0.85
66. Bob Friend 0.55
67. Billy Moran 0.55
68. Bill Freehan 0.70
69. George Altman 0.55
70. Ken Johnson 0.55

SHEET EIGHT

71. Earl Battey 0.55
72. Elston Howard 0.85
73. Billy Williams 1.00
74. Claude Osteen 0.70
75. Jim Gentile 0.70
76. Donn Clendenon 0.55
77. Ernie Brogilo 0.55
78. Hal Woodeshick 0.55
79. Don Drysdale 2.50
80. John Callison 0.70

SHEET NINE

81. Dick Groat 0.70
82. Moe Drabowsky 0.55
83. Frank Howard 0.85
84. Hank Aaron 6.25
85. Al Jackson 0.55
86. Jerry Lumpe 0.55
87. Wayne Causey 0.55
88. Rusty Staub 0.85
89. Ken McBride 0.55
90. Jack Baldschun 0.55

SHEET TEN

91. Sandy Koufax 4.00
92. Camilo Pascual 0.70
93. Ron Hunt 0.55
94. Willie McCovey 2.50
95. Al Kaline 3.10
96. Ray Culp 0.55
97. Ed Mathews 2.50
98. Dick Farrell 0.55
99. Lee Thomas 0.55
100. Vic Davalillo 0.55

1964 WHEATIES STAMPS

No. Player .... Value

1. Aaron, Hank 8.00
2. Allison, Bob 0.75
3. Aparicio, Luis 2.00
4. Bailey, Ed 0.75
5. Barber, Steve 0.75
6. Battey, Eark 0.75
7. Bouton, Jim 1.00
8. Boyer, Ken 1.50

9. Bunning, Jim 1.50
10. Cepeda, Orlando 3.00
11. Clemente, Roberto ... 10.00
12. Culp, Ray 0.75
13. Davis, Tommy 1.00
14. Edwards, John 0.75
15. Ford, Whitey 5.00
16. Fox, Nellie 3.00
17. Friend, Bob 0.75
18. Gilliam, Jim 1.00
19. Groat, Dick 1.50
20. Grant, Jim 0.75
21. Howard, Elston 3.00
22. Jackson, Larry 0.75
23. Javier, Julian 1.00
24. Kaline, Al 5.00
25. Killebrew, Harmon 5.00
26. Leppert, Don 0.75
27. Malzone, Frank 1.00
28. Marichal, Juan 4.00
29. Mays, Willie 8.00
30. McBride, Ken 0.75
31. McCovey, Willie 5.00
32. O'Toole, Jim 0.75
33. Pearson, Albie 0.75
34. Pepitone, Joe 0.75
35. Perranoski, Ron 0.75
36. Pizarro, Juan 0.75
37. Radatz, Dick 0.75
38. Richardson, Bobby 1.50
39. Robinson, Brooks 5.00
40. Santo, Ron 1.50
41. Siebern, Norm 0.75
42. Snider, Duke 6.00
43. Spahn, Warren 5.00
44. Torre, Joe 2.00
45. Tresh, Tom 0.75
46. Versalles, Zoilo 0.75
47. Wagner, Leon 0.75
48. White, Bill 2.50
49. Woodeshick, Hal 0.75
50. Yastrzemski, Carl 5.00

1969 TOPPS STAMPS

No. Player .... Value

ATLANTA BRAVES

1. Hank Aaron 2.50
2. Felipe Alou 0.35
3. Clete Boyer 0.35
4. Tito Francona 0.20
5. Sonny Jackson 0.20
6. Pat Jarvis 0.20
7. Felix Millan 0.20
8. Milt Pappas 0.35
9. Ron Reed 0.20
10. Joe Torre 0.50

BALTIMORE ORIOLES

11. Mark Belanger 0.35
12. Curt Blefary 0.20
13. Don Buford 0.20
14. Jim Hardin 0.20
15. Dave Johnson 0.35
16. Dave McNally 0.35
17. Tom Phoebus 0.20
18. Boog Powell 0.50
19. Brooks Robinson 2.00
20. Frank Robinson 1.50

BOSTON RED SOX

21. Mike Andrews 0.20
22. Ray Culp 0.20
23. Russ Gibson 0.20
24. Ken Harrelson 0.50
25. Jim Lonborg 0.35
26. Rico Petrocelli 0.35
27. Jose Santiago 0.20
28. George Scott 0.35
29. Reggie Smith 0.50
30. Carl Yastrzemski 3.00

CALIFORNIA ANGELS

31. George Brunet 0.20
32. Vic Davalillo 0.20
33. Eddie Fisher 0.20
34. Jim Fregosi 0.20
35. Bobby Knoop 0.35
36. Jim McGlothlin 0.20
37. Rick Reichardt 0.20
38. Roger Repoz 0.20
39. Bob Rodgers 0.20
40. Tom Satriano 0.20

CHICAGO CUBS

41. Ernie Banks 1.50
42. Glenn Beckert 0.20
43. Bill Hands 0.20
44. Randy Hundley 0.20
45. Ferguson Jenkins 0.60
46. Don Kessinger 0.35
47. Adolpho Phillips 0.20
48. Phil Regan 0.20
49. Ron Santo 0.50
50. Billy Williams 0.85

CHICAGO WHITE SOX

51. Sandy Alomar 0.20
52. Luis Aparicio 1.00
53. Ken Berry 0.20
54. Joel Horlon 0.20
55. Tommy John 0.85
56. Duane Josephson 0.20
57. Gary Peters 0.20
58. Gary Wagner 0.20
59. Pete Ward 0.20
60. Wilbur Wood 0.20

CINCINNATI REDS

61. Ted Abernathy 0.20
62. Gerry Arrigo 0.20
63. Johnny Bench 1.50
64. Tommy Helms 0.20
65. Alex Johnson 0.20
66. Jim Maloney 0.35
67. Lee May 0.35
68. Tony Perez 0.60
69. Pete Rose 6.00
70. Bobby Tolan 0.20

CLEVELAND INDIANS

71. Max Alvis 0.20
72. Joe Azcue 0.20
73. Larry Brown 0.20
74. Jose Cardenal 0.20
75. Lee Maye 0.20
76. Sam McDowell 0.35
77. Sonny Siebert 0.20
78. Duke Sims 0.20
79. Luis Tiant 0.35
80. Stan Williams 0.20

DETROIT TIGERS

81. Norm Cash 0.50
82. Bill Freehan 0.35
83. Willie Horton 0.35
84. Al Kaline 1.50
85. Mickey Lolich 0.50
86. Dick McAuliffe 0.20
87. Denny McLain 0.50
88. Bill Northrup 0.20
89. Mickey Stanley 0.20
90. Don Wert 0.20

HOUSTON ASTROS

91. Bob Aspromonte 0.20
92. Larry Dierker 0.20
93. Johnny Edwards 0.20
94. Denver Lemaster 0.20
95. Denis Menke 0.20
96. Joe Morgan 1.00
97. Doug Rader 0.35
98. Rusty Staub 0.50
99. Don Wilson 0.20
100. Jim Wynn 0.35

KANSAS CITY ROYALS

101. Jerry Adair 0.20
102. Wallj Bunker 0.20
103. Moe Drabowsky 0.20
104. Joe Foy 0.20
105. Jackie Hemandez 0.20
106. Roger Nelson 0.20
107. Bob Oliver 0.20
108. Paul Schaal 0.20
109. Steve Whitaker 0.20
110. Hoyt Wilhelm 1.00

LOS ANGELES DODGERS

111. Willie Davis 0.35
112. Don Drysdale 1.50
113. Ron Fairly 0.20
114. Len Gabrielson 0.20
115. Tom Haller 0.20
116. Ron Lefebvre 0.20
117. Claude Osteen 0.35
118. Paul Popovich 0.20
119. Bill Singer 0.20
120. Don Sutton 0.85

MINNESOTA TWINS

121. Bob Allison 0.35
122. Rod Carew 2.00
123. Dean Chance 0.35
124. Jim Kaat 0.60
125. Harmon Killebrew 1.50
126. Tony Oliva 0.50
127. Ron Perranoski 0.20
128. John Roseboro 0.20
129. Cesar Tovar 0.20
130. Ted Uhlaender 0.20

MONTREAL EXPOS

131. Jesus Alou 0.20
132. Bob Bailey 0.20
133. John Bateman 0.20
134. Donn Clondenon 0.20
135. Jim Grant 0.20
136. Larry Jaster 0.20
137. Mack Jones 0.20
138. Manny Mota 0.35
139. Gary Sutherland 0.20
140. Maury Wills 0.60

NEW YORK METS

141. Tommy Ages 0.20
142. Ed Charles 0.20
143. Jerry Grote 0.20
144. Bud Harrelson 0.20
145. Cleon Jones 0.20
146. Jerry Koosman 0.35
147. Ed Kranepool 0.20
148. Tom Seaver 2.00
149. Art Shamsky 0.20
150. Ron Swoboda 0.20

NEW YORK YANKEES

151. Stan Bahnsen 0.20
152. Horace Clarke 0.20
153. Jake Gibbs 0.20
154. Andy Kosko 0.20

No.	Player	Value
155.	Mickey Mantle	6.00
156.	Joe Pepitone	0.35
157.	Bill Robinson	0.20
158.	Mel Stottlemyre	0.35
159.	Tom Tresh	0.35
160.	Roy White	0.35
OAKLAND A'S		
161.	Sal Bando	0.35
162.	Bert Campaneris	0.35
163.	Danny Cater	0.20
164.	Dave Duncan	0.20
165.	Dick Green	0.20
166.	Jim Hunter	0.85
167.	Lew Krausse	0.20
168.	Rick Monday	0.35
169.	Jim Nash	0.20
170.	John Odom	0.20
PHILADELPHIA PHILLIES		
171.	Richie Allen	0.50
172.	John Briggs	0.20
173.	John Callison	0.35
174.	Clay Dalrymple	0.20
175.	Woody Fryman	0.20
176.	Don Lock	0.20
177.	Cookie Rojas	0.20
178.	Chris Short	0.20
179.	Ron Taylor	0.20
180.	Rick Wise	0.20
PITTSBURGH PIRATES		
181.	Gene Alley	0.20
182.	Matty Alou	0.35
183.	Steve Blass	0.35
184.	Jim Bunning	0.70
185.	Roberto Clemente	2.50
186.	Ron Kline	0.20
187.	Jerry May	0.20
188.	Bill Mazeroski	0.60
189.	Willie Stargell	1.50
190.	Bob Veale	0.20
ST. LOUIS CARDINALS		
191.	Nelson Briles	0.20
192.	Lou Brock	1.50
193.	Orlando Cepeda	0.85
194.	Curt Flood	0.50
195.	Bob Gibson	1.50
196.	Julian Javier	0.20
197.	Dal Maxvill	0.20
198.	Tim McCarver	0.35
199.	Vada Pinson	0.35
200.	Mike Shannon	0.35
SAN DIEGO PADRES		
201.	Jose Arcia	0.20
202.	Ollie Brown	0.20
203.	Al Ferrara	0.20
204.	Tony Gonzalez	0.20
205.	Dave Giusti	0.20
206.	Alvin McBean	0.20
207.	Orlando Pena	0.20
208.	Dick Selma	0.20
209.	Larry Stahl	0.20
210.	Zoilo Versalles	0.20
SAN FRANCISCO GIANTS		
211.	Bobby Bolin	0.20
212.	Jim Davenport	0.35
213.	Dick Dietz	0.20
214.	Jim Ray Hart	0.20
215.	Ron Hunt	0.20
216.	Hal Lanier	0.35
217.	Juan Marichal	1.00
218.	Willie Mays	2.50
219.	Willie McCovey	1.50
220.	Gaylord Perry	1.00
SEATTLE PILOTS		
221.	Jack Aker	0.20
222.	Steve Barber	0.20
223.	Gary Bell	0.20
224.	Tommy Davis	0.35
225.	Tommy Harper	0.20
226.	Jerry McNertney	0.20
227.	Mike Mincher	0.20
228.	Roy Oyler	0.20
229.	Rich Rollins	0.20
230.	Chico Salmon	0.20
WASHINGTON SENATORS		
231.	Bernie Allen	0.20
232.	Ed Brinkman	0.20
233.	Paul Casanova	0.20
234.	Joe Coleman	0.20
235.	Mike Epstein	0.20
236.	Jim Hannan	0.20
237.	Dennis Higgins	0.20
238.	Frank Howard	0.35
239.	Ken McMullen	0.20
240.	Camilo Pascual	0.35

1974 TOPPS STAMPS

No.	Player	Value
ATLANTA BRAVES		
1.	Hank Aaron	2.75
2.	Dusty Baker	0.40
3.	Darrell Evans	0.50
4.	Ralph Garr	0.40
5.	Roric Harrison	0.25
6.	Dave Johnson	0.50
7.	Mike Lum	0.25
8.	Carl Morton	0.25
9.	Phil Niekro	0.85
10.	Johnny Oates	0.25
BALTIMORE ORIOLES		
11.	Don Baylor	0.60
12.	Mark Belanger	0.40
13.	Paul Blair	0.40
14.	Tommy Davis	0.40
15.	Bobby Grich	0.50
16.	Grant Jackson	0.25
17.	Dave McNally	0.40
18.	Jim Palmer	1.50
19.	Brooks Robinson	1.50
20.	Earl Williams	0.25
BOSTON RED SOX		
21.	Luis Aparicio	1.00
22.	Orlando Cepeda	0.85
23.	Carlton Fisk	0.85
24.	Tommy Harper	0.40
25.	Bill Lee	0.40
26.	Rick Miller	0.25
27.	Roger Moret	0.25
28.	Luis Tiant	0.50
29.	Rick Wise	0.25
30.	Carl Yastrzemski	2.50
CALIFORNIA ANGELS		
31.	Sandy Alomar	0.25
32.	Mike Epstein	0.25
33.	Bob Oliver	0.25
34.	Vada Pinson	0.40
35.	Frank Robinson	1.50
36.	Ellis Rodriguez	0.25
37.	Nolan Ryan	1.50
38.	Richie Scheinblum	0.25
39.	Bill Singer	0.25
40.	Bobby Valentine	0.50
CHICAGO CUBS		
41.	Glen Beckert	0.25
42.	Jose Cardinal	0.25
43.	Vic Harris	0.25
44.	Burt Hooton	0.25
45.	Randy Hundley	0.25
46.	Don Kessinger	0.40
47.	Rick Monday	0.40
48.	Rick Reuschel	0.40
49.	Ron Santo	0.50
50.	Billy Williams	0.85
CHICAGO WHITE SOX		
51.	Dick Allen	0.50
52.	Stan Bahnsen	0.25
53.	Terry Forster	0.40
54.	Ken Henderson	0.25
55.	Ed Herrmann	0.25
56.	Pat Kelly	0.25
57.	Carlos May	0.25
58.	Bill Melton	0.25
59.	Jorge Orta	0.25
60.	Wilbur Wood	0.25
CINCINNATI REDS		
61.	Johnny Bench	2.00
62.	Jack Billingham	0.25
63.	Pedro Borbon	0.25
64.	Days Concepcion	0.60
65.	Dan Driessen	0.40
66.	Ceasar Geronimo	0.25
67.	Don Gullett	0.40
68.	Joe Morgan	0.85
69.	Tony Perez	0.60
70.	Pete Rose	4.00
CLEVELAND INDIANS		
71.	Buddy Bell	0.50
72.	Chris Chambliss	0.40
73.	Frank Duffy	0.25
74.	Dave Duncan	0.25
75.	John Ellis	0.25
76.	Oscar Gamble	0.40
77.	George Hendrick	0.40
78.	Gaylord Perry	0.85
79.	Charlie Spikes	0.40
80.	Dick Tidrow	0.40
DETROIT TIGERS		
81.	Ed Brinkman	0.25
82.	Norm Cash	0.50
83.	Joe Coleman	0.25
84.	Bill Freehan	0.40
85.	John Hiller	0.40
86.	Willie Horton	0.40
87.	Al Kaline	1.50
88.	Mickey Lolich	0.50
89.	Aurelio Rodriguez	0.25
90.	Mickey Stanley	0.25
HOUSTON ASTROS		
91.	Cesar Cedeno	0.50
92.	Tommy Holms	0.25
93.	Lee May	0.40
94.	Roger Metzger	0.25
95.	Doug Rader	0.40
96.	J.R. Richard	0.50
97.	Dave Roberts	0.25
98.	Jerry Reuss	0.40
99.	Bob Watson	0.40
100.	Jim Wynn	0.40
KANSAS CITY ROYALS		
101.	Steve Bushy	0.40
102.	Fran Healy	0.25
103.	Ed Kirkpatrick	0.25
104.	John Mayberry	0.40
105.	Amos Otis	0.50
106.	Fred Patak	0.25
107.	Marty Pattin	0.25

108. Lou Pinielia 0.50
109. Cookle Rojas 0.25
110. Paul Splittorff 0.25

LOS ANGELES DODGERS

111. Bill Buckner 0.50
112. Ron Cey 0.50
113. Willie Crawford 0.25
114. Willie Davis 0.40
115. Joe Ferguson 0.25
116. Davey Lopes 0.50
117. Andy Messersmith 0.40
118. Claude Osteen 0.40
119. Bill Russell 0.40
120. Don Sutton 0.85

MILWAUKEE BREWERS

121. Jerry Bell 0.25
122. John Briggs 0.25
123. Jim Colborn 0.25
124. Bob Collucio 0.25
125. Pedro Garcia 0.25
126. Dave May 0.25
127. Don Money 0.40
128. Darrell Porter 0.40
129. George Scott 0.40
130. Jim Slaton 0.25

MINNESOTA TWINS

131. Bert Blyleven 0.50
132. Steve Braun 0.25
133. Rod Carew 2.00
134. Ray Corbin 0.25
135. Bobby Darwin 0.25
136. Joe Decker 0.25
137. Jim Holt 0.25
138. Harmon Killebrew 1.25
139. George Mitterwald 0.25
140. Tony Oliva 0.60

MONTREAL EXPOS

141. Bob Bailey 0.25
142. John Boccabolla 0.25
143. Ron Fairly 0.25
144. Tim Foli 0.25
145. Ron Hunt 0.25
146. Mike Jorgensen 0.25
147. Mike Marshall 0.40
148. Steve Renko 0.25
149. Steve Rogers 0.50
150. Ken Singleton 0.50

NEW YORK METS

151. Wayne Garrett 0.25
152. Jerry Grote 0.25
153. Bud Harrelson 0.25
154. Cleon Jones 0.25
155. Jerry Koosman 0.40
156. Jon Matlack 0.40
157. Tug McGraw 0.50
158. Felix Millan 0.25
159. John Milner 0.25
160. Tom Seaver 2.00

NEW YORK YANKEES

161. Ron Blomberg 0.25
162. Sparky Lyle 0.50
163. George Medich 0.40
164. Gene Michaels 0.40
165. Thurman Munson 2.00
166. Bobby Murcer 0.50
167. Graig Nettles 0.70
168. Mel Stottlemyre 0.40
169. Otto Velez 0.25
170. Roy White 0.40

OAKLAND A'S

171. Sal Bando 0.40
172. Vida Blue 0.70
173. Bert Campenaris 0.40
174. Ken Holtzman 0.40
175. Jim Hunter 0.85
176. Reggie Jackson 2.00
177. Deron Johnson 0.25
178. Bill North 0.25
179. Joe Rudi 0.40
180. Gene Tenace 0.40

PHILADELPHIA PHILLIES

181. Bob Boone 0.40
182. Larry Bowa 0.50
183. Steve Carlton 1.60
184. Bill Grabarkewitz 0.25
185. Jim Lonborg 0.40
186. Greg Luzinski 0.50
187. Willie Montanez 0.25
188. Bill Robinson 0.25
189. Wayne Twitchell 0.25
190. Del Unser 0.25

PITTSBURGH PIRATES

191. Nelson Briles 0.25
192. Dock Ellis 0.25
193. Dave Giusti 0.25
194. Richie Hebner 0.25
195. Al Oliver 0.40
196. Dave Parker 1.50
197. Manny Sanguillen 0.40
198. Willie Stargell 1.00
199. Ronnie Stennett 0.25
200. Richie Zisk 0.40

ST. LOUIS CARDINALS

201. Lou Brock 1.75
202. Reggie Cleveland 0.25
203. Jose Cruz 0.40
204. Bob Gibson 1.25
205. Tim McCarver 0.40
206. Ted Simmons 0.50
207. Ted Sizemore 0.25
208. Reggie Smith 0.50
209. Joe Torre 0.60
210. Mike Tyson 0.25

SAN DIEGO PADRES

211. Nate Colbert 0.25
212. Bill Grief 0.25
213. Johnny Grubb 0.25
214. Randy Jones 0.40
215. Fred Kendall 0.25
216. Clay Kirby 0.25
217. Willie McCovey 1.00
218. Jerry Morales 0.25
219. Dave Roberts 0.25
220. Dave Winfield 2.75

SAN FRANCISCO GIANTS

221. Bobby Bonds 0.50
222. Tom Bradley 0.25
223. Ron Bryant 0.25
224. Tito Fuentes 0.25
225. Ed Goodson 0.25
226. Dave Kingman 0.85
227. Garry Maddox 0.40
228. Dave Rader 0.25
229. Elias Sosa 0.25
230. Chris Speier 0.25

TEXAS RANGERS

231. Jim Bibby 0.40
232. Jeff Burroughs 0.40
233. David Clyde 0.25
234. Jim Fregosi 0.40
235. Toby Harrah 0.40
236. Ferguson Jenkins 0.50
237. Alex Johnson 0.25
238. Dave Nelson 0.25
239. Jim Spencer 0.25
240. Bill Sudakis 0.25

1982 FLEER STAMPS

No. Player .... Value

LOS ANGELES DODGERS

1. Fernando Valenzuela (20) 0.22
2. Rick Monday (16) 0.13
3. Ron Cey (9) 0.15
4. Dusty Baker (20) 0.13
5. Burt Hooton (10) 0.07
6. Pedro Guerrero (23) 0.20
7. Jerry Reuss (12) 0.13
8. Bill Russell (7) 0.07
9. Steve Garvey (21) 0.22
10. Davey Lopes (19) 0.13

CINCINNATI REDS

11. Tom Seaver (7) 0.20
12. George Foster (17) 0.15
13. Frank Pastors (12) 0.07
14. Dave Collins (5) 0.13
15. Dave Concepcion (21) 0.14
16. Ken Griffey (6) 0.14
17. Johnny Bench (20) 0.20
18. Ray Knight (16) 0.14
19. Mario Soto (9) 0.14
20. Ron Oester (19) 0.07

ST. LOUIS CARDINALS

21. Ken Oberkfell (21) 0.07
22. Bob Forsch (4) 0.07
23. Keith Hernandez (19) 0.18
24. Dane Iorg (9) 0.07
25. George Hendrick (2) 0.13
26. Gene Tenace (24) 0.07
27. Garry Templeton (12) 0.14
28. Bruce Sutter (18) 0.16
29. Darrell Porter (14) 0.13
30. Tom Herr (3) 0.13

MONTREAL EXPOS

31. Tim Raines (11) 0.20
32. Chris Speier (13) 0.07
33. Warren Cromartie (22) 0.07
34. Larry Parrish (15) 0.13
35. Andre Dawson (1O) 0.19
36. Steve Rogers (1,25) 0.14
37. Jeff Reardon (23) 0.15
38. Rodney Scott (12) 0.07
39. Gary Carter (14) 0.22
40. Scott Sanderson (6) 0.07

HOUSTON ASTROS

41. Cesar Cedeno (7) 0.13
42. Nolan Ryan (1O) 0.20
43. Don Sutton (24) 0.16
44. Terry Puhl (15) 0.13
45. Joe Niekro (13) 0.14
46. Tony Scott (16) 0.07
47. Joe Sambito (1) 0.13
48. Art Howe (9) 0.07
49. Bob Knepper (18) 0.15
50. Jose Cruz (22) 0.15

PHILADELPHIA PHILLIES

51. Pete Rose (16) 0.40
52. Dick Ruthven (12) 0.07
53. Mike Schmidt (l4) 0.30
54. Steve Carlton (17) 0.22
55. Tug McGraw (4) 0.14
56. Larry Bowa (4) 0.14
57. Garry Maddox (18) 0.13
58. Gary Matthews (4) 0.14
59. Manny Trillo (15) 0.13

60. Lonnie Smith (20) 0.14

SAN FRANCISCO GIANTS

61. Vida Blue (11) 0.14
62. Milt May (12) 0.07
63. Joe Morgan (16) 0.17
64. Enos Cabell (8) 0.07
65. Jack Clark (18) 0.16

ATLANTA BRAVES

66. Claudell Washington (19) 0.13
67. Gaylord Perry (16) 0.18
68. Phil Niekro (22) 0.18
69. Bob Horner (7) 0.17
70. Chris Chambliss (11) ... 0.13

1982 Fleer Jose Cruz

PITTSBURGH PIRATES

71. Dave Parker (15) 0.18
72. Tony Pena (11) 0.15
73. Kent Tekulve (23) 0.13
74. Mike Easler (18) 0.14
75. Tim Foli (13) 0.07
76. Willie Stargell (21) 0.18
77. Bill Madlock (5) 0.17
78. Jim Bibby (14) 0.13
79. Omar Moreno (17) 0.13
80. Lee Lacy (2) 0.13

NEW YORK METS

81. Hubie Brooks (24) 0.18
82. Rusty Staub (4) 0.15
83. Ellis Valentine (13) 0.13
84. Neil Allen (1) 0.13
85. Dave Kingman (9) 0.16
86. Mookie Wilson (3) 0.14
87. Doug Flynn (11) 0.07
88. Pat Zachary (8) 0.07
89. John Stearns (6) 0.07
90. Leo Mazzilli (2) 0.07

CHICAGO CUBS

91. Ken Reitz (S23) 0.05
92. Mike Krukow (S11) 0.05
93. Jerry Morales (S1O) 0.05
94. Leon Durham (S22) 0.10
95. Ivan DeJesus (S2) 0.05
96. Bill Buckner (S17) 0.10
97. Jim Tracy (S12) 0.05
98. Steve Henderson (S14) .. 0.05
99. Dick Tidrow (S14) 0.05
100. Mike Tyson (S5) 0.05

SAN DIEGO PADRES

101. Ozzie Smith (S12) 0.10
102. Ruppert Jones (S24) 0.05
103. Broderick Perkins (S1O) . 0.05
104. Gene Richards (S15) ... 0.05
105. Terry Kennedy (S22) 0.05

COMBINATION STAMPS

106. Bibby and Stargell (S4) .. 0.10
107. Rose and Bowa (S21) ... 0.15
108. Valenzuela,Spahn(S1,25) 0.10
109. Rose,Concepcion (S8) .. 0.15
110. Jackson,Winfield (S3) ... 0.15
111. Valenzuela,Lasorda(S4) . 0.10

1982 Fleer Terry Kennedy

NEW YORK YANKEES

112. Reggie Jackson (S6) 0.20
113. Dave Winfield (S3) 0.15
114. Lou Pinielia (S2) 0.10
115. Tommy John (S9) 0.10
116. Rich Gossaage (S1,25) .. 0.10
117. Ron Davis (S1O) 0.05
118. Rick Cerone (S5) 0.05
119. Graig Nettles (S8) 0.10
120. Ron Guldry (S24) 0.15
121. Willie Randolph (S24) ... 0.05

OAKLAND A'S

122. Dwayne Murphy (S15) .. 0.05
123. Rickey Henderson (S16) . 0.15
124. Wayne Gross (S6) 0.05
125. Mike Norris (S8) 0.05
126. Rick Langford (S20) 0.05
127. Jim Spencer (S17) 0.05
128. Tony Armas (S12) 0.10
129. Matt Keough (S7) 0.05
130. Jeff Jones (S19) 0.05
131. Steve McCatty (S3) 0.05

MILWAUKEE BREWERS

132. Rollie Fingers (S7) 0.10
133. Jim Gantner (S15) 0.05
134. Gorman Thomas (S6) ... 0.10
135. Robin Yount (S13) 0.15

136. Paul Molitor (S22) 0.10
137. Ted Simmons (S1O) 0.10
138. Ben Oglivie (S23) 0.05
139. Moose Haas (S21) 0.05
140. Cecil Cooper (S24) 0.10
141. Pete Vuckovich (S1O) ... 0.05

BALTIMORE ORIOLES

142. Doug DeCinces (S21) ... 0.05
143. Jim Palmer (S9) 0.10
144. Steve Stone (S16) 0.05
145. Mike Flanagan (S19) 0.05
146. Rick Dempsey (S9) 0.05
147. Al Bumbry (S14) 0.05
148. Mark Belanger (S8) 0.05
149. Scott McGregor(S23) ... 0.05
150. Ken Singleton (S1O) 0.05
151. Eddie Murray (S5) 0.20

DETROIT TIGERS

152. Lance Parrish (S20) 0.15
153. Dave Rozema (S15) 0.05
154. Champ Summers (S13) .. 0.05
155. Alan Trammell (S2) 0.10
156. Lou Whitaker (S1,25) ... 0.10
157. Milt Wilcox (S5) 0.05
158. Kevin Saucier (S24) 0.05
159. Jack Morris (S14) 0.10
160. Steve Kemp (S7) 0.05
161. Kirk Gibson (S3) 0.15

BOSTON RED SOX

162. Carl Yastrzemski (S3) ... 0.20
163. Jim Rice (S21) 0.15
164. Carney Lansford (S15) .. 0.25
165. Dennis Eckersley (S6) ... 0.15
166. Mike Torrez (S5) 0.05
167. Dwight Evans (S19) 0.10
168. Glenn Hoffman (S18) ... 0.05
169. Bob Stanley (S20) 0.05
170. Tony Perez (S16) 0.10
171. Jerry Remy (S13) 0.05

TEXAS RANGERS

172. Buddy Bell (S5) 0.10
173. Fergie Jenkins (S17) 0.10
174. Mickey Rivers (S9) 0.05
175. Bump Wills (S2) 0.05
176. Jon Matlack (S20) 0.05
177. Steve Comer (S23) 0.05
178. Al Oliver (S1,25) 0.10
179. Bill Stein (S3) 0.05
180. Pat Putnam (S14) 0.05
181. Jim Sundberg (S4) 0.05

CHICAGO WHITE SOX

182. Ron LeFlore (S4) 0.05
183. Carlon Fisk (S11) 0.10
184. Harold Baines (S18) 0.10
185. Bill Almon (S2) 0.05
186. Richard Dotson (S9) 0.05
187. Greg Luzinski (S14) 0.10
188. Mike Squires (S13) 0.05
189. Britt Burns (S19) 0.10
190. LaMarr Hoyt (S6) 0.10

191. Chet Lemon (S22) 0.10

CLEVELAND INDIANS
192. Joe Charboneau (S20) .. 0.05
193. Toby Harrah (S16) 0.05
194. John Denny (S22) 0.10
195. Rick Manning (S8) 0.05
196. Miguel Dilone (S15) 0.05
197. Bo Diaz (S13) 0.05
198. Mike Hargrove (S17) 0.05
199. Bert Blyleven (S11) 0.10
200. Len Barker (S7) 0.05
201. Andre Thornton (S18) ... 0.10

KANSAS CITY ROYALS
202. George Brett (S24) 0.25
203. U.L. Washington (S25) .. 0.05
204. Dan Quisenberry (S17) .. 0.10
205. Larry Gura (S17) 0.05

206. Willie Aikens (S22) 0.05
207. Willie Wilson (S21) 0.10
208. Dennis Leonard (S8) 0.05
209. Frank White (S6) 0.05
210. Hal McRae (S23) 0.05
211. Amos Otis (S18) 0.05

CALIFORNIA ANGELS
212. Don Aase (S23) 0.05
213. Butch Hobson (S6) 0.05
214. Fred Lynn (S18) 0.10
215. Brian Downing (S10) 0.05
216. Dan Ford (S5) 0.05
217. Rod Carew (S5) 0.15
218. Bobby Grich (S19) 0.10
219. Rick Burleson (S11) 0.05
220. Don Baylor (S3) 0.10
221. Ken Forsch (S17) 0.05

SEATTLE MARINERS
222. Bruce Bochte (S20) 0.05
223. Richie Zisk (S21) 0.05
224. Tom Paciorek (S19) 0.05
225. Julio Cruz (S8) 0.05
226. Jeff Burroughs (S23) 0.05

MINNESOTA TWINS
227. Doug Corbett (S8) 0.05
228. Roy Smalley (S24) 0.05
229. Gary Ward (S4) 0.05
230. John Castino (S7) 0.05
231. Rob Wilfong (S12) 0.05

TORONTO BLUE JAYS
232. Dave Stieb (S22) 0.10
233. Otto Velez (S13) 0.05
234. Damaso Garcia (S7) 0.05
235. John Mayberry (S1,25) .. 0.05
236. Alfredo Griffin (S11) 0.05

COMBINATION STAMPS
237. Williams, Yaz (S3) 0.25
238. Nettles,Cerone (S25) ... 0.05
239. Bell and Brett (S25) 0.15
240. Kaat and Carlton (S2) ... 0.10
241. Parker, Carlton (S25) ... 0.15
242. Ryan and Davis (S2) 0.10

1983 FLEER STAMPS

Vertical Strip .... Value
Vertical Strip 1 .... 0.35

1983 Fleer George Brett

Pat Zachry, Chris Speier
Mike Schmidt, George Brett
Gaylord Perry, John Montefusco
Toby Harrah, Bump Wills
Dodgers Logo, A's Logo
Davey Lopes, Ruppert Jones
Dale Berra, Angels Logo
Cardinals Logo, Jack Clark
Craig Swan

Vertical Strip 2 .... 0.35
Tug McGraw, Roy Smalley
Kent Tekulve, Dan Quisenberry
Reggie Smith, Wade Boggs
Rick Sutcliffe, Steve Howe
Brian Downing, Phillies Logo
Cubs Logo, Dick Tidrow
Mario Soto, Ray Knight
Expos Logo, Astros Logo
Neil Allen, Mike Flanagan

Vertical Strip 3 .... 0.35
Warren Cromartie
Fernando Valenzuela
Keith Hernandez, Bob McClure
Jerry Royster, Bill Buckner
Reggie Jackson, Willie Stargell
Rick Monday, Giants Logo
Indians Logo, Ron LeFlore
Lee Mazzilli, Buddy Bell
Pirates Logo, Mets Logo
Dan Driessen, U.L. Washington

Vertical Strip 4 .... 0.35
Don Sutton, Willie Upshaw
Robin Yount, Paul Molitor
Doug DeCinces, Dave Winfield
Ken Forsch, Bob Forsch
Rick Rhoden, White Sox Logo
Red Sox Logo, Gary Lavelle
Harold Baines, Ron Reed
Twins Logo, Orioles Logo
Luis DeLeon, Dave Concepcion

Vertical Strip 5 .... 0.45
Chris Chambliss, Andre Dawson
Dwayne Murphy, Gorman Thomas
Ben Oglivie, Len Barker
Carl Yastrzemski, Pete Rose
Mookie Wilson, Braves Logo
Yankees Logo, Greg Minton
Willie Aikens, Dennis Eckersley
Reds Logo, Tigers Logo
Sixto Lezcano, Ron Guidry

Vertical Strip 6 .... 0.30
Rafael Ramirez, Scott McGregor
Goose Gossage, Bruce Sutter
Ken Oberkfell, Bo Diaz
Jim Rice, Fred Lynn
Jerry Reuss, Angels Logo
Cardinals Logo, Bob Bailor
Eric Show, Dusty Baker
Royals Logo, Mariners Logo
Steve Mura, Tom Underwood

Vertical Strip 7 .... 0.35
Larry Parrish, Jon Matlack
Floyd Bannister, Garth Iorg
Tim Raines, Rickey Henderson
Mark Clear, Expos Logo
Astros Logo, Ken Griffey
Eddie Milner, Hubie Brooks
Indians Logo, Dodgers Logo
Tommy John, Jeff Reardon

Vertical Strip 8 .... 0.35
Tom Brunansky, Tom Hume
Tom Seaver, Jim Palmer
Lance Parrish, George Foster
Al Oliver, Willie Wilson
Jim Sundberg, Pirates Logo
Mets Logo, Jason Thompson
Joe Morgan, Rollie Fingers
Rangers Logo, Phillies Logo
Lou Piniella, John Wockenfuss

Vertical Strip 9 .... 0.30
Jim Beattie, Manny Trillo
Johnny Bench, Ted Simmons
Keith Moreland, Milt Wilcox
Hal McRae, Andre Thornton
Bill Caudill, Twins Logo
Orioles Logo, Bobby Castillo
Manny Sarmiento, Gene Garber
Blue Jay Logo, Giants Logo
John Tudor, Dave Beard

Vertical Strip 10 .... 0.35
Duane Kuiper, Eddie Murray
Art Howe, Dickie Thon
Dave Stieb, Ken Singleton
Cal Ripken, Steve Sax
Bob Watson, Reds Logo
Tigers Logo, Steve Rogers
Bob Stanley, Jerry Mumphrey
Brewers Logo, Chisox Logo
Rick Manning, Darrell Porter

Vertical Strip 11 .... 0.35
Carlton Fisk, Mike Richardt
Alan Ashby, Nolan Ryan
Cecil Cooper, Frank White
Kent Hrbek, Johnny Ray
Burt Hooton, Royals Logo
Mariners Logo, Larry Biittner
Damaso Garcia, Mike Easler
Padres Logo, Braves Logo
Larry Herndon, Al Holland

Vertical Strip 12 .... 0.35
Gary Carter, Garry Maddox
Joe Niekro, Phil Niekro
Bill Laskey, Bob Boone
Rod Carew, Bill Madlock
Jerry Koosman, Indians Logo
Dodgers Logo, Ed VandeBerg
Amos Otis, Dennis Leonard

A's Logo, Angels Logo
Rusty Staub, Dwight Evans

Vertical Strip 13 .... 0.35
Dale Murphy, Larry Christenson
Leon Durham, Greg Luzinski
Gary Matthews, Lou Whitaker
Bruce Kison, Milt May
Randy Martz, Rangers Logo
Phillies Logo, Phil Garner
John Lowenstein, Rick Cerone
Cubs Logo, Pirates Logo
Claudell Washington, Dave Parker

Vertical Strip 14 .... 0.30
Danny Darwin, Tony Pena
Tom Paciorek, Steve Garvey
Charlie Lea, Mike Hargrove
Steve Kemp, Rich Dauer
Al Williams, Blue Jay Logo
Giants Logo, Jim Clancy
Hosken Powell, John Grubb
Expos Logo, Twins Logo
Al Bumbry, Ron Davis

Vertical Strip 15 .... 0.30
Dan Spiliner, Ferguson Jenkins
Enos Cabell, Ken Landreaux
Joaquin Andujar, Don Baylor
Lonnie Smith, Ozzie Smith
Ron Cey, Brewers Logo
White Sox Logo, Willie Randolph
Cesar Cedeno, Richie Zisk
Red Sox Logo, Reds Logo
Ellis Valentine, Atlee Hammaker

Vertical Strip 16 .... 0.30
Jose Cruz, Larry Bowa
Steve Carlton, Pete Vuckovich
Graig Nettles, Bruce Bochte
Tippy Martinez, Dennis Martinez
Ivan DeJesus, Padres Logo
Braves Logo, Gary Ward
Jeff Burroughs, Vida Blue
Yankees Logo, Royals Logo
Carney Lansford, Tom Herr

1972 TOPPS STICKERS (CLOTH)

No.	Player	Value
1.	Aaron, Hank	100.00
2.	Aparicio, Luis IA	25.00
3.	Brown, Ike	8.00
4.	Callison, Johnny	8.00
5.	Checklist 264-319	8.00
6.	Clemente, Roberto	125.00
7.	Concepcion, Dave	10.00
8.	Cook, Ron	8.00
9.	Davis, Willie	9.00
10.	Fitzmorris, Al	8.00
11.	Floyd, Bobby	8.00
12.	Foster, Roy	8.00
13.	Fregosi, Jim KP	9.00
14.	Frisella, Danny IA	8.00
15.	Fryman, Woody	8.00
16.	Harmon, Terry	8.00
17.	Howard, Frank	12.00
18.	Klimkowski, Ron	8.00
19.	LaHoud, Joe	8.00
20.	Lefebvre, Jim	8.00
21.	Maddox, Elliott	8.00
22.	Martinez, Marty	8.00

1972 Topps Hank Aaron

No.	Player	Value
23.	McCovey, Willie	40.00
24.	McRae, Hal	10.00
25.	O'Brien, Syd	8.00
26.	Red Sox Team	12.00
27.	Rodriguez, Aurelio	8.00
28.	Severinsen, Al	8.00
29.	Shamsky, Art	8.00
30.	Stone, Steve	8.00
31.	Swanson, Stan	8.00
32.	Watson, Bob	10.00
33.	White, Roy	10.00

1977 TOPPS STICKERS (CLOTH)

No.	Player	Value
1.	Ashby, Alan	0.25
2.	Bell, Buddy	0.75
3.	Bench, Johnny	10.00
4.	Blue, Vida	1.00
5.	Blyleven, Bert	2.00
6.	Braun, Steve	0.25
7.	Brett, George	8.00
8.	Brock, Lou	6.00

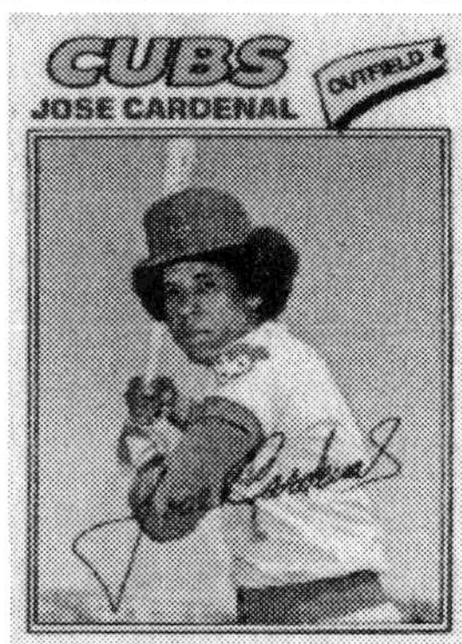

No.	Player	Value
9.	Cardenal, Jose	0.25
10.	Carew, Rod	8.00
11.	Carlton, Steve	10.00
12.	Cash, Dave	0.25
13.	Cedeno, Cesar	1.00
14.	Cey, Ron	1.50
15.	Fidrych, Mark	1.00
16.	Ford, Dan	0.25
17.	Garland, Wayne	0.25
18.	Garr, Ralph	0.50
19.	Garvey, Steve	5.00
20.	Hargrove, Mike	0.75
21.	Hunter, Jim	8.00
22.	Jackson, Reggie	12.00
23.	Jones, Randy	0.25
24.	Kingman, Dave	1.25

No.	Player	Value
25.	Madlock, Bill	1.25
26.	May, Lee	0.50
27.	Mayberry, John	0.25
28.	Messersmith, Andy	0.25
29.	Montanez, Willie	0.25
30.	Montefusco, John	0.25
31.	Morgan, Joe	8.00
32.	Munson, Thurman	8.00
33.	Murcer, Bobby	1.50
34.	Oliver, Al	1.50
35.	Pagan, Dave	0.25
36.	Palmer, Jim	8.00
37.	Perez, Tony	2.00
38.	Rose, Pete	15.00
39.	Rudi, Joe	0.75
40.	Ryan, Nolan	50.00
41.	Schmidt, Mike	15.00
42.	Seaver, Tom	15.00
43.	Simmons, Ted	1.00
44.	Singer, Bill	0.25
45.	Stargell, Willie	6.00
46.	Staub, Rusty	1.00
47.	Sutton, Don	2.00
48.	Tiant, Luis	1.00
49.	Travers, Bill	0.25
50.	Washington, Claudell	1.00
51.	Watson, Bob	1.25
52.	Winfield, Dave	6.00
53.	Yastrzemski, Carl	6.00
54.	Yount, Robin	8.00
55.	Zisk, Richie	0.75

1981 FLEER STICKERS

No.	Player	Value
1.	Steve Garvey	2.00
2.	Ron LeFlore	0.25
3.	Ron Cey	0.45
4.	Dave Revering	0.25
5.	Tony Armas	0.45
6.	Mike Norris	0.25
7.	Steve Kemp	0.35
8.	Bruce Bochte	0.25
9..	Mike Schmidt	2.50
10.	Scott McGregor	0.30
11.	Buddy Bell	0.45
12.	Carney Lansford	0.45
13.	Carl Yastrzemski	2.75
14.	Ben Oglivie	0.30

15. Willie Stargell 0.85
16. Cecil Cooper 0.65
17. Gene Richards 0.25
18. Jim Kern 0.25
19. Jerry Koosman 0.30
20. Larry Bowa 0.30
21. Kent Tekulve 0.25
22. Dan Driessen 0.25
23. Phil Niekro 0.85
24. Dan Quisenberry 0.65
25. Dave Winfield 2.00
26. Dave Parker 0.85
27. Rick Langford 0.25
28. Amos Otis 0.30
29. Bill Buckner 0.30
30. Al Bumbry 0.25
31. Bake McBride 0.25
32. Mickey Rivers 0.25
33. Rick Burleson 0.30
34. Dennis Eckersley 0.30
35. Cesar Cedeno 0.30
36. Enos Cabell 0.25
37. Johnny Bench 2.00
38. Robin Yount 2.00
39. Mark Belanger 0.25
40. Rod Carew 2.00
41. George Foster 0.85
42. Lee Mazzilli 0.25
43. Rose, Bowa, Schmidt . . . 2.00
44. J.R. Richard 0.30
45. Lou Piniella 0.35
46. Ken Landreaux 0.25
47. Rollie Fingers 0.65
48. Joaquin Andujar 0.30
49. Tom Seaver 2.00
50. Bobby Grich 0.35
51. Jon Matlack 0.25
52. Jack Clark 0.45
53. Jim Rice 2.00
54. Rickey Henderson 2.00
55. Roy Smalley 0.25
56. Mike Flanagan 0.30
57. Steve Rogers 0.30
58. Carlton Fisk 0.55
59. Don Sutton 0.60
60. Ken Griffey 0.30
61. Burt Hooton 0.25
62. Dusty Baker 0.30
63. Vida Blue 0.30
64. Al Oliver 0.55
65. Jim Bibby 0.25
66. Tony Perez 0.65
67. Davey Lopes 0.30
68. Bill Russell 0.30
69. Larry Parrish 0.25
70. Garry Maddox 0.25
71. Phil Garner 0.25
72. Graig Nettles 0.55
73. Gary Carter 2.00
74. Pete Rose 4.10
75. Greg Luzinski 0.35
76. Ron Guidry 0.55
77. Gorman Thomas 0.35
78. Jose Cruz 0.35
79. Bob Boone 0.25
80. Bruce Sutter 0.55
81. Chris Chambliss 0.35
82. Paul Molitor 0.35
83. Tug McGraw 0.30
84. Ferguson Jenkins 0.40
85. Steve Carlton 2.00
86. Miguel Dilone 0.25
87. Reggie Smith 0.30
88. Rick Cerone 0.25
89. Alan Trammell 0.65
90. Doug DeCinces 0.40
91. Sparky Lyle 0.30
92. Warren Cromartie 0.25
93. Rick Reuschel 0.25
94. Larry Hisle 0.25
95. Paul Splittorff 0.25
96. Manny Trillo 0.25
97. Frank White 0.30
98. Fred Lynn 0.65
99. Bob Horner 0.65
100. Omar Moreno 0.25
101. Dave Concepcion 0.30
102. Larry Gura 0.25
103. Ken Singleton 0.30
104. Steve Stone 0.25
105. Richie Zisk 0.25
106. Willie Wilson 0.55
107. Willie Randolph 0.30
108. Nolan Ryan 1.50

109. Joe Morgan 0.85
110. Bucky Dent 0.25
111. Dave Kingman 0.30
112. John Castino 0.25
113. Joe Rudi 0.25
114. Ed Farmer 0.25
115. Reggie Jackson 2.50
116. George Brett 2.50
117. Eddie Murray 2.50
118. Rich Gossage 0.65
119. Dale Murphy 3.00
120. Ted Simmons 0.35
121. Tommy John 0.55
122. Don Baylor 0.55
123. Andre Dawson 1.00
124. Jim Palmer 1.00
125. Garry Templeton 0.45
126. Reggie Jackson CL 1.50
127. George Brett CL 1.50
128. Mike Schmidt CL 1.50

1981 TOPPS STICKERS

No. Player Value

1. Steve Stone 0.05
2. John and Norris 0.05
3. Rudy May 0.05
4. Mike Norris 0.05
5. Len Barker 0.05
6. Mike Norris 0.05
7. Don Quisenberry 0.10
8. Rich Gossage 0.10
9. George Brett 0.35
10. Cecil Cooper 0.15
11. Jackson and Oglivie 0.15
12. Gorman Thomas 0.10
13. Cecil Cooper 0.15
14. Brett and Oglivie 0.15
15. Rickey Henderson 0.35
16. Willie Wilson 0.15
17. Bill Buckner 0.10
18. Keith Hernandez 0.15
19. Mike Schmidt 0.30
20. Bob Horner 0.20
21. Mike Schmidt 0.30
22. George Hendrick 0.10
23. Ron Leflore 0.05
24. Omar Moreno 0.05
25. Steve Carlton 0.25
26. Joe Niekro 0.10
27. Don Sutton 0.10
28. Steve Carlton 0.25
29. Steve Carlton 0.25
30. Nolan Ryan 0.25
31. Fingers and Hume 0.10
32. Bruce Sutter 0.15

BALTIMORE ORIOLES

33. Ken Singleton 0.10
34. Eddie Murray 0.30
35. Al Bumbry 0.05
36. Rich Dauer 0.05
37. Scott McGregor 0.10
38. Rick Dempsey 0.10
39. Jim Palmer 0.20
40. Steve Stone 0.05

BOSTON RED SOX

41. Jim Rice 0.25
42. Fred Lynn 0.15
43. Carney Lansford 0.10
44. Tony Perez 0.10
45. Carl Yastrzemski 0.35
46. Carlton Fisk 0.15
47. Dave Stapleton 0.05
48. Dennis Eckersley 0.05

CALIFORNIA ANGELS

49. Rod Carew 0.25
50. Brian Downing 0.05
51. Don Baylor 0.15
52. Rick Burleson 0.10
53. Bobby Grich 0.10
54. Butch Hobson 0.05
55. Andy Hassler 0.05
56. Frank Tanana 0.10

CHICAGO WHITE SOX

57. Chet Lemon 0.10
58. Lamar Johnson 0.05
59. Wayne Nordhagen 0.05
60. Jim Morrison 0.05
61. Bob Molinaro 0.05
62. Rich Dotson 0.10
63. Britt Burns 0.10
64. Ed Farmer 0.05

CLEVELAND INDIANS

65. Toby Harrah 0.10
66. Joe Charboneau 0.10
67. Miguel Dilone 0.05
68. Mike Hargrove 0.05
69. Rick Manning 0.05
70. Andre Thornton 0.10
71. Ron Hassey 0.05
72. Len Barker 0.05

DETROIT TIGERS

73. Lance Parrish 0.20
74. Steve Kemp 0.10
75. Alan Trammell 0.20
76. Champ Summers 0.05
77. Rick Peters 0.05
78. Kirk Gibson 0.25
79. Johnny Wockenfuss 0.05
80. Jack Morris 0.15

KANSAS CITY ROYALS

81. Willie Wilson 0.10
82. George Brett 0.35
83. Frank White 0.10
84. Willie Aikens 0.10
85. Clint Hurdle 0.05
86. Hal McRae 0.10
87. Dennis Leonard 0.10
88. Larry Gura 0.05
89. AL Pennant Winner 0.05
90. AL Pennant Winner 0.05

MILWAUKEE BREWERS

91. Paul Molitor 0.15

92. Ben Oglivie 0.10
93. Cecil Cooper 0.15
94. Ted Simmons 0.15
95. Robin Yount 0.25
96. Gorman Thomas 0.10
97. Mike Caldwell 0.05

1981 Topps Willie Stargell

98. Moose Haas 0.05

MINNESOTA TWINS

99. John Castino 0.05
100. Roy Smalley 0.05
101. Ken Landreaux 0.05
102. Butch Wynegar 0.05
103. Ron Jackson 0.05
104. Jerry Koosman 0.10
105. Roger Erickson 0.05
106. Doug Corbett 0.05

NEW YORK YANKEES

107. Reggie Jackson 0.30
108. Willie Randolph 0.10
109. Rick Cerone 0.05
110. Bucky Dent 0.10
111. Dave Winfield 0.25
112. Ron Guidry 0.15
113. Rich Gossage 0.15
114. Tommy John 0.15

OAKLAND A'S

115. Rickey Henderson 0.35
116. Tony Armas 0.15
117. Dave Revering 0.05
118. Wayne Gross 0.05
119. Dwayne Murphy 0.10
120. Jeff Newman 0.05
121. Rick Langford 0.05
122. Mike Norris 0.05

SEATTLE MARINERS

123. Bruce Bochte 0.05
124. Tom Paciorek 0.05
125. Dan Meyer 0.05
126. Julio Cruz 0.05
127. Richie Zisk 0.05
128. Floyd Bannister 0.10
129. Shane Rawley 0.10

TEXAS RANGERS

130. Buddy Bell 0.15
131. Al Oliver 0.15
132. Mickey Rivers 0.10
133. Jim Sundberg 0.10
134. Bump Wills 0.05
135. Jon Matlack 0.05
136. Danny Darwin 0.05

TORONTO BLUE JAYS

137. Damaso Garcia 0.10
138. Otto Velez 0.05
139. John Mayberry 0.10
140. Alfredo Grfffin 0.05
141. Alvis Woods 0.05
142. Dave Stieb 0.15
143. Jim Clancy 0.05

ATLANTA BRAVES

144. Gary Matthews 0.10
145. Bob Horner 0.20
146. Dale Murphy 0.35
147. Chris Chambliss 0.10
148. Phil Niekro 0.15
149. Glenn Hubbard 0.05
150. Rick Camp 0.05

CHICAGO CUBS

151. Dave Kingman 0.15
152. Bill Caudill 0.05
153. Bill Buckner 0.15
154. Barry Foote 0.05
155. Mike Tyson 0.05
156. Ivan DeJesus 0.05
157. Rick Reuschel 0.10
158. Ken Reitz 0.05

CINCINNATI REDS

159. George Foster 0.15
160. Johnny Bench 0.25
161. Dave Concepcion 0.15
162. Dave Collins 0.10
163. Ken Griffey 0.15
164. Dan Driessen 0.05
165. Tom Seaver 0.25
166. Tom Hume 0.05

HOUSTON ASTROS

167. Cesar Cedeno 0.10
168. Rafael Landestoy 0.05
169. Jose Cruz 0.15
170. Art Howe 0.05
171. Terry Puhl 0.05
172. Joe Sambito 0.05
173. Nolan Ryan 0.25
174. Joe Niekro 0.10

LOS ANGELES DODGERS

175. Dave Lopes 0.10
176. Steve Garvey 0.30
177. Ron Cey 0.15
178. Reggie Smith 0.10
179. Bill Russell 0.05
180. Burt Hooton 0.05
181. Jerry Reuss 0.05
182. Dusty Baker 0.10

MONTREAL EXPOS

183. Larry Parrish 0.10
184. Gary Carter 0.30
185. Rodney Scott 0.05
186. Ellis Valentine 0.05

187. Andre Dawson 0.15
188. Warren Cromartie 0.05
189. Chris Speier 0.05
190. Steve Rogers 0.10

NEW YORK METS

191. Lee Mazzilli 0.05
192. Doug Flynn 0.05
193. Steve Henderson 0.05
194. John Stearns 0.05
195. Joel Youngblood 0.05
196. Frank Taveras 0.05
197. Pat Zachry 0.05
198. Neil Allen 0.05

PHILADELPHIA PHILLIES

199. Mike Schmidt 0.30
200. Pete Rose 0.45
201. Larry Bowa 0.10
202. Bake McBride 0.05
203. Bob Boone 0.05
204. Gary Maddox 0.05
205. Tug McGraw 0.10
206. Steve Carlton 0.25
207. NL Pennant Winner 0.05
208. NL Pennant Winner 0.05

PITTSBURGH PIRATES

209. Phil Garner 0.05
210. Dave Parker 0.15
211. Omar Moreno 0.05
212. Mike Easler 0.10
213. Bill Madlock 0.15
214. Ed Ott 0.05
215. Willie Stargell 0.20
216. Jim Bibby 0.05

ST. LOUIS CARDINALS

217. Garry Templeton 0.15
218. Sixto Lezcano 0.05
219. Keith Hernandez 0.20
220. George Hendrick 0.10
221. Bruce Sutter 0.15
222. Ken Oberkfell 0.05
223. Tony Scott 0.05
224. Darrell Porter 0.05

SAN DIEGO PADRES

225. Gene Richards 0.05
226. Broderick Perkins 0.05
227. Jerry Mumphrey 0.05
228. Luis Salazar 0.05
229. Jerry Turner 0.05
230. Ozzie Smith 0.15
231. John Curtis 0.05
232. Rick Wise 0.05

SAN FRANCISCO GIANTS

233. Terry Whitfield 0.05
234. Jack Clark 0.15
235. Darrell Evans 0.15
236. Larry Herndon 0.05
237. Milt May 0.05
238. Greg Minton 0.05
239. Vida Blue 0.15
240. Eddie Whitson 0.10

FOIL ALL-STARS

241. Cecil Cooper 0.30
242. Willie Randolph 0.25
243. George Brett 0.65
244. Robin Yount 0.55
245. Reggie Jackson 0.65
246. Al Oliver 0.30
247. Willie Wilson 0.30
248. Rick Cerone 0.25
249. Steve Stone 0.25
250. Tommy John 0.30
251. Rich Gossage 0.30
252. Steve Garvey 0.55
253. Phil Garner 0.25
254. Mike Schmidt 0.65
255. Garry Templeton 0.25
256. George Hendrick 0.25
257. Dave Parker 0.35
258. Cesar Cedeno 0.25
259. Gary Carter 0.55
260. Jim Bibby 0.25
261. Steve Carlton 0.55
262. Tug McGraw 0.20

1982 TOPPS STICKERS

No.	Player	Value
1.	Bill Madlock BA LL	0.15
2	C. Lansford BA LL	0.05
3.	Mike Schmidt HR LL	0.25
4.	Armas, Grich, Evans, Murray HR LL	0.15
5.	Mike Schmidt RBI LL	0.25
6.	Eddie Murray RBI LL	0.25
7.	Tim Raines SB LL	0.20
8.	R. Henderson SB LL	0.25
9.	Tom Seaver Win LL	0.15
10.	McCatty, Martinez, Vukovich, Morris Win LL	0.05
11.	F. Valenzuela Ks LL	0.20
12.	Len Barker Ks LL	0.05
13.	Nolan Ryan ERA LL	0.20
14.	Steve McCatty ERA LL	0.05
15.	Bruce Sutter Sv LL	0.10
16.	Rollie Fingers Sv LL	0.10
	ATLANTA BRAVES	
17.	Chris Chambliss	0.05
18.	Bob Horner	0.15
19.	Dale Murphy	0.35
20.	Phil Niekro	0.15
21.	Bruce Benedict	0.05
22.	Claudell Washington	0.10
23.	Glenn Hubbard	0.05
24.	Rick Camp	0.05
	CHICAGO CUBS	
25.	Leon Durham	0.15
26.	Ken Reitz	0.05
27.	Dick Tidrow	0.05
28.	Tim Blackwell	0.05
29.	Bill Buckner	0.10
30.	Steve Henderson	0.05
31.	Mike Krukow	0.05
32.	Ivan DeJesus	0.05
	CINCINNATI REDS	
33.	Dave Collins	0.10
34.	Ron Oester	0.05
35.	John Bench	0.25
36.	Tom Seaver	0.25
37.	Dave Concepcion	0.10
38.	Ken Griffey	0.10
39.	Ray Knight	0.10
40.	George Foster	0.15
	HOUSTON ASTROS	

No.	Player	Value
41.	Nolan Ryan	0.25
42.	Terry Puhl	0.05
43.	Art Howe	0.05
44.	Jose Cruz	0.15
45.	Bob Knepper	0.10
46.	Craig Reynolds	0.05
47.	Cesar Cedeno	0.10
48.	Alan Ashby	0.05
	LOS ANGELES DODGERS	
49.	Ken Landreaux	0.10
50.	Fernando Valenzuela	0.25
51.	Ron Cey	0.15
52.	Dusty Baker	0.10
53.	Burt Hooton	0.05
54.	Steve Garvey	0.30
55.	Pedro Guerrero	0.20
56.	Jerry Reuss	0.10
	MONTREAL EXPOS	
57.	Andre Dawson	0.15
58.	Chris Speier	0.05
59.	Steve Rogers	0.10
60.	Warren Cromartie	0.05
61.	Gary Carter	0.30
62.	Tim Raines	0.20
63.	Scott Sanderson	0.05
64.	Larry Parrish	0.05
65.	Joel Youngblood	0.05
	NEW YORK METS	
66.	Neil Allen	0.05
67.	Lee Mazzilli	0.05
68.	Hubie Brooks	0.15
69.	Ellis Valentine	0.05
70.	Doug Flynn	0.05
71.	Pat Zachry	0.05
72.	Dave Kingman	0.15
	PHILADELPHIA PHILLIES	
73.	Garry Maddox	0.05
74.	Mike Schmidt	0.35
75.	Steve Carlton	0.25
76.	Manny Trillo	0.05
77.	Bob Boone	0.05
78.	Pete Rose	0.50
79.	Gary Matthews	0.10
80.	Larry Bowa	0.10
	PITTSBURGH PIRATES	
81.	Omar Moreno	0.05
82.	Rick Rhoden	0.05
83.	Bill Madlock	0.20
84.	Mike Easler	0.10
85.	Willie Stargell	0.20
86.	Jim Bibby	0.05
87.	Dave Parker	0.20
88.	Tim Foli	0.05
	ST. LOUIS CARDINALS	
89.	Ken Oberkfell	0.05
90.	Bob Forsch	0.05
91.	George Hendrick	0.10
92.	Keith Hernandez	0.20
93.	Darrell Porter	0.05
94.	Bruce Sutter	0.15
95.	Sixto Lezcano	0.05
96.	Garry Templeton	0.10
	SAN DIEGO PADRES	
97.	Juan Eichleberger	0.05
98.	Broderick Perkins	0.05
99.	Ruppert Jones	0.05
100.	Terry Kennedy	0.15
101.	Luis Salazar	0.05
102.	Gary Lucas	0.05
103.	Gene Richards	0.05
104.	Ozzie Smith	0.15
	SAN FRANCISCO GIANTS	
105.	Enos Cabell	0.05
106.	Jack Clark	0.15
107.	Greg Minton	0.05
108.	Johnnie LeMaster	0.05
109.	Larry Herndon	0.10
110.	Milt May	0.05
111.	Vida Blue	0.15
112.	Darrell Evans	0.10
	HIGHLIGHTS (113-120)	
113.	HL: Len Barker	0.05
114.	HL: Julio Cruz	0.05
115.	HL: Billy Martin	0.15
116.	HL: Tim Raines	0.20
117.	HL: Pete Rose	0.35
118.	HL: Bill Stein	0.05
119.	HL: F. Valenzuela	0.25
120.	HL: C. Yastrzemski	0.30
	NL ALL-STARS (121-130)	
121.	Pete Rose AS	0.80
122.	Manny Trillo AS	0.25
123.	Mike Schmidt AS	0.65
124.	Dave Concepcion AS	0.30
125.	Andre Dawson AS	0.40
126.	George Foster AS	0.30
127.	Dave Parker AS	0.35
128.	Gary Carter AS	0.55
129.	Steve Carlton AS	0.50
130.	Bruce Sutter AS	0.30
	AL ALL-STARS (131-140)	
131.	Rod Carew AS	0.55
132.	Jerry Remy AS	0.25
133.	George Brett AS	0.65
134.	Rick Burleson AS	0.25
135.	Dwight Evans AS	0.30
136.	Ken Singleton AS	0.25
137.	Dave Winfield AS	0.55
138.	Carlton Fisk AS	0.30
139.	Jack Morris AS	0.35
140.	Rich Gossage AS	0.35
	BALTIMORE ORIOLES	
141.	Al Bumbry	0.05
142.	Doug DeCinces	0.10
143.	Scott McGregor	0.05
144.	Ken Singleton	0.10
145.	Eddie Murray	0.30
146.	Jim Palmer	0.20
147.	Rich Dauer	0.05
148.	Mike Flanagan	0.10
	BOSTON RED SOX	
149.	Jerry Remy	0.05
150.	Jim Rice	0.25
151.	Mike Torrez	0.05
152.	Tony Perez	0.10
153.	Dwight Evans	0.20
154.	Mark Clear	0.05
155.	Carl Yastrzemski	0.35
156.	Carney Lansford	0.15
	CALIFORNIA ANGELS	
157.	Rick Burleson	0.10
158.	Don Baylor	0.15
159.	Ken Forsch	0.05
160.	Rod Carew	0.25
161.	Fred Lynn	0.20
162.	Bob Grich	0.15
163.	Dan Ford	0.05
164.	Butch Hobson	0.05
	CHICAGO WHITE SOX	
165.	Greg Luzinski	0.10
166.	Rich Dotson	0.10
167.	Billy Almon	0.05
168.	Chet Lemon	0.10
169.	Steve Trout	0.05
170.	Carlton Fisk	0.15
171.	Tony Bernazard	0.05
172.	Ron LeFlore	0.05
	CLEVELAND INDIANS	
173.	Bert Blyleven	0.20
174.	Andre Thornton	0.15
175.	Jorge Orta	0.05
176.	Bo Diaz	0.05
177.	Toby Harrah	0.05
178.	Len Barker	0.05
179.	Rick Manning	0.05
180.	Mike Hargrove	0.05
	DETROIT TIGERS	
181.	Alan Trammell	0.20
182.	Al Cowens	0.05
183.	Jack Morris	0.20
184.	Kirk Gibson	0.20
185.	Steve Kemp	0.10
186.	Milt Wilcox	0.05
187.	Lou Whitaker	0.15
188.	Lance Parrish	0.20
	KANSAS CITY ROYALS	
189.	Willie Wilson	0.15
190.	George Brett	0.35

191. Dennis Leonard 0.05
192. John Wathan 0.05
193. Frank White 0.10
194. Amos Otis 0.10
195. Larry Gura 0.05
196. Willie Aikens 0.05

MILWAUKEE BREWERS

197. Ben Oglivie 0.10
198. Rollie Fingers 0.15
199. Cecil Cooper 0.15
200. Paul Molitor 0.15
201. Ted Simmons 0.15
202. Pete Vuckovich 0.05
203. Robin Yount 0.25
204. Gorman Thomas 0.15

MINNESOTA TWINS

205. Rob Wilfong 0.05
206. Hosken Powell 0.05
207. Roy Smalley 0.05
208. Butch Wynegar 0.05
209. John Castino 0.05
210. Doug Corbett 0.05
211. Roger Erickson 0.05
212. Mickey Hatcher 0.05

NEW YORK YANKEES

213. Dave Winfield 0.25
214. Tommy John 0.15
215. Graig Nettles 0.15
216. Reggie Jackson 0.35
217. Rich Gossage 0.15
218. Rick Cerone 0.05
219. Willie Randolph 0.10
220. Jerry Mumphrey 0.05

OAKLAND A'S

221. Rickey Henderson ... 0.35
222. Mike Norris 0.05
223. Jim Spencer 0.05
224. Tony Armas 0.15
225. Matt Keough 0.05
226. Cliff Johnson 0.05
227. Dwayne Murphy 0.10
228. Steve McCatty 0.05

SEATTLE MARINERS

229. Richie Zisk 0.10
230. Lenny Randle 0.05
231. Jeff Burroughs 0.05
232. Bruce Bochte 0.05
233. Gary Gray 0.05
234. Floyd Bannister 0.05
235. Julio Cruz 0.05
236. Tom Paciorek 0.05

TEXAS RANGERS

237. Danny Darwin 0.05
238. Buddy Bell 0.15
239. Al Oliver 0.15
240. Jim Sundberg 0.10
241. Pat Putnam 0.05
242. Steve Comer 0.05
243. Mickey Rivers 0.10
244. Bump Wills 0.05

TORONTO BLUE JAYS

245. Damaso Garcia 0.15
246. Lloyd Moseby 0.15
247. Ernie Whitt 0.05
248. John Mayberry 0.05
249. Otto Velez 0.05
250. Dave Stieb 0.15
251. Barry Bonnell 0.05
252. Alfredo Griffin 0.05

POSTSEASON (253-260)

253. 1981 NL Playoffs 0.10
254. 1981 NL Playoffs 0.10
255. Dodgers World Champs 0.10
256. Dodgers World Champs 0.10
257. F. Valenzuela WS 0.15
258. Steve Garvey WS 0.15
259. Reuss and Yeager WS 0.10
260. Pedro Guerrero WS .. 0.15

1982 TOPPS INSERTS

No.	Player	Value
17.	Chris Chambliss	0.05
21.	Bruce Benedict	0.05
25.	Leon Durham	0.10
29.	Bill Buckner	0.10
33.	Dave Collins	0.05
37.	Dave Concepcion	0.10
41.	Nolan Ryan	0.15
45.	Bob Knepper	0.10
49.	Ken Landreaux	0.05
53.	Burt Hooton	0.05
57.	Andre Dawson	0.10
61.	Gary Carter	0.20
65.	Joel Youngblood	0.05
69.	Ellis Valentine	0.05
73.	Garry Maddox	0.05
77.	Bob Boone	0.05
81.	Omar Moreno	0.05
85.	Willie Stargell	0.10
89.	Ken Oberkfell	0.05
93.	Darrell Porter	0.07
97.	Juan Eichelberger	0.05
101.	Luis Salazar	0.05
105.	Enos Cabell	0.07
109.	Larry Herndon	0.05
143.	Scott McGregor	0.10
148.	Mike Flanagan	0.10
151.	Mike Torrez	0.05
156.	Carney Lansford	0.10
161.	Fred Lynn	0.10
166.	Rich Dotson	0.05
171.	Tony Bernazard	0.05
176.	Bo Diaz	0.05
181.	Alan Trammell	0.10
186.	Milt Wilcox	0.05
191.	Dennis Leonard	0.07
196.	Willie Aikens	0.05
201.	Ted Simmons	0.10
206.	Hosken Powell	0.05
211.	Roger Erickson	0.05
215.	Graig Nettles	0.10
216.	Reggie Jackson	0.20
221.	Rickey Henderson	0.25
226.	Cliff Johnson	0.05
231.	Jeff Burroughs	0.05
236.	Tom Paciorek	0.05
241.	Pat Putnam	0.05
246.	Lloyd Moseby	0.10
251.	Barry Bonnell	0.05

1983 FLEER STICKERS

Strip .... Value

Strip 1A 0.45
91 Phil Niekro, 223 Terry Kennedy
125 Keith Moreland, 74 Tony Pena
207 Nolan Ryan/Red Sox logo PO
249 Lou Whitaker/Angels logo CL
182 Floyd Bannister
143 Al Oliver/Pete Rose
192 Rickey Henderson
112 Fernando Valenzuela

Strip 1B 0.45
192 Rickey Henderson, 91 Phil Niekro
223 Terry Kennedy, 74 Tony Pena
249 Lou Whitaker/Braves logo CL
207 Nolan Ryan/Expos logo PO
125 Keith Moreland
182 Floyd Bannister
143 Al Oliver/Pete Rose
112 Fernando Valenzuela

Strip 2 .... 0.50
51 Fred Breining, 158 Greg Luzinski
248 Milt Wilcox/Reds Logo PO
239 George Foster, 216 Mario Soto
202 Eddie Murray, 121 Dusty Baker
110 Garth Iorg/Blue Jays Logo CL
78 Lee Lacy, 46 Ken Griffey

Strip 3 .... 0.65
139 Bobby Castillo, 115 Burt Hooten
80 Mike Easter, 49 Reggie Smith
250 Tom Brookens, 29 Geoff Zahn
204 Dickie Thon/Phillies Logo PO
198 Cal Ripken, 174 Pete Rose
140 Dusty Baker/Dale Murphy
xx Royals Logo CL

Strip 4 .... 0.45
59 Tom Burgmeier, 53 Chili Davis
230 Bob Bailor/Brewers Logo PO
258 Woody Fryman, 166 Billy Sample
75 Manny Sarmiento/Robin Yount
185 Bruce Bochte
220 Wayne Krenchiki
114 Rick Monday/Mets Logo CL

Strip 5 .... 0.50
21 Mike Caldwell, 133 Ron Davis
246 Rick Manning/Blue Jays Logo PO
155 Harold Baines, 82 Rick Camp
167 John Grubb, 89 Steve Bedrosian
222 Ruppert Jones/Tigers Logo CL
113 Steve Garvey, 34 Bob Boone

Strip 6 .... 0.45
70 John Candelaria, 177 Bo Diaz
132 Bill Buckner, 10 Ozzie Smith
69 Dwight Evans/Astros Logo PO
263 Bill Guilickson, 196 Rich Dauer
231 Craig Swan/A's Logo CL
134 Jack O'Connor
191 Tom Underwood

Strip 7 .... 0.45
26 Rod Carew, 38 Graig Nettles
189 Dwayne Murphy, 52 Gary Lavelle
108 Jim Clancy/Orioles Logo CL

152 Jerry Koosman/Astro Logo PO
228 Tim Lollar, 212 Alan Ashby
261 Warren Cromartie
15 Ben Oglivie
Strip 8 . . . . 0.50
179 Bill Caudill, 226 Tim Flannery
241 A. Thornton/Yankees Logo PO
257 Chris Speier, 205 Phil Garner
129 Randy Martz, 43 Rick Cerone
25 Tommy John/A's Logo CL
103 Larry Gura, 73 Kent Tekulve
Strip 9 . . . . 0.45
221 Cesar Cedeno, 211 Art Howe
168 Larry Parrish, 251 Chet Lemon
xx Cardinals Logo PO
42 Dave Collins
81 Willie Stargell
107 Jim McLaughlin
227 Garry Templeton
xx Phillies Logo CL
105 Damaso Garcia
186 Jeff Burroughs
Strip 10 . . . . 0.50
99 Amos Otis, xx Twins Logo PO
149 Steve Kemp, 218 Tom Seaver
86 Chris Chambliss
242 Mike Hargrove
178 Gary Matthews
254 John Wockenfuss
xx Rangers Logo CL
20 Gorman Thomas
24 Steve Renko
Strip 11 . . . . 0.45
48 Jack Clark, 83 Bob Watson
23 Cecil Cooper, 122 Ron Cey
44 Willie Randolph/Pirate Logo CL
234 John Stearns, 93 Bob Walk
126 Dick Tidrow/Indians Logo PO
201 Tippy Martinez
163 Charlie Hough
Strip 12 . . . . 0.50
264 Andre Dawson, 209 Terry Puhl
169 Ivan Dejesus, 106 Hosken Powell
141 Nolan Ryan/Alan Ashby
31 Fred Lynn/Reds Logo CL
244 Lary Sorensen, 61 Mark Clear
xx Royals Logo PO
161 Danny Darwin
Strip 13 . . . . 0.45
96 Vida Blue, 138 Tom Brunansky
245 Len Barker, 217 Dan Driessen
124 Bump Wills, 153 Carlton Fisk
47 Ron Guidry/Cubs Logo CL
63 Dennis Eckersley
57 Bill Laskey
180 Ed VandeBerg
xx Dodgers Logo PO
Strip 14 . . . . 0.50
87 Gene Garber, 45 Lou Piniella
173 Garry Maddox, 131 Leon Durham
22 Ted Simmons/Reds Logo CL
100 Dan Quisenberry
xx Padres Logo PO
14 Pete Vuckovich
130 Fergie Jenkins
270 John Montefusco
269 George Hendrick
Strip 15 . . . . 0.45
159 LaMarr Hoyt, 266 Charlie Lea
238 Rusty Staub/Rangers Logo CL
206 Jose Cruz, 162 Lamar Johnson
183 Richie Zisk, 36 Rich Gossage
68 Jerry Remy/Orioles Logo PO
119 Steve Howe, 97 U.L. Washington
Strip 16 . . . . 0.50
58 Duane Kuiper, 11 Bob Forsch
85 Rafael Ramirez/Mets Logo CL
142 Omar Moreno/Lee Lacy
160 George Wright, 187 Dave Beard
247 Toby Harrah, 268 Al Oliver

1983 Fleer Moreno & Lacey

102 Hal McRae, 64 Wade Boggs
xx Expos Logo PO
Strip 17 . . . . 0.45
190 Rick Langford, 128 Larry Bowa
5 Dane Iorg/Expos Logo CL
252 Jack Morris, 156 Britt Burns
193 Mike Flanagan, 184 Al Cowens
12 Gantner/Royals Logo PO
60 Carl Yastrzemski
28 Ken Forsch
Strip 18 . . . . 0.45
150 Rudy Law, 235 Ellis Valentine
181 Gaylord Perry/Red Sox Logo CL
147 Ray Knight/Tom Hume
135 Kent Hrbek, 101 Willie Aikens
13 Rollie Fingers, 71 Bill Madlock
xx Giants Logo PO
67 Carney Lansford
41 Jerry Mumphrey
Strip 19A 0.55
90 Dale Murphy, 260 Steve Rogers
214 Johnny Bench/Mariner Logo PO
262 Gary Carter, 3 Darrell Porter
164 Buddy Bell, 19 Paul Molitor
55 Joe Morgan/Yankees Logo CL
65 Bob Stanley, 33 Don Baylor
Strip 19B 0.55
90 Dale Murphy, 260 Steve Rogers
214 Johnny Bench/Angels Logo PO
262 Gary Carter, 3 Darrell Porter
164 Buddy Bell, 19 Paul Molitor
55 Joe Morgan/Pirates Logo CL
65 Bob Stanley, 33 Don Baylor
Strip 20 . . . . 0.45
210 Joe Niekro, 50 Atlee Hammaker
267 Jeff Reardon, 256 Larry Herndon
127 Bill Campbell/Giants Logo PO
30 Doug DeCinces, 92 Jerry Royster
6 Keith Hernandez
146 Ben Oglivie/Hal McRae
172 Ron Reed/Brewers Logo CL
Strip 21 . . . . 0.45
8 Ken Oberkfell, 56 Al Holland
151 Ron LeFlore, 175 Manny Trillo
232 Dave Kingman/Cubs Logo CL
120 Ken Landreaux
xx White Sox Logo PO
197 John Lowenstein
219 Dave Concepcion
253 Alan Trammell
259 Scott Sanderson
Strip 22 . . . . 0.50
116 Bill Russell, 84 Bob Horner
35 Brian Downing/Tigers Logo PO
2 Willie McGee, 136 Gary Ward

171 Tug McGraw, 236 Neil Allen
255 Lance Parrish, 77 Dale Berra
xx Twins Logo CL
88 Claudell Washington
Strip 23 . . . . 0.45
4 Lonnie Smith, 188 Davey Lopes
215 Larry Biittner/Braves Logo PO
17 Bob McClure, xx Cards Logo CL
54 Greg Minton, 27 Bruce Kison
265 Tim Raines, 200 Jim Palmer
148 Buddy Bell/Carlton Fisk
95 Dennis Leonard
Strip 24 . . . . 0.55
240 Rick Sutcliffe, 237 Pat Zachry
176 Steve Carlton, 157 Tom Paciorek
104 Willie Wilson/Tigers Logo PO
9 John Stuper, 37 Roy Smalley
213 Tom Hume/Dodgers Logo CL
194 Scott McGregor
145 Rose/Schmidt/Knight
Strip 25A 0.65
1 Bruce Sutter, 40 Lee Mazzilli
72 Dave Parker/Padres Logo CL
98 George Brett, 243 Dan Spillner
118 Steve Sax, 144 Rickey Henderson
170 Mike Schmidt, 195 Ken Singleton
233 Mookie Wilson
xx White Sox Logo PO
Strip 25B 0.65
1 Bruce Sutter, 40 Lee Mazzilli
72 Dave Parker/Mariners Logo CL
118 Steve Sax, 144 Rickey Henderson
170 Mike Schmidt, 195 Ken Singleton
233 Mookie Wilson/Twins Logo PO
98 George Brett, 243 Dan Spillner
Strip 26 . . . . 0.45
94 Frank White, 62 Mike Torrez
66 Jim Rice/Indians Logo CL
123 Jerry Reuss, 137 Al Williams
165 Jon Matlack, 76 Johnny Ray
208 Ray Knight/Mets Logo PO
203 Al Bumbry, 225 Eric Show
Strip 27 . . . . 0.55
39 Dave Winfield, 32 Reggie Jackson
16 Don Sutton/Orioles Logo CL
111 Dave Stieb/Pirates Logo PO
7 Juaquin Andujar
117 Pedro Guerrero
154 Salome Barojas
199 Dennis Martinez
109 Barry Bonnell
229 Sixto Lezcano

1983 TOPPS STICKERS

No.	Player	Value
1.	Hank Aaron (foil)	0.60
2.	Babe Ruth (foil)	0.70
3.	Willie Mays (foil)	0.60
4.	Frank Robinson (foil)	0.45
5.	Reggie Jackson	0.30
6.	Carl Yastrzemski	0.30
7.	Johnny Bench	0.25
8.	Tony Perez	0.15
9.	Lee May	0.10
10.	Mike Schmidt	0.30
11.	Dave Kingman	0.15
12.	Reggie Smith	0.10
13.	Graig Nettles	0.15
14.	Rusty Staub	0.10
15.	Willie Wilson	0.15
16.	LaMarr Hoyt	0.10
17.	Jackson and Thomas	0.15
18.	Floyd Bannister	0.10
19.	Hal McRae	0.10
20.	Rick Sutcliffe	0.15
21.	Rickey Henderson	0.35
22.	Dan Quisenberry	0.15

BALTIMORE ORIOLES

23. Jim Palmer (foil) 0.45
24. John Lowenstein 0.10
25. Mike Flanagan 0.10
26. Cal Ripken 0.30
27. Rich Dauer 0.10
28. Ken Singleton 0.10
29. Eddie Murray 0.30
30. Rick Dempsey 0.10

1983 Topps Reggie Jackson

BOSTON RED SOX
31. Carl Yastrzemski (foil) . . . 0.60
32. Carney Lansford 0.15
33. Jerry Remy 0.10
34. Dennis Eckersley 0.15
35. Dave Stapleton 0.10
36. Mark Clear 0.10
37. Jim Rice 0.25
38. Dwight Evans 0.15
CALIFORNIA ANGELS
39. Rod Carew 0.25
40. Don Baylor 0.15
41. Reggie Jackson (foil) . . . 0.60
42. Geoff Zahn 0.10
43. Bobby Grich 0.10
44. Fred Lynn 0.15
45. Bob Boone 0.10
46. Doug DeCinces 0.10
CHICAGO WHITE SOX
47. Tom Paciorek 0.10
48. Britt Burns 0.10
49. Tony Bernazard 0.10
50. Steve Kemp 0.15
51. Greg Luzinski (foil) 0.30
52. Harold Baines 0.20
53. LaMarr Hoyt 0.10
54. Carlton Fisk 0.15
CLEVELAND INDIANS
55. Andre Thornton (foil) 0.30
56. Mike Hargrove 0.10
57. Len Barker 0.10
58. Toby Harrah 0.10
59. Dan Spinner 0.10
60. Rick Manning 0.10
61. Rick Sutcliffe 0.15
62. Ron Hassey 0.10
DETROIT TIGERS
63. Lance Parrish (foil) 0.40
64. John Wockenfuss 0.10
65. Lou Whitaker 0.15
66. Alan Trammell 0.20
67. Kirk Gibson 0.20
68. Larry Herndon 0.10
69. Jack Morris 0.20
70. Dan Petry 0.15
KANSAS CITY ROYALS
71. Frank White 0.10
72. Amos Otis 0.10
73. Willie Wilson (foil) 0.35
74. Dan Quisenberry 0.15
75. Hal McRae 0.10
76. George Brett 0.35
77. Larry Gura 0.10
78. John Wathan 0.10
MILWAUKEE BREWERS
79. Rollie Fingers 0.15
80. Cecil Cooper 0.15
81. Robin Yount (foil) 0.50
82. Ben Oglivie 0.10
83. Paul Molitor 0.15
84. Gorman Thomas 0.10
85. Ted Simmons 0.15
86. Pete Vuckovich 0.10
MINNESOTA TWINS
87. Gary Gaetti 0.15
88. Kent Hrbek (foil) 0.60
89. John Castino 0.10
90. Tom Brunansky 0.15
91. Bobby Mitchell 0.10
92. Gary Ward 0.10
93. Tim Laudner 0.10
94. Ron Davis 0.10
NEW YORK YANKEES
95. Willie Randolph 0.10
96. Roy Smalley 0.10
97. Jerry Mumphrey 0.10
98. Ken Griffey 0.15
99. Dave Winfield (foil) 0.60
100. Rich Gossage 0.15
101. Butch Wynegar 0.10
102. Ron Guidry 0.20
OAKLAND A'S
103. Rickey Henderson(foil) . . 0.60
104. Mike Heath 0.10
105. Dave Lopes 0.10
106. Rick Langford 0.10
107. Dwayne Murphy 0.10
108. Tony Armas 0.15
109. Matt Keough 0.10
110. Danny Meyer 0.10
SEATTLE MARINERS
111. Bruce Bochte 0.10
112. Julio Cruz 0.10
113. Floyd Bannister 0.10
114. Gaylord Perry (foil) 0.40
115. Al Cowens 0.10
116. Richie Zisk 0.10
117. Jim Essian 0.10
118. Bill Caudill 0.10
TEXAS RANGERS
119. Buddy Bell (foil) 0.35
120. Larry Parrish 0.10
121. Danny Darwin 0.10
122. Bucky Dent 0.15
123. Johnny Grubb 0.10
124. George Wright 0.10
125. Charlie Hough 0.15
126. Jim Sundborg 0.10
TORONTO BLUE JAYS
127. Dave Stieb (foil) 0.40
128. Willie Upshaw 0.10
129. Alfredo Griffin 0.15
130. Lloyd Moseby 0.10
131. Ernie Whitt 0.10
132. Jim Clancy 0.10
133. Barry Bonnell 0.10
134. Damaso Garcia 0.15
RECORD BREAKERS
135. RB: Jim Kaat 0.15
136. RB: Jim Kaat 0.15
137. RB: Greg Minton 0.10
138. Re: Greg Minton 0.10
139. RB: Paul Molitor 0.15
140. RB: Paul Molitor 0.15
141. RB: Manny Trillo 0.10
142. RB: Manny Trillo 0.10
143. RB: Joel Youngblood . . . 0.10
144. RB: Joel Youngblood . . . 0.10
145. RB: Robin Yount 0.20
146. RB: Robin Yount 0.20

1983 Topps Tom Seaver

PLAYOFF ACTION
147. Willie McGee 0.15
148. Darrell Porter 0.10
149. Darrell Porter 0.10
150. Robin Yount 0.20
151. Bruce Benedict 0.10
152. Bruce Benedict 0.10
153. George Hendrick 0.10
154. Bruce Benedict 0.10
155. Doug DeCinces 0.10
156. Paul Molitor 0.15
157. Charlie Moore 0.10
158. Fred Lynn 0.15
159. Rickey Henderson 0.35
160. Dale Murphy 0.35
161. Willie Wilson 0.15
162. Jack Clark 0.15
163. Reggie Jackson 0.30
164. Andre Dawson 0.20
165. Dan Quisenberry 0.15
166. Bruce Sutter 0.15
167. Robin Yount 0.25
168. Ozzie Smith 0.15
169. Frank White 0.10
170. Phil Garner 0.10
171. Doug DeCinces 0.10
172. Mike Schmidt 0.30
173. Cecil Cooper 0.15
174. Al Oliver 0.15
175. Jim Palmer 0.20
176. Steve Carlton 0.25
177. Carlton Fisk 0.15
178. Gary Carter 0.30
WORLD SERIES ACTION
179. WS: Joaquin Andujar . . . 0.10
180. WS: Ozzie Smith 0.15
181. WS: Cecil Cooper 0.15
182. WS: Darrell Porter 0.10
183. WS: Darrell Porter 0.10
184. WS: Mike Caldwell 0.10
185. WS: Mike Caldwell 0.10
186. WS: Ozzie Smith 0.15
187. WS: Bruce Sutter 0.15
188. WS: Keith Hernandez . . . 0.15
169. WS: Dane Iorg 0.10
190. WS: Dane Iorg 0.10
RECORD BREAKERS
191. RB: Tony Armas 0.10
192. RB: Tony Armas 0.10
193. RB: Lance Parrish 0.15
194. RB: Lance Parrish 0.15
195. RB: John Wathan 0.10

196. RB: John Wathan 0.10
197. RB: Rickey Henderson .. 0.20
198. RB: Rickey Henderson .. 0.20
199. RB: Rickey Henderson .. 0.20
200. RB: Rickey Henderson .. 0.20
201. RB: Rickey Henderson .. 0.20
202. RB: Rickey Henderson .. 0.20
203. Steve Carlton 0.20
204. Steve Carlton 0.20
205. Al Oliver 0.15
206. Murphy and Oliver 0.15
207. Dave Kingman 0.15
208. Steve Rogers 0.10
209. Bruce Sutter 0.15
210. Tim Raines 0.20

ATLANTA BRAVES

211. Dale Murphy (foil) 0.65
212. Chris Chambliss 0.10
213. Gene Garber 0.10
214. Bob Horner 0.15
215. Glenn Hubbard 0.10
216. Claudell Washington 0.10
217. Bruce Benedict 0.10

218. Phil Niekro 0.15

CHICAGO CUBS

219. Leon Durham (foil) 0.35
220. Jay Johnstone 0.10
221. Larry Bowa 0.10
222. Keith Moreland 0.15
223. Bill Buckner 0.15
224. Fergie Jenkins 0.15
225. Dick Tidrow 0.10
226. Jody Davis 0.15

CINCINNATI REDS

227. Dave Concepcion 0.10
228. Dan Driessen 0.10
229. Johnny Bench (foil) 0.30
230. Ron Oester 0.10
231. Cesar Cedeno 0.10
232. Alex Trevino 0.10
233. Tom Seaver 0.25
234. Mario Soto 0.10

HOUSTON ASTROS

235. Nolan Ryan (foil) 0.60
236. Art Howe 0.10
237. Phil Garner 0.10
238. Ray Knight 0.15
239. Terry Puhl 0.10
240. Joe Niekro 0.15
241. Alan Ashby 0.10
242. Jose Cruz 0.15

LOS ANGELES DODGERS

243. Steve Garvey 0.30
244. Ron Cey 0.15
245. Dusty Baker 0.10
246. Ken Landreaux 0.10
247. Jerry Reuss 0.10
248. Pedro Guerrero 0.20
249. Bill Russell 0.10
250. F. Valenzuela (foil) 0.55

MONTREAL EXPOS

251. Al Oliver (foil) 0.35
252. Andre Dawson 0.20
253. Tim Raines 0.20
254. Jeff Reardon 0.15
255. Gary Carter 0.30
256. Steve Rogers 0.10
257. Tim Wallach 0.15
258. Chris Speier 0.10

NEW YORK METS

259. Dave Kingman 0.15
260. Bob Bailor 0.10
261. Hubie Brooks 0.15
262. Craig Swan 0.10
263. George Foster 0.15
264. John Stearns 0.10
265. Neil Allen 0.10
266. Mookie Wilson (foil) 0.30

PHILADELPHIA PHILLIES

267. Steve Carlton (foil) 0.50
268. Manny Trillo 0.10
269. Gary Matthews 0.10
270. Mike Schmidt 0.30
271. Ivan DeJesus 0.10
272. Pete Rose 0.45
273. Bo Diaz 0.10
274. Sid Monge 0.10

PITTSBURGH PIRATES

275. Bill Madlock (foil) 0.35
276. Jason Thompson 0.10
277. Don Robinson 0.10
278. Omar Moreno 0.10
279. Dale Berra 0.10
280. Dave Parker 0.20
281. Tony Pena 0.15
282. John Candelaria 0.10

ST. LOUIS CARDINALS

283. Lonnie Smith 0.10
284. Bruce Sutter (foil) 0.35
285. George Hendrick 0.10
286. Tom Herr 0.10
287. Ken Oberkfell 0.10
288. Ozzie Smith 0.15
289. Bob Forsch 0.10
290. Keith Hernandez 0.20

SAN DIEGO PADRES

291. Garry Templeton 0.15
292. Broderick Perkins 0.10
293. Terry Kennedy (foil) 0.30
294. Gene Richards 0.10
295. Ruppert Jones 0.15
296. Tim Lollar 0.10
297. John Montefusco 0.10
298. Sixto Lezcano 0.10

SAN FRANCISCO GIANTS

299. Greg Minton 0.10
300. Jack Clark (foil) 0.35
301. Milt May 0.10
302. Reggie Smith 0.10
303. Joe Morgan 0.15
304. John LeMaster 0.10
305. Darrell Evans 0.15
306. Al Holland 0.10

YOUNG STARS

307. Jesse Barfield 0.20
308. Wade Boggs 0.55
309. Tom Brunansky 0.15
310. Storm Davis 0.15
311. Von Hayes 0.20
312. Dave Hostetler 0.10
313. Kent Hrbek 0.25
314. Tim Laudner 0.10
315. Cal Ripken 0.30
316. Andre Robertson 0.10
317. Ed VandeBerg 0.10
318. Glenn Wilson 0.15
319. Chili Davis 0.20
320. Bob Dernier 0.15
321. Terry Francona 0.15
322. Brian Giles 0.10
323. David Green 0.10
324. Atlee Hammaker 0.10
325. Bill Laskey 0.10
326. Willie McGee 0.20
327. Johnny Ray 0.20
328. Ryne Sandberg 0.40
329. Steve Sax 0.20
330. Eric Show 0.10

1984 FLEER STICKERS

No. Player .... Value

GAME WINNING RBI'S

1. Dickie Thon 0.07
2. Ken Landreaux 0.05
3. Darrell Evans 0.07
4. Harold Baines 0.15
5. Dave Winfield 0.25

1984 Fleer Mike Schmidt

BATTING AVERAGE

6. Bill Madlock 0.10
7. Lonnie Smith 0.07
8. Jose Cruz 0.07
9. George Hendrick 0.07
10. Ray Knight 0.05
11. Wade Boggs 0.40
12. Rod Carew 0.25
13. Lou Whitaker 0.15
14. Alan Trammell 0.15

15. Cal Ripken 0.30

HOME RUNS LEADERS

16. Mike Schmidt 0.30
17. Dale Murphy 0.35
18. Andre Dawson 0.15
19. Pedro Guerrero 0.15
20. Jim Rice 0.25
21. Tony Armas 0.07
22. Ron Kittle 0.15
23. Eddie Murray 0.30

HITS LEADERS

24. Jose Cruz 0.07
25. Andre Dawson 0.15
26. Rafael Ramirez 0.05
27. Al Oliver 0.10
28. Wade Boggs 0.40
29. Cal Ripken 0.30
30. Lou Whitaker 0.15
31. Cecil Cooper 0.10

SLUGGING PERCENTAGE

32. Dale Murphy 0.35
33. Andre Dawson 0.15
34. Pedro Guerrero 0.15
35. Mike Schmidt 0.30
36. George Brett 0.30
37. Jim Rice 0.25
38. Eddie Murray 0.30
39. Carlton Fisk 0.15

PINCH HITS

40. Rusty Staub 0.07
41. Duane Walker 0.05
42. Steve Braun 0.05
43. Kurt Bevacqua 0.05

DESIGNATED HITTERS

44. Hal McRae 0.07
45. Don Baylor 0.10
46. Ken Singleton 0.07
47. Greg Luzinski 0.07

ON BASE PERCENTAGE

48. Mike Schmidt 0.30
49. Keith Hernandez 0.20
50. Dale Murphy 0.35
51. Tim Raines 0.25
52. Wade Boggs 0.40
53. Rickey Henderson 0.35

54. Rod Carew 0.25
55. Ken Singleton 0.10

WON LOST PERCENTAGE

56. John Denny 0.10
57. John Candelaria 0.05
58. Larry McWilliams 0.05
59. Pascual Perez 0.05
60. Jesse Orosco 0.07
61. Moose Haas 0.07
62. Richard Dotson 0.07
63. Mike Flanagan 0.07
64. Scott McGregor 0.07

EARNED RUN AVERAGE

65. Atlee Hammaker 0.05
66. Rick Honeycutt 0.05

SAVES LEADERS

67. Lee Smith 0.10
68. Al Holland 0.07
69. Greg Minton 0.05
70. Bruce Sutter 0.10
71. Jeff Reardon 0.07
72. Frank DiPino 0.05
73. Don Quisenberry 0.10
74. Bob Stanley 0.05
75. Ron Davis 0.05
76. Bill Caudill 0.05
77. Peter Ladd 0.05

STRIKEOUTS

78. Steve Carlton 0.25
79. Mario Soto 0.10
80. Larry McWilliams 0.05
81. Fernando Valenzuela ... 0.25

82. Nolan Ryan 0.25
83. Jack Morris 0.20
84. Floyd Bannister 0.10
85. Dave Stieb 0.15
86. Dave Righetti 0.15
87. Rick Sutcliffe 0.15

STEALS LEADERS

88. Tim Raines 0.25
89. Alan Wiggins 0.07
90. Steve Sax 0.10
91. Mookie Wilson 0.05
92. Rickey Henderson 0.35
93. Rudy Law 0.05
94. Willie Wilson 0.10
95. Julio Cruz 0.05

FUTURE HALL OF FAMERS

96. Johnny Bench 0.25
97. Cark Yastrzemski 0.30
98. Gaylord Perry 0.20
99. Pete Rose 0.35
100. Joe Morgan 0.15
101. Steve Carlton 0.25
102. Jim Palmer 0.20
103. Rod Carew 0.25

ROOKIE STARS

104. Darryl Strawberry 0.40
105. Craig McMurtry 0.07
106. Mel Hall 0.15
107. Lee Tunnell 0.07
108. Bill Dawley 0.05
109. Ron Kittle 0.15
110. Mike Boddicker 0.15
111. Julio Franco 0.15
112. Daryl Sconiers 0.05
113. Neal Heaton 0.05

WORLD SERIES BATTING

114. John Shelby 0.05
115. Rick Dempsey 0.05
116. John Lowenstein 0.05
117. Jim Dwyer 0.05
118. Bo Diaz 0.05
119. Pete Rose 0.35
120. Joe Morgan 0.15
121. Gary Matthews 0.10
122. Garry Maddox 0.10

PLAYOFF MANAGERS

123. Paul Owens 0.05
124. Tom Lasorda 0.07
125. Joe Altobelli 0.05
126. Tony LaRussa 0.05

1984 TOPPS STICKERS

1984 Topps Claudell Washington

No.	Player	Value
1.	Steve Carlton (top)	0.25
2.	Steve Carlton (bottom)	0.20
3.	Rickey Henderson (top)	0.20
4.	R. Henderson (bottom)	0.20
5.	Fred Lynn (top)	0.10
6.	Fred Lynn (bottom)	0.07
7.	Greg Luzinski (top)	0.07
8.	Greg Luzinski (bottom)	0.05
9.	Dan Quisenberry (top)	0.10
10.	D. Quisenberry (bottom)	0.07
CHAMPIONSHIP SERIES		
11.	LaMarr Hoyt	0.07
12.	Mike Flanagan	0.05
13.	Mike Boddicker	0.05
14.	Tito Landrum	0.05
15.	Steve Carlton	0.10
16.	Fernando Valenzuela	0.10
17.	Charlie Hudsson	0.05
18.	Gary Matthews	0.05
WORLD SERIES (19-26)		
19.	John Denny	0.05
20.	John Lowenstein	0.05
21.	Jim Palmer	0.10
22.	Benny Ayala	0.05
23.	Rick Dempsey	0.05
24.	Cal Ripken	0.10
25.	Sammy Stewart	0.05
26.	Eddie Murray	0.10
ATLANTA BRAVES		
27.	Dale Murphy	0.30
28.	Chris Chambliss	0.05
29.	Glenn Hubbard	0.05
30.	Bob Horner	0.15
31.	Phil Niekro	0.15
32.	Claudell Washington	0.10
33.	Rafael Ramirez	0.05
34.	Bruce Benedict	0.05

35. Gene Garber 0.05
36. Pascual Perez 0.05
37. Jerry Royster 0.05
38. Steve Bedrosian 0.07

CHICAGO CUBS

39. Keith Moreland 0.05
40. Leon Durham 0.10

41. Ron Cey 0.10
42. Bill Buckner 0.10
43. Jody Davis 0.10
44. Lee Smith 0.07
45. Ryne Sandberg 0.40
46. Larry Bowa 0.07
47. Chuck Rainey 0.05
48. Ferguson Jenkins 0.10
49. Dick Ruthven 0.05
50. Jay Johnstone 0.05

CINCINNATI REDS

51. Mario Soto 0.07
52. Gary Redus 0.10
53. Ron Oester 0.05
54. Cesar Cedeno 0.07
55. Dan Driessen 0.05
56. Dave Concepcion 0.07
57. Dann Bilardello 0.05
58. Joe Price 0.05
59. Tom Hume 0.05
60. Eddie Milner 0.07
61. Paul Householder 0.05
62. Bill Scherrer 0.05

HOUSTON ASTROS

63. Phil Garner 0.07
64. Dickie Thon 0.07
65. Jose Cruz 0.10
66. Nolan Ryan 0.20
67. Terry Puhl 0.05
68. Ray Knight 0.07
69. Joe Niekro 0.07
70. Jerry Mumphrey 0.05
71. Bill Dawley 0.05
72. Alan Ashby 0.05
73. Denny Walling 0.05
74. Frank DiPino 0.05

LOS ANGELES DODGERS

75. Pedro Guerrero 0.20
76. Ken Landreaux 0.05
77. Bill Russell 0.07
78. Steve Sax 0.10
79. Fernando Valenzuela .. 0.15
80. Dusty Baker 0.07
81. Jerry Reuss 0.07
82. Alejandro Pena 0.07
83. Rick Monday 0.05
84. Rick Honeycutt 0.05
85. Mike Marshall 0.10
86. Steve Yeager 0.05

MONTREAL EXPOS

87. Al Oliver 0.10
88. Steve Rogers 0.07
89. Jeff Reardon 0.10
90. Gary Carter 0.30
91. Tim Raines 0.20
92. Andre Dawson 0.15
93. Manny Trillo 0.05
94. Tim Wallach 0.10
95. Chris Speier 0.05
96. Bill Gullickson 0.07
97. Doug Flynn 0.05
98. Charlie Lea 0.05
99. Bill Madlock 0.15
100. Wade Boggs 0.40
101. Mike Schmidt 0.30
102A. Jim Rice 0.30
102B. Reggie Jackson 0.25

NEW YORK METS

103. Hubie Brooks 0.10
104. Jesse Orosco 0.07
105. George Foster 0.10
106. Tom Seaver 0.25
107. Keith Hernandez 0.20
108. Mookie Wilson 0.07
109. Bob Bailor 0.05
110. Walt Terrell 0.07
111. Brian Giles 0.05
112. Jose Oquendo 0.05
113. Mike Torrez 0.05
114. Junior Ortiz 0.05

PHILADELPHIA PHILLIES

115. Pete Rose 0.40
116. Joe Morgan 0.20
117. Mike Schmidt 0.30
118. Gary Matthews 0.07
119. Steve Carlton 0.20
120. Bo Diaz 0.05
121. Ivan DeJesus 0.05
122. John Denny 0.07
123. Garry Maddox 0.05
124. Von Hayes 0.15
125. Al Holland 0.05
126. Tony Perez 0.10

PITTSBURGH PIRATES

127. John Candelaria 0.07
128. Jason Thompson 0.05
129. Tony Pena 0.10
130. Dave Parker 0.20
131. Bill Madlock 0.15
132. Kent Tekulve 0.07
133. Larry McWilliams 0.05
134. Johnny Ray 0.15
135. Marvell Wynne 0.05
136. Dale Berra 0.05
137. Mike Easler 0.07
138. Lee Lacy 0.07

ST. LOUIS CARDINALS

139. George Hendrick 0.07
140. Lonnie Smith 0.07
141. Willie McGee 0.10
142. Tom Herr 0.07
143. Darrell Porter 0.05
144. Ozzie Smith 0.10
145. Bruce Sutter 0.10
146. Dave LaPoint 0.05
147. Neil Allen 0.05
148. Ken Oberkfell 0.05
149. David Green 0.05
150. Andy Van Slyke 0.10

SAN DIEGO PADRES

151. Garry Templeton 0.07
152. Juan Bonilla 0.05
153. Alan Wiggins 0.07
154. Terry Kennedy 0.10
155. Dave Dravecky 0.10
156. Steve Garvey 0.30
157. Bobby Brown 0.05
158. Ruppert Jones 0.05
159. Luis Salazar 0.05
160. Tony Gwynn 0.40
161. Gary Lucas 0.05
162. Eric Show 0.05

SAN FRANCISCO GIANTS

163. Darrell Evans 0.10
164. Gary Lavelle 0.05
165. Atlee Hammaker 0.07
166. Jeff Leonard 0.10
167. Jack Clark 0.15
168. Johnny LeMaster 0.05
169. Duane Kuiper 0.05
170. Tom O'Malley 0.05
171. Chili Davis 0.10
172. Bill Laskey 0.05
173. Joel Youngblood 0.05
174. Bob Brenly 0.10
175. Atlee Hammaker 0.05
176. Rick Honeycutt 0.05
177. John Denny 0.07
178. LaMarr Hoyt 0.07

FOILS (179-198)

179. Tim Raines 0.40
180. Dale Murphy 0.55
181. Andre Dawson 0.35
182. Steve Rogers 0.25
183. Gary Carter 0.50
184. Steve Carlton 0.40
185. George Hendrick 0.25
186. Johnny Ray 0.30
187. Ozzie Smith 0.30
188. Mike Schmidt 0.55
189. Jim Rice 0.40
190. Dave Winfield 0.40
191. Lloyd Moseby 0.30
192. LaMarr Hoyt 0.25
193. Ted Simmons 0.25
194. Ron Guidry 0.30
195. Eddie Murray 0.55
196. Lou Whitaker 0.30
197. Cal Ripken 0.55
198. George Brett 0.65
199. Dale Murphy 0.35
200A. Cecil Cooper 0.10
200B. Jim Rice 0.15
201. Tim Raines 0.20
202. Rickey Henderson 0.30

BALTIMORE ORIOLES

203. Eddie Murray 0.25
204. Cal Ripken 0.25
205. Gary Roenicke 0.05
206. Ken Singleton 0.05
207. Scott McGregor 0.05
208. Tippy Martinez 0.05
209. John Lowenstein 0.05
210. Mike Flanagan 0.05
211. Jim Palmer 0.15
212. Dan Ford 0.05
213. Rick Dempsey 0.05
214. Rich Dauer 0.05

BOSTON RED SOX

215. Jerry Remy 0.05
216. Wade Boggs 0.35
217. Jim Rice 0.00
218. Tony Armas 0.20
219. Dwight Evans 0.10
220. Bob Stanley 0.05
221. Dave Stapleton 0.05
222. Rich Gedman 0.07
223. Glenn Hoffman 0.05
224. Dennis Eckersley 0.07
225. John Tudor 0.07
226. Bruce Hurst 0.05

CALIFORNIA ANGELS

227. Rod Carew 0.25
228. Bobby Grich 0.07
229. Doug DeCinces 0.07
230. Fred Lynn 0.15
231. Reggie Jackson 0.30
232. Tommy John 0.10
233. Luis Sanchez 0.05
234. Bob Boone 0.05
235. Bruce Kison 0.05
236. Brian Downing 0.05
237. Ken Forsch 0.05
238. Rick Burleson 0.05

CHICAGO WHITE SOX

239. Dennis Lamp 0.05
240. LaMarr Hoyt 0.07
241. Richard Dotson 0.05
242. Harold Baines 0.15
243. Carlton Fisk 0.10
244. Greg Luzinski 0.07
245. Rudy Law 0.05
246. Tom Paciorek 0.05
247. Floyd Bannister 0.05

1984 Topps Richard Dotson

248. Julio Cruz 0.05
249. Vance Law 0.05
250. Scott Fletcher 0.05

CLEVELAND INDIANS

251. Toby Harrah 0.05
252. Pat Tabler 0.07
253. Gorman Thomas 0.07
254. Rick Sutcliffe 0.10
255. Andre Thornton 0.07
256. Bake McBride 0.05
257. Alan Bannister 0.05
258. Jamie Easterly 0.05
259. Lary Sorenson 0.05
260. Mike Hargrove 0.05
261. Bert Blyleven 0.10
262. Ron Hassey 0.05

DETROIT TIGERS

263. Jack Morris 0.15
264. Larry Herndon 0.05
265. Lance Parrish 0.15
266. Alan Trammell 0.15
267. Lou Whitaker 0.10
268. Aurelio Lopez 0.05
269. Dan Petry 0.10
270. Glenn Wilson 0.10
271. Chet Lemon 0.07
272. Kirk Gibson 0.15
273. Enos Cabell 0.05
274. Johnny Wockenfuss ... 0.05

KANSAS CITY ROYALS

275. George Brett 0.30
276. Willie Aikens 0.05
277. Frank White 0.05
278. Hal McRae 0.05
279. Dan Quisenberry 0.10
280. Willie Wilson 0.10
281. Paul Splittorff 0.05
282. U.L. Washington 0.05
283. Bud Black 0.07
284. John Wathan 0.05
285. Larry Gura 0.07
286. Pat Sheridan 0.07
287A. Rusty Staub 0.07
287B. Dave Righetti 0.10
288A. Bob Forsch 0.07
288B. Mike Warren 0.07
289. Al Holland 0.07
290. Dan Quisenberry 0.10

MILWAUKEE BREWERS

291. Cecil Cooper 0.10
292. Moose Haas 0.05
293. Ted Simmons 0.10
294. Paul Molitor 0.10
295. Robin Yount 0.20
296. Ben Oglivie 0.07
297. Tom Tellman 0.05
298. Jim Gantner 0.05
299. Rick Manning 0.05
300. Don Sutton 0.15
301. Charlie Moore 0.05
302. Jim Slaton 0.05

MINNESOTA TWINS

303. Gary Ward 0.07
304. Tom Brunansky 0.10
305. Kent Hrbek 0.20
306. Gary Gaetti 0.10
307. John Castino 0.05
308. Ken Schrom 0.05
309. Ron Davis 0.05
310. Lenny Faedo 0.05
311. Darrell Brown 0.05
312. Frank Viola 0.10
313. Dave Engle 0.07
314. Randy Bush 0.05

NEW YORK YANKEES

315. Dave Righetti 0.10
316. Rich Gossage 0.10
317. Ken Griffey 0.07
318. Ron Guidry 0.15
319. Dave Winfield 0.20
320. Don Baylor 0.10
321. Butch Wynegar 0.05
322. Omar Moreno 0.05
323. Andre Robertson 0.05
324. Willie Randolph 0.05
325. Don Mattingly 0.40
326. Graig Nettles 0.10

OAKLAND A'S

327. Rickey Henderson 0.25
328. Carney Lansford 0.10
329. Jeff Burroughs 0.05
330. Chris Codiroli 0.05
331. Dave Lopes 0.05
332. Dwayne Murphy 0.05
333. Wayne Gross 0.05
334. Bill Almon 0.05
335. Tom Underwood 0.05
336. Dave Beard 0.05
337. Mike Heath 0.05
338. Mike Davis 0.07

SEATTLE MARINERS

339. Pat Putnam 0.05
340. Tony Bernazard 0.05
341. Steve Henderson 0.05
342. Richie Zisk 0.07
343. Dave Henderson 0.05
344. Al Cowens 0.07
345. Bill Caudill 0.05
346. Jim Beattie 0.05
347. Rick Nelson 0.05
348. Roy Thomas 0.05
349. Spike Owen 0.07
350. Jamie Allen 0.05

TEXAS RANGERS

351. Buddy Bell 0.10
352. Billy Sample 0.05
353. George Wright 0.05
354. Larry Parrish 0.07
355. Jim Sundberg 0.07
356. Charlie Hough 0.05
357. Pete O'Brien 0.10
358. Wayne Tolleson 0.05
359. Danny Darwin 0.05
360. Dave Stewart 0.07
361. Mickey Rivers 0.07
362. Bucky Dent 0.07

TORONTO BLUE JAYS

363. Willie Upshaw 0.07
364. Damaso Garcia 0.07
365. Lloyd Moseby 0.10
366. Cliff Johnson 0.05
367. Jim Clancy 0.05
368. Dave Stieb 0.10
369. Alfredo Griffin 0.05
370. Barry Bonnell 0.05
371. Luis Leal 0.05
372. Jesse Barfield 0.15
373. Ernie Whitt 0.05
374. Rance Mulliniks 0.05

YOUNG STARS

375. Mike Boddicker 0.07
376. Greg Brock 0.07
377. Bill Doran 0.10
378. Nick Esasky 0.07
379. Julio Franco 0.10
380. Mel Hall 0.10
381. Bob Kearney 0.07
382. Ron Kittle 0.10
393. Carmelo Martinez 0.07
384. Craig McMurtry 0.07
385. Darryl Strawberry 0.50
386. Matt Young 0.07

1985 FLEER STICKERS

1985 Fleer Eddie Murray

No.	Player	Value
1.	Pete Rose	0.40
2.	Pete Rose	0.30
3.	Pete Rose	0.30
4.	Don Mattingly	0.40
5.	Dave Winfield	0.25
6.	Wade Boggs	0.35
7.	Buddy Bell	0.10
8.	Tony Gwynn	0.20
9.	Lee Lacy	0.07
10.	Chili Davis	0.10
11.	Ryne Sandberg	0.10
12.	Tony Armas	0.07
13.	Jim Rice	0.20
14.	Dave Kingman	0.10
15.	Alvin Davis	0.20
16.	Gary Carter	0.25
17.	Mike Schmidt	0.20
18.	Dale Murphy	0.25
19.	Ron Cey	0.07
20.	Eddie Murray	0.20
21.	Harold Baines	0.10
22.	Kirk Gibson	0.10
23.	Jim Rice	0.20
24.	Gary Matthews	0.07
25.	Keith Hernandez	0.20
26.	Gary Carter	0.20
27.	George Hendrick	0.07
28.	Tony Armas	0.07
29.	Dave Kingman	0.10
30.	Dwayne Murphy	0.05
31.	Lance Parrish	0.15
32.	Andre Thornton	0.07
33.	Dale Murphy	0.25
34.	Mike Schmidt	0.20
35.	Gary Carter	0.25
36.	Darryl Strawberry	0.30
37.	Don Mattingly	0.30
38.	Larry Parrish	0.07
39.	George Bell	0.10
40.	Dwight Evans	0.10
41.	Cal Ripken	0.30
42.	Tim Raines	0.20
43.	Johnny Ray	0.10
44.	Juan Samuel	0.20
45.	Ryne Sandberg	0.25

No.	Player	Value
46.	Mike Easler	0.05
47.	Andre Thornton	0.07
48.	Dave Kingman	0.10
49.	Don Baylor	0.10
50.	Rusty Staub	0.05
51.	Steve Braun	0.05
52.	Kevin Bass	0.07
53.	Greg Gross	0.05
54.	Rickey Henderson	0.25
55.	Dave Collins	0.07
56.	Brett Butler	0.10
57.	Gary Pettis	0.07
58.	Tim Raines	0.20
59.	Juan Samuel	0.15
60.	Alan Wiggins	0.05
61.	Lonnie Smith	0.07
ACTION (62-79)		
62.	Eddie Murray SA	0.15
63.	Eddie Murray SA	0.15
64.	Eddie Murray SA	0.15
65.	Eddie Murray SA	0.15
66.	Eddie Murray SA	0.15
67.	Eddie Murray SA	0.15
68.	Tom Seaver SA	0.10
69.	Tom Seaver SA	0.10
70.	Tom Seaver SA	0.10
71.	Tom Seaver SA	0.10
72.	Tom Seaver SA	0.10
73.	Tom Seaver SA	0.10
74.	Mike Schmidt SA	0.15
75.	Mike Schmidt SA	0.15
76.	Mike Schmidt SA	0.15
77.	Mike Schmidt SA	0.15
78.	Mike Schmidt SA	0.15
79.	Mike Schmidt SA	0.15

1985 Fleer Al Holland

No.	Player	Value
80.	Mike Boddicker	0.07
81.	Bert Blyleven	0.07
82.	Jack Morris	0.10
83.	Dan Petry	0.07
84.	Frank Viola	0.07
85.	Joaquin Andujar	0.07
86.	Mario Soto	0.05
87.	Dwight Gooden	0.50
88.	Joe Niekro	0.07
89.	Rick Sutcliffe	0.10
90.	Mike Boddicker	0.07
91.	Dave Stieb	0.10
92.	Bert Blyleven	0.07
93.	Phil Niekro	0.07
94.	Alejandro Pena	0.07
95.	Dwight Gooden	0.50
96.	Orel Hershiser	0.15
97.	Rick Rhoden	0.07
98.	John Candelaria	0.07
99.	Dan Quisenberry	0.10
100.	Bill Caudill	0.05
101.	Willie Hernandez	0.10
102.	Dave Righetti	0.10
103.	Ron Davis	0.05
104.	Bruce Sutter	0.10
105.	Lee Smith	0.07
106.	Jesse Orosco	0.07
107.	Al Holland	0.05
108.	Goose Gossage	0.10
109.	Mark Langston	0.07
110.	Dave Stieb	0.10
111.	Mike Witt	0.10
112.	Bert Blyleven	0.07
113.	Dwight Gooden	0.50
114.	Fernando Valenzuela	0.15
115.	Nolan Ryan	0.15
116.	Mario Soto	0.07
117.	Ron Darling	0.15
118.	Dan Gladden	0.10
119.	Jeff Stone	0.10
120.	John Franco	0.07
121.	Barbaro Garbey	0.05
122.	Kirby Puckett	0.30
123.	Roger Clemens	0.35
124.	Bret Saberhagen	0.15
125.	Sparky Anderson	0.05
126.	Dick Williams	0.05

1985 TOPPS STICKERS

No.	Player	Value
1.	Steve Garvey (top) (foil)	0.35
2.	S. Garvey (bottom, foil)	0.25
3.	Dwight Gooden (top)	0.40
4.	Dwight Gooden (bottom)	0.25
5.	Joe Morgan (top)	0.15
6.	Joe Morgan (bottom)	0.10
7.	Don Sutton (top)	0.15
8.	Don Sutton (bottom)	0.10
9.	Jack Morris ALCS	0.15
10.	Milt Wilcox ALCS	0.05
11.	Kirk Gibson ALCS	0.20
12.	Chicago Cubs NLCS	0.05

1985 Topps Harold Baines

No.	Player	Value
13.	Steve Garvey NLCS	0.15
14.	Steve Garvey NLCS	0.15
15.	Jack Morris WS	0.15
16.	Kurt Bevacqua WS	0.05
17.	Milt Wilcox WS	0.05
18.	Alan Trammell WS	0.10
19.	Kirk Gibson WS	0.15
20.	Alan Trammell WS	0.15
21.	Chet Lemon WS	0.05
ATLANTA BRAVES		
22.	Dale Murphy	0.35
23.	Steve Bedrosian	0.05
24.	Bob Horner	0.15
25.	Claudell Washington	0.07
26.	Rick Mahler (212)	0.05
27.	Rafael Ramirez (213)	0.05
28.	Craig McMurtry (214)	0.05
29.	Chris Chambliss (215)	0.05
30.	Alex Trevino (216)	0.05
31.	Bruce Benedict (217)	0.05
32.	Ken Oberkfell (218)	0.05
33.	Glenn Hubbard (219)	0.05
CHICAGO CUBS		
34.	Ryne Sandberg	0.30
35.	Rick Sutcliffe	0.15
36.	Leon Durham	0.10
37.	Jody Davis	0.10
38.	Bob Dernier (224)	0.05
39.	Keith Moreland (225)	0.05
40.	Scott Sanderson (226)	0.05
41.	Lee Smith (227)	0.05
42.	Ron Cey (228)	0.05
43.	Steve Trout (229)	0.05
44.	Gary Matthews (230)	0.05
45.	Larry Bowa (231)	0.05
CINCINNATI REDS		
46.	Mario Soto	0.07
47.	Dave Parker	0.20
48.	Dave Concepcion	0.07
49.	Gary Redus	0.07
50.	Ted Power (236)	0.05
51.	Nick Esasky (237)	0.05
52.	Duane Walker (238)	0.05
53.	Eddie Milner (239)	0.05
54.	Ron Oester (240)	0.05
55.	Cesar Cedeno (241)	0.05
56.	Joe Price (242)	0.05
57.	Pete Rose (243)	0.20
HOUSTON ASTROS		
58.	Nolan Ryan	0.25
59.	Jose Cruz	0.10
60.	Jerry Mumphrey	0.05
61.	Enos Cabell	0.05
62.	Bob Knepper (248)	0.05
63.	Dickie Thon (249)	0.05
64.	Phil Garner (250)	0.05
65.	Craig Reynolds (251)	0.05
66.	Frank DiPino (252)	0.05
67.	Terry Puhl (253)	0.05
68.	Bill Doran (254)	0.05
69.	Joe Niekro (255)	0.05
LOS ANGELES DODGERS		
70.	Pedro Guerrero	0.20
71.	Fernando Valenzuela	0.20
72.	Mike Marshall	0.10
73.	Alejandro Pena	0.07
74.	Orel Hershiser (260)	0.10
75.	Ken Landreaux (261)	0.05
76.	Bill Russell (262)	0.05
77.	Steve Sax (263)	0.07
78.	Rick Honeycutt (264)	0.05
79.	Mike Scioscia (265)	0.05
80.	Tom Niedenfuer (266)	0.05
81.	Candy Maldonado (267)	0.05
MONTREAL EXPOS		
82.	Tim Raines	0.20
83.	Gary Carter	0.30
84.	Charlie Lea	0.05
85.	Jeff Reardon	0.07
86.	Andre Dawson (272)	0.07
87.	Tim Wallach (273)	0.07
88.	Terry Francona (274	0.05
89.	Steie Rogers (275)	0.05
90.	Bryn Smith (276)	0.05
91.	Bill Gullickson (277)	0.05
92.	Dan Driessen (278)	0.05
93.	Doug Flynn (279)	0.05
QUADRUPLE STICKERS		
94.	M. Schmidt (170/192/280)	0.07
95.	T. Armas (171/193/281)	0.05
96.	D. Murphy (172/194/282)	0.10
97.	R. Sutcliffe(173/195/283)	0.05
NEW YORK METS		
98.	Keith Hernandez	0.20
99.	George Foster	0.15
100.	Darryl Strawberry	0.35
101.	Jesse Orosco	0.07
102.	Mookie Wilson (288)	0.05
103.	Doug Sisk (289)	0.05
104.	Hubie Brooks (290)	0.05
105.	Ron Darling (291)	0.07
106.	Wally Backman (292)	0.05

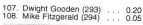

107. Dwight Gooden (293) . . . 0.20
108. Mike Fitzgerald (294) . . . 0.05

109. Walt Terrell (295) 0.05

PHILADELPHIA PHILLIES

110. Ozzie Virgil 0.05
111. Mike Schmidt 0.30
112. Steve Carlton 0.25
113. Al Holland 0.05
114. Juan Samuel (300) 0.07
115. Von Hayes (301) 0.07
116. Jeff Stone (302) 0.05
117. Jerry Koosman (303) . . . 0.05
118. Al Oliver (304) 0.05
119. John Denny (305) 0.05
120. Charles Hudson (306) . . . 0.05
121. Garry Maddox (307) 0.05

PITTSBURGH PIRATES

122. Bill Madlock 0.15
123. John Candelaria 0.07
124. Tony Pena 0.10
125. Jason Thompson 0.05
126. Lee Lacy (312) 0.05
127. Rick Rhoden (313) 0.05
128. Doug Frobel (314) 0.05
129. Kent Tekulve (315) 0.05
130. Johnny Ray (316) 0.05
131. Marvell Wynne (317) 0.05
132. Larry Mcwilliams (318) . . 0.05
133. Dale Berra (319) 0.05

ST LOUIS CARDINALS

134. George Hendrick 0.07
135. Bruce Sutter 0.10
136. Joaquin Andujar 0.07
137. Ozzie Smith 0.10
138. Andy Van Styke (324) . . . 0.05
139. Lonnie Smith (325) 0.05
140. Darrell Porter (326) 0.05
141. Willie McGee (327) 0.07
142. Tom Herr (328) 0.05
143. Dave LaPoint (329) 0.05
144. Neil Allen (330) 0.05
145. David Green (331) 0.05

SAN DIEGO PADRES

146. Tony Gwynn 0.30
147. Rich Gossage 0.10
148. Terry Kennedy 0.07
149. Steve Garvey 0.25
150. Alan Wiggins (336) 0.05
151. Garry Templeton (337) . . 0.05
152. Ed Whitson (338) 0.05
153. Tim Lollar (339) 0.05
154. Dave Dravecky (340) . . . 0.05
155. Graig Nettles (341) 0.07
156. Eric Show (342) 0.05
157. Carmelo Martinez (343) . . 0.05

SAN FRANCISCO GIANTS

158. Bob Brenly 0.07
159. Gary Lavelle 0.05
161. Jeff Leonard 0.07
160. Jack Clark 0.15
162. Chili Davis (348) 0.07
163. Mike Krukow (349) 0.05
164. Johnnie LeMaster (350) . 0.05
165. Atlee Hammaker (351) . . 0.05
166. Dan Gladden (352) 0.05
167. Greg Minton (353) 0.05
168. Joel Youngblood (354) . . 0.05
169. Frank Williams (355) 0.05

QUADRUPLE STICKERS

170. T. Gwynn (94/192/280) . . 0.15
171. D. Mattingly(95/193/281) . 0.20
172. B. Sutter (96/194/282) . . . 0.05
173. Quisenberry(97/195/283) . 0.05

ALL STAR FOILS (174-191)

174. Tony Gwynn (foil) 0.45
175. Ryne Sandberg (foil) 0.45
176. Steve Garvey (foil) 0.45
177. Dale Murphy (foil) 0.60
179. Darryl Strawberry (foil) . . 0.60
180. Gary Carter (foil) 0.55
181. Ozzie Smith (foil) 0.35
182. Charlie Lea (foil) 0.30
183. Lou Whitaker (foil) 0.35
184. Rod Carew (foil) 0.45
185. Cal Ripken (foil) 0.55
186. Dave Winfield (foil) 0.50
187. Reggie Jackson (foil) . . . 0.60
188. George Brett (foil) 0.60
189. Lance Parrish (foil) 0.45
190. Chet Lemon (foil) 0.30
191. Dave Stieb (foil) 0.35

QUADRUPLE STICKERS

192. G. Carter (94/170/280) . . 0.10
193. M. Schmidt (95/171/281) . 0.10
194. T. Armas (96/172/282) . . 0.05
195. M. Witt (97/173/283) 0.07

BALTIMORE ORIOLES

196. Eddie Murray 0.25
197. Cal Ripken 0.25
198. Scott McGregor 0.05
199. Rick Dempsey 0.05
200. Tippy Martinez (360) 0.05
201. Ken Singleton (361) 0.05
202. Mike Boddicker (362) . . . 0.05
203. Rich Dauer (363) 0.05
204. John Shelby (364) 0.05
205. Al Bumbry (365) 0.05
206. John Lowenstein (366) . . 0.05
207. Mike Flanagan (367) 0.05

BOSTON RED SOX

208. Jim Rice 0.25
209. Tony Armas 0.10
210. Wade Boggs 0.35
211. Bruce Hurst 0.05
212. Dwight Evans (26) 0.05
213. Mike Easler (27) 0.05
214. Bill Buckner (28) 0.05
215. Bob Stanley (29) 0.05
216. Jackie Gutierrez (30) 0.05
217. Rich Gedman (31) 0.05
218. Jerry Remy (32) 0.05
219. Marty Barrett (33) 0.05

CALIFORNIA ANGELS

220. Reggie Jackson 0.30
221. Geoff Zahn 0.05
222. Doug DeCinces 0.07
223. Rod Carew 0.25
224. Brian Downing (38) 0.05
225. Fred Lynn (39) 0.07
226. Gary Pettis (40) 0.07
227. Mike Witt (41) 0.07
228. Bob Boone (42) 0.05
229. Tommy John (43) 0.05
230. Bobby Grich (44) 0.05
231. Ron Romanick (45) 0.05

CHICAGO WHITE SOX

232. Ron Kittle 0.10
233. Richard Dotson 0.07
234. Harold Baines 0.20
235. Tom Seaver 0.25
236. Greg Walker (50) 0.10
237. Roy Smalley (51) 0.05
238. Greg Luzinski (52) 0.05
239. Julio Cruz (53) 0.05
240. Scott Fletcher (54) 0.05
241. Rudy Law (55) 0.05

242. Vance Law (56) 0.05
243. Carlton Fisk (57) 0.05

CLEVELAND INDIANS

244. Andre Thornton 0.07
245. Julio Franco 0.10
246. Brett Butler 0.10
247. Bert Blyleven 0.10
248. Mike Hargrove (62) 0.05
249. George Vukovich (63) . . . 0.05
250. Pat Tabler (64) 0.05
251. Brook Jacoby (65) 0.07
252. Tony Bernazard (66) 0.05
253. Ernie Camacho (67) 0.05
254. Mel Hall (68) 0.07
255. Carmen Castillo (69) 0.05

DETROIT TIGERS

256. Jack Morris 0.15
257. Willie Hernandez 0.10
258. Alan Trammell 0.15
259. Lance Parrish 0.20
260. Chet Lemon (74) 0.05
261. Lou Whitaker (75) 0.07
262. Howard Johnson (76) . . . 0.05
263. Barbaro Garbey (77) 0.05
264. Dan Petry (78) 0.07
265. Aurelio Lopez (79) 0.05
266. Larry Herndon (80) 0.05
267. Kirk Gibson (81) 0.10

KANSAS CITY ROYALS

268. George Brett 0.35
269. Dan Quisenberry 0.10
270. Hal McRae 0.05
271. Steve Balboni 0.07
272. Pat Sheridan (86) 0.05
273. Jorge Orta (87) 0.05
274. Frank White (88) 0.05
275. Bud Black (89) 0.05
276. Darryl Motley (90) 0.05
277. Willie Wilson (91) 0.07
278. Larry Gura (92) 0.05
279. Don Slaught (93) 0.05

QUADRUPLE STICKERS

280. D. Gooden (94/170/192) . 0.25
281. M. Langston(95/171/193) . 0.07
282. T. Raines (96/172/194) . . 0.10
283. R. Henderson (97/173/195/283) 0.15

MILWAUKEE BREWERS

284. Robin Yount 0.25
285. Rollie Fingers 0.10
286. Jim Sundberg 0.05
287. Cecil Cooper 0.10
288. Jamie Cocanower 0.05
289. Mike Caldwell (103) 0.05
290. Don Sutton (104) 0.07
291. Rick Manning (105) 0.05
292. Ben Oglivie (106) 0.05
293. Moose Haas (107) 0.05
294. Ted Simmons (108) 0.07
295. Jim Gantner (109) 0.05

MINNESOTA TWINS

296. Kent Hrbek 0.20
297. Ron Davis 0.05
298. Dave Engle 0.05
299. Tom Brunansky 0.15
300. Frank Viola (114) 0.05
301. Mike Smithson (115) 0.05
302. Gary Gaetti (116) 0.07
303. Tim Teufel (117) 0.05
304. Mickey Hatcher (118) . . . 0.05
305. John Butcher (119) 0.05
306. Darrell Brown (120) 0.05
307. Kirby Puckett (121) 0.15

NEW YORK YANKEES

308. Dave Winfield 0.25
309. Phil Niekro 0.15
310. Don Mattingly 0.40
311. Don Baylor 0.10
312. Willie Randolph (126) . . . 0.05
313. Ron Guidry (127) 0.07
314. Dave Righetti (128) 0.07
315. Bobby Meacham (129) . . 0.05
316. Butch Wynegar (130) . . . 0.05
317. Mike Pagliarulo (131) . . . 0.10
318. Joe Cowley (132) 0.05
319. John Montefusco (133) . . 0.05

1985 Topps Jim Gantner

OAKLAND A'S

320. Dave Kingman 0.10
321. Rickey Henderson 0.25
322. Bill Caudill 0.05
323. Dwayne Murphy 0.05
324. Steve McCatty (138) 0.05
325. Joe Morgan (139) 0.07
326. Mike Heath (140) 0.05
327. Chris Codiroli (141) 0.05
328. Ray Burris (142) 0.05
329. Tony Phillips (143) 0.05
330. Carney Lansford (144) . . 0.05
331. Bruce Bochte (145) 0.05

SEATTLE MARINERS

332. Alvin Davis 0.25
333. Al Cowens 0.05
334. Jim Beattie 0.05
335. Bob Kearney 0.05
336. Ed Vandeberg (150) 0.05
337. Mark Langston (151) 0.07
338. Dave Henderson (152) . . . 0.05
339. Spike Owen (153) 0.05
340. Matt Young (154) 0.05
341. Jack Perconte (155) 0.05
342. Barry Bonnell (156) 0.05
343. Mike Stanton (157) 0.05

TEXAS RANGERS

344. Pete O'Brien 0.10
345. Charlie Hough 0.05
346. Larry Parrish 0.05
347. Buddy Bell 0.10
348. Frank Tanana (162) 0.05
349. Curt Wilkerson (163) 0.05
350. Jeff Kunkel (164) 0.05
351. Billy Sample (165) 0.05
352. Danny Darwin (166) 0.05
353. Gary Ward (167) 0.05
354. Mike Mason (168) 0.05
355. Mickey Rivers (169) 0.05

TORONTO BLUE JAYS

356. Dave Stieb 0.15
357. Damaso Garcia 0.07
358. Willie Upshaw 0.07
359. Lloyd Moseby 0.10
360. George Bell (200) 0.07
361. Luis Leal (201) 0.05
362. Jesse Barfield (202) 0.07
363. Dave Collins (203) 0.05
364. Roy Lee Jackson (204) . . 0.05
365. Doyle Alexander (205) . . . 0.05
366. Alfredo Griffin (206) 0.05
367. Cliff Johnson (207) 0.05

YOUNG STARS

368. Alvin Davis 0.25
369. Juan Samuel 0.15
370. Brook Jacoby 0.15
371. Langston and Gooden . . . 0.07
372. Mike Fitzgerald 0.07
373. Jackie Gutierrez 0.05
374. Dan Gladden 0.10
375. Carmelo Martinez 0.07
376. Kirby Puckett 0.35

1986 FLEER STICKERS

No. Player . . . . Value

1. Harold Baines 0.30
2. Jesse Barfield 0.30
3. Don Baylor 0.20
4. Juan Beniquez 0.10
5. Tim Birtsas 0.15
6. Bert Blyleven 0.20
7. Bruce Bochte 0.10
8. Wade Boggs 1.25
9. Dennis Boyd 0.20
10. Phil Bradley 0.30
11. George Brett 0.80
12. Hubie Brooks 0.20
13. Chris Brown 0.80
14. Tom Browning 0.30
15. Tom Brunansky 0.15
16. Bill Buckner 0.15
17. Britt Burns 0.10
18. Brett Butler 0.15
19. Jose Canseco 3.50
20. Rod Carew 0.40
21. Steve Carlton 0.40
22. Don Carman 0.25
23. Gary Carter 0.50
24. Jack Clark 0.20
25. Vince Coleman 2.00
26. Cecil Cooper 0.25
27. Jose Cruz 0.10
28. Ron Darling 0.30
29. Alvin Davis 0.30
30. Jody Davis 0.15
31. Mike Davis 0.15
32. Andre Dawson 0.25
33. Mariano Duncan 0.40
34. Shawon Dunston 0.20
35. Leon Durham 0.15
36. Darrell Evans 0.15
37. Tony Fernandez 0.20
38. Carlton Fisk 0.20
39. John Franco 0.15
40. Julio Franco 0.15
41. Damaso Garcia 0.15
42. Scott Garrelts 0.15
43. Steve Garvey 0.55
44. Rich Gedman 0.15
45. Kirk Gibson 0.30
46. Dwight Gooden 2.50
47. Pedro Guerrero 0.30
48. Ron Guidry 0.25
49. Ozzie Guillen 0.40
50. Tony Gwynn 0.40
51. Andy Hawkins 0.10
52. Von Hayes 0.15
53. Rickey Henderson 0.80
54. Tom Henke 0.15
55. Keith Hernandez 0.30
56. Willie Hernandez 0.15
57. Tommy Herr 0.15
58. Orel Hershiser 0.40
59. Teddy Higuera 0.55
60. Bob Horner 0.30
61. Charlie Hough 0.10
62. Jay Howell 0.10
63. LaMarr Hoyt 0.15
64. Kent Hrbek 0.30
65. Reggie Jackson 0.55
66. Bob James 0.10
67. Dave Kingman 0.15
68. Ron Kittle 0.15
69. Charlie Leibrandt 0.15
70. Fred Lynn 0.25
71. Mike Marshall 0.25
72. Don Mattingly 1.50
73. Oddibe McOowell 0.55
74. Willie McGee 0.30
75. Scott McGregor 0.15
76. Paul Molitor 0.15
77. Charile Moore 0.10
78. Keith Moreland 0.15
79. Jack Morris 0.20
80. Dale Murphy 1.00
81. Eddie Murray 0.80
92. Phil Niekro 0.30
93. Joe Orsulak 0.20
84. Dave Parker 0.30
85. Lance Parrish 0.30
86. Larry Parrish 0.15
87. Tony Pena 0.25
88. Gary Pettis 0.15
89. Jim Presley 0.40
90. Kirby Puckett 0.80
91. Don Quisenberry 0.25
92. Tim Raines 0.30
93. Johnny Ray 0.15
94. Jeff Reardon 0.15
95. Rick Reuschel 0.10
96. Jim Rice 0.30
97. Dave Righetti 0.25
98. Ernest Riles 0.30
99. Cal Ripken 0.55
100. Ron Romanick 0.15
101. Pete Rose 1.25
102. Nolan Ryan 0.55
103. Bret Saberhagen 0.55
104. Mark Salas 0.15
105. Juan Samuel 0.25
106. Ryne Sandberg 0.55
107. Mike Schmidt 0.50
108. Mike Scott 0.15
109. Tom Seaver 0.35
110. Bryn Smith 0.10
111. Dave Smith 0.10
112. Lonnie Smith 0.10
113. Ozzie Smith 0.30
114. Mario Soto 0.15
115. Dave Stieb 0.20
116. Darryl Strawberry 0.80
117. Bruce Sutter 0.25
118. Garry Templeton 0.15
119. Gorman Thomas 0.20
120. Andre Thornton 0.15
121. Alan Trammell 0.30
122. John Tudor 0.20
123. Fernando Valenzuela . . . 0.30
124. Frank Viola 0.15
125. Gary Ward 0.10
126. Lou Whitaker 0.30
127. Frank White 0.15
128. Glenn Wilson 0.15
129. Willie Wilson 0.25
130. Dave Winfield 0.40
131. Robin Yount 0.40
132. Gooden, Murphy CL 1.50

1986 TOPPS STICKERS

No. Player . . . . Value

1. Pete Rose (top) (foil) 0.45
2. Pete Rose (bottom) (foil) . 0.30
3. George Brett (175) 0.15
4. Rod Carew (178) 0.15
5. Vince Coleman (179) ... 0.15
6. Dwight Gooden (180) ... 0.20
7. Phil Niekro (181) 0.10
8. Tony Perez (182) 0.10
9. Nolan Ryan (183) 0.15
10. Tom Seaver (184) 0.15
11. Ozzie Smith NLCS 0.10

12. Bill Madlock NLCS 0.15
13. Cardinals NLCS 0.10
14. Al Oliver ALCS 0.07
15. Jim Sundberg ALCS 0.07
16. George Brett ALCS 0.15
17. Bret Saberhagen WS ... 0.15
18. Dane Iorg WS 0.05
19. Tito Landrum WS 0.05
20. John Tudor WS 0.07
21. Buddy Biancalana WS .. 0.05
22. Darryl Motley WS 0.05
23. Brett and White WS 0.10

HOUSTON ASTROS

24. Nolan Ryan 0.25
25. Bill Doran 0.10
26. Jose Cruz (185) 0.05
27. Mike Scott (188) 0.05
28. Kevin Bass (189) 0.05
29. Glenn Davis (190) 0.15
30. Mark Bailey (191) 0.05
31. Dave Smith (192) 0.05
32. Phil Garner (193) 0.05
33. Dickie Thon (194) 0.05

ATLANTA BRAVES

34. Bob Horner 0.15
35. Dale Murphy 0.30
36. Glenn Hubbard (195) ... 0.05
37. Bruce Sutter (198) 0.10
38. Ken Oberkfell (199) 0.05
39. Claudell Washington (200) 0.05
40. Steve Bedrosian (201) .. 0.05
41. Terry Harper (202) 0.05
42. Rafael Ramirez (203) ... 0.05
43. Rick Mahler (204) 0.05

ST. LOUIS CARDINALS

44. Joaquin Andujar 0.10
45. Willie McGee 0.10
46. Ozzie Smith (205) 0.07
47. Vince Coleman (208) ... 0.10
48. Danny Cox (209) 0.05
49. Tom Herr (210) 0.05
50. Jack Clark (211) 0.07
51. Andy Van Slyke (212) ... 0.07
52. John Tudor (213) 0.05
53. Terry Pendleton (214) ... 0.05

CHICAGO CUBS

54. Keith Moreland 0.07
55. Ryne Sandberg 0.30
56. Lee Smith (215) 0.07
57. Steve Trout (218) 0.05
58. Jody Davis (219) 0.07
59. Gary Matthews (220) ... 0.05
60. Leon Durham (221) 0.07
61. Rick Sutcliffe (222) 0.07
62. Dennis Eckersley (223) .. 0.05
63. Bob Dernier (224) 0.05

LOS ANGELES DODGERS

64. Fernando Valenzuela ... 0.20
65. Pedro Guerrero 0.20
66. Jerry Reuss (225) 0.05
67. Greg Brock (228) 0.05
68. Mike Scioscia (229) 0.05
69. Ken Howell (230) 0.05
70. Bill Madlock (231) 0.07
71. Mike Marshall (232) 0.07
72. Steve Sax (233) 0.07
73. Orel Hershiser (234) 0.10

MONTREAL EXPOS

74. Andre Dawson 0.15
75. Tim Raines 0.20
76. Jeff Reardon (235) 0.07
77. Hubie Brooks (238) 0.07
78. Bill Gullickson (239) 0.05
79. Bryn Smith (240) 0.05
80. Terry Francona (241) ... 0.05
81. Vance Law (242) 0.05
82. Tim Wallach (243) 0.07
83. Herm Winningham (244) . 0.05

SAN FRANCISCO GIANTS

84. Jeff Leonard 0.07
85. Chris Brown 0.30
86. Scott Garretts (245) 0.07
87. Jose Uribe (248) 0.05
88. Manny Trillo (249) 0.05
89. Dan Driessen (250) 0.05
90. Dan Gladden (251) 0.07
91. Mark Davis (252) 0.05
92. Bob Brenly (253) 0.07
93. Mike Krukow (254) 0.05

NEW YORK METS

94. Dwight Gooden 0.50
95. Darryl Strawberry 0.35

96. Gary Carter (255) 0.20
97. Wally Backman (258) ... 0.05
98. Ron Darling (259) 0.10
99. Keith Hernandez (260) .. 0.10
100. George Foster (261) 0.07
101. Howard Johnson (262) .. 0.05
102. Rafael Santana (263) ... 0.05
103. Roger McDowell (264) .. 0.07

SAN DIEGO PADRES

104. Steve Garvey 0.30
105. Tony Gwynn 0.30
106. Craig Nettles (265) 0.07
107. Rich Gossage (268) 0.07
108. Andy Hawkins (269) 0.05
109. Carmelo Martinez (270) .. 0.05
110. Garry Templeton (271) .. 0.05
111. Terry Kennedy (272) 0.05
112. Tim Flannery (273) 0.05
113. LaMarr Hoyt (274) 0.05

PHILADELPHIA PHILLIES

114. Mike Schmidt 0.30
115. Ozzie Virgil 0.10
116. Steve Carlton (275) 0.15
117. Garry Maddox (278) 0.05
118. Glenn Wilson (279) 0.05
119. Kevin Gross (280) 0.05
120. Von Hayes (281) 0.07
121. Juan Samuel (282) 0.07
122. Rick Schu (283) 0.07
123. Shane Rawley (284) 0.05

PITTSBURGH PIRATES

124. Johnny Ray 0.15
125. Tony Pena 0.10
126. Rick Reuschel (285) 0.05
127. Sammy Khalifa (288) ... 0.05
128. Marvell Wynne (289) 0.05
129. Jason Thompson (290) .. 0.05
130. Rick Rhoden (291) 0.05
131. Bill Almon (292) 0.05
132. Joe Orsulak (293) 0.05
133. Jim Morrison (294) 0.05

CINCINNATI REDS

134. Pete Rose 0.40
135. Dave Parker 0.20
136. Mario Soto (295) 0.05
137. Dave Concepcion (298) .. 0.07
138. Ron Oester (299) 0.05
139. Buddy Bell (300) 0.07
140. Ted Power (301) 0.05
141. Tom Browning (302) 0.07
142. John Franco (303) 0.07
143. Tony Perez (304) 0.07
144. Willie McGee (305) 0.10
145. Dale Murphy (306) 0.15

FOILS (146-163)

146. Tony Gwynn (foil) 0.45
147. Tom Herr (foil) 0.30
148. Steve Garvey (foil) 0.50
149. Dale Murphy (foil) 0.50
150. Darryl Strawberry (foil) .. 0.60
151. Graig Nettles (foil) 0.35
152. Terry Kennedy (foil) 0.30
153. Ozzie Smith (foil) 0.35
154. LaMarr Hoyt (foil) 0.30
155. Rickey Henderson (foil) .. 0.60
156. Lou Whitaker (foil) 0.35
157. George Brett (foil) 0.60
158. Eddie Murray (foil) 0.60
159. Cal Ripken (foil) 0.60
160. Dave Winfield (foil) 0.50
161. Jim Rice (foil) 0.45
162. Carlton Fisk (foil) 0.40
163. Jack Morris (foil) 0.35
164. Wade Boggs (307) 0.25
165. Darrell Evans (308) 0.15

OAKLAND A'S

166. Mike Davis 0.07
167. Dave Kingman 0.10
168. Alfredo Griffin (309) 0.05

169. Carney Lansford (310) .. 0.05
170. Bruce Bochte (311) 0.05
171. Dwayne Murphy (312) ... 0.05
172. Dave Collins (313) 0.05
173. Chris Codiroli (314) 0.05
174. Mike Heath (315) 0.05
175. Jay Howell (3) 0.05

CALIFORNIA ANGELS

176. Rod Carew 0.25
177. Reggie Jackson 0.30
178. Doug DeCinces (4) 0.05
179. Bob Boone (5) 0.05
180. Ron Romanick (6) 0.05
181. Bob Grich (7) 0.05
182. Donnie Moore (8) 0.05
183. Brian Downing (9) 0.05
184. Ruppert Jones (10) 0.05
185. Juan Beniquez (26) 0.05

TORONTO BLUE JAYS

186. Dave Stieb 0.15
187. Jorge Bell 0.15
188. Willie Upshaw (27) 0.05
189. Tom Henke (28) 0.07
190. Damaso Garcia (29) 0.05
191. Jimmy Key (30) 0.07
192. Jesse Barfield (31) 0.07
193. Dennis Lamp (32) 0.05
194. Tony Fernandez (33) ... 0.10
195. Lloyd Moseby (36) 0.07

MILWAUKEE BREWERS

196. Cecil Cooper 0.10
197. Robin Yount 0.25
198. Roille Fingers (37) 0.07
199. Ted Simmons (38) 0.07
200. Ben Oglivie (39) 0.05
201. Moose Haas (40) 0.05
202. Jim Gantner (41) 0.05
203. Paul Molitor (42) 0.07
204. Charlie Moore (43) 0.05
205. Danny Darwin (46) 0.05

CLEVELAND INDIANS

206. Brett Butler 0.10
207. Brook Jacoby 0.15
208. Andre Thornton (47) 0.05
209. Tom Waddell (48) 0.05
210. Tony Bernazard (49) 0.05
211. Julio Franco (50) 0.07
212. Pat Tabler (51) 0.05
213. Joe Carter (52) 0.10
214. George Vukovich (53) ... 0.05
215. Rich Thompson (56) 0.05

SEATTLE MARINERS

216. Gorman Thomas 0.07
217. Phil Bradley 0.15
218. Alvin Davis (57) 0.10
219. Jim Presley (58) 0.10
220. Matt Young (59) 0.05
221. Mike Moore (60) 0.05
222. Dave Henderson (61) ... 0.05
223. Ed Nunez (62) 0.05
224. Spike Owen (63) 0.05
225. Mark Langston (66) 0.07

BALTIMORE ORIOLES

226. Cal Ripken 0.30
227. Eddie Murray 0.30
228. Fred Lynn (67) 0.07
229. Lee Lacy (68) 0.05
230. Scott McGregor (69) 0.05
231. Storm Davis (70) 0.05
232. Rick Dempsey (71) 0.05
233. Mike Boddicker (72) 0.05
234. Mike Young (73) 0.07
235. Sammy Stewart (76) 0.05

TEXAS RANGERS

236. Pete O'Brien 0.10
237. Oddibe McDowell 0.25
238. Toby Harrah (77) 0.05
239. Gary Ward (78) 0.05
240. Larry Parrish (79) 0.05
241. Charlie Hough (80) 0.05
242. Burt Hooton (81) 0.05
243. Don Slaught (82) 0.05
244. Curt Wilkerson (83) 0.05
245. Greg Harris (86) 0.05

BOSTON RED SOX

246. Jim Rice 0.25
247. Wade Boggs 0.40
248. Rich Gedman (87) 0.07
249. Dennis Boyd (88) 0.07
250. Marty Barrett (89) 0.05
251. Dwight Evans (90) 0.07
252. Bill Buckner (91) 0.07
253. Bob Stanley (92) 0.05
254. Tony Armas (93) 0.07

255. Mike Easler (96) 0.05

KANSAS CITY ROYALS

256. George Brett 0.30
257. Dan Quisenberry 0.10
258. Willie Wilson (97) 0.07
259. Jim Sundberg (98) 0.05
260. Bret Saberhagen (99) ... 0.10
261. Bud Black (100) 0.05
262. Charlie Leibrandt (101) .. 0.05
263. Frank White (102) 0.05
264. Lonnie Smith (103) 0.05
265. Steve Balboni (106) 0.05

DETROIT TIGERS

266. Kirk Gibson 0.20
267. Alan Trammell 0.20
268. Jack Morris (107) 0.10
269. Darrell Evans (108) 0.05
270. Dan Petry (109) 0.07
271. Larry Herndon (110) 0.05
272. Lou Whitaker (111) 0.10
273. Lance Parish (112) 0.10
274. Chet Lemon (113) 0.05
275. Willie Hernandez (116) .. 0.07

MINNESOTA TWINS

276. Tom Brunansky 0.15
277. Kent Hrbek 0.20
278. Mark Salas (117) 0.05
280. Tim Teufel (119) 0.05
279. Bert Blyleven (118) 0.10
281. Ron Davis (120) 0.04
282. Mike Smithson (121) 0.05
283. Gary Gaetti (122) 0.10
284. Frank Viola (123) 0.07
285. Kirby Puckett (126) 0.30

CHICAGO WHITE SOX

286. Carlton Fisk 0.10
287. Tom Seaver 0.20
288. Harold Baines (127) 0.10
289. Ron Kittle (128) 0.07
290. Bob James (129) 0.05
291. Rudy Law (130) 0.05
292. Britt Burns (131) 0.05
293. Greg Walker (132) 0.07
294. Ozzie Guillen (133) 0.10
295. Tim Hulett (136) 0.05

NEW YORK YANKEES

296. Don Mattingly 0.40
297. Rickey Henderson 0.30
298. Dave Winfield (137) 0.15
299. Butch Wynegar (138) ... 0.05
300. Don Baylor (139) 0.07
301. Eddie Whitson (140) 0.05
302. Ron Guidry (141) 0.07
303. Dave Righetti (142) 0.07
304. Bobby Meacham (143) .. 0.05
305. Willie Randolph (144) ... 0.05

YOUNG STARS

306. Vince Coleman (145) ... 0.20
307. Oddibe McDowell (164) .. 0.10
308. Larry Sheets (165) 0.10
309. Ozzie Guillen (168) 0.10
310. Ernest Riles (169) 0.07
311. Chris Brown (170) 0.20
312. Fisher and McDowell (171) 0.07
313. Tom Browning (172) 0.07
314. Glenn Davis (173) 0.20
315. Mark Salas (174) 0.05

BASKETBALL STICKERS

1971-72 TOPPS STICKERS

No.	Player	Value
1.	Lou Hudson	2.00
2.	Bob Rule	
3.	Calvin Murphy	
4.	Walt Wesley	1.00
5.	Jo Jo White	
6.	Bob Dandridge	
7.	Nate Thurmond	4.00
8.	Earl Monroe	
9.	Spencer Haywood	
10.	Dave DeBusschere	2.00
11.	Bob Lanier	
12.	Tom VanArsdale	
13.	Hal Greer	1.00
14.	Johnny Green	
15.	Elvin Hayes	
16.	Jimmy Walker	0.50
17.	Don May	
18.	Archie Clark	
19.	Happy Hairston	1.00
20.	Leroy Ellis	
21.	Jerry Sloan	
22.	Pete Maravich	8.00
23.	Bob Kauffman	
24.	John Havlicek	
25.	Walt Frazier	3.00
26.	Dick VanArsdale	
27.	Dave Bing	
28.	Bob Love	2.00
29.	Ron Williams	
30.	Dave Cowens	
31.	Jerry West	6.00
32.	Willis Reed	
33.	Chet Walker	

No.	Player	Value
34.	Oscar Robertson	5.00
35.	Wes Unseld	
36.	Bobby Smith	
37.	Connie Hawkins	6.00
38.	Jeff Mullins	
39.	Lew Alcindor	
40.	Billy Cunningham	1.00
41.	Walt Bellamy	
42.	Geoff Petrie	
43.	Wilt Chamberlain	6.00
44.	Gus Johnson	
45.	Gus VanLier	
46.	NBA Logos	1.00

1971-72 ABA STICKERS

No.	Player	Value
1.	James Jones	3.00
2.	Willie Wise	
3.	Dan Issel	
4.	Mack Calvin	1.00
5.	Roger Brown	
6.	Bob Verga	
7.	Bill Melchioni	2.00
8.	Mel Daniels	
9.	Donnie Freeman	
10.	Joe Caldwell	2.00
11.	Louie Dampier	
12.	Mike Lewis	
13.	Rick Barry	5.00
14.	Larry Jones	
15.	Julius Keye	
16.	Larry Cannon	2.00
17.	Zelmo Beatty	
18.	Charlie Scott	
19.	Steve Jones	1.00
20.	George Carter	
21.	John Brisker	
22.	ABA Logos	1.50
23.	ABA Logos	1.50
24.	ABA Logos	1.50

1987-88 Fleer Charles Barkley

1986-87 FLEER STICKERS

No.	Player	Value
1.	Kareem Abdul-Jabbar	5.00
2.	Larry Bird	12.00
3.	Adrian Dantley	1.75
4.	Alex English	1.75
5.	Julius Erving	5.00
6.	Patrick Ewing	15.00
7.	Magic Johnson	16.00
8.	Michael Jordan	60.00
9.	Akeem Olajuwon	9.00
10.	Isiah Thomas	6.00
11.	Dominique Wilkins	8.00

1987-88 FLEER STICKERS

No.	Player	Value
1.	Magic Johnson	10.00
2.	Michael Jordan	33.00
3.	Akeem Olajuwon	4.50
4.	Larry Bird	8.00
5.	Kevin McHale	1.25
6.	Charles Barkley	8.00
7.	Dominique Wilkins	4.00
8.	Kareem Abdul-Jabbar	3.00
9.	Mark Aguirre	1.00
10.	Chuck Person	1.25
11.	Alex English	1.00

1988-89 FLEER STICKERS

No.	Player	Value
1.	Mark Aguirre	0.30
2.	Larry Bird	3.50
3.	Clyde Drexler	3.00
4.	Alex English	0.30
5.	Patrick Ewing	2.50
6.	Magic Johnson	4.00
7.	Michael Jordan	10.00
8.	Karl Malone	2.50
9.	Kevin McHale	0.50
10.	Isiah Thomas	1.00
11.	Dominique Wilkins	1.50

1989-90 FLEER STICKERS

No.	Player	Value
1.	Karl Malone	0.75
2.	Akeem Olajuwon	0.50
3.	Michael Jordan	3.00
4.	Charles Barkley	1.50
5.	Magic Johnson	2.00
6.	Isiah Thomas	0.50
7.	Patrick Ewing	0.75
8.	Dale Ellis	0.20
9.	Chris Mullin	0.75
10.	Larry Bird	1.50
11.	Tom Chambers	0.20

FOOTBALL STAMPS

1964 WHEATIES STAMPS

No.	Player	Value
1.	Adderley, Herb	3.25
2.	Alderman, Grady	1.75
3.	Atkins, Doug	3.25
4.	Baker, Sam	1.75
5.	Barnes, Erich	1.50
6.	Barr, Terry	1.75
7.	Bass, Dick	1.75
8.	Baughan, Maxie	1.75
9.	Berry, Raymond	4.25
10.	Bradshaw, Charles	1.75
11.	Brown, Jim	12.50
12.	Brown, Roger	1.75
13.	Brown, Timmy	2.25
14.	Cogdill, Gail	1.75
15.	Davis, Willie	3.25
16.	Davis, Tommy	1.75
17.	DeMarco, Bob	1.75
18.	Dess, Darrell	1.75
19.	Dial, Buddy	1.75
20.	Ditka, Mike	7.75
21.	Fiss, Galen	1.75
22.	Folkins, Lee	1.75
23.	Fortunato, Joe	1.75
24.	Glass, Bill	1.75
25.	Gordy, John	1.75
26.	Gray, Ken	1.75
27.	Gregg, Forrest	3.25
28.	Hawkins, Rip	1.75
29.	Johnson, Charley	2.25
30.	Johnson, John Henry	3.00
31.	Jordan, Henry	1.50
32.	Katcavage, Jim	1.50
33.	Kramer, Jerry	2.50
34.	Krupa, Joe	1.75
35.	LoVetere, John	1.75
36.	Lynch, Dick	1.50
37.	Marchetti, Gino	3.00
38.	Marconi, Joe	1.75
39.	Mason, Tommy	1.50
40.	Meinert, Dale	1.50
41.	Michaels, Lou	1.75
42.	Minnesota Vikings	1.50
43.	Mitchell, Bobby	3.50
44.	Morrow, John	1.50
45.	New York Giants	1.50
46.	Olsen, Merlin	4.25
47.	Pardee, Jack	2.75
48.	Parker, Jim	3.00
49.	Parrish, Bernie	1.50
50.	Perkins, Don	2.25
51.	Petitbon, Richie	1.50
52.	Pottios, Myron	1.50
53.	Promuto, Vince	1.50
54.	Pyle, Mike	1.50
55.	Retzlaff, Pete	1.50
56.	Ringo, Jim	3.00
57.	Rutgens, Joe	1.75
58.	St. Louis Cardinals	1.50
59.	San Francisco 49ers	1.50
60.	Schafrath, Dick	1.50
61.	Schmidt, Joe	3.00
62.	Shofner, Del	2.00
63.	Sneed, Norm	2.00
64.	Starr, Bart	6.00
65.	Taylor, Jim	5.00
66.	Taylor, Roosevelt	1.50
67.	Thomas, Clendon	1.50
68.	Tittle, Y.A.	6.25
69.	Unitas, John	10.00
70.	Wade, Bill	2.00
71.	Walker, Wayne	1.50
72.	Whittenton, Jesse	1.50
73.	Wilson, Larry	1.50
74.	Woodson, Abe	1.50

1969 GLENDALE STAMPS

No.	Player	Value
1.	Abramowicz, Dan	0.35
2.	Adderley, Herb	1.25
3.	Alderman, Grady	0.25
4.	Alexander, Kermit	0.35
5.	Allen, Chuck	0.25
6.	Alworth, Lance	1.75
7.	Anderson, Donny	0.45
8.	Andrie, George	0.35
9.	Antwine, Houston	0.25
10.	Atkins, Doug	0.80
11.	Atkinson, Al	0.25
12.	Baker, Sam	0.35

13. Bakken, Jim 0.35
14. Ballman, Gary 0.35
15. Barber, Stew 0.25
16. Barnes, Erich 0.35
17. Barney, Lem 0.35
18. Bass, Dick 0.35
19. Baughan, Maxie 0.35
20. Beard, Ed 0.25
21. Beathard, Pete 0.35
22. Beauchamp, Al 0.25
23. Beer, Tom 0.25
24. Beirne, Jim 0.25
25. Bell, Bobby 0.80
26. Bemiller, Al 0.25
27. Berry, Bob 0.55
28. Biletnikoff, Fred 1.25
29. Boozer, Emerson 0.35
30. Bosley, Bruce 0.25
31. Boyette, Garland 0.25
32. Bramlett, John 0.25
33. Brodie, John 1.50
34. Brown, Aaron 0.25
35. Brown, Bill 0.35
36. Brown, Fred 0.25
37. Brown, Roger 0.30
38. Brown, Tom 0.25
39. Brown, Willie 0.80
40. Brumm, Don 0.25
41. Bryant, Charlie 0.25
42. Buchanan, Buck 0.80
43. Bull, Ronnie 0.35
44. Buoniconti, Nick 0.55
45. Burris, Bo 0.25
46. Butkus, Dick 2.25
47. Butler, Jim 0.25
48. Byrd, George 0.30
49. Cadile, Jim 0.25
50. Campbell, Woody 0.25
51. Cannon, Billy 0.55
52. Cappelletti, Gino 0.35
53. Carollo, Joe 0.25
54. Case, Pete 0.25
55. Charles, John 0.25
56. Clancy, Jack 0.25
57. Clark, Mike 0.25
58. Coffey, Junior 0.25
59. Coffey, Lee Roy 0.25
60. Collins, Gary 0.35
61. Concannon, Jack 0.35
62. Conners, Dan 0.25
63. Cox, Fred 0.35
64. Crutcher, Tommy 0.25
65. Csonka, Larry 2.25
66. Current, Mike 0.25
67. Curtis, Mike 0.35
68. Dale, Carroll 0.35
69. Davidson, Ben 0.55
70. Davis, Ben 0.25
71. Davis, Willie 1.25
72. Dawson, Len 1.75
73. DeLong, Steve 0.25
74. DeMarco, Bob 0.25
75. Demarie, John 0.25
76. Denson, Al 0.25
77. Dixon, Hewritt 0.35
78. Douglas, John 0.25
79. Dowler, Boyd 0.35
80. Duranko, Pete 0.25
81. Eaton, Scott 0.25
82. Eddy, Nick 0.35
83. Edgerson, Booker 0.25
84. Eisenhauer, Larry 0.25
85. Elliott, John 0.25
86. Evans, Norm 0.25
87. Evey, Dick 0.25
88. Farr, Mel 0.35
89. Farr, Miller 0.25
90. Flanagan, Ed 0.25
91. Flatley, Paul 0.35
92. Fleming, Marv 0.35
93. Frazier, Willie 0.25
94. Frederickson, Tucker 0.35
95. Gabriel, Roman 0.55
96. Gagner, Larry 0.25
97. Gamble, R.C. 0.25
98. Garrett, Mike 0.35
99. Garrison, Gary 0.30
100. Gaubatz, Dennis 0.25
101. Goeddeke, George 0.25
102. Gogolak, Charlie 0.25
103. Gogolak, Peter 0.25
104. Goode, Irv 0.25
105. Goode, Tom 0.25
106. Gordon, Dick 0.25
107. Gosset, Bruce 0.25
108. Graham, Kenny 0.25
109. Granger, Hoyle 0.25
110. Gray, Ken 0.25
111. Green, Cornell 0.35
112. Griese, Bob 2.25
113. Gros, Earl 0.25
114. Gruneisen, Sam 0.25
115. Gunner, Harry 0.25
116. Hadl, John 0.00
117. Haik, Mac 0.25
118. Hanburger, Chris 0.35
119. Hand, Larry 0.25
120. Hauss, Len 0.25
121. Hayes, Bob 0.55
122. Herman, Dave 0.25
123. Hickerson, Gene 0.25
124. Hill, Fred 0.25
125. Hill, Winston 0.25
126. Hilton, John 0.25
127. Hindman, Stan 0.25
128. Hoak, Dick 0.25
129. Holmes, Robert 0.25
130. Houston, Jim 0.25
131. Houston, Ken 0.80
132. Howley, Chuck 0.35
133. Huard, John 0.25
134. Hubbert, Brad 0.25
135. Hudson, Jim 0.25
136. Huff, Sam 1.25
137. Humphrey, Claude 0.35
138. Hunt, Bobby 0.25
139. Jackson, Richard 0.25
140. Jacobs, Harry 0.25
141. Jaquess, Pete 0.25
142. Jefferson, Roy 0.35
143. Jeter, Bob 0.35
144. Johnson, Bob 0.25
145. Johnson, Charley 0.55
146. Johnson, Jim 0.35
147. Johnson, Randy 0.35
148. Jones, Clint 0.35
149. Jones, David (Deacon) 1.25
150. Jones, Homer 0.35
151. Jordan, Henry 0.35
152. Jordan, Lee Roy 0.80
153. Jurgensen, Sonny 1.75
154. Kammerer, Carl 0.25
155. Kanicki, Jim 0.25
156. Kapp, Joe 0.55
157. Karras, Alex 1.50
158. Katcavage, Jim 0.25
159. Kellermann, Ernie 0.25
160. Kelly, Leroy 0.55
161. Kemp, Jack 5.25
162. Kilmer, Bill 0.55
163. King, Charlie 0.25
164. Koy, Ernie 0.25
165. Krause, Paul 0.35
166. Krueger, Charlie 0.25
167. Lammons, Pete 0.25
168. Lamonica, Daryle 0.55
169. Lanier, Willie 0.80
170. Larsen, Gary 0.25
171. Lassiter, Ike 0.25
172. LeBeau, Dick 0.35
173. Lewis, Gary 0.25
174. Lilly, Bob 1.50
175. Lindsey, Dale 0.25
176. Little, Floyd 0.55
177. Lloyd, Dave 0.25
178. Lockhart, Carl (Spider) 0.25
179. Logan, Jerry 0.25
180. Long, Bob 0.25
181. Lorick, Tony 0.25
182. Lothridge, Billy 0.25
183. Lucci, Mike 0.35
184. Lyles, Lenny 0.25
185. Lynch, Fran 0.25
186. Mack, Tom 0.45
187. Mackey, John 0.55
188. Maher, Bruce 0.25
189. Maples, Bobby 0.25
190. Marsh, Aaron 0.25
191. Marshall, Jim 0.55
192. Martha, Paul 0.35
193. Mason, Tommy 0.35
194. Matson, Pat 0.25
195. Matte, Tom 0.45
196. McCloughan, Kent 0.25
197. McCullouch, Earl 0.25
198. McDole, Ron 0.25
199. McGee, Ben 0.25
200. McMillan, Ernie 0.25
201. McNeil, Clifton 0.25
202. McRae, Bennie 0.25
203. Meador, Ed 0.35
204. Michaels, Lou 0.25
205. Middendorf, Dave 0.25
206. Miller, Clark 0.25
207. Mix, Ron 0.80
208. Morris, Jon 0.25
209. Morton, Craig 0.55
210. Mudd, Howard 0.25
211. Munson, Bill 0.35
212. Namath, Joe 6.25
213. Nance, Jim 0.35
214. Neighbors, Billy 0.35
215. Nelson, Al 0.25
216. Nelsen, Bill 0.35
217. Niland, John 0.25
218. Nix, Kent 0.25
219. Nobis, Tommy 0.55
220. Norton, Rick 0.25
221. O'Bradovich, Ed 0.25
222. O'Donnell, Joe 0.25
223. Olsen, Merlin 1.75
224. Orr, Jimmy 0.35
225. Osborn, Dave 0.25
226. Otto, Jim 1.25
227. Page, Alan 0.80
228. Parks, David 0.35
229. Peters, Floyd 0.25
230. Petitbon, Rich 0.25
231. Philbin, Gerry 0.25
232. Piccolo, Brian 4.25
233. Pitts, Frank 0.25
234. Pitts, John 0.25
235. Post, Dick 0.35
236. Promuto, Vince 0.25
237. Pyle, Mike 0.25
238. Ramsey, Nate 0.25
239. Reaves, Ken 0.25
240. Reed, Alvin 0.25
241. Reeves, Dan 1.25
242. Renfro, Mel 0.35
243. Rentzel, Lance 0.35
244. Rice, Andy 0.25
245. Richardson, Willie 0.35
246. Richter, Pat 0.35
247. Robinson, Dave 0.35
248. Robinson, Johnny 0.45
249. Robinson, Paul 0.25
250. Rock, Walt 0.25
251. Roland, Johnny 0.30

252. Rowe, Dave 0.25
253. Rush, Jerry 0.25
254. Russell, Andy 0.35
255. Saimes, George 0.30
256. Sauer, George 0.35
257. Sayers, Gale 3.25
258. Scarpati, Joe 0.25
259. Schafrath, Dick 0.25

1972 NFLPA Dick Butkus

260. Schoenke, Ray 0.25
261. Schuh, Harry 0.25
262. Shiner, Dick 0.25
263. Shinnick, Don 0.25
264. Shy, Don 0.25
265. Simmons, Jerry 0.35
266. Simpson, O.J. 5.25
267. Smith, Jackie 0.35
268. Snead, Norman 0.45
269. Snell, Matt 0.45
270. St. Jean, Len 0.25
271. Staley, Bill 0.25
272. Stallings, Larry 0.35
273. Starr, Bart 2.75
274. Stenerud, Jan 0.45
275. Stickles, Monty 0.25
276. Stonebreaker, Steve 0.25
277. Stovall, Jerry 0.35
278. Stratton, Mike 0.25
279. Studstill, Pat 0.35
280. Sullivan, Dan 0.25
281. Sweeney, Walt 0.25
282. Taliaferro, Mike 0.25
283. Tarkenton, Fran 4.25
284. Taylor, Otis 0.45
285. Taylor, Roosevelt 0.25
286. Tensi, Steve 0.35
287. Thomas, Aaron 0.25
288. Tingelhoff, Mick 0.45
289. Trull, Don 0.35
290. Trumpy, Bob 0.55
291. Turner, Jim 0.35
292. Twilley, Howard 0.45
293. Tyrer, Jim 0.45
294. Unitas, Johnny 5.25
295. Upshaw, Gene 1.50
296. Van Heusen, Billy 0.25
297. Walker, Wayne 0.25
298. Warren, Jimmy 0.25
299. Webster, George 0.35
300. Westmoreland, Dick 0.25
301. Whalen, Jim 0.25
302. Wilburn, J.R. 0.25
303. Wilcox, Dave 0.35
304. Willard, Ken 0.45
305. Williams, Del 0.25
306. Williams, Maxie 0.25
307. Wilson, Larry 0.80
308. Winston, Roy 0.25
309. Wood, Willie 0.80
310. Woodeshick, Tom 0.25
311. Woodson, Marv 0.25
312. Wyche, Sam 1.25

FOOTBALL STICKERS

1972 NFLPA STICKERS

No.	Player	Value
1.	Anderson, Donny	1.25
2.	Blanda, George	6.25
3.	Bradshaw, Terry	9.00
4.	Brockington, John	1.25
5.	Brodie, John	3.00
6.	Butkus, Dick	5.25
7.	Gordon, Dick	1.00
8.	Greene, Joe	4.00
9.	Hadl, John	1.00
10.	Hayes, Bob	1.25
11.	Johnson, Ron	3.25
12.	Little, Floyd	1.50
13.	Namath, Joe	15.00
14.	Nobis, Tommy	1.50
15.	Page, Alan	4.25
16.	Plunkett, Jim	2.75
17.	Sayers, Gale	6.00
18.	Staubach, Roger	10.25
19.	Unitas, Johnny	9.25
20.	Warfield, Paul	2.75

1981 TOPPS STICKERS

No.	Player	Value
1.	Brian Sipe	0.15
2.	Dan Fouts	0.30
3.	John Jefferson	0.10
4.	Bruce Harper	0.05
5.	J.T. Smith	0.10
6.	Luke Prestridge	0.05
7.	Lester Hayes	0.10
8.	Gary Johnson	0.05
9.	Bert Jones	0.20
10.	Fred Cook	0.05
11.	Roger Carr	0.05
12.	Greg Landry	0.10
13.	Raymond Butler	0.10
14.	Bruce Laird	0.05
15.	Ed Simonini	0.05
16.	Curtis Dickey	0.10
17.	Joe Cribbs	0.15
18.	Joe Ferguson	0.15
19.	Ben Williams	0.05
20.	Jerry Butler	0.10
21.	Roland Hooks	0.05
22.	Fred Smerlas	0.10
23.	Frank Lewis	0.10
24.	Mark Brammer	0.05
25.	Dave Woodley	0.10
26.	Nat Moore	0.10
27.	Uwe Von Schamann	0.05
28.	Vern Den Herder	0.05
29.	Tony Nathan	0.10
30.	Duriel Harris	0.10
31.	Don McNeal	0.10
32.	Delvin Williams	0.10
33.	Stanley Morgan	0.15
34.	John Hannah	0.15
35.	Horace Ivory	0.05
36.	Steve Nelson	0.05
37.	Steve Grogan	0.15
38.	Vagas Ferguson	0.10
39.	John Smith	0.05
40.	Mike Haynes	0.10
41.	Mark Gastineau	0.15
42.	Wesley Walker	0.15
43.	Joe Klecko	0.15
44.	Chris Ward	0.05
45.	Johnny "Lam" Jones	0.10
46.	Marvin Powell	0.10
47.	Richard Todd	0.15
48.	Greg Buttle	0.10
49.	Eddie Edwards	0.05
50.	Dan Ross	0.10
51.	Ken Anderson	0.25
52.	Ross Browner	0.10
53.	Don Bass	0.10
54.	Jim LeClair	0.05
55.	Pete Johnson	0.10
56.	Anthony Munoz	0.15
57.	Brian Sipe	0.15
58.	Mike Pruitt	0.15
59.	Greg Pruitt	0.15
60.	Thom Darden	0.05
61.	Ozzie Newsome	0.25
62.	Dave Logan	0.05
63.	Lyle Alzado	0.15
64.	Reggie Rucker	0.10
65.	Robert Brazile	0.10
66.	Mike Barber	0.10
67.	Carl Roaches	0.10
68.	Ken Stabler	0.20
69.	Gregg Bingham	0.10
70.	Mike Renfro	0.10
71.	Leon Gray	0.10
72.	Rob Carpenter	0.10
73.	Franco Harris	0.35
74.	Jack Lambert	0.25
75.	Jim Smith	0.10
76.	Mike Webster	0.10
77.	Sidney Thornton	0.05
78.	Joe Greene	0.25
79.	John Stallworth	0.20
80.	Tyrone McGriff	0.05
81.	Randy Gradishar	0.15
82.	Haven Moses	0.10
83.	Riley Odoms	0.10
84.	Matt Robinson	0.10
85.	Craig Morton	0.15
86.	Rulon Jones	0.10
87.	Rick Upchurch	0.10
88.	Jim Jensen	0.10
89.	Art Still	0.10
90.	J.T. Smith	0.10
91.	Steve Fuller	0.10
92.	Gary Barbaro	0.10
93.	Ted McKnight	0.05
94.	Bob Grupp	0.05
95.	Henry Marshall	0.05
96.	Mike Williams	0.05
97.	Jim Plunkett	0.20
98.	Lester Hayes	0.15
99.	Cliff Branch	0.15
100.	John Matuszak	0.15
101.	Matt Millen	0.10
102.	Kenny King	0.10
103.	Ray Guy	0.15
104.	Ted Hendricks	0.15

105. John Jefferson 0.15
106. Fred Dean 0.10
107. Dan Fouts 0.30
108. Charlie Joiner 0.15
109. Kellen Winslow 0.15
110. Gary Johnson 0.10
111. Mike Thomas 0.05
112. Louie Kelcher 0.10
113. Jim Zorn 0.15
114. Terry Beeson 0.05
115. Jacob Green 0.10
116. Steve Largent 0.55
117. Dan Doornink 0.05
118. Manu Tuiasosopo 0.05
119. John Sawyer 0.05
120. Jim Jodat 0.05
121. Walter Payton AP foil 1.25
122. Brian Sipe AP foil 0.30
123. Joe Cribbs AP foil 0.35
124. James Lofton AP foil 0.35
125. John Jefferson AP foil 0.30
126. Leon Gray AP foil 0.30
127. Joe DeLamielleure AP foil 0.30
128. Mike Webster AP foil 0.30
129. John Hannah AP foil 0.35
130. Mike Kennn AP foil 0.30
131. Kellen Winslow AP foil 0.35
132. Lee Roy Selmon AP foil 0.35
133. Randy White AP foil 0.35
134. Gary Johnson AP foil 0.30
135. Art Still AP foil 0.30
136. Robert Brazile AP foil 0.30
137. Nolan Cromwell AP foil 0.30
138. Ted Hendricks AP foil 0.30
139. Lester Hayes AP foil 0.30
140. Randy Gradishar AP foil 0.30
141. Lemar Parrish AP foil 0.30
142. Donnie Shell AP foil 0.30
143. Ron Jaworski 0.15
144. Archie Manning 0.20
145. Walter Payton 0.55
146. Billy Simms 0.25
147. James Lofton 0.15

148. Dave Jennings 0.10
149. Nolan Cromwell 0.15
150. Al Baker 0.10
151. Tony Dorsett 0.35
152. Harvey Martin 0.15
153. Danny White 0.25
154. Pat Donovan 0.05
155. Drew Pearson 0.15
156. Robert Newhouse 0.10
157. Randy White 0.20
158. Butch Johnson 0.15
159. Dave Jennings 0.05
160. Brad Van Pelt 0.10
161. Phil Simms 0.25
162. Mike Friede 0.05
163. Billy Taylor 0.10
164. Gary Jeter 0.10
165. George Martin 0.05
166. Earnest Gray 0.05
167. Ron Jaworski 0.15
168. Bill Bergey 0.15
169. Wilbert Montgomery 0.15
170. Charlie Smith 0.05
171. Jerry Robinson 0.10
172. Herman Edwards 0.05
173. Harold Carmichael 0.15
174. Claude Humphrey 0.10
175. Ottis Anderson 0.25
176. Jim Hart 0.20
177. Pat Tilley 0.10
178. Rush Brown 0.05
179. Tom Brahaney 0.05
180. Dan Dierdorf 0.15
181. Wayne Morris 0.05
182. Doug Marsh 0.05
183. Art Monk 0.55
184. Clarence Harmon 0.05
185. Lemar Parrish 0.05
186. Joe Theismann 0.30
187. Joe Lavender 0.05
188. Wilbur Jackson 0.05
189. Dave Butz 0.10
190. Coy Bacon 0.05
191. Walter Payton 1.25
192. Alan Page 0.10
193. Vince Evans 0.10
194. Roland Harper 0.05
195. Dan Hampton 0.20
196. Gary Fencik 0.05
197. Mike Hartenstine 0.05
198. Robin Earl 0.05
199. Billy Sims 0.25
200. Leonard Thompson 0.05
201. Jeff Komlo 0.10
202. Al Baker 0.10
203. Ed Murray 0.05
204. Dexter Bussey 0.05
205. Tom Ginn 0.05
206. Freddie Scott 0.10
207. James Lofton 0.15
208. Mike Butler 0.05
209. Lynn Dickey 0.15
210. Gerry Ellis 0.05
211. Eddie Lee Ivery 0.15
212. Ezra Johnson 0.05
213. Paul Coffman 0.10
214. Aundra Thompson 0.05
215. Ahmad Rashad 0.20
216. Tommy Kramer 0.15
217. Matt Blair 0.10
218. Sammy White 0.10
219. Ted Brown 0.10
220. Joe Senser 0.10
221. Rickey Young 0.10
222. Randy Holloway 0.05
223. Lee Roy Selmon 0.20
224. Doug Williams 0.20
225. Ricky Bell 0.10
226. David Lewis 0.05
227. Gordon Jones 0.10
228. Dewey Selmon 0.10
229. Jimmie Giles 0.10
230. Mike Washington 0.05
231. William Andrews 0.15
232. Jeff Van Note 0.10
233. Steve Bartkowski 0.20
234. Junior Miller 0.10
235. Lynn Cain 0.10
236. Joel Williams 0.05
237. Alfred Jenkins 0.10
238. Kenny Johnson 0.05
239. Jack Youngblood 0.15
240. Elvis Peacock 0.10
241. Cullen Bryant 0.05
242. Dennis Harrah 0.05
243. Billy Waddy 0.05
244. Nolan Cromwell 0.15
245. Doug France 0.10
246. Johnnie Johnson 0.10
247. Archie Manning 0.20
248. Tony Galbreath 0.10
249. Wes Chandler 0.15
250. Stan Brock 0.05
251. Ike Harris 0.05
252. Russell Erxleben 0.05
253. Jimmy Rogers 0.05
254. Tom Myers 0.05
255. Dwight Clark 0.15
256. Earl Cooper 0.05
257. Steve DeBerg 0.15
258. Randy Cross 0.05
259. Freddie Solomon 0.10
260. Jim Miller 0.05
261. Charley Young 0.10
262. Bobby Leopold 0.05

1981 TOPPS RED BORDERS

No.	Player	Value
1.	Steve Bartkowski	0.55
2.	Bert Jones	0.55
3.	Joe Cribbs	0.55
4.	Walter Payton	3.75
5.	Ross Browner	0.35
6.	Brian Sipe	0.45
7.	Tony Dorsett	1.50
8.	Randy Gradishar	0.45
9.	Billy Sims	0.55
10.	James Lofton	0.45
11.	Mike Barber	0.35
12.	Art Still	0.45
13.	Jack Youngblood	0.45
14.	Dave Woodley	0.45
15.	Ahmad Rashad	0.80
16.	Russ Francis	0.45
17.	Archie Manning	0.65
18.	Dave Jennings	0.35
19.	Richard Todd	0.45
20.	Lester Hayes	0.35
21.	Ron Jaworski	0.45
22.	Franco Harris	1.30
23.	Ottis Anderson	0.65
24.	John Jefferson	0.45
25.	Freddie Solomon	0.35
26.	Steve Largent	2.55
27.	Lee Roy Selmon	0.65
28.	Art Monk	1.50

1982 TOPPS COMING SOON

No.	Player	Value
5.	Joe Montana (SB XVI MVP)	0.15
6.	NFC Championship	0.15
9.	Joe Montana (SB XVI)	0.15
71.	Tommy Kramer	0.20
73.	George Rogers	0.20
75.	Tom Skladany	0.15
139.	Nolan Cromwell AP	0.20
143.	Jack Lambert AP	0.35
144.	Lawrence Taylor AP	0.80
150.	Billy Sims AP	0.25
154.	Ken Anderson AP	0.25
159.	John Hannah AP	0.20
160.	Anthony Munoz AP	0.25
220.	Ken Anderson	0.25
221.	Dan Fouts	0.35
222.	Frank Lewis	0.15

1982 TOPPS STICKERS

No.	Player	Value
1.	49ers Super Bowl XVI foil	0.35
2.	49ers Super Bowl XVI foil	0.30
3.	Super Bowl XVI Trophy foil	0.30
4.	Super Bowl XVI Trophy foil	0.30
5.	Montana (SB XVI MVP) foil	2.25
6.	49ers NFC Champs foil	0.30
7.	Bengals AFC Champs foil	0.35
8.	Ken Anderson (SB XVI) foil	0.35
9.	Joe Montana (SB XVI) foil	2.25
10.	Super Bowl XVI foil	0.30
11.	Steve Bartkowski	0.20
12.	William Andrews	0.15
13.	Lynn Cain	0.10
14.	Wallace Francis	0.10
15.	Alfred Jackson	0.10
16.	Alfred Jenkins	0.10
17.	Mike Kenn	0.10

18. Junior Miller 0.10
19. Vince Evans 0.10
20. Walter Payton 1.25
21. Dave Williams 0.05
22. Brian Baschnagel 0.05
23. Rickey Watts 0.05
24. Ken Margerum 0.10
25. Revie Sorey 0.05
26. Gary Fencik 0.05
27. Matt Suhey 0.05
28. Danny White 0.20
29. Tony Dorsett 0.40
30. Drew Pearson 0.15
31. Rafael Septien 0.10
32. Pat Donovan 0.05
33. Herbert Scott 0.05
34. Ed "Too Tall" Jones 0.20
35. Randy White 0.20
36. Tony Hill 0.15
37. Eric Hipple 0.10
38. Billy Sims 0.25
39. Dexter Bussey 0.05
40. Freddie Scott 0.10
41. David Hill 0.05
42. Ed Murray 0.05
43. Tom Skladany 0.05
44. Doug English 0.10
45. Al Baker 0.10
46. Lynn Dickey 0.15
47. Gerry Ellis 0.05
48. Harlan Huckleby 0.10
49. James Lofton 0.15
50. John Jefferson 0.10
51. Paul Coffman 0.05
52. Jan Stenerud 0.10
53. Rich Wingo 0.05
54. Wendell Tyler 0.10
55. Preston Dennard 0.05
56. Billy Waddy 0.05
57. Frank Corral 0.05
58. Jack Youngblood 0.15
59. Pat Thomas 0.05
60. Rod Perry 0.10
61. Nolan Cromwell 0.10
62. Tommy Kramer 0.15
63. Rickey Young 0.10
64. Ted Brown 0.10
65. Ahmad Rashad 0.20
66. Sammy White 0.10
67. Joe Senser 0.10
68. Ron Yary 0.10
69. Matt Blair 0.10
70. Joe Montana foil 1.75
71. Tommy Kramer foil 0.35
72. Alfred Jenkins foil 0.30
73. George Rogers foil 0.35
74. Wendell Tyler foil 0.30
75. Tom Skladany foil 0.30
76. Everson Walls foil 0.30
77. Curtis Greer foil 0.30
78. Archie Manning 0.20
79. Dave Waymer 0.05
80. George Rogers 0.25
81. Jack Holmes 0.05
82. Toussaint Tyler 0.05
83. Wayne Wilson 0.05
84. Russell Erxleben 0.05
85. Elois Grooms 0.05
86. Phil Simms 0.20
87. Scott Brunner 0.10
88. Rob Carpenter 0.10
89. Johnny Perkins 0.05
90. Dave Jennings 0.10
91. Harry Carson 0.15
92. Lawrence Taylor 0.35
93. Beasley Reece 0.05
94. Mark Haynes 0.10
95. Ron Jaworski 0.15
96. Wilbert Montgomery 0.10
97. Hubert Oliver 0.05
98. Harold Carmichael 0.15
99. Jerry Robinson 0.10
100. Stan Walters 0.05
101. Charlie Johnson 0.05
102. Roynell Young 0.05
103. Tony Franklin 0.05
104. Neil Lomax 0.20
105. Jim Hart 0.20
106. Ottis Anderson 0.25
107. Stump Mitchell 0.10
108. Pat Tilley 0.10
109. Rush Brown 0.05

1987 Topps Jerry Gray

110. E.J. Junior 0.10
111. Ken Greene 0.05
112. Mel Gray 0.10
113. Joe Montana 1.25
114. Ricky Patton 0.05
115. Earl Cooper 0.05
116. Dwight Clark 0.15
117. Freddie Solomon 0.10
118. Randy Cross 0.10
119. Fred Dean 0.10
120. Ronnie Lott 0.30
121. Dwight Hicks 0.10
122. Doug Williams 0.20
123. Jerry Eckwood 0.10
124. James Owens 0.10
125. Kevin House 0.10
126. Jimmie Giles 0.10
127. Charley Hannah 0.05
128. Lee Roy Selmon 0.20
129. Hugh Green 0.15
130. Joe Theismann 0.30
131. Joe Washington 0.10
132. John Riggins 0.20
133. Art Monk 0.25
134. Ricky Thompson 0.05
135. Don Warren 0.05
136. Perry Brooks 0.05
137. Mike Nelms 0.10
138. Mark Moseley 0.10
139. Nolan Cromwell AP foil 0.30
140. Dwight Hicks AP foil 0.30
141. Ronnie Lott AP foil 0.50
142. Harry Carson AP foil 0.35
143. Jack Lambert AP foil 0.40
144. Lawrence Taylor AP foil 0.60
145. Mel Blount AP foil 0.40
146. Joe Klecko AP foil 0.30
147. Randy White AP foil 0.40
148. Don English AP foil 0.30
149. Fred Dean AP foil 0.30
150. Billy Sims AP foil 0.35
151. Tony Dorsett AP foil 0.60
152. James Lofton AP foil 0.30
153. Alfred Jenkins AP foil 0.30
154. Ken Anderson AP foil 0.35
155. Kellen Winslow AP foil 0.35
156. Marvin Powell AP foil 0.30
157. Randy Cross AP foil 0.30
158. Mike Webster AP foil 0.35
159. John Hannah AP foil 0.35
160. Anthony Munoz AP foil 0.35
161. Curtis Dickey 0.10
162. Randy McMillan 0.10
163. Roger Carr 0.10
164. Raymond Butler 0.10
165. Reese McCall 0.05
166. Ed Simonini 0.05
167. Herb Orvis 0.05
168. Nesby Glasgow 0.05
169. Joe Ferguson 0.15
170. Joe Cribbs 0.15
171. Jerry Butler 0.10
172. Frank Lewis 0.10
173. Mark Brammer 0.05
174. Fred Smerlas 0.10
175. Jim Haslett 0.05
176. Charles Romes 0.05
177. Bill Simpson 0.05
178. Ken Anderson 0.25
179. Charles Alexander 0.05
180. Pete Johnson 0.10
181. Isaac Curtis 0.10
182. Cris Collinsworth 0.15
183. Pat McInally 0.10
184. Anthony Munoz 0.15
185. Louis Breeden 0.05
186. Jim Breech 0.05
187. Brian Sipe 0.15
188. Charles White 0.15
189. Mike Pruitt 0.10
190. Reggie Rucker 0.10
191. Dave Logan 0.05
192. Ozzie Newsome 0.25
193. Dick Ambrose 0.05
194. Joe DeLamielleure 0.10
195. Ricky Feacher 0.05
196. Craig Morton 0.15
197. Dave Preston 0.05
198. Rick Parros 0.05
199. Rick Upchurch 0.10
200. Steve Watson 0.10
201. Riley Odoms 0.10
202. Randy Gradishar 0.15
203. Steve Foley 0.05
204. Ken Stabler 0.20
205. Gifford Nielsen 0.10
206. Tim Wilson 0.05
207. Ken Burrough 0.10
208. Mike Renfro 0.10
209. Greg Stemrick 0.05
210. Robert Brazile 0.10
211. Gregg Bingham 0.05
212. Steve Fuller 0.15
213. Bill Kenney 0.15
214. Joe Delaney 0.15
215. Henry Marshall 0.05
216. Nick Lowery 0.10
217. Art Still 0.10
218. Gary Green 0.05
219. Gary Barbaro 0.10
220. Ken Anderson foil 0.35
221. Dan Fouts foil 0.45
222. Frank Lewis foil 0.30
222. Steve Watson foil 0.30
223. James Brooks foil 0.45
224. Chuck Muncie foil 0.30
225. Pat McInally foil 0.30
226. John Harris foil 0.30
227. Joe Klecko foil 0.35
228. Dave Woodley 0.15
229. Tony Nathan 0.10
230. Andra Franklin 0.10
231. Nat Moore 0.10
232. Duriel Harris 0.10
233. Uwe von Schamann 0.05
234. Bob Baumhower 0.10
235. Glenn Blackwood 0.05
236. Tommy Vigorito 0.05
237. Steve Grogan 0.15
238. Matt Cavanaugh 0.10
239. Tony Collins 0.10
240. Vagas Ferguson 0.10
241. John Smith 0.05
242. Stanley Morgan 0.15
243. John Hannah 0.15
244. Steve Nelson 0.05

No.	Player	Value
245.	Don Hasselbeck	0.05
246.	Richard Todd	0.15
247.	Bruce Harper	0.10
248.	Wesley Walker	0.15
249.	Jerome Barkum	0.10
250.	Marvin Powell	0.10
251.	Mark Gastineau	0.15
252.	Joe Klecko	0.15
253.	Darrol Ray	0.10
254.	Marty Lyons	0.10
255.	Marc Wilson	0.15
256.	Kenny King	0.10
257.	Mark van Eeghen	0.10
258.	Cliff Branch	0.15
259.	Bob Chandler	0.10
260.	Ray Guy	0.15
261.	Ted Hendricks	0.15
262.	Lester Hayes	0.15
263.	Terry Bradshaw	0.35
264.	Franco Harris	0.30
265.	John Stallworth	0.15
266.	Jim Smith	0.10
267.	Mike Webster	0.10
268.	Jack Lambert	0.25
269.	Mel Blount	0.20
270.	Donnie Shell	0.10
271.	Bennie Cunningham	0.05
272.	Dan Fouts	0.30
273.	Chuck Muncie	0.15
274.	James Brooks	0.20
275.	Charlie Joiner	0.15
276.	Wes Chandler	0.15
277.	Kellen Winslow	0.15
278.	Doug Wilkerson	0.05
279.	Gary Johnson	0.10
280.	Rolf Benirschke	0.10
281.	Jim Zorn	0.15
282.	Theotis Brown	0.10
283.	Dan Doornink	0.05
284.	Steve Largent	1.25
285.	Sam McCullum	0.10
286.	Efren Herrera	0.05
287.	Manu Tuiasosopo	0.05
288.	John Harris	0.05

1983 TOPPS INSERTS

No.	Player	Value
1.	Allen, Marcus	2.75
2.	Anderson, Ken	0.45
3.	Anderson, Ottis	0.35
4.	Andrews, William	0.30
5.	Bradshaw, Terry	0.80
6.	Chandler, Wes	0.25
7.	Clark, Dwight	0.30
8.	Collinsworth, Cris	0.25
9.	Cribbs, Joe	0.30
10.	Cromwell, Nolan	0.25
11.	Dorsett, Tony	0.80
12.	Fouts, Dan	0.80
13.	Gastineau, Mark	0.30
14.	Giles, Jimmie	0.25
15.	Harris, Franco	0.80
16.	Hendricks, Ted	0.45
17.	Hill, Tony	0.30
18.	Jefferson, John	0.30
19.	Lofton, James	0.30
20.	McNeil, Freeman	0.30
21.	Montana, Joe	2.75
22.	Moseley, Mark	0.25
23.	Newsome, Ozzie	0.55
24.	Payton, Walter	2.75
25.	Riggins, John	0.45
26.	Simms, Billy	0.35
27.	Stallworth, John	0.35
28.	Taylor, Lawrence	1.25
29.	Theisman, Joe	0.55
30.	Todd, Richard	0.25
31.	Walker, Wesley	0.30
32.	White, Danny	0.35
33.	Winslow, Kellen	0.30

1983 TOPPS STICKERS

No.	Player	Value
1.	Franco Harris foil	0.60
2.	Franco Harris foil	0.45
3.	Walter Payton foil	1.25
4.	Walter Payton foil	1.25
5.	John Riggins	0.20
6.	Tony Dorsett	0.35
7.	Mark van Eeghen	0.10
8.	Chuck Muncie	0.10
9.	Wilbert Montgomery	0.10
10.	Greg Pruitt	0.10
11.	Sam Cunningham	0.10
12.	Ottis Anderson	0.15
13.	Mike Pruitt	0.10
14.	Dexter Bussey	0.05
15.	Mike Pagel	0.10
16.	Curtis Dickey	0.10
17.	Randy McMillan	0.10
18.	Raymond Butler	0.10
19.	Nesby Glasgow	0.05
20.	Zachary Dixon	0.05
21.	Matt Bouza	0.05
22.	Johnie Cooks	0.10
23.	Curtis Brown	0.05
24.	Joe Cribbs	0.10
25.	Roosevelt Leaks	0.10
26.	Jerry Butler	0.10
27.	Frank Lewis	0.10
28.	Fred Smerlas	0.10
29.	Ben Williams	0.05
30.	Joe Ferguson	0.15
31.	Isaac Curtis	0.10
32.	Cris Collinsworth	0.10
33.	Anthony Munoz	0.15
34.	Max Montoya	0.05
35.	Ross Browner	0.10
36.	Reggie Williams	0.15
37.	Ken Riley	0.10
38.	Pete Johnson	0.10
39.	Ken Anderson	0.25
40.	Charles White	0.10
41.	Dave Logan	0.05
42.	Doug Dieken	0.05
43.	Ozzie Newsome	0.25
44.	Tom Cousineau	0.15
45.	Bob Golic	0.10
46.	Brian Sipe	0.15
47.	Paul McDonald	0.10
48.	Mike Pruitt	0.10
49.	Luke Prestridge	0.05
50.	Randy Gradishar	0.10
51.	Rulon Jones	0.10
52.	Rick Parros	0.05
53.	Steve DeBerg	0.15
54.	Tom Jackson	0.15
55.	Rick Upchurch	0.10
56.	Steve Watson	0.10
57.	Robert Brazile	0.10
58.	Willie Tullis	0.05
59.	Archie Manning	0.15
60.	Gifford Nielsen	0.10
61.	Harold Bailey	0.05
62.	Carl Roaches	0.10
63.	Gregg Bingham	0.10
64.	Daryl Hunt	0.05
65.	Gary Green	0.10
66.	Gary Barbaro	0.10
67.	Bill Kenney	0.15
68.	Joe Delaney	0.10
69.	Henry Marshall	0.05
70.	Nick Lowery	0.10
71.	Jeff Gossett	0.05
72.	Art Still	0.10
73.	Ken Anderson foil	0.35
74.	Dan Fouts foil	0.45
75.	Wes Chandler foil	0.30
76.	James Brooks foil	0.40
77.	Rick Upchurch foil	0.30
78.	Luke Prestridge foil	0.30
79.	Jesse Baker foil	0.30
80.	Freeman McNeil foil	0.35
81.	Ray Guy	0.10
82.	Jim Plunkett	0.15
83.	Lester Hayes	0.10
84.	Kenny King	0.10
85.	Cliff Branch	0.15
86.	Todd Christensen	0.10
87.	Lyle Alzado	0.15
88.	Ted Hendricks	0.15
89.	Rod Martin	0.10
90.	Dave Woodley	0.15
91.	Ed Newman	0.05
92.	Earnie Rhone	0.05
93.	Don McNeal	0.05
94.	Glenn Blackwood	0.05
95.	Andra Franklin	0.05
96.	Nat Moore	0.05
97.	Lyle Blackwood	0.10
98.	A.J. Duhe	0.10
99.	Tony Collins	0.10
100.	Stanley Morgan	0.15
101.	Pete Brock	0.05
102.	Steve Nelson	0.05
103.	Steve Grogan	0.15
104.	Mark van Eeghen	0.10
105.	Don Hasselbeck	0.05
106.	John Hannah	0.15
107.	Mike Haynes	0.10
108.	Wesley Walker	0.10
109.	Marvin Powell	0.10
110.	Joe Klecko	0.15
111.	Bobby Jackson	0.05
112.	Richard Todd	0.15
113.	Lance Mehl	0.10
114.	Johnny "Lam" Jones	0.10
115.	Mark Gastineau	0.15
116.	Freeman McNeil	0.15
117.	Franco Harris	0.30
118.	Mike Webster	0.10
119.	Mel Blount	0.15
120.	Donnie Shell	0.10
121.	Terry Bradshaw	0.30
122.	John Stallworth	0.15
123.	Jack Lambert	0.20
124.	Dwayne Woodruff	0.05
125.	Bennie Cunningham	0.05
126.	Charlie Joiner	0.15
127.	Kellen Winslow	0.15
128.	Rolf Benirschke	0.10
129.	Louie Kelcher	0.10
130.	Chuck Muncie	0.10
131.	Wes Chandler	0.10
132.	Gary Johnson	0.10
133.	James Brooks	0.15
134.	Dan Fouts	0.30
135.	Jacob Green	0.10
136.	Michael Jackson	0.05
137.	Jim Zorn	0.10
138.	Sherman Smith	0.10
139.	Keith Simpson	0.05
140.	Steve Largent	1.25
141.	John Harris	0.05
142.	Jeff West	0.05
143.	Ken Anderson foil	0.35
144.	Ken Anderson foil	0.35
145.	Tony Dorsett foil	0.45
146.	Tony Dorsett foil	0.45

147. Dan Fouts foil 0.45
148. Dan Fouts foil 0.45
149. Joe Montana foil 1.75
150. Joe Montana foil 1.75
151. Mark Moseley foil 0.30
152. Mark Moseley foil 0.30
153. Richard Todd 0.15
154. Butch Johnson 0.10
155. Bill (Gary) Hogeboom 0.15
156. A.J. Duhe 0.10
157. Kurt Sohn 0.05
158. Drew Pearson 0.15
159. John Riggins 0.20
160. Pat Donovan 0.05
161. John Hannah 0.10
162. Jeff Van Note 0.10
163. Randy Cross 0.10
164. Marvin Powell 0.10
165. Kellen Winslow 0.15
166. Dwight Clark 0.15
167. Wes Chandler 0.10
168. Tony Dorsett 0.30
169. Freeman McNeil 0.15
170. Ken Anderson 0.25

171. Mark Moseley 0.10
172. Mark Gastineau 0.15
173. Gary Johnson 0.05
174. Randy White 0.15
175. Ed "Too Tall" Jones 0.15
176. Hugh Green 0.10
177. Harry Carson 0.10
178. Lawrence Taylor 0.25
179. Lester Hayes 0.10
180. Mark Haynes 0.10
181. Dave Jennings 0.10
182. Nolan Cromwell 0.10
183. Tony Peters 0.05
184. Jimmy Cefalo 0.10
185. A.J. Duhe 0.10
186. John Riggins 0.20
187. Charlie Brown 0.15
188. Mike Nelms 0.05
189. Mark Murphy 0.05
190. Fulton Walker 0.05
191. Marcus Allen 1.00
192. Chip Banks 0.10
193. Charlie Brown 0.15
194. Bob Crable 0.10
195. Vernon Dean 0.05
196. Jim McMahon 0.55
197. James Robbins 0.05
198. Luis Sharpe 0.05
199. Rohn Stark 0.05
200. Lester Williams 0.05
201. Leo Wisniewski 0.05
202. Butch Woolfolk 0.10
203. Mike Kenn 0.10
204. R.C. Thielemann 0.05
205. Buddy Curry 0.05
206. Steve Bartkowski 0.15
207. Alfred Jackson 0.05
208. Don Smith 0.05
209. Alfred Jenkins 0.10
210. Fulton Kuykendall 0.05
211. William Andrews 0.15
212. Gary Fencik 0.10
213. Walter Payton 1.00

214. Mike Singletary 0.55
215. Otis Wilson 0.10
216. Matt Suhey 0.05
217. Dan Hampton 0.15
218. Emery Moorehead 0.05
219. Mike Hartenstine 0.05
220. Danny White 0.20
221. Drew Pearson 0.15
222. Rafael Septien 0.05
223. Ed "Too Tall" Jones 0.15
224. Everson Walls 0.10
225. Randy White 0.15
226. Harvey Martin 0.10
227. Tony Hill 0.10
228. Tony Dorsett 0.30
229. Billy Sims 0.25
230. Leonard Thompson 0.05
231. Ed Murray 0.05
232. Doug English 0.10
233. Ken Fantetti 0.05
234. Tom Skladany 0.05
235. Freddie Scott 0.05
236. Eric Hipple 0.10
237. David Hill 0.05
238. John Jefferson 0.10
239. Paul Coffman 0.05
240. Ezra Johnson 0.05
241. Mike Douglass 0.05
242. Mark Lee 0.05
243. John Anderson 0.05
244. Jan Stenerud 0.10
245. Lynn Dickey 0.15
246. James Lotton 0.15
247. Vince Ferragamo 0.15
248. Preston Dennard 0.05
249. Jack Youngblood 0.10
250. Mike Guman 0.05
251. LeRoy Irvin 0.10
252. Mike Lansford 0.05
253. Kent Hill 0.05
254. Nolan Cromwell 0.10
255. Doug Martin 0.05
256. Greg Coleman 0.05
257. Ted Brown 0.10
258. Mark Mullaney 0.05
259. Joe Senser 0.10
260. Randy Holloway 0.05
261. Matt Blair 0.10
262. Sammy White 0.10
263. Tommy Kramer 0.15
264. Joe Theismann foil 0.45
265. Joe Montana foil 1.35
266. Dwight Clark foil 0.35
267. Mike Nelms foil 0.30
268. Carl Birdsong foil 0.30
269. Everson Walls foil 0.30
270. Doug Martin foil 0.30
271. Tony Dorsett foil 0.45
272. Russell Erxleben 0.05
273. Stan Brock 0.05
274. Jeff Groth 0.05
275. Bruce Clark 0.05
276. Ken Stabler 0.20
277. George Rogers 0.15
278. Derland Moore 0.05
279. Wayne Wilson 0.05
280. Lawrence Taylor 0.20
281. Harry Carson 0.10
282. Brian Kelley 0.25
283. Brad Van Pelt 0.10
284. Earnest Gray 0.05
285. Dave Jennings 0.10
286. Rob Carpenter 0.10
287. Scott Brunner 0.10
288. Ron Jaworski 0.15
289. Jerry Robinson 0.10
290. Frank LeMaster 0.05
291. Wilbert Montgomery 0.10
292. Tony Franklin 0.05
293. Harold Carmichael 0.15
294. John Spagnola 0.05
295. Herman Edwards 0.05
296. Ottis Anderson 0.20
297. Carl Birdsong 0.05
298. Doug Marsh 0.10
299. Neil Lomax 0.20
300. Rush Brown 0.05
301. Pat Tilley 0.10
302. Wayne Morris 0.10
303. Dan Dierdorf 0.15
304. Roy Green 0.15
305. Joe Montana 1.25
306. Randy Cross 0.10
307. Freddie Solomon 0.10
308. Jack Reynolds 0.05
309. Ronnie Lott 0.25
310. Renaldo Nehemiah 0.20
311. Russ Francis 0.10
312. Dwight Clark 0.15
313. Doug Williams 0.15
314. Bill Capece 0.05
315. Mike Washington 0.05
316. Hugh Green 0.10
317. Kevin House 0.10
318. Lee Roy Selmon 0.15
319. Neal Colzie 0.05
320. Jimmie Giles 0.10
321. Cedric Brown 0.05
322. Tony Peters 0.05
323. Neal Olkewicz 0.05
324. Dexter Manley 0.10
325. Joe Theismann 0.25
326. Rich Milot 0.05
327. Mark Moseley 0.10
328. Art Monk 0.25
329. Mike Nelms 0.10
330. John Riggins 0.20

1984 TOPPS STICKERS

No.	Player	Value
1.	Plunkett, Allen SB foil	0.35
2.	Plunkett, Allen SB foil	0.30
3.	Plunkett, Allen SB foil	0.30
4.	Plunkett, Allen SB foil	0.30
5.	Marcus Allen SB MVP foil	0.60
6.	Walter Payton	0.55
7.	Mike Richardson (157)	0.05
8.	Jim McMahon (158)	0.10
9.	Mike Hartenstine	0.05
10.	Mike Singletary	0.15
11.	Willie Gault	0.15
12.	Terry Schmidt (162)	0.05
13.	Emery Moorehead (163)	0.05
14.	Leslie Frazier (164)	0.05
15.	Jack Thompson (165)	0.05
16.	Booker Reese (166)	0.05
17.	James Wilder (167)	0.10
18.	Lee Roy Selmon	0.10
19.	Hugh Green	0.10

20. Gerald Carter (170) 0.05
21. Steve Wilson (171) 0.05
22. Michael Morton (172) ... 0.05
23. Kevin House 0.05
24. Ottis Anderson 0.15
25. Lionel Washington (175) . 0.05
26. Pat Tiley (176) 0.05
27. Curtis Greer (177) 0.05
28. Roy Green 0.10
29. Carl Birdsong 0.05
30. Neil Lomax (180) 0.10
31. Lee Nelson (181) 0.05
32. Stump Mitchell (182) 0.05
33. Tony Hill (183) 0.10
34. Everson Walls (184) 0.05
35. Danny White (185) 0.10
36. Tony Dorsett 0.25
37. Ed "Too Tall" Jones 0.15
38. Rafael Septien (188) 0.05
39. Doug Cosbie (189) 0.05
40. Drew Pearson (190) 0.10
41. Randy White 0.15
42. Ron Jaworski 0.15
43. Anthony Griggs (193) ... 0.05
44. Hubert Oliver (194) 0.05
45. Wilbert Montgomery (195) 0.05
46. Dennis Harrison 0.05
47. Mike Quick 0.10
48. Jerry Robinson (198) ... 0.05
49. Michael Williams (199) .. 0.05
50. Herman Edwards (200) .. 0.05
51. Steve Bartkowski (201) .. 0.10
52. Mick Luckhurst (202) 0.05
53. Mike Pitts (203) 0.05
54. William Andrews 0.10
55. R.C. Thielemann 0.05
56. Buddy Curry (206) 0.05
57. Billy Johnson (207) 0.05
58. Ralph Giacomarro (208) . 0.05
59. Mike Kenn 0.05
60. Joe Montana 1.00
61. Fred Dean (211) 0.05
62. Dwight Clark (212) 0.10
63. Wendell Tyler (213) 0.10
64. Dwight Hicks 0.05

1987 Topps Irv Eatman

65. Ronnie Lott 0.20
66. Roger Craig (216) 0.15
67. Fred Solomon (217) 0.05
68. Ray Wersching (218) ... 0.05
69. Brad Van Pelt (219) 0.05
70. Butch Woolfolk (220) 0.05
71. Terry Kinard (221) 0.05
72. Lawrence Taylor 0.20
73. Ali Haji-Sheikh 0.10
74. Mark Haynes (224) 0.05
75. Rob Carpenter (225) 0.05
76. Earnest Gray (226) 0.05
77. Harry Carson 0.10
78. Billy Sims 0.20
79. Ed Murray (229) 0.05
80. William Gay (230) 0.05
81. Leonard Thompson (231) 0.05
82. Doug English 0.10
83. Eric Hipple 0.10
84. Ken Fantetti (234) 0.05
85. Bruce McNorton (235) ... 0.05
86. James Jones (236) 0.10
87. Lynn Dickey (237) 0.10
88. Ezra Johnson (238) 0.05
89. Jan Stenerud (239) 0.05
90. James Lofton 0.10
91. Larry McCarren 0.05
92. John Jefferson (242) 0.05
93. Mike Douglass (243) 0.05
94. Gerry Ellis (244) 0.05
95. Paul Coffman 0.05
96. Eric Dickerson 1.50
97. Jackie Slater (247) 0.05
98. Carl Ekern (248) 0.05
99. Vince Ferragamo (249) .. 0.05
100. Kent Hill 0.05
101. Nolan Cromwell 0.10
102. Jack Youngblood (252) .. 0.05
103. John Misko (253) 0.05
104. Mike Barber (254) 0.05
105. Jeff Bostic (255) 0.05
106. Mark Murphy (256) 0.05
107. Joe Jacoby (257) 0.05
108. John Riggins 0.20
109. Joe Theismann 0.25
110. Russ Grimm (260) 0.05
111. Neal Olkewicz (261) 0.05
112. Charlie Brown (262) 0.05
113. Dave Butz 0.05
114. George Rogers 0.15
115. Jim Kovach (265) 0.05
116. Dave Wilson (266) 0.05
117. Johnnie Poe (267) 0.05
118. Russell Erxleben 0.05
119. Rickey Jackson 0.10

1987 Topps Sylvester Stamps

120. Jeff Groth (270) 0.05
121. Richard Todd (271) 0.10
122. Wayne Wilson (272) 0.05
123. Steve Dils (273) 0.05
124. Benny Ricardo (274) 0.05
125. John Turner (275) 0.05
126. Ted Brown 0.05
127. Greg Coleman 0.05
128. Darrin Nelson (278) 0.05
129. Scott Studwell (279) 0.05
130. Tommy Kramer (280) ... 0.10
131. Doug Martin 0.05
132. N. Cromwell (144)AP foil . 0.20
133. C. Birdsong (145)AP foil . 0.20
134. D. Cherry (146)AP foil ... 0.20
135. R. Lott (147)AP foil 0.30
136. L. Hayes (148)AP foil ... 0.20
137. L. Taylor (149)AP foil ... 0.30
138. J. Lambert (150)AP foil .. 0.25
139. Chip Banks (151) AP foil . 0.20
140. L. Selmon (152) AP foil .. 0.20
141. F. Smerlas (153) AP foil . 0.20
142. D. English (154) AP foil .. 0.20
143. D. Betters (155) AP foil .. 0.20
144. Dan Marino (132) AP foil . 1.00
145. A. Haji-Sheikh(133)AP foil 0.20
146. E. Dickerson(134) AP foil 1.00
147. Curt Warner (135) AP foil 0.25
148. James Lofton (136) AP foil 0.20
149. Christensen (137) AP foil 0.20
150. Collinsworth (138) AP foil 0.20
151. Mike Kenn (139) AP foil . 0.20
152. Russ Grimm (140) AP foil 0.20
153. Jeff Bostic (141) AP foil .. 0.20
154. John Hannah (142) AP foil 0.20
155. A. Munoz (143) AP foil .. 0.20
156. Ken Anderson 0.20
157. Pete Johnson (7) 0.05
158. Reggie Williams (8) 0.10
159. Isaac Curtis (9) 0.05
160. Anthony Munoz 0.10
161. Cris Collinsworth 0.10
162. Charles Alexander (12) .. 0.05
163. Ray Horton (13) 0.05
164. Steve Kreider (14) 0.05
165. Ben Williams (15) 0.05
166. Frank Lewis (16) 0.05
167. Roosevelt Leaks (17) ... 0.05
168. Joe Ferguson 0.10
169. Fred Smerlas 0.10
170. Joe Danelo (20) 0.05
171. Chris Keating (21) 0.05
172. Jerry Butler (22) 0.05
173. Eugene Marve 0.05
174. Louis Wright 0.10
175. Barney Chavous (25) ... 0.05
176. Zack Thomas (26) 0.05
177. Luke Prestridge (27) 0.05
178. Steve Watson 0.10
179. John Elway 1.00
180. Steve Foley (30) 0.05
181. Sammy Winder (31) 0.05
182. Rick Upchurch (32) 0.05
183. Bobby Jones (33) 0.05
184. Matt Bahr (34) 0.05
185. Doug Dieken (35) 0.05
186. Mike Pruitt 0.10
187. Chip Banks 0.10
188. Tom Cousineau (38) 0.05
189. Paul McDonald (39) 0.05
190. Clay Matthews (40) 0.05
191. Ozzie Newsome 0.15
192. Dan Fouts 0.25
193. Chuck Muncie (43) 0.10
194. Linden King (44) 0.05
195. Charlie Joiner (45) 0.10
196. Wes Chandler 0.10
197. Kellen Winslow 0.10
198. James Brooks (48) 0.10
199. Mike Green (49) 0.05
200. Rolf Benirschke (50) 0.05
201. Henry Marshall (51) 0.05
202. Nick Lowery (52) 0.05
203. Jerry Blanton (58) 0.05
204. Bill Kenney 0.10
205. Carlos Carson 0.10
206. Billy Jackson (56) 0.05
207. Art Still (57) 0.05
208. Theotis Brown (58) 0.05
209. Deron Cherry 0.10
210. Curtis Dickey 0.10
211. Nesby Glasgow (61) 0.05
212. Mike Pagel (62) 0.05
213. Ray Donaldson (63) 0.05
214. Raul Allegre 0.05
215. Chris Hinton 0.10
216. Rohn Stark (66) 0.05
217. Randy McMillan (67) 0.05
218. Vernon Maxwell (68) 0.05
219. A.J. Duhe (69) 0.05
220. Andra Franklin (70) 0.05

221. Ed Newman (71) 0.05
222. Dan Marino 1.25
223. Doug Betters 0.10
224. Bob Baumhower (74) ... 0.05
225. Reggie Roby (75) 0.05
226. Dwight Stephenson (76) . 0.05
227. Mark Duper 0.15
228. Mark Gastineau 0.15
229. Freeman McNeil (79) ... 0.10
230. Bruce Harper (80) 0.05
231. Wesley Walker (81) 0.05
232. Marvin Powell 0.10
233. Joe Klecko 0.10
234. Johnny "Lam" Jones (84) 0.05
235. Lance Mehl (85) 0.05
236. Pat Ryan (86) 0.10
237. Florian Kempf (87) 0.05
238. Carl Roaches (88) 0.05
239. Gregg Bingham (89) 0.05

240. Tim Smith 0.05
241. Jesse Baker 0.05
242. Doug France (92) 0.05
243. Chris Dressel (93) 0.05
244. Willie Tuilis (94) 0.05
245. Robert Brazile 0.10
246. Tony Collins 0.10
247. Brian Holloway (97) 0.05
248. Stanley Morgan (98) 0.10
249. Rick Sanford (99) 0.05
250. John Hannah 0.10
251. Rich Camarillo 0.05
252. Andre Tippett (102) 0.10
253. Steve Grogan (103) 0.10
254. Clayton Weishuhn (104) . 0.05
255. Jim Plunkett (105) 0.10
256. Rod Martin (106) 0.05
257. Lester Hayes (107) 0.10
258. Marcus Allen 0.30
259. Todd Christensen 0.10
260. Ted Hendricks (110) 0.10
261. Greg Pruitt (111) 0.10
262. Howie Long (112) 0.10
263. Vann McElroy 0.10
264. Curt Warner 0.30
265. Jacob Green (115) 0.05
266. Bruce Scholtz (116) 0.05
267. Steve Largent (117) 0.55
268. Kenny Easley 0.10
269. Dave Krieg 0.15
270. Dave Brown (120) 0.05
271. Zachary Dixon (121) 0.05
272. Norm Johnson (122) 0.05
273. Terry Bradshaw (123) ... 0.25
274. Keith Willis (124) 0.05
275. Gary Anderson (125) ... 0.05
276. Franco Harris 0.30
277. Mike Webster 0.10
278. Calvin Sweeney (128) ... 0.05
279. Rick Woods (129) 0.05
280. Bennie Cunningham (130) 0.05
281. Jack Lambert 0.20
282. Curt Warner (283) foil ... 0.40
283. T. Christensen (282) foil . 0.20

1985 TOPPS COMING SOON

No.	Player	Value
6.	Ken Anderson	0.20
15.	Greg Bell	0.15
24.	John Elway	0.55
33.	Ozzie Newsome	0.20
42.	Charlie Joiner	0.15
51.	Bill Kenney	0.15
60.	Randy McMillan	0.10
69.	Dan Marino	0.80
77.	Mark Clayton	0.15
78.	Mark Gastineau	0.15
87.	Warren Moon	0.30
96.	Tony Eason	0.15
105.	Marcus Allen	0.25
114.	Steve Largent	0.55
123.	John Stallworth	0.15
156.	Walter Payton	0.80
165.	James Wilder	0.10
174.	Neil Lomax	0.20
183.	Tony Dorsett	0.30
192.	Mike Quick	0.15
201.	William Andrews	0.10
210.	Joe Montana	1.00
214.	Dwight Clark	0.15
219.	Lawrence Taylor	0.25
228.	Billy Sims	0.15
237.	James Lofton	0.15
246.	Eric Dickerson	1.00
255.	John Riggins	0.20
268.	George Rogers	0.15
281.	Tommy Kramer	0.15

1985 TOPPS STICKERS

No.	Player	Value
1.	Super Bowl XIX	0.15
2.	Super Bowl XIX	0.05
3.	Super Bowl XIX	0.05
4.	Super Bowl XIX	0.05
5.	Super Bowl XIX	0.05
6.	Ken Anderson	0.15
7.	M.L. Harris (157)	0.05
8.	Eddie Edwards (157)	0.05
9.	Louis Breeden (159)	0.05
10.	Larry Kinnebrew	0.05
11.	Isaac Curtis (161)	0.05
12.	James Brooks (162)	0.10
13.	Jim Breech (163)	0.05
14.	Boomer Esiason (164)	0.30
15.	Greg Bell	0.10
16.	Fred Smerlas (166)	0.05
17.	Joe Ferguson (167)	0.10
18.	Ken Johnson (168)	0.05
19.	Darryl Talley (169)	0.05
20.	Preston Dennard (170)	0.05
21.	Charles Romes (171)	0.05
22.	Jim Haslett (172)	0.05
23.	Byron Franklin	0.05
24.	John Elway	0.30
25.	Rulon Jones (175)	0.05
26.	Butch Johnson (176)	0.05
27.	Rick Karlis (177)	0.05
28.	Sammy Winder	0.05
29.	Tom Jackson (179)	0.10
30.	Mike Harden (180)	0.05
31.	Steve Watson (181)	0.05
32.	Steve Foley (182)	0.05
33.	Ozzie Newsome	0.15
34.	Al Gross (184)	0.05
35.	Paul McDonald (185)	0.05
36.	Matt Bahr (186)	0.05
37.	Charles White (187)	0.10
38.	Don Rogers (188)	0.05
39.	Mike Pruitt (189)	0.05
40.	Reggie Camp (190)	0.05
41.	Boyce Green	0.05
42.	Charlie Joiner	0.15
43.	Dan Fouts (193)	0.10
44.	Keith Ferguson (194)	0.05
45.	Pete Holohan (195)	0.05
46.	Earnest Jackson	0.10
47.	Wes Chandler (197)	0.05
48.	Gill Byrd (198)	0.05
49.	Kellen Winslow (199)	0.10
50.	Billy Ray Smith (200)	0.05
51.	Bill Kenney	0.10
52.	Herman Heard (202)	0.05
53.	Art Still (203)	0.05
54.	Nick Lowery (204)	0.05
55.	Deron Cherry (205)	0.05
56.	Henry Marshall (206)	0.05
57.	Mike Bell (207)	0.05
58.	Todd Blackledge	0.05
59.	Carlos Carson	0.10

1987 Topps Earnest Jackson

No.	Player	Value
60.	Randy McMillan	0.05
61.	Donnel Thompson (211)	0.05
62.	Raymond Butler (212)	0.05
63.	Ray Donaldson (213)	0.05
64.	Art Schlichter	0.10
65.	Rohn Stark (215)	0.05
66.	Johnie Cooks (216)	0.05
67.	Mike Pagel (217)	0.05
68.	Eugene Daniel (218)	0.05
69.	Dan Marino	0.55
70.	Pete Johnson (220)	0.05
71.	Tony Nathan (221)	0.05
72.	Glenn Blackwood	0.05
73.	Woody Bennett (223)	0.05
74.	Dwight Stephenson (224)	0.05
75.	Mark Duper (225)	0.10
76.	Doug Betters (226)	0.05

1987 Topps Keith Millard

No.	Player	Value
77.	Mark Clayton	0.10

78. Mark Gastineau 0.10
79. Johnny "Lam" Jones (229) 0.05
80. Mickey Shuler (230) 0.05
81. Tony Paige (231) 0.05
82. Freeman McNeil 0.10
83. Russell Carter (233) 0.10
84. Wesley Walker (234) 0.10
85. Bruce Harper (235) 0.05
86. Ken O'Brien (236) 0.10
87. Warren Moon 0.30
88. Jesse Baker (236) 0.05
89. Carl Roaches (239) 0.05
90. Carter Hartwig (240) 0.05
91. Larry Moriarty (241) 0.05
92. Robert Brazile (242) 0.05
93. Oliver Luck (243) 0.05
94. Willie Tullis (244) 0.05
95. Tim Smith 0.05
96. Tony Eason 0.10
97. Stanley Morgan (247) . . . 0.10
98. Mosi Tatupu (248) 0.05
99. Raymond Clayborn (249) 0.05
100. Andre Tippett 0.10
101. Craig James (251) 0.05
102. Derrick Ramsey (252) . . . 0.05
103. Tony Collins (253) 0.05
104. Tony Frankln (254) 0.05
105. Marcus Allen 0.20
106. Chris Bahr (256) 0.05
107. Marc Wilson (257) 0.10
108. Howie Long (258) 0.10
109. Bill Pickel (259) 0.05
110. Mike Haynes (260) 0.05
111. Malcolm Barnwell (261) . . 0.05
112. Rod Martin (262) 0.05
113. Todd Christensen 0.10
114. Steve Largent 0.80

1987 Topps Garin Veris

115. Curt Warner (265) 0.10
116. Kenny Easley (266) 0.10
117. Jacob Green (267) 0.05
118. Daryl Turner 0.10
119. Norm Johnson (269) 0.05
120. Dave Krieg (270) 0.10
121. Eric Lane (271) 0.05
122. Jeff Bryant (272) 0.05
123. John Stallworth 0.10
124. Donnie Shell (274) 0.05
125. Gary Anderson (275) . . . 0.05
126. Mark Malone (276) 0.05
127. Sam Washington (277) . . 0.05
128. Frank Pollard (278) 0.05
129. Mike Merriweather 0.05
130. Walter Abercrombie (280) 0.05
131. Louis Lipps 0.15
132. Mark Clayton (144) 0.10
133. Randy Cross (145) 0.05
134. Eric Dickerson (146) 0.55
135. John Hannah (147) 0.10
136. Mike Kenn (148) 0.05
137. Dan Marino (149) 0.40
138. Art Monk (150) 0.15
139. Anthony Munoz (151 . . . . 0.10
140. Ozzie Newsome (152) . . . 0.10
141. Walter Payton (153) 0.40
142. Jan Stenerud (154) 0.05
143. Dwight Stephenson (155) 0.05
144. Todd Bell (132) 0.05
145. Richard Dent (133) 0.10
146. Kenny Easley (134) 0.10
147. Mark Gastineau (135) . . . 0.10
148. Dan Hampton (136) 0.10
149. Mark Haynes (137) 0.05
150. Mike Haynes (138) 0.10
151. E.J. Junior (139) 0.05
152. Rod Martin (140) 0.05
153. Steve Nelson (141) 0.05
154. Reggie Roby (142) 0.05
155. Lawrence Taylor (143) . . 0.15
156. Walter Payton 0.55
157. Dan Hampton 0.10
158. Willie Gault (8) 0.10
159. Matt Suhey (9) 0.05
160. Richard Dent 0.15
161. Mike Singletary (11) 0.10
162. Gary Fencik (12) 0.05
163. Jim McMahon (13) 0.10
164. Bob Thomas (14) 0.05
165. James Wilder 0.10
166. Steve DeBerg 0.05
167. Mark Cotney (17) 0.05
168. Adger Armstrong (18) . . . 0.05
169. Gerald Carter (19) 0.05
170. David Logan 0.05
171. Hugh Green (21) 0.10
172. Lee Roy Selmon (22) . . . 0.10
173. Kevin House 0.10
174. Neil Lomax 0.15
175. Ottis Anderson (25) 0.10
176. Al Baker (26) 0.05
177. E.J. Junior (27) 0.05
178. Roy Green 0.10
179. Pat Tilley (29) 0.05
180. Stump Mitchell (30) 0.05
181. Lionel Washington (31) . . 0.05
182. Curtis Greer (32) 0.05
183. Tony Dorsett 0.25
184. Gary Hogeboom (34) . . . 0.10
185. Jim Jeffcoat (35) 0.05
186. Danny White (36) 0.10
187. Michael Downs (37) 0.05
188. Doug Cosbie (38) 0.05
189. Tony Hill (39) 0.05
190. Rafael Septien (40) 0.05
191. Randy White 0.10
192. Mike Quick 0.10
193. Ray Ellis (43) 0.05
194. John Spagnola 0.05
195. Dennis Harrison (45) 0.05
196. Wilbert Montgomery 0.10
197. Greg Brown (47) 0.05
198. Ron Jaworski (48) 0.10
199. Paul McFadden (49) 0.05
200. Wes Hopkins (50) 0.05
201. William Andrews 0.10
202. Mike Pitts (52) 0.05
203. Steve Bartkowski (53) . . . 0.10
204. Gerald Riggs (54) 0.10
205. Alfred Jackson (55) 0.05
206. Don Smith (56) 0.05
207. Mike Kenn (57) 0.05
208. Kenny Johnson (58) 0.05
209. Stacey Bailey 0.05
210. Joe Montana 1.00
211. Wendell Tyler (61) 0.05
212. Keena Turner (62) 0.05
213. Ray Wersching (63) 0.05
214. Dwight Clark 0.10
215. Dwaine Board (65) 0.05
216. Roger Craig (66) 0.15
217. Ronnie Lott (67) 0.15
218. Freddie Solomon (68) . . . 0.05
219. Lawrence Taylor 0.20
220. Zeke Mowatt (70) 0.05
221. Harry Carson (71) 0.05
222. Rob Carpenter (72) 0.05
223. Bobby Johnson (73) 0.05
224. Joe Morris (74) 0.10
225. Mark Haynes (75) 0.05
226. Lionel Manuel (76) 0.05
227. Phil Simms 0.15
228. Billy Sims 0.15

1988 Topps Henry Thomas

229. Leonard Thompson (79) . 0.05
230. James Jones (80) 0.05
231. Ed Murray (81) 0.05
232. Wiliam Gay 0.05
233. Gary Danielson (83) 0.05
234. Curtis Green (84) 0.05
235. Bobby Watkins (85) 0.05
236. Doug English (86) 0.05
237. James Lofton 0.10
238. Eddie Lee Ivery (88) 0.05
239. Mike Douglas (89) 0.05
240. Gerry Ellis (90) 0.05
241. Tim Lewis (91) 0.05
242. Paul Coffman (92) 0.05
243. Tom Flynn (93) 0.05
244. Ezra Johnson (94) 0.05
245. Lynn Dickey 0.10
246. Eric Dickerson 1.00
247. Jack Youngblood (97) . . . 0.10
248. Doug Smith (98) 0.05
249. Jeff Kemp (99) 0.05
250. Kent Hill 0.05
251. Mike Lanstord (101) 0.05
252. Henry Ellard (102) 0.05
253. LeRoy Irvin (103) 0.05
254. Ron Brown (104) 0.10
255. John Riggins 0.15
256. Dexter Manley (106) 0.10
257. Darrell Green (107) 0.10
258. Joe Theismann (108) . . . 0.10
259. Mark Moseley (109) 0.05
260. Clint Didier (110) 0.05
261. Vernon Dean (111) 0.05
262. Calvin Muhammad (112) . 0.05
263. Art Monk 0.15
264. Bruce Clark 0.10
265. Hoby Brenner (115) 0.05
266. Dave Wilson (116) 0.05
267. Hokie Gajan (117) 0.05
268. George Rogers 0.15
269. Rickey Jackson (119) . . . 0.05
270. Brian Hansen (120) 0.05
271. Dave Waymer (121) 0.05
272. Richard Todd (122) 0.10
273. Jan Stenerud 0.10
274. Ted Brown (124) 0.05
275. Leo Lewis (125) 0.05
276. Scott Studwell (126) 0.05
277. Alfred Anderson (127) . . . 0.05
278. Rufus Bess (128) 0.05

279. Darrin Nelson (129) 0.05
280. Greg Coleman (130) 0.05
281. Tommy Kramer 0.10
282. Joe Montana (283) 0.55
283. Dan Marino (282) 0.40
284. Brian Hansen (285) 0.05
285. Jim Arnold (284) 0.05

1986 TOPPS STICKERS

No.	Player	Value
1.	Walter Payton (left)	0.55
2.	Walter Payton (right)	0.40
3.	Richard Dent (left)	0.10
4.	Richard Dent (right)	0.10
5.	Richard Dent (SB MVP) foil	0.30
6.	Walter Payton	0.80
7.	William Perry	0.15
8.	Jim McMahon (158)	0.15
9.	Richard Dent (159)	0.10
10.	Jim Covert (160)	0.10
11.	Dan Hampton (161)	0.10
12.	Mike Singletary (162)	0.10
13.	Jay Hilgenberg (163)	0.05
14.	Otis Wilson (164)	0.05
15.	Jimmie Giles	0.10
16.	Kevin House (166)	0.05
17.	Jeremiah Castille (167)	0.05
18.	James Wilder	0.10
19.	Donald Igwebuike (169	0.05
20.	David Logan (170)	0.05
21.	Jeff Davis (171)	0.05
22.	Frank Garcia (172)	0.05
23.	Steve Young (173)	0.10
24.	Stump Mitchell	0.10
25.	E.J. Junior	0.10
26.	J.T. Smith (176)	0.05
27.	Pat Tilley (177)	0.05
28.	Neil Lomax (178)	0.10
29.	Leonard Smith (179)	0.05
30.	Ottis Anderson (180)	0.10
31.	Curtis Greer (181)	0.05
32.	Roy Green (182)	0.05
33.	Tony Dorsett	0.20
34.	Tony Hill (184)	0.05
35.	Doug Cosbie (185)	0.05
36.	Everson Walls	0.10
37.	Randy White (187)	0.10
38.	Rafael Septien (188)	0.05
39.	Mike Renfro (189)	0.05
40.	Danny White (190)	0.10
41.	Ed "Too Tall" Jones (191)	0.10

1988 Topps Howie Long

No.	Player	Value
42.	Earnest Jackson	0.10
43.	Mike Quick	0.10
44.	Wes Hopkins (194)	0.05
45.	Reggie White (195)	0.20
46.	Greg Brown (196)	0.05
47.	Paul McFadden (197)	0.05
48.	John Spagnola (198)	0.05
49.	Ron Jaworski (199)	0.10
50.	Herman Hunter (200)	0.05
51.	Gerald Riggs	0.10
52.	Mike Pitts (202)	0.05
53.	Buddy Curry (203)	0.05
54.	Billy Johnson	0.05
55.	Rick Donnelly (205)	0.05
56.	Rick Bryan (206)	0.10
57.	Bobby Butler (207)	0.05
58.	Mick Luckhurst (208)	0.05
59.	Mike Kenn (209)	0.05
60.	Roger Craig	0.25
61.	Joe Montana	1.00
62.	Michael Carter (212)	0.10
63.	Eric Wright (213)	0.05
64.	Dwight Clark (214)	0.10
65.	Ronnie Lott (215)	0.10
66.	Carlton Williamson (216)	0.05
67.	Wendell Tyler (217)	0.05
68.	Dwaine Board (218)	0.05
69.	Joe Morris	0.15
70.	Leonard Marshall (220)	0.05
71.	Lionel Manuel (221)	0.05
72.	Harry Carson	0.10
73.	Phil Simms (223)	0.10
74.	Sean Landeta (224)	0.05
75.	Lawrence Taylor (225)	0.15
76.	Elvis Patterson (226)	0.05
77.	George Adams (227)	0.05
78.	James Jones	0.10
79.	Leonard Thompson	0.05
80.	William Graham (230)	0.05
81.	Mark Nichols (231)	0.05
82.	William Gay (232)	0.05
83.	Jimmy Williams (233)	0.05
84.	Billy Sims (234)	0.10
85.	Bobby Watkins (235)	0.05
86.	Ed Murray (236)	0.05
87.	James Lofton	0.05
88.	Jessie Clark (238)	0.05
89.	Tim Lewis (239)	0.05
90.	Eddie Lee Ivery	0.10
91.	Phillip Epps (241)	0.05
92.	Ezra Johnson (242)	0.05
93.	Mike Douglass (243)	0.05
94.	Paul Coffman (244)	0.05
95.	Randy Scott (245)	0.05
96.	Eric Dickerson	1.00
97.	Dale Hatcher	0.05
98.	Ron Brown (248)	0.05
99.	LeRoy Irvin 249)	0.05
100.	Kent Hill (20)	0.05
101.	Dennis Harrah (251)	0.05
102.	Jackie Slater (252)	0.05
103.	Mike Wilcher (253)	0.05
104.	Doug Smith (254)	0.05
105.	Art Monk	0.15
106.	Joe Jacoby (256)	0.05
107.	Russ Grimm (257)	0.05
108.	George Rogers	0.10
109.	Dexter Manley (259)	0.10
110.	Jay Schroeder (260)	0.10
111.	Gary Clark (261)	0.05
112.	Curtis Jordan (262)	0.05
113.	Charles Mann (263)	0.05
114.	Morten Andersen	0.10
115.	Rickey Jackson	0.10
116.	Glen Redd (266)	0.05
117.	Bobby Hebert (267)	0.15
118.	Hoby Brenner (268)	0.05
119.	Brian Hansen (269)	0.05
120.	Dave Waymer (270)	0.05
121.	Bruce Clark (271)	0.05
122.	Wayne Wilson (272)	0.05
123.	Joey Browner	0.10
124.	Darrin Nelson (274)	0.05
125.	Keith Millard (275)	0.15
126.	Anthony Carter	0.15
127.	Buster Rhymes (277)	0.10
128.	Steve Jordan (278)	0.05
129.	Greg Coleman (279)	0.05
130.	Ted Brown (280)	0.05
131.	John Turner (281)	0.05
132.	Harry Carson (144) AP foil	0.25
133.	Deron Cherry (145) AP foil	0.20
134.	Richard Dent (146) AP foil	0.25
135.	Mike Haynes (147) AP foil	0.20
136.	Wes Hopkins (148) AP foil	0.20
137.	Joe Klecko (149) AP foil	0.20
138.	L. Marshall (150) AP foil	0.20
139.	Mecklenburg (151) AP foil	0.20
140.	Rohn Stark (152) AP foil	0.20
141.	L. Taylor (153) AP foil	0.25
142.	A. Tippett (154) AP foil	0.20
143.	E. Walls (155) AP foil	0.20
144.	Marcus Allen (132) AP foil	0.30
145.	G. Anderson (133) AP foil	0.20
146.	Doug Cosbie (134) AP foil	0.20
147.	Jim Covert (135) AP foil	0.20
148.	John Hannah (136) AP foil	0.20
149.	Jay Hilgenberg (137) AP foil	0.20
150.	Kent Hill (138) AP foil	0.20
151.	B. Holloway (139) AP foil	0.20
152.	S. Largent (140) AP foil	0.85
153.	Dan Marino (141) AP foil	0.85
154.	Art Monk (142) AP foil	0.30
155.	W. Payton (143) AP foil	0.85
156.	Anthony Munoz	0.20
157.	Boomer Esiason	0.30
158.	Cris Collinsworth (8)	0.05
159.	Eddie Edwards (9)	0.05
160.	James Griffin (10)	0.05
161.	Jim Breech (11)	0.05
162.	Eddie Brown (12)	0.05
163.	Ross Browner	0.05
164.	James Brooks (14)	0.10
165.	Greg Bell	0.10
166.	Jerry Butler (16)	0.05
167.	Don Wilson (17)	0.05
168.	Andre Reed	0.15
169.	Jim Haslett (19)	0.05
170.	Bruce Mathison (20)	0.05
171.	Bruce Smith (21)	0.20
172.	Joe Cribbs (22)	0.10
173.	Charles Romes (23)	0.05
174.	Karl Mecklenburg	0.10
175.	Rulon Jones	0.10
176.	John Elway (26)	0.25
177.	Sammy Winder (27)	0.05
178.	Louis Wright (28)	0.05
179.	Steve Watson (29)	0.05
180.	Dennis Smith (30)	0.05
181.	Mike Harden (31)	0.05
182.	Vance Johnson (32)	0.10
183.	Kevin Mack	0.10
184.	Chip Banks (34)	0.05
185.	Bob Golic (35)	0.05
186.	Earnest Byner	0.10
187.	Ozzie Newsome	0.15
188.	Bernie Kosar	0.30
189.	Don Rogers (39)	0.05
190.	Al Gross (40)	0.05
191.	Clarence Weathers (41)	0.05
192.	Lionel James	0.10
193.	Dan Fouts	0.20
194.	Wes Chandler (44)	0.10
195.	Kellen Winslow (45)	0.10
196.	Gary Anderson (46)	0.10
197.	Charlie Joiner (47)	0.10
198.	Ralf Mojsiejenko (48)	0.05
199.	Bob Thomas (49)	0.05
200.	Tim Spencer (50)	0.05
201.	Deron Cherry	0.10
202.	Bill Maas (52)	0.05
203.	Herman Heard (53)	0.05
204.	Carlos Carson	0.10
205.	Nick Lowery (55)	0.05
206.	Bill Kenney (56)	0.10
207.	Albert Lewis (57)	0.10
208.	Art Still (58)	0.05
209.	Stephone Paige (59)	0.05
210.	Rohn Stark	0.05
211.	Chris Hinton	0.10
212.	Albert Bentley (62)	0.05
213.	Eugene Daniel (63)	0.05
214.	Pat Beach (64)	0.05
215.	Clitt Odom (65)	0.05
216.	Duane Bickett (66)	0.05
217.	George Wonsley (67)	0.05

218. Randy McMillan (68) 0.05

219. Dan Marino 0.40
220. Dwight Stephenson (70) . 0.05
221. Roy Foster (71) 0.05
222. Mark Clayton 0.10
223. Mark Duper (73) 0.05
224. Fuad Reveiz (74) 0.05
225. Reggie Roby (75) 0.05
226. Tony Nathan (76) 0.05
227. Ron Davenport (77) 0.05
228. Freeman McNeil 0.15
229. Joe Klecko 0.10
230. Mark Gastineau (80) 0.10
231. Ken O'Brien (81) 0.10
232. Lance Mehl (82) 0.05
233. Al Toon (83) 0.15
234. Mickey Shuler (84) 0.05
235. Pat Leahy (85) 0.05
236. Wesley Walker (86) 0.10
237. Drew Hill 0.10
238. Warren Moon (88) 0.15
239. Mike Rozier (89) 0.10
240. Mike Munchak 0.10
241. Tim Smth (91) 0.05
242. Butch Woolfolk (92) 0.05
243. Willie Drewrey (93) 0.05
244. Keith Bostic (94) 0.05
245. Jesse Baker (95) 0.05
246. Craig James 0.10
247. John Hannah 0.15
248. Tony Eason (98) 0.10
249. Andre Tippet (99) 0.05
250. Tony Collins (100) 0.05
251. Bran Holloway (101) 0.05
252. Irving Fryar (102) 0.10
253. Raymond Clayborn (103) 0.05
254. Steve Nelson (104) 0.05
255. Marcus Allen 0.20
256. Mike Haynes (106) 0.05
257. Todd Christensen (107) . . 0.05
258. Howie Long 0.10
259. Lester Hayes (109) 0.05
260. Rod Martin (110) 0.05
261. Dokie Williams (111) 0.05
262. Chris Bahr (112) 0.05
263. Bill Pickel (113) 0.05
264. Curt Warner 0.15
265. Steve Largent 0.55
266. Fredd Young (116) 0.10
267. Dave Krieg (117) 0.10
268. Daryl Turner (118) 0.05
269. John Harris (119) 0.05
270. Randy Edwards (120) ... 0.05
271. Kenny Easley (121) 0.05
272. Jacob Green (122) 0.05
273. Gary Anderson 0.05
274. Mike Webster (124) 0.05
275. Walter Abercrombie (125) 0.05
276. Louis Lipps 0.10
277. Frank Pollard (127) 0.05
278. Mike Merriweather (128) . 0.10
279. Mark Malone (129) 0.05
280. Donnie Shell (130) 0.05
281. John Stallworth (131) ... 0.10
282. Marcus Allen (284) foil .. 0.45
283. Ken O'Brien (285) foil ... 0.25
284. Kevin Butler (282) foil ... 0.20
285. Roger Craig (283) foil ... 0.35

1987 TOPPS STICKERS

No.	Player	Value
1.	Phil Simms (SB MVP)	0.30
2.	SB XXI (upper left)	0.05
3.	SB XXI (upper right)	0.05
4.	SB XXI (lower left)	0.05
5.	SB XXI (lower right)	0.05
6.	Mike Singletary	0.20
7.	Jim Covert (156)	0.05
8.	Willie Gault (157)	0.10
9.	Jim McMahon (158)	0.10
10.	Doug Flutie (159)	0.15
11.	Richard Dent (160)	0.10
12.	Kevin Butler (161)	0.05
13.	Wilber Marshall (162)	0.05
14.	Walter Payton	0.55
15.	Calvin Magee	0.05
16.	David Logan (165)	0.05
17.	Jeff Davis (166)	0.05
18.	Gerald Carter (167)	0.05
19.	James Wilder	0.05
20.	Chris Washington (168)	0.05
21.	Phil Freeman (169)	0.05
22.	Frank Garcia (170)	0.05
23.	Donald Igwebuike (171)	0.05
24.	Al Baker (175)	0.05
25.	Vai Sikahema (176)	0.05
26.	Leonard Smith (177)	0.05
27.	Ron Wolfley (178)	0.05
28.	J.T. Smith	0.05
29.	Roy Green (179)	0.05
30.	Cedrick Mack (180)	0.05
31.	Neil Lomax (181)	0.10
32.	Stump Mitchell	0.10
33.	Herschel Walker	0.55
34.	Danny White (184)	0.10
35.	Michael Downs (185)	0.05
36.	Randy White (186)	0.10
37.	Eugene Lockhart (188)	0.05
38.	Mike Sherrard (189)	0.05
39.	Jim Jeffcoat (190)	0.05
40.	Tony Hill (191)	0.05
41.	Tony Dorsett	0.20
42.	Keith Byars (192)	0.05
43.	Andre Waters (193)	0.05
44.	Kenny Jackson (194)	0.05
45.	John Teltschik	0.05
46.	Roynell Young (196)	0.05
47.	Randall Cunningham (197)	0.55
48.	Mike Reichenbach	0.05
49.	Reggie White	0.20
50.	Mike Quick	0.10
51.	Bill Fralic (201)	0.10
52.	Sylvester Stamps (202)	0.05
53.	Bret Clark (203)	0.05
54.	William Andrews (204)	0.05
55.	Buddy Curry (205)	0.05
56.	Dave Archer (206)	0.10
57.	Rick Bryan (207)	0.05
58.	Gerald Riggs	0.10
59.	Charlie Brown	0.10
60.	Joe Montana	1.00
61.	Jerry Rice	1.00
62.	Carlton Williamson (212)	0.05
63.	Roger Craig (213)	0.15
64.	Ronnie Lott (214)	0.15
65.	Dwight Clark (215)	0.10
66.	Jeff Stover (216)	0.05
67.	Charles Haley (217)	0.10
68.	Ray Wersching (218)	0.05
69.	Lawrence Taylor	0.20
70.	Joe Morris	0.15
71.	Carl Banks (221)	0.10
72.	Mark Bavaro (222)	0.10
73.	Harry Carson (223)	0.10
74.	Phill Simms (224)	0.10
75.	Jim Burt (225)	0.05
76.	Brad Benson 26)	0.05
77.	Leonard Marshall (227)	0.05
78.	Jeff Chadwick	0.10
79.	Devon Mitchell (228)	0.05
80.	Chuck Long (229)	0.10
81.	Demetrius Johnson (230)	0.05
82.	Herman Hunter (231)	0.05
83.	Keith Ferguson (232)	0.05
84.	Garry James (233)	0.05
85.	Leonard Thompson (234)	0.05
86.	James Jones	0.10
87.	Kenneth Davis	0.10
88.	Brian Noble (237)	0.05
89.	Al Del Greco (238)	0.05
90.	Mark Lee (239)	0.05
91.	Randy Wright	0.10
92.	Tim Harris (240)	0.10
93.	Phillip Epps (241)	0.05
94.	Walter Stanley (242)	0.10
95.	Eddie Lee Ivery (243)	0.05
96.	Doug Smith (247)	0.05
97.	Jerry Gray (248)	0.05
98.	Dennis Harrah (249)	0.05
99.	Jim Everett (250)	0.80
100.	Jackie Slater (251)	0.05
101.	Vince Newsome (252)	0.05
102.	LeRoy Irvin (253)	0.05
103.	Henry Ellard	0.10
104.	Eric Dickerson	0.80
105.	George Rogers (256)	0.10
106.	Darrell Green (257)	0.10
107.	Art Monk (258)	0.15
108.	Neal Olkewicz (260)	0.05
109.	Russ Grimm (261)	0.05
110.	Dexter Manley (262)	0.05
111.	Kelvin Bryant (263)	0.05
112.	Jay Schroeder	0.10
113.	Gary Clark	0.10
114.	Rickey Jackson	0.10
115.	Eric Martin (264)	0.05
116.	Dave Waymer (265)	0.05
117.	Morten Andersen (266)	0.05
118.	Bruce Clark (267)	0.05
119.	Hoby Brenner (269)	0.05
120.	Brian Hansen (270)	0.05
121.	Dave Wilson (71)	0.05
122.	Rueben Mayes	0.15
123.	Tommy Kramer	0.10
124.	Mark Malone (124)	0.05
125.	Anthony Cartef (275)	0.05
126.	Keith Millard (276)	0.05
127.	Steve Jordan	0.10
128.	Chuck Nelson (277)	0.05
129.	Issiac Holt (278)	0.05
130.	Darrin Nelson (279)	0.05
131.	Gary Zimmerman (280)	0.05

1987 Topps Leonard Smith

132. Mark Bavaro (116) AP foil 0.20
133. Jim Covert (147) AP foil 0.20
134. E. Dickerson (148) AP foil 0.60
135. Bill Fralic (149) AP foil 0.20
136. T. Franklin (150) AP foil 0.20
137. D. Harrah (151) AP foil 0.20
138. Dan Marino (152) AP foil 0.45
139. Joe Morris (153) AP foil 0.25
140. Jerry Rice (154) AP foil 0.60
141. Cody Risien (155) AP foil 0.20
142. D. Stephenson(282)AP foil 0.20
143. Al Toon (283) AP foil 0.25
144. Deron Cherry (284) AP foil 0.20
145. Hanord Dixon (285) AP foil 0.20
146. D. Green (132) AP foil 0.20
147. Ronnie Lott (133) AP foil 0.25
148. Bill Maas (134) AP foil 0.20
149. Dexter Manley (135) AP foil 0.20
150. Mecklenburg (136) AP foil 0.20
151. M. Singletary (137) AP foil 0.25
152. Rohn Stark (138) AP foil 0.20
153. L. Taylor (139) AP foil 0.30
154. Andre Tippett(140) AP foil 0.20
155. Reggie White (141) AP foil 0.30
156. Boomer Esiason (7) 0.15
157. Anthony Munoz (8) 0.10
158. Tim McGee (9) 0.05
159. Max Montoya (10) 0.05
160. Jim Breech (11) 0.05
161. Tim Krumrie (12) 0.05
162. Eddie Brown (13) 0.05
163. James Brooks 0.10
164. Cris Collinsworth 0.10
165. Charles Romes (16) 0.05
166. Robb Riddick (17) 0.05
167. Eugene Marve (18) 0.05
168. Chris Burkett (20) 0.05
169. Bruce Smith (21) 0.10
170. Greg Bell (22) 0.05
171. Pete Metzelaars (23) 0.05
172. Jim Kelly 0.30
173. Andre Reed 0.10
174. John Elway 0.30
175. Mike Harden (24) 0.05
176. Gerald Willhite (25) 0.05

177. Rulon Jones (26) 0.05
178. Ricky Hunley (27) 0.05
179. Mark Jackson (29) 0.05
180. Rich Karlis (30) 0.05
181. Sammy Winder (31) 0.05
182. Karl Mecklenburg 0.10
183. Bernie Kosar 0.45
184. Kevin Mack (34) 0.05
185. Bob Golic (35) 0.05
186. Ozzie Newsome (36) 0.10
187. Brian Brennan 0.10
188. Gerald McNeil 0.05
189. Hanford Dixon (38) 0.05
190. Cody Risien (39) 0.05
191. Chris Rockins (40) 0.05
192. Gill Byrd (42) 0.05
193. Kellen Winslow (43) 0.05
194. Billy Ray Smith (44) 0.05
195. Wes Chandler 0.05
196. Leslie O'Neal (46) 0.05
197. Ralf Mojsiejenko (47) 0.05
198. Lee Williams (48) 0.05
199. Gary Anderson 0.10
200. Dan Fouts 0.20
201. Stephone Paige (51) 0.05
202. Irv Eatman (52) 0.05
203. Bill Kenney (53) 0.05
204. Dino Hackett (54) 0.05
205. Carlos Carson (55) 0.05
206. Art Still (56) 0.05
207. Lloyd Burruss (57) 0.05
208. Deron Cherry 0.10
209. Bill Maas 0.10
210. Gary Hogeboom 0.10
211. Rohn Stark 0.10
212. Cliff Odom (62) 0.05
213. Randy McMillan (63) 0.05
214. Chris Hinton (64) 0.05
215. Matt Bouza (65) 0.05
216. Ray Donaldson (66) 0.05
217. Bill Brooks (67) 0.05
218. Jack Trudeau (68) 0.05
219. Mark Duper 0.10
220. Dan Marino 0.40
221. Dwight Stephenson (71) 0.05
222. Mark Clayton (72) 0.10
223. Roy Foster (73) 0.05
224. John Offerdahl (74) 0.05
225. Lorenzo Hampton (75) 0.05
226. Reggie Roby (76) 0.05
227. Tony Nathan (77) 0.05
228. Johnny Hector (79) 0.05
229. Wesley Walker (80) 0.05
230. Mark Gastineau (81) 0.10
231. Ken O'Brien (82) 0.10
232. Dave Jennings (83) 0.05
233. Mickey Shuler (84) 0.05
234. Joe Klecko (85) 0.05
235. Freeman McNeil 0.10
236. Al Toon 0.15
237. Warren Moon (88) 0.15
238. Dean Steinkuhler (89) 0.05
239. Mike Rozier (90) 0.10
240. Ray Childress (92) 0.05
241. Tony Zendejas (93) 0.05
242. John Grimsley (94) 0.05
243. Jesse Baker (95) 0.05
244. Ernest Givins 0.10
245. Drew Hill 0.10
246. Tony Franklin 0.05
247. Steve Grogan (96) 0.05
248. Garin Veris (97) 0.05
249. Stanley Morgan (98) 0.05
250. Fred Marion (99) 0.05
251. Haymond Clayborn (100) 0.05
252. Mosi Tatupu (101) 0.05
253. Tony Eason (102) 0.05
254. Andre Tippett 0.10
255. Todd Christensen 0.10
256. Howie Long (105) 0.10
257. Marcus Allen (106) 0.15
258. Vann McElroy (107) 0.05
259. Dokie Williams 0.10
260. Mike Haynes (108) 0.05
261. Sean Jones 0.05
262. Jim Plunkett (110) 0.10
263. Chris Bahr (111) 0.05
264. Dave Krieg (115) 0.10
265. Jacob Green (116) 0.05
266. Norm Johnson (117) 0.05
267. Fredd Young (118) 0.05
268. Steve Largent 0.45
269. Dave Brown (119) 0.05
270. Kenny Easley (120) 0.05
271. Bobby Joe Edmonds (121) 0.05
272. Curt Warner 0.15
273. Mike Merriweather 0.10
274. Mark Malone (124) 0.05
275. Bryan Hinkle (125) 0.05
276. Earnest Jackson (126) 0.05
277. Keith Willis (128) 0.05
278. Walter Abercrombie (129) 0.05
279. Donnie Shell (130) 0.05
280. John Stallworth (131) 0.10
281. Louis Lipps 0.15
282. Eric Dickerson (142) foil 0.60
283. Dan Marino (143) foil 0.50
284. Tony Franklin (144) foil 0.20
285. T. Christensen (145) foil 0.20

1988 PANINI STICKERS

No.	Player	Value
1.	Super Bowl XXII Program	0.15
2.	Bills Helmet	0.05
3.	Bills Action	0.05
4.	Cornelius Bennett	0.30
5.	Chris Burkett	0.10
6.	Derrick Burroughs	0.05
7.	Shane Conlan	0.15
8.	Ronnie Harmon	0.10
9.	Jim Kelly	0.25
10.	Buffalo Bills foil	0.15
11.	Mark Kelso	0.10
12.	Nate Odomes	0.05
13.	Andre Reed	0.10
14.	Fred Smerlas	0.10
15.	Bruce Smith	0.15
16.	Uniform	0.05
17.	Bengals Helmet	0.05
18.	Bengals Action	0.05
19.	Jim Breech	0.05
20.	James Brooks	0.15
21.	Eddie Brown	0.10
22.	Cris Collinsworih	0.10
23.	Boomer Esiason	0.30
24.	Rodney Holman	0.15
25.	Bengals foil	0.15
26.	Larry Kinnebrew	0.05
27.	Tim Krumrie	0.05
28.	Anthony Murioz	0.10
29.	Reggie Williams	0.10
30.	Carl Zander	0.05
31.	Uniform	0.05
32.	Browns Helmet	0.05
33.	Browns Action	0.05
34.	Earnest Byner	0.10
35.	Hanford Dixon	0.10
36.	Bob Golic	0.10
37.	Mike Johnson	0.05
38.	Bernie Kosar	0.35
39.	Kevin Mack	0.10
40.	Browns	0.05
41.	Clay Matthews	0.10
42.	Gerald McNeil	0.10
43.	Frank Minnifield	0.10
44.	Ozzie Newsome	0.15
45.	Cody Risien	0.05
46.	Uniform	0.05
47.	Broncos Helmet	0.05
48.	Broncos Action	0.05
49.	Keith Bishop	0.05
50.	Tony Dorsett	0.20
51.	John Elway	0.35
52.	Simon Fletcher	0.10
53.	Mark Jackson	0.10
54.	Vance Johnson	0.10
55.	Broncos foil	0.15
56.	Rulon Jones	0.10
57.	Rich Karlis	0.05
58.	Karl Mecklenburg	0.10
59.	Ricky Nattiel	0.10
60.	Sammy Winder	0.10
61.	Uniform	0.05
62.	Oilers Helmet	0.05
63.	Oilers Action	0.05
64.	Keith Bostic	0.05
65.	Steve Brown	0.05
66.	Ray Childress	0.05
67.	Jeff Donaldson	0.05
68.	John Grimsley	0.05
69.	Robert Lyles	0.05
70.	Oilers foil	0.15
71.	Drew Hill	0.10
72.	Warren Moon	0.25
73.	Mike Munchak	0.10

74. Mike Rozier 0.15
75. Johnny Meads 0.05
76. Uniform 0.05
77. Colts Helmet 0.05
78. Colts Action 0.05
79. Albert Bentley 0.10
80. Dean Biasucci 0.05
81. Duane Bickett 0.10
82. Bill Brooks 0.10
83. Johnie Cooks 0.10
84. Eric Dickerson 0.80
85. Colts foil 0.15
86. Ray Donaldson 0.05
87. Chris Hinton 0.10
88. Cliff Odom 0.10
89. Barry Krauss 0.05
90. Jack Trudeau 0.10
91. Uniform 0.05
92. Chiefs Helmet 0.05
93. Chiefs Action 0.05
94. Carlos Carson 0.10
95. Deron Cherry 0.10
96. Dino Hackett 0.10
97. Bill Kenney 0.10
98. Albert Lewis 0.10
99. Nick Lowery 0.10
100. Chiefs foil 0.10
101. Bill Maas 0.10
102. Christian Okoye 0.80
103. Stephone Paige 0.10
104. Paul Palmer 0.10
105. Kevin Ross 0.10
106. Uniform 0.05
107. Raiders Helmet 0.05
108. Raiders Action 0.05
109. Marcus Allen 0.20
110. Todd Christensen 0.10
111. Mike Haynes 0.10
112. Bo Jackson 1.00
113. James Lofton 0.10
114. Howie Long 0.15
115. Raiders foil 0.15
116. Rod Martin 0.10
117. Vann McElroy 0.10
118. Bill Pickel 0.05
119. Don Mosebar 0.05
120. Stacey Toran 0.05
121. Uniform 0.05
122. Dolphins Helmet 0.05
123. Dolphins Action 0.05
124. John Bosa 0.05
125. Mark Clayton 0.10
126. Mark Duper 0.10
127. Lorenzo Hampton 0.10
128. William Judson 0.05
129. Dan Marino 0.45
130. Dolphins foil 0.15
131. John Offerdahl 0.10
132. Reggie Roby 0.10
133. Jackie Shipp 0.05
134. Dwight Stephenson 0.10
135. Troy Stradford 0.10
136. Uniform 0.05
137. Patriots Helmet 0.05
138. Patriots Action 0.05
139. Bruce Armstrong 0.10
140. Raymond Clayborn 0.10
141. Reggie Dupard 0.10
142. Steve Grogan 0.10
143. Craig James 0.10
144. Ronnie Lippett 0.10
145. Patriots foil 0.15
146. Fred Marion 0.05
147. Stanley Morgan 0.10
148. Mosi Tatupu 0.05
149. Andre Tippett 0.10
150. Garin Veris 0.05
151. Uniform 0.05
152. Jets Helmet 0.05
153. Jets Action 0.05
154. Bob Grable 0.05
155. Mark Gastineau 0.10
156. Pat Leahy 0.05
157. Johnny Hector 0.10
158. Marty Lyons 0.10
159. Freeman McNeil 0.10
160. Jets foil 0.15
161. Ken O'Brien 0.10
162. Mickey Shuler 0.05
163. Al Toon 0.15
164. Roger Vick 0.10
165. Wesley Walker 0.10
166. Uniform 0.05
167. Steelers Helmet 0.05
168. Steelers Action 0.05
169. Walter Abercrombie 0.05

1988 Topps Gary Lee

170. Gary Anderson 0.05
171. Todd Blackledge 0.10
172. Thomas Everett 0.05
173. Delton Hall 0.05
174. Bryan Hinkle 0.05
175. Steelers foil 0.15
176. Earnest Jackson 0.10
177. Louis Lipps 0.10
178. David Little 0.05
179. Mike Merriweather 0.10
180. Mike Webster 0.10
181. Uniform 0.05
182. Chargers Helmet 0.05
183. Chargers Action 0.05
184. Gary Anderson 0.10
185. Chip Banks 0.10
186. Martin Bayless 0.05
187. Chuck Ehin 0.05
188. Vencie Glenn 0.05
189. Lionel James 0.10
190. Chargers foil 0.15
191. Mark Malone 0.10
192. Rolf Mojsiejenko 0.05
193. Billy Ray Smith 0.10
194. Lee Williams 0.10
195. Kellen Winslow 0.10
196. Uniform 0.05
197. Seahawks Helmet 0.05
198. Seahawks Action 0.05
199. Eugene Robinson 0.05
200. Jeff Bryant 0.05
201. Ray Butler 0.10
202. Jacob Green 0.10
203. Norm Johnson 0.05
204. Dave Krieg 0.15
205. Seahawks foil 0.15
206. Steve Largent 0.55
207. Joe Nash 0.10
208. Curt Warner 0.15
209. Bobby Joe Edmonds 0.10
210. Daryl Turner 0.10
211. Uniform 0.05
212. AFC Logo 0.05
213. Bernie Kosar 0.30
214. Curt Warner 0.15
215. Rice, Largent 0.80
216. Bavaro, Munoz 0.15
217. Zimmerman, Bill Fralic 0.10
218. Stephenson, Munchak 0.10
219. Joe Montana 0.80
220. White, Dickerson 0.55
221. Andersen, Sikahema 0.15
222. Smith, White 0.20
223. Carter, McMichael 0.15
224. Jim Arnold 0.10
225. Banks, Tippett 0.10
226. Wilburn, Singletary 0.15
227. Dixon, Minnifield 0.10
228. Lott, Browner 0.15
229. NFC Logo 0.05
230. Gary Clark 0.10
231. Richard Dent 0.15
232. Falcons Helmet 0.05
233. Falcons Action 0.05
234. Rick Bryan 0.10
235. Bobby Butler 0.05
236. Tony Casillas 0.10
237. Floyd Dixon 0.05
238. Rick Donnelly 0.05
239. Bill Fralic 0.10
240. Falcons foil 0.15
241. Mike Gann 0.10
242. Chris Miller 0.30
243. Robert Moore 0.05
244. John Rade 0.05
245. Gerald Riggs 0.10
246. Uniform 0.05
247. Bears Helmet 0.05
248. Bears Action 0.05
249. Neal Anderson 0.25
250. Jim Covert 0.10
251. Richard Dent 0.15
252. Dave Duerson 0.10
253. Dennis Gentry 0.05
254. Jay Hilgenberg 0.10
255. Bears foil 0.15
256. Jim McMahon 0.20
257. Steve MeMichael 0.10
258. Matt Suhey 0.05
259. Mike Singletary 0.15
260. Otis Wilson 0.10
261. Uniform 0.05
262. Cowboys Helmet 0.05
263. Cowboys Action 0.05
264. Bill Bates 0.10
265. Doug Cosbie 0.10
266. Ron Francis 0.10
267. Jim Jeffcoat 0.10
268. Ed Jones 0.15
269. Eugene Lockhart 0.10
270. Cowboys foil 0.15
271. Danny Noonan 0.15
272. Steve Pelluer 0.15
273. Herschel Walker 0.45
274. Everson Walls 0.10
275. Randy White 0.15
276. Uniform 0.05
277. Lions Helmet 0.05
278. Lions Action 0.05
279. Jim Arnold 0.05
280. Jerry Ball 0.10
281. Michael Cofer 0.05
282. Keith Ferguson 0.05
283. Dennis Gibson 0.05
284. James Griffin 0.05
285. Lions foil 0.15
286. James Jones 0.10
287. Chuck Long 0.15
288. Pete Mandley 0.05
289. Eddie Murray 0.05
290. Garry James 0.10
291. Uniform 0.05
292. Packers Helmet 0.05
293. Packers Action 0.05
294. John Anderson 0.05
295. Dave Brown 0.05
296. Alphonso Carreker 0.05
297. Kenneth Davis 0.10
298. Phillip Epps 0.10
299. Brent Fullwood 0.10
300. Packers foil 0.15
301. Tim Harris 0.10

302. Johnny Holland 0.10
303. Mark Murphy 0.05
304. Brian Noble 0.05
305. Walter Stanley 0.10
306. Uniform 0.05
307. Rams Helmet 0.05
308. Rams Action 0.05
309. Jim Collins 0.05
310. Henry Ellard 0.10
311. Jim Everett 0.30
312. Jerry Gray 0.10
313. LeRoy Irvin 0.10
314. Mike Lansford 0.05
315. Los Angeles Rams foil .. 0.15
316. Mel Owens 0.10
317. Jackie Slater 0.05
318. Doug Smith 0.05
319. Charles White 0.05
320. Mike Wilcher 0.05
321. Uniform 0.05
322. Vikings Helmet 0.05
323. Vikings Action 0.05
324. Joey Browner 0.10
325. Anthony Carter 0.15
326. Chris Doleman 0.15
327. D.J. Dozier 0.10
328. Steve Jordan 0.10
329. Tommy Kramer 0.10
330. Vikings foil 0.15
331. Darrin Nelson 0.10
332. Jesse Solomon 0.10
333. Scott Studwell 0.05
334. Wade Wilson 0.20
335. Gary Zimmerman 0.10
336. Uniform 0.05
337. Saints Helmet 0.05
338. Saints Action 0.05
339. Morten Andersen 0.10
340. Bruce Clark 0.10
341. Brad Edelman 0.05
342. Bobby Hebert 0.10
343. Dalton Hilliard 0.20
344. Rickey Jackson 0.10
345. Saints foil 0.15
346. Vaughan Johnson 0.10
347. Rueben Mayes 0.15
348. Sam Mills 0.10
349. Pat Swilling 0.10
350. Dave Waymer 0.05
351. Uniform 0.05
352. Giants Helmet 0.05
353. Giants Action 0.05
354. Carl Banks 0.10
355. Mark Bavaro 0.15
356. Jim Burt 0.05
357. Harry Carson 0.10
358. Terry Kinard 0.10
359. Lionel Manuel 0.10
360. Giants foil 0.10
361. Leonard Marshall 0.10
362. George Martin 0.10
363. Joe Morris 0.15
364. Phil Simms 0.15
365. George Adams 0.10
366. Uniform 0.05
367. Eagles Helmet 0.05
368. Eagles Action 0.05
369. Jerome Brown 0.20
370. Keith Byars 0.10
371. Randall Cunningham 0.30
372. Terry Hoage 0.05
373. Seth Joyner 0.05
374. Mike Quick 0.10
375. Eagles foil 0.15
376. Clyde Simmons 0.05
377. Anthony Toney 0.10
378. Andre Waters 0.05
379. Reggie White 0.15
380. Roynell Young 0.05
381. Uniform 0.05
382. Cardinals Helmet 0.05
383. Cardinals Action 0.05
384. Robert Awalt 0.10
385. Roy Green 0.10
386. Neil Lomax 0.15
387. Stump Mitchell 0.10
388. Niko Noga 0.05
389. Freddie Joe Nunn 0.10
390. Cardinals foil 0.15
391. Luis Sharpe 0.10
392. Vai Sikahema 0.10
393. J.T. Smith 0.10
394. Leonard Smith 0.05
395. Lonnie Young 0.05
396. Uniform 0.05
397. 49ers Helmet 0.05
398. 49ers Action 0.05
399. Dwaine Board 0.05

1988 Topps Sammy Winder

400. Michael Carter 0.15
401. Roger Craig 0.20
402. Jeff Fuller 0.05
403. Don Griffin 0.05
404. Ronnie Lott 0.15
405. 49ers foil 0.15
406. Joe Montana 0.80
407. Tom Rathman 0.30
408. Jerry Rice 0.55
409. Keena Turner 0.05
410. Michael Walter 0.05
411. Uniform 0.05
412. Bucs Helmet 0.05
413. Bucs Action 0.05
414. Mark Carrier 0.15
415. Gerald Carter 0.05
416. Ron Holmes 0.05
417. Rod Jones 0.05
418. Calvin Magee 0.05
419. Ervin Randle 0.05
420. Buccaneers foil 0.15
421. Donald Igwebuike 0.05
422. Vinny Testaverde 0.30
423. Jackie Walker 0.10
424. Chris Washington 0.05
425. James Wilder 0.10
426. Uniform 0.05
427. Redskins Helmet 0.05
428. Redskins Action 0.05
429. Gary Clark 0.10
430. Monte Coleman 0.10
431. Darrell Green 0.10
432. Charles Mann 0.10
433. Kelvin Bryant 0.10
434. Art Monk 0.15
435. Redskins foil 0.15
436. Ricky Sanders 0.10
437. Jay Schroeder 0.10
438. Alvin Walton 0.05
439. Barry Wilburn 0.10
440. Doug Williams 0.15
441. Uniform 0.05
442. Super Bowl action 0.05
443. Super Bowl action 0.10
444. Doug Williams (SB MVP) 0.10
445. Super Bowl action 0.10
446. Super Bowl action 0.10
447. Super Bowl action 0.10

1988 TOPPS STICKERS

No.	Player	Value
1.	D. Williams (SB XXII MVP)	0.15
2.	'Skins v. Broncos(SB XXII)	0.05
3.	'Skins v. Broncos(SB XXII)	0.05
4.	'Skins v. Broncos(SB XXII)	0.05
5.	'Skins v. Broncos(SB XXII)	0.05
6.	Neal Anderson (234)	0.20
7.	Willie Gault (224)	0.10
8.	Dennis Gentry (219)	0.05
9.	Dave Duerson (197)	0.05
10.	Steve McMichael (266)	0.05
11.	Dennis McKinnon (230)	0.05
12.	Mike Singletary (209)	0.10
13.	Jim McMahon	0.15
14.	Richard Dent	0.15
15.	Vinnie Testaverde (167)	0.15
16.	Gerald Carter (187)	0.05
17.	Jeff Smith (185)	0.05
18.	Chris Washington (212)	0.05
19.	Bobby Futrell (231)	0.05
20.	Calvin Magee (182)	0.05
21.	Ron Holmes (169)	0.05
22.	Ervin Randle	0.05
23.	James Wilder	0.10
24.	Neil Lomax	0.15
25.	Robert Awalt (161)	0.10
26.	Leonard Smith (177)	0.05
27.	Stump Mitchell (178)	0.05
28.	Vai Sikahema (280)	0.05
29.	Freddie Joe Nunn (222)	0.05
30.	Earl Farrell (223)	0.05
31.	Roy Green (157)	0.05
32.	J.T. Smith	0.10
33.	Michael Downs	0.05
34.	Herschel Walker	0.40
35.	Roger Ruzek (269)	0.05
36.	Ed "Too Tall" Jones (245)	0.10
37.	Everson Walls (252)	0.05
38.	Bill Bates (213)	0.05
39.	Doug Cosbie (179)	0.05
40.	Eugene Lockhart (186)	0.05
41.	Danny White (205)	0.10
42.	Randall Cunningham	0.25
43.	Reggie White	0.15
44.	Anthony Toney (256)	0.05
45.	Mike Quick (248)	0.10
46.	John Spagnola (235)	0.05
47.	Clyde Simmons (275)	0.05
48.	Andre Waters (261)	0.05
49.	Keith Byars (265)	0.05
50.	Jerome Brown (240)	0.05
51.	John Rade	0.10
52.	Rick Donnelly	0.05
53.	Scott Campbell (160)	0.05
54.	Floyd Dixon (246)	0.05
55.	Gerald Riggs (236)	0.10
56.	Bill Fralic (267)	0.10
57.	Mike Gann (165)	0.05
58.	Tony Casillas (168)	0.10
59.	Rick Bryan (257)	0.05
60.	Jerry Rice	0.30
61.	Ronnie Lott	0.15
62.	Ray Wesching (220)	0.05
63.	Charles Haley (281)	0.05
64.	Joe Montana (190)	0.55
65.	Joe Cribbs (221)	0.10
66.	Mike Wilson (203)	0.05
67.	Roger Craig (251)	0.20
68.	Michael Walter (162)	0.05
69.	Mark Bavaro	0.10
70.	Carl Banks	0.10
71.	George Adams (274)	0.05
72.	Phil Simms (216)	0.10
73.	Lawrence Taylor (181)	0.15
74.	Joe Morris (198)	0.10
75.	Lionel Manuel (204)	0.05
76.	Sean Landeta (210)	0.05
77.	Harry Carson (159)	0.10
78.	Chuck Long (166)	0.10

79. James Jones (259) 0.05
80. Garry James (158) 0.05
81. Gary Lee (176) 0.05
82. Jim Arnold (260) 0.05
83. Dennis Gibson (232) 0.05
84. Mike Cofer (242) 0.05
85. Pete Mandley 0.05
86. James Griffin 0.05
87. Randy Wright (206) 0.10
88. Phillip Epps (191) 0.05
89. Brian Noble (249) 0.05
90. Johnny Holland (258) ... 0.05
91. Dave Brown (156) 0.05
92. Brent Fullwood (207) 0.10
93. Kenneth Davis (194) 0.05
94. Tim Harris 0.15
95. Walter Stanley 0.10
96. Charles White 0.10
97. Jackie Slater 0.05
98. Jim Everett (271) 0.20
99. Mike Lansford 200) 0.05
100. Henry Ellard (199) 0.05
101. Dale Hatcher (170) 0.05
102. Jim Collins (268) 0.05
103. Jerry Gray (214) 0.05
104. LeRoy Irvin (276) 0.05
105. Darrell Green 0.10
106. Doug Williams 0.15
107. Gary Clark (247) 0.05
108. Charles Mann (171 ..... 0.15
109. Art Monk (270) 0.10

110. Barry Wilburn (196) 0.05
111. Alvin Walton (188) 0.05
112. Dexter Manley (233) 0.05
113. Kelvin Bryant (180) 0.10
114. Morten Andersen 0.10
115. Rueben Mayes (244) ... 0.10
116. Brian Hansen (279) 0.05
117. Dalton Hilliard (241) 0.20
118. Rickey Jackson (195) ... 0.05
119. Eric Martin (189) 0.05
120. Mel Gray (278) 0.05
121. Bobby Hebert (215) 0.10
122. Pat Swilling 0.10
123. Anthony Carter 0.15
124. Wade Wilson (225) 0.10
125. Darrin Nelson (250) 0.05
126. D.J. Dozier (239) 0.05
127. Chris Doleman 0.05
128. Henry Thomas (255) 0.05
129. Jesse Solomon (211) ... 0.05
130. Neal Guggemos (243) ... 0.05
131. Joey Browner (208) 0.05
132. Carl Banks (152) AP foil . 0.20
133. J. Browner (145) AP foil . 0.20
134. H. Dixon (147) AP foil ... 0.20
135. R. Donnelly (149) AP foil . 0.20
136. K. Easley (155) AP foil .. 0.20
137. D. Green (151) AP foil .. 0.20
138. Bill Maas (148) AP foil .. 0.20
139. M. Singletary (153) AP foil 0.25
140. Bruce Smith (154) AP foil 0.25
141. Andre Tippett (146) AP foil 0.20
142. Reggie White (150) AP foil 0.25
143. Fredd Young (144) AP foil 0.20
144. M. Andersen (143) AP foil 0.20
145. Mark Bavaro (133) AP foil 0.20
146. E. Dickerson (141) AP foil 0.40
147. John Elway (134) AP foil . 0.40
148. Bill Fralic (138) AP foil .. 0.20
149. Mike Munchak (135) AP foil 0.20
150. A. Munoz (142) AP foil .. 0.20
151. Jerry Rice (137) AP foil .. 0.50
152. Jackie Slater (132) AP foil 0.20
153. J.T. Smith (139) AP foil .. 0.20
154. D. Stephenson (140) AP foil 0.20
155. Charles White (136) AP foil 0.20
156. Larry Kinnebrew (91) ... 0.05
157. Stanford Jennings (31) .. 0.05
158. Eddie Brown (80) 0.05
159. Scott Fulhage (7) 0.05
160. Boomer Esiason (53) ... 0.15
161. Tim Krumrie (25) 0.05
162. Anthony Munoz (68) 0.10
163. Jim Breech 0.05
164. Reggie Williams 0.15
165. Andre Reed (57) 0.10
166. Cornelius Bennett (78) .. 0.15
167. Ronnie Harmon (15) 0.10
168. Shane Conlan 0.10
169. Chris Burkett 0.05
170. Mark Kelso (101) 0.05
171. Robb Riddick (108) 0.05
172. Bruce Smith 0.15
173. Jim Kelly 0.20
174. Jim Ryan 0.05
175. John Elway 0.25
176. Sammy Winder (81) 0.05
177. Karl Mecklenburg (26) ... 0.10
178. Mark Haynes (27) 0.05
179. Rulon Jones (39) 0.05
180. Ricky Nattiel (113) 0.05
181. Vance Johnson (73) 0.05
182. Mike Harden (20) 0.05
183. Frank Minnifield 0.10
184. Bernie Kosar 0.30
185. Earnest Byner (17) 0.05
186. Webster Slaughter (40) .. 0.05
187. Brian Brennan (16) 0.05
188. Carl Hairston (111) 0.05
189. Mike Johnson (119) 0.05
190. Clay Matthews (64) 0.05
191. Kevin Mack (88) 0.05
192. Kellen Winslow 0.10
193. Billy Ray Smith 0.10
194. Gary Anderson (93) 0.05
195. Chip Banks (118) 0.05
196. Elvis Patterson (110) 0.05
197. Lee Williams (9) 0.05
198. Curtis Adams (74) 0.05
199. Vencie Glenn (100) 0.05
200. Ralf Mojsiejenko (99) ... 0.05
201. Carlos Carson 0.10
202. Bill Maas 0.10
203. Christian Okoye (66) 0.55
204. Deron Cherry (75) 0.05
205. Dino Hackett (41) 0.05
206. Mike Bell (87) 0.05
207. Stephone Paige (92) 0.05
208. Bill Kenney (131) 0.05
209. Paul Palmer (12) 0.10
210. Jack Trudeau (76) 0.10
211. Albert Bentley (129) 0.05
212. Bill Brooks (18) 0.05
213. Dean Biasucci (38) 0.05
214. Cliff Odom (108) 0.05
215. Barry Krauss (121) 0.05
216. Mike Prior (72) 0.05
217. Eric Dickerson 0.50
218. Duane Bickett 0.10
219. Dwight Stephenson (8) .. 0.05
220. John Offerdahl (62) 0.05
221. Troy Stradford (65) 0.10
222. John Bosa (29) 0.05
223. Jackie Shipp 0.05
224. Paul Lankford (7) 0.05

1988 Topps Elvis Patterson

225. Mark Duper (124) 0.05
226. Dan Marino 0.35
227. Mark Clayton 0.10
228. Bob Crable 0.05
229. Al Toon 0.15
230. Freeman McNeil (11) ... 0.10
231. Johnny Hector (19) 0.05
232. Pat Leahy (83) 0.05
233. Ken O'Brien (112) 0.10
234. Alex Gordon (6) 0.05
235. Harry Hamilton (46) 0.05
236. Mickey Shuler (55) 0.05
237. Mike Rozier 0.10
238. Al Smith 0.05
239. Ernest Givens (126) 0.10
240. Warren Moon (50) 0.15
241. Drew Hill (117) 0.05
242. Alonzo Highsmith (84) ... 0.15
243. Mike Munchak (130) 0.05
244. Keith Bostic (115) 0.05
245. Sean Jones (36) 0.05
246. Stanley Morgan (54) 0.05
247. Garin Veris (107) 0.05
248. Stephen Starring (45) ... 0.05
249. Steve Grogan (89) 0.10
250. Irving Fryar (125) 0.10
251. Rich Camarillo (67) 0.05
252. Ronnie Lippett (37) 0.05
253. Andre Tippett 0.10
254. Fred Marion 0.05
255. Howie Long (128) 0.10
256. James Lofton (44) 0.05
257. Vance Mueller (59) 0.05
258. Jerry Robinson (90) 0.05
259. Todd Christensen (79) .. 0.10
260. Vann McElroy (82) 0.05
261. Greg Townsend (48) 0.05
262. Bo Jackson 1.50
263. Marcus Allen 0.20
264. Curt Warner 0.15
265. Jacob Green (49) 0.05
266. Norm Johnson (10) 0.05
267. Brian Bosworth (56) 0.15
268. Bobby Joe Edmonds (102) 0.10
269. Dave Krieg (35) 0.10
270. Kenny Easley (109) 0.10
271. Steve Largent (98) 0.40
272. Fredd Young 0.10
273. David Little 0.05
274. Frank Pollard (71) 0.05
275. Dwight Stone (47) 0.05
276. Mike Merriweather (114) . 0.05
277. Earnest Jackson 0.10
278. Delton Hall (120) 0.05
279. Gary Anderson (116) ... 0.05
280. Harry Newsome (28) 0.05
281. Dwayne Woodruff (63) .. 0.05

282. J.T. Smith (283) 0.05
283. Charles White (282) 0.10
284. Reggie White (285) 0.15
285. Morten Andersen (284) . . 0.05

1989 PANINI STICKERS

No.	Player	Value
1.	SB XXIII Program	0.15
2.	SB XXIII Program	0.05
3.	Floyd Dixon	0.05
4.	Tony Casillas	0.10
5.	Bill Fralic	0.10
6.	Aundray Bruce	0.15
7.	Scott Case	0.15
8.	Rick Donnelly	0.05
9.	Atlanta logo foil	0.15
10.	Helmet foil	0.15
11.	Marcus Cotton	0.15
12.	Chris Miller	0.30
13.	Robert Moore	0.05
14.	Bobby Butler	0.05
15.	Rick Bryan	0.10
16.	John Settle	0.25
17.	Jim McMahon	0.15
18.	Neal Anderson	0.25
19.	Dave Duerson	0.05
20.	Steve McMichael	0.10
21.	Jay Hilgenberg	0.10
22.	Dennis McKinnon	0.05
23.	Chicago logo foil	0.15
24.	Helmet foil	0.15
25.	Richard Dent	0.15
26.	Dennis Gentry	0.05
27.	Mike Singletary	0.15
28.	Vestee Jackson	0.10
29.	Mike Tomczak	0.15
30.	Dan Hampton	0.15
31.	Michael Irvin	0.15
32.	Eugene Lockhart	0.10
33.	Herschel Walker	0.30
34.	Kelvin Martin	0.10
35.	Jim Jeffcoat	0.05
36.	Everson Walls	0.05
37.	Dallas logo foil	0.15
38.	Helmet foil	0.15
39.	Danny Noonan	0.10
40.	Ray Alexander	0.10
41.	Gary Cobb	0.05
42.	Ed "Too Tall" Jones	0.15
43.	Kevin Brooks	0.05
44.	Bill Bates	0.05
45.	Detroit logo foil	0.15
46.	Chuck Long	0.10
47.	Jim Arnold	0.05
48.	Michael Cofer	0.05
49.	Eddie Murray	0.05
50.	Keith Ferguson	0.05
51.	Pete Mandley	0.05
52.	Helmet foil	0.15
53.	Jerry Ball	0.10
54.	Bennie Blades	0.25
55.	Dennis Gibson	0.05
56.	Chris Spielman	0.15
57.	Eric Williams	0.05
58.	Lomas Brown	0.10
59.	Johnny Holland	0.10
60.	Tim Harris	0.10
61.	Mark Murphy	0.05
62.	Walter Stanley	0.10
63.	Brent Fullwood	0.20
64.	Ken Ruettgers	0.10
65.	Green Bay logo foil	0.15
66.	Helmet foil	0.15
67.	John Anderson	0.05
68.	Brian Noble	0.05
69.	Sterling Sharpe	0.40
70.	Keith Woodside	0.15
71.	Mark Lee	0.05
72.	Don Majkowski	1.00
73.	Aaron Cox	0.10
74.	LeRoy Irvin	0.10
75.	Jim Everett	0.25
76.	Mike Lansford	0.05
77.	Mike Wilcher	0.05
78.	Henry Ellard	0.10
79.	Rams helmet foil	0.10
80.	Jerry Gray	0.10
81.	Doug Smith	0.05
82.	Tom Newberry	0.10
83.	Jackie Slater	0.05
84.	Greg Bell	0.10
85.	Kevin Greene	0.15
86.	Chris Doleman	0.15
87.	Steve Jordan	0.05
88.	Jesse Solomon	0.05
89.	Randall McDaniel	0.10
90.	Hassan Jones	0.10
91.	Joey Browner	0.10
92.	Vikings logo foil	0.15
93.	Helmet foil	0.15
94.	Anthony Carter	0.15
95.	Gary Zimmerman	0.05
96.	Wade Wilson	0.15
97.	Scott Studwell	0.05
98.	Keith Millard	0.15
99.	Carl Lee	0.15

1988 Topps Jesse Solomon

No.	Player	Value
100.	Morten Andersen	0.10
101.	Bobby Hebert	0.15
102.	Rueben Mayes	0.10
103.	Sam Mills	0.10
104.	Vaughan Johnson	0.10
105.	Pat Swilling	0.10
106.	Saints logo foil	0.15
107.	Helmet foil	0.15
108.	Brad Edelman	0.05
109.	Craig Heyward	0.10
110.	Eric Martin	0.10
111.	Dalton Hilliard	0.15
112.	Lonzell Hill	0.15
113.	Rickey Jackson	0.10
114.	Erik Howard	0.05
115.	Phil Simms	0.20
116.	Leonard Marshall	0.10
117.	Joe Morris	0.15
118.	Bart Oates	0.05
119.	Mark Bavaro	0.10
120.	Giants logo foil	0.15
121.	Helmet foil	0.15
122.	Terry Kinard	0.10
123.	Carl Banks	0.10
124.	Lionel Manuel	0.10
125.	Stephen Baker	0.10
126.	Pepper Johnson	0.05
127.	Jim Burt	0.05
128.	Cris Carter	0.15
129.	Mike Quick	0.10
130.	Terry Hoage	0.10
131.	Keith Jackson	0.35
132.	Clyde Simmons	0.10
133.	Eric Allen	0.15
134.	Eagles logo foil	0.15
135.	Helmet foil	0.15
136.	Randall Cunningham	0.30
137.	Mike Pitts	0.05
138.	Keith Byars	0.10
139.	Seth Joyner	0.05
140.	Jerome Brown	0.15
141.	Reggie White	0.15
142.	Jay Novacek	0.10
143.	Neil Lomax	0.15
144.	Ken Harvey	0.10
145.	Freddie Joe Nunn	0.10
146.	Robert Awalt	0.05
147.	Niko Noga	0.10
148.	Phoenix logo foil	0.15
149.	Helmet foil	0.15
150.	Tim McDonald	0.15
151.	Roy Green	0.10
152.	Stump Mitchell	0.10
153.	J.T. Smith	0.10
154.	Luis Sharpe	0.10
155.	Vai Sikahema	0.10
156.	Jeff Fuller	0.10
157.	Joe Montana	0.80
158.	Harris Barton	0.10
159.	Michael Carter	0.15
160.	Jeff Fuller	0.10
161.	Jerry Rice	0.80
162.	49ers logo foil	0.15
163.	Helmet foil	0.15
164.	Tom Rathman	0.15
165.	Roger Craig	0.20
166.	Ronnie Lott	0.15
167.	Charles Haley	0.10
168.	John Taylor	0.30
169.	Michael Walter	0.05
170.	Ron Hall	0.10
171.	Ervin Randle	0.05
172.	James Wilder	0.10
173.	Ron Holmes	0.10
174.	Mark Carrier	0.15
175.	William Howard	0.05
176.	Tampa Bay logo foil	0.15
177.	Helmet foil	0.15
178.	Lars Tate	0.20
179.	Vinny Testaverde	0.15
180.	Paul Gruber	0.10
181.	Bruce Hill	0.15
182.	Reuben Davis	0.10
183.	Ricky Reynolds	0.10
184.	Ricky Sanders	0.10
185.	Gary Clark	0.10
186.	Mark May	0.10
187.	Darrell Green	0.10
188.	Jim Lachey	0.10
189.	Doug Williams	0.10
190.	Helmet foil	0.15
191.	Redskins logo foil	0.15
192.	Kelvin Bryant	0.10
193.	Charles Mann	0.10
194.	Alvin Walton	0.05
195.	Art Monk	0.15
196.	Barry Wilburn	0.05
197.	Mark Rypien	0.25
198.	NFC logo	0.05
199.	Scott Case	0.15
200.	Herschel Walker	0.30
201.	Walker, Craig	0.30
202.	Ellard, Rice	0.30
203.	Matthews, Newberry	0.10
204.	Zimmerman, Munoz	0.10
205.	Boomer Esiason	0.20
206.	Jay Hilgenberg	0.10
207.	Keith Jackson	0.20
208.	White, Smith	0.15
209.	Millard, Krumrie	0.10
210.	Lee, Minnifield	0.10
211.	Browner, Cherry	0.10
212.	Shane Conlan	0.10
213.	Mike Singletary	0.15
214.	Cornelius Bennett	0.10
215.	AFC logo	0.05
216.	Boomer Esiason	0.20
217.	Erik McMillan	0.20
218.	Jim Kelly	0.20
219.	Cornelius Bennett	0.15

220.	Fred Smerlas	0.10
221.	Shane Conlan	0.10
222.	Scott Norwood	0.10
223.	Mark Kelso	0.05
224.	Bills logo foil	0.15
225.	Helmet foil	0.15

1988 Topps Albert Bentley

226.	Thurman Thomas	0.30
227.	Pete Metzelaars	0.05
228.	Bruce Smith	0.10
229.	Art Still	0.10
230.	Kent Hull	0.10
231.	Andre Reed	0.15
232.	Tim Krumrie	0.10
233.	Boomer Esiason	0.20
234.	Ickey Woods	0.30
235.	Eric Thomas	0.15
236.	Rodney Holman	0.15
237.	Jim Skow	0.10
238.	Bengals helmet foil	0.15
239.	James Brooks	0.15
240.	David Fulcher	0.15
241.	Carl Zander	0.05
242.	Eddie Brown	0.10
243.	Max Montoya	0.10
244.	Anthony Munoz	0.10
245.	Felix Wright	0.05
246.	Clay Matthews	0.10
247.	Hanford Dixon	0.10
248.	Ozzie Newsome	0.15
249.	Bernie Kosar	0.25
250.	Kevin Mack	0.10
251.	Bengals Helmet foil	0.15
252.	Brian Brennan	0.05
253.	Reggie Langhorne	0.05
254.	Cody Risien	0.05
255.	Webster Slaughter	0.05
256.	Mike Johnson	0.10
257.	Frank Minnifield	0.10
258.	Mike Horan	0.05
259.	Dennis Smith	0.10
260.	Ricky Nattiel	0.10
261.	Karl Mecklenburg	0.10
262.	Keith Bishop	0.05
263.	John Elway	0.25
264.	Broncos helmet foil	0.15
265.	Broncos logo foil	0.15
266.	Simon Fletcher	0.10
267.	Vance Johnson	0.10
268.	Tony Dorsett	0.25
269.	Greg Kragen	0.15
270.	Mike Harden	0.05
271.	Mark Jackson	0.05
272.	Warren Moon	0.25
273.	Mike Rozier	0.15
274.	Houston logo foil	0.15
275.	Allen Pinkett	0.10
276.	Tony Zendejas	0.05
277.	Alonzo Highsmith	0.15
278.	Johnny Meads	0.10
279.	Helmet foil	0.10
280.	Mike Munchak	0.10
281.	John Grimsley	0.05
282.	Ernest Givins	0.10
283.	Drew Hill	0.10
284.	Bruce Matthews	0.10
285.	Ray Childress	0.10
286.	Colts logo foil	0.10
287.	Chris Hinton	0.10
288.	Clarence Verdin	0.10
289.	Jon Hand	0.10
290.	Chris Chandler	0.15
291.	Eugene Daniel	0.05
292.	Dean Biasucci	0.05
293.	Helmet foil	0.15
294.	Duane Bicker	0.05
295.	Rohn Stark	0.05
296.	Albert Bentley	0.10
297.	Bill Brooks	0.05
298.	O'Brien Alston	0.10
299.	Ray Donaldson	0.05
300.	Carlos Carson	0.05
301.	Lloyd Burruss	0.05
302.	Steve DeBerg	0.10
303.	Irv Eatman	0.05
304.	Dino Hackett	0.10
305.	Albert Lewis	0.10
306.	Chiefs helmet foil	0.15
307.	Chiefs logo foil	0.15
308.	Deron Cherry	0.10
309.	Paul Palmer	0.10
310.	Neil Smith	0.10
311.	Christian Okoye	0.40
312.	Stephone Paige	0.10
313.	Bill Maas	0.10
314.	Marcus Allen	0.20
315.	Vann McElroy	0.05
316.	Mervyn Fernandez	0.10
317.	Bill Pickel	0.05
318.	Greg Townsend	0.05
319.	Tim Brown	0.30
320.	Raiders logo foil	0.15
321.	Helmet foil	0.15
322.	James Lofton	0.10
323.	Willie Gault	0.15
324.	Jay Schroeder	0.15
325.	Matt Millen	0.05
326.	Howie Long	0.10
327.	Bo Jackson	1.00
328.	Lorenzo Hampton	0.10
329.	Jarvis Williams	0.10
330.	Jim Jensen	0.10
331.	Dan Marino	0.40
332.	John Offerdahl	0.10
333.	Brian Sochia	0.10
334.	Miami logo foil	0.15
335.	Helmet foil	0.15
336.	Ferrell Edmunds	0.15
337.	Mark Brown	0.05
338.	Mark Duper	0.10
339.	Troy Stradford	0.10
340.	T.J. Turner	0.10
341.	Mark Clayton	0.10
342.	Patriots logo foil	0.15
343.	Johnny Rembert	0.15
344.	Garin Veris	0.05
345.	Stanley Morgan	0.10
346.	John Stephens	0.30
347.	Fred Marion	0.05
348.	Irving Fryar	0.10
349.	Helmet foil	0.15
350.	Andre Tippett	0.10
351.	Roland James	0.05
352.	Brent Williams	0.10
353.	Raymond Clayborn	0.05
354.	Tony Eason	0.10
355.	Bruce Armstrong	0.10
356.	Jets logo foil	0.15
357.	Marly Lyons	0.10
358.	Bobby Humphery	0.05
359.	Pat Leahy	0.05
360.	Mickey Shuler	0.05
361.	James Hasty	0.10
362.	Ken O'Brien	0.10
363.	Helmet foil	0.15
364.	Alex Gordon	0.10
365.	Al Toon	0.15
366.	Erik McMillan	0.15
367.	Johnny Hector	0.10
368.	Wesley Walker	0.10
369.	Freeman McNeil	0.10
370.	Steelers logo foil	0.15
371.	Gary Anderson	0.05
372.	Rodney Carter	0.10
373.	Merril Hoge	0.20
374.	David Little	0.10
375.	Bubby Brister	0.35
376.	Thomas Everett	0.15
377.	Helmet foil	0.15
378.	Rod Woodson	0.25
379.	Bryan Hinkle	0.05
380.	Tunch Ilkin	0.10
381.	Aaron Jones	0.10
382.	Louis Lipps	0.10
383.	Warren Williams	0.10
384.	Anthony Miller	0.25
385.	Gary Anderson	0.10
386.	Lee Williams	0.10
387.	Lionel James	0.10
388.	Gary Plummer	0.10
389.	Gill Byrd	0.10
390.	Chargers helmet foil	0.15
391.	Rolf Moisieienko	0.05
392.	Rod Bernstine	0.15
393.	Keith Browner	0.10
394.	Billy Ray Smith	0.10
395.	Leslie O'Neal	0.10
396.	Jamie Holland	0.05
397.	Tony Woods	0.15
398.	Bruce Scholtz	0.05
399.	Joe Nash	0.10
400.	Curt Warner	0.15
401.	John L. Williams	0.20
402.	Bryan Millard	0.10
403.	Seahawks logo foil	0.15
404.	Helmet foil	0.15
405.	Steve Largent	0.55
406.	Norm Johnson	0.05
407.	Jacob Green	0.10
408.	Dave Krieg	0.15
409.	Paul Moyer	0.10
410.	Brian Blades	0.35
411.	SB XXIII	0.10
412.	Jerry Rice	0.55
413.	SB XXIII	0.10
414.	SB XXIII	0.10
415.	SB XXIII	0.10
416.	SB XXIII	0.10

1990 HOF STICKERS

No.	Player	Value
1.	Wilbur Henry	0.10
2.	George Trafton	0.10
3.	Mike Michalske	0.15
4.	Turk Edwards	0.10
5.	Bill Hewitt	0.10
6.	Mel Hein	0.15
7.	Joe Stydahar	0.10
8.	Dan Fortmann	0.10
9.	Alex Wojciechowicz	0.10
10.	George Connor	0.10
11.	Jim Thorpe	0.30
12.	Ernie Nevers	0.20
13.	John McNally	0.15
14.	Ken Strong	0.10
15.	Bronko Nagurski	0.25
16.	Clarke Hinkle	0.10
17.	Ace Parker	0.10
18.	Bill Dudley	0.10
19.	Don Hutson	0.10
20.	Dante Lavelli	0.10
21.	Elroy Hirsch	0.20
22.	Raymond Berry	0.20
23.	Bobby Mitchell	0.20
24.	Don Maynard	0.10
25.	Mike Ditka	0.20
26.	Lance Alworth	0.20

27. Charley Taylor 0.10
28. Paul Warfield 0.20
29. Lou Groza 0.20
30. Art Donovan 0.25
31. Leo Nomellini 0.10
32. Andy Robustelli 0.10
33. Gino Marchetti 0.10
34. Forrest Gregg 0.15
35. Jim Otto 0.10
36. Ron Mix 0.10
37. Deacon Jones 0.15
38. Bob Lilly 0.20
39. Merlin Olsen 0.25
40. Alan Page 0.10
41. Joe Greene 0.20
42. Art Shell 0.10
43. Sammy Baugh 0.30
44. Sid Luckman 0.20
45. Bob Waterfield 0.20
46. Bobby Layne 0.20
47. Norm Van Brocklin 0.20
48. Y.A. Tittle 0.25
49. Johnny Unitas 0.40
50. Bart Starr 0.30
51. Sonny Jorgensen 0.25
52. Joe Namath 0.40
53. Roger Staubach 0.45
54. Terry Bradshaw 0.45
55. Steve Van Buren 0.20
56. Marion Motley 0.20
57. Joe Perry 0.20
58. Hugh McElhenny 0.20
59. Frank Gifford 0.40
60. Jim Brown 0.45
61. Jim Taylor 0.20
62. Gale Sayers 0.30
63. Larry Csonka 0.20
64. Emlen Tunnell 0.10
65. Jack Christiansen 0.10
66. Night Train Lane 0.15
67. Sam Huff 0.10
68. Ray Nitschke 0.15
69. Larry Wilson 0.10
70. Willie Wood 0.10
71. Bobby Bell 0.10
72. Willie Brown 0.10
73. Dick Butkus 0.30
74. Jack Ham 0.10
75. George Halas 0.10
76. Steve Owen 0.10
77. Art Rooney 0.15
78. Bert Bell 0.10
79. Paul Brown 0.10
80. Pete Rozelle 0.15

1990 PANINI STICKERS

No.	Player	Value
1.	SB XXIII Program	0.15
2.	SB XXIII Program	0.15
3.	Bills Crest foil	0.15
4.	Thurman Thomas	0.15
5.	Nate Odomes	0.05
6.	Jim Kelly	0.20
7.	Cornelius Bennett	0.10
8.	Scott Norwood	0.05
9.	Mark Kelso	0.05
10.	Kent Hull	0.10
11.	Jim Ritcher	0.05
12.	Darryl Talley	0.05
13.	Bruce Smith	0.10
14.	Shane Conlan	0.10
15.	Andre Reed	0.10
16.	Jason Buck	0.10
17.	David Fulcher	0.10
18.	Jim Skow	0.10
19.	Anthony Munoz	0.10
20.	Eric Thomas	0.10
21.	Eric Ball	0.10
22.	Tim Krumrie	0.05
23.	James Brooks	0.10
24.	Bengals Crest foil	0.15
25.	Rodney Holman	0.10
26.	Boomer Esiason	0.20
27.	Eddie Brown	0.10
28.	Tim McGee	0.10
29.	Browns Crest foil	0.15
30.	Mike Johnson	0.05
31.	David Grayson	0.05
32.	Thane Gash	0.10
33.	Robert Banks	0.10
34.	Eric Metcalf	0.20
35.	Kevin Mack	0.10
36.	Reggie Langhorne	0.05
37.	Webster Slaughter	0.10
38.	Felix Wright	0.10
39.	Bernie Kosar	0.20
40.	Frank Minnifield	0.10
41.	Clay Matthews	0.10
42.	Vance Johnson	0.10
43.	Ron Holmes	0.10
44.	Melvin Bratton	0.15
45.	Greg Kragen	0.10
46.	Karl Mecklenburg	0.10
47.	Dennis Smith	0.05
48.	Bobby Humphrey	0.30
49.	Simon Fletcher	0.05

1987 Topps Mike Haynes

No.	Player	Value
50.	Broncos Crest foil	0.15
51.	Michael Brooks	0.10
52.	Steve Atwater	0.15
53.	John Elway	0.30
54.	David Treadwell	0.05
55.	Oilers Crest foil	0.15
56.	Bubba McDowell	0.10
57.	Ray Childress	0.10
58.	Bruce Matthews	0.10
59.	Allen Pinkett	0.10
60.	Warren Moon	0.25
61.	John Grimsley	0.05
62.	Alonzo Highsmith	0.15
63.	Mike Munchak	0.10
64.	Ernest Givins	0.10
65.	Johnny Meads	0.10
66.	Drew Hill	0.10
67.	William Fuller	0.05
68.	Duane Bickett	0.05
69.	Jack Trudeau	0.10
70.	Jon Hand	0.10
71.	Chris Hinton	0.10
72.	Bill Brooks	0.10
73.	Donnell Thompson	0.05
74.	Jeff Herrod	0.05
75.	Andre Rison	0.10
76.	Colts Crest foil	0.15
77.	Chris Chandler	0.10
78.	Ray Donaldson	0.05
79.	Albert Bentley	0.10
80.	Keith Taylor	0.10
81.	Chiefs Crest foil	0.15
82.	Leonard Griffin	0.10
83.	Dino Hackett	0.10
84.	Christian Okoye	0.30
85.	Chris Martin	0.10
86.	John Alt	0.10
87.	Kevin Ross	0.10
88.	Steve DeBerg	0.10
89.	Albert Lewis	0.10
90.	Stephone Paige	0.10
91.	Derrick Thomas	0.15
92.	Neil Smith	0.10
93.	Pete Mandley	0.05
94.	Howie Long	0.10
95.	Greg Townsend	0.05
96.	Mervyn Fernandez	0.10
97.	Scott Davis	0.10
98.	Steve Beuerlein	0.10
99.	Mike Dyal	0.10
100.	Willie Gault	0.10
101.	Eddie Anderson	0.10
102.	Raiders Crest foil	0.15
103.	Terry McDaniel	0.10
104.	Bo Jackson	0.45
105.	Steve Wisniewski	0.10
106.	Steve Smith	0.10
107.	Dolphins Crest foil	0.15
108.	Mark Clayton	0.10
109.	Louis Oliver	0.10
110.	Jarvis Willliams	0.10
111.	Ferrell Edmunds	0.10
112.	Jeff Cross	0.10
113.	John Offerdahl	0.10
114.	Brian Sochia	0.10
115.	Dan Marino	0.35
116.	Jim Jensen	0.10
117.	Sammie Smith	0.15
118.	Reggie Roby	0.05
119.	Roy Foster	0.05
120.	Bruce Armstrong	0.10
121.	Steve Grogan	0.10
122.	Hart Lee Dykes	0.10
123.	Andre Tippett	0.10
124.	Johnny Rembert	0.10
125.	Ed Reynolds	0.10
126.	Cedric Jones	0.10
127.	Vincent Brown	0.10
128.	Patriots Crest foil	0.15
129.	Brent Williams	0.10
130.	John Stephens	0.15
131.	Eric Sievers	0.10
132.	Maurice Hurst	0.10
133.	Jets Crest foil	0.15
134.	Johnny Hector	0.05
135.	Eric McMillan	0.10
136.	Jeff Lageman	0.10
137.	Al Toon	0.15
138.	James Hasty	0.10
139.	Kyle Clifton	0.10
140.	Ken O'Brien	0.15
141.	Jim Sweeney	0.10
142.	Jo Jo Townsell	0.10
143.	Dennis Byrd	0.10
144.	Mickey Shuler	0.05
145.	Alex Gordon	0.05
146.	Keith Willis	0.05
147.	Louis Lipps	0.10
148.	David Little	0.10
149.	Greg Lloyd	0.10
150.	Cornell Lake	0.10
151.	Tim Worley	0.10
152.	Dwayne Woodruff	0.10
153.	Gerald Williams	0.10
154.	Steelers Crest foil	0.15
155.	Merril Hoge	0.15
156.	Bubby Brister	0.20
157.	Tunch Ilkin	0.10
158.	Rod Woodson	0.10
159.	Charger Crest foil	0.15
160.	Leslie O'Neal	0.10
161.	Billy Ray Smith	0.10
162.	Marion Butts	0.10
163.	Lee Willliams	0.10
164.	Gil Byrd	0.10
165.	Jim McMahon	0.15
166.	Courtney Hall	0.10
167.	Burt Grossman	0.10
168.	Gary Plummer	0.10
169.	Anthony Miller	0.10

170. Billy Joe Tolliver 0.20
171. Vencie Glenn 0.10
172. Andy Heck 0.10
173. Brian Blades 0.15
174. Bryan Millard 0.05
175. Tony Woods 0.05
176. Rufus Porter 0.05
177. Dave Wyman 0.05
178. John L. Williams 0.10
179. Jacob Green 0.10
180. Seahawks Crest foil 0.15
181. Eugene Robinson 0.05
182. Jeff Bryant 0.05
183. Dave Krieg 0.10
184. Joe Nash 0.10
185. Christian Okoye LL 0.15
186. Felix Wright LL 0.05
187. Rod Woodson LL 0.10
188. Sanders, Okoye AP 0.40
189. Rice, Sharpe AP 0.35
190. Bruce Matthews AP 0.10
191. Jay Hilgenberg AP 0.10
192. Tom Newberry AP 0.10
193. Anthony Munoz AP 0.10
194. Jim Lachey AP 0.10
195. Keith Jackson AP 0.15
196. Joe Montana AP 0.40
197. Fulcher, Lott AP 0.15
198. Lewis, Allen AP 0.10
199. Reggie White AP 0.15
200. Keith Millard AP 0.10
201. Chris Doleman AP 0.10
202. Mike Singletary AP 0.10
203. Tim Harris AP 0.10
204. Lawrence Taylor AP 0.15
205. Rich Camarillo AP 0.05
206. Sterling Sharpe LL 0.20
207. Chris Doleman LL 0.10
208. Barry Sanders LL 0.40
209. Falcons Crest foil 0.15
210. Michael Haynes 0.10
211. Scott Case 0.10
212. Marcus Cotton 0.10
213. Chris Miller 0.15
214. Keith Jones 0.10
215. Tim Green 0.10
216. Deion Sanders 0.20
217. Shawn Collins 0.10
218. John Settle 0.10
219. Bill Fralic 0.10
220. Aundray Bruce 0.10
221. Jessie Tuggle 0.10
222. James Thornton 0.10
223. Dennis Gentry 0.05
224. Richard Dent 0.15
225. Jay Hilgenberg 0.10
226. Steve McMichael 0.10
227. Brad Muster 0.10
228. Donnell Woodford 0.10
229. Mike Singletary 0.10
230. Bears Crest foil 0.15
231. Mark Bortz 0.10
232. Kevin Butler 0.05
233. Neal Anderson 0.15
234. Trace Armstrong 0.10
235. Cowboys Crest foil 0.15
236. Mark Tuinei 0.10
237. Tony Tolbert 0.10
238. Eugene Lockhart 0.10
239. Daryl Johnston 0.15
240. Troy Aikman 0.30
241. Jim Jeffcoat 0.05
242. James Dixon 0.10
243. Jesse Solomon 0.05
244. Ken Norton 0.10
245. Kelvin Martin 0.05
246. Danny Noonan 0.10
247. Michael Irvin 0.10
248. Eric Williams 0.05
249. Richard Johnson 0.05
250. Michael Cofer 0.05
251. Chris Spielman 0.10
252. Rodney Peete 0.15
253. Bennie Blades 0.10
254. Jerry Ball 0.10
255. Eddie Murray 0.05
256. Lions Crest foil 0.15

1987 Topps Neil Olkewicz

257. Barry Sanders 0.40
258. Jerry Holmes 0.05
259. Dennis Gibson 0.05
260. Lomas Brown 0.10
261. Packers Crest foil 0.15
262. Dave Brown 0.05
263. Mark Murphy 0.05
264. Perry Kemp 0.10
265. Don Majkowski 0.35
266. Chris Jacke 0.10
267. Keith Woodside 0.10
268. Tony Mandarich 0.15
269. Robert Brown 0.05
270. Sterling Sharpe 0.20
271. Tim Harris 0.10
272. Brent Fullwood 0.10
273. Brian Noble 0.05
274. Alvin Wright 0.05
275. Flipper Anderson 0.15
276. Jackie Slater 0.10
277. Kevin Greene 0.10
278. Pete Holohan 0.05
279. Tom Newberry 0.05
280. Jerry Gray 0.10
281. Henry Ellard 0.10
282. Rams Crest foil 0.15
283. LeRoy Irvin 0.10
284. Jim Everett 0.30
285. Greg Bell 0.10
286. Doug Smith 0.05
287. Vikings Crest foil 0.15
288. Joey Browner 0.10
289. Wade Wilson 0.15
290. Chris Doleman 0.10
291. Al Noga 0.10
292. Herschel Walker 0.30
293. Henry Thomas 0.10
294. Steve Jordan 0.10
295. Anthony Carter 0.10
296. Keith Millard 0.10
297. Carl Lee 0.10
298. Randall McDaniel 0.10
299. Gary Zimmerman 0.10
300. Morten Andersen 0.10
301. Rickey Jackson 0.10
302. Sam Mills 0.05
303. Hoby Brenner 0.05
304. Dalton Hilliard 0.15
305. Robert Massey 0.10
306. John Fourcade 0.15
307. Lonzell Hill 0.10
308. Saints Crest foil 0.15
309. Jim Dombrowski 0.10
310. Pat Swilling 0.10
311. Vaughan Johnson 0.10
312. Eric Martin 0.10
313. Giants Crest foil 0.15
314. Ottis Anderson 0.15
315. Myron Guyton 0.10
316. Terry Kinard 0.10
317. Mark Bavaro 0.10
318. Phil Simms 0.20
319. Lawrence Taylor 0.15
320. Odessa Turner 0.10
321. Erik Howard 0.10
322. Mark Collins 0.10
323. Dave Meggett 0.25
324. Leonard Marshall 0.10
325. Carl Banks 0.10
326. Anthony Toney 0.05
327. Seth Joyner 0.05
328. Cris Carter 0.10
329. Eric Allen 0.10
330. Keith Jackson 0.15
331. Clyde Simmons 0.10
332. Byron Evans 0.05
333. Keith Byars 0.10
334. Eagles Crest foil 0.15
335. Reggie White 0.15
336. Izel Jenkins 0.10
337. Jerome Brown 0.20
338. David Alexander 0.10
339. Cardinals Crest foil 0.15
340. Rich Camarillo 0.05
341. Ken Harvey 0.10
342. Luis Sharpe 0.05
343. Timm Rosenbach 0.15
344. Tim McDonald 0.15
345. Vai Sikahema 0.10
346. Freddie Joe Nunn 0.05
347. Ernie Jones 0.10
348. J.T. Smith 0.10
349. Eric Hill 0.05
350. Roy Green 0.10
351. Anthony Bell 0.10
352. Kevin Fagan 0.10
353. Roger Craig 0.20
354. Ronnie Lott 0.15
355. Mike Cofer 0.10
356. John Taylor 0.15
357. Joe Montana 0.40
358. Charles Haley 0.10
359. Guy McIntyre 0.10
360. 49ers Crest foil 0.15
361. Pierce Holt 0.10
362. Tom Rathman 0.15
363. Jerry Rice 0.30
364. Michael Carter 0.10
365. Buccaneers Crest foil 0.15
366. Lars Tate 0.15
367. Paul Gruber 0.10
368. Winston Moss 0.10
369. Reuben Davis 0.10
370. Mark Robinson 0.05
371. Bruce Hill 0.10
372. Kevin Murphy 0.10
373. Ricky Reynolds 0.10
374. Harry Hamilton 0.10
375. Vinny Testaverde 0.15
376. Mark Carrier 0.10
377. Ervin Randle 0.05
378. Ricky Sanders 0.10
379. Charles Mann 0.10
380. Jim Lachey 0.10
381. Wilber Marshall 0.10
382. A.J. Johnson 0.10
383. Darrell Green 0.10
384. Mark Rypien 0.15
385. Gerald Riggs 0.10
386. Redskins Crest foil 0.15
387. Alvin Walton 0.10
388. Art Monk 0.15
389. Gary Clark 0.10
390. Ernest Byner 0.10
391. Jerry Rice (SB XXIV foil) 0.30
392. 49ers OL (SB XXIV foil) 0.20
393. T. Rathman (SB XXIV foil) 0.15
394. C. Brooks (SB XXIV foil) 0.15
395. John Elway (SB XXIV foil) 0.25
396. J. Montana (SB XXIV foil) 0.45

REGULAR SEASON BASEBALL TICKETS

by Dennis Goldstein

Baseball tickets go back to the 1860s, if not the late 1850s. Many of the earliest tickets were issued as season passes to team members for their families and friends. By the 1870s, the leading professional and amateur baseball clubs were producing tickets for individual games. This practice continues to the present day.

Most baseball ticket collectors seek World Series and All Star tickets. Finite in number, these tickets are generally much more attractive and of higher quality than regular season tickets. Subsequently, World Series and All Star tickets, especially early ones, command significantly higher prices than most regular season tickets.

A small but growing number of collectors look for regular season baseball tickets for major league teams. These collectors are attracted to the tickets due to their relatively low prices, their lack of attention from other collectors, and the ease with which they are displayed and stored. Many regular season ticket collectors will accept tickets, especially earlier ones, in lesser condition. Tickets are usually not sought for their attractiveness, as many have been badly torn by ball park ticket-takers. Since regular season tickets were not intended as keepsakes, many surviving tickets are not in great shape. Often, early tickets that did survive were glued in scrapbooks.

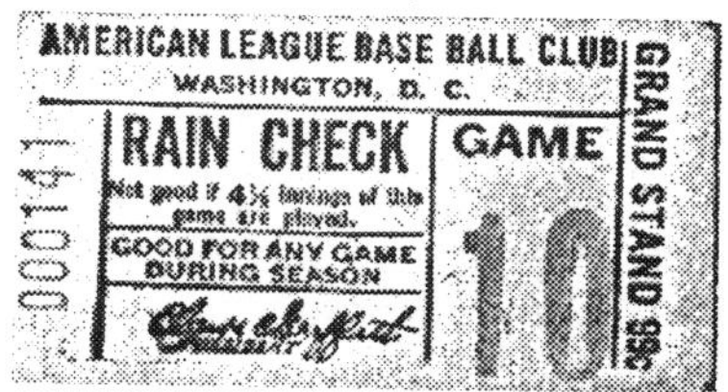

1920s Washington Nationals ticket stub

While many collectors will buy tickets in lesser condition, condition does affect the price to some extent. Full (unused) tickets are generally worth many times more than ticket stubs from the same game. On the other hand, tickets in unusually poor condition are not collectible.

Most regular season ticket collectors focus on a certain aspect of ticket collecting, since it is virtually impossible to collect all old tickets of the major league teams. Many season tickets, especially ones prior to 1930, are not only difficult to find, but also difficult to precisely identify by year, as many are undated and similar in design to other years' tickets. Dated tickets usually are worth considerably more than undated tickets from the same era. Other factors that enhance the value of a regular season ticket are attractiveness and a baseball schedule on the reverse. Many baseball ticket collectors concentrate on a limited area of ticket collecting such as special regular season events; a favorite team or era; or obscure major leagues, such as the Union League (1884), the Player's League (1890), the Federal League (1914-15), and the Negro Leagues (1920s-40s).

Tickets from special events, the obscure major leagues, and pre-1900 tickets generally bring high prices. Sought after special events tickets include the first game of a stadium, city or team, and significant games (such as Roger Maris' 61st-homer game).

The price guide provides a price range for each major team's tickets in excellent condition for each decade. An excellent ticket is free of any significant defects. For reasons similar to those provided in the introduction to regular season baseball programs, price ranges and some open-ended values are provided.

Our price guide contains values for pre-1970 major league teams. Few collectors seek the more recent major or minor league ticket stubs or other baseball tickets such as exhibition, semi-pro, college, high school, and amateur tickets. Most of these tickets are worth very little. Among the non-major league tickets, only very early tickets from the top minor league teams have much value. These tickets are too numerous to list in the price guide.

TICKET STUBS

AUTO RACING TICKET STUBS

DAYTONA 500 STUBS

Date	Winner	Value
1959	Lee Petty	100.00
1960	Junior Johnson	50.00
1961	Marvin Panch	25.00
1962	Fireball Roberts	25.00
1963	Tiny Lund	20.00
1964	Richard Petty	75.00
1965	Fred Lorenzen	15.00
1966	Richard Petty	20.00
1967	Mario Andretti	15.00
1968	Cale Yarborough	8.00
1969	L.R. Yarborough	8.00
1970	Pete Hamilton	8.00
1971	Richard Petty	10.00
1972	A.J. Foyt	10.00
1973	Richard Petty	8.00
1974	Richard Petty	8.00
1975	Benny Parsons	4.00
1976	David Pearson	4.00
1977	Cale Yarborough	4.00
1978	Bobby Allison	5.00
1979	Richard Petty	8.00
1980	Buddy Baker	4.00
1981	Richard Petty	7.00
1982	Bobby Allison	4.00
1983	Cale Yarborough	4.00
1984	Cale Yarborough	4.00
1985	Bill Elliott	4.00
1986	Geoff Bodine	3.00
1987	Bill Elliott	3.00
1988	Bobby Allison	3.00
1989	Darrell Waltrip	3.00
1990	Derrike Cope	3.00
1991	Ernie Irvan	3.00
1992	Davey Allison	3.00

INDY 500 STUBS

Date	Winner	Value
1911	Ray Harroun	250.00
1912	Joe Dawson	225.00
1913	Jules Goux	225.00
1914	Rene Thomas	225.00
1915	Ralph DePalma	225.00
1916	Dario Resta	225.00
1917-18	Race not held due to WWI	
1919	Howard Wilcox	200.00
1920	Gaston Chevrolet	150.00
1921	Tommy Milton	150.00
1922	Jimmy Murphy	150.00
1923	Tommy Milton	150.00
1924	L.L Corum & J. Boyer	150.00
1925	Peter DePaolo	150.00
1926	Frank Lockhart	150.00
1927	George Sounders	150.00
1928	Louis Meyer	150.00
1929	Ray Keech	150.00
1930	Billy Arnold	135.00
1931	Louis Schneider	135.00
1932	Fred Frame	135.00
1933	Louis Meyer	135.00
1934	Bill Cummings	135.00
1935	Kelly Petillo	135.00
1936	Louis Meyer	135.00
1937	Wilbur Shaw	140.00
1938	Floyd Roberts	135.00
1939	Wilbur Shaw	140.00
1940	Wilbur Shaw	135.00
1941	F. Davis & M. Rose	135.00
1942-45	Race not held due to WWII	
1946	George Robson	100.00
1947	Mauri Rose	95.00
1948	Mauri Rose	95.00
1949	Bill Holland	95.00
1950	Johnnie Parsons	80.00
1951	Lee Wallard	75.00
1952	Troy Ruttman	75.00
1953	Bill Vukovich	75.00
1954	Bill Vukovich	75.00
1955	Bob Sweikert	75.00
1956	Pat Flaherty	30.00
1957	Sam Hanks	30.00
1958	Jimmy Bryan	30.00
1959	Rodger Ward	30.00
1960	Jim Rathmann	25.00
1961	A.J. Foyt	30.00
1962	Rodger Ward	25.00
1963	Parnelli Jones	25.00
1964	A.J. Foyt	30.00
1965	Jim Clark	20.00
1966	Graham Hill	20.00
1967	A.J. Foyt	30.00
1968	Bobby Unser	25.00
1969	Mario Andretti	25.00
1970	Al Unser	20.00
1971	Al Unser	20.00
1972	Mark Donohue	15.00
1973	Gordon Johncock	15.00
1974	J. Rutherford	15.00
1975	Bobby Unser	15.00
1976	J. Rutherford	15.00
1977	A.J. Foyt	18.00
1978	Al Unser	15.00
1979	Rick Mears	15.00
1980	J. Rutherford	12.00
1981	Bobby Unser	12.00
1982	Gordon Johncock	12.00
1983	Tom Sneva	13.00
1984	Rick Mears	13.00
1985	Danny Sullivan	12.00
1986	Bobby Rahal	12.00
1987	Al Unser	12.00
1988	Rick Mears	12.00
1989	E. Fittipaldi	10.00
1990	Arie Luyendyk	10.00
1991	Rick Mears	10.00
1992	Al Unser, Jr	10.00

BASEBALL TICKET STUBS

ALL-STAR GAME STUBS

Year	Site	Value
1933	Comiskey Park	600.0

Indianapolis 500 (1961)

All Star Game (1948 & 1956)

Year	Site	Price
1934	Polo Grounds	800.00
1935	Cleveland Stadium	250.00
1936	Braves Field	500.00
1937	Griffith Stadium	450.00
1938	Crosley Field	250.00
1939	Yankee Stadium	250.00
1940	Sportsman's Park	200.00
1941	Briggs Stadium	150.00
1942	Polo Grounds	250.00
1943	Shibe Park	150.00
1944	Forbes Field	200.00
1945	No game	
1946	Fenway Park	150.00
1947	Wrigley Field	100.00
1948	Sportsman's Park	100.00
1949	Ebbets Field	200.00
1950	Comiskey Park	125.00
1951	Briggs Stadium	50.00
1952	Shibe Park	75.00
1953	Crosley Field	100.00
1954	Cleveland Stadium	50.00
1955	County Stadium	50.00
1956	Griffith Stadium	50.00
1957	Busch Stadium	50.00
1958	Memorial Stadium	75.00
1959	Game 1: Forbes Field	50.00
	Game 2: Memorial Coliseum	25.00
1960	Game 1: Mun. Stadium	25.00
	Game 2: Yankee Stadium	30.00
1961	Game 1: Candlestick.	40.00
	Game 2: Fenway Park	25.00
1962	Game 1: D.C. Stadium	15.00
	Game 2: Wrigley Field	15.00
1963	Cleveland Stadium	10.00
1964	Shea Stadium	15.00
1965	Metropolitan Stadium	8.00
1966	Busch Memorial Stadium	6.00
1967	Anaheim Stadium	6.00
1968	The Astrodome	7.00
1969	RFK Stadium	6.00
1970	Riverfront Stadium	5.00
1971	Tiger Stadium	5.00
1972	Atlanta Stadium	5.00
1973	Royals Stadium	5.00
1974	Three Rivers Stadium	5.00
1975	County Stadium	5.00
1976	Veterans Stadium	5.00
1977	Yankee Stadium	5.00
1978	San Diego Stadium	6.00
1979	The Kingdome	5.00
1980	Dodger Stadium	5.00
1981	Cleveland Stadium	5.00
1982	Olympic Stadium	6.00
1983	Comiskey Park	5.00
1984	Candlestick Park	5.00
1985	The Metrodome	5.00
1986	The Astrodome	5.00
1987	Oakland Coliseum	5.00
1988	Riverfront Stadium	5.00
1989	Anaheim Stadium	5.00
1990	Wrigley Field	5.00
1991	SkyDome	5.00
1992	Jack Murphy Stadium	5.00

AMERICAN LEAGUE PLAYOFF STUBS

Year	Team	Price
1969	Baltimore Orioles	10.00
	Minnesota Twins	10.00
1970	Baltimore Orioles	8.00
	Minnesota Twins	8.00
1971	Baltimore Orioles	8.00
	Oakland A's	8.00
1972	Oakland A's	8.00
	Detroit Tigers	6.00
1973	Oakland A's	8.00
	Baltimore Orioles	6.00
1974	Oakland A's	6.00
	Baltimore Orioles	6.00
1975	Boston Red Sox	7.00
	Oakland A's	6.00
1976	New York Yankees	10.00
	Kansas City Royals	6.00
1977	New York Yankees	6.00
	Kansas City Royals	6.00
1978	New York Yankees	6.00
	Kansas City Royals	6.00
1979	Baltimore Orioles	6.00
	California Angels	6.00
1980	Kansas City Royals	6.00
	New York Yankees	6.00
1981	New York Yankees	6.00
	Oakland A's	6.00
1982	Milwaukee Brewers	4.00
	California Angels	4.00
1983	Baltimore Orioles	6.00
	Chicago White Sox	5.00
1984	Detroit Tigers	4.00
	Kansas City Royals	4.00
1985	Kansas City Royals	4.00
	Toronto Blue Jays	5.00
1986	Boston Red Sox	5.00
	California Angels	6.00
1987	Minnesota Twins	4.00
	Detroit Tigers	4.00
1988	Oakland A's	4.00
	Boston Red Sox	4.00
1989	Oakland A's	4.00
	Toronto Blue Jays	4.00
1990	Oakland A's	4.00
	Boston Red Sox	4.00
1991	Minnesota Twins	4.00
	Toronto Blue Jays	4.00
1992	Toronto Blue Jays	4.00
	Oakland A's	4.00

NATIONAL LEAGUE PLAYOFF STUBS

Year	Team	Price
1969	New York Mets	25.00
	Atlanta Braves	15.00
1970	Cincinnati Reds	8.00
	Pittsburgh Pirates	8.00
1971	Pittsburgh Pirates	6.00
	San Francisco Giants	6.00
1972	Cincinnati Reds	8.00
	Pittsburgh Pirates	8.00
1973	New York Mets	10.00
	Cincinnati Reds	8.00
1974	Los Angeles Dodgers	6.00
	Pittsburgh Pirates	6.00
1975	Cincinnati Reds	8.00
	Pittsburgh Pirates	6.00
1976	Cincinnati Reds	8.00
	Philadelphia Phillies	6.00
1977	Los Angeles Dodgers	6.00
	Philadelphia Phillies	6.00
1978	Los Angeles Dodgers	6.00
	Philadelphia Phillies	6.00
1979	Pittsburgh Pirates	8.00
	Cincinnati Reds	6.00
1980	Philadelphia Phillies	6.00
	Houston Astros	5.00
1981	Los Angeles Dodgers	6.00
	Montreal Expos	8.00
1982	St. Louis Cardinals	5.00
	Atlanta Braves	5.00
1983	Philadelphia Phillies	5.00
	Los Angeles Dodgers	5.00
1984	San Diego Padres	5.00
	Chicago Cubs	5.00
1985	St. Louis Cardinals	5.00
	Los Angeles Dodgers	5.00
1986	New York Mets	6.00
	Houston Astros	5.00
1987	St. Louis Cardinals	4.00
	San Francisco Giants	4.00
1988	Los Angeles Dodgers	4.00
	New York Mets	4.00
1989	San Francisco Giants	4.00
	Chicago Cubs	4.00
1990	Cincinnati Reds	4.00
	Pittsburgh Pirates	4.00
1991	Atlanta Braves	5.00
	Pittsburgh Pirates	4.00
1992	Atlanta Braves	5.00
	Pittsburgh Pirates	4.00

REGULAR SEASON GAME TICKET STUBS

ANGELS

1961-69 .... 2.00-5.00

ASTROS (COLT 45s)

1962-69 .... 2.00-5.00

ATHLETICS

Philadelphia Athletics

1901-09 .... 50.00-100.00
1910-19 .... 35.00-50.00
1920-29 .... 20.00-35.00
1930-39 .... 10.00-20.00
1940-49 .... 10.00-15.00
1950-54 .... 5.00-10.00

Kansas City Athletics

1955-59 .... 4.00-8.00
1960-67 .... 2.00-5.00

Oakland Athletics

1968-69 .... 2.00-5.00

BLUE JAYS

1970-79 .... 2.00-4.00

BRAVES

Boston Braves

pre-1900 .... 200.00-350.00
1900-09 .... 75.00-150.00
1910-19 .... 50.00-75.00
1920-29 .... 25.00-50.00
1930-39 .... 15.00-25.00
1940-49 .... 10.00-15.00
1950-52 .... 5.00-10.00

Milwaukee Braves

1953-59 .... 5.00-10.00
1960-65 .... 2.00-5.00

Atlanta Braves

1966-69 .... 2.00-5.00

BREWERS

Seattle Pilots

1969 . . . . . 4.00-10.00

Milwaukee Brewers

1970-79 . . . . . 2.00-5.00

BROWNS
(became ORIOLES in 1954)

pre-1900 . . . . . 200.00-400.00
1902-09 . . . . . 100.00-200.00
1910-19 . . . . . 50.00-100.00
1920-29 . . . . . 25.00-50.00
1930-39 . . . . . 15.00-25.00
1940-49 . . . . . 10.00-15.00
1950-59 . . . . . 8.00-10.00

CARDINALS

pre-1900 . . . . . 200.00-350.00
1900-09 . . . . . 100.00-200.00
1910-19 . . . . . 50.00-100.00
1920-29 . . . . . 25.00-50.00
1930-39 . . . . . 10.00-20.00
1940-49 . . . . . 5.00-10.00
1950-59 . . . . . 4.00-8.00
1960-69 . . . . . 2.00-5.00

CUBS

pre-1900 . . . . . 200.00-350.00
1900-09 . . . . . 100.00-200.00
1910-19 . . . . . 50.00-100.00
1920-29 . . . . . 25.00-50.00
1930-39 . . . . . 15.00-25.00
1940-49 . . . . . 10.00-15.00
1950-59 . . . . . 5.00-10.00
1960-69 . . . . . 2.00-5.00

DODGERS

Brooklyn Dodgers

pre-1900 . . . . . 200.00-350.00
1900-09 . . . . . 100.00-200.00
1910-19 . . . . . 50.00-100.00
1920-29 . . . . . 25.00-50.00
1930-39 . . . . . 15.00-25.00
1940-49 . . . . . 10.00-20.00
1950-57 . . . . . 5.00-15.00

Los Angeles Dodgers

1958-59 . . . . . 5.00-10.00
1960-69 . . . . . 2.00-5.00

EXPOS

1969 . . . . . 4.00-10.00

GIANTS

New York Giants

pre-1900 . . . . . 200.00-350.00
1900-09 . . . . . 75.00-150.00
1910-19 . . . . . 50.00-75.00
1920-29 . . . . . 25.00-40.00
1930-39 . . . . . 15.00-25.00
1940-49 . . . . . 10.00-15.00
1950-57 . . . . . 5.00-10.00

San Francisco Giants

1958-59 . . . . . 5.00-8.00
1960-69 . . . . . 2.00-5.00

INDIANS

pre-1900 . . . . . 200.00-375.00
1900-09 . . . . . 100.00-200.00
1910-19 . . . . . 50.00-100.00
1920-29 . . . . . 25.00-50.00
1930-39 . . . . . 15.00-25.00
1940-49 . . . . . 10.00-15.00
1950-59 . . . . . 5.00-10.00
1960-69 . . . . . 2.00-5.00

MARINERS

1977-79 . . . . . 2.00-5.00

Lou Gehrig Memorial, Yankee Stadium (1941)

METS

1962-69 . . . . . 3.00-10.00

ORIOLES

pre-1900 . . . . . 200.00-400.00
1902-03 . . . . . 200.00-250.00
1954-59 . . . . . 5.00-15.00
1960-69 . . . . . 2.00-5.00

PADRES

1969 . . . . . 4.00-10.00

PHILLIES

pre-1900 . . . . . 200.00-350.00
1900-09 . . . . . 100.00-200.00
1910-19 . . . . . 50.00-100.00
1920-29 . . . . . 25.00-50.00
1930-39 . . . . . 15.00-25.00
1940-49 . . . . . 10.00-15.00
1950-59 . . . . . 5.00-10.00
1960-69 . . . . . 2.00-5.00

PIRATES

pre-1900 . . . . . 200.00-375.00
1900-09 . . . . . 100.00-200.00
1910-19 . . . . . 50.00-100.00
1920-29 . . . . . 25.00-50.00
1930-39 . . . . . 15.00-25.00
1940-49 . . . . . 10.00-15.00
1950-59 . . . . . 5.00-10.00
1960-69 . . . . . 2.00-5.00

RANGERS

1972-79 . . . . . 2.00-5.00

REDS

pre-1900 . . . . . 200.00-375.00
1900-09 . . . . . 100.00-200.00
1910-19 . . . . . 50.00-100.00
1920-29 . . . . . 25.00-50.00
1930-39 . . . . . 15.00-25.00
1940-49 . . . . . 10.00-15.00
1950-59 . . . . . 5.00-10.00
1960-69 . . . . . 2.00-5.00

RED SOX

1901-09 . . . . . 75.00-200.00
1910-19 . . . . . 50.00-100.00
1920-29 . . . . . 25.00-50.00
1930-39 . . . . . 15.00-25.00
1940-49 . . . . . 10.00-15.00
1950-59 . . . . . 5.00-10.00
1960-69 . . . . . 2.00-5.00

ROYALS

1969 . . . . . 4.00-10.00

SENATORS
(became Twins in 1961)
(became Rangers in 1972)

pre-1900 . . . . . 200.00-350.00
1900-09 . . . . . 100.00-200.00
1910-19 . . . . . 50.00-100.00
1920-29 . . . . . 25.00-50.00
1930-39 . . . . . 15.00-25.00
1940-49 . . . . . 10.00-15.00
1950-59 . . . . . 5.00-10.00
1960-69 . . . . . 3.00-10.00

TIGERS

pre-1900 . . . . . 200.00-350.00
1900-09 . . . . . 100.00-200.00
1910-19 . . . . . 50.00-100.00
1920-29 . . . . . 25.00-50.00
1930-39 . . . . . 15.00-25.00
1940-49 . . . . . 10.00-15.00
1950-59 . . . . . 5.00-10.00
1960-69 . . . . . 2.00-5.00

TWINS

1961-69 . . . . . 2.00-10.00

WHITE SOX

1901-09 . . . . . 100.00-200.00
1910-19 . . . . . 75.00-150.00
1920-29 . . . . . 25.00-50.00
1930-39 . . . . . 15.00-25.00
1940-49 . . . . . 10.00-15.00
1950-59 . . . . . 5.00-10.00
1960-69 . . . . . 2.00-5.00

YANKEES

1903-09 . . . . . 100.00-200.00
1910-19 . . . . . 50.00-100.00
1920-29 . . . . . 25.00-75.00
1930-39 . . . . . 15.00-35.00
1940-49 . . . . . 10.00-15.00
1950-59 . . . . . 5.00-15.00
1960-69 . . . . . 2.00-10.00

WORLD SERIES STUBS

Year	Team	Value
1903	Boston A.L.	2,000.00
	Pittsburgh N.L.	2,500.00
1904	No series	
1905	New York N.L.	1,750.00
	Philadelphia A.L.	1,250.00
1906	Chicago N.L.	1,250.00
	Chicago A.L.	1,250.00
1907	Chicago N.L.	1,000.00
	Detroit A.L.	1,000.00
1908	Chicago N.L.	900.00
	Detroit A.L.	1,000.00
1909	Detroit A.L.	800.00
	Pittsburgh N.L.	800.00
1910	Chicago N.L.	750.00
	Philadelphia A.L.	750.00
1911	New York N.L.	800.00
	Philadelphia A.L.	800.00
1912	Boston A.L.	750.00

Yankee Stadium World Series (1928 & 1937) and a 1932 Wrigley Field stub

Year	Team	Price
	New York N.L.	800.00
1913	New York N.L.	750.00
	Philadelphia A.L.	700.00
1914	Boston N.L.	700.00
	Philadelphia A.L.	700.00
1915	Boston A.L.	650.00
	Philadelphia N.L.	650.00
1916	Boston A.L.	650.00
	Brooklyn N.L.	650.00
1917	Chicago A.L.	600.00
	New York N.L.	600.00
1918	Boston A.L.	600.00
	Chicago N.L.	600.00
1919	Chicago A.L.	1,000.00
	Cincinnati N.L.	800.00
1920	Brooklyn N.L.	600.00
	Cleveland A.L.	500.00
1921	New York Both	650.00
1922	New York Both	650.00
1923	New York A.L.	600.00
	New York N.L.	600.00
1924	New York N.L.	600.00
	Washington A.L.	400.00
1925	Pittsburgh N.L.	350.00
	Washington A.L.	350.00
1926	New York A.L.	400.00
	St. Louis N.L.	250.00
1927	New York A.L.	400.00
	Pittsburgh N.L.	250.00
1928	New York A.L.	400.00
	St. Louis N.L.	350.00
1929	Chicago N.L.	300.00
	Philadelphia A.L.	300.00
1930	Philadelphia A.L.	200.00
	St. Louis N.L.	200.00
1931	Philadelphia A.L.	150.00
	St. Louis N.L.	150.00
1932	Chicago N.L.	200.00
	New York A.L.	350.00
1933	New York N.L.	150.00
	Washington A.L.	150.00
1934	Detroit A.L.	150.00
	St. Louis N.L.	150.00
1935	Chicago N.L.	125.00
	Detroit A.L.	125.00
1936	New York N.L.	125.00
	New York A.L.	150.00
1937	New York N.L.	100.00
	New York A.L.	100.00
1938	Chicago N.L.	50.00
	New York A.L.	75.00
1939	Cincinnati N.L.	50.00
	New York A.L.	60.00
1940	Cincinnati N.L.	50.00
	Detroit A.L.	50.00
1941	Brooklyn N.L.	50.00
	New York A.L.	75.00
1942	New York A.L.	75.00
	St. Louis N.L.	50.00
1943	New York A.L.	50.00
	St. Louis N.L.	45.00
1944	St. Louis A.L.	45.00
	St. Louis N.L.	40.00
1945	Chicago N.L.	40.00
	Detroit A.L.	50.00
1946	Boston A.L.	35.00
	St. Louis N.L.	35.00
1947	Brooklyn N.L.	40.00
	New York A.L.	35.00
1948	Boston N.L.	40.00
	Cleveland A.L.	25.00
1949	Brooklyn N.L.	35.00
	New York A.L.	30.00
1950	New York A.L.	30.00
	Philadelphia N.L.	25.00
1951	New York A.L.	40.00
	New York N.L.	40.00
1952	Brooklyn N.L.	35.00
	New York A.L.	35.00
1953	Brooklyn N.L.	35.00
	New York A.L.	35.00
1954	Cleveland A.L.	30.00
	New York N.L.	30.00
1955	Brooklyn N.L.	35.00
	New York A.L.	30.00
1956	Brooklyn N.L.	35.00
	New York A.L.	30.00
1957	Milwaukee N.L.	25.00
	New York A.L.	30.00
1958	Milwaukee N.L.	25.00
	New York A.L.	25.00
1959	Chicago A.L.	20.00
	Los Angeles N.L.	20.00
1960	New York A.L.	30.00
	Pittsburgh N.L.	25.00
1961	Cincinnati N.L.	25.00
	New York A.L.	35.00
1962	New York A.L.	35.00
	San Francisco N.L.	25.00
1963	Los Angeles N.L.	20.00
	New York A.L.	25.00
1964	New York A.L.	20.00
	St. Louis N.L.	15.00
1965	Los Angeles N.L.	15.00
	Minnesota A.L.	15.00
1966	Baltimore A.L.	20.00
	Los Angeles N.L.	15.00
1967	Boston A.L.	15.00
	St. Louis N.L.	15.00
1968	Detroit A.L.	15.00
	St. Louis N.L.	10.00
1969	Baltimore A.L.	25.00
	New York N.L.	60.00
1970	Baltimore A.L.	15.00
	Cincinnati N.L.	10.00
1971	Baltimore A.L.	10.00
	Pittsburgh N.L.	10.00
1972	Cincinnati N.L.	15.00
	Oakland A.L.	10.00
1973	New York N.L.	15.00
	Oakland A.L.	10.00
1974	Los Angeles N.L.	10.00
	Oakland A.L.	10.00
1975	Boston A.L.	10.00
	Cincinnati N.L.	10.00
1976	Cincinnati N.L.	10.00
	New York A.L.	10.00
1977	Los Angeles N.L.	15.00
	New York A.L.	15.00
1978	Los Angeles N.L.	10.00
	New York A.L.	10.00
1979	Baltimore A.L.	10.00
	Pittsburgh N.L.	10.00
1980	Kansas City A.L.	8.00
	Philadelphia N.L.	8.00
1981	Los Angeles N.L.	8.00
	New York A.L.	8.00
1982	Milwaukee A.L.	8.00
	St. Louis N.L.	8.00
1983	Baltimore A.L.	10.00
	Philadelphia N.L.	8.00
1984	Detroit A.L.	8.00
	San Diego N.L.	8.00
1985	Kansas City A.L.	8.00
	St. Louis N.L.	8.00
1986	Boston A.L.	8.00
	New York N.L.	8.00
1987	Minnesota A.L.	10.00
	St. Louis N.L.	8.00
1988	Los Angeles N.L.	10.00
	Oakland A.L.	8.00
1989	Oakland A.L.	8.00
	San Francisco N.L.	8.00
1990	Cincinnati N.L.	8.00
	Oakland A.L.	8.00
1991	Atlanta N.L.	10.00
	Minnesota A.L.	10.00
1992	Atlanta N.L.	10.00
	Toronto A.L.	10.00

BASKETBALL TICKET STUBS

NBA ALL-STAR GAME

Year	Site	Value
1951	Boston	50.00
1952	Boston	35.00
1953	Fort Wayne	25.00
1954	New York	25.00
1955	New York	25.00
1956	Rochester	25.00
1957	Boston	25.00
1958	St. Louis	25.00
1959	Detroit	25.00
1960	Philadelphia	25.00
1961	Syracuse	20.00
1962	St. Louis	20.00
1963	los Angeles	20.00
1964	Boston	20.00
1965	St. Louis	20.00
1966	Cincinnati	20.00
1967	San Francisco	15.00
1968	New York	15.00
1969	Baltimore	20.00
1970	Philadelphia	10.00
1971	San Diego	10.00
1972	Los Angeles	8.00
1973	Chicago	8.00
1974	Seattle	8.00
1975	Phoenix	8.00
1976	Philadelphia	8.00
1977	Milwaukee	8.00
1978	Atlanta	8.00
1979	Detroit	8.00
1980	Washington	15.00
1981	Cleveland	8.00
1982	New Jersey	8.00
1983	Los Angeles	8.00
1984	Denver	8.00
1985	Indiana	8.00
1986	Dallas	8.00
1987	Seattle	8.00
1988	Chicago	8.00
1989	Houston	8.00
1990	Miami	8.00
1991	Charlotte	8.00
1992	Orlando	8.00

NCAA DIVISION I FINAL FOUR STUBS

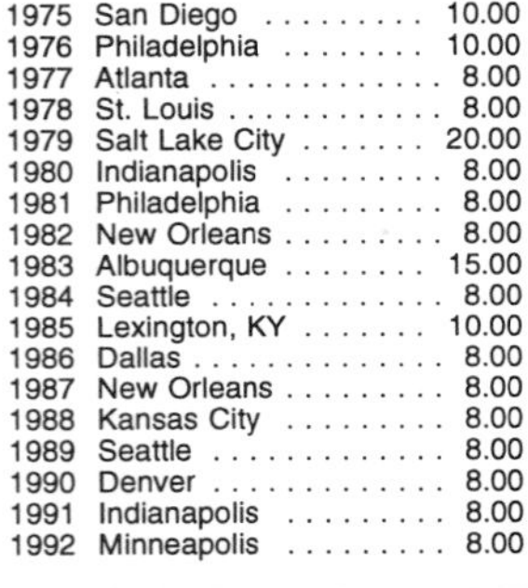

Year	Site	Value
1952	Seattle	75.00
1953	Kansas City	50.00
1954	Kansas City	25.00
1955	Kansas City	50.00
1956	Evanston, IL	50.00
1957	Kansas City	25.00
1958	Louisville	20.00
1959	Louisville	20.00
1960	San Francisco	15.00
1961	Kansas City	15.00
1962	Louisville	15.00
1963	Louisville	15.00
1964	Kansas City	20.00
1965	Portland	20.00
1966	College Park, MD	15.00
1967	Louisville	15.00
1968	Los Angeles	15.00
1969	Louisville	20.00
1970	College Park, MD	20.00
1971	Houston	15.00
1972	Los Angeles	15.00
1973	St. Louis	15.00
1974	Greensboro, NC	10.00
1975	San Diego	10.00
1976	Philadelphia	10.00
1977	Atlanta	8.00
1978	St. Louis	8.00
1979	Salt Lake City	20.00
1980	Indianapolis	8.00
1981	Philadelphia	8.00
1982	New Orleans	8.00
1983	Albuquerque	15.00
1984	Seattle	8.00
1985	Lexington, KY	10.00
1986	Dallas	8.00
1987	New Orleans	8.00
1988	Kansas City	8.00
1989	Seattle	8.00
1990	Denver	8.00
1991	Indianapolis	8.00
1992	Minneapolis	8.00

BOXING TICKET STUBS

HEAVYWEIGHT BOUTS

Date	Bout	Value
09/07/92	Corbett/Sullivan	1,000.00
01/25/94	Corbett/Mitchell	500.00
03/17/97	Fitzsimmons/Corbett	600.00
06/09/99	Jeffries/Fitzsimmons	750.00
11/03/99	Jeffries/Sharkey	600.00
04/06/00	Jeffries/Finnegan	500.00
05/11/00	Jeffries/Corbett	650.00
11/15/01	Jeffries/Ruhlin	450.00
07/25/02	Jeffries/Fitzsimmons	500.00
08/14/03	Jeffries/Corbett	600.00
08/25/04	Jeffries/Munroe	400.00
10/02/06	Burns/Flynn	300.00
11/28/06	Burns/O'Brien	300.00
05/08/07	Burns/O'Brien	300.00
12/26/08	Johnson/Burns	600.00
03/10/09	Johnson/McLaglen	400.00
05/19/09	Johnson/O'Brien	400.00
06/30/09	Johnson/Ross	400.00
09/09/09	Johnson/Kaufman	300.00
10/16/09	Johnson/Ketchel	400.00
07/04/10	Johnson/Jeffries	450.00
07/04/12	Johnson/Flynn	250.00
12/19/13	Johnson/Jm. Johnson	200.00
06/27/14	Johnson/Moran	250.00
04/05/15	Willard/Johnson	250.00
03/25/16	Willard/Moran	200.00
07/04/19	Dempsey/Willard	500.00
09/06/20	Dempsey/Miske	350.00
12/14/20	Dempsey/Brennan	350.00
07/02/21	Dempsey/Carpentier	400.00
07/04/23	Dempsey/Gibbons	450.00
09/14/23	Dempsey/Firpo	300.00
09/23/26	Tunney/Dempsey	450.00
07/21/27	Dempsey/Sharkey	300.00
09/22/27	Tunney/Dempsey	400.00
07/26/28	Tunney/Heeney	150.00
06/12/30	Schmeling/Sharkey	125.00
07/03/31	Schmeling/Stribling	100.00
06/21/32	Sharkey/Schmeling	100.00
09/26/32	Schmeling/Walker	125.00
06/25/35	Louis/Carnera	250.00
09/24/35	Louis/M. Baer	200.00
06/19/36	Schmeling/Louis	250.00
08/18/36	Louis/Sharkey	200.00
06/22/37	Louis/Braddock	175.00
06/22/38	Louis/Schmeling	225.00
07/13/39	Conn/Bettina	125.00
09/25/39	Conn/Bettina	100.00
11/17/39	Conn/Lesnevich	100.00
06/05/40	Conn/Lesnevich	100.00
05/23/41	Louis/B. Baer	200.00
06/18/41	Louis/Conn	200.00
01/09/42	Louis/B. Baer	200.00
06/19/46	Louis/Conn	175.00
12/05/47	Louis/Walcott	150.00
06/25/48	Louis/Walcott	150.00
06/22/49	Charles/Walcott	75.00
09/27/50	Charles/Louis	100.00
03/07/51	Charles/Walcott	50.00
07/18/51	Walcott/Charles	50.00
10/26/51	Marciano/Louis	150.00
06/05/52	Walcott/Charles	50.00
09/23/52	Marciano/Walcott	100.00
05/15/53	Marciano/Walcott	100.00
06/17/54	Marciano/Charles	100.00
09/17/54	Marciano/Charles	100.00
05/16/55	Marciano/Cockell	100.00
09/21/55	Marciano/Moore	100.00
11/30/56	Patterson/Moore	100.00
06/26/59	Johansson/Patterson	80.00
06/20/60	Patterson/Johansson	75.00

1978, 1958, 1930 and 1976 World Series

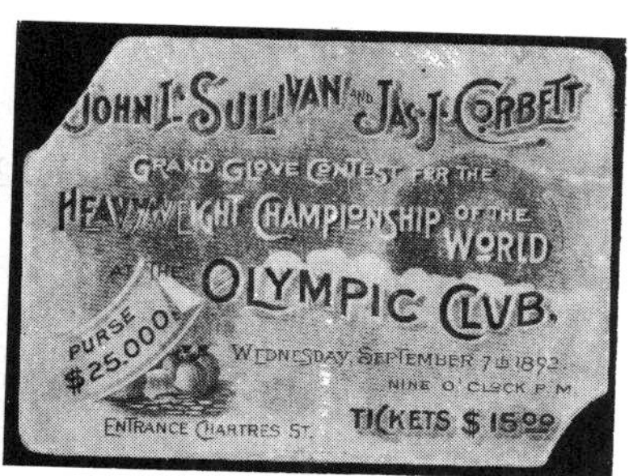

Flynn vs. Jackson (1912), Sullivan vs. Corbett (1892), La Motta vs. Graziano (1950), Ali vs. Norton (1976)

03/13/61 Patterson/Johansson 75.00
09/25/62 Liston/Patterson . . . 80.00
11/15/62 Clay/Moore 250.00
07/22/63 Liston/Patterson . . 125.00
02/25/64 Clay/Liston 200.00
05/25/65 Ali/Liston 100.00
11/22/65 Ali/Patterson 75.00
03/04/68 Frazier/Mathis 35.00
11/28/70 Frazier/Foster 50.00
03/08/71 Frazier/Ali 75.00
09/20/72 Ali/Patterson 65.00
11/21/72 Ali/Foster 50.00
01/22/73 Foreman/Frazier . . . 65.00
03/31/73 Norton/Ali 60.00
09/01/73 Foreman/Roman . . . 40.00
09/10/73 Ali/Norton 50.00
01/28/74 Ali/Frazier 65.00
03/26/74 Foreman/Norton . . . 50.00
10/30/74 Ali/Foreman 45.00
10/01/75 Ali/Frazier 50.00
06/15/76 Foreman/Frazier . . . 40.00
09/28/76 Ali/Norton 35.00
09/29/77 Ali/Shavers 45.00
02/15/78 Spinks/Ali 45.00
06/09/78 Holmes/Norton 20.00
09/15/78 Ali/L. Spinks 40.00
10/02/80 Holmes/Ali 30.00
06/12/81 Holmes/L. Spinks . . 15.00
06/11/82 Holmes/Cooney 15.00
05/20/83 Holmes/Witherspoon 25.00
09/21/85 Spinks/Holmes 15.00
04/19/86 Spinks/Holmes 10.00
11/22/86 Tyson/Berbick 45.00
03/07/87 Tyson/B. Smith 30.00
05/30/87 Tyson/Thomas 25.00
05/30/87 Tucker/Douglas 25.00
08/01/87 Tyson/Tucker 30.00
10/16/87 Tyson/Biggs 20.00
01/22/88 Tyson/Holmes 25.00
03/20/88 Tyson/Tubbs 25.00
06/27/88 Tyson/M. Spinks . . . 25.00
02/25/89 Tyson/Bruno 30.00
07/21/89 Tyson/Williams 15.00
02/10/90 Douglas/Tyson 50.00
10/25/90 Holyfield/Douglas . . 15.00
03/18/91 Tyson/Ruddock 20.00
04/19/91 Holyfield/Foreman . . 15.00
06/28/91 Tyson/Ruddock 15.00
10/18/91 Mercer/Morrison 8.00
11/23/91 Holyfield/Cooper 8.00
02/07/92 Holmes/Mercer 8.00
05/15/92 Moorer/Cooper 8.00
06/19/92 Holyfield/Holmes 8.00
07/18/92 Bowe/Coetzer 10.00
10/31/92 Lewis/Ruddock 10.00
11/13/92 Bowe/Holyfield 10.00

LIGHT HEAVYWEIGHT BOUTS

01/13/22 Tunney/Levinsky . . 125.00
01/30/23 Greb/Loughran . . . 100.00
05/23/22 Greb/Tunney 100.00
02/23/23 Tunney/Greb 60.00
12/10/23 Tunney/Greb 60.00
07/24/24 Tunney/Carpentier . . 50.00
09/17/24 Tunney/Greb 50.00
01/07/25 Walker/McTigue . . . 40.00
03/27/25 Tunney/Greb 50.00
06/05/25 Tunney/Gibbons . . . 50.00
03/28/29 Loughran/Walker . . . 30.00
11/03/33 Rosenbloom/Walker 30.00
07/13/39 Conn/Bettina 25.00
09/25/39 Conn/Bettina 25.00
11/17/39 Conn/Lesnevich . . . 25.00
06/05/40 Conn/Lesnevich . . . 25.00
06/25/52 Maxim/Robinson . . . 25.00
12/17/52 A. Moore/Maxim . . . 25.00
06/24/53 A. Moore/Maxim . . . 20.00
01/27/54 A. Moore/Maxim . . . 20.00

MIDDLEWEIGHT BOUTS

10/16/09 J. Johnson/Ketchel 200.00
08/31/23 Greb/Wilson 65.00
07/02/25 Greb/Walker 65.00
10/02/42 Robinson/LaMotta . . 75.00
02/05/43 LaMotta/Robinson . . 50.00
02/26/43 Robinson/LaMotta . . 50.00
02/23/45 Robinson/LaMotta . . 50.00
09/26/45 Robinson/LaMotta . . 50.00
02/14/51 Robinson/LaMotta . . 50.00
07/10/51 Turpin/Robinson . . . 40.00
09/12/51 Robinson/Turpin . . . 35.00
03/13/52 Robinson/Olson . . . 30.00
04/16/52 Robinson/Graziano . 40.00
04/02/54 Olson/Gavilan 20.00
09/23/57 Basilio/Robinson . . . 25.00
03/25/58 Robinson/Basilio . . . 25.00
09/25/71 Monzon/Griffith 8.00
11/11/72 Monzon/Briscoe 8.00
06/02/73 Monzon/Griffith 8.00
02/09/74 Monzon/Napoles 8.00
09/27/80 Hagler/Minter 8.00
11/10/83 Hagler/Duran 10.00
03/18/85 Hagler/Hearns 10.00
06/11/86 Hearns/Duran 10.00
04/06/87 Leonard/Hagler 10.00
02/24/89 Duran/Barkley 8.00
12/07/89 Leonard/Duran 10.00

WELTERWEIGHT BOUTS

07/18/21 Walker/Britton 100.00
11/01/22 Walker/Britton 100.00
12/20/46 Robinson/T. Bell . . . 30.00
06/24/47 Robinson/Doyle 30.00
12/19/47 Robinson/Taylor . . . 25.00
02/27/48 Williams/Gavilan . . . 20.00
06/28/48 Robinson/Docusen . 25.00
09/23/48 Robinson/Gavilan . . 25.00
01/28/49 Gavilan/Williams . . . 20.00
04/01/49 Gavilan/Williams . . . 20.00
07/11/49 Robinson/Gavilan . . 25.00
09/18/53 Gavilan/Basilio 15.00
10/12/69 Napoles/Griffith 15.00
11/30/79 Leonard/Benitez . . . 10.00

03/31/80	Leonard/Green	10.00
06/20/80	Duran/Leonard	15.00
11/25/80	Leonard/Duran	15.00
03/28/81	Leonard/Bonds	9.00
09/16/81	Leonard/Hearns	10.00
02/15/82	Leonard/Finch	8.00
10/29/87	Hearns/Roldan	8.00
06/06/88	Hearns/Barkley	8.00
11/04/88	Hearns/Kinchen	8.00
06/12/89	Leonard/Hearns	10.00

LIGHTWEIGHT BOUTS

09/29/77	Arguello/Artis	10.00
06/20/81	Arguello/Watt	8.00
10/03/81	Arguello/Mancini	8.00

FEATHERWEIGHT BOUTS

10/29/48	Saddler/Pep	40.00
02/11/49	Pep/Saddler	25.00
09/08/50	Saddler/Pep	25.00
09/26/51	Saddler/Pep	25.00

COLLEGE FOOTBALL TICKET STUBS

ALL-AMERICAN BOWL

Hall-of-Fame Classic from 1977-84

All games played in December

1977	Maryland/Minnesota	8.00
1978	Texas A&M/Iowa St.	5.00
1979	Missouri/S. Carolina	5.00
1980	Arkansas/Tulane	4.00
1981	Mississippi St./Kansas	4.00
1982	Air Force/Vanderbilt	4.00
1983	W. Virginia/Kentucky	4.00
1984	Kentucky/Wisconsin	4.00
1985	Georgia Tech/Mich. St.	2.00
1986	Florida St./Indiana	2.00
1987	Virginia/BYU	2.00
1988	Florida/Illinois	2.00
1989	Texas Tech/Duke	2.00
1990	N.C. State/So. Miss.	2.00

ALOHA BOWL

All games played in December

1982	Washington/Maryland	6.00
1983	Penn St./Washington	4.00
1984	SMU/Notre Dame	4.00
1985	Alabama/USC	4.00
1986	Arizona/N. Carolina	2.00
1987	UCLA/Florida	2.00
1988	Washington St./Houston	2.00
1989	Michigan St./Hawaii	2.00
1990	Syracuse/Arizona	2.00
1991	Georgia Tech/Stanford	2.00

BLOCKBUSTER BOWL

All games played in December

1990	Florida St./Penn St.	5.00
1991	Alabama/Colorado	4.00

BLUEBONNET BOWL

All games played in December

1959	Clemson/TCU	15.00
1960	Alabama/Texas	10.00
1961	Kansas/Rice	10.00
1962	Missouri/Georgia Tech	8.00
1963	Baylor/LSU	8.00
1964	Tulsa/Mississippi	8.00
1965	Tennessee/Tulsa	8.00
1966	Texas/Mississippi	6.00
1967	Colorado/Miami, FL	6.00
1968	SMU/Oklahoma	6.00
1969	Houston/Auburn	6.00
1970	Alabama/Oklahoma	5.00
1971	Colorado/Houston	5.00
1972	Tennessee/LSU	5.00
1973	Houston/Tulane	5.00
1974	Houston/N.C. State	5.00
1975	Texas/Colorado	5.00
1976	Nebraska/Texas Tech	5.00
1977	USC/Texas A&M	5.00
1978	Stanford/Georgia	4.00
1979	Purdue/Tennessee	4.00
1980	N. Carolina/Texas	4.00
1981	Michigan/UCLA	4.00
1982	Arkansas/Florida	4.00
1983	Okahoma St./Baylor	4.00
1984	W. Virginia/TCU	2.00
1985	Air Force/Texas	2.00
1986	Baylor/Colorado	2.00
1987	Texas/Pittsburgh	2.00

CALIFORNIA BOWL

All games played in December

1981	Toledo/San Jose St.	6.00
1982	Fresno St./Bowl. Green	4.00
1983	N. Illinois/Cal St. Full.	4.00
1984	UNLV/Toledo	4.00
1985	Fresno St./Bowl. Green	4.00
1986	San Jose St./Miami, OH	2.00
1987	E. Michigan/San Jose St.	2.00
1988	Fresno St./W. Michigan	2.00
1989	Fresno St./Ball St.	2.00
1990	San Jose St./Cent. Mich.	2.00
1991	Bowl. Green/Fresno St.	2.00

COPPER BOWL

All games played in December

1989	Arizona/N.C. State	5.00
1990	California/Wyoming	2.00
1991	Indiana/Baylor	2.00

COTTON BOWL

Games played in January, except for December games indicated by an "*"

1937	TCU/Marquette	100.00
1938	Rice/Colorado	50.00
1939	St. Mary's/Texas Tech	50.00
1940	Clemson/B.C.	25.00
1941	Texas A&M/Fordham	25.00
1942	Alabama/Texas A&M	20.00
1943	Texas/Georgia Tech	20.00
1944	Randolph Field/Texas	20.00
1945	Oklahoma A&M/TCU	15.00
1946	Texas/Missouri	15.00
1947	Arkansas/LSU	15.00
1948	Penn St./SMU	15.00
1949	SMU/Oregon	15.00
1950	Rice/N. Carolina	10.00
1951	Tennessee/Texas	10.00
1952	Kentucky/TCU	10.00
1953	Texas/Tennessee	10.00
1954	Rice/Alabama	10.00
1955	Georgia Tech/Arkansas	10.00
1956	Mississippi/TCU	10.00
1957	TCU/Syracuse	10.00
1958	Navy/Rice	10.00
1959	Air Force/TCU	10.00
1960	Syracuse/Texas	8.00
1961	Duke/Arkansas	8.00
1962	Texas/Mississippi	8.00
1963	LSU/Texas	8.00
1964	Texas/Navy	8.00
1965	Arkansas/Nebraska	8.00
1966	LSU/Arkansas	8.00
*1966	Georgia/SMU	5.00
1968	Texas A&M/Alabama	6.00
1969	Texas/Tennessee	6.00
1970	Texas/Notre Dame	8.00
1971	Notre Dame/Texas	6.00
1972	Penn St/Texas	5.00
1973	Texas/Alabama	5.00
1974	Nebraska/Texas	5.00
1975	Penn St./Baylor	5.00
1976	Arkansas/Georgia	4.00
1977	Houston/Maryland	4.00
1978	Notre Dame/Texas	5.00
1979	Notre Dame/Houston	5.00
1980	Houston/Nebraska	4.00
1981	Alabama/Baylor	4.00
1982	Texas/Alabama	4.00
1983	SMU/Pittsburgh	2.00
1984	Georgia/Texas	2.00
1985	Boston College/Houston	2.00
1986	Texas A&M/Auburn	2.00
1987	Ohio St./Texas A&M	2.00
1988	Texas A&M/Notre Dame	4.00
1989	UCLA/Arkansas	2.00
1990	Tennessee/Arkansas	2.00
1991	Miami, FL/Texas	2.00
1992	Florida St./Texas A&M	2.00

FIESTA BOWL

Games played in January, except for December games indicated by an "*"

*1971	Arizona St./Florida St.	10.00
*1972	Arizona St./Missouri	8.00
*1973	Arizona St./Pitt.	5.00
*1974	Oklahoma St./BYU	5.00
*1975	Arizona St./Nebraska	5.00
*1976	Oklahoma/Wyoming	5.00
*1977	Penn St./Arizona St.	5.00
*1978	Arkansas/UCLA	5.00
*1979	Pittsburgh/Arizona	4.00
*1980	Penn St./Ohio St.	5.00
1982	Penn St./USC	5.0
1983	Arizona St./Oklahoma	4.0
1984	Ohio St./Pittsburgh	4.0
1985	UCLA/Miami, FL	5.0
1986	Michigan/Nebraska	4.0
1987	Penn St./Miami, FL	5.0
1988	Florida St./Nebraska	4.0
1989	Notre Dame/W. Virginia	5.0
1990	Florida St./Nebraska	4.0
1991	Louisville/Alabama	2.0
1992	Penn St./Tennessee	2.0

FLORIDA CITRUS BOWL

Tangerine Bowl from 1947-82

Games played in January, except fo December games indicated by an "

1947	Catawba/Maryville	20.0
1948	Catawba/Marshall	15.0
1949	Murray St./S. Ross St.	10.0
1950	St. Vin./Emory & Henry	10.0
1951	M. Harvey/E. & Henry	10.0
1952	Stetson/Arkansas St.	10.0
1953	E. Texas St./Tenn. Tech	10.0
1954	Arkansas St./E. Tex. St.	10.0
1955	Neb.-Omaha/E. Kentucky	10.0
1956	Juniata/Missouri Valley	10.0
1957	W. Texas St./So. Miss	10.0
1958	E. Texas St./So. Miss	8.
*1958	E. Texas St./Miss. Valley	8.
1960	Mid. Tenn. St./Presb.	8.
*1960	Citadel/Tennessee Tech	8.
*1961	Lamar/Mid. Tenn. St.	8.
*1962	Houston/Miami, OH	8.
*1963	W. Ken./Coast Guard	8.
*1964	E. Carolina/Mass.	8
*1965	E. Carolina/Maine	6
*1966	Morgan St./Westchester	6
*1967	Tenn.-Martin/West.	6
*1968	Richmond/Ohio U.	6
*1969	Toledo/Davidson	6
*1970	Toledo/William & Mary	6
*1971	Toledo/Richmond	6
*1972	Tampa/Kent St.	5

*1973 Miami, OH/Florida 5.00
*1974 Miami, OH/Georgia 5.00
*1975 Miami, OH/S. Carolina . 5.00
*1976 Oklahoma/BYU 5.00
*1977 Florida St./Texas Tech . 5.00
*1978 N.C. State/Pittsburgh .. 4.00
*1979 LSU/Wake Forest 4.00
*1980 Florida/Maryland 4.00
*1981 Missouri/So. Mississippi 4.00
*1982 Auburn/Boston College . 4.00
*1983 Tennessee/Maryland ... 2.00
*1984 Florida St./Georgia 4.00
*1985 Ohio St./BYU 2.00
1987 Auburn/USC 2.00
1988 Clemson/Penn St. 2.00
1989 Clemson/Oklahoma ... 2.00
1990 Illinois/Virginia 2.00
1991 Geo. Tech/Nebraska ... 2.00
1992 California/Clemson 2.00

FREEDOM BOWL

All games played in December

1984 Iowa/Texas 6.00
1985 Washington/Colorado .. 5.00
1986 UCLA/BYU 2.00
1987 Arizona St./Air Force ... 2.00
1988 BYU/Colorado 2.00
1989 Washington/Florida 2.00
1990 Colorado St./Oregon ... 2.00
1991 Tulsa/San Diego St. ... 2.00

GATOR BOWL

Games played in January, except for December games indicated by an "*"

1946 Wake Forest/S.Carolina 20.00
1947 Oklahoma/N.C. State . 15.00
1948 Georgia/Maryland 15.00
1949 Clemson/Missouri 10.00
1950 Maryland/Missouri 10.00
1951 Wyoming/W & L 15.00
1952 Miami, FL/Clemson ... 15.00
1953 Florida/Tulsa 10.00
1954 Texas Tech/Auburn .. 10.00
*1954 Auburn/Baylor 10.00
*1955 Vanderbilt/Auburn 8.00
*1956 Georgia Tech/Pitt. 8.00
*1957 Tennessee/Texas A&M . 8.00
*1958 Mississippi/Florida 8.00
1960 Arkansas/Georgia Tech . 8.00
*1960 Florida/Baylor 8.00
*1961 Penn St./Georgia Tech . 8.00
*1962 Florida/Penn St. 8.00
*1963 N. Carolina/Air Force .. 8.00
1965 Florida St./Oklahoma .. 8.00
*1965 Geo. Tech/Tex. Tech .. 8.00
*1966 Tennessee/Syracuse .. 8.00
*1967 Florida St./Penn St. ... 8.00
*1968 Missouri/Alabama 6.00
*1969 Florida/Tennessee 6.00
1971 Auburn/Mississippi 6.00
*1971 Georgia/N. Carolina ... 6.00
*1972 Auburn/Colorado 5.00
*1973 Texas Tech/Tenn. 5.00
*1974 Auburn/Texas 5.00
*1975 Maryland/Florida 5.00
*1976 Notre Dame/Penn St. .. 5.00
*1977 Pittsburgh/Clemson 4.00
*1978 Clemson/Ohio St. 4.00
*1979 N. Carolina/Michigan ... 4.00
*1980 Pittsburgh/S. Carolina .. 4.00
*1981 N. Carolina/Arkansas .. 4.00
*1982 Florida St./W. Virginia .. 4.00
*1983 Florida/Iowa 2.00
*1984 Okla. St./S. Carolina ... 2.00
*1985 Florida St./Okla. St. ... 2.00
*1986 Clemson/Stanford 2.00
*1987 LSU/S. Carolina 2.00
1989 Georgia/Michigan St. .. 2.00
1990 Clemson/W. Virginia ... 2.00
1991 Michigan/Mississippi ... 2.00
*1991 Oklahoma/Virginia 2.00

HALL-OF-FAME BOWL

Games played in January, except for December games indicated by an "*"

*1986 Boston Col./Georgia ... 5.00
1988 Michigan/Alabama 4.00
1989 Syracuse/LSU 4.00
1990 Auburn/Ohio St. 2.00
1991 Clemson/Illinois 2.00
1992 Syracuse/Ohio St. 2.00

HOLIDAY BOWL

All games played in December

1978 Navy/BYU 8.00
1979 Indiana/BYU 5.00
1980 BYU/SMU 5.00
1981 BYU/Washington St. ... 5.00
1982 Ohio St./BYU 5.00
1983 BYU/Missouri 4.00
1984 BYU/Michigan 4.00
1985 Arkansas/Arizona St. .. 4.00
1986 Iowa/San Diego St. 4.00
1987 Iowa/Wyoming 2.00
1988 Oklahoma St./Wyoming . 2.00
1989 Penn St./BYU 2.00
1990 Texas A&M/BYU 2.00
1991 Iowa/BYU 2.00

INDEPENDENCE BOWL

All games played in December

1976 McNeese St./Tulsa 6.00
1977 La. Tech/Louisville 4.00
1978 E. Carolina/La. Tech ... 4.00
1979 Syracuse/McNeese St. . 4.00
1980 So. Miss./McNeese St. . 4.00
1981 Texas A&M/Okla. St. .. 4.00
1982 Wisconsin/Kansas St. .. 4.00
1983 Air Force/Mississippi ... 2.00
1984 Air Force/Va. Tech 2.00
1985 Minnesota/Clemson 2.00
1986 Mississippi/Tex. Tech .. 2.00
1987 Washington/Tulane 2.00
1988 So. Miss./UTEP 2.00
1989 Oregon/Tulsa 2.00
1990 La. Tech/Maryland 2.00
1991 Georgia/Arkansas 2.00

JOHN HANCOCK BOWL

Known as Sun Bowl from 1936-86

Games played in December, except for January games indicated by an "*"

*1936 Hardin-Sim./N.Mex. St. 40.00
*1937 Hardin-Sim./Tex. Mines 30.00
*1938 W. Virginia/Texas Tech 25.00
*1939 Utah/New Mexico 20.00
*1940 Arizona St./Catholic U. 15.00
*1941 W. Reserve/Arizona St. 15.00
*1942 Tulsa/Texas Tech 15.00
*1943 Air Force/Hardin-Sim. . 15.00
*1944 SW Texas/New Mexico 15.00
*1945 SW Texas/New Mexico 10.00
*1946 New Mexico/Denver .. 10.00
*1947 Cincinnati/Virg. Tech .. 10.00
*1948 Miami, OH/Texas Tech 10.00
*1949 W. Virginia/Tex. Mines 10.00
*1950 Tex.Western/Georgetown 8.00
*1951 West Texas/Cincinnati . 8.00
*1952 Texas Tech/Pacific 8.00
*1953 Pacific/So. Miss. 8.00
*1954 Tex. Western/So. Miss. . 8.00
*1955 Tex. Western/Florida St. 8.00
*1956 Wyoming/Texas Tech .. 8.00
*1957 G. Wash./Tex.Western . 8.00
*1958 Louisville/Drake 6.00
1958 Wyoming/Hard.-Simmons 6.00
1959 New Mex. St./N. Texas . 6.00
1960 New Mex. St./Utah St. . 6.00
1961 Villanova/Wichita 6.00
1962 West Texas/Ohio U. ... 6.00
1963 Oregon/SMU 6.00
1964 Georgia/Georgia Tech .. 6.00
1965 Texas Western/TCU .. 6.00
1966 Wyoming/Florida St. ... 6.00
1967 UTEP/Mississippi 5.00
1968 Auburn/Arizona 6.00
1969 Nebraska/Georgia 6.00
1970 Ga. Tech/Texas Tech .. 5.00
1971 LSU/Iowa St. 5.00
1972 N. Carolina/Texas Tech 5.00
1973 Missouri/Auburn 5.00
1974 Miss. St./N. Carolina ... 4.00
1975 Pittsburgh/Kansas 4.00
*1977 Texas A&M/Florida 4.00
1977 Stanford/LSU 4.00
1978 Texas/Maryland 4.00
1979 Washington/Texas 4.00
1980 Nebraska/Miss. St. 4.00
1981 Oklahoma/Houston 4.00
1982 N. Carolina/Texas 2.00
1983 Alabama/SMU 2.00
1984 Maryland/Tennessee ... 2.00
1985 Arizona/Georgia 2.00
1986 Alabama/Washington .. 2.00
1987 Okla. St./W. Virginia ... 2.00
1988 Alabama/Army 2.00

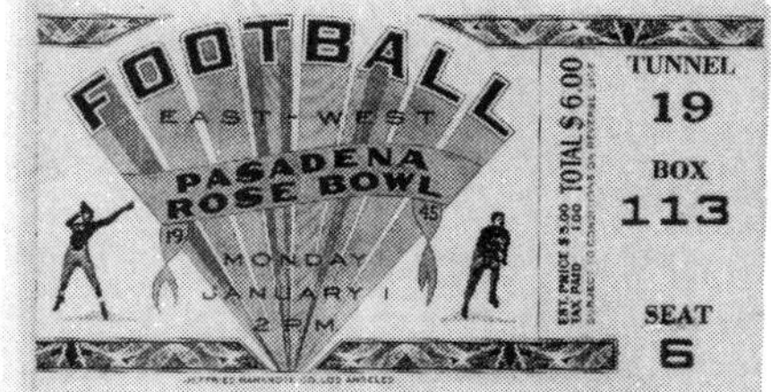

Rose Bowl (1945), Orange Bowl (1952)

Year	Game	Price
1989	Pittsburgh/Texas A&M	2.00
1990	Michigan St./USC	2.00
1991	UCLA/Illinois	2.00

LIBERTY BOWL

All games played in December

Year	Game	Price
1959	Penn St./Alabama	25.00
1960	Penn St./ Oregon	15.00
1961	Syracuse/Miami, FL.	20.00
1962	Oregon St./Villanova	15.00
1963	Miss. St./N.C. State	15.00
1964	Utah/W. Virginia	10.00
1965	Mississippi/Auburn	10.00
1966	Miami, FL/Va. Tech	10.00
1967	N.C. State/Georgia	8.00
1968	Mississippi/Va. Tech	8.00
1969	Colorado/Alabama	8.00
1970	Tulane/Colorado	8.00
1971	Tennessee/Arkansas	6.00
1972	Geo. Tech/Iowa St.	6.00
1973	N.C. State/Kansas	6.00
1974	Tennessee/Maryland	5.00
1975	USC/Texas A&M	5.00
1976	Alabama/UCLA	5.00
1977	Nebraska/N. Carolina	5.00
1978	Missouri/LSU	4.00
1979	Penn St./Tulane	4.00
1980	Purdue/Missouri	4.00
1981	Ohio St./Navy	4.00
1982	Alabama/Illinois	2.00
1983	N. Dame/Boston Col.	4.00
1984	Auburn/Arkansas	2.00
1985	Baylor/LSU	2.00
1986	Tennessee/Minnesota	2.00
1987	Georgia/Arkansas	2.00
1988	Indiana/S. Carolina	2.00
1989	Mississippi/Air Force	2.00
1990	Air Force/Ohio St.	2.00
1991	Air Force/Miss. St.	2.00

ORANGE BOWL

All games played in January

Year	Game	Price
1935	Bucknell/Miami, FL	125.00
1936	Catholic/Mississippi	75.00
1937	Duquesne/Miss. St.	50.00
1938	Auburn/Michigan St.	50.00
1939	Tennessee/Oklahoma	25.00
1940	Georgia Tech/Missouri	25.00
1941	Miss. St./Georgetown	25.00
1942	Georgia/TCU	20.00
1943	Alabama/B.C.	20.00
1944	LSU/Texas A&M	20.00
1945	Tulsa/Georgia Tech	20.00
1946	Miami, FL/Holy Cross	25.00
1947	Rice/Tennessee	15.00
1948	Georgia Tech/Kansas	15.00
1949	Texas/Georgia	15.00
1950	Santa Clara/Kentucky	15.00
1951	Clemson/Miami, FL	20.00
1952	Georgia Tech/Baylor	10.00
1953	Alabama/Syracuse	10.00
1954	Oklahoma/Maryland	10.00
1955	Duke/Nebraska	10.00
1956	Oklahoma/Maryland	12.00
1957	Colorado/Clemson	12.00
1958	Oklahoma/Duke	10.00
1959	Oklahoma/Syracuse	10.00
1960	Georgia/Missouri	8.00
1961	Missouri/Navy	8.00
1962	LSU/Colorado	8.00
1963	Alabama/Oklahoma	10.00
1964	Nebraska/Auburn	8.00
1965	Texas/Alabama	8.00
1966	Alabama/Nebraska	8.00
1967	Florida/Georgia Tech	8.00
1968	Oklahoma/Tennessee	8.00
1969	Penn St./Kansas	6.00
1970	Penn St./Missouri	6.00
1971	Nebraska/LSU	6.00
1972	Nebraska/Alabama	6.00
1973	Nebraska/Notre Dame	10.00
1974	Penn St./LSU	5.00
1975	Notre Dame/Alabama	8.00
1976	Oklahoma/Michigan	5.00
1977	Ohio St./Colorado	4.00
1978	Arkansas/Oklahoma	4.00
1979	Oklahoma/Nebraska	4.00
1980	Oklahoma/Florida St.	4.00
1981	Oklahoma/Florida St.	4.00
1982	Clemson/Nebraska	2.00
1983	Nebraska/LSU	2.00
1984	Miami, FL/Nebraska	4.00
1985	Washington/Oklahoma	2.00
1986	Oklahoma/Penn St.	2.00
1987	Oklahoma/Arkansas	2.00
1988	Miami, FL/Oklahoma	4.00
1989	Miami, FL/Nebraska	4.00
1990	Notre Dame/Colorado	4.00
1991	Colorado/Notre Dame	4.00
1992	Miami, FL/Nebraska	2.00

PEACH BOWL

Games played in December, except for January games indicated by an "*"

Year	Game	Price
1968	LSU/Florida St.	20.00
1969	W. Virginia/S. Carolina	10.00
1970	Ariz. St./N. Carolina	6.00
1971	Mississippi/Geo. Tech	6.00
1972	N.C. State/W. Virginia	6.00
1973	Georgia/Maryland	6.00
1974	Texas Tech/Vanderbilt	5.00
1975	W. Virginia/N.C. State	5.00
1976	Kentucky/N. Carolina	5.00
1977	N.C. State/Iowa St.	5.00
1978	Purdue/Georgia Tech	4.00
1979	Baylor/Clemson	4.00
*1981	Miami, FL/Virginia Tech	6.00
1981	W. Virginia/Florida	4.00
1982	Iowa/Tennessee	4.00
1983	Florida St./N. Carolina	4.00
1984	Virginia/Purdue	2.00
1985	Army/Illinois	2.00
1986	Virginia Tech/N.C. St.	2.00
*1988	Tennessee/Indiana	2.00
1988	N.C. State/Iowa	2.00
1989	Syracuse/Georgia	2.00
1990	Auburn/Indiana	2.00
*1992	E. Carolina/N.C. State	2.00

ROSE BOWL

All games played in January

Year	Game	Price
1902	Michigan/Stanford	1,500.00
1916	Washington St./Brown	500.00
1917	Oregon/Penn	350.00
1918	Mare Island/Camp Lewis	350.00
1919	Grt. Lakes/Mare Island	300.00
1920	Harvard/Oregon	250.00
1921	California/Ohio St.	250.00
1922	Cal./Wash. & Jeff.	200.00
1923	USC/Penn St.	250.00
1924	Navy/Washington	150.00
1925	Notre Dame/Stanford	200.00
1926	Alabama/Washington	150.00
1927	Alabama/Stanford	150.00
1928	Stanford/Pittsburgh	150.00
1929	Georgia Tech/Cal.	100.00
1930	USC/Pittsburgh	100.00
1931	Alabama/Washington St.	75.00
1932	USC/Tulane.	50.00
1933	USC/Pittsburgh	60.00
1934	Columbia/Stanford	40.00
1935	Alabama/Stanford	40.00
1936	Stanford/SMU	35.00
1937	Pitt./Washington	30.00
1938	California/Alabama	30.00
1939	USC/Duke	30.00
1940	USC/Tennessee	30.00
1941	Stanford/Nebraska	25.00
1942	Oregon St./Duke game played in Durham	150.00
1943	Georgia/UCLA	25.00
1944	USC/Washington	20.00
1945	USC/Tennessee	25.00
1946	Alabama/USC	20.00
1947	Illinois/UCLA	20.00
1948	Michigan/USC	25.00
1949	Northwestern/Cal.	20.00
1950	Ohio St./Cal.	20.00
1951	Michigan/Cal.	20.00
1952	Illinois/Stanford	15.00
1953	USC/Wisconsin	15.00
1954	Michigan St./UCLA	15.00
1955	Ohio St./USC	15.00
1956	Michigan St./UCLA	12.00
1957	Iowa/Oregon St.	12.00
1958	Ohio St./Oregon	12.00
1959	Iowa/California	12.00
1960	Washington/Wisconsin	12.00
1961	Washington/Minnesota	12.00
1962	Minnesota/UCLA	10.00
1963	USC/Wisconsin	10.00
1964	Illinois/Washington	10.00
1965	Michigan/Oregon St.	12.00
1966	UCLA/Michigan St.	10.00
1967	Purdue/USC	10.00
1968	USC/Indiana	8.00
1969	Ohio St./USC	8.00
1970	USC/Michigan	10.00
1971	Stanford/Ohio St.	8.00
1972	Stanford/Michigan	10.00
1973	USC/Ohio St.	5.00
1974	Ohio St./USC	5.00
1975	USC/Ohio St.	5.00
1976	UCLA/Ohio St.	5.00
1977	USC/Michigan	6.00
1978	Washington/Michigan	5.00
1979	USC/Michigan	5.00
1980	USC/Ohio St.	4.00
1981	Michigan/Washington	4.00
1982	Washington/Iowa	2.00
1983	UCLA/Michigan	4.00
1984	UCLA/Illinois	2.00
1985	USC/Ohio St.	2.00
1986	UCLA/Iowa	2.00
1987	Arizona St./Michigan	2.00
1988	Michigan St./USC	2.00
1989	Michigan/USC	2.00
1990	USC/Michigan	2.00
1991	Washington/Iowa	2.00
1992	Washington/Michigan	2.00

SUGAR BOWL

Games played in January, except for December games indicated by an "*"

Year	Game	Price
1935	Tulane/Temple	125.00
1936	TCU/LSU	65.00
1937	Santa Clara/LSU	50.00
1938	Santa Clara/LSU	50.00
1939	TCU/Carnegie Tech	40.00
1940	Texas A&M/Tulane	40.00
1941	B.C./Tennessee	30.00
1942	Fordham/Missouri	25.00
1943	Tennessee/Tulsa	25.00
1944	Georgia Tech/Tulsa	15.00
1945	Duke/Alabama	25.00
1946	Okla. A&M/St. Mary's	15.00
1947	Georgia/N. Carolina	15.00
1948	Texas/Alabama	20.00
1949	Oklahoma/N. Carolina	15.00
1950	Oklahoma/LSU	15.00
1951	Kentucky/Oklahoma	10.00
1952	Maryland/Tennessee	10.00
1953	Georgia Tech/Miss.	10.00
1954	Geo. Tech/W. Virginia	10.00
1955	Navy/Mississippi	10.00
1956	Geo. Tech/Pittsburgh	8.00
1957	Baylor/Tennessee	8.00

1958	Mississippi/Texas	8.00
1959	LSU/Clemson	8.00
1960	Mississippi/LSU	8.00
1961	Mississippi/Rice	8.00
1962	Alabama/Arkansas	12.00
1963	Mississippi/Arkansas	8.00
1964	Alabama/Mississippi	10.00
1965	LSU/Syracuse	8.00
1966	Missouri/Florida	8.00
1967	Alabama/Nebraska	12.00
1968	LSU/Wyoming	6.00
1969	Arkansas/Georgia	6.00
1970	Mississippi/Arkansas	6.00
1971	Tennessee/Air Force	6.00
1972	Oklahoma/Auburn	6.00
*1972	Oklahoma/Penn St.	6.00
*1973	Notre Dame/Alabama	10.00
*1974	Nebraska/Florida	6.00
*1975	Alabama/Penn St.	6.00
1977	Pittsburgh/Georgia	5.00
1978	Alabama/Ohio St.	6.00
1979	Alabama/Penn St.	6.00
1980	Alabama/Arkansas	6.00
1981	Georgia/Notre Dame	8.00
1982	Pittsburgh/Georgia	4.00
1983	Penn St./Georgia	4.00
1984	Auburn/Michigan	4.00
1985	Nebraska/LSU	4.00
1986	Tennessee/Miami, FL	5.00
1987	Nebraska/LSU	4.00
1988	Auburn/Syracuse	4.00
1989	Florida St./Auburn	4.00
1990	Miami, FL/Alabama	4.00
1991	Tennessee/Virginia	2.00
1992	Notre Dame/Florida	4.00

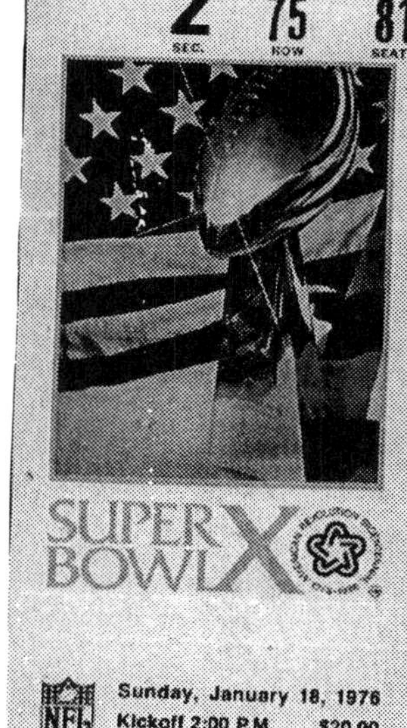

Super Bowl X

PRO FOOTBALL TICKET STUBS

CHAMPIONSHIP GAMES

1933	NFL Championship	250.00
1934	NFL Championship	200.00
1935	NFL Championship	200.00
1936	NFL Championship	200.00
1937	NFL Championship	200.00
1938	NFL Championship	175.00
1939	NFL Championship	175.00
1940	NFL Championship	250.00
1941	NFL Championship	150.00
1942	NFL Championship	150.00
1943	NFL Championship	150.00
1944	NFL Championship	150.00
1945	NFL Championship	150.00
1946	NFL Championship	125.00
1947	NFL Championship	100.00
1948	NFL Championship	100.00
1949	NFL Championship	100.00
1950	NFL Championship	80.00
1951	NFL Championship	80.00
1952	NFL Championship	80.00
1953	NFL Championship	75.00
1954	NFL Championship	75.00
1955	NFL Championship	65.00
1956	NFL Championship	65.00
1957	NFL Championship	65.00
1958	NFL Championship	60.00
1959	NFL Championship	60.00
1960	NFL Championship	50.00
	AFL Championship	75.00
1961	NFL Championship	50.00
	AFL Championship	60.00
1962	NFL Championship	40.00
	AFL Championship	50.00
1963	NFL Championship	35.00
	AFL Championship	40.00
1964	NFL Championship	35.00
	AFL Championship	30.00
1965	NFL Championship	20.00
	AFL Championship	20.00
1966	NFL Championship	15.00
	AFL Championship	10.00
	Super Bowl I	**150.00**
1967	NFL Championship	8.00
	AFL Championship	8.00
	Super Bowl II	**125.00**
1968	NFL Championship	8.00
	AFL Championship	8.00
	Super Bowl III	**85.00**
1969	NFL Championship	8.00
	AFL Championship	8.00
	Super Bowl IV	**75.00**
1970	AFC Championship	5.00
	NFC Championship	5.00
	Super Bowl V	**50.00**
1971	AFC Championship	5.00
	NFC Championship	5.00
	Super Bowl VI	**45.00**
1972	AFC Championship	5.00
	NFC Championship	5.00
	Super Bowl VII	**35.00**
1973	AFC Championship	5.00
	NFC Championship	5.00
	Super Bowl VIII	**30.00**
1974	AFC Championship	8.00
	NFC Championship	5.00
	Super Bowl IX	**25.00**
1975	AFC Championship	8.00
	NFC Championship	5.00
	Super Bowl X	**25.00**
1976	AFC Championship	6.00
	NFC Championship	5.00
	Super Bowl XI	**25.00**
1977	AFC Championship	5.00
	NFC Championship	5.00
	Super Bowl XII	**25.00**
1978	AFC Championship	5.00
	NFC Championship	5.00
	Super Bowl XIII	**20.00**
1979	AFC Championship	5.00
	NFC Championship	4.00
	Super Bowl XIV	**20.00**
1980	AFC Championship	3.00
	NFC Championship	4.00
	Super Bowl XV	**20.00**
1981	AFC Championship	4.00
	NFC Championship	5.00
	Super Bowl XVI	**20.00**
1982	AFC Championship	3.00
	NFC Championship	4.00
	Super Bowl XVII	**20.00**
1983	AFC Championship	3.00
	NFC Championship	4.00
	Super Bowl XVIII	**20.00**
1984	AFC Championship	3.00
	NFC Championship	3.00
	Super Bowl XIX	**20.00**
1985	AFC Championship	2.00
	NFC Championship	4.00
	Super Bowl XX	**15.00**
1986	AFC Championship	4.00
	NFC Championship	2.00
	Super Bowl XXI	**15.00**
1987	AFC Championship	4.00
	NFC Championship	2.00
	Super Bowl XXII	**15.00**
1988	AFC Championship	2.00
	NFC Championship	2.00
	Super Bowl XXIII	**15.00**
1989	AFC Championship	2.00
	NFC Championship	2.00
	Super Bowl XXIV	**15.00**
1990	AFC Championship	2.00
	NFC Championship	2.00
	Super Bowl XXV	**15.00**
1991	AFC Championship	2.00
	NFC Championship	2.00
	Super Bowl XXVI	**15.00**
1992	AFC Championship	2.00
	NFC Championship	2.00
	Super Bowl XXVII	**15.00**

PRO BOWL STUBS

1951	L.A. Coliseum	75.00
1952	L.A. Coliseum	40.00
1953	L.A. Coliseum	40.00
1954	L.A. Coliseum	25.00
1955	L.A. Coliseum	25.00
1956	L.A. Coliseum	25.00
1957	L.A. Coliseum	20.00
1958	L.A. Coliseum	15.00
1959	L.A. Coliseum	15.00
1960	L.A. Coliseum	15.00
1961	L.A. Coliseum	15.00
1962	L.A. Coliseum	15.00
1963	L.A. Coliseum	10.00
1964	L.A. Coliseum	10.00
1965	L.A. Coliseum	10.00
1966	L.A. Coliseum	10.00
1967	L.A. Coliseum	10.00
1968	L.A. Coliseum	10.00
1969	L.A. Coliseum	10.00
1970	L.A. Coliseum	6.00
1971	L.A. Coliseum	6.00
1972	L.A. Coliseum	6.00
1973	Texas Stadium	6.00
1974	Arrowhead Stadium	6.00
1975	Orange Bowl	6.00
1976	Superdome	6.00
1977	Kingdome	6.00
1978	Tampa Stadium	5.00
1979	L.A. Coliseum	5.00
1980	Aloha Stadium	4.00
1981	Aloha Stadium	4.00

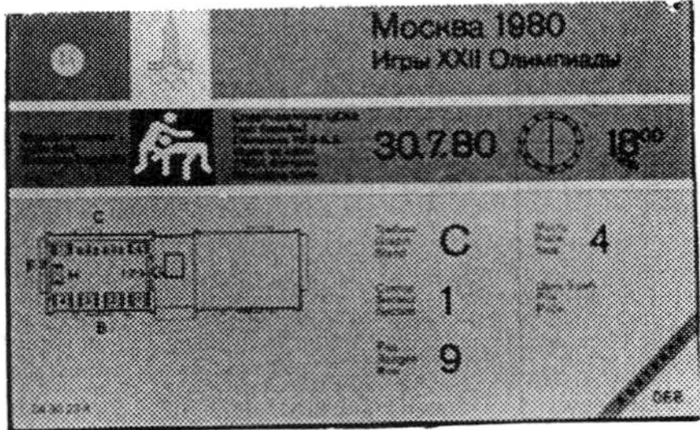

Olympics:Los Angeles (1932), Moscow (1980)

1982 thru 1992 Aloha	4.00

HOCKEY TICKET STUBS

NHL ALL-STAR GAME

Year	Site	Value
1947	Toronto	100.00
1948	Chicago	50.00
1949	Toronto	50.00
1950	Detroit	45.00
1951	Toronto	45.00
1952	Detroit	45.00
1953	Montreal	40.00
1954	Detroit	25.00
1955	Detroit	25.00
1956	Montreal	25.00
1957	Montreal	25.00
1958	Montreal	25.00
1959	Montreal	15.00
1960	Montreal	15.00
1961	Chicago	10.00
1962	Toronto	8.00
1963	Toronto	8.00
1964	Toronto	8.00
1965	Montreal	8.00
1966	Game moved to mid-season	
1967	Montreal	8.00
1968	Toronto	6.00
1969	Montreal	6.00
1970	St. Louis	5.00
1971	Boston	5.00
1972	Minnesota	5.00
1973	New York	5.00
1974	Chicago	5.00
1975	Montreal	5.00
1976	Philadelphia	4.00
1977	Vancouver	4.00
1978	Buffalo	4.00
1979	New York (Challenge Cup)	5.00
1980	Detroit	4.00
1981	Los Angeles	4.00
1982	Washington	4.00
1983	N.Y. Islanders	4.00
1984	New Jersey	4.00
1985	Calgary	4.00
1986	Hartford	4.00
1987	Quebec (Rendez-Vous'87)	5.00
1988	St. Louis	4.00
1989	Edmonton	4.00
1990	Pittsburgh	4.00
1991	Chicago	4.00
1992	Philadelphia	4.00

STANLEY CUP PLAYOFFS

Year	Champion/runner-up	Value
1930	Canadiens/Boston	200.00
1931	Canadiens/Chicago	150.00
1932	Toronto/N.Y. Rangers	100.00
1933	N.Y. Rangers/Toronto	150.00
1934	Chicago/Detroit	100.00
1935	Maroons/Toronto	75.00
1936	Detroit/Toronto	75.00
1937	Detroit/N.Y. Rangers	75.00
1938	Chicago/Toronto	75.00
1939	Boston/Toronto	75.00
1940	N.Y. Rangers/Toronto	100.00
1941	Boston/Detroit	75.00
1942	Toronto/Detroit	50.00
1943	Detroit/Boston	45.00
1944	Montreal/Chicago	45.00
1945	Toronto/Detroit	40.00
1946	Montreal/Boston	45.00
1947	Toronto/Montreal	40.00
1948	Toronto/Detroit	40.00
1949	Toronto/Detroit	35.00
1950	Detroit/N.Y. Rangers	35.00
1951	Toronto/Montreal	30.00
1952	Detroit/Montreal	30.00
1953	Montreal/Boston	30.00
1954	Detroit/Montreal	25.00
1955	Detroit/Montreal	25.00
1956	Montreal/Detroit	25.00
1957	Montreal/Boston	25.00
1958	Montreal/Boston	25.00
1959	Montreal/Toronto	20.00
1960	Montreal/Toronto	20.00
1961	Chicago/Detroit	15.00
1962	Toronto/Chicago	8.00
1963	Toronto/Detroit	8.00
1964	Toronto/Detroit	8.00
1965	Montreal/Chicago	10.00
1966	Montreal/Detroit	10.00
1967	Toronto/Montreal	10.00
1968	Montreal/St. Louis	8.00
1969	Montreal/St. Louis	8.00
1970	Boston/St. Louis	6.00
1971	Montreal/Chicago	6.00
1972	Boston/N.Y. Rangers	6.00
1973	Montreal/Chicago	5.00
1974	Philadelphia/Boston	5.00
1975	Philadelphia/Buffalo	5.00
1976	Montreal/Philadelphia	5.00
1977	Montreal/Boston	5.00
1978	Montreal/Boston	5.00
1979	Montreal/N.Y. Rangers	5.00
1980	Islanders/Philadelphia	6.00
1981	Islanders/Minnesota	5.00
1982	Islanders/Vancouver	5.00
1983	Islanders/Edmonton	8.00
1984	Edmonton/Islanders	5.00
1985	Edmonton/Philadelphia	5.00
1986	Montreal/Calgary	5.00
1987	Edmonton/Philadelphia	5.00
1988	Edmonton/Boston	5.00
1989	Calgary/Montreal	5.00
1990	Edmonton/Boston	5.00
1991	Pittsburgh/Minnesota	5.00
1992	Pittsburgh/Chicago	5.00

OLYMPIC TICKET STUBS

Olympic stub values are for common event stubs.

SUMMER OLYMPICS STUBS

Year	Site	Value
1900	Paris, France	150.00
1904	St. Louis, Missouri	100.00
1908	London, England	150.00
1912	Stockholm, Sweden	150.00
1920	Antwerp, Belgium	100.00
1924	Paris, France	80.00
1928	Amsterdam, Holland	40.00
1932	Los Angeles, California	40.00
1936	Berlin, Germany	40.00
1948	London, England	30.00
1952	Helsinki, Finland	20.00
1956	Melbourne, Australia	15.00
1956	Stockholm, Sweden	75.00
1960	Rome, Italy	20.00
1964	Tokyo, Japan	20.00
1968	Mexico City, Mexico	20.00
1972	Munich, Germany	10.00
1976	Montreal, Quebec	10.00
1980	Moscow, Soviet Union	10.00
1984	Los Angeles, California	5.00
1988	Seoul, South Korea	5.00
1992	Barcelona, Spain	2.00

WINTER OLYMPICS STUBS

Year	Site	Value
1932	Lake Placid, New York	50.00
1936	Garmisch-Partenkirchen, Germany	150.00
1948	St. Moritz, Switzerland	45.00
1952	Oslo, Norway	35.00
1956	Cortina d'Ampezzo, Italy	35.00
1960	Squaw Valley, California	25.00
1964	Innsbruck, Austria	25.00
1968	Grenoble, France	25.00
1972	Sapporo, Japan	25.00
1976	Innsbruck, Austria	15.00
1980	Lake Placid, New York	5.00
1984	Sarajevo, Yugoslavia	10.00
1988	Calgary, Alberta	5.00
1992	Albertville, France	2.00

TEAM PUBLICATIONS

AUTO RACING YEARBOOKS

INDIANAPOLIS 500 YEARBOOKS
FLOYD CLYMER'S
(Hard Covers Add $5-10.00)

Year	Cover	Contents	Value

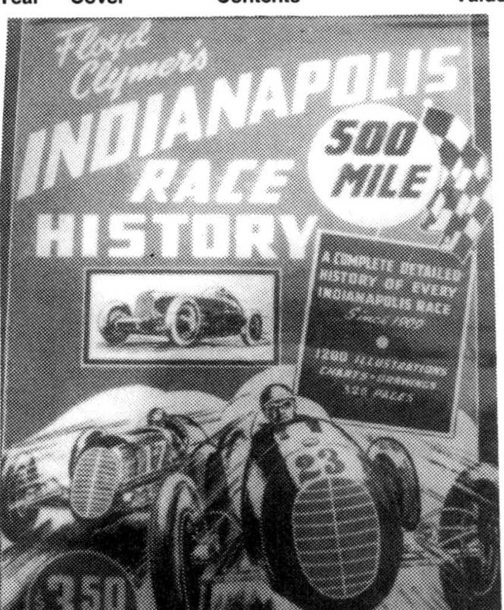

Floyd Clymer's 1945 Indianapolis 500 Yearbook

1945 Two Cars Race history from 1909-1941. $3.50 cover price. 100.00
1946 Two Cars Supplement, features winner-George Robson. 50.00
1947 Mauri Rose Feature on Mauri Rose, comments by Russ Catlin. 50.00
1948 Mauri Rose Supplement, features Mauri Rose & Bill Holland 50.00
1949 Bill Holland Feature on Bill Holland, interview w/ Lou Moore 50.00
1950 J. Parsons Feature on Parsons winning race in 345 miles 55.00
1951 Lee Wallard Feature on Wallard, technical features inc. NOVI 60.00
1952 Troy Ruttman Ruttman wins when Vukovich breaks down in final 8 laps 175.00
1953 Bill Vukovich Feature on Vukovich, Scarborough dies in race from heat 50.00
1954 Bill Vukovich Vukovich wins second, Jimmy Bryan finishes second. 50.00
1955 Bob Sweikert Sweikert wins/Vulkovich crashes & dies on back stretch 50.00
1956 Pat Flaherty Flaherty wins for John Zink & A.J. Watson. New Museum 125.00
1957 Sam Hanks Hanks victory, how to drive the 500, by Jim Bryan. 40.00
1958 Jimmy Bryan Features Bryan victory, Pat O'Connor fatally injured 250.00
1959 Rodger Ward Ward's win, pre-race activity, by Jack Fox 35.00
1960 Jim Rathman Rathman wins closely over Ward, Hurubise rookie/year 200.00
1961 A.J. Foyt Golden anniversary, Foyt's first win, Sach's second. 65.00
1962 Rodger Ward Ward's second win, stories on Foyt, Thompson 45.00
1963 Parnelli Jones Jones victory featured, articles on the Lotus & Novis 45.00
1964 A.J. Foyt Foyt's second win. Sachs & McDonald fatally injured. 65.00
1965 Jimmy Clark Clark's win first with rear engine car, 30 pages technical 50.00
1966 Graham Hill Hill's victory, 50 year history, Personalities & celebs 50.00
1967 A.J. Foyt Foyt's third victory, story on Leo Goossen- car designer 200.00
1968 Bobby Unser Last Clymer. Unser's win, Familiar faces, born losers. 50.00

author changes to CARL HUNGNESS in 1971

1972 Al Unser, Mario Andretti, Mark Donohue four yearbooks in one, 292 pages 150.00
1973 Gordon Johncock Kurtis cars, Pocono & Ontario 500's.Profile of Sid Collins 100.00
1974 J. Rutherford Articles on 1924 & 1954 races; Sampson Schraeder 25.00
1974 "Donald Davidson Yearbook" 25.00
1975 B. Unser/eagle Profiles on Unser, Dan Gurney, Don Brown, ... 25.00
1976 Borg-Warner/Rutherford New Indy cars,Profiles on Ralph Ligouri, Herb Porter, Wally Meskowski 25.00
1977 A.J. Foyt CRA sends its best, tribute to Sid Collins; 1937 race 30.00
1978 Al Unser Tony Hulman; Speedway Safety Patrol, Clint Brawner. 25.00
1979 Rick Mears Studebaker at Indy; Jackie Stewart, 60 years ago. 30.00
1980 J. Rutherford 1941 winner restored. The greatest debacle in racing 25.00
1981 Bobby Unser The hearing: Re-reversal, Ron Burton, artist 25.00
1982 Gordon Johncock Profiles on Roger Penske, A.J.Foyt, Desire Wilson, ... 25.00
1983 Tom Sneva The Meyer family, Dick, Greene, Patrick Racing Team 25.00
1984 Rick Mears New records, Mears-Penske win again, details of race 30.00
1985 Danny Sullivan Sullivan's spin and win, garage area nostalgia, ... 25.00
1986 Bobby Rahal Relive Rahal's glory days, tribute to Jim Trueman 25.00
1987 Al Unser Unser's historic 4th win, Cummins day in Columbus 25.00
1988 Rick Mears Practice, qualifications, race day, rookies & engines 30.00
1989 Emerson Fittipaldi Customary stories, Brazilian champ, spins & wrecks 25.00
1990 Arie Luyendyk Luyendyck wins at record breaking 185.981 mph. 25.00
1991 Rick Mears Feature on Mears' fourth Indy victory. 30.00

BASEBALL YEARBOOKS LEAGUE ISSUED

AMERICAN LEAGUE RED BOOKS

1943 Blue "V," (First Red Book) 100.00
1944 Blue baseball w/ red seams 80.00
1945 Blue baseball w/ red seams 75.00

1992 Blue Jays yearbook

1992 Braves yearbook

1982 Dodgers yearbook

1989 Indians yearbook

1973 Mets yearbook

1972 Orioles Yearbook

1991 Reds yearbook

1988 Twins yearbook

1962 Yankees yearbook

American League Red Book 1964

1946 Blue baseball w/ title 65.00
1947 Baseball in upper right corner 55.00
1948 Title & year 45.00
1949 Title & year 45.00
1950 Title & year (1st glossy cover) 40.00
1951 AL Golden Anniversary 40.00
1952 "Play Ball!" (w/ Ted Williams) 40.00
1953 8 AL Stars (Fox, Shantz, Wynn, others) 40.00
1954 Rosen, Kuenn, Vernon, Stengel 40.00
1955 AL All-Star Team photo 35.00
1956 Lemon, Stengel, 6 other AL managers 35.00
1957 8 AL Team logos 35.00
1958 50th Anniversary of BBWAA 35.00
1959 Tiger sliding into home 35.00
1960 Ruth, DiMaggio, Fox, Cobb, Gehrig, others . . 40.00
1961 4 players w/arms liked (Min., Cal.) 30.00
1962 Mantle, Maris, other AL homerun leaders . . . 40.00
1963 10 AL Team pennants 30.00
1964 Yastrzemski,Killebrew,G.Peters,E.Howard . . 30.00
1965 D.Chance, Oliva, Powell, others 30.00
1966 T.Conigliaro,McDowell,Blefary,Versailles . . . 25.00
1967 Frank Robinson "Triple Crown" 30.00
1968 Carl Yastrzemski "MVP & Triple Crown" 30.00
1969 Ruth, Cobb, W.Johnson HOF plaques 30.00
1970 Harmon Killebrew 22.50
1971 Boog Powell 20.00
1972 12 AL Team logos and ML logo 20.00

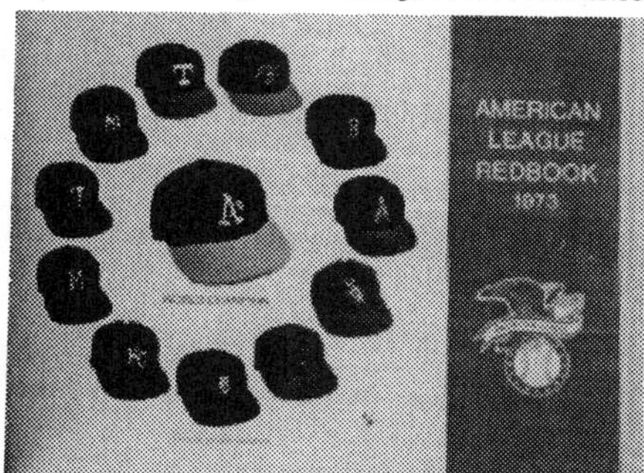

American League Red Book 1973

1973 12 AL Team hats w/Oakland in center 20.00
1974 12 AL Team logos and ML logo 20.00
1975 12 AL Team logos 16.00
1976 Carlton Fisk Word Series Homer sequence . 20.00
1977 14 AL Logos, featuring Seattle & Toronto. . . 16.00
1978 Yastrzemski, Carew, Murray, Nettles, others . 16.00
1979 Carew, Guidry, Rice, Dent, Staub, Whitaker . 16.00
1980 Eddie Murray & Orioles leaving dugout 12.00
1981 Brett, Charboneau, Boddicker 12.00
1982 1981 Playoffs team pictures 12.00
1983 Ripken, Yount, P.Vukovich 14.00
1984 Ripken, Kittle, Quisenberry, L.Hoyt 12.00
1985 14 AL Stars & Tigers World Series celebration 8.00
1986 Newspaper Headlines (Seaver, Boggs,etc.) . 10.00
1987 Clemens, Mattingly, Canseco, Boggs, Barfield 9.00
1988 Twins World Series celebration 8.00
1989 1988 AL Media Guide covers 8.00
1990 1980's Red Book covers 8.00

NATIONAL LEAGUE GREEN BOOKS

1935 Date January 30, 1935 (First Green Book) . . 75.00
1936 60th Birthday Edition, date Feb. 2, 1936 . . . . 60.00
1937 Title & date February 5, 1937 . . . . . . 60.00
1938 Title & year 60.00
1939 Centennial Edition 1839-1939 . . . . . . 55.00

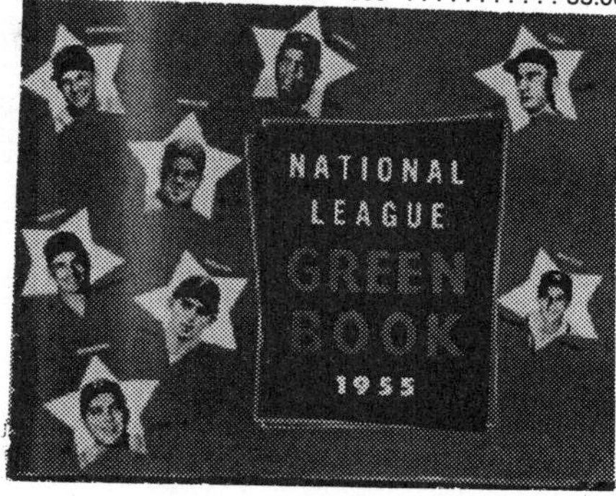

National League Green Book 1955

1940 Title & year 55.00
1941 Title & year 55.00
1942 Baseball diamond 100.00
1943 Title & year 100.00
1944 Title & year 80.00
1945 Title & year 75.00
1946 BBWAA logo 65.00
1947 Title & year in diamond shape 55.00
1948 Runner thrown out at first base 45.00
1949 8 Pennants w/ NL team logos 45.00
1950 8 Baseballs w/ NL team logos 40.00
1951 Ball in Glove, "75th Anniversary" 40.00
1952 8 NL cities, "Our 76th Year" 40.00

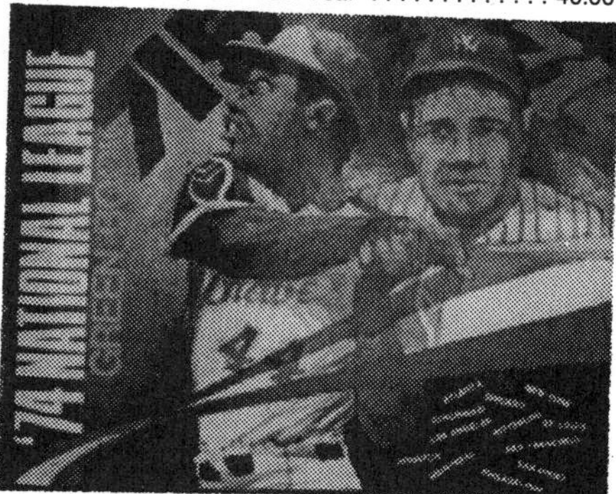

National League Green Book 1974

1953 8 NL cities, "Our 78th Year" 40.00
1954 NL All-Star Team (1st glossy cov.) 40.00
1955 8 NL stars (Mays, Musial, Spahn) 40.00
1956 Dodgers' celebration photos 35.00
1957 NL logo "82nd Season" 35.00
1958 NL salutes the BBWAA 35.00
1959 Stan Musial & Warren Spahn clippings 37.50
1960 Musial, Roberts, McCovey, Banks, Snider,etc. 40.00
1961 Groat,F.Robinson,F.Howard,Burdette,Spahn . 35.00
1962 Map of U.S. w/ 10 NL logos 30.00
1963 1958-1962 League Champs' parks 30.00

1964	Stan Musial "...so long, Stan"	35.00
1965	List of past NL Champions	30.00
1966	7 Stadiums of 1960's	25.00
1967	1962-1966 Attendance figures	25.00
1968	1967 Highlights news clippings	25.00
1969	1869 Cincinnati Red Stockings	25.00
1970	Hodges, McCovey, Sizemore, Rose, Mets	22.50
1971	Baseball w/ 12 NL team names	20.00
1972	12 bats w/ NL team names	20.00
1973	Roberto Clemente memorial	25.00
1974	Hank Aaron & Babe Ruth bust	25.00
1975	Brock, Aaron, Schmidt, Garvey, M.Marshall	18.00
1976	Bench, McEnaney, Reds World Series celebration	16.00
1977	12 NL Team logos	16.00
1978	12 NL Stars	16.00
1979	12 NL Team helmets & 4 baseball bats	16.00
1980	Baseball	12.00
1981	Schmidt, McGraw, All-Stars, Astros	12.00
1982	Rose, Schmidt, Ryan, Valenzuela	15.00
1983	D.Murphy, Carlton, Sax, Oliver, D.Porter	12.00
1984	12 NL team pennants	12.00
1985	Sandberg,Sutcliffe,Garvey,Gooden	9.00
1986	Ryan, Gooden, McGee, Rose	10.00
1987	Raines,Scott,Schmidt,Worrell,Mets	8.00
1989	Gibson, Hershiser, Hatcher, LA celebration	8.00
1990	NL MVP's & Cy Youngs of 1980's	8.00

BASEBALL TEAM MEDIA GUIDES & YEARBOOKS

Angels 1962 Year Book

ANGELS' MEDIA GUIDES

Los Angeles Angels

1961	Player coming out of baseball	30.00
1962	Baby w/ Angels logo	15.00
1963	Haney, Rigney, Angels logo	15.00
1964	Angels in action	15.00
1965	Dean Chance & Cy Young Trophy	18.00

California Angels

1966	Anaheim Stadium	15.00
1967	ML Team Logos & Anaheim Stad.	12.00
1968	Anaheim Stadium & logo	12.00
1969	New Look AL West	12.00
1970	Player & Press box	12.00
1971	4 Angels in California	12.00
1972	Del Rice	12.00
1973	Nolan Ryan	20.00
1974	Anaheim Stadium	10.00
1975	Dick Williams	10.00
1976	Angels baseball cards	12.00
1977	Frank Tanana	12.00
1978	Nolan Ryan, J. Rudi, F. Tanana	14.00
1979	Anaheim Stadium	10.00
1980	Don Baylor	7.00
1981	Angels equipment	7.00
1982	Angels logos	7.00
1983	Angels in action (w/ Reggie)	8.00
1984	Angels celebrating (w/ Reggie)	7.00
1986	DeCinces, Downing, Schofield	6.00
1987	Donnie Moore	6.00
1988	Brian Downing & Wally Joyner	5.00
1989	All-Star Game logo	5.00
1990	Angels Stars (w/Finley, Joyner)	5.00
1991	Finley in action art & logo	5.00
1992	Bryan Harvey	5.00

ANGELS' YEARBOOKS

Los Angeles Angels

1962	Angels baby w/ cake	85.00
1963		60.00
1964	Angels in action	45.00
1965	Angels in action	45.00

California Angels

1966		40.00
1967	"All About the Angels" w/ logo	40.00
68-82	Not issued.	
1983	Jackson, Carew, Lynn, others	12.00
1984	Anaheim Stadium	9.00
1985	Silver Anniversary	8.00
86-91	Yearbook/program	5.00
1992	Langston, Abbott, Finley & Harvey	5.00

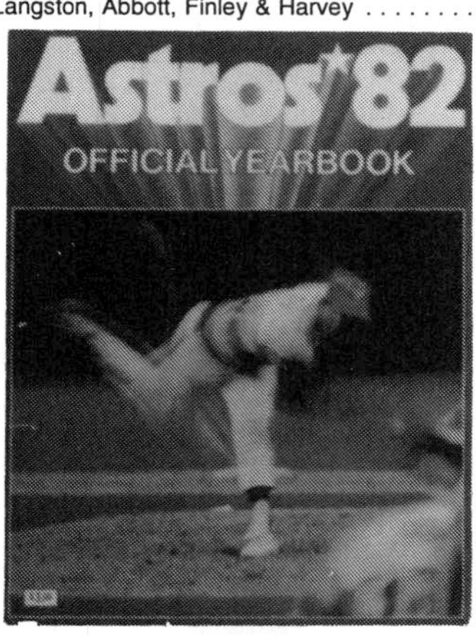

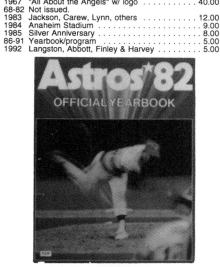

Astros 1982 Yearbook

ASTROS' MEDIA GUIDES

Houston Colt 45s

1962	45's logo	55.00
1963	45's logo	25.00
1964	Player art	20.00

Houston Astros

1965	New logo	15.00
1966	Catcher's mask	15.00
1967	Astro turf	12.00
1968	Astrodome art	12.00
1969	Baseball anniversary	12.00
1970	Entire Astro roster	12.00
1971	Lockerroom art	12.00
1972	Bat/ball as pool cue	12.00
1973	Zodiac signs	12.00
1974	Big orange	10.00
1975	Equipment	10.00
1976	Bicentennial logo	10.00
1977	Player art	10.00
1978	Art	10.00
1979	Art	10.00
80-90		6.00
1991	Helmet, bat & ball	5.00
1992	Biggio, Harnisch & Bagwell	5.00

ASTROS' YEARBOOKS

Houston Colt 45s

1962	Pistol, baseball, Texas	175.00
1963	Not issued.	
1964		125.00

Houston Astros

1965	"Inside the Astrodome"	100.00
66-81	Not issued.	
1982	Nolan Ryan	20.00
83-91	Yearbook/program	5.00
1992	Luis Gonzalez	5.00

Athletics 1958 Year Book

ATHLETICS' MEDIA GUIDES

Philadelphia Athletics

1930	Elephant mascot	75.00
1931	Elephant mascot	70.00
1932	Elephant mascot	65.00
1933	Elephant mascot	60.00
1934	Elephant mascot	60.00
1935	Elephant mascot	55.00
1936	Elephant mascot	55.00
1937	Elephant mascot	50.00
1938	Elephant mascot	50.00
1939	Elephant & "A's"	50.00
1940	Elephant w/ pennant	45.00
1941	Baseball & "A's"	45.00
1942		45.00
1943	Elephant w/ flag	40.00
1944	Elephant w/ flag	40.00
1945		40.00
1946	Connie Mack	45.00
1947		35.00
1948	Elephant & baseball	35.00
1949		30.00
1950	Connie Mack (Golden Jubilee)	45.00
1951		30.00
1952	Elephant mascot	25.00
1953		25.00
1954	Eddie Joost	25.00

Kansas City Athletics

1955	K.C. Municipal Stadium	40.00
1956	Elephant logo	20.00
1957	Elephant logo	20.00
1958	Elephant logo	20.00
1959	"A's" baseball	20.00
1960	A's hat & baseball	20.00
1961	K.C. Municipal Stadium	15.00
1962		15.00
1963	Baseball & player sliding	15.00
1964	A's logo & year	15.00
1965	A's logo & year	15.00
1966	A's logo & year	15.00
1967	A's logo & year	12.00

Oakland Athletics

1968	Oakland Stadium, ball w/ logo	25.00
1969	Hunter, Bando, Campenaris	18.00
1970	Player swinging bat	12.00
1971	A's logo & year	12.00

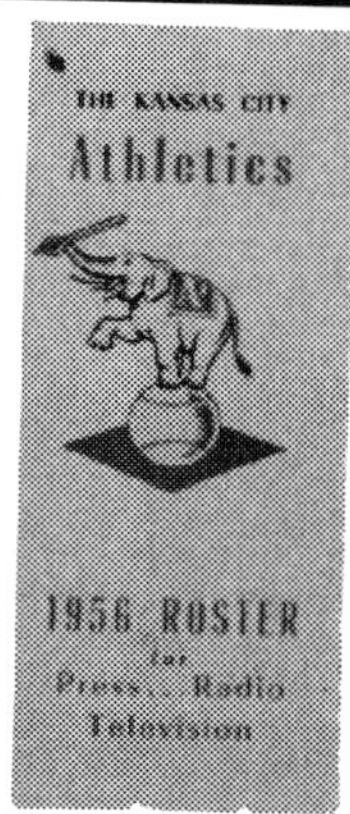

Athletics 1946 & 1956 Media guides

1972	A's logo & year	14.00
1973	A's logo & year	14.00
1974	A's logo & year	14.00
1975	A's logo & year	10.00
1976	A's logo & year	10.00
1977	A's logo & year	10.00
1978	A's logo & year	10.00
1979	A's logo & year	10.00
1980	A's logo & year	7.00
1981	BillyBall baseball	9.00
1982	Running cleats	7.00
1983	A's jukebox	7.00
1984	Oakland sportswriters	6.00
1985	Athletics memorabilia	6.00
1986		6.00
1987	All-Athletics Team	7.00
1988	Batter swinging	5.00
1989	Canseco, Weiss, Eckersley	6.00
1990	World Series Trophy	5.00
1991		5.00
1992	25th anniversary	6.00

ATHLETICS' YEARBOOKS

Philadelphia Athletics

1949	Connie Mack	135.00
1950	Connie Mack Golden Jubilee	135.00
1951	Elephant mascot	110.00
1952	Elephant mascot w/ hat	110.00
1953	Elephant pitching "53" ball	100.00
1954	Play at first base	95.00

Kansas City Athletics

1955	A's batter ripping through map	160.00
1956	Elephant mascot w/ cake	100.00
1957	Kansas City Municipal Stadium	90.00
1958	Play at first base	85.00
1959	Kansas City Municipal Stadium	75.00
1960	Athletics hat on baseball	60.00
1961	Pitcher & baseball	45.00
1962	Athletics in action	45.00
1963		45.00
1964	Player making catch	40.00
1965	A's donkey w/ Charlie O. flag	45.00
1966		75.00
1967	Athletics pitcher	50.00

Oakland Athletics

1968	Oakland Coliseum	100.00
1969	Connie Mack	60.00
1970	Jackson, Monday, Odom, others	45.00
1971	Bert Campenaris and Sal Bando	35.00
1972	Vida Blue and Dick Williams	25.00
1973	Williams, Rudi, Hunter, Fingers	22.50
1974	"One More in 74" w/ 2 trophies	22.50
1975	"Keep it Alive in 75"	20.00
1976	Bicentennial celebration	15.00
1977	A's logo w/ arch of balls	15.00
1978		18.00
1979	"The Swingin' A's" w/ logo	18.00
1980		15.00

Year	Description	Price
1981	Not issued.	
1982	Billy Ball baseball	15.00
1983	A's baseball card collage	10.00
84-present	Yearbook/program	5.00

BLUE JAYS' MEDIA GUIDES

Year	Description	Price
1977	Toronto Exhibition Stadium	20.00
1978	Blue Jays pitcher	10.00
1979	Blue Jays in action	10.00
1980	Alfredo Griffin	7.00
1981	Blue Jays equipment	7.00
1982	Bobby Cox & Blue Jays in action	7.00
1983	Blue Jays hat & equipment	7.00
1984	Blue Jays in action	6.00
1985	Blue Jays logo	6.00
1986	Blue Jays 10th Anniversary	6.00
1987	Bell, Barfield, Eichorn, Fernandez	6.50
1988	George Bell	6.00
1989	Blue Jays stars (w/ McGriff)	5.50
1990	Blue Jays (w/ Gruber, McGriff)	5.50
1991	Dave Steib	5.00
1992		5.00

BLUE JAYS' YEARBOOKS

Year	Description	Price
1977	Fans; "The First Year"	35.00
1978	Not issued.	
1979		15.00
1980		12.00
1981	Jim Clancy & Ernie Whitt	12.00
1982	Whitt, B. Martinez, Moseby	10.00
1983	Blue Jays baseball cards	10.00
1984	Exhibition Stadium	10.00
1985	Logo & year	10.00
1986	AL baseball & bat	10.00
1987	Whitt, Clancy, Barfield	9.00
1988	George Bell	9.00
1988	Blue Jay batting	8.00
1989		8.00
1990	George Bell	8.00
1991		5.00
1992	Roberto Alomar	5.00

Braves 1960 Media Guide

BRAVES' MEDIA GUIDES

Boston Braves

Year	Description	Price
1931	Indian Head, player roster	80.00
1932	Indian Head	60.00
1933	Indian Head	60.00
1934	Indian Head	55.00
1935	Indian Head	55.00
1936	Player rosters	55.00
1937	Player rosters	50.00
1938	"Bees" baseball	50.00
1939		50.00
1940	Casey Stengel	60.00
1941	Casey Stengel	60.00
1942	Indian Head	45.00
1943	Indian Head	40.00
1944	Airplane, flag, baseball bat	40.00
1945	Indian Head	40.00
1946	Billy Southworth	40.00
1947	Billy Southworth	40.00
1948	Bob Elliott	40.00
1949	Billy Southworth	35.00
1950	Braves Logo	30.00
1951		30.00
1952	Indian head & baseball	25.00

Milwaukee Braves

Year	Description	Price
1953	State of Florida	35.00
1954		25.00
1955		20.00
1956		20.00
1957		25.00
1958		25.00
1959		20.00
1960	Indian head & pennant	20.00
1961	Indian head & pennant	15.00
1962	Indian head & pennant	15.00
1963	Indian head & pennant	15.00
1964	Aaron, Spahn, Mathews, Alou	20.00
1965	Felipe Alou & Bobby Bragan	17.50

Atlanta Braves

Year	Description	Price
1966	Player swinging bat	22.50
1967	Felipe Alou	14.00
1968	Hands gripping bat	12.00
1969	Players in action	12.00
1970	Henry Aaron	18.00
1971	Foot sliding into base	12.00
1972	Players in action	12.00
1973	Players in action	12.00
1974	Players in action	10.00
1975	"Knit" baseballs	10.00
1976	Dave Bristol	10.00
1977	Braves hat	10.00
1978	Atlanta-Fulton Co. Stadium	10.00
1979	Phil Niekro & All-Stars	12.00
1980	Stadium & baseball	7.00
1981	Dale Murphy & Bob Horner	8.00
1982	Joe Torre	7.00
1983	Murphy, Niekro, Torre, Bedrosian	7.00
1984	Braves Logo	6.00
1985	Dale Murphy & Bruce Sutter	6.00
1986	Bobby Cox & Chuck Tanner	6.00
1987	Braves uniform	6.00
1988		5.00
1989	Perry, Glavine, Gant, Smith, Thomas	5.50
1990	25th Anniversary Logo	5.00
1991	Gant & Justice	5.50
1992	Olsen & Smoltz celebrating	5.00

BRAVES' YEARBOOKS

Boston Braves

Year	Description	Price
1946		300.00
1947	Billy Southworth	200.00
48-49	Not issued.	
1950	Smiling Brave	150.00
1951	Baseball diamond & ball	150.00
1952	Braves players talking	150.00

Milwaukee Braves

Year	Description	Price
1953	Runner sliding into home	175.00
1954	"To the People of Milwaukee"	100.00
1955	Fans and stadium	90.00
1956	Cartoon of Braves fans	80.00
1957	Braves logo in crystal ball	85.00
1958	Brave raising W.S. Pennant	80.00
1959	Brave in hot-air balloon	70.00
1960	Brave w/ 2 baseball bats	60.00
1961	Brave w/ other NL players	45.00
1962	Braves logo	45.00
1963	Brave w/ other NL players	40.00
1964	Aaron, Spahn, Mathews, Torre, etc.	55.00
1965	Felipe Alou & Bobby Bragan	35.00

Atlanta Braves

Year	Description	Price
1966	Aaron, Mathews, others	60.00
1967	Play at home plate	35.00
1968	Play at second base	25.00
1969	Braves infielder	25.00
1970	Braves in action	20.00
1971	Babe Ruth & Hank Aaron	22.50
1972	Five Braves	18.00

Year	Description	Price
1973	Braves pitcher	18.00
1974	Babe Ruth & Hank Aaron	20.00
1975	Four Braves	15.00
1976	Aaron, Cepeda, Niekro, others	18.00
1977	Former Braves, inc. Aaron	15.00
1978	Spahn, Niekro, Burdette	12.00
1979	G. Garber stopping Rose streak	15.00
1980	Bobby Cox & Bob Horner	10.00
1981	Dale Murphy, Bob Horner, others	10.00
1982	Horner, Aaron, Spahn, others	12.00
1983	P. Niekro in Uncle Sam outfit	10.00
1984	Horner, Murphy, Aaron	8.00
1985	Aaron, Murphy, 20th Anniv.	8.00
1986	Chuck Tanner & Dale Murphy	8.00
1987	Dale Murphy	9.00
1988	"Braves Illustrated"	8.00
1989	Not issued.	
1990	25 Years in Atlanta	6.00
1991		5.00
1992	NL Champs celebration	5.00

BREWERS' MEDIA GUIDES

Seattle Pilots

Year	Description	Price
1969	Pilots logo	75.00

Milwaukee Brewers

Year	Description	Price
1970		20.00
1971	Newspaper clipping	20.00
1972	State of Wisconson	15.00
1973	Del Crandall & George Scott	12.00
1974	Brewers mascot	12.00
1975	Brewers mascot	10.00
1976	Baseball glove	10.00
1977	Robin Yount	15.00
1978	Larry Hisle	10.00
1979	George Bamberger	10.00
1980	G. Thomas, Cooper, Lezcano	8.00
1981	Oglivie, Cooper, Yount	8.00
1982	Rollie Fingers	7.00
1983	Yount, Vukovich, Kuenn	8.00
1984	County Stadium	6.00
1985	Brewers uniform #85	6.00
1986	Brewers pitcher in action	6.00
1987	Ted Higuera	6.00
1988	Player running	5.00
1989	20th Anniversary logo	5.00
1990	Player running	5.00
1991		5.00
1992	Phil Garner	5.00

BREWERS' YEARBOOKS

Seattle Pilots

Year	Description	Price
1969	Pilot logo w/ 10 pictures	175.00

Milwaukee Brewers

Year	Description	Price
1970	First year, Brewers hitter	75.00
71-78	Not issued.	
1979	Larry Hisle	13.00
1980	Gorman Thomas	10.00
1981	Yount, Fingers, Molitor, other	12.00
1982	Crowd celebrating	10.00
1983	Robin Yount & fans	12.00
1984	County Stadium	10.00
1985	George Bamberger & fans	9.00
1986	Brewers locker room	8.00
1987	Brewers baseball cards	8.00
1988	Paul Molitor hologram	10.00
1989	Brewer greats (w/ Aaron)	7.00
1990	Brewers logo & city skyline	6.00
1991		6.00
1992	Gantner, Molitor & Yount	5.00

CARDINALS' MEDIA GUIDES

Year	Description	Price
1930	Logo & year	75.00
1931		70.00
1932	Logo & year (WS Champions)	65.00
1933	Logo & year	60.00
1934	Logo & year	60.00
1935	Logo & year (WS Champions)	55.00
1936	Logo & year	55.00
1937	Logo & year	50.00
1938		50.00
1939	Name & year	50.00
1940	Logo & year	45.00
1941	Logo & year	45.00
1942	Statue of Liberty & logo	45.00

Cardinals 1971 Yearbook

Year	Description	Price
1943	Logo & flag (WS Champions)	40.00
1944	Logo & Victory "V"	40.00
1945	Logo & year (WS Champions)	40.00
1946		35.00
1947	Logo (WS Champions)	35.00
1948	Baseball & logo	35.00
1949	Baseball & logo	30.00
1950	Cardinals & baseball	30.00
1951	25th Anniversary of WS Champs	30.00
1952	Cardinals logo	25.00
1953	"It's the Cardinals"	25.00
1954	Cardinals logo	25.00
1955	Cardinals logo	20.00
1956	Cardinals logo	20.00
1957	Cardinals logo	20.00
1958	Cardinal mascot	20.00
1959	Stan Musial	35.00
1960	Cardinal mascot	20.00
1961	McDaniel, Broglio, Sadecki, Simmons	15.00
1962	Stan Musial	30.00
1963	Art player in action	15.00
1964	White, Javier, Groat, Boyer	20.00
1965	Cardinals logo (WS Champions)	15.00
1966	Cardinals logo & Busch Stadium	15.00
1967	Busch Stadium	12.00
1968	World Series Trophy	12.00
1969	Bob Gibson	16.00
1970	Joe Torre	14.00
1971	Bob Gibson & Joe Torre	18.00
1972	Red Schoendienst & Joe Torre	15.00
1973	Torre, Gibson, Brock, Simmons	16.00
1974	Cardinals hat & uniform	10.00
1975	Lou Brock & Cardinals logo	15.00
1976	Busch Stadium	10.00
1977	Vern Rapp & Lou Brock	12.00
1978	Cardinals equipment	10.00
1979	St. Louis Arch	10.00
1980	Keith Hernandez	8.00
1981	Whitey Herzog	7.50
1982	Whitey Herzog	7.50
1983	World Series Celebration	7.00
1984	Player running	6.00
1985	Busch Stadium & St. Louis Arch	6.00
1986	McGee, Coleman, Herzog	6.50
1987	Whitey Herzog & past managers	6.00
1988	N.L. Champions Celebration	5.00
1989	Whitey Herzog & action photos	5.00
1990	Card logo, A.A Busch	5.00
1991	Joe Torre	5.00
1992	100th anniversary, with Ozzie	5.00

CARDINALS' YEARBOOKS

Year	Description	Price
1951	Cardinal in bottom right	200.00
1952	Cardinal and soldier	110.00
1953	Stan Musial	75.00
1954	Red Schoendienst	95.00
1955	Cardinal pitcher getting sign	85.00

1956 Cardinal pitcher getting sign 85.00
1957 Cardinal circling the bases 55.00
1958 Cardinal circling the base 50.00
1959 Stan Musial 45.00
1960 Cardinal catching a ball 40.00
1961 Simmons, Sadecki and others 35.00
1962 Stan Musial and his milestones 35.00
1963 Musial sliding into second 30.00
1964 Boyer, White, Groat and Javier 40.00
1965 Bob Gibson 45.00
1966 New Busch Stadium photo 35.00
1967 World Champs 50.00
1968 Horizontal w/ Busch Stadium 40.00
1969 Gibson, Brock, Flood and more 30.00
1970 Five Cardinal drawings 20.00
1971 Gibson, Brock, Torre, others 25.00
1972 Cardinals fielder 20.00
1973 Cardinals batter 18.00
1974 Torre, T. Simmons and others 20.00
1975 Gibson, Brock and others 18.00
1976 Centennial Yearbook 15.00
1977 Brock and Cobb 15.00
78-87 Not issued.
1988 Wraparound team photo 8.00
1989 Coleman and Worrell 9.00
1990 Herzog and Busch Stadium 7.00
1991 Lee Smith 6.00
1992 Guerrero, Jose, Lankford 5.00

Cubs 1946 & 1963 Media Guides

CUBS' MEDIA GUIDES

1926 Blank w/ year 70.00
1927 Blank w/ year 70.00
1928 Blank w/ year 65.00
1929 Blank w/ year 65.00
1930 Blank w/ year 65.00
1931 Rogers Hornsby 75.00
1932 Rogers Hornsby 75.00
1933 Cub mascot 60.00
1934 Cub mascot 55.00
1935 Cub mascot 55.00
1936 Cub mascot 55.00
1937 Cub mascot throwing ball 50.00
1938 Cub mascot swinging bat 50.00
1939 Cub mascot holding pennant 50.00
1940 . . . . 45.00
1941 Jimmy Wilson 45.00
1942 . . . . 45.00
1943 . . . . 40.00
1944 . . . . 40.00
1945 . . . . 40.00
1946 Charlie Grimm 35.00
1947 Cub mascot 35.00
1948 . . . . 35.00
1949 . . . . 30.00
1950 . . . . 30.00
1951 . . . . 30.00
1952 . . . . 25.00
1953 . . . . 25.00
1954 . . . . 25.00
1955 . . . . 20.00
1956 . . . . 20.00
1957 . . . . 20.00
1958 Cubs logo 20.00
1959 Cubs logo 20.00
1960 Cubs logo 20.00
1961 Cubs logo 15.00
1962 Cubs logo 15.00
1963 Cubs logo 15.00
1964 Cubs logo 15.00
1965 Cubs logo 15.00
1966 Cubs logo 15.00
1967 Cubs logo 12.00
1968 Cubs logo 12.00
1969 Cubs logo 12.00
1970 Cubs logo 12.00
1971 Cubs logo 12.00
1972 Cubs logo 12.00
1973 Cubs logo 12.00
1974 Cubs logo 10.00
1975 Cubs logo 10.00
1976 Cubs logo 10.00
1977 Cubs logo 10.00
1978 Cubs logo 10.00
1979 Cubs logo 10.00
1980 Cubs logo 7.00
1981 Cubs logo 7.00
1982 Cubs logo 7.00
1983 Wrigley Field, Fan celebration 7.00
1984 Autographed baseballs 6.00
1985 Frey, Sandberg, Sutcliffe, Green 7.00
1986 Cub Secondbasemen (Sandberg) 6.00
1987 Billy Williams 7.00
1988 Andre Dawson 5.50
1989 Wrigley Field 5.00
1990 Wrigley Field 5.00
1991 Sandberg 5.50
1992 Wrigley Field at night 5.00

CUBS' YEARBOOKS

1934 Wraparound batting scene 275.00
1939 "Player's Records" 200.00
1941 "Player's history & rec. book" 175.00
1942 "Player roster & record book" 150.00
1948 Logo and large, blue "1948" 115.00
1949 Logo and large, blue "1949" 100.00
1950 Hat and red "1950" 90.00
1951 Ball in center of red glove 90.00
1952 Logo w/ blue "5" and red "2" 80.00
1953 Cubs logo 80.00
1954 Name & year 70.00
1955 Name & year 70.00
1956 Overlapping "195" & "6" 65.00
1957 Head with Cubs hat 65.00
58-84 Not issued.
1985 Wrigley photo 10.00
1986 70th Anniversary w/ Sandberg 10.00
1987 Sandberg and B. Williams 10.00
1988 Andre Dawson 9.00
1989 . . . . 8.00
1990 Photo of players' bats 7.00
1991 Ryne Sandberg 6.00
1992 Montage of players in action 5.00

DODGERS' MEDIA GUIDES

Brooklyn Dodgers

1928 Name & year 80.00
1929 Name & year 75.00
1930 Name & year 75.00
1931 Name & year 70.00
1932 Name & year 70.00
1933 Logo & year 65.00
1934 Logo & year 65.00
1935 Logo & year 60.00
1936 Logo & year 55.00
1937 Logo & year 55.00
1938 Logo & year 50.00
1939 100th Anniversary logo 50.00
1940 50th Anniversary in Brooklyn 45.00
1941 Airplane 45.00
1942 "V" logo 45.00
1943 . . . . 40.00
1944 . . . . 40.00
1945 . . . . 40.00
1946 . . . . 35.00
1947 . . . . 35.00
1948 . . . . 35.00
1949 . . . . 30.00

1950 "The Bum" 30.00
1951 "The Bum" 30.00
1952 . . . . . 25.00
1953 "The Bum" 25.00
1954 . . . . . 25.00
1955 Walt Alston 25.00
1956 Walt Alston 25.00
1957 Walt Alston 25.00

Dodgers 1975 Yearbook

Los Angeles Dodgers

1958 Walt Alston 45.00
1959 L.A. Coliseum 20.00
1960 Drawing of Dodger Stadium 20.00
1961 Dodger Stadium 15.00
1962 Airplane & players cartoon 15.00
1963 Koufax, Wills, Drysdale, T. Davis 20.00
1964 Players celebrating 15.00
1965 Championship pennants 15.00
1966 Mascot climbing mountain 15.00
1967 Mascot juggling crowns 12.00
1968 Walt Alston 16.00
1969 100th Anniversary 12.00
1970 W.Davis, Sizemore, Singer, Osteen 12.00
1971 Dodgers in action 12.00
1972 Dodgers in action 12.00
1973 Dodgers in action 12.00
1974 Dodgers in action 10.00
1975 Steve Garvey HR sequence 12.00
1976 Garvey, Cey, Sutton, Buckner, Lopes 14.00
1977 Tom Lasorda 12.00
1978 Garvey, Cey, Baker, Smith 14.00
1979 Dodger Stadium 10.00
1980 Dodgers logo 7.00
1981 1980 Highlights 7.00
1982 Howe, Yeager, W.S. Trophy 8.00
1983 Sax, Guerrero, Valenzuela 8.00
1984 Fireworks over Dodger Stadium 6.00
1985 Bill Russell 6.00
1986 Player swinging bat 6.00
1987 Dodger Stadium 6.00
1988 Baseballs 5.00
1989 W.S. Trophy 5.00
1990 100th Anniversary hats & pins 5.00
1991 Logo 5.00
1992 Logo 5.00

DODGERS' YEARBOOKS

Brooklyn Dodgers

1947 . . . . . 275.00
1949 N.L. Champs 225.00
1950 . . . . . 200.00
1951 . . . . . 175.00
1952 "The Bum" holding sign 150.00
1953 "The Bum" holding bat 150.00
1954 "The Bum" w/ saw and hammer 125.00
1955 "The Bum" reaching for star 175.00
1956 "The Bum" holding #6 . . . . . 150.00
1957 "The Bum" holding pennants 150.00

Los Angeles Dodgers

1958 Autographed team ball 150.00
1959 Play at second base 95.00
1960 Dodger Stadium drawing 50.00
1961 . . . . . 35.00
1962 . . . . . 35.00
1963 Maury Wills 50.00
1964 1963 World Champions banner 30.00
1965 Dodger Stadium 50.00
1966 Walter Alston 30.00
1967 Dodger juggling crowns 25.00
1968 Koufax, Drysdale, others 25.00
1969 Baseball's Centennial logo 35.00
1970 Dodger & Met mascots 25.00
1971 10th Anniversary of Stadium 22.00
1972 Dodger Stadium 22.00
1973 Walter Alston & Maury Wills 25.00
1974 Jimmy Wynn 20.00
1975 Steve Garvey (N.L. Champions) 18.00
1976 Davey Lopes 18.00
1977 20th Anniversary (Koufax, etc.) 22.00
1978 Cey, Garvey, Lasorda, others 15.00
1979 Tom Lasorda 12.00
1980 Dodger baseball cards 10.00
1981 Steve Garvey & Dusty Baker 12.00
1982 World Seris trophy 12.00
1983 25th Anniversary in L.A. 10.00
1984 Lasorda, "A Winning Tradition" 10.00
1985 Garvey, Valenzuela, Russell 10.00
1986 Hershiser, Guerrero, Marshall 10.00
1987 24 past L.A. yearbooks 10.00
1988 "Blueprint for Success" 8.00
1989 World Series trophy 7.00
1990 . . . . . 6.00
1991 . . . . . 5.00
1992 30 years in Dodger stadium 5.00

EXPOS' MEDIA GUIDES

1969 Expos logo 20.00
1970 Jarry Park 15.00
1971 Baseball 12.00
1972 Jarry Park & action photos 12.00
1973 Montreal photos 12.00
1974 Gene Mauch 10.00
1975 Expos in action 10.00
1976 Expos in action 10.00
1977 D.Williams, Cash, Perez, McEnaney 10.00
1978 Gary Carter & Andre Dawson 14.00
1979 Expos logo 10.00
1980 Locker w/ Expos uniform 7.00
1981 Pennant 7.00
1982 Expos in action 7.00
1983 Hands gripping bat 7.00
1984 Expos hats 6.00
1985 Olympic Stadium w/ dome 6.00
1986 Expos logo & baseball 6.00
1987 Olympic Stadium w/ dome 6.00
1988 20th Anniversary bat 5.00
1989 Hands Hi-Fiving 5.00
1990 Expos logo 5.00
1991 Logo 5.00
1992 Denny Martinez 5.00

EXPOS' YEARBOOKS

1969 Larry Jaster 45.00
1970 Expos equipment & fan 25.00
1971 Fan w/ Expos pennant 20.00
1972 Four Different Covers, ea. 20.00
73-81 Not issued.
1982 Expos celebration & A.S. logo 10.00
1983 Carter, Oliver, Dawson, others 12.00
1984 Dawson, Rose, Raines, others 12.00
1985 Dawson, Raines, Wallach, others 10.00
1986 . . . . . 8.00
87-91 Yearbook/program. 5.00
1992 Gary Carter 5.00

GIANTS' MEDIA GUIDES

New York Giants

1927 Name & Year 90.00
1928 Name & Year 85.00
1929 Name & Year 80.00
1930 Name & Year 75.00
1931 Name & Year 70.00
1932 Name & Year 65.00
1933 Name & Year 65.00
1934 Name & Year (WS Champions) 60.00

Year	Description	Price
1935	Name & Year	60.00
1936	Name & Year (Felt cover)	55.00
1937	Name & Year (Felt cover)	55.00
1938	Name & Year	50.00
1939	New York World's Fair	50.00
1940	Name & Year	45.00
1941	Name & Year	45.00
1942	Name & Year	45.00
1943	Name & Year	40.00
1944	Name & Year	40.00
1945	Name & Year	40.00
1946	Name & Year	35.00
1947	Baseball w/ year	35.00
1948	Baseball w/ year	35.00
1949	Baseball w/ year	30.00
1950	Polo Grounds	30.00
1951	Giants logo	30.00
1952	"The Giant" & Leo Durocher	30.00
1953	Polo Grounds	25.00
1954	Giants logo	25.00
1955	"The Giant" (WS Champions)	20.00
1956	Giants hat	20.00
1957	Giants hat	20.00

San Francisco Giants

Year	Description	Price
1958	Candlestick Park drawing	40.00
1959	Giants in action	20.00
1960	Giants logo	20.00
1961	Giants in action	15.00
1962	Giants in action	15.00
1963	Candlestick Park	15.00
1964	Candlestick Park	15.00
1965	Candlestick Park	15.00
1966	Giants logo & baseball	15.00
1967	Giants logo	12.00
1968	Giants logo	12.00
1969	Giants logo	12.00
1970	Willie Mays & Willie McCovey	20.00
1971	Year of the Fox	12.00
1972	"Best in the West"	12.00
1973	Candlestick Park	12.00
1974	Bonds, Bryant, Matthews	15.00
1975	Giants logo	10.00
1976	Giants logo	10.00
1977	J. Altobelli & John Montefusco	10.00
1978	Giants in action	10.00
1979	Giants Management, Blue, Clark	11.00
1980	On deck circle w/ Giants logo	7.00
1981	Golden Gate Bridge	7.00
1982	25th Anniversary in S.F.	7.00
1983	Giants logo	7.00
1984	Giants logo	6.00
1985	Giants logo	6.00
1986	Giants logo	6.00
1987	Giants logo	6.00
1988	Giants logo	5.00
1989	Giants logo	5.00
1990	Giants logo	5.00
1991	Giants logo 3D	5.00
1992	Uniform art	5.00

GIANTS' YEARBOOKS

New York Giants

Year	Description	Price
1947		185.00
48-50	Not issued.	
1951		100.00
1952	Durocher and Giant	100.00
1953	Polo Grounds photo	75.00
1954	Giant cutting "1951" book	125.00
1955	Giant holding other mascots	100.00
1956	Giants cap	90.00
1957	Photo of play at second	85.00

San Francisco Giants

Year	Description	Price
1958	Giant with load of books	250.00
1959	Photo of a play at third	85.00
1960	Al Dark and a play at first	75.00
1961	Giants hat	55.00
1962	N.L. Champs	45.00
1963	Trolley car w/ Giants pennant	40.00
1964	Child looking at Candlestick	40.00
1965	Painting of a play at second	40.00
1966	Willie Mays w/ S.F. baseball	45.00
1967	Mays, Marichal and more	45.00
1968	Willie Mays	35.00
1969	Mays, McCovey, Bonds and more	35.00
1970	3 photos each of Mays, McCovey	30.00
1971	Willie McCovey	27.50
1972	Willie Mays sliding into third	26.00
1973	Marichal, Bonds and Speier	22.00
1974	"Young Giants '74"	18.00
1975	G. Matthews, Caldwell and more	15.00
1976		15.00
77-79	Not issued.	
1980	Giant batter	10.00
1981	Frank Robinson	14.00
1982	Silver Anniversary yearbook	10.00
1983	Frank Robinson & Jim Mutrie	12.00
1984	Giants All-Star memorabilia	10.00
1985	Horizontal "A History of ..."	9.00
86-91	Yearbook/program.	5.00
1992	Will Clark hologram	7.50

Indians 1984 Yearbook

INDIANS' MEDIA GUIDES

Year	Description	Price
1936	Indian chief & year	55.00
1937	Indian chief & year	50.00
1938	Indian chief & year	50.00
1939	Indian chief & year	50.00
1940	Indian chief & year	45.00
1941	Indian chief & year	45.00
1942	Lou Boudreau	55.00
1943	Lou Boudreau	50.00
1944	Indians mascot & year	40.00
1945	Indians mascot & year	40.00
1946	Lou Boudreau	45.00
1947	Indians mascot	35.00
1948	Indians mascot w/ media	35.00
1949	Indian mascot	30.00
1950	Indian mascot batting	30.00
1951	Indian mascots	30.00
1952	Feller, Garcia, Lemon, Wynn	35.00
1953	Press box and media	25.00
1954	Al Rosen	35.00
1955		20.00
1956		20.00
1957	Mgr. Kirby Farrell	20.00
1958	Frank Lane & Bobby Bragan	25.00
1959	Rocky Colavito	25.00
1960	Tito Francona	22.50
1961	Jim Perry	17.50
1962	Indian mascot	15.00
1963	Indians uniform #20	15.00
1964	Indian mascot	15.00
1965	Indian mascot	15.00
1966	Baseball w/ feather	15.00
1967	Cleveland Stadium	12.00
1968	Autographed baseball	12.00
1969	100th Anniversary w/ mascot	12.00
1970	Indian mascot	12.00
1971	Indians hat w/ feather	12.00
1972	Indians in action	12.00
1973	Indians logo	12.00
1974	Indians logo	10.00
1975	Frank Robinson	10.00
1976	Baseball w/ feather	16.00
1977	Player batting	10.00

1978	Baseball w/ logo & glove	10.00
1979	Indians logo	10.00
1980	Fireworks over Cleveland Stad.	7.00
1981	Indians logo	7.00
1982	Cleveland Stadium	7.00
1983	Indians logo	7.00
1984	Indians memorabilia	6.00
1985	Bert Blyleven & Andre Thornton	6.00
1986	Past Indians uniforms	6.00
1987	Joe Carter	6.50
1988	Indians uniform #88	5.00
1989	Swindell, Candiotti, Farrell, Jones	5.00
1990	90 Years of Cleveland baseball	5.00
1991	Jacoby, Jones & Alomar Jr.	5.00
1992	60 years years Indian baseball	5.00

INDIANS' YEARBOOKS

1948	World Champs	100.00
1949	Logo wearing crown	65.00
1950	Fans entering stadium	100.00
1951	50th Anniversary w/ logo	190.00
1952	Chain w/ Indians logo	85.00
1953	Umpire yelling "Play ball"	80.00
1954	Lemon, Wynn, Doby, Garcia, Rosen	110.00
1955	Indian wearing crown	90.00
1956	Indian mascot	75.00
1957	Indian mascot w/ "57" on chest	75.00
1958	Herb Score	95.00
1959	Indians logo	60.00
1960	Jim Perry & Indians pitchers	55.00
1961		75.00
1962		75.00
1963		75.00
1964	Indian sliding into home	40.00
1965	Past & present uniforms	40.00
1966	Sam McDowell	40.00
1967	Picture Set	50.00
1968	Baseball & year	25.00
1969	Runner sliding into base	25.00
1970	Sam McDowell	22.50
1971	Indians in action	20.00
1972	Indians in action	20.00
73-83	Not issued.	
1984	Sutcliffe, Franco, others	10.00
85-88	Not issued.	
1989	Autographed team ball	7.00
1990	90th Anniversary in Cleveland	6.00
1991		6.00
1992	Hargrove art	5.00

MARINERS' MEDIA GUIDES

1977	Kingdome	20.00
1978	Baseball w/ Mariners logo	10.00
1979	Kingdome	10.00
1980	Mariners equipment	7.00
1981	Maury Wills	7.00
1982	Mariners logo	7.00
1983	Gaylord Perry & M's equipment	8.00
1984	Mariners logo	6.00
1985	Beattie, Langston, Davis, Hendu	7.00
1986	Mariners memorabilia	6.50
1987	Mariners logo	6.00
1988	Mariners bat	5.00
1989	Kingdome & baseball w/ logo	5.00
1990	AL Baseballs w/ M's logo	5.00
1991		5.00
1992	Mariners logo	5.00

MARINERS' YEARBOOKS

77-84	Not issued.	
1985	Langston, Davis, Beattie tuxes	10.00
86-present	Not issued.	

METS' MEDIA GUIDES

1964	Shea Stadium	35.00
1965	Mr. Met	20.00
1966	3 Mass media	15.00
1967	G. Weiss & D. Grant	12.00
1968	Gil Hodges/shea stadium crowd	12.00
1969	Gil Hodges	18.00
1970	W.S. Ticket & action photos	12.00
1971	Scoreboard	12.00
1972	Tom Seaver	18.00
1973	Yogi Berra & pennant	15.00
1974	N.L. Champ flag	10.00
1975	5 Met GMs	10.00
1976	Mgr. Joe Frazier	10.00
1977	Met uniform #77	10.00
1978	Mets logo, hat, glove	10.00
1979	Willie Mays	12.00
1980	Mets logo	7.00
1981	Baseball, New York City	7.00
1982	George Bamberger locker	7.00
1983	Tom Seaver & others	8.00
1984	Davey Johnson at computer	6.00
1985	Mets Stars (w/ Seaver)	7.00
1986	R. Craig, Gooden, Shea Stadium	7.00
1987	World Series Ring	6.00
1988	Shea 25th Anniversary	5.00
1989	Howard Johnson & Frank Cashen	5.50
1990	Howard Johnson	5.00
1991	Harrelson & Hodges	5.00
1992	Torborg, Bonilla & Murray	5.00

Mets 1983 Yearbook

METS' YEARBOOKS

1962	First year	300.00
1963		125.00
1964	Mullin Cartoon	85.00
1965		60.00
1966		60.00
1967	Mullin Cartoon	45.00
1968	Gil Hodges	45.00
1969	World Champs	85.00
1970	Film strips & W.S. celebration	25.00
1971	Play at the plate	20.00
1972	Seaver, McGraw, Harrelson, etc	30.00
1973	All-Star Gallery w/Seaver, Mays	45.00
1974	N.L. Champions pennant	20.00
1975	Tom Seaver	20.00
1976	Mr. Met	15.00
1977	Jerry Koosman	18.00
1978		15.00
1979	Mets logo	12.00
1980	Mazzilli w/ fan, others	15.00
1981	Joe Torre & All-Time Mets	10.00
1982	G. Foster & G. Bamberger	12.00
1983	Foster, Seaver, M. Wilson	15.00
1984	Strawberry, Hernandez, Orosco	15.00
1985	Gooden, Hernandez, D. Johnson	15.00
1986	25th Anniversary logo	12.00
1987	World Champions logo	10.00
1988	Strawberry, Gooden, HoJo, etc.	9.00
1989	Strawberry, Gooden, Carter, etc.	8.00
1990	6 Mets starters (Gooden, etc.)	7.00
1991		6.00
1992		6.00

ORIOLES' MEDIA GUIDES

St. Louis Browns

1927	Name & year	80.00
1928	Name & year	75.00

Orioles 1955 Yearbook

Year	Description	Price
1929		75.00
1930		75.00
1931	Sportsman's Park	70.00
1932	Sportsman's Park	70.00
1933	Sportsman's Park	70.00
1934		65.00
1935		65.00
1936	Rogers Hornsby	80.00
1937	Browns logo	60.00
1938		60.00
1939		60.00
1940	Fred Haney	55.00
1941	Statue & year	55.00
1942		55.00
1943	Browns logo	50.00
1944		50.00
1945		50.00
1946	Browns logo	45.00
1947	Baseball w/ logo	45.00
1948	"Meet the Brownies"	40.00
1949		40.00
1950	Browns logo	30.00
1951	Browns logo	30.00
1952	Browns mascot	25.00
1953	Browns mascot	25.00

Baltimore Orioles

Year	Description	Price
1954	Orioles mascot	45.00
1955	Orioles mascot	25.00
1956	Orioles mascot	25.00
1957	Orioles mascot	20.00
1958	Orioles mascot	20.00
1959	Orioles mascot	20.00
1960	Orioles mascot	20.00
1961	Orioles mascot	15.00
1962	Orioles mascot	15.00
1963	Orioles mascot	15.00
1964	Orioles mascot	15.00
1965	Hank Bauer	17.50
1966	Orioles mascot	15.00
1967	Brooks Robinson & Dave McNally	18.00
1968	Memorial Stadium	12.00
1969	View from press box	12.00
1970	Orioles dugout	12.00
1971	World Series Celebration	12.00
1972	Orioles mascot w/ pennants	12.00
1973	Player face drawing	12.00
1974	Orioles Award Winners	10.00
1975	Orioles in action	10.00
1976	Orioles logo	10.00
1977	Belanger, L. May, Palmer	12.00
1978	Earl Weaver	12.00
1979	25th Anniversary Hats	10.00
1980	Players celebrating	7.00
1981	Orioles locker room	7.00
1982	Orioles logo & mascot	8.00
1983	Frank & Brooks Robinson	8.00
1984	World Series Celebration	6.00
1985	Palmer, Bumbry, Singleton	7.00
1986	Eddie Murray & Cal Ripken	7.00
1987	Cal Ripken Sr.	6.00
1988	Orioles logo	5.00
1989	New Orioles uniforms	5.00
1990	1989 Highlights	5.00
1991	"Season to remember"	5.00
1992	Cal Ripken & stadium art	5.00

ORIOLES' YEARBOOKS

St. Louis Browns

Year	Description	Price
1944		300.00
1945		275.00
1946		250.00
1947		225.00
1948		200.00
1949		200.00
1950	Browns sketchbook	175.00
1951	Browns logo	175.00
52-53		150.00

Baltimore Orioles

Year	Description	Price
1954	Orioles mascot in spotlight	225.00
1955	Oriole mascot batting	125.00
1956	Oriole mascot on deck	100.00
1957	Oriole mascot pitching	85.00
1958	Oriole mascot riding rocket	80.00
1959	Oriole mascot w/ report	75.00
1960	Oriole mascot sitting on eggs	70.00
1961	Oriole mascot hitting opponent	70.00
1962	Jim Gentile (oversized)	60.00
1963	(oversized)	50.00
1964	Orioles catcher (oversized)	40.00
1965	Bunker, Bauer, B. Robinson (oversized)	45.00
1966	Robinsons, Powell, Blefary (oversized)	40.00
1967	Frank Robinson & fans	40.00
1968	Brooks & Frank Robinson	37.50
1969	Dave McNally	30.00
1970	Boog Powell	22.00
1971	B.Robinson, Palmer, others	25.00
1972	Palmer, Cuellar, McNally	25.00
1973	Orioles player	18.00
1974	Orioles jukebox (special 20th yearbook)	18.00
1975		15.00
76-79	Not issued.	
1980	Orioles mascot	12.00
1981	Orioles players	10.00
1982	Earl Weaver & Frank Robinson	12.00
1983	Brooks Robinson	12.00
1984	30th Anniversary in Baltimore	10.00
1985		9.00
1986	Robinsons, Ripken, Murray	10.00
87-91	Yearbook/program.	5.00
1992		5.00

Orioles 1983 Yearbook

PADRES' MEDIA GUIDES

Year	Description	Price
1969	Preston Gomez & J.M. Stadium	25.00
1970	Jack Murphy Stadium	15.00
1971	Jack Murphy Stadium	12.00
1972	S.D. vs L.A., 7/3/71	12.00
1973	Nate Colbert	14.00
1974	Player swinging bat	10.00
1975	Padres in action	10.00
1976	Randy Jones	10.00
1977	Randy Jones & Butch Metzger	10.00

Year	Description	Price
1978	Pitcher, hitter in action	10.00
1979	Roger Craig & star Padres	10.00
1980	Jerry Coleman & Dave Winfield	8.00
1981	Frank Howard & J.M. Stadium	8.00
1982	Dick Williams	7.00
1983	Padres memorabilia	7.00
1984	Padres logo, Ray Kroc memorial	6.50
1985	N.L. Champions trophy	6.00
1986	Padres logo	6.00
1987	Larry Bowa	6.00
1988	Tony Gwynn & Benito Santiago	6.00
1989	Padres logo & J.M. Stadium	5.00
1990	Padres in action	5.00
1991	New uniform	5.00
1992	Allstar game	5.00

PADRES' YEARBOOKS

Year	Description	Price
1969	Jack Murphy Stadium	75.00
70-78	Not issued	
1979	Dave Winfield	14.00
1980	Dave Winfield	14.00
1981	Not issued.	
1982		10.00
1983	Steve Garvey & Dick Williams	10.00
1984	Garvey, Williams, Templeton, etc.	10.00
1985	Padres hat & N.L. Champs ring	9.00
1986	Padres memorabilia	9.00
87-91	Yearbook/program	5.00
1992	Fernandez, Gwynn, Santiago	5.00

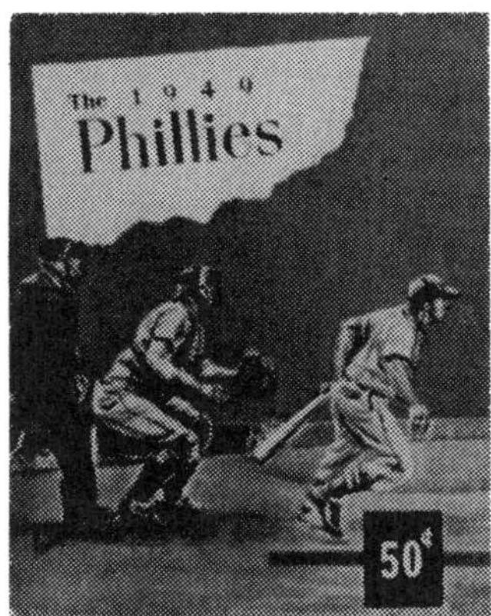

Phillies 1949 Yearbook

PHILLIES' MEDIA GUIDES

Year	Description	Price
1930	Phillies logo	75.00
1931		70.00
1932	Phillies logo	65.00
1933	Phillies golden anniversary	60.00
1934	Phillies logo	60.00
1935	Phillies logo	55.00
1936	Phillies logo	55.00
1937	Phillies logo	50.00
1938		50.00
1939		50.00
1940		45.00
1941	Player swinging bat	45.00
1942	Soldier w/ crossed bats	45.00
1943		40.00
1944		40.00
1945		40.00
1946	Shibe Park & Phillies logo	35.00
1947	Shibe Park & Phillies logo	35.00
1948	Shibe Park & Phillies logo	35.00
1949		30.00
1950		30.00
1951		30.00
1952	Shibe Park	25.00
1953	Player swinging bat	25.00
1954	Robin Roberts	35.00
1955	"Get Set To Go In 55"	20.00
1956	Crowd photo	20.00
1957	Crowd photo	20.00
1958	Crowd photo	20.00
1959	Phillies logo	20.00
1960	Phillies logo	20.00
1961	Phillies logo	15.00
1962		15.00
1963		15.00
1964	Phillies hat logo	15.00
1965	Phillies hat logo	15.00
1966	Phillies hat logo	15.00
1967	Phillies hat logo	12.00
1968	Phillies hat logo	12.00
1969	Phillies hat logo	12.00
1970	Phillies "P"	12.00
1971	Frank Luchessi	12.00
1972	Phillies logo	12.00
1973	Steve Carlton & Cy Young award	18.00
1974	Phillies in action	10.00
1975	Phillies in action	10.00
1976	Phillies in action	10.00
1977	Division champs pennant	10.00
1978	Fireworks over Veterans Stad.	10.00
1979	Phillies logo	10.00
1980	Baseball & Phillies logo	8.00
1981	World Series trophy	7.00
1982	Basket of baseballs	7.00
1983	100th Anniversary logo	7.00
1984	N.L. Championship Trophy	6.00
1985	Hands gripping bat	6.00
1986	Home plate w/ Phillies logo	6.00
1987	Mike Schmidt & trophies	7.00
1988	Mike Schmidt & Steve Bedrosian	6.50
1989	Nick Leyva & Lee Thomas	5.00
1990	Schmidt, Carlton, Roberts, Ashburn	5.50
1991	Equipment	5.00
1992	Phillies memorabilia	5.00

PHILLIES' YEARBOOKS

Year	Description	Price
1949	Red batting scene	175.00
1950	3/4 size Phillie & sheet music	150.00
1951	3/4 size w/ 6 player drawings	500.00
1952	Color stadium photo	110.00
1953	Phillie batter	100.00
1954	Smiling Phillie (head only)	100.00
1955	Phillie pitcher	85.00
1956	Ashburn and Roberts	100.00
1957	Ball w/ Phillie hat	75.00
1958	Hat on pinstriped background	75.00
1959	Five balls - one w/ logo	60.00
1960	"New Faces of 1960":11 photos	60.00
1961	1st edition	250.00
1961	2nd edition	75.00
1962	Four balls and logo	45.00
1963	Bat, ball and logo	40.00
1964	1st or 2nd edition	40.00
1964	3rd edition - Bunning and 10 other Phillies	80.00
1965	4 photos incl. Bunning & Allen	40.00
1966	Stadium photo	35.00
1967	Child eating a hot dog	35.00
1968	Phillie ballplayers	25.00
1969	Connie Mack Stadium Mem. issue	30.00
1970	Veterans Stadium in tree bark	20.00
1971	Veterans Stadium drawing	20.00
1972	Stadium, fans and players	20.00
1973	12 drawings incl. Carlton	22.50
1974	12 drawings w/ Carlton & Bowa	22.50
1975	7 photos w/ Schmidt & Carlton	20.00
1976	8 drawings w/Schmidt & Carlton	20.00
1977	Bowa photo	15.00
1978	14 photos w/ Schmidt & Carlton	18.00
1979	Schmidt, Rose, Carlton & more	18.00
1980	Schmidt, Rose, Carlton & more	16.00
1981	World Series ring photo	10.00
1982	Schmidt, Rose and Carlton	12.00
1983	Centennial celebration	10.00
1984	Schmidt, Carlton and 20 others	12.00
1985	Schmidt, Carlton, Samuel, Hayes	12.00
1986	Mike Schmidt at bat	12.00
1987	Schmidt, Samuel and others	12.00
1988	Veterans Stadium photo	8.00
1989	Schmidt,V.Hayes, Jordan & more	9.00
1990	Photo of Kruk's equipment	7.00

Year	Description	Price
1991	Fireworks over Veterans	6.00
1992	New logo, Williams, Kruk	5.00

Pirates 1987 Yearbook

PIRATES' MEDIA GUIDES

Year	Description	Price
1930	Pirate & year	75.00
1931	Pirate & year	65.00
1932	Pirate & year	65.00
1933	Pirate & year	60.00
1934	Pirate & year	60.00
1935	Pirate & year	55.00
1936	Pirate & year	55.00
1937	Pirate & year	50.00
1938	Pirate & year	50.00
1939	100th Anniversary & Pirate	50.00
1940	Pirate & year	45.00
1941	Pirate & year	45.00
1942	Pirate (Remember Pearl Harbor)	45.00
1943	Pirate (Buy War Bonds, Stamps)	40.00
1944	Pirate & year	40.00
1945	Pirate & year	40.00
1946	Pirate (Buy Victory Bonds)	35.00
1947	Billy Herman	40.00
1948	William Meyer	40.00
1949	40th Anniversary	30.00
1950	Baseballs	30.00
1951	Logo & year	30.00
1952	Baseball & year	25.00
1953	Fred Haney	25.00
1954	Honus Wagner statue	40.00
1955	Year & baseball diamond	20.00
1956	Pirate cartoon	20.00
1957	Pirate cartoon	20.00
1958	Danny Murtaugh	25.00
1959	Pirate cartoon	20.00
1960	Pirate cartoon	20.00
1961	Pirate cartoon	15.00
1962	Pitcher	15.00
1963	Baseballs	15.00
1964	Logo & year	15.00
1965	Harry Walker	18.00
1966	Pirate cartoon	15.00
1967	Pirate cartoon	12.00
1968	Larry Shepard & coaches	12.00
1969	100th Anniversary & Forbes	12.00
1970	3 River stadium model	12.00
1971	Danny Murtaugh	12.00
1972	World Series Celebration	12.00
1973	Clemente Memorial	25.00
1974	Three Rivers Stadium	10.00
1975	Championship Stars & Logo	10.00
1976	Rennie Stennett	10.00
1977	Pirates in action	10.00
1978	Three Pirates	10.00
1979	Pirates uniform	10.00
1980	Willie Stargell	9.00
1981	Pirates logo	7.00
1982	Pirates hat	7.00
1983	Pirates logo	7.00
1984	Bill Madlock	6.00
1985	Tony Pena	6.00
1986	Three Rivers Stadium	6.00
1987	100th Anniversary Logo	6.00
1988	Pirates memorabilia	5.00
1989	Bonilla, VanSlyke, LaValliere	6.00
1990	Bonilla, Bonds, Drabek, VanSlyke	5.50
1991	1990 East Disiov Champs	5.00
1992	Drabek & Slaught celebrate	5.00

PIRATES' YEARBOOKS

Year	Description	Price
1951	Forbes Field photo	175.00
1952	Pirate w/ sword and pistol	125.00
1953	"Buc youngster" in sailboat	110.00
1954	Honus Wagner statue	100.00
1955	Pirate batter "It's a hit!"	95.00
1956	Pirate swinging at "1956" ball	85.00
1957	Pirate winding up	85.00
1958	Pirate head between two bats	80.00
1959	Pirate with "Pa Pitt"	70.00
1960	Pirate in sailboat	65.00
1961	Pirate on a treasure chest	60.00
1962	Ball wearing bandana and cap	55.00
1963	Pirate batter	50.00
1964	Pirate sliding into third	45.00
1965	Manager Harry Walker w/roaches	45.00
1966	Wraparound Forbes Field photo	40.00
1967	Clemente, Mazeroski and others	50.00
1968	Clemente, Stargell and others	45.00
1969	Wraparound Forbes Field photo	30.00
1970	Three Rivers Stadium	25.00
1971	Same as '70 w/"Revised 1971"	20.00
1972	Clemente, Stargell and others	35.00
1973	Clemente, Stargell and others	35.00
1974	Stargell, Parker and others	25.00
1975	5 Pirate historical photos	16.00
1976	Yosemite Sam cartoon	16.00
1977	Pirate baseball cards	15.00
1978		15.00
1979	Dave Parker	15.00
1980	"The Family of Stars"	14.00
1981	Madlock, Lacy, Rhoden & others	10.00
1982	Stargell, Madlock and others	12.00
1983	Chuck Tanner	10.00
1984	Madlock, Pena, Ray, others	10.00
1985	Painting of Maz's '60 homer	12.00
1986	Pena, Ray, Leyland, M.Brown	9.00
1987	Centennial yearbook	8.00
1988	Bonds, Bonilla, Van Slyke, others	9.00
1989	Photo of official N.L. balls	8.00
1990	Van Slyke bat, Leyland uniform	7.00
1991	Stargell, Kiner, Bonds & more	6.00
1992	Uniforms	5.00

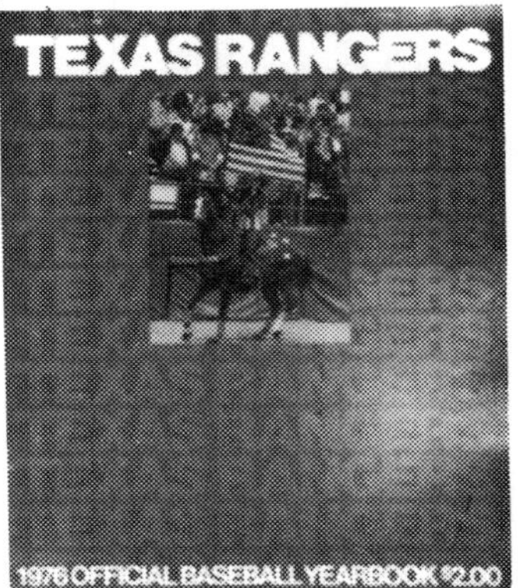

Rangers 1976 Yearbook

RANGERS' MEDIA GUIDES

Year	Description	Price
1972	Rangers logo	20.00
1973	Herzog, Short, Burke	15.00
1974	Billy Martin	15.00
1975	Martin, Jenkins, Jenkins, Hargrove	14.00
1976	Toby Harrah & oldtimers	10.00

1977 Rangers hat & equipment 10.00
1978 Billy Hunter 10.00
1979 Baseball & year 10.00
1980 Rangers catcher 7.00
1981 Fireworks over scoreboard 7.00
1982 Baseball w/ logo 7.00
1983 Baseball glove 7.00
1984 Buddy Bell & others 6.00
1985 Rangers hat 6.00
1986 Arlington Stadium 6.00
1987 Bobby Valentine 6.00
1988 Rangers logo & baseball 5.00
1989 Rangers uniforms (inc. Ryan) 7.00
1990 Home plate w/ Rangers logo 5.00
1991 5.00
1992 Julio Franco 5.00

RANGERS' YEARBOOKS

72-75 Not issued.
1976 Rangers cowgirl on horse 20.00
1977 Autographed Rangers ball 15.00
1978 15.00
1979 Jenkins, Oliver, 4 others 14.00
1980 Arlington Stadium 12.00
1981 Rangers hitter 12.00
1982 Rangers baseball 10.00
1983 Not issued.
1984 George Wright 10.00
1985 Pete O'Brien equipment 9.00
86-89 Not issued.
1990 Rangers helmet rack 6.00
1991 5.00
1992 5.00

Reds 1941 Media Guide

REDS' MEDIA GUIDES

1930 Reds logo 65.00
1931 Reds logo 60.00
1932 Reds logo 60.00
1933 60.00
1934 Cincinnati Reds 55.00
1935 Reds logo 55.00
1936 Reds logo 55.00
1937 Reds logo 50.00
1938 Bill McKechnie 50.00
1939 1869 Reds 50.00
1940 Reds logo 45.00
1941 Baseball & Champions pennant 45.00
1942 Eagle & Reds logo 45.00
1943 Eagle & Reds logo 40.00
1944 Reds logo & batter 40.00
1945 Eagle & baseball 40.00
1946 Hitter & catcher 35.00
1947 Eagle & baseball 35.00
1948 Reds logo & batter 35.00
1949 Reds logo & city 30.00
1950 Cartoon sportswriter 30.00
1951 75th Anniversary Logo 30.00
1952 Eagle & Reds logo 25.00
1953 25.00
1954 25.00
1955 Reds mascot 20.00
1956 Birdie Tebbetts 20.00
1957 Schedule 20.00
1958 Reds mascot hitting 20.00
1959 Mayo Smith 20.00
1960 Fred Hutchinson 20.00
1961 F. Hutchinson & GM W. DeWitt 18.00
1962 Reds mascot 15.00
1963 Reds mascot 15.00
1964 Reds mascot 15.00
1965 Reds mascot 15.00
1966 Reds mascot 15.00
1967 Reds mascot 12.00
1968 3 Mass media 12.00
1969 100th Anniversary Logo 12.00
1970 NL Hats 12.00
1971 3 Mass media 12.00
1972 Baseball field 12.00
1973 Sparky Anderson 12.00
1974 D. Gullett & J. Billingham 10.00
1975 Johnny Bench 14.00
1976 Joe Morgan & MVP Trophy 12.00
1977 Johnny Bench 14.00
1978 George Foster 10.00
1979 John McNamara 10.00
1980 Riverfront Stadium 7.00
1981 Reds players in action 7.00
1982 Reds uniform 7.00
1983 Russ Nixon 7.00
1984 Reds logo 6.00
1985 Riverfront Stadium 6.00
1986 Pete Rose 7.50
1987 NL Logos 6.00
1988 A.S. Game logo 5.00
1989 Autographed bats 5.00
1990 Lou Piniella 5.00
1991 World Series trophy 5.00
1992 Reds equipment 5.00

REDS' YEARBOOKS

1948 Ray Lamanno & Ewell Blackwell 200.00
1949 Harry Gumbert & Bucky Walters 175.00
1950 Not issued.
1951 75th Anniversary of N.L. 125.00
1952 Crosley Field 115.00
1953 Reds mascot leaning on bat 100.00
1954 Reds mascot swinging bat 95.00
1955 Reds mascot riding on bat 90.00
1956 Reds mascot swinging bat 90.00
1957 Reds mascot in space ship 80.00
1958 Reds mascot in orbit 65.00
1959 VanDerMeer, Lombardi, others 60.00
1960 Reds mascot, Goodman, Rixey 55.00
1961 Reds mascot running after ball 45.00
1962 Reds mascot raising pennant 45.00
1963 Reds mascot yelling "Charge" 45.00
1964 Reds mascot in action 35.00
1965 Reds mascot making catch 35.00
1966 Reds mascot reaching for ball 30.00
1967 Reds mascots & Crosley Field 30.00
1968 Autographed team ball 25.00
1969 Bench, Rose, Perez, others 30.00
1970 Johnny Bench 25.00
1971 Rose, Bench, Anderson, others 25.00
1972 Bench, Perez, other film strips 25.00
1973 Morgan, Bench, others 25.00
1974 Pete Rose sliding into home 25.00
1975 Joe Morgan 20.00
1976 Morgan, Rose, Perez 18.00
1977 Morgan, Bench, Foster, others 15.00
1978 Pete Rose 12.00
1979 Bench, Perez, Griffey, Foster 14.00
1980 Reds equipment 10.00
1981 Riverfront Stadium & baseball 10.00
1982 Binoculars on stadium seat 10.00
1983 Red player signing autographs 10.00
1984 4 bats & baseball equipment 10.00
1985 Pete Rose & Ty Cobb 12.00

Year	Cover	Price
1986	Not issued.	
1987	Rose, Parker, E.Davis, others	9.00
1988	All-Star Game logo	8.00
1989	Baseball w/ Reds logo	7.00
1990	Red player w/ fans	6.00
1991		5.00
1992	Bats & Hat	5.00

Red Sox 1974 Yearbook

RED SOX' MEDIA GUIDES

Year	Cover	Price
1939	Jimmie Foxx	70.00
1940	Red Sox logo	45.00
1941	Fenway Park	45.00
1942	Baseball bats & year	45.00
1943	Tufts College batting cage	40.00
1944		40.00
1945	Name & year	40.00
1946	Player in action	35.00
1947	World Series Pennant	35.00
1948	Joe McCarthy	45.00
1949		30.00
1950	Red Sox mascot	30.00
1951	Oldtimer & current player	30.00
1952	Fenway Park	25.00
1953	Red Sox logo	25.00
1954	Red Sox logo	25.00
1955	Red Sox logo	20.00
1956	Name & year	20.00
1957	Red Sox in action	20.00
1958	Red Sox media	20.00
1959	Player in mirror	20.00
1960	Player on horse	20.00
1961	Baseball glove & ball	15.00
1962	Yastrzemski & others	22.50
1963	Johnny Pesky	15.00
1964	Red Sox logo	15.00
1965	Red Sox logo	15.00
1966	Showerhead & Red Sox logo	15.00
1967	Red Sox logo	18.00
1968	A.L. Championship Pennant	12.00
1969	100th Anniversary	12.00
1970	Fenway Park	12.00
1971	Red Sox stars	12.00
1972	Cheering fan	12.00
1973	Red Sox in action	12.00
1974	Darrell Johnson	10.00
1975	Fenway Park	10.00
1976	A.L. Championship Pennant	10.00
1977	Don Zimmer	12.00
1978	Red Sox stars (w/ Yaz, Rice)	15.00
1979	Jim Rice	11.00
1980	Carl Yastrzemski	12.00
1981	Ralph Houk	7.00
1982	Ralph Houk & players	7.00
1983	Bob Stanley & Dwight Evans	7.00
1984	Jim Rice & Wade Boggs	7.00
1985	Tony Armas	6.00
1986	Gedman, Buckner, Boggs, Boyd	6.00
1987	Roger Clemens & John McNamara	7.00
1988	Roger Clemens & Dwight Evans	6.00
1989	Joe Morgan	5.00
1990	Fenway Park	5.00
1991	Burks & Penn	5.00
1992	Hobson & Clemens	5.00

RED SOX' YEARBOOKS

Year	Cover	Price
1951	Fenway Park	175.00
1952	Red Sox sliding into home	175.00
53-54	Not issued.	
1955	Red Sox fielder	100.00
1956	Red Sox owners	80.00
1957	Fenway Park	80.00
1958	Red Sox signing autograph	70.00
1959	Red Sox pitcher	70.00
1960	Gary Geiger	60.00
1961	Red Sox batter	45.00
1962	Yaz	45.00
1963		40.00
1964		40.00
1965	Dick Radatz	40.00
1966	Fenway Park	35.00
1967	Yastrzemski,Scott, T.Conigliaro	75.00
1968	Yastrzemski, D.Williams, Lonborg	45.00
1969	Fenway Park	25.00
1970	Yaz, Lyle, Petrocelli, 8 others	30.00
1971	Yaz, Scott, Petrocelli, 6 others	30.00
1972	Carl Yastrzemski and fans	30.00
1973	Carlton Fisk and fans	25.00
1974	Carlton Fisk (w/ Munson)	25.00
1975	Foxx, Williams, Yaz, Fisk, others	22.50
1976	Fred Lynn	15.00
1977	Carl Yastrzemski	17.50
1978	Jim Rice	12.00
1979	Carl Yastrzemski	12.00
1980	Fred Lynn	10.00
1981	Rice, Yaz, Eckersley, others	12.00
1982	Yaz, Evans, Rice, Lansford, others	12.00
1983	Carl Yastrzemski	12.00
1984	Jim Rice	10.00
1985	Tony Armas	10.00
1986	Wade Boggs	10.00
1987	Roger Clemens & Fenway Park	9.00
1988	Roger Clemens & Wade Boggs	9.00
1989	Dwight Evans	6.00
1990	Ellis Burks & Mike Greenwell	6.00
1991		5.00
1992	Viola, Clemens & Rearden	5.00

ROYALS' MEDIA GUIDES

Year	Cover	Price
1969	Royals logo	20.00
1970	Player batting	15.00
1971	Royals bat rack	12.00
1972	Royals Stadium	12.00
1973	Royals in action	12.00
1974	Royals Stadium	10.00
1975	Player batting	10.00
1976	Whitey Herzog	10.00
1977	Royals in action	10.00
1978	Players pitching, hitting	10.00
1979	'76-'78 AL West Champions	10.00
1980	Royals logo & scoreboard	7.00
1981	Royals in action & logo	7.00
1982	Royals logo & pitcher	7.00
1983	Statue of batter	6.00
1984	George Brett & fans	7.00
1985	Scoreboard (AL West Champions)	6.00
1986	World Series Trophy	6.00
1987	Royals in action (w/ Brett)	7.00
1988	Fireworks over scoreboard	5.00
1989	Royals equipment	5.00
1990	Royals in action	5.00
1991	George Brett art	5.00
1992	Logo equipment	5.00

ROYALS' YEARBOOKS

Year	Cover	Price
1969	Pitcher inside large "R"	50.00
1970	Piniella, Otis, 7 others	25.00
1971	Piniella, Otis, 2 others	25.00
1972	Catcher's mitt w/ face	22.00
1973	Mayberry, Splittorf, 2 others	20.00
1974	Otis, Mayberry, Splittorf	18.00
1975	Killebrew, McRae, Mayberry, etc.	18.00
76-82	Not issued.	
1983	Bronze Royals statue	10.00
1984	Royals jacket & equipment	10.00

1985	Division champs celebration	10.00
1986	Hand wearing W.S. Ring	10.00
1987	Royals championship pennants	8.00
1988	Fireworks over Royals Stadium	8.00
1989	Royals player locker	7.00
1990	Royals in action	6.00
1991		5.00
1992	Newspaper headlines	5.00

SENATORS' MEDIA GUIDES

1933	Capitol & year	80.00
1934	Capitol & year	80.00
1935	Capitol & year	75.00
1936	Capitol & year	75.00
1937	Capitol & year	75.00
1938	Capitol & year	70.00
1939	Capitol & year	70.00
1943	Capitol & year	70.00
1941	Capitol & year	65.00
1942	Capitol & year	65.00
1943	Capitol & year	65.00
1944	Capitol & year	60.00
1945	Capitol & year	60.00
1946	Capitol & year	60.00
1947	Capitol & year	55.00
1948	Capitol & year	55.00
1949	Capitol & year	55.00
1950	Capitol & year	50.00
1951	Capitol & year	50.00
1952	Capitol & year	50.00
1953	Capitol, baseball, bat	45.00
1954	Capitol, baseball, bat	45.00
1955	Capitol, baseball, bat	45.00
1956	Sportswriter	40.00
1957	Senators mascot pitching	40.00
1958	Golden Anniversary of BBWAA	40.00
1959	Mascot blowing out candles	35.00
1960	HR Congratulations	35.00

Becomes Minnesota Twins

1961	Doherty, Vernon, Quesada	35.00
1962	Senators Logo & Stadium	30.00
1963	Senators Logo & Stadium	30.00
1964	Senators Logo & Stadium	30.00
1965	Senators Logo & Stadium	25.00
1966	Senators Logo & Stadium	25.00
1967	Pitcher & baseball	25.00
1968	Hitter & baseball	22.00
1969	Frank Howard	25.00
1970	Bob Short & Ted Williams	25.00
1971	Senators Logo & Stadium	18.00

Becomes Texas Rangers

SENATORS' YEARBOOKS

1947		250.00
1949		150.00
1950		125.00
1952	National's batter	95.00
1953	Capitol building & baseball	95.00
1954	Bob Porterfield, Mickey Vernon	100.00
1955	National w/ 4 bats	85.00
1956	Clark C. Griffith memorial	85.00
1957	Senators pitcher	95.00
1958	Roy Sievers	90.00
1959		80.00
1960	Harmon Killebrew	80.00

Becomes Minnesota Twins

1961	"A Team is Born"	65.00
1962	Washington Stadium	55.00
1963	Red cover w/ dedication	55.00
1964	"Off the Floor in '64"	50.00
1965	Senator signing autograph	50.00
1966	Senators in action	45.00
1967	Capitol & Washington Monument	45.00
1968	Pitcher delivering	35.00
1969	Ted Williams	45.00
1970-71	Not issued.	

Becomes Texas Rangers

TIGERS' MEDIA GUIDES

1933	Tiger head & year	60.00
1934	Tiger head & year	55.00
1935	Tiger head & year	55.00
1936	Tiger head & year	55.00
1937		50.00
1938	Tiger head & year	50.00
1939	Tiger head & year	50.00
1940		45.00
1941	Briggs Stadium	45.00
1942	Flag over Briggs Stadium	45.00
1943	Tiger head & year	40.00
1944	Tiger head & year	40.00
1945	Tiger head & year	40.00
1946	Tiger head & year	35.00
1947	Tiger head & year	35.00
1948	Tiger head & year	35.00
1949	Tiger head	30.00
1950	Tiger head & year	30.00
1951	Tiger head & year	30.00
1952	Tiger head & year	25.00
1953	Tiger head & year	25.00

Senators 1969; Twins 1970; White Sox 1972 Media Guides

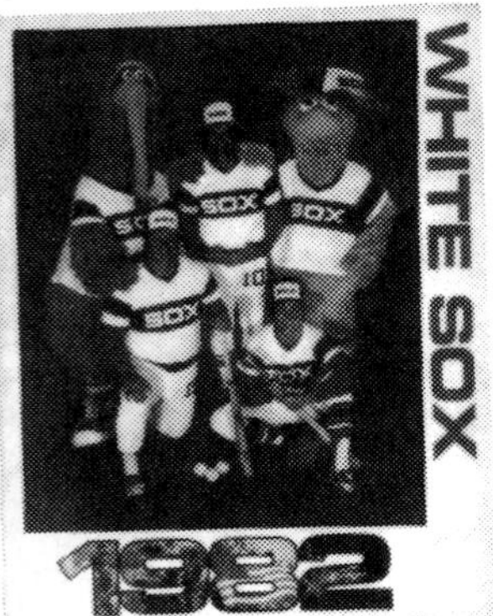

Twins 1961; White Sox 1982; Yankees 1954 Yearbooks

Year	Description	Price
1954	Tiger head & year	25.00
1955	Tiger head & year	20.00
1956	Al Kaline & Ray Boone	25.00
1957	Frank Lary	20.00
1958	Jim Bunning	25.00
1959	Tiger head & year	20.00
1960	Tiger head & year	20.00
1961	Tiger Stadium	15.00
1962	Tigers logo & players	15.00
1963	Tigers logo	15.00
1964	Tigers logo	15.00
1965	Tigers logo	15.00
1966	Tigers mascot & year	15.00
1967	Tigers mascot & year	12.00
1968	Tigers mascot & year	12.00
1969	Tigers mascot (WS Champions)	12.00
1970	Tigers mascot fielding	12.00
1971	Tigers mascot throwing	12.00
1972	Tigers mascot fielding	12.00
1973	Tigers mascot fielding	12.00
1974	Tigers mascot sliding	10.00
1975	Tigers mascot in field	10.00
1976	Tigers mascot pitching	10.00
1977	Tigers mascot catching	10.00
1978	Tigers mascot batting	10.00
1979	Tigers logo & year	10.00
1980	Tigers mascot in action	7.00
1981	Tiger jumping	7.00
1982	Tigers logo	7.00
1983	Greenberg & Gehringer uniforms	8.00
1984	Tigers mascot boxing	6.00
1985	Tigers logo & W.S. Trophy	6.00
1986	Tigers mascot in stadium	6.00
1987	Tiger & baseball	6.00
1988		5.00
1989	"The Press Guide" & logo	5.00
1990	Uniform "D"	5.00
1991	Star Wars theme	5.00
1992	Trammell, Whitaker art	5.00

TIGERS' YEARBOOKS

Year	Description	Price
1955		250.00
1956	Not issued.	
1957	Tiger sliding into home	125.00
1958	Tiger HOFs (w/ Cobb)	135.00
1959	Tiger batting & logo	85.00
1960	Tiger Stadium	70.00
1961	Tiger head & 5 baseballs	55.00
1962	Tiger head & 9 players	55.00
1963	Tiger head	45.00
1964	Tiger head	45.00
1965	Bill Freehan	40.00
1966	Willie Horton	35.00
1967	Denny McLain	40.00
1968	Al Kaline	40.00
1969	World Series Trophy	30.00
1970	Tiger hat, bats, baseballs	20.00
1971	Billy Martin, Kaline, Horton	25.00
1972	Mickey Lolich	15.00
1973		15.00
1974		12.00
1975		12.00
1976	75th Anniversary	15.00
1977	Fidrych, Staub, LeFlore	12.00
1978		12.00
1979	Alan Trammell & Lou Whitaker	18.00
1980	Trammell, Whitaker, Morris, etc.	15.00
1981	Trammell, Whitaker, Morris, etc.	15.00
1982	Clubhouse photo (w/ Gibson)	12.00
1983	Gehringer and Greenberg	10.00
1984	Morris, Whitaker, Trammell, etc.	10.00
1985	World Championship Trophy	10.00
1986	Sparky Anderson	10.00
1987	Tiger on top of baseball	8.00
1988	Tiger face "Eye of the Tiger"	8.00
1988	"Intend-a-Pennant"	7.00
1990	Roaring into the 90's Tiger	6.00
1991	Five heads of players	5.00
1992	Sparky Anderson and Casey	5.00

TWINS' MEDIA GUIDES

Year	Description	Price
1961	Metropolitan Stadium drawing	30.00
1962	Metropolitan Stadium	20.00
1963	Player batting	15.00
1964	Baseball & year	15.00
1965	All-Star Game hosts	15.00
1966	Player fielding (A.L. Champs)	15.00
1967	Twins uniform	12.00
1968	Pitcher delivering	12.00
1969	Metropolitan Stadium	12.00
1970	Twins stars (w/ Carew)	16.00
1971	Jim Perry	12.00
1972	Minnesota media	12.00
1973	Rod Carew	16.00
1974	Baseballs	10.00
1975	Rod Carew & Ty Cobb	15.00
1976	24 Twins (w/ Carew, Killebrew)	14.00
1977	Old Press Guide covers	10.00
1978	Rod Carew	12.00
1979	Metropolitan Stadium	10.00
1980	Twins baseball cards	7.00
1981	Twins hats & uniforms, bats	7.00
1982	Metrodome	7.00
1983	Kent Hrbek	7.00
1984	Twins uniforms	6.00
1985	All-Star Game logo	6.00
1986	25th Anniversary logo	6.00
1987	Gary Gaetti & Kirby Puckett	6.00
1988	World Series Trophy	5.00
1989	Frank Viola & Kirby Puckett	6.00
1990	Puckett, Carew, Oliva	5.00
1991	30 years, Carew, Killebrew (HOF)	5.00
1992	World Series trophy celebration	5.00

TWINS' YEARBOOKS

Year	Description	Price
1961	Twins batters	200.00

Year	Cover	Price
1962	Metropolitan Stadium	50.00
1963	Harmon Killebrew	55.00
1964	Gloved hand & baseball	40.00
1965	Autographed Twins ball	40.00
1966	Tony Oliva (AL Champions)	45.00
1967	Killebrew, Oliva, Kaat	40.00
1968	Jim Kaat & Harmon Killebrew	35.00
1969	Killebrew, Carew, Oliva, others	35.00
1970	Rod Carew	30.00
1971	Carew, Killebrew, Oliva, others	30.00
1972	Tony Oliva & Harmon Killebrew	30.00
1973	Frank Quilici	20.00
1974	Rod Carew	22.50
1975	Rod Carew	20.00
1976	Rod Carew	20.00
1977	Past Twins yearbooks	16.00
1978	Rod Carew	12.00
1979	Twins batting helmet	12.00
1980	Twins baseball cards	10.00
1981	20th Anniversary (w/ Carew)	12.00
1982	Metrodome	10.00
83-84	Not issued.	
1985	Yearbook/scorecard	10.00
1986	25th Anniversary celebration	10.00
1987	Twins uniforms	8.00
1988	World Champions celebration	8.00
1989	Puckett, Reardon, Viola, Gaetti	7.00
1990	Puckett, Carew, Oliva	6.00
1991		5.00
1992	World Series trophy	5.00

WHITE SOX' MEDIA GUIDES

Year	Cover	Price
1933	Name & year	60.00
1934	Name & year	55.00
1935	Name & year	55.00
1936	Name & year	55.00
1937	Name & year	50.00
1938	Name & year	50.00
1939	Name & year	50.00
1940	Name & year	45.00
1941	Ted Lyons	50.00
1942	Jimmy Dykes	45.00
1943	Buy More War Bonds	40.00
1944	Back the Attack	40.00
1945		40.00
1946	Name & year	35.00
1947	Ted Lyons	40.00
1948	Mascot & year	35.00
1949	White Sox logo & year	30.00
1950	Luke Appling	35.00
1951	Paul Richards	30.00
1952	Minoso, Fox, Rogovin, Carrasquel	30.00
1953	White Sox in action	25.00
1954	White Sox mascot	25.00
1955	White Sox mascot	20.00
1956	White Sox mascot	20.00
1957	White Sox mascot	20.00
1958	White Sox mascot	20.00
1959	White Sox mascot	20.00
1960	White Sox mascot	20.00
1961	Name & year	15.00
1962	White Sox in action	15.00
1963	White Sox in action	15.00
1964	White Sox in action	15.00
1965	Pitcher delivering	15.00
1966	Batter swinging	15.00
1967	White Sox in action	12.00
1968	Batter at home plate	12.00
1969	Batter swinging	12.00
1970	Fielder in action	12.00
1971	Chuck Tanner	12.00
1972	White Sox in action	12.00
1973	Wood, Tanner, Allen	14.00
1974	White Sox logo	10.00
1975	AL 75th Anniversary	10.00
1976	White Sox logo	10.00
1977	White Sox logo	10.00
1978	Batter & White Sox logo	10.00
1979	Don Kessinger	10.00
1980	Fans in crowd	7.00
1981	Pitcher in action	7.00
1982	White Sox logo	7.00
1983	Sportswriter equipment	7.00
1984	Scoreboard, AL West Champs	6.00
1985	Comiskey Park	6.00
1986	Aparicio, Appling, Guillen	7.00
1987	New White Sox uniform #87	6.00
1988	White Sox in action	5.00
1989	Past White Sox stars	5.00
1990	Comiskey Park 80 years	5.00
1991	Equipment art	5.00
1992	Logo in black/silver	5.00

WHITE SOX' YEARBOOKS

Year	Cover	Price
1952		100.00
1953	Comiskey Park	95.00
1954	White Sox batter	85.00
1955	White Sox batter	80.00
1956	White Sox sliding into home	75.00
1957	White Sox fielder	75.00
1958	White Sox batter	65.00
1959	White Sox mascot w/ hat	80.00
1960	White Sox fielding	55.00
1961	White Sox pitching	45.00
1962	White Sox batting	45.00
1963	White Sox fielding	40.00
1964	Fireworks over Comiskey Park	40.00
1965	White Sox uniform #80	35.00
1966	White Sox batter swinging	35.00
1967	White Sox in action	30.00
1968	White Sox batter at plate	25.00
1969	Tommy John	25.00
1970	White Sox in action	20.00
71-81	Not issued.	
1982	Fisk, Luzinski, LaRussa	10.00
1983	All-Star Game w/ Fisk, others	10.00
1984	LaRussa, Luzinski, Kittle, Hoyt	10.00
1985	Not issued.	
1986	J.Davis, Baines, Guillen, Walker	9.00
1987	Not issued.	
1988	White Sox memorabilia	8.00
1989	Not issued.	
1990		6.00
1991		5.00
1992	"Good guys wear Black Sox"	5.00

YANKEES' MEDIA GUIDES

Year	Cover	Price
1936	Joe McCarthy	70.00
1937	Joe McCarthy	65.00
1938	Joe McCarthy	65.00
1939	Joe McCarthy	65.00
1940	Joe McCarthy	60.00
1941	Joe McCarthy	60.00
1942	Joe McCarthy	60.00
1943		45.00
1944		45.00
1945	Victory "V" & year	40.00
1946	Yankees logo & year	40.00
1947	Yankees logo & year	35.00
1948	Yankees logo & year	35.00
1949	Yankees logo & year	30.00
1950	Yankees logo & year	30.00
1951	Yankees logo & year	30.00
1952	Yankees logo & year	25.00
1953	Yankees logo & year	25.00
1954	Yankees logo & year	25.00
1955	Yankees logo & year	20.00
1956	Yankees logo & year	20.00
1957	Yankees logo & year	20.00
1958	Yankees logo & year	20.00
1959	Yankees logo & year	20.00
1960	Yankee stadium	20.00
1961	Yankees logo & year	15.00
1962	Yankees logo & year	15.00
1963	Yankees logo & year	15.00
1964	Yogi Berra & logo	18.00
1965	Yankees logo	15.00
1966	Yankee Stadium & logo	15.00
1967	Batter & Yankees logo	12.00
1968	Yankee Stadium	12.00
1969	Yankee hat & glove	12.00
1970	Mel Stottlemyre	12.00
1971	Yankees in action & logo	12.00
1972	Roy White & Bobby Murcer	14.00
1973	Yankee Stadium	12.00
1974	Mickey Mantle & Whitey Ford	18.00
1975	Catfish Hunter & Bobby Bonds	15.00
1976	Yankee Stadium	10.00
1977	Chris Chambliss & Thurman Munson	12.00
1978	Babe Ruth & Reggie Jackson	15.00

Year	Cover	Price
1979	Goose Gossage & Thurman Munson	12.00
1980	Gene Michael & Dick Howser	7.00
1981	Yankees logo	7.00
1982	Yankees logo	7.00
1983	Billy Martin w/ umpire	8.00
1984	Righetti & Yankee no-hitters	7.00
1985	Don Mattingly	7.00
1986	Henderson, Mattingly, Guidry, Niekro	7.00
1987	Lou Piniella & team	6.00
1988	Yankees logo	5.00
1989	Dallas Green	5.00
1990	Baseball bat & ball	5.00
1991	Sax, Mattingly, Kelly, Maas	5.00
1992	Art, Yankee greats.	5.00

YANKEES' YEARBOOKS

Year	Cover	Price
1950	Big League Books	275.00
1951	Big League Books	250.00
1952	Big League Books	250.00
1953	Big League Books	225.00
1954	Yankee w/ 6 World Series bats; B.L. Books	200.00
1955	3 Yankees; Big League Books	175.00
1956	Yankee sliding into home; B.L. Books	150.00
1957	Yankee batting; Big League Books	125.00
1958	Yankee fielding; Big League Books	100.00
1959	Big League Books	90.00
1960	Art- batter; Big League Books	90.00
1961	Art- pitcher; Big League Books	75.00
1961	Official	125.00
1962	Mantle & Maris; Big League Books	60.00
1962	Yankee Stadium; Official	65.00
1963	Yankee holding 6 bats; Big League Books	45.00
1963	Official	60.00
1964	Big League Books	35.00
1964	Berra & Houk; Official	60.00
1965	Big League Books	30.00
1965	Official	50.00
1966	Two autographed balls	50.00
1967	Mickey Mantle	70.00
1968	Mantle, Stottlemyre, others	50.00
1969	Mantle, Stottlemyre, others	45.00
1970	Murcer, Stottlemyre, others	30.00
1971	Murcer, White, others	25.00
1972	Murcer, White, Stottlemyre	25.00
1973	DiMaggio, Ruth, Gehrig, Mantle	35.00
1974	Thurman Munson & Bobby Murcer	25.00
1975	25th Annual w/ Past yearbooks	15.00
1976	Yankee Stadium	25.00
1977	Chris Chambliss	20.00
1978	World Series Trophy	15.00
1979	World Series Celebration	15.00
1980	Yankee Stadium	12.00
1981	Yankees Big Apple	12.00
1982	Winfield, Gossage, Guidry, others	12.00
1983	Billy Martin	15.00
1984	Baseball cards	10.00
1985	Ruth, Gehrig, Mantle, Maris, etc.	12.00
1986	Yankees MVP's	12.00
1987	Gehrig, Mattingly, Mantle, Rickey	12.00
1988	Mattingly, Rickey, Clark, Randolph	10.00
1989	Yankee Memorabilia	8.00
1990	Don Mattingly	7.00
1991		5.00
1992	Don Mattingly	5.00

BASKETBALL PUBLICATIONS

BLAZERS' MEDIA GUIDES

Year	Cover	Price
70-71	Rick Adelman	15.00
71-72	Geoff Petrie	8.00
72-73	Sidney Wicks	8.00
73-74	Coach Jack McCloskey	8.00
74-75	Bill Walton	10.00
75-76	Lenny Steele	5.00
76-77	Bill Walton	8.00
77-78	Bill Walton, NBA Champs!	10.00
78-79	Maurice Lucas in action	7.50
79-80	Radio announcer, Walton, Ramsey	7.50
80-81	Billy Bates	5.00
81-82	Jim Paxson	5.50
82-83	Mychal Thompson	5.00

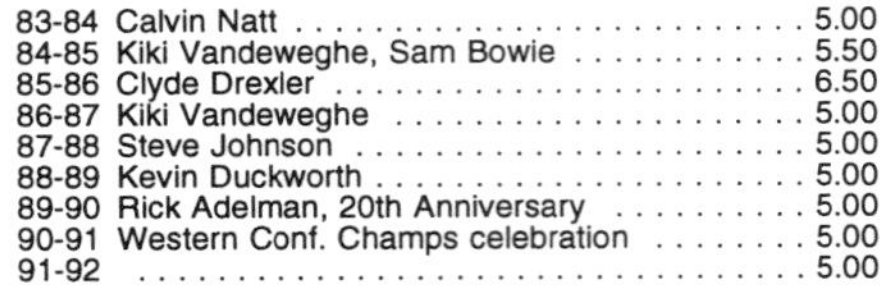

Year	Cover	Price
83-84	Calvin Natt	5.00
84-85	Kiki Vandeweghe, Sam Bowie	5.50
85-86	Clyde Drexler	6.50
86-87	Kiki Vandeweghe	5.00
87-88	Steve Johnson	5.00
88-89	Kevin Duckworth	5.00
89-90	Rick Adelman, 20th Anniversary	5.00
90-91	Western Conf. Champs celebration	5.00
91-92		5.00

BLAZERS' YEARBOOKS

No separate yearbooks issued; see media guide listings for all years

Bullets 1986-87 Media Guide

BUCKS' MEDIA GUIDES

Year	Cover	Price
68-69	Bucks vs. Royals w/ Embry	15.00
69-70	Bucks logo	8.00
70-71	Kareem in action	12.50
71-72	Kareem in action vs. Bullets	12.50
72-73	Kareem in action vs. Suns	10.00
73-74	Lucius Allen in action	8.00
74-75	Kareem, Milwaukee skyline	10.00
75-76	Bucks vs. Bulls action	6.00
76-77	Gary Brokaw vs. Bulls	6.00
77-78	Brian Winters vs. Suns	6.00
78-79	Marques Johnson art	5.00
79-80	Starting 5 art (front & back)	6.50
80-81	Team art (front & back)	6.00
81-82	Sidney Moncreif art	5.50
82-83	Bucks art	5.00
83-84	Nelson, Moncreif, M. Johnson art	5.50
84-85	"Super Sid" Moncreif	5.50
85-86	Paul Pressey	5.00
86-87	Moncreif, Milwaukee skyline	5.50
87-88	20th Anniversary art, headlines	5.50
88-89	Bucks vs.Rockets full court photo	5.00
89-90	Del Harris	5.00
90-91	Bucks action photos	5.00

91-92 . . . . 5.00

BUCKS' YEARBOOKS

69-70 See Media Guides
No other yearbooks issued; see media guide listings for other years

BULLETS' MEDIA GUIDES

Baltimore Bullets

64-65 Gus Johnson in action 25.00
65-66 Media Equipment 15.00
66-67 Media Equipment 10.00
67-68 20 yrs of Basketball in Baltimore 10.00
68-69 Bullets action 8.00
69-70 W. Unseld, G. Shue, E. Monroe art 10.00
70-71 Wes Unseld 10.00
71-72 Bullets art 8.00
72-73 Bullets action 8.00

Washington Bullets

73-74 KC Jones & starting five 8.00
74-75 Elvin Hayes 7.50
75-76 Unseld, Hayes, Chenier 7.00
76-77 Dick Motta 5.00
77-78 Hayes, Unseld, Kupchak, others art 6.50
78-79 "The Fat Lady Sang, " NBA Champs 6.00
79-80 Championship Trophy 5.00
80-81 Unseld, Hayes, Shue, Porter 5.50
81-82 Action photos 5.00
82-83 Lucas, Ruland, Ballard art 5.00
83-84 Jeff Ruland, Rick Mahorn art 5.00
84-85 Ruland, Ballard, Mahorn, Robinson art 5.00
85-86 Action art 5.00
86-87 Moses Malone art 5.50
87-88 Moses Malone, Wash. Monument 5.50
88-89 Wes Unseld 5.00
89-90 Unseld, Hammonds, B. King, others 5.00
90-91 Unseld, B. King, Hammonds 5.00
91-92 . . . . 5.00

BULLETS' YEARBOOKS

74-75 See Media Guides
88-89 Wes Unseld 7.00
89-90 Wes Unseld 7.00
No other yearbooks issued; see media guide listings for other years

BULLS' MEDIA GUIDES

66-67 Bulls logo 25.00
67-68 Bulls logo 15.00
68-69 Bulls logo 10.00
69-70 Bulls logo 10.00
70-71 Bulls logo 8.00
71-72 Bulls logo, action 7.50
72-73 Chet Walker in action 6.00
73-74 Chet Walker in action 6.00
74-75 Bulls logo, action photos 5.00
75-76 Bulls logo, Jerry Sloan 5.00
76-77 Bulls art 5.00
77-78 Action photos 5.00
78-79 Artis Gilmore in action 5.00
79-80 Artis Gilmore & Jerry Sloan action 5.00
80-81 Reggie Theus in action 5.00
81-82 Gilmore, Greenwood in action vs. Celtics 5.00
82-83 Rod Thorn & Paul Westhead 5.00
83-84 Kevin Loughery in Chicago 5.00
84-85 O. Woolridge & Michael Jordan 10.00
85-86 O. Woolridge, M. Jordan, S. Albeck 10.00
86-87 Michael Jordan art 10.00
87-88 Action photos (w/ Jordan), AS logo 8.00
88-89 B.Cartwright, M.Jordan, H.Grant art 7.50
89-90 Bulls comics 6.00
90-91 25th Anniversary art 6.00
91-92 . . . . 5.00

BULLS' YEARBOOKS

69-70, 71-72, 72-73, 75-76 thru 87-88
See Media Guides
No other yearbooks issued; see media guide listings for other years

CAVALIERS' MEDIA GUIDES

70-71 Cavaliers logo & year 12.50
71-72 Cavaliers logo & year 8.00
72-73 Cavaliers logo & year 7.00

Cavs 1984-85 Yearbook

73-74 Cavalier action art 6.00
74-75 Cavaliers logo & year, action art 6.00
75-76 Cleveland Coliseum 5.00
76-77 Cavaliers team photo 5.50
77-78 Cavaliers mascot & logo 5.00
78-79 "C'mon Cavaliers" 5.00
79-80 "A New Era...Cavaliers II" 5.00
80-81 Cavaliers action photos 5.00
81-82 Mike Mitchell action art 5.00
82-83 Ron Brewer, Cleveland skyline 5.00
83-84 New Cavaliers logo 5.00
84-85 15th season Cavs basketball cards 5.00
85-86 Cavaliers art 5.00
86-87 Lenny Wilkens 5.00
87-88 Williams, Harper, Dougherty 5.50
88-89 Cavaliers vs. Bulls action 5.00
89-90 20th Season - Wilkens, action photos 5.00
90-91 Cavalier uniform & action photos 5.00
91-92 . . . . 5.00

CAVALIERS' YEARBOOKS

77-78 thru 81-82, 84-85, 85-86
See Media Guides
No other yearbooks issued; see media guide listings for other years

CELTICS' MEDIA GUIDE

51-52 Folder report - plain brown cover 125.00
52-53 . . . . 25.00
53-54 . . . . 25.00
54-55 Individual Celtics photos 50.00
55-56 Bob Cousy art 55.00
56-57 Team photos 50.00
57-58 Individual Celtics photos 45.00
58-59 Frank Ramsey in action 40.00
59-60 Gene Conley 35.00
60-61 Boston Garden 30.00
61-62 Red Auerbach & starting five 40.00
62-63 Bob Cousy 40.00

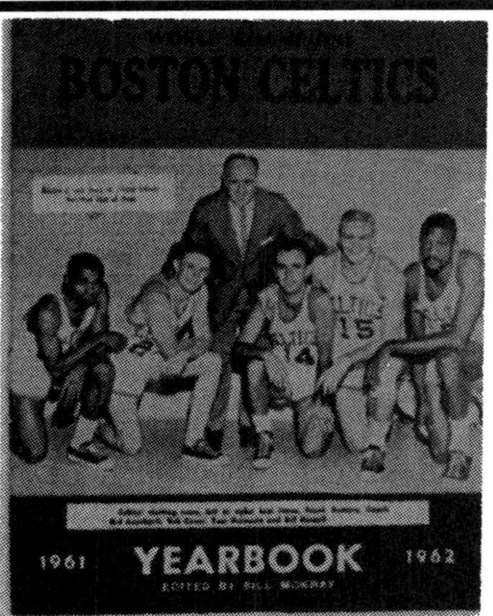

Celtics 1961-62 Yearbook

63-64 Tom Heinsohn in action 35.00
64-65 Boston Garden 15.00
65-66 . . . . 10.00
66-67 Bill Russell 15.00
67-68 John Havlicek in action 15.00
68-69 Bill Russell & Red Auerbach art 15.00
69-70 Celtics mascot 7.50
70-71 Cowens, White, Nelson, others 8.50
71-72 Cowens, Havlicek, White in action 10.00
72-73 Cowens, Havlicek in action vs. Lakers 10.00
73-74 Cowens, Havlicek, White art 10.00
74-75 John Havlicek & Paul Silas 10.00
75-76 John Havlicek & Dave Cowens 10.00
76-77 Championship trophy 8.50
77-78 John Havlicek 8.50
78-79 Dave Cowens in action 7.50
79-80 M.L. Carr, Larry Bird art 20.00
80-81 L. Bird, B. Fitch, R. Auerbach 15.00
81-82 Championship banner & trophy 7.50
82-83 Celtics art (w/ Bird) 10.00
83-84 Celtics vs. Hawks action 5.00
84-85 Championship trophy 5.00
85-86 Larry Bird in action vs. Lakers 7.50
86-87 Larry Bird photos 7.50
87-88 Starting 5 photos (w/ Bird) 7.50
88-89 Celtics historical photos 5.00
89-90 Red Auerbach 5.00
90-91 Celtics art (Bird, Auerbach, etc) 7.00
91-92 . . . . 5.00

CELTICS' YEARBOOKS

55-56 thru 73-74 See Media Guides
74-75 Paul Silas 25.00
75-76 John Havlicek 25.00
76-77 Jo Jo White 20.00
77-78 Dave Cowens 20.00
78-79 . . . . 18.00
79-80 . . . . 18.00
80-81 Larry Bird 30.00
81-82 Larry Bird 25.00
82-83 McHale, Bird, Parish, others 20.00
83-84 Robert Parish 12.00
84-85 Bird v. Magic, Championship banner 18.00
85-86 Larry Bird 16.00
86-87 Championship banner 14.00
87-88 Bird, Parish, McHale, others 12.00
88-89 Larry Bird 10.00
89-90 Robert Parish 8.00
90-91 Larry Bird 9.00
91-92 . . . . 5.00

CLIPPERS' MEDIA GUIDES

Buffalo Braves

70-71 Braves logo 15.00
71-72 Braves logo 8.00
72-73 Elmore Smith in action vs. Chamberlain 10.00
73-74 Braves action photo 7.50
74-75 Braves vs. Kings action 7.00
75-76 Braves action 7.00
76-77 Four action photos 7.00
77-78 Buffalo skyline photo 7.00

SD Clippers

78-79 Randy Smith 7.00
79-80 Bill Walton 6.50
80-81 Paul Silas 6.00
81-82 Freeman Williams 5.00
82-83 Tom Chambers 5.50
83-84 Terry Cummings 5.00

LA Clippers

84-85 Logo, LA Memorial Sports Arena 5.00
85-86 Derek Smith photos 5.00
86-87 Benoit Benjamin dunking 5.00
87-88 Cage, Nixon, Benjamin photos 5.00
88-89 D. Manning, others action 5.50
89-90 Benjamin, Manning, others art 5.50
90-91 Manning, Kimble, C. Smith photos 5.50
91-92 . . . . 5.00

CLIPPERS' YEARBOOKS

No separate yearbooks issued; see media guide listings for all years

HAWKS' MEDIA GUIDES

68-69 Hawks mascot 12.50
69-70 Lou Hudson 8.50
70-71 Atlanta skyline, Hawks art 7.50
71-72 Richie Guerin, Hawks bench 6.00
72-73 Hawks logo 5.00
73-74 Overhead shot of Omni court 5.00
74-75 Lou Hudson 5.00
75-76 Tom Van Ardsdale 5.00
76-77 John Drew 5.00
77-78 Hawks logo and art 5.00
78-79 Hawks logo, newspaper clips 5.00
79-80 H. Brown, J. Drew, Armond Hill 5.00
80-81 Dan Roundfield vs. Kareem art 5.50
81-82 Action art 5.00
82-83 Dan Roundfield 5.00
83-84 Hawks action art 5.00
84-85 Dominique Wilkins art 8.00
85-86 Dominique Wilkins 7.50
86-87 Dominique Wilkins 7.00
87-88 Dominique Wilkins 7.00
88-89 Dominique Wilkins 6.50
89-90 Wilkins, Malone, Rivers art 6.00
90-91 "Let's Run One" 5.00
91-92 . . . . 5.00

HAWKS' YEARBOOKS

89-90 Wilkins, Rivers, Malone 8.50
90-91 Dominique Wilkins 7.50
No other yearbooks issued; see media guide listings for other years

HEAT MEDIA GUIDES

88-89 Heat logo 8.00
89-90 Rory Sparrow w/ fan art 5.00
90-91 House w/ basketball in driveway 5.00
91-92 . . . . 5.00

HEAT YEARBOOKS

No separate yearbooks issued; see media guide listings for all years

HORNETS' MEDIA GUIDES

88-89 Stern, G. Shinn, Hornets uniform 8.00
89-90 NBA Attendance champions banner 5.00
90-91 3 Gene Little photos 5.00
91-92 . . . . 5.00

HORNETS' YEARBOOKS

No separate yearbooks issued until 91-92; see media guide listings for all years

JAZZ MEDIA GUIDES

New Orleans Jazz

74-75 New Orleans scene, logo 8.50
75-76 . . . . 6.00
76-77 Pete Maravich 10.00
77-78 . . . . 6.00
78-79 Maravich, L. Robinson art 8.50

Utah Jazz

79-80 Salt Palace 6.00
80-81 Tom Nissalke, Adrian Dantley 5.00
81-82 Adrian Dantley 5.00
82-83 F. Layden, A. Dantley, D. Griffith 5.00
83-84 Rickey Green, Mark Eaton 5.00
84-85 "A Winning Combination" 5.00
85-86 K. Malone, T. Bailey, J. Stockton 9.50
86-87 Mark Eaton 5.00
87-88 Malone, Eaton, Bailey, others 6.00
88-89 Malone, others 10th Anniversary 6.50
89-90 Jazz logo 5.00
90-91 Jerry Sloan photos 5.00
91-92 . . . . 5.00

JAZZ YEARBOOKS

78-79 thru 87-88 See Media Guides
No other yearbooks issued; see media guide listings for other years

KINGS' MEDIA GUIDES

Cincinnati Royals

57-58 World wearing Royals crown 45.00
58-59 Basketball wearing Royals crown 20.00
59-60 Basketball wearing Royals crown 20.00
60-61 Royals mascot cartoon 15.00
61-62 Royal masct w/ snake charmer 15.00
62-63 Royal mascot w/ briefcase 15.00
63-64 . . . . 10.00
64-65 . . . . 10.00
65-66 . . . . 10.00
66-67 . . . . 10.00
67-68 Coach Ed Tucker art 10.00
68-69 Oscar Robertson & W. Chamberlain 17.50
69-70 Coach Bob Cousy art 10.00
70-71 T.Van Ardsdale, Archibald, Van Lier 7.50
71-72 Royals patch & pins 7.50

KC-Omaha Kings

72-73 Kings logo art 7.00
73-74 Archibald & Cousy 7.50
74-75 Action art, coach Phil Johnson 7.00

Kansas City Kings

75-76 Johnson, Archibald art 7.00
76-77 Starting 5 art (front & back) 5.00
77-78 Birdsong, Burleson, Allen art (f & b) 5.00
78-79 Kings logo 5.00
79-80 Kings logo, player art 5.00
80-81 S. Wedman, R. King, action photos 5.00
81-82 Phil Ford 5.00
82-83 GM Axelson, Fitzsimmons, scoreboard 5.00
83-84 Kings logo 5.00
84-85 Kings team photo 5.00

Sacramento Kings

85-86 Kings logo 6.00
86-87 Kings fans in crowd 5.00
87-88 "We're Building Together" photo 5.00
88-89 Kenny Smith 5.00
89-90 Ainge, Tisdale, McCray, etc. 5.00
90-91 Simmons, Mays, Bonner, others 5.50
91-92 . . . . 5.00

KINGS' YEARBOOKS

69-70, 89-90 thru 90-91 See Media Guides
No other yearbooks issued; see media guide listings for other years

KNICKS' MEDIA GUIDES

58-59 . . . . 75.00
59-60 . . . . 35.00
60-61 . . . . 30.00
61-62 . . . . 25.00
62-63 . . . . 25.00
63-64 . . . . 15.00
64-65 . . . . 15.00

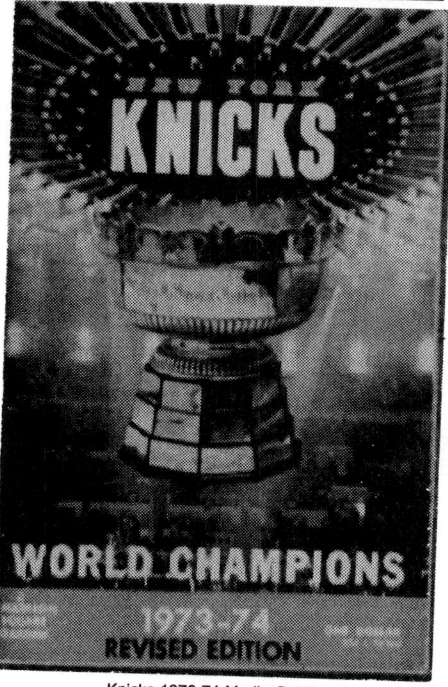

Knicks 1973-74 Media Guide

65-66 . . . . 10.00
66-67 Cartoon player 10.00
67-68 . . . . 10.00
68-69 . . . . 10.00
69-70 Willis Reed, Dave DeBeusschere 15.00
70-71 . . . . 7.50
71-72 . . . . 7.50
72-73 . . . . 7.50
73-74 Championship trophy 10.00
74-75 Bill Bradley uniform 8.50
75-76 . . . . 7.50
76-77 . . . . 7.50
77-78 Willis Reed 8.50
78-79 M. Webster, Monroe, others 8.00
79-80 Bill Cartwright 6.50
80-81 Cartwright, Richardson, Holzman, etc 6.50
81-82 NYC skyline 6.00
82-83 Hubie Brown 6.00
83-84 Knicks action 6.00
84-85 Action art 6.00
85-86 King, Ewing, Cartwright, others art 10.00
86-87 Uniforms & locker 6.00
87-88 Rick Pitino & Al Bianchi 6.50
88-89 P. Ewing, C. Oakley, M. Jackson 7.50
89-90 M. Jackson, S. Jackson, P. Ewing 7.00
90-91 Patrick Ewing art 6.50
91-92 . . . . 5.00

KNICKS' YEARBOOKS

78-79 thru 90-91 See Media Guides
No other yearbooks issued; see media guide listings for other years

LAKERS' MEDIA GUIDES

60-61 Name & year art 75.00
61-62 . . . . 20.00
62-63 . . . . 15.00
63-64 . . . . 10.00
64-65 . . . . 10.00

65-66 . . . . 10.00
66-67 Lakers logo 10.00
67-68 Logo & year 8.50
68-69 Chamberlain, E.Baylor, J.Wilkes 12.50
69-70 . . . . 8.50
70-71 . . . . 8.00
71-72 . . . . 7.50
72-73 Championship trophy 7.50
73-74 Gail Goodrich in action vs. Phoenix 7.50
74-75 Gail Goodrich 7.00
75-76 Kareem art 10.00
76-77 J. West action photos & as GM 6.00
77-78 Laker girl wearing uniform #1 . . . . 6.00
78-79 Kareem action vs. Detroit 8.00
79-80 Magic & Kareem 25.00
80-81 Kareem & Magic art 15.00
81-82 Forum & art (Magic, Kareem, etc) 12.50
82-83 Magic, Kareem, Nixon, others art 12.50
83-84 The Forum 6.00
84-85 Kareem art (by L. Niemann) 10.00
85-86 Kareem & championship trophy 8.00
86-87 Chick Hearn 6.00
87-88 Magic, Kareem, Worthy, etc., trophy art 8.00
88-89 Kareem uniform & locker 8.00
89-90 Magic multiple photos 8.00
90-91 Magic, Worthy, Perkins, others art 7.50
91-92 . . . . 5.00

LAKERS' YEARBOOKS

No separate yearbooks known; see media guide listings for all years

MAGIC MEDIA GUIDES

89-90 Magic art 8.00
90-91 Matt Goukas photos 5.00
91-92 . . . . 5.00

MAGIC YEARBOOKS

No separate yearbooks known; see media guide listings for all years

MAVERICKS' MEDIA GUIDES

80-81 Mavericks uniform art 8.00
81-82 Dallas Reunion Arena 5.00
82-83 Dick Motta art 5.00
83-84 Mark Aguirre art 5.50
84-85 Rolando Blackman art 5.50
85-86 Action art 5.00
86-87 Derek Harper, action photos 5.00
87-88 Donaldson, MacLoed, Mavs logo 5.00
88-89 Roy Tarpley 6.00
89-90 Brad Davis, 10th Anniversary 5.00
90-91 D. Harper, R. Blackman, F. Lever 5.50
91-92 . . . . 5.00

MAVERICKS' YEARBOOKS

80-81 thru 82-83 See Media Guides
87-88 Mark Aguirre 7.00
88-89 Roy Tarpley 6.00
No other yearbooks issued; see media guide listings for other years

NETS' MEDIA GUIDES

New York Nets

68-69 Nets action photo 15.00
69-70 . . . . 10.00
70-71 Player going to hoop 7.50
71-72 Rick Barry, others art 8.50
72-73 "Eastern Division Playoff Champs" 8.00
73-74 Dr. J in doctor's outfit (rare) 40.00
74-75 President Rowe & GM Debusschere 7.50
75-76 Dr. J 15.00
76-77 Dr. J 15.00

New Jersey Nets

77-78 State of New Jersey & Nets art 7.50
78-79 B.King, Williamson, Jordan photos 7.50
79-80 "The Excitement is Building" art 6.00
80-81 "Up & Coming" action photos 6.00
81-82 "A New Era" logo 5.00
82-83 Dawkins, Gminski, others 5.50
83-84 Action art 5.00
84-85 Daryl Dawkins dunking 7.00
85-86 Buck Williams 6.50
86-87 Mike Gminski photos 5.00

Mavericks 1983-84 Media Guide

87-88 Woolridge, Gminski, Williams 5.50
88-89 Reed, Hinson, Williams, etc. photos 5.00
89-90 Roy Hinson 5.00
90-91 Action art 5.00
91-92 . . . . 5.00

NETS' YEARBOOKS

75-76 Dr. J and Bill Melchionni 25.00
78-79 thru 80-81, 83-84 thru 90-91
See Media Guides
No other yearbooks issued; see media guide listings for other years

NUGGETS' MEDIA GUIDES

Denver Rockets

67-68 . . . . 15.00
68-69 . . . . 8.50
69-70 Nuggets art 8.50
70-71 . . . . 7.50
71-72 Ralph Simpson 6.00
72-73 Alex Hannum 6.00
73-74 Team photo 6.50

Denver Nuggets

74-75 C. Scheer, L. Brown, M. Calvin 6.00
75-76 Thompson, Issel, Moe, Scheer, etc 6.50
76-77 Action art 5.00
77-78 White on white logo & year 5.00
78-79 Nuggets mascot 5.00
79-80 David Thompson 5.50
80-81 Dan Issel 5.00
81-82 Thompson, English, Issel 5.00
82-83 Nuggets logo 5.00
83-84 10th Anniversary action photos 5.50
84-85 Action art 5.00
85-86 Alex English & Calvin Natt art 5.00
86-87 Alex English, Nuggets logo 5.00
87-88 A. English, F. Lever, C. Natt art 5.00
88-89 Moe, English, Lever 5.00

89-90	Alex English, Denver skyline	5.00
90-91	C. Scheer & B. Bickerstaff	5.00
91-92		5.00

NUGGETS' YEARBOOKS

No separate yearbooks issued; see media guide listings for all years

PACERS' MEDIA GUIDES

67-68	No media guide	
68-69	Mel Daniels	17.50
69-70	Mel Daniels	12.50
70-71	Roger Brown	8.00
71-72	Bob Leonard cartoon	6.00
72-73	Daniels, McGinnis, Leonard, others	6.00
73-74	3 ABA trophies	6.00
74-75	Market Square Arena	5.00
75-76	Pacers logo	5.00
76-77	Billy Knight in action vs. Dr. J.	7.50
77-78	Coach Bob Leonard, logo	5.00
78-79	Market Square Arena	5.00
79-80	Pacers logo	5.00
80-81	"Year of Excitement"	5.00
81-82	Coach Jack McKinney artwork	5.00
82-83	Herb Williams art	5.00
83-84	Indianapolis artwork	5.00
84-85	"Pacer Pride" basketball	5.00
85-86	Uniform, ball, sneaker art	5.00
86-87	Herb Williams art	5.00
87-88	Jack Ramsey, player art	5.00
88-89	S. Stipanovich in action vs. Ewing	5.50
89-90	Reggie Miller action photos	6.50
90-91	Action art	5.00
91-92		5.00

PACERS' YEARBOOKS

No separate yearbooks issued; see media guide listings for all years

Pistons 1976-77 Media Guide

PISTONS' MEDIA GUIDES

69-70	Happy Hairston action	20.00
70-71		10.00
71-72		8.00
72-73	Coach Earl Lloyd	8.00
73-74		7.50
74-75	Pistons logo & year	7.50
75-76	Action art, logo (front & back)	7.00
76-77	Douglas, Money, Porter, Rowe art	6.00
77-78	Pistons action art	6.00
78-79	Pistons action art	6.00
79-80	Silverdome, Pistons logo	5.00
80-81		5.00
81-82	Kent Benson, Isiah Thomas art	8.50
82-83		6.50
83-84	K. Tripucka, I. Thomas photos	6.50
84-85	Isiah Thomas in Detroit	6.50
85-86	Laimbeer, Thomas photos	6.00
86-87	Isiah Thomas art	6.00
87-88	Adrian Dantley in action vs. Celtics	5.00
88-89	The Palace	5.00
89-90	Championship celebration photo	5.50
90-91	Dumars, Thomas photos, 2 trophies	5.50
91-92		5.00

PISTONS' YEARBOOKS

69-70, 75-76 thru 78-79 See Media Guides
No other yearbooks issued; see media guide listings for other years

ROCKETS' MEDIA GUIDES

San Diego Rockets

67-68	Rockets logo & basketball	12.50
68-69	Rockets logo	8.00
69-70	Elvin Hayes	8.00
70-71	Elvin Hayes	8.00

Houston Rockets

71-72	Rockets action art	7.50
72-73	Rockets action art	6.00
73-74	Tomjanovich, Newlin v. Chamberlain	7.00
74-75	Rudy Tomjanovich	5.00
75-76	Mike Newlin	5.00
76-77	Cal Murphy, Coach Tom Nissalke	5.00
77-78	R. Tomjanovich, J. Lucas art	5.00
78-79	Barry, Malone, Tomjanovich art	7.00
79-80	Moses Malone art	7.00
80-81	Rockets action art	5.00
81-82	Moses Malone in action vs. Celtics	6.00
82-83	Elvin Hayes in action vs. Denver	5.00
83-84	Ralph Sampson art	5.00
84-85	A. Olajuwon, B. Fitch, R. Sampson	9.00
85-86	McCray, Olajuwon, Sampson in action	6.50
86-87	Reid, Sampson, Olajuwon vs. Denver	6.00
87-88	Olajuwon in action vs. Sonics	6.00
88-89	Tomjanovich, Chaney, Dawson	5.00
89-90	Thorpe, Floyd, Olajuwon photos	6.00
90-91	20th Anniversary logo foldout	7.50
91-92		5.00

ROCKETS' YEARBOOKS

No separate yearbooks issued; see media guide listings for all years

SIXERS' MEDIA GUIDES

66-67		25.00
67-68	Billy Cunningham & W. Chamberlain	20.00
68-69	Hal Greer	10.00
69-70	H. Greer, B. Cunningham photos	10.00
70-71	Team pictures art	8.00
71-72	Sixers mascot	7.50
72-73	F.Carter, B.Bridges, J.Block photos	7.00
73-74	Gene Shue art	6.00
74-75	Shue, Cunningham, others art	6.00
75-76	Cunningham, McGinnis, Catchings art	5.00
76-77	George McGinnis & Doug Collins	5.00
77-78	Dr. J art	15.00
78-79	Dr. J, Collins, B. Jones art	12.50
79-80	Dr. J art	12.50
80-81	76ers basketball	5.00
81-82	Dr. J w/ trophies art	10.00
82-83	Dr. J dunking art	10.00
83-84	Dr. J & Moses Malone	10.00
84-85	Dr. J "Poetry in Motion"	8.50
85-86	Moses in action vs. Kareem	7.50
86-87	Barkley in action vs. Bullets	8.50
87-88	25th Anniversary, Cheeks photo	7.00
88-89	Mo Cheeks & Charles Barkley	7.00
89-90	Charles Barkley	6.50
90-91	Charles Barkley	6.00
91-92		5.00

SIXERS' YEARBOOKS

No separate yearbooks issued; see media guide listings for all years

SONICS' MEDIA GUIDES

67-68 Sonics name & year 15.00
68-69 B. Rule, T. Meschery, R. Thorn 7.50
69-70 Lenny Wilkens 8.00
70-71 Basketball & year 5.00
71-72 Sonics action 5.00
72-73 Spencer Haywood 5.00
73-74 Seattle city skyline 5.00
74-75 S. Watts, B. Russell, F. Brown 6.00
75-76 Action photos montage 5.00
76-77 Sonics basketball 5.00
77-78 "Great Stuff!" 5.00
78-79 John Johnson, Jack Sikma 5.00
79-80 Dennis Johnson 7.50
80-81 Lonnie Shelton 5.00
81-82 Jack Sikma 5.00
82-83 Gus Williams 5.00
83-84 Fred Brown 5.00
84-85 Sonics logo 5.00
85-86 Sonics art 5.00
86-87 Tom Chambers & Xavier McDaniel 6.00
87-88 Bernie Bickerstaff 5.00
88-89 Sonics equipment & locker 5.00
89-90 Derrick McKey 5.00
90-91 K.C. Jones 5.00
91-92 . . . . 5.00

SONICS' YEARBOOKS

No separate yearbooks issued; see media guide listings for all years

SPURS' MEDIA GUIDES

73-74 Hemisfair Arena 10.00
74-75 Spurs logo 6.00
75-76 Gervin, Silas, others 8.50
76-77 James Silas 6.00
77-78 George Gervin art 7.50
78-79 Billy Paultz 5.00
79-80 White on white logo 5.00
80-81 Stan Albeck art 5.00
81-82 Gervin, "Bruise Brothers" 6.50
82-83 Mitchell, Gervin, Gilmore 6.00
83-84 Artis Gilmore 5.50
84-85 Cotton Fitzsimmons 5.00
85-86 Mike Mitchell 5.00
86-87 Alvin Robertson 5.00
87-88 Johnny Moore & Alvin Robertson 5.00
88-89 Larry Brown 5.00
89-90 D. Robinson, S. Elliott, T. Cummings 10.00
90-91 David Robinson 8.00
91-92 . . . . 5.00

SPURS' YEARBOOKS

88-89 thru 89-90 See Media Guides
No separate yearbooks issued; see media guide listings for all years

SUNS' MEDIA GUIDES

68-69 Suns logo & year 12.50
69-70 Suns logo & year 7.50
70-71 Suns logo 5.00
71-72 Connie Hawkins in action 6.50
72-73 3 action photos 5.00
73-74 Neil Walk & Charlie Scott 5.00
74-75 Suns logo & year 5.00
75-76 Suns logo & year 5.00
76-77 Alvin Adams 5.50
77-78 Paul Westphal 5.00
78-79 W. Davis, Westphal, Ron Lee art 5.00
79-80 John MacLoed 5.00
80-81 A. Adams opening tip vs. Atlanta 5.00
81-82 Computer graphics player dunking 5.00
82-83 Basketball 5.00
83-84 Larry Nance dunking vs. Bucks 6.00
84-85 Walter Davis 5.00
85-86 "Catch our Fire, " logo 5.00
86-87 Suns artwork 5.00
87-88 Suns basketball 5.00
88-89 Chambers, Hornacek, others photos 5.50
89-90 Chambers, Johnson, Fitzsimmons 5.50

Suns 1977-78 Media Guide

90-91 Suns basketball 5.00
91-92 . . . . 5.00

SUNS' YEARBOOKS

No separate yearbooks issued; see media guide listings for all years

TIMBERWOLVES' MEDIA GUIDES

89-90 Timberwolves logo 7.50
90-91 Timberwolves basketball 5.00
91-92 . . . . 5.00

TIMBERWOLVES' YEARBOOKS

89-90 Timberwolves uniform #1 . . . . 15.00
90-91 Starting lineup (P.Richardson, etc) 10.00
91-92 . . . . 5.00

WARRIORS' MEDIA GUIDES

San Francisco Warriors

62-63 . . . . 40.00
63-64 . . . . 15.00
64-65 . . . . 15.00
65-66 . . . . 10.00
66-67 . . . . 10.00
67-68 . . . . 10.00
68-69 Warriors logo & year 8.00
69-70 Nate Thurmond 9.50
70-71 Nate Thurmond in action vs. Knicks 9.50

Golden State Warriors

71-72 Coach Al Attles 7.50
72-73 Nate Thurmond art 7.50
73-74 Nate Thurmond art 7.50
74-75 Warriors art 5.00
75-76 NBA Champions trophy 6.00
76-77 Al Attles 5.00
77-78 Warriors action art 5.00
78-79 Warriors action photo 5.00
79-80 Warriors logos 5.00
80-81 Warriors logo 5.00
81-82 Al Attles 5.00
82-83 Basketball & year 5.00
83-84 "Still the Best Game in Town" art 5.00
84-85 Warriors action art 5.00
85-86 Mullin, Short, Floyd, etc. photos 7.50
86-87 "The New Warriors" 5.00
87-88 Larry Smith 5.00
88-89 Ralph Sampson 5.00
89-90 Chris Mullin action photo 6.50

90-91	Warriors action art	5.00
91-92		5.00

WARRIORS' YEARBOOKS

68-69 thru 72-73 See Media Guides
No other yearbooks issued; see media guide listings for other years

FOOTBALL PUBLICATIONS

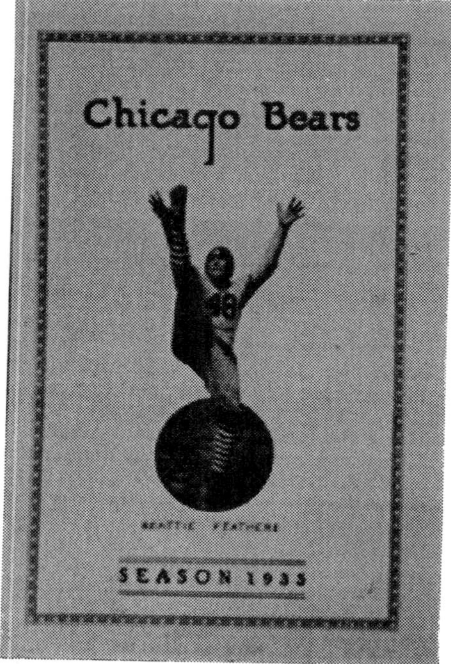

Bears 1933 Media Guide

BEARS' MEDIA GUIDES

Year	Cover	Price
1934	Name & year	65.00
1935	Beattie Feathers	60.00
1936	Jack Manders	60.00
1937		55.00
1938		55.00
1939		50.00
1940		50.00
1941	Bears in action	45.00
1942	Bears in action	45.00
1943	Bears in action	45.00
1944		40.00
1945	Bears team picture	40.00
1946	Name & year	40.00
1947		35.00
1948	Bears mascot	35.00
1949	Bears mascot	35.00
1950	Bears mascot	30.00
1951	Bears mascot	30.00
1952	Bears mascot	30.00
1953	Bears mascot	25.00
1954	Name & year	25.00
1955	Bears in action	25.00
1956	Bears in action	20.00
1957	Bears in action	20.00
1958	Bears mascot	20.00
1959	Bears team picture	20.00
1960	Bears mascot	18.00
1961	Bears mascot	18.00
1962	Bear in action	18.00
1963	Bears mascot & year	18.00
1964	World Champions banner	15.00
1965	Bear in action	15.00
1966	Bears action photos	15.00
1967	Bear in action	15.00
1968	Bears helmet & year	12.00
1969	Golden Anniversary helmets	12.00
1970	Helmet & year	12.00
1971	Helmet & year	12.00
1972	Helmet & year	10.00
1973	Abe Gibron	10.00
1974	Helmet & year	10.00
1975	Buffone, Rives, Harris, Knox	10.00
1976	Helmet & year	9.00
1977	Jack Pardee	9.00
1978	Logo & year	9.00
1979	Bears in action	9.00
1980	George Halas	9.00
1981	"Home of the Bears"	7.00
1982	Mike Ditka	7.00
1983	Mike Ditka & George Halas	7.00
1984	Walter Payton	8.50
1985	Bears in action	7.00
1986	Bears in action	6.00
1987	Payton, Sayers, Nagurski, Grange	7.50
1988	Bears helmet	6.00
1989	Bears equipment	6.00
1990	Bears helmet	6.00
1991		5.00
1992		5.00

BEARS' YEARBOOKS

Year	Cover	Price
1986	Locker w/ Super Bowl Trophy	9.00

BENGALS' MEDIA GUIDES

Year	Cover	Price
1968	Paul Brown	20.00
1969	Riverfront Stadium	15.00
1970	"Date Book & Media Guide, " year	12.00
1971	"Date Book & Media Guide, " year	12.00
1972	"Date Book & Media Guide, " year	12.00
1973	"Date Book & Media Guide, " year	10.00
1974	Cincinnati	10.00
1975	Bengal in action	10.00
1976	Ken Anderson	9.50
1977	Riverfront Stadium	9.00
1978	Riverfront Stadium field	9.00
1979	Bengals helmets	9.00
1980	Tiger, Bengals in action	9.00
1981	New uniform	7.00
1982	Anderson, Bush, Lapham, tiger	7.00
1983	Bengals helmet	7.00
1984	Ken Anderson	7.00
1985	Cris Collinsworth	7.00
1986	Boomer Esiason	7.00
1987	Esiason, Brooks, Brown, others	6.50
1988	Tiger	6.00
1989	Tiger	6.00
1990	Tiger	6.00
1991		5.00
1992		5.00

BILLS' MEDIA GUIDES

Year	Cover	Price
1960	Bills logo & year	25.00
1961	Bills mascot & year	20.00
1962	Bills mascot & year	18.00
1963	Bills mascot & year	18.00
1964	Bills logo & year	18.00
1965	Bills logo & year	15.00
1966	Bills team picture	15.00
1967	Action pictures	15.00
1968	Action pictures	12.00
1969	John Rauch	12.00
1970	O.J. Simpson	14.00
1971	Dennis Shaw	12.00
1972	O.J. Simpson & Dennis Shaw	12.00
1973	Bills Stadium	10.00
1974	O.J. Simpson	12.50
1975	Tony Greene	10.00
1976	Bills helmet	9.00
1977	Bills logo	9.00

Bills 1965 Yearbook

1978	Chuck Knox	9.00
1979	20th Anniversary photos	9.00
1980	Ferguson, Haslett, Butler	9.00
1981	Cribbs, East Div. Champs celeb.	7.00
1982	Bills helmet	7.00
1983	Buffalo	7.00
1984	25th Anniversary logo	7.00
1985	Past & present Bills helmets	7.00
1986	Scott Norwood	7.00
1987	Bills helmet	6.00
1988	Kelly, Smith, Bennett, others	6.00
1989	Scott Norwood, others	6.00
1990	Bills helmet & uniform	6.00
1991		5.00
1992		5.00

BILLS' YEARBOOKS

1965	Bills vs. Chiefs action	35.00
1969	Rushing player w/ O.J. Simpson	27.50
1989	Bills logo, Bills in action	6.00
1990		6.00
1991		5.00
1992		5.00

BRONCOS' MEDIA GUIDES

1960		25.00
1961		20.00
1962		18.00
1963	Broncos mascot logo	18.00
1964	Lionel Taylor	18.50
1965	Broncos mascot logo	15.00
1966	Lionel Taylor in action	15.00
1967	Lou Saban	15.00
1968	Broncos helmet	12.00
1969	Broncos mascot logo	12.00
1970	Mike Haffner in action	12.00
1971	F.Little, R.Jackson, L.Saban	12.50
1972	Floyd Little & John Ralston	10.50
1973	Offensive huddle	10.00
1974	Broncos helmet, huddle	10.00
1975	Otis Armstrong	10.00
1976	Riley Odoms	9.00
1977	Orange Crush defense	10.00
1978	Mile High Stadium	9.00
1979	Broncos helmet	9.00
1980	Broncos helmet	9.00
1981	Broncos uniform #81	7.00
1982	Dan Reeves	7.00
1983	Broncos in action	7.00
1984	John Elway & Broncos QB	7.50
1985	Bronco silhouette	7.00
1986	Broncos in action	6.00
1987	John Elway	6.50
1988	Karl Mecklenburg	6.00
1989	Football stitching	6.00
1990	Broncos headquarters	6.00
1991		5.00
1992		5.00

BRONCOS' YEARBOOKS

1974	"The Making of a Contender"	20.00
1986	Louis Wright in action	9.00

BROWNS' MEDIA GUIDES

1949	Browns mascot	35.00
1950	Cleveland Stadium & crowd	30.00
1951	Name & year	30.00
1952	Paul Brown	32.00
1953	Cartoon Brown	25.00
1954	Media equipment	25.00
1955	Cartoon reporter	25.00
1956	Cartoon reporter	20.00
1957	Coach & Browns player	20.00
1958	Browns in action	20.00
1959	Browns in action	20.00
1960	Browns mascot & helmet	18.00
1961	Browns mascot & helmet	18.00
1962	Jim Brown	22.50
1963	Jim Brown in action	22.50
1964	Jim Brown	22.50
1965	Browns helmet	15.00
1966	Action pictures	15.00
1967	Leroy Kelly in action	15.00
1968	Browns helmet	12.00
1969	Browns helmet	12.00
1970	Browns helmet	12.00
1971	Browns helmet	12.00
1972	Browns helmet	10.00
1973	Browns helmet	10.00
1974	Browns helmet	10.00
1975	Browns helmet	10.00
1976	Browns helmet	9.00
1977	Browns helmet	9.00
1978	Browns helmet	9.00
1979	Browns in action	9.00
1980	Sam Rutigliano	9.00
1981	Brian Sipe	7.50
1982	Browns helmet & Cleveland	7.00
1983	Browns defense in action	7.00
1984	Ozzie Newsome	7.50
1985	M. Schottenheimer & C. Mathews	7.00
1986	Kevin Mack & Ernest Byner	6.50
1987	Bernie Kosar celebrating	6.00
1988	Kosar & Byner in action	6.50
1989	Bernie Kosar in action	6.50
1990	W. Slaughter & R. Langhorne	6.00
1991		5.00
1992		5.00

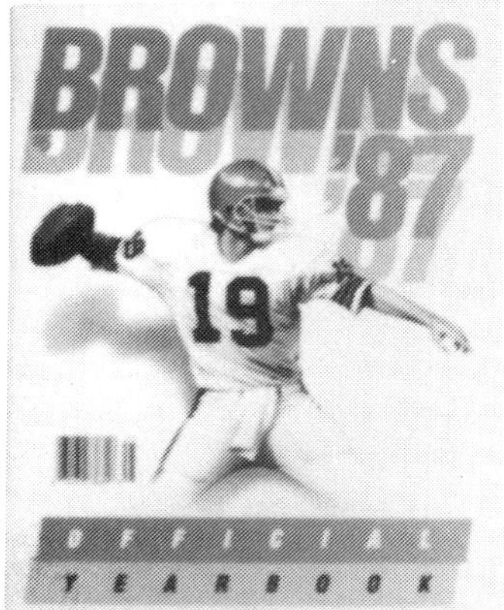

Browns 1987 Yearbook

BROWNS' YEARBOOKS

1987	Bernie Kosar	7.50

BUCCANEERS' MEDIA GUIDES

1976 6 Buccaneer helmets 15.00
1977 LeeRoy Selmon, Dave Pear in action 12.00
1978 John McKay 10.00
1979 Bucs helmet, John McKay 9.00
1980 Jimmy Giles, fans celebration 9.00
1981 John McKay 9.00
1982 Hugh Culverhouse & John McKay 7.00
1983 Buccaneers in action 7.00
1984 McKay, Green, Selmon 7.00
1985 Leeman Bennett & James Wilder 7.50
1986 Buccaneers in action 6.00
1987 .... 6.00
1988 Don Perkins & Vinny Testaverde 6.50
1989 Buccaneers in action 6.00
1990 Mark Carrier 6.00
1991 .... 5.00
1992 .... 5.00

CARDINALS' MEDIA GUIDES

Chicago Cardinals

1947 Logo & year 40.00
1948 Logo & year 40.00
1949 Logo & year 35.00
1950 Logo & year 35.00
1951 Logo & year 30.00
1952 Logo & year 30.00
1953 Logo & year 30.00
1954 Logo & year 25.00
1955 Logo & year 25.00
1956 Logo & year 25.00
1957 Logo & year 20.00
1958 Logo & year 20.00
1959 Logo & year 20.00

St. Louis Cardinals

1960 Mascot & year 22.00
1961 Mascot & year 18.00
1962 Mascot & year 18.00
1963 Wally Lemm & Charley Johnson 18.00
1964 Bobby Joe Conrad in action 15.00
1965 Jim Bakeen in action 15.00
1966 Busch Stadium field 15.00
1967 Larry Wilson 15.00
1968 Hart, Roland, OL in action 12.50
1969 Dave Williams in action 12.00
1970 Cardinals in action 12.00
1971 Cardinals helmets 12.00
1972 Cardinals helmet, StL arch 10.00
1973 Bakeen kicking FG 10.00
1974 Busch Stadium field 10.00
1975 J.Hart, T.Metcalf, D.Coryell 12.00
1976 Jim Hart, offense in action 10.00
1977 Cardinals vs. Cowboys 9.00
1978 Cardinals greats (Matson, etc.) 9.50
1979 Cardinals in action 9.00
1980 Cardinals in action 9.00
1981 Cardinals in action 7.00
1982 Stump Mitchell 7.00
1983 Cardinals helmets 7.00
1984 25th Anniversary in St. Louis 7.00
1985 Cardinals mascot & StL arch 7.00
1986 Gene Stallings 6.00
1987 Cardinals uniform #87 .... 6.00

Phoenix Cardinals

1988 Lomax, Sikahema, Sharpe, etc. 7.00
1989 Cardinals in desert 6.00
1990 Cardinal defense 6.00
1991 .... 5.00
1992 .... 5.00

CARDINALS' YEARBOOKS

St. Louis Cardinals

1967 Team Photo 30.00

Phoenix Cardinals

1988 .... 8.50
1989 Cardinals' Helmet in desert 6.50
1990 .... 6.00
1991 .... 5.00
1992 .... 5.00

CHARGERS' MEDIA GUIDES

Los Angeles Chargers

1960 Logo & year 25.00

San Diego Chargers

1961 Logo & year 22.00
1962 Logo & year 18.00
1963 Logo & year 18.00
1964 Logo & year 18.00
1965 Mascot & year 15.00
1966 Charger in action 15.00
1967 Jack Murphy Stadium 15.00
1968 Chargers in action 12.00
1969 John Hadl, offensive line 13.50
1970 Lance Alworth in action 13.50
1971 Chargers in action 12.00
1972 John Hadl 12.00
1973 Dennis Partee 10.00
1974 New Chargers uniform 10.00
1975 Don Woods 10.00
1976 Dan Fouts in action 12.00
1977 Dan Fouts in action 12.00
1978 Joe Washington in action 9.00
1979 Chargers in action 9.00
1980 Chargers in action 9.00
1981 Cliff McGee, Greg McCrary 7.00
1982 Charger airplanes 7.00
1983 Chargers helmet 7.00
1984 25th Anniversary logo 7.00
1985 Dan Fouts, Charlie Joiner 8.50
1986 L.James, others celebration 6.00
1987 Chargers helmet 6.00
1988 Chargers logo 6.00
1989 Chargers action photos 6.00
1990 A.Miller, L.O'Neal, L.Williams 6.00
1991 .... 5.00
1992 .... 5.00

CHIEFS' MEDIA GUIDES

1960 .... 25.00
1961 .... 20.00
1962 .... 18.00
1963 L.Dawson, H.Stram, C.McClinton 20.00
1964 Curtis McClinton in action 18.00
1965 L.Dawson, H.Stram, J.Mays 16.00
1966 Chiefs in action 15.00
1967 L. Hunt, H. Stram, AFL Trophy 15.00
1968 Chiefs in action 12.00
1969 Willie Lanier in action 12.00
1970 Hank Stram, Chiefs celebration 12.00
1971 Ed Podolak 12.00
1972 Arrowhead Stadium 10.00
1973 L.Dawson, H.Stram, O.Taylor 12.00
1974 Chiefs action photos 10.00
1975 Chiefs helmet 10.00
1976 .... 9.00
1977 Paul Wiggin & Mike Livingston 9.00
1978 Chiefs helmet & football 9.00
1979 Chiefs T-wing offense 9.00
1980 Marv Levy, Chiefs in action 9.00
1981 A.Still, G.Barbaro, J.T. Smith 7.00
1982 Joe Delaney & Jack Rudnay 7.00
1983 John Mackovic & Carlos Carson 7.00
1984 25th Anniversary logo 7.00
1985 John Mackovic & helmet 7.00
1986 Stephone Paige 6.00
1987 Cherry, Burruss, Lewis, Ross 6.00
1988 N.Lowery, P.Palmer, A.Lewis 6.00
1989 M.Schottenheimer & C. Peterson 6.00
1990 Center gripping ball 6.00
1991 .... 5.00
1992 .... 5.00

CHIEFS' YEARBOOKS

1972 Ed Podolak in action 20.00

COLTS' MEDIA GUIDES

Baltimore Colts

1950 Colts logo 30.00
1951 .... 30.00
1952 .... 30.00
1953 Colts mascot logo 25.00
1954 Colts mascot logo 25.00
1955 Colts mascot logo 25.00
1956 Colts mascot logo 20.00
1957 Colts logo 20.00
1958 Memorial Stadium 20.00
1959 Colts logo 20.00
1960 '58 & '59 World Champs pennant 18.00
1961 Colts helmet & logo 18.00
1962 Colts helmet & logo 18.00

Colts 1953 Media Guide

1963	Colts in action	18.00
1964	Offensive huddle	15.00
1965	Colts offense (w/ Unitas)	16.00
1966	Colts cheerleaders	15.00
1967	Kickoff formation	15.00
1968	John Unitas in action	16.00
1969	Colts sideline	12.00
1970	Colts offense (w/ Unitas)	12.50
1971	Super Bowl Trophy	12.00
1972	"The Baltimore Colts"	10.00
1973	Ted Hendricks	10.00
1974	Colt in action	10.00
1975	Lydell Mitchell	10.00
1976	Bert Jones	9.50
1977	Bert Jones in huddle	9.50
1978	Bert Jones, Colts in action	9.50
1979	Colts helmet	9.00
1980	Colts helmet	9.00
1981	Colts helmet	7.00
1982	Championship pennants	7.00
1983	Mike Pagel	7.00
	Indianapolis Colts	
1984	Colts in action	8.00
1985	Colts helmet, Hoosierdome	7.00
1986	Colts helmet, NFL flag	6.00
1987	Colts helmet	6.00
1988	Colts helmet	6.00
1989	Colts helmet	6.00
1990	Colts helmet	6.00
1991		5.00
1992		5.00

COLTS' YEARBOOKS

Baltimore Colts

1953	10th Anniversary Helmet	60.00
1958	Memorial Stadium	45.00
1959		45.00
1960		40.00
1961	Weeb Eubank, Colts sideline	40.00
1962	Colts helmet	40.00
1963		35.00
1964	John Unitas in action	35.00
	Indianapolis Colts	
1988	Eric Dickerson in action	7.50

COWBOYS' MEDIA GUIDES

1960	Cowboys mascot	27.50
1961	L.G. Dupre in action	22.00
1962	2 players, uniform #s 19 & 62	18.00

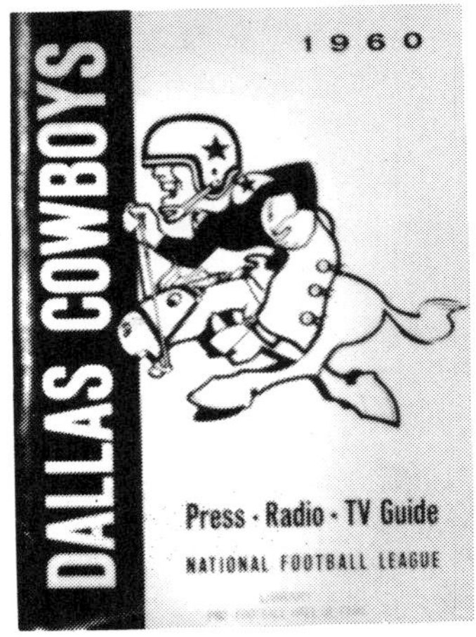

Cowboys 1960 Media Guide

1963	Bill Howton	18.00
1964	Cowboys helmet	18.00
1965	Bob Lilly	18.00
1966	Bob Hayes in action	16.50
1967	Don Meredith in action	15.00
1968	Don Perkins	16.00
1969	Tom Landry	15.00
1970	Calvin Hill	12.50
1971	Texas Stadium	12.00
1972	Landry, Schram, Murchison, trophy	10.00
1973	Mel Renfro	10.00
1974	Cornell Green	10.00
1975	Roger Staubach in action	12.00
1976	Cliff Harris	9.00
1977	Drew Pearson	9.00
1978	R.White, H.Martin, 2 trophies	9.50
1979	20th Anniversary	9.00
1980	Tony Dorsett	9.50
1981	Randy White	7.50
1982	Tom Landry	7.50
1983	Texas Stadium & Cowboys star	7.00
1984	25th Anniversary logo	7.00
1985	Randy White in action	7.50
1986	Tom Landry & Tony Dorsett	7.50
1987	Tony Dorsett & Herschel Walker	8.00
1988	Cowboys star	6.00
1989	Jimmy Jones & Jimmy Johnson	6.00
1990	Eugene Lockhart	6.00
1991		5.00
1992		5.00

COWBOYS' YEARBOOKS

1967	Don Meredith	42.00
1968	Bob Hayes	36.00
1969	Bob Lilly	38.00
1970	Calvin Hill	30.00
1971	Walt Garrison	30.00
1972	Roger Staubach	30.00
1973	Tom Landry	27.50

DOLPHINS' MEDIA GUIDES

1966	George Wilson	20.00
1967	Dolphins helmet	15.00
1968	Orange Bowl	15.00
1969	B.Griese, K.Noonan, J.Clancy	13.50
1970	Dolphins logo & year	12.00
1971	Shula, Griese, Warfield, others	13.50
1972	Garo Yepremian	10.00
1973	Super Bowl trophy	10.00
1974	Helmet & 2 Super Bowl trophies	10.00
1975	Bob Griese & Don Shula	12.00
1976	Kuechenberg, Langer, Malone	9.00
1977	Bob Griese	10.00
1978	Nat Moore	9.00

Year	Cover	Price
1979	Delvin Williams	9.00
1980	Vern DenHerder	9.00
1981	David Woodley	7.00
1982	Tony Nathan	7.00
1983	Andra Franklin	7.00
1984	Dan Marino	8.50
1985	D.Marino, M.Duper, M.Clayton	8.00
1986	Joe Robbie, Dwight Stephenson	6.00
1987		6.00
1988	Dan Marino	7.50
1989	Dolphins logo	6.00
1990	25th Anniversary logo	6.00
1991		5.00
1992		5.00

EAGLES' MEDIA GUIDES

Year	Cover	Price
1947	Season schedule	35.00
1948		35.00
1949	Earle Neale & title touchdown	35.00
1950	Steve VanBuren	30.00
1951	Eagle	30.00
1952	Eagle in action	30.00
1953	Jim Trimble	25.00
1954	Eagle	25.00
1955	Eagle	25.00
1956	Hugh Devore	20.00
1957	25th Anniversary Eagle	20.00
1958	L. "Buck" Shaw	20.00
1959	Eagle & Franklin Field	20.00
1960	Franklin Field	18.00
1961	Eagle wearing crown	18.00
1962	Baby eagle hatching from ball	18.00
1963	Eagle & goalposts	18.00
1964	Franklin Field	15.00
1965	Norm Snead in action	16.00
1966	Tim Brown scoring TD	15.00
1967	Harold Wells in action	15.00
1968	Norm Snead & offensive line	14.00
1969	Apollo XI logo	12.00
1970	Zodiac symbols	12.00
1971	Eagles history	12.00
1972	Eddie Khayat	10.00
1973	Gabriel, McCormack, Bradley	10.50
1974	Gabriel, Carmichael, others	12.00
1975	Eagles in action	10.00
1976	Dick Vermiel	9.00
1977	Vermiel & Eagles action photos	9.00
1978	Harold Carmichael in action	10.00
1979	Carmichael, Montgomery, others	9.00
1980	Dick Vermiel & coaches	9.00
1981	Eagles helmet	7.00
1982	50th Anniversary logo	7.00
1983	Marion Campbell	7.00
1984	Mike Quick	7.00
1985	Norman Braman	7.00
1986	Buddy Ryan	6.00
1987	Reggie White	6.50
1988	Mike Quick	6.00
1989	Randall Cunningham	7.00
1990	Cunningham, Jackson, huddle	6.50
1991		5.00
1992		5.00

EAGLES' YEARBOOKS

Year	Cover	Price
1972	Eagles vs. Cowboys	30.00
1973	Eagles vs. Chiefs	20.00
1974	R. Gabriel & H. Carmichael	22.00
1975	Eagles in action	15.00
1976	Dick Vermiel	15.00
1977		15.00
1978-80		12.00
1981	NFC Champions ring	10.00
1982	Eagles memorabilia	10.00
1983	H. Carmichael & W. Montgomery	11.00
1984-85		9.00
1986	Mike Quick	9.00
1987		7.00
1988	Mike Quick	7.00
1989	William Frizzell, others	6.00
1990	Randall Cunningham	7.00
1991		5.00
1992		5.00

FALCONS' MEDIA GUIDES

Year	Cover	Price
1966	Randy Johnson in action vs. Falcons	20.00
1967	Falcons helmet	15.00
1968	Nobis, Lothridge, Johnson, others	15.00
1969	4 Falcons linemen	12.00
1970	Falcons QB in action	12.00
1971	Falcon in action	12.00
1972	Bob Berry in action	10.00
1973	Falcons logos	10.00
1974	Bob Lee & Falcons off. line	10.00
1975	Marion Campbell	10.00
1976	Jim Mitchell in action	9.00
1977	Steve Bartkowski in action	9.00
1978	Falcons new training complex	9.00
1979	Falcons def. line in action	9.00
1980	Falcons in action	9.00
1981	Falcons off. line in action	7.00
1982	3 Falcons in action	7.00
1983	Falcons helmet, Atl. skyline	7.00
1984	W.Andrews, B.Curry, B.Johnson	7.00
1985	R.Bryan, S.Bailey, G.Riggs	7.00
1986	Falcons helmet & falcon	6.00
1987	Falcons media equipment	6.00
1988	"Putting it all Together"	6.00
1989	Chris Miller	6.00
1990	25th Anniversary logo	6.00
1991		5.00
1992		5.00

FALCONS' YEARBOOKS

Year	Cover	Price
1966	Logo & year	45.00
1967	Logo & year	35.00
1968	Logo & year	30.00
1969	Logo & year	25.00
1970-71		25.00
1972		20.00
1973	Dave Hampton, Falcons helmet	20.00
1974	Tommy Nobis in action	20.00
1975		15.00
1976	Steve Bartkowski, others	15.00
1977		15.00

Forty Niners 1954 Media Guide

49ERS' MEDIA GUIDES

Year	Cover	Price
1950	Three Cartoon reporters	30.00
1951	49ers mascot	30.00
1952	Three 49ers mascots	30.00
1953	49ers mascot	25.00
1954	49ers mascot	25.00
1955	49er in action & mascot	25.00
1956	49ers mascot	20.00
1957	Three 49ers mascots	20.00
1958		20.00
1959	49ers mascot	20.00
1960	Red Hickey	18.00
1961	49ers mascot	18.00
1962	49ers mascot	18.00

Year	Description	Price
1963	49ers mascot	18.00
1964	49ers mascot	15.00
1965	49ers mascot	15.00
1966	49ers mascot	15.00
1967	49ers in action	15.00
1968	49er on sideline	12.00
1969	John Brodie & Gary Lewis in action	12.50
1970	John Brodie & Frankie Albert	12.50
1971	Candlestick Park	12.00
1972	49ers helmet & Candlestick	10.00
1973	Dick Nolan	10.00
1974	49ers helmet, Golden Gate, etc	10.00
1975	Footballs, 49er helmet	10.00
1976	Monte Clark	9.00
1977	E.DeBartolo, J.Thomas, K.Meyer	9.00
1978	Golden Gate Bridge	9.00
1979	O.J. Simpson	12.00
1980	Paul Hofer, John Ayers in action	9.00
1981	Joe Montana, Fred Solomon in action	8.50
1982	"The Catch, " Super Bowl trophy	8.00
1983		7.00
1984	Hand holding helmet	7.00
1985	Wendell Tyler, Randy Cross in action	7.00
1986	40th Anniversary logo	6.00
1987	Joe Montana	7.50
1988	Tom Rathman in action	6.00
1989	Joe Montana, Jerry Rice	7.50
1990	Roger Craig in action	6.00
1991		5.00
1992		5.00

49ERS' YEARBOOKS

Year	Description	Price
1958	49ers mascot shooting guns	45.00
1963	John Brodie in action	36.00
1985	Bill Walsh, Super Bowl celeb..	9.50
1986	Joe Montana	12.00
1987-88		7.00
1989	3 Super Bowl trophies	6.00
1990		6.00
1991		5.00
1992		5.00

Giants 1966 Media Guide

GIANTS' MEDIA GUIDES

Year	Description	Price
1945	Ward Cuff	40.00
1946	Giant in action	40.00
1947	Giant in action	35.00
1948	Giants logo	35.00
1949	1925 Giants	35.00
1950	Polo Grounds	30.00
1951	Polo Grounds	30.00
1952	Radio microphone	30.00
1953	Steve Owens, others	25.00
1954	Giants logo	25.00
1955	Giants logo	25.00
1956	Giants logo	20.00
1957	Giants logo	20.00
1958	Giants logo	20.00
1959	Giants logo	20.00
1960	Giants logo & year	18.00
1961	Giants logo & year	18.00
1962	Giants logo & year	18.00
1963	Giants logo & year	18.00
1964	Giants logo & year	15.00
1965	Giants logo & year	15.00
1966	Giants mascot & year	15.00
1967	Giants helmet & year	15.00
1968	Giants helmet & year	12.00
1969	Giants helmet & year	12.00
1970	Giants helmet & year	12.00
1971	Giants helmet & year	12.00
1972	Giants helmet & year	10.00
1973	Giants helmet & year	10.00
1974	Giants logo	10.00
1975	Giants helmet	10.00
1976	Giants Stadium construction	9.00
1977	Giants Stadium opening day	9.00
1978	Giants offensive line in action	9.00
1979	Harry Carson	9.00
1980	Taylor, Carson, Simms, others	9.50
1981	Phil Simms & offensive line	7.00
1982	Lawrence Taylor & Harry Carson	8.00
1983	Taylor, Carson, Simms, others	7.50
1984	Giants Greats (w/ Gifford)	7.50
1985	Taylor, Carson, Simms, others	7.50
1986	Taylor, Carson, Simms, others	6.50
1987	Simms, Super Bowl tickets	6.00
1988	Taylor, Banks, Marshall in action	6.50
1989	Giants Stadium & past homes	6.00
1990	Taylor, Simms, Bavaro, others	6.50
1991		5.00
1992		5.00

GIANTS' YEARBOOKS

Year	Description	Price
1964	Y.A. Tittle, Alex Webster in action	35.00
1965	Giants OL in action	35.00
1966	Tucker Frederickson	30.00
1967	Giants vs. Cardinals	30.00
1968	Fran Tarkenton	30.00
1969	Fran Tarkenton in action	25.00
1970	Joe Morrison in action	25.00
1976	John Mendenhall in action	15.00
1986	Phil Simms	9.00

JETS' MEDIA GUIDES

Year	Description	Price
1960		25.00
1961		20.00
1962		18.00
1963		18.00
1964	Jets logo & year	18.00
1965	Jets logo & year	15.00
1966	Jets logo & year	15.00
1967	Jets logo & year	15.00
1968	Jets logo & year	12.00
1969	Jets logo & year	15.00
1970	Jets logo & year	12.00
1971	Jets logo & year	12.00
1972	Jets logo & year	10.00
1973	Jets logo & year	10.00
1974	Jets logo & year	10.00
1975	Jets logo & year	10.00
1976	Jets logo & year	9.00
1977	Jets logo & year	9.00
1978	Jets helmet & logo	9.00
1979	Jets defensive line in action	9.00
1980	Todd, Powell, Statue of Liberty	9.00
1981	Bruce Harper & Marvin Powell	7.00
1982	Mark Gastineau, others	7.00
1983	Freeman McNeil, others	7.00
1984	25th Anniversary logo	7.00
1985	Namath, Gastineau, McNeil	8.50
1986	McNeil, Gastineau, Klecko, etc	6.00
1987	D.Maynard, A.Toon, M.Shuler	6.50
1988	Al Toon	6.50
1989	A.Toon, M.Shuler, E.McMillan	6.50
1990	Dick Steinberg & Bruce Coslet	6.00
1991		5.00
1992		5.00

JETS' YEARBOOKS

Year	Description	Price
1960		80.00
1961	"Titans" AFL	60.00
1962		50.00

Jets 1987 Media Guide; Chargers 1982 Media Guide

1963		45.00
1964	Snell, McDaniel, Grantham, etc	45.00
1965	Matt Snell in action	40.00
1966	Joe Namath in action	45.00
1967	Jets vs. Chargers	35.00
1968	Joe Namath, Emerson Boozer in action	45.00
1969	Joe Namath in action	50.00
1970	Don Maynard	32.00
1971-72		25.00
1973-74		20.00
1975	Jets in action	15.00
1976		15.00
1977	Todd, Gaines, Buttle, others	15.00

LIONS' MEDIA GUIDES

1946	Lions mascot	40.00
1947	Name & year	35.00
1948	Bo McMillin	35.00
1949	A: Lions mascot (40 pgs.)	35.00
	B: Bo McMillin (20 pgs.)	30.00
1950	Name & year	30.00
1951	A: Doak Walker (48 pgs.)	32.00
	B: Lions mascot (48 pgs.)	30.00
1952	Name & year	30.00
1953	Mascot w/ World Champs pennant	25.00
1954	Mascot w/ World Champs pennant	25.00
1955	Mascot, West Div. Champs banner	25.00
1956	Briggs Stadium	20.00
1957	Lions in action	20.00
1958	Team picture	20.00
1959	Name & year	20.00
1960	Lion in action	18.00
1961	Jim Gibbons	18.00
1962	Briggs Stadium	18.00
1963	Lions mascot	18.00
1964	Lion in action	15.00
1965	Lions helmet	15.00
1966	2 players, uniform #s 19 & 66	15.00
1967	Lions logo	15.00
1968	Lions in action	12.00
1969	Lions in action	12.00
1970	Lions in action	12.00
1971	Lions helmet	12.00
1972	Lions logo	10.00
1973	Lions logo	10.00
1974	Lions logo	10.00
1975	Lions in action	10.00
1976	Lions helmet	9.00
1977	Lions in action	9.00
1978	Lions in action	9.00
1979	Monte Clark & Gary Danielson	9.00
1980	Lions in action	9.00
1981	Billy Sims in action	7.50
1982	Lions in action	7.00
1983	50th Anniversary logo	7.00
1984	Lions helmet	7.00
1985	James Jones	7.00
1986	Thomas, Ford, Rogers, helmet	6.00
1987	Lion	6.00
1988	Lion	6.00
1989	Wayne Fontes	6.00
1990	B.Sanders, Spielman, Murray, Ball	6.50
1991		5.00
1992		5.00

OILERS' MEDIA GUIDES

1960		25.00
1961	Oilers mascot	20.00
1962	Ivy, Jamison, Husmann	18.00
1963	Oilers in action	18.00
1964	Sammy Baugh, Oilers in action	18.50
1965	Oilers helmets	15.00
1966	Talmini, Hicks, Burrell, etc	15.00
1967	Astros logo	15.00
1968	Astrodome	12.00
1969	Astrodome	12.00
1970	Oilers artwork	12.00
1971	Oilers sculpture	12.00
1972	Oilers helmet	10.00
1973	Oilers helmet	10.00
1974	Sid Gillman, Oilers in action	10.00
1975	Oilers in action	10.00
1976	Cheering fans	9.00
1977	Oilers logo	9.00
1978	Oilers in action	9.00
1979	20th Anniversary, Oilers in action	9.00
1980	Bum Phillips	9.00
1981	Oiler in action	7.00
1982	Oiler helmets	7.00
1983	Oiler helmet	7.00
1984		7.00
1985	Moon, Munchak, Steinkuhler	7.50
1986		6.00
1987	Givins, Hill, Grimsley, Childress	6.00
1988	Oilers helmet & field	6.00
1989	Oilers helmet	6.00
1990	Moon, Givins, Hill	6.50
1991		5.00
1992		5.00

OILERS' YEARBOOKS

1965	Oilers vs. Chargers	35.00

PACKERS' MEDIA GUIDES

1947	Curly Lambeau & champion teams	35.00
1948	Curly Lambeau	35.00
1949	"Home of the Packers"	35.00
1950	Name & year	30.00
1951	State of Wisconson	30.00
1952	State of Wisconson	30.00
1953	Name & year	25.00
1954	Name & year	25.00
1955	State of Wisconson	25.00
1956	State of Wisconson	20.00
1957	Green Bay Stadium	20.00
1958	Green Bay Stadium	20.00
1959	Vince Lombardi & Stadium	22.00
1960	Packers in action	18.00
1961	"West Division Champs 1960"	18.00
1962		18.00
1963	"World Champions"	18.00
1964	Packers logo	15.00
1965	Jim Taylor in action	15.00
1966	Bart Starr in action	16.00
1967	Elijah Pitts in action	15.00
1968	Willie Davis in action	12.00
1969	Donny Anderson in action	12.00
1970	Packers in action	12.00
1971	Packers training	12.00
1972	John Brockington in action	10.00
1973	Packers defense vs. Bears	10.00
1974	John Brockington	10.00
1975	Bart Starr	12.00
1976	Bart Starr & Dave Hanner	10.50
1977	Lynn Dickey	9.00
1978	Packers running onto field	9.00

Packers 1964 Yearbook

Year	Description	Price
1979	Bart Starr & Vince Lombardi	12.00
1980	Packers celebration	9.00
1981	Mike Douglass	7.00
1982	Jan Stenerud	7.00
1983	Larry McCarren	7.00
1984	Forrest Gregg	7.00
1985	Lynn Dickey in action	7.00
1986	Packers defense vs. Dolphins	6.00
1987	Mark Lee	6.00
1988	Lindy Infante	6.00
1989	Lindy Infante	6.00
1990	Tim Harris	6.00
1991		5.00
1992		5.00

PACKERS' YEARBOOKS

Year	Description	Price
1960	Paul Hornung & Jerry Kramer in action	50.00
1961	Forrest Gregg	42.00
1962	Vince Lombardi	50.00
1963	Jim Taylor in action	36.00
1964	Bart Starr	40.00
1965	Vince Lombardi & Curly Lambeau	42.00
1966		30.00
1967	Packers vs. Chiefs	30.00
1968	Ray Nitschke	32.00
1969	Donny Anderson in action	25.00
1970	Travis Williams	25.00
1971	Dan Devine	25.00
1972	John Brockington	20.00
1973	Chestor Marcol & Ron Widby	20.00
1974		20.00
1975	Bart Starr	18.00
1976	Fred Carr sacking Bradshaw	15.00
1977		15.00
1978	Johnny Gray	12.00
1979	T. Middleton & D. Whitehurst	12.00
1980	Rich Wingo	12.00
1981	Gerry Ellis & Eddie Lee Ivery	10.00
1982	John Jefferson & James Lofton	10.00
1983	Mike Douglass	10.00
1984	25th Anniversary (w/ F. Gregg)	9.00
1985	Paul Coffmann	9.00
1986	Randy Scott	9.00
1987	Randy Wright	7.00
1988	Lindy McDaniel	7.00
1989	Tim Harris	6.00
1990		6.00
1991		5.00
1992		5.00

PATRIOTS' MEDIA GUIDES

Boston Patriots

Year	Description	Price
1960		25.00
1961		20.00
1962		18.00
1963	Cartoon Patriot & reporters	18.00
1964	Patriots helmet	18.00
1965	B. Parilli & G. Cappeletti	16.00
1966	Nick Buoniconti	16.00
1967	Jim Nance in action	16.00
1968	Patriots logo	12.00
1969	Clive Rush	12.00
1970	Patriots action photos	12.00
	New England Patriots	
1971	Foxboro Stadium	12.00
1972	J.Plunkett, J.Adams, R.Vataha	10.00
1973	Patriots coaching staff	10.00
1974	Patriots action photos	10.00
1975	Patriots fans	10.00
1976	"Patriots of '76"	9.00
1977	Chuck Fairbanks	9.00
1978	Super-hero Patriot cartoon	9.00
1979	Patriots in action	9.00
1980	Stanley Morgan	9.00
1981	Ron Erhardt & action photos	7.00
1982	Ron Meyer	7.00
1983	Boston sites	7.00
1984	Steve Grogan	7.50
1985	Patriots helmet	7.00
1986	Andre Tippett	6.00
1987	Stanley Morgan	6.00
1988	Raymond Clayborn	6.00
1989	Patriots in action	6.00
1990	Rod Rust	6.00
1991		5.00
1992		5.00

PATRIOTS' YEARBOOKS

Boston Patriots

Year	Description	Price
1965	Gino Cappelletti & Babe Parilli	36.00
1966	J.D. Garrett & Jim Nance in action	32.00
1967	Jim Nance in action	32.00
	New England Patriots	
1980	Rod Shoate in action	12.00
1985	Tony Eason, Craig James, others	9.00

RAIDERS MEDIA GUIDES

Year	Description	Price
1960		25.00
1961	Raiders mascot	20.00
1962		18.00
1963	Bo Roberson	18.00
1964	Raiders helmet	18.00
1965	Oakland-Alameda Co. Stadium	15.00
1966	Raiders helmet	15.00
1967	Raider in action	15.00
1968	AFL Champions ring	12.00
1969	Dan Birdwell	12.00
1970	Raiders offensive huddle	12.00
1971	Raiders offense (w/ LaMonica)	12.00
1972	Raiders logo & year	10.00
1973	Raiders in action	10.00
1974	Pre-game huddle	10.00
1975	Raiders action photos	10.00
1976	Raider player on sideline	9.00
1977	Super Bowl XI ring	9.00
1978	Dave Caspar in action	9.00
1979	20th Anniversary memorabilia	9.00
1980	Raiders third decade	9.00
1981	Super Bowl XV ring	7.00
	Los Angeles Raiders	
1982	Raider player on sideline	8.00
1983	Raiders in action	7.00
1984	Super Bowl XVIII ring	7.00
1985	Helmet, 3 Super Bowl trophies	7.00
1986	Raiders logo	6.00
1987	Matt Millen holding helmet	6.00
1988	Van McElroy in action	6.00
1989	Raiders helmet	6.00
1990	Raiders helmet	6.00
1991		5.00
1992		5.00

RAMS MEDIA GUIDES

Year	Description	Price
1945	Bob Waterfield	40.00
1946		40.00
1947	Bob Waterfield	35.00
1948		35.00
1949	Ram's head logo & year	35.00
1950	Ram's head logo & year	30.00

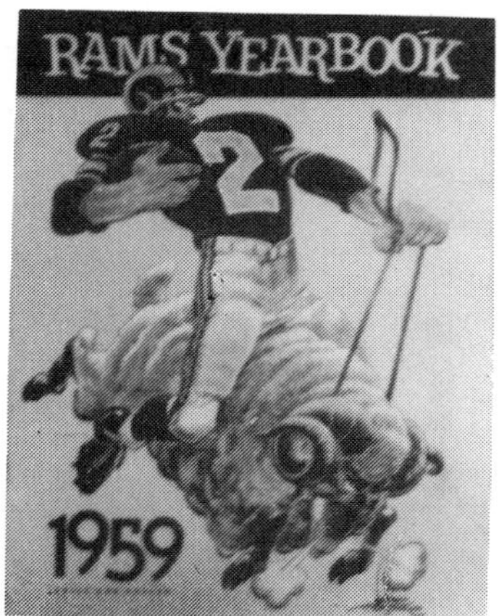

Rams 1959 Yearbook

Year	Cover	Price
1951	Ram's head logo & year	30.00
1952	Ram's head logo & year	30.00
1953	Ram's head logo & year	25.00
1954	Ram's head logo & year	25.00
1955	Ram's head logo & year	25.00
1956	Ram's head logo & year	20.00
1957	Ram's head logo & year	20.00
1958	Ram's head logo & year	20.00
1959	Ram's head logo & year	20.00
1960	Ram's head logo & year	18.00
1961	Ram's head logo & year	18.00
1962	Ram's head logo & year	18.00
1963	Ram's head logo & year	18.00
1964	Ram's head logo & year	15.00
1965	Ram's head logo & year	15.00
1966	Ram's head logo & year	15.00
1967	Ram's head logo & year	15.00
1968	Ram's head logo & year	12.00
1969	Ram's head logo & year	12.00
1970	Ram's head logo & year	12.00
1971	Ram's head logo & year	12.00
1972	Ram's head logo & year	10.00
1973	Rams in action	10.00
1974	Rams helmet	10.00
1975	Rams helmet	10.00
1976	Rams helmet	9.00
1977	Rams helmet	9.00
1978	Rams helmets past & present	9.00
1979	Carroll Rosenbloom	9.00
1980	Rams in action	9.00
1981	Ram wearing uniform #81	7.00
1982	Los Angeles sites	7.00
1983	Rams helmet	7.00
1984	Rams players coming onto field	7.00
1985	40th Anniversary logo	7.00
1986	Eric Dickerson	6.50
1987		6.00
1988	Rams in action	6.00
1989	Rams helmet & equipment	6.00
1990	Ram wearing uniform #90	6.00
1991		5.00
1992		5.00

RAMS YEARBOOK

Year	Cover	Price
1958	Cartoon running back	45.00
1959	Cartoon mascot riding ram	45.00
1960	Cartoon ram chewing helmet	40.00
1961	Cartoon ram butting "NFL"	40.00
1962	Jon Arnett	40.00
1963	Dick Bass in action	35.00

REDSKINS MEDIA GUIDES

Year	Cover	Price
1947	Name & Indian mascot	35.00
1948	Indian mascot & year	35.00
1949	Indian mascot & year	35.00
1950	Indian mascot & year	30.00
1951	Indian mascot & year	30.00
1952	Indian mascot & year	30.00
1953	Indian mascot & year	25.00
1954	Indian mascot & year	25.00
1955	Redskins in action	25.00
1956	Redskins in action	20.00
1957	Redskins in action	20.00
1958	Year & name	20.00
1959	Redskins helmet, pennant	20.00
1960	Football w/ year 1960	18.00
1961	Silver Anniversary	19.00
1962	Football	18.00
1963	Capitol Building	18.00
1964	Tomahawk & drum	15.00
1965	Redskins helmet	15.00
1966	Teepee & D.C. Stadium	15.00
1967	Teepee & D.C. Stadium	15.00
1968	Teepee & D.C. Stadium	12.00
1969	Teepee & D.C. Stadium	12.00
1970	Teepee & D.C. Stadium	12.00
1971	Teepee & D.C. Stadium	12.00
1972	Redskins helmet	10.00
1973	Redskins logo, D.C. sites	10.00
1974	Redskins helmet, Capitol	10.00
1975	Pre-game huddle	10.00
1976	Redskins logo, George Allen	9.00
1977	Redskins in action	9.00
1978	Mark Moseley kicking FG	9.00

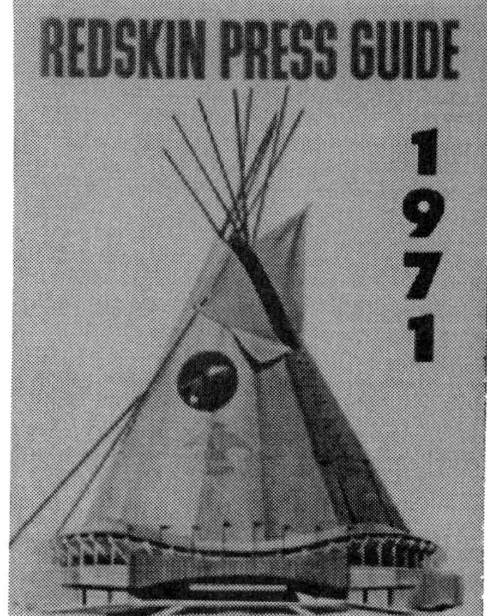

Redskins 1971 Media Guide

Year	Cover	Price
1979	Indian, Redskins in action	9.00
1980	Redskins helmet	9.00
1981	Redskins logo	7.00
1982	"Redskins" & helmet	7.00
1983	Helmet & Super Bowl trophy	7.00
1984	Joe Theismann	7.50
1985	John Riggins & Joe Theismann	7.50
1986	50th Anniversary logo	6.00
1987	Art Monk & Gary Clark	6.00
1988	Super Bowl XXII ring	6.00
1989	Art Monk in action	6.00
1990	Charles Mann	6.00
1991		5.00
1992		5.00

REDSKINS YEARBOOKS

Year	Description	Price
1973	George Allen & Chris Hanburger	32.00
1986	50th Anniversary logo	9.50
1987		7.00
1988	Super Bowl action photos	7.00
1989	Rypien, Williams, Bryant, Sanders	6.50
1990		6.00
1991		5.00
1992		5.00

SAINTS MEDIA GUIDES

Year	Description	Price
1967	Saint in action	20.00
1968	Band playing at stadium	15.00
1969	Saints defense in action	12.00
1970	Dan Abramowicz in action	12.00
1971	Tom Dempsey 63 yd. FG	13.50
1972	Manning, Strong, Kupp in action	10.00
1973	Bob Pollard in action	10.00
1974	Saints defense	10.00
1975	Saints in action	10.00
1976	Hank Stram	9.00
1977	H.Stram, C.Muncie, Superdome	9.00
1978	Superdome	9.00
1979	Dick Nolan & Joe Federspiel	9.00
1980	Saints helmet & uniform	9.00
1981	Bum Phillips & Archie Manning	7.50
1982	George Rogers in action	7.00
1983	Saints logo	7.00
1984	Bum Phillips chalk talk	7.00
1985	Saints helmet & Louisiana	7.00
1986	Saints logo, helmet, uniform	6.00
1987	R. Mayes, J. Mora, R. Jackson	6.00
1988	Saints helmet	6.00
1989	Saints helmet	6.00
1990	Dalton Hilliard	6.00
1991		5.00
1992	Superdome crowd	5.00

SAINTS YEARBOOK

Year	Description	Price
1968	Dan Abramowicz	30.00

SEAHAWKS MEDIA GUIDES

Year	Description	Price
1976	Seahawks helmet	15.00
1977	Zorn, Patera, Niehaus	12.00
1978	Sherman Smith	10.00
1979	Jim Zorn, Steve Largent	12.00
1980	Jack Patera	9.00
1981	Steve Largent & hawk	10.50
1982	Steve Largent in action	12.00
1983	Chuck Knox & Kingdome	7.00
1984	Chuck Knox	7.00
1985	Players coming onto field	7.00
1986	Steve Largent in action	9.00
1987	Referee signalling TD	6.00
1988	Ron Heller & Johnny Holloway	6.00
1989	Largent, Williams, Krieg, etc.	7.50
1990	Uniform #90 & equipment	6.00
1991		5.00
1992		5.00

SEAHAWKS YEARBOOK

Year	Description	Price
1976	Seahawks helmet & NFL pennants	25.00
1989	Seahawks helmet	6.00

STEELERS MEDIA GUIDES

Year	Description	Price
1947	Name & year	35.00
1948	Cartoon reporters	35.00
1949	Cartoon reporters	35.00
1950	Cartoon reporters	30.00
1951	John P. Michelosen	30.00
1952	Cartoon steelworker	30.00
1953	Steeler kicker	25.00
1954	City of Pittsburgh	25.00
1955	Steelers in action	25.00
1956	Steelers in action	20.00
1957	Brovelli, Nickel	20.00
1958	Steelers in action	20.00
1959	Steelers mascot & logo	20.00
1960	Steelers in action	18.00
1961	Steelers helmet	18.00
1962	Steelers uniform	18.00
1963	Steelers helmet & year	18.00
1964	Steelers helmet & year	15.00
1965	City of Pittsburgh	15.00

Steelers 1958 Media Guide

Year	Description	Price
1966	City of Pittsburgh	15.00
1967	Steelers in action	15.00
1968	Steelers helmet	12.00
1969	Three Rivers Stadium	12.00
1970	Steelers in action	12.00
1971	Black & yellow stripes	12.00
1972	Steelers helmet	10.00
1973	Joe Greene	12.00
1974	Steelers helmet	10.00
1975	F.Harris, T.Bradshaw, R.Blier	12.00
1976	Steelers helmet	9.00
1977	Steelers helmet	9.00
1978	Steelers helmet	9.00
1979	Steelers helmet	9.00
1980	"Steelers 1980" football	9.00
1981	Football	7.00
1982	50th Anniversary logo	7.00
1983	Steelers helmet	7.00
1984	Franco Harris	8.00
1985	Steelers helmet	7.00
1986	Steelers helmet	6.00
1987	Steelers helmet	6.00
1988	Chuck Noll	6.00
1989	Steelers helmet, Pittsburgh	6.00
1990	"Steelers '90" logo	6.00
1991		5.00
1992		5.00

STEELERS YEARBOOKS

Year	Description	Price
1979	Terry Bradshaw	15.00
1990	Lipps, Woodson, Brister, others	6.00
1991		5.00
1992		5.00

VIKINGS MEDIA GUIDES

Year	Description	Price
1961	Vikings logo	25.00
1962	Vikings logo	20.00
1963	Vikings logo	18.00
1964	Vikings logo	18.00
1965	Vikings logo	15.00
1966	Fran Tarkenton	16.00
1967	Vikings in action	15.00
1968	Joe Kapp	12.00
1969	Bud Grant	12.00
1970	Fred Cox	12.00

1971	Jim Marshall	12.00
1972	Alan Page	12.00
1973	Fan in Viking costume	10.00
1974	Players during National anthem	10.00
1975	Fans cheering	10.00
1976	Fran Tarkenton in action	10.00
1977	Vikings logo	9.00
1978	Chuck Foreman	9.00
1979	Ahmad Rashad	10.00
1980	Vikings new offices & facility	9.00
1981	T.Kramer, A.Rashad, S.White	8.00
1982	Vikings in action	7.00
1983	Blair, Martin, Studwell, Johnson	7.00
1984	Les Steckel	7.00
1985	25th Anniversary logo	7.00
1986	Jerry Burns	6.00
1987	Tommy Kramer, others	6.00
1988	Doleman, Millard, Browner, others	6.00
1989	Tim Irwin, others	6.00
1990	30th Anniversary logo	6.00
1991		5.00
1992		5.00

VIKINGS' YEARBOOKS

1961	2 Cartoon Vikings & referee	55.00

HOCKEY PUBLICATIONS

BARONS MEDIA GUIDES

76-77	Logo & year, Premier Edition	20.00
77-78	Starting five: Maruk, Meloche, etc	15.00

BLACKHAWKS MEDIA GUIDES

60-61		75.00
61-62		20.00
62-63		15.00
63-64		15.00
64-65		15.00
65-66		15.00
66-67		15.00
67-68	Hull, Mikita, Chairman A. Wirtz	15.00
68-69	Hull, Mikita, President W. Wirtz	15.00
69-70	Black Hawks logo & year	10.00
70-71	Mascot & Wales Trophy	8.00
71-72	Logo & year, W. Division Champs	8.00
72-73	Black Hawks mascot	8.00
73-74	Black Hawks logo & art	8.00
74-75	Black Hawks art	8.00
75-76	50th Anniversary art	10.00
76-77	Black Hawks logo & year	8.00
77-78	Black Hawks logo, action art	8.00
78-79	Black Hawks logo & crossed sticks	8.00
79-80	Black Hawks logo	8.00
80-81	T.Esposito, others, logo & year	8.00
81-82	Denis Savard & Darryl Sutter	8.00
82-83	Doug Wilson w/ Norris Trophy	8.00
83-84	Celebration photos	6.00
84-85	Logo, Savard, Secord, others	6.00
85-86	"Chicago has Fans" slogan	6.00
86-87	Savard, Murray, Secord art	6.00
87-88	Coach Bob Murdock & coaches art	6.00
88-89	D. Savard action photos & locker	6.00
89-90	Celebration photos	6.00
90-91	All-Star Game logo	6.00
91-92		6.00
92-93	Clarence S. Campbell bowl	6.00

BLUES MEDIA GUIDES

67-68	Schock, Keenan, Martin, others	20.00
68-69	Glenn Hall	10.00
69-70	Vezina & Campbell Trophies	10.00
70-71	Campbell Trophy	8.00
71-72	Blues action photos	8.00
72-73	St. Louis Arena	8.00
73-74	Action photos	8.00
74-75	Garry Unger, Andy Hebenton	8.00
75-76	Hall, Gratton, Johnston, others	8.00
76-77	Emile Francis	8.00
77-78	Blues art	5.00
78-79	Blues art	5.00
79-80	Ed Staniowski art	5.00
80-81	Blues art	5.00
81-82	Mike Liut art	5.00
82-83	Emile Francis art	5.00
83-84	Brian Sutter	5.00
84-85	Blues jersey	5.00
85-86	Blues logo	5.00
86-87	Blues memorabilia	5.00
87-88	Blues art	5.00
88-89	B.Sutter, Berry, J.Micheletti art	5.00
89-90	Dan Kelly	5.00
90-91	Brett Hull & Rick Meagher	6.00
91-92		5.00
92-93	Brett Hull	5.00

Bruins 1947-48 Media Guide

BRUINS MEDIA GUIDES

46-47		150.00
47-48		125.00
48-49		100.00
49-50		75.00
50-51		50.00
51-52	Bruins logo & year	50.00
52-53	Bear's head art	40.00
53-54	Bear's head art	40.00
54-55	Bear's head art	40.00
55-56	Bruins name & year	35.00
56-57	Bruins name & year	35.00
57-58	Bruins name & year	35.00
58-59	Bruins name & year	35.00
59-60	Bear head cartoon	30.00
60-61	Bruin cartoon	20.00
61-62	Bruins mascot & year	20.00
62-63	Wayne Connelly	20.00
63-64	John Bucyk	25.00
64-65	G. Dornhofer & R. Leiter	15.00
65-66	Ed Johnston	15.00
66-67	Murray Oliver	15.00
67-68	Bobby Orr	20.00
68-69	Bruins action vs. Canadiens	10.00
69-70	Esposito, Hodge vs. Black Hawks	15.00
70-71	Bruins action vs. Black Hawks	10.00
71-72	Pre-game anthems w/ Canadiens	10.00
72-73	Stanley Cup trophy	10.00
73-74	50th Anniv. w/ Espo, Orr, etc.	15.00
74-75	John Bucyk art	8.00
75-76	Terry O'Reilly photos	8.00
76-77	Cherry, Ratelle, Park art	8.00
77-78	Gerry Cheevers photos	10.00
78-79	Bob Schmautz	8.00
79-80	Rick Middleton	8.00
80-81	Ray Bourque art	10.00

81-82	Wayne Cashman	5.00
82-83	Steve Kaspar w/ Selke Trophy	5.00
83-84	60th Anniv., P. Peeters w/ Vezina	5.00
84-85	Barry Pederson art	5.00
85-86	Bruins hockey pucks	5.00
86-87	Gord Kluzak photos	5.00
87-88	Ray Bourque w/ Norris Trophy	6.00
88-89	Cam Neely photos	5.00
89-90	R. Lemelin & A. Moog photos	5.00
90-91	Bruins art	5.00
91-92		5.00
92-93	Fred Cusick	5.00

CANADIENS MEDIA GUIDES

53-54	Canadiens' logo	150.00
54-55	Canadiens' logo	125.00
55-56	Canadiens' logo	75.00
56-57		40.00
57-58		30.00
58-59		25.00
59-60		25.00
60-61		25.00
61-62		20.00
62-63	Claude Provost, Henri Richard	25.00
63-64		20.00
64-65		20.00
65-66		15.00
66-67		15.00
67-68		15.00
68-69		15.00
69-70		15.00
70-71	Canadiens art	10.00
71-72	Canadiens logo	10.00
72-73	Canadiens logo	10.00
73-74	Canadiens art	10.00
74-75	50th Anniversary art	15.00
75-76	Lafleur, Pollack, Bowman	15.00
76-77	Lafleur, Dryden, Cournoyer	15.00
77-78	Serge Savard	10.00
78-79	Yvan Cournoyer	10.00
79-80	Serge Savard	10.00
80-81	Guy Lafleur & Pierre Larouche	10.00
81-82	Bob Gainey	10.00
82-83	Guy Lafleur & others	10.00
83-84	Mario Tremblay	8.00
84-85	Guy Carbonneau	8.00
85-86	Steve Penney	8.00
86-87	Stanley Cup celebration	8.00
87-88	Mats Naslund	8.00
88-89	Nasland, Roy, Richer, others	10.00
89-90	Stanley Cup celebration	6.00
90-91	Patrick Roy, Stephane Richer	8.00
91-92		6.00
92-93	Patrick Roy	6.00

CANUCKS MEDIA GUIDES

70-71	Logo, action photo	15.00
71-72	Logo, action art	8.00
72-73	Canucks logo	8.00
73-74	Canucks puck & stick	8.00
74-75	Celebration vs. Black Hawks art	8.00
75-76	Canucks art	8.00
76-77	Action photos	6.00
77-78	Don Lever, others	6.00
78-79	New Canucks logo	6.00
79-80	Glen Hanlon	6.00
80-81	Canucks vs. North Stars action	5.00
81-82	Darcy Rota vs. Capitals	5.00
82-83	Fans celebrating	5.00
83-84	Action photos	5.00
84-85	Canucks logo	5.00
85-86	Canucks new uniform art	5.00
86-87	Action photos	5.00
87-88	Execs. Quinn, Burke, MacCammon	5.00
88-89	Stan Smyl	5.00
89-90	Trevor Linden	6.00
90-91	Canucks jerseys & equipment	5.00
91-92		5.00
92-93	Bure, McLean, Walter & Quinn	6.00

CAPITALS MEDIA GUIDES

74-75	Capitals locker room	10.00
75-76	Ron Low	6.00
76-77	Tony White	6.00
77-78	Capitals art	6.00
78-79	Guy Charron art (foldout)	8.00
79-80	Ryan Walter	6.00
80-81	Gartner, Maruk, Walter, others	8.00
81-82	Mike Palmateer art	6.00
82-83	Dennis Maruk art	6.00
83-84	Rod Langway photos	6.00
84-85	Rod Langway, others	6.00
85-86	Mike Gartner & Bobby Carpenter	6.00
86-87	Capital Building & Caps puck	5.00
87-88	Larry Murphy & Bob Gould art	5.00
88-89	15th Anniversary, Scott Stevens	8.00
89-90	Ridley, Ciccarelli, Courtnall	5.00
90-91	Langway, Druce photos/headlines	6.00
91-92		6.00
92-93	Dale Hunter	7.00

Devils 1982-83 Media Guide

DEVILS MEDIA GUIDES

82-83	Devils art	10.00
83-84	Team in tuxedos	8.00
84-85	Mel Bridgman w/ Devils' kids	6.00
85-86	D.Sulliman, T.Higgins, G.Adams	6.00
86-87	Kirk Muller	6.00
87-88	Kid's Devils art	5.00
88-89	Aaron Broten, Kirk Muller	5.00
89-90	Sean Burke art	5.00
90-91	John McClean	5.00
91-92		5.00
92-93		5.00

FLAMES MEDIA GUIDES

Atlanta Flames

72-73	Flames logo	15.00
73-74	Logo, Phil Myre	8.00
74-75		8.00
75-76	Logo, action photos	6.00
76-77	Daniel Bouchard	6.00
77-78	W.Plett, E.Vail, T.Lysiak art	6.00
78-79	Flames uniform, puck, equipment	6.00
79-80	Guy Chouinard art	6.00

Calgary Flames

80-81	Flames logo	8.00
81-82	Kent Nilsson	6.00
82-83	Flames logo	6.00
83-84	Lanny McDonald	7.00
84-85	McDonald goal v. Edm. celebration	7.00
85-86	Goalie gloving puck	6.00
86-87	Campbell Conference trophy	6.00
87-88	Joe Mullen	6.00
88-89	Joe Nieuwendyk & Hakan Loob	6.00
89-90	Stanley Cup trophy	6.00

90-91	Al MacInnis & Sergei Makarov	6.00
91-92		6.00
92-93		6.00

FLYERS MEDIA GUIDES

67-68	Flyers art	20.00
68-69	Campbell Trophy	10.00
69-70	Flyers art	8.00
70-71	Flyers logo & NHL pucks	8.00
71-72	TV camera	5.00
72-73	Gene Hart, Dan Earle	6.00
73-74	Flyers art	6.00
74-75	Stanley Cup art	6.00
75-76	Trophies	6.00
76-77	Clarke, Leach, Barber	8.00
77-78	Flyers equipment	5.00
78-79	Flyers art	5.00
79-80	Action photos	5.00
80-81	Flyers logo & action photos	5.00
81-82	Flyers' faces	5.00
82-83	Action photos	5.00
83-84	Bobby Clarke	6.00
84-85	Brian Propp	6.00
85-86	Pelle Lindbergh art	8.00
86-87	Mark Howe	6.00
87-88	Ron Hextall	6.00
88-89	Flyers action art	5.00
89-90	Flyers action art	5.00
90-91	Flyers equipment	5.00
91-92		6.00
92-93	Flyers art featuring Lindros & others	6.00

Islanders 1972-73 Yearbook

ISLANDERS MEDIA GUIDES

72-73	Islanders logo	15.00
73-74	Billy Harris	8.00
74-75	Syl Apps, Denis Potvin	10.00
75-76		8.00
76-77	Chico Resch, Denis Potvin	8.00
77-78	Ed Westfall	6.00
78-79	Mike Bossy	8.00
79-80	Bryan Trottier	8.00
80-81	Stanley Cup Champions	8.00
81-82	Stanley Cup Champions	8.00
82-83	Bryan Trottier w/ Stanley Cup	8.00
83-84	Potvin, Trottier, Smith, Tonelli	8.00
84-85	Mike Bossy 400th goal	8.00
85-86	Bossy, Trottier, Sutter, Tonelli	8.00
86-87	Terry Simpson & Al Arbour art	5.00
87-88		5.00
88-89	Trottier, LaFontaine, others	6.00
89-90	David Volek	5.00
90-91	Pat LaFontaine	6.00
91-92		5.00
92-93	"The New Ice Age"	5.00

JETS MEDIA GUIDES

72-73		15.00
73-74		8.00
74-75		8.00
75-76	Jets team photos	8.00
76-77		8.00
77-78		8.00
78-79	WHA Championship trophy	8.00
79-80	Lars-Erik Sjoberg w/ WHA trophy	8.00
80-81	Dave Christian	6.00
81-82	Dave Babych	6.00
82-83	Dale Hawerchuk & Calder Trophy	6.00
83-84	Dale Hawerchuk, others art	6.00
84-85	Hawerchuk, Carlyle, Boschman	6.00
85-86	Dale Hawerchuk & Jets puck	6.00
86-87	Action photos	5.00
87-88	"Lightning on Ice"	5.00
88-89	Winnipeg city skyline	5.00
89-90	Ashton, Elynuik, others	5.00
90-91	"Winnipeg Style"	5.00
91-92		5.00
92-93	Troy Murray, Essensa art	5.00

KINGS MEDIA GUIDES

68-69	Kings art	15.00
69-70	Gerry Desjardins	10.00
70-71	Kings logo	6.00
71-72	Bob Pulford	8.00
72-73	Butch Goring	8.00
73-74	"Go Kings" art	6.00
74-75	Butch Goring vs. Bruins	8.00
75-76	Pulford, Dionne, Vachon art	8.00
76-77	Butch Goring art	8.00
77-78	Goring, Dionne, Vachon	8.00
78-79	Marcel Dionne vs. Canadiens	8.00
79-80	Vachon, Dionne, Goring, Taylor	8.00
80-81	Simmer, Dionne, Taylor art	8.00
81-82	Mario Lessard	5.00
82-83	Steve Bozek celebration photo	5.00
83-84	Dionne jersey & action photos	6.00
84-85	Coach P. Quinn & GM R. Vachon	5.00
85-86	Dionne, Taylor, Nicholls, others	6.00
86-87	20th Anniversary logo	6.00
87-88	Robitaille, Nicholls, others	6.00
88-89	Gretzky & Robitaille art	8.00
89-90	Kings black logo	5.00
90-91	Fan photos & logo	5.00
91-92		6.00
92-93		6.00

LIGHTNING MEDIA GUIDES

92-93		6.00

MAPLE LEAFS MEDIA GUIDES

62-63	George Armstrong	25.00
63-64	Frank Mahovlich	25.00
64-65	Action photos	15.00
65-66	Johnny Bower	15.00
66-67	Dave Keon	15.00
67-68	Dave Keon	15.00
68-69		10.00
69-70	Maple Leafs action	6.00
70-71	Maple Leafs art	6.00
71-72	Maple Leafs art	6.00
72-73	Maple Leafs Garden & logo	6.00
73-74		6.00
74-75	Maple Leafs logo	6.00
75-76	Maple Leafs logo	6.00
76-77	Sittler, Salming, others art	10.00
77-78	Sittler, Salming, Horton, others	10.00
78-79	Darryl Sittler	8.00
79-80	Borje Salming	8.00
80-81	Borje Salming	8.00
81-82	50th Anniversary photos	8.00
82-83	Rick Vaive 50th goal	6.00
83-84	Viave, Poddubny, Gingras, others	6.00
84-85	Rick Vaive, Allan Bester	6.00
85-86	Maple Leafs action	6.00
86-87	Goal celebration	6.00

87-88	Wendell Clark	6.00
88-89	Maple Leafs logo	6.00
89-90	Vincent Damphousse	6.00
90-91	Leeman, Olczyk, Damphousse	6.00
91-92		6.00
92-93		6.00

NORDIQUES MEDIA GUIDES

74-75		10.00
75-76		6.00
76-77	Nordiques fleur-de-lis logo	6.00
77-78		6.00
78-79		6.00
79-80	Nordiques art	5.00
80-81	Nordiques art	5.00
81-82	Stastny brothers art	8.00
82-83	Nordiques art	5.00
83-84	Stastnys, Hunter, Goulet, others	6.00
84-85	Nordiques memorabilia	5.00
85-86	Nordiques art	5.00
86-87	Nordiques logo	5.00
87-88	Nordiques action	5.00
88-89	Goal celebration	5.00
89-90	Media equipment	5.00
90-91	Lafleur, Sakic, Petit	6.00
91-92		5.00
92-93	Nolan, Sakic and Sundin	5.00

North Stars 1972-73 Yearbook & Kings 1988-89 Yearbook

NORTH STARS MEDIA GUIDES

67-68	North Stars logo	15.00
68-69	Cesare Maniago	8.00
69-70	Danny Grant & Calder Trophy	8.00
70-71	Danny O'Shea faceoff	8.00
71-72	North Stars vs. Bruins action	6.00
72-73	Cesare Maniago & Gump Worsley	6.00
73-74	Dennis Hextall art	6.00
74-75	Bill Goldsworthy	6.00
75-76	North Stars action	6.00
76-77	North Stars vs. Flames action	6.00
77-78	Sharpley, Pirus, Eriksson, Jensen	6.00
78-79	North Stars & Barons uniforms	5.00
79-80	Action art	5.00
80-81	Al MacAdam & Steve Payne	5.00
81-82	Don Beaupre, others	6.00
82-83	Celebration photo vs. Blues	5.00
83-84	Asst. GM John Mariucci art	5.00
84-85	Neal Broten	6.00
85-86	Announcer A.Shaver, action photos	5.00
86-87	Neal Broten w/ trophies	5.00
87-88	Dino Ciccarelli	5.00
88-89	Celebration photo	5.00
89-90	Player skate-stopping	5.00
90-91	Broten, Casey, Bellows	5.00
91-92		5.00
92-93		5.00

OILERS MEDIA GUIDES

75-76	Fight vs. Cleveland	20.00
76-77	Oilers action photo	8.00
77-78		8.00
78-79	Dave Dryden, Hamilton, others	8.00
79-80	Dave Dryden & Wayne Gretzky	15.00
80-81	Blair McDonald & Wayne Gretzky	15.00
81-82	Andy Moog & Wayne Gretzky	15.00
82-83	Oilers puck	8.00
83-84	Andy Moog & Mark Messier art	8.00
84-85	Oilers uniforms & Stanley Cup	6.00
85-86	Wayne Gretzky w/ trophies	10.00
86-87	Gretzky, Coffey w/ trophies	10.00
87-88	Wayne Gretzky, Cup celebration	10.00
88-89	10th Anniversary logo	7.00
89-90	Oilers logo	5.00
90-91	Mark Messier & trophy	7.00
91-92		5.00
92-93	Stanley Cup memorabilia	5.00

PENGUINS MEDIA GUIDES

68-69	Les Binkley	20.00
69-70	Penguins art	10.00
70-71	Red Kelly	8.00
71-72	Penguins logo	8.00
72-73	Penguins logo	8.00
73-74	Ken Schinkel	8.00
74-75	Syl Apps	8.00
75-76	Ron Schock	7.00
76-77	P.LaRouche, S.Apps, J.Pronovost	7.00
77-78	Syl Apps	7.00
78-79	Orest Kindrachuck	6.00
79-80	George Ferguson & Randy Carlyle	7.00
80-81	Rick Kehoe	7.00
81-82	Rick Kehoe & Randy Carlyle	7.00
82-83	Michael Dian	6.00
83-84	Goal celebration	6.00
84-85	Mike Bullard	6.00
85-86	Mario Lemieux art	10.00
86-87	Penguins memorabilia	6.00
87-88	Mario Lemieux	7.00
88-89	Mario Lemieux art	7.00
89-90	Lemieux, Coffey, Barrasso, Brown	7.00
90-91	C.Patrick,S.Bowman,B.Johnson art	6.00
91-92		6.00
92-93		6.00

RANGERS MEDIA GUIDES

47-48	"Inside the Blue Shirt"	200.00
48-49	Buddy O'Connor	175.00
49-50	Edgar Laprade	125.00
50-51	Chuck Rayner, 25th Anniversary	125.00
51-52	Don Raleigh	75.00
52-53		50.00
53-54		50.00
54-55	Muzz Patrick, Ivan Irwin art	50.00
55-56		40.00
56-57		40.00
57-58		30.00
58-59		30.00
59-60		25.00
60-61		15.00
61-62		15.00
62-63		15.00
63-64	Jacques Plante	15.00
64-65	Rod Gilbert	10.00
65-66	Harry Howell vs. Stan Mikita	10.00
66-67	Bob Nevin	8.00
67-68	Ed Giacomin	10.00
68-69	Jean Ratelle	10.00
69-70	Arnie Brown vs. Bobby Hull	10.00
70-71	Brad Park, Ed Giacomin	10.00
71-72	Gilles Villemure & Ed Giacomin	10.00
72-73	Vic Hadfield 50th goal	8.00
73-74	Ed Giacomin	8.00
74-75	Brad Park, Ted Irvine	8.00
75-76	50th Anniversary logo	10.00
76-77	Rangers jersey art	6.00
77-78	Phil Esposito, others	8.00
78-79	Fred Shero	6.00
79-80	John Davidson	6.00
80-81	Action photos	6.00
81-82	Action photos	6.00
82-83	Action photos	6.00
83-84	Madison Square Garden	6.00
84-85	Rangers jersey	6.00
85-86	Empire State Building	6.00
86-87	Statue of Liberty	6.00
87-88	Phil Esposito, Bergeron	6.00
88-89	Action photos	6.00
89-90	Tony Granato, Brian Leetch	7.00
90-91	Leetch, Nicholls, Gartner	6.00
91-92	Richter, Leetch & past Rangers	6.00

Rangers 1967-68 Blue Book; Rangers 1974-75 Yearbook; Red Wings 1976-77 Media Guide

92-93		6.00

RED WINGS MEDIA GUIDES

60-61	Cartoon	35.00
61-62		25.00
62-63	Red Wings logos	25.00
63-64		25.00
64-65		20.00
65-66		20.00
66-67	Delvecchio, Crozier, Howe	20.00
67-68		15.00
68-69	Gordie Howe art	15.00
69-70		10.00
70-71	Gordie Howe 25th season art	15.00
71-72	Alex Delvecchio	10.00
72-73	A. Delvecchio & historical photos	10.00
73-74	M. Redmond & A. Delvecchio	10.00
74-75	GM/Coach Alex Delvecchio	10.00
75-76	50th season goalie mask	10.00
76-77	50th Anniversary photos	8.00
77-78	Goalie mask & logos	6.00
78-79	Action photos w/ headlines	6.00
79-80	Olympia Stad. & Joe Louis Arena	6.00
80-81	Action art	6.00
81-82	Reed Larson	6.00
82-83	Management art, team art	6.00
83-84	Goalie net, Red Wings jersey	6.00
84-85	Logo, action photos	6.00
85-86	John Ogrodnick	6.00
86-87	Klima, Yzerman, Coach Demers	8.00
87-88	Demers, celebration photos	6.00
88-89	Demers, Yzerman, G. Gallant	7.00
89-90	Logo & management photos	6.00
90-91	Steve Yzerman & Shawn Burr	7.00
91-92		6.00
92-93	Racine, Ysebaert & others	6.00

ROCKIES MEDIA GUIDES

Colorado Rockies

76-77	Rockies logo	15.00
77-78	Mountains photo, logo	8.00
78-79	Mountains, stream, logo	8.00
79-80	20 Don Cherry photos	8.00
80-81	Lanny McDonald	10.00
81-82	Action photos, logo	8.00

became New Jersey Devils in 1982-83

SABRES MEDIA GUIDES

70-71	Sabres logo & year	15.00
71-72	Action photo	8.00
72-73	Roger Crozier	8.00
73-74	Gil Perreault action	10.00
74-75	Richard Martin	8.00
75-76	Rene Robert	6.00
76-77	Danny Gare	6.00
77-78	Gerry Desjardins	6.00
78-79	Don Edwards	6.00
79-80	Craig Ramsay	6.00
80-81	Danny Gare	6.00
81-82	Danny Gare, others	6.00
82-83	Gil Perreault, "The First Sabre"	6.00
83-84	Mike Ramsey	6.00
84-85	Tom Barrasso	6.00
85-86	Sauve, Barrasso, others	6.00
86-87	Action photos vs. Habs, Whalers	6.00
87-88	Sabres bench & logo	6.00
88-89	Tom Barrasso	6.00
89-90	Phil Housley	6.00
90-91	Pierre Turgeon	6.00
91-92		6.00
92-93		6.00

SEALS MEDIA GUIDES

Oakland Seals

68-69	Seals action	25.00
69-70	Seals art	15.00
70-71	Bay Area's Hockey Team art	10.00

California Golden Seals

71-72	Seals art	10.00
72-73	Seals art	8.00
73-74	Seals art	8.00
74-75		8.00
75-76	Seals action	8.00

SENATORS MEDIA GUIDES

92-93	Senators history art	5.00

SHARKS MEDIA GUIDES

91-92		7.00
92-93	Die-cut Shark fin	7.00

WHALERS MEDIA GUIDES

New England Whalers

72-73		15.00
73-74	Ted Green w/ WHA trophy	10.00
74-75	Al Smith, Hartford Civic Center	10.00

Hartford Whalers

75-76	Number "5" with Whaler photos	8.00
76-77	Ley, Webster, others	6.00
77-78		6.00
78-79	Gordie Howe	8.00
79-80	Rick Ley	6.00
80-81	Dave Keon	6.00
81-82	Coach Larry Pleau	6.00
82-83	Whalers pucks	5.00
83-84	Stoughton, Francis, Johnson	6.00
84-85	Logo, Greg Millen photos	5.00
85-86	Ron Francis	6.00
86-87	Francis, Dineen, Liut art	6.00
87-88	Mike Liut	5.00
88-89	Ulf Samuelsson & Dave Tippett	5.00
89-90	Kevin Dineen action photo	5.00
90-91	Ron Francis	5.00
91-92		5.00
92-93	Closeup of blue Whaler jersey	5.00

HALLS OF FAME

AUTO RACING HALL OF FAME

Aitken, Johny 1981
Anderson, Gil 1983
Andretti, Mario 1986
Baker, Cannonball . 1981
Banks, Henry 1985
Bergere, Cliff 1976
Bettenhausen, Tony 1968
Boyer, Joe 1985
Bruce-Brown, David 1980
Burman, Bob ... 1953-54
Bryan, Jimmy 1973
Chevrolet, Gaston .. 1964
Chevrolet, Louis ... 1952
Clark, Jimmy 1988
Cooper, Earl 1953-54
Cummings, Bill 1970
Dawson, Joe 1976
DePalma, Ralph . 1953-54
DePaolo, Peter 1963
Durant, Cliff 1983
Fengler, Harlan 1983
Foyt, A.J. 1978
Frame, Fred 1984
Goux, Jules 1989
Gant, Harry 1982
Gurney, Dan 1988
Hanks, Sam 1981
Harroun, Ray 1952
Hartz, Harry 1963
Hearne, Eddie 1964
Hepburn, Ralph ... 1970
Holland, Bill 1992
Horn, Ted 1964
Jones, Parnelli 1985
Keech, Ray 1984
Lockhart, Frank ... 1965
Mays, Rex 1963
McGrath, Jack 1987
Meyer, Louis 1963
Milton, Tommy .. 1953-54
Moore, Lou 1969
Mulford, Ralph .. 1953-54
Murphy, Jimmy 1964
Nalon, Dennis 1983
Oldfield, Barney ... 1952
Parsons, Johnnie .. 1986
Resta, Dario 1953-54
Richenbacker, Ed .. 1954
Roberts, Floyd 1985
Rose, Mauri 1967
Ruby, Lloyd 1991
Rutherford, Jon 1987
Ruttman, Troy 1992
Shaw, Wilbur 1963
Snyder, Jimmy 1981
Stevens, Myron ... 1982
Strang, Lewis 1982
Unser, Al 1986
Unser, Bobby 1990
Vukovich, Bill 1972
Ward, Rodger 1981
Wilcox, Howard ... 1963

BASEBALL HALL OF FAME

Aaron, Hank 1982
Alexander, Grover .. 1938
Alston, Walter 1983
Anson, Cap 1939
Aparicio, Luis 1984
Appling, Luke 1964
Averill, Earl 1975
Baker, Frank 1955
Bancroft, Davey ... 1971
Banks, Ernie 1977
Barlick, Al 1989
Barrow, Ed 1953
Beckley, Jake 1971
Bell, Cool Papa ... 1974
Bench, Johnny 1989
Bender, Chief 1953
Berra, Yogi 1972
Bottomley, Jim 1974
Boudreau, Lou 1970
Bresnehan, Roger .. 1945
Brock, Lou 1985
Brouthers, Dan 1945
Brown, Mordecai ... 1949
Bulkeley, Morgan .. 1937
Burkett, Jesse 1946
Campanella, Roy .. 1969
Carew, Rod 1991
Carey, Max 1961
Cartwright, Alex ... 1938
Chadwick, Henry .. 1938
Chance, Frank 1946
Chandler, Happy ... 1982
Charleston, O 1976
Chesbro, Jack 1946
Clarke, Fred 1945
Clarkson, John 1963
Clemente, Rob 1973
Cobb, Ty 1936
Cochrane, Mickey .. 1947
Collins, Eddie 1939
Collins, Jimmy 1945
Combs, Earle 1970
Comiskey, Charles . 1939
Conlan, Jocko 1974
Connolly, Tom 1953
Connor, Roger 1976
Coveleski, Stan ... 1969
Crawford, Sam 1957
Cronin, Joe 1956
Cummings, Candy . 1939
Cuyler, Kiki 1968
Dandridge, Ray ... 1987
Dean, Dizzy 1953
Delahanty, Ed 1945
DiMaggio, Joe 1955
Dickey, Bill 1954
Dihigo, Martin 1977
Doerr, Bobby 1986
Drysdale, Don 1984
Duffy, Hugh 1945
Evans, Billy 1973
Evers, Johnny 1946
Ewing, Buck 1939
Faber, Red 1964
Feller, Bob 1962
Ferrell, Rick 1984
Fingers, Rollie 1992
Flick, Elmer 1970
Ford, Whitey 1974
Foster, Rube 1981
Foxx, Jimmie 1951
Frick, Ford 1970
Frisch, Frankie 1947
Galvin, Pud 1965
Gehrig, Lou 1939
Gehringer, C 1949
Gibson, Bob 1981
Gibson, Josh 1972
Giles, Warren 1979
Gomez, Lefty 1972
Goslin, Goose 1968
Greenberg, Hank .. 1956
Griffith, Clark 1946
Grimes, Burleigh ... 1964
Grove, Lefty 1947
Hafey, Chick 1971
Haines, Jesse 1970
Hamilton, Billy 1961
Harridge, Will 1972
Harris, Buckey 1975
Hartnett, Gabby ... 1955
Heilmann, Harry ... 1952
Herman, Billy 1975
Hooper, Harry 1971
Hornsby, Rogers ... 1942
Hoyt, Waite 1969
Hubbard, Cal 1976
Hubbell, Carl 1947
Huggins, Miller 1964
Hunter, Catfish 1987
Irvin, Monte 1973
Jackson, Reggie ... 1993
Jackson, Travis ... 1982
Jenkins, Ferguson . 1991
Jennings, Hugh ... 1945
Johnson, Ban 1937
Johnson, Judy 1975
Johnson, Walter ... 1936
Joss, Addie 1978
Kaline, Al 1980
Keefe, Tim 1964
Keeler, Willie 1939
Kell, George 1983
Kelley, Joe 1971
Kelly, George 1973
Kelly, King 1945
Killebrew, H 1984
Kiner, Ralph 1975
Klein, Chuck 1980
Klem, Bill 1953
Koufax, Sandy 1972
Lajoie, Nap 1937
Landis, Kenesaw .. 1944
Lazzeri, Tony 1991
Lemon, Bob 1976
Leonard, Buck 1972
Lindstrom, Fred ... 1976
Lloyd, John 1977
Lyons, Ted 1955
MacPhail, Larry ... 1978
Mack, Connie 1937
Mantle, Mickey 1974
Manush, Heinie ... 1964
Maranville, R 1954
Marichal, Juan 1983
Marquard, Rube ... 1971
Mathews, Eddie ... 1978
Mathewson, Chris .. 1936
Mays, Willie 1979
McCarthy, Joe 1957
McCarthy, Tommy . 1946
McCovey, Will 1986
McGinnity, Joe ... 1946
McGraw, John 1937
McKechnie, Bill 1962
Medwick, Joe 1968
Mize, Johnny 1981
Morgan, Joe 1990
Musial, Stan 1969
Nichols, Kid 1949
O'Rourke, Jim 1945
Ott, Mel 1951
Paige, Satchel 1971
Palmer, Jim 1990
Pennock, Herb 1948
Perry, Gaylord 1991
Plank, Eddie 1946
Radbourn, Hoss ... 1939
Reese, Pee Wee .. 1984
Rice, Sam 1963
Rickey, Branch 1967

Rixey, Eppa 1963
Roberts, Robin 1976
Robinson, Brooks . . 1983
Robinson, Frank . . . 1982
Robinson, Jackie . . 1962
Robinson, Wilbert . . 1945
Roush, Edd 1962
Ruffing, Red 1967
Rusie, Amos 1977
Ruth, Babe 1936
Schalk, Ray 1955
Schoendienst, Red . 1989
Seaver, Tom 1992
Sewell, Joe 1977
Simmons, Al 1953
Sisler, George 1939
Slaughter, Enos . . . 1985
Snider, Duke 1980
Spahn, Warren 1973
Spalding, Al 1939
Speaker, Tris 1937
Stargell, Willie 1988
Stengel, Casey 1966
Terry, Bill 1954
Thompson, Sam . . . 1974
Tinker, Joe 1946
Traynor, Pie 1948
Vance, Dazzy 1955
Vaughn, Arky 1985
Veeck, Bill 1991
Waddell, Rube 1946
Wagner, Honus . . . 1936
Wallace, Bobby . . . 1953
Walsh, Ed 1946
Waner, Lloyd 1967
Waner, Paul 1952
Ward, John M. 1964
Weiss, George 1971
Welch, Mickey 1973
Wheat, Zack 1959
Wilhelm, Hoyt 1985
Williams, Billy 1987
Williams, Ted 1966
Wilson, Hack 1979
Wright, George 1937
Wright, Harry 1953
Wynn, Early 1972
Yastrzemski, Carl . . 1989
Yawkey, Tom 1980
Young, Cy 1937
Youngs, Ross 1972

BASKETBALL HALL OF FAME

Archibald, Nate 1991
Arizin, Paul 1977
Auerbach, Red 1968
Barlow, Thomas . . . 1980
Barry, Rick 1987
Baylor, Elgin 1976
Beckman, John 1972
Bee, Clair 1967
Bellamy, Walt 1993
Bing, Dave 1990
Borgmann, Bennie . 1961
Bradley, Bill 1982
Brennan, Joseph . . 1974
Cervi, Alfred 1984
Chamberlain, Wilt . . 1978
Cooper, Charles . . . 1976
Cousy, Bob 1970
Cowens, Dave 1991
Cunningham, Billy . . 1986
Davies, Robert 1969
DeBernardi, F 1961
DeBusschere, D . . . 1982
Dehnert, Henry 1968
Erving, Julius 1993
Endacott, Paul 1971
Foster, Bud 1964
Frazier, Walt 1987
Friedman, Marty . . . 1971
Fulks, Joe 1977
Gaines, Clarence . . 1981
Gale, Laddie 1976
Gallatin, Harry 1991
Gates, William 1989
Gola, Tom 1975
Greer, Hal 1981
Gruenig, Robert . . . 1963
Hagan, Cliff 1977
Hanson, Victor 1960
Havlicek, John 1983
Hayes, Elvin 1990
Heinsohn, Tommy . . 1986
Holman, Nat 1964
Holzman, Red 1986
Houbregs, Robert . . 1987
Hyatt, Chuck 1959
Iba, Henry 1968
Issel, Dan 1993
Johnson, William . . 1976
Johnston, Neil 1990
Jones, K.C. 1989
Jones, Sam 1983
Knight, Bobby 1991
Krause, Edward . . . 1975
Kurland, Bob 1961
Lapchick, Joe 1966
Lovellette, Clyde . . . 1988
Lucas, Jerry 1979
Luisetti, Hank 1959
Macauley, Ed 1960
Maravich, Pete 1987
Martin, Slater 1981
McCracken, Branch 1960
McCracken, Jack . . 1962
McDermott, Bobby . 1988
McGuire, Dick 1993
McGuire, Frank 1976
Meyer, Ray 1978
Mikan, George 1959
Mokray, William . . . 1965
Monroe, Earl 1990
Murphy, Calvin 1993
Murphy, Charles . . . 1960
Myers, Ann 1993
Naismith, James . . . 1959
Page, Harlan 1962
Pettit, Bob 1970
Phillip, Andy 1961
Podoloff, Maurice . . 1973
Pollard, Jim 1977
Ramsey, Frank 1981
Reed, Willis 1981
Robertson, Oscar . . 1979
Roosma, John 1961
Rupp, Adolph 1968
Russell, Bill 1974
Saperstein, Abe . . . 1970
Schayes, Dolph . . . 1972
Schmidt, Ernest . . . 1973
Schommer, John . . 1959
Sedran, Barney . . . 1962
Semjanova, Uljana . 1993
Sharman, Bill 1975
Smith, Dean 1982
Stagg, Alonzo 1959
Steinmetz, Chris . . . 1961
Thompson, John . . . 1962
Thurmond, Nate . . . 1984
Twyman, Jack 1982
Unseld, Wes 1988
Vandivier, Robert . . 1974
Wachter, Edward . . 1961
Walton, Bill 1993
Wanzer, Robert . . . 1987
West, Jerry 1979
Wilkens, Lenny 1989
Wooden, John 1960
Woolpert, Phil 1992

Women

Harris, Lucy 1992
White, Nera 1992

Coaches

Anderson, Harry . . . 1984
Auerbach, Red 1968
Barry, Sam 1978
Blood, Ernest 1960
Cann, Howard 1967
Carlson, Henry 1959
Carnesecca, Lou . . 1992
Carnevale, Ben 1969
Case, Everett 1981
Dean, Everett 1966
Diddie, Ed 1971
Drake, Bruce 1972
Gaines, Clarence . . 1981
Gardner, Jack 1983
Gill, Amory 1967
Harshman, Marv . . . 1984
Hickey, Ed 1978
Hobson, Howard . . . 1965
Holzman, Red 1986
Iba, Hank 1968
Julian, Alvin 1967
Keaney, Frank 1960
Keagan, George . . . 1961
Knight, Bob 1991
Lambert, Ward 1960
Litwack, Harry 1975
Leoffler, Ken 1964
Lonborg, Dutch 1972
McCutchan, Arad . . 1980
McGuire, Al 1992
McGuire, Frank 1976
Meanwell, Walter . . 1959
Meyer, Ray 1978
Miller, Ralph 1988
Ramsay, Jack 1992
Rupp, Adolph 1968
Sachs, Leonard . . . 1961
Shelton, Everett . . . 1979
Smith, Dean 1982
Taylor, Fred 1985
Wade, Margaret . . . 1984
Watts, Stan 1985
Wooden, John 1972

BOXING HALL OF FAME

Modern Era

Ali, Muhammad . . . 1990
Arguello, Alexis 1992
Armstrong, Henry . . 1990
Basilio, Carmen . . . 1990
Benvenuti, Nino . . . 1992
Burley, Charley 1992
Cerden, Marcel 1991
Charles, Ezzard . . . 1990
Conn, Billy 1990
Foster, Bob 1990
Frazier, Joe 1990
Fullmer, Gene 1991
Gavilan, Kid 1990
Graham, Billy 1992
Graziano, Rocky . . . 1991
Griffith, Emile 1990
Jack, Beau 1991
Jofre, Eder 1992
LaMotta, Jake 1990
Liston, Sonny 1991
Louis, Joe 1990
Marciano, Rocky . . . 1990
Monzon, Carlos . . . 1990
Moore, Archie 1990
Napoles, Jose 1990
Norton, Ken 1992
Olivares, Ruben . . . 1991
Ortiz, Carlos 1991
Patterson, Floyd . . . 1991
Pep, Willie 1990
Robinson, S.R. 1990
Saddler, Sandy 1990
Sanchez, Sal 1991
Schmeling, Max . . . 1992
Tiger, Dick 1991
Walcott, Jersey J . . 1990
Williams, Ike 1990
Zale, Tony 1991

Old-Timers

Ambers, Lou 1992
Atell, Abe 1990
Britton, Jack 1990
Brown, Panama Al . 1992
Canzoneri, Tony . . . 1990
Carpentier, G 1991

- Chocolate, Kid 1991
- Corbett, James J 1990
- Dempsey, Jack 1990
- Dempsey, Jack 1992
- Dixon, George 1990
- Driscoll, Jim 1990
- Dundee, Johnny 1991
- Fitzsimmons, Bob 1990
- Gans, Joe 1990
- Gibbons, Mike 1992
- Greb, Harry 1990
- Griffo, Young 1991
- Jackson, Peter 1990
- Jeffries, James J 1990
- Johnson, Jack 1990
- Ketchel, Stanley 1990
- Langford, Sam 1990
- Leonard, Benny 1990
- Lewis, Ted (Kid) 1992
- Loughran, Tommy 1991
- McCoy, Charles 1991
- McFarland, Packey 1992
- McGovern, Terry 1990
- McLarnin, Jimmy 1991
- Nelson, Battling 1992
- Ross, Barney 1990
- Ryan, Tommy 1991
- Tunney, Gene 1990
- Walker, Mickey 1990
- Walcott, Joe 1991
- Wilde, Jimmy 1990
- Wills, Harry 1992

Pioneers

- Belcher, Jem 1992
- Broughton, Jack 1990
- Burke, James 1992
- Cribb, Tom 1991
- Figg, James 1992
- Jackson, John 1992
- King, Tom 1992
- Langham, Nat 1992
- Mace, Jem 1990
- Mendoza, Daniel 1990
- Sayers, Tom 1990
- Spring, Tom 1992
- Sullivan, John L 1990
- Thompson, William 1991

Non-Participants

- Andrews, Thomas S 1992
- Arcel, Ray 1991
- Blackburn, Jack 1992
- Chambers, John 1990
- Coffroth, James W 1991
- Dundee, Angelo 1992
- Egan, Pierce 1991
- Fleischer, Nat 1990
- Goldman, Charley 1992
- Jacobs, Mike 1990
- Kearns, Jack 1990
- Liebling, A.J. 1992
- Lansdale, Lord 1990
- Markson, Harry 1992
- Parnassus, George 1991
- Queensberry, M 1990
- Rickard, Tex 1990
- Walker, James J. 1992

FOOTBALL HALL OF FAME

- Adderley, Herb 1980
- Alworth, Lance 1961
- Atkins, Doug 1952
- Badgro, Red 1981
- Battles, Cliff 1931
- Baugh, Sammy 1936
- Bednarik, Chuck 1948
- Bell, Bert 1963
- Bell, Bobby 1962
- Berry, Raymond 1973
- Bidwill, Charles 1967
- Biletnikoff, Fred 1964
- Blanda, George 1981
- Blount, Mel 1989
- Bradshaw, Terry 1989
- Brown, Jim 1971
- Brown, Paul 1967
- Brown, Roosevelt 1975
- Brown, Willie 1984
- Buchanan, Buck 1990
- Butkus, Dick 1964
- Campbell, Earl 1977
- Canadeo, Tony 1974
- Carr, Joe 1963
- Chamberlin, Guy 1915
- Christiansen, J 1970
- Clark, Dutch 1963
- Connor, George 1947
- Conzelman, Jimmy 1964
- Csonka, Larry 1967
- Davis, Willie 1981
- Dawson, Len 1987
- Ditka, Mike 1960
- Donovan, Art 1968
- Driscoll, John 1917
- Dudley, Bill 1941
- Edwards, Turk 1931
- Ewbank, Weeb 1978
- Fears, Tom 1947
- Flaherty, Ray 1976
- Ford, Len 1976
- Fortmann, Daniel 1935
- Fouts, Dan 1993
- Gatski, Frank 1985
- George, Bill 1974
- Gifford, Frank 1951
- Gillman, Sid 1983
- Graham, Otto 1943
- Grange, Red 1925
- Greene, Joe 1968
- Gregg, Forrest 1977
- Griese, Bob 1966
- Groza, Lou 1974
- Guyon, Joe 1918
- Halas, George 1963
- Ham, Jack 1970
- Hannah, John 1991
- Harris, Franco 1990
- Healey, Ed 1916
- Hein, Mel 1930
- Hendricks, Ted 1968
- Henry, Wilbur 1919
- Herber, Arnie 1966
- Hewitt, Bill 1971
- Hinkle, Clarke 1937
- Hirsch, Elroy 1943
- Hornung, Paul 1956
- Houston, Ken 1986
- Hubbard, Cal 1926
- Huff, Sam 1955
- Hunt, Lamar 1972
- Hutson, Don 1934
- Johnson, John H 1903
- Jones, Deacon 1980
- Jones, Stan 1991
- Jurgensen, Sonny 1983
- Kiesling, Walt 1966
- Kinard, Bruiser 1937
- Lambeau, Curley 1963
- Lambert, Jack 1990
- Landry, Tom 1990
- Lane, Dick 1974
- Langer, Jim 1987
- Lanier, Willie 1986
- Lary, Yale 1979
- Lavelli, Dante 1975
- Layne, Bobby 1947
- Leemans, Tuffy 1978
- Lilly, Bob 1960
- Little, Larry 1993
- Lombardi, Vince 1971
- Luckman, Sid 1938
- Lyman, Link 1964
- Mara, Tim 1963
- Marchetti, Gino 1972
- Marshall, George 1963
- Matson, Ollie 1972
- Maynard, Don 1987
- McAfee, George 1939
- McCormack, Mike 1984
- McElhenny, Hugh 1951
- McNally, John 1963
- Michalske, Mike 1964
- Millner, Wayne 1968
- Mitchell, Bobby 1983
- Mix, Ron 1979
- Moore, Lenny 1975
- Motley, Marion 1968
- Musso, George 1982
- Nagurski, Bronko 1963
- Namath, Joe 1985
- Neale, Earle 1969
- Nevers, Ernie 1963
- Nitschke, Ray 1978
- Nomellini, Leo 1969
- Olsen, Merlin 1982
- Otto, Jim 1980
- Owen, Steve 1966
- Page, Alan 1988
- Parker, Ace 1972
- Parker, Jim 1973
- Payton, Walter 1993
- Perry, Joe 1969
- Pihos, Pete 1970
- Ray, Hugh 1966
- Reeves, Dan 1967
- Ringo, Jim 1981
- Robustelli, Andy 1971
- Rooney, Art 1964
- Rozelle, Pete 1985
- St.Clair, Bob 1990
- Sayers, Gale 1977
- Schmidt, Joe 1973
- Schramm, Tex 1991
- Shell, Art 1989
- Simpson, O.J. 1985
- Starr, Bart 1977
- Staubach, Roger 1985
- Stautner, Ernie 1969
- Strong, Ken 1967
- Stydahar, Joe 1967
- Tarkenton, Fran 1986
- Taylor, Charley 1976
- Taylor, Jim 1976
- Thorpe, Jim 1963
- Tittle, Y.A. 1971
- Trafton, George 1964
- Trippi, Charlie 1968
- Tunnell, Emlen 1967
- Turner, Bulldog 1966
- Unitas, Johnny 1979
- Upshaw, Gene 1987
- Van Brocklin, N 1971
- Van Buren, Steve 1965
- Walker, Doak 1986
- Walsh, Bill 1993
- Warfield, Paul 1983
- Waterfield, Bob 1965
- Weinmeister, A 1984
- Willis, Bill 1977
- Wilson, Larry 1978
- Wojciechowicz, A 1968
- Woll, Chuck 1993
- Wood, Willie 1989

GOLF HALL OF FAME

Men

- Anderson, Wille 1975
- Armour, Tommy 1976
- Ball, John Jr. 1977
- Barnes, Jim 1989
- Boros, Julius 1982
- Braid, James 1976
- Casper, Billy 1978
- Cooper, Harry 1992
- Cotton, Thomas 1980
- Demaret, Jimmy 1983
- DeVicenzo, Rob 1989
- Evans, Chick 1975
- Floyd, Ray 1989
- Guldahl, Ralph 1981
- Hagen, Walter 1974
- Hilton, Harold 1978
- Hagan, Ben 1974
- Irwin, Hale 1992
- Jones, Bobby 1974
- Little, Lawson 1980

Littler, Gene 1990
Locke, Bobby 1977
Middlecoff, Cary . . . 1986
Morris, Tom, Sr. . . . 1976
Morris, Tom, Jr 1975
Nelson, Byron 1974
Nicklaus, Jack 1974
Ouimet, Francis . . . 1974
Palmer, Arnold 1974
Player, Gary 1974
Runyan, Paul 1990
Sarazen, Gene 1974
Smith, Horton 1990
Snead, Sam 1974
Taylor, John 1975
Thomson, Peter . . . 1988
Travers, Jerry 1976
Travis, Walter 1979
Trevina, Lee 1981
Vardon, Harry 1974
Watson, Tom 1988

Women

Berg, Patty 1974
Howe, Dorothy 1978
Carner, JoAnne . . . 1985
Lopez, Nancy 1989
Rawls, Betsy 1987
Suggs, Louise 1979
Vare, Glenna 1975
Wethered, Joyce . . . 1975
Whitworth, Kathy . . 1982
Wright, Mickey 1976
Zaharias, Babe 1974

Contributors

Campbell, William . . 1990
Corcoran, Fred 1975
Crosby, Bing 1978
Dey, Joe 1975
Graffis, Herb 1977
Harlow, Robert 1988
Hope, Bob 1983
Jones, Robert 1987
Roberts, Clifford . . . 1978
Rodriguez, C.C 1992
Ross, Donald 1977
Tufts, Richard 1992

HOCKEY HALL OF FAME

Abel, Sid 1969
Adams, Jack 1959
Allen, Keith 1993
Apps, Syl 1961
Armstrong, George . 1975
Bailey, Ace 1975
Bain, Dan 1945
Baker, Hobey 1945
Barber, Bill 1990
Barry, Marty 1965
Bathgate, Andy 1978
Beliveau, Jean 1972
Benedict, Clint 1965
Bentley, Doug 1964
Bentley, Max 1966
Blake, Toe 1966
Boivin, Leo 1986
Boon, Dickie 1952
Bossy, Mike 1991
Bouchard, Butch . . . 1966
Boucher, Frank 1958
Boucher, Buck 1960
Bower, John 1976
Bowie, Russell 1945
Brimsek, Francis . . . 1966
Broadbent, Punch . . 1962
Broda, Turk 1967
Bucyk, John 1981
Burch, Billy 1974
Cameron, Harry . . . 1962
Cheevers, Gerry . . . 1985
Clancy, King 1958
Clapper, Dit 1947
Clarke, Bobby 1987
Cleghorn, Sprague . 1958
Colville, Neil 1967
Conacher, Charles . 1961
Connell, Alex 1958
Cook, William 1952
Coulter, Arthur 1974
Cournoyer, Yvan . . . 1982
Cowley, Bill 1968
Crawford, Rusty . . . 1962
Darragh, Jack 1962
Davidson, Scotty . . . 1950
Day, Hap 1961
Delvecchio, Alex . . . 1977
Denneny, Cy 1959
Dion, Marcel 1993
Drillon, Gordie 1975
Drinkwater, C 1950
Dryden, Ken 1983
Dumart, Woody . . . 1993
Dunderdale, Tom . . 1974
Durnan, Bill 1964
Dutton, Red 1958
Dye, Babe 1970
Esposito, Phil 1984
Esposito, Tony 1988
Farrell, Arthur 1965
Flaman, Fern 1990
Foyston, Frank 1958
Frederickson, F . . . 1958
Gadsby, Bill 1970
Gainey, Bob 1993
Gardiner, Chuck . . . 1945
Gardiner, Herb 1958
Gardner, Jimmy . . . 1962
Geoffrion, B 1972
Gerard, Eddie 1945
Giacomin, Eddie . . . 1987
Gilbert, Rod 1982
Gilmour, Billy 1962
Goheen, Moose . . . 1952
Goodfellow, Ebbie . . 1963
Grant, Mike 1952
Green, Shorty 1962
Griffis, Si 1950
Hainsworth, G 1961
Hall, Glenn 1975
Hall, Joe 1961
Harvey, Doug 1973
Hay, George 1958
Horn, Riley 1977
Hextall, Bryan 1969
Holmes, Hap 1972
Hooper, Tom 1962
Horner, Red 1965
Horton, Tim 1977
Howe, Gordie 1972
Howe, Sydney 1965
Howell, Harry 1979
Hull, Bobby 1983
Hutton, Bouse 1962
Hyland, Harry 1962
Irvin, Dick 1958
Jackson, Harvey . . . 1971
Johnson, Bob 1993
Johnson, Ching . . . 1958
Johnson, Moose . . . 1952
Johnson, Thomas . . 1970
Joliat, Aurel 1947
Keats, Duke 1958
Kelly, Red 1969
Kennedy, Teeder . . 1966
Keon, Dave 1986
Lach, Elmer 1966
Lafleur, Guy 1988
Lalonde, Newsy . . . 1950
Laperriere, Jacq . . . 1987
Laviolette, Jack 1962
Lehman, Hugh 1958
Lemaire, Jacques . . 1984
LeSueur, Percy 1961
Lewis, Herb 1989
Lindsay, Ted 1966
Lumley, Harry 1980
MacKay, Mickey . . . 1952
Mahovlich, Frank . . 1981
Malone, Joe 1950
Mantha, Sylvio 1960
Marshall, Jack 1965
Mathers, Frank 1993
Maxwell, Steamer . . 1962
McDonell, Lanny . . . 1993
McGee, Frank 1945
McGimsie, Billy 1962
McNamara, George 1958
Mikita, Stan 1983
Moore, Richard 1974
Moran, Paddy 1958
Morenz, Howie 1945
Mosienko, Bill 1965
Nighbor, Frank 1947
Noble, Reg 1962
O'Connor, Buddy . . 1988
Oliver, Harry 1967
Olmstead, Bert 1985
Orr, Bobby 1979
Parent, Bernie 1984
Park, Brad 1988
Patrick, Joseph 1980
Patrick, Lester 1947
Perreault, Gil 1990
Phillips, Tommy . . . 1945
Pilote, Pierre 1975
Pitre, Pit 1962
Plante, Jacques . . . 1978
Potvin, Denis 1991
Pratt, Babe 1966
Primeau, Joe 1963
Pronovost, Marcel . . 1978
Pulford, Bob 1991
Pulford, Harvey 1973
Quackenbush, Bill . . 1976
Rankin, Frank 1961
Ratelle, Jean 1985
Rayner, Chuck 1973
Reardon, Ken 1966
Richard, Henri 1979
Richard, Maurice . . 1961
Richardson, G 1950
Roberts, Gordon . . . 1971
Ross, Art 1945
Russel, Blair 1965
Russell, Ernest 1965
Ruttan, Jack 1962
Savard, Serge 1986
Sawchuck, Terry . . . 1971
Scanlan, Fred 1965
Schmidt, Milt 1961
Schriner, Sweeny . . 1962
Seibert, Earl 1964
Seibert, Oliver 1961
Shore, Eddie 1947
Siebert, Babe 1964
Simpson, Joe 1962
Sittler, Darryl 1989
Smith, Alfred 1962
Smith, Clint 1991
Smith, Hooley 1972
Smith, Thomas 1973
Stanley, Allan 1945
Stanley, Barney . . . 1962
Stewart, Jack 1964
Stewart, Nelson . . . 1962
Stuart, Bruce 1961
Stuart, Hod 1945
Taylor, Cyclone . . . 1947
Thompson, Tiny . . . 1959
Tretiak, Vlad 1989
Trihay, Harry 1950
Ullman, Norm 1982
Vezina, Georges . . . 1945
Walker, Jack 1960
Walsh, Marty 1962
Watson, Harry 1962
Weiland, Cooney . . 1971
Westwick, Harry . . . 1962
Whitcroft, Fred 1962
Wilson, Phat 1962
Worsley, Gump 1980
Worters, Roy 1969

LPGA HALL OF FAME

Berg, Patty 1951
Bradley, Pat 1991
Carner, JoAnne . . . 1982

Hall of Fame Inductees

Haynie, Sandra 1977
Jameson, Betty 1951
Lopez, Nancy 1987
Mann, Carol 1977
Rawls, Betsy 1960
Suggs, Louise 1951
Whitworth, Kathy .. 1975
Wright, Mickey 1964
Zaharias, Babe 1951

TENNIS HALL OF FAME

Men

Adee, George 1964
Alexander, Fred ... 1961
Alison, Wilmer 1963
Alansa, Manuel 1977
Ashe, Arthur 1985
Behr, Karl 1969
Borg, Bjorn 1987
Borotra, Jean 1976
Bromwich, John ... 1984
Brookes, Norman .. 1977
Brugnon, Jacques .. 1976
Budge, Don 1964
Campbell, Oliver ... 1955
Chace, Malcolm ... 1961
Clark, Clarence 1983
Clark, Joseph 1955
Clothier, William ... 1956
Cochet, Henri 1976
Cooper, Ashley 1991
Crawford, Jack 1979
Doeg, John 1962
Doherty, Lawrence . 1980
Doherty, Reginald .. 1980
Drobry, Jaroslav ... 1983
Dwight, James 1955
Emerson, Ray 1982
Etchebaster, P 1978
Falkenburg, Bob ... 1974
Fraser, Neale 1984
Garland, Chuck ... 1969
Gonzales, Pancho . 1968
Grant, Bryan 1972
Griffin, Clarence ... 1970
Hackett, Harold 1961
Hewitt, Bob 1992
Hoad, Lew 1980
Havey, Fred 1974
Hunt, Joe 1966
Hunter, Frank 1961
Johnston, Bill 1958
Jones, Perry 1970
Kodes, Jan 1990
Kramer, Jack 1968
Lacoste, Rene 1976
Larned, William 1956
Larsen, Art 1976
Laver, Rod 1981
Lott, George 1964
Mako, Gene 1973
McKinley, Chuck ... 1986
McLoughlin, M 1957
McMillan, Frew 1992
McNeil, Don 1965
Mulloy, Gardnar ... 1972
Murray, Lindley 1958
Myrick, Julian 1963
Nastase, Ilie 1991
Newcombe, John .. 1991
Nielsen, Arthur 1971
Olmedo, Alex 1987
Osuna, Rafael 1979
Parker, Frank 1966
Patterson, Gerald .. 1989
Patty, Budge 1977
Perry, Fred 1975
Pettit, Tom 1982
Peitrangeli, N 1986
Quist, Adrian 1984
Ralston, Dennis ... 1987
Renshaw, Ernest .. 1983
Renshaw, William .. 1983
Richards, Vincent .. 1961
Riggs, Bobby 1967
Rache, Tony 1986
Rosewall, Ken 1980
Santana, Manuel .. 1984
Savitt, Dick 1976
Schroeder, Ted 1966
Sears, Richard 1955
Sedgman, Frank ... 1979
Segura, Pancho ... 1984
Seixas, Vic 1971
Shields, Frank 1964
Slocum, Henry 1955
Smith, Stan 1987
Stolle, Fred 1985
Talbert, Bill 1967
Tilden, Bill 1959
Trabert, Tony 1970
Van Ryn, John 1963
Vilas, Guillermo ... 1991
Vines, Elsworth 1962
Von Cramm, G 1977
Ward, Halcombe ... 1956
Washburn, Watson . 1965
Whitman, Malcolm . 1955
Wilding, Anthony ... 1978
Williams, Rich 1957
Wood, Sidney 1964
Wrenn, Robert 1955
Wright, Beals 1956

Women

Atkinson, Julie 1974
Austin, Tracy 1992
Barger-Wallach, M . 1958
Bertz Addie, Paul .. 1965
Brough Clapp, L ... 1967
Browne, Mary 1957
Bueno, Maria 1978
Bjurstedt, Molla 1958
Cahill, Mabel 1976
Connolly, Maureen . 1968
Dod, Charlotte 1983
Douglas, Dorothy .. 1981
Fry Irvin, S 1970
Gibson, Althea 1971
Hansell, Ellen 1965
Hard, Darlene 1973
Hart, Doris 1969
Hayden Jones, Ann 1985
Heldman, Gladys .. 1979
Hotchkiss, Hazel ... 1957
Jacobs, Helen 1962
King, Billie Jean ... 1987
Lenglen, Suzanne .. 1978
Marble, Alice 1964
McKane, Kitty 1978
Moore, Elisabeth ... 1971
Nuthall, Betty 1977
Osborne, Margaret . 1967
Paffrey, Sarah 1963
Roosevelt, Ellen ... 1975
Round, Dorothy ... 1986
Ryan, Elizabeth ... 1972
Sears, Eleanora ... 1968
Smith, Margaret ... 1979
Sutton, May 1956
Townsend, Bertha .. 1974
Wade, Virginia 1989
Wagner, Marie 1969
Wills Roark, H 1969

Contributors

Baker, Lawrence ... 1975
Chatrier, Phil 1992
Cullman, Joe 1990
Danzig, Allison 1968
Davis, Dwight 1956
Gray, David 1985
Gustaf, V 1980
Hester, W.E. 1981
Hopman, Harry 1978
Laney, Al 1979
Martin, Alastair 1973
Martin, William 1982
Outerbridge, Mary .. 1981
Pell, Theodore 1966
Van Alen, James .. 1965

U.S. OLYMPIC HALL OF FAME

Bobsled

Eagan, Eddie 1983

Boxing

Clay, Cassius 1983
Eagan, Eddie 1983
Foreman, George .. 1990
Frazier, Joe 1989
Leonard, Sugar R .. 1985
Patterson, Floyd ... 1987

Diving

Lee, Sammy 1990
Louganis, Greg 1985
McCormick, Pat ... 1985

Figure Skating

Albright, Tenley ... 1988
Button, Dick 1983
Fleming, Peggy ... 1983
Hamill, Dorothy 1991
Hamilton, Scott 1990

Gymnastics

Conner, Bart 1991
Retton, Mary Lou .. 1985
Vidmar, Peter 1991

Rowing

Kelly, Jack Sr. 1990

Speed Skating

Heiden, Eric 1983

Swimming

Babashoff, S 1987
Caulkins, Tracy 1990
Daniels, Charles ... 1988
De Varona, Donna . 1987
Kahanamaku, D ... 1984
Meyer, Debbie 1986
Naber, John 1984
Schallander, D 1983
Spitz, Mark 1983
Weissmuller, Jon .. 1983

Track & Field

Beamon, Bob 1983
Baston, Ralph 1985
Calhoun, Lee 1991
Davenport, Wil 1991
Davis, Glenn 1986
Didrikson, Babe ... 1983
Dillard, Harry 1983
Evans, Lee 1989
Ewry, Ray 1983
Jenner, Bruce 1986
Johnson, Rafer 1983
Kraenzlein, Alvin ... 1985
Lewis, Carl 1985
Mathias, Bob 1983
Mills, Billy 1984
Morrow, Bob 1989
Moses, Edwin 1985
O'Brien, Parry 1984
Oerter, Al 1983
Owens, Jesse 1983
Paddock, Charley .. 1991
Richards, Bob 1983
Rudolph, Wilma ... 1983
Sheppard, Mel 1989
Shorter, Frank 1984
Thorpe, Jim 1983
Toomey, Bill 1984
Tyus, Wyomia 1985
Whitfield, Mal 1988
Wykoff, Frank 1984

Weight Lifting

Davis, John 1989
Kono, Tommy 1990

Wrestling

Gable, Dan 1985

Contributors

Arledge, Roone ... 1989
Brundage, Avery ... 1983
Bushnell, Asa 1990
Iba, Hank 1985
Kane, Robert 1986
McKay, Jim 1988
Miller, Don 1984
Simon, William 1991
Walker, Leroy 1987

SPORTS ADDRESSES

AUTO RACING

Formula One
8 Place de la Concorde
75008 Paris, France

Indianapolis Motor Speedway Hall of Fame
4790 West 16th St.
Indianapolis, IN 46222

International Motorsports Hall of Fame
P.O. Box 1018
Talladega, Al 35160

Motor Sports Hall of Fame of America
P.O. Box 194
Novi, MI 48050

NASCAR
P.O. Box 2875
Daytona Beach, FL 32120

BASEBALL

National Baseball Hall of Fame
P.O. Box 590
Cooperstown, NY 13326

Baltimore Orioles
333 West Camden St.
Baltimore, MD 21202

Boston Red Sox
Fenway Park
4 Yawkey Way
Boston, Ma 02215

California Angels
P.O. Box 2000
Anaheim, CA 92803

Chicago White Sox
Comiskey Park
333 W. 35th St.
Chicago, IL 60616

Cleveland Indians
Cleveland Stadium
Cleveland, OH 44114

Colorado Rockies
1700 Lincoln St. Suite 3710
Denver, CO 80203

Detroit Tigers
Tiger Stadium
Detroit, MI 48216

Florida Marlins
2269 NW 199th St.
Miami, FL 33056

Kansas City Royals
P.O. Box 419969
Kansas City, MO 64141

Milwaukee Brewers
County Staduim
201 S. 46th St.
Milwaukee, WI 53214

Minnesota Twins
Hubert H. Humphrey Metrodome
501 Chicago Ave. So.
Minneapolis, MN 55415

New York Yankees
Yankee Stadium
Bronx, NY 10451

Oakland Athletics
Oakland-Alameda County Coliseum
Oakland, CA 94621

Seattle Mariners
P.O. Box 4100
Seattle, WA 98104

Texas Rangers
P.O. Box 90111
Arlington, TX 76004

Toronto Blue Jays
SkyDome
300 Bremner Blvd.
Suite 3200
Toronto, Ontario M5V 3B3

BASKETBALL

Naismith Memorial Basketball Hall of Fame
1150 West Columbus Ave.
Springfield, MA 01105

Atlanta Hawks
One CNN Center
South Tower Suite 405
Atlanta, GA 30303

Boston Celtics
151 Merrimac St.
5th Floor
Boston, MA 02114

Charlotte Hornets
One Hive Drive
Charlotte, NC 28217

Chicago Bulls
One Magnificent Mile
980 N. Michigan Ave.
Suite 1600
Chicago, IL 60611

Cleveland Cavaliers
2923 Streetsboro Rd.
Richfield, OH 44286

Dallas Mavericks
Reunion Arena
777 Sports St.
Dallas, TX 75207

Denver Nuggets
1635 Clay St.
Denver, CO 80204

Detroit Pistons
The Palace of Auburn Hills
Two Championship Dr.
Auburn Hills, MI 48326

Golden State Warriors
Oakland Coliseum Arena
Oakland, CA 94621

Houston Rockets
The Summit
10 Greenway Plaza East
Houston, TX 77277

Indiana Pacers
300 East Market St.
Indianapolis, IN 46204

Los Angeles Clippers
L.A. Sports Arena
3939 S. Figueroa St.
Los Angeles, CA 90037

Los Angeles Lakers
Great Western Forum
3900 W. Manchester Blvd.
Inglewood, CA 90306

Miami Heat
Miami Arena
Miami, FL 33136

Milwaukee Bucks
Bradley Center
1001 N. Forth St.
Milwaukee, WI 53203

Minnesota Timberwolves
Target Center
600 First Ave. N.
Minneapolis, MN 55403

New Jersey Nets
Meadowlands Arena
East Rutherford, NJ 07073

New York Knickerbockers
Madison Square Garden
4 Pennsylvania Plaza
New York, NY 10121

Orlando Magic
Orlando Arena
1 Magic Place
Orlando, FL 32801

Philadelphia 76ers
Veterans Stadium
Broad St. & Pattison Ave.
Philadelphia, PA 19148

Phoenix Suns
P.O. Box 1369
Phoenix, AZ 85001

Portland Trail Blazers
Suite 600
Lloyd Building
700 N.E. Multnomah St.
Portland, OR 97232

Sacramento Kings
One Sports Parkway
Sacremento, CA 95834

San Antonio Spurs
600 East Market St.
Suite 102
San Antonio, TX 78205

Seattle Supersonics
190 Queene Anne Ave. N.
Seattle, WA 98109

Utah Jazz
Delta Center
301 West South Temple
Salt Lake City, UT 84101

Washington Bullets
One Harry S Truman Dr.
Landover, MD 20785

BOXING

International Boxing Federation
134 Evergreen Pl., 9th Fl.
East Orange, NJ 07018

International Boxing Hall of Fame
1 Hall of Fame Dr.
Canastota, NY 13032

World Boxing Association
Centro Comercial Ciudad Turmero
Local #21, Piso #2
Calle Petion Cruce Con Urdaneta Turmero
2115 Estado Aragua, Venezuela

FOOTBALL

College Football Hall of Fame
5440 Kings Island Dr.
Kings Island, OH 45034
Pro Football Hall of Fame
2121 George Halas Dr. NW
Canton, OH 44708

AFC

Buffalo Bills
One Bills Drive
Orchard Park, NY 14127

Cincinnati Bengals
200 Riverfront Stadium
Cincinnati, OH 45202

Cleveland Browns
80 First Avenue
Berea, OH 44017

Denver Broncos
13655 Broncos Parkway
Englewood, CO 80112

Houston Oilers
6910 Fannin St.
Houston, TX 77030

Indianapolis Colts
P.O. Box 535000
Indianapolis, IN 46253

Kansas City Chiefs
One Arrowhead Drive
Kansas City, MO 64129

Los Angeles Raiders
332 Center St.
El Segundo, CA 90245

Miami Dolphins
Joe Robbie Stadium
2269 NW 199th St.
Miami, FL 33056

New England Patriots
Foxboro Stadium

Route 1
Foxboro, MA 02035

New York Jets
1000 Fulton Ave.
Hempstead, NY 11550

Pittsburgh Steelers
300 Stadium Circle
Pittsburgh, PA 15212

San Diego Chargers
Box 609609
San Diego, CA 92160

Seattle Seahawks
11220 NE 53rd St.
Kirkland, WA 98033

NFC

Atlanta Falcons
2745 Burnett Rd.
Suwanee, GA 30174

Chicago Bears
Halas Hall
250 N. Washington
Lake Forest, IL 60045

Dallas Cowboys
Cowboys Center
One Cowboys Parkway
Irving, TX 75063

Detroit Lions
Pontiac Silverdome
1200 Featherstone Rd
Pontiac, MI 48342

Green Bay Packers
P.O. Box 10628
Green Bay, WI 54307

Los Angeles Rams
2327 West Lincoln Ave.
Anaheim, CA 92801

Minnesota Vikings
9520 Viking Drive
Eden Prairie, MN 55344

New Orleans Saints
6928 Saints Drive
Metairie, LA 70003

New York Giants
Giants Stadium
East Rutherford, NJ 07073

Philadelphia Eagles
Veterans Stadium
Broad St. & Pattison Ave.
Philadelphia, PA 19148

Phoenix Cardinals
P.O. Box 888
Phoenix, AZ 85001

San Francisco 49ers
4949 Centennial Blvd.
Santa Clara, CA 95054

Tampa Bay Buccaneers
1 Buccaneer Place
Tampa, FL 33607

Washington Redskins
21300 Redskin Park Drive
Ashburn, VA 22011

GOLF

LPGA Hall of Fame
LPGA Headquaters
2570 Volusia Ave.
Suite B
Daytona Beach, FL 32114

LPGA Tour
2570 Volusia Ave.
Daytona Beach, FL 32114

PGA of America
100 Avenue of the Champions
Palm Beach Gardens, FL 33418

PGA Tour
Sawgrass
Ponte Vedra, FL 32082

PGA World Golf Hall of Fame
PGA Boulevard
P.O. Box 1908
Pinehurst, NC 28374

USGA
P.O. Box 708
Liberty Corner Road
Far Hills, NJ 07931

HOCKEY

Hockey Hall of Fame
BCE Place
Toronto, Ontario M6K 3C3

Boston Bruins
Boston Garden
150 Causeway St.
Boston, MA 02114

Buffalo Sabres
Memorial Auditorium
140 Main St.
Buffalo, NY 14202

Calgary Flames
Olympic Saddledome
P.O. Box 1540 Station M
Calgary, Alberta T2P 3B9

Chicago Blackhawks
Chicago Stadium
1800 West Madison St.
Chicago, IL 60612

Detroit Red Wings
Joe Louis Sports Arena
600 Civic Center Drive
Detroit, MI 48226

Edmonton Oilers
Northlands Coliseum
Edmonton, Alberta T5B 4M9

Hartford Whalers
242 Trumbull St.
8th Floor
Hartford, CT 06103

Los Angeles Kings
Great Western Forum
3900 West Manchester Blvd.
Inglewood, CA 90306

Minnesota North Stars
Metropolitan Sports Center
7901 Cedar Ave. S.
Bloomington, MN 55425

Montreal Canadiens
Montreal Forum
2313 Catherine St. W.
Montreal, Quebec H3H 1N2

New Jersey Devils
Meadowlands Arena
P.O. Box 504
East Rutherford, NJ 07073

New York Islanders
Nassau Veterans' Memorial Coliseum
Uniondale, NY 11553

New York Rangers
4 Penn Plaza
4th Floor
New York, NY 10001

Ottawa Senators
301 Moodie Drive
Suite 200
Nepean, Ontario K2H 9C4

Philadelphia Flyers
The Spectrum
Pattison Place
Philadelphia, PA 19148

Pittsburgh Penguins
Civic Arena
Pittsburgh, PA 15219

Quebec Nordiques
Colisee de Quebec
2205 Ave. du Colisee
Quebec City, Quebec
G1L 4W7

St. Louis Blues
St. Louis Arena
5700 Oakland Ave.
St. Louis, MO 63110

San Jose Sharks
10 Almaden Blvd.
Suite 600
San Jose, CA 95113

Tampa Bay Lightning
501 E. Kennedy Blvd.
Suite 175
Tampa, FL 33602

Toronto Maple Leafs
Maple Leaf Gardens
60 Carlton St.
Toronto, Ontario M5B 1L1

Vancouver Canucks
Pacific Coliseum
100 North Renfrew St.
Vancouver, Brit. Columbia V5K 3N7

Washington Capitals
Capital Centre
Landover, MD 20785

Winnipeg Jets
Winnipeg Arena
15-1430 Maroons Rd
Winnipeg, Manitoba
R3G OL5

HORSE RACING

National Horse Racing Hall of Fame
Union Ave.
Saratoga Springs, NY 12866

Thoroughbred Racing Associations
420 Fair Hill Dr.
Suite 1
Elkton, MD 21921

OLYMPICS

International Olympic Committee
Chateau de Vidy
CH-1007 Lausanne
Switzerland

1994
Lillehammer Olympic Organizing Committee
Elve Gaten 19
P.O. Box 106
N-2601 Lillehammer, Norway

1996
Atlanta Committee for the Olympic Games
250 Williams St.
Suite 6000
Atlanta, GA 30303

U.S. Olympic Hall of Fame
U.S. Olympic Committee
1750 E. Boulder St.
Colarado Springs, CO

United States Olympic Committee
1750 E. Boulder St.
Colorado Springs, CO 80909

SOCCER

United States Soccer Federation
Soccer House
1801-1811 South Prairie Ave.
Chicago, IL 60616

World Cup USA 1994
U.S. Organizing Committee
1270 Ave. of Americas, #220
New York, NY 10020

TENNIS

Association of Tennis Professionals
200 ATP Tour Blvd.
Ponte Vedra Beach, FL 32082

International Tennis Hall of Fame
194 Bellevue Ave.
Newport, RI 02840

International Tennis Federation
Pallisert Rd.
Barons Court
London, England W14 9EN

United States Tennis Association
1212 Ave. of the Americas
12th Floor
New York, NY 10036

Women's Tennis Association
133 First St. NE
St. Petersburg, FL 33701

WRESTLING

World Wrestling Federation
P.O. Box 3857
1241 E. Main St.
Stamford, CT 06902

BIBLIOGRAPHY

Ainslie, Michael. *Sotheby's Important Baseball Cards and Sports Memorabilia.* Sotheby's Holdings Inc., New York, NY, 1991.

Baker, Mark Allen. *Baseball Autograph Handbook.* Krause Publications Inc., Iola, Wisconsin, 1990.

Beckett, Dr. James. *The Sport Americana Football Card Price Guide.* Edgewater Book Company Inc., Cleveland, OH, 1990.

Beckett, Dr. James. *The Sport Americana Price Guide to Baseball Collectibles.* Edgewater Book Company Inc., Cleveland OH, 1986.

Beckett, Dr. James. *The Sport Americana Football Card Price Guide.* Edgewater Book Company Inc., Cleveland, OH, 1991.

Butler, Don & Ellingboe, Steve. *Football Baseball & Hockey Price Guide.* Krause Publications Inc, Iola, WI, 1991.

Chase, Aaron & Falvey, William. *The Official Collector's Guide to Kentucky Derby Mint Julep Glasses.* Louisville Manufacturing Co., Louisville, Kentucky, 1991.

Didinger, Ray. *America's Greatest Game.* Simon and Shuster, New York, NY, 1990.

Dinger, Ralph & Duplacey, James. *The National Hockey League Official Guide & Recorded Book.* The National Hockey League, Caledon, Ontario, 1992.

Flynn, Patrick. *Bobbin' Head Dolls Hartland Statues Price Guide.* Minnie Memories, Mankato, MN.

Fusselle, Warner. *The Baseball Encyclopedia (Eighth Edition).* Macmillan Publishing Co., New York, NY, 1990.

Garrett, Duane B. *Public Auction No. 167.* Richard Wolffers Auctions, Inc., San Francisco, CA, 1992.

Goldburg, Larry & Gutierrez, Mike & Applebaum, Steve. *The Official 13th Annual National Sports Collectors Convention Auction.* Superior Galleries, Beverly Hills, CA, 1992.

Goldman, Herbert G. *The Ring 1984 Record Book and Boxing Encyclopedia.* The Ring Publishing Corp., 1984.

Hake, Ted & Steckler, Roger. *An Illustrated Price Guide to Non-Paper Sports Collectibles.* Hake's Americana & Collectible Press, York, PA, 1986.

Hollander, Zander & Sachare, Alex. *The Official NBA Basketball Ecyclopedia.* Villard Books,

New York, 1989.

Hunter, Tim. *Bobbin Head Guide 18th Edition.* Golddust Dr., Sparks, NV, 1993.

Kaye, Allan. *Sports Cards News & Price Guides.* Allan Kaye Publications Inc., St. Louis, Mo, 1992.

King, Whit. *Collector's World.* Richmond Racing Promotions Inc., Mechanicsville, VA 1993.

Kozak, Karl M. *Cartwrights Journal of Baseball Collectibles.* Sports and Information Media Group Inc., San Diego, CA, 1992.

Kurowski, Jeff. *Standard Catalog of Baseball Cards (Third Edition).* Krause Publications, Iola, WI, 1992.

Larson, Mark A. *Sports Collectors Digest's Complete Guide to Baseball Memorabilia.* Krause Publications, Iola, Wisconsin, 1992.

Meserole, Mike. *1993 Sports Almanac.* Publication Services, Inc., Boston, MA, 1993.

Reed, Debbie. *Die Cast Digest.* Die Cast Digest Inc., Knoxville, TN, 1993.

Slater, Thomas D. *Auction #5 - Auction #11.* The Political Gallery, Indianapolis, IN, 1991-92.

Slocum, Frank & Foley, Red. *The Complete Collection: Topps Baseball Cards.* Topps Chewing Gum, Inc., New York, NY, 1985.

Sugar, Bert Randolph. *The Sports Collectors Bible.* The Bobbs-Merrill Company, Inc., New York, 1975.

Tocco, Paul. *Legends Sports Memorabilia Price Guide. Vol. 4, No. 2.* Legends Sports Memorabilia Inc., San Diego, CA, 1991.

Tocco, Paul. *Legends Sports Memorabilla. Vol. 5, No. 4.* Legends Sports Memorabilla Inc., San Diego, CA 1992.

Tocco, Paul. *Legends Sports Memorabilla.* Vol. 6, No. 1. Legends Sports Memorabilla Inc., San Diego, CA 1993.

Tremblay-Matte, Cecile. *Histoire du PIN'S Olympique 1896-1992.* Cecile Matte Inc., Paris, France 1992.

Turner, Dane. *Racing Collectibles Price Guide.* SportsStar Inc., Orlando, FL, 1993.

Wallechinsky, David. *The Complete Book of the Olympics.* Little, Brown and Company, Canada, 1992.

White, Ernie. *Tuff Stuff.* Tuff Stuff Publications Inc., Glen Allen, VA, 1993.

DIRECTORY OF CONTRIBUTORS

AUTO RACING

Thom Dixon
5349 N. Keystone
Indianapolis, IN 46220

Ted Knorr
c/o Turn 4 Collectibles
P.O. Box 24594
Speedway, IN 46224

David Sassman
P.O. Box 24072
Indianapolis, IN 46224

AUTOGRAPHS

Rich Altman
c/o Hollywood Collectibles
4912 Arthur St.
Hollywood, FL 33021

Bob Eaton
c/o R & R Enterprises
P.O. Box 2000
S. Amherst, NH 03031

Mark Jordan
First National Bank Building
1600 Airport Freeway, Suite 506
Bedford, TX 76022

Jay Kemplin
c/o Upperdeck Sportscard
1717 S. Philo Rd. #213
Urban, IL 61801

Mark Kimball
81 Water St.
Hallowell, ME 04347

Paul Kinzer
c/o Blue Chip Sports Collectibles
4820 Spanish Oak Dr.
Douglasville, GA 30135

Greg Manning Co., Inc.
115 Main Rd.
Montville, NJ 07045

Richard Moody
c/o Moody's Sports Memorabilia
319 Wake Forest Dr., #T204
Warner Robins, GA 31093-1094

Ralph Paticchio
P.O. Box 129
Everett, MA 02149

Pat Quinn
c/o Sports Collectors Store
9 S. La Grange Rd.
La Grange, IL 60525

Lew Scalia Jr.
c/o East Coast Sports
2060 S.W. 71st Terr.
Bldg. E-5 Davie, FL 33317

Jim Stinson
c/o Sports Collectibles
1290 W. Diamond Valley Dr.
St. George, UT 84770

Dave Stuart
6735 E. Pepperwood CT
Wichita, KS 67226

Greg Tucker
P.O. Box 909
Broken Arrow, OK 74013-0909

BOBBIN' HEAD DOLLS

Pat Flynn
c/o MinneMemories
122 Shadywood Ave.
Mankato, MN 56001

Tim Hunter
1668 Golddust Dr.
Sparks, NV 89436

CEREAL BOXES

Bud Tompkins
c/o The Minnesota Connection
17773 Kenwood Trail
Lakeville, MN 55044

DIE-CAST CARS

Die Cast Digest
P.O. Box 12510
Knoxville, TN 37912-0510

Racing Collectibles Price Guide
P.O. Box 607785
Orlando, FL 32860-7785

EQUIPMENT

Mitchell & Ness Nostalgia Co.
1229 Walnut St.
Philadelphia, PA 19107

George R. Charabowski
30 Karen Avenue
Stratford, Conn 06497

Murf Denny
Box 127
Brule, WI 54820

Hartel Sports Inc.
1004 Glenview Drive
P.O. Box 3
Steeleville, IL 62288

Phil Wood
c/o Diamond Duds
P.O. Box 10153
Silver Spring, Maryland 20904-0153

Jordan Yuter
6329 Fariston Dr.
Philladelphia, PA 19120

FIGURINES

Tim Hunter
1668 Golddust Dr.
Sparks, NV 89436

Bud Tompkins
c/o The Minnesota Connection
17773 Kenwood Trail
Lakeville, MN 55044

The Sports Alley, Inc.
15545 E. Whittier Blvd.
Whittier, CA 90603

GAMES

Mark W. Cooper
518 Sussex Rd.
Wynnewood, PA 19096

Debby & Marty Krim
New England Auction Gallery
P.O. Box 2273
West Peabody, MA 01960

Rich R. La Rocca
P.O. Box 426
Canfield, OH 44406

Alex G. Malloy
P.O. Box 38
South Salem, NY 10590

HORSE RACING

Dick Hering
202 Brookshire Lane
Wilmington, NC 28409

OLYMPICS

Harvey Abrams
P.O. Box 732
State College, PA 16804

Jonathan Becker
165 Danbury Rd.
Ridgefield, CT 06877

Don Bigsby
P.O. Box 2325
Albany, NY 12220

Bob Christianson
483 80th Street
Brooklyn, NY 11209-3902

Jim Greensfelder
5825 Squire Hill Ct.
Cincinnati, OH 45421

Eiran Harris
5912 Clanranald
Montreal, Quebec H3X 2T1

PENNANTS

Patricia Denny
Box 127
Brule, WI 54820

Noel Emerling
5133 Arnold Ct.
Hamburg, NY 14075

Steve Prieur
c/o WinCraft Incorporated
1205 E. Sanborn St.
Winona, MN 55987

PINS

Richard Galasso
289 Pascack Rd., #484
Washington Township, NJ 07675

Daniel Lovegrove
P.O. Box 1011
Darien, CT 06820

Bill Nelson
P.O. Box 41630
Tuscon, AZ 85717-1630

POCKET SCHEDULES

Judy Bartolett
7421 Gleason Rd.
Edina, MN 55439

Marty Falk
c/o The Sked Notebook
8 Fillmore Place
Lawrenceville, NJ 08648

Paul Jarrell
4675 Lottie Place
College Park, GA 30337

Clay Marston
Box 73600
509 St. Clair Ave. West
Toronto, Ontario M6C 1C0
Canada

POSTERS

Bob Manning
c/o Big League Cards
21175 Tomball Parkway #222
Houston, TX 77070

Don Scott
c/o Boxing Collector's Newsletter
59 Bosson St.
Revere, MA 02151

PRICE GUIDES

Mark Wollin
c/o Doris' Collectibles
P.O. Box 183
St. Peter, IL 62880

PROGRAMS

Dennis Goldstein
516 Manford Rd., SW
Atlanta, GA 30310

Kenrich Co.
9418 E. Las Tunas Dr., #248
Temple City, CA 91780

Mike Wamsley
c/o B&W Sports Cards
2526 North Main
Hutchinson, KS 67502

PUBLICATIONS

Bob Adelson
c/o Adelson Sports
13610 N. Scottsdale Rd., #10
Scottsdale, AZ 85254

B & E Collectibles
12 Marble Ave.
Thornwood, NY 10594

Beryl Blatt
c/o Beulah Sports
Glenview Plaza
1877 Waukegan Rd.
Glenview, IL 60025

Anthony M. Bruno
One Gillridge Pkwy
Middletown, NJ 07743

Robert Crestohl
4732 Circle Rd.
Montreal, Quebec H3W 1Z1
Canada

Jeff Goldstein
c/o The Shortstop Sports Shop
10825 Washington Blvd.
Culver City, CA 90232

Tom Goldstein
c/o TG Sports Enterprises
99 Snelling Ave. N
St. Paul, MN 55104

Michael Jaspersen
1814 Litchfield Ave.
Long Beach, CA 90815

Lou Madden
4545 E. Shea Blvd., #210
Phoenix, AZ 85028

Pat Quinn
c/o Sports Collectors Store
9 S. LaGrange Road
LaGrange, IL 60525

Tom Sarro
P.O. Box 193
Brooklyn, NY 11209

Lloyd E. Williams
c/o Sports Publications
1205 Hazel
Oshikosh, WI 54901

Toni Zufferli
3050 Orleans Rd.
Unit 53
Mississauga, Ontario L5L 5P7

INDEX

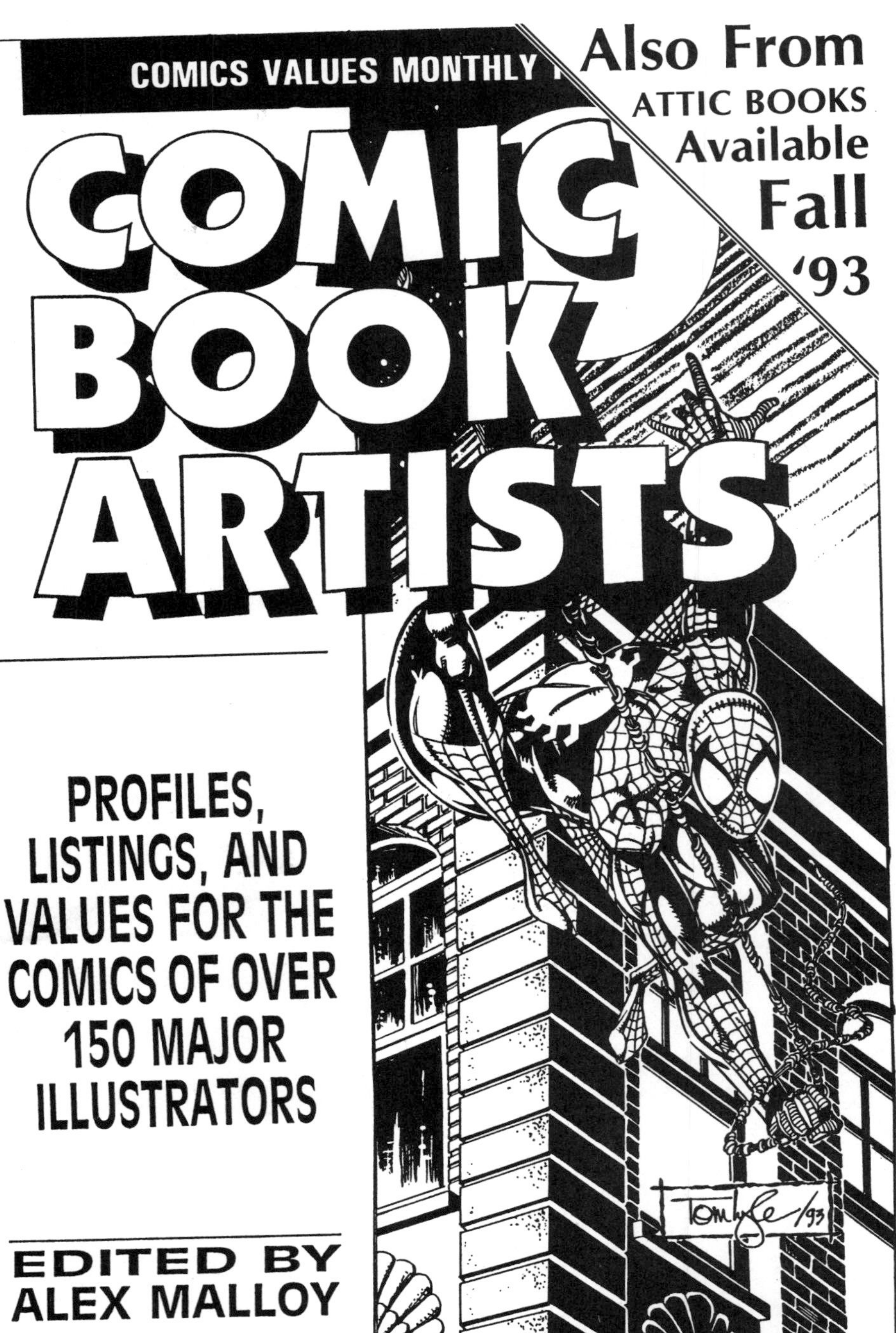
COMICS VALUES MONTHLY
Also From
ATTIC BOOKS
Available
Fall
'93
COMIC
BOOK
ARTISTS
PROFILES,
LISTINGS, AND
VALUES FOR THE
COMICS OF OVER
150 MAJOR
ILLUSTRATORS
EDITED BY
ALEX MALLOY